# California Practice Guide

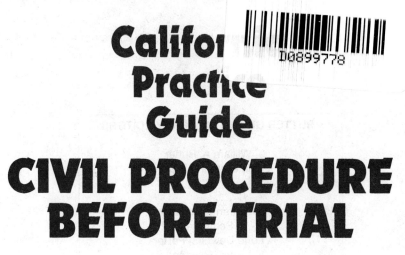

# CIVIL PROCEDURE BEFORE TRIAL

Chapters 1-7

## JUDGE ROBERT I. WEIL (Ret.)
Los Angeles Superior Court

## JUDGE IRA A. BROWN, JR. (Ret.)
San Francisco Superior Court

### SUPERVISING EDITOR
**Justice William F. Rylaarsdam**, Calif. Court of Appeal, 4th App. Dist.

### CONTRIBUTING EDITORS
**Justice Paul A. Turner**, Calif. Court of Appeal, 2nd App. Dist.
**Judge Anthony J. Mohr**, Los Angeles Superior Court
**Judge Lee Smalley Edmon**, Los Angeles Superior Court

## 2004

CONTINUING LEGAL EDUCATION **TRG** PROGRAMS AND PUBLICATIONS

# THE RUTTER GROUP™
A DIVISION OF WEST

Copyright© 1983, 1984, 1985, 1986, 1987, 1988, 1989, 1990, 1991, 1992, 1993, 1994, 1995, 1996, 1997, 1998, 1999, 2000, 2001, 2002, 2003, 2004 by THE RUTTER GROUP, A DIVISION OF WEST

Permission is hereby granted for the copying of pages or portions of pages of this book by photocopy, Xerox or other similar process, or by manual transcription, by or under the direction of licensed attorneys solely for use in the practice of law. Otherwise, all rights reserved; no copying for in-house training distribution or other use is permitted which will infringe the copyright without the express written consent of The Rutter Group, A Division of West.

(For information, contact The Rutter Group at 15760 Ventura Blvd./Suite 630, Encino, CA 91436; or phone (818) 990-3260, tollfree (800) 747-3161.)

This book should be cited as Weil & Brown, CAL. PRAC. GUIDE: CIV. PRO. BEFORE TRIAL (The Rutter Group 2004).

*Please note:* Programs and publications by The Rutter Group (TRG), A Division of West, are intended to provide attorneys with current and accurate information about the subjects covered. However, such information may not be sufficient in dealing with a client's particular legal problem, and TRG does not warrant or represent its suitability for such purpose. Attorneys attending programs presented by TRG or using its publications do so with the understanding that TRG is not engaged in the practice of law and does not render legal, accounting or other professional services; and that the information published by TRG should not be relied upon as a substitute for independent research to original sources of authority.

# ABOUT THE AUTHORS

**Judge Robert I. Weil** (Ret.) is well known to California lawyers. As a judge of the Los Angeles Superior Court, he served over five years in the Law & Motion Departments and was Supervising Judge of the Law Departments. He was later assigned to a settlement calendar and successfully handled numerous complex cases.

Judge Weil is a graduate of USC School of Law and practiced real estate and entertainment law before his appointment to the bench. He has taught civil procedure courses to hundreds of judges and thousands of lawyers statewide. He is currently engaged in dispute resolution as a private judge.

## IN MEMORIAM

**Judge Ira A. Brown, Jr.** was one of the original authors of this Practice Guide. He was regarded as one of the finest law and motion judges in California.

Judge Brown graduated from the University of Michigan Law School and practiced law both in Michigan and California.

He served in the Law and Motion Department of the San Francisco Superior Court for over 10 years and was also Presiding Judge of that court.

Judge Brown is fondly remembered by lawyers and judges throughout California from his many appearances in continuing education programs.

# PREFACE TO FIRST EDITION

This Practice Guide is designed for, and dedicated to, the civil litigators of the California Bar.

We feel they are entitled to a bit of compassion and assistance. They frequently have to deal with unsympathetic judges, unreasonable adversaries, and unhappy clients—sometimes, all at once!

Added to this balancing act is the pressure of trying to catch up with the latest changes in the fields in which they practice, while running a busy law office.

Then, of course, they are supposed to know all the ground rules governing the litigation process . . . rules that are constantly being rewritten, refined and generally tinkered with by the Legislature, the Judicial Council and our courts.

This Practice Guide is designed to offer some reliable help with the rules governing civil litigation before trial.

- Our focus is on practice in the metropolitan courts of California.

- Our approach is to cover each stage of pretrial proceedings, setting forth the applicable rules as clearly and simply as possible, with key illustrations of their application.

- Our aim is to keep this Guide "on target" by rewriting it frequently, to eliminate obsolete material and to catch the new trends as they develop.

Obviously, no book can substitute for independent research and analysis in a particular case. But we think you will find herein the basic information needed to handle problems commonly encountered in civil litigation before trial . . and also, some pointers that will enable you to practice more confidently and successfully!

ROBERT I. WEIL (Ret.)
Judge of the Superior Court
Los Angeles County

IRA A. BROWN, JR. (Ret.)
Judge of the Superior Court
San Francisco City and County

# TABLE OF CONTENTS

See front of each chapter for detailed summaries of contents

Chapter 1:            PRELAWSUIT CONSIDERATIONS

Chapter 2:            PARTIES TO THE ACTION

Chapter 3:            JURISDICTION AND VENUE

Chapter 4:            SUMMONS

Chapter 5:            DEFAULTS: HOW TO OBTAIN THEM AND
                      HOW TO CURE THEM

Chapter 6:            PLEADINGS

Chapter 7:            ATTACKING THE PLEADINGS

Chapter 8:            DISCOVERY

Chapter 9, Part I:    LAW AND MOTION

Chapter 9, Part II:   PROVISIONAL  REMEDIES

Chapter 9, Part III:  SANCTIONS

Chapter 10:           SUMMARY JUDGMENT

Chapter 11:           DISMISSALS

Chapter 12, Part I:   CASE MANAGEMENT AND TRIAL SETTING

Chapter 12, Part II:  SETTLEMENT PROCEDURES

Chapter 13:           JUDICIAL ARBITRATION AND MEDIATION

Chapter 14:           REPRESENTATIVE AND CLASS ACTIONS

Tables:               CASES, STATUTES AND COURT RULES

INDEX

# CHAPTER 1

# PRELAWSUIT CONSIDERATIONS

## CONTENTS

Page

**A. ACCEPTING A NEW CASE** ................................................... 1-1
  1.  First Contact With Client ............................................ 1-1
    a.  Take the call personally ...................................... 1-2
    b.  Determine basic information .............................. 1-2
    c.  Determine referral source .................................. 1-3
    d.  Set up office interview ....................................... 1-3
    e.  Confirm decision to decline case in writing ............... 1-3
  2.  First Meeting With Client............................................ 1-3
    a.  Preparing for the meeting .................................. 1-3
      (1) Do some preliminary research ....................... 1-3
      (2) Block out time ........................................... 1-3
    b.  Handling the meeting ......................................... 1-4
      (1) Ascertain essential facts ............................... 1-4
        (a) Interview techniques .............................. 1-4
          1)  Narrative .................................... 1-4
          2)  Question and answer................ 1-4
        (b) Take good notes ................................... 1-4
      (2) Determine whether dispute subject to
          arbitration ................................................ 1-5
      (3) Discuss the law generally .............................. 1-5
      (4) Discuss any deadlines applicable ................... 1-5
      (5) Discuss strategy alternatives ........................ 1-6
        (a) Doing nothing ...................................... 1-6
        (b) Seeking early settlement ....................... 1-6
        (c) Limited litigation .................................. 1-6
        (d) "All-out" litigation ................................. 1-6
          1)  Caution—ethical limitations .............. 1-6
          2)  Caution—risk of sanctions ............... 1-7
          3)  Caution—risk of attorney fee award ....... 1-7
      (6) Discuss ADR ............................................. 1-7
      (7) Discuss timing ........................................... 1-7
      (8) Discuss yourself ......................................... 1-8
      (9) Discuss potential negatives........................... 1-8
      (10) If potential client has been sued, consider
           insurance coverage .................................. 1-9
      (11) Consider insurance consequences of cross-
           complaint................................................ 1-9

(12) Be careful about allowing third persons to "sit in" on conference ............................................... 1-9

    c.  Confidential communications protected even if attorney not retained ............................................. 1-9

3.  Determining Whether to Take the Case ......................... 1-10

    a.  Ethical considerations—conflict of interest limitations ............................................................... 1-10

      (1)  California Rules of Professional Conduct ............ 1-10

        (a)  Interests to be disclosed ............................. 1-10

        (b)  Relationship with opposing counsel to be disclosed ...................................................... 1-11

        (c)  Interests requiring clients' informed consent ....................................................... 1-11

        (d)  Where confidential information acquired through representation ............................... 1-11

      (2)  "Informed written consent" ............................. 1-11

        (a)  Actual vs. potential conflicts ...................... 1-12

        (b)  Consent to future conflicts upheld .............. 1-12

      (3)  Effect .............................................................. 1-12

      (4)  Conflicts between present clients (*concurrent* representation) ................................................ 1-13

        (a)  Application .................................................. 1-13

        (b)  Dropping one client no cure ("hot potato rule") ......................................................... 1-14

      (5)  Conflicts between present and former clients (*successive* representation) .............................. 1-15

        (a)  Knowledge of confidential information conclusively presumed ............................... 1-15

        (b)  What constitutes "substantial relationship" ... 1-15

          1)  Factors considered .............................. 1-15

      (6)  Vicarious disqualification of law firm? ............. 1-15

        (a)  Compare—successive representation cases ......................................................... 1-16

      (7)  Procedure to disqualify lawyer or law firm for conflict ........................................................... 1-16

    b.  Ethical considerations—disqualification based on matters other than conflict of interests ...................... 1-16

      (1)  Hiring expert previously consulted by opposing party .............................................................. 1-16

      (2)  Attorney as potential witness .......................... 1-17

        (a)  Rule of Professional Conduct ...................... 1-17

        (b)  Exceptions ................................................. 1-17

    c.  Merits of case ..................................................... 1-17

      (1)  Overrides duty to client .................................. 1-18

      (2)  Lack of merit appearing after case filed ............ 1-18

      (3)  No malpractice liability for refusing to handle case ............................................................... 1-18

        (a)  Refusal made clear ..................................... 1-18

      (4)  Competence to handle case ............................ 1-19

        (a)  Handling cases beyond own expertise .......... 1-19

Rev. #1 2004

    d.  Time and resources, as consideration ...................... 1-20
    e.  Financial costs, as consideration .............................. 1-20
        (1) Special costs considerations ............................. 1-20
            (a) Nonresident plaintiff or foreign corporation ... 1-20
                1)  Timing ..................................................... 1-20
                2)  Procedure ............................................... 1-21
            (b) Malpractice actions ............................... 1-21
            (c) Other actions requiring security ................... 1-21
        (2) Waiver of court costs for indigents .................... 1-22
            (a) Only court costs and fees waivable ............. 1-22
    f.  Nature of case or client, as considerations ............... 1-22
        (1) Interesting case? ............................................. 1-22
        (2) Interesting client? ............................................ 1-22
        (3) Potential for further business? ........................... 1-22
        (4) Potential for enhancing attorney's
            reputation? ..................................................... 1-23
4.  Fee Considerations ..................................................... 1-23
    a.  Client responsibility for attorney fees ........................ 1-23
        (1) Limitation—representing minors ......................... 1-24
        (2) Cases where fees recoverable from opposing
            party ............................................................. 1-24
            (a) Compare—attorney fees as tort
                damages ..................................................... 1-24
            (b) Compare—attorney fees as losses
                covered by "hold harmless" agreements ....... 1-25
    b.  Fee arrangements with client ................................... 1-25
        (1) Types of fee arrangements ................................ 1-25
            (a) Hourly rate ................................................. 1-25
                1)  Compare—blended rates ....................... 1-25
                2)  Compare—discounted rates ................... 1-26
            (b) Fixed fee ................................................... 1-26
            (c) Contingent fee .......................................... 1-26
            (d) Combination fee ........................................ 1-26
                1)  "Capped fee" ..................................... 1-26
                2)  "Target fee" ........................................ 1-26
                  3)  "Task billing" ...................................... 1-27
                  4)  "Value billing" ..................................... 1-27
                  5)  Partial contingency ............................. 1-27
             (e) Litigation budgets ...................................... 1-27
        (2) Which type is appropriate ................................. 1-28
        (3) Evaluating hourly rate cases ............................. 1-28
        (4) Evaluating flat rate cases ................................. 1-30
        (5) Evaluating contingent fee cases ........................ 1-30
            (a) Liability ..................................................... 1-30
            (b) Damages ................................................. 1-31
            (c) Collectibility .............................................. 1-31
            (d) Likelihood of early settlement ...................... 1-31
    c.  Fees recoverable from opposing party pursuant
      to contract.................................................................. 1-32
        (1) Conditions precedent enforced .......................... 1-32

    (2)  Claims covered ................................... 1-32
        (a)  Under provision limited to "actions on
            contract"...................................... 1-33
            1)  Compare—defending against tort
                claim ...................................... 1-33
            2)  Compare—successful and unsuccessful
                contract claims ....................... 1-33
        (b)  Under broader ("arising out of") fee
            provision .................................... 1-34
    (3)  Reciprocal right under Civ.C. §1717 .......... 1-34
        (a)  Limited to fees on contract claims.......... 1-34
        (b)  Where contract held invalid or
            unenforceable ............................. 1-35
            1)  Compare—illegal contracts ......... 1-35
        (c)  Determining "prevailing party" .............. 1-35
            1)  No "prevailing party" where plaintiff
                voluntarily dismisses.................. 1-35
                a)  Contract vs. tort claims ..................... 1-36
            2)  Defendant may "prevail" by tendering
                amount due ............................. 1-36
            3)  Net recovery may be determinative ........ 1-36
                a)  Noncontract claims disregarded ....... 1-36
                b)  Several contract claims .................... 1-37
                c)  Earlier recoveries considered ........... 1-37
            4)  Court's discretion ........................... 1-37
                a)  Where plaintiff loses on contract
                    claim but wins on others.................. 1-38
                b)  No discretion where unqualified win
                    on contract claim ........................ 1-38
                  1/  Equitable considerations
                      disregarded ......................... 1-38
    (4)  Nonsignatory's right to fees................... 1-38
        (a)  Nonsignatory plaintiffs .................... 1-38
            1)  Application ............................... 1-39
            2)  Compare.................................. 1-39
        (b)  Nonsignatory defendants ................. 1-39
            1)  Application ............................... 1-40
            2)  Compare.................................. 1-40
    (5)  Nonsignatory plaintiff's *liability* for fees .............. 1-40
        (a)  Assignee ..................................... 1-41
        (b)  Third party beneficiary ................... 1-41
    (6)  Amount of fee award ......................... 1-42
        (a)  Fee arrangements with client not
            controlling .................................. 1-42
        (b)  Factors considered in determining
            "reasonable" fee .......................... 1-43
    (7)  Procedure to obtain fee award .............. 1-43
        (a)  Noticed motion............................. 1-43
        (b)  Pleading requirement?.................... 1-43
  d.  Fee awards authorized by statute................. 1-44

Rev. #1 2004

| | | |
|---|---|---|
| (1) | In general | 1-44 |
| (2) | No reciprocal right | 1-44 |
| (3) | Not limited to fees owed by client | 1-44 |
| (4) | Mixed actions | 1-45 |
| (5) | Determining "prevailing" party | 1-45 |
| (6) | Not a limit on negotiated fees | 1-46 |
| (7) | Limited by negotiated fee? | 1-46 |
| (8) | Procedure to fix statutory fees | 1-47 |
| | (a) No interim awards | 1-47 |
| (9) | Pilot program (Riverside County only)—fee award for refusing CCP §998 settlement offer | 1-47 |
| (10) | Statutory fee award belongs to client or attorney? | 1-48 |
| | (a) Comment | 1-48 |
| | (b) Effect of client's settlement waiving fees? | 1-48 |
| | (c) Validity of splitting court-ordered fees with client? | 1-49 |

e. Fees under court's equitable powers ........................ 1-49
    (1) Common fund doctrine .................................... 1-49
    (2) Substantial benefit doctrine ............................ 1-49
    (3) "Private attorney general" doctrine .................. 1-50
f. Proof requirements for fee awards ........................ 1-50
    (1) Fee schedules as presumptive amount.............. 1-50
    (2) Billing records ............................................. 1-51
    (3) Expert opinion ............................................. 1-51
    (4) Attorney's testimony alone may suffice .............. 1-51
        (a) Compare—federal practice ............................ 1-51
g. Discovery by opposing party ................................ 1-52

5. Formalizing the Attorney-Client Relationship ................... 1-52
a. When to formalize ............................................ 1-52
b. Matters to be agreed upon ................................ 1-53
    (1) Identity of client ............................................. 1-53
    (2) Work to be done ............................................. 1-53
    (3) Authority conferred ......................................... 1-53
        (a) Implied authority re "procedural" matters ...... 1-54
        (b) No implied authority re "substantive rights" ........................................................ 1-54
            1) Application ............................................. 1-54
            2) Unauthorized acts void ............................ 1-55
                a) Compare—ratification ...................... 1-55
            3) Opposing counsel cannot rely on "apparent" authority ............................... 1-55
            4) Attorney personally liable for unauthorized acts ................................... 1-56
        (c) Test for when client authorization required ........................................................ 1-56
            1) Effect ...................................................... 1-56
            2) Factors considered ................................... 1-56

        (d)  Effect of agreement conferring settlement
authority on attorney .......................................1-57
          1)  Compare—provisions prohibiting
client from "settling around" attorney ......1-57
    (4)  Fee arrangement................................................1-57
    (5)  How costs are to be paid..................................1-57
    (6)  Security arrangements for fees and costs ..........1-57
  c.  When writing required ..............................................1-57
    (1)  Required contents ............................................1-57
    (2)  Exceptions to written agreement requirement.....1-59
        (a)  Emergencies............................................1-59
        (b)  Prior dealings...........................................1-59
        (c)  Waiver......................................................1-59
        (d)  Corporate clients ....................................1-59
    (3)  Type of writing ..................................................1-60
        (a)  Letter agreements...................................1-60
        (b)  Formal retainer agreements......................1-60
        (c)  State Bar Sample Forms .........................1-60
    (4)  Signed copy to client upon execution .................1-60
    (5)  Additional requirements re billings ....................1-60
    (6)  Effect of failure to comply .................................1-61
        (a)  Effect of promissory note given as security .....1-61
        (b)  Compare—quantum meruit recovery for
services rendered ...................................1-62
          1)  Includes referral fees ...............................1-62
        (c)  Compare—recovery of statutory fees ...........1-62
        (d)  Compare—certain civil rights actions ...........1-62
        (e)  Compare—class actions ..............................1-62
    (7)  Compare—privileged communication .................1-63
  d.  Special requirements re contingency fee contracts ...1-63
    (1)  Contents.............................................................1-63
        (a)  Not limited to litigation matters .....................1-64
        (b)  Scope of services ..........................................1-64
        (c)  Right to fees on discharge or withdrawal? ....1-83
        (d)  Must fee be negotiated? ...............................1-83
        (e)  Sanctions and fee awards as part of
recovery? ..................................................1-84
        (f)  Effect of defendant's cross-complaint on
contingency fee? ......................................1-84
    (2)  Signed copy to client upon execution .................1-84
    (3)  Effect of failure to comply .................................1-84
        (a)  Example.....................................................1-84
        (b)  Compare—statutory fees .............................1-84
    (4)  Compare—workers' compensation claims ..........1-85
    (5)  Compare—claims between merchants ...............1-85
        (a)  "Merchants"...............................................1-85
        (b)  Limits on contingency fees .........................1-85
    (6)  Effect of provision obligating client to accept
designated amount in settlement? ......................1-85
    (7)  Special limitations on contingency fees in
medical malpractice cases ...............................1-86

|   |   | (a) Not waivable by client | 1-86 |
|   |   | (b) Hybrid actions | 1-87 |
| e. | | Ethical considerations re fees | 1-87 |
|   | (1) | Unconscionable or illegal fees | 1-87 |
|   |   | (a) "Unconscionable" fees | 1-88 |
|   |   | 1) Factors considered | 1-88 |
|   |   | (b) "Illegal" fees | 1-89 |
|   |   | (c) No "unilateral increases" | 1-89 |
|   |   | (d) Adequate records required | 1-89 |
|   | (2) | Fee splitting | 1-89 |
|   | (3) | Unearned fees to be deposited in trust account? | 1-90 |
|   |   | (a) Nonrefundable fees ("retainers") | 1-90 |
|   |   | (b) Refundable fees ("advance fees") | 1-90.1 |
| f. | | Credit terms | 1-90.1 |
|   | (1) | Truth-in-lending laws | 1-90.1 |
|   |   | (a) Requirements | 1-90.2 |
|   |   | (b) Effect of failure to comply | 1-90.2 |
| g. | | Provisions for payment of costs | 1-90.2 |
|   | (1) | Authority to incur expenses | 1-90.2 |
|   |   | (a) Prior approval of extraordinary expenses | 1-90.2 |
|   | (2) | Client's responsibility for costs | 1-90.3 |
|   |   | (a) Advances from client | 1-90.3 |
|   |   | 1) Ethical limitation | 1-90.3 |
|   |   | (b) Advances to client | 1-90.3 |
|   |   | 1) Repayment may be contingent | 1-90.3 |
| h. | | Security for payment of costs and fees | 1-90.4 |
|   | (1) | Lien on cause of action and recovery | 1-90.4 |
|   | (2) | Third party guarantee | 1-90.4 |
|   | (3) | Security interest in real or personal property | 1-90.4 |
|   |   | (a) *Caution*—CRPC limitations | 1-90.4 |
|   |   | (b) Application to security interests | 1-90.5 |
|   |   | (c) Compare—unsecured promissory note | 1-90.5 |
| i. | | Arbitration of disputes? | 1-90.5 |
|   | (1) | Ethical considerations | 1-90.6 |
|   | (2) | Limitation—*fees and costs disputes* subject to State Bar arbitration rules | 1-91 |
|   |   | (a) State Bar "mandatory fees/costs arbitration" | 1-91 |
|   |   | 1) Attorney must notify client of right to arbitration | 1-91 |
|   |   | 2) Effect of failure to give notice | 1-92 |
|   |   | (b) Predispute agreement for binding arbitration of fees/costs disputes invalid | 1-92 |
|   |   | 1) Comment | 1-92 |
|   |   | 2) Federal preemption? | 1-92 |
|   |   | (c) Compare—postdispute agreements for binding arbitration | 1-93 |
|   |   | 1) Limited to State Bar arbitrators | 1-93 |

        2) No waiver ............................................................... 1-93
        3) Federal preemption? ............................. 1-93
    (3) Other disputes subject to binding arbitration ....... 1-93
       (a) Voluntariness ............................................ 1-94
       (b) No special form required .............................. 1-94
       (c) No express jury waiver required ................... 1-94
       (d) Explanations not required ........................... 1-94
6.  Dealing With Prior Counsel ............................................ 1-94
  a.  Discharging the prior lawyer .................................. 1-94
  b.  Prior lawyer's right to fees ................................... 1-95
    (1) Right to fees where client discharges
        attorney ................................................................ 1-95
       (a) Contingency fee cases .................................. 1-96
          1) Portion of fee earned .............................. 1-96
          2) Costs advanced .................................... 1-96.1
       (b) Liens to secure fees ................................. 1-96.1
          1) Validity dependent upon contract ........ 1-96.1
          2) Priority over later liens ......................... 1-96.2
            a) May be given for past or future
               services ........................................... 1-96.2
            b) "Secret" lien ................................... 1-96.2
            c) Adjudicating competing lien
               claims ............................................. 1-96.3
            d) Equities favoring other creditors .... 1-96.3
            e) Effect of client's bankruptcy ........... 1-96.3
          3) Independent action required to
            enforce attorney's lien ......................... 1-96.3
            a) Not enforceable in underlying
               action ............................................. 1-96.4
          4) Notice of attorney's lien filed in
            underlying action .................................. 1-96.4
            a) Not required ................................... 1-96.4
            b) Tort liability for "settling around"
               attorney's lien ................................. 1-96.5
    (2) No right to fees where attorney abandons
        case ..................................................................... 1-96.5
       (a) Example ...................................................... 1-96.5
       (b) Compare—withdrawal after performance
          of services ................................................ 1-96.6
    (3) Right to fees where "good cause" shown
        for withdrawal .................................................... 1-96.6
       (a) Withdrawal mandatory under ethical
          rules ......................................................... 1-96.6
       (b) Withdrawal permissive under ethical
          rules ......................................................... 1-96.6
          1) Refusal to settle NOT cause ................... 1-97
    (4) Effect of order relieving counsel ......................... 1-97
    (5) Effect of retainer agreement authorizing
        attorney to withdraw at will? ............................... 1-97
  c.  Obtaining signed substitution and client's file ........... 1-98

Rev. #1 2004

        (1) Prior lawyer's duty to sign substitution and
            deliver client's file .................................................. 1-98
            (a) Not essential to court appearance ................ 1-98
        (2) Refusal as ground for disciplinary action ............. 1-98
        (3) Fee agreement exacted as condition of
            turning over files invalid ....................................... 1-99
        (4) Contract liens on file invalid .............................. 1-99
        (5) Contents of file to be delivered ........................... 1-99
    d. Taking case from prior lawyer as tort ...................... 1-100
        (1) Breach of fiduciary duty to former firm ............. 1-100
        (2) Interference with contract relationship............... 1-100
    e. Compare—former partnership or employment
       agreements restricting representation ...................... 1-101

**B. PRELAWSUIT INVESTIGATIONS, RESEARCH AND
ANALYSIS** ................................................................... 1-101
  1. Sources for Investigation ............................................... 1-101
    a. Client ........................................................................ 1-101
    b. Client's files ............................................................. 1-102
    c. Patient's medical records......................................... 1-102
      (1) Costs ................................................................. 1-102
    d. Third parties ............................................................. 1-102
      (1) Witnesses ......................................................... 1-102
        (a) *Caution re discovery* ............................... 1-103
      (2) Experts............................................................. 1-103
        (a) Prelawsuit consultation required in
            certain malpractice cases ......................... 1-103
        (b) Consultations generally shielded from
            discovery.................................................... 1-103
        (c) Caution re contacting opposing party's
            experts ....................................................... 1-104
      (3) Compare—opposing party's medical
        providers ........................................................... 1-104
      (4) Opposing party or counsel ............................... 1-104
        (a) Ethical ban on communicating with parties
            represented by counsel.............................. 1-104
          1) Actual knowledge required ................... 1-105
            a) Rationale ........................................ 1-105
            b) Knowledge tested objectively ......... 1-105
          2) Ban applies to indirect
            communications ................................... 1-105
            a) Compare—parties
              communicating with each other ...... 1-105
      (5) Opposing party a corporation, partnership or
        association ......................................................... 1-106
        (a) Officers, directors and managers ................ 1-106
          1) Dissidents ............................................ 1-106
          2) Lower level managers........................... 1-106
          3) Violation as ground for disqualification
            of counsel? ............................................ 1-106
        (b) Employees ................................................. 1-107

           1) Not dependent on managerial status.... 1-107
           2) Communications unrelated to
                employee's own acts or omissions? ..... 1-108
           3) Not limited to matters in litigation ......... 1-108
           4) Compare—before knowledge of
                representation ................................... 1-109
        (c) Compare—*former* officers and
             employees ..................................................... 1-110
           1) Ex parte contact permitted ................... 1-111
               a) Shareholder status immaterial ....... 1-111
               b) "Control group" status
                  immaterial? ......................................... 1-111
           2) No inquiry re privileged
               communications ..................................... 1-112
           3) Corporation's remedy ............................ 1-112
     (6) Disqualification of offending counsel? .............. 1-113
        (a) Factors favoring disqualification ................... 1-113
        (b) Factors favoring retention ......................... 1-113
     (7) Vicarious disqualification of entire firm? ........... 1-113
        (a) Compare—federal approach ..................... 1-114
        (b) "Gag" orders to offending counsel ............. 1-114
  2. Use of Illegally Obtained Evidence? ............................ 1-114
    a. Records stolen by client from opposing party ......... 1-114
     (1) Remedy .................................................................. 1-115
  3. Prelawsuit Legal Research ....................................... 1-115
  4. Alternative Dispute Resolution ("ADR") ..................... 1-115
    a. Particular procedures ............................................. 1-116
     (1) Negotiation ............................................................ 1-116
     (2) Mediation ............................................................... 1-116
     (3) Nonbinding arbitration or neutral evaluation ...... 1-116
     (4) Court-sponsored settlement conference before
        suit filed ............................................................... 1-116
     (5) Binding (contractual) arbitration ......................... 1-117
        (a) Distinguish "judicial arbitration" ................... 1-117
        (b) Judge as arbitrator? ..................................... 1-117
     (6) Judge pro tem ....................................................... 1-117
        (a) Caution—no power over nonsignatories ..... 1-117
        (b) Compare—power over parties .................... 1-118
     (7) "Reference" by agreement .................................. 1-118
        (a) Compare—court-ordered reference ............ 1-118
    b. Advantages vs. disadvantages ............................. 1-118
  5. Litigation Planning ................................................... 1-119
    a. Plaintiff's considerations ....................................... 1-119
     (1) Parties .................................................................. 1-119
        (a) Substantive law ........................................... 1-119
         1) *Caution re malicious prosecution* ......... 1-119
        (b) Joinder problems ........................................ 1-120
        (c) Tactical considerations ............................... 1-120
        (d) Prop. 51 considerations ............................. 1-120
        (e) Claims against governmental entities ......... 1-121

Rev. #1 2004

(2) WHEN to sue? ............................................... 1-121
(3) WHERE to sue? ............................................. 1-121
(4) File as limited or unlimited civil case? .............. 1-121
(5) CHOICE OF LAW considerations ..................... 1-122
(6) WHAT THEORIES or claims? .......................... 1-122
  (a) Ethical considerations ................................. 1-122
  (b) Malpractice considerations ......................... 1-122
  (c) Caution—potential liability "traps" for
    lawyer and client ....................................... 1-123
    1) Malicious prosecution ........................... 1-123
      a) Compare—lack of merit discovered
        *after* suit filed ............................... 1-124
    2) Abuse of process .................................. 1-124
      a) Limitation—filing and
        maintenance of suit insufficient ...... 1-124
    3) Sanctions for unfounded tort action
      against government or on indemnity
      claim (CCP §1038) ............................. 1-124
    4) Sanctions for violation of "certificate
      of merit" (CCP §128.7) ......................... 1-125
      a) Effect ............................................ 1-125
    5) Costs and fees on SLAPP suits ............ 1-126
  (d) Tactical considerations re choice of
    theories ...................................................... 1-126
    1) Recoverability of punitive damages ...... 1-126
    2) Insurance coverage ............................. 1-127
      a) Compare—"malicious" and
        "wilful" conduct .............................. 1-127
    3) Recoverability of attorney fees ............. 1-127
    4) Availability of provisional remedies ....... 1-127
    5) Priority in obtaining trial date ................ 1-127
b. Defendant's considerations ..................................... 1-128
(1) Right court? ................................................... 1-128
(2) When to appear ............................................. 1-128
(3) What defenses and counter-attacks are
  available against plaintiff? ............................... 1-128
  (a) Preserving right to sue for malicious
    prosecution ................................................ 1-128
  (b) Frivolous denials, defenses or cross-
    claims as basis for sanctions ..................... 1-128
    1) Certificate of merit ............................... 1-129
  (c) Cross-complaints as basis for sanctions or
    tort claim ................................................... 1-129
    1) Malicious prosecution ........................... 1-129
    2) Sanctions............................................. 1-129
(4) Who else should be brought into the action? .... 1-129

C. **PRELAWSUIT NOTICES, CLAIMS AND DEMANDS** ........ 1-130
1. Communications to Opposing Party Generally ............. 1-130
  a. Not represented by counsel..................................... 1-130
  b. Demand for preservation of evidence ..................... 1-130

c. Demand letters; improper threats .......................... 1-130
   (1) Threats of criminal charges improper ............... 1-131
   (2) Threats of civil action ....................................... 1-131
   (3) Potential tort liability—"litigation privilege"
       available? ....................................................... 1-131
       (a) Purposes ................................................. 1-132
       (b) Requirements ......................................... 1-132
           1) Compare—no intent or motives
              requirement ........................................ 1-132
           2) Compare—no "interest of justice"
              requirement ........................................ 1-132
           3) Compare—absolute vs. qualified
              privilege ............................................. 1-133
           4) Compare—nonlitigants cannot claim
              derivative privilege ............................ 1-133
       (c) Judicial or "quasi-judicial" proceedings ....... 1-133
       (d) Conduct outside U.S. ................................. 1-134
       (e) Which statements privileged ..................... 1-134
           1) "Logical relation to action" ................ 1-134
           2) Statements made in court or in
              pleadings ........................................... 1-134
              a) Application ................................. 1-135
              b) Compare—notice of lien on
                 judgment ..................................... 1-135
           3) Statements outside court ................... 1-136
              a) Correspondence ........................... 1-136
              b) Recording lien ............................. 1-136
              c) Recording lis pendens .................. 1-136
           4) Prelawsuit communications ................ 1-137
              a) Nature of prelawsuit
                 communication ............................. 1-137
              b) Requirements for privilege ........... 1-137
                 1/ Does not affect absolute
                    nature of privilege ................... 1-138
                 2/ Separate "imminency"
                    requirement? ............................. 1-138
              c) Factors considered ...................... 1-138
           5) Statements made during
              settlement .......................................... 1-140
           6) Compare—statements made *after*
              litigation over ................................... 1-140
           7) Statements by and to
              nonparticipants ................................. 1-140
           8) Statements to news media ................ 1-141
              a) Background ................................. 1-141
              b) Privilege still limited to statements
                 "furthering objects of litigation" ....... 1-141
       (f) Compare—privilege not applicable to
           conduct ....................................................... 1-142
           1) Unauthorized recording ..................... 1-142

Rev. #1 2004

   2) Unauthorized reading and
       dissemination of confidential
       information ............................................. 1-142
   3) Financing litigation ............................... 1-142
   4) Filing contract claim with public
       agency .................................................... 1-142
 (g) Which actions barred by privilege .............. 1-143
   1) Except malicious prosecution ............... 1-144
   2) Abuse of process? ............................... 1-144
     a) Distinction between
         communications and conduct? ....... 1-144
   3) Actions to enjoin tort or statutory
       violation ................................................ 1-144
   4) Compare—privilege no defense to
       other liability ......................................... 1-145
     a) Criminal charges ........................... 1-145
     b) Disciplinary charges ...................... 1-145
     c) Malpractice actions ....................... 1-145
     d) Unauthorized disclosure of trade
         secret ............................................ 1-145
 (h) Statutory exceptions ................................... 1-146
   1) Exception for marital dissolution
       actions naming third parties ................. 1-146
   2) Exception for concealing insurance
       coverage ............................................... 1-146
     a) Compare—misrepresentations
         re terms of insurance ................... 1-146
     b) Compare—misrepresentation to
         insured or third party
         beneficiary .................................... 1-147
   3) Exception for planning destruction
       or alteration of evidence ...................... 1-147
     a) Compare—instructions to lie or
         conceal evidence privileged ........... 1-147
   4) Exception for slander of title based
       on improper lis pendens ...................... 1-148
 (i) Exception for violation of constitutional
       right to privacy? ..................................... 1-148
   1) Contra authority ................................. 1-148
 (4) Requirements re collection letters (Fair Debt
     Collection Practices Act) ........................... 1-149
2. Claims Against Government Entities ........................... 1-149
 a. General considerations ............................................. 1-150
 (1) Purpose ............................................................. 1-150
 (2) Constitutionality ................................................. 1-150
 (3) Entities protected ............................................... 1-150
 (4) Pleading requirement? ....................................... 1-150
 (5) Effect of failure to comply ................................. 1-150.1
   (a) Action against public employees also
       barred ........................................................... 1-150.1

   b.  Claims excepted ....................................... 1-150.1
       (1) Claims based on federal law ..................... 1-150.2
       (2) Claims having different claims-filing
           procedures ...................................... 1-150.2
           (a) FEHA claims ................................. 1-150.2
           (b) Claims against State Compensation
               Insurance Fund ............................. 1-150.2
           (c) Claims against Foster Home Insurance
               Fund ....................................... 1-150.2
       (3) Claims by another public entity ................ 1-150.3
       (4) "Redundant" claims ............................. 1-150.3
       (5) "Defensive cross-complaints" ................... 1-150.3
       (6) Claims for return of improperly confiscated
           property ........................................ 1-150.4
   c.  Circumstances under which claims filing
       excused ............................................. 1-150.4
       (1) Public entity's failure to file identifying
           information ..................................... 1-150.4
           (a) Effect of letterhead identification ........ 1-150.5
       (2) Advance payment by public entity .............. 1-150.5
       (3) Estoppel against public entity ................ 1-150.5
           (a) Requirements ............................... 1-150.5
           (b) Application ................................. 1-150.6
               1)  Misleading statements .................. 1-150.6
               2)  Inducing delay ......................... 1-150.6
               3)  Intimidation ........................... 1-150.7
       (4) Mental incapacity .............................. 1-150.7
       (5) Minor in custody as dependent of juvenile
           court ........................................... 1-150.7
   d.  Procedural requirements ............................ 1-150.8
       (1) Content of claim ............................... 1-150.8
           (a) Additional data not required ............... 1-150.8
           (b) "Substantial compliance" sufficient ........ 1-150.8
               1)  Test ................................... 1-150.8
               2)  Application ............................ 1-150.9
               3)  "Intent to sue" letter in medical
                   malpractice cases ...................... 1-150.10
           (c) Compare—entity's duty to warn claimant
               of defects in claim ....................... 1-150.11
               1)  Caution re earlier cases .............. 1-150.11
           (d) Compare—omitted claims .................... 1-150.11
           (e) Amendments ................................. 1-150.12
       (2) Presentation to governmental entity ........... 1-150.12
           (a) Presentation to wrong office .............. 1-150.12
           (b) Presentation to wrong entity ............. 1-150.13
           (c) Entity's failure to provide up-to-date
               information excuses compliance with
               claims requirement ........................ 1-150.13
       (3) Suit following rejection of claim ............. 1-151
           (a) Suit must be based on facts stated in
               claim ...................................... 1-151

(b) Application ........................................... 1-151
(c) Compare—immaterial variance ................ 1-151
e. Time limits ................................................ 1-152
(1) Time limit on presentation of claim—6
months or 1 year ..................................... 1-152
(a) Accrual of cause of action..................... 1-152
1) Accrual dependent on discovery of
injury.................................................. 1-152
a) Compare—minors' malpractice
claims ............................................. 1-153
2) Delayed accrual based on late
discovery of cause of injury ................. 1-153
a) Facts required ............................... 1-153
3) Effect of discouraging legal advice ....... 1-154
4) Claims by minors, insane persons;
tolling of statute of limitations .............. 1-154
a) Effect of "delayed discovery" by
parents or guardian? ..................... 1-155
b) Compare—equitable discovery ...... 1-155
c) Compare—rules governing leave
to file late claims ........................... 1-155
(b) Claims for indemnification..................... 1-155
(c) Claims by person presently charged
with crime ............................................. 1-156
(d) Public works claims .............................. 1-156
(2) Time limit for action by public entity—45
days .......................................................... 1-156
(a) Extension for service by mail ................ 1-157
(3) Notice of rejection ................................... 1-157
(a) Form of notice...................................... 1-157
(b) Manner of giving notice......................... 1-158
(4) Time limit for filing suit after notice of
rejection—6 months ................................. 1-158
(a) Measuring 6-month period .................... 1-158
(b) No exception for minors ........................ 1-159
(c) Proof of service unnecessary ................ 1-159
(d) Amended claims ................................... 1-159
1) Example ............................................ 1-159
2) Compare—unnecessary amendment ... 1-159
3) Compare—original claim barred .......... 1-160
(e) Serving entity as "Doe" after 6 months ....... 1-160
(f) Serving public employee as "Doe" after
6 months ............................................... 1-160
(g) Equitable tolling of statute .................... 1-161
1) Requirements ................................... 1-161
(5) Compare—statute of limitations .............. 1-162
(a) Suit required within 6 months after
rejection even if statute has not run ........... 1-162
(b) Suit within 6 months after rejection
timely even if statute has run ..................... 1-162

      (c) Compare—actions filed in federal court ...... 1-162
         1) Waiver and estoppel doctrines ............. 1-163
  f. Relief for late claims ............................................. 1-163
    (1) Statutory notice to claimant required ............... 1-163
    (2) Application to present late claim ....................... 1-164
      (a) Personal delivery or mailing ...................... 1-164
      (b) Time limit jurisdictional ............................. 1-164
      (c) Tolling for certain minors only ................... 1-164
      (d) Entity must permit if grounds for relief
         shown ........................................................ 1-165
         1) "Excusable neglect" ............................ 1-165
      (e) Deemed denied unless granted within 45
         days .......................................................... 1-165
         1) Extension for service by mail ............... 1-166
    (3) Petition to court if application denied;
      6-month limit ................................................... 1-166
      (a) Timeliness ................................................ 1-166
      (b) Grounds for relief .................................... 1-166
         1) "Mistake, surprise, excusable
           neglect" .............................................. 1-166
           a) Attorney "affidavit of fault"
             insufficient ................................... 1-167
         2) Minority alone excuses ........................ 1-167
         3) Incapacity as excuse ........................... 1-167
      (c) Procedure ................................................ 1-168
         1) Service ................................................ 1-168
         2) Effect of delay in service ..................... 1-168
      (d) Burden of proof ....................................... 1-168
         1) Example .............................................. 1-169
         2) Burden on public entity to prove
           prejudice .............................................. 1-169
      (e) Determination .......................................... 1-169
         1) Liberal policy ....................................... 1-170
         2) Prejudice to public entity as
           consideration ....................................... 1-170
         3) Denials strictly scrutinized on
           appeal ................................................. 1-170
         4) Showings sufficient for relief ................ 1-170
         5) Showings NOT sufficient for relief ........ 1-172
      (f) Filing suit on claim; 30-day limit .............. 1-172.2
         1) Time limit strictly applied ..................... 1-173
           a) Runs from date court "makes"
             order .......................................... 1-173
           b) No tolling for minors ....................... 1-174
         2) Effect of suit filed before relief
           granted? ............................................... 1-174
         3) Compare—estoppel .............................. 1-175
      (g) Effect of denial ........................................ 1-175
      (h) Denial as bar to action alleging claim
         timely filed? .............................................. 1-175

Rev. #1 2004

      1)  View that denial no bar ........................ 1-175

      2)  View that denial may bar separate
          lawsuit .................................................. 1-176

3.  Claims Against Decedent's Estate ............................. 1-176

   a.  Creditor's claim in probate proceedings ................. 1-176

     (1)  Which "claims" ..................................... 1-177

     (2)  Essential element of cause of action .............. 1-177

     (3)  Compare—must be raised before judgment ..... 1-177

     (4)  Exceptions ......................................... 1-177

   b.  Procedure ................................................. 1-177

     (1)  Contents ............................................ 1-177

        (a)  Written demand may be accepted as
            claim ........................................... 1-178

     (2)  Filing ............................................... 1-178

   c.  Time limit for filing creditor's claim ...................... 1-178

     (1)  Extension for creditors unaware of claim or
         estate administration ............................. 1-178

   d.  Time limit for suit following rejection .................... 1-179

     (1)  3-month statute of limitations on rejected
         claims .............................................. 1-179

     (2)  Compare—1-year statute of limitations on
         claims against decedent ........................... 1-179

   e.  Exceptions to claim filing requirement ................... 1-180

     (1)  Claims covered by liability insurance .............. 1-180

     (2)  Secured claims .................................... 1-180

     (3)  Claims by public entities ........................... 1-180

4.  Particular Causes of Action Requiring Notice or
  Demand Before Suit ......................................... 1-181

   a.  "Demand" promissory notes and similar
     obligations ............................................... 1-181

   b.  Rescission of contract ................................... 1-181

     (1)  Complaint as notice ............................... 1-181

   c.  Breach of warranty ...................................... 1-181

   d.  Consumer Legal Remedies Act .......................... 1-182

     (1)  Form of notice .................................... 1-182

     (2)  Compare—injunction actions ...................... 1-182

   e.  Defamation actions—demand for retraction ........... 1-182

     (1)  Form of demand .................................. 1-182

     (2)  Service on publisher or broadcaster ............... 1-182

   f.  Benefits conferred by mistake ........................... 1-182

   g.  Conversion by bailee .................................... 1-183

   h.  Certain environmental claims ............................ 1-183

5.  Medical Malpractice Action—Notice of Intent to Sue ..... 1-183

   a.  Actions for "professional negligence" .................... 1-183

     (1)  Actions "based on" professional negligence ...... 1-184

     (2)  Elder abuse ....................................... 1-184

        (a)  Compare—claims seeking punitive
            damage ........................................ 1-184

   b.  Effect of failure to give notice ........................... 1-185

     (1)  Disciplinary proceeding ............................ 1-185

(2) No pleading requirement ................................. 1-185
  c.  Content of notice ...................................... 1-185
    (1) Specificity required ............................... 1-185
      (a) Effect of failure to specify all injuries .......... 1-186
    (2) Different from notice of claim against public
       entity ..................................................... 1-186
  d.  Service ...................................................... 1-186
    (1) By mail ................................................. 1-186
      (a) Compare—improper addresses ................. 1-187
      (b) Service effective upon mailing .................... 1-187
        1)  Actual notice not required .................... 1-187
      (c) Effect on 90-day notice period? ................. 1-187
  e.  Tolling of statute of limitations where notice
    served during last 90 days ............................. 1-188
    (1) Example ................................................ 1-188
    (2) Compare—no relief under CCP §473(b) for
       untimely notice .................................... 1-189
    (3) Other grounds for tolling 3-year statute ............. 1-189
    (4) No tolling as to intentional tort claims .............. 1-189
    (5) No tolling as to doctors not named or served
       with notice ........................................... 1-189
    (6) Tolling as to "Doe" defendants ..................... 1-190
  f.  Compare—medical information release
    required for prelawsuit settlement ...................... 1-190
 6.  New Home Construction Defect Claims ...................... 1-190
  a.  Compare—contractual ADR procedures not
    affected .................................................... 1-191
  b.  Prelawsuit notice requirement .......................... 1-191
    (1) "Builder" .............................................. 1-191
      (a) Compare—residential construction
        standards not limited to "builder" ................. 1-191
    (2) Manner of service ................................... 1-192
      (a) Service on designated agent ..................... 1-192
    (3) Contents ............................................. 1-192
    (4) Compare—notice not required for customer
       service requests ................................... 1-192
  c.  Postnotice procedures (optional with builder) ....... 1-192.1
    (1) Acknowledgment of receipt ......................... 1-192.1
    (2) Document disclosure ................................ 1-192.1
    (3) Election to inspect .................................. 1-192.1
    (4) Offer to repair ...................................... 1-192.1
      (a) Homeowner's response ......................... 1-192.2
    (5) Additional provisions ................................ 1-192.2
  d.  Statutes of limitations extended ........................ 1-192.2
**D.  PRELAWSUIT CONSULTATION REQUIREMENT IN
CERTAIN PROFESSIONAL NEGLIGENCE ACTIONS** .... 1-192.2
 1.  Certificate Required on Filing Action ...................... 1-192.2
  a.  Purpose .................................................... 1-192.2
  b.  Enforcement ............................................... 1-192.3
 2.  Actions Subject to Certificate Requirement ............... 1-192.3

      a.   Actions against certain construction
           professionals ........................................................ 1-192.3
   3.  Contents of Certificate ................................................ 1-192.3
      a.   Prelawsuit consultation showing merit................. 1-192.3
          (1)  Qualified consultant ...................................... 1-192.3
      b.   Excuse for lack of consultation ............................ 1-192.4
          (1)  Inability to obtain consultation ...................... 1-192.4
          (2)  Intent to rely solely on res ipsa loquitur .......... 1-192.4
          (3)  Imminent running of statute of limitations ...... 1-192.4
   4.  Filing and Service ...................................................... 1-192.4
   5.  Procedures for Attacking Lack of Certificate ............... 1-192.4
      a.   Comment ............................................................. 1-192.5
      b.   Compare—defective certificate ........................... 1-192.5
      c.   Attorney fees ...................................................... 1-192.5
          (1)  May include paralegal fees............................ 1-192.5
          (2)  Includes fees in obtaining award ................... 1-192.5
   6.  Consultation Privileged .............................................. 1-192.5
      a.   Not discoverable ................................................. 1-192.5
      b.   Exception—after judgment for defendant ............ 1-192.5
          (1)  Not applicable to settlements ....................... 1-192.6
   7.  Compare—Prelawsuit Notice to "Health Care
      Provider" .................................................................... 1-192.6
      a.   Compare—statute of limitations impact ............... 1-192.6

E.  **PRELAWSUIT ADR REQUIREMENT** ........................... 1-192.6
   1.  Enforcement of CC&Rs in "Common Interest
      Developments" (Condos, etc.) ..................................... 1-192.6
      a.   Application............................................................ 1-192.6
          (1)  "Common interest development" .................... 1-192.6
          (2)  Which actions............................................... 1-192.6
      b.   Procedure for requesting ADR ............................ 1-192.7
      c.   Certificate to accompany complaint ..................... 1-192.7
      d.   Effect of failure to comply ................................... 1-192.7
      e.   Attorney fees ...................................................... 1-192.7
   2.  Construction Claims by "Common Interest
      Developments" Against Builder ................................... 1-192.8
      a.   Notice to builder ................................................. 1-192.8
          (1)  Effect on statute of limitations ...................... 1-192.9
          (2)  Effect of commencing suit without notice ....... 1-192.9
      b.   Builder's response .............................................. 1-192.9
      c.   Settlement offers ................................................ 1-192.10
      d.   Members to be notified of settlement offer ......... 1-192.10
      e.   Time limits .......................................................... 1-192.10
      f.    Privileges (cases filed after 6/30/02) ................. 1-192.10
      g.   Trial priority (cases filed after 6/30/02) .............. 1-192.11

F.  **EXHAUSTION OF OTHER REMEDIES** ...................... 1-192.11
   1.  Exhaustion of Administrative Remedy ........................ 1-192.11
      a.   Jurisdictional....................................................... 1-192.11
          (1)  Waiver ......................................................... 1-192.11
          (2)  Estoppel ...................................................... 1-192.11

b. Compare—statutes creating both administrative and judicial remedies ........................................ 1-192.12
c. "Exhaustion" .................................................... 1-192.12
   (1) Compare—seeking rehearing before administrative tribunal ............................... 1-192.12
   (2) Compare—several administrative remedies available ...................................................... 1-192.13
d. Exceptions to exhaustion doctrine ..................... 1-192.13
   (1) Remedy inadequate, unavailable or futile .... 1-192.13
   (2) Challenge to constitutionality of administrative body ...................................... 1-192.13
   (3) Federal civil rights claims ........................... 1-192.13
e. Compare—exhaustion of *judicial* remedies ........ 1-192.13
f. Compare—"primary jurisdiction doctrine" .......... 1-192.14
   (1) Rationale .................................................... 1-192.14
   (2) Discretionary ............................................. 1-192.14
2. Exhaustion of Internal Grievance Procedures ......... 1-192.15
a. Application ...................................................... 1-192.15
   (1) Discipline, expulsion .................................. 1-192.15
   (2) Related damage claims .............................. 1-192.15
b. Limited judicial review (mandamus) .................... 1-192.15
c. Compare—where no hearing held ...................... 1-192.16
3. Contractual Arbitration ............................................. 1-192.16

**G. PRIOR COURT ORDER REQUIRED FOR CERTAIN PLEADINGS** ............................................................. 1-192.16
1. Statutes Restricting "Pleadability" of Certain Claims .................................................................... 1-192.16
a. Effect .............................................................. 1-192.17
2. Actions for Childhood Sexual Abuse ....................... 1-192.17
a. Claims against third parties barred if plaintiff age 26 or older ............................................... 1-192.17
b. Procedural requirements where plaintiff age 26 or older .......................................................... 1-192.17
   (1) Complaint naming "Doe" defendants ........... 1-192.17
   (2) Certificate of merit .................................... 1-192.17
   (3) Amendment of complaint; certificate of corroborative fact ........................................ 1-192.18
   (4) Effect of failure to comply ......................... 1-192.18
3. Actions by Vexatious Litigants ................................. 1-192.18
a. Notice and hearing required ............................. 1-192.18
b. Persons subject to statute .............................. 1-192.18
   (1) Persons controlling litigation ...................... 1-192.18
   (2) Present representation by counsel immaterial ...................................................... 1-192.19
c. Based on number of unsuccessful suits filed ..... 1-192.19
   (1) "Finally determined adversely" ................... 1-192.19
   (2) "Immediately preceding" seven-year period .......................................................... 1-192.19
d. Bond requirement ............................................ 1-192.20
   (1) No "reasonable probability" of recovery ........ 1-192.20

    (2) Financial ability immaterial .......................... 1-192.20

**H. FILING FEE CONSIDERATIONS** .................. 1-192.20
  1. Bounced Check Problem .......................... 1-192.21
    a. Effect on pending hearings ................ 1-192.21
    b. Relief under CCP §473? ................ 1-192.21

**FORMS**
- Letter Agreement for Hourly Rate Fee .................. 1-193
- State Bar Sample Written Fee Agreement—Hourly Litigation .................. 1-197
- State Bar Sample Written Fee Agreement—Hourly Non-Litigation .................. 1-200
- State Bar Sample Written Fee Agreements—Other Clauses of Interest in Fee Agreements .................. 1-200.3
- Guarantee Agreement .................. 1-200.5
- Contingency Fee Agreement .................. 1-201
- State Bar Sample Contingency Fee Agreement .................. 1-206
- Notice of Lien .................. 1-207
- Petition to Confirm, Correct, or Vacate Attorney-Client Fee Arbitration Award .................. 1-208.1
- Rejection of Award and Request for Trial After Attorney-Client Fee Arbitration .................. 1-208.4
- Claim Against Governmental Entity (City of Los Angeles) .................. 1-209
- Claim Against Governmental Entity (California State Board of Control) .................. 1-211
- Application for Permission to Present Late Claim Against Governmental Entity .................. 1-213
- Petition for Order Permitting Late Claim Against Governmental Entity .................. 1-214
- Checklist: Petition for Relief From Requirement to File a Government Claim .................. 1-216
- Creditor's Claim Against Decedent's Estate .................. 1-217
- Notice of Rescission .................. 1-219
- Notice of Breach of Warranty .................. 1-220
- Notice of Intent to Commence Action Against Health Care Provider .................. 1-221
- Certificate of Merit (Professional Negligence Actions) .................. 1-222

**RESERVED**

# PRELAWSUIT CONSIDERATIONS

---

### STRATEGY CONSIDERATIONS

[1:1]

This Chapter covers various preliminary considerations in handling a civil lawsuit: the initial client contact and interview; the determination whether to take the case, and on what fee basis; initial investigation of the facts and legal research; early tactical planning; initial contact with the opposing party or counsel; and (where required) prefiling notices, claims and demands.

These prefiling considerations may impact the lawsuit in a variety of ways:

- First of all, careful investigation, research and analysis are crucial to successful litigation. Poor investigation or analysis leads to poor case selection, increasing the risk of loss. On the other hand, careful analysis at the outset enables the lawyer to choose the most effective strategies and tactics for resolution of the lawsuit.

- Initial interviews with the client set the *tone* for the attorney-client relationship. Particularly where attorney and client are new to each other, their prelawsuit conferences are the groundwork upon which the client gains confidence in the attorney's recommendations.

- Prelawsuit contacts with opposing counsel also set the tone for their dealings throughout the case. Again, particularly where they are new to each other, their initial discussions and correspondence may form impressions as to whether the opposing counsel is well-prepared, cooperative, reasonable, etc.

- Finally, in certain cases, prelawsuit notices and demands may affect the client's right to proceed; *see* ¶*1:567 ff.*

---

## A. ACCEPTING A NEW CASE

1. **[1:2]** **First Contact With Client:** The first contact with a prospective client is usually by telephone. The client's purpose is to determine whether you are interested in handling his or her case. Your purpose should be to determine whether to meet personally with the prospective client to consider taking the case.

a. [1:3] **Take the call personally:** When you receive a telephone call from a prospective client, it is good practice to speak with the caller yourself, rather than simply have a secretary set up an appointment. Prospective clients usually appreciate a show of personal concern from the lawyer at the outset. Moreover, after having spoken with you on the telephone, they may find it easier to communicate with you during the office interview.

b. [1:4] **Determine basic information:** Take the time during this initial phone call to learn a few basic facts about the prospective client and his or her case:

   (1) *Why* he or she wants to see you (e.g., the client has been injured; or has been served with a summons and complaint).

   (2) In very general terms, the *nature of the case* (e.g., whether and how the caller has been damaged).

   (3) *When* the operative facts occurred, so that you will be able to determine possible statute of limitations problems.

   (4) *Who else is involved* (e.g., the names of potential opposing or coparties or important witnesses). Such information may disclose obvious conflicts of interest (¶*1:39 ff.*). It also may be helpful in determining whether some third person should attend the first office interview with the client.

   (5) *What documents* are necessary for the first meeting. Often, unless requested to do so, prospective clients fail to bring crucial contracts, letters, accident reports, etc.

   (6) Whether *any lawsuit has been commenced.* People often wait until the last minute to deal with legal problems. If a deadline is imminent, and there is not enough time to meet with the client, you may have to call opposing counsel and ask for a continuance or an extension of time to plead, etc.

   ☞[1:4.1] *PRACTICE POINTER: Make it clear* both to the caller *and to the opposing counsel that you have not yet been retained.* You should tell opposing counsel when you expect to know whether you will represent the potential client. If a continuance is granted on such terms, confirm the arrangement with a letter. Be sure to send copies to the prospective client, clearly stating that you have *not* yet agreed to assume representation, so that the client will be aware of the possible need to hire other counsel.

c. **[1:5] Determine referral source:** Finding out how the client was referred to you enables you to send a thank you note to the person who made the referral. This is not only a matter of common courtesy, but also an excellent way of encouraging future referrals.

d. **[1:6] Set up office interview:** If the case appears worthwhile, you should invite the caller to meet with you. Usually, the meeting should be scheduled *as soon as possible*, as most prospective clients will be concerned about their problems and will be seeking prompt advice.

⊏⟩**[1:7] *PRACTICE POINTER:*** If you are pressed for time, don't hesitate to suggest "creative" scheduling— e.g., early mornings, lunch hours, evenings, etc. Such flexibility favorably impresses potential clients.

e. **[1:7.1] Confirm decision to decline case in writing:** If you decide not to take the case (either at the time of the initial telephone call or after an office interview), *send a letter* to the prospective client confirming that fact and *warning of any apparent deadlines* for taking legal action (e.g., statute of limitations, time to file claim or answer, etc.). Doing so may avoid misunderstandings and later claims by the prospective client that you agreed to take the case and failed to file suit before the statute of limitations had run, etc.

2. **[1:8] First Meeting With Client:** The purpose of the first meeting is *not* to figure out all the problems and issues in the case. Rather, it is basically to enable the *client* to decide whether you can and should represent him or her; and to enable *you* to decide whether you can and should represent this person.

a. **Preparing for the meeting**

(1) **[1:9] Do some preliminary research:** You will know from your initial telephone conversation the general nature of the prospective client's problem. Brush up on the relevant law in that area. Also, if possible, find out what you can about whatever business or industry the client is engaged in, if relevant to the problem. (The Internet may be a valuable resource for such research.) The more conversant you are with the factual and legal issues, the better questions you will ask, and the better your chances for a successful first meeting.

(2) **[1:10] Block out time:** As a rule of thumb, set aside 30-60 minutes for your initial interview (more, if your telephone contact indicates this may be necessary). In any event, do whatever you can to *avoid interruptions*. Interruptions not only distract you, but also may cause

the potential client to think you are too busy to handle his or her problem.

b.  [1:11]  **Handling the meeting:**  It is up to the lawyer to guide the conversation. Here are the matters that need to be covered:

(1) [1:12]  **Ascertain essential facts:**  Obviously, the first thing you need to know is what has happened to the client to cause him or her to seek legal advice.

(a) [1:13]  **Interview techniques:**  There are two interview techniques that may be used to ascertain what happened. Effective interviewing often combines both methods:

1) [1:14]  **Narrative:**  Ask the prospective client to tell you what happened. You mainly listen and interrupt only to clarify. This technique allows you to hear a complete story put in the person's own words. It also often has a cathartic benefit for the prospective client, who is anxious to tell the story from the beginning to end.

2) [1:15]  **Question and answer:**  This allows the attorney to control the scope of the conversation, and reduces digressions by the prospective client. The danger is that the attorney may appear overbearing, or may not ask all of the right questions!

⇨[1:15.1]  *PRACTICE POINTER:*  Usually, the most effective technique is the narrative approach *followed by* questions and answers. The follow-up questions enable the attorney to confirm his or her understanding of the client's story and to fill in gaps in the client's narration.

(b) [1:16]  **Take good notes:**  You will want to prepare a memorandum following the interview. In addition, your note-taking usually will convey to the client the impression that you are well-organized and are concerned about the matter.

⇨[1:17]  *PRACTICE POINTER:*  Client interview sheets and checklists of standard interview questions should be utilized wherever applicable. They help you ask the necessary questions and record the client's answers. For certain types of recurrent litigation (i.e., auto accident, wrongful termination), *questionnaires* to be filled out by the prospective client may be useful.

Some lawyers prefer to *tape-record* the initial conference (with the client's consent of course). Doing so captures everything the client says and may protect the lawyer in the event a question later arises regarding what was said at the meeting. (Bear in mind, however, that in the event of a dispute with the client, the tape recording will be *discoverable* by both the client and the State Bar. See CCP §2018(e) & (f).)

(2) [1:17.1] **Determine whether dispute subject to arbitration:** More and more contracts contain arbitration clauses. In the course of the review of relevant documents, be sure to look for such a clause and discuss its effect with the prospective client.

(3) [1:18] **Discuss the law generally:** After the salient facts are ascertained, the client will expect to know what you think about his or her case. You should discuss rights and liabilities *generally*, because further investigation and legal analysis usually will be necessary. Avoid premature conclusions on liability or the value of a case. Instead, make it clear that such matters will *depend on proving* whatever facts are essential to the claim or defense.

   (a) [1:19] Some clients (particularly those who have been "shopping" attorneys) may press you to venture an opinion as to the value of their case at the initial interview. *Avoid* doing so. "Shooting from the hip" can be embarrassing later on. It may even harm the client and expose you to claims of malpractice if the case turns out differently than the opinion you expressed.

   (b) [1:20] Do not be afraid to tell the client you will need to investigate the facts further or to research the law in order to form an opinion regarding the case. Most prospective clients will understand and appreciate a cautious approach.

   (c) [1:21] Obviously, if the matter is outside your field, you will need to associate or consult with other counsel before expressing *any* opinion. (Or, alternatively, turn down the case!) [See Rule 3-110 of the California Rules of Professional Conduct, *discussed at ¶1:172-174*]

(4) [1:22] **Discuss any deadlines applicable:** You should have ascertained any deadlines during your initial telephone conversation. Go over them again with

the client. If dealing with a prospective plaintiff, be specific as to statutes of limitation, deadlines on filing administrative claims, etc. If dealing with a prospective defendant, focus on dates for filing responsive pleadings, etc.

(5) [1:23] **Discuss strategy alternatives:** It is not necessary (or prudent) to *decide* which course of action to pursue at this first meeting. But the range of alternatives should be presented to the prospective client, as it may affect his or her decision regarding employing counsel. Among the possible alternatives to consider are:

(a) [1:24] **Doing nothing:** If the client's claim is tenuous or too expensive to pursue, or if litigation might cause other problems (e.g., adverse publicity), the client may decide to abandon the claim.

(b) [1:25] **Seeking early settlement:** The client should be given an estimate of the cost, time and effort likely to be incurred in litigation. The possibility of early negotiations toward settlement and other alternative dispute resolution ("ADR") procedures should be explored (*see* ¶*1:31, 1:478*). Seeking settlement should *not* be viewed as a sign of weakness, but rather as an intelligent evaluation of the risks vs. benefits of litigation.

If suit is filed, counsel must discuss settlement and other matters with opposing counsel at least 30 days before the case management conference (*see* ¶*12:77.5 ff.*). The court will inquire at the case management conference whether a settlement conference should be scheduled and whether the case is suitable for ADR. [CRC 121(e)(6),(7); *see* ¶*1:478, 12:82 ff.*]

(c) [1:26] **Limited litigation:** The client should be told that litigation is not necessarily an "all-out war" that cannot be controlled. Rather, the possibility of a limited, cost-conscious approach should be discussed. Of course, the client must be advised that the opposition may escalate the lawsuit and take control out of your hands.

(d) [1:27] **"All-out" litigation:** Many clients *want* "all-out war" in every lawsuit. They expect the attorney to prosecute or defend their case vigorously and to assert every conceivable claim and defense. The costs and risks of such "all-out" litigation must be explained to the client.

1) [1:28] **Caution—ethical limitations:** You walk a difficult line when dealing with clients

who insist on "all-out" warfare in civil litigation. You should not be (or appear to be) afraid to assert all plausible claims or defenses. But there are ethical limitations against asserting nonmeritorious claims and defenses (*see* ¶*1:166*). These ethical limitations *supersede* any obligation to your client. Violation thereof may expose you to professional discipline (¶*1:167*).

2) **[1:29] Caution—risk of sanctions:** Adhering slavishly to the client's demands, rather than exercising independent judgment, could also prove costly: By signing pleadings, *counsel certifies* (subject to sanctions) that:
— the pleading is *not* being presented primarily for an improper purpose;
— the claims, defenses and legal contentions are warranted by existing law or by a *nonfrivolous* argument for the extension, modification, or reversal of existing law or the establishment of new law; and
— the allegations, factual contentions or denials of factual contentions have *evidentiary support* or, if specifically so identified, are likely to have such support. [CCP §128.7; *see discussion at* ¶*9:1135 ff.*]

3) **[1:30] Caution—risk of attorney fee award:** If there is a contract or statute authorizing fee awards to the prevailing party (*see* ¶*1:224 ff.*), your client could end up paying the opposing party's attorney fees if you lose the case. "Scorched earth" litigation tactics which run up legal fees on both sides of the case increase the downside of losing the case!

(6) **[1:31] Discuss ADR:** The client should be made aware of alternative forms of dispute resolution (ADR) that might be utilized to reach the legal objective sought: e.g., mediation, arbitration, neutral fact-finding, etc. If such procedures would be appropriate to the case, they should be explained to the client and evaluated as viable alternatives to a lawsuit. *See discussion at* ¶*1:478 ff.*

(7) **[1:32] Discuss timing:** Most clients are concerned not only with what will happen, but also with *when* it will happen. Therefore, the attorney should rough out a likely timetable for the lawsuit . . . e.g., how long it will take to get a complaint (or answer) on file; to complete discovery; to get to trial; the time involved if the opposing party appeals a judgment in the client's favor, etc.

⇨[1:33]  **PRACTICE POINTER:**  Be careful not to promise more than you can deliver on timing: i.e., avoid committing yourself to getting a pleading on file "within the next 2 weeks" unless you are *sure* you can do so. The client may assume that delays later in the lawsuit are your fault if you are unable to meet your commitments at the outset.

(8) [1:34]  **Discuss yourself:**  The prospective client must decide whether to employ you. He or she therefore will probably want to ask questions concerning your background, experience, ability and the resources available through you (access to investigators, experts, etc.). You should invite such questions, and answer them directly and completely. The prospective client probably will be measuring such intangibles as your personality and demeanor in response to his or her questions.

A brochure describing your firm and its experience (or similar information on a Web site) may inspire a prospective client's confidence in your capabilities.

You also will need to discuss the matter of *fees and costs; see* ¶*1:199 ff.*

[1:34.1-34.4]  *Reserved.*

(9) [1:34.5]  **Discuss potential negatives:**  The prospective client should be made aware, at the earliest possible time, of potential negative effects of the proposed litigation. For example:

- [1:34.6]  If the client loses, he or she will usually be liable for the opposing party's *court costs*; and, if the action is one in which attorney fees are awardable (*see* ¶*1:224 ff.*), he or she will also be liable for the opposing party's *attorney fees.* The client should be aware of this risk, including the *dollar amounts* that may be involved.

- [1:34.7]  Likewise, if there is any basis for a *cross-complaint* against your client, this risk should be discussed and evaluated.

- [1:34.8]  Advise the prospective client that litigation may take a long time, maybe several years, especially if an appeal is involved. Is the prospective client prepared to remain emotionally and *financially* committed to the litigation for this long a time period? (This may lead to further consideration of early settlement or ADR; *see* ¶*1:31.*)

- [1:34.9]  If the client's claims affect "free speech" rights in connection with public matters, plaintiff may be exposed to liability under the anti-SLAPP statute (CCP §425.16) for defendant's costs and attorney fees (*see ¶7:207 ff.*).

(10) [1:34.10]  **If potential client has been sued, consider insurance coverage:**  Many claims against prospective clients are or may be covered under liability insurance. If there is even a *potential* for such coverage, the insurer is usually required to provide a defense at no cost to the insured. Therefore, analyze available insurance coverage before undertaking defense of a prospective client.

Because a potential for coverage may exist in situations beyond those with which many lawyers are familiar, it may be good practice to *consult an insurance law specialist*. Failure to do so may be malpractice because failing to turn the matter over to the client's insurer exposes the client to unnecessary expense.

(11) [1:34.11]  **Consider insurance consequences of cross-complaint:**  In representing defendants, there is a natural tendency to look for possible bases for a cross-complaint. Be careful, however, about asserting claims that could trigger liability insurance coverage. This will bring in counsel to defend the cross-complaint at no cost to the plaintiff, which may run up the cost of the cross-complaint and defending the lawsuit generally.

[1:34.12-34.14]  *Reserved.*

(12) [1:34.15]  **Be careful about allowing third persons to "sit in" on conference:**  The attorney-client privilege may be jeopardized if third persons are present during the conference unless their presence is *necessary to further the client's interest* (e.g., parent, spouse) or to facilitate communication with the lawyer (e.g., interpreter). [See Ev.C. §952—no privilege for information transmitted in presence of unnecessary third persons; see also *Marshall v. Marshall* (1956) 140 CA2d 475, 480, 295 P2d 131, 134]

c.  [1:35]  **Confidential communications protected even if attorney not retained:**  Conversations and communications between an attorney and prospective client are protected by the *attorney-client privilege*, so long as confidential in nature and made in order to obtain legal advice. This is true even if the attorney consulted is *not* ultimately retained to represent the client. [Ev.C. §954; *Sullivan v. Sup.Ct. (Spingola)* (1972) 29 CA3d 64, 69, 105 CR 241, 243] (Except where necessary to prevent the client from committing a criminal act likely to cause death or serious bodily harm; see Ev.C. §956.5.)

Likewise privileged are communications *from the lawyer* to the client relating to the matter in question, even though the client has not yet decided to retain counsel. [*Benge v. Sup.Ct. (Mac Machines)* (1982) 131 CA3d 336, 347, 182 CR 275, 280]

(1) **[1:36]** **Rationale:** Unless a prospective client makes known to the lawyer *all* the facts, the advice which follows will be useless, if not misleading. Any lawsuit filed might be conducted along improper lines, and the trial might be full of surprises, resulting in much wasted litigation. Moreover, unless the prospective client knows that the lawyer cannot be compelled to reveal what is told to him, the client may suppress what he or she thinks to be unfavorable facts. [*City & County of San Francisco v. Sup.Ct.* (1951) 37 C2d 227, 235, 231 P2d 26, 30]

⇨**[1:37]** *PRACTICE POINTER:* Tell the client at the outset of the interview of the existence of the privilege and how it works. Make sure he or she understands that the privilege can be *waived* if he or she *discloses to third parties* whatever was said during the interview.

3. **[1:38]** **Determining Whether to Take the Case:** There are a variety of considerations affecting the attorney's decision whether to accept representation of a prospective client in a particular case. The following are the considerations applicable to all cases:

a. **[1:39]** **Ethical considerations—conflict of interest limitations:** First and foremost, an attorney may be barred from accepting or continuing to represent a client by conflict of interest limitations. *The following is a broad overview* of those limitations.

*Cross-refer:* For detailed discussion, see Vapnek, Tuft, Peck & Wiener, *Cal. Prac. Guide: Professional Responsibility* (TRG), Ch. 4.

(1) **[1:40]** **California Rules of Professional Conduct:** The following provisions of the California Rules of Professional Conduct ("CRPC") may be relevant in determining whether an attorney is disqualified from representing a client because of conflicting interests:

(a) **[1:41]** **Interests to be disclosed:** "A member shall not accept or continue representation of a client without providing written disclosure to the client where:

— "the member has or had a legal, business, *financial, professional, or personal relationship* with a *party or witness* in the same matter," which relationship would affect the member's representation; or

— the member has or had a similar relationship with another person or entity the member knows or reasonably should know *would be affected substantially* by resolution of the matter; or

— the member has or had a "legal, business, financial, or professional interest" in the *subject matter* of the representation. [CRPC 3-310(B) (emphasis added)]

(b) [1:42] **Relationship with opposing counsel to be disclosed:** Similarly, "(a) member shall not represent a client in a matter in which another party's lawyer is a *spouse, parent, child or sibling of the member*, lives with the member, is a client of the member, or has an *intimate personal relationship with the member*, unless the member informs the client in writing of this relationship." [CRPC 3-320 (emphasis added)]

(c) [1:43] **Interests requiring clients' informed consent:** "A member shall not, without the informed written consent of each client":

— accept or continue representation of more than one client in a matter in which the clients' interests *actually or potentially* conflict; or

— represent a client in a matter "and at the same time *in a separate matter* accept as a client a person or entity whose interest in the first matter is *adverse* to the client in the first matter." [CRCP 3-310(C) (emphasis added)]

(d) [1:44] **Where confidential information acquired through representation:** Similarly, "(a) member shall not, without the informed written consent of the client or former client, accept *employment adverse to the client or former client* where, by reason of the representation of the client or former client, the member has obtained *confidential information material* to the employment." [CRPC 3-310(E) (emphasis added)]

(2) [1:45] **"Informed written consent":** "Informed written consent" means the client's or former client's written agreement to the representation after *full disclosure* of all relevant circumstances and of "the *actual and foreseeable adverse consequences* to the client or former client." [CRPC 3-210(A) (emphasis added)]

⇨ [1:46] *PRACTICE POINTER:* Any consent you prepare should provide the client with enough information to make an intelligent choice on whether to retain you as counsel; e.g., the specific ways in which your representation of both clients might impair the rights of one over the other. Broad, general, all-encompassing "consents" do not suffice.

(a) [1:47]   **Actual vs. potential conflicts:**   If the conflict is merely potential (there being no existing dispute between the clients in question), the attorney may accept the case with full disclosure to and informed written consent of both clients. [*Klemm v. Sup.Ct. (County of Fresno)* (1977) 75 CA3d 893, 899, 142 CR 509, 512]

If the potential conflict later develops into an actual conflict, the attorney must obtain an *additional* written consent, describing in particular the conflict that has arisen. [See CRCP 3-310 "Discussion"]

(b) [1:48]   **Consent to future conflicts upheld:**   A law firm representing multiple clients may ask each to agree that in the event a conflict arises with another of the firm's clients, the firm may continue to represent one against the other. By signing such agreement, the client (whom the firm now opposes) waives its right to disqualify the firm based on any presumption of breach of confidence arising from the "substantial relationship" between the former representation and the current litigation. [*Elliott v. McFarland Unified School Dist.* (1985) 165 CA3d 562, 573, 211 CR2d 802, 809; see *Zador Corp. v. Kwan* (1995) 31 CA4th 1285, 1300-1301, 37 CR2d 754, 761—joint clients' agreement not to disqualify Attorneys "notwithstanding any adversity that may develop" included cross-claims between them]

[1:49]   *Reserved.*

(3) [1:50]   **Effect:**   The above limitations may apply where:

- The interests of *present clients* conflict;

- The interests of *present and former clients* conflict;

- The *lawyer's relationship with third parties* (e.g., parties, witnesses, opposing counsel) creates a conflict;

- The lawyer's *personal interests* or relationships creates a conflict;

- The lawyer has *business or financial dealings* with the client;

- The lawyer received *confidential information* while previously representing the opposing party.

⮕[1:51] *PRACTICE POINTER:* It is essential that you create and maintain a system enabling you to *identify and cross-reference:*
— clients you and your firm represent or have represented;
— parties who have consulted you for potential representation;
— parties who have economic ties to you or your firm;
— parties to mediations and arbitrations where you or a member of your firm has acted as the mediator or abitrator;
— witnesses interviewed; and
— experts consulted.

This is *absolutely necessary* because the duty to disclose arises not only when the conflict is known but also when the lawyer "should have known."

[1:52-54] *Reserved.*

(4) [1:55] **Conflicts between present clients (*concurrent* representation):** Absent "informed written consent" (*see ¶1:45*), a lawyer may not concurrently represent clients who have *actual or potential* conflicts; nor may the lawyer represent one client against another in an *unrelated* matter. It is *immaterial whether the lawyer possesses confidential information* that could be misused to the prejudice of either client. [*Truck Ins. Exchange v. Fireman's Fund Ins. Co.* (1992) 6 CA4th 1050, 1054, 8 CR2d 228, 230]

The rule of disqualification in such cases is "per se and automatic" [*Flatt v. Sup.Ct. (Daniel)* (1994) 9 C4th 275, 284, 36 CR2d 537, 542]

*Cross-refer:* See detailed discussion in Vapnek, Tuft, Peck & Wiener, *Cal. Prac. Guide: Professional Responsibility* (TRG), Ch. 4.

(a) **Application**

- [1:56] In a shareholder derivative suit (shareholder suing on behalf of corporation for wrongs done to the corporation), a lawyer may not simultaneously represent the directors who are being sued for alleged misconduct and the corporation itself, absent informed written consent. The corporation's interests are aligned with the plaintiff and thus adverse to the directors. [*Forrest v. Baeza* (1997) 58 CA4th 65, 75, 67 CR2d 857, 863]

- **[1:57]** Attorneys representing Husband in a personal injury action could not represent Wife in marriage dissolution proceedings. [*Jeffry v. Pounds* (1977) 67 CA3d 6, 9-10, 136 CR 373, 376]

    [1:58-59] *Reserved.*

(b) **[1:60] Dropping one client no cure ("hot potato rule"):** The attorney cannot avoid disqualification by dropping one client in favor of the other (like a "hot potato"). The client dropped does not become a "former client" for purposes of assessing the conflict (lesser standards apply to "former" clients; *see* ¶1:65 ff.). [*Truck Ins. Exchange v. Fireman's Fund Ins. Co.*, supra, 6 CA4th at 1059, 8 CR2d at 233]

⇨[1:61] *PRACTICE POINTERS:* Be aware of the *potential* for conflict when you agree to represent two or more parties whose interests appear to be the same at the outset of the representation *but may later diverge.*

- For example, if two partners ask you to represent them in defense of a contract claim, there is a potential conflict because if either is forced to pay the claim, he or she will have indemnity rights against the other. Therefore, you may represent both *only* if you first obtain their *informed written consent.*

- Similarly, potential conflicts also exist when you are asked to represent simultaneously both a business entity and one or more of the persons who control that entity. [See CRPC 3-310(C)(1)]

In such cases, be sure you disclose *in writing* to each client all areas of potential conflict, including:
- conflicting client instructions;
- divergent client objectives;
- the need to advocate inconsistent positions;
- potential future areas of dispute (e.g., indemnity);
- possibility that one client may demand that certain information not be disclosed to another.

    [1:62-64] *Reserved.*

(5) [1:65]  **Conflicts between present and former clients (*successive* representation):**  Absent "informed written consent" (*see* ¶1:45), a lawyer may not represent a client in litigation against a former client that bears a "substantial relationship" to the earlier proceedings. [*Jessen v. Hartford Cas. Ins. Co.* (2003) 111 CA4th 698, 712, 3 CR3d 877, 887]

*Cross-refer:* See detailed discussion in Vapnek, Tuft, Peck & Wiener, *Cal. Prac. Guide: Professional Responsibility* (TRG), Ch. 4.

(a) [1:66]  **Knowledge of confidential information conclusively presumed:**  Where a "substantial relationship" exists between the present and former litigation, *and* the nature of the employment was such that confidential information material to the case *would normally* be imparted, such knowledge is conclusively presumed and disqualification is mandatory. [*Flatt v. Sup.Ct. (Daniel)* (1994) 9 C4th 275, 283, 36 CR2d 537, 541]

(b) [1:67]  **What constitutes "substantial relationship":**  A "substantial relationship" exists whenever the "subject matter" of the prior and the current representations are linked in some rational manner. [*Flatt v. Sup.Ct. (Daniel)*, supra, 9 C4th at 283, 36 CR2d at 541]

"Subject matter" includes information material to the "evaluation, prosecution, settlement or accomplishment of the litigation or transaction." [*Jessen v. Hartford Cas. Ins. Co.*, supra, 111 CA4th at 712, 3 CR3d at 884-887]

1) [1:68]  **Factors considered:**  In determining whether the same "subject matter" is involved, courts consider the following:
— similarities between the two factual situations;
— similarities between the legal question posed; and
— the nature and extent of the attorney's involvement with the two cases. [*Morrison Knudsen Corp. v. Hancock, Rothert & Bunshoft* (1999) 69 CA4th 223, 234, 81 CR2d 425, 432; see also *Jessen v. Hartford Cas. Ins. Co.*, supra, 111 CA4th at 709, 3 CR3d at 884-885]

[1:69-79]  *Reserved.*

(6) [1:80]  **Vicarious disqualification of law firm?**  Where an attorney is disqualified from *concurrent* rep-

resentation, the entire law firm is vicariously disqualified. [*Henriksen v. Great American Sav. & Loan* (1992) 11 CA4th 109, 114, 14 CR2d 184, 187; ABA Model Code DR 5-105(D)]

The imputed disqualification applies even if the attorney with the conflict is "of counsel" to the firm. [*People ex rel. Department of Corporations v. SpeeDee Oil Change Systems, Inc.* (1999) 20 C4th 1135, 1156, 86 CR2d 816, 830]

   (a) **[1:81]** **Compare—successive representation cases:** A law firm may also be vicariously disqualified if one of its members *previously represented* the adverse party. A *presumption* of shared confidences applies. But this presumption may be rebutted by:

      • **[1:82]** Showing the firm had *effective screening procedures in place* to prevent passing information from the disqualified lawyer to others in the firm. [*People ex rel. Department of Corporations v. SpeeDee Oil Change Systems, Inc.*, supra, 20 C4th at 1150-1152, 86 CR2d at 826-828]

      • **[1:83]** Where although formerly employed by a law firm that represented the adverse party, the member did *not personally* handle the case and was *not reasonably likely to have obtained confidential information* regarding the adverse party. [See *Adams v. Aerojet-General Corp.* (2001) 86 CA4th 1324, 1339, 104 CR2d 116, 126]

      **[1:84-89]** *Reserved.*

   *Cross-refer:* See detailed discussion in Vapnek, Tuft, Peck & Wiener, *Cal. Prac. Guide: Professional Responsibility* (TRG), Ch. 4.

   (7) **[1:90]** **Procedure to disqualify lawyer or law firm for conflict:** If the conflict exists in a pending suit, the procedure to disqualify counsel is to file and serve a motion to disqualify or "recuse" counsel; *see* ¶9:406.5. (If no lawsuit is pending, a separate suit to *enjoin* the representation must be initiated.)

   **[1:91-94]** *Reserved.*

  b. **Ethical considerations—disqualification based on matters other than conflict of interests**

   (1) **[1:95]** **Hiring expert previously consulted by opposing party:** A law firm may be disqualified where

it retains an expert *knowing* the expert had previously been consulted (though not necessarily retained) by the opposing party. A rebuttable presumption arises that the expert shared confidential information obtained from the opposing party. [*Shadow Traffic Network v. Sup.Ct. (Metro Traffic Control, Inc.)* (1994) 24 CA4th 1067, 1084-1085, 29 CR2d 693, 702-703]

(2) **[1:96]** **Attorney as potential witness:** An attorney may be required to decline or withdraw from representation where the attorney will be called as a witness (by either the client or the opposing party) if the case goes to a jury trial. The risk is that the attorney's credibility as a witness may become an issue, thereby impairing his or her effectiveness as an advocate.

  (a) **[1:97]** **Rule of Professional Conduct:** An attorney "shall not act as an advocate" *before a jury* that will hear the attorney's testimony . . . unless the client gives "informed, written consent." [CRPC 5-210(C)]

  (b) **[1:98]** **Exceptions:** Client consent to continued employment in a civil case need not be obtained if the lawyer's testimony will relate solely to:

- An uncontested matter or a mere formality (e.g., identifying documents) (CRPC 5-210(A)); or

- The nature and value of legal services rendered in the case (e.g., to support an award of attorney fees) (CRPC 5-210(B)).

*Cross-refer:* See detailed discussion in Vapnek, Tuft, Peck & Wiener, *Cal. Prac. Guide: Professional Responsibility* (TRG), Ch. 4.

[1:99-165] *Reserved.*

c. **[1:166]** **Merits of case:** An attorney is prohibited from accepting employment if he or she knows or *should* know that the case lacks merit.

- An attorney's duty is to maintain "only such actions as appear to him legal or just . . ." [Bus. & Prof.C. §6068(c)]

- An attorney must refrain from accepting cases or conducting a defense "without probable cause *and* for the purpose of harassing or maliciously injuring any person." [CRPC 3-200(A)]

- Further, an attorney must refrain from presenting any claim or defense that is "not warranted under existing law, unless it can be supported by good faith argument for an extension, modification or reversal of existing law." [CRPC 3-200(B)]

- Finally, an attorney's signature on a pleading or other court paper *constitutes a certificate of merit:*
  — that the paper is not presented primarily for an improper purpose;
  — that the claims or defenses are warranted by existing law (or nonfrivolous argument for extension or change of existing law); and
  — that the claims or defenses have evidentiary support (or, if so identified that they are likely to have evidentiary support after reasonable opportunity for discovery). [CCP §128.7 (applicable to cases filed on or after 1/1/95); *see detailed discussion at ¶9:1135 ff.*]

(1) **[1:167] Overrides duty to client:** The attorney's public obligation to refuse nonmeritorious actions supersedes and prevails over the duty of "zealous" representation of the client's interests. [*Kirsch v. Duryea* (1978) 21 C3d 303, 309, 146 CR 218, 222]

(2) **[1:168] Lack of merit appearing after case filed:** If the attorney only discovers the lack of merit after the case has already been filed, the attorney should promptly ask to be relieved as counsel. An attorney is authorized to withdraw from a case whenever the client insists upon presenting a claim or defense that the attorney is ethically barred from handling (i.e., a claim or defense neither warranted under existing law nor supported by good faith argument for extension, modification or reversal thereof). [CRPC 3-200(B)]

(3) **[1:169] No malpractice liability for refusing to handle case:** An attorney who declines or withdraws from a case because he or she believes it lacks merit is ordinarily *not* liable in damages if it turns out the attorney was mistaken. Provided the client had time to secure other counsel, the attorney is generally protected against malpractice claims by the client. The attorney's choice to honor the public obligation "must be shown to have been so manifestly erroneous that no prudent attorney would have done so." [*Kirsch v. Duryea*, supra]

(a) **[1:170] Refusal made clear:** To avoid potential malpractice claims, the attorney's decision not to accept the case must be made clear to the prospective client . . . particularly where pleading or other deadlines are facing the client.

➯ **[1:171] *PRACTICE POINTER:*** Send a letter, fax or other formal notification following any meeting with a potential client in which you have declined to accept a case. Your letter should *warn the client regarding any deadline* and what action needs to be taken. Be sure to enclose and return any documents, photographs or other evidence received from the client (retaining photocopies if appropriate).

(4) **[1:172]** **Competence to handle case:** An attorney must not "intentionally, recklessly, or repeatedly fail to perform legal services with competence." [CRPC 3-110(A)]

To perform legal services "with competence" means to apply the *diligence, learning and skill,* and *mental, emotional* and *physical ability* "reasonably necessary" for the performance of the service. It includes the duty to *supervise* subordinates. [See CRPC 3-110(B), and accompanying "Discussion"]

(a) **[1:173]** **Handling cases beyond own expertise:** If lacking sufficient learning and skill (either on taking the case or during the course of representation), the attorney must either:

- *Associate* another lawyer reasonably believed to be competent;

- Where appropriate, professionally *consult* with another lawyer reasonably believed to be competent (this is limited to cases in which mere consultation can "fill the gap" in the attorney's learning or skill); or

- "Gear up" to handle the case—i.e., *acquire sufficient learning and skill* before performance is required (this alternative is appropriate of course only if the attorney has the time, resources and ability to do so). [CRPC 3-110(C)]

➡**[1:174]** *CAUTION:* Attorneys are notoriously poor judges of their own limitations, and often tend to take on more than they can handle.

It may be tempting to accept a big case with a big fee potential. But such cases are likely to draw opposing counsel who are more experienced than you are, and this may inhibit your client's chances for success.

Therefore, be *extremely careful* about deciding to learn a new field of law in order to handle a case offered to you. There is a substantial risk of malpractice liability and professional discipline in this situation!

[1:175-179] *Reserved.*

*Cross-refer:* See detailed discussion in Vapnek, Tuft, Peck & Wiener, *Cal. Prac. Guide: Professional Responsibility* (TRG), Ch. 6.

d. [1:180] **Time and resources, as consideration:** Even assuming there is no question as to the attorney's competence (or other ethical limitations on accepting the case), busy lawyers often decline representation because they lack the time or resources to handle the matter.

Experience teaches that mistakes usually are made because the lawyer has overextended himself or herself, so that there simply was not enough time to give each case the proper attention. Thus, experienced practitioners carefully evaluate their existing commitments before accepting new cases—in order to avoid disservice to the new client, to their existing clients, and to themselves!

e. [1:181] **Financial costs, as consideration:** Each new case in the office requires support staff (secretaries, paralegals, other lawyers) and overhead (filing, bookkeeping, etc.). In addition, there may be litigation costs to consider (filing fees, discovery expenses, expert witness fees, etc.).

If these costs are to be paid currently by the client, they should have little effect on the decision whether to take the case. But if not, the attorney must consider the amount of such costs, and how long it is likely to be before he or she will be compensated.

(1) [1:182] **Special costs considerations:** Certain types of cases involve special costs considerations:

(a) [1:183] **Nonresident plaintiff or foreign corporation:** If plaintiff resides outside California or is a foreign corporation, the court *may* order plaintiff to post an undertaking for any court costs and attorney fees that may be awarded to the defendant. [See CCP §1030; and *Shannon v. Sims Service Center, Inc.* (1985) 164 CA3d 907, 914, 210 CR 861, 865—constitutionality upheld; but see also *Baltayan v. Estate of Getemyan* (2001) 90 CA4th 1427, 1433, 110 CR2d 72, 77—court has discretion *not* to order undertaking where nonresident plaintiff is indigent]

1) [1:184] **Timing:** Such order may be made on defendant's motion any time before trial.

However, it is advantageous for defendant to move within 30 days after service because the court then has discretion to *stay all proceedings* pending determination of the motion. [CCP §1030(e)]

2) [1:185] **Procedure:** The motion must be supported by points and authorities and affidavits showing:

- plaintiff's nonresidency;

- a "reasonable possibility" defendant will prevail in the action; and

- the nature and amount of costs and fees defendant is likely to incur in the action. [CCP §1030(b)]

Granting or denial is discretionary; and the court's ruling is nonappealable. If an undertaking is ordered, it must be posted within 30 days or the action may be dismissed (*see* ¶11:280.1*). [CCP §1030(d),(g)]

(b) [1:186] **Malpractice actions:** In malpractice actions against hospitals, health care professionals, architects, engineers, etc., plaintiff may be ordered to file an undertaking for up to $500 to secure payment of defense costs ($1,000 if more than one defendant). Defendant must move for such an order within six months after service of summons (30 days if defendant is an architect, engineer, etc.), and must present affidavits showing that plaintiff's claim is "frivolous." If an undertaking is ordered, the action is subject to dismissal if not posted by plaintiff within the time allowed by the court. [See CCP §§1029.5, 1029.6; ¶11:280.4*]

(c) [1:187] **Other actions requiring security:** An undertaking or other security may be required in other actions as well, including:
— for issuance of a *preliminary injunction* (CCP §529 et seq., *see* ¶9:640*);
— shareholder's derivative actions (Corps.C. §800(c) ($50,000 limit regardless of number of defendants); and see *Hale v. Southern Calif. IPA Med. Group* (2001) 86 CA4th 919, 926, 103 CR2d 773, 778);
— actions to enforce fair political practices (Gov.C. §91012).

If you're being asked to undertake a matter involving any of these situations, check the applicable security bond statutes (CCP §995.010 et seq.).

(2) **[1:188]** **Waiver of court costs for indigents:** Indigent persons may apply for a waiver of court fees and costs (i.e., "to proceed in forma pauperis"). Such application must be on forms provided by the Judicial Council (Judicial Council Form Nos. 982(a)(17)-982(a)(20)). These forms require a showing that either:
— applicant is a welfare recipient; or
— family income is less than 125% of poverty line income established under federal law (based on number of dependents); or
— family income is otherwise insufficient to pay both for necessaries of life and court fees and costs. [Gov.C. §68511.3; CRC 985] (The application is confidential; see CRC 985(h).)

The application and accompanying pleadings must be accepted for filing even before the court rules on the application. The application is granted within five court days after it is filed unless acted upon by the court during that time. [CRC 985(e)]

Before denying the fee waiver petition, a hearing must be held. [*Simpson v. Sup.Ct.* (2001) 92 CA4th Supp. 1, 6, 111 CR2d 819, 822]

Persons granted *in forma pauperis* status must notify the court promptly of any change in financial status. Court staff may require additional documentation and may periodically request updated financial information. [CRC 985(g)]

(a) **[1:188.1]** **Only court costs and fees waivable:** Indigent persons may also obtain waivers for other court costs and fees, including jury, witness and reporter's fees. But they may still have to pay for other litigation expenses, such as deposition transcripts, expert witnesses, etc.

f. **[1:189]** **Nature of case or client, as considerations:** Often the decision whether to take a new matter may be based on intangible factors, such as:

(1) **[1:190]** **Interesting case?** Will the case be enjoyable, challenging, educational, professionally enriching or otherwise worthwhile to handle?

(2) **[1:191]** **Interesting client?** Will the attorney be *able* to work with the prospective client? If so, will the attorney *enjoy* working with the client?

(3) **[1:192]** **Potential for further business?** Sometimes a case will be accepted because it may lead to more business for the lawyer. The present case offered may be otherwise unacceptable to the attorney, but the

attorney may decide that the client could provide better cases in the future. Similarly, acceptance of a case from a good referral source could precipitate further referrals.

(4) **[1:193]** **Potential for enhancing attorney's reputation?** Sometimes the decision on accepting a case may depend in part on whether the outcome might enhance the attorney's reputation. (E.g., establishing a new theory of recovery or defense.)

4. **Fee Considerations**

a. **[1:194]** **Client responsibility for attorney fees:** In most cases, the attorney's compensation is a matter of contract, express or implied, with the client. [See CCP §1021—"Except as attorney's fees are specifically provided for by statute, the measure and mode of compensation of attorneys . . . is left to the agreement, express or implied, of the parties . . ."]

Further, except as noted below, the successful party *cannot* recover attorney fees as costs from the opposing party. [*Summers v. Newman* (1999) 20 C4th 1021, 1031, 86 CR2d 303, 309; see also *Young v. Redman* (1976) 55 CA3d 827, 835, 128 CR 86, 91]

*Cross-refer:* For detailed discussion of attorney fee agreements and fee considerations, see Vapnek, Tuft, Peck & Wiener, *Cal. Prac. Guide: Professional Responsibility* (TRG), Ch. 5.

⟱**[1:195]** *PRACTICE POINTER:* You owe an ethical obligation to explain the economic risks involved to your clients. It often comes as a surprise to them that they cannot force the opposing party to pay your legal fees. It may be a real shock for them to find out that a supposed "victory" in court could turn out to be an economic disaster because your legal fees exceed the amount recovered!

Therefore, make sure your clients understand from the outset that win, lose or draw, they are responsible for your fees. This may result in their taking a more realistic view of the case!

Where the prospective plaintiff's claim is for a relatively small sum, and your fees could cost a good deal, your best advice may be for the client to file in *small claims court* without a lawyer. Even if the claim exceeds small claims jurisdiction ($5,000; *see ¶3:41 ff.*), the client is sometimes better off waiving the excess and avoiding legal fees entirely.

(1) [1:196] **Limitation—representing minors:** A guardian ad litem must be appointed to represent the interest of a minor (who is not otherwise a ward or conservatee). Any settlement is subject to court approval and the court must determine the attorney fees payable out of such settlement. [See Prob.C. §1003; *and discussion at* ¶12:572 ff.]

(2) [1:197] **Cases where fees recoverable from opposing party:** There are cases in which courts are authorized to order the opposing party to pay all or part of the attorney's compensation. This may encourage the attorney to accept a case where the client's own financial resources are limited. Such alternative fee sources exist where:

- **Contract with opposing party authorizes fees award:** *See* ¶1:224.

- **Statute authorizes fee award:** *See* ¶1:287 ff.

- **Fee award authorized under court's equitable powers:** *See* ¶1:294.

⇨ [1:197.1] *PRACTICE POINTER:* Litigation costs (including any potential fee award) can be enormous, sometimes rivaling or even exceeding the amount of the claim. Therefore, in commencing or responding to litigation, it is critical to determine whether a statute, a common-law theory or a contractual provision may provide some method of shifting the fee burden to the opposing party. Sometimes, the mere threat of an attorney fees award alters the dynamics of the litigation. As noted by one court, "(t)he prospect of court-awarded attorney fees plays a significant part in determining a strategy for initiating or defending litigation." [*International Billing Services, Inc. v. Emigh* (2000) 84 CA4th 1175, 1187, 101 CR2d 532, 539]

(a) [1:198] **Compare—attorney fees as tort damages:** Attorney fees incurred by the client in instituting or defending an action as a direct result of the opposing party's tortious conduct may be recoverable as damages from the tort. [*Prentice v. North American Title Guar. Corp.* (1963) 59 C2d 618, 620-621, 30 CR 821, 823; see *Sindell v. Gibson, Dunn & Crutcher* (1997) 54 CA4th 1457, 1472, 63 CR2d 594, 602-603, and cases cited therein]

- [1:198.1] D's *fraudulent misrepresentations* caused P to incur attorney fees in pursuing meritless claim against TP. The fees incurred may be recoverable as damages from the fraud. [See *Gray v. Don Miller & Associates, Inc.* (1984) 35 C3d 498, 505, 198 CR 551, 556— real estate agent's fraud caused purchaser to believe his offer had been accepted and to sue seller for specific performance; see also *Shapiro v. Sutherland* (1998) 64 CA4th 1534, 1551, 76 CR2d 101, 111]

- **[1:198.2]** Lawyers allegedly were negligent in failing to document a community property waiver. As a result, Clients were forced to defend litigation that would have been avoided had the waiver been obtained. Fees incurred in the litigation may be recoverable as damages in Clients' malpractice action against Lawyers. [See *Sindell v. Gibson, Dunn & Crutcher,* supra, 54 CA4th at 1470, 63 CR2d at 602]

  **[1:198.3-198.4]** *Reserved.*

(b) **[1:198.5]** **Compare—attorney fees as losses covered by "hold harmless" agreements:** Attorney fees may also be recoverable where another person or entity has agreed to *indemnify* ("hold harmless") the client against specified claims or losses. (E.g., building contractors often agree to indemnify the property owner against claims asserted by subcontractors or others doing work on the property.) [See Civ.C. §2778(3)—indemnity against claims includes costs of defense; see also *Heppler v. J.M. Peters Co., Inc.* (1999) 73 CA4th 1265, 1297, 87 CR2d 497, 521]

b. **Fee arrangements with client**

(1) **[1:199]** **Types of fee arrangements:** There are four basic fee arrangements normally utilized by attorneys handling civil litigation:

(a) **[1:200]** **Hourly rate:** The client pays for the attorney's time, and often for support staff time (paralegal assistants, investigators, etc.) at designated hourly rates. Such fees are payable regardless of the outcome of the case.

1) **[1:200.1]** **Compare—blended rates:** Firms whose members have different billing rates sometimes quote a uniform rate no matter who works on the case. This rate is obtained by blending the anticipated proportion of work to be done by the persons charging the highest

rates with the percentage of work to be performed by persons charging the lower rates.

The problem with this arrangement is that clients sometimes feel the firm is assigning too many younger members and not enough partners to the case.

    2)  **[1:200.2]** **Compare—discounted rates:** Lawyers often offer discounted rates to attract new business. Discounts can also be offered on a *volume* basis; e.g., 10% discount on billings over $10,000 a month, etc.

(b)  **[1:201]** **Fixed fee:** The attorney charges a flat fee for the services to be rendered in the case, again regardless of the outcome.

Profitability depends on the lawyer's ability to estimate hours accurately and to work efficiently. The client gets the benefit of cost certainty.

(c)  **[1:202]** **Contingent fee:** The attorney's compensation is dependent upon the result achieved; usually, a percentage of what the plaintiff recovers, or what the defendant saves. Often, the attorney is required to advance costs in connection with such fee arrangement.

    •  There are also *reverse* contingency fees in which *defense counsel* are paid a share of the damages *avoided* on monetary claims against their clients.

(d)  **[1:203]** **Combination fee:** Sometimes, the fee arrangement will combine several of the above. For example, an attorney may charge a reduced hourly rate for his time *plus* a percentage of the recovery. Or, the arrangement may be for a contingent fee, *limited* to a fixed maximum amount.

    1)  **[1:203.1]** **"Capped fee":** The matter is handled on an hourly basis at standard rates but with a maximum fee (or "cap") to complete the job even if more hours are required.

    This arrangement protects the client but exposes the lawyer to considerable risk if the fee cap proves insufficient.

    2)  **[1:203.2]** **"Target fee":** The matter is handled on an hourly fee at standard rates up to a target estimated by the attorney. If the attorney is able to complete the work for less than the estimate, the attorney gets some percentage

(e.g., 50%) of the savings. Conversely, if the hours exceed the target, any billings thereafter are at a discounted rate (e.g., 50% discount from standard).

This arrangement encourages lawyer efficiency and still gives the lawyer some protection against conditions that require more hours than anticipated.

3) **[1:203.3]** **"Task billing":** To curb open-ended hourly billings, some corporate and insurance company clients insist on a fixed fee for *specified services.* (E.g., X dollars for filing an answer; Y dollars for preparing a routine set of interrogatories; Z dollars for preparing a summary judgment motion, etc.) This arrangement makes sense where attorneys can use relatively standardized pleadings and procedures (e.g., answers and interrogatories often used by defense counsel in personal injury cases).

4) **[1:203.4]** **"Value billing":** Some companies pay their lawyers a negotiated fixed fee, subject to an agreed upon increase or decrease *depending upon the result* achieved by counsel.

5) **[1:203.5]** **Partial contingency:** The lawyer's compensation depends in part on the outcome of the matter. Work is billed on an hourly basis (or even fixed fee) but there is a "kicker" provision for additional compensation that depends on the results.

(e) **[1:204]** **Litigation budgets:** Many clients now require firms representing them in litigated matters to furnish budgets itemizing the costs and fees likely to be expended *at each stage* of the litigation.

▷**[1:204.1]** *PRACTICE POINTER:* Whether or not required by the client, it is good practice to prepare such a budget and discuss it with the client at the outset of any litigation matter. Doing so may make the client more amenable to early settlement negotiations or ADR (*see* ¶*1:478*); and, if the client decides to go forward, the client is less apt to be unpleasantly surprised by and dispute your billings.

A litigation budget is good practice even in *contingency fee* cases (at least where litigation costs come off the top). Clients often have no idea of the costs and expenses that may be incurred and that will reduce their recovery.

[1:205]  *Reserved.*

(2) [1:206]  **Which type is appropriate:**  In some cases, it could be appropriate to consider several of the above as alternatives for handling a new case. In most situations, however, the choice is dictated by the nature of the case (e.g., most personal injury cases are handled on a contingent fee basis); or the nature of the client (e.g., most businesses will hire attorneys only on an hourly or flat fee basis, and will *not* pay contingent fees); or by the attorney's usual practice (e.g., an attorney handling a large volume of unlawful detainer cases can routinize his or her procedures and charge a fixed fee for each).

Once the appropriate type of fee arrangement is known, the particular case must be evaluated in light of the fee potential.

(a) [1:207]  For public policy reasons, contingency fee arrangements are not allowed in certain kinds of cases; e.g., marital dissolution cases if the services required would be "promotive of dissolution." [See State Bar Ethics Comm. Formal Opn.No. 1983-72]

(b) [1:208]  Governmental bodies may employ private attorneys on a contingency fee basis for certain kinds of cases (e.g., to recover damages), but *not* where private counsel is acting, in effect, as a public prosecutor (e.g., public nuisance abatement action against seller of allegedly obscene materials). In the latter case, due process demands "absolute neutrality" on the part of the lawyer (prosecutor) representing the government. [*People ex rel. Clancy v. Sup.Ct. (Ebel)* (1985) 39 C3d 740, 746-747, 218 CR 24, 27-28]

(3) [1:209]  **Evaluating hourly rate cases:**  Hourly rate cases are the easiest to evaluate. The only real consideration is whether the client is likely to pay the bill in a timely manner. This includes not only the client's *ability* to pay (financial condition), but the client's relative sophistication and *experience* in paying attorney fees on an hourly basis. I.e., a client who has never previously paid an hourly rate may be unprepared for the high legal fees likely to be incurred in civil litigation.

⇨[1:210]  *PRACTICE POINTERS*

• First of all, if the client has been referred to your office, it is not inappropriate to ask the referral source in a discreet manner if the client pays his or her bills.

- Any doubts as to payment habits can be allayed by *obtaining a retainer in advance.* Indeed, many lawyers require a sizable retainer for *all* litigation matters, because it impresses upon the client that litigation is expensive.

- *Don't be afraid to ask for a healthy retainer.* It forces the client to weigh the importance of the case, and the funds that will have to be committed to pursue it. One much-used rule of thumb is to request a retainer that will cover *at least* the first month's estimated fees. (If such a request scares off a prospective client, you are probably in luck . . . since that is the kind of client who is not likely to pay fees when billed!)

- If you are wary of the client's ability or willingness to pay fees after the retainer is used up, by all means include in your fee contract a provision requiring the client to renew the retainer after it is used up . . . so there will always be funds paid in advance.

- If handling the case on an hourly rate, tell the client your actual rate (rather than vague references to "customary" rates), so the client will not be surprised by your billings. Where written fee agreements are required, your hourly rate must be specified in the agreement (*see* ¶1:330).

- Be sure to prepare and discuss with the client a *litigation budget* covering the costs and fees likely to be incurred at each stage of the litigation (*see* ¶1:204). Also make sure the client understands that these are only estimates and that the expense could go higher. (For example: "It is impossible to know in advance what the total fees and costs will be. Much of our work may depend on the opposing party's willingness to cooperate and other uncertainties in litigation. However, this is our best estimate at present.")

- Be careful about taking *security* for payment of your fees (trust deeds, collateral, etc.). Unless certain precautions are taken, you may be violating the Rules of Professional Conduct (*see* ¶1:400).

- Payment by credit card is becoming more common. Consider contacting VISA, Mastercard, etc. for details.

(4) [1:211] **Evaluating flat rate cases:** Setting a flat rate requires knowing:

- What time is *ordinarily* required to do the work in question;

- What risks exist that the time required in the particular case may *exceed* the time ordinarily required; and

- What controls the attorney will have to minimize such risks.

(a) [1:212] The answers to these questions are usually derived after the attorney has had considerable experience in handling cases in a particular field, so that he or she will be able to anticipate problems.

(b) [1:213] Flat rates generally work best when the attorney is handling many similar cases for the same client. Losses resulting from problem cases are then offset by the higher profits from the "run of the mill" cases.

⇨[1:214] *PRACTICE POINTER:* Avoid flat rates for nonroutinized cases. Whatever rate you set will usually turn out to be too low (meaning loss to you), or too high (usually meaning an unhappy client!). And, fees grossly disproportionate to the work done may violate ethical rules against "unconscionable" fees. [CRPC 4-200; *see ¶1:373*]

(5) [1:215] **Evaluating contingent fee cases:** These are the most difficult cases to evaluate. A good starting point, at least, is to break the case down into the following components, and to evaluate each separately:

(a) [1:216] **Liability:** Evaluating liability requires knowing enough about the facts and law to make an intelligent appraisal. This is often difficult to do at the time of the initial client interview. It therefore often will be in the attorney's interest to expend time doing further investigation or research before deciding whether to accept the case. Doing so avoids poor case selection.

⇨[1:217] *CAUTION:* Remember the ethical ban on accepting nonmeritorious cases (¶*1:166*).

➪[1:218] *CAUTION:* Remember also that if you take a case, and then drop it because you think it's a loser, you are not entitled to *any* fees—even if the client ultimately recovers! (*See ¶1:448.*)

(b) [1:219] **Damages:** The extent of plaintiff's damages, and problems in proving (or disproving) plaintiff's claims must be considered. Some damages are easily calculable (e.g., medical expenses in a personal injury case). But others are difficult (e.g., pain and suffering, damage to the goodwill of a business).

➪[1:220] *PRACTICE POINTER:* One excellent way of evaluating damages is to research what similar cases have brought in the way of judgments in local courts. Jury verdicts in personal injury cases are reported and analyzed by several publishers (e.g., "Jury Verdicts Weekly," Santa Rosa, "Tri-Service Trial Reports," Los Angeles). To be sure, each case is unique; but patterns in jury verdicts do exist, and give some guidance for the attorney seeking to evaluate a case.

(c) [1:221] **Collectibility:** A judgment for damages is worthless unless the defendant is insured or has adequate assets. Therefore, the enforceability of any judgment recovered must be considered.

➪[1:222] *PRACTICE POINTER:* If there is no insurance, you must also consider whether the defendant is likely to file *bankruptcy* if a substantial judgment is obtained against him or her.

(d) [1:223] **Likelihood of early settlement:** Realistically, most cases settle before trial. But some cases settle sooner than others, resulting in earlier fees and less work for the attorney. In determining settlement potential, the attorney should look at:

• How *clear* the questions of liability;

• How *grievous* the damage;

• The amount of work and expense likely to be necessary, taking into account the resistance likely to be encountered;

- The opposing party's probable attitude toward early settlement (e.g., some insurance companies are notorious for not settling); and

- Any unique circumstances favoring, or hindering, settlement (e.g., a defendant may want to avoid unfavorable publicity).

c. **[1:224]** **Fees recoverable from opposing party pursuant to contract:** One of the exceptions to the "no attorneys' fees as costs or damages" rule (¶1:194) is that the court may award fees to the prevailing party where the parties have provided by contract for a fee award to either party. [See Civ.C. §1717(a)] (Such attorney fees provisions are common in promissory notes, leases, construction contracts, etc.)

➡️**[1:225]** *PRACTICE POINTERS:* Carefully review any documents involved for such provisions. Clients are often unaware of such provisions in contracts they sign. Or, they may never have seen the document in which the attorney fee provision appears; e.g., in a trust deed or other instrument of record affecting property they have purchased, and to which they are bound as successors in interest. [See *Mackinder v. OSCA Develop. Co.* (1984) 151 CA3d 728, 736-737, 198 CR 864, 870—non-assuming grantee of property bound by recorded deed restrictions creating right to attorney fees]

Also carefully consider whether, if the suit is unsuccessful, *the client may be liable for the opponent's fees* under such contract provisions or under statute or case law. If such potential liability exists, be sure to *warn* the client (preferably in writing) and evaluate the scope of this risk *before* initiating suit. Failure to do so may lead to a malpractice claim if the client loses.

[1:225.1-225.4] *Reserved.*

(1) **[1:225.5]** **Conditions precedent enforced:** Contractual conditions precedent to a fee award are enforceable; e.g., a provision that allows a fee award to a prevailing party only if that party first sought to resolve the dispute through mediation. [*Leamon v. Krajkiewcz* (2003) 107 CA4th 424, 432, 132 CR2d 362, 367—no fee award to prevailing party who did not satisfy contract provision requiring mediation before suit]

(2) **[1:226]** **Claims covered:** Civ.C. §1717(a) authorizes such awards "(i)n any action on a contract." [See *Milman v. Shukhat* (1994) 22 CA4th 538, 543-545, 27

CR2d 526, 529-530—includes declaratory relief actions]

Where noncontract claims (e.g., tort claims) are joined in "an action on a contract," the court's power to award fees on the noncontract claims depends on the *wording* of the attorney fees provision:

(a) [1:227] **Under provision limited to "actions on contract":** Where the provision covers only actions *"on the contract"* or "to enforce the contract," only fees for services relating to the contract cause of action are recoverable. [*Loube v. Loube* (1998) 64 CA4th 421, 430, 74 CR2d 906, 911—provision for fees in action "to enforce terms of the parties' agreement" did *not* authorize fee award in malpractice action]

Where noncontract (tort) causes of action are joined, an apportionment is required. [*Reynolds Metals Co. v. Alperson* (1979) 25 C3d 124, 129, 158 CR 1, 3; *Exxess Electronixx v. Heger Realty Corp.* (1998) 64 CA4th 698, 708-709, 75 CR2d 376, 383—where lease authorized fee award in action "to enforce the terms of the contract," lessee who prevailed in tort action (failure to disclose defects) not entitled to fees]

1) [1:228] **Compare—defending against tort claim:** Fee apportionment may be proper where the contract and tort claims are unrelated but *not* where a party must defend against a tort claim *in order to prevail on its contract* claim. (E.g., P sues to enforce contract; D cross-complains for rescission and fraud.) In such cases, the party prevailing on the contract claim is entitled to recover *all* of its fees. [*Siligo v. Castellucci* (1994) 21 CA4th 873, 879-880, 26 CR2d 439, 443]

[1:228.1-228.4] *Reserved.*

2) [1:228.5] **Compare—successful and unsuccessful contract claims:** Fee apportionment may also be required where plaintiff wins on one contract claim but loses another. Apportionment is not necessary, however, for representation on an issue *common to both* claims. [See *Acree v. General Motors Accept. Corp.* (2001) 92 CA4th 385, 400, 112 CR2d 99, 115]

[1:229] *Reserved.*

(b) [1:230]   **Under broader ("arising out of") fee provision:**   Most attorney fee provisions are worded more broadly than the above. The typical clause extends to disputes "arising out of the contract." Such a provision authorizes a fee award on tort as well as contract claims. [*Santisas v. Goodin* (1998) 17 C4th 599, 608, 71 CR2d 830, 836]

- [1:231]   Real estate sales agreement provided for attorney fees "in any litigation *arising out of* the execution of the agreement or the sale" of the property. This facially valid provision "embraces all claims, *both tort and breach of contract* . . . because all are claims 'arising out of' the execution of the agreement or the sale." [*Santisas v. Goodin,* supra, 17 C4th at 608, 71 CR2d at 836 (emphasis added)]

⇨[1:232]   *PRACTICE POINTER:*   For broadest possible coverage, the following wording is suggested:

"The prevailing party shall be entitled to attorneys fees in any action or proceeding *arising out of* this agreement and/or in any action or proceeding *to enforce a judgment* based on a cause of action arising out of this agreement."

(3) [1:233]   **Reciprocal right under Civ.C. §1717:**   A contract provision stating fees and costs incurred *to enforce the contract* are recoverable by one of the contracting parties (e.g., "Landlord shall be entitled to attorney's fees . . .") is read as a matter of law to authorize a fee award to *whichever* party prevails "*in any action on a contract.*" [Civ.C. §1717(a) (emphasis added)]

This reciprocal right cannot be waived in the contract. [Civ.C. §1717(a) (last para.)]

⇨[1:234]   *CAUTION:*   This makes every attorney's fee provision a "two-edged sword": Even if the contract states only your client is entitled to a fee award, if your client loses the case, your fee claim will fail . . . *and* the opposing party will be entitled to a fee award *against* your client!

[1:235]   *Reserved.*

(a) [1:236]   **Limited to fees on contract claims:** The reciprocal fee right under §1717(a) is not as broad as fees recoverable by the prevailing party under a broad attorney's fee clause (e.g., actions "*arising out of* the contract"). An award under §1717(a) is limited to fees and costs incurred in actions *to enforce the contract*, not tort claims. [*Moallem v. Coldwell Banker Comm'l Group, Inc.* (1994) 25 CA4th 1827, 1832, 31 CR2d 253, 255-256]

- [1:236.1] An action for *fraud* sounds in tort and is not "on the contract" for purposes of Civ.C. §1717, even where the alleged fraud occurred in connection with the contract containing the attorney fee clause. [*Stout v. Turney* (1978) 22 C3d 718, 730, 150 CR 637, 644]

(b) [1:237] **Where contract held invalid or unenforceable:** The validity or existence of the contract is not a prerequisite to an award of attorney fees under Civ.C. §1717: "(A) party is entitled to attorney fees under section 1717 even when the party prevails on grounds the contract is inapplicable, *invalid, unenforceable or nonexistent,* if the other party would have been entitled to attorney's fees if it had prevailed." [*Hsu v. Abbara* (1995) 9 C4th 863, 870, 39 CR2d 824, 828 (emphasis added; internal quotes omitted)]

1) [1:237.1] **Compare—illegal contracts:** A different rule applies where the *object* of the contract is illegal. In that event, the parties are in pari delicto and neither can enforce the contract. Therefore, there is no right to reciprocal fees. [*Bovard v. American Horse Enterprises, Inc.* (1988) 201 CA3d 832, 843, 247 CR 340, 346]

(c) [1:238] **Determining "prevailing party":** Fees may be awarded to the "prevailing party on the contract" if the case ends either in judgment or involuntary dismissal. The court, however, may also determine there is *no* prevailing party for purposes of a fee award. [Civ.C. §1717(b)(1)]

Any dispute as to which party "prevailed" must be determined on noticed motion, regardless of whether the action proceeds to judgment. [Civ.C. §1717(b)(1)]

The procedure to fix the *amount* of the fee award is discussed at ¶1:282 ff.

1) [1:239] **No "prevailing party" where plaintiff voluntarily dismisses:** If plaintiff voluntarily dismisses the action (including a voluntary

dismissal pursuant to settlement), there is no prevailing party for purposes of §1717 fees. [Civ.C. §1717(b)(2); *see detailed discussion at ¶11:39 ff.*]

a) **[1:240]** **Contract vs. tort claims:** Civ. C. §1717(b)(2) bars defendants from recovering fees in "any action on a contract." But it does not affect defendant's right to fees under a contract provision for fees to the *"prevailing party."* Under such a provision, defendant may be awarded fees incurred in connection with *tort* claims asserted alone or in conjunction with a contract claim. [*Santisas v. Goodin* (1998) 17 C4th 599, 617, 71 CR2d 830, 842; *see discussion at ¶11:39.20*]

2) **[1:241]** **Defendant may "prevail" by tendering amount due:** If defendant alleges and proves it tendered the *full amount* due prior to suit, it will be deemed the prevailing party. (The amount must be deposited with the court; and the court will order it invested in an insured interest-bearing account.) [Civ.C. §1717(b)(2)]

3) **[1:242]** **Net recovery may be determinative:** Where each party asserts contract claims against the other (complaint and cross-complaint), the party who recovers *more* than the other is the "prevailing" party. [Civ.C. §1717 (b)(1); *Haire v. Stevenson* (1987) 196 CA3d 1249, 1251-1252, 242 CR 433, 435]

However, "(t)he prevailing party determination is to be made only upon final resolution of the contract claims and only by a comparison of the extent to which each party has succeeded and failed to succeed in its contentions." [*Hsu v. Abbara* (1995) 9 C4th 863, 876, 39 CR2d 824, 833]

The party recovering "greater relief" is not necessarily the party receiving the greater monetary judgment. E.g., where one party has received earlier payments or other recoveries, the court has discretion to determine that he or she is the "prevailing" party even if required to pay a nominal net judgment. [*Sears v. Baccaglio* (1998) 60 CA4th 1136, 1154-1155, 70 CR2d 769, 781]

a) **[1:243]** **Noncontract claims disregarded:** If tort claims are joined in the same action, the "prevailing party" is determined with reference only to the *contract* claims. [Civ.C. §1717(b)(1)]

Effect: For fee purposes, P's recovery of $1,000 on a promissory note makes him or her the "prevailing party" notwithstanding D's recovery of $100,000 against P on a tort cross-complaint!

Of course, for judgment purposes, the contract claim would merely be an offset against the tort claim, and a net judgment would be entered in favor of D. [See Civ.C. §1717(c)]

Thus, D would be the "prevailing party" for *court* costs purposes under CCP §1032 (a) . . . while P would be the "prevailing party" for contract attorney fee purposes under Civ.C. §1717(b)!

b) **[1:244] Several contract claims:** In actions on several contracts, a party may "prevail" on one contract and not another. In such cases, the court may (discretionary) *offset* fee awards under one contract against amounts due under the other. [*Hunt v. Fahnestock* (1990) 220 CA3d 628, 633, 269 CR 614, 617]

c) **[1:245] Earlier recoveries considered:** The court has discretion to determine that a party who ends up having to pay a nominal net judgment is nevertheless the "prevailing" party under Civ.C. §1717 because of *earlier payments, settlements, insurance proceeds or other recovery.* [*Sears v. Baccaglio* (1998) 60 CA4th 1136, 1154-1155, 70 CR2d 769, 781]

4) **[1:246] Court's discretion:** The trial court has broad discretion in determining the "prevailing party"; and may determine there is *no* prevailing party for purposes of contract fee awards. [Civ.C. §1717(b)(1)]

In determining litigation success, courts respect substance rather than form and may be guided by equitable considerations: "For example, a party who is denied direct relief on a claim may nonetheless be found to be a prevailing party if it is clear that the party has otherwise achieved its main litigation objective." [*Hsu v. Abbara* (1995) 9 C4th 863, 877, 39 CR2d 824, 833]

On the other hand, where there *is* a clear winner, it is an abuse of discretion to find that the party is not the "prevailing party." [*Pacific Custom Pools, Inc. v. Turner Const. Co.* (2000) 79 CA4th 1254, 1257, 94 CR2d 756, 769]

a) **[1:247]** **Where plaintiff loses on contract claim but wins on others:** Where plaintiff asserts both contract and non-contract claims, and *loses* on the contract claim, the court has discretion to treat *defendant* as the prevailing party . . . even if plaintiff wins a judgment on the noncontract claim! [See *Korech v. Hornwood* (1997) 58 CA4th 1412, 1422, 68 CR2d 637, 643—P sued for breach of contract and to foreclose mechanic's lien; P won lien foreclosure but lost on contract claim; court held D was prevailing party]

b) **[1:248]** **No discretion where unqualified win on contract claim:** The court has *no* discretion to deny fees when the single contract claim presented results in an unqualified win for one party (i.e., "purely good news for one party and bad news for the other"). That party is the prevailing party as a matter of law. [*Hsu v. Abbara*, supra, 9 C4th at 875-876, 39 CR2d at 832]

　　1/ **[1:249]** **Equitable considerations disregarded:** In such cases, the court may not invoke equitable considerations unrelated to litigation success, such as the parties' behavior during settlement negotiations or discovery proceedings, to deny fees. [*Hsu v. Abbara*, supra, 9 C4th at 877, 39 CR2d at 833; see *Deane Gardenhome Ass'n v. Denktas* (1993) 13 CA4th 1394, 1398, 16 CR2d 816, 819]

(4) **[1:250]** **Nonsignatory's right to fees:** One not a party to a contract may recover fees as prevailing party in an action on the contract, *if it would have been liable* for such fees had it lost the action. [*Reynolds Metals Co. v. Alperson* (1979) 25 C3d 124, 128, 158 CR 1, 3]

(a) **[1:251]** **Nonsignatory plaintiffs:** A non-signatory suing to enforce a contract (e.g., as assignee or third party beneficiary) may recover fees as prevailing party under Civ.C. §1717 *if it would have been liable* for such fees had it lost the case. [*Steve Schmidt & Co. v. Berry* (1986) 183 CA3d 1299, 1315-1317, 228 CR 689, 699-700]

1) **Application**

- [1:252] Cooperating Broker sued to obtain commission due under listing agreement between Listing Broker and Owner. Cooperating Broker was entitled to attorney fees as prevailing party although not a party to the listing agreement. It was enough that he would have been *liable* for fees under the listing agreement had he lost his suit. [*Steve Schmidt & Co. v. Berry,* supra]

  [1:253-254] *Reserved.*

2) [1:255] **Compare:** But if the nonsignatory plaintiff is *not* liable for attorney fees under the contract, it cannot recover fees as prevailing party. [See *Leach v. Home Sav. & Loan Ass'n* (1986) 185 CA3d 1295, 1307, 230 CR 553, 561—trust beneficiary unsuccessfully sued to enjoin foreclosure of loan on trust property, held not liable for fees because she would have had no right to fees against lender had she won the action]

  - [1:256] Blue Cross contracted to reimburse Hospital for care furnished to Blue Cross subscribers. The contract contained an attorney fees clause. Hospital prevailed in a billing dispute with Patient, a Blue Cross subscriber. Hospital was not entitled to a fee award against Patient because Patient was neither a signatory to Hospital's contract with Blue Cross *nor a third party beneficiary* as to Blue Cross' promise to reimburse Hospital's charges. [*Whiteside v. Tenet Healthcare Corp.* (2002) 101 CA4th 693, 709, 124 CR2d 580, 590-591]

  [1:257-259] *Reserved.*

(b) [1:260] **Nonsignatory defendants:** Similarly, a nonsignatory defendant's right to recover fees as prevailing party turns on whether he or she would have been liable for fees had the other side won. [*Reynolds Metals Co. v. Alperson* (1979) 25 C3d 124, 128-129, 158 CR 1, 3]

1) **Application**

- [1:261] A nonsignatory who is sued *as if a party* to the contract (e.g., as alter ego or partner or coventurer of signatory corporation) can recover fees as prevailing party. Since the nonsignatory *would have been liable* for fees had it lost, it can recover fees when it wins. [*Reynolds Metals Co. v. Alperson*, supra; *Republic Bank v. Marine Nat'l Bank* (1996) 45 CA4th 919, 925, 53 CR2d 90, 93—sublease "incorporated by reference" terms of master lease, including fee provision, thus authorizing fee award against sublessee]

- [1:262] Defendants sued by Bank as "guarantors" of a promissory note were held not liable because they never signed the guaranty. They were entitled to recover attorney fees from Bank because, under the terms of the guaranty, Bank would have been entitled to attorney fees if it had prevailed. [*Rainier Nat'l Bank v. Bodily* (1991) 232 CA3d 83, 85-86, 282 CR 926, 927]

  [1:263-264] *Reserved*

2) [1:265] **Compare:** Purchaser of property lost suit against Seller's Broker for fraud in connection with purchase. Seller's Broker was *not* entitled to a fee award against Purchaser because it was not a party to the main body of the purchase contract containing the attorney fee provision. [*Super 7 Motel Associates v. Wang* (1993) 16 CA4th 541, 546, 20 CR2d 193, 197]

   But the result was different where the purchase contract *expressly provided* for a fee award in any dispute by *or against* the broker. This made Broker a party to that portion of the contract. [*Pacific Preferred Properties, Inc. v. Moss* (1999) 71 CA4th 1456, 1463, 84 CR2d 500, 504]

   [1:266-267] *Reserved.*

(5) [1:268] **Nonsignatory plaintiff's *liability* for fees:** Where plaintiff sues as an *assignee* or *third party beneficiary* to enforce a contract with an attorney fee provision, but loses the action, plaintiff's liability for fees depends on whether it could have enforced the attorney fee provision if it prevailed: "(T)he signatory defendant

is entitled to attorney fees only if the nonsignatory plaintiff would have been entitled to its fees if the plaintiff had prevailed." [*Sessions Payroll Management, Inc. v. Noble Const. Co., Inc.* (2000) 84 CA4th 671, 679, 101 CR2d 127, 132 (internal quotes omitted)]

(a) [1:269] **Assignee:** An assignee is normally entitled to enforce a provision for attorney fees in the assigned contract. Therefore, a party who unsuccessfully claims to be an assignee or who loses an action to enforce the contract may be held liable under Civ.C. §1717 for the defendant's attorney fees. [See *Heppler v. J.M. Peters Co., Inc.* (1999) 73 CA4th 1265, 1289, 87 CR2d 497, 518; *California Wholesale Material Supply, Inc. v. Norm Wilson & Sons, Inc.* (2002) 96 CA4th 598, 605, 117 CR2d 390, 394]

- [1:270] Subcontractor's Assignee sued to collect amounts allegedly owed by General Contractor. The subcontract contained an attorney fees clause. Assignee lost because General Contractor proved it paid the money in question to senior creditors. Assignee, although a nonsignatory to the subcontract, was liable for General Contractor's attorney fees pursuant to the subcontract. [*California Wholesale Material Supply, Inc. v. Norm Wilson & Sons, Inc.*, supra, 96 CA4th at 605, 117 CR2d at 394]

(b) [1:271] **Third party beneficiary:** Whether a third party beneficiary can enforce an attorney fee clause in the contract *depends on the contracting parties' intent.* If the provision was not intended to benefit the third party beneficiary, it cannot be enforced by or against him or her. [See *Sessions Payroll Management, Inc. v. Noble Const. Co., Inc.*, supra, 84 CA4th at 680, 101 CR2d at 133]

- [1:272] General Contractor's contract with Subcontractor contained an attorney fee provision and provided that Payroll Service would handle all payrolls. Even if Payroll Service was a third party beneficiary (which was doubtful), there was no indication that the attorney fee provision was intended for its benefit. Thus, when Payroll Service sued Subcontractor and lost, it could not be held liable for defendant's attorney fees under Civ.C. §1717. [*Sessions Payroll Management, Inc. v. Noble Const. Co., Inc.*, supra, 84 CA4th at 680, 101 CR2d at 133]

- [1:273] Sublessee sued Lessor for breach of the original lease that contained an attorney fee provision, and in which *Lessor expressly agreed to a sublease.* Because Sublessee was entitled to enforce the attorney fee provision against Lessor, upon losing the action it was liable for Lessor's attorney fees under Civ.C. §1717. [*Real Property Services Corp. v. City of Pasadena* (1994) 25 CA4th 375, 383-384, 30 CR2d 536, 541-542]

    [1:274] *Reserved.*

(6) [1:275] **Amount of fee award:** Contracts providing for "reasonable" expenses and attorney fees rely upon the court to determine the amount. Such awards are governed by equitable principles. [*PLCM Group, Inc. v. Drexler* (2000) 22 C4th 1084, 1095, 95 CR2d 198, 206; *Hunt v. Fahnestock* (1990) 220 CA3d 628, 633, 269 CR 614, 617]

    (a) [1:276] **Fee arrangements with client not controlling:** In determining a "reasonable fee," the court may consider the lawyer's fee arrangement with his or her client as some evidence of the value of the legal services rendered. But it is *not* controlling, and the court may properly award a lesser sum. [*Vella v. Hudgins* (1984) 151 CA3d 515, 521, 198 CR 725, 729]

    The result, of course, is that the victorious client may be obligated to pay his or her lawyer far more than the court has awarded. [*Vella v. Hudgins,* supra—contingency fee agreement obligated client to pay lawyer $100,000, but after considering all relevant factors, court ordered other party to pay only $50,000]

    ⇨[1:277] *PRACTICE POINTER:* This is a difficult point for many clients to grasp. They assume that since the lease or promissory note, etc. authorizes recovery of attorney fees, *any* fee you charge the client will have to be paid by the opposing party. They are usually surprised to learn that the fees awardable by the court (*if* they win) may not cover your billings.

    Therefore, be sure to explain to your clients at the outset that they are fully responsible for your fees (either as billed or whenever else agreed upon), notwithstanding the possibility that the court may order the opposing party to pay fees. It is a good idea to include a provision to this effect in your retainer agreement:

— "Any fees awarded by the court, pursuant to statute or contract, in connection with the subject matter of this representation, shall be paid to Attorney and shall apply against Client's fee obligation under this Agreement, but *shall not limit or discharge* Client's fee obligation." *(See Forms 1:A & 1:B.)*

[1:278-279] *Reserved.*

(b) **[1:280] Factors considered in determining "reasonable" fee:** The criteria used by courts to fix the amount of "reasonable" attorney fees (under contract or a statutory provision for fee awards) is beyond the scope of this Practice Guide.

*Cross-refer:* See detailed discussion in Wegner, Fairbank, Epstein & Chernow, *Cal. Prac. Guide: Civil Trials & Evidence* (TRG), Ch. 17.

[1:281] *Reserved.*

(7) **[1:282] Procedure to obtain fee award:** Fee awards based on contract clauses are recoverable as part of the *costs of suit.* [CCP §1033.5(a)(10)]

(a) **[1:283] Noticed motion:** Unless the parties stipulate otherwise, the amount must be fixed *on noticed motion*; or in default cases, upon entry of default judgment. [CCP §1033.5(c)(5)]

However, where the fee can be fixed *without the necessity of a court determination* (e.g., the contract provides for a fee of "$2,500 or 10% of the unpaid principal balance, whichever is greater"), it can be claimed in the costs memorandum; no court order is necessary. [CRC 870.2(e)]

*Cross-refer:* See detailed discussion in Wegner, Fairbank, Epstein & Chernow, *Cal. Prac. Guide: Civil Trials & Evidence* (TRG), Ch. 17.

[1:284] *Reserved.*

(b) **[1:285] Pleading requirement?** In the past, it was customary to plead contract attorney fees as *damages* and request an award of such fees in the complaint. CCP §1033.5(c)(5) now authorizes award of contract attorney fees as *"costs of suit"* . . . which *seems* to say that such fees can be awarded even if *not* specifically demanded in the complaint. However, there is as yet no case authority so holding.

⟹[1:286] **PRACTICE POINTER:** Until the issue is resolved, *continue to plead* contract attorney fees as damages and as part of the prayer for relief in the complaint.

d. **Fee awards authorized by statute**

(1) [1:287] **In general:** Literally hundreds of California statutes authorize court awards of attorney fees in specific types of actions. Some statutes merely authorize an award in the court's discretion (i.e., the court "may" award same; see CCP §386.6, dealing with interpleader actions). Other statutes, however, are mandatory (the court "shall" award fees; see CCP §1036, dealing with inverse condemnation actions; and CCP §425.16(c), dealing with SLAPP motions, ¶7:259).

Even where the statute is only permissive, an exercise of discretion is required and the court must state its reasons for denial of fees. [*Moran v. Oso Valley Greenbelt Ass'n* (2001) 92 CA4th 156, 160-161, 111 CR2d 636, 639]

There are also numerous *federal* statutes under which fees may be awarded by federal or state courts. E.g., prevailing parties in *civil rights litigation* are entitled to an award of reasonable attorney fees "unless special circumstances would render such an award unjust." [42 USC §1988; see *Choate v. County of Orange* (2000) 86 CA4th 312, 322, 103 CR2d 339, 345-346—fees ordinarily awarded to prevailing plaintiffs under federal civil rights statute, but prevailing *defendants* can recover fees only where plaintiff's claim was "objectively frivolous, unreasonable or groundless" or plaintiff continued to litigate after it clearly became so]

(2) [1:288] **No reciprocal right:** Statutory fees are recoverable only as provided by the statute. Thus, a statute stating a winning plaintiff may recover fees in a particular kind of case does not authorize an award to defendant if it wins. I.e., the principle of "reciprocity" applicable to contract fees (Civ.C. §1717(a)) does *not* apply to statutory fees! [*Covenant Mut. Ins. Co. v. Young* (1986) 179 CA3d 318, 323-324, 225 CR 861, 863-864; *Earley v. Sup.Ct. (Washington Mut. Bank)* (2000) 79 CA4th 1420, 1430, 95 CR2d 57, 62]

(3) [1:288.1] **Not limited to fees owed by client:** Statutory fees are not limited to cases in which a client is represented on a fee-for-service basis. Statutory fee awards may compensate for legal work provided at no personal expense to the client (e.g., services rendered

by client's in-house counsel, or by counsel appearing pro bono). [See *Lolley v. Campbell* (2002) 28 C4th 367, 373, 121 CR2d 571, 575]

[1:288.2-288.4]   *Reserved.*

(4) [1:288.5]   **Mixed actions:**   When a cause of action for which attorney fees are provided by statute is joined with other causes of action for which attorney fees are not permitted, the prevailing party may recover only on the statutory cause of action. Such fees need not be apportioned, however, on issues *common* to both causes of action; i.e., all expenses incurred on the common issues qualify for an award. [*Akins v. Enterprise Rent-A-Car Co. of San Francisco* (2000) 79 CA4th 1127, 1133, 94 CR2d 448, 452]

(5) [1:289]   **Determining "prevailing party":**   Normally, the prevailing party is the one in whose favor a *net judgment* is entered. [See *Smith v. Rae-Venter Law Group* (2002) 29 C4th 345, 354, 127 CR2d 516, 532]

But a decision on the merits is not always necessary. Which party "prevailed" is determined *pragmatically.* [See *Winick Corp. v. Safeco Ins. Co.* (1986) 187 CA3d 1502, 1507-1508, 232 CR 479, 481-482; *Galan v. Wolfriver Holding Corp.* (2000) 80 CA4th 1124, 1129, 96 CR2d 112, 115]

- [1:289.1]   For example, where the statute authorizes fees to a "prevailing" defendant, a dismissal for failure to prosecute makes defendant the "prevailing" party. [*Winick Corp. v. Safeco Ins. Co., supra,* 187 CA3d at 1508, 232 CR at 482]

- [1:289.2]   But the court may find there is no prevailing party where a dismissal follows a settlement or for other reasons the merits of the dispute were not resolved. [*Galan v. Wolfriver Holding Corp., supra,* 80 CA4th at 1129, 96 CR2d at 116—defendant "waited the plaintiff out" betting plaintiff would voluntarily dismiss]

  [1:289.3]   *Reserved.*

- [1:289.4]   D was the "prevailing party" for purposes of a statutory fee award where it obtained summary judgment based on evidence showing P had *released* his claim against D, and therefore his lawsuit was "frivolous." [*Linsley v. Twentieth Century Fox Films Corp.* (1999) 75 CA4th 762, 767, 89 CR2d 429, 435—fee award under FEHA]

- [1:289.5]   But fee awards should not be made to defendants who "prevail" only as the result of a *ju-*

*risdictional* defect, rather than on the merits of the claim. [See *Hon v. Marshall* (1997) 53 CA4th 470, 477, 62 CR2d 11, 15—summary judgment against P for *failure to exhaust administrative remedies* under FEHA did *not* entitle D to fees as "prevailing" party]

(6) [1:290] **Not a limit on negotiated fees:** Except where expressly provided otherwise (e.g., probate, workers' compensation cases), statutory fees awarded in litigation are *not* exclusive; i.e., they do not affect counsel's right to negotiate his or her own fees with the client. (Again, this is a point that should be explained clearly to the client!)

For example, a fee award to plaintiff's attorney under the Federal Civil Rights Act (42 USC §1988) does *not* excuse a contingency fee agreement requiring plaintiff to pay the attorney more than the statutory award. The statute merely regulates what the losing defendant must pay, not what the plaintiff must pay his or her lawyer pursuant to contract. [*Venegas v. Mitchell* (1990) 495 US 82, 89-90, 110 S.Ct. 1679, 1684]

☞ [1:290.1] *PRACTICE POINTER:* This comes as a surprise to many clients. They assume a fee award by the court excuses whatever fee obligation they incurred by contract; see ¶1:277.

To avoid such misunderstanding, in taking cases for which a fee award is authorized by statute or contract, include a provision to the following effect in your retainer agreement:
— "Any fees awarded by the court, pursuant to statute or contract, in connection with the subject matter of this representation, shall be paid to Attorney and shall apply against Client's fee obligation under this agreement, but *shall not limit or discharge* Client's fee obligation." (*See Forms 1:A & 1:B.*)

(7) [1:291] **Limited by negotiated fee?** Conversely, an attorney-client fee agreement does not limit the amount of fees a court may award where statutes authorize "reasonable fee" awards. [See *Blanchard v. Bergeron* (1989) 489 US 87, 91, 109 S.Ct. 939, 943—client recovered $10,000 for civil rights violation: court could award additional $7,500 attorney fees although contingency fee agreement was for 40% of recovery]

Conversely, where the statute provides for reimbursement of fees "*incurred*," a court may not award fees in excess of those for which the party is obligated. The party claiming fees must present evidence of the fees incurred, and this is a ceiling the court may not exceed when fixing "reasonable attorney fees." [*Andre v. City of West Sacramento* (2001) 92 CA4th 532, 537, 111 CR2d 891, 895]

(8) **[1:292]** **Procedure to fix statutory fees:** Like contract attorney fees, statutory fees are recoverable as *costs of suit.* [CCP §1033.5(c)(5)]

The amount may be fixed either:
— in the court's statement of decision;
— upon application supported by affidavit accompanying a memorandum of costs;
— upon noticed motion; or
— in default cases, upon entry of default judgment. [CCP §1033.5(c)(5)]

If a noticed motion is utilized, it must be filed within the time allowed for filing a notice of appeal—i.e., 60 days after mailing or service of notice of entry of judgment (or appealable order); otherwise, within 180 days after entry. [*Los Angeles Times v. Alameda Corridor Transp. Auth.* (2001) 88 CA4th 1381, 1389, 107 CR2d 29, 36]

⇨**[1:292.1]** *PRACTICE POINTER:* Unless the court states its reasons for granting or denying fees, the prevailing party on the issue should request permission to *file a proposed written order* articulating the court's reasons. [See *Moran v. Oso Valley Greenbelt Ass'n* (2001) 92 CA4th 156, 160-161, 111 CR2d 636, 639]

[1:292.2-292.4] *Reserved.*

(a) **[1:292.5]** **No interim awards:** There is generally no basis for an interim award of attorney fees under California statutes (except possibly under CCP §1021.5, the "private attorney general" statute, ¶*1:298*). [*Bell v. Farmers Ins. Exch.* (2001) 87 CA4th 805, 832, 105 CR2d 59, 79—noting different result under federal civil rights statutes]

(9) **[1:293]** **Pilot program (Riverside County only)—fee award for refusing CCP §998 settlement offer:** An experimental program is in effect in Riverside County under which reasonable attorney fees *may* (discretionary) be awarded against a party who fails to obtain at trial what could have been obtained before trial through a CCP §998 settlement offer. Fees are awardable only for services rendered after the offer. Such an award does not diminish other fees to which a party is entitled

under statute or contract. But there are important exceptions and limitations. [See CCP §1021.1 (1/1/05 "sunset" provision)]

[1:293.1-293.9]  *Reserved.*

(10) [1:293.10]  **Statutory fee award belongs to client or attorney?**  Absent an agreement to the contrary, *legislative intent determines* whether a statutory fee award belongs to the client or the attorney. [See *Flannery v. Prentice* (2001) 26 C4th 572, 590, 110 CR2d 809, 823—unless parties have agreed otherwise, fee awards in actions under California Fair Employment and Housing Act (Gov.C. §12965) *belong to attorney* to the extent award exceeds fees already paid by client; and same result with fee awards under CCP §1021.5 ("private attorney general" statute)]

(a) [1:293.11]  **Comment:**  The holding in *Flannery,* above, is based on what the Court found to be *legislative intent* with respect to the particular statute involved (FEHA). *The result may be different as to other statutory fee awards.*

(b) [1:293.12]  **Effect of client's settlement waiving fees?**  It is unclear whether the attorney's right to FEHA fees affects the client's right to settle the case and *waive* statutory fees.

*Flannery* suggests it does not. It cites with apparent approval a Ninth Circuit case stating (with respect to a *federal* fee statute): "the attorneys' right does not come into being until the client exercises that power; the defendant's liability will only arise if that power is exercised." [*United States ex rel. Virani v. Jerry M. Lewis Truck Parts & Equip., Inc.* (9th Cir. 1996) 89 F3d 574, 577]

[1:293.13-293.14]  *Reserved.*

⇨[1:293.15]  *PRACTICE POINTER:*  Because of remaining uncertainty whether attorney fees awarded under a statute belong to the attorney or client, the issue should be addressed in your initial contract with the client. (Attempts to resolve the issue later will create a conflict of interest.) For example:

— "In consideration of Attorney accepting a lower fee from Client than otherwise would be charged for the services to be rendered by Attorney under this Agreement, Client hereby irrevocably assigns to Attorney any fees that may be awarded by the court in connection with the subject matter of this representation. Such fee award shall belong exclusively to Attorney. Client further agrees not to take any action that would impair Attorney's right to such an award from the court, and that *Attorney's right to seek such an award shall be preserved in any settlement or compromise of Client's claims."*

[1:293.16-293.19] *Reserved.*

(c) [1:293.20] **Validity of splitting court-ordered fees with client?** It is unclear whether a contingency fee agreement that splits court-awarded attorney fees with the client violates CRPC 1-320(A) (prohibiting a lawyer from sharing legal fees with a person who is *not* a lawyer). [See *Flannery v. Prentice* (2001) 26 C4th 572, 586, 110 CR2d 809, 820—noting but not deciding whether allowing litigants to keep a portion of FEHA fee awards "would amount . . . to improper sharing of legal fees by nonlawyers" in violation of CRPC 1-320(A)]

e. [1:294] **Fees under court's equitable powers:** There are a few cases in which the court is deemed to have inherent equitable authority to order fees payable to the prevailing party or counsel:

(1) [1:295] **Common fund doctrine:** Where the lawsuit has resulted in the recovery of a fund or property benefiting others as well as plaintiff (e.g., a class action), the court has inherent equitable power to order plaintiff's attorney fees paid out of such common fund or property. This assures that all those benefitted by the litigation pay their fair share of obtaining the recovery. [See *Serrano v. Priest* (1977) 20 C3d 25, 35, 141 CR 315, 318; but see *Dunk v. Ford Motor Co.* (1996) 48 CA4th 1794, 1809, 56 CR2d 483, 493—"common fund doctrine" of questionable validity in California and, even if valid, applies only where recovery consists of *ascertainable amount*]

The "common fund" doctrine is codified in certain areas (e.g., Lab.C. §3856, involving employer/employee claims against third party tortfeasor).

(2) [1:296] **Substantial benefit doctrine:** Even when no common fund or property has been recovered, the court has equitable power to order fees where:
— plaintiff has sued in a representative capacity on behalf of others;
— plaintiff's efforts have created a substantial *pecuniary or nonpecuniary* benefit to members of an ascertainable class; and

— the court's jurisdiction over the subject matter makes possible an award which spreads the cost proportionately among the members of the benefitted class. [*Ciani v. San Diego Trust & Sav. Bank* (1994) 25 CA4th 563, 578, 30 CR2d 581, 590—doctrine rests on concepts of unjust enrichment]

- **[1:297]** The court may order the persons benefitted to pay a share of plaintiff's counsel fees out of their own pockets; or it may order such fees payable by the defendant. [See *Fletcher v. A.J. Industries, Inc.* (1968) 266 CA2d 313, 324, 72 CR 146, 150—corporation ordered to pay fees to plaintiff's lawyer in shareholder's derivative suit against corporation]

(3) **[1:298] "Private attorney general" doctrine:** Attorney fees may be awarded to the successful party against an opposing party in any action that has resulted in enforcement of an important right affecting the public interest if:
— a significant benefit, pecuniary or otherwise, has been conferred on the *general public* or a *large class* of persons; and
— the necessity and financial burden of private enforcement are such as to make a fee award appropriate; and
— in the "interest of justice," such fees should be paid by the opposing party rather than out of the recovery. [CCP §1021.5]

*Cross-refer:* See detailed discussion of this "private attorney general" doctrine in Wegner, Fairbank, Epstein & Chernow, *Cal. Prac. Guide: Civil Trials & Evidence* (TRG), Ch. 17.

**[1:299-301]** *Reserved.*

f. **[1:302] Proof requirements for fee awards:** The attorney bears the burden of proof as to "reasonableness" of any fee claim (whether under contract or statute) not based upon the court's established schedule of attorney fees. [CCP §1033.5(c)(5)]

This burden requires *competent evidence* as to the nature and value of the services rendered. [*Martino v. Denevi* (1986) 182 CA3d 553, 559, 227 CR 354, 358—attorney's testimony he had billed client $40,000 "for services rendered" was *insufficient* by itself to support fee award in that amount]

(1) **[1:303] Fee schedules as presumptive amount:** Many courts have adopted attorney fee schedules by local rule (*see ¶1:276*). These schedules *presumptively*

establish a "reasonable" fee for routine cases. [See L.A. Sup.Ct. Rule 3.2(a); Orange Sup.Ct. Rule 366; San Diego Sup.Ct. Rule 2.53]

The burden is on the applicant to justify any award above the fee schedule. Some rules require that such application be accompanied by an *itemized statement* of the services rendered. [See L.A. Sup.Ct. Rule 3.2(a),(d)]

(2) **[1:304]** **Billing records:** Unless relying on such fee schedules, the attorney should submit *contemporaneous* time and billing records that accurately reflect the work done: I.e., the number of hours worked, the lawyer's billing rates, the types of issues dealt with and appearances made on the client's behalf. [*Martino v. Denevi*, supra, 182 CA3d at 559, 227 CR at 358]

➡️ **[1:305]** *PRACTICE POINTER:* Such records may not be absolutely essential to fee recovery in state practice (see below). But it is foolhardy to practice without such records!

Moreover, it is your *professional responsibility* to limit your fees to "reasonable" charges (*see* ¶1:374), and such records are essential to establishing "reasonableness" and to enabling the client to evaluate the worth of the services provided. [*Martino v. Denevi*, supra]

(3) **[1:306]** **Expert opinion:** In addition to detailed billing records, expert opinion evidence should be presented by the applicant and other lawyers as to what is a "reasonable fee" for such services . . . *unless* the trial court is already aware of the nature and extent of the attorney's services (from observation of the trial proceedings and case file). [*Martino v. Denevi*, supra]

(4) **[1:307]** **Attorney's testimony alone may suffice:** However, detailed time and billing records are *not* absolutely essential: "Testimony of an attorney as to the number of hours worked on a particular case is sufficient evidence to support an award of attorney fees, *even in the absence of detailed time records.*" [*Martino v. Denevi*, supra, 182 CA3d at 559, 227 CR at 358 (emphasis added)]

(a) **[1:308]** **Compare—federal practice:** The result may be contra in some federal courts, in which detailed time and billing records are held *essential* to any recovery of attorney fees. [See discussion in

*Martino v. Denevi,* supra, 182 CA3d at 559, 227 CR at 358]

[1:308.1-308.4]   *Reserved.*

g.  [1:308.5]   **Discovery by opposing party:**   Defendant may conduct limited discovery to determine whether plaintiff's interest in the outcome of the litigation is such that would preclude an attorney fee award under CCP §1021.5. [*Save Open Space Santa Monica Mountains v. Sup.Ct. (County of Los Angeles)* (2000) 84 CA4th 235, 253-254, 100 CR2d 725, 733-735]

5.  [1:309]   **Formalizing the Attorney-Client Relationship:**   A clear understanding by both attorney and client of the business relationship between them is essential. Each must understand his or her obligations to the other. The attorney must know what he or she is being retained to accomplish, and how far his or her authority extends. The client must know what information and assistance he or she is expected to provide, and the scope of his or her financial obligations to the lawyer.

*Cross-refer:* For detailed discussion of attorney fee agreements and fee considerations, see Vapnek, Tuft, Peck & Wiener, *Cal. Prac. Guide: Professional Responsibility* (TRG), Ch. 5.

⇨[1:309.1]   *PRACTICE POINTER:*   Most lawyers make it a regular practice to *document all* significant dealings with a client, not just fee agreements. Failure to do so may lead to misunderstandings and disagreements.

Here are some suggestions:

• Avoid relying on personal or telephone conversations to communicate important information to the client (e.g., deposition dates, settlement offers); follow up with a fax or letter explaining such information clearly.

• Prepare a "memo to the file" following *all* significant personal or telephone conversations regarding the case, including conversations with the client, opposing counsel or anyone else. Send copies of your memo to the client if appropriate.

• Send the client *copies of all written communications* received or sent by you regarding the case, with notations where appropriate.

• Be careful about making "courtesy appearances" for other attorneys; this may create an attorney-client relationship, imposing a duty of care.

a.  [1:310]   **When to formalize:**   The attorney-client relationship should be formalized as early as possible. Too often, attorneys start providing services on an "informal" basis, only to find a lack of understanding with the client on some essential point. Therefore, as soon as the attorney decides to take the case, a formal agreement with the client should be entered into.

b. **[1:311] Matters to be agreed upon:** Specific agreements should be reached on the following matters in all cases:

(1) **[1:311.1] Identity of client:** The fee agreement should always identify *whom* you agree to represent . . . and conversely whom you do *not* represent.

⇨**[1:311.2] *PRACTICE POINTER:*** The identity of the client becomes critically important where, for example:

— the party for whom you are to provide services is an *organization or entity* (e.g., corporation or partnership) but others may also be looking to you for representation *individually* (e.g., members, partners, officers, directors, etc.);

— husband and wife ask you to represent one of them in a personal injury or similar matter, but the other spouse may also expect you to protect his or her interests (e.g., claims for loss of consortium);

— one party agrees to *pay or guarantee* payment for your services in representing another;

— you agree to represent two or more parties concurrently, because there may be a *potential conflict* of interest (*see* ¶*1:40 ff.*).

*Cross-refer:* For detailed discussion of these issues, see Vapnek, Tuft, Peck & Wiener, *Cal. Prac. Guide: Professional Responsibility* (TRG), Ch. 3.

(2) **[1:312] Work to be done:** The agreement should spell out specifically the scope of the employment. Particularly where the case is being handled on a contingency fee, it must be made clear exactly how far the attorney is obligated to go to earn the fee. (For example, is the fee earned upon obtaining a judgment; or is the attorney also obligated to perform additional services *after* judgment *without additional fees*, such as on a motion for new trial or on appeal?)

(3) **[1:313] Authority conferred:** The agreement should specify how the relationship will function; e.g., to whom the attorney should report, how decisions are to be made, etc.

(a) **[1:314]** **Implied authority re "procedural" matters:** An attorney retained to represent a client in litigation is clothed with certain implied or ostensible authority by virtue of the relationship. This includes authority to bind the client by stipulation as to "procedural" matters arising during the course of the action. [See *Blanton v. Womancare, Inc.* (1985) 38 C3d 396, 404, 212 CR 151, 156]

   1) **[1:315]** **Application:** The following are actions which an attorney may take without the client's consent (and even over the client's objection):
   — deciding which witnesses to call at trial;
   — granting extensions of time to opposing counsel;
   — stipulating that a witness if called would give substantially the same testimony as a prior witness;
   — stipulating that a temporary judge, rather than a regular judge, may hear a nonjury matter. [See *Linsk v. Linsk* (1969) 70 C2d 272, 276, 74 CR 544, 547; and *Marriage of Crook* (1991) 235 CA3d 30, 33-34, 286 CR 537, 539]

(b) **[1:316]** **No implied authority re "substantive rights":** However, absent express authority from the client, the attorney has no power to impair the client's "substantive rights." [See *Blanton v. Womancare, Inc.*, supra, 38 C3d at 404, 212 CR at 156]

Although CCP §283 provides that an attorney has authority by stipulation filed in open court or with the clerk "to bind his client *in any of the steps of an action or proceeding,*" this is construed as limited to procedural, not substantive, matters. [*Linsk v. Linsk*, supra, 70 C2d at 276, 74 CR at 546]

*Caution:* This issue is involved in a case presently before the California Supreme Court, *Haynes v. Farmers Ins. Exch.*, Case No. S104851.

   1) **[1:317]** **Application:** Thus, the attorney has *no implied authority* merely on the basis of his or her employment and without the client's consent:
   — to settle or compromise the claim;
   — to dismiss with prejudice;
   — to stipulate to a matter which would eliminate an essential element of the claim or defense;

— to stipulate to entry of default judgment or summary judgment against the client;

— to stipulate that the judge can decide the case based on record made in a previous trial before a different judge;

— to stipulate to binding arbitration. [See *Linsk v. Linsk*, supra, 70 C2d at 276, 74 CR at 547; *Blanton v. Womancare, Inc.*, supra, 38 C3d at 407, 212 CR at 158; *In re Horton* (1991) 54 C3d 82, 94, 284 CR 305, 312; *Levy v. Sup.Ct. (Golant)* (1995) 10 C4th 578, 583-584, 41 CR2d 878, 881]

2) **[1:318]** **Unauthorized acts void:** An attorney's unauthorized actions or stipulations do not affect the client's substantive rights and *may be set aside at any time.* [*Romadka v. Hoge* (1991) 232 CA3d 1231, 1236-1237, 283 CR 878, 881—unauthorized dismissal could be set aside even after time limits for relief under CCP §473]

*Caution:* This issue is involved in a case presently before the California Supreme Court, *Haynes v. Farmers Ins. Exch.*, Case No. S104851.

a) **[1:318.1]** **Compare—ratification:** Even unauthorized acts may be binding upon a client who has *ratified* the attorney's acts. [*Caro v. Smith* (1997) 59 CA4th 725, 731, 69 CR2d 306, 310—although client did not sign attorney's stipulation to binding arbitration, she ratified it by voluntarily participating in arbitration and orally agreeing that award would be "binding"]

☞ **[1:318.2]** *CAUTION:* Misrepresenting your authority to stipulate on the client's behalf and then reneging on the stipulation for lack of authority is a *highly improper* tactic and will destroy your reputation as a lawyer. [See *Caro v. Smith,* supra, 59 CA4th at 731, 69 CR2d at 310—"No lawyer should be a person of two truths, his own and his client's"]

3) **[1:319]** **Opposing counsel cannot rely on "apparent" authority:** It follows that opposing counsel cannot rely on stipulations affecting a client's "substantive" right unless they are in

fact authorized by the client: "When an attorney undertakes to bind his client by an agreement to compromise his client's substantive rights, *the opposing party must ascertain at his peril* whether the attorney has authority to make the settlement." [*Blanton v. Womancare, Inc.*, supra, 38 C3d at 407, 212 CR at 158 (emphasis added)]

4) **[1:320]** **Attorney personally liable for unauthorized acts:** By impliedly warranting authority he or she does not have, the attorney may become *personally* liable for detriment suffered by others in reliance thereon: e.g., legal fees incurred by opposing parties in an unsuccessful attempt to enforce whatever settlement had been promised by the lawyer. [See *Covenant Mut. Ins. Co. v. Young* (1986) 179 CA3d 318, 322, 225 CR 861, 863; see also Civ.C. §3318]

(c) **[1:321]** **Test for when client authorization required:** The terms "substantive" and "procedural" do not provide real guidance. The test is whether the matters stipulated to are *central to the controversy*: "If the dispute is *substantially resolved* by virtue of the stipulation, it is tantamount to . . . (a) settlement and dismissal . . . On the other hand, if the substantial portion of the case remains to be litigated, the stipulation represents largely a winnowing of the issues . . ." (so that even an unauthorized stipulation is effective). [*Marriage of Helsel* (1988) 198 CA3d 332, 339, 243 CR 657, 661]

1) **[1:322]** **Effect:** This may uphold unauthorized stipulations on matters that are more than merely "tactical" or "procedural." But the client has adequate remedies against an attorney who makes unauthorized agreements (i.e., malpractice suit, disciplinary proceedings). [*Marriage of Helsel*, supra, 198 CA3d at 339, 243 CR at 661]

2) **[1:323]** **Factors considered:** In determining whether the stipulation is "central to the controversy," the court may compare the extent to which the stipulation *differs* from the positions claimed by each party beforehand.

The court may also consider the *economic value* of the stipulation, both in absolute terms and in relation to the total value of the disputed issues in the case. [*Marriage of Helsel*, supra, 198 CA3d at 340, 243 CR at 662]

[1:324]   *Reserved.*

(d) [1:325]   **Effect of agreement conferring settlement authority on attorney:**   The retainer agreement may expressly authorize the attorney to settle a claim without further consent from the client. Such provision may be valid from the standpoint of agency law, but whether it would be upheld in the attorney-client relationship is unclear.

☞[1:326]   *PRACTICE POINTER:*   Most lawyers recommend *against* including such provisions in your retainer agreement. There is too great a likelihood of misunderstanding with the client should you attempt to settle a case without the client's knowledge and consent.

1)   [1:327]   **Compare—provisions prohibiting client from "settling around" attorney:** Some retainer agreements include provisions seeking to prohibit the *client* from settling without the lawyer's consent. Such provisions appear to be *improper*, as they would impair the client's sole and exclusive authority re a "substantive right."

(4)   **Fee arrangement:**   *See ¶1:199 ff.*

(5)   **How costs are to be paid:**   *See ¶1:391 ff.*

(6)   **Security arrangements for fees and costs:**   *See ¶1:400 ff.*

c.   [1:328]   **When writing required:**   A written fee agreement is required in contingency fee cases (Bus. & Prof.C. §6147, *see ¶1:351*).

It is also required in any other case in which it is "*reasonably foreseeable* that the *total expense to the client*" (fees and costs) *will exceed $1,000.* [Bus. & Prof.C. §6148(a)]

*Compare—fee-sharing upon referral:* The client must consent in writing to a fee-sharing agreement with another lawyer or law firm, after full disclosure of the terms of the agreement, and the fee charged to the client may not be increased by reason of the referral. [See CRPC 2-200(A)]

(1)   [1:329]   **Required contents:**   The contents required in contingency fee contracts are discussed at *¶1:351.* All other fee contracts that are required to be in writing must contain all of the following:

- Any basis of compensation including, but not limited to, hourly rates, statutory fees or flat fees, and other standard rates, fees and charges applicable to the case;

- The general nature of the legal services to be provided to the client; and

- The respective responsibilities of the attorney and the client as to the performance of the contract. [Bus. & Prof.C. §6148(a)]

➡ [1:330] **PRACTICE POINTERS:** Be very specific about fees and expenses because the agreement will be strictly interpreted against you!

- [1:331] *"Standard" rates, fees and charges:* A provision calling for the client to pay your "standard" rates, fees and charges may not be enforceable unless the client had knowledge of those rates and fees *when the agreement was entered into.*

  Therefore, include your rates in sufficient detail to avoid misunderstanding. (E.g., "$200 per hour for partner's time, $150 per hour for associate's time, $40 per hour for paralegal's time" etc.)

  Also, if it is your policy to bill a minimum number of minutes per telephone call, or a minimum fee for court appearances, or a flat amount for travel time, etc., these should be specified in the agreement.

  Likewise, if you bill for word processing, photocopying, etc., the billing rates should be disclosed in the agreement. (E.g., "$35 per hour for word processing; $.25 per page for photocopying" etc.)

- [1:332] *Right to change rates:* Your agreement should expressly reserve your right to change the billing rates for both your services and any other charges (e.g., word processing) upon notice to the client of such changes. This is especially important where your representation is likely to stretch over several years. Failure to include such provisions may result in your being bound to charge only your former (lower) rates. [See *Severson & Werson v. Bolinger* (1991) 235 CA3d 1569, 1572-1573, 1 CR2d 531, 533—agreement to pay attorney's "regular hourly rates" did not obligate clients to pay later increases in rates without notice to clients]

(2) [1:333] **Exceptions to written agreement requirement:** The requirement that fee agreements be in writing is subject to the following exceptions:

(a) [1:334] **Emergencies:** Fees for legal services rendered in an emergency to avoid foreseeable prejudice to the client's interest "or where a writing is otherwise impractical"; [Bus. & Prof.C. §6148(d)(1)]

(b) [1:335] **Prior dealings:** Fee arrangements *implied* by the fact that the attorney's services are "of the same general kind" as previously rendered to and paid for by the client; [Bus. & Prof.C. §6148(d)(2)]

☞[1:336] *PRACTICE POINTER:* Don't rely too heavily on this exception! The vagueness of the statutory language ("of the same general kind") is likely to cause problems in interpretation . . . especially where you have handled several matters for a client, some of which involved fees *under* $1,000 (so that no writing was required under the statute).

Many attorneys send out "pick up letters" to existing clients, for approval and signature, to formalize continued representation in accordance with the statute. (*See Form 1:A.1 for suggested form for this purpose.*)

(c) [1:337] **Waiver:** Where the client knowingly and *in writing* waives compliance with the written fee contract requirement; [Bus. & Prof.C. §6148(d)(3)]

(d) [1:338] **Corporate clients:** Fee agreements with corporations. [Bus. & Prof.C. §6148(d)(4)]

Thus, an oral agreement with a corporate client regarding hourly rates and charges and the general nature of the legal services is enforceable.

*Caution:* The enforceability of an *oral* agreement for a *charging lien* on a corporate client's prospective recovery is presently before the California Supreme Court in *Fletcher v. Davis*, Case No. S114715.

☞[1:339] *PRACTICE POINTER:* Even where not required by statute, your fee arrangements should be in writing wherever possible. It is simply good practice to keep your dealings with a client on a business-like basis.

(3) **[1:340]** **Type of writing:** The statute does not prescribe the form or type of writing required. Lawyers commonly use either of the following:

(a) **[1:341]** **Letter agreements:** Particularly when accepting a new case from an existing client, the attorney may use a simple letter agreement "confirming" the oral understanding reached. Such letters may be informal in tone, but must spell out each of the matters required to be included in a fee contract (above).

- **FORM:** Letter Agreement for Hourly Rate Fee, *see Form 1:A.*

(b) **[1:342]** **Formal retainer agreements:** Some attorneys prefer to use formal written contracts for their fee agreements. The formal contract has the advantage of impressing upon the client the details of the client's rights and obligations; and it usually spells out the attorney's rights in greater detail should the client fail to pay for the services rendered.

(c) **[1:343]** **State Bar Sample Forms:** The State Bar has published sample fee agreements suitable for use in both litigation and nonlitigation matters.

- **FORMS:** State Bar Sample Written Fee Agreements:
  — Hourly Litigation, *see Form 1:A.1.*
  — Hourly Non-Litigation, *see Form 1:A.2.*
  — Other Clauses of Interest in Fee Agreements, *see Form 1:A.3.*

  **[1:344]** *Reserved.*

(4) **[1:345]** **Signed copy to client upon execution:** The attorney must provide the client with a duplicate of the contract *signed by both* the attorney and client. [Bus. & Prof.C. §6148(a)]

(5) **[1:346]** **Additional requirements re billings:** The following statutory requirements apply to client billings (Bus. & Prof.C. §6148(b)):

- All bills rendered by an attorney to a client must *clearly state the basis* thereof (e.g., hours spent for hourly billing, etc.).

- The fee portion of any bill must state *the amount, rate,* basis for calculation, or other method of determining the attorney's fees and costs.

- The cost and expense portion of the bill must clearly identify the costs and expenses incurred and the amount of the costs and expenses.

- The client is entitled to request a bill at intervals of no less than 30 days. The attorney must provide a bill within 10 days following the client's initial request (unless a bill was provided within 31 days prior to such request, in which case the attorney may provide a bill within 31 days after the most recent bill was provided).

- In responding to client requests for billing information, the attorney may use billing data effective on the date of the client's request. If any fees or costs to that date cannot be accurately determined, they shall be described and estimated.

- [1:346.1]  The statute does not specifically require that the billing disclose the date upon which the services were rendered. I.e., so-called "block" billings (e.g., "Services rendered January 1 through March 31, . . ., including . . .").

  However, many clients expect the attorney to provide the date upon which services were rendered for purposes of internal control and audit. They require individual services performed each day to be spelled out in detail so that the total cost of a particular task can be computed.

(6) [1:347]  **Effect of failure to comply:**  Fee agreements or billings which fail to meet the statutory requirements are *voidable* by the client. In such cases, the attorney is entitled to collect only a "reasonable" fee for the services rendered. [Bus. & Prof.C. §6148(c); see *Iverson, Yoakum, Papiano & Hatch v. Berwald* (1999) 76 CA4th 990, 995, 90 CR2d 665, 669—where complaint showed fee agreement did not comply with §6148, client's demurrer constituted an option to void the agreement]

(a) [1:347.1]  **Effect of promissory note given as security:**  Where a promissory note is given to secure payment of fees, the attorney's failure to comply with §6148 also renders the promissory note unenforceable. [*Iverson, Yoakum, Papiano & Hatch v. Berwald,* supra, 76 CA4th at 996, 90 CR2d at 670]

(b) [1:347.2] **Compare—quantum meruit recovery for services rendered:** Even where a written fee agreement is required and noncompliance renders the agreement voidable by the client, the attorney may sue for a "reasonable fee" for services rendered. [See Bus. & Prof.C. §§6147(b), 6148(c); *Flannery v. Prentice* (2001) 26 C4th 572, 589, 110 CR2d 809, 822]

    1) [1:347.2a] **Includes referral fees:** Failure to secure the client's written consent to a fee-sharing agreement with counsel to whom a case is referred (as required by CRPC 2-200(A), *see ¶1:328*) renders the agreement unenforceable. Nonetheless, the referring attorney may recover the reasonable value of his or her services from the attorney to whom the case was referred: "(R)ule 2-200 does not apply where there is no direct division of client-paid fees." [*Huskinson & Brown, LLP v. Wolf* (2004) 32 C4th 453, 459-460, 9 CR3d 693, 697-698—referring attorney awarded $5,000 for 20 hours of services instead of 25% contingency fee orally agreed upon with other counsel]

(c) [1:347.3] **Compare—recovery of statutory fees:** Failure to obtain a written fee agreement with the client does not affect the attorney's right to statutory fees *to which the attorney is entitled* (e.g., statutory fee awards under the FEHA; *see ¶1:293.10*). [*Flannery v. Prentice, supra,* 26 C4th at 586-587, 110 CR2d at 820]

(d) [1:347.4] **Compare—certain civil rights actions:** Written fee agreements may not be required in many civil rights cases: "The realities of pro bono litigation often involve attorneys from several firms or pro bono organizations banding together . . . Such cases may be brought on an emergency basis, or involve relatively small damages. Indeed, injunctive relief may be the primary goal of such litigation. A retainer agreement that covers all such counsel or circumstances may not be practical or feasible in light of time and resource constraints." [*Flannery v. Prentice, supra,* 26 C4th at 590, 110 CR2d at 822, fn. 17]

(e) [1:347.5] **Compare—class actions:** Similarly, in class actions, a written fee agreement with the entire class is usually not feasible; and any fee agreement class attorneys have with named plaintiffs does not bind other class members or the court. [*Flannery v. Prentice,* supra, 26 C4th at 590, 110 CR2d at 822, fn. 17]

(7) [1:348] **Compare—privileged communication:** A fee agreement between attorney and client is "deemed to be a confidential communication," which the attorney is bound "to maintain inviolate" and is protected by the attorney-client privilege. [Bus. & Prof.C. §6149]

(a) [1:349] **Comment:** However, this would not prevent either from suing to enforce the agreement. The privilege does not apply where an issue is raised as to breach of duty (by either party) arising out of the lawyer-client relationship. [Ev.C. §958]

d. [1:350] **Special requirements re contingency fee contracts:** A contingency fee agreement must be in writing, and must also comply with the following additional statutory requirements:

(1) [1:351] **Contents:** The written agreement must state (see Bus. & Prof.C. §6147(a)):

• The contingency fee rate agreed upon;

• How disbursements and costs incurred will affect the contingency fee and the client's recovery (i.e., whether the contingency fee is based on the gross or net recovery);

• To what extent, if any, the client could be required to pay additional compensation for related matters *not covered* by the contingency fee agreement— e.g., additional fees for defending against *cross-complaints*, or on motion for new trial, or on appeal, or in proceedings to enforce the judgment;

• A statement that the contingency fee is not set by law and is *negotiable* between attorney and client . . . except that in *malpractice* actions against health care providers, it must state that a *maximum* rate is set by Bus. & Prof.C. §6146 (*see* ¶*1:368*), and a lower rate may be negotiated between attorney and client.

[1:352] *Reserved.*

**FORMS**

• Contingency Fee Agreement, *see Form 1:B.*

• State Bar Sample Contingency Fee Agreement, *see Form 1:B.1.*

• Other Clauses of Interest in Fee Agreements, *see Form 1:A.3.*

(a) [1:353] **Not limited to litigation matters:** As originally enacted, §6147(a) used the word "plaintiff" and was held to apply only to litigation matters. [See *Franklin v. Appel* (1992) 8 CA4th 875, 886, 10 CR2d 759, 765]

But the statute now uses the word "client," making clear that it covers *all* contingency fee contracts, including those unrelated to litigation. [Bus. & Prof.C. §6147(a)]

(b) [1:354] **Scope of services:** Although not specifically required by statute, a contingency fee agreement should of course specify the claim or claims undertaken by the attorney.

*(Text cont'd on p. 1-83)*

**PAGES 1-65 THROUGH 1-82 ARE RESERVED FOR FUTURE USE**

Rev. #1 2004

It should also specify any claim that the attorney is *not* responsible for pursuing—even if related to the claim undertaken (e.g., a workers' compensation claim or disability insurance claim related to the personal injury claim).

➪[1:355] *PRACTICE POINTER:* It is a good idea to include the client's version of the key facts in your retainer agreement. Doing so may avoid future disputes with the client as to the matters undertaken. It may also provide grounds for withdrawal if investigation and discovery show the client's version is not sustainable.

(c) [1:356] **Right to fees on discharge or withdrawal?** The written agreement must state "to what extent, if any, the client could be required to pay any compensation to the attorney for *related matters that arise out of their relationship* not covered by their contingency contract." [Bus. & Prof.C. §6147(a)(3) (emphasis added)]

Arguably, this may require a statement of the attorney's right to *quantum meruit recovery* out of any subsequent recovery by the client where the client discharges the attorney (*see ¶1:421*), or the attorney withdraws for good cause (*see ¶1:441*).

➪[1:357] *PRACTICE POINTER:* To avoid any question, include appropriate provisions in your contingency fee contract. *See Form 1:B.*

(d) [1:358] **Must fee be negotiated?** Some lawyers argue that the statutory requirement that contingency fees be "negotiable" does not mean they actually have to be negotiated. Thus, they believe that even a preprinted percentage fee agreement would be enforceable.

➪[1:359] *PRACTICE POINTER:* Until the matter is clarified, it is better practice not to use retainer agreement forms with preprinted percentages. A client seeking to avoid the fee agreement after a successful recovery will have a more difficult time doing so if it is shown that the percentage was written in at the time the agreement was signed.

(e) [1:360] **Sanctions and fee awards as part of recovery?** Whether sanctions or fees awarded against the opposing party should be treated as part of the gross recovery to be split with the client, or belong exclusively to the client or exclusively to counsel, is unclear.

⇨ **[1:360.1]** *PRACTICE POINTER:* This matter should be covered in the contingency fee contract: e.g., by stating that any such sanctions or fee awards shall belong exclusively to counsel for the extra effort involved; or shall be applied against the client's fee obligation; or otherwise as agreed. *See Form 1:B.*

[1:360.2-360.4] *Reserved.*

(f) [1:360.5] **Effect of defendant's cross-complaint on contingency fee?** A contingency fee agreement should also state whether the fee is to be based on the recovery attributable to plaintiff's claims *without regard to* any setoffs or counterclaims asserted by defendant, or only on plaintiff's net recovery after setoffs. The former, of course, is more favorable to the attorney. *See Form 1:B.*

(2) [1:361] **Signed copy to client upon execution:** A duplicate copy of the agreement, signed both by the attorney and client (or guardian or representative), must be delivered to the client *at the time the contract is entered into.* [Bus. & Prof.C. §6147(a)]

(3) [1:362] **Effect of failure to comply:** Failure to comply with any of the above statutory requirements renders the contingency fee agreement "voidable" at the option of the client. In such event, the attorney is entitled to collect only a "reasonable fee." [Bus. & Prof.C. §6147(b)]

(a) [1:363] **Example:** Client was not bound by contingency fee agreement that did not state how costs disbursements would affect the fee, and did not state that the percentage was not set by law and was negotiable. Attorney could recover only a reasonable fee for work done. [*Alderman v. Hamilton* (1988) 205 CA3d 1033, 1038, 252 CR 845, 848]

[1:363.1-363.4] *Reserved.*

(b) [1:363.5] **Compare—statutory fees:** Notwithstanding Bus. & Prof.C. §6147, absence of a written retainer agreement does not affect a lawyer's right to statutory attorney fees, at least in FEHA actions under Gov.C. §12965. [*Flannery v.*

*Prentice* (2001) 26 C4th 572, 588-589, 110 CR2d 809, 823]

(4) [1:364] **Compare—workers' compensation claims:** The statutory requirements above (¶*1:351*) do not apply to contingency fee agreements in workers' compensation cases. [Bus.& Prof.C. §6147(c)]

(5) [1:365] **Compare—claims between merchants:** Nor do the above statutory requirements apply to contingency fee contracts on claims between *merchants* where:
— the claim arises from the sale or lease of goods or services rendered, or money loaned for use, in a business or profession; and
— the plaintiff merchant employs 10 or more persons. [Bus. & Prof.C. §6147.5(a)]

(a) [1:366] **"Merchants":** This term refers to persons *dealing* in goods of the kind involved (or holding themselves out as having the knowledge or skill which such a dealer would have). [See Bus. & Prof.C. §6147.5(a); and Comm'l C. §2104(1)]

(b) [1:367] **Limits on contingency fees:** While no written contract for legal services is required, the statute limits the contingency fee that an attorney may charge in the absence of a written contract:
— 20% of the first $300 collected;
— 18% of the next $1,700 collected; and
— 13% of any amount exceeding $2,000. [Bus. & Prof.C. §6147.5(b)]

[1:367.1-367.4] *Reserved.*

(6) [1:367.5] **Effect of provision obligating client to accept designated amount in settlement?** According to one court, there is "nothing unconscionable or unfair" about a retainer agreement obligating the client to accept a designated amount in settlement, provided it represents a *reasonable assessment* of the value of the claim and the attorney agrees to attempt to obtain a greater amount: "Indeed, a promise by a client to accept a reasonable amount in settlement promotes the important public policy favoring settlement of claims." [*Ramirez v. Sturdevant* (1994) 21 CA4th 904, 918, 26 CR2d 554, 561]

(a) [1:367.6] **Comment:** It is usually difficult to make a "reasonable assessment" of a case's worth at the outset. Therefore, a court may be reluctant to force the client to settle for the designated amount later on, finding it was *not* a "reasonable" assessment.

The problem is compounded where the contingency agreement purports to limit the client's right to settle for *less than* the designated sum (e.g., "Client agrees to settle *for no less than* $150,000"). If the client wants to settle for less, and the *attorney wants to hold out for more*, a court might find the agreement void as contrary to public policy favoring settlement.

(7) **[1:368]** **Special limitations on contingency fees in medical malpractice cases:** Under the Medical Injury Compensation Reform Act ("MICRA"), the maximum fee chargeable in malpractice actions against "health care providers" is 40% of the first $50,000, 33 1/3% of next $50,000, 25% of next $500,000, and 15% of any amount in excess of $600,000. [Bus. & Prof.C. §6146 (constitutionality upheld in *Roa v. Lodi Medical Group* (1985) 37 C3d 920, 211 CR 77)]

The limits apply to the claim as a whole regardless of the number of claimants. Thus, in a wrongful death action where the same attorney represents all the heirs, the fee is based on the total recovery for the wrongful death, not on each heir's share. [*Yates v. Law Offices of Samuel Shore* (1991) 229 CA3d 583, 590, 280 CR 316, 321]

Nor may a separate or additional fee be charged for handling an appeal from the judgment. [*Yates v. Law Offices of Samuel Shore*, supra, 229 CA3d at 591, 280 CR at 321]

*Compare:* In addition to the contingency fee to an attorney, a *medical-legal consulting firm* may also receive a contingency fee for reviewing medical records and locating expert witnesses. However, to the extent its services involve those normally performed by an attorney, its fee would have to be allocated as part of the maximum contingent attorney fee allowable under MICRA. [*Ojeda v. Sharp Cabrillo Hosp.* (1992) 8 CA4th 1, 19-20, 10 CR2d 230, 242-243]

*Cross-refer:* See detailed discussion in Flahavan, Rea & Kelly, *Cal. Prac. Guide: Personal Injury* (TRG), Ch. 1.

(a) **[1:369]** **Not waivable by client:** The purpose of the Act was to reduce costs of medical malpractice insurance, and the limitations therefore are not subject to waiver by the client: "A law established for a public reason cannot be contravened by a private agreement." [*Fineberg v. Harney & Moore* (1989) 207 CA3d 1049, 1055, 255 CR 299, 303]

(b) [1:370] **Hybrid actions:** If a nonmalpractice claim is joined in the complaint, the MICRA fee limitations do not apply to recovery on the non-MICRA claims (e.g., fraud, intentional infliction of emotional distress, etc.).

Nor do they apply if the case is settled without specifying the theory of recovery: "Where a plaintiff knowingly chooses to proceed on both non-MICRA and MICRA causes of action, and obtains a recovery that *may* be based on a non-MICRA theory, the limitations of section 6146 should not apply." [*Waters v. Bourhis* (1985) 40 C3d 424, 437, 220 CR 666, 675 (emphasis added)]

1) [1:371] **Caution:** This may lead to fee disputes with the client. The client may take the position the recovery is attributable solely to the malpractice claim so that the MICRA limitations apply. [See *Waters v. Bourhis*, supra]

⇨[1:372] *PRACTICE POINTER:* Avoid this problem! As explained by the Supreme Court: "Because the amount of a client's attorney fee may be affected by whether an action is pursued on a MICRA or non-MICRA basis, and because there may be a *potential conflict of interest* between the attorney and client on this matter, we believe that an attorney . . . must:

- *specifically advise* the client or potential client of the pros and cons of alternative litigation strategies, including potential attorney fees, and

- *obtain the client's (written) consent to* pursue and settle a non-MICRA action as well as a MICRA claim." [*Waters v. Bourhis*, supra, 40 C3d at 438, 220 CR at 676 (paragraphs, bullets, parentheses and emphasis added)]

In addition, it is good practice *before negotiating settlement* to review the fee arrangement with the client and obtain the client's consent to the proposed fee allocations if the settlement is effected!

e. **Ethical considerations re fees**

(1) [1:373] **Unconscionable or illegal fees:** An attorney is subject to discipline and the fee agreement is un-

enforceable, if the fee agreed upon with the client is held by a court to be "unconscionable" or "illegal." [CRPC 4-200(A)]

(a) [1:374] **"Unconscionable" fees:** Unconscionability is determined from "all the facts and circumstances existing at the time the agreement is entered into" (except where the parties contemplate the fee will be determined by later events). [CRPC 4-200(B)]

1) [1:375] **Factors considered:** Various factors are considered, where appropriate, in determining "conscionability" (reasonableness) including:

- Whether the fee was fixed or contingent;

- Amount involved and results obtained;

- Amount of the fee in proportion to the *value* of the services performed;

- Time and labor required;

- Informed consent of the client to the fee arrangement;

- Relative sophistication of the attorney and client;

- Nature and length of the professional relationship with the client;

- Novelty and difficulty of the questions involved and the skill required to deal with them properly;

- Experience, reputation and ability of the attorney performing the services;

- Likelihood (if apparent to the client) that the attorney's acceptance of the case would preclude other employment; and

- Time limitations, if any, imposed by the client or circumstances. [CRPC 4-200(B) (former Rule 2-107(B)); and see *Serrano v. Priest* (1977) 20 C3d 25, 48, 141 CR 315, 328]

2) [1:376] **Application:** A fee is not unconscionable simply because it is more than other lawyers might have charged for the same work. It must be "so exorbitant and disproportionate to the services performed as to shock the conscience of lawyers of ordinary prudence prac-

ticing in the same community." [*Champion v. Sup.Ct. (Boccardo)* (1988) 201 CA3d 777, 782, 247 CR 624, 626 (quoting *former* CRPC 2-107(B))]

(b) **[1:377]** **"Illegal" fees:** The Rules of Professional Conduct do not define an "illegal" fee, and determinations are therefore left to case law. [See *In re Goldstone* (1931) 214 C 490, 499, 6 P2d 513, 516—charging fee "so wholly disproportionate" to services performed "as to shock to conscience" warrants discipline]

Where fees are set by statute (e.g., probate cases; workers' compensation claims; or the contingency fee limits in medical malpractice cases, *see* ¶*1:368*), an attorney charging more than the statutory fee would no doubt be subject to discipline for exacting an "illegal" fee.

(c) **[1:378]** **No "unilateral increases":** A fixed fee agreement cannot be unilaterally increased by the attorney, even if the work turns out to be more onerous than anticipated. The attorney is subject to discipline for charging fees beyond those agreed upon with the client for the same work. [*Grossman v. State Bar* (1983) 34 C3d 73, 75, 192 CR 397, 399]

(d) **[1:379]** **Adequate records required:** Even if the fee agreement is reasonable and proper, it may be unenforceable if the lawyer has failed to maintain records that substantiate the amounts billed.

Moreover, failure to maintain adequate records reflecting handling of *monies received* on behalf of the client is also ground for disciplinary action against the lawyer. [*Fitzsimmons v. State Bar* (1983) 34 C3d 327, 331-332, 193 CR 896, 899]

(2) **[1:380]** **Fee splitting:** Dividing fees with another lawyer (who is not a partner or associate) is permissible *only if* the client *consents* in *writing* to the employment of the other lawyer, after full written *disclosure* that fees will be divided. In addition, the total fee must *not* exceed "reasonable compensation" for the services rendered, and must not be increased by reason of the fee-splitting agreement. [CRPC 2-200(A); see *Scolinos v. Kolts* (1995) 37 CA4th 635, 640, 44 CR2d 31, 33—agreement not so disclosed held void as against public policy; *Margolin v. Shemaria* (2000) 85 CA4th 891, 899, 102 CR2d 502, 507—oral fee-sharing agreement unen-

forceable despite defendant attorney's promise to obtain client's written consent]

The prohibition is not limited to "referral fees." The client's written consent to fee-sharing is required even where an outside lawyer works on the case under an agreement to share a contingent fee. [*Chambers v. Kay* (2002) 29 C4th 142, 148, 126 CR2d 536, 541; *but see* ¶*1:347.2a* (quantum meruit recovery available]

(3) [1:381] **Unearned fees to be deposited in trust account?** CRPC 4-100 requires trust account deposit of "all funds received or held for the benefit of clients . . ." Although not entirely clear (see below), this apparently includes *unearned fees* that are *refundable* to the client.

Whether fee prepayments are refundable depends, of course, on the fee agreement in each case.

(a) [1:382] **Nonrefundable fees ("retainers"):** If the *entire* amount prepaid presently "belongs" to the attorney, it should *not* be deposited in the trust account. [CRPC 4-100(A)]

This refers to the classic "retainer" fee: "A retainer is a sum of money paid by a client to secure an attorney's availability over a given period of time. Thus, such a fee is earned by the attorney *when paid* since the attorney is entitled to the money regardless of whether he actually performs any services under the agreement." [*Baranowski v. State Bar* (1979) 24 C3d 153, 164, 154 CR 752, 757, fn. 4 (emphasis added)]

1) [1:383] **Comment:** Courts are unlikely to treat fees paid in advance as a nonrefundable "retainer" unless it is *perfectly clear* that this is what the client intended. Otherwise, fee agreements are interpreted to allow refunds where services are not performed.

*(Text cont'd on p. 1-90.1)*

Even if a true "retainer" was intended, if the amount collected is disproportionate to the work done, it could be challenged by the client as an "unconscionable" fee (see ¶1:373).

(b) [1:384] **Refundable fees ("advance fees"):** On the other hand, funds "belonging in part to a client and in part *presently or potentially* to the member (attorney) . . ." must be deposited in the trust account. [CRPC 4-100(A) (emphasis added)]

Under this arrangement, the attorney may initially withdraw only whatever portion *presently* belongs to the attorney. Thereafter, further amounts may be withdrawn when the attorney's interest becomes "fixed." [CRPC 4-100(A); see *Securities & Exch. Comm'n v. Interlink Data Network of Los Angeles, Inc.* (9th Cir. 1996) 77 F3d 1201, 1206, fn. 4 (applying Calif. law)—agreement that advance payments be deposited in trust account, to be withdrawn as services rendered, is strong indication that unearned portion belongs to client, not attorney]

1) [1:385] **Comment:** This probably applies to most fee prepayments: i.e., the fee is not earned and the attorney's right to withdraw is not "fixed" until the work is done and billed; and the client expects a refund for services not performed.

However, the Supreme Court has expressly left open the question whether such "advance fees" must be deposited in the attorney's trust account. [See *Baranowski v. State Bar,* supra, 24 C3d at 164, 154 CR at 757] (But one lower court has held such funds must be segregated in a trust account until earned; see *T & R Foods, Inc. v. Rose* (1996) 47 CA4th Supp. 1, 7, 56 CR2d 41, 44.)

f. [1:386] **Credit terms:** The agreement should specify when the fee is payable (otherwise it will be deemed payable only upon completion of all services). If payment is to be made in installments, a schedule of payments for each installment should be included, together with a specification of any interest charges.

(1) [1:387] **Truth-in-lending laws:** If the fee is for "personal, family or household" purposes, and by written agreement is payable in *more than four installments, or* interest is charged, and the attorney "regularly" extends such credit, the attorney may have to comply with federal truth-in-lending laws ("Regulation Z" requirements). [See 12 CFR §226.2(a)]

Compare: These requirements do *not* apply to fees owed by a corporation or partnership; nor to amounts owed by an individual client for fees in connection with a "business, commercial or agricultural purpose." [Regulation Z, 12 CFR §226.3]

(a) [1:388] **Requirements:** Under Regulation Z, the debtor must be furnished with a written disclosure statement detailing the interest rate, the dollar cost of credit provided, a payment schedule, an itemization of interest and late charges, etc. (See detailed requirements in Regulation Z, 12 CFR §226.18.)

(b) [1:389] **Effect of failure to comply:** Noncompliance may subject an attorney to civil penalties, including any actual damages to the debtor and twice the amount of any finance charge; plus criminal penalties if the failure was "willful." [15 USC §§1640, 1611]

Comment: It may also subject the attorney to *disciplinary proceedings* because Rule of Professional Conduct 4-200(A) provides that a member of the State Bar "shall not enter into an agreement for, charge or collect an *illegal* or unconscionable fee." Arguably, a fee agreement violating Regulation Z is an "illegal" fee within the meaning of this Rule.

➪[1:390] *PRACTICE POINTER:* You can avoid these problems by *billing periodically* as time accrues rather than negotiating a fee payable in installments.

g. [1:391] **Provisions for payment of costs:** Further, the agreement should address counsel's authority to incur court costs and related expenses essential to effective representation (e.g., investigation costs, filing fees, expert fees, deposition costs, jury and witness fees, etc.); and the client's obligation to pay or reimburse counsel therefor.

(1) [1:392] **Authority to incur expenses:** It is generally advisable to specify that counsel has the client's *advance* consent to incur necessary litigation costs and expenses. (Advance approval on every expense-related decision is usually impractical and time-consuming.)

(a) [1:393] **Prior approval of extraordinary expenses:** The client may, however, request a right of prior approval of expenses above a certain amount. This is particularly common in regard to hiring of experts . . . whose fees may run into thousands of dollars. Counsel should forewarn the client of this possibility, and if advance approval is requested, the agreement should so indicate.

(2) [1:394] **Client's responsibility for costs:** The agreement must make clear the client's responsibility for costs and expenses incurred by counsel in handling the case (and in contingency fee cases, how cost disbursements will affect the client's recovery; *see ¶1:351*).

(a) [1:395] **Advances from client:** The client may be able to *advance* funds toward payment of these costs. In such event, it may be appropriate to require the client to deposit with counsel sufficient sums to cover the estimated costs and to replenish this deposit as necessary.

1) [1:396] **Ethical limitation:** Such deposits must be kept in a *client trust account*, maintained separately from the attorney's personal and office accounts. Commingling with other funds, or an unjustified draw against the deposit, is ground for State Bar discipline. [See CRPC 4-100(A)]

(b) [1:397] **Advances to client:** Alternatively, counsel can agree to advance on behalf of the client costs and expenses in prosecuting or defending an action or otherwise protecting the client's interests. [CRPC 4-210(A)(3)]

1) [1:398] **Repayment may be contingent:** Repayment of the costs advanced may be made contingent on the outcome of the case. [CRPC 4-210(A)(3)]

*Caution:* This applies only to expenses incurred in providing legal service to the client (in litigation or otherwise). It does *not* permit an attorney to make repayment of personal loans or advances to the client contingent on the outcome of the client's case.

➪[1:399] *PRACTICE POINTER:* Contingency fee agreements sometimes provide that costs advanced by the lawyer are to be "reimbursed out of any recovery." But that may prove unfair where the client discharges the lawyer; i.e., the discharged lawyer has to wait until the case is settled or a judgment obtained (*see ¶1:424*).

To avoid this result, your retainer agreement should require the client to reimburse you for costs advanced "upon demand." (*See Form 1:B.*)

h. **[1:400]** **Security for payment of costs and fees:** If the client is to provide some form of security for his or her obligation to pay fees and costs, it must be clearly covered in the written agreement.

**[1:400.1-400.4]** *Reserved.*

(1) **[1:400.5]** **Lien on cause of action and recovery:** The most common form of security for fees and costs is for the client to agree that the attorney shall have a lien on the client's cause of action and any judgment or settlement obtained. *See detailed discussion at ¶1:426 ff.*

(2) **[1:401]** **Third party guarantee:** Where the client's financial situation is not strong enough to assure payment of the fees and costs, the attorney may insist upon a third party guarantee. For example, an attorney asked to represent a new corporation with limited assets may require the principal shareholders of the corporation to guarantee payment of the corporation's legal bills. In such cases, the *fee agreement with the client should be contingent* on execution of the guarantee.

⇨ **[1:402]** *PRACTICE POINTER:* A separate guarantee (either a separate document or a separate guarantee clause following the client's signature on the retainer agreement) is preferable to having the guarantor simply sign the retainer agreement. The latter raises questions as to whether the guarantor is a client to whom you owe duties.

• *FORM:* Guarantee Agreement, *see Form 1:A.4.*

(3) **[1:403]** **Security interest in real or personal property:** The client's obligation to pay fees and costs may be secured; e.g., by a pledge of personal property or by a trust deed on real property.

(a) **[1:404]** *Caution—CRPC limitations:* The California Rules of Professional Conduct impose special limitations on dealings with a client whereby the attorney acquires an interest "adverse" to the client. *Each* of the following requirements must be satisfied:

• The transaction must be "fair and reasonable" to the client; *and*

- The terms must be "fully disclosed and transmitted in writing" in a manner that can be "reasonably understood by the client"; *and*

- The client must be *specifically advised in writing* that he or she may seek advice by *independent counsel*, and given a *reasonable opportunity* to do so; *and*

- The client must thereafter *consent in writing* to the terms of the transaction. [CRPC 3-300]

(b) **[1:405] Application to security interests:** The above Rules apply to the attorney's taking a promissory note and trust deed from the client to secure payment of fees. The trust deed is an "adverse interest" because it can be used to summarily extinguish the client's interest in the property through private foreclosure proceedings. [*Hawk v. State Bar* (1988) 45 C3d 589, 601, 247 CR 599, 606—discipline imposed]

    1) **[1:406] Comment:** Although the attorney is subject to discipline, it is unclear whether courts would refuse enforcement of a security interest violating the CRPC. The Rules specifically state that their violation does *not* automatically give rise to a civil cause of action. [See "Discussion" following CRPC 1-100]

(c) **[1:407] Compare—unsecured promissory note:** By contrast, an unsecured promissory note is *not* an "adverse interest" because "it does not give the attorney any *present* right in the client's property which the attorney can summarily realize." [*Hawk v. State Bar*, supra, 45 C3d at 601, 247 CR at 606]

*Caution:* Whether an *oral* agreement for a *charging lien* on a cause of action is an "adverse interest" subject to CRPC 3-300 is presently before the California Supreme Court in *Fletcher v. Davis*, Case No. S114715.

i. **[1:408] Arbitration of disputes?** An increasing number of attorneys include in their retainer agreements provisions for arbitration of any dispute with the client, specifically including malpractice claims.

*FORMS:* A suggested arbitration provision is included in both *Form 1:A* ("Letter Agreement for Hourly Rate Fee") and *Form 1:B* ("Contingency Fee Agreement").

➪**[1:408.1]** *PRACTICE POINTER:* Whether to include an arbitration provision in your retainer fee agreement is a highly personal decision. Some lawyers feel it is professionally improper to foreclose clients' access to the courts.

The *advantages* of arbitration may be its privacy and expediency, and avoidance of "runaway" jury verdicts on malpractice claims.

The *disadvantages* include limited discovery and limited judicial review.

If you decide to include an arbitration clause, *check first with your malpractice insurer!* Make sure the carrier agrees to defend and indemnify you in *arbitration* as well as judicial proceedings.

(1) [1:408.2] **Ethical considerations:** Arbitration provisions are not per se ethically improper. Thus, an attorney may properly refuse to represent potential clients who object to arbitration. [*Powers v. Dickson, Carlson & Campillo* (1997) 54 CA4th 1102, 1115, 63 CR2d 261, 269—arbitration clause in initial retainer agreement did not create conflict of interest and thus *not* subject to stricter scrutiny than other provisions]

Nor is there any ethical bar to binding arbitration agreements with *existing clients*. [See *Powers v. Dickson, Carlson & Campillo*, supra, 54 CA4th at 1115, 63 CR2d at 269—no need to advise existing client to seek independent counsel before signing amendment to fee agreement containing arbitration clause] (*Caution:* The result might be contra if amendments to an existing arbitration agreement are *adverse* to the client; and conflict of interest rules may apply to arbitration provisions in connection with separate financial transactions with the client.)

(*Text cont'd on p. 1-91*)

(2) [1:409]  **Limitation—*fees and costs disputes* subject to State Bar arbitration rules:**  Retainer agreement provisions for arbitration of fees and costs disputes are limited by statutes giving the client the right to submit such disputes to *nonbinding* arbitration under State Bar rules. [See *Alternative Systems, Inc. v. Carey* (1998) 67 CA4th 1034, 1042-1043, 79 CR2d 567, 572]

(a) [1:409.1]  **State Bar "mandatory fees/costs arbitration":**  Upon timely *demand by the client*, any dispute between attorney and client over fees or costs, or both, must be submitted to *nonbinding* arbitration pursuant to Rules adopted by the State Bar. These Rules provide for mediation and arbitration of such disputes under systems sponsored by local bar associations. [See Bus. & Prof.C. §6200(d)]

Fees/costs dispute arbitration is "mandatory" for the attorney but it is optional for the client (unless the client otherwise agrees in writing). [See Bus. & Prof.C. §§6200(c), 6201(a), 6204(a)]

The arbitrator's award is *not binding* (unless the parties otherwise agree in writing after the dispute has arisen; *see ¶1:410.5*). Either party may petition the court for a *trial de novo* within 30 days after notice of the arbitrator's award. [Bus. & Prof.C. §6204(a)]

When the attorney is retained by one person to provide legal services to another, the one who has agreed to pay the lawyer's bills is the one entitled to arbitrate any fees and/or costs dispute. [*Wager v. Mirzayance* (1998) 67 CA4th 1187, 1189, 79 CR2d 661, 662]

*FORMS*

• Petition to Confirm, Correct, or Vacate Attorney-Client Fee Arbitration Award, *see Form 1:B.3.*

• Rejection of Award and Request for Trial After Attorney-Client Fee Arbitration, *see Form 1:B.4.*

1) [1:409.2]  **Attorney must notify client of right to arbitration:**  The attorney must give the client *written notice* of the client's right to arbitration under the State Bar program (above). [Bus. & Prof.C. §6201(a); *Wager v. Mirzayance*, supra, 67 CA4th at 1190-1191, 79 CR2d at 663]

Such notice must be given before or concurrently with service of summons in any suit for fees/costs, or prior to or at the time of commencing any other proceeding (e.g., contractual arbitration through AAA or JAMS) to collect fees and/or costs. Failure to do so is ground for dismissal of the action or proceeding. [Bus. & Prof.C. §6201(a)]

The notice must be given *after* a fees/costs dispute has arisen; i.e., it is not sufficient if given in the retainer agreement or before there was any dispute. [*Huang v. Cheng* (1998) 66 CA4th 1230, 1234, 78 CR2d 550, 552]

2) **[1:409.3]** **Effect of failure to give notice:** Failure to give such notice is ground for *dismissal* of whatever action or proceeding is initiated by the attorney to collect fees and/or costs. [Bus. & Prof.C. §6201(a)]

(b) **[1:410]** **Predispute agreement for binding arbitration of fees/costs disputes invalid:** No agreement for binding arbitration of a dispute over fees or costs may be made in the retainer agreement. *Nor may the retainer agreement waive* the parties' right to trial de novo following a State Bar fee arbitration. [See Bus. & Prof.C. §6204(a); *Alternative Systems, Inc. v. Carey* (1998) 67 CA4th 1034, 1042-1043, 79 CR2d 567, 572]

1) **[1:410.1]** **Comment:** This has a curious effect. Clients may be bound in the retainer agreement to arbitrate *malpractice* claims against their attorneys but not disputes over fees and/or costs! It is not clear what happens when a fee dispute is intertwined with claims of malpractice or breach of fiduciary duty (e.g., client claims fee charged was "unconscionable").

*Caution:* Whether a client who opposed arbitration under the mandatory fee arbitration scheme is estopped from claiming the arbitrator exceeded his or her powers by arbitrating a malpractice as well as a fee claim is presently before the California Supreme Court in *Aguilar v. Lerner*, Case No. S099667.

2) **[1:410.2]** **Federal preemption?** The Federal Arbitration Act (9 USC §1 et seq.) governs contractual arbitration in written contracts involving *interstate commerce.* Because the Act embodies a strong federal policy favoring arbitration, it *preempts conflicting state laws.* [*Southland Corp. v. Keating* (1984) 465 US 1,

12, 104 S.Ct. 852, 859] (See detailed discussion in Knight, Fannin, Chernick & Haldeman, *Cal. Prac. Guide: Alternative Dispute Resolution* (TRG), Ch. 5.)

Comment: If the attorney-client agreement affects interstate commerce (and that term is interpreted broadly), the ban on binding predispute arbitration would appear to be preempted by the FAA.

[1:410.3-410.4] *Reserved.*

(c) [1:410.5] **Compare—postdispute agreements for binding arbitration:** *After* such a dispute has arisen, the parties may agree to be bound *by the award of arbitrators appointed under the State Bar rules.* [Bus. & Prof.C. §6204(a)]

1) [1:410.6] **Limited to State Bar arbitrators:** This provision has been interpreted to *preempt* contractual arbitration provisions requiring clients to submit fee disputes to *any other entity* (e.g., to private arbitration providers such as AAA or JAMS): "(T)his is a closed system and the binding arbitration agreed to in writing is the arbitration conducted by local bar associations under the (State Bar rules), not some other private alternative dispute resolution provided by another forum." [*Alternative Systems, Inc. v. Carey,* supra, 67 CA4th at 1042-1043, 79 CR2d at 572 (parentheses added) (dictum because court was dealing with predispute agreement)]

2) [1:410.7] **No waiver:** This system is for protection of the public and therefore a client does *not* waive its right to trial de novo under the State Bar rules by signing a fee agreement calling for binding arbitration with the AAA or other private arbitration provider. [*Alternative Systems, Inc. v. Carey,* supra, 67 CA4th at 1044, 79 CR2d at 573]

3) [1:410.8] **Federal preemption?** It is unclear whether this "closed system" for binding fees/costs arbitration conflicts with, and is therefore preempted by, the Federal Arbitration Act *(see ¶1:410.2).*

(3) [1:411] **Other disputes subject to binding arbitration:** Although fees and costs disputes are excluded (see above), the retainer agreement may provide for binding arbitration of other disputes between attorney

and client; e.g., malpractice claims, breach of fiduciary duty re investments, etc.

(a) [1:411.1] **Voluntariness:** Retainer agreements are *not* contracts of adhesion; i.e., they are not a standardized contract offered on a take-it-or-leave-it basis by a party of superior bargaining strength. Therefore, arbitration provisions in the retainer agreement are not considered involuntary. [*Powers v. Dickson, Carlson & Campillo* (1997) 54 CA4th 1102, 1110, 63 CR2d 261, 266]

(b) [1:411.2] **No special form required:** The arbitration provision need not comply with the statutory requirements for arbitration of medical malpractice claims (see CCP §1295, requiring specific language in large bold red type, etc.). [*Powers v. Dickson, Carlson & Campillo*, supra, 54 CA4th at 1114, 63 CR2d at 268—*rejecting* contrary suggestion in State Bar Form.Opn. 1989-116, fn. 5]

(c) [1:411.3] **No express jury waiver required:** Nor is it necessary for the arbitration provision to contain an express waiver of the client's right to jury trial. [*Powers v. Dickson, Carlson & Campillo*, supra, 54 CA4th at 1115, 63 CR2d at 269]

(d) [1:411.4] **Explanations not required:** It has been suggested that the attorney must fully disclose to the client the terms and consequences of the arbitration provision; i.e., no right to jury trial, limited appellate review, etc. [See State Bar Form.Opn. 1989-116]

It is doubtful, however, that this is necessary since a retainer agreement is *not* an adhesion contract and unambiguous provisions for arbitration are enforceable. [*Powers v. Dickson, Carlson & Campillo*, supra, 54 CA4th at 1115, 63 CR2d at 269]

⇨[1:411.5] *PRACTICE POINTER:* Even if not required, it is good practice to discuss such matters with the client; and to *include the client's acknowledgment* of such explanation in the retainer agreement. The client should be asked to sign or initial the acknowledgment. *See the suggested arbitration provisions in Forms 1:A and 1:B.*

[1:412-415] *Reserved.*

6. [1:416] **Dealing With Prior Counsel:** Clients may want to switch lawyers in the middle of the case. This can pose special problems for the new lawyer:

- The client's right to discharge the prior lawyer (*see* ¶*1:417*);

- The prior lawyer's right to fees (*see* ¶*1:419*);

- The prior lawyer's obligation to sign the substitution of attorneys and to deliver the client's file (*see* ¶*1:448*); and

- Under certain circumstances, the new lawyer's taking the case from the prior lawyer may be actionable as a tort (interference with the prior lawyer's contract relationship with the client) (*see* ¶*1:456*).

a. **[1:417]** **Discharging the prior lawyer:** The client has the absolute right to discharge his or her lawyer at any time—with or without cause. The fact that the attorney may have rendered valuable services or that the client is indebted to him therefor does not deprive the client of the right. [*Fracasse v. Brent* (1972) 6 C3d 784, 790-791, 100 CR 385, 389; *Santa Clara County Counsel Attys. Ass'n v. Woodside* (1994) 7 C4th 525, 555, 28 CR2d 617, 634]

**[1:418]** *Reserved.*

b. **[1:419]** **Prior lawyer's right to fees:** The prior lawyer's right to fees depends on the contractual relationship with the client, and whether the attorney withdrew or was discharged by the client.

⟹ **[1:420]** *PRACTICE POINTER:* It is always a good idea to call the prior lawyer to verify his or her fee arrangements with the client *before* you accept the case.

You may discover that the prior lawyer has a contractual lien on the cause of action. This may affect your decision on whether to accept the case.

Also, it is customary in some communities to reimburse prior counsel for out-of-pocket costs advanced on behalf of the client. In such communities, you need to know how much money will be expected from your firm if you take over the case.

In addition to financial considerations, talking with the prior lawyer may reveal his or her evaluation of the case and of the client. Particularly where the client has already had several lawyers on the case, it may help you decide whether you *really* want to take the case!

(1) **[1:421]** **Right to fees where client discharges attorney:** As stated above, a client has the absolute right to discharge counsel at any time. Thus, the client's discharging the prior lawyer is not a breach of contract.

But the former attorney is entitled to recover in quasi-contract for the *reasonable value* of services rendered before discharge—whether such discharge was *with or without cause. [Fracasse v. Brent* (1972) 6 C3d 784, 792, 100 CR 385, 390]

Unless a contingency fee is agreed upon, the attorney is normally compensated at a reasonable hourly rate for the number of hours worked . . . but in no event more than a "reasonable fee" for the services performed. [See *Cazares v. Saenz* (1989) 208 CA3d 279, 287, 256 CR 209, 213-214]

(a) **[1:422] Contingency fee cases:** However, where the case was being handled on a contingency fee basis, the discharged lawyer is entitled to recover only upon occurrence of the contingency— i.e., when the client settles or obtains judgment. If the client recovers nothing, the discharged attorney gets nothing. [*Fracasse v. Brent*, supra]

1) **[1:423] Portion of fee earned:** "Reasonable value" in contingency fee cases is not limited to an hourly rate. An enhanced fee is justified by the risk involved, the delay in receiving payment, etc.

The discharged attorney's pro rata share of the recovery is determined by comparing the value of his or her services to the value of the total services rendered. This is by no means limited to "straight time" (i.e., how many hours spent by each attorney). The court may adjust "for difficulty of the work or other relevant factors." [*Cazares v. Saenz* (1989) 208 CA3d 279, 288-289, 256 CR 209, 215—dealing with dispute between attorneys on referral fees]

This pro rata approach is proper even in "windfall" cases—i.e., where the discharged attorney's pro rata share *exceeds* the reasonable value of his or her services: "In essence, having contracted with the lawyer or firm to pay a particular fee, (the client or successor attorney) is estopped to deny that the pro rata contract price accurately measures the reasonable value of the services rendered." [*Cazares v. Saenz*, supra, 208 CA3d at 290, 256 CR at 216]

An attorney discharged shortly before conclusion of the case may be entitled to the *entire* contingent fee as the appropriate quantum meruit recovery. [See *Fracasse v. Brent*, supra, 6 C3d at 791, 100 CR at 390]

2) **[1:424] Costs advanced:** If the contingency fee agreement provides that costs advanced will be "reimbursed out of the gross recovery," the discharged attorney must wait for reimbursement until the case settles or a judgment is obtained. If the case is still pending, the attorney's suit for reimbursement is premature. [*Kroff v. Larson* (1985) 167 CA3d 857, 860-861, 213 CR 526, 528]

> ➡ **[1:425] *PRACTICE POINTER:*** To avoid this result, your retainer agreement should provide that costs advanced are repayable by the client "upon demand" (*see ¶1:399*).
>
> As mentioned earlier, it is customary in some communities for the lawyer taking over the case to reimburse the discharged lawyer for costs advanced (*see ¶1:420*). But, there is probably no way of compelling the new lawyer to do so. So, the matter should be covered in the retainer agreement with the client.

(b) **[1:426] Liens to secure fees:** The fee agreement with the discharged lawyer may provide for a lien on the client's cause of action to secure payment of fees and costs advanced (*see Form 1:B.1*).

The lien need not be expressly created; and, the word "lien" need not be used. A lien may be implied where the fee agreement indicates the attorney is to look to the judgment for payment of his or her fees. [See *Cetenko v. United Calif. Bank* (1982) 30 C3d 528, 531, 179 CR 902, 904]

An attorney with a lien is regarded as "an *equitable assignee of the judgment or settlement* to the extent of fees and costs which are due him for services." [*Levin v. Gulf Ins. Group* (1999) 69 CA4th 1282, 1286, 82 CR2d 228, 230 (emphasis added; internal quotes omitted)]

1) **[1:427] Validity dependent upon contract:** Such contractual liens are valid and enforceable; the contract is treated as an equitable assignment *pro tanto* of the client's recovery. [*Bandy v. Mt. Diablo Unified School Dist.* (1976) 56 CA3d 230, 235, 126 CR 890, 893]

Absent a valid contract with the client, no lien can be claimed. The common law general retaining lien and special charging lien are *not* recognized in California. [See *Isrin v. Sup.Ct. (County of Los Angeles)* (1965) 63 C2d 153, 157, 45 CR 320, 323]

And the mere fact that the attorney has performed services on a case does *not* entitle him or her to a lien. (I.e., an attorney's lien is *not* like a mechanic's or materialman's lien!) [*Trimble v. Steinfeldt* (1986) 178 CA3d 646, 651, 224 CR 195, 197—lawyer who performed services on case, but who was never attorney of record and had no contract with client, *not* entitled to lien]

2) **[1:428] Priority over later liens:** Where the contract gives the attorney a lien on the client's cause of action, it *arises upon execution* of the contract. Thus, "other things being equal," an attorney's lien takes priority over later liens (e.g., an attachment or judgment creditor's lien). [Civ.C. §2897; see *Cetenko v. United Calif. Bank* (1982) 30 C3d 528, 533, 179 CR 902, 905; *Pangborn Plumbing Corp. v. Carruthers & Skiffington* (2002) 97 CA4th 1039, 1052, 119 CR2d 416, 424]

It may also be entitled to priority, depending on the equities of the case, over a later acquired *offset* against the client (e.g., claims acquired by the defendant against the plaintiff). [*Brienza v. Tepper* (1995) 35 CA4th 1839, 1849, 42 CR2d 690, 695—Attorney's contractual lien on Client's claim against Debtor was protected despite fact that Debtor had obtained assignment of Bank's claim against Client in a greater amount]

a) **[1:429] May be given for past or future services:** The lien may be given for past or future services. It may even secure payment of services *unrelated to the action* on which the lien is given. [*Bluxome Street Associates v. Fireman's Fund Ins. Co.* (1988) 206 CA3d 1149, 1153-1155, 254 CR 198, 200-202—upholding attorneys' lien on client's action handled by other attorneys]

b) **[1:430] "Secret" lien:** Unlike other liens, an attorney's lien on a tort cause of action may be a "secret" lien. Notice of the lien is *not* required to be given to the client's creditors. [See *Cetenko v. United Calif. Bank,* supra, 30 C3d at 533, 179 CR at 905]

The UCC filing provisions applicable to liens generally (Comm'l C. §9-104) do *not* apply to liens on *tort* causes of action. [See *Bluxome Street Associates v. Fireman's Fund Ins. Co.,* supra, 206 CA3d at 1155, 254 CR at 202]

c) **[1:431] Adjudicating competing lien claims:** Upon proof of the existence of an attorney's contractual lien on the judgment, the court may *stay enforcement* of a judgment creditor's lien on the judgment until there is a judicial determination of lien priority in an independent action (*see ¶1:433*). Indeed, it may be "an abuse of discretion for the trial court to direct payment of the judgment proceeds . . . without giving (the attorney) a fair opportunity to first litigate the validity of his lien claim in a separate action." [*Brown v. Sup.Ct. (Cyclon)* (2004) 116 CA4th 320, 335, 9 CR3d 912, 925 (parentheses added); *see ¶1:433*]

d) **[1:432] Equities favoring other creditors:** The attorney's lien is entitled to priority over later liens only when "other things (are) equal" (Civ.C. §2897). Thus, in appropriate cases, the court has power to deny priority to an attorney's lien in favor of a later creditor. [See *Del Conte Masonry Co. v. Lewis* (1971) 16 CA3d 678, 681, 94 CR 439, 441—where attorney delayed obtaining contractual lien until after judgment creditor filed motion for lien, equities favored judgment creditor]

e) **[1:432.1] Effect of client's bankruptcy:** A valid attorney's lien on a prospective recovery survives the client's bankruptcy. Bankruptcy may discharge the client's obligation to pay for prebankruptcy legal services but does not prevent the attorney from enforcing a lien for those services. [*Saltarelli & Steponovich v. Douglas* (1995) 40 CA4th 1, 5-6, 46 CR2d 683, 686—notice of lien need not be filed in underlying action]

3) **[1:433] Independent action required to enforce attorney's lien:** A contractual lien for

attorney fees is not self-executing. In the face of an objection by any party, the lien must be enforced in a separate action. (In contingency fee matters, of course, the action lies only after the client obtains a judgment or settlement; see above.) [*Carroll v. Interstate Brands Corp.* (2002) 99 CA4th 1168, 1176, 121 CR2d 532, 538]

Normally, the independent action is for *declaratory relief* to establish the *validity* and *amount* of the attorney's lien and *priority* as to any competing liens on the judgment (*see ¶1:428*). Any competing judgment lienholders must be joined as parties to the action. [See *Brown v. Sup.Ct. (Cyclon)* (2004) 116 CA4th 320, 333, 9 CR3d at 923]

a) **[1:433.1]** **Not enforceable in underlying action:** An attorney claiming a lien on a client's cause of action and judgment may *not* intervene or file a motion in the underlying action to enforce the lien. The court in that action has *no jurisdiction* to establish the validity, amount or priority of the attorney's lien. [*Carroll v. Interstate Brands Corp.,* supra, 99 CA4th at 1176, 121 CR2d at 538; *Bandy v. Mt. Diablo Unified School Dist.* (1976) 56 CA3d 230, 234, 126 CR 890, 893]

4) **[1:434]** **Notice of attorney's lien filed in underlying action:** Although the court in the underlying action cannot enforce the lien, discharged attorneys can prevent the client from "settling around" their lien by filing a *notice* of lien in the underlying action. [*Valenta v. Regents of Univ. of Calif.* (1991) 231 CA3d 1465, 1469-1470, 282 CR2d 812, 814-815]

**FORM:** Notice of Lien, *see Form 1:B.2*

a) **[1:435]** **Not required:** Filing such notice of lien in the pending action is "permissible and even advisable" (and indeed, it is common practice). [*Valenta v. Regents of Univ. of Calif.*, supra, 231 CA3d at 1470, 282 CR at 815]

But a discharged attorney is not required to file such notice in order to establish his or her lien. I.e., even if no notice is filed, the attorney's "secret" lien on the judgment is enforceable; and it is entitled to *priority* against the client's subsequent creditors or assignees. [See *Hansen v. Haywood* (1986) 186 CA3d 350, 356, 230 CR 580, 584]

➪ [1:436] ***PRACTICE POINTER:*** Even if not required, a discharged attorney will usually file such notice. It effectively prevents plaintiff from "settling around" the lien . . . because, to avoid getting involved in the dispute, defendant or its insurer will almost certainly make any settlement draft payable jointly to the client, the new attorney *and* the discharged attorney.

The settlement proceeds will thus be tied up until everyone involved can agree on how the money should be divided . . . or until one or the other brings an *independent* action for declaratory relief. [See *Carroll v. Interstate Brands Corp.*, supra, 99 CA4th at 1176, 121 CR2d at 538 (citing text)]

[1:436.1-436.4] *Reserved.*

b) [1:436.5] **Tort liability for "settling around" attorney's lien:** Defendants and their attorneys risk tort liability in paying a judgment or settlement to the plaintiff or others in disregard of a discharged attorney's *known* lien. [*Levin v. Gulf Ins. Group* (1999) 69 CA4th 1282, 1287-1288, 82 CR2d 228, 231—upholding claim for intentional interference with prospective economic advantage against defendant's insurer and its attorneys]

(2) [1:437] **No right to fees where attorney abandons case:** Prior counsel has no right to a lien or fee in a contingency fee case if he or she *withdrew without good cause.* [*Hensel v. Cohen* (1984) 155 CA3d 563, 567-568, 202 CR 85, 87-88; see *Rus, Miliband & Smith v. Conkle & Olesten* (2003) 113 CA4th 656, 673-674, 6 CR3d 612, 623-624]

(a) [1:438] **Example:** Attorney took a case on a contingency fee basis, but later decided it was a "dead bang loser" and told the client to get another lawyer. The client did so. Attorney was entitled to *nothing* for the work done prior to withdrawal. I.e., having abandoned the case, Attorney had no right of recovery, either on a contract or quasi-contract basis. [*Hensel v. Cohen*, supra]

(b) **[1:439] Compare—withdrawal after performance of services:** But if the attorney has *fully* performed the services required by the contract, the attorney's withdrawal from the case does not prejudice his or her right to fees already earned under the contract. [*Joseph E. Di Loreto, Inc. v. O'Neill* (1991) 1 CA4th 149, 157-158, 1 CR2d 636, 640-641]

    1) **[1:440] Example:** Attorney's contingency fee agreement covered only services in obtaining a judgment in the trial court. After obtaining a $600,000 judgment, he told Client additional fees would be required to handle the appeal. When Client refused, Attorney told Client he would not represent her further. His withdrawal from case did *not* affect his right to the contingency fee already earned. [*Joseph E. Di Loreto, Inc. v. O'Neill*, supra, 1 CA4th at 157, 1 CR2d at 640-641]

(3) **[1:441] Right to fees where "good cause" shown for withdrawal:** On the other hand, if the attorney *has* "good cause" for withdrawal, the court may allow quantum meruit recovery for services rendered prior to withdrawal. [See *Estate of Falco v. Decker* (1987) 188 CA3d 1004, 1016, 233 CR 807, 814]

(a) **[1:442] Withdrawal mandatory under ethical rules:** "Good cause" certainly exists where the attorney's withdrawal is *mandated under ethical rules*: e.g., CRPC 3-200 and 3-400(B) mandate withdrawal where counsel should know the client is acting "without probable cause and for the purpose of harassing or maliciously injuring any person." [See also *Estate of Falco v. Decker*, supra, 188 CA3d at 1016, 233 CR at 814]

(b) **[1:443] Withdrawal permissive under ethical rules:** "Good cause" may (or may not) exist in cases involving *permissive withdrawal*: E.g., CRPC 3-700(C)(1)(d) permits an attorney to withdraw where the client refuses to cooperate or otherwise makes it "*unreasonably difficult*" for the lawyer to carry out his or her employment effectively.

In such cases, "it is within the discretion of the trial court, with heightened scrutiny consistent with the standards articulated here, to determine *whether counsel's withdrawal was justified for the purpose of awarding fees.*" [*Estate of Falco v. Decker*, supra, 188 CA3d at 1016, 233 CR at 814, fn. 12 (emphasis added)]

Such justification may be difficult to establish in *contingency fee cases:* "To allow an attorney under a contingency fee agreement to withdraw without compulsion and still seek fees from any future recovery is to shift the time, effort and risk of obtaining the recovery . . . from the attorney, who agreed to bear those particular costs in the first place, to the client . . . (I)t is unassailably unfair to allow him or her to escape that labor absent the *most compelling* of permissive reasons." [*Rus, Miliband & Smith v. Conkle & Olesten* (2003) 113 CA4th 656, 675-676, 6 CR3d 612, 625-626 (emphasis and parentheses added)]

*(Text cont'd on p. 1-97)*

**RESERVED**

1) **[1:444] Refusal to settle NOT cause:** The client has an absolute right to reject settlement, even though the attorney strongly recommends it. Therefore, refusal to settle by itself does *not* constitute cause for withdrawal for the purpose of awarding fees. [*Estate of Falco v. Decker*, supra, 188 CA3d at 1018, 233 CR at 815]

2) **Application**

- **[1:445]** Because Clients refused Attorney's recommendation to settle a contingency fee case on "any terms I can put together," Attorney moved to withdraw as counsel. The motion was granted (on ground of breakdown of attorney-client relationship). Clients then settled the case in pro per for a large amount. Their refusal to settle did *not* justify Attorney's withdrawal and Attorney therefore was not entitled to any share of the recovery. [*Estate of Falco v. Decker,* supra, 188 CA3d at 1014, 233 CR at 813]

- **[1:445.1]** On the other hand, if after refusing to settle, Clients later *accepted terms negotiated* by Attorney, Attorney might be entitled to recover on a theory of unjust enrichment. [*Estate of Falco v. Decker,* supra, 188 CA3d at 1019, 233 CR at 816]

(4) **[1:446] Effect of order relieving counsel:** An order relieving counsel (e.g., substituting client in pro per) establishes only a breakdown of the attorney-client relationship. It does *not* determine that counsel had justifiable cause for withdrawal so as to be entitled to fees. [*Estate of Falco v. Decker*, supra, 188 CA3d at 1014, 233 CR at 813]

*Cross-refer:* The procedure to be relieved as attorney of record is discussed at ¶9:385.

(5) **[1:447] Effect of retainer agreement authorizing attorney to withdraw at will?** Some contingency fee contracts purport to authorize Attorney to withdraw at any time, with or without cause; and obligate Client to pay for services rendered prior to withdrawal. The validity of such provisions is unclear.

Arguably, such attempts by the attorney to "hedge his or her bet" may be held void as contrary to public policy ... except perhaps where the attorney did not have adequate opportunity to investigate the case before accepting it (e.g., where statute of limitations was about to run out).

c. **[1:448]** **Obtaining signed substitution and client's file:** The client has the absolute right to substitute one attorney for another at any time and for any reason. It is immaterial that the client owes the former attorney money (for fees or costs advanced), or that the substitution will work to the purported detriment of the former attorney. [*Kallen v. Delug* (1984) 157 CA3d 940, 950, 203 CR 879, 885]

(1) **[1:449]** **Prior lawyer's duty to sign substitution and deliver client's file:** Any delay in effecting the substitution may put the client's interests at risk. Therefore, once notified of the client's wishes to substitute new counsel, the prior lawyer must comply *promptly* with the client's wishes. The prior lawyer has *no* right to refuse to sign a substitution or to withhold the file until his or her fees are paid or secured. [*Kallen v. Delug*, supra, 157 CA3d at 951, 203 CR at 885]

☞**[1:449.1]** *PRACTICE POINTER:* Before turning the client's file over to new counsel, the prior lawyer should make and retain *copies* of all relevant documents. Failure to retain such copies may prove to be a substantial handicap if the prior lawyer is subsequently sued for malpractice.

Also, don't quibble with new counsel over the cost of copying the file. Plan to pay that cost yourself!

☞**[1:449.2]** *FURTHER PRACTICE POINTER:* If you are the new attorney on the case, make sure you file the substitution of attorneys *promptly.* Until this has been done, the other attorney remains the "attorney of record" . . . which means that the opposing party can continue to serve papers on the prior attorney!

(a) **[1:450]** **Not essential to court appearance:** If authorized by the client, the new attorney may file pleadings on the client's behalf even before a substitution of attorneys is obtained: "Where the actual authority of the new attorney appears, courts regularly excuse the absence of a formal substitution . . . particularly where the adverse party has not been misled or otherwise prejudiced." [*Baker v. Boxx* (1991) 226 CA3d 1303, 1309, 277 CR 409, 412]

(2) **[1:451]** **Refusal as ground for disciplinary action:** Delay or refusal to turn over a client's file after being

notified of the substitution is ground for disciplinary action against the prior lawyer (and possible civil liability if it results in harm to the client). [See CRPC 3-700(D) & 4-100(B)(4); and L.A. County Bar Ass'n Ethics Comm. Opn. Nos. 48, 103, 197, 253 and 330; and S.F. Bar Ass'n Ethics Comm. Opn. No. 1975-4]

(3) **[1:452]** **Fee agreement exacted as condition of turning over files invalid:** Since the prior lawyer cannot refuse to sign the substitution and turn over the client's files, he or she cannot exact any consideration for doing so. I.e., the prior lawyer's promise to do that which he or she is already ethically obligated to do is *illegal* consideration. Any contract based on such a promise is void as contrary to public policy. [*Kallen v. Delug*, supra, 157 CA3d at 951, 203 CR at 885]

(4) **[1:453]** **Contract liens on file invalid:** Even if the fee agreement gives the prior attorney a lien on the client's files, he or she cannot refuse to turn over the files to new counsel. I.e., prior counsel has no contractual right to damage the client's case. Thus, where the client's files have no economic value to the attorney, and are being used only to extort disputed fees, the lien is void as contrary to public policy. [*Academy of Calif. Optometrists v. Sup.Ct. (Damir)* (1975) 51 CA3d 999, 1006, 124 CR 668, 672]

(5) **[1:454]** **Contents of file to be delivered:** Disputes sometimes arise as to what documents in the prior attorney's file must be delivered to new counsel:

The Rules of Professional Conduct require release to the client (or delivery at the client's request) of "correspondence, pleadings, deposition transcripts, exhibits, physical evidence, expert's reports, *and other items reasonably necessary* to the client's representation, *whether the client has paid for them or not . . ."* [CRPC 3-700(D) (emphasis added)]

➡️**[1:455]** *PRACTICE POINTER:* Obtaining the client's files and a signed substitution is sometimes a point of friction with prior counsel. Notwithstanding the authorities cited above, some lawyers insist on retaining the file until their costs are reimbursed and their fees secured.

Since delay in obtaining the file could be prejudicial to the client, *it is your duty* to compel prior counsel to sign the substitution and deliver the file.

As a first step, you should send a letter to the prior lawyer citing the above authorities. (Send him or her photocopies of these pages, if you choose!)

If this does not work promptly, file a motion to recuse him or her as counsel (*see ¶9:382*) *without further delay.*

d. **[1:456]** **Taking case from prior lawyer as tort:** Under certain circumstances, the new lawyer's taking a case from the prior lawyer may be actionable as a tort. [*Rosenfeld, Meyer & Susman v. Cohen* (1983) 146 CA3d 200, 221-222, 194 CR 180, 193]

(1) **[1:457]** **Breach of fiduciary duty to former firm:** Upon dissolution of a law partnership, a partner may accept *new* business from clients of the former firm. But he or she may not appropriate *unfinished* business (cases in progress) belonging to the firm. The fees generated thereby must be shared with the other members of the former partnership. [*Rosenfeld, Meyer & Susman v. Cohen*, supra, 146 CA3d at 216-217, 194 CR at 189-190—Client had engaged Law Partnership to handle major antitrust case on contingency fee basis; just before settlement, the partner handling the case withdrew from the firm and took the client with him, and then settled the case, reaping for himself a huge fee]

(2) **[1:458]** **Interference with contract relationship:** Moreover, an attorney who obtains employment by *persuading the client to discharge* present counsel may be liable for interfering with a contract relationship, unless justification for such interference is shown. [*Rosenfeld, Meyer & Susman v. Cohen*, supra, 146 CA3d at 216-217, 194 CR at 193]

Even though the client has the absolute right to discharge his or her lawyer at any time (*Fracasse v. Brent*, supra), another lawyer has no right or privilege to *cause* the client to do so! [*Rosenfeld, Meyer & Susman v. Cohen*, supra, 146 CA3d at 221-222, 194 CR at 193]

➩**[1:459]** **PRACTICE POINTER:** Watch out for this problem in dealing with persons presently represented by other counsel!

You are certainly justified in accepting a case where the client comes to you after having already made up his or her mind to discharge existing counsel. But you are *not* justified in encouraging a client to "ditch" existing counsel with whom there was no prior dissatisfaction.

Be particularly careful in dealing with persons who say they are "unhappy" with existing counsel, but who have not yet discharged such counsel. In

Rev. #1 2001

such cases, *call the existing counsel,* and give him or her an opportunity to solve the client's "unhappiness" *before* accepting the case. Doing so should deter any claim that you caused the client to discharge existing counsel. (It should also enhance your reputation with the other lawyer!)

e. **[1:460] Compare—former partnership or employment agreements restricting representation:** Law partnership and employment agreements often obligate lawyers who leave the firm to pay some portion of *fees derived from future representation* of the firm's clients. So long as not unreasonable in amount, such provisions appear to be enforceable; i.e., they are *not* unlawful penalties or restrictions on the right to practice. [See *Howard v. Babcock* (1993) 6 C4th 409, 425, 25 CR2d 80, 90—partnership agreement forfeiting withdrawing partners' share of accounts receivable if they competed with partnership not void as against public policy, but case remanded for determination of "reasonableness" of forfeiture]

## B. PRELAWSUIT INVESTIGATIONS, RESEARCH AND ANALYSIS

[1:461]  Having accepted the case, the attorney will usually embark on legal research and investigations of the facts in order to define and analyze the client's problems. Sometimes, of course, it is absolutely imperative to file a lawsuit immediately (e.g., the client contacts the lawyer the day before the statute of limitations will run). However, in any other situation, the attorney should not proceed to court without sufficient factual and legal foundation.

1. **[1:462] Sources for Investigation:** Prelawsuit investigations usually involve a number of sources:

   a. **[1:463] Client:** The client is obviously the first and best source of factual information. Much of the initial client interview is normally used for determining the critical facts. Follow-up communications and correspondence with the client may be necessary to tie down the details. Sometimes, further office interviews will be required with the client or with others assisting him (family, friends, employees, etc.).

   ➡**[1:464] *PRACTICE POINTER:*** As stated earlier, client-interview questionnaires and fact sheets are often helpful in digging out all the factual information required in various kinds of cases. In other cases, it may be helpful to utilize a cassette recorder to supplement your note-taking. (Always ask the client's permission to record the interview or conversation before doing so.) The recording will be privileged against disclosure to the opposing side; *see ¶1:35-37.* (Remember, however, that the recording will not be privileged from discovery by the client and the State Bar in the event of a later dispute with the client! See CCP §2018(e) & (f).)

b. [1:465] **Client's files:** The client's own documents and records will usually be the first thing the opposition wants to examine. Thus, it is essential that you go through them *carefully before filing suit.* Such documents and records may alert you to pitfalls and issues that need further investigation or research in order to evaluate the case.

Be sure to examine contractual documents to determine whether the parties agreed to submit the dispute to arbitration.

➡️[1:465.1] *PRACTICE POINTER:* In larger organizations, there is usually a designated employee who has a good, overall understanding of how that business keeps its records. Often, your initial client contact will be with someone higher up. Therefore, always ask who has the best knowledge regarding the contents and organization of the client's records, and try to talk to that person, in order to identify what records should be submitted for your review.

c. [1:466] **Patient's medical records:** Whenever an attorney presents a signed written authorization from the client (patient), a medical provider is required to make all patient records under the provider's control available for inspection and copying. If the requesting attorney employs a professional photocopier, the medical provider must allow that person to do the copying. [See Ev.C. §1158]

   (1) [1:466.1] **Costs:** The medical provider may, however, impose "reasonable charges" (subject to statutory limits) for locating and making the records available. [See Ev.C. §1158]

d. [1:467] **Third parties:** Interviews with the client and review of the client's files should identify any third persons who can provide essential information:

   (1) [1:468] **Witnesses:** First-hand witnesses should always be interviewed *before* a lawsuit is filed, if possible. Their testimony is likely to have a large impact on the outcome of the case, and it is best to know where they stand. Also, you may be able to interview them before your opponent, in which event you may be able to extract more information from "unfriendly" witnesses.

Rev. #1 2001

➡️[1:469] *PRACTICE POINTER:* Always ask the witness to sign a statement based on your interview. You should explain that statements are necessary because memories are imperfect, and that you will be relying on the information obtained in advising your client and preparing the case for trial. Even if such statements are inadmissible as evidence, they may serve to refresh the witness' memory before trial (and to impeach the witness who changes his or her story during the course of the litigation).

To lessen the likelihood that a witness statement may be discoverable, consider inserting a clause following the witness' signature, as follows:

—"This witness statement was taken by an attorney. It contains the responses of the witness to questions formulated by the attorney based upon the attorney's legal analysis, and hence reflects the impressions, conclusions, opinions, legal research and theories of the attorney within the meaning of CCP §2018(c). This document is absolutely protected attorney work product. (Signature by Attorney)."

(a) [1:469.1] *Caution re discovery:* Third party witness statements may be discoverable by the opposing party if good cause is shown. Witness statements are *not* protectible as "attorney work product" even if a great deal of "work" went into obtaining them. *See discussion at ¶8:245 ff.*

[1:469.2-469.4] *Reserved.*

(2) [1:469.5] **Experts:** If the case involves medical or other scientific or technical problems, it is often prudent to consult an expert *before* filing suit. Doing so will help you evaluate the case more accurately, and may point out problems of which you would otherwise be unaware.

(a) [1:469.6] **Prelawsuit consultation required in certain malpractice cases:** In cases involving claims of malpractice by architects, engineers, etc., such consultation with an expert is a prerequisite to filing suit (*see ¶1:874 ff.*).

(b) [1:469.7] **Consultations generally shielded from discovery:** Experts retained solely for consultation purposes (as opposed to those employed to testify at trial) are generally shielded from discovery. Their identity and reports are treated as the attorney's "work product"; *see ¶8:246 ff.*

(c) **[1:469.8] Caution re contacting opposing party's experts:** It is improper to obtain information from an expert engaged as a *consultant* by the opposing party. An attorney who does so must be recused (disqualified) from the case. [*County of Los Angeles v. Sup.Ct. (Hernandez)* (1990) 222 CA3d 647, 658, 271 CR 698, 705; *see discussion at ¶1:95, 8:263.1*]

**[1:469.9]** *Reserved.*

(3) **[1:469.10] Compare—opposing party's medical providers:** Without the opposing party's authorization, an attorney may *not* seek privileged information from an opposing party's doctor or health insurer. [*Torres v. Sup.Ct. (Daily)* (1990) 221 CA3d 181, 188, 270 CR 401, 405; see *Province v. Center for Women's Health & Family Birth* (1993) 20 CA4th 1673, 1685-1686, 25 CR2d 667, 674; see also Civ.C. §56.10]

(4) **[1:470] Opposing party or counsel:** Do not overlook the opposing party as a possible source of additional factual information. If the opposing party is not yet represented by an attorney, you may wish to contact him or her directly, and ask for whatever information is relevant to your client's claim.

➡ **[1:471]** *PRACTICE POINTER:* It is usually a good idea to contact opposing counsel shortly after being retained to introduce yourself and discuss the case preliminarily. You can explain that you have just been retained and are anxious to get as much information as possible in order to evaluate the case.

The opposing party may be anxious to settle and willing to provide whatever information you need to evaluate your client's case. Even if no settlement is in prospect, opposing counsel may be willing to provide you with important documents or other evidence, and to disclose key elements of the opposing party's position . . . all of which will lead to a more rapid and accurate evaluation of your client's case.

(a) **[1:471.1] Ethical ban on communicating with parties represented by counsel:** Once the attorney learns that the opposing party is represented by counsel, all further communications with that party relating to a "subject of controversy" must be through counsel, unless he or she otherwise agrees: "A member of the State Bar shall not communicate *directly or indirectly* with a party whom he knows to be represented by counsel upon a subject of controversy without the express consent of such counsel . . ." [CRPC 2-100(A) (emphasis added)]

*Cross-refer:* See detailed discussion in Vapnek, Tuft, Peck & Wiener, *Cal. Prac. Guide: Professional Responsibility* (TRG), Ch. 8.

1) [1:471.2] **Actual knowledge required:** Rule 2-100 refers to *actual,* not constructive, knowledge that the person interviewed is represented by counsel. [*Truitt v. Sup.Ct. (Atchison, Topeka & S.F. Ry. Co.)* (1997) 59 CA4th 1183, 1188, 69 CR2d 558, 561-562]

   a) [1:471.3] **Rationale:** "A bright line rule is absolutely necessary in this situation . . . Lawyers should not be at risk of disciplinary action . . . because they 'should have known' that the opposing party was represented or would be represented at some future time." [*Truitt v. Sup.Ct. (Atchison Topeka & S.F. Ry. Co.),* supra, 59 CA4th at 1188, 69 CR2d at 561-562]

   b) [1:471.4] **Knowledge tested objectively:** The attorney's knowledge that the opposing party is represented by counsel is determined objectively, not subjectively; i.e., the attorney cannot claim lack of knowledge where such knowledge is apparent from surrounding circumstances. [See Cal. State Bar Form.Opn. 1996-145]

2) [1:471.5] **Ban applies to indirect communications:** It is improper for an attorney to use the client to "lure" the opposing party into a conference with the attorney behind opposing counsel's back (e.g., "Ask him to meet you at my office to work this thing out"). [*Abeles v. State Bar* (1973) 9 C3d 603, 607, 108 CR 359, 361]

   a) [1:471.6] **Compare—parties communicating with each other:** But Rule 2-100 does *not* prevent the *parties themselves* from communicating with each other. Nor does it prevent a lawyer from *advising* the client to do so. (E.g., "Why don't you talk to him directly and ask what he will take to settle the case?") [See "Discussion" following CRPC 2-100]

   [1:471.7-471.9] *Reserved.*

(5) [1:471.10] **Opposing party a corporation, partnership or association:** The ethical ban on communicating with parties represented by counsel extends to:

- An *officer, director* or *managing agent* of a corporation or association;

- A *partner* or *managing agent* of a partnership; and

- An association member or *employee* of the corporation, partnership or association "if the subject of the communication is *an act or omission of such person* . . . which may be binding upon or imputed to the organization for purposes of *civil or criminal liability* or whose statement may constitute an admission on the part of the organization." [CRPC 2-100(B) (emphasis added)]

(a) [1:471.11] **Officers, directors and managers:** Contact with *any* present officer, director, partner or managing agent of an adverse party is improper under Rule 2-100(B). It makes no difference whether the person contacted is a member of the "control group" or has the power to speak on behalf of the corporation.

1) [1:471.12] **Dissidents:** It makes no difference that the director or officer contacted is involved in a dispute with the corporation. This may create a conflict of interest for corporate counsel, but it does *not* justify opposing counsel "going behind corporate counsel's back." [See *Mills Land & Water Co. v. Golden West Refining Co.* (1986) 186 CA3d 116, 128, 230 CR 461, 467—lawyer disqualified for talking with dissenting director of company suing his client without consent of company's lawyers]

2) [1:471.13] **Lower level managers:** The mere fact that an employee has been designated as a "manager" or holds a similar title is not controlling. The prohibition only applies to those employees who "exercise substantial discretionary authority over significant aspects" of the organization's business. [*Snider v. Sup.Ct. (Quantum Productions, Inc.)* (2003) 113 CA4th 1187, 1209, 7 CR3d 119, 134]

3) [1:471.14] **Violation as ground for disqualification of counsel?** Although *Mills* upheld disqualification on this ground, other courts have questioned whether counsel can be disqualified or evidence sanctions imposed solely

for improper ex parte contacts: "(W)e question whether a protective or suppression order is warranted by showing only a violation of rule 2-100, without an additional showing that the violation led to the disclosure of confidential communications protected by the attorney client privilege . . . or created an unfair advantage, or impacted the fairness of the trial or the integrity of the judicial system." [*Continental Ins. Co. v. Sup.Ct. (Commercial Bldg. Maint. Co.)* (1995) 32 CA4th 94, 111, 37 CR2d 843, 853, fn. 5; *see further discussion at ¶1:471.46 ff.*]

(b) [1:471.15] **Employees:** Rule 2-100(B) prohibits ex parte contact with an employee of a corporation or partnership if:

- the subject of the communication is "*any act or omission of such person* . . . which may be *binding upon or imputed to* the organization for purposes of civil or criminal liability"; or

- the employee is one "whose statement may constitute an *admission* on the part of the organization." [CRPC 2-100(B)(2) (emphasis added)]

1) [1:471.16] **Not dependent on managerial status:** The ban on contacting employees whose statement may constitute "an admission" apparently refers to those having managerial status (to speak on behalf of the corporation). However, ex parte contact with even middle and lower level employees is prohibited *if* it relates to *their own acts or omissions* and their statement might be damaging to the corporation.

Reasons: It is difficult for counsel to ascertain who is a manager or member of the "control group"; *any* employee may be prejudiced by the ex parte contact (reprisals, etc.); the corporation has an interest in preventing disclosure to an opponent of knowledge or information that would be protected in communication between the employee and the corporation's counsel. [See *Mills Land & Water Co. v. Golden West Refining Co.* (1986) 186 CA3d 116, 130, 230 CR 461, 468-469, citing with approval L.A. Co. Bar Ass'n Ethics Comm. Formal Opn. No. 410 (1983)]

2) **[1:471.17]** **Communications unrelated to employee's own acts or omissions?** Rule 2-100(B) bars ex parte contact with nonmanagerial employees where the subject is the employee's own "act or omission" . . . but it does not deal with *other* knowledge or information of such employees: e.g., instructions received, conversations overheard, acts or omissions of *other* employees, etc.

The propriety of such ex parte communication is therefore left to case law (see "Discussion" following CRPC 1-100). Unfortunately, there is little case law in point:

a) **[1:471.18]** One case, in dictum, has adopted a "bright line" position barring ex parte contact with *all employees* of an opposing corporate party *regarding the matter in controversy* (not just communications regarding the employee's own acts or omissions). [See *Mills Land & Water Co. v. Golden West Refining Co.*, supra, 186 CA3d at 130, 230 CR at 468-469, citing with approval L.A. Co. Bar Ass'n Ethics Comm. Formal Opn. No. 410 (1983)]

3) **[1:471.19]** **Not limited to matters in litigation:** The ban on contacting current employees is not limited to matters already in litigation. Thus, if the attorney *knows* such employees are already represented by counsel, interviewing them violates CRPC 2-100 even with respect to matters not yet in litigation. [See *Triple A Machine Shop, Inc. v. State of Calif.* (1989) 213 CA3d 131, 138-140, 261 CR 493, 497-498]

⇨ **[1:471.20]** *PRACTICE POINTER:* If in doubt about the status of an opposing party's employees, counsel "would be well advised" to conduct discovery on this issue before initiating ex parte contact. In addition, once actual contact is made, counsel should first ask questions that establish the employee's status within the organization before moving to substantive matters. [See *Snider v. Sup.Ct. (Quantum Productions, Inc.)* (2003) 113 CA4th 1187, 1215, 7 CR3d 119, 139]

**[1:471.21-471.24]** *Reserved.*

4) **[1:471.25] Compare—before knowledge of representation:** The Rule is not violated, however, merely because the attorney "should know" such employees *will be* represented *after* an action is filed. [*Jorgensen v. Taco Bell Corp.* (1996) 50 CA4th 1398, 1401, 58 CR2d 178, 180; *Truitt v. Sup.Ct. (Atchison, Topeka & S.F. Ry. Co.)* (1997) 59 CA4th 1183, 1188, 69 CR2d 558, 561-562; *see ¶1:471.2*]

Nor does knowledge that a corporation has full or part-time "house counsel" trigger application of Rule 2-100 . . . unless the attorney *knows in fact* that such counsel represents the person being interviewed. [*Jorgensen v. Taco Bell Corp.*, supra, 50 CA4th at 1402, 58 CR2d at 181]

- **[1:471.26]** P's counsel retained private investigator to interview D's employees before filing a sexual harassment lawsuit against D and one of its officers. P's counsel was not disqualified despite D's contention that she "should have known" the employees interviewed would be represented by counsel after suit was filed. Such "routine prelitigation investigation activities*" do not violate* CRPC 2-100. [*Jorgensen v. Taco Bell Corp.*, supra, 50 CA4th at 1402, 58 CR2d at 180—interviews not a subterfuge for violation because conducted 7 months before suit filed]

- **[1:471.26a]** Attorney interviewed Employee after serving a complaint on Employer but *before Defense Counsel answered* on Employer's behalf. Rule 2-100 was not violated because Attorney had *no actual knowledge* of such representation when the interview occurred. [*Truitt v. Sup.Ct. (Atchison Topeka & S.F. Ry. Co.),* supra, 59 CA4th at 1188, 69 CR2d at 561-562]

  "Vague declarations" by Employer claimed Attorney knew that Employer "always" referred such matters "immediately" to in-house or outside counsel. Even if true, this was *not* sufficient to establish Attorney's actual knowledge of representation in a particular case. [*Truitt v. Sup.Ct. (Atchison Topeka & S.F. Ry. Co.),* supra, 59 CA4th at 1188, 69 CR2d at 561-562]

⇨[1:471.27]  **PRACTICE POINTER FOR PLAINTIFFS:**  First of all, don't play games about whether you knew or had reason to know the employee was represented by counsel. *Ask* at the outset of the interview. If you fail to do so, opposing counsel can always claim that you had "reason to know" and should be disqualified.

If in fact you have no knowledge or reason to believe the person is represented, interviewing defendant's employees may be very helpful in evaluating plaintiff's claims. Doing so may avoid unnecessary litigation and expensive discovery. [See *Jorgensen v. Taco Bell Corp.,* supra, 50 CA4th at 1402, 58 CR2d at 181]

At the same time, it's risky to base your case on helpful information given by such employees orally in informal interviews. Plan to write out and ask them to sign their statements; or, better yet, ask them if they object to having you tape record their statements. Either way, you should also depose them as soon as possible in order to solidify and preserve helpful testimony.

⇨[1:471.28]  **PRACTICE POINTER FOR DEFENDANTS:**  If you represent the defendant entity and are aware of a potential claim, advise defendant to instruct its employees *not* to speak to the claimant's investigators. Or, better yet, write a letter to the claimant's counsel advising that you represent the defendant's employees in connection with the matter and that they may not be interviewed without your consent! [See *Jorgensen v. Taco Bell Corp.,* supra, 50 CA4th at 1403, 58 CR2d at 181]

[1:471.29]  *Reserved.*

(c)  [1:471.30]  **Compare—*former* officers and employees:**  Rule 2-100 is not intended to apply to communications with persons no longer holding office or employed by an adverse party: "Paragraph (B) is intended to apply only to persons employed at the time of the communication." [See "Discussion" following CRPC 2-100; and *Triple A Machine Shop, Inc. v. State of Calif.* (1989) 213 CA3d 131, 140, 261 CR 493, 498]

1) **[1:471.31] Ex parte contact permitted:** Rule 2-100(B) applies only to persons employed at the time of the ex parte contact. Therefore, it is not a violation or ground for disqualification for counsel to interview an opposing party's former employees (who are not themselves represented by counsel) without opposing counsel's knowledge or consent. [*State Farm Fire & Cas. Co. v. Sup.Ct. (Taylor)* (1997) 54 CA4th 625, 652, 62 CR2d 834, 852; *Continental Ins. Co. v. Sup.Ct. (Commercial Bldg. Maint. Co.)* (1995) 32 CA4th 94, 118-119, 37 CR2d 843, 857-858; see also *Mills Land & Water Co. v. Golden West Refining Co.*, supra, 186 CA3d at 129-130, 230 CR at 468]

[1:471.32] *Reserved.*

a) **[1:471.33] Shareholder status immaterial:** Ex parte contact is proper even if the former officer, director, etc. is still a minority shareholder in the adverse party. [*Nalian Truck Lines, Inc. v. Nakano Warehouse & Transp. Corp.* (1992) 6 CA4th 1256, 1264, 8 CR2d 467, 472, fn. 9]

b) **[1:471.34] "Control group" status immaterial?** One court has stated in dictum that ex parte contact is *improper* with former employees who "remain members of the corporation's control group as that term is defined in *Upjohn Co. v. United States.*" [*Bobele v. Sup.Ct. (Valley Hilton Hotel)* (1988) 199 CA3d 708, 714, 245 CR 144, 148]

But later cases reject this limitation: "Counsel representing a client opposing a corporate defendant has a right to meet ex parte with ex-employees of the corporation, even if they were managerial employees." [*State Farm Fire & Cas. Co. v. Sup.Ct. (Taylor)* (1997) 54 CA4th 625, 652, 62 CR2d 834, 852; *Nalian Truck Lines, Inc. v. Nakano Warehouse & Transp. Corp.* (1992) 6 CA4th 1256, 1264, 8 CR2d 467, 472]

1/ **[1:471.35] Comment:** The latter cases seem correct. A "bright line" test (present employment) is essential because it enables the attorney to determine beforehand whether *ex parte* conduct is permissible. Otherwise, zealous representation could be "chilled" by fear of disqualification. [*Nalian Truck Lines, Inc. v. Nakano Warehouse & Transp. Corp.*, supra, 6 CA4th at 1264, 8 CR2d at 472]

[1:471.36-471.38] *Reserved.*

2) [1:471.39] **No inquiry re privileged communications:** While counsel may inquire regarding any relevant fact, it is improper to inquire about privileged communications. [*State Farm Fire & Cas. Co. v. Sup.Ct. (Taylor)* (1997) 54 CA4th 625, 652, 62 CR2d 834, 852]

   a) [1:471.39a] **Comment:** This can create problems. If privileged communications are in fact divulged, the opposing party is likely to accuse counsel of soliciting the disclosure and demand that counsel be disqualified. It could also lead to counsel and the former employee giving contradictory accounts of the interview, again exposing counsel to the risk of disqualification.

3) [1:471.40] **Corporation's remedy:** According to several cases, it is incumbent upon the corporation which knows that its former employees possess privileged information to seek a *protective order* against disclosure. [*Nalian Truck Lines, Inc. v. Nakano Warehouse & Transp. Corp.*, supra, 6 CA4th at 1264, 8 CR2d at 472; *Bobele v. Sup.Ct. (Valley Hilton Hotel)*, supra, 199 CA3d at 714, 245 CR at 148]

   a) [1:471.41] **Comment:** Not many employers are likely to seek such protective orders. First of all, doing so is time-consuming and expensive. Moreover, it may backfire by tipping off adverse parties to sources of information of which they are otherwise unaware.

▷[1:471.42] *PRACTICE POINTER:* In actions against a corporation or other entity, its former officers and employees are sometimes the *best available* source of information regarding unprivileged events. [See *State Farm Fire & Cas. Co. v. Sup.Ct. (Taylor)* (1997) 54

CA4th 625, 638, 62 CR2d 834, 843 (citing text)]

Moreover, former officers and employees can sometimes provide information that is arguably shielded from discovery by *privacy or privilege* (attorney-client, trade-secret, attorney work product, etc.).

However, it may be improper for an attorney to *inquire* about privileged information because the attorney has a duty to uphold the law (Bus. & Prof.C. §6068(a)). Obtaining such information also raises the risk of adverse protective orders, evidence sanctions, etc.

[1:471.43-471.45]   *Reserved.*

(6) [1:471.46]   **Disqualification of offending counsel?** Violation of Rule 2-100 exposes counsel to disciplinary charges. However, whether the attorney is to be disqualified from representing the client in the present case lies within the *discretion* of the trial court. [*Chronometrics, Inc. v. Sysgen, Inc.* (1980) 110 CA3d 597, 607-608, 168 CR 196, 202-203; *Mills Land & Water Co. v. Golden West Refining Co.* (1986) 186 CA3d 116, 126, 230 CR 461, 466]

(a) [1:471.47]   **Factors favoring disqualification:** Disqualification may be proper if counsel's misconduct is *likely to have a continuing effect* on the proceedings; e.g., enabling counsel to cross-examine opposing witnesses more effectively. [*Chronometrics, Inc. v. Sysgen, Inc.*, supra, 110 CA3d at 607, 168 CR at 202]

(b) [1:471.48]   **Factors favoring retention:**   However, an attorney cannot be disqualified *solely* for punishment purposes. If the transgression is not likely to have any continuing effect on the proceedings, the party has the right to be represented by counsel of choice. [See *Chronometrics, Inc. v. Sysgen, Inc.*, supra, 110 CA3d at 608, 168 CR at 203]

(7) [1:471.49]   **Vicarious disqualification of entire firm?** Even if the offending counsel is to be disqualified, this does not mean that his or her entire law firm should also be disqualified.

A *balancing of interests* is required: Any potential prejudice to the opposing party may be *outweighed* by the client's interest in being represented by counsel of its own choosing. And, where *no* prejudice is shown, disqualification is clearly improper. [*Mills Land & Water Co. v. Golden West Refining Co.*, supra]

(a) [1:471.50] **Compare—federal approach:** Language in some federal cases suggests that "any doubt" be resolved in favor of disqualifying the entire law firm. But this is inconsistent with California's "balancing of interests" approach (above). [See *Mills Land & Water Co. v. Golden West Refining Co.*, supra, 186 CA3d at 133, 230 CR at 471]

(b) [1:471.51] **"Gag" orders to offending counsel:** Where a member of a law firm is disqualified, but the firm is not, the court may order the offending counsel not to disclose to other members of the firm any information obtained through the improper, ex parte contact. "We cannot assume compliance with this restriction is unrealistic." [*Mills Land & Water Co. v. Golden West Refining Co.*, supra, 186 CA3d at 137, 230 CR at 473]

But such an order is proper only on a showing that offending counsel obtained information from the opposing party that was otherwise not available (e.g., through discovery) and that is likely to have a substantial, continuing effect on the proceedings. [*Mills Land & Water Co. v. Golden West Refining Co.*, supra]

1) [1:471.52] **Comment:** "Gag" orders to the offending counsel seem an unrealistic solution. If unfair advantage has been taken by one member of the firm, his or her knowledge should be imputed to other members of the firm, and the *entire firm disqualified.*

2. [1:472] **Use of Illegally Obtained Evidence?** The attorney's duty to uphold the law (Bus. & Prof.C. §6068(a)) clearly bars the attorney from directing or encouraging the client or any third person to obtain evidence in an illegal manner (e.g., illegal tape recordings). But there appears to be no bar to an attorney's use of records or information obtained in this manner without the attorney's involvement. [See *Evens v. Sup.Ct. (Los Angeles Unified School Dist.)* (1999) 77 CA4th 320, 325, 91 CR2d 497, 499—California's privacy laws and statute prohibiting unauthorized recording of classroom teachers do not prevent use of such recordings in teacher disciplinary proceedings]

a. [1:472.1] **Records stolen by client from opposing party:** An attorney may not retain confidential records taken from an opposing party's files by its employees and delivered to the attorney for use in potential litigation against the employer. The fact that such records are not privileged and may be subject to discovery during litigation does *not* justify "self help evidence gathering" by the client. [*Pillsbury, Madison & Sutro v. Schectman* (1997) 55 CA4th 1279, 1288, 64 CR2d 698, 705]

    (1) **[1:472.2]** **Remedy:** An injunction ordering the attorney to return the records is the *"least sanction"* appropriate in such cases. [*Pillsbury, Madison & Sutro v. Schectman,* supra, 55 CA4th at 1288, 64 CR2d at 705]

    (2) **[1:472.3]** **Comment:** Presumably, the court could also order return of any *copies* of the wrongfully obtained records; and limit use of information obtained therefrom unless the documents were obtained through proper discovery procedures. (However, if the records would be discoverable in any event, such return would merely create unnecessary work.)

    **[1:473-475]** *Reserved.*

3. **[1:476]** **Prelawsuit Legal Research:** Based on the facts ascertained through interviews and investigations, the attorney has to research the applicable law in order to determine the issues likely to be involved in the litigation. Of particular importance will be:

- What theories of recovery (or defense) are available to the client?

- What are the essential elements (e.g., prima facie case) for each such theory?

- What theories are the opposing parties likely to rely upon?

- What are the essential elements for each of the opposing party's theories?

- Who has the burden of proof as to each of the matters identified?

- Are there any special evidentiary requirements applicable?

    ⇨**[1:477]** *PRACTICE POINTER:* From the outset, start a legal memo or research file. Identify each major issue in the case, and add to it whatever authorities or citations you come across through your research. This will give you a head start toward preparing points and authorities if you need them in court, and toward preparing a trial brief. Your research and mental impressions are generally completely protected. (*See "Attorney Work Product," Ch. 8.*)

4. **[1:478]** **Alternative Dispute Resolution ("ADR"):** "Alternative dispute resolution" (ADR) usually refers to procedures other than negotiation or litigation for resolving a dispute. These procedures usually involve appointment of a neutral person or

persons and may consist of mediation, arbitration, judicial fact-finding, appointment of referee or private judge, etc.

*Cross-refer:* See detailed discussion of these various procedures in Knight, Fannin, Chernick & Haldeman, *Cal. Prac. Guide: Alternative Dispute Resolution* (TRG).

Attorneys generally should consider and discuss ADR with their clients before filing suit (see ¶*1:31*). In any event, the court will make an "ADR information package" available to plaintiff when suit is filed, which plaintiff must serve on each defendant along with the complaint. The ADR "package" explains the potential advantages and disadvantages of ADR and describes the principal ADR processes. [See CRC 201.9]

In addition, the parties must be prepared to discuss with the court at the case management conference (¶*12:77.5 ff.*) whether the case should be referred to any form of ADR. [CRC 212(e)(6); see ¶*12:83*]

Compliance with contract provisions requiring ADR may be a condition precedent to judicial enforcement of the contract. [See *Leamon v. Krajkiewcz* (2003) 107 CA4th 424, 432, 132 CR2d 362, 367—court refused contractual fee award to prevailing party that failed to satisfy contract provision requiring mediation before suit]

a. **[1:479] Particular procedures:** There are various alternative dispute resolution ("ADR") procedures to consider:

(1) **[1:480] Negotiation:** Direct settlement negotiations with the opposing party or counsel (or insurer).

(2) **[1:481] Mediation:** Mediation is a process in which a neutral person or persons facilitate communication between disputants to assist them in reaching a mutually acceptable agreement. [CRC 1580(c)]

Mediations may be either "facilitative" (mediator does not evaluate the case) or "evaluative" (mediator attempts to promote settlement by offering evaluations), or a combination of the two.

In some courts, mediation may be ordered in lieu of "judicial arbitration" (*see* ¶*13:11 ff.*).

(3) **[1:481.1] Nonbinding arbitration or neutral evaluation:** Parties agree to present their evidence and arguments (usually in shortened and informal form) to a privately-selected neutral who provides a nonbinding evaluation that the parties can use as an aid in their settlement negotiations.

(4) **[1:482] Court-sponsored settlement conference before suit filed:** Some courts provide prelitigation voluntary settlement conferences with a settlement

judge or other judicial officer. The judge's evaluation is not binding on either party.

(5) [1:483] **Binding (contractual) arbitration:** By agreement before or after a dispute arises, parties may agree *to accept and be bound* by an arbitrator's award. Arbitration pursuant to such agreements is referred to as "*contractual arbitration.*"

    (a) [1:484] **Distinguish "judicial arbitration":** Despite lack of agreement to arbitrate, certain cases must be "arbitrated" before a trial date is assigned. But the arbitrator's award is not binding (either party may demand a trial de novo). *See Ch. 13.*

    (b) [1:485] **Judge as arbitrator?** Sometimes parties involved in litigation ask the judge to whom the case is assigned (or other settlement judge) to resolve specific issues holding up settlement. (E.g., parties ask judge to determine whether particular items of damage are recoverable.)

    A judge is prohibited by law from accepting private employment and therefore cannot serve as a contract arbitrator. But litigants can enter into stipulations which may have the same effect; e.g., for a "final and binding" decision by the judge and waiving the right to appeal. [See *Elliott & Ten Eyck Partnership v. City of Long Beach* (1997) 57 CA4th 495, 505, 67 CR2d 140, 145; *Heenan v. Sobati* (2002) 96 CA4th 995, 1002, 117 CR2d 532, 537—parties waived court reporter and right to appeal]

(6) [1:486] **Judge pro tem:** By stipulation of the parties, any member of the State Bar may be appointed a "temporary judge" and empowered to act until final disposition of the case. (A *court commissioner* may be designated in such stipulations.) [Cal. Const. Art. VI, §21; CRC 244] (Different rules apply in small claims cases; see CRC 1727.)

This is the provision under which retired judges are often chosen to adjudicate (so-called "rent-a-judge" programs). The parties are responsible for the judge's fees, which usually run between $250-$500 per hour. It is customary to split the cost.

    (a) [1:487] **Caution—no power over nonsignatories:** A temporary judge's powers are limited to parties who have signed the stipulation *or otherwise submitted* to his or her power to act as a judge. Otherwise, a temporary judge has no power to hold nonsignatory *witnesses or attorneys* in contempt or to impose sanctions against them. [See *In re Plotkin* (1976) 54 CA3d 1014, 1016-1017, 127 CR 190, 192; and *Nierenberg v. Sup.Ct.* (1976) 59 CA3d 611, 619, 130 CR 847, 851-852]

(b) [1:487.1] **Compare—power over parties:** Temporary judges who act under stipulation have "full judicial powers" until final determination of the cause. This includes the power to *cite a party for contempt* and to summarily adjudicate the contempt. [*Fine v. Sup.Ct. (DeFlores)* (2002) 97 CA4th 651, 664-665, 119 CR2d 376, 386-387]

(7) [1:488] **"Reference" by agreement:** Upon stipulation of the parties, the court may appoint a referee to try any or all of the *issues* in the case (whether of fact or law) and to report a decision to the court. The court, rather than the referee, renders judgment. [CCP §638; CRC 244.1; see *City of Shasta Lake v. County of Shasta* (1999) 75 CA4th 1, 24, 88 CR2d 863, 878 (citing text)]

Unlike judge pro tems (above), the referee need not be a member of the State Bar. This is often helpful where the entire case turns on some technical issue; e.g., whether there was a construction defect can be determined by a referee who is a construction expert.

(a) [1:489] **Compare—court-ordered reference:** *Under narrow, specified circumstances,* the court may order a reference in certain types of proceedings: e.g., accounting issues, discovery disputes. [See CCP §639; CRC 244.2; *and discussion at* ¶*8:746.1 ff. & 9:183*]

b. [1:490] **Advantages vs. disadvantages:** The advantages of ADR are obvious: avoiding the publicity, costs and delays of litigation; avoiding rigors of "fast track" rules and judicial intervention in case management; and generally reducing the level of hostilities and stress of litigation. Speed is an important factor for plaintiffs' attorneys handling claims on a contingency fee, because the quicker the case settles, the sooner the attorney gets paid!

But there are also disadvantages to consider. ADR may not be appropriate where:

• Damages are not yet fully ascertained so that not enough is known to evaluate the case properly (in which event, plaintiffs' attorneys usually prefer to file suit to avoid any statute of limitations problem, and discuss settlement later); or

• Plaintiff's attorney wants a jury trial because the case has distinct jury appeal; or

- Novel issues of law or public policy are involved so that a public trial is required and the right to appellate review is crucial.

Also, rightly or wrongly, there is a perception that many arbitrators tend to "split things down the middle," rather than make hard decisions.

*Cross-refer:* See detailed discussion of ADR procedures in Knight, Fannin, Chernick & Haldeman, *Cal. Prac. Guide: Alternative Dispute Resolution* (TRG), Chs. 1-6.

5. **[1:491] Litigation Planning:** Filing a lawsuit (or responding to one already filed by the opposing party) commits you to a certain course of action: i.e., certain theories, certain defenses, certain claims. Under modern practice, these initial choices are rarely irrevocable, but they are not always easy to change. Consequently, careful practitioners attempt to plan *before* initiating suit or undertaking the defense the specific directions they wish to take in the litigation.

   a. **[1:492] Plaintiff's considerations:** Attorneys representing plaintiffs will usually focus on the following considerations:

   (1) **[1:493] Parties:** Deciding whom to join as plaintiffs and whom to sue as defendants is the first step in planning the lawsuit.

   (a) **[1:494] Substantive law:** First of all, the attorney has to identify which parties can be held liable under the substantive law for the injuries, damages or losses sustained. (E.g., in a product liability action, the retailer, the distributor, the manufacturer, the designer, the government, etc.)

   In addition, the attorney has to identify what persons may have been acting in concert with the defendant (e.g., conspirators in intentional wrongdoing); or who are otherwise responsible for their acts because of the relationship between them (e.g., employer-employee).

   1) **[1:494.1] *Caution re malicious prosecution:*** Naming persons as defendants before you have sufficient evidence to uphold a judgment against them could expose you and your client to liability for malicious prosecution (*see* ¶*1:522*).

   ➡ **[1:494.2] *PRACTICE POINTER:*** If you lack sufficient evidence to prove a cause of action, *name "Doe" defendants* to prevent running of the statute of limitations. (An amendment naming the real defendants will normally "relate back" to commencement of the action; *see ¶6:736.*) [See CCP §474; *Puryear v. Golden Bear Ins. Co.* (1998) 66 CA4th 1188, 1194-1197, 78 CR2d 507, 512]

(b) **[1:495]** **Joinder problems:** Which persons *must* be joined as parties-plaintiff or defendant in the action ("indispensable" vs. "necessary" parties)? And, which persons *may* be joined therein ("proper" parties)? Should the action be maintained as a representative suit or class action on behalf of nonparties? (*See detailed discussion at ¶2:150 ff.*)

(c) **[1:496]** **Tactical considerations:** There may be tactical reasons for naming, or *not* naming, a particular person as defendant in the action:

　1) **[1:497]** Joining a local resident as codefendant may *destroy diversity* of citizenship (should plaintiff be considering filing in federal court; or should plaintiff want to prevent removal from state to federal court; *see ¶3:623-629*).

　2) **[1:498]** Joining a nonresident as a codefendant may raise jurisdictional problems or grounds for staying the action (*see "Personal Jurisdiction," ¶3:130 ff., and "Inconvenient Forum," ¶3:407 ff.*).

　3) **[1:499]** Joining a particular codefendant may enable plaintiff to establish *venue* in a county where it otherwise would not be proper (*see ¶3:450 ff.*).

　4) **[1:500]** *Not* joining a particular person as a codefendant may facilitate more favorable testimony from that person at trial.

(d) **[1:501]** **Prop. 51 considerations:** In actions for *personal injury, property damage or wrongful death*, comparative fault principles apply to the recovery of "noneconomic damages" (e.g., pain and suffering, emotional distress, etc.). [Civ.C. §1431.2, enacted as "Proposition 51"]

Comparative fault does not, however, apply to *economic* damages (e.g., wage losses). These are still recoverable in full from *any* tortfeasor under the doctrine of joint and several liability. [Civ.C. §1431]

Thus, where Prop. 51 applies, a defendant can limit its liability for noneconomic damages by proving some other tortfeasor was partly or entirely to blame for plaintiff's injuries. To avoid the so-called "empty chair" defense, plaintiff will usually want to join *everyone* who might possibly be at fault in causing his or her injuries.

➡️**[1:502]** ***PRACTICE POINTER:*** If you represent plaintiff, serve interrogatories on defendant at the outset of the litigation, asking *whether it contends* any other person or entity is responsible in any way for plaintiff's injuries.

You can then amend your complaint to name and join whomever the defendant blames. Unless patently invalid, the joinder of someone whom the defendant blames is almost certainly *not* a "frivolous" joinder.

    (e) **[1:503]** **Claims against governmental entities:** If there are reasonable grounds for asserting a claim against a public entity, there are special claims procedures and procedural requirements to consider at the outset. *See ¶1:646 ff.*

(2) **[1:504]** **WHEN to sue?** If there is a statute of limitations about to run, obviously suit should be filed immediately. Otherwise, however, plaintiff's attorney *may* find it advantageous to delay filing suit—e.g., for settlement purposes, to complete investigations or to obtain evidence before alerting the opposing party, to delay defendant's right to obtain discovery from plaintiff. Defendant may have difficulty "catching up" after suit is filed because of time pressures under "fast track" rules (*¶12:4 ff.*).

(3) **[1:505]** **WHERE to sue?** In which state or states is the defendant subject to personal jurisdiction? Is the matter one which could or must be filed in federal court? Are there any tactical advantages in suing in state or federal court? (*See detailed discussion in Ch. 3.*)

If suit is to be filed in a California court, in what county or counties is venue "proper"? And if filed there, what are the chances that the court might later transfer the action to another county on "convenience" grounds? (*See ¶3:450 ff.*)

(4) **[1:506]** **File as limited or unlimited civil case?** Exaggerating a claim in order to file it as a general (unlimited) civil case (*see ¶3:2.1 ff.*) may not be a good idea for several reasons:

    • **[1:507]** The court has discretion to *deny costs* whenever plaintiff recovers a judgment of less than $25,000. [CCP §1033(a)]

- **[1:508]** The court may order the case reclassified as a *limited* civil case upon finding to a legal certainty that a judgment over $25,000 cannot be obtained. [CCP §§396, 403.040(a); *see discussion at* ¶*3:112 ff.*]

  Such reclassification may result in a transfer to another department of the court and is likely to delay getting to trial. (As a practical matter, cases involving no more than $25,000 are often disposed of through judicial arbitration; *see* ¶*13:1 ff.*)

(5) **[1:509]** **CHOICE OF LAW considerations:** Assuming jurisdiction and venue requirements are satisfied, are there any choice of law issues? I.e., if the case involves persons, property or transactions located outside California, *which state's laws* is a California court likely to apply?

**[1:510]** *Reserved.*

(6) **WHAT THEORIES or claims?**

(a) **[1:511]** **Ethical considerations:** Plaintiff's lawyer owes the client the duty to assert all claims which a competent lawyer would assert; i.e., a lawyer possessing the learning and skill necessary to handle the client's case. [CRPC 3-110(A)]

  But there are also limitations: The attorney must *not* assert a claim "without probable cause *and* for the purpose of harassing or maliciously injuring any person." Nor may an attorney assert a claim "not warranted under existing law, unless it can be supported by good faith argument for extension, modification or reversal of existing law." [CRPC 3-200(A),(B)]

  An attorney in a civil case is *not* a "hired gun" required to carry out every direction of the client. If the client insists on pursuing frivolous claims, the attorney has no alternative but to withdraw from the representation. [*Young v. Rosenthal* (1989) 212 CA3d 96, 134, 260 CR 369, 393]

  Indeed, an attorney's signature on a pleading or other court paper constitutes a *certificate of merits* to the court under CCP §128.7 (*see discussion at* ¶*1:529*).

(b) **[1:512]** **Malpractice considerations:** The attorney owes a duty to pursue all claims available, even those not clearly valid under existing law: i.e., if a sizeable number of other lawyers or judges in the community would regard a cause of action as tenable, it may be malpractice to ignore it!

"(E)ven with respect to an unsettled area of the law, we believe an attorney assumes an obligation to his client to undertake *reasonable research* in an effort to ascertain relevant legal principles and to make an *informed decision* as to a course of conduct based upon an *intelligent assessment* of the problem." [*Smith v. Lewis* (1975) 13 C3d 349, 359, 118 CR 621, 627 (emphasis added) (disapproved on another point in *Marriage of Brown* (1976) 15 C3d 838, 851, 126 CR 633, 641, fn. 14)]

But "(p)leading a claim *unsupported* by probable cause is more likely to constitute malpractice than the opposite. This is so because it *exposes the client* to a *malicious prosecution* claim" (below). [*Mabie v. Hyatt* (1998) 61 CA4th 581, 595, 71 CR2d 657, 666]

(c) **[1:513] Caution—potential liability "traps" for lawyer and client:** But this does not mean that the lawyer or client can assert with impunity any claim whatsoever against an adversary.

    1) **[1:514] Malicious prosecution:** If a lawsuit is initiated "with malice" and "without probable cause" and results in a judgment in favor of the defendant, plaintiff may be liable for malicious prosecution. [*Bertero v. National General Corp.* (1974) 13 C3d 43, 50, 118 CR 184, 189]

    The action may also lie against *plaintiff's lawyer* if he or she *knows* plaintiff's claims are false. Otherwise, the lawyer is entitled to rely on information furnished by the client, and is not liable for malicious prosecution if that information turns out to be untrue. [*Swat-Fame, Inc. v. Goldstein* (2002) 101 CA4th 613, 625, 124 CR2d 556, 564; *Morrison v. Rudolph* (2002) 103 CA4th 506, 513, 126 CR2d 747, 752]

    Joinder of a meritorious claim will not prevent liability for malicious prosecution of other claims that are frivolous. [*Crowley v. Katleman* (1994) 8 C4th 666, 679, 34 CR2d 386, 392—probable cause must support *each* cause of action; *Citi-Wide Preferred Couriers, Inc. v. Golden Eagle Ins. Corp.* (2003) 114 CA4th 906, 8 CR3d 199, 205—although some small amount of money was owed, most of amount claimed in prior action lacked probable cause]

Nor will pleading the frivolous claim "on information and belief." [*Mabie v. Hyatt*, supra, 61 CA4th at 596, 71 CR2d at 667, fn. 9—"no one can obtain a license to maliciously prosecute a lawsuit simply by reciting 'information and belief'"]

a) **[1:515] Compare—lack of merit discovered** *after* **suit filed:** It is not clear whether an attorney who, after filing a lawsuit, discovers that it lacks probable cause may be liable for malicious prosecution for *continuing* the suit.

*Caution:* This issue is presently before the California Supreme Court in *Zamos v. Stroud,* Case No. S118032.

**[1:516-526]** *Reserved.*

2) **[1:527] Abuse of process:** Similarly, an abuse of process claim may lie where defendant willfully uses court processes improperly (e.g., obtaining an injunction on the basis of false affidavits) and for an "ulterior purpose" (e.g., to compel payment of money not due). [See *Spellens v. Spellens* (1957) 49 C2d 210, 232-233, 317 P2d 613, 626-627]

Lack of probable cause must also be shown. Otherwise, it could seriously "chill" the right to seek judicial relief and allow evasion of the probable cause requirement in malicious prosecution actions. [*Oren Royal Oaks Venture v. Greenberg, Bernhard, Weiss & Karma, Inc.* (1986) 42 C3d 1157, 1169, 232 CR 567, 575]

a) **[1:528] Limitation—filing and maintenance of suit insufficient:** The "process" misused must be something other than a summons and complaint: "(T)he mere filing *or maintenance* (continued prosecution) of a lawsuit—even for an improper purpose—is not a proper basis for an abuse of process action." [*Oren Royal Oaks Venture v. Greenberg, Bernhard, Weiss & Karma, Inc.*, supra, 42 C3d at 1169, 232 CR at 575 (emphasis and parentheses added)]

**[1:529-540]** *Reserved.*

3) **[1:541] Sanctions for unfounded tort action against government or on indemnity claim (CCP §1038):** Sanctions may be

awarded: in a tort action against a governmental entity, or in an action for express or implied indemnity or contribution, if the court finds the action was "not brought in good faith and with reasonable cause." [CCP §1038(a); *see* ¶*9:1265 ff.*]

If defendant obtains summary judgment or nonsuit in such an action, the court is empowered to order plaintiff to pay "defense costs," including reasonable attorney fees. [*Gamble v. Los Angeles Dept. of Water & Power* (2002) 97 CA4th 253, 259, 118 CR2d 271, 275; see CCP §1038(a),(b); *see also discussion at ¶10:337 ff.*]

Note: A defendant seeking an award under this statute *waives* any right to sue for damages for malicious prosecution. [CCP §1038(c)]

4) **[1:542]** **Sanctions for violation of "certificate of merit" (CCP §128.7):** In actions filed *after 1/1/95,* the attorney's (or unrepresented party's) signature on a pleading or other court paper constitutes a certificate that:

- *No improper purpose:* "It is not being presented primarily for an improper purpose, such as to harass or to cause unnecessary delay or needless increase in the cost of litigation";

- *Legal merit:* "The claims, defenses and other legal contentions therein are *warranted by existing law* or by a nonfrivolous argument for the extension, modification, or reversal of existing law or the establishment of new law";

- *Evidentiary support:* "The allegations and other factual contentions have *evidentiary support* or, if specifically so identified, are likely to have evidentiary support after a reasonable opportunity for further investigation or discovery." [CCP §128.7(b)(1),(2) & (3) (emphasis added)]

a) **[1:543]** **Effect:** This statute embodies Federal Rule of Civil Procedure 11, with minor modifications. The effect is that the attorney may *not* rely entirely on the client's version of the facts if there is time to investigate before filing the complaint. Violating this certificate exposes the attorney and/or party to appropriate sanctions.

*See detailed discussion at ¶9:1135 ff.*

b) **[1:543.1] Limitation:** However, this section is of limited usefulness because of a cumbersome 21-day "safe harbor" provision, which permits the offending party to correct its sanctionable conduct. [CCP §128.7(c)(1); *see discussion at ¶9:1196*]

**[1:543.2-543.4]** *Reserved.*

5) **[1:543.5] Costs and fees on SLAPP suits:** A special statute (CCP §425.16, *see ¶7:207 ff.*) applies to lawsuits brought primarily to "chill" defendants' exercise of *constitutionally-protected rights* of speech and petition—so-called "strategic litigation against public participation" (SLAPP). (E.g., tort actions by land developers against environmental activists or neighborhood groups opposing their plans, in which plaintiffs attempt to use the cost of litigation to "bludgeon" defendants into silence.) A special *motion to strike* is authorized that forces plaintiffs to prove a *"probability" of success* on the merits at the outset of litigation. If plaintiffs are unable to do so, defendants are *entitled* to their *attorney fees and court costs* on the motion to strike (CCP §425.16(c); *see ¶7:207 ff.*).

➪**[1:543.6]** *CAUTION:* This SLAPP statute is *broadly* construed and may reach lawsuits complaining of activities not normally thought to involve "free speech" (*see ¶7:208.5 ff.*).

Therefore, before filing a lawsuit that could even *conceivably* "chill" a defendant's First Amendment rights, advise plaintiffs of the risk of a nonmeritorious complaint; i.e., that they may end up having to pay *defense fees and costs* on a SLAPP motion!

(d) **[1:544] Tactical considerations re choice of theories:** Where the claim could be asserted on one of several theories, plaintiff's lawyer will have to evaluate the advantages and disadvantages of proceeding on each or all of these theories. For example, here are some of the factors that should be taken into consideration:

1) **[1:545] Recoverability of punitive damages:** If the claim can be asserted in a cause

of action that allows for punitive damages, it will usually be in plaintiff's interest to pursue this.

[1:546]   *Reserved.*

2)  [1:547]   **Insurance coverage:**   Likewise, if the claim can be asserted in a cause of action covered by liability insurance, plaintiff will usually choose to do so.

   a)  [1:548]   **Compare—"malicious" and "wilful" conduct:**   Sometimes plaintiff will be tempted to proceed on the theory that defendant was acting "maliciously" or was "wanton and wilful," in order to recover punitive damages. But such allegations may cause defendant's liability insurance carrier to deny coverage (Ins.C. §533 bars coverage for "wilful" acts and most policies expressly exclude such coverage). Thus, plaintiff could end up with an empty verdict. (Or, even if the carrier defends, it may do so on a reservation-of-rights basis, making settlement more difficult.)

3)  [1:549]   **Recoverability of attorney fees:**   If a cause of action can be asserted under which attorney fees can be awarded to plaintiff's attorney, it will usually be advantageous to proceed on this basis. For example, attorney fees may be recoverable pursuant to:

   • *Contract* provisions authorizing fee awards (¶*1:224*);

   • *Statutes* authorizing fees in particular actions (¶*1:287*);

   • Court's *equitable power* to order fees in "common fund," "substantial benefit" and "private attorney general" cases (¶*1:294*).

4)  [1:550]   **Availability of provisional remedies:**   Plaintiff's lawyer should also consider whether it is advisable to obtain a lien on defendant's property before judgment in order to assure collectibility of the judgment. If so, the claim will have to be asserted by a cause of action as to which prejudgment seizure or liens are permissible. (*See discussion of "attachment," "claim and delivery," and other provisional remedies, ¶9:500 ff.*)

5)  [1:551]   **Priority in obtaining trial date:** Some causes of action are entitled by statute to

early trial dates; e.g., unlawful detainer, declaratory relief. (*See* ¶*12:240 ff.*)

b. **[1:552] Defendant's considerations:** Attorneys representing defendants will usually focus on the following considerations before filing their first appearances in an action:

(1) **[1:553] Right court?** Has plaintiff filed suit in a court having subject matter and personal jurisdiction, and is it the "proper" court for venue purposes? If it is a diversity of citizenship case, would there be an advantage to removing it to federal court? Is there a basis to stay or dismiss on forum non conveniens grounds; or to transfer the action from one county to another (either on "wrong court" or "convenience of witnesses" grounds)?

(2) **[1:554] When to appear:** Defendants may need to obtain extensions of time to plead in order to avoid default. Assuming an extension is available, is it advantageous to pursue informal investigations and settlement negotiations before appearing; or is it more advantageous to file a vigorous answer and take advantage of the defendant's "first crack" at discovery (¶*8:439 ff.*)?

(3) **[1:555] What defenses and counter-attacks are available against plaintiff?** The same considerations applicable to a plaintiff's theories and claims against defendant (¶*1:511 ff.*) apply here as well.

(a) **[1:556] Preserving right to sue for malicious prosecution:** Choice of defenses is crucial where defendant is thinking malicious prosecution (i.e., plaintiff's claim appears to be brought "maliciously" and "without probable cause"). To preserve the right to sue for malicious prosecution, defendant must obtain a judgment establishing its *innocence* rather than winning on technical grounds (e.g., statute of limitations). [ *Lackner v. LaCroix* (1979) 25 C3d 747, 751-752, 159 CR 693, 695; *Warren v. Wasserman, Comden & Casselman* (1990) 220 CA3d 1297, 1303, 271 CR 579, 583]

(b) **[1:557] Frivolous denials, defenses or cross-claims as basis for sanctions:** Just as plaintiffs may be sanctioned for filing frivolous lawsuits, defendants may be sanctioned for asserting non-meritorious cross-complaints or denials and defenses in their answers—e.g., answers containing dozens of affirmative defenses (waiver, estoppel, laches, unclean hands, etc.) for which there is no evidentiary support. [See CCP §128.5 for cases filed prior to 1/1/95 (¶*9:1010 ff.*); or CCP §128.7 for cases filed after that date (¶*9:1135 ff.*)]

1) [1:558] **Certificate of merit:** Under CCP §128.7 (applicable where complaint filed after 1/1/95), defense counsel's (or an unrepresented defendant's) signature on the answer is a *certificate* that "denials of factual contentions are warranted on the evidence or, if specifically so identified, are reasonably based on a lack of information or belief." [CCP §128.7(b)(4)]

Sanctions for violation of this certificate include striking of nonmeritorious denials or defenses.

*See detailed discussion at ¶9:1135 ff.*

[1:559-562] *Reserved.*

(c) [1:563] **Cross-complaints as basis for sanctions or tort claim:** The same liability "traps" discussed with respect to plaintiff's complaint (¶1:513 *ff.*) apply to claims asserted in a cross-complaint. [See *Bertero v. National General Corp.* (1974) 13 C3d 43, 53, 118 CR 184, 192]

1) [1:564] **Malicious prosecution:** To stall a municipal court collection action, defendants filed a frivolous cross-complaint for $5 million, compelling transfer to superior court. Defendants thus "used the legal system in an attempt to club a legitimate creditor into submission by extending this litigation when they in fact had no valid defenses." [*National Secretarial Service, Inc. v. Froehlich* (1989) 210 CA3d 510, 525, 258 CR 506, 515, fn. 13]

2) [1:565] **Sanctions:** Sanctions for a frivolous cross-complaint may be imposed under CCP §128.7 (*see ¶1:542*).

(4) [1:566] **Who else should be brought into the action?** First of all, are there any third parties who may be responsible, in whole or in part, for whatever damage plaintiff is claiming? Or, against whom defendant may have a claim that is related in some way to the claim being asserted by plaintiff? If so, would it be advantageous to proceed against such third parties by cross-complaint in the present action; or should a separate lawsuit be filed?

Also, are there any third persons who should be *joined* with *plaintiff* in the action, but who are not named in the complaint? Would it be advantageous to file a motion to compel their joinder, or would it be better to "let sleeping dogs lie"?

## C. PRELAWSUIT NOTICES, CLAIMS AND DEMANDS

### 1. Communications to Opposing Party Generally

a. **[1:567]** **Not represented by counsel:** As long as the opposing party is not yet represented by counsel, the attorney may communicate with him or her personally. I.e., there is nothing wrong with a lawyer communicating with a lay person (provided no improper threats or demands are made; *see ¶1:598-603*).

CRPC 2-100 (prohibiting contact with opposing party represented by counsel) requires *actual knowledge* that the party is represented by counsel. [*Truitt v. Sup.Ct. (Atchison, Topeka & Santa Fe Ry. Co.)* (1997) 59 CA4th 1183, 1188, 69 CR2d 558, 561]

▷**[1:568]** *PRACTICE POINTER:* Even so, to avoid risks of misunderstanding, many lawyers limit themselves to *written* communications when dealing with an opposing party who has no lawyer. This avoids questions as to what was said, and minimizes the possibility that the attorney might have to testify as a witness (e.g., to refute the opposing party's claims that a "deal" was made with the attorney, etc.) . . . in which event, the attorney might have to withdraw from the case (*see ¶1:96-98*).

b. **[1:569]** **Demand for preservation of evidence:** If litigation is likely, it is good practice to put the opposing party on notice of what records or other evidence will be needed in that litigation, and to demand their preservation for that purpose. This is particularly true as to computer records and other electronically-stored evidence. Many businesses periodically recycle their back-up electronic storage media, destroying prior versions of the information.

It would be foolhardy for the opposing party to ignore such demand. Destruction of evidence *in anticipation of a discovery request* "would surely be a misuse of discovery within the meaning of CCP §2023"—exposing that party to a wide range of sanctions, including default and dismissal. [See *Cedars-Sinai Med. Ctr. v. Sup.Ct. (Bowyer)* (1998) 18 C4th 1, 12, 74 CR2d 248, 254]

**[1:570-597]** *Reserved.*

c. **[1:598]** **Demand letters; improper threats:** Clients often want their lawyers to write belligerent letters to the opposing party or counsel, threatening dire consequences unless the clients' demands are met promptly. The attorney must use restraint, however:

(1) **[1:599]** **Threats of criminal charges improper:**
Threats to "call the district attorney's office" or otherwise
use the criminal process unless the opposing party
complies with some demand, may subject the attorney
to discipline and civil liability. [CRPC 5-100—"A member of the State Bar shall not threaten to present criminal, administrative or disciplinary charges to obtain an
advantage in a civil action . . . "]

Threats to present charges to an administrative agency
or disciplinary board are treated the same as threats of
criminal charges. [See CRPC 5-100]

- **[1:599.1]** Collection attorneys who send demand
letters threatening to initiate criminal proceedings
violate the above Rule. [See *Nguyen v. Proton Technology Corp.* (1999) 69 CA4th 140, 152, 81 CR2d
392, 399]

- **[1:599.2]** It is likewise improper for an attorney to
*contact an adversary's parole officer* in an attempt
to gain advantage in civil litigation. [See *Nguyen v.
Proton Technology Corp.*, supra, 69 CA4th at 152-
153, 81 CR2d at 399—such conduct not privileged
under Civ.C. §47(b)]

**[1:600-601]** *Reserved.*

(2) **[1:602]** **Threats of civil action:** On the other hand,
there is nothing improper with threatening civil action if
the client's demands are not met. Such threats do not
violate any statutory or disciplinary rule.

➡️**[1:603]** *PRACTICE POINTER:* However, such
threats are not always a good tactic. Belligerent
letters generally evoke belligerent responses. If it
is your purpose in writing to pursue an out-of-court
settlement, the tone of your correspondence
should be conciliatory, not belligerent!

(3) **[1:604]** **Potential tort liability—"litigation privilege"
available?** Prelawsuit demands and communications
to opposing parties or counsel may give rise to tort
claims; e.g., intentional infliction of emotional distress,
defamation, invasion of privacy, etc.

However, a so-called "litigation privilege" protects statements made in the course of judicial proceedings.
[Civ.C. §47(b)(2)—"A privileged publication . . . is one
made . . . in any judicial proceeding"; *Dove Audio, Inc.
v. Rosenfeld, Meyer & Susman* (1996) 47 CA4th 777,
783, 54 CR2d 830, 834—privilege also applies to statements made *in preparation for* sending complaint to
Attorney General]

A similar privilege protects communications "in any other official proceeding authorized by law." [Civ.C. §47(b)(3); see *Passman v. Torkan* (1995) 34 CA4th 607, 616, 40 CR2d 291, 296—defendant's letter to district attorney, accusing plaintiff of criminal conduct and designed to prompt a criminal prosecution, was absolutely privileged]

(a) [1:605] **Purposes:** To free litigants and witnesses from fear of harassment for what they say in litigation; to encourage zealous advocacy by counsel; and to "avoid an unending roundelay of litigation." [*Silberg v. Anderson* (1990) 50 C3d 205, 213, 266 CR 638, 642-643]

(b) [1:606] **Requirements:** Even fraudulent and malicious statements are *absolutely* privileged if:

- Made in a judicial or quasi-judicial proceeding (not necessarily in the courthouse);

- By litigants or other participants authorized by law;

- To further the *objects* of the litigation; and

- Having some connection or logical relation to the action. [*Silberg v. Anderson*, supra, 50 C3d at 213-214, 266 CR at 642; see *Rothman v. Jackson* (1996) 49 CA4th 1134, 1141, 57 CR2d 284, 288]

1) [1:607] **Compare—no intent or motives requirement:** The third requirement above (communication must further the objects of the litigation) is *not* a test of defendant's motives or purposes. It is simply part of the requirement that the communication have some logical relation to the litigation. I.e., as long as the communication is *relevant* to the litigation, it is absolutely privileged . . . regardless of defendant's selfish or evil motives. [*Silberg v. Anderson*, supra, 50 C3d at 220, 266 CR at 643-645; *Rothman v. Jackson*, supra, 49 CA4th at 1141, 57 CR2d at 288]

2) [1:608] **Compare—no "interest of justice" requirement:** Earlier cases that also required the communication to have been made "in the interest of justice" have been overruled. (Such a requirement would *undo* the privilege because tortious conduct is rarely "in the interest of justice.") [*Silberg v. Anderson,* supra, 50 C3d at 216-217, 266 CR at 645-647]

3) **[1:609] Compare—absolute vs. qualified privilege:** The litigation privilege is *absolute.* Unlike a qualified privilege, which can be lost if defendant acted maliciously, the litigation privilege confers immunity regardless of defendant's motive (see above). [*Aronson v. Kinsella* (1997) 58 CA4th 254, 263, 68 CR2d 305, 311]

But a *balancing of interests* analysis applies in determining whether the litigation privilege bars an action for *invasion of privacy* under Calif. Const. Art. I, §1. *See* ¶1:644.5.

**[1:609.1-609.4]** *Reserved.*

4) **[1:609.5] Compare—nonlitigants cannot claim derivative privilege:** Persons who are not participants in the litigation cannot claim the privilege for communications to the litigants. [*Wise v. Thrifty Payless, Inc.* (2000) 83 CA4th 1296, 100 CR2d 437, 443—where Husband invaded Wife's privacy by obtaining information from Pharmacy for use in litigation, Husband was immune from liability because of §47(b) privilege but Pharmacy was not; *Schoendorf v. U.D. Registry, Inc.* (2002) 97 CA4th 227, 243, 118 CR2d 313, 324 (citing text)]

(c) **[1:610] Judicial or "quasi-judicial" proceedings:** The litigation privilege applies to "quasi-judicial proceedings" as well as proceedings in court. "Quasi-judicial" covers proceedings by which an administrative body or agency holds hearings and decides issues by application of law to facts. [*Pettus v. Cole* (1996) 49 CA4th 402, 437, 57 CR2d 46, 69-70]

This has been interpreted to include:

- **[1:610.1]** *Contractual arbitration proceedings . . .* "(b)ecause such a proceeding is designed to serve a function analogous to . . . the court system." [*Moore v. Conliffe* (1994) 7 C4th 634, 643, 29 CR2d 152, 157]

- **[1:610.2]** Communications made to agents of the federal Internal Revenue Service, an official administrative agency, designed to initiate appropriate investigative and enforcement proceedings. [*Tiedemann v. Sup.Ct. (Nair)* (1978) 83 CA3d 918, 926, 148 CR 242, 247]

- **[1:610.3]** Because a workers' compensation proceeding is a quasi-judicial proceeding, a medical examiner's report to the workers' compensation insurer is absolutely privileged under Civ.C. §47(b)(2). [*Harris v. King* (1998) 60 CA4th 1185, 1187-1188, 70 CR2d 790, 791— report allegedly defamed injured worker]

[1:610.4-610.9]  *Reserved.*

(d) [1:610.10]  **Conduct outside U.S.:**  The litigation privilege applies to proceedings in foreign countries. [*Beroiz v. Wahl* (2000) 84 CA4th 485, 494, 100 CR2d 905, 910-911—torts allegedly committed in connection with eviction proceedings in Mexico]

(e) [1:611]  **Which statements privileged:**  The Civ.C. §47(b) privilege extends to communications made in *furtherance of the objects* of the litigation and having some *logical relation* to the action. [*Silberg v. Anderson*, supra, 50 C3d at 214, 266 CR at 642]

1) [1:611.1]  **"Logical relation to action":** The mere fact the communication concerns the same subject matter as the lawsuit is *not* enough. The communication *must further the objects* of the litigation; i.e., it "must *function as a necessary or useful step* in the litigation process and must serve its purposes." [*Rothman v. Jackson* (1996) 49 CA4th 1134, 1147, 57 CR2d 284, 292 (emphasis added)]

"(I)f *Silberg's* 'furtherance' test is to serve its purpose, the test can be satisfied only by communications which function *intrinsically*, and apart from any consideration of the speaker's intent, to advance a litigant's case." [*Rothman v. Jackson*, supra, 49 CA4th at 1148, 57 CR2d at 293 (emphasis added)]

2) [1:611.2]  **Statements made in court or in pleadings:**  It is very difficult to establish the *lack* of "logical relationship" between a defamatory statement and the objects of the litigation where the statement was made in court or in papers filed with the court. The defamation must be "so *palpably irrelevant* to the subject matter of the action that *no reasonable person* can doubt its irrelevance." [*Sacramento Brewing Co. v. Desmond, Miller & Desmond* (1999) 75 CA4th 1082, 1090, 89 CR2d 760, 766 (emphasis added)]

Indeed, one case states that since a party's pleadings "obviously" further the object of the litigation, statements contained in such pleadings *necessarily* satisfy the "logical relationship" test, even if false and defamatory. [*Rothman v. Jackson*, supra, 49 CA4th at 1148, 57 CR2d at 293]

a) **Application**

- [1:611.3]  Attorney sent creditors of "*Summit* Brewing Co.," a bankrupt debtor, a notice of motion that misidentified the debtor as "*Sacramento* Brewing Co." A real company by that name, a stranger to the proceedings, sued for defamation. The erroneous identification in the notice of motion was absolutely privileged under §47(b) because the communication involved (the notice of motion) was "logically related" to the object of the bankruptcy action. [*Sacramento Brewing Co. v. Desmond, Miller & Desmond,* supra, 75 CA4th at 1090, 89 CR2d at 766]

- [1:611.4]  Psychologist who had been retained to conduct a child custody evaluation and was appointed by the court as an expert witness was immune from various contract and tort claims based on her report and recommendations to the court. [*Laborde v. Aronson* (2001) 92 CA4th 459, 464, 112 CR2d 119, 122]

  [1:611.5-611.9]  *Reserved.*

b) [1:611.10]  **Compare—notice of lien on judgment:**  The litigation privilege does *not* protect every document filed in a lawsuit. A notice of lien on the judgment or settlement proceeds is nonprivileged because it bears *no logical relationship to the issues* or subject matter of the lawsuit, and is not designed to further the objects of any party to the litigation. [*Limandri v. Judkins* (1997) 52 CA4th 326, 345-346, 60 CR2d 539, 549]

  *Caution:*  This issue may be involved in a case presently before the California Supreme Court, *McMeans v. Scripps Health, Inc.,* Case No. S109573.

3) **[1:612]** **Statements outside court:** The requirement that the statement be made "in" a judicial or quasi-judicial proceeding does not limit the privilege to courthouse proceedings. The privilege extends to publications required or permitted by law "*to achieve the objects of the litigation*, even though the publication is made outside the courtroom and no function of court or its officers is invoked." [*Albertson v. Raboff* (1956) 46 C2d 375, 380-381, 295 P2d 405, 408 (emphasis added); *Wilton v. Mountain Wood Homeowners Ass'n, Inc.* (1993) 18 CA4th 565, 569, 22 CR2d 471, 473]

a) **[1:612.1]** **Correspondence:** The requirement of a "logical relation" to the objects of the action is satisfied "by demand letters and like communications between litigants or their attorneys which are directed towards settlement of a pending or anticipated lawsuit." [*Rothman v. Jackson* (1996) 49 CA4th 1134, 1148, 57 CR2d 284, 293]

b) **[1:613]** **Recording lien:** Recording a lien in the county recorder's office is privileged under Civ.C. §47(b) if authorized by law and related to an action to foreclose the lien. [*Wilton v. Mountain Wood Homeowners Ass'n, Inc.*, supra, 18 CA4th at 570, 22 CR2d at 474—assessment lien filed by homeowners' association for fees due to association by homeowner; see also *Limandri v. Judkins* (1997) 52 CA4th 326, 346, 60 CR2d 539, 550—same rule for mechanics' liens]

It makes no difference that the lienholder has the alternative of enforcing the lien by private sale. The litigation privilege applies because of the possibility of a judicial foreclosure action. [*Wilton v. Mountain Wood Homeowners Ass'n, Inc.*, supra, 18 CA4th at 570, 22 CR2d at 474]

c) **[1:614]** **Recording lis pendens:** A lis pendens imparts constructive notice of a lawsuit affecting real property. The litigation privilege applies if the lis pendens was authorized by law—i.e., one that identifies an action on file in a court of competent jurisdiction that affects title or right to possession of real property. [Civ.C. §47(b)(4); see *Palmer v. Zaklama* (2003) 109 CA4th 1367, 1380, 1 CR3d 116, 125]

*Cross-refer:* See detailed discussion in Greenwald & Asimow, *Cal. Prac. Guide: Real Property Transactions* (TRG), Ch. 11.

[1:615] *Reserved.*

4) [1:616] **Prelawsuit communications:** Although one of the requirements is that the publication be made "in" a judicial proceeding, several cases have extended the privilege to statements made before suit is filed. It is sufficient that the communications have "some relation" to an *anticipated* lawsuit. [*Rubin v. Green* (1993) 4 C4th 1187, 1194, 17 CR2d 828, 832—resident of mobilehome park (an attorney) warned owner of intent to sue for enumerated defects and "solicited" other residents as clients in the anticipated litigation]

a) [1:617] **Nature of prelawsuit communication:** As long as the purposes of the litigation privilege are served thereby, the privilege extends to such prelawsuit communication as:
— *demand letters* from an attorney to a potential adversary;
— statements made during investigative interviews with private individuals prior to a hearing; or
— correspondence to persons with potential claims seeking support for filing a lawsuit. [*Dove Audio, Inc. v. Rosenfeld, Meyer & Susman* (1996) 47 CA4th 777, 781-782, 54 CR2d 830, 833]

b) [1:618] **Requirements for privilege:** The statements must have "some relation to a proceeding contemplated in *good faith* and under *serious consideration*" by a possible party to the proceeding. [*Aronson v. Kinsella* (1997) 58 CA4th 254, 262, 68 CR2d 305, 310; see also *Laffer v. Levinson, Miller, Jacobs & Phillips* (1995) 34 CA4th 117, 123-124, 40 CR2d 233, 237-238, and cases cited therein]

"Good faith" and "serious consideration of litigation" are addressed to the *Silberg* requirement that the statement have some "connection or logical relation to the action" (¶*1:606*). [*Aronson v. Kinsella*, supra, 58 CA4th at 265, 68 CR2d at 312]

1/ [1:618.1] **Does not affect absolute nature of privilege:** One case states these requirements render the litigation privilege for prelawsuit statements "qualified" rather than absolute. [*Laffer v. Levinson, Miller, Jacobs & Phillips*, supra, 34 CA4th at 124, 40 CR2d at 238]

But that is inaccurate because qualified privileges can be defeated by proof of malice (¶*1:609*). If "good faith" and "serious consideration" are shown, defendant's motives are immaterial; the privilege is *absolute*. [*Aronson v. Kinsella*, supra, 58 CA4th at 265, 68 CR2d at 312]

*Caution:* Whether *good faith* is in fact a requirement of the litigation privilege is presently before the California Supreme Court in *Balser v. Wells Fargo Bank*, Case No. S101833.

2/ [1:618.2] **Separate "imminency" requirement?** Some cases state as a separate requirement that the contemplated litigation be "imminent" and impending when the statement is made, rather than merely a possibility. [See *Edwards v. Centex Real Estate Corp.* (1997) 53 CA4th 15, 35, 61 CR2d 518, 521]

But other cases reject this as a separate requirement; i.e., it is enough that litigation was under "serious consideration." [See *Aronson v. Kinsella*, supra, 58 CA4th at 268, 68 CR2d at 314]

c) [1:619] **Factors considered:** In determining whether a prelawsuit statement was made in "good faith" and in "serious consideration of litigation," or merely a negotiating tactic, courts consider such factors as:

- the strength or weakness of the claim asserted;

- the claimant's subsequent failure to file the threatened action (*Laffer v. Levin-*

*son, Miller, Jacobs & Phillips,* supra, 34 CA4th at 124, 40 CR2d at 238; but see *Aronson v. Kinsella,* supra, 58 CA4th at 268, 68 CR2d at 314—privilege upheld where lawsuit never filed);

- whether the statement was made to resolve a *bona fide dispute* rather than merely a means of obtaining a settlement (see *Edwards v. Centex Real Estate Corp.* (1997) 53 CA4th 15, 35, 61 CR2d 518, 531);

- the proximity *in time* between the statement and the litigation (see *Edwards v. Centex Real Estate Corp.,* supra, 53 CA4th at 35, 61 CR2d at 521—statements made many years before litigation commenced held not privileged).

But there is *no* requirement that a complaint be drafted or in the process of being drafted for the privilege to apply. [See *Aronson v. Kinsella,* supra, 58 CA4th at 268, 68 CR2d at 314—*rejecting* any separate "imminency" requirement]

[1:619.1-619.5]    *Reserved.*

d) **Application**

- [1:619.6]    An attorney *demand letter threatening suit* if a claim is not settled is protected by the litigation privilege only if made in *good faith* contemplation of a lawsuit. I.e., there is no privilege if the letter is merely a negotiating tactic sent in hopes of inducing settlement (a factual question in each case). [*Edwards v. Centex Real Estate Corp.,* supra, 53 CA4th at 35, 61 CR2d at 530, fn. 10]

- [1:619.6a]    Attorney's demand letter accused Competitor of raiding Client's employees, stating the raiding was being done by X who formerly "was in prison for violently assaulting his wife." The reference to X's prior criminal history was *not* privileged because not logically connected to the alleged raiding of employees: "*(A)dverting to criminal law matters in the course of purely civil disputes is strongly discouraged."* [*Nguyen v. Proton Technology Corp.* (1999) 69 CA4th 140, 152, 81 CR2d 392, 399, fn. 11 (emphasis added)]

- **[1:619.7]** Where the person receiving the demand *complies* with it, there is no need to file suit. Therefore, a demand made in good faith while litigation was under consideration is privileged *even though no lawsuit was ever filed.* [*Aronson v. Kinsella,* supra, 58 CA4th at 268, 68 CR2d at 314]

  **[1:619.8-619.9]** *Reserved.*

5) **[1:619.10] Statements made during settlement:** Statements made during settlement negotiations are privileged under §47(b) where the statements bear a "clear relation" to the action and were made "to achieve the objects of the suit." [*Asia Investment Co. v. Borowski* (1982) 133 CA3d 832, 842-843, 184 CR 317, 324]

   But a false statement as to the *amount of insurance coverage* available is expressly not protected, so that the settlement may be rescinded if the other party relied on this misrepresentation. [Civ.C. §47(b)(3); *see ¶1:638*]

6) **[1:620] Compare—statements made *after* litigation over:** The privilege does *not* extend at all to statements made *after* conclusion of a judicial proceeding (e.g., after an action has been settled and dismissed). [See *Laffer v. Levinson, Miller, Jacobs & Phillips* (1995) 34 CA4th 117, 123, 40 CR2d 233, 237—accusations of fraud in connection with lawsuit settlement]

7) **[1:621] Statements by and to nonparticipants:** Statements made by or to nonparticipants in the action are generally *not* privileged under Civ.C. §47(b), and thus are actionable unless privileged on some other basis (e.g., as communications to news media, see below). [See *Silberg v. Anderson* (1990) 50 C3d 205, 219, 266 CR 638, 647; *Rothman v. Jackson* (1996) 49 CA4th 1134, 1143, 57 CR2d 284, 290]

- **[1:621.1]** False accusations of child molestation made in court pleadings in a domestic relations proceeding are absolutely privileged. But the same accusations made to police officers are not: "The privilege for statements made in a 'judicial proceeding' does not apply to statements made outside of the courtroom to nonparties unconnected to the proceedings." [*Begier v. Strom* (1996) 46 CA4th 877, 882, 54 CR2d 158, 161]

- **[1:621.2]** A creditor of one of the parties does not become a "litigant or other participant" merely by filing a notice of lien against any judgment or settlement proceeds that party may obtain. [*Limandri v. Judkins* (1997) 52 CA4th 326, 345, 60 CR2d 539, 549]

8) **[1:622]** **Statements to news media:** Communications to a "public journal" of "a judicial proceeding . . . or anything in the course thereof" are privileged, unless they violate a court order, the CRPC or other confidentiality requirements imposed by law. [Civ.C. §47(d)]

   a) **[1:622.1]** **Background:** The statute was amended specifically to *abrogate* a case (*Shahvar v. Sup.Ct. (ASP Computer Products, Inc.)* (1994) 25 CA4th 653, 30 CR2d 597) holding unprivileged a lawyer's faxing a copy of a civil complaint to a newspaper. [See Stats. 1996, Ch. 1055, §1 (statement of legislative intent)]

   **[1:622.2-622.4]** *Reserved.*

   b) **[1:622.5]** **Privilege still limited to statements "furthering objects of litigation":** Even so, the litigation privilege protects only communications that "further the objects" of the litigation. [*Rothman v. Jackson*, supra, 49 CA4th at 1143, 57 CR2d at 291, fn. 3]

   Therefore, press releases regarding *anticipated* civil litigation ("We *are going to sue* P for plagiarism and theft") are *not* privileged. Such statements do not "further" the objects of the lawsuit; they are designed instead for public relations purposes. Attorneys who choose to "litigate in the press" do so at their own risk. [*Rothman v. Jackson*, supra, 49 CA4th at 1149, 57 CR2d at 294;

see *Susan A. v. County of Sonoma* (1991) 2 CA4th 88, 95, 3 CR2d 27, 31—"trial by press is a universally condemned practice"]

[1:623-624] *Reserved.*

(f) [1:625] **Compare—privilege not applicable to conduct:** The Civ.C. §47(b) privilege protects statements, publications and other communications, not conduct. [*Kimmel v. Goland* (1990) 51 C3d 202, 212, 271 CR 191, 197]

1) [1:626] **Unauthorized recording:** The unauthorized recording of private telephone conversations may be actionable as an invasion of privacy despite the fact it was done in anticipation of litigation. [*Kimmel v. Goland,* supra, 51 C3d at 212, 271 CR at 197—lawyer may be sued for aiding client's recording]

2) [1:626.1] **Unauthorized reading and dissemination of confidential information:** A party's or counsel's unauthorized reading and dissemination of confidential information regarding the opposing party (e.g., mental health records) are noncommunicative *acts.* The litigation privilege does not bar a suit for invasion of privacy or personal injuries arising from this conduct. [*Mansell v. Otto* (2003) 108 CA4th 265, 272-275, 133 CR2d 276, 282-284—no action lies, however, where information obtained through judicial process]

3) [1:627] **Financing litigation:** "(W)hile it could be argued that an exhortation to sue (communication) might be privileged, *financing* and otherwise promoting the litigation (conduct) would not be." [*Pacific Gas & Elec. Co. v. Bear Stearns* (1990) 50 C3d 1118, 1132, 270 CR 1, 8, fn. 12 (emphasis and parentheses added)]

4) [1:628] **Filing contract claim with public agency:** Filing a claim with a public entity for overages on a public work project is not protected by the litigation privilege, even if the contractor planned to sue upon denial of the claim: "The litigation privilege was never meant to spin out from judicial action a party's performance and course of conduct under a contract." [*Stacy & Witbeck, Inc. v. City & County of San Francisco* (1996) 47 CA4th 1, 8, 54 CR2d 530, 534]

[1:628.1-628.4] *Reserved.*

5) [1:628.5] **Comment:** The distinction between "communications" and "conduct" is often
difficult to draw. The test appears to be whether
the conduct *causes injury at the time it occurs*
(in which event, no privilege) or only when evidence obtained thereby is used in a judicial
proceeding (privilege applies).

[1:629-633] *Reserved.*

(g) [1:634] **Which actions barred by privilege:**
The privilege extends to *all* tort actions based on
the communication *except* as noted below.

Thus, it may be asserted as a defense to:
— abuse of process;
— defamation;
— fraud;
— invasion of privacy;
— intentional infliction of emotional distress;
— intentional interference with contract or prospective advantage;
— negligent misrepresentation;
— negligence;
— assertion of statutorily authorized lien (*Olszewski v. Scripps Health* (2003) 30 C4th 798, 832,
135 CR2d 1, 29); or
— "unfair competition" under Bus. & Prof.C.
§17200. [*Rubin v. Green* (1993) 4 C4th 1187,
1203, 17 CR2d 828, 838; see *Silberg v. Anderson*, supra, 50 C3d at 216, 266 CR at 644]

It also extends to suits for wrongful conduct outside
the scope of traditional tort claims. [*Carden v.
Getzoff* (1987) 190 CA3d 907, 913, 235 CR 698,
701—action against expert witness for "manufacturing false evidence"; *California Physicians' Service
v. Sup.Ct. (Landa)* (1992) 9 CA4th 1321, 1325-
1326, 12 CR2d 95, 97—action against defendant
insurer for "malicious defense" to complaint]

And it extends to suits to *enjoin tortious conduct*
apart from any damages claim. Civ.C. §47(b) cannot be avoided by "putting a new label on the complaint." [See *Rubin v. Green* (1993) 4 C4th 1187,
1203, 17 CR2d 828, 837-838—litigation privilege
barred suit to enjoin attorneys from "unfair competition" by allegedly misrepresenting facts to potential clients regarding anticipated litigation]

*Compare—breach of contract claims:* The privilege
is generally described as one that "precludes liabil-

ity in tort, not liability for breach of contract." [*Navellier v. Sletten* (2003) 106 CA4th 763, 773-774, 131 CR2d 201, 209-210]

1) **[1:635]** **Except malicious prosecution:** Statements made in the course of a judicial proceeding are admissible to show the action was maliciously prosecuted. I.e., one may not institute litigation without probable cause in order to obtain a privilege to defame others! [See *Ribas v. Clark* (1985) 38 C3d 355, 364, 212 CR 143, 149]

2) **[1:636]** **Abuse of process?** Arguably, for the same reason, the privilege should not bar claims for abuse of process. But numerous cases hold that it does. [See cases cited in *Silberg v. Anderson*, supra, 50 C3d at 215, 266 CR at 644; *O'Keefe v. Kompa* (2000) 84 CA4th 130, 134, 100 CR2d 602, 605—privilege applied to post-trial collection efforts; *Brown v. Kennard* (2001) 94 CA4th 40, 48, 113 CR2d 891, 897—abuse of process action against judgment creditor's attorney who levied on holder's bank account barred by litigation privilege]

a) **[1:636a]** **Distinction between communications and conduct?** Some courts draw a distinction between a party's *application* for a court process (e.g., writ of execution) and *levies* made thereunder. The application is treated as a privileged "communication" but the *levies* are "conduct" not protected by the litigation privilege and therefore subject to an abuse of process action. [*Drum v. Bleau, Fox & Assocs.* (2003) 107 CA4th 1009, 1027-1028, 132 CR2d 602, 615-616]

Other courts treat both the application and levy as privileged and hence not actionable. [*Brown v. Kennard* (2001) 94 CA4th 40, 48-49, 113 CR2d 891, 898]

3) **[1:636.1]** **Actions to enjoin tort or statutory violation:** Civ.C. §47(b) cannot be avoided by pleading a claim for injunctive relief rather than for damages. "The salutary purpose of the privilege should not be frustrated by putting a new label on the complaint." [See *Rubin v. Green* (1993) 4 C4th 1187, 1203, 17 CR2d 828, 837-838]

Rev. #1 2004

- [1:636.2] Thus, a suit to *enjoin* attorneys from "unfair competition" (Bus. & Prof.C. §17200) based on "wrongful solicitation" and "misrepresenting" facts to potential clients regarding anticipated litigation against plaintiff was properly dismissed. Prelawsuit discussions with potential clients clearly fall within the Civ.C. §47(b) privilege (*see* ¶*1:616*). The privilege is not lost because "wrongful solicitation" violates various statutes; the State Bar and prosecuting authorities may pursue that matter. [*Rubin v. Green*, supra, 4 C4th at 1204, 17 CR2d at 833-835]

   [1:636.3-636.4] *Reserved.*

4) [1:636.5] **Compare—privilege no defense to other liability:** The litigation privilege applies only to tort claims based on statements made in judicial proceedings. It does not protect against the following:

   a) [1:636.6] **Criminal charges:** Civ.C. §47(b) does not preclude criminal liability for perjury, subornation of perjury, etc. [*Silberg v. Anderson*, supra, 50 C3d at 219, 266 CR at 647]

   b) [1:636.7] **Disciplinary charges:** Nor does it shield a witness from disciplinary proceedings based on testimony given in a court proceeding. [*Silberg v. Anderson*, supra, 50 C3d at 219, 266 CR at 647; *Budwin v. American Psychological Ass'n* (1994) 24 CA4th 875, 881, 29 CR2d 453, 457—expert witness may be censured by professional society for false testimony]

   c) [1:636.8] **Malpractice actions:** The litigation privilege does not shield an attorney or expert witness from liability to the party who hired the expert for negligence in preparation or presentation of the case. [See *Mattco Forge, Inc. v. Arthur Young & Co.* (1992) 5 CA4th 392, 406, 6 CR2d 781, 790]

   d) [1:636.9] **Unauthorized disclosure of trade secret:** The litigation privilege does not protect the unauthorized disclosure of trade secret information to a competitor or potential competitor of the trade secret's owner, even in the course of litigation. [See Civ.C. §3426.11]

(h) **Statutory exceptions**

1) [1:637] **Exception for marital dissolution actions naming third parties:** There is no privilege for tortious statements in pleadings or affidavits in marital dissolution actions concerning a nonparty (e.g., allegations that spouse's lover is child abuser) *unless* such statements are:

— relevant to the action;
— made *under oath* and without malice; and
— based on *probable cause* to believe the statement was true. [See Civ.C. §47(b)(1)]

2) [1:638] **Exception for concealing insurance coverage:** The litigation privilege does not shield statements made in a judicial proceeding "knowingly concealing the existence of an insurance policy or policies." [Civ.C. §47(b)(3)]

This may apply, for example, where P settles and releases D for a nominal sum in reliance on D's statement that he had no liability insurance. If P later discovers D had insurance, the litigation privilege does not bar an action to rescind the settlement on grounds of fraud. [See *Home Ins. Co. v. Zurich Ins. Co.* (2002) 96 CA4th 17, 24-25, 116 CR2d 583, 589]

a) [1:639] **Compare—misrepresentations re terms of insurance:** This exception does not apply to misrepresentations regarding the *terms* of a liability insurance policy (e.g., the policy limits). As long as the *existence* of the policy is known, it is up to plaintiff to use discovery or other methods to ferret out the terms of the insurance. [*Home Ins. Co. v. Zurich Ins. Co.*, supra, 96 CA4th at 25-26, 116 CR2d at 589; *Morales v. Cooperative of American Physicians, Inc., Mutual Protection Trust ("CAP-MPT")* (9th Cir. 1999) 180 F3d 1060, 1063-1064 (applying Calif. Law)—interrogatory response disclosing existence of policy and its limits, but failing to reveal that policy was "excess" rather than "primary," was not statement concealing existence of insurance policy within meaning of exception to litigation privilege]

- **[1:639.1]** This may apply, for example, where in order to induce plaintiff to settle an earlier lawsuit, defendant (or its insurer) intentionally understates the amount of insurance coverage available to satisfy the claim. The litigation privilege would bar a subsequent fraud action against the defendant (or its insurer) in such cases. [See *Morales v. Cooperative of American Physicians, Inc., Mutual Protection Trust ("CAP-MPT")*, supra, 180 F3d at 1064]

b) **[1:640] Compare—misrepresentation to insured or third party beneficiary:** There is no litigation privilege for an insurer (or its attorney) to defraud its own insured or a person standing in the shoes of the insured: e.g., a judgment creditor of an insured defendant entitled to enforce the policy as third party beneficiary under Ins.C. §11580. The rights afforded by §11580 *prevail* over the litigation privilege. [*Shafer v. Berger, Kahn, Shafton, Moss, Figler, Simon & Gladstone* (2003) 107 CA4th 54, 80-81, 131 CR2d 777, 798—injured party may pursue fraud claim against insurer's coverage counsel]

3) **[1:641] Exception for planning destruction or alteration of evidence:** There is no privilege for communications made to further the *intentional* destruction or alteration of *physical evidence* in order to deprive a party of the use of such evidence. [Civ.C. §47(b)(2)]

(E.g., in preparing discovery responses, party instructs his secretary to shred harmful documents or destroy damaging photographs to prevent having to disclose them.)

a) **[1:642] Compare—instructions to lie or conceal evidence privileged:** By its terms, the above exception applies only to communications re destruction or alteration of *physical* evidence. Thus, it would not apply to the situation where a party or counsel (or insurer) *directs a witness to lie* or *conceal* harmful evidence in order to evade liability. [See *Doctors' Co. v. Sup.Ct. (Marchand)* (1990) 225 CA3d 1284, 1294, 275 CR 674, 680]

Such communications are clearly privileged. [*Kupiec v. American Int'l Adjustment Co.* (1991) 235 CA3d 1326, 1333, 1 CR2d 371, 374—privilege bars action against liability insurer for *instructing its insured not to tell the truth* during discovery]

- • [1:643] **Comment:** This seems to stretch the Civ.C.§47(b) privilege to the breaking point! But it avoids the unending litigation that would result if disgruntled litigants could sue adverse witnesses for lying or concealing evidence; and the person guilty of such conduct may be subject to criminal liability.

4) [1:644] **Exception for slander of title based on improper lis pendens:** A person who files a lis pendens when the underlying action is *not related to the real property* may be subject to a slander of title action: "A recorded lis pendens is not a privileged publication unless it identifies an action previously filed with a court of competent jurisdiction which affects the title or right of possession of real property, as authorized or required by law." [Civ.C. §47(b)(4); *see discussion at ¶9:421 ff.*]

Comment: However, CCP §405.32 authorizes the property owner to file a *motion to expunge* an improper lis pendens. This motion allows the court to evaluate the underlying real property claim on its merits (*see ¶9:429 ff.*). Failure to make such motion arguably would constitute a failure to mitigate damages resulting from the improper lis pendens.

[1:644.1-644.4] *Reserved.*

(i) [1:644.5] **Exception for violation of constitutional right to privacy?** The right to privacy recognized in Calif. Const. Art. I, §1 may trump the litigation privilege. A *balancing of interests analysis* applies where the litigation privilege is asserted as a defense to a claim based upon invasion of the constitutional right to privacy. [See *Jeffrey H. v. Imai, Tadlock & Keeney* (2001) 85 CA4th 345, 360, 101 CR2d 916, 926—claim against lawyers for violating opposing party's privacy in prior litigation (by unnecessarily disclosing his HIV status)]

1) [1:644.6] **Contra authority:** Not all courts agree with this result. "Weighing" the constitu-

tional right to privacy against the interests promoted by the litigation privilege "clearly conflicts with the absolute nature of the privilege." [See *Wise v. Thrifty Payless, Inc.* (2000) 83 CA4th 1296, 1303, 100 CR2d 437, 442, fn. 1]

(4) **[1:645]** **Requirements re collection letters (Fair Debt Collection Practices Act):** Lawyers who "regularly" do consumer debt collection work are "debt collectors" within the meaning of the federal "Fair Debt Collection Practices Act" (15 USC §§1601, 1692-1692a(6)).

The Act requires "debt collectors" to furnish debtors with written notice containing:
* Amount of debt;
* Name of creditor;
* Unless debtor notifies it of dispute re validity within 30 days, debt will be presumed valid by collector (whether this puts a "hold" on legal proceedings for 30 days is unclear);
* Promise to obtain verification of any matter debtor claims to be in dispute; and
* Upon request by debtor, to obtain name of original creditor (if different from current creditor). [15 USC §1692g(a)]

If the debtor notifies the attorney within the 30-day period that the debt is disputed, collection efforts must cease until verification of the debt is sent to the debtor.

No further contact with the debtor (other than a lawsuit) is permitted if the debtor declines in writing to pay the debt, or asks the attorney to stop contacting him. Moreover, contacting third parties (employers, etc.) is prohibited.

Violations of the Act subject the "debt collector" to liability for actual damages, statutory damages (up to $1,000 per violation), and legal fees for debtor's counsel. In addition, such violations expose the attorney to *disciplinary action* (Bus. & Prof.C. §6077.5 embodies the same requirements). (See comprehensive treatment of the Fair Debt Collection Practices Act in Ahart, *Cal. Prac. Guide: Enforcing Judgments & Debts* (TRG), Ch. 2.)

2. **[1:646]** **Claims Against Government Entities:** In general, no suit for money or damages may be maintained against a governmental entity unless a formal claim has been presented to such entity, and has been rejected (or is deemed rejected by the passage of time). [Gov.C. §§945.4, 912.4; see *Munoz v. State of Calif.* (1995) 33 CA4th 1767, 1776, 39 CR2d 860, 864]

The claims requirement applies only to *monetary claims*. It is not a prerequisite to other types of judicial relief (e.g., injunction, writ of mandate, etc.). [*Minsky v. City of Los Angeles* (1974) 11 C3d 113, 121, 113 CR 102, 108]

The claims requirement applies to *any monetary claim* even if it is merely incidental to other relief sought. [*TrafficSchoolOnline, Inc. v. Clarke* (2003) 112 CA4th 736, 742, 5 CR3d 408, 412; *Gatto v. County of Sonoma* (2002) 98 CA4th 744, 763, 120 CR2d 550, 564]

Although commonly referred to as the "Tort Claims Act," this is a misnomer because the claims presentation requirement also applies to *contract claims* against the state and local public agencies (see Gov.C. §§905, 905.2, 945.4). [*Baines Pickwick Limited v. City of Los Angeles* (1999) 72 CA4th 298, 303-304, 85 CR2d 74, 77] (But many contract claims are *exempt; see* ¶*1:658.*)

a. **General considerations**

   (1) [1:647] **Purpose:**   The purpose of the claims statutes is "to provide the public entity sufficient information to enable it to adequately investigate claims and to settle them, if appropriate, without the expense of litigation." [*City of San Jose v. Sup.Ct. (Lands Unlimited)* (1974) 12 C3d 447, 455, 115 CR 797, 802]

   (2) [1:648] **Constitutionality:**   The claims filing statutes have been repeatedly upheld against challenges on "due process" and "equal protection" grounds. [See *Harrison v. County of Del Norte* (1985) 168 CA3d 1, 9, 213 CR 658, 663]

   (3) [1:649] **Entities protected:**   With few exceptions, the claims filing statutes apply to claims against every public entity in the State. This includes the State and every political subdivision, every agency and department thereof, and every special purpose district (public schools, public hospitals, public transportation, etc.). [See Gov.C. §900 et seq.]

   [1:650] *Reserved.*

   (4) [1:651] **Pleading requirement?**   It is presently unclear whether compliance with the claims statute is an essential element of the cause of action that must be pleaded in the complaint.

   **Caution:**   This issue is presently before the California Supreme Court in *State of Calif. v. Sup.Ct. (Bodde)*, Case No. S114171.

   ➪[1:652] *PRACTICE POINTER:*   Until the Supreme Court holds otherwise, plaintiffs should plead compliance with the claims statute. Most trial courts will follow earlier cases requiring such pleading. [See *Del Real v. City of Riverside* (2002) 95 CA4th 761, 767, 115 CR2d 705, 709; and *Wood v. Riverside Gen. Hosp.* (1994) 25 CA4th 1113, 1119, 31 CR2d 8 11]

(5) **[1:653]** **Effect of failure to comply:** Failure to comply with the claims statute bars the claim against the public entity. [*Kim v. Walker* (1989) 208 CA3d 375, 384, 256 CR 223, 228—treated as "jurisdictional defect"]

(a) **[1:654]** **Action against public employees also barred:** If action against the public entity is barred by failure to file a timely claim, suit against a public employee for causing injury in the scope of his or her employment is also barred. [Gov.C. §950.2]

1) **[1:655]** **Rationale:** Otherwise, the protection provided to the public entity by the claim requirement would be meaningless . . . because public employees are entitled to *indemnification* from the public entity for liability incurred in the course and scope of their employment (Gov.C. §§825-825.6). [*Briggs v. Lawrence* (1991) 230 CA3d 605, 613, 281 CR 578, 582]

2) **Application**

- **[1:656]** City Official defamed Union Leader in the course of official meetings. Union Leader sued City Official for defamation, but did not file claim against City. Held: The filing of a timely claim against City was a condition precedent to a tort action against *either* City or City Official. [*Mazzola v. Feinstein* (1984) 154 CA3d 305, 310, 201 CR 148, 150-151]

- **[1:657]** Client sued County Public Defender for malpractice. Suit was properly dismissed because Client failed to comply with tort claims statute. Public Defender was a *salaried, full-time* public employee, not an independent contractor, and hence claim filing with County was required. [*Briggs v. Lawrence* (1991) 230 CA3d 605, 613-615, 281 CR 578, 583-586]

b. **[1:658]** **Claims excepted:** As will be seen, many types of claims are exempt from the claims filing procedures.

Gov.C. §905 exempts a broad variety of *nontort* claims for which adequate claims procedures are already available: e.g., claims for tax refunds, salary due, retirement benefits, bond payments, unemployment insurance benefits, etc. [See *Blue v. Los Angeles Unified School Dist.* (1994) 26 CA4th Supp. 12, 14, 31 CR2d 923, 924—no claim required prior to suing for benefits payable on public employee's death]

The exclusions enumerated in §905 are not exclusive. Various other exceptions are recognized by case law.

(1) **[1:659]** **Claims based on federal law:** The Supremacy Clause of the U.S. Constitution (Art. VI, cl. 2) protects federal rights from impairment by state rules of procedure. Thus, claims filing requirements of state law cannot defeat a claim arising under federal law.

For example, claims against a public entity based on the Federal Civil Rights Act (42 USC §1983) need *not* be presented to the public entity prior to suit in state (or federal) court. [*Felder v. Casey* (1988) 487 US 131, 134, 108 S.Ct. 2302, 2304-2305; *Williams v. Horvath* (1976) 16 C3d 834, 842, 129 CR 453, 459]

(2) **[1:660]** **Claims having different claims-filing procedures:** No claim under the Tort Claims Act is required where statutes prescribe different claims filing procedures. For example:

(a) **[1:660.1]** **FEHA claims:** Employment discrimination claims against a public entity under the California Fair Employment and Housing Act (Gov.C. §12900 et seq.) are not subject to claims filing requirements. Reason: The FEHA has its own procedures that assure adequate notice to the public entity. Therefore, no claims presentation under the Tort Claims Act is required. [*Snipes v. City of Bakersfield* (1983) 145 CA3d 861, 865, 193 CR 760, 762]

(b) **[1:660.2]** **Claims against State Compensation Insurance Fund:** A special statute (Ins.C. §11873) *excludes* the State Compensation Insurance Fund from the Tort Claims Act. Thus, there is no claims filing requirement in actions against the State Fund. [*Maxon Industries, Inc. v. State Comp. Ins. Fund* (1993) 16 CA4th 1387, 1391, 20 CR2d 730, 731]

(c) **[1:660.3]** **Claims against Foster Home Insurance Fund:** The Legislature has created a "Foster Home and Small Family Home Insurance Fund" to pay claims against foster parents for acts arising from the foster-care relationship. Plaintiffs must file a claim *with the Fund* before commencing a civil action against a foster parent for which the Fund may be liable (Health & Saf.C. §1527.6(d)). Compliance with the Tort Claims Act (e.g., by filing a claim with the Victim Compensation and Government Claims Board; see ¶1:694) is not necessary and does *not* satisfy this requirement. [*Becerra v. Gonzales* (1995) 32 CA4th 584, 592, 38 CR2d 248, 253]

(3) **[1:661]** **Claims by another public entity:** Governmental entities normally can sue each other without complying with the Tort Claims Act. [Gov.C. §905(i)]

But the Act also authorizes public entities to enact *their own claims procedures* which may apply to claims by other public entities. [Gov.C. §935; *City of Ontario v. Sup.Ct. (Department of Transp.)* (1993) 12 CA4th 894, 901-903, 16 CR2d 32, 36-37—State's equitable indemnity claim against City barred by its failure to file claim as required by City ordinance]

(4) **[1:662]** **"Redundant" claims:** No filing is required as to claims *necessarily included* in a claim already filed with the public entity.

- **[1:663]** For example, a claim filed by an employee for on-the-job injury necessarily includes any claim the employer (or workers' comp insurer) may have for benefits paid the employee on account of such injury. [*San Diego Unified Port Dist. v. Sup.Ct. (Campbell)* (1988) 197 CA3d 843, 847, 243 CR 163, 165]

- **[1:664]** Likewise, a liability insurer who pays a claim against its insured is *subrogated* to the insured's right to seek indemnification from third persons. Thus, where the insured has already filed an indemnification claim with a public entity, no additional claim need be filed by the insurer. [*Smith v. Parks Manor* (1987) 197 CA3d 872, 881, 243 CR 256, 261]

- **[1:665]** *Compare:* But the "redundant" claim doctrine does *not* cover *completely separate* injuries. Thus, where Parents sought damages for emotional distress caused by Public Hospital's negligent treatment of their Child, Parents could not rely on a tort claim filed on Child's behalf. Their injuries were separate and distinct from those of Child. [*Nguyen v. Los Angeles County/Harbor UCLA Med. Center* (1992) 8 CA4th 729, 734, 10 CR2d 709, 712]

(5) **[1:666]** **"Defensive cross-complaints":** No claims filing is required as to a cross-complaint that:

— is filed in response to a *public entity's initiation* of the action;

— arises out of the same transaction or event; and

— is *defensive in nature* (no affirmative relief requested). [*Krainock v. Sup.Ct. (Poway Unified School Dist.)* (1990) 216 CA3d 1473, 1478, 265 CR 715, 718]

(a) **[1:666.1]** **Example:** Student injured in school-yard scuffle sued Other Student for assault and School District for negligent supervision. School District cross-complained for indemnity against Other Student who in turn cross-complained for indemnity against School District. Other Student's cross-complaint against School District was not subject to the claims filing requirement. [*Krainock v. Sup.Ct. (Poway Unified School Dist.)*, supra, 216 CA3d at 1475-1476, 265 CR at 718]

(b) **[1:667]** **Rationale:** The purpose of the claims statute is satisfied where the public entity has had an opportunity to investigate and evaluate the matter: "(T)he act should not be allowed to become a snare for the unwary litigant if its statutory purpose is satisfied." [*Krainock v. Sup.Ct. (Poway Unified School Dist.)*, supra, 216 CA3d at 1477, 265 CR at 717]

**[1:667.1-667.4]** *Reserved.*

(6) **[1:667.5]** **Claims for return of improperly confiscated property:** Plaintiffs seeking return of specific property confiscated by the government are not subject to the claims filing requirements applicable to damage claims. [*Long v. City of Los Angeles* (1998) 68 CA4th 782, 784, 80 CR2d 583, 584]

It follows that where the government has lost or destroyed the confiscated property, it is not permitted to invoke the Tort Claims Act as a defense to what has become, by virtue of its own misconduct, a damages action. [*Long v. City of Los Angeles,* supra, 68 CA4th at 786, 80 CR2d at 585—City was ordered to return to plaintiff several hundred birds wrongfully seized, but half were lost or destroyed]

c. **[1:668]** **Circumstances under which claims filing excused:** In addition to the various types of claims excepted from the claims filing statutes (above), there are circumstances under which the filing requirements are excused:

(1) **[1:669]** **Public entity's failure to file identifying information:** Public agencies are required to file iden-

tifying information with the Secretary of State and County Clerk (see Gov.C. §53051). If they fail to do so, the claimant is *excused* from filing a claim or suing within the time limits discussed below. [*Wilson v. San Francisco Redevelopment Agency* (1977) 19 C3d 555, 560, 138 CR 720, 723]

(a) [1:670] **Effect of letterhead identification:** Public entities are required to identify themselves as such in dealings with the public. This is satisfied if the words "public agency," "district," "city," etc. appear on the entity's letterhead stationery and identification cards used by its representatives. Absent such identification, however, a written application for leave to file a late claim "shall be granted" if the claimant acted with reasonable diligence. [See Gov.C. §7530]

- [1:671] If the letterhead is proper, further identification is *not required*. For example, a county hospital whose letterhead identified it as a public agency was *not* also required to put this information on its patient's medical records. [*Rojes v. Riverside General Hosp.* (1988) 203 CA3d 1151, 1165, 250 CR 435, 442]

(2) [1:672] **Advance payment by public entity:** If the entity (or an insurance carrier on its behalf) makes a partial or advance payment of damages to the injured party, without notifying of the claims filing requirement, such filing is excused. [Ins.C. §11583; see *Maisel v. San Francisco State Univ.* (1982) 134 CA3d 689, 693-694, 184 CR 694, 696-697—remanded for determination whether University's furnishing medical care to injured student constituted advance payment of damages]

(3) [1:673] **Estoppel against public entity:** "A public entity may be estopped from asserting the limitations of the claims statute where its agents or employees have *prevented or deterred* the filing of a timely claim by some affirmative act." [*John R. v. Oakland Unified School Dist.* (1989) 48 C3d 438, 445, 256 CR 766, 769 (emphasis added)]

(a) [1:674] **Requirements:** To establish such estoppel, however, the claimant would have to show that:

- Claimant was ignorant of the true facts (i.e., public entity's responsibility for damage or injury);
- Public entity was apprised of the true facts;

- Public entity *intended* its statements or conduct be relied upon (or claimant had the right to believe it so intended);

- Claimant reasonably relied on the public entity's statements or conduct to its detriment. [See *Driscoll v. City of Los Angeles* (1967) 67 C2d 297, 305, 61 CR 661, 666; *Ortega v. Pajaro Valley Unified School Dist.* (1998) 64 CA4th 1023, 1044, 75 CR2d 777, 789]

(b) **Application**

1) [1:675] **Misleading statements:** An estoppel may be based on misleading statements by a public officer about the need for or advisability of filing a claim. Actual fraud or intent to mislead is *not* required. [*John R. v. Oakland Unified School Dist.*, supra, 48 C3d at 445, 256 CR at 769]

- [1:676]   The following were sufficient to allege an estoppel:

   D's real name was "Oak Valley Hospital District" but it *did business as* "Oak Valley *District Hospital*";

   P was misled thereby, and on checking with the Secretary of State, *was told there was no public entity* under D's *business name*;

   P relied on this information and failed to file a timely claim. [*Elmore v. Oak Valley Hosp. Dist.* (1988) 204 CA3d 716, 723-724, 251 CR 405, 409-410]

2) [1:677] **Inducing delay:** Estoppel may also be invoked where a public entity induces a reasonably prudent person to avoid seeking legal advice or commencing litigation. [*Bertorelli v. City of Tulare* (1986) 180 CA3d 432, 440, 225 CR 582, 586]

- [1:678]   Public Entity leased premises to Lessee for construction of improvements without disclosing third party claims affecting Lessee's use of the premises. When Lessee found out, Public Entity assumed responsibility for the third party claims, thereby inducing Lessee not to take action and to proceed with construction. Public Entity was estopped to assert the claims statute as a defense: "The claims statute may not be invoked to penalize a plaintiff who at the behest of a public entity has been induced not to take action." [*Ocean Services Corp. v. Ventura Port Dist.* (1993) 15 CA4th 1762, 1776, 19 CR2d 750, 757]

3) **[1:679] Intimidation:** Acts of violence or intimidation on the part of a public entity that are intended to prevent the filing of a claim may also create an estoppel. [*John R. v. Oakland Unified School Dist.*, supra, 48 C3d at 445, 256 CR at 769]

- **[1:680]** Where the claim is for sexual molestation of a minor by a public school teacher, no actual threat by the teacher may be necessary. The teacher's warning the child "not to tell" may constitute a sufficient implied threat (of retaliation) to invoke an estoppel. [*Christopher P. v. Mojave Unified School Dist.* (1993) 19 CA4th 165, 173, 23 CR2d 353, 359]

[1:680.1-680.4] *Reserved.*

(4) **[1:680.5] Mental incapacity:** The time within which to file a late claim against a governmental entity is tolled if the claimant is mentally incapacitated and does not have a conservator. [Gov.C. §911.4]

Even if a mentally incapacitated claimant *has* a conservator, the statute is tolled when the conservator does not and could not have known of the claim. [*Favorite v. County of Los Angeles* (1998) 68 CA4th 835, 839, 80 CR2d 656, 658—conservator had no reason to know mentally incapacitated ward had been sexually abused while drugged]

[1:680.6-680.9] *Reserved.*

(5) **[1:680.10] Minor in custody as dependent of juvenile court:** The statute is also tolled for the period of time a minor is detained by or adjudged to be a dependent child of the juvenile court if:
- the minor is in the *custody or control of a public agency* against which a claim of injury or abuse is made;
- that agency was *aware* of the injury or abuse claimed by the minor and failed to report it to the minor's attorney or the court as required by law. [See Gov.C. §911.4(d)]

d. **Procedural requirements**

(1) [1:681] **Content of claim:** The claim must be in writing and must show:

- The name and address of the claimant;

- The date and place of the accident or event out of which the claim arose;

- A general description of the damage, loss or indebtedness incurred;

- The names of any public employees allegedly responsible; and

- The amount of the claim *if it totals under $10,000.* Claims over that amount must not state an amount, but only whether the case would be filed as a "limited civil case." [Gov.C. §910(f); see *Poway Unified School Dist. v. Sup.Ct. (Copley Press)* (1998) 62 CA4th 1496, 1503, 73 CR2d 777, 781 (citing text)]

*FORMS:* The public entity must provide forms specifying the above information. Those forms must be used by the claimant; otherwise, the claim may be rejected and must be resubmitted on the proper form. [Gov.C. §910.4]

The following forms are representative:

- City of Los Angeles claim form: "Claim for Damages to Person or Property," *see Form 1:C.*

- State of California claim form: "Government Claim," *see Form 1:D.*

(a) [1:682] **Additional data not required:** A claim that provides the above information satisfies the claims act, even if it omits other information requested on the claim form provided by the public entity. [*Blair v. Sup.Ct. (Dept. of Transp.)* (1990) 218 CA3d 221, 225, 267 CR 13, 16—Board of Control claim form asked "what particular act or omission caused accident"]

(b) [1:683] **"Substantial compliance" sufficient:** Technical defects will not invalidate a claim so long as there has been "substantial compliance" with the claims filing requirement. [See *Phillips v. Desert Hosp. Dist.* (1989) 49 C3d 699, 706, 263 CR 119, 124]

1) [1:684] **Test:** The test is whether sufficient information is disclosed "to enable a public

entity to investigate and evaluate the claim to determine whether settlement is appropriate." [*Phillips v. Desert Hosp. Dist.*, supra, 49 C3d at 706, 263 CR at 124]

But there cannot be "substantial" compliance without *some* compliance with *each* of the requirements for a valid claim (¶1:681). [*City of San Jose v. Sup.Ct. (Lands Unlimited)* (1974) 12 C3d 447, 456-457, 115 CR 797, 803]

Note: Even a *defective* claim, however, obligates the public entity to *warn* the claimant of the defects (*see* ¶1:688). [*Phillips v. Desert Hosp. Dist.*, supra, 49 C3d at 707, 263 CR at 124]

2) **Application**

- [1:685] Plaintiff was injured by a Sanitation District bulldozer. Plaintiff's attorney sent a letter to the bulldozer operator, *with a copy to the Sanitation District,* stating plaintiff's name and the date and place of the accident, asking re insurance. The District acknowledged the correspondence and directed the attorney to contact its insurer. This was sufficient compliance with the claims filing provisions (making it incumbent on District to specify any defects in the information provided, see below). [*Foster v. McFadden* (1973) 30 CA3d 943, 949, 106 CR 685, 689 (cited with approval in *Phillips v. Desert Hosp. Dist.,* below); see also *Wilson v. Tri-City Hosp.* (1990) 221 CA3d 441, 449, 270 CR 436, 440-441]

- [1:686] Patient's Mother wrote a letter to Public Hospital detailing mistreatment of Patient. This was *not* "substantial compliance" with the claim filing requirement because there was *no* compliance with several statutory requirements: i.e., no monetary claim was made, and the letter was not sent to the statutorily designated agent. [*Wood v. Riverside Gen. Hosp.* (1994) 25 CA4th 1113, 1118, 31 CR2d 8, 10]

  [1:686.1] *Reserved.*

- [1:686.2] Contractor's letter to public agency's General Manager outlining history of Contractor's work, dispute over fees and seeking General Manager's personal involvement in resolving the matter, did *not* constitute substantial compliance with the claims statute: "The letter's import was merely to provide information and to request negotiation of an ongoing dispute, rather than to advise of imminent litigation over a 'claim.'" [*Schaefer Dixon Assocs. v. Santa Ana Watershed Project Authority* (1996) 48 CA4th 524, 534, 55 CR2d 698, 704]

3) [1:687] **"Intent to sue" letter in medical malpractice cases:** Medical malpractice plaintiffs must notify health care providers in writing at least 90 days before filing suit (CCP §364, *see ¶1:856*).

Such notice may also serve as a "claim" under the governmental claims act (making it incumbent on the public entity to notify the plaintiff of any defect or omission; see below). The document need only disclose "the existence of a claim that if not paid or otherwise resolved will result in litigation" against the entity. [*Phillips v. Desert Hosp. Dist.* (1989) 49 C3d 699, 707, 263 CR 119, 125—immaterial that plaintiff was unaware health care provider was public entity]

a) [1:687.1] But, a governmental tort claim based upon a public health care provider's negligence does *not* necessarily satisfy CCP §364. The notice of intent to sue under CCP §364 must describe the injury in greater detail than required for a governmental tort claim (*¶1:861*). [See *Munoz v. State of Calif.* (1995) 33 CA4th 1767, 1784, 39 CR2d 860, 869—failure to timely file tort claim not excused because claimant lacked sufficient information to serve notice of intent to sue under CCP §364]

b) [1:687.2] Moreover, a governmental tort claim cannot also serve as a CCP §364 notice where the claimant *did not intend* to combine them. [See *Wurts v. County of Fresno* (1996) 44 CA4th 380, 387-388, 51 CR2d 689, 693-694—claimant sent both notice and claim; *and discussion at ¶1:861*]

⇨ [1:687.3] *PRACTICE POINTER:* When asserting a medical malpractice claim against a public agency, file a tort claim (under Gov.C. §810 et seq.) and an intent to sue letter (under CCP §364) *separately.* Doing so avoids the kinds of problems noted above.

(c) [1:688] **Compare—entity's duty to warn claimant of defects in claim:** If the public entity deems the claim as presented defective or incomplete, it may notify the claimant *within 20 days*, specifying the defects (see Gov.C. §910.8). Otherwise, *the public entity waives any defense* based on such defects or omissions. [Gov.C. §911; *Phillips v. Desert Hosp. Dist.* (1989) 49 C3d 699, 705, 263 CR 119, 123]

1) [1:689] **Caution re earlier cases:** Be careful about relying on cases decided before *Phillips v. Desert Hosp.*, above. Earlier cases sometimes treated defective claims as totally ineffective (i.e., thus barring lawsuit) *without considering the public entity's duty to warn* the claimant of the defects. (See, e.g., *Loehr v. Ventura Community College Dist.* (1983) 147 CA3d 1071, 1083, 195 CR 576, 583—discharged employee's letter demanding reinstatement and threatening suit for defamation not "substantial compliance" with claims statute because it did not specify defamation or damage; no discussion of Gov.C. §910.8 duty to specify defect in claim.)

While not specifically overruled in *Phillips*, these cases seem inconsistent with its approach.

(d) [1:690] **Compare—omitted claims:** The doctrine of "substantial compliance" and the public entity's duty to warn of defects do not apply where the claim presented to the public entity relates to *different matters* than the claim ultimately sued upon. In such cases, the claim submitted is ineffective. [*State ex rel. Dept. of Transp. v. Sup.Ct. (Hall)* (1984) 159 CA3d 331, 336, 205 CR 518, 520]

1) [1:691] **Example:** Landowners filed claim for diminution in value of their property due to a mudslide. No mention was made of any physical injuries or emotional distress. These claims could *not* be saved under the doctrine of "substantial compliance." [*State ex rel. Dept. of Transp. v. Sup.Ct. (Hall)*, supra, 159 CA3d at 337-338, 205 CR at 521; see also *Nguyen v.*

*Los Angeles County Harbor/UCLA Med. Center* (1992) 8 CA4th 729, 734, 10 CR2d 709, 712—minor's claim made no mention of parents' claim for emotional distress]

2) [1:692] **Comment:** The lawsuit is barred in such cases because the public entity had no opportunity to investigate or evaluate the omitted matters. Moreover, because the claim as presented was complete on its face (i.e., *not* a "defective" claim), the public entity had no duty to warn the claimant of possible defects in the claim.

(e) [1:693] **Amendments:** A claim may be amended any time before expiration of the time for presentation of the claim (¶*1:710*), provided it "relates to the same transaction or occurrence which gave rise to the original claim . . ." [Gov.C. §910.6(a)]

(2) [1:694] **Presentation to governmental entity:** Claims against the state must be delivered or mailed to an office of the Victim Compensation and Government Claims Board. Claims against local governmental entities must be delivered or mailed to the clerk, secretary, auditor or governing body of such entity at its principal office. [Gov.C. §915]

Claims against *judicial branch* entities (e.g., superior courts) are subject to special filing requirements. [See Gov.C. §915(c)]

⇨[1:695] *PRACTICE POINTER:* It is sometimes difficult to ascertain the correct names and addresses of local entities (e.g., mosquito abatement districts, etc.) and their officers. This information can always be obtained from the *Roster of Public Agencies* maintained by the Secretary of State. In addition, every county clerk maintains a similar roster for public agencies located within the county. [See Gov.C. §§53050, 53051(c)]

Delivery or mailing to the entity listed satisfies the claims presentation requirement. [Gov.C. §915(e)]

(a) [1:696] **Presentation to wrong office:** Cases are split on whether there is "substantial compliance" with Gov.C. §915 where the claim is addressed to the correct public entity but is filed in the wrong office or agency (e.g., a claim that deals with an agency of the City of Los Angeles is presented to Los Angeles County).

- [1:697]   One view finds substantial compliance on the theory it is the *duty of the officer or employee* receiving the claim to forward it to the proper office. Under this approach, it is immaterial whether the claim was actually received by the proper office. [*Jamison v. State of Calif.* (1973) 31 CA3d 513, 517, 107 CR 496, 498— claim filed with State Department of Water Resources should have been filed with Board of Control]

- [1:698]   But other cases hold there is no substantial compliance *unless the claim is timely received* by the proper office. [*Life v. County of Los Angeles* (1991) 227 CA3d 894, 901, 278 CR 196, 201—claim filed with County Hospital's "legal office" should have been filed with Board of Supervisors]

(b) [1:699]   **Presentation to wrong entity:**   A claim is not properly presented if filed with the wrong entity. (Still, if a reasonable effort was made during the 6-month period to determine the proper entity, permission to file a late claim may be granted, or the court may grant relief under Gov.C. §946.6; see *Bettencourt v. Los Rios Comm. College Dist.* (1986) 42 C3d 270, 277, 228 CR 190, 193, *discussed at ¶1:791.*)

But "substantial compliance" is found where both entities have identical officers and directors, and one is a *subordinate* of, or is *ultimately controlled* by, the other. Such filing adequately apprises the responsible entity of the claim, satisfying the purpose of the claims statute. [*Carlino v. Los Angeles Co. Flood Control Dist.* (1992) 10 CA4th 1526, 1533, 13 CR2d 437, 441—claim against County Flood Control District incorrectly filed with County Board of Supervisors: same persons members of both boards]

(c) [1:700]   **Entity's failure to provide up-to-date information excuses compliance with claims requirement:**   If the public entity has failed to provide up-to-date information to the Secretary of State and County Clerk (above), compliance with the claims statute may be totally excused. [Gov.C. §946.4(a); see *Banfield v. Sierra View Local Dist. Hosp.* (1981) 124 CA3d 444, 456-457, 177 CR 290, 296]

**RESERVED**

Rev. #1 2004

(3) [1:701] **Suit following rejection of claim:** If the public body rejects the claim (or fails to act on the claim within the time limits below), the claimant may then file suit.

(a) [1:702] **Suit must be based on facts stated in claim:** The lawsuit cannot interject new or different claims. Plaintiff is limited to the matters set forth in the claim for which relief was denied. [*Nelson v. State of Calif.* (1982) 139 CA3d 72, 75-76, 188 CR 479, 481; *Donohue v. State of Calif.* (1986) 178 CA3d 795, 804, 224 CR 57, 62]

(b) **Application**

- [1:703] P was injured by a motorist taking driving test with DMV examiner. P's claim to State alleged DMV examiner was negligent in allowing unlicensed motorist *to take driving test.* Following rejection of claim, P filed lawsuit alleging DMV examiner had negligently *instructed* motorist during the driving test. Held: These were different acts of negligence than set forth in the claim. [*Donohue v. State of Calif.*, supra—motion for judgment on pleadings granted]

  [1:704] *Reserved.*

- [1:705] State fair shooting victim sued State for failure to warn or take adequate precautions against anticipated gang-related violence and reckless conduct of security officers in firing the shot which hit plaintiff. These allegations did not support a cause of action based on inadequate lighting in the parking lot as a basis for the dangerous condition of the property. [*Turner v. State of Calif.* (1991) 232 CA3d 883, 890, 284 CR 349, 352]

(c) [1:706] **Compare—immaterial variance:** But a complaint based on "essentially the same foundation" as the claim is proper although it *elaborates* on matters stated in the claim . . . particularly where those matters *need not have been included* in the claim originally. [*Blair v. Sup.Ct. (Dept. of Transp.)* (1990) 218 CA3d 221, 225-226, 267 CR 13, 16; *see* ¶*1:682*]

- [1:707] Claim form asked for "each particular act or omission" that caused the accident. (This is *not required* information; *see* ¶*1:681.*) Claimant answered "negligent maintenance and construction of highway; failure to sand and care for highway." Following rejection of the claim, P's complaint alleged the accident was caused by "lack of guard rails . . . dangerous slope of the road . . . failure to warn of ice build up." This was the same accident described in the claim; any variance was immaterial. [*Blair v. Sup.Ct. (Dept. of Transp.)*, supra]

- [1:708] P's notice of claim against City alleged false arrest, battery, etc. by Police Officer. Her subsequent lawsuit added claims that City was reckless in hiring, training and supervising its police officers. This was not a material variance because there was *no change in the fundamental facts giving rise to injury.* The allegations re reckless hiring, training, etc. merely sought to show City's direct responsibility for Police Officer's misconduct. [*White v. Sup.Ct. (City & County of San Francisco)* (1990) 225 CA3d 1505, 1511, 275 CR 706, 709-710]

  [1:709] *Reserved.*

e. **Time limits**

(1) [1:710] **Time limit on presentation of claim—6 months or 1 year:** Any claim against a public entity for *personal injury or death,* or for *damage to personal property* or crops must be presented to the governmental entity within *6 months* of accrual of the cause of action. All other claims must be presented *within 1 year.* [Gov.C. §911.2]

If mailed, the claim is deemed presented and received when mailed (i.e., when placed in a properly addressed, sealed, postage prepaid envelope and deposited in the U.S. mail). [Gov.C. §915.2]

(a) [1:711] **Accrual of cause of action:** The time limit runs from the date the claimant's right to sue arises. This is the date upon which the statute of limitations would begin to run if there were no claim-filing requirement. [Gov.C. §901; see *Colores v. Board of Trustees of Calif. State Univ.* (2003) 105 CA4th 1293, 1320, 130 CR2d 347, 367-368]

1) [1:712] **Accrual dependent on discovery of injury:** Most actions accrue on the date of injury (e.g., personal injury actions; CCP §335.1). However, some actions accrue only when the injury is *discovered* (e.g., medical malpractice actions; CCP §340.5).

*Caution:* The scope of the discovery rule in *defamation* cases is presently before the California Supreme Court in *Shively v. Bozanich,* Case No. S094467.

a) [1:713] **Compare—minors' malpractice claims:** While an adult's malpractice claim accrues only on discovery (above), a minor's claim must be commenced within 3 years of the alleged *"wrongful act"* (CCP §340.5) (which could be sooner than the date the injury is discovered).

For purposes of the claims statutes, however, a minor's medical malpractice action against County accrues only when the child's *parent or guardian* knew or reasonably should have known that a "wrongful act" (e.g., negligent medical care) caused the child's injuries. [*Torres v. County of Los Angeles* (1989) 209 CA3d 325, 335, 257 CR 211, 217]

2) [1:714] **Delayed accrual based on late discovery of cause of injury:** In some situations, although plaintiff was aware of injury, the cause of action accrues when plaintiff first became aware, or through reasonable diligence *could have become aware,* that defendant's negligence was a cause of such injury. [*Leaf v. City of San Mateo* (1980) 104 CA3d 398, 408, 163 CR 711, 716; *Scott v. County of Los Angeles* (1977) 73 CA3d 476, 482-484, 140 CR 785, 788-789]

"The belated discovery rule protects the plaintiff ... when, despite diligent investigation, he is *blamelessly ignorant* of the cause of his injuries. It also protects the defendant, who is spared precipitous litigation." [*Bastian v. San Luis Obispo County* (1988) 199 CA3d 520, 529, 245 CR 78, 82]

a) [1:715] **Facts required:** To raise the issue of belated discovery, plaintiff must state:

• when the discovery was made;

• the circumstances behind the discovery; and

• facts showing the failure to discover earlier was *reasonable* (rather than the result of a failure to investigate or act diligently). [*Norgart v. Upjohn Co.* (1999) 21 C4th 383, 397, 87 CR2d 453, 463; *Bastian v. San Luis Obispo County,* supra, 199 CA3d at 527, 245 CR at 80-81]

b) **[1:716] Example:** County-operated clinic prescribed "Dalkon shield" birth control device for Plaintiff. She delivered a deformed child. She claimed she attributed this to natural causes until publication of an FDA report finding the "Dalkon shield" unsafe. If proved, these facts would justify application of the delayed accrual rule. [*Dujardin v. Ventura County Gen. Hosp.* (1977) 69 CA3d 350, 358, 138 CR 20, 23]

**[1:717]** *Reserved.*

3) **[1:718] Effect of discouraging legal advice:** A limitations period dependent on discovery of a cause of action begins to run when plaintiff *first seeks* legal advice . . . even if the advice is wrong: "(T)he risk that discouraging legal advice will lead to loss of a cause of action must fall upon the plaintiff who obtains that advice, rather than upon a wholly uninvolved defendant . . ." [*Reyes v. County of Los Angeles* (1988) 197 CA3d 584, 592, 243 CR 35, 39]

4) **[1:719] Claims by minors, insane persons; tolling of statute of limitations:** Where defendant is not a public entity, the time for filing suit on claims accruing while a person is a minor or insane is *tolled* until he or she is no longer a minor or insane. [CCP §352(a); see *Alcott Rehabilitation Hosp. v. Sup.Ct. (Smith)* (2001) 93 CA4th 94, 101, 112 CR2d 807, 811— "insane" means a person is "incapable of caring for his or her property or transacting business or understanding the nature or effects of his or her acts"]

But the claimant's minority or insanity is *not* ground for tolling a lawsuit against a public entity on causes of action for which a claim must be presented under the Government Code. I.e., the statute of limitations *continues to run notwithstanding* the claimant's minority or insanity. [CCP §352(b); see *John R. v. Oakland Unified School Dist.* (1989) 48 C3d 438, 444, 256 CR 766, 768, fn. 3]

a) [1:720] **Effect of "delayed discovery" by parents or guardian?** It is unclear whether the "delayed discovery" rule applies to such claims; e.g., whether the statute of limitations on claims for injuries or abuse of a minor is extended until his or her parents or guardian reasonably should have known of the injury. [See *John R. v. Oakland Unified School Dist.*, supra, 48 C3d at 444, 256 CR at 768 (noting but not deciding this issue)]

b) [1:721] **Compare—equitable discovery:** Where a minor's claim is involved, courts may be more willing to estop the public entity from asserting the claims statute as a defense. *See discussion at ¶1:673 ff.*

c) [1:721.1] **Compare—rules governing leave to file late claims:** Even if the statute of limitations is tolled, there is generally *no tolling* of the time for seeking leave to file a late claim. *See discussion at ¶1:761.*

(b) [1:722] **Claims for indemnification:** A claim against a public entity for indemnification accrues when the party seeking indemnification is *served* in the lawsuit by the injured party. [Gov.C. §901] (Earlier rule was that claim accrued only when party seeking indemnification was forced to pay; see *People ex rel. Dept. of Transp. v. Sup.Ct. (Frost)* (1980) 26 C3d 744, 756, 163 CR 585, 592.)

Example: Victim sues Driver for injuries arising out of intersection accident. Driver wants to cross-complain against City for equitable indemnification on theory traffic controls were improper. Driver must file formal claim with City within six months (formerly 100 days) after Driver is served in Victim's lawsuit. [*People v. Sup.Ct. (Shortstop)* (1983) 143 CA3d 754, 759-760, 192 CR 198, 201-202—late discovery of facts does not extend statute]

1) [1:723] **Comment:** Gov.C. §901 may operate very unfairly: When served with the complaint, defendant may not know or have reason to know that a public entity may have contributed to plaintiff's injuries. Defendant may only discover this after considerable investigation and discovery. But it will be too late then to file a claim! The rule has been criticized. [See *Greyhound Lines, Inc. v. County of Santa Clara*

(1986) 187 CA3d 480, 488, 231 CR 702, 706 (conc. opn.)]

(c) **[1:724] Claims by person presently charged with crime:** A criminal defendant cannot maintain a damages action against a police officer (or the governmental employer) for conduct relating to the pending criminal charges. The statute of limitations on the civil action is tolled while the criminal charges are pending. [Gov.C. §945.3; see *McAlpine v. Sup.Ct. (Francois)* (1989) 209 CA3d 1, 8, 257 CR 32, 37—statute of limitations tolled until date of judgment and sentence]

*But the claims filing requirement is not!* Thus, any claim for personal injury, death or damage to personal property must be presented within 6 months after the cause of action accrues . . . even though the pending criminal charges bar prosecution of the civil remedy. [Gov.C. §945.3; see *McMartin v. County of Los Angeles* (1988) 202 CA3d 848, 859-860, 249 CR 53, 58-59—upholding constitutionality]

The ban on damages actions against police officers does not apply to actions against other defendants (e.g., civilians). The statute of limitations is not excused as to such defendants. [*Damjanovic v. Ambrose* (1992) 3 CA4th 503, 509, 4 CR2d 560, 563]

➪ **[1:725] *PRACTICE POINTER:*** If a client claims "police brutality" or "false arrest" in connection with pending criminal charges, file a notice of claim *immediately* with the appropriate governmental entity. *Do not wait until the criminal charges are disposed of* to decide whether to pursue a civil action. It may be too late!

(d) **[1:726] Public works claims:** Special statutes require local agencies, upon demand, to meet informally for settlement purposes with contractors having construction claims against the agency for less than $375,000. The time limit for filing a claim against the agency is *tolled* while this "meet and confer" process is under way. [See Pub. Contract C. §20104.2]

**Cross-refer—relief for late claims:** See ¶1:757 ff.

(2) **[1:727] Time limit for action by public entity—45 days:** The governmental entity has only 45 days

within which to either accept or reject the claim (unless extended by stipulation with the claimant). If it fails to act within the 45-day period, the claim is *deemed rejected* by operation of law. [Gov.C. §912.4]

(a) [1:727.1]  **Extension for service by mail:**  If the claim was presented by mail, the public entity has an additional time period to respond: 5 days if the "place of address" is in California, 10 days if in another state, 20 days if in another country. [Gov.C. §915.2]

(3) [1:728]  **Notice of rejection:**  The public entity is required to give written notice of its rejection or of its inaction (which is deemed a rejection; see above). [Gov.C. §913]

Failure to do so waives the public entity's defense based on untimeliness even if the claim is otherwise insufficient (unless it contained no address to which notice could be sent). [Gov.C. §911.3(b); *Phillips v. Desert Hosp. Dist.* (1989) 49 C3d 699, 706, 263 CR 119, 123]

(a) [1:729]  **Form of notice:**  The notice *must* warn the claimant of the 6-month statute of limitations on filing suit after rejection (in "substantially the . . . form" set forth in the statute). [Gov.C. §913(b); see *Chalmers v. County of Los Angeles* (1985) 175 CA3d 461, 464, 221 CR 19, 20—failure to include such warning would extend time for filing suit to 2 years from time of accrual]

[1:730]  A suggested form notice of rejection is contained in the statute (Gov.C. §913(a)). However, use of the statutory form is optional, and a notice may be sufficient although it contains less information than would have been provided by the statutory form. [*Chalmers v. County of Los Angeles*, supra, 175 CA3d at 465, 221 CR at 20-21]

1) [1:731]  **Example:**  County's letter to P stated her claim had been rejected, and warned of the 6-month limit on suit, but *failed* to state certain information that would have been provided by the statutory form:

- the date P's claim was filed;
- the date of its rejection; and
- the fact that rejection was by operation of law (resulting from County's failure to act within 45 days after filing).

The notice was sufficient, and suit barred because not filed within 6 months. [*Chalmers v.*

*County of Los Angeles*, supra—omission of date of rejection irrelevant because 6-month limit runs from date of mailing; *see* ¶*1:734*]

2) [1:732] **Compare:** P mistakenly thought his claim was not timely, and therefore filed an application for leave to file a late claim along with his claim. County notified him that it was denying leave to file a *late* claim (no mention of the underlying claim). This was *not* adequate notice of rejection of the main claim . . . so the 6-month limit on filing suit did not apply. [*Jenkins v. County of Contra Costa* (1985) 167 CA3d 152, 156, 213 CR 126, 128]

(b) [1:733] **Manner of giving notice:** Notice of rejection may be given either by personally delivering the notice to the claimant, or by mailing to the claimant at whatever address is designated in the claim. (No notice need be given if no address is given in the claim.) [See Gov.C. §§913(a), 915.4]

(4) [1:734] **Time limit for filing suit after notice of rejection—6 months:** If proper notice of rejection is given (above), suit must be commenced within *6 months* after *delivery* or *mailing* of the notice of rejection. [Gov.C. §945.6(a)(1)]

Compare: If no notice or improper notice was given, claimant has *2 years from the accrual* of the cause of action within which to sue. [Gov.C. §945.6(a)(2); *Mandjik v. Eden Township Hosp. Dist.* (1992) 4 CA4th 1488, 1497, 6 CR2d 582, 585]

(a) [1:735] **Measuring 6-month period:** The 6-month period runs from the date the notice is personally delivered or *deposited* in the mail. [Gov.C. §945.6(a)(1)]

1) [1:735.1] The "6-month period" consists of 6 calendar months or 182 days, whichever is longer. [*Gonzales v. County of Los Angeles* (1988) 199 CA3d 601, 604, 245 CR 112, 113]

2) [1:736] If the 6 months ends on a Saturday, Sunday or holiday, it is extended to the next day that is not a holiday. [CCP §12a; *DeLeon v. Bay Area Rapid Transit Dist.* (1983) 33 C3d 456, 460-461, 189 CR 181, 183-184]

3) [1:737] There is no five-day extension for mailed notices; CCP §1013(a) does *not* apply to notices of rejection of claims. [*Cole v. Los An-*

*geles Unified School Dist.* (1986) 177 CA3d 1,
4-5, 222 CR 426, 428-429]

[1:737.1-737.4] *Reserved.*

(b) [1:737.5] **No exception for minors:** The 6-
month statute of limitations cannot be extended by
provisions outside the Tort Claims Act. Hence, although minors are generally entitled to far longer
statutes of limitations, they are bound by §945.6's
6-month limit in actions against public entities.
[*Martell v. Antelope Valley Hosp. Med. Ctr.* (1998)
67 CA4th 978, 983, 79 CR2d 329, 332]

(c) [1:738] **Proof of service unnecessary:** The
notice must warn the claimant that suit must be filed
within 6 months after the notice was mailed (see
above). But the notice itself need not state the date
of mailing; nor need there be a proof of service by
mail. It is the claimant's duty to investigate the exact date on which the notice of rejection was mailed!
[*Dowell v. County of Contra Costa* (1985) 173 CA3d
896, 901-902, 219 CR 341, 344]

(d) [1:739] **Amended claims:** Where both an original and amended claim (¶1:693) have been filed
within the claims-filing period, and the entity has
separately rejected both claims, the 6-month period
runs from notice of rejection of the *amended* claim.
[*Norwood v. Southern Calif. Rapid Transit Dist.*
(1985) 164 CA3d 741, 743, 211 CR 6, 7]

1) [1:740] **Example:** One of several heirs filed
a wrongful death claim with the transit district.
It promptly sent notice of rejection. Later—
but still within the claims-filing period—an
amended claim was filed on behalf of all heirs.
Again, the entity sent notice of rejection. Suit
filed within 6 months of the latter notice was
timely even as to the heir whose individual
claim had been rejected *more* than 6 months
previously. It was the amended claim which
notified defendant "for the first time of the legally
correct plaintiffs to the action." [*Norwood v.
Southern Calif. Rapid Transit Dist.*, supra, 164
CA3d at 743, 211 CR at 8]

2) [1:741] **Compare—unnecessary amendment:** But the rule is different where the
amended claim is unnecessary. E.g., P filed
timely claim against City, but failed to commence suit within 6 months after it was rejected; instead, P sought leave to file late claim

naming City employees responsible for his injury. But this was unnecessary to the claim against City (nor was it necessary to a suit against the employees individually). "In essence, it amounts to no more than an attempt to amend the original claim . . . (Since the amendment was unnecessary) *the amendment relates back* to the date the *original* claim was filed." As a consequence, the 6-month statute of limitations ran from the *date the original claim was rejected, not* the date of the amendment. [*Julian v. San Diego* (1986) 183 CA3d 169, 175, 229 CR 664, 668 (emphasis added)]

3) [1:742] **Compare—original claim barred:** An amended claim alleging additional injuries has *no effect* where the original claim was rejected as untimely and the claimant has not applied for leave to present a late claim. [*Dixon v. City of Turlock* (1990) 219 CA3d 907, 913, 268 CR 510, 513—immaterial that public entity *responded* to amended claim as long as no waiver of lack of timeliness]

Comment: In appropriate cases, courts might *construe* an amended claim as an application to present a *late claim*. (This could not be done in *Dixon* because the 1-year period for such applications had already expired; see ¶1:759.)

(e) [1:743] **Serving entity as "Doe" after 6 months:** A defendant whose identity is unknown when suit is filed may be sued by a fictitious name ("Doe"); and the complaint can be later amended to substitute its real name. [See CCP §474, *discussed at* ¶6:79 ff.]

Such amendments are generally *not* permitted in actions against public entity defendants . . . because plaintiffs were *aware* of the entity's identity when suit was filed (having presented a tort claim to the entity). [*Olden v. Hatchell* (1984) 154 CA3d 1032, 1036-1037, 201 CR 715, 719; *Chase v. State of Calif.* (1977) 67 CA3d 808, 813, 136 CR 833, 835-836]

(f) [1:744] **Serving public employee as "Doe" after 6 months:** It is not clear whether the same rule applies to joinder of public employees as "Doe" defendants after expiration of the 6-month period.

1) [1:745] **Comment:** As a matter of fairness, if joinder of the employee as a "Doe" is otherwise proper (under CCP §474, *see* ¶6:79 ff.),

the amendment *should* relate back to satisfy the 6-month statute. The reason is that it is often difficult for P to ascertain the true names of the responsible employees until after discovery proceedings that may extend beyond the 6-month deadline. [See *Olden v. Hatchell* (1984) 154 CA3d 1032, 1037, 201 CR 715, 719]

(g) **[1:746]** **Equitable tolling of statute:** The statute may be "equitably tolled" where the entity has received timely notification of the first of two proceedings, and plaintiff was acting reasonably in proceeding on one claim and not the other. [See *Elkins v. Derby* (1974) 12 C3d 410, 417, 115 CR 641, 645, fn. 3]

1) **[1:747]** **Requirements:** Such tolling may be found where:

- The claimant has *several* distinct claims against the *same* entity; and

- An action on the first claim was filed *within* the statutory period; and

- The facts of both claims are so *similar* that the entity's investigation of the first claim will enable it to fairly defend against the second—i.e., *no prejudice* to defendant from the delay in filing the other claim; and

- The claimant acted reasonably and in good faith in suing on the first claim and not the other. [*Collier v. Pasadena* (1983) 142 CA3d 917, 923-926, 191 CR 681, 684-686]

2) **Application**

- **[1:748]** Fireman, permanently injured on duty, filed timely claim against City for workers' compensation benefits; but failed to sue for disability pension within statutory time limit because unaware that City had denied his application for such pension. Since same injury was involved in both claims, delay in filing did not prejudice City. [*Collier v. Pasadena*, supra]

- **[1:748.1]** Filing suit in federal court suspended running of the 6-month limitation period where (i) plaintiff filed the federal action well within the 6-month statute of limitations; (ii) defendants were notified of the action and thus had the opportunity to begin gathering evidence and preparing a defense; and (iii) no prejudice to defendants was shown because plaintiff filed his state action one week before the federal court dismissed the federal action without prejudice to pursuing the claims in state court. [*Addison v. State of Calif.* (1978) 21 C3d 313, 316, 146 CR 224, 225]

(5) [1:749] **Compare—statute of limitations:** The two-year statute of limitations on personal injury actions (CCP §335.1) usually has little effect in actions against public entities, for several reasons:

(a) [1:750] **Suit required within 6 months after rejection even if statute has not run:** The 6-month period provided for filing suit after notice of rejection (Gov.C. §945.6, ¶1:734) *supersedes* other applicable statutes of limitations. Thus, suit more than 6 months after rejection is barred even if the statute of limitations on the claim has not yet run. [*Anson v. County of Merced* (1988) 202 CA3d 1195, 1202, 249 CR 457, 461—CCP §340.5 1-year limit on suit following discovery of medical malpractice by public entity]

(b) [1:751] **Suit within 6 months after rejection timely even if statute has run:** Conversely, suit filed within 6 months after notice of rejection is timely even if the statute has then run. Compliance with §945.6 *exempts* a claimant from the statute of limitations. [*Schmidt v. Southern Calif. Rapid Transit Dist.* (1993) 14 CA4th 23, 30, 17 CR2d 340, 344]

This applies both to suits against the public entity and to suits against the public employees whose acts are the subject of the claim involved. [*Massa v. Southern Calif. Rapid Transit Dist.* (1996) 43 CA4th 1217, 1222, 51 CR2d 164, 167]

• [1:752] P sued Police Officer and Public Agency for injuries resulting from alleged police brutality. Although the statute of limitations had run, the suit was timely both as as to Public Agency *and Police Officer* because it was filed within 6 months after Public Agency denied P's claim. [*Massa v. Southern Calif. Rapid Transit Dist.,* supra, 43 CA4th at 1222, 51 CR2d at 167 (dealing with former 1-year statute of limitations on personal injury actions)]

(c) [1:753] **Compare—actions filed in federal court:** The 6-month deadline on filing suit after notice of rejection applies only to claims based on state law, not claims based on federal law. Some federal statutes (e.g., federal Civil Rights Act, 42 USC §1983) "borrow" state law (e.g., California's two-year statute on personal injury actions). Claims under these statutes are subject only to the "borrowed" statute of limitations (e.g., two-years) without regard to the 6-month period governing presentation of claims to public agencies. [*Silva v. Crain* (9th Cir. 1999) 169 F3d 608, 610-611]

1) **[1:754] Waiver and estoppel doctrines:** However, as with the statute of limitations defense generally, waiver and estoppel principles may apply. [See *Halus v. San Diego County Assessment Appeals Board* (SD CA 1992) 789 F.Supp. 327, 328-329]

[1:755] *Reserved.*

⇨**[1:756] PRACTICE POINTER:** As seen from the above, any of *three* deadlines may cut off plaintiff's right to proceed against a public entity:

- The "6-month or 1-year" deadline on presentation of claims; or

- The 6-month deadline on filing suit following notice of rejection; or

- Where federal statutes "borrow" California's statute of limitations (above), the applicable state law limitations period (e.g., two years) *without regard* to any shorter or longer period provided for actions on claims presented to public entities.

To avoid slip-ups on any case against a public entity defendant, enter *all three* deadlines in your case control or tickler file!

f. **[1:757] Relief for late claims:** There is considerable flexibility in application of the time limit on filing claims (¶*1:710*).

(1) **[1:758] Statutory notice to claimant required:** First of all, when a claim is filed late, the public entity *must* send a specific notice to the claimant within *45 days* after the filing. (The notice basically states that the claim is returned as untimely, but that the claimant may apply promptly to the public entity for leave to file a late claim.) [Gov.C. §911.3(a)]

If the public entity fails to give such notice within 45 days after such late claim is filed, it *waives* the defense that the claim is untimely (unless the claim contained no address to which the notice could be sent). [Gov.C. §911.3(b)]

(2) **[1:759]** **Application to present late claim:** The claimant has up to *1 year* after accrual of the cause of action to apply in writing to the public entity for permission to file a late claim. The application must state the reason for the delay and be accompanied by a copy of the proposed claim. [Gov.C. §911.4]

(a) **[1:759.1]** **Personal delivery or mailing:** The application must be personally delivered or deposited in the mail, *properly addressed,* within the 1-year period. [Gov.C. §§915(b), 915.2]

If mailed, the application is deemed presented and received when mailed (i.e., when placed in a properly addressed, sealed, postage prepaid envelope and deposited in the U.S. mail). [Gov.C. §915.2]

A *misaddressed* application is invalid unless actually received by the public entity within the 1-year period. [See Gov.C. §915(c); *Munoz v. State of Calif.* (1995) 33 CA4th 1767, 1780, 39 CR2d 860, 866— application to State Board of Control timely mailed but misaddressed and not received until after 1-year deadline held insufficient]

(b) **[1:760]** **Time limit jurisdictional:** The requirement that the application to present a late claim be made no later than 1 year after accrual of the claim is jurisdictional in nature. The public entity cannot grant an application for such relief filed after the 1-year period; nor can the court grant relief in a late claim-relief petition under Gov.C. §946.6. [*Santee v. Santa Clara County Office of Education* (1990) 220 CA3d 702, 713, 269 CR 605, 611; *Dixon v. City of Turlock* (1990) 219 CA3d 907, 911, 268 CR 510, 512]

(c) **[1:761]** **Tolling for certain minors only:** The 1-year deadline is not tolled merely because the claimant is a minor. [See Gov.C. §911.4(c)]

Rather, the 1-year deadline is tolled only if the minor:

— is *mentally incapacitated* and no guardian or conservator has been appointed (see Gov.C. §911.4(c)); or

— is in the *custody or control* of the public entity against which the claim is to be filed and that entity has failed to report the injury or abuse as required by law (see Gov.C. §911.4(d)).

- [1:761.1] There is no basis for tolling the 1-year time limit where the minor has a *parent or another adult* responsible for the child's care because that person can present a claim on the child's behalf. A guardian ad litem is *not* necessary in order to file a tort claim under the Tort Claims Act. [*Hernandez v. County of Los Angeles* (1986) 42 C3d 1020, 1025, 232 CR 519, 522]

[1:762] *Reserved.*

**FORM:** Application for Permission to Present Late Claim Against Governmental Entity, *see Form 1:E.*

(d) [1:763] **Entity must permit if grounds for relief shown:** The public entity must grant a timely application for leave to file a late claim if any of the following statutory grounds is shown:

- *"Mistake, inadvertence, surprise or excusable neglect"* and the public entity was *not prejudiced* by the claimant's failure to file the claim within the time allowed by §911.2 (¶*1:710*);

- Claimant was a *minor* throughout the time allowed for filing such claims;

- Claimant was *physically or mentally incapacitated* throughout the claims-filing period and for this reason failed to present a timely claim; or

- Claimant *died* during the claims-filing period. [Gov.C. §911.6(b)]

1) [1:764] **"Excusable neglect":** The showing required for relief because of "mistake, inadvertence, surprise or excusable neglect" is the same as required under CCP §473(b) for relieving a party from a default judgment. [*Ebersol v. Cowan* (1983) 35 C3d 427, 435, 197 CR 601, 606]

It generally must appear that plaintiffs acted diligently to retain counsel within the 6-month claims-filing period and that the failure to file in time resulted from "relatively minor" negligent conduct by counsel. [*Munoz v. State of Calif.* (1995) 33 CA4th 1767, 1782, 39 CR2d 860, 868]

(e) [1:765] **Deemed denied unless granted within 45 days:** The public entity has only 45 days within which to act on an application for permission to file a late claim. Otherwise, it is deemed denied by operation of law. [Gov.C. §911.6(c)]

1) **[1:765.1]** **Extension for service by mail:** If the application for leave to file a late claim was presented by mail, the public entity has an additional time period to act: 5 days if the "place of address" is in California, 10 days if in another state, 20 days if in another country. [Gov.C. §915.2]

(3) **[1:766]** **Petition to court if application denied; 6-month limit:** If the public entity denies the application to file a late claim (or it is deemed denied because the entity fails to act on it within the 45-day limit *above*), claimant may petition the court for relief within *6 months* after the application was denied. [Gov.C. §946.6(b); *City of Los Angeles v. Sup.Ct. (Katz)* (1993) 14 CA4th 621, 629, 17 CR2d 703, 708]

(a) **[1:767]** **Timeliness:** The 6-month period in which to petition the court for relief runs from the *date the application is denied* . . . not from the date notice thereof is mailed or delivered to the claimant. [See Gov.C. §946.6(b)]

Thus, tardy notice does not extend the 6-month period. On the other hand, if the delay is "considerable," due process may *estop* the public entity from objecting to timeliness of the suit. [*Rason v. Santa Barbara City Housing Authority* (1988) 201 CA3d 817, 825, 247 CR 492, 497]

(b) **[1:768]** **Grounds for relief:** The statutory grounds for relief are:

- "Mistake, inadvertence, surprise or excusable neglect" . . . *unless* the public entity proves it would be *prejudiced* in defense of the claim by the granting of such relief;

- Claimant was a *minor* throughout the claims-filing period;

- Claimant was physically or mentally incapacitated throughout the claims-filing period and for this reason unable to file a timely claim; or

- Claimant died during the claims-filing period. [Gov.C. §946.6(c)]

1) **[1:769]** **"Mistake, surprise, excusable neglect":** The most common ground for relief is excusable neglect. The showing required is the same as required for discretionary relief from default under CCP §473(b) (*see ¶5:282*

ff.). [*Lutz v. Tri-City Hosp.* (1986) 179 CA3d 807, 810, 224 CR 787, 789-790; *Munoz v. State of Calif.* (1995) 33 CA4th 1767, 1783-1784, 39 CR2d 860, 869]

For relief on any or all of these grounds "it must be shown that one's misconception was *reasonable* . . . Plaintiff must show more than that she did not discover a fact until too late; she must establish that in the use of *reasonable diligence* she failed to discover it." [*Cole v. City of Los Angeles* (1986) 187 CA3d 1369, 1376, 232 CR 624, 627; *Department of Water & Power v. Sup.Ct. (Dzhibinyan)* (2000) 82 CA4th 1288, 1294, 99 CR2d 173, 177]

    a)  **[1:770]  Attorney "affidavit of fault" insufficient:** CCP §473(b) requires trial courts to grant relief from a default or dismissal where the application is accompanied by an attorney's "affidavit of fault" (*see* ¶5:292*). This statute does not apply, however, to dismissals caused by failure to comply with applicable statutes of limitation, including suit on government tort claims. [*Castro v. Sacramento County Fire Protection Dist.* (1996) 47 CA4th 927, 933, 55 CR2d 193, 196]

    2)  **[1:771]  Minority alone excuses:** "Excusable neglect" is *not* required where the party seeking relief is a minor. Minority is a separate ground for relief. Thus, a minor is not penalized for inexcusable delays in filing caused by his or her parents or attorneys. [*Hernandez v. County of Los Angeles* (1986) 42 C3d 1020, 1027-1028, 232 CR 519, 524]

But the minor's application for relief under Gov.C. §911.4 must still be made "within a *reasonable* time" (not to exceed one year from accrual of the action). [Gov.C. §946.6(c); see *Rousseau v. City of San Carlos* (1987) 192 CA3d 498, 501-502, 236 CR 373, 374-375—7-month delay from time counsel retained held "not unreasonable" in the case of a brain-damaged minor (parents' lack of diligence disregarded)]

    3)  **[1:772]  Incapacity as excuse:** Physical or mental incapacity is an excuse if the injured person was *both* disabled during the claim-filing period *and* such disability was the *reason*

for the failure to file. [*Draper v. City of Los Angeles* (1990) 52 C3d 502, 508-509, 276 CR 864, 868-869]

Indeed, where such disability is shown, relief may be required even if a claim *filed* on the injured person's behalf during the statutory period proves defective. Courts may conclude that a person so disabled *could not have authorized* the defective claim. [*Draper v. City of Los Angeles,* supra, 52 C3d at 507, 276 CR at 868]

(c) **[1:773] Procedure:** Copies of the petition and any supporting affidavits must be served on the public entity, with a notice of hearing on the petition, at least 15 days before the hearing date. [Gov.C. §946.6(d); CCP §1005(b)]

1) **[1:774] Service:** If a local public entity is involved, the papers must be served on its "clerk or secretary or board." [Gov.C. §946.6(d)]

In proceedings against the State, the papers must be served at any office of the Attorney General (or on the Director of Transportation in Sacramento if the claim relates to that Department's activities). [See Gov.C. §946.6(d)]

Judicial branch entities are subject to special service rules. [See Gov.C. §946.6(d)]

2) **[1:774.1] Effect of delay in service:** There is no specific time within which the petition must be served on the public entity and a hearing set. But unreasonable delay creates a *presumption of prejudice* to the public entity, justifying denial of the petition. [*Han v. City of Pomona* (1995) 37 CA4th 552, 560, 43 CR2d 616, 620—petition for relief timely filed in April 1991 but not served and no hearing set until Oct. 1993]

**FORMS**

• Petition for Order Permitting Late Claim Against Governmental Entity (Gov.C. §946.6), *see Form 1:F.*

• Checklist re Petition for Relief From Requirement to File Government Claim, *see Form 1:G.*

(d) **[1:775] Burden of proof:** The petitioner has the burden of proving one of the statutory grounds for relief, above, by a preponderance of the evidence.

Rev. #1 2004

[*Rodriguez v. County of Los Angeles* (1985) 171 CA3d 171, 175, 217 CR 69, 71]

1) **[1:776] Example:** For example, where relief is sought on grounds of "excusable neglect," there must be proof of the *specific reasons* why the claim was not discovered and filed within the claims-filing period. Mere allegations that the claimant was "unaware" of the public entity's negligence in time to file do not suffice. [*Rodriguez v. County of Los Angeles*, supra]

2) **[1:777] Burden on public entity to prove prejudice:** If the claimant meets the burden of showing "mistake, inadvertence, surprise or excusable neglect," the burden shifts to the public entity to prove prejudice. I.e., it must prove that granting such relief would *prejudice its defense of the claim*. [Gov.C. §946.6(c)(1); see *Moore v. State of Calif.* (1984) 157 CA3d 715, 726-727, 203 CR 847, 855]

However, abstract claims of prejudice and equivocal evidence do not suffice. [*Ramariz v. County of Merced* (1987) 194 CA3d 684, 691, 239 CR 774, 778]

- **[1:778] Example:** Governmental investigators stated P's delay in claims filing *prevented them from finding witnesses* to the accident in which P was seriously injured. This was *not* sufficient proof that public entity would be prejudiced in defense of the action, because there was *no showing such witnesses existed* or would have been discoverable if a timely claim had been filed. [*Ramariz v. County of Merced*, supra]

- **[1:779] Comment:** Public entities often reject claims *without* any investigation or attempt to settle and thus are in no position to claim prejudice from delay in filing the claim. Judges who are aware of this practice are more likely to grant motions for leave to file late claims. If the public entity claims prejudice, the court may allow discovery to determine what the public entity would have done had it been given timely notice of the claim.

(e) **[1:780] Determination:** The court will make an *independent* determination as to whether the claimant has shown grounds for relief (i.e., minority, disability, "excusable neglect," etc.) based on the petition, attached affidavits and any evidence received at the hearing. [Gov.C. §946.6(e); *Bettencourt v. Los Rios Comm. College Dist.* (1986) 42 C3d 270, 275, 228 CR 190, 192]

1) **[1:781] Liberal policy:** Courts exercise their power to grant relief liberally, so as to preserve meritorious claims wherever possible. Any doubts are to be resolved in favor of permitting the suit to proceed. [*Viles v. California* (1967) 66 C2d 24, 28-29, 56 CR 666, 671-672; *Bettencourt v. Los Rios Comm. College Dist.*, supra, 42 C3d at 276, 228 CR at 192]

2) **[1:782] Prejudice to public entity as consideration:** Prejudice to the public entity is relevant only where relief is sought on the ground of "mistake, surprise or excusable neglect." The other grounds (physical incapacity, minority, etc.) carry no such condition.

   • [1:783] Thus, for example, if P establishes that he or she was physically or mentally incapacitated during the claims-filing period, P is entitled to relief *even though the public entity was prejudiced* by the delay. [*County of Alameda v. Sup.Ct. (Moos)* (1987) 196 CA3d 619, 625, 242 CR 215, 218, fn. 3]

3) **[1:784] Denials strictly scrutinized on appeal:** The trial court's decision will not be disturbed on appeal except for abuse of discretion. However, denial of relief is subject to "stricter scrutiny" than its allowance. Where uncontradicted evidence shows adequate cause for relief, the denial constitutes an abuse of discretion. [*Bettencourt v. Los Rios Comm. College Dist.*, supra]

4) **[1:785] Showings sufficient for relief:** In general, cases granting relief on the basis of excusable neglect involve plaintiffs who acted diligently to retain counsel within the claims-filing period. It is usually the neglectful conduct of counsel which is determined to be excusable. [*Ebersol v. Cowan* (1983) 35 C3d 427, 435, 197 CR 601, 606]

In deciding whether "excusable neglect" has been shown, the court must consider not only the nature of the particular mistake or neglect, but also *whether counsel was otherwise diligent* in investigating and pursuing the claim. [*Bettencourt v. Los Rios Comm. College Dist.*, supra, 42 C3d at 276, 228 CR at 193]

The claimant was held entitled to relief under Gov.C. §946.6 *as a matter of law* in the following cases, so that the denial of relief was an abuse of discretion:

- [1:786]   P made diligent efforts to obtain counsel during the claims-filing period following her injuries. She consulted with 10 different lawyers before finding one who determined that the public entity might be liable and agreed to represent her. [*Ebersol v. Cowan*, supra]

- [1:787]   Cases are split on whether P's *failure to discover* the facts showing a possible cause of action against the public entity constitutes "excusable neglect":

  — [1:788]   One line of cases holds that mere ignorance of the possible basis for an action against a public entity is *not* a reasonable excuse for P's failure to act. [*Tsingaris v. State of Calif.* (1979) 91 CA3d 312, 314, 154 CR 135, 136]

  — [1:789]   But other cases grant relief if P was otherwise diligent. [*Syzemore v. County of Sacramento* (1976) 55 CA3d 517, 524, 127 CR 741, 745—abuse of discretion to deny relief to lay person "unlearned in the law, ignorant of the claim requirement ... and *unaware of the existence of a tenable cause of action*"]

- [1:790]   P timely hired counsel, but the lawyer made a mathematical error in computing the claims-filing period so that P's claim was filed one day late. [See *Ebersol v. Cowan*, supra, 35 C3d at 436, 197 CR at 606, fn. 9, and cases cited therein]

- [1:791]   P timely hired counsel, but counsel filed claim with *wrong* entity because he erroneously assumed City College employees were State employees. (Even so, the College District had *actual notice* of the claim within the claims-filing period.) It was error to deny relief because it was "not unreasonable for counsel to assume that Sacramento City College was part of the statewide higher education system." [*Bettencourt v. Los Rios Comm. College Dist.*, supra, 42 C3d at 277, 228 CR at 193]

- [1:792]   P's counsel inadvertently forgot to open a file on P's case, and as a result the claim was filed 23 days late. This was held to be a "minor error." [*Flores v. Board of Supervisors* (1970) 13 CA3d 480, 483, 91 CR 717, 718]

  [1:793-796]   *Reserved.*

- [1:797]   *Ongoing settlement discussions* throughout the claims-filing period may, under some circumstances, *estop* the public entity from asserting the claims statute as a defense. E.g., Adjuster representing City *paid* P's property damage claim and "continuously" discussed settlement of personal injury claim without mentioning claims-filing requirement. Under these circumstances, P's failure to consult an attorney and resulting delay in filing was excusable: "A reasonably prudent person would believe that nothing further need be done to preserve his or her claim." [*Bertorelli v. City of Tulare* (1986) 180 CA3d 432, 441, 225 CR 582, 587]

5) [1:798]   **Showings NOT sufficient for relief:** In contrast, relief will generally be *denied* where the plaintiff failed to take any action to pursue his or her claim during the claims-filing period; or where the conduct of plaintiff's retained counsel was *unreasonable* or dilatory. [See *Ebersol v. Cowan*, supra, 35 C3d at 436, 197 CR at 607, fns. 10, 11, and cases cited therein]

  The following excuses have been held *insufficient* as a matter of law to entitle a claimant to relief under Gov.C. §946.6:

- [1:799]   P was ignorant of the claims-filing requirement and the claims-filing time limit. [*El Dorado Irrig. Dist. v. Sup.Ct.* (1979) 98 CA3d 57, 62, 159 CR 267, 270]

- [1:800]   P's "mental and emotional preoccupation" with his physical injuries delayed his calling a lawyer and filing suit. [*Drummond v. County of Fresno* (1987) 193 CA3d 1406, 1411, 238 CR 613, 616]

- [1:800.1] Where P did nothing for seven months to retain counsel or investigate potential liability for his wife's death, his failure to file a timely claim was not excusable. [*People ex rel. Department of Transp. v. Sup.Ct. (Isenhower)* (2003) 105 CA4th 39, 44, 129 CR2d 60, 63]

- [1:801] Cases are *split* on whether an injured worker's delay in consulting with an attorney is excusable because he mistakenly thought workers' compensation was his only remedy:

  [1:802] One case holds this insufficient as a matter of law: "Ignorance of the possible cause of action against the public entity is insufficient to constitute excusable neglect." [*Harrison v. County of Del Norte* (1985) 168 CA3d 1, 4, 213 CR 658, 661]

  [1:803] Another holds to the contrary: "(R)eliance on the theory that workers' compensation was his sole remedy was reasonable ... It follows, therefore, that his failure to seek advice of counsel (within the claims-filing period) was excusable . . ." [*Powell v. City of Long Beach* (1985) 172 CA3d 105, 110, 218 CR 97, 100]

  [1:804-807]   *Reserved.*

- [1:808] P's first lawyer concluded that she had no reasonable chance for recovery against the public entity and therefore decided *not* to file a claim. P's second lawyer concluded otherwise. The first lawyer's decision not to file was neither "excusable neglect" nor "positive misconduct" (except in the eyes of the second lawyer!). [*Mitchell v. State of Calif.* (1985) 163 CA3d 1016, 1022-1023, 210 CR 266, 270] (For discussion of "positive misconduct," *see* ¶5:355.)

  [1:809-811]   *Reserved.*

- [1:812] A city clerk's misstatement to claimant as to the deadline for filing was held *not* to estop City from asserting the claims-filing limitation, because the claim form that had been mailed to the claimant clearly stated when it was due. Her failure to read the form did not constitute "mistake, inadvertence, surprise or excusable neglect" under Gov.C. §946.6. [*Cole v. City of Los Angeles* (1986) 187 CA3d 1369, 1376, 232 CR 624, 627]

- **[1:813]** P's counsel failed to do anything within 6 months on claim against City that was properly calendared in both his manual and computerized tickler file. [*Tackett v. City of Huntington Beach* (1994) 22 CA4th 60, 65, 27 CR2d 133, 136]

(f) **[1:814]** **Filing suit on claim; 30-day limit:** If the court grants the petition for relief, claimant must file suit on the claim against the public entity *within 30 days* thereafter. [Gov.C. §946.6(f)]

*(Text cont'd on p. 1-173)*

Rev. #1 2003

The court has no power to order the public entity to accept filing of a late claim, but only the power to allow timely filing (within 30 days) of a lawsuit *without the filing of a claim* at all. [*Ard v. County of Contra Costa* (2001) 93 CA4th 339, 343, 112 CR2d 886, 889]

(Note that the claimant does *not* go back before the public entity. The court's order relieves claimant of any further presentation of the claim to the governmental agency.)

1) **[1:815]** **Time limit strictly applied:** Although a liberal policy is followed in granting relief from failure to file a timely claim (*above*), the 30-day limit on filing suit after such relief is granted is *strictly* applied:

   a) **[1:816]** **Runs from date court "makes" order:** The 30 days runs from the date the court "makes an order" granting relief. [Gov.C. §946.6(f)]

   Unless the parties waive notice or the court orders otherwise, an attorney order is required on any motion. [See CRC 391, *discussed in Ch. 9(I)*]

   The 30-day period runs from the date the court *signs* the formal order. [See *County of Nevada v. Sup.Ct. (Bylinda)* (1986) 183 CA3d 806, 809, 228 CR 447, 449]

   *Compare:* Where an attorney order is waived or excused by the court, the 30 days runs from the date of the court's *minute order.* [See *Mandjik v. Eden Township Hosp. Dist.* (1992) 4 CA4th 1488, 1497, 6 CR2d 582, 585—decided before CRC 391 effective]

   ⇨**[1:817]** *PRACTICE POINTER FOR DEFENDANT:* Many judges prefer to use *minute orders* rather than formal attorney orders. But whether a minute order starts the 30-day clock running is unclear.

   Therefore, to avoid any question, defense counsel should *insist on a formal written order* signed by the judge or a formal waiver of this requirement signed by the claimant. Otherwise, the 30-day period could extend indefinitely!

☞[1:817.1] *PRACTICE POINTER FOR PLAINTIFF:* To avoid uncertainty regarding when the 30-day filing period commences, plaintiff should either file within 30 days of entry of the minute order or request a formal order. Obtaining a formal order will provide the added benefit of at least a few extra days to file.

b) [1:818] **No tolling for minors:** The fact plaintiff is a minor does *not* toll the 30-day limit for filing suit after relief is granted. [*Rivera v. Carson* (1981) 117 CA3d 718, 726, 173 CR 4, 8]

2) [1:819] **Effect of suit filed before relief granted?** Courts are split on whether a lawsuit filed *before* the court grants relief under Gov.C. §946.6(f) (e.g., suit filed to avoid running of the 1-year statute of limitations on personal injury claims) constitutes a timely filing:

- [1:819.1] One view is that compliance with claim requirements is an *essential element of a cause of action* for damages against a public entity. Therefore, a premature complaint is ineffective (fails to state a cause of action) and cannot be saved by an amendment filed after the court grants relief under §946.6(f). [*Wilson v. People By & Through Dept. of Pub. Works* (1969) 271 CA2d 665, 668-669, 76 CR 906, 908]

- [1:819.2] But later decisions are more liberal and may uphold complaints filed *before* relief under §946.6(f) was granted. [See *Savage v. State of Calif.* (1970) 4 CA3d 793, 797, 84 CR 650, 653—complaint filed against state to protect against running of statute of limitations stated application for leave to file late claim was pending; *Bell v. Tri-City Hosp. Dist.* (1987) 196 CA3d 438, 444, 241 CR 796, 799—prematurely-filed complaint satisfied §946.6(f) because tort claims requirements are merely a procedural predicate to suit and *not* an element of cause of action]

[1:819.3-819.4] *Reserved.*

Rev. #1 2002

3) **[1:819.5] Compare—estoppel:** A governmental entity may be estopped from relying on the 30-day limit where it has prevented or deterred timely filing; e.g., where its attorneys have *misled* plaintiff's attorney regarding the 30-day window after the court granted leave to file a late claim. [*Ard v. County of Contra Costa* (2001) 93 CA4th 339, 347, 112 CR2d 886, 892]

(g) **[1:820] Effect of denial:** The court's denial of a petition for relief under Gov.C. §946.6 is a determination that there was not a sufficient excuse for the delay in filing the claim. [*Ngo v. County of Los Angeles* (1989) 207 CA3d 946, 951, 255 CR 140, 143]

The denial is an appealable order because it may effectively foreclose further relief on the claim. [*Dockter v. City of Santa Ana* (1968) 261 CA2d 69, 74, 67 CR 686, 690]

(h) **[1:821] Denial as bar to action alleging claim timely filed?** Cases are split on whether the trial court's denial of relief under Gov.C. §946.6 bars plaintiff from proceeding on the theory that the original claim was *timely*. I.e., does the denial *collaterally estop* plaintiff from litigating the issue of timeliness in a separate lawsuit?

Example: P was treated in a public hospital more than 1 year ago. He claims he recently discovered injuries from the treatment received. His notice of claim to the public entity is rejected as untimely; and so is his application for leave to present a late claim. The court then denies P's petition for relief under Gov.C. §946.6. Does the court's denial bar P from suing the public entity on the theory his original claim *was timely* (i.e., that his action accrued on discovery and therefore there was no need for permission to file late claim)?

1) **[1:822] View that denial no bar:** One line of cases holds the trial court has no power in a §946.6 proceeding to determine whether the original claim was timely (or the related issue of substantial compliance) ... because, by definition, the claim-relief proceeding assumes that a claim was *not* timely filed. [*Ngo v. County of Los Angeles* (1989) 207 CA3d 946, 950-951, 255 CR 140, 143; *Rason v. Santa Barbara City Housing Authority* (1988) 201 CA3d 817, 827-828, 247 CR 492]

Indeed, under this view, plaintiff may proceed *simultaneously* seeking late-claim relief in a §946.6 proceeding and filing a complaint alleging timely compliance with the claims statute! [*Ngo v. County of Los Angeles*, supra, 207 CA3d at 952, 255 CR at 143; *Mandjik v. Eden Township Hosp. Dist.* (1992) 4 CA4th 1488, 1500, 6 CR2d 582, 587-588]

2) **[1:823] View that denial may bar separate lawsuit:** Another line of cases holds the court *has* jurisdiction in a late claim-relief proceeding to make factual determinations that may collaterally estop a separate lawsuit on the claim. I.e., in denying relief under Gov.C. §946.6, the court *may* determine the timeliness of the claim or substantial compliance with claim presentation requirements. (Of course, there may also be cases in which relief is denied without such factual determinations.) [*Santee v. Santa Clara County Office of Education* (1990) 220 CA3d 702, 711, 269 CR 605, 610]

Some cases go even further, and treat a §946.6 petition as an *election of remedies* that precludes petitioner from filing and pursuing a separate complaint alleging timely compliance. [*Reyes v. County of Los Angeles* (1988) 197 CA3d 584, 593-594, 243 CR 35, 41, fn. 5]

⇨ **[1:824] *PRACTICE POINTER:*** Where there is any question concerning compliance with claim presentation requirements, careful practitioners should go both ways: i.e., if appropriate, file a lawsuit alleging compliance with claim presentation requirements, while simultaneously petitioning for relief under Gov.C. §946.6. [See *Santee v. Santa Clara County Office of Education*, supra, 220 CA3d at 712, 269 CR at 610, fn. 6]

## 3. Claims Against Decedent's Estate

a. **[1:825] Creditor's claim in probate proceedings:** In general, no lawsuit may be maintained against a decedent's estate (and no lawsuit pending against the decedent at time of death may be continued against the estate) unless the plaintiff has filed a timely creditor's claim in the probate proceedings. [Prob.C. §9002]

No suit may be maintained on a cause of action against the decedent unless the claim has been first presented to and rejected by the decedent's estate representative. [Prob.C. §9351]

There are time limits on filing a creditor's claim in the probate proceedings (Prob.C. §9100; see ¶1:832). And, if the claim is rejected, there are time limits on filing a lawsuit on the claim (Prob.C. §9353; see ¶1:837).

(1) [1:826] **Which "claims":** This applies to *all liabilities of the decedent*, whether arising in *contract, tort or otherwise*. It includes demands that are not yet due, or that are contingent or unliquidated in amount, as well as fixed, accrued liabilities. [Prob.C. §9000]

- It even includes claims arising *after* the decedent's death from a *liability* incurred by decedent during his or her lifetime. (E.g., where Decedent negligently injured Victim, and Victim dies *after* Decedent, Victim's heirs' wrongful death claim arises after Decedent's death.)

- However, *disputes regarding decedent's title* to assets in the estate are *not* "claims" within the meaning of the creditor claim statutes (Prob.C. §9000(b)). Likewise, failure to file a claim does not affect a *lienholder's* right to foreclose its lien on assets in the estate (provided no recourse is sought against other assets of the estate); see ¶1:841.

(2) [1:827] **Essential element of cause of action:** The timely filing of a creditor's claim is an essential element of the cause of action against the decedent's estate. It must be affirmatively pleaded as part of the complaint, and proved at trial. Failure to do so is ground for dismissal of the action.

(3) [1:828] **Compare—must be raised before judgment:** Failure to file a creditor's claim does not destroy the court's jurisdiction. If defendant does not raise the defect until after the judgment has become final, the defect is waived. [*Rogers v. Hirschi* (1983) 141 CA3d 847, 851-852, 190 CR 575, 577]

(4) [1:829] **Exceptions:** There are some exceptions under which filing a creditor's claim is not required; see ¶1:838 ff.

b. **Procedure**

(1) [1:830] **Contents:** The creditor's claim must be under oath, must state the claimant's name and address, the facts supporting the claim, and that it is a "just claim"; and:

- If the claim is due, it must state the amount of the claim and that all payments and offsets have been credited;

- If based on a written instrument, the original or a copy of the instrument with all endorsements must be attached to the claim (except that if it is a recorded trust deed or similar lien, it is sufficient to describe the instrument and state the book and page number where recorded). [Prob.C. §§9151-9153]

The creditor's claim may be made either by the creditor or someone acting on the creditor's behalf; but in the latter event, the reason must be stated. [Prob.C. §9151]

- *FORM:* Creditor's Claim Against Decedent's Estate, *see Form 1:H.*

  The Official Form *is not* mandatory. But its use is "deemed to comply" with the form and content requirements of the Probate Code. [See Prob.C. §§1001(b), 9153]

(a) **[1:831] Written demand may be accepted as claim:** A written demand for payment within the time limit for filing a claim (below) may be accepted by the personal representative. Formal defects are *waived* if the personal representative *pays* the amount demanded within 30 days after expiration of the 4-month time limit for filing claims (below) . . . provided the debt was actually due (over and above all prior payments and offsets), was paid in good faith, and the estate is solvent. [See Prob.C. §9154]

(2) **[1:832] Filing:** The claim is filed with the court in which the decedent's estate is being administered. In addition, a copy must be mailed to decedent's personal representative. Failure to mail a copy does not invalidate the claim, but any loss caused by such failure must be borne by the creditor. [Prob.C. §9150]

c. **[1:833] Time limit for filing creditor's claim:** The deadline for filing a creditor's claim is the *later* of the following:

- 4 months after issuance of letters to the decedent's personal representative (letters testamentary or letters of administration); or

- 60 days after the creditor is given notice of administration (see Prob.C. §9100(a)) and within one year of the date of death. [CCP §366.2]

(1) **[1:834] Extension for creditors unaware of claim or estate administration:** Upon petition, the court may

allow a claim to be filed after the deadline if it appears that neither the creditor nor attorney representing the creditor had actual knowledge of the *estate administration* within 15 days before expiration of the Prob.C. §9100 deadline, and the petition was filed within 30 days after either the creditor or creditor's attorney had actual knowledge of the administration, whichever occurred first; *or* neither the creditor nor attorney representing the creditor had knowledge of the *existence of the claim* within 15 days before expiration of the Prob.C. §9100 deadline, and the petition was filed within 30 days after either the creditor or creditor's attorney had knowledge of the existence of the claim, whichever occurred first. [Prob.C. §9103(a)]

Limitation: In any event, the creditor's claim must be filed *within 1 year after letters of administration are first issued* to decedent's general personal representative, and *before an order for final distribution* of the estate. [Prob.C. §9103(b)]

This is not as open-ended as it may seem. Decedent's representative cannot approve claims barred by the statute of limitations (Prob.C. §9103(b)). And, for claims against decedents dying after 1992, there is a *1-year statute of limitations* running from the date of decedent's death (CCP §366.2, *see* ¶1:837). Thus, as a practical matter, any creditor's claim must be filed within 1 year of the decedent's death.

d. **[1:835] Time limit for suit following rejection:** If the claim is rejected, written notice must be given by the executor or administrator. (If the personal representative fails to act on the claim, the creditor has the option to treat the claim as rejected 30 days after filing; see Prob.C. §9256.)

(1) **[1:836] 3-month statute of limitations on rejected claims:** As stated earlier, proper filing of a creditor's claim (or a Prob.C. §9103 petition to file late claim) *tolls* the statute of limitations on a claim against the decedent until the claim is allowed, approved or rejected by the personal representative (Prob.C. §9352, *see* ¶1:825).

If a claim is due when rejected, the creditor must commence suit (or arbitration, where applicable) *within 3 months* after notice of rejection is given ... *regardless of whether the statute of limitations otherwise applicable* (see below) will expire before or after that time. (For claims not yet due, suit must be commenced within 3 months after they become due.) [Prob.C. §9353]

(2) **[1:837] Compare—1-year statute of limitations on claims against decedent:** For decedents dying after

1992, there is a uniform 1-year statute of limitations on claims that survive the decedent's death. The nature of the claim is immaterial: i.e., contract and tort claims alike are subject to this uniform 1-year limitations period. [CCP §366.2] (A similar 1-year limitations period applies to decedents dying after 1990 and before 1993; see former CCP §353(b).)

As stated above, the 1-year statute is *tolled* by the timely filing of a creditor's claim until the claim is allowed, approved or rejected. Once rejected, the 3-month statute (Prob.C. §9353) applies.

e. **[1:838]** **Exceptions to claim filing requirement:** There are some exceptions under which plaintiff may sue directly without filing any creditor's claim.

(1) **[1:839]** **Claims covered by liability insurance:** No creditor's claim may be required on claims covered by liability insurance. The injured party (e.g., the victim of auto accident caused by decedent's negligence and in which decedent perished) may sue the decedent's estate without first filing a claim. The action may be served upon the liability insurer or someone designated by it. However, any recovery in such action is limited to the *insurance proceeds* (unless a probate claim was timely filed and the personal representative joined as a defendant). [Prob.C. §§550-555, 9390]

➡**[1:840]** *PRACTICE POINTER FOR PLAINTIFFS:* This makes it essential for plaintiffs to investigate and discover the policy limits and whether coverage is disputed on any claim against a decedent. (Such information is subject to discovery; *see ¶8:91.*)

Also be sure to find out whether the decedent's estate is being probated. If it is, that *may* be an indication of assets, and a claim in the probate estate could preserve another source of potential recovery!

(2) **[1:841]** **Secured claims:** The holder of a mortgage or lien on property belonging to the decedent's estate may enforce same without filing a creditor's claim, provided no recourse is sought against other assets of the estate. [Prob.C. §9391; see *Cosentino v. Coastal Const. Co.* (1994) 30 CA4th 1712, 1716, 36 CR2d 444, 446]

(3) **[1:842]** **Claims by public entities:** Failure to file a claim will not bar a public entity's claim for taxes and certain other liabilities owed by the decedent, whether

assessed before or after the decedent's death (unless the public entity is requested in writing to file a claim in the estate administration proceeding and fails timely to do so). [See Prob.C. §§9200-9201]

   f.   **Cross-refer:** For detailed coverage of claims against decedents' estates and creditor notice and claim filing rules, see Ross, *Cal. Prac. Guide: Probate* (TRG), Ch. 8.

4.  [1:843] **Particular Causes of Action Requiring Notice or Demand Before Suit:** There are a number of causes of action in which plaintiff is required to give some sort of notice or demand to the defendant before filing suit. These are really not procedural requirements, but rather substantive law requirements—usually, for the purpose of affording the defendant an opportunity to mitigate damage or liability. In any event, the prelawsuit notice or demand is an essential element of the cause of action, and must be affirmatively alleged in the complaint and proved at trial.

The following are some of the more common causes of action in which prelawsuit notice or demand is required:

   a.   [1:844] **"Demand" promissory notes and similar obligations:** Whenever a promissory note or other obligation is due "upon demand," no cause of action arises until demand for performance is made; and the complaint must allege such demand *prior* to filing suit.

   b.   [1:845] **Rescission of contract:** A party seeking to rescind a contract must, upon discovering the facts entitling him or her to rescind, promptly give *notice of rescission* to the other party, and restore or offer to restore everything of value received under the contract. [Civ.C. §1691]

      (1) [1:846] **Complaint as notice:** However, if notice has not previously been given, plaintiff's complaint for rescission "shall be deemed to be" the requisite notice of rescission and offer to restore. [Civ.C. §1691]

     •  *FORM:* (Prelawsuit) Notice of Rescission, *see Form 1:I.*

   c.   [1:847] **Breach of warranty:** To recover for breach of warranty (express or implied) after receipt of goods, the buyer must notify the seller of the claimed breach. The notice must be given within whatever time is stated in the contract; and if none, within a reasonable time after discovery of the breach. Failure to give timely notice may *bar* any action for such breach. [Comm'l C. §2607(3)(A); see *Vogel v. Thrifty Drug Co.* (1954) 43 C2d 184, 188, 272 P2d 1, 4]

     •  *FORM:* Notice of Breach of Warranty, *see Form 1:J.*

d. **[1:848] Consumer Legal Remedies Act:** To recover *damages* for unfair or deceptive practices under the Consumer Legal Remedies Act (Civ.C. §1750 et seq.), the consumer must notify the seller at least 30 days before filing suit, of the allegedly unfair or deceptive practice and give the seller an opportunity to repair or replace the goods or services involved, or make a suitable adjustment. [See Civ.C. §1782(a)]

(1) **[1:849] Form of notice:** Such notice and demand must be in writing, and must be sent by registered or certified mail, return receipt requested. [Civ.C. §1782(a)]

(2) **[1:850] Compare—injunction actions:** Prelawsuit notice is required only where the action is for *damages*. It is *not* required where the plaintiff sues only for injunctive relief under the Act. [Civ.C. §1782(d)] (Plaintiff may amend his injunction complaint without leave of court within 30 days of filing to add a request for damages; but, in such event, he must allege compliance with the notice and demand provision above. See Civ.C. §1782(d).)

e. **[1:851] Defamation actions—demand for retraction:** In a defamation action against a *newspaper publisher* or *radio broadcaster*, plaintiff must make a demand for retraction prior to filing suit, in order to recover general or exemplary damages. (Absent such demand, plaintiff is limited to special damages.) [Civ.C. §48a]

(1) **[1:852] Form of demand:** Such demand must be in writing, and must *specify* the statements claimed to be defamatory, and demand retraction thereof.

(2) **[1:853] Service on publisher or broadcaster:** The notice and demand must be served on the publisher or broadcaster within 20 days after "knowledge" of the defamatory publication. [Civ.C. §48a]

Service on the "publisher" may be made by serving:
— the publisher personally or;
— *someone designated* by the publisher to receive requests for correction; or
— someone else employed at the newspaper *if the publisher acquires actual knowledge* thereof within the 20-day period. [*Freedom Newspapers, Inc. v. Sup.Ct. (Gould)* (1992) 4 C4th 652, 658, 14 CR2d 839, 842—service on newspaper editor upheld on both grounds]

f. **[1:854] Benefits conferred by mistake:** Where property or services have been conferred by one person upon another *by mistake*, the party rendering such services or property must demand restitution from the other party before filing suit (to allow the other opportunity to adjust the matter out of court). [See *Mitchell v. California Pac. Title Ins. Co.* (1926) 79 CA 45, 52, 248 P 1035, 1038]

g. **[1:855] Conversion by bailee:** To recover damages for conversion against a bailee or other person to whom possession of personal property was entrusted, the owner must allege a demand for return of the property prior to filing suit. [See Civ.C. §1823]

[1:855.1-855.4] *Reserved.*

h. **[1:855.5] Certain environmental claims:** Before a private party may sue to enforce the Safe Drinking Water and Toxic Enforcement Act ("Proposition 65") (Health & Saf.C. §25249.6 et seq.), 60-day notice must be given to the alleged offender and to the Attorney General, the District Attorney and the City Attorney. [Health & Saf.C. §25249.7 (d); 22 Cal.C.Regs. §12903(b)(2)]

The notice must contain "*sufficient facts* to facilitate and encourage the alleged polluter to comply with the law, and to encourage the public attorney charged with enforcement to undertake its duty." [*Yeroushalmi v. Miramar Sheraton* (2001) 88 CA4th 738, 750, 106 CR2d 332, 341 (emphasis added)—boilerplate notice "regurgitating" language of statute and regulations inadequate]

5. **[1:856] Medical Malpractice Action—Notice of Intent to Sue:** An attorney contemplating an action for "professional negligence" against a "health care provider" (doctor, hospital, etc.) is required to give the potential defendant at least 90 days' notice of the intent to commence such action. A copy must also be sent to the Medical Board of California or Board of Podiatric Medicine, if applicable. [CCP §§364, 364.1]

(CCP §364 was enacted in response to the medical malpractice insurance crises of the mid-1970s. It supposedly enables doctors and hospitals—and their insurers—to settle meritorious claims before suit, thereby avoiding unfavorable publicity and expense.)

[1:856.1-856.4] *Reserved.*

a. **[1:856.5] Actions for "professional negligence":** By its terms, CCP §364 applies only to actions for "professional negligence."

This term has been interpreted by some courts to *exclude* causes of action for *intentional* torts (e.g., battery). [*Noble v. Sup.Ct. (Katz)* (1987) 191 CA3d 1189, 1192, 237 CR 38, 40; *Perry v. Shaw* (2001) 88 CA4th 658, 668, 106 CR2d 70, 77]

However, in a different context (the CCP §425.13 non-MICRA provisions limiting punitive damage claims against health care providers, ¶6:329), the Supreme Court has interpreted "professional negligence" more broadly: "(A)n action for damages arises out of the professional negligence of a health care provider if the injury for which damages are sought is *directly related to the professional services provided* by the health care provider." [*Central Pathology Service Med. Clinic, Inc. v. Sup.Ct. (Hull)* (1992) 3 C4th 181, 187, 10 CR2d 208, 212 (emphasis added)]

Comment: Although ultimately declining to decide whether "professional negligence" as defined by MICRA encompasses *intentional torts*, the Supreme Court has indicated that *Central Pathology's* expansive interpretation (above) would *not* apply in the MICRA context: "*Central Pathology* did not purport to define the meaning of the term 'professional negligence' as used in MICRA." [*Barris v. County of Los Angeles* (1999) 20 C4th 101, 116, 83 CR2d 145, 154-155—meaning of "professional negligence" varies depending upon legislative history and purpose of underlying statute]

[1:856.6–856.9]   *Reserved.*

(1) [1:856.10]   **Actions "based on" professional negligence:**   MICRA's notice of intent to sue requirement is not limited to a patient's medical malpractice action against a doctor.

- [1:856.11]   A liability insurer paying a third party for damages caused by its insured tortfeasor may sue other tortfeasors involved for *equitable indemnity*. Where equitable indemnity is sought for "professional negligence" by a doctor in treating the injured party, the action is subject to MICRA's notice of intent to sue requirement (although not subject to MICRA's statute of limitations). [*Preferred Risk Mut. Ins. Co. v. Reiswig* (1999) 21 C4th 208, 217, 87 CR2d 187, 193]

(2) [1:856.12]   **Elder abuse:**   An action against a nursing home under the Elder Abuse and Dependent Adult Civil Protection Act (Welf. & Inst.C. §15600 et seq.) for "reckless neglect" of an elderly patient is *distinct* from an action for professional negligence under MICRA, and thus notice of intent to sue is *not* required. [*Delaney v. Baker* (1999) 20 C4th 23, 41, 82 CR2d 610, 622]

(a) [1:856.13]   **Compare—claims seeking punitive damage:**   Although no notice of intent to sue is required, MICRA's heightened procedural requirements for punitive damage claims against health care providers (e.g., leave of court required; CCP §425.13; *see ¶6:329*) have been held to apply to elder abuse claims seeking punitive damages. [*Community Care & Rehab. Ctr. v. Sup.Ct. (DeGrood)* (2000) 79 CA4th 787, 794-795, 94 CR2d 343, 348]

**Caution:** This holding may be affected by a case presently before the California Supreme Court, *Covenant Care, Inc. v. Sup.Ct. (Inclan)*, Case No. S098817.

[1:856.14-856.19] *Reserved.*

➡️[1:856.20] **PRACTICE POINTER:** Because of the uncertainty as to MICRA's applicability to certain types of actions against health care providers, give notice of intent to sue whenever time permits. But do *not* rely on the 90-day tolling rule (*¶1:863*) in doubtful cases!

b. [1:857] **Effect of failure to give notice:** Unlike other requirements for prelawsuit notice to the opposing party, failure to give the notice required by CCP §364 does *not* affect the plaintiff's right to proceed with the malpractice action. CCP §365 expressly provides that such failure "shall not invalidate any proceedings of any court . . . nor shall it affect the jurisdiction of the court to render a judgment therein."

(1) [1:858] **Disciplinary proceeding:** Rather, such failure is simply ground for disciplinary proceedings by the State Bar against plaintiff's attorney. [CCP §365]

(2) [1:859] **No pleading requirement:** It is not necessary to allege in the complaint that such notice was given; and the failure to give such notice is *not* ground for striking the complaint. [*Toigo v. Hayashida* (1980) 103 CA3d 267, 269, 162 CR 874, 875]

c. [1:860] **Content of notice:** Although no particular form is required, the notice must specify the "legal basis of the claim" and the "type of loss sustained including the specific injuries suffered." [CCP §364(b)]

• **FORM:** Notice of Intent to Commence Action Against Health Care Provider (CCP §364), *see Form 1:K.*

(1) [1:860.1] **Specificity required:** The notice must notify defendant "with specificity (of) *the nature of the injuries* suffered." [CCP §364(b) (emphasis and parentheses added)]

The purpose of this requirement is to give the parties "a meaningful opportunity to settle the claim and thus reduce the number of medical negligence suits in our courts." [*Edwards v. Sup.Ct. (Kirianoff)* (2001) 93 CA4th 172, 179, 112 CR2d 838, 843]

(a) [1:860.2] **Effect of failure to specify all injuries:** Omitting one of several injuries suffered as a result of the same negligence is not fatal. Failure to specify *all* injuries suffered "cannot bar a plaintiff from including the injury unintentionally omitted from the notice in the lawsuit against the medical practitioner." [See *Edwards v. Sup.Ct. (Kirianoff)*, supra, 93 CA4th at 179-180, 112 CR2d at 843-844]

(2) [1:861] **Different from notice of claim against public entity:** In malpractice claims against a public entity, two different prelawsuit notices are required:

- a notice of claim under Gov.C. §911.2 (¶*1:681*); and

- a notice of intent to sue under CCP §364.

A notice of intent to sue under CCP §364 may satisfy the notice of "claim" against a public entity required by Gov.C. §911.2. [*Phillips v. Desert Hosp. Dist.* (1989) 49 C3d 699, 707, 263 CR 119, 125; *see* ¶*1:687*]

However, the notice of claim may not satisfy the requirement of a notice of intent to sue. This is because the notice of claim against a public entity need only provide a *general description* of the injuries, whereas a §364 notice of intent to sue must describe the "*specific* injuries" suffered (see above). Thus, absent specificity in the governmental claim, a *separate* §364 notice of intent to sue is required. [*Anson v. County of Merced* (1988) 202 CA3d 1195, 1204, 249 CR 457, 462—because notice of claim was general, subsequent notice of intent to sue was not redundant and therefore extended time to sue]

In any event, a governmental tort claim will not serve as notice of intent to sue under CCP §364 where the claimant did *not intend* to combine them. [See *Wurts v. County of Fresno* (1996) 44 CA4th 380, 387-388, 51 CR2d 689, 693-694—deadline for MICRA action measured from §364 notice, not from earlier governmental tort claim, even though both documents contained similar information]

d. [1:862] **Service:** The notice must be in writing and be served in the manner required by CCP §1010 et seq. for service of notice in civil proceedings (includes service by mail). [CCP §364(c)]

(1) [1:862.1] **By mail:** Service by mail is authorized to the physician's *residence* or *business* address (see CCP §1012).

Rev. #1 2002

(a) [1:862.2] **Compare—improper addresses:** A notice of intent to sue is ineffective (i.e., no 90-day extension on statute of limitations) if mailed to some other address and the physician never receives it. (E.g., notice mailed in care of a hospital where the services were performed, or to a billing service that is clearly *not* the physician's residence or business address.) Plaintiffs *cannot rely on third parties* to forward the notice to the doctor's home or office. [See *Derderian v. Dietrick* (1997) 56 CA4th 892, 899, 65 CR2d 800, 804-805—notice addressed to doctor in care of medical group that billed for his services was ineffective because he was independent contractor and medical group's address was neither his home nor office]

☞[1:862.3] *PRACTICE POINTER FOR PLAINTIFFS:* If plaintiff lacks first-hand knowledge of the physician's business or residence address, you can obtain it from the State Medical Board, Division of Medical Quality, in Sacramento. (Physicians are required to keep a current mailing address on file with the Board.)

(b) [1:862.4] **Service effective upon mailing:** Service is complete when the notice is deposited in the mail, not when it is received. [*Silver v. McNamee* (1999) 69 CA4th 269, 283, 81 CR2d 445, 453—notice mailed during 1-year period effective even if not received until after expiration]

1) [1:862.5] **Actual notice not required:** As long as the sender has complied with the statutory requirements for service by mail, it need not be proved that the health care provider actually received the mailed notice. [*Silver v. McNamee*, supra, 69 CA4th at 285, 81 CR2d at 455—certified mail notice effective although deliberately refused by doctor]

[1:862.6-862.9] *Reserved.*

(c) [1:862.10] **Effect on 90-day notice period?** CCP §1013(a) provides an extension of time for "any period of notice . . . prescribed by statute" where papers are served by mail (*see ¶9:87.4*). This does *not* delay the effective date of service of a §364 notice; i.e., service is still "complete" upon mailing. [*Silver v. McNamee*, supra, 69 CA4th at 283, 81 CR2d at 453]

Service by mail may, however, entitle the physician to *additional notice* of plaintiff's intent to sue (5 days, if mailed to an address in California), and plaintiff would be barred from commencing suit before expiration of the *extended* notice period. [*Silver v. McNamee,* supra, 69 CA4th at 280-281, 81 CR2d at 452 & fn.12 (dictum)] (Again, however, the only sanction for premature filing is professional discipline; *see* ¶1:858.)

e.  **[1:863]  Tolling of statute of limitations where notice served during last 90 days:**  The statute of limitations in medical malpractice cases is *either:*
— 3 years from the date of injury; *or*
— 1 year after plaintiff discovers the injury, *whichever comes first.* [See CCP §340.5]

(For *minors*, the statutory period is 3 years from the wrongful act; or, if the minor was under age 6, until his 8th birthday *if longer.* See CCP §340.5, 3rd sent.)

If notice of intent to sue is served during the last 90 days of the *1-year* period, the statute is tolled for 90 days. ("Tolled" means the statute ceases to run, so that an additional 90 days is added to the 1-year period.) Suit therefore is timely if filed within 1 year and 90 days after discovery of the injury. [CCP §364(d); *Woods v. Young* (1991) 53 C3d 315, 325, 279 CR 613, 619; *Davis v. Marin* (2000) 80 CA4th 380, 384, 94 CR2d 896, 900—tolling rule applies even where defendant initially served as "Doe"]

Likewise, if notice of intent to sue is served during the last 90 days of the *3-year* period, the statute is tolled for 90 days; i.e., suit therefore is timely if filed within 3 years and 90 days after the date of injury. [*Russell v. Stanford Univ. Hosp.* (1997) 15 C4th 783, 788, 64 CR2d 97, 99; and see *Newman v. Burnett* (1997) 54 CA4th 722, 728, 62 CR2d 175, 178— intent-to-sue notice tolls separate statute of limitations for malpractice claims by minors (above)]

(1)  **[1:864]  Example:**  P suffers *and* discovers medical malpractice injury on January 15 (i.e., 1-year statute applies):

• If P serves notice of intent to sue on February 15, the statute of limitations continues to run and is unaffected. CCP §364(a) bars suit during the 90 days following P's notice, but P will still have approximately 8 months to sue.

• But if P serves notice of intent to sue on December 15, the statute is tolled for 90 days (i.e., P has until 1 year and 90 days after January 15 to sue). CCP §364(a) bars suit during the 90 days after P's December 15 notice, but P will still have 30 days to sue. I.e., whatever period of time remained before the tolling commenced is still available after the 90-day waiting period. [See *Woods v. Young*, supra, 53 C3d at 326, 279 CR at 619, fn. 3]

- *Compare:* If P had filed a notice of intent to sue on February 15 and then a *second* notice on December 15, the latter would *not* toll the statute of limitations: "The tolling provision . . . applies only to plaintiffs who have served their *original* notice of intent to sue within 90 days of the expiration of the applicable limitations period." [*Bennett v. Shahhal* (1999) 75 CA4th 384, 389, 89 CR2d 272, 275 (emphasis added)]

(2) **[1:865] Compare—no relief under CCP §473(b) for untimely notice:** Plaintiff's failure to serve notice of intent to sue within the last 90 days (so as to extend the 1-year statute of limitations) *cannot* be excused on grounds of "mistake, inadvertence or excusable neglect" under CCP §473(b) (*see* ¶5:276 ff.). [*Hanooka v. Pivko* (1994) 22 CA4th 1553, 1561, 28 CR2d 70, 75]

(3) **[1:866] Other grounds for tolling 3-year statute:** CCP §340.5 sets the "outside" limitation at 3 years after the injury (except for minors). The statute expressly provides, however, that this 3-year period can be extended for *fraud, intentional concealment,* or the presence of a *foreign object* in the patient's body. [See CCP §340.5; and detailed discussion in Flahavan, Rea & Kelly, *Cal. Prac. Guide: Personal Injury* (TRG), Ch. 5]

(4) **[1:867] No tolling as to intentional tort claims:** The 90-day tolling applies only to claims for "professional negligence." There is no tolling for intentional tort claims, even though based on the same facts as the negligence claim. [*Noble v. Sup.Ct. (Katz)* (1987) 191 CA3d 1189, 1192-1194, 237 CR 38, 40-41—plaintiff alleged surgery was performed both negligently and without her consent (thus battery)]

(5) **[1:868] No tolling as to doctors not named or served with notice:** The statute of limitations is not tolled as to treating doctors known to plaintiff but not named in the notice of intent to sue. It is immaterial they were agents of the provider named in the notice. [*Godwin v. City of Bellflower* (1992) 5 CA4th 1625, 1631, 7 CR2d 524, 527—notice addressed to Hospital only did not extend statute as to treating doctors employed by Hospital]

(a) **[1:869]** Plaintiff cannot rely on the hospital to forward §364(a) notices to individual doctors whose identity and location is known to plaintiff. Serving the hospital alone does not extend the statute of limitations as to the individual doctors named in the notice. [*Hanooka v. Pivko* (1994) 22 CA4th 1553, 1560, 28 CR2d 70, 74]

(6) **[1:870]** **Tolling as to "Doe" defendants:** CCP §364(e) says the section does not apply to "Doe" defendants joined under CCP §474. But this refers to the requirement of notice before suit. When such notice is given to named defendants within the last 90 days of the limitations period, the statute is tolled against *both* the named defendants and the Doe defendants. [*Grimm v. Thayer* (1987) 188 CA3d 866, 870-871, 233 CR 687, 689; *Camarillo v. Vaage* (2003) 105 CA4th 552, 567, 130 CR2d 26, 37 (citing text)]

➪**[1:871]** *PRACTICE POINTER:* If you plan to join intentional tort claims, *send your intent-to-sue letter more than 90 days* before the end of the statutory period.

Otherwise, if you serve the letter within the last 90 days, you will have a lot of extra work! You'll have to sue right away on the intentional tort claims; wait until after the 90-day period to sue on the negligence claim; and then move to consolidate the separate suits.

f.   **[1:872]** **Compare—medical information release required for prelawsuit settlement:** Once a lawsuit is filed, defendant can generally obtain through discovery the medical records it needs to evaluate the claim. There is no right to discovery before suit is filed; but any *settlement demand* made before service of the complaint *must be accompanied by a medical information release form* to enable the defendant or insurer to obtain the necessary records. [Civ.C. §56.105]

➪**[1:872.1]** *PRACTICE POINTER:* Prior to filing suit against a health care provider, plaintiff's counsel has the right to obtain copies of the patient's medical records promptly upon presentation of the client's authorization. This right is enforceable by an order to show cause and monetary sanctions (*see ¶8:1805.40 ff.*). [See Ev.C. §1158; CCP §1985.7]

**[1:872.2-872.9]** *Reserved.*

6.   **[1:872.10]** **New Home Construction Defect Claims:** Various statutory procedures must be followed before a homeowner may sue a "builder" for defects in construction of a new home (individual dwelling unit) sold after 2002. [Civ.C. §§910-938]

Note: These statutes apply only to *construction defect* claims, not claims for breach of contract, fraud or personal injury.

a.  **[1:872.11]   Compare—contractual ADR procedures not affected:**   The statutory procedures below do not supplant any *binding* dispute resolution procedure provided in the sale agreement ("contractual arbitration, judicial reference, or similar procedures requiring a binding resolution"). [Civ.C. §914(b)]

   Thus, if the sale agreement provides for binding arbitration of construction defect disputes, either party may demand arbitration without regard to the prelawsuit notice requirement below. [See Civ.C. §914(b)]

   (1)  **[1:872.12]**   Similarly, if the sale agreement calls for *mediation* or any other "*nonadversarial* procedure," the *builder* (but apparently not the homeowner) may commence such contractual procedures as an *alternative* to the procedures below. [See Civ.C. §914(a)]

      **[1:872.13-872.14]**   *Reserved.*

b.  **[1:872.15]   Prelawsuit notice requirement:**   Before filing suit on a construction defect claim, the homeowner must give written notice to the "builder" specifying the construction standard allegedly violated. [Civ.C. §910]

   (1)  **[1:872.16]   "Builder":**   "Builder" means the *developer or original seller* of a new home sold after 2002 if that person or entity was *in the business* of building residential units for public purchase. "Builder" does *not* include a general contractor or subcontractor who is not otherwise affiliated with the "builder." [Civ.C. §911 (amended 2003)]

      (a)  **[1:872.16a]   Compare—residential construction standards not limited to "builder":**   Although prelawsuit notice is required only for actions against the "builder," Civ.C. §896 enumerates detailed "building standards for original construction" that apply both to the "builder" and others involved in construction of new homes; i.e., general contractors, subcontractors, material suppliers, design professionals and product manufacturers. [See Civ.C. §896]

         These Civ.C. §896 "building standards" apply only in construction defect actions based on negligence or breach of contract. They do not affect other claims or remedies against such persons (e.g., strict liability). [See Civ.C. §936]

(2) [1:872.17] **Manner of service:** The claimant's notice must be served by certified mail, overnight mail, or personal delivery to the builder. [Civ.C. §910(a)]

    (a) [1:872.18] **Service on designated agent:** The builder is required to maintain the name and address of an agent to receive such notice with the Secretary of State. Alternatively, if the builder has contracted with a third party to accept claims and act on the builder's behalf, and has so notified the homeowner in the original sales agreement, the builder may elect to use that party to receive the notice. [See Civ.C. §912(e)]

    *Comment:* The statute does not say that the claimant's notice *must* be served on the designated agent. Therefore, presumably this is merely an *alternative* method for serving the prelawsuit notice on the builder.

    [1:872.19] *Reserved.*

(3) [1:872.20] **Contents:** The notice must include:

- the claimant's *name, address, and preferred method of contact* (if the claim is made by a group of homeowners or an association, the notice may identify the individual claimants by address or such other description as will enable the builder to identify the locations);

- a statement that the claimant alleges a construction defect against the builder ("a violation pursuant to this part") and that the construction of his or her residence violates one or more of the *building standards set forth set forth in Civ.C. §896*;

    — Note: Civ.C. §896 sets forth "building standards for original construction intended to be sold as an individual dwelling unit." There are over 50 detailed standards covering soil issues, structural issues, water issues, fire protection issues, plumbing and sewer issues, electrical system issues and issues regarding other areas of construction.

- *reasonable detail* sufficient to identify the nature and location of the defect, to the extent known. [Civ.C. §910(a)]

    [1:872.21-872.24] *Reserved.*

(4) [1:872.25] **Compare—notice not required for customer service requests:** The above notice is not required where a homeowner utilizes any "applicable

normal customer service procedure" set forth in any contract, warranty or other builder-generated document. Such customer service requests, however, do *not* satisfy the prelawsuit notice requirement above. [Civ.C. §910(b)]

[1:872.26-872.29]   *Reserved.*

c.   [1:872.30]   **Postnotice procedures (optional with builder):**   The statutory scheme provides various procedures that a builder may utilize to attempt to resolve the homeowner's construction defect claim, and a timetable for each procedure. These procedures are *optional* with the builder. The only consequence of the builder's failure to comply, or delay in compliance, is that the homeowner may commence suit against the builder. [Civ.C. §915]

[1:872.31]   *Caution:*   The discussion below is merely a broad outline of the statutory procedures and does not contain important details. Careful review of the applicable statutes is required.

To the extent these procedures overlap with those required under Civ.C. §1375 (governing damage actions against builders of "common interest developments"), these procedures also satisfy §1375. [Gov.C. §935]

(1)   [1:872.32]   **Acknowledgment of receipt:**   Within 14 days after receipt of the notice of claim, the builder must send written acknowledgment of such receipt. [Civ.C. §913]

(2)   [1:872.33]   **Document disclosure:**   Within 30 days after the homeowner's written request therefor (the time limit is extended for documents lost or destroyed), the builder must provide, at the homeowner's expense, copies of:
— relevant plans and specifications and other documents relating to structure, fire safety or soils standards affecting the homeowner's residence;
— all maintenance and preventative maintenance recommendations pertaining to the residence;
— all maintenance and warranty information pertaining to manufactured products; and
— all limited warranties in effect at the time the home was sold. [Civ.C. §912(a)-(d)]

(3)   [1:872.34]   **Election to inspect:**   The builder is permitted to inspect the claimed defects upon written request within 14 days after sending the acknowledgment of claim. [See Civ.C. §916]

(4)   [1:872.35]   **Offer to repair:**   Within 30 days after the inspection, the builder may make a written offer to repair

the defect. The offer must contain detailed information, including the scope of the repair, completion dates, identity of and other information relating to contractors who will effect the repairs; and must be accompanied by an offer to *mediate* the dispute if the owner so chooses. [See Civ.C. §§917, 919]

    (a) **[1:872.36]** **Homeowner's response:** The homeowner has 30 days to authorize the builder to proceed with the repairs; or alternatively to request the builder to provide the names of other contractors to perform the repairs. [See Civ.C. §918]

  (5) **[1:872.37]** **Additional provisions:** There are further statutory provisions governing:
— partial repairs (see Civ.C. §924);
— cash offers in lieu of repairs (see Civ.C. §929);
— documentation pertaining to the repairs (see Civ.C. §923);
— effect of failure to complete the repairs on time (see Civ.C. §925); and
— prohibition on builder demanding a release in return for a promise to repair (see Civ.C. §926).

    **[1:872.38-872.39]** *Reserved.*

  d. **[1:872.40]** **Statutes of limitations extended:** Statutes of limitations are extended if they expire during this prelitigation process. [See Civ.C. §927]

## D. PRELAWSUIT CONSULTATION REQUIREMENT IN CERTAIN PROFESSIONAL NEGLIGENCE ACTIONS

**[1:873]** Reasonable prefiling investigation of the merits is required as to *all* lawsuits filed after 1994; see CCP §128.7, *discussed at ¶9:1135 ff.* In addition, specific consultation requirements apply to certain professional negligence actions:

1. **[1:874]** **Certificate Required on Filing Action:** In actions for malpractice against certain professionals (¶1:878), plaintiff's or cross-complainant's attorney must file and serve a "certificate of merit" showing that he or she has consulted with and received an opinion from an expert in the field; or an adequate excuse for not doing so. (No such certificate is required in actions filed in pro per.) [CCP §411.35]

  a. **[1:875]** **Purpose:** The obvious purpose of §411.35 is to require plaintiffs (and cross-complainants) to obtain independent support for the merits of their claims against certain professionals . . . and to *refrain* from suit unless the expert opines that the action is meritorious. [See *Adams v. Roses* (1986) 183 CA3d 498, 504, 228 CR 339, 342 (upholding constitutionality)]

b. [1:876] **Enforcement:** Failure to file the certificate renders the complaint subject to special demurrer, and in certain cases to a motion to strike (*see ¶1:887*).

In addition, violation may constitute "unprofessional conduct" and be ground for *professional discipline* against plaintiff's attorney. [CCP §411.35(f)]

2. [1:877] **Actions Subject to Certificate Requirement:** The certificate described below is required in actions for *professional negligence* against any of the following professionals if they are validly licensed:

a. [1:878] **Actions against certain construction professionals:** Actions for damages, *or cross-complaints for equitable indemnity, based on professional negligence* (whether or not "negligence" or "professional negligence" is alleged) against either:

- Architects;

- Professional engineers; and

- Land surveyors. [CCP §411.35]

[1:879] *Reserved.*

3. [1:880] **Contents of Certificate:** Basically, the attorney's certificate must show either prelawsuit consultation (a "certificate of merit") or reasonable excuse for lack of consultation.

a. [1:881] **Prelawsuit consultation showing merit:** The attorney must declare that he or she reviewed the facts of the case personally and with a professional licensed to practice and practicing or teaching in the same field as the defendant; that the consultant is not a party to the action; that the attorney reasonably believes that the consultant is knowledgeable on the issues involved in the particular case; and that, based on such consultation, the attorney has concluded the case is meritorious. [CCP §411.35(b)(1)]

In addition, in actions against *construction professionals*, the certificate must state that the person consulted has rendered an opinion that the named defendant or cross-defendant was (or was not) negligent in the performance of the applicable professional services. [See CCP §411.35(b)(1)]

(1) [1:881.1] **Qualified consultant:** Prelawsuit consultation is required with someone "in the same discipline" as the defendant. [CCP §411.35(b)]

- [1:881.2] A prelawsuit consultation with a structural engineer suffices for a malpractice action against an architect "because their services frequently overlap." [*Ponderosa Ctr. Partners v.*

*McClellan/Cruise/Gaylord & Assocs.* (1996) 45 CA4th 913, 916, 53 CR2d 64, 66]

[1:881.3-881.4] *Reserved.*

(2) [1:881.5] **Comment:** The statute does not require a *written* opinion. Moreover, the opinion may state either that defendant "was negligent *or was not negligent*" (see CCP §411.35(b)(1)). This seems to indicate an action may be maintained despite an adverse opinion. In such event, however, the attorney's certificate would have to state circumstances *apart* from the consultation to establish "a reasonable and meritorious cause for the filing of the action."

- **FORM:** Certificate of Merit (Professional Negligence Action), *see Form 1:L.*

b. [1:882] **Excuse for lack of consultation:** Alternatively, the attorney's certificate must show one of the following as an excuse for lack of such consultation:

(1) [1:883] **Inability to obtain consultation:** Attorney certifies that he or she contacted at least 3 professionals, all of whom refused to consult. (The court may require disclosure of their names.) [CCP §411.35(b)(3)]

(2) [1:884] **Intent to rely solely on res ipsa loquitur:** Attorney certifies that in filing the complaint he or she is relying exclusively on res ipsa or defendant's failure to inform the plaintiff of the consequences of the procedure, or both. [CCP §411.35(d)]

(3) [1:885] **Imminent running of statute of limitations:** Attorney certifies that there is lack of time to consult because statute of limitations is about to run. (But in this event, a certificate of merit must be filed within 60 days after the complaint is served.) [CCP §411.35(b)(2)]

4. [1:886] **Filing and Service:** The certificate of merit must be filed and served "on or before the date" on which "any defendant" is served with the complaint. [CCP §411.35]

a. [1:886.1] **Comment:** This may create problems where there are several defendants who cannot be served on the same day. The statute seems to say that the certificate of merit must be served on *each* defendant before "any defendant" is served with the complaint. However, as long as the certificate is filed and served *along with* the complaint, most courts will probably find substantial compliance with the statute.

5. [1:887] **Procedures for Attacking Lack of Certificate:** Failure to file the certificate required by CCP §411.35 is ground for *special demurrer* to the complaint. [CCP §430.10(h); *see* ¶7:95-97]

It is *also* ground for a *motion to strike*. [CCP §411.35(g); *see* ¶*7:173*]

   a. **[1:888] Comment:** It is not clear why a motion to strike is necessary, since a special demurrer is also available. In any event, if a court grants either, it will almost certainly also grant leave to amend. [See *Price v. Dames & Moore* (2001) 92 CA4th 355, 359, 112 CR2d 65, 69]

   b. **[1:889] Compare—defective certificate:** The Code provides no special procedure for attacking incomplete or defective certificates. Presumably, therefore, the same procedures would be available as where no certificate at all has been filed (i.e., special demurrer or motion to strike; see above).

   c. **[1:889.1] Attorney fees:** The court may order plaintiff or plaintiff's counsel or both "to pay any *reasonable expenses*, including attorney's fees" incurred by defendant as a result of failure to attach a certificate of merit. [CCP §411.35(h)]

     (1) **[1:889.2] May include paralegal fees:** Where the prevailing practice is for attorneys to bill separately for paralegal services, reasonable paralegal expenses are awardable as part of the defendant's "attorney fees." Otherwise, the award of attorney fees would not fully compensate for the legal expenses incurred. [*Guinn v. Dotson* (1994) 23 CA4th 262, 269-270, 28 CR2d 409, 414]

     (2) **[1:889.3] Includes fees in obtaining award:** Defendant can also recover attorney (and paralegal) fees incurred in the successful pursuit of a fee award under CCP §411.35(h) . . . because these expenses are the continuing result of plaintiff's failure to attach a certificate of merit to the complaint. [*Guinn v. Dotson*, supra, 23 CA4th at 271, 28 CR2d at 414-415]

6. **[1:890] Consultation Privileged:** If a certificate of merit is filed, the attorney has a privilege to refuse to disclose the *identity* of the expert with whom he consulted. Moreover, both the attorney and the expert are privileged to refuse to disclose the content of the consultation. [CCP §411.35(e)]

   a. **[1:891] Not discoverable:** The identities and opinions of experts consulted solely to evaluate a case (as opposed to those who will testify at trial) are generally protected as "attorney work product" (*see Ch. 8*). Moreover, statutory procedures for expert witness discovery specifically exclude experts consulted for purposes of obtaining a certificate of merit. [CCP §2018(c)]

   b. **[1:892] Exception—after judgment for defendant:** If defendant obtains a "favorable conclusion" (i.e., wins the lawsuit), the trial court *may* "verify compliance" with the statute by ordering plaintiff's attorney to identify the consultant relied upon in preparing the certificate of merit. The disclosure shall be made in an in-camera proceeding at which defendant may *not* be present. If the court finds a failure to comply with the statute, it may order plaintiff or plaintiff's attorney or both to pay the reasonable expenses, including attorney fees, incurred by defendant as a result of such failure to comply. [CCP §411.35(h); see *Guinn v. Dotson* (1994) 23 CA4th 262, 268, 28 CR 409, 413—"attorneys' fees" include reasonable paralegal fees billed to prevailing civil engineer sued for malpractice]

    (1) [1:893] **Not applicable to settlements:** Disclosure of consultants may be ordered only upon a "favorable conclusion" for the defendant. Settlement and dismissal of the malpractice action do not qualify. [*Korbel v. Chou* (1994) 27 CA4th 1427, 1433, 33 CR2d 190, 192—"favorable conclusion" similar to "favorable termination" for malicious prosecution purposes]

7. [1:894] **Compare—Prelawsuit Notice to "Health Care Provider":** At least 90 days' notice must be given before filing a malpractice action against *any* "health care provider" (including doctors and dentists); see ¶1:856.

    a. [1:895] **Compare—statute of limitations impact:** The time required to give notice to the "health care provider" *extends* the statute of limitations (*see* ¶1:863). However, the time required for prelawsuit *consultation* to determine the merits of the case *does not extend* the limitations period.

    [1:896-898] *Reserved.*

## E. PRELAWSUIT ADR REQUIREMENT

1. [1:899] **Enforcement of CC&Rs in "Common Interest Developments" (Condos, etc.):** Before suing to enforce CC&Rs or other documents governing a "common interest development," the parties must attempt to resolve their dispute through some form of Alternative Dispute Resolution (ADR), either binding or nonbinding. A certificate of compliance must be filed along with the complaint (see below). [See Civ.C. §1354]

    a. **Application**

        (1) [1:900] **"Common interest development":** A "common interest development" means a condominium project, a planned unit development or a cooperative apartment project. [See Civ.C. §1351(b)]

        (2) [1:901] **Which actions:** The prelawsuit ADR requirement applies to actions for declaratory or injunctive relief or for such relief in conjunction with a claim for

*money damages up to $5,000* (applicable to association assessments only if the disputed amount is tendered under protest) relating to enforcement of the association's governing documents. [Civ.C. §§1354(b), 1366.3]

It does *not* apply, however, to actions by the association to enforce liens based on such assessments. [See Civ.C. §1354(b)]

Nor does it apply to cross-complaints. [Civ.C. §1354(e)]

b. **[1:902]** **Procedure for requesting ADR:** Either the association or any unit owner may initiate the process by serving a "Request for Resolution" that:
— describes the dispute;
— requests resolution through ADR; and
— notifies the other party it must respond within 30 days or the request is deemed denied. [See Civ.C. §1354(b)]

If the other party refuses or does not respond within 30 days, the aggrieved party may proceed to file suit. If the other party *accepts*, the ADR process must be completed within 90 days of the request (unless extended by written stipulation). [See Civ.C. §1354(b)]

c. **[1:903]** **Certificate to accompany complaint:** Any complaint to enforce the CC&Rs or other documents governing the condominium development must be accompanied by plaintiff's certificate stating *either* that:
— the ADR procedure discussed above has been *completed*; or
— an opposing party has *refused* to participate in ADR; or
— *preliminary or injunctive relief* is necessary; or
— the statute of limitations will run within the next 120 days. [See Civ.C. §1354(c)]

d. **[1:904]** **Effect of failure to comply:** Failure to file such certificate is ground for a demurrer pursuant to CCP §430.10 or a motion to strike pursuant to CCP §455 . . . *unless* the court finds dismissal for such failure "would result in substantial prejudice to one of the parties." [See Civ.C. §1354(c)]

e. **[1:905]** **Attorney fees:** The prevailing party in any such action is entitled to an award of attorney fees. But in determining the amount of the award, the court may consider that party's refusal to participate in ADR before the lawsuit was filed. [Civ.C. §1354(f)]

• **[1:905.1]** To support a fee award, the action must be one to enforce the *governing documents*. But this is interpreted broadly. It includes an action *to determine the validity of an election* of directors of a homeowner's association. [*Kaplan v. Fairway Oaks Homeowners Ass'n* (2002) 98 CA4th 715, 721,120 CR2d 158, 161-162—fee award under §1354(f) upheld although statute authorizing court to determine election's validity (Corps.C. §7616) did not provide for fee award to prevailing party]

[1:905.2-905.4]  *Reserved.*

2.  [1:905.5]  **Construction Claims by "Common Interest Developments" Against Builder:**  A condo owners' association may be required to participate in ADR before commencing suit against the developer for defective design or construction of the development. [See Civ.C. §1375 (applies only to projects of at least 20 units)]

There are *two separate sets of procedures*, depending upon whether the action was commenced before or after July 1, 2002. (Civ.C. §1375 was amended and §1375.05 was added effective that date and with a sunset date of 1/1/11.)

The post-6/30/02 procedures *mandate prefiling ADR* with a dispute resolution facilitator and compilation of data pertaining to defects and exchanges of lists of defects. If parties fail to comply, the action may be stayed for up to 90 days to allow a noncomplying party to establish substantial compliance. If that party does not comply, the action may be dismissed without prejudice or other remedies may be fashioned by the court. [Civ.C. §1375.05(g)]

Note: Under the new procedures, different rules apply to *peripheral* parties (exposure under $25,000) and *nonperipheral* parties. (See statute for details.)

[1:905.5a]  *Compare—overlap with new home construction defect claims:* If an action is commenced under §1375, the parties are excused from performing substantially similar requirements that have been enforced under Civ.C. §910 et seq., relating to new home construction defect claims (¶*1:872.10 ff.*). [Civ.C. §935]

[1:905.5b-905.5c]  *Reserved.*

[1:905.5d]  **Comment:**  If you are contemplating asserting construction claims on behalf of "common interest developments" or represent parties subject to such claims, carefully review the procedures and time limits described in Civ.C. §§1375 and 1375.05. The discussions of these sections below are merely summaries and do not contain all of the statutory details and requirements.

a.  [1:905.6]  **Notice to builder:**  Before suing the "builder" (i.e., developer) of a common interest development for defective design or construction, the homeowner's association must give written notice to the builder listing the alleged defects and summarizing the results of any testing performed or surveys of the condo residents regarding the defects. [See Civ.C. §1375(a),(b)]

*For cases filed after 6/30/02:* Before a complaint may be filed, plaintiffs must serve a *"notice of commencement of legal proceedings"* on the general contractor. The notice must contain the name and location of the project, an initial list of defects, a summary of the damages resulting from the defects, and the results of any tests conducted. [Civ.C. §1375(a),(b)]

(1) [1:905.7] **Effect on statute of limitations:** The association's notice to the builder tolls all statutes of limitations for 150 days. But the builder may cancel further tolling of the statute by notice to the homeowner's association, in which event the association is excused from further compliance with the statute. [See Civ.C. §1375(b)(3)]

*For cases filed after 6/30/02:* Service of "notice of the commencement of legal proceedings" tolls the statute of limitations for 180 days. The homeowners' association and "nonperipheral" parties (see Civ.C. §1375(e)(3)) may *agree* to an additional extension of up to 180 days. Further extensions require the agreement of *all parties.* [Civ.C. §1375(b),(c)]

(2) [1:905.8] **Effect of commencing suit without notice:** Although the association is not required to file a certificate of compliance before filing suit, a court may be requested to stay the action pending compliance or dismiss the action altogether. [See Civ.C. §1375(h)(3) (B)]

[1:905.9] *Reserved.*

b. [1:905.10] **Builder's response:** Upon receipt of the notice, the builder and the owners' association "shall attempt to settle the dispute or attempt to agree to submit it to alternative dispute resolution." [Civ.C. §1375(b)(2)]

If the builder is unwilling to negotiate the dispute, the association is excused from further compliance with the statute. [See Civ.C. §1375(c)(1)]

*For cases filed after 6/30/02:* "Nonperipheral" parties and insurers must attend a case management meeting, select a dispute resolution facilitator, perform testing, collect and exchange data and documents, including detailed defect lists, and participate in facilitated dispute resolution. The court may order discovery, resolve disputes, and rule on good faith motions. [Civ.C. §1375.05(f)]

[1:905.11] *Reserved.*

c. **[1:905.12] Settlement offers:** After inspection and testing (at its own expense), the builder may make a written settlement offer or proposal to submit the dispute to ADR. The offer must include a copy of the builder's test results and must indicate that the builder has access to sufficient funds to pay the amount offered in settlement. [See Civ.C. §1375(e)]

The builder and the homeowners' association board of directors are required to meet and confer concerning the builder's settlement offer or proposed ADR resolution. [See Civ.C. §1375(e)]

*For cases filed after 6/30/02:* The general contractor may submit a written settlement offer. The offer must state that the contractor has sufficient funds to pay the offered amount. The general contractor may meet with the association's board of directors to discuss the settlement proposal. [Civ.C. §1375(k)]

**[1:905.13-905.14]** *Reserved.*

d. **[1:905.15] Members to be notified of settlement offer:** If the association's board of directors rejects the builder's settlement offer, it shall either hold a special meeting of the members (at the builder's expense) to discuss the offer; or, if the association's performance has been excused, it shall communicate with the members identifying the defect list, the various available options and a statement that if 5% of the membership requests a special meeting then such meeting shall be held to discuss the matter. [See Civ.C. §1375(g)]

*For cases filed after 6/30/02:* The association's board must meet and confer and, if it decides to reject the settlement offer, must conduct a meeting open to each member of the association at least 15 days before suit is filed. The complete text of any settlement offer and a concise explanation of the terms of the offer shall be sent to each member of the association at the contractor's expense. [Civ.C. §1375(k)]

e. **[1:905.16] Time limits:** The statute sets various time limits for each of the above procedures (which may be extended by the parties). If either party fails to meet these deadlines, the other is excused from further compliance with the statute. [See Civ.C. §1375(b)-(f)]

*For cases filed after 6/30/02:* The statute should be consulted for the many time limits it now contains. Noncompliance with these time limits is not excused.

**[1:905.17-905.19]** *Reserved.*

f. **[1:905.20] Privileges (cases filed after 6/30/02):** All defect lists, demands, communications, offers and negotiations made in the course of the prelitigation dispute resolution process are privileged. [Civ.C. §1375(*l*)]

[1:905.21-905.24] *Reserved.*

g. [1:905.25] **Trial priority (cases filed after 6/30/02):** If, after compliance with the mandatory prefiling dispute resolution, the case does not settle, the case must be given trial priority, with some specified exceptions, additional testing and inspections are prohibited, expert witnesses must be disclosed (association's experts first) and expert depositions may be taken before the depositions of percipient witnesses. [Civ.C. §1375.05]

## F. EXHAUSTION OF OTHER REMEDIES

[1:906] In some cases, claimants may be obligated by statute or contract to utilize remedies other than litigation to resolve a dispute. Where such obligation exists and the nonlitigation remedy provides adequate notice and hearing, courts will not adjudicate the claim.

1. [1:906.1] **Exhaustion of Administrative Remedy:** Where an administrative tribunal is created by law to adjudicate the issue sought to be presented to the court, claimants must exhaust the administrative remedy before seeking judicial relief: "In brief, the rule is that where an administrative remedy is provided by statute, relief must be sought from the administrative body and this remedy exhausted before the courts will act." [*Abelleira v. District Court of Appeal* (1941) 17 C2d 280, 292, 109 P2d 942, 948]

   a. [1:906.2] **Jurisdictional:** Where an adequate administrative remedy is provided by statute, resort to that forum is a "jurisdictional" prerequisite to judicial consideration of the claim. [*Styne v. Stevens* (2001) 26 C4th 42, 56, 109 CR2d 14, 26]

      (1) [1:906.3] **Waiver:** "Jurisdictional" is used here in the sense of *reversible error,* not in the sense of the court's power to adjudicate (subject matter jurisdiction) or to bind the parties to its adjudication (personal jurisdiction). Therefore, the exhaustion requirement can be waived. [See *Keiffer v. Bechtel Corp.* (1998) 65 CA4th 893, 897, 76 CR2d 827, 829—exhaustion defect waived if no timely objection]

      [1:906.4-906.5] *Reserved.*

      (2) [1:906.6] **Estoppel:** An administrative agency may also be estopped from challenging plaintiff's failure to exhaust administrative remedies based on its conduct (e.g., correspondence or verbal assurances that the agency would settle without the necessity of plaintiff

filing a formal claim). [See *J.H. McKnight Ranch, Inc. v. Franchise Tax Bd.* (2003) 110 CA4th 978, 990, 2 CR3d 339, 348-349]

[1:906.7-906.9] *Reserved.*

b. **[1:906.10] Compare—statutes creating both administrative and judicial remedies:** Some statutes provide both administrative and judicial remedies. In such cases, the exhaustion requirement depends on the wording of the statute:

- **[1:906.11]** For example, the California Fair Employment and Housing Act (FEHA) (Gov.C. §12900 et seq.) provides that persons claiming violations must file an administrative complaint with the Department of Fair Employment and Housing (DFEH) and obtain a "right to sue" letter from the DFEH *before* commencing a civil action based on such violations. [Gov.C. §§12960, 12965(b)]

  The timely filing of an administrative complaint is a jurisdictional *prerequisite* to the bringing of a civil action for damages under FEHA. [*Romano v. Rockwell Int'l, Inc.* (1996) 14 C4th 479, 492, 59 CR2d 20, 27]

- **[1:906.12]** But California's wage and hour laws provide that an aggrieved employee may seek either administrative or judicial relief; i.e., an administrative complaint is *optional* and does not affect the claimant's right to sue for wage and hour violations. [Lab.C. §§1194, 98.3; see *Cuadra v. Millan* (1998) 17 C4th 855, 858, 72 CR2d 687, 689]

  [1:906.13-906.19] *Reserved.*

c. **[1:906.20] "Exhaustion":** To satisfy the exhaustion requirement, a party must take advantage of every stage of the administrative grievance process provided. [See *Sea & Sage Audubon Society, Inc. v. Planning Comm'n* (1983) 34 C3d 412, 418, 194 CR 357, 360; *Gutkin v. University of Southern Calif.* (2002) 101 CA4th 967, 979, 125 CR2d 115, 124]

(1) **[1:906.21] Compare—seeking rehearing before administrative tribunal:** But where a statute merely provides that a claimant *may* seek a rehearing or reconsideration by the administrative tribunal, there is no exhaustion requirement. [*Sierra Club v. San Joaquin Local Agency Formation Comm'n* (1999) 21 C4th 489, 494, 87 CR2d 702, 705—"We simply see no necessity that parties file pro forma requests for reconsideration raising issues already fully argued before the agency and decided in the administrative decision"]

(2) [1:906.22] **Compare—several administrative remedies available:** Where a claim is subject to review by two separate administrative agencies, plaintiff *need not* exhaust his or her remedies before both agencies prior to bringing suit. [*Schifando v. City of Los Angeles* (2003) 31 C4th 1074, 1089, 6 CR3d 457, 467—city employee claiming employment-related discrimination was not required to exhaust city's internal remedies after exhausting administrative remedy under FEHA]

[1:906.23-906.24] *Reserved.*

d. [1:906.25] **Exceptions to exhaustion doctrine:** Various exceptions are recognized to the exhaustion of remedies doctrine:

(1) [1:906.26] **Remedy inadequate, unavailable or futile:** The failure to pursue administrative remedies does not bar judicial relief where the administrative remedy is *inadequate* or *unavailable*, or where it would be *futile to pursue* the remedy. [See *Yamaha Motor Corp. v. Sup.Ct. (Van Nuys Cycle, Inc.)* (1986) 185 CA3d 1232, 1241, 230 CR 382, 386; *Joel v. Valley Surgical Ctr.* (1998) 68 CA4th 360, 365-366, 80 CR2d 247, 250]

(2) [1:906.27] **Challenge to constitutionality of administrative body:** A party is excused from exhausting the administrative remedy where the challenge is to the *constitutionality* of the administrative body itself or to its *procedures.* [*Unnamed Physician v. Board of Trustees of St. Agnes Med. Ctr.* (2001) 93 CA4th 607, 621, 113 CR2d 309, 319—claim that organization's bylaws violated due process]

[1:906.28-906.29] *Reserved.*

(3) [1:906.30] **Federal civil rights claims:** Generally, a plaintiff is not required to exhaust state administrative or judicial remedies before suing under federal civil rights statutes. [*Felder v. Casey* (1988) 487 US 131, 147, 108 S.Ct. 2302, 2311; *McDaniel v. Board of Ed. of Mountain View School Dist.* (1996) 44 CA4th 1618, 1622, 52 CR2d 448, 450]

e. [1:906.31] **Compare—exhaustion of *judicial* remedies:** Where an administrative decision is quasi-judicial in nature (notice and hearing provided) and is *subject to judicial review,* such review must be sought. Otherwise, the administrative findings may bar any civil action on the claim: "(U)nless a party to a quasi-judicial proceeding challenges the agency's adverse findings made in that proceeding, by means of a mandate action in superior court, those findings are binding in later civil actions." [*Johnson v. City of Loma Linda* (2000) 24 C4th 61, 65, 99 CR2d 316, 319]

(1) **[1:906.32] Rationale:** The rationale for exhaustion of judicial remedies is the doctrine of collateral estoppel (issue preclusion): "The doctrine of collateral estoppel bars the relitigating of issues which were previously resolved in an administrative hearing by an agency acting in a judicial capacity." [*Risam v. County of Los Angeles* (2002) 99 CA4th 412, 419, 121 CR2d 267, 272 (internal quotes omitted)]

f. **[1:907] Compare—"primary jurisdiction" doctrine:** "Primary jurisdiction" is the flip side of the rule requiring exhaustion of administrative remedies. It applies where a claim is cognizable in the first instance *in court* but involves issues within the special competency of an administrative body. In such cases, the trial court may (discretionary) *suspend* the judicial proceedings and refer the issues to the agency for its views. [*Farmers Ins. Exch. v. Sup.Ct. (People)* (1992) 2 C4th 377, 390-391, 6 CR2d 487, 496]

Thus, the primary jurisdiction doctrine creates a *timing* issue, *not a jurisdictional* issue. [*Farmers Ins. Exch. v. Sup.Ct. (People),* supra, 2 C4th at 387, 6 CR2d at 493, fn. 7; *Piscioneri v. City of Ontario* (2002) 95 CA4th 1037, 1051, 116 CR2d 38, 48]

"The agency, in effect, becomes a kind of special master for the trial court." [*Miller v. Sup.Ct. (American Honda Motor Co., Inc.)* (1996) 50 CA4th 1665, 1669, 58 CR2d 584, 586]

(1) **[1:907.1] Rationale:** Referring complex technical issues to administrative agencies with special competence promotes efficiency in decisionmaking and helps assure uniform application of regulatory laws. [*Farmers Ins. Exch. v. Sup.Ct. (People)*, supra, 2 C4th at 391, 6 CR2d at 496]

(2) **[1:907.2] Discretionary:** Even so, application of the primary jurisdiction doctrine is discretionary and will not be applied where contrary to the interests of justice in the particular case. Thus, courts must consider the expense and delay to the litigants, and the adequacy of administrative remedies for the claims involved. [*Farmers Ins. Exch. v. Sup.Ct. (People)*, supra, 2 C4th at 392, 6 CR2d at 496, fns. 9, 10; *Miller v. Sup.Ct. (American Honda Motor Co., Inc.)* (1996) 50 CA4th 1665, 1667, 58 CR2d 584, 591]

(3) **Application**

- **[1:907.3]** The primary jurisdiction doctrine does *not* justify referral to a regulatory agency of *common law contract and tort claims* as to which courts are clearly competent. Any technical issues can be resolved at trial through expert and percipient witnesses. [*Southbay Creditors Trust v. General Motors Accept. Corp.* (1999) 69 CA4th 1068, 1081-1082, 82 CR2d 1, 9]

2. [1:908] **Exhaustion of Internal Grievance Procedures:** A similar exhaustion doctrine applies where an organization's constitution or bylaws (e.g., labor union, hospital, voluntary private or professional association, or public entity) provide an internal grievance procedure for its members. If that procedure provides adequate procedural safeguards, members may be bound to utilize it before suing the organization in court. [See *Rojo v. Kliger* (1990) 52 C3d 65, 86, 276 CR 130, 143; *Bockover v. Perko* (1994) 28 CA4th 479, 486, 34 CR2d 423, 427]

"It is a general and well-established rule that a plaintiff cannot seek judicial review of a grievance against an organization of which the plaintiff is a member without first exhausting the administrative remedies provided by that organization." [*Joel v. Valley Surgical Ctr.* (1998) 68 CA4th 360, 365, 80 CR2d 247, 249; *Palmer v. Regents of Univ. of Calif.* (2003) 107 CA4th 899, 904, 132 CR2d 567, 571—applies to wrongful termination actions against private or public entities]

*Caution:* Whether a *public* employee must exhaust an internal administrative remedy provided by a public entity employer is presently before the California Supreme Court in *Campbell v. Regents of Univ. of Calif.*, Case No. S113275.

a. **Application**

(1) [1:908.1] **Discipline, expulsion:** This "internal grievance procedure" exhaustion requirement applies to expulsion or discipline of members in fraternal organizations, labor unions, and hospital medical staffs. [See *Westlake Comm. Hosp. v. Sup.Ct. (Kaiman)* (1976) 17 C3d 465, 478, 131 CR 90, 94—doctor denied hospital staff privileges must exhaust all available internal remedies before instituting judicial action]

(2) [1:908.2] **Related damage claims:** This exhaustion requirement extends to related common law claims, such as a claim for damages, even if the organization's internal review procedures do not provide a damages remedy. Rationale: This promotes judicial efficiency by unearthing the relevant evidence and providing a record that the court may review. [*Westlake Comm. Hosp. v. Sup.Ct. (Kaiman)*, supra, 17 C3d at 476, 131 CR at 96]

[1:908.3-908.9] *Reserved.*

b. [1:908.10] **Limited judicial review (mandamus):** If the organization has conducted a quasi-judicial hearing as provided in its bylaws, the aggrieved member's only remedy is a *mandamus* proceeding to set aside whatever action was taken against him or her. Unless the member first succeeds in the mandamus action, he or she cannot pursue a tort remedy against the association. [See *Westlake Comm. Hosp. v. Sup.Ct. (Kaiman),* supra, 17 C3d at 484-485, 131 CR at 101—after doctor's hospital staff privileges were revoked, she exhausted hospital's internal grievance procedures and then, without seeking judicial review, sued in tort for damages: failure to seek judicial review *barred* her tort action]

⇨ **[1:908.11]** ***PRACTICE POINTER:*** Keep in mind that in order to obtain mandamus relief, plaintiff must prove that the board's action was *not supported by substantial evidence.* This is usually a difficult burden to meet and makes these cases very difficult to win!

[1:908.12-908.14]  *Reserved.*

c. **[1:908.15]** **Compare—where no hearing held:** On the other hand, when the association takes action against a member (e.g., denying hospital staff privileges to a doctor) *without affording the basic procedural protection* to which he or she is legally entitled, the member may maintain an *immediate* action for tort damages (e.g., fraud, intentional infliction of emotional distress, etc.) arising from expulsion or exclusion. [*Westlake Comm. Hosp. v. Sup.Ct. (Kaiman),* supra, 17 C3d at 478, 131 CR at 97]

[1:908.16-908.19]  *Reserved.*

3. **[1:908.20]** **Contractual Arbitration:** An agreement to arbitrate a dispute may be specifically enforced under either federal or state law. Where a valid arbitration agreement covers plaintiff's claim, plaintiff may be compelled to arbitrate rather than litigate. Unless defendant waives the arbitration agreement, any action to enforce the claim will be stayed pending the arbitration. [See 9 USC §2; CCP §1281 et seq.]

*Cross-refer:* See detailed discussion of contractual arbitration in Knight, Fannin, Chernick & Haldeman, *Cal. Prac. Guide: Alternative Dispute Resolution* (TRG), Ch. 5.

## G. PRIOR COURT ORDER REQUIRED FOR CERTAIN PLEADINGS

1. **[1:909]** **Statutes Restricting "Pleadability" of Certain Claims:** Statutes restrict the "pleadability" of certain claims by imposing a threshold requirement that a court order be obtained *before* such claims may be filed. These claims include:

• Punitive damages claims against health providers (CCP §425.13(a); *see* ¶6:327 ff.);

- Punitive damages claims against religious corporations (CCP §425.14; see ¶6:346 ff.);

- Claims against attorneys for conspiracy with their clients (Civ.C. §1714.10(a); see ¶6:354 ff.); and

- Negligence claims against volunteer directors or officers of nonprofit corporations (CCP §425.15; see ¶6:377 ff.).

    a. **[1:910] Effect:** These statutes operate like a demurrer or summary judgment *in reverse:* i.e., instead of forcing defendant to challenge such claims for lack of legal or factual merit, plaintiff must demonstrate in advance that the claim has sufficient factual and legal merit to proceed to trial. [See *College Hosp., Inc. v. Sup.Ct. (Crowell)* (1994) 8 C4th 704, 719, 34 CR2d 898, 907, *discussed at* ¶6:344]

    **[1:911]** *Reserved.*

2. **[1:912] Actions for Childhood Sexual Abuse:** Actions for damages for childhood sexual abuse may be brought within 8 years after the plaintiff becomes an adult, or 3 years after discovering that an injury or illness suffered as an adult was caused by childhood sexual abuse, whichever is later. [CCP §340.1; see *Doyle v. Fenster* (1996) 47 CA4th 1701, 1707, 55 CR2d 327, 330]

    a. **[1:913] Claims against third parties barred if plaintiff age 26 or older:** Plaintiffs age 26 or older can sue only the person who committed the childhood sexual abuse; suits against third persons whose negligent or intentional acts were allegedly the cause of the abuse are barred, unless that person or entity was on notice of the abuse and failed to guard against it. [CCP §340.1(b)]

    b. **[1:913.1] Procedural requirements where plaintiff age 26 or older:** Special procedures are required in actions by a plaintiff who is 26 or older for childhood sexual abuse:

    (1) **[1:913.2] Complaint naming "Doe" defendants:** The person charged with the abuse may not be named and may be referred to only as a "Doe" in the original complaint filed with the court. [CCP §340.1(m)]

    (2) **[1:913.3] Certificate of merit:** Before serving any defendant, plaintiffs must file a certificate of merit with the court as to *each defendant* allegedly responsible for the abuse. The certificate must show that, in the opinion of both plaintiff's attorney and a qualified mental health practitioner, there is reason to believe plaintiff was subject to the childhood sexual abuse alleged in the complaint. [CCP §340.1(g)-(i)]

    The court must review such certificates *in camera* to determine if there is a "reasonable and meritorious cause for the filing of the action" against each particular defendant. If such finding is made, the duty to serve that defendant arises. [CCP §340.1(j)]

    (3) **[1:913.4] Amendment of complaint; certificate of corroborative fact:** Plaintiff must apply to the court for leave to amend the complaint to name the defendant. Such application must be accompanied by a "certificate of corroborative fact" executed by plaintiff's attorney. [CCP §340.1(n); *see discussion at ¶6:617.5*]

    (4) **[1:913.5] Effect of failure to comply:** Failure to comply with the above requirements is ground for demurrer or motion to strike the complaint and for *disciplinary action against plaintiff's attorney.* [CCP §340.1(k),(*l*)]

3.  **[1:914] Actions by Vexatious Litigants:** Plaintiffs who litigate in propria persona and repeatedly file frivolous pleadings or motions, or attempt to relitigate issues previously determined against them, may be barred from filing new lawsuits without prior leave of court. Alternatively, defendant in the action may move for an order requiring the pro per plaintiff to furnish security in an amount determined by the court. [See CCP §§391-391.7; see *Wolfgram v. Wells Fargo Bank* (1997) 53 CA4th 43, 59-60, 61 CR2d 694, 704-705—rejecting various constitutional challenges]

In appropriate cases, courts may bar vexatious litigants from instituting new litigation either in pro per *or through an attorney.* [*In re Shieh* (1993) 17 CA4th 1154, 1167, 21 CR2d 886, 895— "these attorneys who ostensibly 'represent' (litigant) serve as mere puppets"]

    a.  **[1:914.1] Notice and hearing required:** Although the statute is silent on the subject, a party may not be declared to be a "vexatious litigant" without a noticed motion and hearing "which includes the right to oral argument and presentation of evidence." [*Bravo v. Ismaj* (2002) 99 CA4th 211, 225, 120 CR2d 879, 890]

    b.  **[1:915] Persons subject to statute:** Any person who commences, institutes or maintains an action, including an *attorney at law acting in pro per,* may be determined to be a vexatious litigant. [CCP §391(d); see *In re Shieh* (1993) 17 CA4th 1154, 1166, 21 CR2d 886, 894]

        (1)  **[1:916] Persons controlling litigation:** Likewise, anyone who has *caused* an action to be commenced, instituted or maintained by another in pro per is subject to the statute. [CCP §391(d)]

        A *corporation* was held to be a vexatious litigant where its sole shareholder, who had previously been held a vexatious litigant, was using the corporate shield to avoid the statute. [*Say & Say, Inc. v. Ebershoff* (1993) 20 CA4th 1759, 1770, 25 CR2d 703, 711]

(2) [1:917] **Present representation by counsel immaterial:** The fact plaintiff is presently represented by counsel does not prevent a finding he or she is a vexatious litigant based on *previous* litigation conducted in pro per. [*Camerado Ins. Agency, Inc. v. Sup.Ct. (Stolz)* (1993) 12 CA4th 838, 842, 16 CR2d 42, 44; *In re Shieh*, supra, 17 CA4th at 1166, 21 CR2d at 894]

c.　[1:918] **Based on number of unsuccessful suits filed:** One measure of a "vexatious" litigant is having commenced or *maintained* more than five in pro per lawsuits (other than small claim actions) within the "immediately preceding" seven-year period that have been "finally determined adversely" to the person (excluding small claims actions). [CCP §391(b)(1)]

(1) [1:919] **"Finally determined adversely":** Whether the prior lawsuits were "finally determined adversely" to plaintiff is ordinarily a question of fact; i.e., the court is required to take judicial notice of the court files and judgments in the earlier actions.

- [1:920] "Finally determined" means that all avenues for direct review (appeal) have been exhausted or the time for appeal has expired. [*Childs v. PaineWebber, Inc.* (1994) 29 CA4th 982, 994, 35 CR2d 93, 100—plaintiff cannot be adjudged "vexatious litigant" while earlier lawsuits still on appeal]

- [1:921] Another court's finding that plaintiff is a "vexatious litigant" based on the same lawsuits during the same 7-year period may *collaterally estop* plaintiff from relitigating the issue. [*Stolz v. Bank of America* (1993) 15 CA4th 217, 222-223, 19 CR2d 19, 22]

- [1:921.1] Cases voluntarily dismissed without prejudice by a *pro se* plaintiff count for the purpose of the vexatious litigant statute because they still burden the judicial system and the target of the litigation. [*Tokerud v. Capitol Bank Sacramento* (1995) 38 CA4th 775, 779, 45 CR2d 345, 347]

(2) [1:922] **"Immediately preceding" seven-year period:** Where defendant moves for security on the ground plaintiff is a "vexatious litigant," that seven-year period is measured retroactively from the date the motion is filed (rather than the date the lawsuit was filed). [*Stolz v. Bank of America*, supra, 15 CA4th at 224, 19 CR2d at 23]

[1:923-924] *Reserved.*

☞[1:925]  **PRACTICE POINTERS:**  When defending actions brought by a plaintiff in pro per, check both with your local court clerk *and the Judicial Council.* The Judicial Council is required to maintain records of persons subject to prefiling orders in *any* state court (CCP §391.7(d)).

Also, check any appropriate *federal* district court to see if the pro per plaintiff has been declared a vexatious litigant in any proceeding based on the same transaction (CCP §391(b)(4)).

d.  [1:926]  **Bond requirement:**  Defendant may move the court for an order requiring plaintiff to post a bond on the ground that plaintiff is a vexatious litigant and "there is not a reasonable probability that he will prevail in the litigation against the moving defendant." [CCP §391.1]

(1)  [1:927]  **No "reasonable probability" of recovery:** To satisfy this burden, defendant must show either:
— that plaintiff's recovery is foreclosed *as a matter of law*; or
— that there are insufficient facts to support recovery by plaintiff on its legal theories even if all of plaintiff's allegations are accepted as true. [*Devereaux v. Latham & Watkins* (1995) 32 CA4th 1571, 1582, 38 CR2d 849, 855]

(2)  [1:928]  **Financial ability immaterial:**  The vexatious litigant's impecunious (and in pro per) status does not excuse compliance with the bond requirement. [*Devereaux v. Latham & Watkins*, supra, 32 CA4th at 1587-1588, 38 CR2d at 858]

[1:929-949]  *Reserved.*

## H. FILING FEE CONSIDERATIONS

[1:950]  A fee must be paid to the Clerk of the Court for filing the complaint and most subsequent papers in a civil action. [See Gov.C. §§26830, 68090.7, 72055 et seq.]

Except as stated below, payment of filing fees is "both *mandatory and jurisdictional.*" [*Hu v. Silgan Containers Corp.* (1999) 70 CA4th 1261, 1269, 83 CR2d 333, 338 (emphasis added); *Duran v. St. Luke's Hosp.* (2003) 114 CA4th 457, 460, 8 CR3d 1, 2—court clerk properly refused to accept complaint tendered for filing on eve of statute of limitations because check for filing fee was $3 short]

☞[1:950.1]  **PRACTICE POINTER:**  Check your court's Web site to determine applicable filing fees. Local court Web sites may be accessed through the California Judicial Council home page at "www.courtinfo.ca.gov".

1.  **[1:951]** **Bounced Check Problem:** Where a filing fee is paid by check and that check is later returned unpaid by the bank (e.g., for insufficient funds), the clerk must notify the party by mail that he or she has *20 days* to pay the fee. If the payment is not received within 20 days, "the clerk shall *void* the filing." [CCP §411.20(b) (emphasis added)]

    a.  **[1:952]** **Effect on pending hearings:** If a trial or hearing is scheduled to be heard within the 20-day period above, the fee must be paid *before* the hearing. Otherwise, the court "must *void* the filing and proceed as if (the fee) had not been paid." [CCP §411.20(d) (emphasis and parentheses added)]

    b.  **[1:953]** **Relief under CCP §473?** CCP §473 authorizes the court to relieve a party from any "proceeding" resulting from the party's "mistake, inadvertence, surprise or excusable neglect." [CCP §473(b); *see* ¶5:282 ff.]

        But this generally does not permit relief where an action has been "voided" for nonpayment of fees: "(T)here is no relief under section 473 for *jurisdictional errors* such as (party's) failure to timely pay her filing fees . . ." [*Hu v. Silgan Containers Corp.*, supra, 70 CA4th at 1269, 83 CR2d at 338 (emphasis and parentheses added)—court could not "reinstate" complaint that had been voided by clerk for nonpayment of filing fee]

        (1) **[1:954]** **Compare:** On the other hand, relief may be available under CCP §473 if the fees *had actually been paid* within the time limit, or if plaintiff had been prevented from paying the fees by fraud or some other conduct perpetrated by the defendant. [*Hu v. Silgan Containers Corp.*, supra, 70 CA4th at 1269, 83 CR2d at 338]

**RESERVED**

# LETTER AGREEMENT FOR HOURLY RATE FEE

Date:_____

_____  *(client's name and address)*

_____

_____

    Re:_____  *(name of case or description of transaction)*

Dear_____:

This letter will set forth the terms and conditions under which we agree to represent you in connection with the above-referenced matter or transaction.

1.    <u>Services to be rendered by us</u>: Our law firm will render the following legal services on your behalf:_____

_____

_____

No other legal services are covered by this agreement. We make no promise or guarantee regarding the outcome of the matter upon which we are to represent you.

We reserve complete discretion as to assigning your work to attorneys within the firm. We will endeavor to keep your legal expenses down by utilizing paralegals and law clerks to handle tasks appropriate to their skills.

2.    <u>Fees to be paid by you</u>: The hourly rates for attorneys in our firm presently range from $_____ to $_____; the hourly rates for our paralegals is presently $_____; and the hourly rates for our law clerks is presently $_____. *(OPTIONAL: our rates for time spent in court are $_____ per day, or $_____ per half day.)* Our billings will include telephone conferences in relation to the matter we are handling for you.

Our estimate is that the above matter will involve fees of approximately $_____, in addition to costs and expenses described in the following paragraph.

We reserve the right to change our fee rates at any time by written notice to you. Services rendered after the date of such notice shall be billed at the changed rate.

Any fee awarded by the court, pursuant to statute or contract, in connection with the subject matter of this representation, shall be paid to Attorney and shall be applied against Client's fee obligation under this Agreement, but shall not limit or discharge Client's fee obligation.

3.    <u>Costs and expenses to be paid by you</u>: You authorize us to incur on your behalf whatever costs and expenses are reasonably required in connection with the services to be rendered by us under this Agreement. *(OPTIONAL, except that we agree to obtain your prior approval before incurring any cost or expense exceeding $_____.)* Without limitation, this may include any or all of the following:

- court filing fees

- process serving fees

- fees and mileage to private investigators

- fees to photographers or graphic artists

- fees to experts for consultation and/or appearance at deposition or trial

- fees for obtaining attendance of other witnesses at deposition or trial

- fees to court reporters for taking deposition or copies of transcripts

- jury fees

- messenger and mail expenses

- travel and lodging expenses

- long distance telephone charges

- photocopying charges (at $._____) per page

- word processing charges (at $._____) per page

We reserve the right to change the above rates for photocopying and word processing at any time by written notice to you.

You shall pay and hold us harmless from all such costs and expenses incurred by us on your behalf. We may, but shall not be obligated to, advance funds on your behalf to pay such costs and expenses. In such event, you agree to reimburse us upon demand for the amounts so advanced.

4.      Billings: We shall bill you for our services and for any costs and expenses advanced on your behalf. Such billings shall be on a monthly or other convenient basis. You shall also have the right to request a current bill at any time covering our fees and costs to date, and we agree to provide same within 10 days of your request.

You agree to notify us promptly, and in writing, if you dispute any entry on such billing; and that if you fail to do so within 30 days after receipt thereof, all such entries shall be acknowledged as correct, as between us.

5.      Interest on unpaid bills: All of our billing shall be due and payable immediately upon receipt by you. In the event any bill remains unpaid for more than 30 days after receipt, interest thereon at the rate of _____% shall be due and payable from the date of the bill until the date of ultimate payment.

6.      Delay in payment as excusing services: Further, in the event that any of our bills remains unpaid for more than 30 days after receipt by you, we shall have the right to discontinue rendering further services to you in connection with any other matter then being handled for you by our firm, until the amount of such billing (and interest thereon) is paid in full.

7.      Deposit against fees and costs: Upon execution of this Agreement, you shall pay us the sum of $_____ as a deposit against the legal fees and costs and expenses to be incurred. We will deposit these funds in a Trust Account. You hereby authorize us to withdraw such funds to pay our legal fees as

billed, and costs and expenses as incurred. Any unexpended balance shall be returned to you upon termination of our services under this agreement.

*(OPTIONAL: When the deposit is exhausted, you shall pay us an additional deposit in such amount as we deem reasonably necessary within ____ days following our written request to you. Your failure to do so shall excuse us from any further obligation to render services under this Agreement.)*

8.      Termination of agreement: Either of us shall have the right to terminate this agreement at any time upon notification in writing to the other. Upon such termination, you shall remain responsible for any unpaid billings for services rendered or costs advanced by us. You agree to execute, upon request, a stipulation in such form as to permit us to withdraw as your attorneys of record in any legal action then pending.

9.      Insurance Disclosure:    Our firm maintains errors and omissions (malpractice) insurance coverage.

*(OR* "Our firm does not maintain errors and omissions insurance coverage but has filed with the Sate Bar a written agreement guaranteeing payment of client claims for errors and omissions in the amount specified in Rule IV, Section B, paragraph 1(c), of the Law Corporation Rules of the State Bar.")

*(OR* "Our firm is a law corporation that has provided security for client claims for errors and omissions in one of the manners provided in Rule IV, Section B, of the Law Corporation Rules of the State Bar.")

*(OR* "Our firm does not maintain errors and omissions insurance coverage or meet any of the criteria set forth in Business & Professions Code §6148(a)(4).")

10.     Action to enforce payment: In the event it is necessary for our firm to file legal action to enforce this Agreement, the prevailing party in such action shall be entitled to recover all costs and expenses incurred in connection with such legal action, including reasonable attorney fees and court costs. If our firm represents itself in such action without counsel and is the prevailing party, you agree to compensate our firm for all time reasonably expended in connection with such litigation.

11.     (OPTIONAL) Arbitration of disputes:   Any dispute arising between Attorney and Client as to fees or costs shall be arbitrated pursuant to the provisions of Business & Professions Code §6200 et. seq. (No agreement for binding arbitration of such disputes can be made until after such a dispute has arisen; see Bus. & Prof.C. Sec 6204.)

*Any other dispute arising under this Agreement or in connection with Attorney's services hereunder, including any claim for malpractice, shall be resolved by binding arbitration in accordance with the rules of _____ (e.g., American Arbitration Association, or JAMS, or CCP §1280 et seq.) and in accordance with the following provisions:*

*The arbitrator shall be empowered to order the losing party in the arbitration to reimburse the prevailing party for all expenses incurred in connection with the arbitration, including without limitation the arbitrator's fees and reasonable attorney fees and costs.*

*Attorney has explained to Client regarding such arbitration that:*
*--the parties are waiving their right to a jury trial and to seek remedies*
*available in court proceedings;*
*--prearbitration discovery is generally more limited than and different from*
*court proceedings;*
*--the arbitrator's award is not required to include factual findings or legal*
*reasoning; and*
*--any party's right to appeal or to seek modification of the award is strictly*
*limited and that the award is final and binding on the parties.*

**YOUR INITIALS**          *You acknowledge that we have explained to you*
**BELOW SIGNIFY**          *that such binding arbitration may deprive you*
**ACKNOWLEDGMENT**         *of various rights that you otherwise might have*
**OF THIS EXPLANATION**    *in a legal action, including without limitation the*
                      *right to a jury trial, the right to appeal, and full*
                      *discovery rights.*

_____
(Client's initials)


Please contact the undersigned if you have any questions regarding any matter stated above. If you find everything in order, kindly sign and return the original to us, together with your check for $_____ in payment of the deposit against fees and costs. The enclosed copy of this letter is for your files.

Very truly yours,


By:_____


I HEREBY APPROVE AND AGREE to each of the terms and conditions set forth above, and acknowledge receipt of a copy of this letter agreement.


/s/_____          Dated:_____

# STATE BAR SAMPLE WRITTEN FEE AGREEMENT
# HOURLY LITIGATION

**Form No. 1**
**Sample Written Fee Agreement**
**Hourly Litigation**
**CRANE, GARCIA & MOORE**
**441 Bauchet Street**
**Los Angeles, CA 90012**
**(213) 680-9600**
_____, 19__

## ATTORNEY-CLIENT FEE AGREEMENT

This is the written fee agreement ("Agreement") that California law requires attorneys to have with their clients. Crane, Garcia & Moore ("Attorney") will provide legal services to Stella King ("Client") on the terms set forth below.

**1. CONDITIONS.** This Agreement will not take effect, and Attorney will have no obligation to provide legal services, until Client returns a signed copy of this Agreement and pays the initial deposit called for under Paragraph 5.

**2. SCOPE OF SERVICES.** Client hires Attorney to provide legal services in the following matter:_____ [describe matter]. Attorney will provide those legal services reasonably required to represent Client. Attorney will take reasonable steps to keep Client informed of progress and to respond to Client's inquiries. If a court action is filed, Attorney will represent Client through trial and post-trial motions. This Agreement does not cover representation on appeal or in execution proceedings after judgment. Separate arrangements must be agreed to for those services. Services in any matter not described above will require a separate Agreement.

**3. INSURANCE DISCLOSURE.** (To be included only if the requirements of Business and Professions Code section 6148(a) (4) have not been met.)

Attorney does not meet any of the criteria for errors and omissions (malpractice) coverage set forth in Business and Professions Code section 6148.

**4. CLIENT'S DUTIES.** Client agrees to be truthful with Attorney, to cooperate, to keep Attorney informed of any information or developments which may come to Client's attention, to abide by this agreement, to pay Attorney's bills on time and to keep Attorney advised of Client's address, telephone number and whereabouts. Client will assist Attorney in providing necessary information and documents and will appear when necessary at legal proceedings.

**5. DEPOSIT.** Client agrees to pay Attorney an initial deposit of $_____ by _____. The hourly charges will be credited against the deposit. The initial deposit, as well as any future deposit, will be held in a trust account. Client authorizes Attorney to use that fund to pay the fees and other charges as they are incurred. Payments from the fund will be made upon remittance to client of a billing statement. Client acknowledges that the deposit is not an estimate of total fees and costs, but merely an advance for security.

Whenever the deposit is exhausted, Attorney reserves the right to demand further deposits, each up to a maximum of $_____. Once a trial or arbitration date is set, Client shall pay all sums then owing and deposit the attorneys' fees estimated to be incurred in preparing for and completing the trial or arbitration, as well as the jury fees or arbitration fees, expert witness fees and other costs likely to be assessed. Those sums may exceed the maximum deposit.

Client agrees to pay all deposits after the initial deposit within ____ days of Attorney's demand. Unless otherwise agreed in writing, any unused deposit at the conclusion of Attorney's services will be refunded.

**6. LEGAL FEES AND BILLING PRACTICES.** Client agrees to pay by the hour at Attorney's prevailing rates for all time spent on Client's matter by Attorney's legal personnel. Current hourly rates for legal personnel are as follows:

| | |
|---|---|
| Senior partners | _____/hour |
| Partners | _____/hour |
| Associates | _____/hour |
| Paralegals | _____/hour |
| Law clerks | _____/hour |

These sample written fee agreement forms are intended to satisfy the basic requirements of Business & Professions Code Section 6148 but may not address varying contractual obligations which may be present in a particular case. The State Bar makes no representation of any kind, express or implied, concerning the use of these forms.

1

The rates on this schedule are subject to change on 30 day written notice to client. If Client declines to pay any increased rates, Attorney will have the right to withdraw as Attorney for Client.

The time charged will include the time Attorney spends on telephone calls relating to Client's matter, including calls with Client, witnesses, opposing counsel or court personnel. The legal personnel assigned to Client's matter may confer among themselves about the matter, as required and appropriate. When they do confer, each person will charge for the time expended, as long as the work done is reasonably necessary and not duplicative. Likewise, if more than one of the legal personnel attends a meeting, court hearing or other proceeding, each will charge for the time spent. Attorney will charge for waiting time in court and elsewhere and for travel time, both local and out of town.

Time is charged in minimum units of one tenth (.1) of an hour. The following have higher minimum charges:

Telephone calls: _____

Letters: _____

Other: _____

## 7. COSTS AND OTHER CHARGES.

*(a) In General* Attorney will incur various costs and expenses in performing legal services under this Agreement. Client agrees to pay for all costs, disbursements and expenses in addition to the hourly fees. The costs and expenses commonly include, service of process charges, filing fees, court and deposition reporters' fees, jury fees, notary fees, deposition costs, long distance telephone charges, messenger and other delivery fees, postage, photocopying and other reproduction costs, travel costs including parking, mileage, transportation, meals and hotel costs, investigation expenses, consultants' fees, expert witness, professional, mediator, arbitrator and/or special master fees and other similar items. Except for the items listed below, all costs and expenses will be charged at Attorney's cost.

In-office photocopying _____ /page

Facsimile charges _____ /page

Mileage _____ /mile

Other: _____

*(b) Out of Town Travel* Client agrees to pay transportation, meals, lodging and all other costs of any necessary out-of-town travel by Attorney's personnel. Client will also be charged the hourly rates for the time legal personnel spend travelling.

*(c) Experts, Consultants and Investigators* To aid in the preparation or presentation of Client's case, it may become necessary to hire expert witnesses, consultants or investigators. Client agrees to pay such fees and charges. Attorney will select any expert witnesses, consultants or investigators to be hired and Client will be informed of persons chosen and their charges.

Additionally, Client understands that if the matter proceeds to court action or arbitration, Client may be required to pay fees and/or costs to other parties in the action. Any such payment will be entirely the responsibility of Client.

**8. BILLING STATEMENTS.** Attorney will send Client periodic statements for fees and costs incurred. Each statement will be payable within _____ days of its mailing date. Client may request a statement at intervals of no less than 30 days. If Client so requests, Attorney will provide one within 10 days. The statements shall include the amount, rate, basis of calculation or other method of determination of the fees and costs, which costs will be clearly identified by item and amount.

**9. LIEN.** Client hereby grants Attorney a lien on any and all claims or causes of action that are the subject of the representation under this Agreement. The lien will be for any sums owing to Attorney at the conclusion of services performed. The lien will attach to any recovery Client may obtain, whether by arbitration award, judgment, settlement or otherwise.

**10. DISCHARGE AND WITHDRAWAL.** Client may discharge Attorney at any time. Attorney may withdraw with Client's consent or for good cause. Good cause includes Client's breach of this agreement, refusal to cooperate or to follow Attorney's advice on a material matter or any fact or circumstance that would render Attorney's continuing representation unlawful or unethical. When Attorney's services conclude, all unpaid charges will immediately become due and payable. After services conclude, Attorney will, upon Client's request, deliver Client's file, and property in Attorney's possession, whether or not Client has paid for all services.

2

**11. DISCLAIMER OF GUARANTEE AND ESTIMATES.** Nothing in this agreement and nothing in Attorney's statements to Client will be construed as a promise or guarantee about the outcome of the matter. Attorney makes no such promises or guarantees. Attorney's comments about the outcome of the matter are expressions of opinion only. Any estimate of fees given by Attorney shall not be a guarantee. Actual fees may vary from estimates given.

**12. ENTIRE AGREEMENT.** This Agreement contains the entire Agreement of the parties. No other agreement, statement, or promise made on or before the effective date of this Agreement will be binding on the parties.

**13. SEVERABILITY IN EVENT OF PARTIAL INVALIDITY.** If any provision of this Agreement is held in whole or in part to be unenforceable for any reason, the remainder of that provision and of the entire Agreement will be severable and remain in effect.

**14. MODIFICATION BY SUBSEQUENT AGREEMENT.** This Agreement may be modified by subsequent Agreement of the parties only by an instrument in writing signed by both of them or an oral agreement only to the extent that the parties carry it out.

**15. EFFECTIVE DATE.** This Agreement will govern all legal services performed by Attorney on behalf of Client commencing with the date Attorney first performed services. The date at the beginning of this Agreement is for reference only. Even if this agreement does not take effect, Client will be obligated to pay Attorney the reasonable value of any services Attorney may have performed for Client.

THE PARTIES HAVE READ AND UNDERSTOOD THE FOREGOING TERMS AND AGREE TO THEM AS OF THE DATE ATTORNEY FIRST PROVIDED SERVICES. IF MORE THAN ONE CLIENT SIGNS BELOW, EACH AGREES TO BE LIABLE, JOINTLY AND SEVERALLY, FOR ALL OBLIGATIONS UNDER THIS AGREEMENT. CLIENT SHALL RECEIVE A FULLY EXECUTED DUPLICATE OF THIS AGREEMENT.

DATED: _____  _____
                                Stella King

                                Address: _____

                                _____

                                Telephone: _____


DATED: _____  CRANE, GARCIA & MOORE

                                By: _____
                                Linda H. Garcia, Partner

# STATE BAR SAMPLE WRITTEN FEE AGREEMENT
# HOURLY NON-LITIGATION

**Form No. 2**
**Hourly Non-Litigation Agreement**
**CRANE, GARCIA & MOORE**
**441 Bauchet Street**
**Los Angeles, CA 90012**
**(213) 680-9600**
**_____, 19__**

### ATTORNEY-CLIENT FEE AGREEMENT

This is the written fee agreement ("Agreement") that California law requires attorneys to have with their clients. Crane, Garcia & Moore ("Attorney") will provide legal services to Stella King ("Client") on the terms set forth below.

**1. CONDITIONS.** This Agreement will not take effect, and Attorney will have no obligation to provide legal services, until Client returns a signed copy of this Agreement and pays the initial deposit called for under Paragraph 5.

**2. SCOPE OF SERVICES.** Client hires Attorney to provide legal services in the following matter:_____ [describe matter]. Attorney will provide those legal services reasonably required to represent Client. Attorney will take reasonable steps to keep Client informed of progress and to respond to Client's inquiries. This Agreement does not cover litigation services of any kind, whether in court, arbitration, administrative hearings, or government agency hearings. Separate arrangements must be agreed to for those services. Services in any matter not described above will require a separate Agreement.

**3. INSURANCE DISCLOSURE.** (To be included only if the requirements of Business and Professions Code section 6148(a) (4) have not been met.)

Attorney does not meet any of the criteria for errors and omissions (malpractice) coverage set forth in Business and Professions Code section 6148.

**4. CLIENT'S DUTIES.** Client agrees to be truthful with Attorney, to cooperate, to keep Attorney informed of any information or developments which may come to Client's attention, to abide by this agreement, to pay Attorney's bills on time and to keep Attorney advised of Client's address, telephone number and whereabouts. Client will assist Attorney in providing information and documents necessary for the representation in the described matter.

**5. DEPOSIT.** Client agrees to pay Attorney an initial deposit of $_____ by _____.
The hourly charges will be credited against the deposit. The initial deposit, as well as any future deposit, will be held in a trust account. Client authorizes Attorney to use that fund to pay the fees and other charges as they are incurred. Payments from the fund will be made upon remittance to client of a billing statement. Client acknowledges that the deposit is not an estimate of total fees and costs, but merely an advance for security.

Whenever the deposit is exhausted, Attorney reserves the right to demand further deposits, each up to a maximum of $_____.

Client agrees to pay all deposits after the initial deposit within ____ days of Attorney's demand. Unless otherwise agreed in writing, any unused deposit at the conclusion of Attorney's services will be refunded.

**6. LEGAL FEES AND BILLING PRACTICES.** Client agrees to pay by the hour at Attorney's prevailing rates for all time spent on Client's matter by Attorney's legal personnel. Current hourly rates for legal personnel are as follows:

| Senior partners | _____/hour |
|---|---|
| Partners | _____/hour |
| Associates | _____/hour |
| Paralegals | _____/hour |
| Law clerks | _____/hour |

---

These sample written fee agreement forms are intended to satisfy the basic requirements of Business & Professions Code Section 6148 but may not address varying contractual obligations which may be present in a particular case. The State Bar makes no representation of any kind, express or implied, concerning the use of these forms.

1

The rates on this schedule are subject to change on 30 day written notice to client. If Client declines to pay any increased rates, Attorney will have the right to withdraw as Attorney for Client.

The time charged will include the time Attorney spends on telephone calls relating to Client's matter, including calls with Client and other parties and attorneys. The legal personnel assigned to Client's matter may confer among themselves about the matter, as required and appropriate. When they do confer, each person will charge for the time expended, as long as the work done is reasonably necessary and not duplicative. Likewise, if more than one of the legal personnel attends a meeting or other proceeding, each will charge for the time spent. Attorney will charge for waiting time and for travel time, both local and out of town.

Time is charged in minimum units of one tenth (.1) of an hour. The following have higher minimum charges:

Telephone calls: _____

Letters: _____

Other: _____

### 7. COSTS AND OTHER CHARGES.

*(a) In General* Attorney will incur various costs and expenses in performing legal services under this Agreement. Client agrees to pay for all costs, disbursements and expenses in addition to the hourly fees. The costs and expenses commonly include fees fixed by law or assessed by public agencies, long distance telephone charges, messenger and other delivery fees, postage, photocopying and other reproduction costs, travel costs including parking, mileage, transportation, meals and hotel costs, investigation expenses and consultants' fees and other similar items. Except for the items listed below, all costs and expenses will be charged at Attorney's cost.

In-office photocopying _____ /page

Facsimile charges _____ /page

Mileage _____ /mile

Other: _____

*(b) Out of Town Travel* Client agrees to pay transportation, meals, lodging and all other costs of any necessary out-of-town travel by Attorney's personnel. Client will also be charged the hourly rates for the time legal personnel spend travelling.

*(c) Consultants and Investigators* To aid in the representation in Client's matter, it may become necessary to hire consultants or investigators. Client agrees to pay such fees and charges. Attorney will select any consultants or investigators to be hired and Client will be informed of persons chosen and their charges.

**8. BILLING STATEMENTS.** Attorney will send Client periodic statements for fees and costs incurred. Each statement will be payable within _____ days of its mailing date. Client may request a statement at intervals of no less than 30 days. If Client so requests, Attorney will provide one within 10 days. The statements shall include the amount, rate, basis of calculation or other method of determination of the fees and costs, which costs will be clearly identified by item and amount.

**9. DISCHARGE AND WITHDRAWAL.** Client may discharge Attorney at any time. Attorney may withdraw with Client's consent or for good cause. Good cause includes Client's breach of this agreement, refusal to cooperate or to follow Attorney's advice on a material matter or any fact or circumstance that would render Attorney's continuing representation unlawful or unethical. When Attorney's services conclude, all unpaid charges will immediately become due and payable. After services conclude, Attorney will, upon Client's request, deliver Client's file, and property in Attorney's possession, whether or not Client has paid for all services.

**10. DISCLAIMER OF GUARANTEE AND ESTIMATES.** Nothing in this agreement and nothing in Attorney's statements to Client will be construed as a promise or guarantee about the outcome of the matter. Attorney makes no such promises or guarantees. Attorney's comments about the outcome of the matter are expressions of opinion only. Any estimate of fees given by Attorney shall not be a guarantee. Actual fees may vary from estimates given.

**11. ENTIRE AGREEMENT.** This Agreement contains the entire Agreement of the parties. No other agreement, statement, or promise made on or before the effective date of this Agreement will be binding on the parties.

**12. SEVERABILITY IN EVENT OF PARTIAL INVALIDITY.** If any provision of this Agreement is held in whole or in part to be unenforceable for any reason, the remainder of that provision and of the entire Agreement will be severable and remain in effect.

2

**13. MODIFICATION BY SUBSEQUENT AGREEMENT.** This Agreement may be modified by subsequent Agreement of the parties only by an instrument in writing signed by both of them or an oral agreement only to the extent that the parties carry it out.

**14. EFFECTIVE DATE.** This Agreement will govern all legal services performed by Attorney on behalf of Client commencing with the date Attorney first performed services. The date at the beginning of this Agreement is for reference only. Even if this agreement does not take effect, Client will be obligated to pay Attorney the reasonable value of any services Attorney may have performed for Client.

**THE PARTIES HAVE READ AND UNDERSTOOD THE FOREGOING TERMS AND AGREE TO THEM AS OF THE DATE ATTORNEY FIRST PROVIDED SERVICES. IF MORE THAN ONE CLIENT SIGNS BELOW, EACH AGREES TO BE LIABLE, JOINTLY AND SEVERALLY, FOR ALL OBLIGATIONS UNDER THIS AGREEMENT. THE CLIENT SHALL RECEIVE A FULLY EXECUTED DUPLICATE OF THIS AGREEMENT.**

DATED: _____    _____
                                  Stella King

                                  Address: _____

                                  _____

                                  Telephone: _____

DATED: _____    CRANE, GARCIA & MOORE

                                  By: _____
                                  Linda H. Garcia, Partner

3

# STATE BAR SAMPLE WRITTEN FEE AGREEMENTS
# OTHER CLAUSES OF INTEREST IN FEE AGREEMENTS

## OTHER CLAUSES OF INTEREST IN FEE AGREEMENTS

### 1. ARBITRATION CLAUSE

By initialing this arbitration provision, Client and Attorney are agreeing to have any and all disputes (except where Client may request arbitration of a fee dispute by the State Bar or local bar association as provided by Business and Professions Code Sections 6200, et seq.), that arise out of, or relate to this Agreement, including but not limited to claims of negligence or malpractice arising out of or relating to the legal services provided by Attorney to Client, decided only by binding arbitration in accordance with the rules of [insert name of arbitration provider] and not by court action, except as provided by California law for judicial review of arbitration proceedings. Judgment upon the award rendered by the arbitrator(s) may be entered in any court having jurisdiction thereof. Attorney and Client shall each have the right of discovery in connection with any arbitration proceeding in accordance with Code of Civil Procedure Section 1283.05.

In agreeing to this arbitration provision, ATTORNEY AND CLIENT ARE SPECIFICALLY GIVING UP:

    (I) ALL RIGHTS ATTORNEY AND CLIENT MAY POSSESS TO HAVE SUCH DISPUTES DECIDED IN A COURT OR JURY TRIAL; AND,

    (II) ALL JUDICIAL RIGHTS, INCLUDING THE RIGHT TO APPEAL FROM THE DECISION OF THE ARBITRATOR(S).

IF EITHER ATTORNEY OR CLIENT SHOULD REFUSE TO SUBMIT TO ARBITRATION, EITHER ATTORNEY OR CLIENT MAY BE COMPELLED TO ARBITRATE UNDER CALIFORNIA LAW. ATTORNEY AND CLIENT ACKNOWLEDGE THE ABOVE, AND THAT THIS MUTUAL AGREEMENT FOR BINDING ARBITRATION IS VOLUNTARY.

By initialing below, Client confirms that Client has read and understands this provision, and voluntarily agrees to binding arbitration. In doing so, Client voluntarily gives up important constitutional rights to trial by judge or jury, as well as rights to appeal. Client is advised that Client has the right to have independent counsel review this arbitration provision, and this entire agreement, prior to initialling this provision or signing this Agreement.

_____    _____
    (Client Initial Here)        (Attorney Initial Here)

[In addition to the foregoing clause in the body of the agreement, the following language should appear immediately above the signature line of the retainer agreement]

ARBITRATION NOTICE TO CLIENT:    IF THE ARBITRATION CLAUSE IN THIS AGREEMENT HAS BEEN INITIALED, CLIENT IS AGREEING TO HAVE ISSUES INCLUDING MALPRACTICE DECIDED BY BINDING ARBITRATION AND CLIENT IS GIVING UP CLIENT'S RIGHT TO A COURT OR JURY TRIAL FOR SUCH DISPUTES.

### 2. MEDIATION CLAUSE

If a dispute arises out of or relating to any aspect of this Agreement between Client and Attorney, or the breach thereof, and if the dispute cannot be settled through negotiation, Attorney and Client agree to discuss in good faith the use of mediation before resorting to arbitration, litigation, or any other dispute resolution procedure.

### 3. INTEREST CHARGES

If a billing statement is not paid when due, interest will be charged on the principal balance (fees, costs, and disbursements) shown on the statement. Interest will be calculated by multiplying the unpaid balance by the periodic rate of .833% per month (TEN PERCENT [10%] ANNUAL PERCENTAGE RATE). The unpaid balance will bear interest until paid.

[Interest may not be compounded without compliance with Civil Code section 1916-2.]

### 4. REPLENISHING DEPOSIT

To commence the representation, Client has provided [must provide] Attorney with a $_____ deposit. Attorney will hold the deposit in Attorney's trust account and apply it to each statement when rendered by Attorney. Client will pay any additional balance due upon receipt of Attorney's statements each month and also will replenish the deposit each month in the amount of all payments made to Attorney from the deposit. At the conclusion of the matter, the deposit will be applied to the final statement, in which event Client will be responsible for any amount due over and above the deposit or be entitled to a refund of any amount remaining after the final statement is satisfied in full.

1

## 5. SECURITY DEPOSIT

Attorney's obligation to render services to Client will be subject to Attorney's receipt of a refundable security deposit of $_____.
Attorney will apply $_____ of that deposit to the first fees and costs billed to Client pursuant to this Agreement, and will retain the remainder of the deposit in Attorney's trust account as security for Client's obligations to make timely payment of fees and costs pursuant to this Agreement. Attorney will thereafter apply the remaining deposit against what appears to be the last billing for the services rendered to Client pursuant to this Agreement. Client agrees to provide an additional security deposit of $_____ at least 120 days prior to the first scheduled trial date of the _____ matter.

## 6. ATTORNEYS' FEES CLAUSE

The prevailing party in any action or proceeding arising out of or to enforce any provision of this Agreement, with the exception of a fee arbitration or mediation under Business and Professions Code Sections 6200-6206, will be awarded reasonable attorneys' fees and costs incurred in that action or proceeding, or in the enforcement of any judgment or award rendered.

## 7. OTHER PAYOR CLAUSE—INSURANCE

Client has informed Attorney that Client may have insurance coverage which may pay for some or all of Attorney's fees which may become due under this Agreement. Attorney will make a claim with the insurer for compensation. It is understood, however, that if the insurance provider refuses or fails to pay Attorney for any reason, Client shall remain responsible for paying all Attorney's statements as they are rendered upon the billing and payment terms set forth in this Agreement. Should the insurance provider pay only a portion of the fees and costs, Client shall be responsible for the balance.

## 8. OTHER PAYOR CLAUSE—PERSONAL

Client has informed Attorney that Client has arranged for [employer/relative-name and relationship] to be responsible for some or all of Attorney's fees which may become due under this Agreement. It is understood that should [name] fail for any reason to pay Attorney's statements as they become due, Client shall remain responsible for paying all Attorney's statements as they are rendered upon the billing and payment terms set forth in this Agreement.

It is understood that the attorney/client relationship will only exist between Attorney and Client, and that [employer/relative-name] will have no right to information regarding the representation of Client by Attorney, and have no right to control or direct the Attorney in providing the services under this Agreement, unless specifically approved by Client.

[Provide signature line for employer/relative in Agreement.]

## 9. FIXED FEE CLAUSE

Client agrees to pay a fixed fee of $_____ for Attorney's services under this Agreement. The fixed fee is due by _____. Attorney shall have no obligation to provide services to Client until the fixed fee is paid in full. Unless Attorney withdraws before the completion of the services or otherwise fails to perform services contemplated under this Agreement, the fixed fee will be earned in full and no portion of it will be refunded once any material services have been performed.

## 10. "OTHER ATTORNEY" CLAUSE–CONTINGENCY

It is agreed that Attorney will associate with another attorney, [name], who will assist Attorney regarding the representation. [Name] will be compensated out of the fees which Attorney otherwise will earn under this Agreement based upon the effort and time he/she puts into the case. His/her compensation, however, will not increase the fee due from Client should Attorney obtain a recovery on behalf of Client.

## 11. "OTHER ATTORNEY" CLAUSE–HOURLY

It is agreed that Attorney will associate with another attorney, [name], who will assist Attorney regarding the representation. [Name] will be compensated by Attorney on an hourly basis at a rate of $____ per hour. These charges will be billed by Attorney to Client as a cost as defined in this Agreement. [or "billed directly to Client by the other attorney."]

2

Rev. #1 1998

# GUARANTEE AGREEMENT

GUARANTEE AGREEMENT

FOR AND IN CONSIDERATION OF .............................. ("Attorney") performing legal services on behalf of and extending credit to ................................... ("Client"), we ("Guarantors") guarantee to pay Attorney any indebtedness now or hereafter incurred by Client to Attorney under or in connection with the retainer agreement entered into between said Attorney and Client dated ..................... (OPTIONAL: *a copy of which is attached hereto*).

Said payment shall be made upon demand by Attorney and regardless of whether action is taken by Attorney to enforce payment of said indebtedness by Client.

This guarantee shall continue in full force and effect until we deliver written notice to Attorney not to extend further credit to Client. Delivery of such notice shall prevent liability on our part for any future indebtedness by Client to Attorney, but we shall remain fully liable upon all indebtedness then existing.

We understand and agree that our liability for payment of Client's obligations to Attorney (1) does not create an attorney-client relationship between us and Attorney; (2) does not entitle us to control the litigation or matters described in said retainer agreement; and (3) does not entitle us to notice of any proceedings, or to inspection of Attorney's files, or to information concerning Client's case.

In the event we fail to perform this guarantee agreement, we agree to pay in addition to any other sum due hereunder all costs reasonably incurred in enforcement of this guarantee agreement, including without limitation attorney fees and court costs.

Executed this .......... day of .........................., at ............................., California.


_____          _____
GUARANTOR                                       GUARANTOR

**RESERVED**

# CONTINGENCY FEE AGREEMENT

THIS IS AN AGREEMENT between_____*(name of client)*, hereafter referred to as "Client," and _____*(name of attorney)*, hereafter referred to as "Attorney." Unless a different Agreement is made *in writing*, this Agreement alone shall govern their respective rights and responsibilities.

1. **Claims Covered by Agreement:** Client retains Attorney to represent Client in connection with a claim for damages or other appropriate relief against whomever is responsible for the injury or loss suffered by Client arising out of the following incident or transaction:_____

   _____*(identify accident or other liability-creating facts by date, place, etc.)*

   This Agreement *does not cover* other related claims that may arise and may require legal services. (For example, workers' compensation claims; disputes with Client's own insurance company regarding coverage or amount of loss or reimbursement for benefits paid; disputes with health care providers regarding amount owed or reimbursement for benefits provided.) If such matters arise, separate agreements for legal services will be required if Client wishes Attroney to handle such matters.

2. **Services to be performed by Attorney:** Attorney agrees to perform the following legal services, if necessary, with respect to the claims described above:

   -- investigation of claims;
   -- determining responsible parties;
   -- preparation and filing of lawsuit;
   -- settlement procedures and negotiations;
   -- prosecution of claim by arbitration or legal action until award or judgment is obtained; and
   -- if judgment is obtained in Client's favor, opposing a motion for new trial by an opposing party.

   Attorney is authorized to associate or employ, at Attorney's own expense, other counsel to assist in performing the services required by this Agreement, and to appear on client's behalf in any proceeding or lawsuit.

3. **Services Not Covered by This Agreement:** If additional services are necessary in connection with Client's claims, and Client requests Attorney to perform such services, additional fee arrangements must be made between Attorney and Client. Such additional services may be required, for example:

   -- in defense of any lawsuit, cross-complaint or other cross-demand filed against Client in connection with the above matter or otherwise;
   -- if the judgment obtained is *not* in Client's favor, or the amount thereof is unsatisfactory to Client;
   -- if the judgment obtained is in Client's favor, and an opposing party appeals from the judgment;
   -- if a retrial is ordered after a motion for new trial or mistrial, or reversal of the judgment on appeal; or
   -- in judgment enforcement proceedings.

4. **No Guarantee as to Result:** Client acknowledges that Attorney has made no guarantee as to the outcome or the amounts recoverable in connection with Client's claims.

5. **Litigation Costs and Expenses:** Attorney is authorized to incur reasonable costs and expenses in performing legal services under this Agreement. Client agrees to pay for such costs and expenses in addition to the contingency fee discussed below. *(OPTIONAL: Attorney agrees to obtain Client's prior approval before incurring any costs or expenses exceeding $_____)*

    (a) *Particular costs and expenses:* The costs and expenses necessary in this case may include any or all of the following items. (The list is not exclusive; other items may also be necessary; and the rates shown are subject to change on prior written notice to client.)

        -- court filing fees
        -- process serving fees
        -- fees to private investigators
        -- fees to photographers or graphic artists
        -- fees to experts for consultation and/or for appearance at deposition or trial
        -- jury fees
        -- mail, messenger and other delivery charges
        -- parking and other local travel at\_\_\_\_/mile
        -- transportation, meals, lodging and all other costs of necessary out-of-town travel
        -- long distance telephone charges
        -- photocopying (in office) at\_\_\_\_/page
        -- word processing charges at\_\_\_\_/page
        -- computerized legal research at\_\_\_\_/hour
        -- other computer time at\_\_\_\_/hour

    (b) *Client's responsibility re costs:* Attorney may advance such costs and expenses on Client's behalf, but is not obligated to do so. Client agrees to reimburse Attorney upon demand for any such advances. Client is responsible for such reimbursement regardless of the status or outcome of the litigation, or the amount of any recovery.

6. **Contingency Fee to Attorney:** Client acknowledges that he/she has been advised by Attorney and is aware that contingency fee arrangements are not set by law, and that a contingency fee between Attorney and Client is negotiable. *(OPTIONAL: except that contingency fees in claims against health care providers may not exceed limits contained in Bus. & Prof.C. §6146).*

Bearing in mind that the contingency fee is negotiable, Client agrees that the following fee arrangement is fair and reasonable, and to pay Attorney the following amount:

    If the matter is settled before a lawsuit is filed, an amount equal to \_\_\_\_percent (\_\_%) of any recovery obtained by way of settlement, judgment or compromise, as computed below.

    If the matter is settled after a lawsuit is filed, but before the case is first assigned a trial date, an amount equal to \_\_\_\_percent (\_\_%) of any such recovery.

    Thereafter, an amount equal to \_\_\_\_percent (\_\_%) of any such recovery.

    (a) *Costs and expenses as affecting contingency fee:* Costs and expenses paid in connection with Client's claim shall be reimbursed before the contingency fee is computed. (For example, if the claim is settled for $1,000, and $100 has been expended for litigation costs, the net recovery is $900, and the contingency fee shall be based on that amount.) Client's share of the recovery shall be the balance remaining after reimbursement of such costs and expenses and payment of the contingency fee.

(b) *Setoffs and cross-complaints do not affect contingency fee:* The amount of recovery for purpose of this agreement shall be computed without regard to any setoff, counterclaim, cross-complaint or other demand for affirmative relief asserted by any party against Client, whether or not related to the claims covered by this agreement.

(c) *Form of recovery as affecting contingency fee:* If the recovery consists of payments to be made over a period of time, or other property not entirely cash or cash-equivalent, the contingency fee shall be based on the *present cash value* of the recovery as determined by generally recognized accounting and appraisal standards. (For example, if the recovery consists of $1,000 payable at $100/year over 10 years, its present value may be approximately $380, depending on prevalent interest rates.) The contingency fee shall be paid out of *the first funds or property received* by Client.

(d) *Sanctions awards not part of recovery:* Monetary sanctions awarded to Attorney during the course of this litigation shall not be considered part of Client's recovery in this action. Such sanctions shall be deemed compensation to counsel for extraordinary time and effort expended as a result of an opposing party's bad faith conduct or failure to comply with discovery demands, court orders or similar obligations. But if the sanctions award includes a costs item (such as the filing fee for making a motion), the amount thereof shall be credited to Client's costs account when received by Attorney.

(e) *Fee award by court not a limit on contingency fee:* Any fee awarded by the court, pursuant to statute or contract, in connection with the subject matter of this representation, shall be paid to Attorney and shall be applied against Client's fee obligation under this Agreement, but shall not limit or discharge Client's fee obligation.

7. **Effect of Withdrawal by Attorney:** Attorney may withdraw as counsel for Client for good cause. "Good cause" shall include without limitation, Client's failure to cooperate with Attorney, failure to comply with this Agreement, or requesting Attorney to act in a manner that would violate the Rules of Professional Conduct of the State Bar of California. Such withdrawal shall not affect Client's obligation to reimburse Attorney for costs previously incurred. In addition, Attorney shall be entitled to the reasonable value of legal services performed prior to withdrawal, to be paid by Client from any subsequent recovery on the claims covered by this Agreement.

The reasonable value of Attorney's services prior to withdrawal shall be based on the following factors: the number of hours expended; Attorney's hourly rates; Attorney's experience, reputation and ability; the amount of recovery; and the extent to which Attorney's services have contributed to the recovery.

8. **Effect of Discharge by Client:** Client shall have the right to discharge Attorney at any time upon written notice to Attorney. Such discharge shall not affect Client's obligation to reimburse Attorney for costs incurred prior to

such discharge. In addition, Attorney shall be entitled to the reasonable value of legal services performed prior to such discharge to be paid by Client from any subsequent recovery on claims covered by this Agreement. Such reasonable value shall be based on the factors enumerated in the preceding paragraph.

9. **Attorney's Lien:** To secure payment to attorney of all sums due under this Agreement for services rendered or costs advanced, Client hereby grants Attorney a lien on Client's claim and any cause of action or lawsuit filed thereon, and to any recovery Client may obtain, whether by settlement, judgment or otherwise.

10. **Insurance Disclosure:** Our firm maintains errors and omissions (malpractice) insurance coverage.

(*OR* "Our firm does not maintain errors and omissions insurance coverage but has filed with the State Bar a written agreement guaranteeing payment of client claims for errors and omissions in the amount specified in Rule IV, Section B, paragraph 1(c), of the Law Corporation Rules of the State Bar.")

(*OR* "Our firm is a law corporation that has provided security for client claims for errors and omissions in one of the manners provided in Rule IV, Section B, of the Law Corporation Rules of the State Bar.")

(*OR* "Our firm does not maintain errors and omissions insurance coverage or meet any of the other criteria set forth in Business & Professions Code §6147(a)(6).")

11. (OPTIONAL) **Arbitration of Disputes:** *Any dispute arising between Attorney and Client as to fees or costs shall be arbitrated pursuant to the provisions of Business & Professions Code §6200 et seq.* (No agreement for binding arbitration of such disputes can be made until after such a dispute has arisen; see Bus. & Prof.C. §6204.)

*Any other dispute arising under this Agreement or in connection with Attorney's services hereunder, including any claim for malpractice, shall be resolved by binding arbitration in accordance with the rules of* _____ (e.g., American Arbitration Association, or JAMS, or CCP §1280 et seq.) *and in accordance with the following provisions:*

*The arbitrator shall be empowered to order the losing party in the arbitration to reimburse the prevailing party for all expenses incurred in connection with the arbitration, including without limitation the arbitrator's fees and reasonable attorney fees and costs.*

*Attorney has explained to Client regarding such arbitration that:*
*--the parties are waiving their right to a jury trial and to seek remedies available in court proceedings;*
*--prearbitration discovery is generally more limited than and different from court proceedings;*
*--the arbitrator's award is not required to include factual findings or legal reasoning; and*
*--any party's right to appeal or to seek modification of the award is strictly limited and that the award is final and binding on the parties.*

*You acknowledge that we have explained to you that such binding arbitration may deprive you of various rights that you otherwise might have in a legal action, including without limitation the right to a jury trial, the right to appeal, and full discovery rights.*

_____
(Client's initials)

12.      **Client's Receipt of Agreement and Knowledge of Terms:**    Client acknowledges that he/she has read and fully understands all of the terms and conditions of this Agreement before signing it, and has received a copy of this Agreement upon execution thereof.

Executed at _____*(place)* on _____.

CLIENT                              ATTORNEY


_____        _____


_____        _____
Address                            Address

_____        _____


_____        _____
Telephone                          Telephone


(OPTIONAL)

WITNESSED BY:


_____


_____
Address


_____
Telephone

# [FORM 1:B.1]

# STATE BAR SAMPLE CONTINGENCY FEE AGREEMENT

**Form No. 3**
**Contingency Fee Agreement**
**CRANE, GARCIA & MOORE**
**441 Bauchet Street**
**Los Angeles, CA 90012**
**(213) 680-9600**
**_____, 19 __**

### ATTORNEY-CLIENT CONTINGENCY FEE AGREEMENT

This is the written fee agreement (the "Agreement") that California law requires attorneys to have with their clients. CRANE, GARCIA & MOORE ("Attorney"), will provide legal services to STELLA KING ("Client"), on the terms set forth below.

**1. CONDITIONS.** This Agreement will not take effect, and Attorney will have no obligation to provide legal services, until Client returns a signed copy of this Agreement and pays the initial deposit, if any, called for under Paragraph 8.

**2. SCOPE OF SERVICES.** Client is hiring Attorney to represent Client in the matter of Client's claims against _____ _____ [and possibly others as future investigation may indicate], arising out of _____. which occurred on or about _____.

If a court action is filed, Attorney will represent Client until a settlement or judgment, by way of arbitration or trial, is reached. Attorney will oppose any motion for a new trial or any other post-trial motions filed by an opposing party, or will make any appropriate post-trial motions on Client's behalf. After judgment Attorney will not represent Client on any appeal, or in any proceedings designed to execute on the judgment, without such additional compensation as may be agreed upon in a separate Agreement.

**3. INSURANCE DISCLOSURE.** (To be included only if the requirements of Business and Professions Code section 6147(a)(6) have not been met.) Attorney does not meet any of the criteria for errors and omissions (malpractice) coverage set forth in Business and Professions Code section 6147.

**4. RESPONSIBILITIES OF THE PARTIES.** Attorney will provide those legal services reasonably required to represent Client in prosecuting the claims described in paragraph 2 and will take reasonable steps to keep Client informed of progress and developments, and to respond promptly to inquiries and communications. Client agrees to be truthful with Attorney, to cooperate, to keep Attorney informed of any information and developments which may come to Client's attention, to abide by this Agreement, to pay Attorney's bills for costs on time, and to keep Attorney advised of Client's address, telephone number and whereabouts. Client agrees to appear, at all legal proceedings when Attorney deems it necessary, and to generally cooperate fully with Attorney in all matters related to the preparation and presentation of Client's claims.

**5. LEGAL FEES.** Attorney will only be compensated for legal services rendered if a recovery is obtained for Client. If no recovery is obtained, Client will be obligated to pay only for costs, disbursements and expenses, as described in Paragraph 7.

The fee to be paid to Attorney will be a percentage of the "net recovery," depending on the stage at which the settlement or judgment is reached. The term "net recovery" means: (1) the total of all amounts received by settlement, arbitration award or judgment, including any award of attorneys fees, (2) minus all costs and disbursements set forth in Paragraph 9. [Net recovery shall also include the reasonable value of any non-monetary proceeds.]

Attorney's fee shall be calculated as follows:

(i) If the matter is resolved before filing a lawsuit or formal initiation of proceedings, then Attorney's fee will be __ percent (_%) of the net recovery;

(ii) If the matter is resolved prior to [____] days before the date initially set for the trial or arbitration of the matter then Attorney's fee will be _____ percent (_%) of the net recovery; and

(iii) If the matter is resolved after the times set forth in (i) and (ii), above, then Attorney's fee will be _____ percent (_%) of the net recovery.

In the event of Attorney's discharge or withdrawal as provided in Paragraph 13, Client agrees that, upon payment of the settlement,

---

These sample written fee agreement forms are intended to satisfy the basic requirements of Business & Professions Code Section 6147 but may not address varying contractual obligations which may be present in a particular case. The State Bar makes no representation of any kind, express or implied, concerning the use of these forms.

1

Rev. #1 2001

arbitration award or judgment in Client's favor in this matter. Attorney shall be entitled to be paid by Client a reasonable fee for the legal services provided. Such fee shall be determined by considering the following factors:

(1) the actual number of hours expended by Attorney in performing legal services for Client;

(2) Attorney's hourly rates;

(3) the extent to which Attorney's services have contributed to result obtained;

(4) the amount of the fee in proportion to the value of the services performed;

(5) the amount of recovery obtained;

(6) time limitations imposed on Attorney by Client or by the circumstances; and

(7) the experience, reputation and ability of personnel performing the services.

**6. NEGOTIABILITY OF FEES.** The rates set forth above are not set by law, but are negotiable between an attorney and client.

**7. COSTS AND LITIGATION EXPENSES.** Attorney will incur various costs and expenses in performing legal services under this Agreement. Client agrees to pay for all costs, disbursements and expenses paid or owed by Client in connection with this matter, or which have been advanced by Attorney on Client's behalf and which have not been previously paid or reimbursed to Attorney. Costs, disbursements and litigation expenses commonly include court fees, jury fees, service of process charges, court and deposition reporters' fees, photocopying and reproduction costs, notary fees, long distance telephone charges, messenger and other delivery fees, postage, deposition costs, travel costs including parking, mileage, transportation, meals and hotel costs, investigation expenses, consultant, expert witness, professional mediator, arbitrator and/or special master fees and other similar items. Except for the items listed below, costs and expenses will be charged at our cost.

In-office photocopying _____ /page

Facsimile charges _____ /page

Mileage _____ /mile

Other: _____

Client understands that, as set forth in Paragraph 8, below, a deposit for costs may be required before the expenditure is made by Attorney.

To aid in the preparation or presentation of Client's case, it may become necessary to hire expert witnesses, consultants or investigators. Attorney will select any expert witnesses, consultants or investigators to be hired and Client will be informed of persons chosen and their charges.

Client authorizes Attorney to incur all reasonable costs and to hire any investigators, consultants or expert witnesses reasonably necessary in Attorney's judgment unless one or both of the clauses below are initialed by Attorney.

_____ Attorney shall obtain Client's consent before incurring any costs in excess of $_____.

_____ Attorney shall obtain Client's consent before retaining outside investigators, consultants, or expert witnesses.

If an award of fees and/or costs is sought on Client's behalf in this action, Client understands that the amount which the court may order as fees and/or costs is the amount the court believes the party is entitled to recover, and does not determine what fees and/or costs Attorney is entitled to charge its clients or that only the fees and/or costs which were allowed were reasonable. Client agrees that, whether or not attorneys fees or costs are awarded by the court in Client's case, Client will remain responsible for

2

the payment, in full, of all attorney's fees and costs in accordance with this Agreement.

Additionally, Client understands that if Client's case proceeds to court action or arbitration, Client may be required to pay fees and/or costs to other parties in the action. Any such award will be entirely the responsibility of Client.

**8. DEPOSIT.** Client agrees to pay Attorney an initial deposit for costs of $_____ , to be returned with this signed Agreement. Attorney will hold this initial deposit in a trust account. Client hereby authorizes Attorney to use that deposit to pay the costs, disbursements and other expenses incurred under this Agreement.

When Client's deposit is exhausted, Attorney reserves the right to demand further deposits, each up to a maximum of $_____ . Once a trial or arbitration date is set, Attorney will require Client to pay all sums then owing, and to deposit the costs Attorney estimates will be incurred in preparing for and completing the trial or arbitration, as well as the jury fees or arbitration fees likely to be assessed. Those sums may exceed the maximum deposit.

Client agrees to pay all deposits required under this Agreement within 10 days of Attorney's demand. Any deposit that is unused at the conclusion of Attorney's services will be refunded.

**9. MONTHLY BILLING STATEMENTS.** Attorney will send Client monthly billing statements for costs, disbursements and expenses incurred in connection with this matter. Each statement is to be paid in full within 15 days after the date of such statement.

**10. APPROVAL NECESSARY FOR SETTLEMENT.** Attorney will not make any settlement or compromise of any nature of any of Client's claims without Client's prior approval. Client retains the absolute right to accept or reject any settlement. Client agrees to seriously consider any settlement offer Attorney recommends before making a decision to accept or reject such offer. Client agrees not to make any settlement or compromise of any nature of any of Client's claims without prior notice to Attorney.

**11. LIMITATION OF REPRESENTATION.** Attorney is representing Client only on the matter described in paragraph 2. Attorney's representation does not include independent or related matters that may arise, including, among other things, claims for property damage, workers' compensation, disputes with a health care provider about the amount owed for their services, or claims for reimbursement (subrogation) by any insurance company for benefits paid under an insurance policy.

This Agreement also does not include defending Client against, or representing Client in any claims that may be asserted against Client as a cross-claim or counter-claim in Client's case. This Agreement does not apply to any other legal matters. If any such matters arise later, Attorney and Client will either negotiate a separate Agreement if Client and Attorney agree that Attorney will perform such additional legal work or Client will engage separate counsel with respect to the cross-claim or counter-claim or additional legal work.

**12. DISCHARGE AND WITHDRAWAL.** Client may discharge Attorney at any time, upon written notice to Attorney. Attorney may withdraw from representation of Client (a) with Client's consent (b) upon court approval, or (c) if no court action has been filed, for good cause and upon reasonable notice to Client. Good cause includes Client's breach of this contract, Client's refusal to cooperate with Attorney or to follow Attorney's advice on a material matter or any other fact or circumstance that would render Attorney's continuing representation unlawful or unethical.

Notwithstanding Attorney's withdrawal or Client's notice of discharge, and without regard to the reasons for the withdrawal or discharge, Client will remain obligated to pay Attorney for all costs incurred prior to the termination and, in the event that there is any net recovery obtained by Client after conclusion of Attorney's services, Client remains obligated to pay Attorney for the reasonable value of all services rendered from the effective date of this Agreement to the date of discharge.

**13. CONCLUSION OF SERVICES.** When Attorney's services conclude, all unpaid charges will immediately become due and payable. Attorney is authorized to use any funds held in Attorney's trust account as a deposit against costs to apply to such unpaid charges. After Attorney's services conclude, upon request, Client's file and property will be delivered to Client, Client's Attorney's whether or not Client has paid any fees and/or costs owed to Attorney.

**14. LIEN.** Client hereby grants Attorney a lien on any and all claims or causes of action that are the subject of Attorney's representation under this Agreement. Attorney's lien will be for any sums owing to Attorney for any unpaid costs, or attorneys' fees, at the conclusion of Attorney's services. The lien will attach to any recovery Client may obtain, whether by arbitration award, judgment, settlement or otherwise.

**15. RECEIPT OF PROCEEDS.** All proceeds of Client's case shall be deposited into Attorney's trust account for disbursement in accordance with the provisions of this Agreement.

**16. DISCLAIMER OF GUARANTEE.** Nothing in this Agreement and nothing in Attorney's statements to Client will be construed as a promise or guarantee about the outcome of this matter. Attorney makes no such promises or guarantees. There can be no assurance that Client will recover any sum or sums in this matter. Attorney's comments about the outcome of this matter are expressions of opinion only. Client acknowledges that Attorney has made no promise or guarantees about the outcome.

3

**17. ENTIRE AGREEMENT.** This Agreement contains the entire agreement of the parties. No other agreement, statement or promise made on or before the effective date of this Agreement will be binding on the parties.

**18. SEVERABILITY IN EVENT OF PARTIAL INVALIDITY.** If any provision of this Agreement is held in whole or in part to be unenforceable for any reason, the remainder of that provision and of the entire Agreement will be severable and remain in effect.

**19. MODIFICATION BY SUBSEQUENT AGREEMENT.** This Agreement may be modified by subsequent agreement of the parties only by an instrument in writing signed by both of them or an oral agreement only to the extent that the parties carry it out.

**20. EFFECTIVE DATE.** This Agreement will govern all legal services performed by Attorney on behalf of Client commencing with the date Attorney first performed services. The date at the beginning of the Agreement is for reference only. Even if this Agreement does not take effect, Client will be obligated to pay Attorney the reasonable value of any services Attorney may have performed for Client.

**THE PARTIES HAVE READ AND UNDERSTOOD THE FOREGOING TERMS AND AGREE TO THEM, AS OF THE DATE ATTORNEY FIRST PROVIDED SERVICES. IF MORE THAN ONE CLIENT SIGNS BELOW, EACH AGREES TO BE LIABLE JOINTLY AND SEVERALLY FOR ALL OBLIGATIONS UNDER THIS AGREEMENT. THE CLIENT SHALL RECEIVE A FULLY EXECUTED DUPLICATE OF THIS AGREEMENT.**

DATED: _____     _____
                                   Stella King

                                   Address: _____

                                   telephone: _____

DATED: _____     CRANE, GARCIA & MOORE

                                   By: _____
                                   Linda H. Garcia, Partner

4

# NOTICE OF LIEN

```
1   ..........................
    ..........................
2   ..........................
    ..........................
3   State Bar No.:............

4

5   Former Attorney of Record
    for Plaintiff ............
6

7

8           SUPERIOR COURT OF THE STATE OF CALIFORNIA

9                   COUNTY OF ..........

10

11  ..........................., )    Case No: .....................
                                  )
12          Plaintiff,            )
                                  )
13  vs.                           )    NOTICE OF LIEN
                                  )
14  ..........................,   )
                                  )
15          Defendants.           )
    _____)
16
```

17      TO ALL PARTIES AND TO THEIR COUNSEL, AND TO ALL OTHER PERSONS

18  OR ENTITIES INTERESTED IN THIS ACTION.

19      PLEASE TAKE NOTICE THAT the undersigned law firm was formerly

20  the attorney of record herein for .............. *(name of client)*

21  ...................................; but has been relieved as said

22  party's attorney of record by ............ *(court order dated; or*

23  *substitution of counsel filed)* ................. .

24      PLEASE TAKE FURTHER NOTICE THAT by virtue of a written fee

25  agreement with said party dated ......................, the under-

26  signed law firm has and claims a lien ahead of all others on the

27  said party's claims and causes of action asserted herein, and on

28  any judgment rendered in favor of said party, to secure payment for

                                1

                          NOTICE OF LIEN

legal services rendered *(and costs and expenses advanced on behalf of said party)*, all in accordance with the terms of the fee agreement aforesaid.

Dated: ..........................

/s/ _____

Rev. #1 2004

# PETITION TO CONFIRM, CORRECT, OR VACATE ATTORNEY-CLIENT FEE ARBITRATION AWARD

ADR-103

| ATTORNEY OR PARTY WITHOUT ATTORNEY *(Name, State Bar number, and address )*: | FOR COURT USE ONLY |
|---|---|
| TELEPHONE NO.      FAX NO. *(Optional)*: <br> E–MAIL ADDRESS *(Optional)*: <br> ATTORNEY FOR *(Name)*: | |

**SUPERIOR COURT OF CALIFORNIA, COUNTY OF**
STREET ADDRESS:
MAILING ADDRESS:
CITY AND ZIP CODE:
BRANCH NAME:

PETITIONER:

RESPONDENT:

**PETITION TO** ☐ **CONFIRM** ☐ **CORRECT** ☐ **VACATE**
**ATTORNEY-CLIENT FEE ARBITRATION AWARD**

**Jurisdiction** *(check all that apply):*

☐ **Action is a limited civil case**
    Amount demanded  ☐ does not exceed $10,000
                    ☐ exceeds $10,000, but does not exceed $25,000

☐ **Action is an unlimited civil case** (exceeds $25,000)

CASE NUMBER:

**NOTICE: Please read Alternative Dispute Resolution form ADR-105,** *Information Regarding Rights After Attorney-Client Fee Arbitration,* **promptly and before completing this form. There are short deadlines for requesting court relief after an attorney-client fee arbitration award. Do not use this form to reject a nonbinding attorney-client fee arbitration award and request a trial; use form ADR-104 instead.**

1. **Petitioner and respondent.** Petitioner *(name each):*

    alleges and requests relief against respondent *(name each):*

2. **Attorney-client fee dispute arbitration.** This petition is being filed after an attorney-client fee arbitration conducted under Business and Professions Code sections 6200–6206. Petitioner was
    a. ☐ the attorney involved in the fee dispute.
    b. ☐ the client involved in the fee dispute.

3. **Pending or new action.**
    a. ☐ A court case is already pending, and this is a petition filed in that action. *(If so, proceed to item 4.)*
    b. ☐ This petition commences a new action. *(If so, complete items 3b(1) through 3b(4).)*

        (1) **Petitioner's capacity.** Each petitioner named in item 1 is an individual,
            ☐ except petitioner *(state name and complete one or more of the following):*
            (a) ☐ is a corporation qualified to do business in California.
            (b) ☐ is an unincorporated entity *(specify):*
            (c) ☐ is a representative *(specify):*
            (d) ☐ is *(specify other capacity):*

        (2) **Respondent's capacity.** Each respondent named in item 1 is an individual,
            ☐ except petitioner *(state name and complete one or more of the following):*
            (a) ☐ is a business organization, form unknown.
            (b) ☐ is a corporation.
            (c) ☐ is an unincorporated entity *(specify):*
            (d) ☐ is a representative *(specify):*
            (e) ☐ is *(specify other capacity):*

Page 1 of 3

Form Approved for Optional Use
Judicial Council of California
ADR-103 [Rev. January 1. 2004]

PETITION TO CONFIRM, CORRECT, OR VACATE
ATTORNEY-CLIENT FEE ARBITRATION AWARD
(Alternative Dispute Resolution)

Business and Professions Code, § 6200 et seq.;
Code of Civil Procedure, § 1285 et seq.

| PETITIONER: | CASE NUMBER: |
|---|---|
| RESPONDENT: | |

3. b.    (3) **Amount or property in dispute.** This petition involves a dispute over *(check and complete all that apply):*

      (a) ☐ the following amount of money *(specify amount):* $

      (b) ☐ property *(if the dispute involves property, complete both of the following):*

         (i)   consisting of *(identify property in dispute):*

         (ii)  having a value of *(specify value of property in dispute):* $

    (4) **Venue.** This court is the proper court because *(complete (a) or (b)):*

      (a) ☐ this is the court in the county in which the arbitration was held.

      (b) ☐ the arbitration was not held exclusively in any county of California, **and**

         (i)   ☐ this is the court in the county where the agreement was made.

         (ii)  ☐ this is the court in the county where the agreement is to be performed.

         (iii) ☐ the agreement does not specify a county where it is to be performed and was not made in any county in California, and the following party resides or has a place of business in this county *(name of party):*

         (iv) ☐ the agreement does not specify a county where it is to be performed and was not made in any county in California, and no party to this action resides or has a place of business in California.

4. **Arbitrator.** The following person was duly selected or appointed as arbitrator *(name of each arbitrator):*

5. **Arbitration hearing.** The arbitration hearing was conducted as follows *(complete both of the following):*
   a. **Date** *(each date of arbitration):*
   b. **Location** *(city and state where arbitration was conducted):*

6. **Arbitration award.**
   a. **Date of award.** The arbitration award was made on *(date):*
   b. **Terms of award.** The arbitration award *(complete one or more of the following):*

      (1) ☐ requires ☐ the attorney ☐ the client   to pay the other party this amount: $

      (2) ☐ requires neither the attorney nor the client to pay the other anything.

      (3) ☐ provides *(specify other terms or check item 6(c) and attach a copy of the award):*

   c. ☐ **Attachment of Award.** A copy of the award is submitted as Attachment 6(c).

7. **Notice of award.** The notice of the arbitration award indicates that it was mailed to petitioner on *(date):*

8. **Binding award.** The arbitration award is binding because *(check all that apply):*
   a. ☐ after the fee dispute arose, the parties agreed in writing that the arbitration award would be binding.
   b. ☐ more than 30 days have passed since notice of the award was mailed, and no party has filed a rejection of the award and request for trial.

9. ☐  **Willful nonappearance.** Thirty days have not passed since notice of the award was mailed; however, respondent willfully failed to appear at the arbitration hearing. The award ☐ does ☐ does not  refer to respondent's nonappearance.

10. **Petitioner requests that the court** *(check all that apply):*
   a. ☐ **Confirm the award and enter judgment according to it.**
   b. ☐ **Correct the award and enter judgment according to the corrected award, as follows:**

     (1) The award should be corrected because *(check all that apply):*

      (a) ☐ the amount of the award was not calculated correctly, or a person, thing, or property was not described correctly.

      (b) ☐ the arbitrator exceeded his or her authority.

      (c) ☐ the award is imperfect as a matter of form.

**PETITION TO CONFIRM, CORRECT, OR VACATE
ATTORNEY-CLIENT FEE ARBITRATION AWARD
(Alternative Dispute Resolution)**

| PETITIONER: | CASE NUMBER: |
|---|---|
| RESPONDENT: | |

**10. b.**  (2)  The facts supporting the grounds for correcting the award alleged in item 10b(1) are as follows *(if additional space is required, check here* ☐ *and submit facts on an attachment labeled 10b(2)):*

(3)  The award should be corrected as follows *(if additional space is required, check here* ☐ *and describe requested correction on an attachment labeled 10b(3)):*

**c.** ☐ **Vacate (cancel) the award.**

(1) The award should be vacated because *(check all that apply):*
    (a) ☐ the award was obtained by corruption, fraud, or other unfair means.
    (b) ☐ an arbitrator was corrupt.
    (c) ☐ the misconduct of a neutral arbitrator substantially prejudiced petitioner's rights.
    (d) ☐ the arbitrator exceeded his or her authority, and the award cannot be fairly corrected.
    (e) ☐ the arbitrator unfairly refused to postpone the hearing or to hear evidence useful to settle the dispute.
    (f) ☐ an arbitrator failed to disclose within the time for disclosure a ground for disqualification of which the arbitrator was then aware.
    (g) ☐ an arbitrator should have disqualified himself or herself after petitioner made a demand to do so.

(2) The facts supporting the grounds for vacating the award alleged in item 10c(1) are as follows *(if additional space is required, check here* ☐ *and submit facts on an attachment labeled 10c(2)):*

(3) Petitioner ☐ does ☐ does not request a new arbitration hearing.

**d.** ☐ **Award petitioner interest** from *(date):*
    (1) ☐ at the statutory rate.
    (2) ☐ at the rate of ____ % per year.

**e.** ☐ **Award petitioner costs of suit:**
    (1) ☐ in the amount of: $
    (2) ☐ according to proof.

**f.** ☐ **Award petitioner attorney fees incurred in this action** *(attorney fees incurred in preparation for or in the course of the fee arbitration proceeding are not recoverable):*
    (1) ☐ in the amount of: $
    (2) ☐ according to proof.

**g.** ☐ **Award petitioner the following other relief** *(describe relief requested; if additional space is required, check here* ☐ *and describe relief on an attachment labeled 10g):*

**11. Pages and attachments.** Number of pages attached:

Date:

▶

_____
(TYPE OR PRINT NAME)

_____
(SIGNATURE OF PETITIONER OR ATTORNEY)

ADR-103 [Rev. January 1  2004]

**PETITION TO CONFIRM, CORRECT, OR VACATE
ATTORNEY-CLIENT FEE ARBITRATION AWARD
(Alternative Dispute Resolution)**

Page 3 of 3

**[FORM 1:B.4]**

# REJECTION OF AWARD AND REQUEST FOR TRIAL
# AFTER ATTORNEY-CLIENT FEE ARBITRATION

**ADR-104**

| | |
|---|---|
| ATTORNEY OR PARTY WITHOUT ATTORNEY *(Name, State Bar number, and address)* | *FOR COURT USE ONLY* |

TELEPHONE NO:          FAX NO *(Optional)*:
E-MAIL ADDRESS *(Optional)*:
ATTORNEY FOR *(Name)*:

**SUPERIOR COURT OF CALIFORNIA, COUNTY OF**
  STREET ADDRESS
  MAILING ADDRESS
  CITY AND ZIP CODE
  BRANCH NAME

PETITIONER:

RESPONDENT:

| | |
|---|---|
| **REJECTION OF AWARD AND REQUEST FOR TRIAL AFTER ATTORNEY-CLIENT FEE ARBITRATION** | |
| **Jurisdiction** *(check all that apply):* | |
| ☐ **Action is a limited civil case** | |
| Amount demanded ☐ does not exceed $10,000 | |
| ☐ exceeds $10,000, but does not exceed $25,000 | CASE NUMBER: |
| ☐ **Action is an unlimited civil case** (exceeds $25,000) | |

**NOTICE: Please read Alternative Dispute Resolution form ADR-105, *Information Regarding Rights After Attorney-Client Fee Arbitration*, promptly and before completing this form. There are short deadlines for requesting court relief after an attorney-client fee arbitration award. Do not use this form to confirm, correct, or vacate an attorney-client fee arbitration award; use form ADR-103 instead.**

1. **Petitioner and respondent.** Petitioner *(name each)*:

   alleges and requests relief against respondent *(name each)*:

2. **Attorney-client fee dispute arbitration.** This *Rejection of Award and Request for Trial* concerns an arbitration to determine disputed attorney fees that was conducted under Business and Professions Code sections 6200–6206. Petitioner was
   a. ☐ the attorney involved in the fee dispute.
   b. ☐ the client involved in the fee dispute.

3. **Pending or new action.**
   a. ☐ **Pending action.** A court case concerning the attorney-client fee dispute involved in the arbitration is already pending, and this *Rejection of Award and Request for Trial* is being filed in that action.
   b. ☐ **New action.** This *Rejection of Award and Request for Trial* is being filed with a complaint commencing a new action. *(A request for trial must be filed in a pending case or with a complaint commencing a new action.)*

Form Approved for Optional Use
Judicial Council of California
ADR-104 [New January 1, 2004]
**REJECTION OF AWARD AND REQUEST FOR TRIAL
AFTER ATTORNEY-CLIENT FEE ARBITRATION
(Alternative Dispute Resolution)**
Business and Professions Code, § 6200 et seq.;
Code of Civil Procedure, § 1285 et seq.

4. **Arbitration hearing.** The arbitration hearing was conducted as follows *(complete each of the following):*
   a. **Date** *(each date of arbitration):*

   b. **Location** *(city and state where arbitration was conducted):*
   c. **Appearances at the arbitration.** The arbitration hearing was conducted as follows *(check one of the following):*
      (1) ☐  Petitioner appeared at the arbitration hearing in person or by counsel.
      (2) ☐  Petitioner did not appear at the arbitration hearing. Petitioner's failure to appear was not willful because *(explain reasons for not appearing).*

5. **Arbitration award.**
   a. **Date of award.** The arbitration award was made on *(date):*
   b. **Amount of award.** The arbitration award *(complete one of the following):*
      (1) ☐  requires ☐ the attorney ☐ the client   to pay the other party this amount: $
      (2) ☐  requires neither the attorney nor the client to pay the other anything.
   c. ☐ **Failure to appear.** The arbitrator found that the following party willfully failed to appear at the arbitration hearing:
      (1) ☐  Petitioner *(name each):*
      (2) ☐  Respondent *(name each):*
   d. ☐ **Other provisions of award.** The award also provides *(specify other terms or complete item 5e and attach a copy of the award):*

   e. ☐ **Attachment of award.** A copy of the arbitration award is submitted as Attachment 5(e).

6. **Notice of award.** This *Rejection of Award and Request for Trial* is being filed within 30 days after notice of the award was mailed to petitioner. *(A trial after arbitration is available only if it is requested within 30 days after the notice of award was mailed to the party requesting the trial.)*
   a. The notice of the award indicates that it was mailed to petitioner on *(date):*
   b. ☐  Petitioner alleges that the award was actually mailed on *(date):*

7. **Nonbinding arbitration.** The parties did not agree in writing, at any time after the dispute over attorney fees or costs arose, to be bound by the arbitration award. *(A trial after arbitration is not available if the parties agreed in writing after the dispute arose that the award would be binding.)*
8. **Rejection of award and request for trial.** Petitioner rejects the arbitration award and requests a trial ("hearing de novo") in court to resolve the dispute over attorney fees and costs.
9. **Amount in dispute.** The amount of attorney fees and costs in dispute is *(amount):* $

10. **Pages and attachments.** Number of pages attached:

Date:

▶

_____
(TYPE OR PRINT NAME)

_____
(SIGNATURE OF PETITIONER OR ATTORNEY)

ADR-104 [New January 1, 2004]    **REJECTION OF AWARD AND REQUEST FOR TRIAL**    Page 2 of 2
**AFTER ATTORNEY-CLIENT FEE ARBITRATION**
**(Alternative Dispute Resolution)**

Rev. #1 2004                                                          1-208.5

**RESERVED**

**[FORM 1:C]**

# CLAIM AGAINST GOVERNMENTAL ENTITY
# (CITY OF LOS ANGELES)

FORM CONT. 100-A (Rev. 7/01)

| | |
|---|---|
| # CLAIM FOR DAMAGES<br>## TO PERSON OR PROPERTY | RESERVE FOR FILING STAMP<br><br>CLAIM NO. ———————— |

### INSTRUCTIONS

1. Claims for death, injury to person or to personal property must be filed not later than six months after the occurrence. (Gov. Code Sec. 911.2)
2. Claims for damages relating to any other type of occurrence must be filed not later than one year after the occurrence. (Gov. Code Sec. 911.2)
3. Read entire claim before filing. Claim can be mailed or filed in person. No faxes accepted.
4. See Page 2 for diagram upon which to locate place of accident.
5. This claim form must be signed on Page 2 at bottom.
6. Attach separate sheets, if necessary, to give full details. SIGN EACH SHEET.
7. Fill out in duplicate. ONE COPY TO BE RETAINED BY CLAIMANT.
8. Claim must be filed with CITY CLERK, (Gov. Code Sec. 915a)
   200 NORTH SPRING STREET, ROOM 395, CITY HALL, LOS ANGELES, CA 90012

TO: CITY OF LOS ANGELES

| Name of Claimant | | Age of Claimant |
|---|---|---|
| Home address of Claimant | City, State and Zip Code | Home Telephone Number |
| Business address of Claimant | City, State and Zip Code | Business Telephone Number |

Give address to which you desire notices or communications to be sent regarding this claim:

How did DAMAGE or INJURY occur? Please include as much detail as possible.

When did DAMAGE or INJURY occur? Please include the date and time of the damage or injury.

Where did DAMAGE or INJURY occur? Please describe fully, and locate on the diagram on the reverse side of this sheet. Where appropriate, please give street names and addresses or measurements from specific landmarks:

What particular ACT or OMISSION do you claim caused the injury or damage? Please give names of City employees causing the injruy or damage and identify any vehicles involved by license plate number, if known.

Please list the names and address of Witnesses, Doctors and Hospitals:

SEE PAGE 2 (OVER)                    THIS CLAIM MUST BE SIGNED ON REVERSE SIDE

What DAMAGE or INJURIES do you claim resulted? Please give full extent of injuries or damages claimed:

What is the AMOUNT of your claim? Please itemize your damages:

If you have received any insurance payments, please give the names of the insurance companies:

    For all accidents claims please place on the following diagram the names of the streets where the accident occurred and the nearest cross-streets; indicate the place of the accident by an "X" and by showing the nearest address and distances to street corners. Please indicate where North is on the diagram.

    Note: If the diagram does not fit the situation, please attach your own diagram.

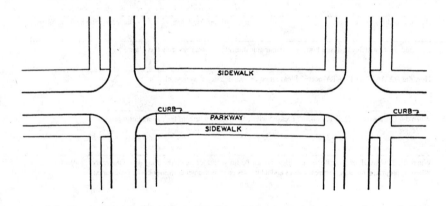

Signature of Claimant or person filing      Typed Name:      Date:
on claimant's behalf giving relationship
to claimant:

# CLAIM AGAINST GOVERNMENTAL ENTITY
## (CALIFORNIA STATE BOARD OF CONTROL)

State of California
Board of Control

## GOVERNMENT CLAIM

SBOC-GC-0002 (Rev. 6/00)

**Please read "Instructions for Filing a Claim"**

If you are filing this claim beyond six months from the incident date, please see instructions for filing a late claim application on the opposite page.

G_____

### Section 1: Claimant Information

Name of Claimant

Telephone Number (include area code)
( )

Mailing Address          City          State          Zip Code

### Section 2: Claim Information

Is the claim filed on behalf of a minor? ❏ Yes ❏ No  If yes, please indicate: Relationship to the minor_____  Date of birth of the minor_____

| Name of State Agency against which this claim is filed | Incident Date          Dollar Amount of Claim |
|---|---|
| | Month     Day     Yr. |
| If the amount exceeds $10,000, indicate type of civil case:<br><br>❏ Limited Civil Case    ❏ Non-Limited Civil Case | Explain how the dollar amount claimed was computed. (Attach three copies of the supporting documentation for the amount claimed with this form.) |
| Describe the specific damage or injury incurred as a result of the incident. | |
| | Location of the incident (If applicable, include street address, city or county, highway number, post mile number and direction of travel.) |
| | Preferred Hearing Location (If an appearance is necessary):<br>❏ Sacramento    ❏ Los Angeles<br>❏ Oakland    ❏ San Diego |

Explain the circumstances that led to the alleged damage or injury. State all facts that support your claim against the State of California, and why you believe the State is responsible for the alleged damage, or injury. If known, provide the name(s) of the State employee(s) who allegedly caused the injury, damage or loss. (If more space is needed, please attach additional sheets.)

_____
_____
_____
_____
_____
_____
_____
_____
_____
_____

State of California
Board of Control

# GOVERNMENT CLAIM

SBOC-GC-0002 (Rev. 6/00) Reverse

Submit completed claim form and three copies to:
STATE BOARD OF CONTROL
GOVERNMENT CLAIMS BRANCH
P.O. Box 3035
Sacramento, CA 95812-3035

## Section 3: Insurance Information (must be completed if claim involves a motor vehicle)

| Has the claim for the alleged damage/injury been filed or will it be filed with your insurance carrier? ☐ Yes ☐ No | Policy Number | Telephone number (include area code) ( ) |
|---|---|---|
| Mailing Address | City | State | Zip Code |
| Name of insurance carrier | Amount of Deductible $ |

Are you the registered owner?
☐ Yes ☐ No

Make:_____ Model:_____ Year:_____

## Section 4: FOR STATE AGENCY USE ONLY (must be completed by the State agency presenting claim)

| Name of State agency | Budget Act Appropriation or Item Number and the appropriate Schedule if applicable. |
|---|---|
| | Name of fund or account |
| Name of agency budget officer or representative | Title | CALNET Number |
| Signature of agency budget officer or representative | Date |

## Section 5: Representative Information (must be completed if claim is being filed by an attorney or authorized representative)

| Name of Attorney/Representative | Telephone Number (include area code) ( ) |
|---|---|
| Mailing Address | City | State | Zip |

## Section 6: Notice and Signature

Section 72 of the Penal Code provides that "every person who, with intent to defraud, presents for allowance or for payment to any State Board or Officer, or to any county, town, city, district, ward, or village, board or officer, authorized to allow or pay the same if genuine, any false or fraudulent claim, bill, account, voucher, or writing, is guilty of a felony."

Signature of Claimant                                      Date

Signature of Attorney/Representative                       Date

Rev. #1 2003

# APPLICATION FOR PERMISSION TO PRESENT LATE CLAIM AGAINST GOVERNMENTAL ENTITY

1 . . . . . . . . . . . . . . . . . . . . . . . . . . . . . . .
. . . . . . . . . . . . . . . . . . . . . . . . . . . . . . .
2 . . . . . . . . . . . . . . . . . . . . . . . . . . . . . . .
. . . . . . . . . . . . . . . . . . . . . . . . . . . . . . .
3 . . . . . . . . . . . . . . . . . . . . . . . . . . . . . . .
State Bar No. . . . . . . . . . . . . . . . . . .
4

5 Attorney for . . . . . . . . . . . . . . . . . . . . .

6

7

8 In the matter of the Claim of                    )
                                                   )   APPLICATION FOR PERMISSION
9 . . . . . . . . . . . . . . . . . . . . . . . . . )   TO PRESENT LATE CLAIM
                                                   )
10 against                                          )   [Gov.C. §911.4]
                                                   )
11 . . . . . . . . . . . . . . . . . . . . . . . . )
                                                   )
12                                                  )

13

14      TO: . . . . . . . . . . . (name of public entity) . . . . . . . . . . . . . . . . . .

15      Application is hereby made for permission to present the attached claim

16 after expiration of the time limit provided in Government Code §911.2.

17      (1) As stated in the attached claim, claimant's cause of action accrued

18 on or about . . . . . . . . . . . . . . . . . . . . . .

19      (2) The time for presentation of such claim under Government Code §911.2

20 expired on or about . . . . . . . . . . . . . . . . . .

21      (3) The reason for the failure to present such claim within the time

22 provided in Government Code §911.2 was as follows: . . . . . . *(facts showing one*

23 *or more of the grounds contained in Gov.C. §911.6: minority, disability,*

24 *"mistake, inadvertence, excusable neglect" AND no prejudice to public entity*

25 *from delay.)* . . . . . . . . . . . . . . . . . . . . . . . . . . . . . . . . . . . . . . . . . . . . .

26      I certify and declare under penalty of perjury under the laws of the

27 State of California that the foregoing is true and correct.

28 DATED: . . . . . . . . . . . . .          . . . . . . . . . . . . . . . . . . . . . . . . . . . . . . . . . . .
                                                           Claimant

---

APPL. FOR PERMISSION TO FILE LATE CLAIM
AGAINST GOVERNMENTAL ENTITY

# PETITION FOR ORDER PERMITTING LATE CLAIM AGAINST GOVERNMENTAL ENTITY

```
 1   .............................
     .............................
 2   .............................
     .............................
 3   .............................
     State Bar No. ..................
 4
 5   Attorney for Petitioner .........
 6
 7
 8               SUPERIOR COURT OF THE STATE OF CALIFORNIA
 9                        COUNTY OF .........
10
11   ..........................,    )    CASE NO.: .............
            Petitioner,             )
12                                  )    PETITION FOR ORDER
                                    )    PERMITTING LATE CLAIM
13   vs.                            )    AGAINST GOVERNMENTAL
                                    )    ENTITY
14   ..........................,    )    [Gov.C. §946.6]
                                    )
15          Respondents.            )
```

16      Petitioner ...... *(name)* ...... hereby petitions this Court for an order

17 relieving him from the provisions of Government Code Section 945.4 on account

18 of failure to file a timely claim against Respondent ...... *(name of*

19 *governmental entity)* ......, and in support thereof alleges as follows:

20      (1) Petitioner has a claim against Respondent arising out of the

21 following facts, circumstances or transactions: ............... *(detail)* .....

22 ..............................................................................

23 ..............................................................................

24      (2) Petitioner's cause of action against Respondent accrued on or about

25 ........ *(date)* ........ .

26      (3) Petitioner failed to present a claim against Respondent within the

27 time limits provided by Government Code Section 911.2.

28

1

PETN. FOR ORDER PERMITTING LATE CLAIM<br>AGAINST GOVERNMENTAL ENTITY

1    (4) On or about ...... *(date)* ......, Petitioner made written

2 application to Respondent for permission to file a late claim in accordance

3 with the provisions of Government Code Section 911.4. A true and correct copy

4 of said application is attached hereto as Exhibit "A" and incorporated herein

5 by reference. Attached and part of said application is a claim form containing

6 full information regarding said claim, signed by Petitioner.

7    (5) Petitioner's application for permission to file a late claim was

8 denied by Respondent on or about ...... *(date)* ......, as follows: ...... *(by*

9 *notice of rejection, or by failure to act within 45-day time limit specified*

10 *in Government Code §911.6(c))* ......

11    (6) The reason for Petitioner's failure to present a claim to Respondent

12 within the time limits provided by Government Code Section 911.2 are as

13 follows: ...... *(facts showing claimant disabled or minor throughout period*

14 *in question; or "mistake, inadvertence, surprise or excusable neglect" AND*

15 *no prejudice to Respondent from delay)* .................................................

16 ...........................................................

17    (7) The information required by Government Code Section 910 relative to

18 Petitioner's claim is set forth in the claim form attached as Exhibit "A" to

19 this Petition.

20    I declare under penalty of perjury under the laws of the State of

21 California that the foregoing is true and correct.

22    Executed this .......... day of .........., at.........................

23 California.

24

25                              ...............................
                                 Petitioner

26

27

28

2

PETN. FOR ORDER PERMITTING LATE CLAIM
AGAINST GOVERNMENTAL ENTITY

**[FORM 1:G]**

# CHECKLIST
# PETITION FOR RELIEF FROM REQUIREMENT TO
# FILE A GOVERNMENT CLAIM

*[Ed. Note: This form or similar forms are used by many courts. Counsel should use this as a checklist in preparing a motion or opposition because it may raise factors of concern to the court. Declarations or points and authorities should be prepared to address each of the points on the checklist.]*

Discovery Cut-off: _____     Calendar: _____

Motion Cut-off: _____     Date: _____

Trial Date: _____     Notice: _____

### PETITION FOR RELIEF FROM REQUIREMENT
### TO FILE A GOVERNMENT CLAIM
### (Gov't Code § 946.6)
### (CONFIDENTIAL COURT DOCUMENT WHEN COMPLETED)

MOVING PARTY: _____

RESPONDING PARTY: _____

SERVICE OF PETITION (Gov't Code § 946.6(d)): _____

    ❑ 21- day lapse between service and hearing (CCP § 1005(a)(9)): _____
    ❑ Proof of Service of moving papers timely filed (5 cal. days -- CRC   317(c)): _____
    ❑ Correct Address (CCP §§ 1013, 1013a): _____

____/____/____     Date cause of action accrued (Gov't Code § 901)

____/____/____     6-month deadline to file § 910 Claim (Gov't Code § 911.2)

____/____/____     Date § 911.4 Application for Leave to Present Late Claim was filed with government entity
    (reasonable time not to exceed 1 year -- Gov't Code § 911.4(b))

____/____/____     Date Application denied, or deemed denied
    (45 days -- Gov't Code § 911.6(c))

____/____/____     Date § 946.6 Petition filed with court
    (within 6 months after Application denied -- Gov't Code § 946.6(b))

    ❑ Petition verified (CCP §2015.5)

    ❑ Reason for failure to present Claim within § 911.2, 6-month period (Government Code section 946.6(b)).
_____

    ❑ Name of claimant, mail address (§ 910(a), (b)) _____

    ❑ Date, place, circumstances of claim (§ 910(c))
_____
    (If Petition was not filed in proper judicial district for trial, pursuant to § 946.6(a) transfer this
    proceeding on the motion of any party)

    ❑ Description of injury, damages (§ 910(d))

    ❑ Names of public employee(s) involved, if known (§ 910(e)) _____

    ❑ Indication whether jurisdiction would rest in the Limited Jurisdiction of Superior Court (§ 910(f); CCP §§85-88)
_____

As grounds for relief pursuant to § 946.6(c) from the requirement to file a § 910 Claim imposed by § 945.4,
Petition alleges:
    ❑ Application was made in a reasonable time not to exceed 1 year
_____ ; and
    ❑ mistake, inadvertence, surprise or excusable neglect and no prejudice to public entity (§ 946.6(c)(1))

or     ❑ person suffering injury or damage was a minor during entire § 911.2, 6-month claim period (§ 946.6(c)(2))

or     ❑ person suffering injury or damage was physically or mentally incapacitated by that disability during
    entire § 911.2, 6-month claim period (§ 946.6(c)(3))

or     ❑ person died within § 911.2, 6-month claim period (§ 946.6(c)(4))
_____

DECLARATION(S) SUPPORTING PETITION (CCP § 2015.5; CRC 315(a))

OPPOSITION (Burden on RP to show prejudice. Weil & Brown, Civ. Pro. Bef. Trial (TRG 2002) ¶1:777)

T/R:     ❑ GRANT

    ❑ DENY

        ❑ without PREJUDICE

        ❑ with PREJUDICE

DECLARATION(S) SUPPORTING PETITION (CCP § 2015.5; CRC 315(a))


OPPOSITION  (Burden on RP to show prejudice (Weil & Brown, §1:777)      Service proper _____


T/R:      ❑ GRANT

          ❑ DENY

                    ❑ without PREJUDICE

                    ❑ with PREJUDICE

WTWR0697 001 wpd

**RESERVED**

# CREDITOR'S CLAIM AGAINST DECEDENT'S ESTATE

**DE-172**

| ATTORNEY OR PARTY WITHOUT ATTORNEY *(Name, state bar number, and address)* | TELEPHONE AND FAX NOS.: | FOR COURT USE ONLY |
|---|---|---|
| | | |

ATTORNEY FOR *(Name)*

**SUPERIOR COURT OF CALIFORNIA, COUNTY OF**

STREET ADDRESS

MAILING ADDRESS

CITY AND ZIP CODE

BRANCH NAME

ESTATE OF *(Name)*:

DECEDENT

| **CREDITOR'S CLAIM** | CASE NUMBER: |
|---|---|

You must file this claim with the court clerk at the court address above before the LATER of (a) four months after the date letters (authority to act for the estate) were first issued to the personal representative, or (b) sixty days after the date the *Notice of Administration* was given to the creditor, if notice was given as provided in Probate Code section 9051. You must also mail or deliver a copy of this claim to the personal representative and his or her attorney. A proof of service is on the reverse.

**WARNING:** Your claim will in most instances be invalid if you do not properly complete this form, file it on time with the court, and mail or deliver a copy to the personal representative and his or her attorney.

1. Total amount of the claim: $
2. Claimant *(name)*:
    a. ☐ an individual
    b. ☐ an individual or entity doing business under the fictitious name of *(specify)*:

    c. ☐ a partnership. The person signing has authority to sign on behalf of the partnership.
    d. ☐ a corporation. The person signing has authority to sign on behalf of the corporation.
    e. ☐ other (specify):
3. Address of claimant *(specify)*:

4. Claimant is ☐ the creditor ☐ a person acting on behalf of creditor *(state reason)*:

5. ☐ Claimant is ☐ the personal representative ☐ the attorney for the personal representative.
6. I am authorized to make this claim which is just and due or may become due. All payments on or offsets to the claim have been credited. Facts supporting the claim are ☐ on reverse ☐ attached.

I declare under penalty of perjury under the laws of the State of California that the foregoing is true and correct.

Date:

►

_____          _____
(TYPE OR PRINT NAME AND TITLE)                         (SIGNATURE OF CLAIMANT)

## INSTRUCTIONS TO CLAIMANT

A. On the reverse, itemize the claim and show the date the service was rendered or the debt incurred. Describe the item or service in detail, and indicate the amount claimed for each item. Do not include debts incurred after the date of death, except funeral claims.
B. If the claim is not due or contingent, or the amount is not yet ascertainable, state the facts supporting the claim.
C. If the claim is secured by a note or other written instrument, the original or a copy must be attached *(state why original is unavailable.)* If secured by mortgage, deed of trust, or other lien on property that is of record, it is sufficient to describe the security and refer to the date or volume and page, and county where recorded. *(See Prob. Code, § 9152.)*
D. Mail or take this original claim to the court clerk's office for filing. If mailed, use certified mail, with return receipt requested.
E. Mail or deliver a copy to the personal representative and his or her attorney. Complete the *Proof of Mailing or Personal Delivery* on the reverse.
F. The personal representative or his or her attorney will notify you when your claim is allowed or rejected.
G. Claims against the estate by the personal representative and the attorney for the personal representative must be filed within the claim period allowed in Probate Code section 9100. See the notice box above.

(Continued on reverse)

| Form Approved by the Judicial Council of California DE-172 [Rev. January 1, 1998] | **CREDITOR'S CLAIM** (Probate) | Probate Code, §§ 9000 et seq., 9153 |
|---|---|---|

| ESTATE OF *(Name)* | | | CASE NUMBER |
|---|---|---|---|
| | DECEDENT | | |

| Date of item | FACTS SUPPORTING THE CREDITOR'S CLAIM <br> ☐ **See attachment** *(if space is insufficient)* <br> Item and supporting facts | Amount claimed |
|---|---|---|
| | | |
| | | **TOTAL:** $ |

**PROOF OF** ☐ **MAILING** ☐ **PERSONAL DELIVERY   TO PERSONAL REPRESENTATIVE**
*(Be sure to mail or take the original to the court clerk's office for filing)*

1. I am the creditor or a person acting on behalf of the creditor. At the time of mailing or delivery I was at least 18 years of age.
2. My residence or business address is *(specify)*:

3. I mailed or personally delivered a copy of this *Creditor's Claim* to the personal representative as follows *(check either a or b below)*:
   a. ☐ **Mail.** I am a resident of or employed in the county where the mailing occurred.
       (1) I enclosed a copy in an envelope AND
          (a) ☐ **deposited** the sealed envelope with the United States Postal Service with the postage fully prepaid.
          (b) ☐ **placed** the envelope for collection and mailing on the date and at the place shown in items below following our ordinary business practices. I am readily familiar with this business' practice for collecting and processing correspondence for mailing. On the same day that correspondence is placed for collection and mailing, it is deposited in the ordinary course of business with the United States Postal Service in a sealed envelope with postage fully prepaid.
       (2) The envelope was addressed and mailed first-class as follows:
          (a) Name of personal representative served:
          (b) Address on envelope:

          (c) Date of mailing:
          (d) Place of mailing *(city and state)*:
   b. ☐ **Personal delivery.** I personally delivered a copy of the claim to the personal representative as follows:
       (1) Name of personal representative served:
       (2) Address where delivered:

       (3) Date delivered:
       (4) Time delivered:

I declare under penalty of perjury under the laws of the State of California that the foregoing is true and correct.
Date:

▶

_____
(TYPE OR PRINT NAME OF CLAIMANT)

_____
(SIGNATURE OF CLAIMANT)

DE-172 [Rev. January 1, 1998]

**CREDITOR'S CLAIM**
(Probate)

Page two

Rev. #1 1998

# NOTICE OF RESCISSION

NOTICE OF RESCISSION

To:  .......... *(parties as to whom contract rescinded)* .........

YOU ARE HEREBY NOTIFIED that ........ *(name)* ........ rescinds that certain ........ *(written/oral)* ....... contract

entered into on or about ..... *(date)* ..... between ................... *(names)* ......................., pertaining to ......

*(subject matter)* ...... .

This rescission is upon the following grounds, among others: .......... *(one or more of grounds enumerated*

*in Civil Code §1689)* ......................................................................................................................................

The undersigned herewith offers to restore to you everything of value that has been received by the

undersigned from you under the aforesaid contract, to wit: ............................................ *(money, specific*

*description of property, etc.)* ...............................................................................................

...................................................... upon condition that you restore to the undersigned everything of value that

you have received from the undersigned under the said contract, to wit:

....................................................... *(money, specific description of property, etc.)* ..........................

..................................................................

DATED: ......................        ..............................
                                                   *(Name of Rescinding Party)*

**[FORM 1:J]**

# NOTICE OF BREACH OF WARRANTY

NOTICE OF BREACH OF WARRANTY

DATED: ................................................

TO: .......... *(seller, manufacturer)* ..........

YOU ARE HEREBY NOTIFIED that the goods you delivered to me on or about .......... *(date)* .......... under the contract of sale dated ..................... are defective in the following regards, among others: ........................... *(detail)* ...............................................................................................................................
.........................................................................................................................................................................
.........................................................................................................................................................................
.....................................

Such defects breach the .......... *(express/implied)* .......... warranties contained in the aforesaid contract as follows: .......... *(e.g., merchantability, fitness for particular purpose, etc.)* .........................................................
.........................................................................................................................................................................
.............................................................. .

DATED: ................................................          ...............................................................

          *(Name of Buyer)*

# NOTICE OF INTENT TO COMMENCE ACTION
# AGAINST HEALTH CARE PROVIDER

NOTICE OF INTENT TO COMMENCE ACTION
AGAINST HEALTH CARE PROVIDER
(CODE OF CIVIL PROCEDURE SECTION 364)


TO:  ............. *(name of health care provider)* ...............

YOU ARE HEREBY NOTIFIED pursuant to the provisions of California Code of Civil Procedure Section 364, that ....... *(name of proposed plaintiff)* .......... intends to, and will, commence a legal action against you ninety (90) days or more after the date of service of this notice.


The legal basis for such action will be that you and the other defendants to be named in such action were negligent in the examination, diagnosis, care and treatment of .......... *(name of proposed plaintiff)* ..... on or about ................. *(dates of alleged negligence)* ................ .


As the result of the foregoing negligence, ............ *(proposed plaintiff)* ...... has sustained injuries, damages and losses of the following types presently known:

    Physical injuries consisting of ................. *(describe specifically)* ..................

    Medical and related expenses

    Impairment of future earning capacity

    Pain and suffering, emotional distress, and impairment of enjoyment of life

    Other damages and losses consisting of ............... *(if applicable)* ......


All of the foregoing is based on facts as presently known, and there may be other and additional injuries, damages, losses and expenses still to ascertained.


DATED: ........................., 19....                     ....................................................

                                              Attorney for ...............................

**[FORM 1:L]**

# CERTIFICATE OF MERIT
# (PROFESSIONAL NEGLIGENCE ACTIONS)

```
 1   ............................................
     ............................................
 2   ............................................
     ............................................
 3   ............................................
     State Bar No. .....................
 4
 5   Attorney for Plaintiff .............
 6
 7
 8              SUPERIOR COURT OF THE STATE OF CALIFORNIA
 9                       COUNTY OF .........
10
11   ............................,    )  NO. ........................
                                     )
12          Plaintiff,               )  CERTIFICATE OF MERIT
                                     )  [CCP §411.35]
13   vs.                             )
                                     )
14   ............................,    )
                                     )
15          Defendants.              )
                                     )
16   _____)
17
18        ...... (name of plaintiff's attorney) ...... declares as follows:
19        1. I am the attorney of record for the plaintiff herein.
20        2. Prior to commencing this action, I personally reviewed the facts of
21   this case, and also consulted with ..........................., who is a
22   person licensed by the State of California to practice and is engaged in
23   practice as a ................. (or teaches said subject at an accredited
24   college or university), which is the same profession or discipline as the
25   defendant in this action. The said person with whom I consulted is not a
26   party to this action.
27        3. I am informed and reasonably believe that such person is knowledge-
28   able as to the relevant issues in this action.
```

1

CERTIFICATE OF MERIT

1     4. The person with whom I consulted has rendered the opinion that

2 defendant .......... (name) .......... was negligent in the performance of

3 the professional duties that are the subject of the complaint in this action.

4     5. Based upon my personal review of the facts of this case, and my

5 consultation with the aforesaid person, I have concluded that there is

6 reasonable and meritorious cause for the filing of the complaint in this

7 action.

8     I declare under penalty of perjury under the laws of the State of

9 California that the foregoing is true and correct.

10     Executed on ........................, .....

11

12                ..............................

               Attorney for Plaintiff

13

14

15

16

17

18

19

20

21

22

23

24

25

26

27

28

2

CERTIFICATE OF MERIT

Rev. #1 1999

# CHAPTER 2

# PARTIES TO THE ACTION

## CONTENTS

Page

A. STANDING TO SUE — "REAL PARTY IN INTEREST"
REQUIREMENT ............................................................. 2-1
  1. "Real Party in Interest" Defined ................................. 2-1
    a. May sue under assumed name ............................... 2-2
    b. Compare—capacity to sue .................................... 2-2
  2. Purpose of Requirement ....................................... 2-2
  3. Application ..................................................... 2-2
    a. Claims held by estate or trust ............................. 2-2
      (1) Application ........................................... 2-3
      (2) Successor fiduciary's standing to sue for advice
         given former administrator? ........................... 2-3
      (3) Beneficiaries cannot sue on behalf of trust ......... 2-3
        (a) Compare—beneficiaries may sue for breach
            of trustee's duties ............................... 2-3
      (4) Trustee in Chapter 7 bankruptcy ................... 2-4
        (a) Compare—actions accruing *after* bankruptcy
            filing ............................................. 2-5
        (b) Compare—actions relating to exempt
            property ......................................... 2-5
        (c) Compare—creditors' claims against
            bankrupt corporation's officers, directors ....... 2-5
        (d) Compare—effect of debtor's failure to
            disclose claim in bankruptcy ................... 2-6
           1) Unintentional nondisclosure
              distinguished ............................... 2-6
           2) Good faith nondisclosure distinguished ... 2-6
      (5) Trust deed trustees ............................... 2-6
        (a) Beneficiaries may also sue .................... 2-6
        (b) Compare—actions by prior lienholders ......... 2-6
          1) Problems with numerous beneficiaries .... 2-7
      (6) Compare—holder of power of attorney ............. 2-7
      (7) Limitation—trustee or executor must be
        represented by attorney ........................... 2-7
    b. Corporate claims ............................................ 2-7
      (1) Application ......................................... 2-8
      (2) Compare—derivative suits .......................... 2-8

      (3) Compare—homeowners' associations ............... 2-8
  c.  Partnership claims .................................................. 2-9
  d.  Claims assigned ..................................................... 2-9
      (1) Assignments for collection only .......................... 2-9
      (2) Partial assignments ........................................2-10
        (a) Effect of nonjoinder ...................................2-10
        (b) Judgment on part of claim as bar to action
            on balance .................................................2-10
        (c) Compare—plaintiff's "syndication" of
            recovery ....................................................2-10
      (3) Assignments conditional on obligor's consent .....2-10
      (4) Assignor lacks standing to sue .......................2-11
        (a) Ground for reversal? ...................................2-11
        (b) Compare—assignment made after suit
            filed .........................................................2-11
  e.  Claims based on subrogation ...............................2-11
      (1) Subrogee may sue in own name .......................2-11
      (2) Alternatively, subrogee may sue in name of
          subrogor ...................................................2-12
      (3) Partial subrogation .......................................2-12
  f.  Decedent's causes of action ................................2-12
      (1) Declaration by "successor in interest" ...............2-12
        (a) Effect of failure to file ...............................2-13
      (2) Compare—wrongful death actions .....................2-13
  g.  Contract claims ....................................................2-14
      (1) Contracts made by agent ...............................2-14
        (a) Undisclosed agency ...................................2-14
      (2) Third party beneficiary contracts .....................2-14
        (a) Compare—incidental beneficiaries .............2-14
      (3) Insurance policies .........................................2-14
        (a) Compare—indirect beneficiaries .................2-15
        (b) Joint insureds ...........................................2-15
        (c) Additional insureds ....................................2-15
        (d) Judgment creditor of insured .....................2-15
        (e) Compare—liability insurer's standing to
            challenge default judgment .....................2-16
      (4) Collective bargaining agreements .....................2-16
  h.  Validation proceedings .........................................2-16
  i.  Cartwright Act violations .......................................2-16
  j.  Actions for unfair competition ...............................2-17
  k.  Actions under Telephone Consumer Protection Act
      (TCPA) ................................................................2-17
  *l.*  Crime victims ......................................................2-17
  m.  Standing to challenge statute (constitutional
      standing) ............................................................2-17
      (1) Sufficient injury .............................................2-17
4.  Exceptions—Suit Permitted by Other Than Real Party
  in Interest .............................................................2-18
  a.  Parents suing for injury to child .............................2-18
      (1) Caution—parent-child conflict of interest
          concerns .....................................................2-18

  b. Representative suits ....................................... 2-18
  c. Mandamus actions—"public right/public duty"
    cases ...................................................... 2-19
   (1) Example .............................................. 2-19
   (2) Environmental protection suits ................ 2-19
   (3) Representative suits ............................... 2-20
  d. Taxpayers' actions ...................................... 2-20
   (1) Tax must be "assessed" ......................... 2-20
  e. County suing for child support ..................... 2-20.1
  f. Defendant spouses ...................................... 2-20.1
  g. Shareholders of dissolved corporation ......... 2-20.1
  h. Protection against workplace violence ......... 2-21
 5. Procedure for Challenging Standing to Sue ......... 2-21
  a. Defect not waived by failure to object ......... 2-21
  b. Jury trial required where facts disputed ......... 2-21
 6. Effect of Lack of Standing to Sue ...................... 2-21

**B. CAPACITY TO SUE OR DEFEND** ......................... 2-22
 1. Nature of Requirement ................................. 2-22
  a. Compare—standing to sue ......................... 2-22
 2. Application ................................................ 2-22
  a. Minors, incompetents ................................ 2-22
   (1) Appointment of guardian ad litem ......... 2-22
    (a) Cannot act in pro per ...................... 2-22.1
     1) Compare—can voluntarily dismiss ...... 2-22.1
    (b) Exceptions ................................ 2-22.1
     1) Minors age 12 or older—seeking or
      opposing protective or restraining
      orders ...................................... 2-22.1
     2) Minors under age 12—seeking or
      opposing protective or restraining
      orders ...................................... 2-23
    (c) Procedure for appointment ................ 2-23
    (d) Due process required for incompetent
     adults ...................................... 2-24
    (e) Effect of no appointment .................. 2-24
   (2) Emancipated minors .......................... 2-25
   (3) Tolling of statute of limitations for minors
    and "insane" persons ......................... 2-25
  b. Compare—disabled persons ......................... 2-25
   (1) No tolling of statute of limitations ......... 2-25
  c. Corporations ............................................ 2-26
   (1) Suspended corporations ..................... 2-26
    (a) Purpose ................................... 2-26
     1) Strictly construed ...................... 2-26
    (b) Application .............................. 2-27
    (c) Foreign corporations .................... 2-27
    (d) Revivor ................................... 2-27
     1) Continuance to obtain revivor ............... 2-28
     2) Substantive defenses not affected by
      revivor ................................... 2-28

|  |  |  | a) | Statute of limitations | 2-28 |
|  |  |  | b) | Compare—statute of limitations waived by cross-complaint | 2-28 |
|  |  | 3) | Procedural acts validated by revivor | | 2-28 |
|  |  | 4) | Contracts executed during suspension | | 2-29 |
|  |  |  | a) | Voidable only in judicial proceedings | 2-29 |
|  | (e) | Compare—surety's rights not affected | | | 2-30 |
| (2) | Nonqualified foreign corporations | | | | 2-30 |
|  | (a) | Capacity to sue prior to qualification | | | 2-30 |
|  |  | 1) | Matter of abatement | | 2-30 |
|  |  |  | a) | Showing required | 2-30 |
|  |  | 2) | Qualification allows pending action to continue | | 2-31 |
|  |  | 3) | Actions previously dismissed may be refiled | | 2-31 |
|  |  | 4) | Compare—actions commenced *after* qualification not subject to statute | | 2-31 |
|  | (b) | Capacity to defend without qualification | | | 2-32 |
|  |  | 1) | Compare—foreign insurers | | 2-32 |
| (3) | Appearance through counsel | | | | 2-32 |
|  | (a) | Exceptions | | | 2-32 |
|  |  | 1) | As to small claims actions | | 2-32 |
|  |  | 2) | As to small claims appeals | | 2-33 |
|  | (b) | Compare—effect of ordering relieving attorney of record | | | 2-33 |
|  | (c) | Compare—appeal from administrative ruling | | | 2-33 |
| (4) | Dissolved corporations | | | | 2-33 |

d. Partnerships and other unincorporated associations ... 2-34

| (1) | Limited partnerships | | | | 2-34.1 |
|  | (a) | Effect of failure to file certificate | | | 2-35 |
|  |  | 1) | Effect of statute banning action | | 2-35 |
| (2) | "Unincorporated association" | | | | 2-35 |
|  | (a) | Limited liability companies | | | 2-35 |
|  | (b) | Compare—business trusts | | | 2-35 |
| (3) | Joinder of members | | | | 2-36 |
| (4) | Appearance through counsel required | | | | 2-36 |

e. Estates ... 2-36

| (1) | Claims against estate covered by liability insurance | | | | 2-36 |
|  | (a) | Substitution of personal representative or consolidation | | | 2-36 |
| (2) | Actions pending against decedent at death | | | | 2-36 |
| (3) | Appearance through counsel | | | | 2-37 |

f. Building contractors ... 2-37

| (1) | No exception for contractors licensed elsewhere | | | | 2-37 |
| (2) | Claims barred | | | | 2-38 |

        (a) Fraud claims ............................................... 2-38

        (b) Compare—unrelated claims ...................... 2-38

        (c) Compare—setoffs ...................................... 2-38

        (d) Express indemnity claims against
            subcontractors and suppliers ...................... 2-38

            1) Compare—equitable (comparative)
               indemnity ................................................. 2-39

            2) Compare—negligence claims ................. 2-39

      (3) Compare—no bar on recovery for work done
         outside California ..................................... 2-39

    g. Fugitives, persons in contempt ...................... 2-39

  3. Procedures to Challenge Party's Capacity ..................... 2-40

    a. Plaintiff's lack of capacity .............................. 2-40

      (1) Defect waived if not raised ..................... 2-40

        (a) Incapacity arising during litigation ............... 2-40

        (b) Relief from waiver? ...................................... 2-40

      (2) Compare—plaintiff's lack of standing to sue ....... 2-40

    b. Defendant's lack of capacity .......................... 2-41

  4. Amendment of Pleadings to Substitute Party Having
    Capacity ..................................................................... 2-41

**C. JOINDER OF PARTIES** ....................................................... 2-41

  1. Compulsory Joinder ..................................................... 2-41

    a. Joinder rules based on practical considerations ........ 2-42

      (1) Plaintiff must join all persons necessary for
         just adjudication ...................................... 2-42

        (a) Comment ...................................................... 2-42

        (b) If such persons not joined, explanation
           required ...................................................... 2-43

        (c) Involuntary plaintiffs may be joined as
           defendants ................................................ 2-43

      (2) Joinder will be ordered if feasible ................ 2-43

        (a) Procedure for compelling joinder .................. 2-43

      (3) If joinder not feasible, court must decide
         whether action should continue .......................... 2-43

        (a) Determinative factors ................................. 2-43

          1) Comment ............................................. 2-44

          2) Compare—case law ............................. 2-44

        (b) Weighing process ..................................... 2-44

    b. Application ..................................................... 2-44

      (1) Claimants to common fund .................... 2-44.1

      (2) Heirs in wrongful death action ............... 2-45

        (a) Effect of failure to join ............................. 2-45

      (3) Conflicting claims among co-owners ................. 2-46

        (a) Compare—claims against third persons ....... 2-46

        (b) Compare—claims of secured lenders .......... 2-46

      (4) Partial assignments ................................... 2-46

        (a) Partial subrogation ..................................... 2-47

        (b) Compare—beneficial interests ...................... 2-47

      (5) Risk of multiple liability ............................... 2-47

        (a) "Substantial risk" ....................................... 2-47

      (6) Suit to set aside contract ....................................2-48
         (a) Application ...............................................2-48
         (b) Exceptional cases ....................................2-48
      (7) Permissive use liability .................................2-48
      (8) Challenging government approvals to third
         parties ............................................................2-48
         (a) Application ...............................................2-49
         (b) Compare—absent party's interest
            adequately represented .......................2-49
      (9) Declaratory relief as to liability insurance
         coverage ........................................................2-49
      (10) Claims against spouses; community vs.
         separate property ...........................................2-50
      (11) Claims against joint tortfeasors .......................2-50
      (12) Judicial foreclosure actions .............................2-50
      (13) Quiet title actions ............................................2-51
  c. Procedure for challenging nonjoinder of party ..........2-51
      (1) Objection must be raised by demurrer or
         answer .............................................................2-51
      (2) Motion to dismiss .........................................2-51
         (a) Ruling may be deferred.............................2-52
      (3) Motion to compel joinder ..............................2-52
         (a) Effect of delay in making motion ..................2-52
      (4) Order compelling joinder ...............................2-52
      (5) Order for dismissal .......................................2-52
         (a) After order for joinder ...............................2-52
  d. Defendant may waive right to compel joinder ...........2-52
  e. Compare—absent party's right to challenge
    judgment ....................................................................2-53
      (1) Example ........................................................2-53
      (2) No laches or estoppel ...................................2-53
2. Permissive Joinder...............................................................2-54
  Strategies and Tactics Re Joinder ...................................2-54
  a. Any person claiming interest in property or
    controversy .................................................................2-55
      (1) Quiet title actions .........................................2-55
         (a) Compare—notice to unknown defendants ....2-56
  b. Any person involved in transaction sued upon .........2-56
      (1) "Relief sought jointly, severally, or in the
         alternative" .....................................................2-56
         (a) Defendants joined in the alternative.............2-56
         (b) Compare—defendants against whom no
            relief sought ...........................................2-57
      (2) "Same transaction or series of transactions" .......2-58
         (a) Application ...............................................2-58
         (b) Defendants joined in the alternative.............2-59
      (3) "Common question of law or fact" ...................2-59
         (a) Single question sufficient ...........................2-59
         (b) Unrelated claims may be joined...................2-60
            1) Contrast—federal rule ...........................2-60

(4) Limitations ............................................2-60
    (a) Insurer cannot be joined in suit against
       insured ..........................................2-60
       1) Compare—validity of release ................2-60
       2) Compare—breach of settlement
          agreement ....................................2-61
       3) Compare—insurer fraud delaying suit ....2-61
       4) Compare—insurance issues intertwined
          with other issues ...............................2-61
  c. Limitation—power of court to order separate trials ....2-62
  d. Procedure for challenging improper joinder ..............2-62
  e. Defect may be waived ..................................2-62
3. Alternative Joinder Procedures in Multi-Defendant
  Cases ......................................................2-62

**D. CLASS ACTIONS** ........................................2-62.1

**E. INTERVENTION** ...........................................2-63
1. Intervention as Right........................................2-63
  a. Statutory right to intervene .............................2-63
  b. Party whose joinder compulsory ...........................2-63
    (1) Effect...............................................2-63
    (2) Test ................................................2-64
       (a) Compare—nonparty's interest adequately
          represented by existing parties ...................2-64
2. Permissive Intervention ....................................2-65
  a. Intervenor's interest in litigation .......................2-65
    (1) Test ................................................2-65
    (2) Court's discretion ....................................2-66
    (3) Application .........................................2-66
    (4) Compare—effect of party's failure to
       prosecute or defend ................................2-69
  b. No new issues ........................................2-69
  c. Reasons for intervention...............................2-69
3. Procedure .................................................2-69
  a. "Timely" application for leave to intervene ...............2-69
    (1) Where statute specifies time for intervention ......2-70
       (a) Compare—possible challenges ..................2-70
    (2) Diligence requirement .............................2-70
    (3) Even after judgment ...............................2-70
  b. Application ex parte or by noticed motion................2-70
  c. Complaint in intervention ..............................2-71
  d. Service of complaint in intervention.....................2-71
  e. Challenging intervention ...............................2-71
4. Effect of Intervention .....................................2-72
  a. Effect of dismissal of plaintiff's claim ...................2-72
  b. No "relation back" for statute of limitations
    purposes .............................................2-72
    (1) Application .........................................2-72
    (2) Compare—employer-employee intervention .......2-72
       (a) Statute ......................................2-73

(b) Effect ..................................................2-73
(c) Compare—employee's action subject to
   dismissal ............................................2-73
   1) Effect of D's answer to complaint in
      intervention ...................................2-74
(d) Employee's right to "intervene back in"
   after employer intervention? ..............2-74
   1) View allowing intervention after
      dismissal ......................................2-74
   2) View barring intervention by employee
      after dismissal ..............................2-74
c. Court costs ..............................................2-75
d. Attorney fees ..........................................2-75
5. Effect of Failure to Intervene .........................2-75

**F. INTERPLEADER** ..............................................2-76
1. When Interpleader Proper .............................2-76
   a. Nature of stakeholding ..........................2-77
   b. Nature of conflicting claims ...................2-77
      (1) Partial conflict sufficient ................2-77
      (2) Limitation—claims to same debt or thing ...........2-77
   c. Partial vs. total interpleader ................2-78
   d. Stakeholder need not attempt to resolve dispute ......2-78
   e. No malicious prosecution liability .............2-78
   f. No insurance "bad faith" liability .............2-78
2. Procedure ....................................................2-79
   a. Interpleader by complaint .....................2-79
      (1) Pleading .......................................2-79
      (2) Deposit in court .............................2-79
   b. Interpleader by defendant ...................2-80
      (1) Interpleader cross-complaint ............2-80
         (a) Verification required ..................2-80
         (b) Deposit in court.........................2-80
      (2) Motion for discharge from liability .......2-80
         (a) Affidavit required ......................2-80
         (b) Notice to all claimants required ......2-80
   c. No cross-complaints against stakeholder ........2-81
      (1) Exception to compulsory cross-complaint
         statute? .........................................2-81
   d. Hearing on right to interplead ...............2-81
      (1) Substitution and discharge ...............2-81
         (a) NO objection to discharge ............2-81
      (2) Other actions restrained .................2-81
   e. Costs and attorney fees to stakeholder .......2-82
      (1) Stakeholder own lawyer ..................2-82

**G. SUBSTITUTION OF PARTIES** ...........................2-82
1. Death of Party ..............................................2-82
   a. Orders for substitution .........................2-82
      (1) Procedure ....................................2-82
      (2) Statement required from successor in
         interest ........................................2-83

(3) Local rules ..................................................................2-83

    b.  Exception—deceased defendants covered by insurance ........................................................................2-83

    c.  Effect of failure to substitute representative ............2-83

  2.  Transfer of Interest .........................................................2-84

    a.  Effect .......................................................................2-84

      (1) Compare—trustee in bankruptcy ......................2-84

      (2) Substitution of counsel ......................................2-84

    b.  Opposing party may compel substitution ..................2-84

    c.  Procedure .................................................................2-85

    d.  Compare—cause of action retained by transferor ................................................................2-85

**FORMS**

- Ex Parte Application and Order for Leave to Intervene ..........2-87
- Complaint In Intervention .....................................................2-90
- Checklist: Intervention .......................................................2-92.1
- Complaint In Interpleader....................................................2-93
- Checklist: Interpleader .......................................................2-95
- Notice of Motion for Discharge From Liability......................2-96
- Declaration in Support of Motion for Discharge From Liability ..............................................................................2-98
- Ex Parte Application for Order Substituting Party ...............2-100
- Checklist: Substitute Estate of Decedent ...........................2-103
- Application and Order for Appointment of Guardian Ad Litem ................................................................................2-105

**RESERVED**

# PARTIES TO THE ACTION

---

**Chapter Scope:** This Chapter deals with the procedures by which a person may become a party to a civil action.

The initial choice, of course, is with plaintiff. Plaintiff's complaint identifies the plaintiff (or coplaintiffs) and the defendant (or codefendants). In making this initial choice, plaintiff's lawyer may have to consider:

- real party in interest requirement (*¶2:1 ff.*);

- rules on party capacity (*¶2:80 ff.*);

- rules on permissive joinder (*¶2:205 ff.*); and

- where appropriate, class action rules (*Ch. 14*).

Ultimately, plaintiff's choice of parties is likely to be based on *jurisdictional* and *tactical* considerations (*¶2:206*).

Plaintiff's choice of parties is not final, however. On defendant's motion, or its own, the court may order joinder of other persons, as plaintiffs or defendants, whose presence it finds necessary for a just adjudication ("necessary" or "indispensable" parties, *¶2:151 ff.*).

Defendant also has the right, by cross-complaint, to join third persons whose liability relates to the subject of plaintiff's complaint (*see ¶6:500 ff.*).

Finally, under certain circumstances, *nonparties* may *intervene* in an action pending between others (*¶2:400 ff.*); or be *substituted* as a party thereto (*¶2:500 ff.*). And, the special remedy of *interpleader* may enable a nonparty to join conflicting claimants to funds or personal property in his or her possession (*¶2:470 ff.*).

---

## A. STANDING TO SUE—"REAL PARTY IN INTEREST" REQUIREMENT

[2:1] First of all, plaintiff must be the "real party in interest" with respect to the claim sued upon. Except as otherwise provided by statute, "every action must be prosecuted in the name of the real party in interest . . ." [CCP §367; see *Cloud v. Northrop Grumman Corp.* (1998) 67 CA4th 995, 1004, 79 CR2d 544, 549 (citing text)]

1. [2:2] **"Real Party in Interest" Defined:** Generally, the real party in interest is the person who has the *right to sue under the*

*substantive law.* It is the person who owns or holds *title to the claim or property* involved, as opposed to others who may be interested or benefited by the litigation. [*Gantman v. United Pac. Ins. Co.* (1991) 232 CA3d 1560, 1566, 284 CR 188, 192]

Real party in interest issues are often discussed in terms of plaintiff's "standing to sue." [See *Powers v. Ashton* (1975) 45 CA3d 783, 787, 119 CR 729, 732; *Windham at Carmel Mtn. Ranch Ass'n v. Sup.Ct. (Presley)* (2003) 109 CA4th 1162, 1172, 135 CR2d 834, 841; *O'Flaherty v. Belgum* (2004) 115 CA4th 1044, , 9 CR3d 286, 326 (citing text)]

   a.  **[2:3]**  **May sue under assumed name:**  The real party in interest may sue in his or her own name, or under any *assumed* name by which he or she is "known and recognized." [*Cabrera v. McMullen* (1988) 204 CA3d 1, 4, 251 CR 34, 35]

   b.  **[2:3.1]**  **Compare—capacity to sue:**  Capacity to sue deals with *disabilities* (e.g., minority or incompetency) affecting a party's right to represent his or her own interests in court (*see ¶2:81 ff.*). A plaintiff's lack of capacity is waived by defendant's failure to object (*see ¶2:139*).

On the other hand, *standing to sue*—the real party in interest requirement—goes to the *existence of a cause of action*; i.e., whether plaintiff has a right to relief. Lack of standing is not waived by failure to object (*see ¶2:77*). [*Pillsbury v. Karmgard* (1994) 22 CA4th 743, 757-758, 27 CR2d 491, 498; *American Alternative Energy Partners II, 1985 v. Windridge, Inc.* (1996) 42 CA4th 551, 559, 49 CR2d 686, 691 (citing text)]

2.  **[2:4]**  **Purpose of Requirement:**  The purpose of the real party in interest requirement is to assure that any judgment rendered will bar the owner of the claim sued upon from relitigating. "It is to save a defendant, against whom a judgment may be obtained, from further harassment or vexation at the hands of some other claimant to the same demand." [*Giselman v. Starr* (1895) 106 C 651, 657, 40 P 8, 10; *Cloud v. Northrop Grumman Corp.* (1998) 67 CA4th 995, 1003, 79 CR2d 544, 549, fn. 2 (citing text); *O'Flaherty v. Belgum*, supra, 115 CA4th at , 9 CR3d at 300 (citing text)]

3.  **[2:5]**  **Application:**  The following are the more common situations in which a party's standing to sue as the real party in interest may be raised:

   a.  **[2:6]**  **Claims held by estate or trust:**  An estate or trust is *not* a legal entity, and therefore has neither capacity nor standing to sue (*see also ¶2:126*). Title to estate or trust assets is held by the executor, administrator or trustee, on behalf of the beneficiaries. Thus, as to claims held by an estate or trust, the executor, administrator or trustee is the real party in interest. Such fiduciary has the right to sue—without joining the persons for whose benefit he or she holds title. [CCP §369(a); *O'Flaherty v. Belgum, supra,* 115 CA4th at    , 9 CR3d at 300 (citing text)]

*Compare—trusts with same persons as both trustees and beneficiaries:* Where the same persons are both the trustees and the beneficiaries of a trust, they may sue *in their own name* without mentioning the trust. [*Hassoldt v. Patrick Media Group, Inc.* (2000) 84 CA4th 153, 170, 100 CR2d 662, 675]

*Compare—decedent's causes of action:* Claims belonging to a decedent at the time of death may be maintained by the decedent's personal representative; or if none, by the decedent's successor in interest. *See discussion at* ¶2:31.5.

## (1) Application

* **[2:6.1]** Trustee of Physician's bankruptcy estate had standing to sue Physician's malpractice Insurer (for fraud and breach of fiduciary duty) in connection with the defense Insurer had provided to Physician in a malpractice action that preceded his bankruptcy. [*Mosier v. Southern Calif. Physicians Ins. Exch.* (1998) 63 CA4th 1022, 1039-1040, 74 CR2d 550, 562]

## (2) [2:6.2] Successor fiduciary's standing to sue for advice given former administrator?

It is not clear whether a successor fiduciary has standing to sue for malpractice by a law firm that advised the estate's *former* administrators while they were handling the estate.

*Caution:* This issue is presently before the California Supreme Court in *Borissoff v. Taylor & Faust,* Case No. S105600.

**[2:6.3-6.4]** *Reserved.*

## (3) [2:6.5] Beneficiaries cannot sue on behalf of trust:

The beneficiary of a trust generally is not the real party in interest on claims belonging to the trust and may not sue in the name of the trust. [*Saks v. Damon Raike & Co.* (1992) 7 CA4th 419, 427, 8 CR2d 869, 875—immaterial that trustee disqualified by conflict of interest; *City of Atascadero v. Merrill Lynch, Pierce, Fenner & Smith, Inc.* (1998) 68 CA4th 445, 462, 80 CR2d 329, 341]

### (a) [2:6.6] Compare—beneficiaries may sue for breach of trustee's duties:

If the trustee's refusal to enforce a valid trust claim against a third person breaches its duties to the trust (e.g., duty to preserve and protect trust assets, etc.), the beneficiaries have several possible remedies:

> — suit to compel the trustee to sue the third party (or to remove the trustee and appoint a trustee ad litem to maintain the action);
>
> — sue the trustee to recover profits or recoup losses resulting from its breach of fiduciary duties; or
>
> — sue the third party directly for any loss caused by the trustee's breach of fiduciary duty *if the third party participated with the trustee in the breach of trust.* [See *Wolf v. Mitchell, Silberberg & Knupp* (1999) 76 CA4th 1030, 1039, 90 CR2d 792, 797—suit to recover property transferred by trustee to third party in breach of trust; *Harnedy v. Whitty* (2003) 110 CA4th 1333, 1342, 2 CR3d 798, 805]

(4) **[2:7]** **Trustee in Chapter 7 bankruptcy:** All causes of action belonging to a bankrupt at the time of filing a Chapter 7 bankruptcy petition (liquidation) become part of the bankruptcy estate. The trustee in bankruptcy therefore is the real party in interest as to such causes of action (unless the trustee chooses to abandon them). [*Curtis v. Kellogg & Andelson* (1999) 73 CA4th 492, 505, 86 CR2d 536, 546; *Cloud v. Northrop Grumman Corp.* (1998) 67 CA4th 995, 1004, 79 CR2d 544, 549 (citing text)]

Even claims that are *nonassignable* under state law (e.g., legal malpractice claims) pass to the debtor's trustee in bankruptcy. [*Office of Statewide Health Planning & Develop. v. Musick, Peeler & Garrett* (1999) 76 CA4th 830, 834, 90 CR2d 705, 707]

With respect to actions commenced *prior* to bankruptcy, courts are split on whether the trustee must be substituted in as plaintiff. (Parties may be substituted upon transfer of interest under CCP §368.5; *see* ¶2:504.) [*ABA Recovery Services, Inc. v. Konold* (1988) 198 CA3d 720, 726, 244 CR 27, 31—*substitution of trustee optional:* prebankruptcy action may continue in name of debtor despite transfer of interest; compare *Bostanian v. Liberty Sav. Bank* (1997) 52 CA4th 1075, 1083, 61 CR2d 68, 73 (contra)—*substitution required:* debtor out of possession has no standing to prosecute cause of action that has passed to bankruptcy estate unless abandoned by trustee]

*Compare—Chapter 11 proceedings:* In Chapter 11 (reorganization) proceedings, where no trustee has been appointed, the *debtor in possession* is the real party in interest. [*Bostanian v. Liberty Sav. Bank*, supra, 52 CA4th at 1078-1079, 61 CR2d at 70]

*Compare—Chapter 13 proceedings:* Similarly, in a Chapter 13 proceeding, where the debtor remains in possession of the property of the estate, the debtor has standing to pursue the claim. [*Kelsey v. Waste Management of Alameda County* (1999) 76 CA4th 590, 596, 90 CR2d 510, 513—not affected by debtor's failure to disclose claim in bankruptcy proceeding]

[2:7.1-7.4]   *Reserved.*

(a) [2:7.5]   **Compare—actions accruing *after* bankruptcy filing:**   Cases are split on whether causes of action accruing after a bankruptcy petition is filed become part of the bankruptcy estate. [See *Bostanian v. Liberty Sav. Bank* (1997) 52 CA4th 1075, 1083, 61 CR2d 68, 73—wrongful foreclosure cause of action accruing subsequent to Chapter 11 filing was property of bankruptcy estate; but see *Haley v. Dow Lewis Motors, Inc.* (1999) 72 CA4th 497, 504, 85 CR2d 352, 356-357 (contra)—wrongful discharge cause of action accruing after employee's bankruptcy filing was *not* property of bankruptcy estate so that debtors entitled to sue in their own names]

(b) [2:8]   **Compare—actions relating to exempt property:**   However, the debtor is the real party in interest on claims for recovery or damage to property determined to be exempt in the bankruptcy proceedings (e.g., debtor's household furnishings). [*Amstone v. Peninsular Fire Ins. Co.* (1991) 226 CA3d 1019, 1026-1027, 277 CR 260, 264—insurance claim for household furnishings lost in fire after bankruptcy filing]

(c) [2:8.1]   **Compare—creditors' claims against bankrupt corporation's officers, directors:**   Creditors of a bankrupt corporation do *not* have standing to sue its officers or directors for mismanagement, "looting" or other acts causing its bankruptcy. Such claims *belong to the corporation* and may be pursued only by its trustee in bankruptcy. [See *Practice Service Corp. v. Clark* (1995) 37 CA4th 1003, 1006, 44 CR2d 104, 106]

But the corporation's creditors may sue its officers and directors for *fraudulent misrepresentations* as to the corporation's financial condition. Such claims belong to the creditors, not the corporation, and are not affected by the corporation's bankruptcy (i.e., no automatic stay). [*Practice Service Corp. v. Clark*, supra, 37 CA4th at 1007-1008, 44 CR2d at 106]

[2:8.2-8.4]   *Reserved.*

(d) [2:8.5] **Compare—effect of debtor's failure to disclose claim in bankruptcy:** A debtor who *intentionally* fails to disclose a claim in bankruptcy proceedings may be *judicially estopped* (*see* ¶6:456.1) from later suing on that claim. [*Thomas v. Gordon* (2000) 85 CA4th 113, 119, 102 CR2d 28, 33; *International Engine Parts, Inc. v. Feddersen & Co.* (1998) 64 CA4th 345, 350, 75 CR2d 178, 182]

    1) [2:8.6] **Unintentional nondisclosure distinguished:** A plaintiff who unintentionally failed to schedule her prepetition claim for wrongful termination as an asset in her bankruptcy action lacked standing to sue. However, the defect could be cured by *substituting the bankruptcy trustee* as the real party in interest or obtaining the trustee's abandonment of the claim. Judicial estoppel does *not* arise absent a finding of *bad faith*. [*Cloud v. Northrop Grumman Corp.* (1998) 67 CA4th 995, 1000, 1019-1020, 79 CR2d 544, 547, 560; see also *Kelsey v. Waste Management of Alameda County* (1999) 76 CA4th 590, 599, 90 CR2d 510, 516]

    2) [2:8.7] **Good faith nondisclosure distinguished:** A plaintiff who failed to schedule her prepetition claim for wrongful termination based on her attorney's advice the claim was probably worthless was not judicially estopped from pursuing the claim. [*Haley v. Dow Lewis Motors, Inc.* (1999) 72 CA4th 497, 511, 85 CR2d 352, 361]

(5) [2:9] **Trust deed trustees:** A trustee with power of sale under a deed of trust or mortgage is *not* the "trustee of an express trust" for standing to sue purposes (CCP §369(a)). Nevertheless, such trustee has standing to maintain *judicial foreclosure proceedings* on behalf of the trust deed beneficiaries. [See CCP §§369(b), 725a]

(a) [2:10] **Beneficiaries may also sue:** The trustee under a deed of trust is not the sole real party in interest in judicial foreclosure proceedings. The trust deed beneficiaries also have standing to maintain such proceedings; and the trustee cannot complain if they do so. [CCP §725a; and see *Monterey S.P. Partnership v. W.L. Bangham, Inc.* (1989) 49 C3d 454, 460, 261 CR 587, 590]

(b) [2:11] **Compare—actions by prior lienholders:** The trust deed beneficiaries, as well as the trustee, are real parties in interest in any action brought by a senior lienholder challenging the existence or priority of the trust deed lien. Therefore, each of the beneficiaries, as well as the trustee, *must be named and served as defendants* in such actions. [*Monterey S.P. Partnership v. W.L. Bangham, Inc.*, supra, 49 C3d at 461, 261 CR at 591—mechanics' lien foreclosure: default judgment against trustee not binding on trust deed beneficiaries]

    1) **[2:12] Problems with numerous beneficiaries:** If there are too many beneficiaries to serve individually, class actions and other alternatives exist for maintaining an action on their behalf; *see* ¶2:233. [*Monterey S.P. Partnership v. W.L. Bangham, Inc.*, supra, 49 C3d at 461, 261 CR at 591, fn. 4]

(6) **[2:13] Compare—holder of power of attorney:** The holder of a power of attorney is merely an agent of the party who appointed him or her, not a trustee. Thus, the holder is *not* the real party in interest as to rights belonging to the principal (property owner), and cannot sue to enforce those rights. Nor can the holder sue derivatively for damages suffered by the owner. [*Arnolds Management Corp. v. Eischen* (1984) 158 CA3d 575, 581, 205 CR 15, 19]

**[2:13.1-13.4]** *Reserved.*

(7) **[2:13.5] Limitation—trustee or executor must be represented by attorney:** A trustee or executor who is not a lawyer *cannot appear in pro per* in legal proceedings to protect assets of the estate or trust . . . "because in this capacity such trustee *would be representing interests of others* and would therefore be engaging in the unauthorized practice of law." [*Ziegler v. Nickel* (1998) 64 CA4th 545, 548, 75 CR2d 312, 314-315 (emphasis added); *Hansen v. Hansen* (2003) 114 CA4th 618, 621, 7 CR3d 688, 691 (citing text); see Bus. & Prof.C. §6125 (unauthorized practice of law)]

  b. **[2:14] Corporate claims:** Claims for injury or damage to a corporation or its property belong to the corporation, not its stockholders. They have no standing to sue for such wrongs even if the value of their stock is disminished. The loss suffered by the stockholder is deemed incidental to the wrong suffered by the corporation. [See *Jones v. H.F. Ahmanson & Co.* (1969) 1 C3d 93, 107, 81 CR 592, 598]

Similarly, a member of a *limited liability company* formed under Corps.C. §17300 cannot sue individually for fraudulent transfer of the company's assets. The *entity* is the real party in interest. If it refuses to sue, however, the member may bring a derivative suit on behalf of the entity (¶2:15). [*PacLink Communications Int'l, Inc. v. Sup.Ct. (Yeung)* (2001) 90 CA4th 958, 964-965, 109 CR2d 436, 439-440]

### (1) Application

- **[2:14.1]** Members of nonprofit association lacked standing to enforce the association's rights under an insurance policy. [*Gantman v. United Pac. Ins. Co.* (1991) 232 CA3d 1560, 1568, 284 CR 188, 192]

- **[2:14.2]** Sole Shareholder lacked standing to sue for antitrust injury to Corporation. [*Vinci v. Waste Management, Inc.* (1995) 36 CA4th 1811, 1815, 43 CR2d 337, 339]

  **[2:14.3]** *Reserved.*

- **[2:14.4]** Minority Shareholder could not sue Majority Shareholder for breaching fiduciary duties to the corporation (negligence in managing corporation's business), even if the breach also damaged Minority Shareholder individually (damage to her reputation, emotional distress and loss of other employment opportunities). These damages were *incidental* to the corporation's injury and *not* a result of the violation of any special duty owed to Minority Shareholder. [*Nelson v. Anderson* (1999) 72 CA4th 111, 127, 84 CR2d 753, 762]

### (2) [2:15] Compare—derivative suits:

But if the corporation refuses to enforce a claim against third persons for damage to the corporation (e.g., against directors for breach of fiduciary duty), a stockholder may under certain circumstances maintain a derivative suit *on the corporation's behalf.* The corporation is named as a *defendant* (or involuntary plaintiff) in such actions because of its refusal to sue as plaintiff. Nonetheless, the corporation is the real party in interest in the claim sued upon. [*Jones v. H.F. Ahmanson & Co.*, supra, 1 C3d at 107, 81 CR at 598]

The principles of derivative lawsuits applicable to corporations likewise apply to limited liability companies. [*PacLink Communications Int'l, Inc. v. Sup.Ct. (Yeung)* (2001) 90 CA4th 958, 963, 109 CR2d 436, 439]

*Cross-refer:* Derivative suit requirements are discussed in detail in Friedman, *Cal. Prac. Guide: Corporations* (TRG), Ch. 6.

### (3) [2:15.1] Compare—homeowners' associations:

A homeowners' association is the real party in interest

and may sue in its own name without joining the individual owners with respect to claims relating to:
— enforcement of governing documents ("CC&Rs"); or
— damage to common areas or separate areas the association is obligated to maintain;
— damage to separate areas that "arise out of or is integrally related to" the above damages. [See CCP §383(a), *discussed at ¶14:232 ff.*]

[2:15.2-15.4] *Reserved.*

c. [2:15.5] **Partnership claims:** The partnership entity is the owner of partnership property and the real party in interest on claims for damage to partnership property. Individual partners may not sue for damage to the partnership property or to their individual "beneficial interest" in the property. [*Mayer v. C.W. Driver* (2002) 98 CA4th 48, 60, 120 CR2d 535, 542; *O'Flaherty v. Belgum* (2004) 115 CA4th 1044, , 9 CR3d 286, 300 (citing text)]

But a partner may maintain a *derivative suit* on behalf of the partnership where the partnership itself fails or refuses to sue (e.g., suit against general partner for breach of fiduciary duty). [*Everest Investors 8 v. McNeil Partners* (2003) 114 CA4th 411, 425, 8 CR3d 31, 40]

d. [2:16] **Claims assigned:** Once a claim has been assigned, the assignee is the owner and has the right to sue thereon. The assignee is the real party in interest, and can maintain suit in his or her own name, without joining the assignor. [See *National Reserve Co. of America v. Metropolitan Trust Co. of Calif.* (1941) 17 C2d 827, 833, 112 P2d 598, 602; and CCP §368.5—"an action or proceeding does not abate by the transfer of an interest"]

Bear in mind, however, that not all claims are assignable. E.g., a purely personal tort claim is *non*assignable. [*Murphy v. Allstate Ins. Co.* (1976) 17 C3d 937, 942, 132 CR 424, 426; see also *Curtis v. Kellogg & Andelson* (1999) 73 CA4th 492, 505, 86 CR2d 536, 544—legal malpractice claim not assignable]

(1) [2:17] **Assignments for collection only:** The above rule applies even to assignments for collection only, in which the assignor retains an interest. The assignee has legal title to the claim, and the right to sue thereon, and is therefore the "real party in interest"—notwithstanding the assignor's retained interest. [*National Reserve Co. of America v. Metropolitan Trust Co. of Calif.*, supra]

[2:18] *Reserved.*

(2) [2:19] **Partial assignments:** If less than the entire claim is assigned (e.g., $10,000 assigned out of $50,000 coming due under contract), the partial assignee gets title only to the part assigned. He or she is entitled to sue as to that part, and therefore is a "real party in interest." But, in any such action, the partial assignee *must join* the assignor and any other partial assignee as parties to the action. The purpose is to protect the debtor from the harassment and expense of having to defend multiple lawsuits. [*Bank of the Orient v. Sup.Ct. (San Francisco Fed. Sav. & Loan Ass'n)* (1977) 67 CA3d 588, 594-595, 136 CR 741, 744-745; *see ¶2:171*]

(a) [2:20] **Effect of nonjoinder:** Failure to join the assignor and all other partial assignees constitutes an impermissible "splitting" of the cause of action on the debt. Upon proper objection by the defendant-debtor, the joinder of such parties is *compulsory* (*see ¶2:171*). But if defendant does not object, the defect is waived (*see ¶2:185*). [See *Ferraro v. William Lyles Const. Co.* (1980) 102 CA3d 33, 44, 162 CR 238, 244]

(b) [2:21] **Judgment on part of claim as bar to action on balance:** Similarly, a *judgment* obtained on *part* of an indivisible claim bars any later action on the balance. [See *Purcell v. Colonial Ins. Co.* (1971) 20 CA3d 807, 814, 97 CR 874, 878]

(c) [2:22] **Compare—plaintiff's "syndication" of recovery:** Plaintiff's agreement with third persons *to share any recovery* from the lawsuit is treated differently than a partial assignment. (E.g., to finance his lawsuit, P sells shares of any potential recovery to Investors.)

In such cases, the third parties are not assignees because they have no right against the defendant (plaintiff alone retains the right to sue). Thus, defendant cannot compel their joinder nor challenge the validity of their agreement with plaintiff. [See *Killian v. Millard* (1991) 228 CA3d 1601, 1604, 279 CR 877, 878]

(3) [2:23] **Assignments conditional on obligor's consent:** Some contract rights are assignable only with the consent of the other contracting party (e.g., leases and franchises often contain such provisions). The other party's refusal to consent does not affect the assignee's standing to enforce the contract as the real party in interest. Otherwise, an obligor could insulate itself from suit by arbitrarily withholding consent . . . "an outrageous

concept." (The reasonableness of the obligor's withholding consent is an issue to be determined in the suit.) [*Don Rose Oil Co. v. Lindsley* (1984) 160 CA3d 752, 759-760, 206 CR 670, 674—assignee of franchise had standing to enforce franchise despite franchisor's refusal to consent to assignment]

[2:24] *Reserved.*

(4) [2:25] **Assignor lacks standing to sue:** Once the transfer has been made, the assignor is no longer the real party in interest and therefore lacks standing to sue. [*Purcell v. Colonial Ins. Co.* (1971) 20 CA3d 807, 814, 97 CR 874, 878]

    (a) [2:26] **Ground for reversal?** But if the assignee "expressly consents that the suit be brought by his assignor, an objection that the assignor is not the real party in interest will not be ground for reversal because the defendant is fully protected from future action..." [*Greco v. Oregon Mut. Fire Ins. Co.* (1961) 191 CA2d 674, 687, 12 CR 802, 809-810]

    (b) [2:27] **Compare—assignment made after suit filed:** Different rules apply where a lawsuit was already on file when the transfer was made. In such cases, the court may permit the assignee to be substituted in place of the assignor; *or the action may be continued in the name of the assignor.* [CCP §368.5; *see* ¶2:504]

e. [2:28] **Claims based on subrogation:** A person obligated to pay for a loss caused by another may, by virtue of his or her payment, become subrogated to whatever claim the payee has against the person causing the loss. (Typical examples: Insurance company pays its insured for injuries caused by a third person; or a surety, pursuant to contract, pays a debtor's obligations to his creditors.)

Such payment entitles the payor to become subrogated (substituted) to the payee's claims against the person whose debt or liability is discharged. In effect, there is an *assignment by operation of law* of the payee's claims. And, as with assignments generally, the subrogee (assignee) is thereafter the real party in interest with respect to the claim. [See *Automobile Ins. Co. v. Union Oil Co.* (1948) 85 CA2d 302, 304-305, 193 P2d 48, 49-50]

(1) [2:29] **Subrogee may sue in own name:** As the real party in interest, the subrogee may file action in its own name alone. [See *United States v. Aetna Cas. & Surety Co.* (1949) 338 US 366, 372, 70 S.Ct. 207, 211]

(2) [2:30] **Alternatively, subrogee may sue in name of subrogor:** Alternatively, the subrogee may if it chooses (and it almost always will) sue in the name of the payee rather than its own name. The purpose, of course, is to permit the subrogee (usually an insurance company) to avoid any prejudice which it might encounter if it sued in its own name; and to take advantage of any sympathy which the payee may have garnered. [See *Lebet v. Cappobiacho* (1940) 38 CA2d Supp. 771, 102 P2d 1109, 1110—insurance policy authorized insurer to sue in name of insured; and *Anheuser-Busch v. Starley* (1946) 28 C2d 347, 351-352, 170 P2d 448, 451]

(3) [2:31] **Partial subrogation:** Partial subrogation claims (as where insurance carrier pays only part of the loss) are treated the same as partial assignments, above. I.e., *neither* the subrogor (insured) nor partial subrogee (insurance carrier) can sue without joining the other. Suit by either alone against the party causing the loss, would constitute an "impermissible splitting of the cause of action." [*Ferraro v. William Lyles Const. Co.* (1980) 102 CA3d 33, 43, 162 CR 238, 243]

[2:31.1-31.4] *Reserved.*

f.   [2:31.5] **Decedent's causes of action:** A cause of action that survives the decedent's death may be commenced by the decedent's personal representative. (Certain damages claims do not survive: e.g., pain, suffering and disfigurement, except elder abuse; see CCP §377.34 & Welf. & Inst.C. §15657(b).)

If no representative has been appointed, suit may be commenced by the decedent's *"successors in interest"* (persons entitled to inherit claim). [CCP §377.30]

This allows decedent's heirs to pursue claims belonging to the decedent where there are no assets to be probated or after the probate proceedings are closed. [*Parsons v. Tickner* (1995) 31 CA4th 1513, 1523-1524, 37 CR2d 810, 815]

(1) [2:31.6] **Declaration by "successor in interest":** A person seeking to commence an action as a decedent's "successor in interest" must execute and file an affidavit or declaration stating (CCP §377.32):

- Decedent's name.

- Date and place of decedent's death (a certified copy of the decedent's death certificate must also be attached to the declaration).

- "No proceeding is now pending in California for administration of the decedent's estate."

- (If the estate has been administered, include a copy of the final order showing decedent's claim *has been distributed* to the successor in interest.)

- *Either of the following,* as appropriate, *with facts* in support:

    "*Declarant is* the decedent's successor in interest as defined in CCP §377.11 and succeeds to the decedent's interest in the action or proceeding."

    OR

    "Declarant is *authorized to act on behalf of* the decedent's successor in interest as defined in CCP §377.11 with respect to the decedent's interest in the action or proceeding."

- "No other person has a superior right to commence the action or proceeding or to be substituted for the decedent in the pending action or proceeding."

- "The affiant or declarant affirms or declares under penalty of perjury under the laws of the State of California that the foregoing is true and correct." [CCP §377.32; see *In re A.C.* (2000) 80 CA4th 994, 1002-1003, 96 CR2d 79, 84-85]

(a) [2:31.7]  **Effect of failure to file:**  The statute does *not* require that the declaration be filed before commencing the action. "However, failure to file the affidavit could possibly subject the action to a *plea in abatement.*" [*Parsons v. Tickner* (1995) 31 CA4th 1513, 1524, 37 CR2d 810, 815 (emphasis added)]

[2:31.8-31.9]  *Reserved.*

(2) [2:31.10]  **Compare—wrongful death actions:**  Any of the following persons have standing to sue for wrongful death of a decedent:
  — decedent's personal representative (administrator or executor of decedent's estate);
  — decedent's surviving spouse, registered domestic partner (see Fam.C. §297), children and issue of deceased children, or if none, persons who would be entitled to decedent's property by intestate succession; and/or
  — if dependent on the decedent, his or her putative spouse, children of a putative spouse, stepchildren or parents. [CCP §377.60; *Cheyanna M. v. A.C. Nielson Co.* (1998) 66 CA4th 855, 858, 78 CR2d

335, 336—"children" includes child born after father's death who can prove paternity by clear and convincing evidence; *Welch v. State of Calif.* (2000) 83 CA4th 1374, 1377, 100 CR2d 430, 432—person lacking objective good faith belief in validity of marriage cannot maintain wrongful death action as "putative spouse"; *Rosales v. Battle* (2003) 113 CA4th 1178, 1185, 7 CR3d 13, 18—person determined to be a "concubina" (concubine) under Mexican law not a putative spouse]

*Cross-refer:* See detailed discussion Flahavan, Rea & Kelly, *Cal. Prac. Guide: Personal Injury* (TRG), Ch. 3.

### g. Contract claims

(1) **[2:32] Contracts made by agent:** Whether or not actually named in the contract, the employer (principal) is the real party in interest as to claims arising from contracts made on his or her behalf by his or her employee (agent), who was understood to be acting as such in making the contract.

(a) **[2:33] Undisclosed agency:** A contract made by an agent for an undisclosed principal is generally treated as the contract of the principal, so that it may sue thereon. [*Ikerd v. Warren T. Merrill & Sons* (1992) 9 CA4th 1833, 1839, 12 CR2d 398, 401, fn. 6]

The other contracting party may sue *either* the principal *or* the agent; but it cannot sue both. [*Ikerd v. Warren T. Merrill & Sons*, supra, 9 CA4th at 1839, 12 CR2d at 401, fn. 6]

(2) **[2:34] Third party beneficiary contracts:** A contract made "expressly for the benefit of a third person" may be enforced by that person. [Civ.C. §1559]

The person to be benefited need not be named in the contract. But the contracting parties' *intent* to benefit that person must appear in the terms of the agreement. [*Johnson v. Sup.Ct. (Calif. Cryobank, Inc.)* (2000) 80 CA4th 1050, 1064, 95 CR2d 864, 873]

(a) **[2:34.1] Compare—incidental beneficiaries:** On the other hand, persons who are only incidentally or remotely benefited by an agreement between others cannot enforce it. [*Lucas v. Hamm* (1961) 56 C2d 583, 590, 15 CR 821, 825]

(3) **[2:35] Insurance policies:** A person *entitled to benefits* under an insurance policy—as either a named insured, additional insured, or a third party beneficiary—

may sue in his or her own name for such benefits. [*Bass v. John Hancock Mut. Life Ins. Co.* (1974) 10 C3d 792, 797, 112 CR 195, 198, fn. 4; *Harper v. Wausau Ins. Co.* (1997) 56 CA4th 1079, 1087, 66 CR2d 64, 68—slip-and-fall victim on insured premises can sue insurer as third party beneficiary of policy's medical payments coverage which does not require proof that insured was at fault] (Where proof of fault is required, a noninsured must first recover a judgment against the insured; see *Shaolian v. Safeco Ins. Co.* (1999) 71 CA4th 268, 275, 83 CR2d 702, 706.)

*Cross-refer:* Persons entitled to sue for medical benefits under another's liability insurance (usually a homeowner's policy) is discussed in Croskey, Kaufman et al., *Cal. Prac. Guide: Insurance Litigation* (TRG), Ch. 7H.

(a) [2:36] **Compare—indirect beneficiaries:** It is not enough that a person benefits *indirectly* from payment of a claim.

For example, shareholders benefit indirectly when a claim is paid under a property insurance policy issued to their corporation. But the corporation (named insured) is the real party in interest on such claim, not the shareholders. [*Republic Indem. Co. of America v. Schofield* (1996) 47 CA4th 220, 225-226, 54 CR2d 637, 640-641; *Gantman v. United Pac. Ins. Co.* (1991) 232 CA3d 1560, 1566-1568, 284 CR 188, 191-192—policy insuring homeowners' association did not insure members individually; *see ¶2:14*]

(b) [2:37] **Joint insureds:** The result is different, of course, where shareholders are named as *joint insureds* with the corporation. They are real parties in interest. [See *Truestone, Inc. v. Travelers Ins. Co.* (1976) 55 CA3d 165, 171, 127 CR 386, 390]

(c) [2:38] **Additional insureds:** A landlord, creditor or other obligee may insist upon being named as an "additional insured" under its tenant's, debtor's or obligor's liability insurance. Additional insureds are entitled to enforce the insurance contract as *third party beneficiaries* (see above). [*Merced County Mut. Fire Ins. Co. v. State of Calif.* (1991) 233 CA3d 765, 775, 284 CR 680, 686; *Kotlar v. Hartford Fire Ins. Co.* (2000) 83 CA4th 1116, 1121, 100 CR2d 246, 249, fn. 3]

[2:38.1-38.4] *Reserved.*

(d) [2:38.5] **Judgment creditor of insured:** Persons injured by a defendant who is insured against liability normally *cannot* sue the liability insurer. The insurer's duties to defend and indemnify flow only to the insured defendant; persons injured by the insured are at most incidental beneficiaries.

But if such persons obtain a final *judgment* against the insured, they become entitled to enforce the liability policy; i.e., they are treated as third party beneficiaries of the insurer's promise to indemnify the insured against such judgments. [See Ins.C. §11580(b)(2); *Harper v. Wausau Ins. Co.* (1997) 56 CA4th 1079, 1086, 66 CR2d 64, 68]

*Cross-refer:* See detailed discussion in Croskey, Kaufman et al., *Cal. Prac. Guide: Insurance Litigation* (TRG), Ch. 15.

[2:38.6-38.9]  *Reserved.*

(e) **[2:38.10]  Compare—liability insurer's standing to challenge default judgment:**  An insurer that may be obligated to pay a judgment against its insured may have standing to move to set aside a default judgment against its insured; *see* ¶5:289.

(4) **[2:39]  Collective bargaining agreements:**  Collective bargaining agreements often provide that employee grievances can be submitted to arbitration *only* by the union or management. In such event, an individual employee has no standing to compel arbitration or to set aside an arbitrator's award. [*Melander v. Hughes Aircraft Co.* (1987) 194 CA3d 542, 547, 239 CR 592, 595]

[2:39.1-39.4]  *Reserved.*

h. **[2:39.5]  Validation proceedings:**  Public agencies may sue to determine the validity of contemplated public actions, such as bond issues. [See CCP §860 et seq.]

If they fail to do so, "any interested person" may bring such an action (but standing is strictly construed). [See CCP §863; *Torres v. City of Yorba Linda* (1993) 13 CA4th 1035, 1042-1043, 17 CR2d 400, 403-404—nonresident of city lacks standing to challenge community redevelopment project]

[2:39.6-39.9]  *Reserved.*

i. **[2:39.10]  Cartwright Act violations:**  The Cartwright Act (Bus. & Prof.C. §16700 et seq.) sets forth California's version of the Sherman Antitrust Act. Plaintiffs suing under the Cartwright Act must be within the "target area" of the antitrust violation to have standing to sue; i.e., they must have suffered direct injury as a result of the anticompetitive conduct. [See Bus. & Prof.C. §16750(a); *Cellular Plus, Inc. v. Sup.Ct. (U.S. West Cellular)* (1993) 14 CA4th 1224, 1232, 18 CR2d 308, 312; *Vinci v. Waste Management, Inc.* (1995) 36 CA4th 1811, 1815, 43 CR2d 337, 339]

j.  [2:39.11] **Actions for unfair competition:**  In an action for unfair competition under Bus. & Prof.C. §17200 et seq., private parties have standing to sue *on behalf of the general public*. [*Stop Youth Addiction, Inc. v. Lucky Stores, Inc.* (1998) 17 C4th 553, 562, 71 CR2d 731, 736; *see ¶2:41, 14:226 ff.*]

But where those allegedly injured are not part of the "general public," an uninjured party has no standing to sue for unfair competition. [*Rosenbluth Int'l, Inc. v. Sup.Ct. (Serrano)* (2002) 101 CA4th 1073, 1079, 124 CR2d 844, 848—where allegedly injured parties were large Fortune 1000 corporations that had individually negotiated contracts with defendant, plaintiff (not a party to any such contract) lacked standing to bring action under §17200]

[2:39.12]  *Reserved.*

k.  [2:39.13] **Actions under Telephone Consumer Protection Act (TCPA):**  Private individuals have a private right of action and therefore standing to sue for "junk fax" transmissions in violation of the federal Telephone Consumer Protection Act (47 USC §227(b)(3)). [*Kaufman v. ACS Systems, Inc.* (2003) 110 CA4th 886, 896, 2 CR3d 296, 305—state courts have *exclusive jurisdiction* of TCPA claims]

[2:39.14]  *Reserved.*

l.  [2:39.15] **Crime victims:**  Civil actions lie in favor of crime victims. Violation of a criminal statute embodying a public policy is generally actionable even though the statute contains no civil remedy. Any injured member of the public for whose benefit the statute is enacted may bring an action. [*Angie M. v. Sup.Ct. (Hiemstra)* (1995) 37 CA4th 1217, 1223, 44 CR2d 197, 202—minor female may sue for violation of statute making unlawful seduction of minor a crime]

[2:39.16-39.17]  *Reserved.*

m.  [2:39.18] **Standing to challenge statute (constitutional standing):**  To challenge a statute on due process or equal protection grounds, a party must show that the statute has caused or threatens to cause such party "with *an injury of sufficient magnitude* to reasonably assure the relevant facts and issues will be adequately presented." [*City of Irvine v. Irvine Citizens Against Overdevelopment* (1994) 25 CA4th 868, 874, 30 CR2d 797, 799 (emphasis added)]

(1)  [2:39.19] **Sufficient injury:**  A party seeking to enjoin enforcement of a state law must show an invasion of a legally protected interest that is:

— *concrete and particularized;* and
— *actual or imminent* (not conjectural or hypothetical). [*Cornelius v. Los Angeles Co. Metropolitan Transp. Authority* (1996) 49 CA4th 1761, 1768, 57 CR2d 618, 622]

[2:39.20-39.24] *Reserved.*

(2) **Application**

- [2:39.25] Party contractually obligated to pay business tax credit had sufficient standing to challenge statute imposing the tax. [*City of Cupertino v. City of San Jose* (1995) 33 CA4th 1671, 1675, 40 CR2d 171, 173]

- [2:39.26] Party developing new strain of cotton had standing to challenge statutory scheme under which it would be assumed into the public domain. [*B.C. Cotton, Inc. v. Voss* (1995) 33 CA4th 929, 948, 39 CR2d 484, 497]

4. [2:40] **Exceptions—Suit Permitted by Other Than Real Party in Interest:** There are several exceptions recognized to the real party in interest requirement, some by statute and others by case law.

a. [2:40.1] **Parents suing for injury to child:** The parents of a legitimate, unmarried child may sue the person responsible for injuries to their child *unless a guardian* for the child has been appointed, in which event the guardian must maintain the action. (If either parent refuses to join, the other may sue alone, naming the refusing parent as a codefendant.) [CCP §376]

Parents also may sue for wrongful death damages when there is no surviving issue of a deceased child. [See CCP §377.60(a)]

*Cross-refer:* A minor lacks *capacity to sue* in his or her own name; *see ¶2:83.*

(1) [2:40.1a] **Caution—parent-child conflict of interest concerns:** If the parent was injured in the same accident, there may be a potential conflict of interest between the parent and child (e.g., claims of fault, competing claims for available policy limits, etc.). The parent should not be considered for appointment as guardian ad litem in such cases.

b. [2:41] **Representative suits:** A person or entity may sue *on behalf of* the real parties in interest "where justified by considerations of *necessity, convenience and justice.*" [*Salton City Area Prop. Owners Ass'n v. M. Penn Phillips Co.* (1977) 75 CA3d 184, 191, 141 CR 895, 899]

This includes:

- *class actions (¶14:9 ff.)*;

- *shareholder derivative* suits *(¶14:241)*;

- statutory actions in which plaintiff may sue *on behalf of the general public* or other large class of persons (e.g., unfair competition under Bus. & Prof.C. §17200) *(¶14:225 ff.)*; and

- other *public interest* lawsuits in which a right to sue in a representative capacity has been recognized *(¶14:200 ff.)*.

*Cross-refer:* See detailed discussion of this topic in *Ch. 14, "Representative and Class Actions."*

[2:42-65]   *Reserved.*

c. **[2:66]   Mandamus actions—"public right/public duty" cases:**   Ordinarily, a plaintiff seeking a writ of mandamus must show that he or she is beneficially interested in the outcome. [See CCP §1086]

"To have standing to seek a writ of mandate, a party must be 'beneficially interested' . . . i.e., have some special interest to be served or some particular right to be preserved or protected over and above the interest held in common with the public at large." [*Associated Builders & Contractors, Inc. v. San Francisco Airports Comm'n* (1999) 21 C4th 352, 361-362, 87 CR2d 654, 659 (internal quotes omitted)]

However, where the question is one of *public right*, and the writ would compel enforcement of a *public duty*, plaintiff need not show any special interest in the result. "It is sufficient that he is interested as a citizen in having the laws executed and the duty in question enforced." [*Green v. Obledo* (1981) 29 C3d 126, 144, 172 CR 206, 216; *Tobe v. City of Santa Ana* (1995) 9 C4th 1069, 1116-1117, 40 CR2d 402, 430-431]

(1) **[2:67]   Example:**   A property owner, taxpayer or elector has standing to sue the City to compel enforcement of environmental laws. Standing is conferred by the plaintiff's "geographical nexus" with the challenged project. Moreover, the "geographical nexus" may be attenuated (i.e., beyond the City limits) . . . because the "effects of environmental abuse are not contained by political lines." [*Citizens Ass'n for Sensible Development of Bishop Area v. County of Inyo* (1985) 172 CA3d 151, 159, 217 CR 893, 897]

(2) **[2:68]   Environmental protection suits:**   Standing requirements may be liberalized for private individuals

suing to enforce environmental protection statutes. [*Laidlaw Environmental Services, Inc., Local Assessment Comm. v. County of Kern* (1996) 44 CA4th 346, 354, 51 CR2d 666, 670; see *Kane v. Redevelopment Agency* (1986) 179 CA3d 899, 904, 224 CR 922, 924— P alleged he was "within class of persons beneficially interested" in City Redevelopment Agency's compliance with CEQA (California Environmental Quality Act), and "resident of County in which City was located"; held sufficient to confer standing in public interest lawsuit to enforce provisions of Act]

(3) [2:69]  **Representative suits:**  A public interest group entity may maintain a mandamus action to challenge conduct that occurred *before the group was formed:* "(T)he fact a petitioner did not exist at the time a governmental agency began disregarding its statutory obligations is not a persuasive reason to entirely excuse a governmental agency's failure to meet these obligations." [*Hogar Dulce Hogar v. Community Develop. Comm'n of City of Escondido* (2003) 110 CA4th 1288, 1295, 2 CR3d 497, 501]

d.  [2:70]  **Taxpayers' actions:**  A taxpayer may sue to prevent a public official from waste or illegal expenditure of public funds. The plaintiff must be:

— a *resident* of the state, city, county or other public entity involved, or a *corporation*; and

— *assessed for and liable to pay* a tax to the public entity or have paid such tax within the past year. [CCP §526a]

The purpose is to permit challenges to governmental action which might otherwise go unchallenged because of standing requirements (i.e., that plaintiff must be directly injured by the program or policy in order to have standing to sue). [*Blair v. Pitchess* (1971) 5 C3d 258, 267-268, 96 CR 42, 49]

(1) [2:70.1]  **Tax must be "assessed":**  Taxpayer standing depends on payment of taxes that are "assessed"; e.g., ad valorem taxes on real or personal property. [See *Cornelius v. Los Angeles Co. Metropolitan Transp. Authority* (1996) 49 CA4th 1761, 1775, 57 CR2d 618, 626-627; *Blair v. Pitchess, supra*, 5 C3d at 269, 96 CR at 50]

• [2:70.2]  Taxpayer standing *cannot* be based on payment of *gasoline* or *sales taxes.* Such taxes are not "assessed" to the consumer. They are really taxes on retailers and distributors, rather than on the consumer to whom the retailer passes the burden. [*Cornelius v. Los Angeles Co. Metropolitan Transp. Authority, supra*, 49 CA4th at 1777, 57 CR2d at 628]

• [2:70.3]  Nor is taxpayer standing conferred by payment of *state income taxes,* at least where the challenged program is only partially or indirectly supported by the taxes paid. Otherwise, local public agencies could be sued for implementing state programs financed indirectly or in part by the state income tax. [*Cornelius v. Los Angeles Co. Metropolitan Transp. Authority*, supra, 49 CA4th at 1777, 57 CR2d at 628]

e.  [2:71]  **County suing for child support:**  A county may sue on behalf of minor children (real parties in interest) to compel parental support. Even if *paternity* is at issue and will be adjudicated in such action, the child need not be made a formal party to the action (no guardian ad litem need be appointed). The child's interests are deemed the same as the county's and therefore receive effective representation by the county. [Fam.C. §17404; *County of Tulare v. Boggs* (1983) 146 CA3d 236, 243, 194 CR 80, 84]

[2:72]  Likewise, where a public assistance recipient's child support rights have been assigned to the county, the county is an indispensable party in proceedings by the support obligor to modify child support. [*Marriage of Mena* (1989) 212 CA3d 12, 19, 260 CR 314, 319; and see detailed discussion in Hogoboom & King, *Cal. Prac. Guide: Family Law* (TRG), Chs. 3 & 6]

f.  [2:73]  **Defendant spouses:**  By statute, in suits against husband and wife, each is the real party in interest as to his or her own interest, and also as to the *other spouse's interest* if he or she neglects to defend the action. [CCP §371]

(Note: The statute apparently is *not* limited to spouses who are living together; nor to claims enforceable against community property.)

g.  [2:74]  **Shareholders of dissolved corporation:**  Shareholders having received assets of a dissolved corporation are liable for its debts (*see ¶2:118*). "As a matter of procedure," they *may be sued in the name of the corporation* upon any cause of action against the corporation. [Corps.C. §2011(a)(3)]

(1)  [2:75]  **Comment:**  How this will work in practice is unclear! Due process normally forbids entry of judgment against persons *not named* in the summons and complaint.

(Text cont'd on p. 2-21)

**RESERVED**

⇨[2:76]  *PRACTICE POINTER:*   Avoid the problem! *Name each shareholder* of the dissolved corporation in both the summons and complaint. Use "Doe" allegations if necessary.

h.  [2:76.1]  **Protection against workplace violence:** Where an employee has suffered violence while at work, or such violence has been threatened, the *employer may sue on behalf of the employee* for a temporary restraining order or injunction prohibiting such violence or threat. [CCP §527.8]

5.  [2:77]  **Procedure for Challenging Standing to Sue:**   A complaint filed by someone other than the real party in interest is subject to *general demurrer* if the defect appears on the face of the complaint: i.e., it fails to state a cause of action by the plaintiff, because the claim sued upon belongs to somebody else. [*Carsten v. Psychology Examining Comm. of Bd. of Med. Qual. Assur.* (1980) 27 C3d 793, 796, 166 CR 844, 846; see *Powers v. Ashton* (1975) 45 CA3d 783, 789, 119 CR 729, 733]

If plaintiff's lack of standing to sue does *not* appear on the face of the complaint, the defect must be raised as an affirmative defense in the answer. *See ¶6:430 ff.*

a.  [2:78]  **Defect not waived by failure to object:**   Plaintiff's lack of standing to sue on the claim is treated as a "jurisdictional" defect and is *not waived* by defendant's failure to raise it by demurrer or answer: "(C)ontentions based on a lack of standing involve jurisdictional challenges and may be raised at any time in the proceeding." [*Common Cause of Calif. v. Board of Supervisors* (1989) 49 C3d 432, 438, 261 CR 574, 577—lack of standing can be raised for first time on appeal; *Associated Builders & Contractors, Inc. v. San Francisco Airports Comm'n* (1999) 21 C4th 352, 361, 87 CR2d 654, 659]

(1)  [2:78.1]  **Rationale:**   Standing to sue affects the right to relief and goes to the *existence of a cause of action* against the defendant. [See CCP §430.80; *Killian v. Millard* (1991) 228 CA3d 1601, 1605, 279 CR 877, 879]

[2:78.2-78.4]  *Reserved.*

b.  [2:78.5]  **Jury trial required where facts disputed:** Where a party's standing depends on disputed facts or credibility determinations (e.g., ownership or possession of property), the parties are entitled to a jury trial on the issue. [*People v. Sup.Ct. (Plascencia)* (2002) 103 CA4th 409, 424, 126 CR2d 793, 804-805]

6.  [2:79]  **Effect of Lack of Standing to Sue:**   When a party lacks standing to sue, the action must be dismissed, unless the complaint can be amended by substituting a party who has

standing. [*Cloud v. Northrop Grumman Corp.* (1998) 67 CA4th 995, 1004-1011, 79 CR2d 544, 549-554]

## B. CAPACITY TO SUE OR DEFEND

[2:80]   In addition to the requirement of *standing to* sue (real party in interest with respect to the claim involved), a party must also have *capacity* to sue (or defend) the action.

1. [2:81]   **Nature of Requirement:**   The rules regarding party capacity are designed to assure that whatever judgment is rendered will be binding on the parties involved, and thus effectively resolve the litigation. However, lack of capacity is not a jurisdictional defect, and must be properly raised or the objection may be waived (¶2:139). [*American Alternative Energy Partners II, 1985 v. Windridge, Inc.* (1996) 42 CA4th 551, 559, 49 CR2d 686, 691 (citing text)]

   a. [2:81.1]   **Compare—standing to sue:**   "There is a difference between the *capacity* to sue, which is the right to come into court, and the *standing* to sue, which is the right to relief in court." [*Color-Vue, Inc. v. Abrams* (1996) 44 CA4th 1599, 1604, 52 CR2d 443, 446 (emphasis in original)]

   Lack of standing negates existence of a cause of action and is not waived by failure to object; it can even be raised for the first time on appeal. Lack of capacity to sue, on the other hand, is *not* an element of the cause of action; it is a technical objection that must be timely raised or is waived (*see* ¶2:139). [*Color-Vue, Inc. v. Abrams*, supra, 44 CA4th at 1605, 52 CR2d at 446]

2. [2:82]   **Application:**   In general, any person or entity has capacity to sue or defend a civil action in California courts. This includes both natural and artificial "persons" (corporations, partnerships, associations, governmental entities, etc.). [*American Alternative Energy Partners II, 1985 v. Windridge, Inc.* (1996) 42 CA4th 551, 559, 49 CR2d 686, 691 (citing text)]

   But there are a few situations in which the plaintiff or defendant may lack capacity to be a party to a civil action. The following are the most common situations in which capacity to sue or defend may be challenged:

   a. [2:83]   **Minors, incompetents:**   Subject to exceptions discussed below (¶2:84.5 ff.), minors and incompetents lack capacity to sue in their own names, or to defend an action brought against them. Instead, litigation must be conducted through a *guardian, conservator of the estate* or *guardian ad litem*. [CCP §372(a)]

      (1) [2:84]   **Appointment of guardian ad litem:**   Except as noted below, if a guardian or conservator has not previously been appointed for the minor or incompetent,

one must be appointed for the purpose of the litigation (guardian ad litem). Moreover, even if there is an existing guardianship or conservatorship, a guardian ad litem may be appointed if the court deems it expedient to do so. [CCP §372] (A guardian ad litem is *mandatory* in paternity actions; see Fam.C. §7635.)

A guardian ad litem is *not a party* to the action but rather the representative of record of a party (the minor) who lacks capacity to represent himself or herself. [*J.W. v. Sup.Ct.* (1993) 17 CA4th 958, 964, 22 CR2d 527, 529-530]

(a) [2:84.1] **Cannot act in pro per:** Except as discussed below, counsel must appear on behalf of the minor or incompetent. A nonattorney appointed as guardian ad litem *cannot* act in pro per. Doing so would constitute the unlawful practice of law (Bus. & Prof.C. §6125). [*J.W. v. Sup.Ct.*, supra, 17 CA4th at 965, 22 CR2d at 530—mother appointed as guardian ad litem for minor child in paternity proceedings could not represent child in pro per (although she could appear in her own right in pro per)]

   1) [2:84.2] **Compare—can voluntarily dismiss:** Where the attorney has been relieved or removed as counsel of record, a nonattorney guardian ad litem *can* voluntarily dismiss the action without prejudice. E.g., where the opposing party's motion for summary judgment is pending, allowing the guardian ad litem to dismiss is "the only fair remedy." [*Mossanen v. Monfared* (2000) 77 CA4th 1402, 1410, 92 CR2d 459, 464]

   [2:84.3-84.4] *Reserved.*

(b) [2:84.5] **Exceptions:** There are some statutory exceptions to the above rules:

   1) [2:84.6] **Minors age 12 or older—seeking or opposing protective or restraining orders:** A minor 12 years of age or older may

*(Text cont'd on p. 2-23)*

**RESERVED**

appear *without a guardian or counsel* for the purpose of requesting or opposing:

— an injunction or TRO to prevent harassment under CCP §527.6 (*see ¶9:697 ff.*) or against workplace violence under CCP §527.8 (*see ¶9:679 ff.*); or

— domestic violence protective orders under Fam.C. §§6200 et seq., 7710 and 7720. [CCP §372(b)(1)]

However, the court may appoint a guardian ad litem in such cases, provided it does not delay issuance or denial of the order sought. [CCP §372(b)(1)]

In making a decision concerning the appointment of a particular guardian ad litem, the court must consider whether the interests of the minor and guardian are adverse. [CCP §372(b)(1)]

2) [2:84.7] **Minors under age 12—seeking or opposing protective or restraining orders:** A minor under 12 years of age, accompanied by a guardian ad litem, may appear *without counsel* for the limited purposes described above (*see ¶2:84.6*). [CCP §374(a)]

In making a decision concerning the appointment of a particular guardian ad litem, the court must consider whether the minor and guardian have divergent interests. [CCP §374(b)]

(c) **Procedure for appointment**

- [2:85] No independent guardianship proceeding is necessary. The guardian ad litem can be appointed as part of the same lawsuit to which the minor or incompetent is a party. [*Sarracino v. Sup.Ct. (Sarracino)* (1974) 13 C3d 1, 12, 118 CR 21, 29]

- [2:86] A minor 14 years old or more may apply to the court directly for appointment of a guardian ad litem. For other minors or incompetents, any relative or friend may apply for such appointment. [CCP §373(a)]

- [2:86.1] If the minor and his or her family fail to seek appointment of a guardian ad litem, "any other party to the action" may do so; or, the court may act sua sponte. [CCP §373(b)]

- [2:86.2] *Local rules:* There may be additional limitations under local rules. For example, local rules may restrict appointment of a parent as guardian ad litem when the parent also asserts personal claims in the same action. [See San Diego Sup.Ct. Rule 2.37A]

[2:86.3-86.4]  *Reserved.*

**FORM:**  Petition and Order for Appointment of Guardian Ad Litem, *see Form 2:I.* (Use of this Judicial Council form is mandatory.)

(d) [2:86.5]  **Due process required for incompetent adults:**  A guardian ad litem may be appointed for an incompetent adult only if (i) he or she *consents* to the appointment or (ii) upon notice and hearing. [*In re Jessica G.* (2001) 93 CA4th 1180, 1187-1188, 113 CR2d 714, 719]

*Comment:* It is not clear how an incompetent person can give effective "consent" to the appointment of a guardian (possibly by not contesting the petition).

A formal hearing is not required. What is necessary is that the court or counsel explain to the party the purpose of the guardian ad litem appointment, the authority the guardian will have, and why it is believed the appointment should be made. The party is entitled to an evidentiary hearing on the issue of competency if he or she so desires: "At a minimum, the court should make an inquiry sufficient to satisfy it that the (party) is, or is not, competent; i.e., whether the (party) understands the nature of the proceedings and can assist the attorney in protecting his/her rights. The court's decision on this issue should be stated on the record." [*In re Jessica G.,* supra, 93 CA4th at 1187-1188, 113 CR2d at 719 (parentheses added)]

(e) [2:87]  **Effect of no appointment:**  Failure to appoint a guardian ad litem for a minor is *not* a defect affecting the court's jurisdiction. Thus, a judgment rendered in favor or against an unrepresented minor is *not* void; it is merely *voidable by the minor.* [*Field v. Hughes* (1933) 131 CA 144, 146, 20 P2d 990, 991; see *Medical Legal Consulting Services, Inc. v. Covarrubias* (1991) 234 CA3d 80, 87-88, 285 CR 559, 563-564 (dictum); see also Fam.C. §6710—minor has right to "disaffirm" contracts (and, if the minor is dead, so can his or her heirs or personal representative)]

The effect is that litigating with an unrepresented minor is usually a "no win" situation for the opposing party: i.e., the minor can *enforce* the judgment if he or she wins, and can disaffirm it if he or she loses!

⇨[2:87.1]  *PRACTICE POINTER FOR PLAIN-TIFFS:*  If the defendant is a minor and his or her family fails to seek appointment of a guardian ad litem, *plaintiff can seek the appointment* (see CCP §373(b)—"any other party to the action").

(2) [2:88]  **Emancipated minors:**  If parents relinquish control of their minor child and his or her earnings, the child may be deemed emancipated under Fam.C. §7504. In such cases, the minor may sue or be sued in his or her own name, without appointment of a guardian ad litem. [See *Jolicoeur v. Mihaly* (1971) 5 C3d 565, 582, 96 CR 697, 707, fn. 12]

(3) [2:88.1]  **Tolling of statute of limitations for minors and "insane" persons:**  If a person is a minor or "*insane*" (not merely incompetent) when a cause of action accrues, the statute of limitations generally is tolled during the party's disability. [See CCP §352(a); *Alcott Rehabilitation Hosp. v. Sup.Ct. (Smith)* (2001) 93 CA4th 94, 100, 112 CR2d 807, 811]

Thus, failure to appoint a guardian for a minor or *insane* person normally does not affect the person's right to sue. The statute *does not begin to run* until the person reaches the age of majority or is no longer "insane." (Note, however, that this does *not* extend the time for filing notice of claim against a governmental entity; CCP §352(b), *see ¶1:719.*)

[2:88.2-88.4]  *Reserved.*

b.  [2:88.5]  **Compare—disabled persons:**  An action "does not abate" by reason of a party's "disability." Rather, on motion, the court must allow the action to be maintained by, or continued against, the party's representative. [CCP §375]

(1) [2:88.6]  **No tolling of statute of limitations:**  The statute of limitations is *not* tolled for disabled persons (as it is for minors and "insane" persons, above). [See CCP §352(a)]

(2) [2:88.7]  **Effect:**  Apparently, the only effect of a party's "disability" is that the court, on motion, *must* allow the action to be continued by or against a representative for the "disabled" party. [See CCP §375]

(3) [2:88.8] **Comment:** The effect of failure to appoint a representative is unclear. It remains to be seen whether an adverse judgment or verdict can be attacked on the ground the losing party was "disabled" and no representative had been appointed.

c. [2:89] **Corporations:** A corporation is a legal entity and therefore normally has capacity to sue or defend. [Corps.C. §207] But there are some circumstances in which its capacity may be challenged:

(1) [2:90] **Suspended corporations:** A corporation whose powers have been suspended for nonpayment of the corporate franchise tax lacks capacity *to sue* in California courts; and, if sued, it lacks capacity *to defend.* [Rev. & Tax.C. §23301; *Reed v. Norman* (1957) 48 C2d 338, 342, 309 P2d 809, 811; see *Color-Vue, Inc. v. Abrams* (1996) 44 CA4th 1599, 1603-1604, 52 CR2d 443, 446—"suspension of corporate powers results in a lack of *capacity* to sue, not a lack of *standing* to sue" (emphasis in original)]

Similarly, a corporation suspended under Corps.C. §2205 for failure to file the biennial statement required by Corps.C. §1502 lacks capacity to sue or defend itself. [*Palm Valley Homeowners Ass'n, Inc. v. Design MTC* (2000) 85 CA4th 553, 560, 102 CR2d 350, 354-355]

⇨[2:90.1] *CAUTION re representing suspended corporation:* Anyone who purports to exercise the rights and powers of a suspended corporation—possibly including a lawyer who appears on its behalf—is guilty of a misdemeanor. [Rev. & Tax.C. §19719]

In addition, a lawyer who *knowingly* represents a suspended corporation and conceals this fact from the court may be subject to *sanctions.* [*Palm Valley Homeowners Ass'n, Inc. v. Design MTC*, supra, 85 CA4th at 563, 102 CR2d at 357]

(a) [2:91] **Purpose:** The purpose of the rule is to enhance tax collections (not to assure enforceability of judgments, as with other rules on party capacity). [*American Alternative Energy Partners II, 1985 v. Windridge, Inc.* (1996) 42 CA4th 551, 562-563, 49 CR2d 686, 693 (citing text); *Color-Vue, Inc. v. Abrams*, supra, 44 CA4th at 1605, 52 CR2d at 447—defendants are only "incidental beneficiaries" of the rule]

1) [2:91.1] **Strictly construed:** A plea in abatement based on plaintiff's lack of capacity

is *not* favored in law and will be strictly construed. [*Color-Vue, Inc. v. Abrams*, supra, 44 CA4th at 1604, 52 CR2d at 446]

[2:91.2-91.4]  *Reserved.*

(b) **Application**

- [2:91.5]  During the period that a corporation is suspended for failure to pay taxes, it may not prosecute or defend an action, *appeal* from an adverse judgment, or seek a writ of mandate. [See *Grell v. Laci Le Beau Corp.* (1999) 73 CA4th 1300, 1306, 87 CR2d 358, 362]

- [2:91.6]  Nor may a suspended corporation invoke the statutory mechanism for *renewing a judgment* obtained while it was in good standing. [*Timberline, Inc. v. Jaisinghani* (1997) 54 CA4th 1361, 1367, 64 CR2d 4, 7—"Renewal of a judgment requires judicial intervention for its validity, regardless how minimal the activity"]

- [2:91.7]  *Compare—suit against corporation:* A suspended corporation may be sued. Service of process is effected in the same manner as upon a corporation that is not suspended. A default judgment may be entered upon its failure to respond. [See CCP §§416.10, 416.20; *Grell v. Laci Le Beau Corp.*, supra, 73 CA4th at 1306, 87 CR2d at 362—statute of limitations not tolled for either party while corporate powers are suspended]

(c) [2:92]  **Foreign corporations:**  A foreign corporation whose powers have been suspended *in its home state* for nonpayment of corporate taxes there, also lacks capacity to sue in California. [*CM Record Corp. v. MCA Records, Inc.* (1985) 168 CA3d 965, 968-969, 214 CR 409, 411]

(d) [2:93]  **Revivor:**  Once the delinquent taxes (plus interest and penalties) are paid, the corporation's powers are restored, thus "reviving" its capacity to sue or defend. But such revivor is "without prejudice to any action, defense or right which has accrued by reason of the original suspension ..." [Rev. & Tax.C. §§23305, 23305a; see *Electronic Equipment Express, Inc. v. Donald H. Seiler & Co.* (1981) 122 CA3d 834, 843, 176 CR 239, 244]

Even before official revivor, a corporation may sue or defend after *substantial compliance* with the revival statute. But this requires payment of *all* taxes, *interest and penalties* due. [*Sade Shoe Co. v. Oschin & Snyder* (1990) 217 CA3d 1509, 1513, 266 CR 619, 623-624]

1) **[2:93.1]** **Continuance to obtain revivor:** Where the complaint is viable, it is an abuse of discretion to deny the corporation's request for a continuance of trial in order to pay delinquent taxes and obtain a certificate of revivor. [See *Color-Vue, Inc. v. Abrams* (1996) 44 CA4th 1599, 1606, 52 CR2d 443, 447—defendant who delayed raising defect until time of trial waived right to object]

2) **[2:94]** **Substantive defenses not affected by revivor:** Substantive defenses that have accrued during suspension are not affected by revivor. For example:

   a) **[2:95]** **Statute of limitations:** The statute of limitations is a substantive defense. Thus, if the statute of limitations runs on a claim belonging to the corporation while its powers are suspended, the claim is time-barred. I.e., revivor of the corporation's powers does *not* revive the claim. [*United Med. Management Ltd. v. Gatto* (1996) 49 CA4th 1732, 1738, 57 CR2d 600, 602]

   *Compare—suit against corporation:* Suspension of corporate status does *not* toll the statute of limitations in an action *against* the corporation; *see* ¶2:91.7.

   b) **[2:96]** **Compare—statute of limitations waived by cross-complaint:** Defendant waives the statute of limitations as a defense by filing a cross-complaint to a complaint by a suspended corporation (seeking affirmative relief in the same action). This allows the corporation, upon its revival, to proceed with its original action. [*Electronic Equipment Express, Inc. v. Donald H. Seiler Co.* (1981) 122 CA3d 834, 847, 176 CR 239, 246; *American Alternative Energy Partners II, 1985 v. Windridge, Inc.* (1996) 42 CA4th 551, 564-565, 49 CR2d 686, 694]

   **[2:97-99]** *Reserved.*

3) **[2:100]** **Procedural acts validated by revivor:** On the other hand, revivor of a corporation's powers validates any procedural step

taken on its behalf while it was under suspension: "Procedural acts ... are validated *retroactively* by corporate revival." [*Benton v. County of Napa* (1991) 226 CA3d 1485, 1489-1490, 277 CR 541, 544]

    a) [2:101] **Application:** Most litigation activity is characterized as "procedural" for purposes of corporate revival. [*Benton v. County of Napa*, supra, 226 CA3d at 1490, 277 CR at 545]

    For example, a *notice of appeal* filed by the corporation while suspended is validated retroactively when it obtains a certificate of revivor. [*Peacock Hill Ass'n v. Peacock Lagoon Const. Co.* (1972) 8 C3d 369, 371, 105 CR 29, 31; see also *Rochin v. Pat Johnson Mfg. Co.* (1998) 67 CA4th 1228, 1236-1237, 79 CR2d 719, 724]

    b) [2:102] **Rationale:** The purpose of the suspension is to put pressure on the corporation to pay its taxes. "There is little purpose in imposing additional penalties after the taxes have been paid." [*Peacock Hill Ass'n v. Peacock Lagoon Const. Co.*, supra, 8 C3d at 371, 105 CR at 30]

4) [2:103] **Contracts executed during suspension:** Contracts entered into by a corporation while suspended are *voidable* at the option of the other party.

Effect: Subsequent revivor of the corporation's powers does not automatically validate contracts entered into during suspension. The other party can still disavow the contract. [*Damato v. Slevin* (1989) 214 CA3d 668, 675, 262 CR 879, 883—no estoppel unless other party *knew* of suspension and corporation did not]

    a) [2:104] **Voidable only in judicial proceedings:** However, a contract entered into during suspension can be declared void only in judicial proceedings (e.g., suit to rescind the contract). Such relief cannot be granted unless (i) the corporation was allowed a "reasonable opportunity" to obtain revivor; and (ii) the corporation *receives full restitution* of benefits conferred by it under the contract. [Rev. & Tax.C. §§23304.5, 23305a]

[2:104.1-104.4]  *Reserved.*

(e) [2:104.5]  **Compare—surety's rights not affected:**  Although a corporation is suspended for nonpayment of franchise tax, the corporation's surety may still raise all defenses and set-offs available to the corporation. [*Reliance Ins. Co. v. Sup.Ct. (Wells)* (2000) 84 CA4th 383, 388, 100 CR2d 807, 810-811]

(2) [2:105]  **Nonqualified foreign corporations:**  Foreign (out-of-state) corporations are prohibited from transacting intrastate business in California without obtaining a "certificate of qualification" from the Secretary of State (which requires filing certain papers and paying certain fees). [See Corps.C. §2105]

But, unlike suspended corporations, they are *not* disabled from suing or defending themselves in California courts:

(a) [2:106]  **Capacity to sue prior to qualification:**  Foreign corporations that have not so "qualified" may not "*maintain* any action or proceeding . . . commenced prior to compliance with Section 2105" upon intrastate business. [Corps.C. §2203(c)]

But this does *not* affect their capacity to *file a lawsuit.* Unlike a corporation whose powers have been suspended (above), nonqualified foreign corporations *do not* lack capacity to sue. Section 2203(c), above, merely bars "maintaining" an action based on intrastate business transacted in California. [*United Med. Management Ltd. v. Gatto* (1996) 49 CA4th 1732, 1739, 57 CR2d 600, 603]

1) [2:106.1]  **Matter of abatement:**  Although the corporation may *commence* such an action *without* qualifying, its failure to qualify is a matter of abatement: i.e., defendants may raise as a *defense* that the foreign corporation lacks capacity *to* "maintain" the action. If this is shown, an action commenced before qualification must be abated until the corporation qualifies. [*United Med. Management Ltd. v. Gatto,* supra, 49 CA4th at 1740, 57 CR2d at 604]

a) [2:106.2]  **Showing required:**  To establish this defense, defendant must show that:

— the action *arises out of* transaction of intrastate business by a foreign corporation; and

— the action was *commenced* by the foreign corporation *prior* to qualifying to transact business here. [*United Systems of Arkansas, Inc. v. Stamison* (1998) 63 CA4th 1001, 1007, 74 CR2d 407, 409]

2) [2:106.3] **Qualification allows pending action to continue:** If the foreign corporation subsequently qualifies to do business here—*and pays fees, penalties and taxes due* as required by Corps.C. §2203(c)—it may then "maintain" an action commenced before qualification. [See Corps.C. §2203(c)]

Qualification thus "restores the foreign corporation to full legal competency and its prior transactions are given full effect." [*United Med. Management Ltd. v. Gatto*, supra, 49 CA4th at 1740, 57 CR2d at 604 (internal quotes omitted)]

[2:106.4] *Reserved.*

3) [2:106.5] **Actions previously dismissed may be refiled:** Where an earlier action was dismissed because of the foreign corporation's failure to qualify, it may commence a new action after qualifying (assuming no statute of limitations problem). The earlier dismissal on procedural grounds is not res judicata. [*United Med. Management Ltd. v. Gatto*, supra, 49 CA4th at 1740, 57 CR2d at 604]

4) [2:106.6] **Compare—actions commenced *after* qualification not subject to statute:** By its terms, Corps.C. §2203 bars nonqualified foreign corporations from "maintaining" actions "commenced prior to compliance with Section 2105." *It does not apply* to actions commenced *after* qualification! [*United Med. Management Ltd. v. Gatto*, supra, 49 CA4th at 1740, 57 CR2d at 604—"Section 2203(c) is to be narrowly construed to effect its remedial purpose"]

Thus, in actions commenced *after* the corporation qualified to transact business here, it need not be shown that the corporation paid *the fees, penalties and taxes* required by §2203(c). [*United Med. Management Ltd. v. Gatto*, supra, 49 CA4th at 1740, 57 CR2d at 604]

[2:107] *Reserved.*

(b) [2:108] **Capacity to defend without qualification:** A foreign corporation transacting business in California which has failed to qualify with the Secretary of State may nevertheless *defend* an action brought against it in California courts without qualifying. (I.e., Corps.C. §2203(c)'s ban on "maintaining" an action or proceeding does not apply to defending them.) [*United Med. Management Ltd. v. Gatto*, supra, 49 CA4th at 1739, 57 CR2d at 603]

[2:109] *Reserved.*

1) [2:110] **Compare—foreign insurers:** A different statute, however, applies to nonadmitted foreign or alien insurers. They *lack capacity to defend* themselves in California courts until they *either:*

— obtain a certificate of authority to transact insurance business in California; or

— *give a bond* in an amount to be fixed by the court to secure the payment of any judgment that may be rendered in the action against them. [Ins.C. §1616; see *Ludgate Ins. Co. v. Lockheed Martin Corp.* (2000) 82 CA4th 592, 611, 98 CR2d 277, 290—insurer can avoid bond requirement by showing adequate assets in U.S. to pay judgment]

[2:111] *Reserved.*

(3) [2:112] **Appearance through counsel:** Although it has capacity to sue and defend, a corporation is not a natural person, and therefore *cannot* appear in an action *in propria persona*. It can appear only through counsel. [*Merco Construction Engineers, Inc. v. Mun.Ct. (Sully Miller Contracting Co.)* (1978) 21 C3d 724, 731, 147 CR 631, 635]

This prohibition stems from the notion a corporate representative who would likely appear on behalf of the corporation would be engaged in the unlicensed practice of law. [*Gamet v. Blanchard* (2001) 91 CA4th 1276, 1284, 111 CR2d 439, 445, fn. 5]

[2:113] *Reserved.*

(a) **Exceptions**

1) [2:114] **As to small claims actions:** A different rule applies in small claims actions, because attorneys are not allowed to represent

clients in such actions (CCP §116.530(a)). Therefore, a corporation is allowed to appear in small claims court through an officer, director or employee. [See CCP §116.540(b), upheld in *Merco Construction Engineers, Inc. v. Mun.Ct., (Sully Miller Contracting Co.)*, supra]

2) [2:115] **As to small claims appeals:** Likewise, on an appeal to superior court from a small claims judgment, corporations may appear through a director, officer or employee (although an attorney may participate as well). [CCP §116.770(c)]

- [2:116] **Comment:** The validity of this statute is unclear. It would seem to be subject to the same constitutional challenge upheld in the *Merco* case, above: i.e., violating the separation of powers clause of the California Constitution, because only courts have the power to determine who is qualified to appear before them.

[2:116.1-116.4] *Reserved.*

(b) [2:116.5] **Compare—effect of order relieving attorney of record:** The ban on corporate self-representation does not prevent a court from granting a motion to withdraw as attorney of record (*see ¶9:385*) *even if it leaves the corporation without representation.* "Such an order puts pressure on the corporation to obtain new counsel or risk forfeiting important rights through nonrepresentation." [*Gamet v. Blanchard* (2001) 91 CA4th 1276, 1284, 111 CR2d 439, 445, fn. 5]

(c) [2:117] **Compare—appeal from administrative ruling:** A nonlawyer agent of the corporation may file a valid notice of appeal from an administrative ruling to secure a de novo court hearing. True, the notice invokes the judicial process, but it is not like a pleading: It is a "form document . . . that requires no legal training or acumen to prepare . . . *Its sole purpose is to give notice* of the de novo hearing request." [*Rogers v. Mun.Ct. (Solar Elec. Engr., Inc.)* (1988) 197 CA3d 1314, 1318-1319, 243 CR 530, 532 (emphasis added)]

(4) [2:118] **Dissolved corporations:** Dissolved corporations have capacity to sue and be sued in the process of winding up their affairs. [Corps.C. §2010(a); see *Penasquitos, Inc. v. Sup.Ct. (Barbee)* (1991) 53 C3d

1180, 1185, 283 CR 135, 138—dissolved corporations continue to exist for purposes of prosecuting and defending lawsuits]

Before a corporation is permitted to dissolve, provision must be made for all known claims. [Corps.C. §§1905, 2004; *Penasquitos, Inc. v. Sup.Ct. (Barbee)*, supra, 53 C3d at 1191, 283 CR at 142]

Claims against the corporation, whether arising (first discovered) before or after its dissolution, may be enforced as follows:

- **[2:119]** *Action against corporation:* Suit may be maintained against the corporation itself to the extent of any undistributed assets, *including insurance.* [Corps.C. §2011(a)]

  (For rules governing *service of summons* on a dissolved corporation, see Corps.C. §2011(b) & CCP §416.20(b), *discussed at ¶4:154.*)

- **[2:120]** *Suit against shareholders:* Alternatively, the shareholders of the dissolved corporation may be sued if any of the corporation's assets have been distributed to them. Each shareholder is liable to the extent of the assets received or their pro rata share of the claim, whichever is less. [Corps.C. §2011(a)]

  Note: "(S)hareholders of the dissolved corporation *may be sued in the corporate name* of the (dissolved) corporation." [Corps.C. §2011(a)(3)]

- **[2:120.1]** *Suit against surviving corporation in merger:* A surviving corporation after a merger may be responsible for the dissolved corporation's liabilities, even if unknown. This is so even when the acquired corporation ceased business long before the merger and existed only as a "shell." [See *Petrini v. Mohasco Corp.* (1998) 61 CA4th 1091, 1094-1099, 71 CR2d 910, 912-915—surviving corporation could be liable for asbestos-related death]

- **[2:120.2]** *Suit against buyer of corporate assets:* In some situations (e.g., product line tort liability), the buyer of a dissolved corporation's assets may be liable as a corporate successor. [See *Henkel Corp. v. Hartford Acc. & Indemn. Co.* (2003) 29 C4th 934, 941, 129 CR2d 828, 833; *Ray v. Alad Corp.* (1977) 19 C3d 22, 28-33, 136 CR 574, 579-581]

  **[2:121]** *Reserved.*

d. **[2:122] Partnerships and other unincorporated associations:** A partnership or other unincorporated association (profit or non-profit) has capacity both to sue and be *sued* in the entity name, and to defend any such action against it. [CCP §369.5(a); *American Alternative Energy Partners II, 1985 v. Windridge, Inc.* (1996) 42 CA4th 551, 49 CR2d 686, 691]

(1) [2:122.1] **Limited partnerships:** As with other partnerships, a limited partnership may sue or be sued in

*(Text cont'd on p. 2-35)*

**RESERVED**

the name it has assumed or by which it is known. [See CCP §369.5]

(a) [2:122.2]  **Effect of failure to file certificate:**  Filing a certificate of limited partnership with the Secretary of State is a precondition to *existence* of a limited partnership formed since 1984 (see Corps.C. §15621(a)). Absent such certificate, a limited partnership is not formed and any entity purporting to be a limited partnership is treated as a *general partnership*, exposing the members to personal liability. [*American Alternative Energy Partners II, 1985 v. Windridge, Inc.* (1996) 42 CA4th 551, 560-561, 49 CR2d 686, 691-692]

> 1) [2:122.3]  **Effect of statute banning action:** By statute, a limited partnership may not "maintain" any action, suit or proceeding in California courts until the requisite certificate is filed (see Corps.C. §15712(b)(4)).
>
> But this statute has been interpreted narrowly; it does not prevent *commencement* of an action. [*American Alternative Energy Partners II, 1985 v. Windridge, Inc.,* supra, 42 CA4th at 562, 49 CR2d at 693]

(2) [2:123]  **"Unincorporated association":**  This term covers any group whose members share a common purpose and who function under a common name. This includes *churches*, labor *unions*, political parties, professional or trade associations, social clubs, homeowners' associations, etc. [See *Barr v. United Methodist Church* (1979) 90 CA3d 259, 266, 153 CR 322, 328; see *Tenants Ass'n of Park Santa Anita v. Southers* (1990) 222 CA3d 1293, 1300, 272 CR 361, 364—unincorporated association of past and present tenants of mobilehome park had capacity to sue]

(a) [2:123a]  **Limited liability companies:**  A limited liability company has the power to "sue, be sued, complain and defend . . . in its own name" any action or proceeding. [Corps.C. §17003(b)]

(b) [2:123.1]  **Compare—business trusts:**  A business trust is usually treated as an unincorporated association.

But business trusts organized *outside* California are treated the same as foreign corporations (see Corps.C. §§171, 170). Thus, if transacting business here, they must "qualify" with the Secretary of State to have capacity to sue; *see ¶2:105 ff.*

(3) [2:124] **Joinder of members:** In an action against a partnership or other unincorporated association, any member may be joined and served as an individual defendant; in which event, any judgment obtained against the entity may also be binding upon the member individually. [CCP §369.5(b); *and see "joinder of parties,"* ¶2:150 ff.]

(4) [2:125] **Appearance through counsel required:** An unincorporated association is more like a corporation than an individual (may sue or be sued in entity name, etc.). Therefore, like a corporation, an unincorporated association can appear in court (other than small claims court) only through a licensed attorney. [*Clean Air Transport Systems v. San Mateo Co. Transit Dist.* (1988) 198 CA3d 576, 578-579, 243 CR 799, 800]

e. [2:126] **Estates:** A probate or trust estate is not a legal entity; it is simply a collection of assets and liabilities. As such, it has no capacity to sue or be sued, or to defend an action. Any litigation must be maintained by, or against, the executor or administrator of the estate. [See *Tanner v. Best* (1940) 40 CA2d 442, 445, 104 P2d 1084, 1086; *Galdjie v. Darwish* (2003) 113 CA4th 1331, 1344, 7 CR3d 178, 188 (citing text); *and see* ¶2:6 ff.]

(1) [2:127] **Claims against estate covered by liability insurance:** But an action may be filed or continued against the "Estate of (decedent)" to establish the decedent's liability for damages for which he or she was covered by liability insurance. [See Prob.C. §§550, 9390] (By doing so, however, the claimant waives any claims not covered under the insurance policy or in excess of the policy limit unless a claim has been filed against the estate; see Prob.C. §554.)

*Cross-refer:* See further discussion in Ross, *Cal. Prac. Guide: Probate* (TRG), Ch. 8.

(a) [2:127.1] **Substitution of personal representative or consolidation:** If an action is brought against the estate in these circumstances, the court may (i) appoint and substitute the personal representative as defendant, or (ii) consolidate the actions against the estate and the personal representative. [Prob.C. §552(b),(c); see *Blue Ridge Ins. Co. v. Stanewich* (9th Cir. 1998) 142 F3d 1145, 1150 (applying Calif. law)]

(2) [2:128] **Actions pending against decedent at death:** An action pending against a decedent at the time of death may be *continued* against decedent's personal representative, thus exposing decedent's estate

to potential liability in excess of any liability insurance, provided:

- a formal creditor's claim is first properly filed and rejected by the representative; and

- plaintiff substitutes the representative as a party to the action within 3 months after rejection of the claim (provided the notice of rejection expressly advises plaintiff of this requirement). [See Prob.C. §9370(a)]

(a) [2:129] **Purpose:** This section obviates the necessity of filing a new action and, at the same time, keeps the personal representative apprised of claims affecting the estate.

(3) [2:130] **Appearance through counsel:** An executor or administrator cannot appear in pro per in matters outside the probate proceedings (e.g., in actions by or against the estate). Any such appearance must be through counsel. (Of course, if the executor or administrator is a licensed attorney, he or she can act as such counsel.) [*City of Downey v. Johnson* (1968) 263 CA2d 775, 779, 69 CR 830, 833; *Hansen v. Hansen* (2003) 114 CA4th 618, 621, 7 CR3d 688, 691 (citing text)]

f. [2:131] **Building contractors:** Building contractors are required to be licensed by the State; unlicensed persons may not sue for compensation for their services. [Bus. & Prof.C. §7031(a)]

Licensure is required *when the services were rendered* and *cannot* be excused under the judicial doctrine of substantial compliance. [Bus. & Prof.C. §7031(d); *Construction Fin'l, LLC v. Perlite Plastering Co., Inc.* (1997) 53 CA4th 170, 180-181, 61 CR2d 574, 579-580] (Exceptions apply where lack of license is due to circumstances beyond the contractor's control; see Bus. & Prof.C. §7031(d).)

The statute applies to anyone contracting to perform work in California, either as a contractor *or subcontractor*. I.e., the statute protects both owners and general contractors in dealing with unlicensed persons. [*Hydrotech Systems, Ltd. v. Oasis Waterpark* (1991) 52 C3d 988, 997, 277 CR 517, 522]

(1) [2:132] **No exception for contractors licensed elsewhere:** If not licensed in California, an out-of-state contractor cannot recover for work done here. It is immaterial that he or she was licensed where the contract was negotiated and that the work done here was an "isolated transaction," or that "extraordinary circum-

stances" existed. [*Hydrotech Systems, Ltd. v. Oasis Waterpark*, supra, 52 C3d at 992, 277 CR at 519]

(2) **[2:133] Claims barred:** Bus. & Prof.C. §7031 bars all actions, however characterized, which effectively seek "compensation" for unlicensed contract work. Thus, an unlicensed contractor cannot recover either the contract price or the reasonable value of labor and materials. [*Hydrotech Systems, Ltd. v. Oasis Waterpark*, supra, 52 C3d at 995-997, 277 CR at 521-522]

  (a) **[2:133.1] Fraud claims:** An unlicensed contractor cannot escape §7031 by alleging the owner "fraudulently" promised to pay (i.e., promised to pay without intending to pay) for the unlicensed work. As long as the *primary relief* sought is *compensation* for unlicensed work, recovery is barred. [*Hydrotech Systems, Ltd. v. Oasis Waterpark*, supra, 52 C3d at 1002, 277 CR at 526]

  (b) **[2:133.2] Compare—unrelated claims:** On the other hand, plaintiff's "incidental" or "peripheral involvement" in unlicensed work does not shield defendants from tort liability "external" to the construction work and thus unrelated to any protective concern of the licensing law. [*Hydrotech Systems, Ltd. v. Oasis Waterpark*, supra, 52 C3d at 1001, 277 CR at 526]

  Nor does lack of a license affect a contractor's right to sue under federal civil rights laws for racial discrimination during performance of the contract. [*Holland v. Morse Diesel Int'l, Inc.* (2001) 86 CA4th 1443, 1450, 104 CR2d 239, 244]

  [2:133.3-133.4] *Reserved.*

  (c) **[2:133.5] Compare—setoffs:** Some cases permit the unlicensed contractor to assert a setoff based on a contract for building services that otherwise would be unenforceable. Rationale: Section 7031 does not bar assertion of a valid defense. [See *Ranchwood Communities v. Jim Beat Const. Co.* (1996) 49 CA4th 1397, 1411, 57 CR2d 386, 393]

  [2:133.6-133.9] *Reserved.*

  (d) **[2:133.10] Express indemnity claims against subcontractors and suppliers:** An unlicensed general contractor who is being held liable for construction defects cannot enforce *indemnification agreements* by its subcontractors and suppliers. Reason: "But for" the illegal construction contract, there would be no subcontracts for indemnity or otherwise. [See *Ranchwood Communities v. Jim Beat Const. Co.*, supra, 49 CA4th at 1418, 57 CR2d at 397—causes of action for express indemnity, breach of warranties and declaratory relief barred]

1) **[2:133.11] Compare—equitable (comparative) indemnity:** But an unlicensed contractor acting as a developer of mass-produced homes may obtain comparative indemnity or contribution from negligent suppliers and subcontractors for construction defects (for which the developer is strictly liable). Banning comparative indemnity in such cases would be a windfall to the negligent suppliers and subcontractors "and would not be within the protective purpose of the licensing statute." [*Ranchwood Communities v. Jim Beat Const. Co.*, supra, 49 CA4th at 1420-1421, 57 CR2d at 399]

2) **[2:133.12] Compare—negligence claims:** Likewise beyond the scope of the licensing law are the contractor's *negligence* claims against its subcontractors and suppliers. [*Ranchwood Communities v. Jim Beat Const. Co.*, supra, 49 CA4th at 1420-1421, 57 CR2d at 399]

(3) **[2:134] Compare—no bar on recovery for work done outside California:** On the other hand, the licensing law does not bar recovery for work done *outside* the State ... even if the contract was entered into here by a person whose residence and principal place of business is here. [*Mechanical Wholesale Corp. v. Fuji Bank, Ltd.* (1996) 42 CA4th 1647, 1653, 50 CR2d 466, 469, fn. 6]

g. **[2:135] Fugitives, persons in contempt:** Fugitives from justice or persons in contempt of court lack capacity to *initiate* civil proceedings ("disentitlement" doctrine). But they have the right to *defend* actions against them; due process of law protects their right to be heard (through counsel) and to present their defenses. [*Doe v. Sup.Ct. (Polanski)* (1990) 222 CA3d 1406, 1410, 272 CR 474, 476-477]

**[2:136] *PRACTICE POINTER:*** Even so, the right to defend may be forfeited if such defendant fails to appear for deposition or trial. A CCP §2025(c) notice of deposition, or a CCP §1987(b) "notice to appear" at trial, has the same effect as a subpoena. Defendant's disobedience may support an order striking the answer and entering a default judgment (CCP §2023(b)(4)).

3. **[2:137]** **Procedures to Challenge Party's Capacity:** Lack of capacity to sue or defend is *not* a jurisdictional defect. Therefore, unless the objection is properly raised, the court may proceed to adjudicate and render judgment notwithstanding the defect. The following are the proper procedures for raising the objection:

    a. **[2:138]** **Plaintiff's lack of capacity:** If plaintiff's lack of capacity appears on the face of his or her complaint (a rare case), defendant can raise the objection by *special demurrer* (see CCP §430.10(b), ¶*7:70-71*); or alternatively, as an affirmative defense in the answer. More frequently, lack of capacity does not appear on the face of the complaint, and the objection therefore can only be raised as a defense in the answer. The affirmative defense is in the nature of a *plea in abatement* (*see* ¶*6:475*). [*Color-Vue, Inc. v. Abrams* (1996) 44 CA4th 1599, 1604, 52 CR2d 443, 446]

        (1) **[2:139]** **Defect waived if not raised:** If not raised either by demurrer or answer, plaintiff's lack of capacity to sue is deemed waived, so that a valid judgment can be rendered notwithstanding. [CCP §430.80, ¶*7:32*; see *Color-Vue, Inc. v. Abrams*, supra, 44 CA4th at 1605, 52 CR2d at 447—court is "rarely justified in permitting the defense to be made later"]

            (a) **[2:139.1]** **Incapacity arising during litigation:** Where plaintiff's lack of capacity to sue arises or occurs *after the time to demur or answer* (e.g., corporation suspended for nonpayment of franchise tax), defendant should move for leave to file an amended answer asserting the plea in abatement. [*Color-Vue, Inc. v. Abrams*, supra, 44 CA4th at 1604, 52 CR2d at 446, fn. 5]

            (b) **[2:139.2]** **Relief from waiver?** Under "unusual" circumstances, defendants who have waived the lack-of-capacity plea may be allowed to raise it later. [*Color-Vue, Inc. v. Abrams*, supra, 44 CA4th at 1605, 52 CR2d at 447]

                • **[2:139.3]** For example, if the plaintiff corporation, suspended for nonpayment of taxes, announces that it does not intend to pay its delinquent taxes, the court "may properly relieve defendant from his waiver and permit him to assert the corporation's lack of capacity to sue." [*Color-Vue, Inc. v. Abrams*, supra, 44 CA4th at 1605, 52 CR2d at 447—no basis for relieving defendant of waiver, however, where corporation expresses willingness to pay taxes]

        (2) **[2:140]** **Compare—plaintiff's lack of standing to sue:** But if plaintiff is not the real party in interest on

the claim, the defect is "jurisdictional," and is *not* waived
by defendant's failure to assert it by demurrer or answer
(¶*2:78*). [*Color-Vue, Inc. v. Abrams*, supra, 44 CA4th at
1604, 52 CR2d at 446]

    b.  [2:141]  **Defendant's lack of capacity:**  This is *not*
ground for demurrer to the answer (see CCP §430.20,
¶*7:35*). As there is no responsive pleading to an answer, a
defendant's lack of capacity to defend may be challenged
by a *motion for summary judgment* (see CCP §437c, *Ch.
10*). [*Mediterranean Exports, Inc. v. Sup.Ct. (Harvard Invest.
Co.)* (1981) 119 CA3d 605, 615-616, 174 CR 169, 175]

  4.  [2:142]  **Amendment of Pleadings to Substitute Party Having Capacity:**  If the court sustains an objection to a party's capacity to sue or defend, it may grant leave to *substitute* a party
or entity having the requisite capacity. [*Lazar v. Estate of Lazar*
(1962) 208 CA2d 554, 561, 25 CR 354, 358; *American Alternative Energy Partners II, 1985 v. Windridge, Inc.* (1996) 42 CA4th
551, 49 CR2d 686, 691]

    a.  [2:143]  **Example:**  Action filed against "Estate of Jones";
complaint may be amended to substitute executors of the
estate as defendants. [*Lazar v. Estate of Lazar*, supra, 208
CA2d at 561, 25 CR at 358; also see "amendment of pleadings," ¶*6:602 ff.*]

    b.  [2:144]  **Limitation:**  Substitution of plaintiffs is not allowed where it would affect a defendant's meritorious defense. [*Sade Shoe Co. v. Oschin & Snyder* (1990) 217 CA3d
1509, 1517, 266 CR 619, 624]

      (1)  [2:145]  **Example:**  XYZ Corp. filed suit while its powers were suspended for nonpayment of franchise taxes.
Because of the suspension, the suit did not toll the statute of limitations (*see* ¶*2:95*). After the statute had run,
the corporation sought to amend the complaint to substitute its directors as plaintiffs. Substitution was denied
because it would defeat the statute of limitations defense. [*Sade Shoe Co. v. Oschin & Snyder*, supra]

      [2:146-149]  *Reserved.*

## C.  JOINDER OF PARTIES

[2:150]  Plaintiff's attorney must decide at the outset of the action
which persons *must* be joined as plaintiffs or defendants (compulsory joinder); and, which persons *may* be joined if plaintiff wishes
(permissive joinder).

  1.  [2:151]  **Compulsory Joinder:**  Plaintiff must join as parties
to the action all persons whose interests are so directly involved
that the court cannot render a fair adjudication in their absence.

Merely being named as a party to the action is not enough. A
party is not properly "joined" unless properly *served with sum-*

*mons and complaint.* [*Ruttenberg v. Ruttenberg* (1997) 53 CA4th 801, 808, 62 CR2d 78, 82]

[2:152-154] *Reserved.*

a. [2:155] **Joinder rules based on practical considerations:** The common law distinctions between "necessary" and "indispensable" parties have been abandoned (although the term "indispensable" continues to be used; see below). Modern joinder rules are based on the practical considerations discussed in this section.

The current Code provisions are derived from Rule 19 of the Federal Rules of Civil Procedure. Federal precedents therefore may be pertinent in resolving joinder disputes. [*Countrywide Home Loans, Inc. v. Sup.Ct. (HP Lemona II)* (1999) 69 CA4th 785, 792, 82 CR2d 63, 66]

(1) [2:156] **Plaintiff must join all persons necessary for just adjudication:** Plaintiff is required to join as parties to the action any person whose interest is such that:

- In his or her absence, *complete relief cannot be accorded* among those already parties to the action; *or*

- Any judgment rendered in his or her absence might either (a) *prejudice* his or her ability to protect his or her interest in later litigation; or (b) leave any of the parties before the court exposed to a *risk of additional liability or inconsistent obligations.* [CCP §389(a); see *Olszewski v. Scripps Health* (2003) 30 C4th 798, 808-809, 135 CR2d 1, 10—"(A) person is an indispensable party . . . when the judgment to be rendered necessarily must affect his rights"]

(a) [2:156.1] **Comment:** Courts rarely apply the "complete relief" clause as the *sole* basis for finding an absentee necessary. In most cases, this clause is used in connection with some other basis for compulsory joinder (i.e., where nonjoinder may harm the interests of an absentee or expose an existing party to multiple liability). [See *Countrywide Home Loans, Inc. v. Sup.Ct. (HP Lemona II)*, supra, 69 CA4th at 794, 82 CR2d at 68]

As to the second clause, a nonjoined party's ability to protect its interest is not impaired or impeded as a practical matter *where a joined party has the same interest* in the litigation. [See *Deltakeeper v. Oakdale Irrig. Dist.* (2001) 94 CA4th 1092, 1102, 115 CR2d 244, 252]

(b) [2:157] **If such persons not joined, explanation required:** If any such persons are *not* named as parties to the lawsuit, the complaint must state their names (if known), and the *reasons* why they have not been joined. [CCP §389(c)]

(c) [2:158] **Involuntary plaintiffs may be joined as defendants:** If any such person is allied in interest with plaintiff, but refuses to join as coplaintiff, he or she may be sued as a *defendant* (or "involuntary plaintiff"). In such cases, the complaint must state the reasons why such person was so joined. [CCP §382]

(2) [2:159] **Joinder will be ordered if feasible:** Wherever plaintiff fails to join some person necessary for a just adjudication, the court shall order that person be made a party to the action. [CCP §389(a)]

(a) **Procedure for compelling joinder:** *See ¶2:185 ff.*

(3) [2:160] **If joinder not feasible, court must decide whether action should continue:** If such person *cannot* be joined (either because he cannot be located, or is not subject to service of process, or the statute of limitations has run, etc.), the court must then decide whether—"in equity and in good conscience"—the action should proceed without him, or should be dismissed without prejudice (the absent party thus being regarded as *indispensable*). [CCP §389(b); see also *Koster v. County of San Joaquin (Cose & Assocs.)* (1996) 47 CA4th 29, 44, 54 CR2d 565, 574 (citing text); *Kaczorowski v. Mendocino County Bd. of Supervisors* (2001) 88 CA4th 564, 570, 106 CR2d 14, 19]

It is thus seen that failure to join an indispensable party is really *not* a "jurisdictional" defect in the fundamental sense of lacking power to adjudicate. Rather, it is for reasons of equity and good conscience that the court *should not* proceed in the absence of such a party. [*County of San Joaquin v. State Water Resources Control Bd.* (1997) 54 CA4th 1144, 1151-1153, 63 CR2d 277, 282-283]

(a) [2:161] **Determinative factors:** The court's decision on whether the action should proceed without the absent party will be based on the following factors:

- The extent to which its judgment may prejudice the absent party or the parties already before the court;

- The extent to which such prejudice may be lessened or avoided by protective provisions in the judgment, or other measures;

- Whether a judgment rendered in such person's absence will provide an *adequate* remedy to the parties before the court; and

- Whether, if the action is dismissed for nonjoinder, the plaintiff will have an adequate remedy elsewhere. [CCP §389(b); see *Deltakeeper v. Oakdale Irrig. Dist.* (2001) 94 CA4th 1092, 1106-1108, 115 CR2d 244, 256-257; *Olszewski v. Scripps Health* (2003) 30 C4th 798, 808, 135 CR2d 1, 10—that adverse ruling against defendants might have a financial impact on state (absent party) "does not make the state an indispensable party"]

  1) [2:162] **Comment:** CCP §389(a) also mentions the possibility that joinder might "deprive the court of jurisdiction over the subject matter of the action." This language was adopted intact from the Federal Rule (FRCP 19), but is rarely applicable . . . because subject matter jurisdiction of California courts depends on the nature and amount in controversy, not on the residence of the parties. (*See discussion of subject matter jurisdiction at ¶3:2 ff.*)

  2) [2:162.1] **Compare—case law:** Some cases bypass the above factors (relying on case law predating CCP §389(b)):

  — "The controlling test for determining whether a person is an indispensable party is where the plaintiff seeks some type of affirmative relief which, if granted, *would injure or affect the interest of a third person not joined*, that third person is an indispensable party." [*Save Our Bay, Inc. v. San Diego Unified Port Dist.* (1996) 42 CA4th 686, 692, 49 CR2d 847, 850 (emphasis added; internal quotes omitted)]

  (b) [2:163] **Weighing process:** The court has "considerable discretion" in considering and weighing these factors. No one factor is determinative or outweighs the other. [*County of San Joaquin v. State Water Resources Control Bd.*, supra, 54 CA4th at 1154, 63 CR2d at 283]

  b. [2:164] **Application:** The following cases illustrate the compulsory joinder issue and application of the rules stated above:

(1) [2:165]  **Claimants to common fund:**  Where a number of persons have an undetermined interest in the same property or fund, each is an indispensable party to any action by the other to obtain his share of the property or fund. Rationale: The judgment obtained by any one claimant for part of the property or fund would *necessarily determine the amount remaining available* for the others. [*Bank of Calif. v. Sup.Ct.* (1940) 16 C2d 516, 521, 106 P2d 879, 883]

*(Text cont'd on p. 2-45)*

**RESERVED**

(a) **Examples**

1) [2:166]   In an action by one creditor against the assignee for benefit of creditors to obtain payment of his share of the debtor's assets, all other creditors are indispensable parties. [See *Bank of Calif. v. Sup.Ct.*, supra]

2) [2:167]   In an action by the lessor of an oil and gas lease to set aside purported assignments of his interest on the ground of forgery, and to recover royalties due under the lease, the assignees of the lease are indispensable parties. [*Atlantic Richfield Co. v. Sup.Ct. (Anderson)* (1975) 51 CA3d 168, 176, 124 CR 63, 67]

(2) [2:168]   **Heirs in wrongful death action:**   A wrongful death cause of action belongs to *all* the decedent's heirs, and therefore they are all "necessary" parties. (There is no common fund, however. Each heir's damages are separate and any judgment must be apportioned among the plaintiffs in the action; see CCP §377.61.) [*Ruttenberg v. Ruttenberg* (1997) 53 CA4th 801, 808, 62 CR2d 78, 82]

Any heir who refuses to join as a coplaintiff may be joined as a defendant so that all heirs are before the court in the same action. [*Ruttenberg v. Ruttenberg,* supra, 53 CA4th at 808, 62 CR2d at 82—"An heir named as a defendant in a wrongful death action is, in reality, a plaintiff"]

(a) [2:168.1]   **Effect of failure to join:**   Nonjoinder of one or more heirs does not affect the court's power to adjudicate the wrongful death action; i.e., they are *not* "indispensable" parties. [*Ruttenberg v. Ruttenberg,* supra, 53 CA4th at 808, 62 CR2d at 81]

However, a judgment rendered in the wrongful death action bars claims by the omitted heirs against the tortfeasor responsible for the decedent's death. Therefore, the plaintiffs who obtained the judgment are personally liable to the omitted heirs for whatever *damages they could have recovered* if they had been joined in the action against the tortfeasor. [*Ruttenberg v. Ruttenberg,* supra, 53 CA4th at 810, 62 CR2d at 83]

Similarly, a *settlement* between defendant and some of the heirs in a wrongful death action bars any subsequent action by the other heirs, unless defendant knew or should have known of their existence before the settlement. [*Gonzales v. South-*

*ern Calif. Edison Co.* (1999) 77 CA4th 485, 489, 91 CR2d 530, 532]

*Cross-refer:* See further discussion in Flahavan, Rea & Kelly, *Cal. Prac. Guide: Personal Injury* (TRG), Ch. 3.

(3) [2:169] **Conflicting claims among co-owners:** If an action seeks to determine conflicting claims to ownership or possession of property among its owners, all the owners should be joined as parties. If some owner cannot be made a party to the action, the court may be unable to afford complete relief to the parties before the court. In such a case, the absent party would be regarded as "indispensable," and the action dismissed without prejudice. Examples: suits to dissolve a partnership; or for partition of real property. [See *Kraus v. Willow Park Public Golf Course* (1977) 73 CA3d 354, 369, 140 CR 744, 753]

(a) [2:170] **Compare—claims against third persons:** But where one of several co-owners sues for damage to commonly-held property, the other co-owners are *not* "indispensable." They will not be bound by the judgment and can protect themselves by relitigating the matter. [*Kraus v. Willow Park Public Golf Course,* supra—several investors in large limited partnership sued general partners and others to impose constructive trust on funds invested; other limited partners should have been joined if feasible, but were *not* "indispensable"]

[2:170.1-170.4] *Reserved.*

(b) [2:170.5] **Compare—claims of secured lenders:** A homeowners association suing a developer for construction defects need not join secured lenders, even though the lenders' security might have been impaired as a result of the defects. [*Harboring Villas Homeowners Ass'n v. Sup.Ct.* (*Ce Mar Las Vegas IX, Inc.*) (1998) 63 CA4th 426, 428, 73 CR2d 646, 647]

Likewise, Lender with a lien on Tenant's leasehold interest was not an indispensable party in an unlawful detainer action based on Tenant's failure to pay the rent, *absent any agreement by Landlord* to permit Lender to cure Tenant's default. [*Glendale Fed'l Bank v. Hadden* (1999) 73 CA4th 1150, 1154, 87 CR2d 102, 105]

(4) [2:171] **Partial assignments:** Where there has been a partial assignment of a claim, the assignor and

assignee are regarded as "indispensable" parties in any action to enforce the claim against the debtor. Allowing either to proceed without joining the other would *prejudice* the debtor by exposing him or her to the harassment and expense of having to defend multiple lawsuits on the same debt. [See *Bank of the Orient v. Sup.Ct. (San Francisco Fed. Sav. & Loan Ass'n)* (1977) 67 CA3d 588, 595, 136 CR 741, 745; *and ¶2:19 ff.*]

(a) [2:172]  **Partial subrogation:**  The same reasoning and rule applies where there has been a partial subrogation of a claim (e.g., insurance company pays insured for part of loss caused by third party). Neither the subrogor nor partial subrogee can sue without joining the other. [*Ferraro v. William Lyles Const. Co.* (1980) 102 CA3d 33, 43, 162 CR 238, 243; *and see ¶2:31*]

(b) [2:173]  **Compare—beneficial interests:**  Transfer of a promissory note to a trustee or custodian for others is *not* a partial assignment because only the holder may sue on the note. Persons with beneficial interests therefore are neither proper nor indispensable parties in an action on the note. [*Niederer v. Ferreira* (1987) 189 CA3d 1485, 1496, 234 CR 779, 785]

(5) [2:174]  **Risk of multiple liability:**  Joinder may also be ordered if an existing party is exposed to a "substantial risk" of multiple liability or otherwise inconsistent obligations because of the absent party's claimed interest in the subject matter of the litigation. [CCP §389(a)(2)(ii)]

(a) [2:175]  **"Substantial risk":**  Whatever risk of multiple liability is created by the nonjoinder must be "substantial"—i.e., a *real* risk, not a hypothetical one. [*Union Carbide Corp. v. Sup.Ct. (Villmar Dental Labs, Inc.)* (1984) 36 C3d 15, 21, 201 CR 580, 583]

(b) [2:176]  **Example:**  Plaintiffs, users of natural gas, sued Gas Producers for price-fixing in violation of state law. Plaintiffs did not join the various suppliers and distributors through whom they had purchased the gas. Producers claimed the nonjoinder exposed them to a "risk of multiple liability" . . . because these intermediate parties could sue them for the same conduct. Held: Since none of the suppliers or distributors had yet made any such claim against Producers, and there was a short statute of limitations on such claims, the risk of multiple liability was *not* "substantial." (If such claims were later filed, the court could at that time order joinder of such parties.) [*Union Carbide Corp. v. Sup.Ct. (Villmar Dental Labs, Inc.)*, supra]

(6) [2:177] **Suit to set aside contract:** Ordinarily, all parties to a contract are *necessary* parties in an action involving rights under the contract. But they are not always indispensable: "Indeed, if a party to a contract were always indispensable in a suit to set aside the contract, it would eliminate the exercise of discretion accorded to the trial court" under CCP §389(b). [*Deltakeeper v. Oakdale Irrig. Dist.* (2001) 94 CA4th 1092, 1106-1106, 115 CR2d 244, 255]

(a) **Application**

- [2:177.1] The immediate seller is a necessary party in an action to rescind even though a preceding seller, rather than the immediate seller, breached a duty to disclose a known problem with the house. [*Shapiro v. Sutherland* (1998) 64 CA4th 1534, 1552, 76 CR2d 101, 112]

(b) [2:178] **Exceptional cases:** There are exceptional cases, however, in which courts will adjudicate suits to set aside a contract despite inability to join one of the contracting parties. [See *People ex rel. Lungren v. Community Redevelop. Agency for City of Palm Springs* (1997) 56 CA4th 868, 882, 65 CR2d 786, 795—action challenging Indian Tribe's purchase of property from local governmental agency would not be dismissed although Indian Tribe was indispensable party and could not be joined because of sovereign immunity; there was strong public interest in reviewing the agency's action because the transfer would put the property beyond state's power to regulate]

[2:178.1-178.4] *Reserved.*

(7) [2:178.5] **Permissive use liability:** The owner of a motor vehicle is liable for injuries caused by permissive users up to statutory limits (see Veh.C. §17150). However, in any action against the owner, the permissive user "shall be made a party defendant if service of process can be made in a manner sufficient to secure personal jurisdiction . . ." [Veh.C. §17152] (Personal jurisdiction can be obtained in many cases by service outside California; *see* Ch. 3.)

(8) [2:179] **Challenging government approvals to third parties:** Where plaintiff seeks to enjoin the government from issuing permits, variances, etc. to third par-

ties, those third parties may be "indispensable" to the lawsuit. [*Sierra Club, Inc. v. California Coastal Comm'n* (1979) 95 CA3d 495, 501, 157 CR 190, 194]

(a) **Application**

- [2:180] Plaintiff sued Coastal Commission to set aside a building permit without joining the developer to whom the permit had been issued. The developer was an indispensable party because its interests would be directly affected and injured if the permit were set aside. [*Sierra Club, Inc. v. California Coastal Comm'n* (1979) 95 CA3d 495, 501, 157 CR 190, 194—action dismissed because applicable statute of limitations had run by the time plaintiff sought to bring developer into the case]

  [2:180.1-180.4] *Reserved.*

(b) [2:180.5] **Compare—absent party's interest adequately represented:** But an absent party may not be considered "indispensable" where parties already before the court *adequately* represent the absent party's interests in connection with the governmental permit in question. In such cases, as a practical matter, the absent party's ability to protect his or her interest has not been impaired. [See *Citizens Ass'n for Sensible Development of Bishop Area v. County of Inyo* (1985) 172 CA3d 151, 161, 217 CR 893, 899—landowner would have been a proper party but was *not* indispensable because developer had been joined and had "ably argued" on behalf of the owner's interests]

(9) [2:181] **Declaratory relief as to liability insurance coverage:** All persons who may be affected by the relief sought in a declaratory relief action should be joined as parties. Indeed, it may be an abuse of discretion to grant such relief in their absence. [See *Aetna Cas. & Sur. Co. v. Aceves* (1991) 233 CA3d 544, 554, 284 CR 477, 484]

Thus, injured third parties, as well as the insured, are proper defendants in a declaratory relief action by an insurance company to determine whether the accident was covered. [*State Farm Mut. Auto. Ins. Co. v. Crane* (1990) 217 CA3d 1127, 1135, 266 CR 422, 426-427]

(a) [2:182] **Example:** After Victim sued Insured for personal injury, Insurance Co. sued for declaratory relief that Insured's policy did not cover accident. Victim was *proper* defendant in the declaratory relief action, although not an insured. Reason: Coverage determinations may affect Victim's rights to enforce against Insurance Co. any judgment obtained against Insured. [*State Farm Mut. Auto. Ins. Co. v. Crane*, supra, 217 CA3d at 1135, 266 CR at 426-427]

[2:183]   *Reserved.*

(10) [2:184]   **Claims against spouses; community vs. separate property:**   Either spouse may be sued on a joint obligation without joinder of the other spouse; and a judgment against either is enforceable against the *community property.* [See Fam.C. §910]

But, if plaintiff seeks to reach the *separate property* of either spouse, that spouse is a necessary party to the action. [See *Credit Bureau of Santa Monica Bay Dist., Inc. v. Terranova* (1971) 15 CA3d 854, 860, 93 CR 538, 542—action against nondebtor spouse for other spouse's "necessaries of life" under Fam.C. §914; see also *Reynolds & Reynolds Co. v. Universal Forms, Labels & Systems, Inc.* (CD CA 1997) 965 F.Supp. 1392, 1396 (applying Calif. law)]

*Cross-refer:* For further discussion, see Hogoboom & King, *Cal. Prac. Guide: Family Law* (TRG), Ch. 8.

[2:184.1-184.4]   *Reserved.*

(11) [2:184.5]   **Claims against joint tortfeasors:**   Joint tortfeasors are not necessary parties. Plaintiff may choose which tortfeasors to sue. [*Countrywide Home Loans, Inc. v. Sup.Ct. (HP Lemona II)* (1999) 69 CA4th 785, 796-797, 82 CR2d 63, 69—error to sustain demurrers on ground of misjoinder of parties]

⇨[2:184.6]   *PRACTICE POINTER:*   Plaintiffs usually join everyone who might possibly be at fault. It is risky to omit one of several tortfeasors because the named defendants are likely to blame everything on the absentee (the "empty chair defense").

As a practical matter, even if plaintiff opts not to sue one of several tortfeasors, defendants can join the absentee by a third party cross-complaint for indemnity.

[2:184.7-184.9]   *Reserved.*

(12) [2:184.10]   **Judicial foreclosure actions:**   All parties holding an interest in real property are "necessary"

parties in a judicial foreclosure action, but they are *not* "indispensable." A foreclosing party who inadvertently fails to name a necessary party retains a right of foreclosure against the party not named. The unnamed party is entitled to an equitable right of redemption in a subsequent quiet title proceeding. [See *Diamond Benefits Life Ins. Co. v. Troll* (1998) 66 CA4th 1, 5-9, 77 CR2d 581, 584-586—easement holder not named in foreclosure action not bound by judgment]

[2:184.11-184.14] *Reserved.*

(13) [2:184.15] **Quiet title actions:** In an action to quiet title, plaintiff *must* name as defendants all persons having an adverse claim to the property, either known to plaintiff or disclosed by the record or apparent from an inspection of the property. (Such persons are thus regarded as "indispensable" party defendants.) [CCP §§762.010, 762.060(b)] (For joinder of permissive party defendants, *see* ¶2:207.5.)

c. **Procedure for challenging nonjoinder of party**

(1) [2:185] **Objection must be raised by demurrer or answer:** Nonjoinder of a party must be raised at the outset of the action or defendant waives the defect (*see* ¶2:196-198). If it appears on the face of the complaint that some person with a material interest in the subject of the action has not been joined, defendant may object either by special demurrer on this ground, or by affirmative defense in the answer. [CCP §430.10(d)—demurrer for "defect or misjoinder of parties"]

But defendant's waiver of the defect does *not* affect the *absent party's* rights. It is not bound by a judgment in an action to which it is not a party; *see* ¶2:199.

(a) [2:186] Plaintiff is required to set forth in the complaint the names of all persons having such an interest who have not been joined, and the reasons for their nonjoinder. [CCP §389(c), ¶2:157]

(b) [2:187] If plaintiff fails to do so, defendant will probably be unable to demur to the complaint, as nonjoinder of a party rarely appears from the face of the complaint. In such cases, defendant must raise the objection by affirmative defense in his answer. Such defense will be in the nature of a *plea in abatement; see* ¶6:475.

(2) [2:188] **Motion to dismiss:** If nonjoinder *is* raised by demurrer, it may be coupled with a motion to dismiss on the ground that "justice requires that the action not

proceed" in the party's absence. [*Union Carbide Corp. v. Sup.Ct. (Villmar Dental Labs, Inc.)* (1984) 36 C3d 15, 22, 201 CR 580, 584] (This is one of the few situations in which a motion to dismiss can be used to challenge pleadings; *see ¶7:370 ff.*)

(a) [2:189]  **Ruling may be deferred:**  Where such a motion is made at the pleading stage, the court may not have adequate information as to the relationship of the absent party to the action and the practical effects of an adjudication upon him and others. In such cases, the court may properly defer its ruling on the motion until the case is further advanced. [*Union Carbide Corp. v. Sup.Ct. (Villmar Dental Labs, Inc.)*, supra]

(3) [2:190]  **Motion to compel joinder:**  As long as the objection has been raised as a defense in the answer, defendant may move the court any time prior to trial for an order compelling the joinder of the absent party. [CCP §389(a); and see *Bank of the Orient v. Sup.Ct. (San Francisco Fed. Sav. & Loan Ass'n)* (1977) 67 CA3d 588, 595, 136 CR 741, 745]

(a) [2:191]  **Effect of delay in making motion:** However, if the moving party is seeking to compel joinder to protect himself or herself against a later suit by the absent person, undue delay in making the motion may be a reason for *denying* the motion. [See *Union Carbide Corp. v. Sup.Ct. (Villmar Dental Labs, Inc.)*, supra]

(4) [2:192]  **Order compelling joinder:**  If the court determines that the absent party is subject to service of process, and "in equity and in good conscience" should be joined as a party to the action, it will order his or her joinder. [CCP §389(a)] (Note the considerable discretion vested in the trial court in deciding the joinder issue.)

(5) [2:193]  **Order for dismissal:**  If such party cannot be joined (e.g., because not subject to jurisdiction), the court must decide whether to dismiss the action without prejudice, the absent person being thus regarded as "indispensable." [CCP §389(b)]

(a) [2:194]  **After order for joinder:**  It may be error for a court to dismiss without first ordering joinder of the absent party. [*Haller v. Burbank Community Hosp. Foundation* (1984) 149 CA3d 650, 659, 197 CR 45, 51]

[2:195]  *Reserved.*

d. [2:196]  **Defendant may waive right to compel joinder:** As stated above, nonjoinder of a party must be raised by demurrer or answer at the outset of the action, or the objection is waived. [CCP §430.80]

If defendant only discovers the existence of the absent party later in the litigation, defendant should *seek leave to amend the answer* to raise nonjoinder as an affirmative defense. [See *Bank of the Orient v. Sup.Ct. (San Francisco Fed. Sav. & Loan Ass'n)*, supra]

[2:197-198] *Reserved.*

e. [2:199] **Compare—absent party's right to challenge judgment:** Indispensable parties cannot be bound by a judgment in an action in which they are not joined as parties. Such a judgment "is subject to later *collateral attack* (in a separate lawsuit) by the nonjoined indispensable party." [See *Save Our Bay, Inc. v. San Diego Unified Port Dist.* (1996) 42 CA4th 686, 693, 49 CR2d 847, 851 (emphasis and parentheses added)]

(1) [2:200] **Example:** P sued City Director of Finance to compel processing of a license application; but P did *not* join City. Court purported to grant relief both against Director and City (ordering City to issue the license applied for). The court "lacked subject matter jurisdiction" to render such a judgment because City was not a party to the action. [*Welch v. Bodeman* (1986) 176 CA3d 833, 849, 222 CR 435, 440]

- [2:201] **Comment:** Failure to join an indispensable party is really *not* a defect in subject matter jurisdiction. The court's power to render a judgment is not being challenged: "It is for reasons of *equity and convenience*, and *not* because it is without power to proceed, that the court should not proceed with a case where it determines that an 'indispensable' party is absent and cannot be joined." [*Save Our Bay, Inc. v. San Diego Unified Port Dist.* (1996) 42 CA4th 686, 693, 49 CR2d 847, 851 (emphasis added; internal quotes omitted); *see also ¶2:160*]

[2:202] *Reserved.*

(2) [2:203] **No laches or estoppel:** The absent party's *knowledge* of the action affecting its rights does not make it a party thereto. Nor is it obliged to intervene or challenge the defective pleadings. Laches and estoppel cannot validate a judgment against an absent indispensable party. [*Inland Counties Regional Center, Inc. v. Office of Admin. Hearings (Mionske)* (1987) 193 CA3d 700, 706, 238 CR 422, 425]

[2:204] *Reserved.*

2. **[2:205]** **Permissive Joinder:** The rules discussed in the preceding section determine which parties *must* be joined in the action (compulsory joinder). Next to be considered is the question of which parties the plaintiff *may* join, if he or she chooses—i.e., the rules governing *permissive* joinder of plaintiffs and defendants.

---

### STRATEGIES AND TACTICS RE JOINDER

#### [2:206]

As will be seen below, California law permits joinder of plaintiffs and defendants as long as there is a *single* common question of law or fact affecting each of the persons joined. But there are both advantages and disadvantages to consider in joining multiple parties:

**Suing on behalf of several coplaintiffs in single action**

- **Advantages:** The several coplaintiffs can often share legal fees and expenses; e.g., discovery and pretrial preparation are usually far less costly than in separate lawsuits. Their demands can be aggregated, if necessary, to avoid the action being classified as a "limited civil case" (*see* ¶3:105). And, such aggregation may create a more formidable lawsuit to defend against . . . perhaps prompting more favorable settlement offers from the defendant.

  Where a jury trial is contemplated, plaintiffs often name a "deep pocket" defendant as the *first*-named defendant. The advantage is that whenever the clerk or judge calls the case, that defendant's name will be used! (But there is always a risk that that defendant's financial status may worsen by the time of trial and the jury may be aware of this.)

- **Disadvantages:** The more parties, the more there is a possibility of confusing the issues. Plaintiffs with independent claims run the risk that their separate claims may not be separately evaluated by the jury; particularly, that weaknesses or defenses as to one plaintiff's claim may "muddy up" the liability as to the others' claims as well. And, if each plaintiff has his or her own lawyer, there may be disagreements on strategies and tactics, making it more difficult to try the case. Also, it is sometimes more difficult to settle several plaintiffs' claims simultaneously; if defendant makes a "lump-sum" offer, it may place plaintiffs' lawyer in a conflict of interest situation trying to negotiate with each plaintiff as to his or her claim's settlement value.

- **Defense tactics:** If joinder is merely permissive, defendant *cannot compel* plaintiff to join others with similar claims as coplaintiffs in a single action. Defendant's rem-

---

---

**STRATEGIES AND TACTICS RE JOINDER**
**(Cont'd)**

edy when faced with multiple suits by plaintiffs with similar claims is a *motion to consolidate* (CCP §1048(a), *see* ¶12:347*)*; or, if the actions are pending in different courts, a *motion to coordinate* (CCP §404, *see* ¶12:371*)*.

**Joining several codefendants in single action**

- **Advantages:** It is usually less costly to sue several defendants in a single lawsuit than separately. If there are several defendants, plaintiff may choose whichever one's residence is best for venue purposes (¶3:487*)*. If the defendant is a nonresident, joining a resident defendant will prevent removal to federal court on diversity grounds (¶3:624*)*. There is always a possibility that one defendant may start blaming the other for the damages claimed by plaintiff, and end up proving plaintiff's lawsuit for him. And, the more potential contributors to any settlement or judgment, the easier it may be to reach a settlement. It also prevents the "empty chair" defense at trial (where defendant blames a nonjoined party; *see discussion at* ¶1:501-502*)*.

- **Disadvantages:** Defendants can pool their resources too; and thus perhaps mount a more effective defense than they could afford individually. There is also the risk of confusing the issues; i.e., different defendants raising different defenses may confuse the trier of fact and dilute or defeat plaintiff's claims. Finally, if any of the defendants is a nonresident, there is an increased risk of jurisdictional challenges that may delay the litigation.

- **Defense tactic:** Where such joinder would be *prejudicial* or *inconvenient* to a particular defendant, its remedy is a *motion to sever* (CCP §1048(b), *see* ¶12:407*)*.

---

a. **[2:207]** **Any person claiming interest in property or controversy:** First of all, anyone may join as coplaintiff, or be sued as a defendant, if they have or claim an interest "in the property or controversy which is the subject of the action." [CCP §§378(a)(2), 379(a)(2)]

Such persons are clearly proper parties to the action. Indeed, in most cases, such persons would be subject to the rules of compulsory joinder discussed above ("parties *necessary* for a just adjudication"; *see* ¶2:156 ff.).

[2:207.1-207.4] *Reserved.*

(1) **[2:207.5]** **Quiet title actions:** In an action to quiet title to property, plaintiff *must* name as defendants

all persons having an adverse claim to the property; they are "indispensable" parties (CCP §§762.010, 762.060(b), see ¶2:184.10).

Plaintiff may also name the rest of the world as defendants ("permissive" party defendants) in the following manner:
— "all persons unknown, claiming any legal or equitable right, title, estate, lien, or interest in the property described in the complaint adverse to plaintiff's title, or any cloud upon plaintiff's title thereto." [CCP §762.060(a)]

(a) **[2:207.6]** **Compare—notice to unknown defendants:** Upon a showing of diligence in seeking to ascertain the identity of such unknown persons, the court may order that they be served *by publication* of the summons and complaint. [CCP §763.010]

Where service by publication is ordered, plaintiff must *also:*
— post a copy of the summons and complaint on the property in issue; and
— record a *lis pendens.* [CCP §763.020]

*Cross-refer: Service by publication* is discussed at ¶4:245 ff.

b. **[2:208]** **Any person involved in transaction sued upon:** In addition, any person may join as coplaintiff, or be joined as a defendant, if:

• A right to relief is asserted by, or against, them jointly, severally, or in the alternative; and

• The right to relief arises out of the *same transaction or series of transactions*; and

• There is at least one question of law or fact common to all parties joined. [CCP §§378(a)(1), 379(a)(1)]

(1) **[2:209]** **"Relief sought jointly, severally, or in the alternative":** Note that it is *not* necessary that each plaintiff or defendant be involved in every cause of action in the complaint. Thus, for example, if there are several plaintiffs (e.g., driver and passenger in auto accident), each may seek *separate* relief. Likewise, if there are several defendants, relief may be sought against them separately, or jointly. [CCP §§378(b), 379(b)]

(a) **[2:210]** **Defendants joined in the alternative:** Where plaintiff is *in doubt* as to which of several persons is liable for his or her injuries, he or she may join them all as defendants in the action so that their respective liabilities may be determined. In such cases, the complaint *must allege facts* showing why plaintiff is "in doubt." [CCP §379(c); *Landau v. Salam* (1971) 4 C3d 901, 907, 95 CR 46, 51]

- [2:210a] **Comment:** This seems consistent with CCP §128.7, which makes the pleader's signature a certification that *evidentiary support exists* for the matters alleged (or is likely to exist after reasonable opportunity for discovery); *see ¶9:1135 ff.*

(b) [2:210.1] **Compare—defendants against whom no relief sought:** Persons against whom *no relief* is sought cannot properly be joined as defendants. It is not enough that they support the defendant in the lawsuit and would benefit indirectly if the defendant wins: "(I)t is fundamental that a person should not be compelled to defend himself in a lawsuit when no relief is sought against him." [*Pinnacle Holdings, Inc. v. Simon* (1995) 31 CA4th 1430, 1437, 37 CR2d 778, 782 (internal quotes omitted)]

- [2:210.2] Example: Landlord sued City for declaration of its right to increase rents under local rent control ordinance. Tenants who had voiced opposition to rent increases were not properly joined as codefendants because no relief was sought against them. [*Pinnacle Holdings, Inc. v. Simon*, supra, 31 CA4th at 1437, 37 CR2d at 782]

  Note: "SLAPP" suit sanctions might be available in such cases under CCP §425.16; *see ¶7:207 ff.* [*Pinnacle Holdings, Inc. v. Simon*, supra, 31 CA4th at 1437, 37 CR2d at 782]

  [2:210.3-210.4] *Reserved.*

- [2:210.5] *Compare:* A parent corporation was properly joined in an action against its subsidiaries under the Unfair Competition Law (UCL) (Bus. & Prof.C. §17200) *despite having sold control* to another entity. Joinder was proper because "(i)njunctive relief is available under the UCL . . . and the court could order (parent corporation) *not to engage in similar allegedly unlawful conduct* in the future." [*AICCO, Inc. v. Insurance Co. of North America* (2001) 90

CA4th 579, 598, 109 CR2d 359, 374 (emphasis and parentheses added)]

(2) [2:211] **"Same transaction or series of transactions":** The requirement that the right to relief arise from the "same transaction or series of transactions" is construed broadly. It is sufficient if there is any *factual relationship* between the claims joined (and this tends to merge with the "common question" requirement, below). [*Kraft v. Smith* (1944) 24 C2d 124, 128, 148 P2d 23, 25; *State Farm Fire & Cas. Co. v. Sup.Ct. (Allegro)* (1996) 45 CA4th 1093, 1113, 53 CR2d 229, 241 (citing text)]

(a) [2:212] **Application:** A right to relief arising out of the "same transaction or series of transactions" has been found in the following cases:

- [2:213] Over 200 employees and their family members claimed injuries resulting from the employees having been exposed to hazardous chemicals over a period of years at their place of employment. The fact that each employee was not exposed on every occasion any other employee was exposed did not destroy the community of interest linking the plaintiffs. [*Anaya v. Sup.Ct. (Dow Chem. Co.)* (1984) 160 CA3d 228, 233-234, 206 CR 520, 523-524]

[2:214-216] *Reserved.*

- [2:216.1] Numerous policyholders who sustained earthquake losses sued Insurance Co. for not giving them adequate notice of reductions in the scope of their coverage. The inadequate notice was a common fact central to all claims.

The fact plaintiffs also alleged improper claims handling practices did not render the joinder improper: "While not every plaintiff may have been victimized by the same claims handling practice, that is a matter which can be resolved in discovery; and the trial court will always retain the right to sever the claims of particular plaintiffs in order to prevent prejudice to (Insurance Co.)." [*State Farm Fire & Cas. Co. v. Sup.Ct. (Allegro)* (1996) 45 CA4th 1093, 1113-1114, 53 CR2d 229, 241 (parentheses added)]

- [2:217] *Compare:* But the right to relief did *not* arise out of the "same transaction or series of transactions" where three chiropractors sued for trespass to their separate and distinct premises, and there was *no* allegation of any community of interest among the plaintiffs, or any common scheme by the defendants. [*Coleman v. Twin Coast Newspapers* (1959) 175 CA2d 650, 654, 346 P2d 488, 490]

- [2:218] Nor was it proper for Farmers Insurance Company to join 300 policyholders in a suit for declaratory relief on whether their homeowners' insurance covered damages from a rainstorm. The mere fact that all claims resulted from the *same storm* did *not* show they arose out of the "same transaction or occurrence": "We find it improper to label the damage herein to innumerable types of structures, occurring at widely separated locations within the state, resulting from a myriad of causes, and under various conditions as the 'same transaction or occurrence' within the meaning of CCP §379." [*Farmers Ins. Co. v. Adams* (1985) 170 CA3d 712, 723, 216 CR 287, 294 (disapproved on other grounds in *Garvey v. State Farm Fire & Cas. Co.* (1989) 48 C3d 395, 411, 257 CR 292, 302, fn. 10)]

(b) [2:219] **Defendants joined in the alternative:** Where defendants have been joined in the alternative because plaintiff is "in doubt" as to which defendant caused his injuries, the *injury issue itself supplies the requisite relationship* . . . even if the defendants' acts were otherwise unrelated. Example: P claims permanent back injury after having been involved in two separate traffic accidents, and is "in doubt" as to which accident caused his injury. He may properly join both drivers as defendants, so that the injury issue may be determined. [*Landau v. Salam* (1971) 4 C3d 901, 906-907, 95 CR 46, 50-51]

(3) [2:220] **"Common question of law or fact":** The final requirement is that there be a *single* question of law or fact common to all parties joined. But this does not add much, because the claims have to be factually related to start off with (arising out of the "same transaction or series of transactions"; see above).

(a) [2:221] **Single question sufficient:** For example, in an auto accident case, Passenger and Driver may join as plaintiffs. The "common question" is whether the driver of the other car was negligent. This is sufficient for joinder purposes, even though there are also many *separate* questions involved; e.g., injuries and losses sustained by each plaintiff, comparative negligence of Driver, etc. [See *Anaya v. Sup.Ct. (Dow Chem. Co.)* (1984) 160 CA3d 228, 233, 206 CR 520, 523]

(b) [2:222] **Unrelated claims may be joined:** As long as there is a "common question" involving each of the parties joined, the joinder of parties rules are satisfied. This being so, plaintiff may then join *any other causes of action* he or she has against any of the defendants joined. I.e., wide-open joinder of claims is permitted, once the party-joinder rules are satisfied. [CCP §427.10(a); *discussed at ¶6:268*]

Example: In an auto accident case, P sues D1 as driver of car causing his injury, and D2 as owner of the car. The "common question" of liability satisfies the party-joinder rules. P may, if he wishes, join an unrelated cause of action he has against D2 (e.g., for nonpayment of a promissory note).

1) [2:223] **Contrast—federal rule:** In federal practice, all claims joined must arise out of the *same transaction* or series of transactions. [FRCP 20(a)]

(4) [2:224] **Limitations:** For policy reasons, there are certain limitations on party joinder, notwithstanding the existence of a "common question":

(a) [2:225] **Insurer cannot be joined in suit against insured:** Plaintiff generally cannot join an insurance carrier as a party to his or her action against the insured tortfeasor. The injured party has no direct claim against the liability insurer until *after* a judgment is first obtained against the insured. [Ins.C. §11580(b)(2); see *McKee v. National Union Fire Ins. Co.* (1993) 15 CA4th 282, 285-290, 19 CR2d 286, 287-291]

1) [2:226] **Compare—validity of release:** But if the claim against the insurance carrier goes to the validity of a *release* signed by plaintiff, that claim *may* be joined in the personal injury action against the insured. The court's power to bifurcate issues at trial is deemed sufficient to safeguard against prejudicial use of evidence of the liability insurance. [*Johnson v. Threats* (1983) 140 CA3d 287, 291, 189 CR 447, 449— P claimed that D's insurer had obtained release by fraud]

2) **[2:227] Compare—breach of settlement agreement:** Likewise, an injured plaintiff may join a cause of action against the defendant's insurance carrier for breach of contract; i.e., *reneging on an oral agreement to settle* the underlying personal injury claim. The risk of prejudicing the liability claim with evidence of the alleged settlement can be avoided by *bifurcating* these issues at trial. [*Ahmed v. Peterson* (1986) 186 CA3d 374, 377, 230 CR 636, 637]

3) **[2:228] Compare—insurer fraud delaying suit:** To get around a statute of limitations defense, plaintiffs may claim they delayed suit in reliance on the insurer's fraudulent promises to settle. In such cases, a *fraud* claim against the insurer may be joined with the negligence claim against the insured. Such joinder appears proper because the negligence claim against the insured is barred unless plaintiff first proves the fraud claim against the insurer.

But the insurer can prevent such joinder by having its insured *waive the statute of limitations* defense. In such event, the insurer's alleged fraud in delaying suit becomes irrelevant to the automobile accident. [*Geraci v. United Services Auto. Ass'n* (1987) 188 CA3d 1245, 1251, 233 CR 896, 899]

➡️ **[2:229] *PRACTICE POINTER FOR DEFENDANT:*** Bifurcation may not prevent the jury from learning that the alleged tortfeasor is insured (i.e., the insurance company will still be a named defendant in the action). And, discovery initiated by plaintiff against the insurer could conceivably hamper its defense of the insured.

Therefore, defense counsel should try to get rid of the cause of action against the insurance carrier at the earliest possible time: by demurrer, motion for summary judgment, etc.

**[2:229.1-229.4]** *Reserved.*

4) **[2:229.5] Compare—insurance issues intertwined with other issues:** A liability insurer may be joined where insurance coverage issues are "inextricably intertwined" with liability issues, creating a potential for prejudice if the insurer is not a party to the action. [*Royal*

*Surplus Lines Ins. Co. v. Ranger Ins. Co.* (2002) 100 CA4th 193, 199, 122 CR2d 459, 463—Landowner could join Subcontractor's liability insurer in suit claiming Subcontractor had contractual obligation to defend and indemnify Landowner, because issues involved in interpretation of subcontract and Subcontractor's insurance policy were inextricably intertwined]

c. **[2:230] Limitation—power of court to order separate trials:** The liberal rules on party-joinder, and the wide-open rule on joinder of claims, may lead to unduly complicated proceedings. To avoid unfairness or hardship to any party, therefore, the court has power to order separate trials on any of the causes of action joined; or to make any other order to prevent embarrassment, delay or undue expense to any party. [CCP §379.5; *Anaya v. Sup.Ct. (Dow Chem. Co.)* (1984) 160 CA3d 228, 234, 206 CR 520, 524]

d. **[2:231] Procedure for challenging improper joinder:** Misjoinder of parties can be challenged either by *demurrer* to the complaint or by raising the objection as an affirmative defense in the answer. [CCP §430.10(d), ¶6:475, 7:78-83]

e. **[2:232] Defect may be waived:** Any objection as to misjoinder of parties must be raised at the outset of the case. Failure to object by demurrer or answer *waives* the defect. [CCP §430.80, ¶7:83]

3. **[2:233] Alternative Joinder Procedures in Multi-Defendant Cases:** The Supreme Court has noted various alternatives where the defendants are too numerous to be sued and served individually. [*Monterey S.P. Partnership v. W.L. Bangham, Inc.* (1989) 49 C3d 454, 461, 261 CR 587, 591, fn. 4—involving 252 trust deed beneficiaries who were real parties in interest; *see* ¶2:11]

- *Class actions:* Suing all defendants as a class under CCP §382 ("defendant class actions," *see* ¶14:58);

- *Service on agents:* "Serving any . . . individual designated as 'attorney-in-fact' for the beneficiaries" under CCP §416.90 (providing for service of summons upon a "person authorized . . . to receive service of process");

- *Service by publication:* "(R)equesting permission from the trial court to serve a summons on the beneficiaries by publication" under CCP §415.50 (*see* ¶4:245 ff.).

a. **[2:234] Comment:** Easier said than done! Defendant class actions are subject to rigid procedural requirements (¶14:9 ff.). Service on "attorneys in fact" is effective only if they have *actual* authority to accept service (¶4:128). And, service by publication is available only after reasonable diligence to serve personally (¶*4:249*). [See conc.opn. in *Monterey S.P. Partnership v. W.L. Bangham, Inc.*, supra, 49 C3d at 466, 261 CR at 593-594—calling for legislative consideration]

[2:235-249]   *Reserved.*

## D. CLASS ACTIONS

[2:250]   The class action device is an extension of the permissive joinder rules discussed above. The existence of a "common question" may permit suit to be maintained by a *representative* on behalf of a group of persons if the procedure is both necessary and superior to separate lawsuits.

*Cross-refer:* The rules and procedures governing class actions involve much more than party joinder issues, and are therefore dealt

*(Text cont'd on p. 2-63)*

**RESERVED**

with in a separate chapter. *See Ch. 14, "Representative and Class Actions."*

[2:251-399]  *Reserved.*

## E. INTERVENTION

[2:400]  Intervention is the procedure whereby someone not named as a party to an action (or ordered joined as a party) may nevertheless become a party. An intervention takes place when the court grants leave to a nonparty to join the plaintiff in claiming what is sought by the complaint; or to unite with the defendant in resisting the plaintiff's claims; or to demand anything adverse to both parties. [CCP §387(a)]

1.  [2:401]  **Intervention as Right:**  If the proper procedure is followed (¶2:436 ff.), the court must allow a nonparty to intervene in the following cases. It makes no difference that such intervention will expand the issues in the case and impinge on the right of the original parties to litigate the matter in their own fashion.

    a.  [2:402]  **Statutory right to intervene:**  There are a number of statutes entitling a nonparty to intervene in litigation pending between others. Examples:

        (1)  [2:403]  In class actions under the Consumer Legal Remedies Act, any member of the consumer class may appear through counsel. [Civ.C. §1781(e)(3)]

        (2)  [2:404]  A shareholder or creditor of a corporation may intervene in involuntary dissolution proceedings against the corporation [Corps.C. §1800(c)]; and a creditor may also intervene in actions by the corporation against a shareholder to enforce subscription agreements. [Corps.C. §414]

        (3)  [2:405]  Any person having a "legal or equitable interest" in property that is the subject of a pending condemnation action may intervene as a defendant therein. [CCP §1250.230]

        [2:406]  *Reserved.*

    b.  [2:407]  **Party whose joinder compulsory:**  In addition, a nonparty has the right to intervene in litigation between others where he claims an *interest in the property or transaction* involved in such litigation, and is so situated that any judgment rendered in his absence "may as a practical matter impair or impede his ability to protect that interest . . ." [CCP §387(b)]

        (1)  [2:408]  **Effect:**  Intervention under this provision is a counterpart to the compulsory joinder rule of CCP §389, *discussed at ¶2:156 ff.* It gives the nonparty the *right* to intervene in cases where his or her joinder has not yet

been ordered, but could be, under the joinder rules previously discussed.

(2) [2:409] **Test:** The party claiming a right to intervene must show an interest in the "property or transaction" that is the subject of the litigation, that would be *substantially prejudiced* by any judgment rendered in his or her absence (see test for compulsory joinder, ¶2:161).

(a) [2:409.1] **Compare—nonparty's interest adequately represented by existing parties:** There is no right to intervene if the court finds that the nonparty's interests are being *adequately* represented by one or more of the existing parties to the litigation. [CCP §387(b)]

(3) **Application**

- [2:410] An employer who has paid *workers' compensation benefits* to an employee injured on the job has the *right* to intervene in the employee's lawsuit against the person causing such injury. Having paid such benefits, the employer has a subrogation *interest in the employee's cause of action*, and any judgment rendered in his absence might impair that interest. [See Lab.C. §3853; *Bailey v. Reliance Ins. Co.* (2000) 79 CA4th 449, 454, 94 CR2d 149, 153]

- [2:411] But a health care insurer has *no* absolute *right* to intervene in its subscriber's personal injury action. The insurer may have a right to reimbursement from the subscriber if he or she recovers, but it has *no interest in the subscriber's cause of action* against the person causing the injuries. Hence, there is no basis for mandatory intervention. [*California Physicians' Serv. v. Sup.Ct. (Gilmore)* (1980) 102 CA3d 91, 96, 162 CR 266, 270]

- [2:412] Nor does an automobile insurer which has paid benefits to its insured for injuries caused by another have an absolute right to intervene in its insured's action against the party responsible for such injuries. Unless the insurer has *retained* a right of subrogation in the insurance policy, it has no interest in the insured's cause of action, and thus no right to intervene. [*Knight v. Alefosio* (1984) 158 CA3d 716, 726-727, 205 CR 42, 48—"income continuation benefits" paid to insured, who sued other driver for loss of income; insurer had no right of subrogation because none reserved in policy]

- [2:413] Nor does a nonparty have the right to intervene merely to assert a privilege to prevent disclosure of confidential information. An evidentiary privilege is *not* "an interest in the property or transaction" involved in the litigation within the meaning of §387(b). The privilege can be asserted without the holder becoming a party to the action. [*Mylan Laboratories, Inc. v. Soon-Shiong* (1999) 76 CA4th 71, 79, 90 CR2d 111, 116—former director accused of wrongdoing in minority shareholder's derivative suit against other directors could not intervene to prevent disclosure of memo protected by attorney-client privilege that had come into possession of other directors]

**⟹[2:413.1]** ***PRACTICE POINTER:*** Rather than intervene, the proper procedure for a nonparty who wishes to assert a privilege is to seek a protective order under CCP §2025(i) as an "affected natural person or organization." Alternatively, if the issue arises while the nonparty is being deposed, he or she can simply refuse to answer the question or to produce the document and then oppose any later motion to compel.

2. **[2:414] Permissive Intervention:** If proper procedures are followed (¶*2:438 ff.*), the court has *discretion* to permit a nonparty to intervene in litigation pending between others, provided:

- The nonparty has a *direct and immediate interest* in the litigation; and

- The intervention will *not enlarge* the issues in the case; and

- The *reasons* for intervention *outweigh* any opposition by the existing parties. [See CCP §387(a); and *Truck Ins. Exch. v. Sup.Ct. (Transco Syndicate #1)* (1997) 60 CA4th 342, 346, 70 CR2d 255, 257 (citing text)]

a. **[2:415] Intervenor's interest in litigation:** First of all, the party seeking intervention must have an "interest in the matter in litigation, or in the success of either of the parties, or an interest against both . . . " [CCP §387(a)]

(1) **[2:416] Test:** The party seeking to intervene must have a *direct and immediate* interest in the *outcome* of the litigation; i.e., he or she *must stand to gain or lose by direct operation of the judgment.* [*Fireman's Fund Ins.Co. v. Gerlach* (1976) 56 CA3d 299, 303-305, 128 CR 396, 398-399; *US Ecology, Inc. v. State of Calif.* (2001) 92 CA4th 113, 140, 111 CR2d 689, 710]

(a) **[2:417]** However, the party need *not* have any *pecuniary* interest in the dispute, nor a specific interest in the "property or transaction" involved in the litigation (as is required for intervention by right; ¶2:409). [*Simpson Redwood Co. v. State of Calif.* (1987) 196 CA3d 1192, 1201, 242 CR 447, 451]

(b) [2:418]   Nor need it be shown that such interest will inevitably be affected by the outcome of the litigation . . . a *substantial probability* is sufficient. [*Timberidge Enterprises, Inc. v. Santa Rosa* (1978) 86 CA3d 873, 881, 150 CR 606, 611]

(c) [2:419]   *Bottom line:* Whether the interest is sufficiently "direct" and "substantial" must be decided on the facts of each case. But CCP §387 is to be construed *liberally* in favor of intervention. [*Simpson Redwood Co. v. State of Calif.* (1987) 196 CA3d 1192, 1201, 242 CR 447, 451—error to refuse intervention by conservation league in title dispute between timber company and State dealing with parklands which league had donated to State, because its *reputation* could be adversely affected by outcome]

(2) [2:420]   **Court's discretion:**   A trial court has discretion to deny intervention even when a "direct interest" is shown, if the interests of the original litigants *outweigh* the intervenor's concerns. For example, intervention will not be allowed when it would retard the principal suit, or require a reopening of the case for further evidence, or delay the trial of the action, or change the position of the original parties. [See *Marriage of Kerr* (1986) 185 CA3d 130, 134, 229 CR 610, 612]

(3) **Application**

(a) [2:421]   *Members of a class or association* are generally permitted to intervene in an action to which the class or association is a party. Since each member is entitled to a share of any recovery in such action, they have a direct and immediate interest in the outcome. [See *Mann v. Sup.Ct. (Gans)* (1942) 53 CA2d 272, 280, 127 P2d 970, 974]

(b) [2:422]   But a *creditor of a party* generally may *not* intervene in an action by or against his or her debtor. Even if the debtor-party will be rendered unable to pay the debt if he or she loses the lawsuit, the creditor does *not* have a sufficiently "direct" interest in the outcome to permit intervention therein. [*Continental Vinyl Products v. Mead Corp.* (1972) 27 CA3d 543, 550-551, 103 CR 806, 811]

1) [2:423]   However, where a creditor has obtained a *lien* on the debtor's assets, and that

lien could be jeopardized by the proceedings, the creditor may be permitted to intervene to protect his or her lien. [*Marriage of Kerr*, supra—judgment creditor holding lien on Wife's property permitted to intervene in dissolution action where the property was alleged to be community property]

[2:424]   ***PRACTICE POINTER:***   A creditor holding a *judgment* (from another lawsuit) does not have to intervene. It can simply file and serve a "notice of lien" together with a certified copy of the judgment (CCP §708.410). This establishes the creditor's right to payment from any recovery by the judgment debtor in the present action.

On the other hand, filing a notice of lien does not ensure the judgment debtor will pursue the action diligently (and often has the opposite effect). To ensure diligent prosecution, the judgment creditor should consider intervening in the action as permitted by CCP §708.430.

(c)  [2:425]   Nor will a *shareholder of a corporate party* usually be permitted to intervene in an action by or against the corporation. The shareholder's interest in any judgment rendered is only "indirect" or "consequential." [*Continental Vinyl Products v. Mead Corp.*, supra, 27 CA3d at 553, 103 CR at 813]

1)  [2:426]   But where suit is filed against both the corporation and its officers, and there is a *potential conflict of interest* between them, shareholders may be permitted to intervene on behalf of the corporation to insure a good faith defense. [*Montgomery v. Bio-Med Specialties, Inc.* (1986) 183 CA3d 1292, 1294, 228 CR 709, 710]

(d)  [2:427]   An *insurance carrier* that has paid benefits to its insured for losses caused by a third party may be *subrogated* by operation of law to the insured's claim against such third party, to the extent of its payments. As subrogee, it has a direct pecuniary interest in the outcome of the litigation, and may be permitted to intervene therein. [*Deutschmann v. Sears, Roebuck & Co.* (1982) 132 CA3d 912, 915, 183 CR 573, 575]

1)  [2:428]   *Compare:* But a *health care provider*, which has only the right to reimbursement from

its subscriber if and when the subscriber recovers for his or her injuries, is *not* entitled to intervene in the subscriber's personal injury action. I.e., the health care provider is *not* subrogated to the subscriber's claim, and is really only a potential creditor. [*California Physicians' Serv. v. Sup.Ct. (Gilmore)* (1980) 102 CA3d 91, 96, 162 CR 266, 270]

[2:429] *Reserved.*

(e) [2:430]  A *liability insurer* normally *cannot* intervene in a tort action against its insured to contest whether the claim against the insured is covered under its policy. The judgment in the tort action collaterally estops the insurer only on issues necessarily adjudicated therein—i.e., the insured's liability and the amount of the injured party's damages. It does not bind the insurer on coverage issues. [*Kuperstein v. Sup.Ct. (Allstate)* (1988) 204 CA3d 598, 600, 251 CR 385, 387]

1) [2:430.1]  A liability insurer may be permitted to intervene, however, where the insured is *barred* from defending itself. In such cases, intervention is necessary to protect the insurer's own interests because it may be obligated to pay any judgment rendered against its insured (assuming no coverage defenses). [*Reliance Ins. Co. v. Sup.Ct. (Wells)* (2000) 84 CA4th 383, 386-387, 100 CR2d 807, 810—insurer entitled to intervene where insured barred from defending because its corporate status had been suspended for nonpayment of franchise tax; *Jade K. v. Viguri* (1989) 210 CA3d 1459, 1468, 258 CR 907, 912—insurer permitted to intervene and file motion to set aside default judgment where insured defendant was in jail]

(f) [2:431]  State sued to invalidate County ordinances banning spraying of toxic herbicides. *Members of the public* were permitted to intervene because invalidation of the ordinances could have a direct and immediate effect on their health. No pecuniary interest need be shown. [*People v. Trinity County* (1983) 147 CA3d 655, 661-662, 195 CR 186, 189-190]

(g) [2:432]  A *joint tortfeasor* who has entered into a good-faith settlement pursuant to CCP §877.6 and is dismissed from the action may thereafter intervene to pursue a declaratory relief action for equitable indemnity against the nonsettling joint tort-feasor. [*Bolamperti v. Larco Mfg.* (1985) 164 CA3d 249, 255-256, 210 CR 155, 159]

(4) [2:433] **Compare—effect of party's failure to prosecute or defend:** What might otherwise be an insufficient interest to permit intervention, may become a "direct and immediate" interest where an existing party is failing to prosecute or defend the action in good faith. [*Continental Vinyl Products v. Mead Corp.*, supra, 27 CA3d at 551, 103 CR at 811]

(a) [2:434] Thus, for example, if the officers and directors of a corporation fail to exercise good faith in defending an action against it, a shareholder (whose interest is otherwise insufficient) may be permitted to intervene, in order to assert defenses on the corporation's behalf. [*Continental Vinyl Products v. Mead Corp.*, supra]

(b) [2:435] Similarly, where the defendant has *defaulted*, third parties may be permitted to intervene in order to set aside the default and to raise defenses on the defendant's behalf where they have a "direct and immediate interest" in contesting the defendant's liability. [See *Jade K. v. Viguri* (1989) 210 CA3d 1459, 1468-1470, 258 CR 907, 912-914—D's liability insurer permitted to intervene to litigate fault and damage issues; and *Fireman's Fund Ins. Co. v. Gerlach* (1976) 56 CA3d 299, 303, 128 CR 396, 398—D's judgment creditor permitted to intervene; *Nasongkhla v. Gonzalez* (1994) 29 CA4th Supp. 1, 4, 34 CR2d 379, 381]

b. [2:436] **No new issues:** Where intervention is of right, new issues may be interjected (¶2:401). But where permissive only, intervention is not proper if it would enlarge the issues in the case. [*Fireman's Fund Ins. Co. v. Gerlach,* supra; see also *Kuperstein v. Sup.Ct. (Allstate)* (1988) 204 CA3d 598, 600-601, 251 CR 385, 387—liability insurer precluded from intervening to contest coverage in action against its insured]

c. [2:437] **Reasons for intervention:** Most importantly, the purposes served by allowing the nonparty to intervene must *outweigh* the original parties' interest in conducting their own lawsuit on their own terms. [*People v. Trinity County* (1983) 147 CA3d 655, 661, 195 CR 186, 189]

3. **Procedure**

a. [2:438] **"Timely" application for leave to intervene:** Whether intervention is of right, or only permissive, the party seeking to intervene must make "timely" application to the court. [CCP §387(a)]

Whether intervention is permissive or mandatory, a petition seeking leave to intervene is required; without permission from the court, a party lacks any standing in the action. [*Lohnes v. Astron Computer Products* (2001) 94 CA4th 1150, 1153, 115 CR2d 34, 36]

(1) [2:438.1] **Where statute specifies time for intervention:** Where a statute authorizes intervention "at *any time* before trial" (e.g., Lab.C. §3853, *see ¶2:454*), the words are given literal effect: i.e., an intervention is "timely" even on the eve of trial and although a settlement has been reached between existing parties! [*Mar v. Sakti Int'l Corp.* (1992) 9 CA4th 1780, 1785, 12 CR2d 388, 392—employer moved to intervene in employee's action against wrongdoer to recover benefits paid employee: motion timely although made just 4 days before trial, and after parties had settled (but action not dismissed because another complaint in intervention pending)]

   (a) [2:438.2] **Compare—possible challenges:** Once filed, the complaint in intervention may be subject to various defenses and challenges as a result of delay: e.g., *dismissal for delay in prosecution*. [*Mar v. Sakti Int'l Corp.*, supra, 9 CA4th at 1785, 12 CR2d at 392]

(2) [2:439] **Diligence requirement:** Except in cases such as the above, what is and is not "timely" ultimately rests in the court's discretion. Unreasonable delay after learning of the action or the ground for intervention may therefore result in denial of leave to intervene: "Aside from the statutory limitation . . . it is the general rule that a right to intervene should be asserted within a reasonable time and that the intervenor must not be guilty of an unreasonable delay after knowledge of the suit." [See *Allen v. California Water & Tel. Co.* (1947) 31 C2d 104, 108, 187 P2d 393, 395—decided under former statute allowing intervention "before trial"]

(3) [2:440] **Even after judgment:** Leave to intervene may be granted at any time—even after judgment has been rendered—if the court finds the application was "timely" under the circumstances, and intervention is otherwise appropriate. [*Mallick v. Sup.Ct. (County of Marin)* (1979) 89 CA3d 434, 437, 152 CR 503, 505—members of class may intervene in class action after judgment, in order to remove class representative]

b. [2:441] **Application ex parte or by noticed motion:** A nonparty may seek leave to intervene by ex parte application to the court (*see ¶9:345 ff.*); or by a regular noticed motion served on the existing parties. In either event, copies of the proposed complaint in intervention (below) should be attached to the application. [*Adoption of Lenn E.* (1986) 182 CA3d 210, 217, 227 CR 63, 67]

(1) **FORMS**

- Application and Order for Leave to Intervene, *see Form 2:A.*

- Checklist on Motion for Leave to Intervene, *see Form 2:C.*

➪[2:442] **PRACTICE POINTER:** A noticed motion gives the existing parties time to settle and dismiss the action before your motion can be heard. This would cut off your right to intervene, and could bar relief entirely if the statute of limitations has run. Consequently, it may be preferable to apply *ex parte* for leave to intervene (although some judges are hostile to ex parte motions generally). But you will have to notify opposing parties by telephone prior to making the *ex parte* application (CRC 379; *see ¶9:352*).

c. [2:443] **Complaint in intervention:** The intervenor's pleading (whether it supports plaintiff's claims, or defendant, or claims adversely to both) is captioned "Complaint In Intervention." [See *Timberidge Enterprises, Inc. v. Santa Rosa* (1978) 86 CA3d 873, 879, 150 CR 606, 609]

It must comply with the rules applicable to pleadings generally (*see Ch. 6*). In addition, it must set forth the *grounds upon which the intervention rests*; i.e., the facts which show that intervention is a matter of right (*¶2:401 ff.*), or the basis for permissive intervention (*¶2:414*).

- **FORM:** Complaint In Intervention, *see Form 2:B.*

d. [2:444] **Service of complaint in intervention:** A complaint in intervention must be served on any parties who have not yet appeared in the action, in the same manner as the complaint (*¶4:180 ff.*). Service on parties who have appeared is made through service (by mail or other permitted methods) on their attorneys of record. [CCP §387(a)]

e. [2:445] **Challenging intervention:** Unless a noticed motion for leave to intervene was utilized (*¶2:441*), the existing parties' first opportunity to challenge the intervention is normally by *demurrer* or *motion to strike* the complaint in intervention. [See *Timberidge Enterprises, Inc. v. Santa Rosa*, supra]

(1) **[2:446]** Any objection to the intervention is deemed *waived*, unless raised by the existing parties at their earliest opportunity to do so. [See *Bloom v. Waxman* (1941) 48 CA2d 646, 120 P2d 509, 510]

4. **[2:447]** **Effect of Intervention:** If leave to intervene is granted, the intervenor becomes an independent party to the action. Thereafter, he or she has the same rights as any other party—e.g., to demand a jury trial; to object to the jurisdiction of the court, or to the sufficiency of the pleadings; or to disqualify a judge. [See *Deutschmann v. Sears, Roebuck & Co.* (1982) 132 CA3d 912, 916, 183 CR 573, 575]

a. **[2:448]** **Effect of dismissal of plaintiff's claim:** Where the intervenor is subrogated to all or a portion of plaintiff's cause of action, the dismissal of plaintiff's complaint will *not* affect the intervenor. The intervenor has an independent interest in the litigation. [*Deutschmann v. Sears, Roebuck & Co.*, supra—plaintiff's complaint dismissed for failure to serve and return summons within statutory time limit; intervenor entitled to continue action]

(1) **[2:449]** Of course, if the case goes to trial, the intervenor's claim (based on subrogation) is no better than the plaintiff's. Thus, if plaintiff fails to recover on the merits, so would the intervenor. [See *Deutschmann v. Sears, Roebuck & Co.*, supra]

b. **[2:450]** **No "relation back" for statute of limitations purposes:** A complaint in intervention, like any other complaint, is subject to the defense of the statute of limitations. Thus, if it asserts a new cause of action from that already before the court, the application for leave to intervene must be filed within the statutory period. [*Andersen v. Barton Memorial Hosp., Inc.* (1985) 166 CA3d 678, 682, 212 CR 626, 629]

(1) **Application**

(a) **[2:451]** Heir A filed complaint in intervention in wrongful death action timely filed by Heir B, after statute had run on any independent action. The wrongful death statute (CCP §377.60) requires that all claims be determined in a single action, so that omitted heirs must join pending action. But each heir's claim is still a "personal and *separate cause of action.*" Since Heir A's cause of action was barred by statute, he could not join other heir's action, and his complaint in intervention had to be dismissed. [*Andersen v. Barton Memorial Hosp., Inc.*, supra]

**[2:452]** *Reserved.*

(2) **[2:453]** **Compare—employer-employee intervention:** A different rule applies in actions brought by

either employee or employer (or the employer's insurer) against a third party for injuries caused to the employee. "Substantively, as well as procedurally ... regardless of who brings the action (employee, employer or insurer), it is *essentially the same lawsuit*. The defendant is therefore put on notice of the claim, and the purpose of the statute of limitations is served." [See *Andersen v. Barton Memorial Hosp., Inc.*, supra, 166 CA3d at 684, 212 CR at 630]

(a) **[2:454] Statute:** Labor Code §3853 specifically provides that when an action is brought by either employer or employee against a third party who has caused injuries to the employee, "the other (employer or employee) may, *at any time before trial on the facts*, join as party plaintiff." (And, the workers' compensation insurer has the same rights to join as the employer; see Lab.C. §3850(b).)

(b) **[2:455] Effect:** This permits a complaint in intervention to be filed *even after the statute of limitations has run* on any independent action on the employer's or employee's claim. [*Jordan v. Sup.Ct. (Associated Indem. Corp.)* (1981) 116 CA3d 202, 207-208, 172 CR 30, 32; *Home Ins. Co. v. Southern Calif. Rapid Transit Dist.* (1987) 196 CA3d 522, 525-526, 241 CR 858, 859—action against governmental tortfeasor]

   1) **[2:456] Example:** Insurer sued D who had injured Employee to recover disability benefits paid to Employee on account of such injuries. Employee filed complaint in intervention for general damages for such injuries after expiration of the statute of limitations. Although Employee's claim would have been time-barred in an independent action, it was properly asserted by intervention in Insurer's action, pursuant to Labor Code §3853. [*Jordan v. Sup.Ct. (Associated Indem. Corp.)*, supra, 116 CA3d at 207-208, 172 CR at 32]

(c) **[2:457] Compare—employee's action subject to dismissal:** However, an employer or insurer cannot intervene after expiration of the 3-year period for service of summons (CCP §583.210, ¶11:51). The employee's action is subject to *mandatory* dismissal, and a complaint in intervention cannot "breathe life back into a case already dead." [*Chambers v. Santa Cruz City School Dist.* (1987) 193 CA3d 518, 522, 238 CR 356, 358; see also *Taito v. Owens Corning* (1992) 7 CA4th 798, 803, 9

CR2d 687, 689—no intervention allowed where worker's complaint had been dismissed for failure to name and serve defendant within 1-year limitations period]

1) **[2:458]  Effect of D's answer to complaint in intervention:**  Nor can the employee avoid dismissal based on D's answer to the employer's complaint in intervention within the 3-year period. That does *not* constitute an appearance in the employee's action. (To this extent at least, the employee's and employer's actions are regarded as separate.) [*Duckett v. Sup.Ct. (Skelton)* (1989) 207 CA3d 1419, 1424-1425, 255 CR 733, 736]

(d) **[2:459]  Employee's right to "intervene back in" after employer intervention?**  Cases are split on whether an employer's *timely* intervention in an action allows the employee to "intervene back in" where his or her earlier action was *dismissed for failure to prosecute.*

Example: Employee sues Third Party for injuries suffered on the job. Complaint is dismissed for failure to serve summons within 3 years. Employer's workers' comp carrier had intervened before the dismissal. Employee now seeks to intervene in the same action.

1) **[2:460]  View allowing intervention after dismissal:**  At least one case holds the insurer's intervention keeps the door open for the employee to reenter the action. Rationale: Labor Code §3853 gives employer and employee the "*unconditional right* to intervene" in each other's action *anytime before trial.* [*Buell v. CBS, Inc.* (1982) 136 CA3d 823, 826, 186 CR 455, 457]

2) **[2:461]  View barring intervention by employee after dismissal:**  However, more recent cases refuse to allow an employee who fails to comply with mandatory service statutes to avoid the dismissal penalty by intervening back into the very litigation he or she set in motion after the statute of limitations has run. Such "procedural leapfrog" could go on forever (dilatory employer could be dismissed and re-intervene, etc.)! [*Bishop v. Silva* (1991) 234 CA3d 1317, 1327, 285 CR 910, 916; *Fairmont*

*Ins. Co. v. Frank* (1996) 42 CA4th 457, 461, 49
CR2d 670, 671]

[2:462]   *Reserved.*

c.   [2:463]   **Court costs:**   As a party to the action, the intervenor is subject to the same procedural rights, remedies and
liabilities as original parties, including the right to recover or
suffer an award of court costs. Thus, if the intervenor voluntarily *dismisses* the complaint before trial, or *loses* at trial,
it may be held liable for costs incurred by opposing parties
during the period of intervention. [*Catello v. I.T.T. General
Controls* (1984) 152 CA3d 1009, 1014-1015, 200 CR 4, 8;
see *Garcia v. Hyster Co.* (1994) 28 CA4th 724, 732, 34
CR2d 283, 287—error to award costs from date complaint
filed]

[2:463.1-463.4]   *Reserved.*

d.   [2:463.5]   **Attorney fees:**   An intervenor may also recover
or suffer an award of attorney fees where a statute or contract authorizes a fee award. [See *Big Bear Mun. Water Dist.
v. Bear Valley Mut. Water Co.* (1989) 207 CA3d 363, 386,
254 CR 757, 770-771]

- [2:463.6]   Subcontractor's Insurer intervened in
Employee's personal injury action against General
Contractor, in order to recoup workers' compensation
benefits Insurer had paid to Employee. Insurer "stands
in the shoes of the subcontractor" and is bound by the
terms of its subcontract, including an attorney fees provision. Thus, if General Contractor prevails, Subcontractor's Insurer may be liable for fees. [*Employers
Mut. Liab. Ins. Co. v. Tutor-Saliba Corp.* (1998) 17 C4th
632, 641-642, 71 CR2d 851, 856-857]

5.   [2:464]   **Effect of Failure to Intervene:**   Intervention is never
mandatory. Thus, a person may choose to "sit on the sidelines"
even if pending litigation clearly affects his or her interests.

It is unclear, however, whether such "sideline sitters" run the risk
of *collateral estoppel*—i.e., whether they may be barred from
relitigating issues adversely decided in the prior litigation:

- [2:465]   **View supporting collateral estoppel:**   One
case held an employee collaterally estopped from suing
third parties for injury suffered in a work-related accident because the employee had failed to intervene in an earlier
*federal* action by his employer against the same parties for
benefits paid the employee and for property damage suffered in the same accident. [*Lewis v. County of Sacramento*
(1990) 218 CA3d 214, 217-219, 266 CR 678, 680-681—employee had *testified on employer's behalf* in the prior action:
court stressed the "identity of interest" between the employer

and employee, suggesting collateral estoppel might also be based on concepts of *privity*]

- [2:466] **View rejecting collateral estoppel:** In federal practice, *nonparties* are *not* subject to collateral estoppel: "Joinder as a party, rather than knowledge of a lawsuit and an opportunity to intervene, is the method by which potential parties are subjected to the jurisdiction of the court and bound by a judgment or decree." [*Martin v. Wilks* (1989) 490 US 755, 756, 109 S.Ct. 2180, 2184]

- [2:467] **Comment:** *Lewis v. County of Sacramento* may not be reliable precedent because the prior action involved in that case *was* a *federal* action. The scope and effect given to a federal judgment is normally governed by federal law; and, as stated above, federal law *rejects* collateral estoppel based on failure to intervene.

    [2:468-469] *Reserved.*

## F. INTERPLEADER

[2:470] Interpleader is a procedure whereby a person holding money or personal property to which conflicting claims are being made by others, can join the adverse claimants and force them to litigate their claims among themselves. (For example, an escrowholder who receives conflicting demands from the parties to the escrow regarding the funds or documents he or she holds.) [*Hancock Oil Co. v. Hopkins* (1944) 24 C2d 497, 508, 150 P2d 463, 469; *City of Morgan Hill v. Brown* (1999) 71 CA4th 1114, 1122, 84 CR2d 361, 365]

Once the stakeholder's right to interplead is established, and he or she deposits the money or personal property in court, he or she may be discharged from liability to any of the claimants. This enables the stakeholder to avoid multiplicity of actions, and the risk of inconsistent results if each of the claimants were to sue him or her separately. [*Cantu v. Resolution Trust Corp.* (1992) 4 CA4th 857, 874, 6 CR2d 151, 160; *City of Morgan Hill v. Brown*, supra, 71 CA4th at 1122, 84 CR2d at 365-366]

"An interpleader action is traditionally viewed as two suits: one between the stakeholder and the claimants to determine the stakeholder's right to interplead, and the other among the claimants to determine who shall receive the funds interpleaded . . . As against the stakeholder, claimants may raise only matters which go to whether the suit is properly one for interpleader; i.e., whether the elements of an interpleader action are present." [*State Farm Fire & Cas. Co. v. Pietak* (2001) 90 CA4th 600, 612, 109 CR2d 256, 264]

1. [2:471] **When Interpleader Proper:** Interpleader is proper whenever "double or multiple claims are asserted . . . by two or more persons . . . such that they may expose (the person against

whom the claims are asserted) . . . to double or multiple liability . . ." [CCP §386(b)]

a. **[2:472]** **Nature of stakeholding:** Interpleader is proper where a person holds money or chattels for another, or is indebted to another under contract or otherwise. Typical situations include:

(1) **[2:473]** Life insurance benefits held by an insurer, where conflicting claims thereto are being made by the named beneficiary and someone else. [*Union Mutual Life Ins. Co. v. Broderick* (1925) 196 C 497, 501, 238 P 1034, 1036]

(2) **[2:474]** Liability insurer whose insured is faced with several third party claims exceeding the policy limits. [*Lehto v. Allstate Ins. Co.* (1994) 31 CA4th 60, 71, 36 CR2d 814, 820]

(3) **[2:475]** Bank holding funds (deposits, checks, escrows, etc.), where conflicting claims are being made by its depositor and others. [*Conner v. Bank of Bakersfield* (1920) 183 C 199, 202, 190 P 801, 802]

**[2:476]** *Reserved.*

b. **[2:477]** **Nature of conflicting claims:** Interpleader is proper regardless of the nature or source of the conflicting claims. Under modern law, the conflicting claims need *not* be of common origin; i.e., they may arise from completely independent dealings with the stakeholder. They may arise from contract, property or other transactions of any kind. They may be liquidated or unliquidated in amount; and the stakeholder's liability on the claims need not have yet arisen. [CCP §386(b); *City of Morgan Hill v. Brown* (1999) 71 CA4th 1114, 1123, 84 CR2d 361, 366]

(1) **[2:478]** **Partial conflict sufficient:** Interpleader is proper even though the conflicting claims are not identical or mutually exclusive. A partial conflict is sufficient (e.g., Bank holding $10,000, of which A claims the entire amount, and B claims only $2,000). [CCP §386(b); *City of Morgan Hill v. Brown*, supra, 71 CA4th at 1123, 84 CR2d at 366]

**[2:478.1-478.4]** *Reserved.*

(2) **[2:478.5]** **Limitation—claims to same debt or thing:** But interpleader will not lie where each of the claimants asserts the right to a *different* thing, debt or duty. [*City of Morgan Hill v. Brown*, supra, 71 CA4th at 1123, 84 CR2d at 366]

• **[2:478.6]** Attorney was a member of Law Firm that represented City. When Attorney was terminated by

Law Firm, she demanded her share of a large fee owed by City. City interpleaded the money because of conflicting demands from Attorney and Law Firm. Interpleader was *improper* because Attorney and Law Firm were *not claiming the same thing.* Attorney had no direct claim against City for fees; her claim was against Law Firm. [*City of Morgan Hill v. Brown*, supra, 71 CA4th at 1123, 84 CR2d at 366]

c. **[2:479]** **Partial vs. total interpleader:** Interpleader is proper if any part of the money or property held is subject to conflicting demands from others. Thus, interpleader lies if the person holding the money or property is not a totally disinterested stakeholder. I.e., he or she may claim some portion of the funds or property in dispute for himself or herself. [CCP §386(a); see *City of Morgan Hill v. Brown*, supra, 71 CA4th at 1123, 84 CR2d at 366]

[2:479.1-479.4] *Reserved.*

d. **[2:479.5]** **Stakeholder need not attempt to resolve dispute:** The stakeholder has the right to interplead the disputed funds on receipt of conflicting demands. It owes no duty to attempt to resolve the dispute between warring claimants before incurring the expense of interpleader. [*Cantu v. Resolution Trust Corp.* (1992) 4 CA4th 857, 876, 6 CR2d 151, 161]

e. **[2:479.6]** **No malicious prosecution liability:** Stakeholders incur no tort liability to the claimants named in an interpleader action. Claimants are *not defendants* from whom affirmative relief is sought. They are offered the *opportunity* to assert a right but can ignore the complaint or disclaim any interest if they choose. Therefore, claimants cannot sue the stakeholder for malicious prosecution. [*Cantu v. Resolution Trust Corp.*, supra, 4 CA4th at 875, 6 CR2d at 160]

f. **[2:479.7]** **No insurance "bad faith" liability:** Where competing third party claims asserted against an insured exceed the insured's liability insurance policy limits, the insurance company may file an interpleader action to apportion the policy proceeds among the competing claimants. The fact the insurer's purpose was to reduce its costs of defending the insured against the multiple claims "does not render resort to the (interpleader) procedure an act of bad faith" toward the insured. [*Lehto v. Allstate Ins. Co.* (1994) 31 CA4th 60, 71, 36 CR2d 814, 819 (parentheses added); *Schwartz v. State Farm Fire & Cas. Co.* (2001) 88 CA4th 1329, 1341, 106 CR2d 523, 529—same rule for excess insurer]

2. **[2:480] Procedure:** The stakeholder (party against whom conflicting claims are being made) may interplead the money or personal property in court in various ways:

    a. **[2:481] Interpleader by complaint:** The stakeholder may take the initiative and file a lawsuit against the various conflicting claimants, requiring them to litigate their respective claims to the money or property he or she holds. [CCP §386(b)]

    A *two-step procedure* is generally followed:

    — First, the court must determine whether plaintiff may bring the suit and force the claimants to interplead; and

    — Second, if it is so determined, the court will discharge plaintiff from liability and then determine the rights of the various claimants to the property that has been deposited with the court. [*City of Morgan Hill v. Brown*, supra, 71 CA4th at 1126-1127, 84 CR2d at 368]

    ⇨**[2:482] *PRACTICE POINTER:*** Taking the initiative in this manner makes particular sense where the stakeholder is obligated to pay interest on the funds held, or has been threatened with a suit for damages for wrongful detention of the property involved. The sooner the stakeholder can deposit the money or property in court, the sooner he or she will be relieved from further liability (¶*2:484*).

    (1) **[2:483] Pleading:** The stakeholder may simply allege that he or she is holding money or property to which others are making conflicting demands; that he or she is unable to determine the validity of the respective claims, and fears exposure to multiple liability if he or she delivers the money or property to any of the claimants; and therefore requests a court order determining to whom the money or property belongs. [See *Fidelity Sav. & Loan Ass'n v. Rodgers* (1919) 180 C 683, 684, 182 P 426, 427]

    (a) *FORMS*

      • Complaint In Interpleader, *see Form 2:D.*

      • Checklist on Interpleader, *see Form 2:E.*

    (2) **[2:484] Deposit in court:** Any amount which the plaintiff-stakeholder admits owing may be deposited with the court clerk at the time of filing the complaint, without the necessity of a court order (which is required for deposits later). Such deposit has the effect of terminating any obligation for interest, or for damages for detention of property, after the date of the deposit. [CCP

§386(c)] Funds so deposited will be ordered invested in an insured, interest-bearing account. [CCP §386.1]

b. **[2:485] Interpleader by defendant:** If the stakeholder has already been sued by one or more of the adverse claimants, and wishes to interplead the other claimants, he or she has several alternatives:

(1) **[2:486] Interpleader cross-complaint:** The defendant-stakeholder may file a verified cross-complaint joining the other adverse claimants, with allegations similar to the complaint in intervention, above. [CCP §386(b)]

(a) **[2:487] Verification required:** Although there is no requirement that a complaint in intervention be verified, the statute does require verification of an interpleader cross-complaint. [CCP §386(b)] The purpose apparently is to assure the defendant's good faith in raising this as a means of avoiding payment of his obligation. (*See "verification of pleadings,"* ¶6:309 *ff.*)

(b) **[2:488] Deposit in court:** As with interpleader complaints (above), any amount which the stakeholder admits owing may be deposited with the court clerk at time of filing the cross-complaint, without necessity of a court order. Again, this terminates any ongoing liability for interest or damages for detention of property. [CCP §386(c)]

(2) **[2:489] Motion for discharge from liability:** If the defendant-stakeholder claims no interest in the funds or property held, he or she need not file an interpleader cross-complaint. He or she may simply apply to the court for permission to deposit the money or property with the court clerk, and for an order discharging him or her from further liability to the adverse claimants. Such order will also *substitute the adverse claimants as parties* to the action; or, if only money is involved, simply *dismiss* the stakeholder. [CCP §§386(a), 386.5]

(a) **[2:490] Affidavit required:** In either event, the motion must be supported by an affidavit by the stakeholder establishing the ground for interpleader. [CCP §§386(a), 386.5]

(b) **[2:491] Notice to all claimants required:** Notice of the motion must be served on each of the adverse claimants to the funds or property. [CCP §§386(a), 386.5] (Those who are not parties to the action will have to be served personally; *see* ¶4:76-81.)

**FORMS**

- Notice of Motion for Discharge From Liability, *see Form 2:F.*

- Declaration in Support of Motion for Discharge From Liability, *see Form 2:G.*

c. **[2:491.1]** **No cross-complaints against stakeholder:** Defendants in an interpleader action may cross-complain against each other, but no cross-complaint lies against the stakeholder. Unless the stakeholder waives this limitation (e.g., by failure to object), the only relief available to a defendant against the stakeholder is to have the interpleader action *dismissed.* [*State Farm Fire & Cas. Co. v. Pietak* (2001) 90 CA4th 600, 613, 109 CR2d 256, 265]

(1) **[2:491.2]** **Exception to compulsory cross-complaint statute?** "At the very least, it is arguable that section 386 (the interpleader statute) is an exception to the compulsory cross-complaint rule of section 426.30" (¶6:511 ff.). [*State Farm Fire & Cas. Co. v. Pietak,* supra, 90 CA4th at 615, 109 CR2d at 266 (parentheses added)]

d. **[2:492]** **Hearing on right to interplead:** Regardless which procedure is utilized by the stakeholder, a hearing is usually held at the outset of the action to determine the propriety of the interpleader.

(1) **[2:493]** **Substitution and discharge:** If the stakeholder claims no interest in the money or property, he or she is normally permitted to deposit same with the court clerk (if he or she has not already done so), and is thereupon discharged from liability. If the adverse claimants are not already parties to the action, they will be ordered joined at this point.

(a) **[2:494]** **NO objection to discharge:** The adverse claimants cannot prevent the stakeholder from being discharged by claiming the funds should have been paid to them. To pursue such claims, they must file an independent action against the stakeholder. [*Pacific Loan Management Corp. v. Sup.Ct. (Armstrong)* (1987) 196 CA3d 1485, 1489, 242 CR 547, 549]

(2) **[2:495]** **Other actions restrained:** The court may also restrain the adverse claimants from instituting or further prosecuting any other action in any state court involving the same fund or property. [CCP §386(f)]

This includes enjoining the enforcement of a judgment already obtained in the other action. [*Surety Co. of the*

Pacific v. Piver (1983) 149 CA3d Supp. 29, 31-32, 197 CR 531, 532]

e. **[2:496] Costs and attorney fees to stakeholder:** Regardless which procedure is utilized by the stakeholder, he or she may seek reimbursement for his or her costs and reasonable attorney fees incurred. [*UAP-Columbus JV 326132 v. Nesbitt* (1991) 234 CA3d 1028, 1036, 285 CR 856, 861]

The court may (discretionary) order payment thereof out of the funds deposited by the stakeholder. (Ultimately, such payment may be charged to one or more of the adverse claimants in the final judgment.) [CCP §386.6]

(1) **[2:497] Stakeholder own lawyer:** Such costs and fees may be awarded to the stakeholder even though he or she is an attorney, has appeared in pro se, and performed his or her own legal services. [CCP §386.6(b)]

[2:498-499] *Reserved.*

## G. SUBSTITUTION OF PARTIES

1. **[2:500] Death of Party:** A pending action does not abate by reason of the death of a party if the cause of action survives. [CCP §377.21]

(Basically, all causes of action survive death *except* as provided by statute; see CCP §377.20. But no damages are recoverable for *decedent's* pain, suffering or disfigurement, except in elder abuse cases; see CCP §377.34 & Welf. & Inst.C. §15657(b). And, no punitive or exemplary damages are recoverable *against* a decedent's estate; see CCP §377.42. See more detailed discussion of the damages issues in Flahavan, Rea & Kelly, *Cal. Prac. Guide: Personal Injury* (TRG), Ch. 3.)

a. **[2:501] Orders for substitution:** The court may make appropriate orders substituting the decedent's personal representative or successor in interest as plaintiff on claims belonging to the decedent. Alternatively, it may appoint the successor in interest as a special administrator or guardian ad litem on such claims. [CCP §377.33]

On claims *against* the decedent, the court may order the decedent's personal representative substituted as defendant or, to the extent provided by statute, the decedent's successor in interest. (However, the court may not permit an action to be continued against decedent's personal representative unless proof of compliance with the Prob.C. §9000 et seq. creditor claims statutes is first made.) [CCP §377.41]

(1) **[2:501.1] Procedure:** An order substituting the decedent's representative or successor in interest may be obtained "on motion." Apparently, either a noticed

motion or *ex parte application* may be utilized (*see* ¶*9:349*). [CCP §377.31]

Although the statute is silent on the point, the motion apparently can be made by any party to the proceeding or by the representative or successor in interest.

(2) [2:501.2] **Statement required from successor in interest:** A successor in interest (person entitled to inherit claim) who seeks to be substituted as plaintiff in place of the decedent must execute and file a declaration in statutory form. [CCP §377.32; *see discussion at* ¶*2:31.6*]

(3) [2:501.3] **Local rules:** Local rules in some courts require plaintiff's attorney to notify the court and opposing parties within 10 days after learning of plaintiff's death. Proceedings are then suspended for 90 days, after which the case may be dismissed unless plaintiff's counsel shows the cause of action survives. [See S.D. Sup.Ct. Rule 2.46]

*FORMS*

- Ex Parte Application and Order Substituting Party, *see Form 2:H.*

- Checklist—Substitute Estate of Decedent, *see Form 2:H.1.*

b. [2:502] **Exception—deceased defendants covered by insurance:** No such substitution may be necessary where the defendant in a personal injury or wrongful death action dies during the course of the litigation. The action can be continued against the original defendant if there is adequate liability insurance covering plaintiff's claim. [CCP §377.50; Prob.C. §§550-555] (This avoids the expense of having an executor or administrator appointed and a probate estate kept open throughout the litigation.)

However, if the substitution is not made, plaintiff is deemed to have waived any damages not covered by the insurance policy. [See Prob.C. §554]

c. [2:503] **Effect of failure to substitute representative:** Unless the decedent's personal representative is made a party, a judgment should not be rendered for or against a decedent, nor for or against the representative. [See *Sacks v. FSR Brokerage, Inc.* (1992) 7 CA4th 950, 957, 9 CR2d 306, 310; *Sellery v. Cressey* (1996) 48 CA4th 538, 541, 55 CR2d 706, 707, fn. 2]

However, the failure to substitute decedent's representative *does not automatically void* an ensuing judgment. The issue in each case is whether the decedent's estate has been *prejudiced* by failure to join the decedent's representative. [*Sacks v. FSR Brokerage, Inc.*, supra, 7 CA4th at 959, 9 CR2d at 311—one of several defendants died before defense summary judgment motion filed: not ground for reversal of summary judgment *in decedent's favor*]

On the other hand, of course, a judgment *against* a decedent may not be enforceable against the decedent's estate if no notice of the claim was filed within the time permitted by law. [Prob.C. §§9002, 9100]

2. **[2:504] Transfer of Interest:** If during the course of the lawsuit, plaintiff or defendant transfers his or her interest therein to another, the court may allow the transferee to be substituted as a party to the action, OR *the action may be continued in the name of the original party.* [CCP §368.5; see *Casey v. Overhead Door Corp.* (1999) 74 CA4th 112, 121, 87 CR2d 603, 609]

   a. **[2:505] Effect:** The transferee has the *option* either to appear as a party of record or to allow the action to continue in the name of the transferor (and any judgment rendered accordingly). [*Luster v. Collins* (1993) 15 CA4th 1338, 1345, 19 CR2d 215, 219]

      (1) **[2:506] Compare—trustee in bankruptcy:** Courts are split on whether the trustee in Chapter 7 bankruptcy proceedings *must* be substituted as plaintiff in state court proceedings commenced prior to bankruptcy, or whether such substitution is *optional* and the proceedings can continue in the debtor's name (*see* ¶2:7 ff.).

      (2) **[2:507] Substitution of counsel:** The attorney for the transferor/assignor does not automatically cease to be attorney of record; a formal substitution of the transferee's attorney is normally required. But that formality may be excused where the transferee's attorney assumed control of the case and prosecuted it to judgment, and the opposing party was aware of the transfer and was not misled or prejudiced thereby. [*Casey v. Overhead Door Corp.* (1999) 74 CA4th 112, 122, 87 CR2d 603, 610]

➪ **[2:508] *PRACTICE POINTER:*** If you represent the transferee, be sure to *get a substitution of attorneys signed by the transferor* at the time of the transfer, substituting your firm as attorney of record for the transferor . . . and, file it *immediately*. That way, if your client does decide to continue the action in the name of the transferor, there won't be any risk of a dismissal or default entered without your knowledge!

   b. **[2:509] Opposing party may compel substitution:** The transferee's right to continue the action in the name of the transferor is limited by the fact that any other party to the action may apply for an order substituting the transferee as a party. [See *Higgins v. Kay* (1914) 168 C 468, 472, 143 P 710, 711]

➪[2:510]  *PRACTICE POINTER:*  This is good practice if you represent the opposing party. Otherwise, you run the risk that any judgment obtained for costs or damages may not be enforceable against the transferee. Or, the transferee may claim it is not bound by an adverse judgment. (That claim is not valid if the transferee controlled the litigation, but it is easier to avoid the problem by substituting the transferee *before* judgment!)

c.  [2:511]  **Procedure:**  An order substituting the transferee may be obtained on noticed motion. Where sought by the transferee, many courts will grant the order ex parte.

•  *FORM:*  Ex Parte Application and Order Substituting Party, *see Form 2:H.*

d.  [2:512]  **Compare—cause of action retained by transferor:**  The rules are different, of course, where plaintiff retains the *cause of action* sued upon notwithstanding transfer of the property.

Example: Plaintiff had standing to sue a contractor for damages for defective construction of her condominium even after selling it to another. I.e., she was still the real party in interest as to the *damages* cause of action. [*Vaughn v. Dame Const. Co.* (1990) 223 CA3d 144, 148-149, 272 CR 261, 263-264—sale of condo after suit filed did not affect standing to sue for presale damage]

**RESERVED**

# EX PARTE APPLICATION AND ORDER
# FOR LEAVE TO INTERVENE

```
   State Bar No.:.................
 2 ...............................
   ...............................
 3 ..............................

 4

 5 Attorney for .................

 6

 7

 8           SUPERIOR COURT OF STATE OF CALIFORNIA

 9                  COUNTY OF .........

10

11 ..........................., )      NO.: ...................
                                )
12           Plaintiff,          )
                                )      EX PARTE APPLICATION FOR
13 vs.                           )      LEAVE TO INTERVENE
                                )      [CCP §387]
14 ..........................., )
                                )
15           Defendants.        )
   _____)

17      .......... (name) .......... hereby applies for leave of court

18 to intervene in this action by filing the Complaint in Intervention

19 attached to this Application and incorporated herein by this

20 reference.

21      This Application is made upon the ground that ...............

22 ......... (EITHER:   "I have an interest in the matter in

23 litigation, or in the success of either of the parties, or an

24 interest against both, within the meaning of CCP §387(a)" OR "I

25 claim an interest relating to the property or transaction which is

26 the subject of this action and am so situated that disposition of

27 this action may as a practical matter impair or impede my ability

28 to protect that interest, within the meaning of CCP §387(b)") .....
```

1

APPL. FOR LEAVE TO INTERVENE

1      2.   In support of this Application, I make the following

2 statements of fact, all of which are based on matters of which I

3 have personal knowledge, and as to which I can testify competently

4 as a witness: .................. *(Facts showing applicant's right*

5 *to intervene under CCP §387(b), or interest permitting intervention*

6 *under CCP §387(a))* .......................................................

7 ...................................

8      3.   I have notified or caused to be notified all parties who

9 have appeared in this action that this Application for Leave to

10 Intervene would be presented to this Court ex parte.   Such notice

11 was given on ............. in the following manner ..............

12 ...........................................................................

13      4.   I declare under penalty of perjury under the laws of the

14 State of California that the foregoing is true and correct.

15 Executed on ......................... at ......................

16

17                         .....................................

                              Proposed Plaintiff in Intervention

18

19

20

21

22

23

24

25

26

27

28

APPL. FOR LEAVE TO INTERVENE

Rev. #1 2001

```
 1        ORDER GRANTING LEAVE TO INTERVENE

 2        Upon reading and considering the foregoing Ex Parte Appli-

 3   cation for Leave to Intervene, and the proposed Complaint in Inter-

 4   vention attached thereto, and good cause appearing:

 5        IT IS HEREBY ORDERED THAT ............... (name) ...........

 6   is hereby granted leave to intervene in this action, and to file

 7   the Complaint in Intervention aforesaid.

 8   DATED: .............        /s/_____
                                Judge
 9

10

11

12

13

14

15

16

17

18

19

20

21

22

23

24

25

26

27

28
```

3

APPL. FOR LEAVE TO INTERVENE

**[FORM 2:B]**

# COMPLAINT IN INTERVENTION

```
 1  ................................
    State Bar No.:.................
 2  ................................
    ................................
 3  ................................
 4
 5  Attorney for .................
 6
 7
 8          SUPERIOR COURT OF STATE OF CALIFORNIA
 9               COUNTY OF ..........
10
11  ......................., )      NO.: ....................
                             )
12           Plaintiff,      )
                             )      COMPLAINT IN INTERVENTION
13  vs.                      )
                             )
14  ......................., )
                             )
15           Defendants.     )
    _____)
16
17  ......................., )
                             )
18           Intervenor,     )
                             )
19  vs.                      )
                             )
20  ....................... )
              (if appropriate)   )
21  _____)
22       By leave of court, ............... (name) .......... hereby
23  intervenes in this action, and does hereby .......... (EITHER:
24  "join with plaintiff(s) in claiming what is sought by the
25  complaint" OR "unite with defendant(s) in resisting the claims of
26  the plaintiff(s)" OR "demand adversely to both plaintiff(s) and
27  defendant(s)") ................. as follows:
28  /////
```

1.   This action was commenced by plaintiff ..... *(name)* .....
against defendant ...... *(name)* ...... on ...... *(date)* ....... and
seeks recovery as follows: .......................................

2.   Defendant ........... *(name)* .............. has appeared
in this action as follows: ......... *(e.g., "by answer filed on*
*(date) setting forth general denials and the following affirmative*
*defenses (describe)"; or "by answer and cross-complaint against*
*plaintiff asserting a cause of action for (describe) and seeking*
*recovery of (describe)"; or "has failed to answer the complaint or*
*appear in this action," etc.)* ..........

3.   *(Use EITHER of the following paragraphs:)*

Intervenor has the right to intervene in this action
under Code of Civil Procedure Section 387(b) by virtue of the
following facts: ........................................................
..........................................................................

*(OR)*

Intervenor claims an interest in the matter in litigation
as follows by reason of which intervention is proper under Code of
Civil Procedure Section 387(a) ....................................
..........................................................................

4.   Intervenor alleges that ..... *(insert claims, defense or*
*demands as in any other pleading)*................................

WHEREFORE, Intervenor prays for judgment as follows: .........
..........................................................................
and for costs of suit and such other relief as the Court deems
just.

.............................
Attorney for Intervenor

2

COMPLAINT IN INTERVENTION

**RESERVED**

# CHECKLIST
# INTERVENTION

*[Ed. Note: This form or similar forms are used by many courts. Counsel should use this as a checklist when preparing a motion or opposition because it may raise factors of concern to the court. Declarations or points and authorities should be prepared to address each of the points on the checklist.]*

Discovery Cut-off: _____  Calendar: _____

Motion Cut-off: _____  Date: _____

Trial Date: _____  Notice: _____

**INTERVENTION**
**(CCP §§ 387, 1250.230)**
**(CONFIDENTIAL COURT DOCUMENT WHEN COMPLETED)**

NAME OF MOVING PARTY: _____

NAME OF RESPONDING PARTY: _____

CORRECT ADDRESS IN PROOF OF SERVICE (CCP §§ 1013, 1013a): _____

21-DAY LAPSE (CCP § 1005): _____

INTERVENTION ON SIDE OF:  ❑ PLAINTIFF  ❑ DEFENDANT  ❑ OTHER _____

**CONDITIONS**

❑ SHOWING OF <u>INTEREST</u>:

❑ INTEREST RELATING TO PROPERTY OR TRANSACTION SUBJECT OF ACTION:

❑ PERSON SITUATED THAT DISPOSITION MAY IMPAIR OR IMPEDE ABILITY TO PROTECT INTEREST:

    ❑ UNLESS INTEREST ADEQUATELY REPRESENTED:

❑ CAUSE OF ACTION OR DEFENSE STATED:

❑ DILIGENCE IN BRINGING INTERVENTION:

❑ NEW PARTIES OR ISSUES ADDED:

❑ COMPULSIVE OR PERMISSIVE:

❑ DECLARATION (CCP § 2015.5, CRC 315(a)):

OPPOSITION:

RECOMMENDED RULING:

    ❑ GRANT      ❑ DENY

**RESERVED**

# COMPLAINT IN INTERPLEADER

```
1    ..............................
     State Bar No.:.................
2    ..............................
     ..............................
3    ..............................

4

5    Attorney for .................

6

7

8              SUPERIOR COURT OF STATE OF CALIFORNIA

9                    COUNTY OF .........

10

11   ..........................., )        NO.: ...................
                                   )
12            Plaintiff,           )
                                   )        COMPLAINT IN INTERPLEADER
13   vs.                           )
                                   )
14   ..........................., )
                                   )
15            Defendants.          )
     _____)
16

17        Plaintiff alleges as follows:

18        1.  Plaintiff is now in possession of the following described

19   money or property: ......................................................

20   ..........................................................

21        2.  Defendants and each of them have made conflicting demands

22   upon plaintiff to the aforesaid money or property, as follows: ....

23   ..........................................................

24   ........................................

25        3.  Plaintiff is unable to determine the validity of the

26   conflicting demands made by defendants as aforesaid, and cannot

27   determine to whom said money or property belongs.

28   /////
```

1

COMPLAINT IN INTERPLEADER

1    4.    Plaintiff claims no interest in the money or property
2  aforesaid (except as follows: ...............................
3  ...............................................)
4    5.    Concurrently with filing this complaint, plaintiff shall
5  deposit the aforesaid money or property with the clerk of this
6  Court pursuant to Code of Civil Procedure Section 386(c).
7    6.    Plaintiff has incurred costs and reasonable attorney's
8  fees in connection with these proceedings in the sum of $.........
9  and may incur additional costs and fees hereafter.
10    WHEREFORE plaintiff prays judgment as follows:
11    (1)    That defendants and each of them be ordered to interplead
12  and litigate their claims to the money or property described in
13  this complaint; (2) that plaintiff be discharged from liability to
14  each of said defendants with respect to said money or property; and
15  (3) that plaintiff be awarded costs and reasonable attorney's fees
16  to be paid to plaintiff from the funds deposited with the court
17  clerk as aforesaid; and (4) for such other and further relief as
18  the Court deems just.
19  DATED: .................       ...............................
20                                 Attorney for Plaintiff
21
22
23
24
25
26
27
28

---

2

COMPLAINT IN INTERPLEADER

# CHECKLIST
# INTERPLEADER

*[Ed. Note: This form or similar forms are used by many courts. Counsel should use this as a checklist when preparing a motion or opposition because it may raise factors of concern to the court. Declarations or points and authorities should be prepared to address each of the points on the checklist.]*

Discovery Cut-off: _____

Motion Cut-off: _____

Trial Date: _____

Calendar: _____

Date: _____

Notice: _____

### INTERPLEADER
### (CCP § 386)
### (CONFIDENTIAL COURT DOCUMENT WHEN COMPLETED)

NAME OF MOVING PARTY: _____

NAME OF RESPONDING PARTY: _____

CORRECT ADDRESS IN PROOF OF SERVICE (CCP §§ 1013, 1013a): _____

21-DAY LAPSE UNDER CCP § 1005: _____

### FACTORS

Claims relating to personal property or
    contract: _____

Allegation that moving party has no claim to
    subject matter: _____

Allegation that defendants make conflicting claims: _____

Allegation that moving party cannot determine which
    claim is valid: _____

Moving party deposited
    $ or property in court or deposit offered: _____

Demand for attorney's fees: _____

Answers or defaults filed (*id.*) _____

DECLARATION OF MOVING PARTY (CCP § 2015.5; CRC 315(a)):

OPPOSITION:

RECOMMENDED RULING:

    ❑ Grant

    ❑ Deny

    ❑ Restraining Order (CCP § 386(f))

    ❑ Dismiss and Discharge Liability

# NOTICE OF MOTION FOR
# DISCHARGE FROM LIABILITY

```
1   ...........................
    ...........................
2   State Bar No.:...............
    ...........................
3   ...........................
    ...........................
4
5   Attorney for: ...............
6
7
8                SUPERIOR COURT OF STATE OF CALIFORNIA
9                     COUNTY OF .........
10  ..........................,   ) CASE NO. ....................
                                  )
11         Plaintiff,             ) HEARING DATE/TIME: ..........
                                  ) DEPT. NO. ...................
12         vs.                    ) HEARING JUDGE: ...... (if known)
                                  )
13  ..........................,   ) NOTICE OF MOTION FOR ORDER
                                  ) DISCHARGING DEFENDANT STAKEHOLDER
14         Defendant.             ) FROM LIABILITY; AWARDING COSTS AND
                                  ) FEES; AND FOR SUBSTITUTION OF
15                                ) PARTIES (or dismissal);
                                  ) DECLARATION OF .....; POINTS AND
16                                ) AUTHORITIES; PROPOSED ORDER
                                  )
17                                ) DATE ACTION FILED: ..........
                                  ) DATE SET FOR TRIAL: ....(if set)
18  _____)
```

19        TO:  EACH PARTY OF THIS ACTION, AND TO THE ATTORNEY OF RECORD FOR

20   EACH PARTY; and

21        TO: ....... (names of adverse claimants who are not already

22   parties to the action) ........

23        YOU ARE HEREBY NOTIFIED THAT on ....... (date) ....... at .......

24   (time) ........ or as soon thereafter as the matter can be heard, in

25   Department ........ of this Court, located at ....... (address)

26   ......., California, defendant ......(stakeholder) (moving party)

27   ...... will move the court for an order that: (1) Said Defendant

28   deposit with the Clerk of the Court forthwith the following described

                                  1

                  MOTION FOR DISCHARGE FROM LIABILITY

1 *(money or property)* ........., less the sum of $ ........ as the costs

2 and reasonable attorney's fees incurred by said defendant in

3 connection with these proceedings; and (2) That upon making such

4 deposit, said defendant be discharged from any further liability to

5 any party to this action or to ..... *(name of adverse claimants not*

6 *already parties)* ...... with respect to the *(money or property)* so

7 deposited; and (3) *(EITHER)* That a judgment of dismissal thereupon be

8 entered in favor of said defendant *(OR)* That the following persons

9 thereupon be substituted as defendants in this action: ..... *(names of*

10 *adverse claimants not already parties)* ..... instead of and in place

11 of ...... *(moving party)* ......

12     Said motion will be made upon the ground that the defendant .....

13 *(moving party)* ..... is a stakeholder only, and has no interest in the

14 *(money or property)* sought to be deposited as aforesaid; that

15 conflicting demands to said *(money or property)* have been made or may

16 be made by each of the parties to whom this notice of motion is given;

17 that the moving party is unable to determine the validity of said

18 demands and therefore wishes to deposit said *(money or property)* and

19 interplead said claimants; and that said moving party has incurred

20 cost and attorney's fees in the amount of $ ...... in connection with

21 these proceedings.

22     Said motion will be based on this notice, the attached

23 declaration of ............, the points and authorities set forth

24 below, and the complete files and records of this action.

25 DATED: ............, ......

26     /s/_____
    Attorney for ................

27     POINTS AND AUTHORITIES IN SUPPORT OF MOTION

28     *(Follow suggestions in Law and Motion Chapter, ¶9:64-81)*

2

MOTION FOR DISCHARGE FROM LIABILITY

# DECLARATION IN SUPPORT OF
# MOTION FOR DISCHARGE FROM LIABILITY

```
 1  . . . . . . . . . . . . . . . . . . . . . . . . . . .
 2  State Bar No.: . . . . . . . . . . . . .
 3  . . . . . . . . . . . . . . . . . . . . . . . . . . . . . .
 4  . . . . . . . . . . . . . . . . . . . . . . . . . . . .
 5  Attorney for: . . . . . . . . . . . . .
 6
 7
 8              SUPERIOR COURT OF STATE OF CALIFORNIA
 9                     COUNTY OF . . . . . . . . .
10
11  . . . . . . . . . . . . . . . . . . . . . . . . . ,  ) CASE NO. . . . . . . . . . . . . . . . . . . . .
                                                       )
12                      Plaintiff,                     ) HEARING DATE/TIME: . . . . . . . . . . .
                                                       ) DEPT. NO. . . . . . . . . . . . . . . . . . . .
13           vs.                                       ) HEARING JUDGE: . . . . . . (if known)
                                                       )
14  . . . . . . . . . . . . . . . . . . . . . . . . . ,  ) NOTICE OF MOTION FOR ORDER
                                                       ) DISCHARGING DEFENDANT-
15                      Defendant.                     ) STAKEHOLDER FROM LIABILITY;
                                                       ) DECLARATIONS OF . . . . . . . . . . . . ;
16                                                     ) POINTS AND AUTHORITIES;
                                                       ) PROPOSED ORDER;
17                                                     )
                                                       ) DATE ACTION FILED: . . . . . . . . . . .
18  _____ ) TRIAL DATE: . . . . . . . . . (if set)
```

19      I, the undersigned, declare as follows:

20      1.   I am the . . . . . . . . . . . . in this action, and have

21  personal knowledge of each fact stated herein, and can testify

22  competently as a witness thereto.

23      2.   Summons and complaint in this action were served on

24  defendant . . . . . . . . . . . . on or about . . . . . . . . . . . . No answer has

25  yet been filed by said defendant, and the time to answer has not

26  yet expired.

27      3.   The complaint seeks recovery by plaintiff from said

28  defendant of the following described *(money or property)* . . . . . . . .

1

DECL'N OF . . . . . . . . IN SUPPORT OF
MOTION FOR DISCHARGE FROM LIABILITY

1 ........................................................

2 ...............................................

3     4.  Said defendant holds said *(money or property)* solely as

4 stakeholder by reason of the following facts: .................

5 ...............................................

6     5.  Conflicting demands to said *(money or property)* have been

7 made on said defendant by other persons, to wit: .................

8 ...............................................

9     6.  Said defendant is unable to determine the validity of the

10 conflicting demands and is exposed to the risk of double or

11 multiple liability if he pays the amount demanded by plaintiff in

12 this action without interpleading the other claimants named above.

13     7.  Said defendant claims no interest in the *(money or*

14 *property)* described above, and wishes to deposit same in court and

15 be discharged from any further liability to any of said claimants.

16     8.  As a result of being sued in this action, and the

17 necessity of filing the attached motion, and in connection with the

18 hearing thereon, said defendant has incurred costs and attorney

19 fees in the sum of $ ............ consisting of the following: ....

20 .......... *(detail services rendered and costs incurred)* ........

21     I declare under penalty of perjury under the laws of the State

22 of California that the foregoing is true and correct.

23     Executed on ............... at ..........................

24     ..............................

25                      Declarant

26

27

28

---

2

DECL'N OF ....... IN SUPPORT OF
MOTION FOR DISCHARGE FROM LIABILITY

**[FORM 2:H]**

# EX PARTE APPLICATION
# FOR ORDER SUBSTITUTING PARTY

1  ...........................
   State Bar No. ..............
2  ...........................
   ...........................
3  ...........................

4

5  Attorney for ..............

6

7

8              SUPERIOR COURT OF STATE OF CALIFORNIA

9                      COUNTY OF .........

10

11 ..............................,  ) No. ...............
                                    )
12           Plaintiff,             )
                                    )
13 vs.                              ) EX PARTE APPLICATION FOR ORDER
                                    ) SUBSTITUTING PARTY [CCP §377.31]
14 ..............................,  )
                                    )
15           Defendant.             )

16

17      ......... (name of declarant) ....... hereby applies for an order by

18 this Court substituting ........ (name of party) ........ as a party to this

19 action instead and in place of ....... (name of former party) ........... In

20 support of this Application, I make the following statements of fact, all of

21 which are based on matters of which I have personal knowledge, and as to which

22 I can testify competently as a witness:

23      1.    The decedent's name was ...................

24      2.    The decedent died on ........ (date) ....... at ...... (place)

25 .....................

26      3.    No proceeding is now pending in California for administration of

27 the decedent's estate.

28 /////

                                    1
_____
                 APPL. FOR ORDER SUBSTITUTING PARTY

1    4.    *(If the decedent's estate was administered)* Attached hereto is a
2  copy of a final order showing distribution of the decedent's cause of action
3  in this lawsuit or proceeding to ................................. as the
4  decedent's successor in interest.
5    5.    The undersigned is *(or is authorized to act on behalf of)* the
6  decedent's successor in interest as defined in Section 377.11 of the
7  California Code of Civil Procedure with respect to the decedent's interest in
8  this lawsuit or proceeding.
9    6.    No other person has a superior right to commence this lawsuit or
10 proceeding or to be substituted for decedent in the pending action or
11 proceeding.
12    I declare under penalty of perjury under the laws of the State of
13 California that the foregoing is true and correct.
14    Executed on ............. at ...................................
15                                         /s/_____
                                           Declarant
16
17
18
19
20
21
22
23
24
25
26
27
28

2

APPL. FOR ORDER SUBSTITUTING PARTY

ORDER SUBSTITUTING PARTY

On reading and considering the foregoing Application for Order Substituting Party, and good cause appearing:

IT IS HEREBY ORDERED THAT ...... *(name of new party)* ...... be and hereby is substituted as a party to this action instead and in place of ...... *(name of former party)* ......

DATED: ....................          /s/ _____
                                     Judge

1
2
3
4
5
6
7
8
9
10
11
12
13
14
15
16
17
18
19
20
21
22
23
24
25
26
27
28

3

APPL. FOR ORDER SUBSTITUTING PARTY

# CHECKLIST
# SUBSTITUTE ESTATE OF DECEDENT

*[Ed. Note: This form and similar forms are used by many other courts. Counsel should use this as a checklist when preparing a motion or opposition because it may raise factors of concern to the court. Declarations or points and authorities should be prepared to address each of the points on the checklist.]*

Discovery Cut-off: _____     Calendar: _____

Motion Cut-off: _____       Date: _____

Trial Date: _____           Notice: _____

**SUBSTITUTE ESTATE OF DECEDENT**
**(PROBATE CODE §§ 550 et seq.; CCP § 377.10 et seq.)**
**(CONFIDENTIAL COURT DOCUMENT WHEN COMPLETED)**

NAME OF MOVING PARTY: _____

NAME OF RESPONDING PARTY: _____

CORRECT ADDRESS IN PROOF OF SERVICE (CCP §§ 1013, 1013a): _____

21- DAY LAPSE (CCP § 1005): _____

Successor in interest, Representative, Beneficiary _____

Statement (CCP § 377.32) _____

Insured Decedent's estate (CCP § 377.50) _____

DECLARATION OF MOVING PARTY (CCP § 2015.5; CRC 315(a)):

OPPOSITION:

RECOMMENDED RULING:

    ❑ Grant

    ❑ Deny

        ❑ w/o prejudice

    ❑ Other just order (CCP § 377.33) _____

**RESERVED**

# APPLICATION AND ORDER FOR
# APPOINTMENT OF GUARDIAN AD LITEM

982(a)(27)

| ATTORNEY OR PARTY WITHOUT ATTORNEY *(Name, State Bar number, and address):* | FOR COURT USE ONLY |
|---|---|
| TELEPHONE NO.:　　　　　FAX NO. *(Optional):* | |
| E-MAIL ADDRESS *(Optional):* | |
| ATTORNEY FOR *(Name):* | |

**SUPERIOR COURT OF CALIFORNIA, COUNTY OF**
　　　STREET ADDRESS:
　　　MAILING ADDRESS:
　　　CITY AND ZIP CODE:
　　　BRANCH NAME:

　　PLAINTIFF/PETITIONER:

DEFENDANT/RESPONDENT:

| APPLICATION AND ORDER FOR APPOINTMENT OF GUARDIAN AD LITEM—CIVIL　　☐ EX PARTE | CASE NUMBER: |
|---|---|

**Note: This form is for use in civil proceedings in which a party is a minor, an incapacitated person, or a person for whom a conservator has been appointed. A party who seeks the appointment of a guardian ad litem in a family law proceeding should use form FL-935. A party who seeks the appointment of a guardian ad litem in a probate proceeding should use form DE-350/GC-100. An individual may not act as a guardian ad [item unless he or she is represented by an attorney or is an attorney.**

1. Applicant *(name):*　　　　　　　　　　　　　　is
　　a. ☐ the parent of *(name):*
　　b. ☐ the guardian of *(name):*
　　c. ☐ the conservator of *(name):*
　　d. ☐ a party to the suit.
　　e. ☐ the minor to be represented *(if the minor is 14 years of age or older).*
　　f. ☐ another interested person *(specify capacity):*

2. This application seeks the appointment of the following person as guardian ad litem *(state name, address, and telephone number):*

3. The guardian ad litem is to represent the interests of the following person *(state name, address, and telephone number):*

4. The person to be represented is:
　　a. ☐ a minor *(date of birth):*
　　b. ☐ an incompetent person.
　　c. ☐ a person for whom a conservator has been appointed.

5. The court should appoint a guardian ad litem because:
　　a. ☐ the person named in item 3 has a cause or causes of action on which suit should be brought *(describe):*

　　☐ Continued on Attachment 5a.

Page 1 of 2

| Form Adopted for Mandatory Use Judicial Council of California 982(a)(27) [Rev. January 1, 2004] | **APPLICATION AND ORDER FOR APPOINTMENT OF GUARDIAN AD LITEM—CIVIL** | Code of Civil Procedure, § 372 et seq. |
|---|---|---|

5. b. ☐ more than 10 days have elapsed since the summons in the above-entitled matter was served on the person named in item 3, and no application for the appointment of a guardian ad litem has been made by the person identified in item 3 or any other person.

c. ☐ the person named in item 3 has no guardian or conservator of his or her estate.

d. ☐ the appointment of a guardian ad litem is necessary for the following reasons (specify):

☐ Continued on Attachment 5d.

6. The proposed guardian ad litem's relationship to the person he or she will be representing is:

a. ☐ related (state relationship):

b. ☐ not related (specify capacity):

7. The proposed guardian ad litem is fully competent and qualified to understand and protect the rights of the person he or she will represent and has no interests adverse to the interests of that person. (If there are any issues of competency or qualification or any possible adverse interests, describe and explain why the proposed guardian should nevertheless be appointed):

☐ Continued on Attachment 7.

▶

_____           _____
(TYPE OR PRINT NAME)                        (SIGNATURE OF ATTORNEY)

I declare under penalty of perjury under the laws of the State of California that the foregoing is true and correct.
Date:

▶

_____           _____
(TYPE OR PRINT NAME)                        (SIGNATURE OF APPLICANT)

## CONSENT TO ACT AS GUARDIAN AD LITEM

I consent to the appointment as guardian ad litem under the above petition.
Date:

▶

_____           _____
(TYPE OR PRINT NAME)                        (SIGNATURE OF PROPOSED GUARDIAN AD LITEM)

## ORDER ☐ EX PARTE

**THE COURT FINDS** that it is reasonable and necessary to appoint a guardian ad litem for the person named in item 3 of the application, as requested.

**THE COURT ORDERS** that (name):
is hereby appointed as the guardian ad litem for (name):
for the reasons set forth in item 5 of the application.
Date:

_____
JUDICIAL OFFICER

☐ SIGNATURE FOLLOWS LAST ATTACHMENT

# CHAPTER 3

# JURISDICTION AND VENUE

## CONTENTS

|  | Page |
|---|---|
| **STRATEGY RE CHOOSING COURT** | 3-1 |
| **A. SUBJECT MATTER JURISDICTION (COMPETENCY)** | 3-2 |
|    1. Background—Trial Court Unification | 3-2 |
|      a. Limited vs. unlimited civil cases | 3-2 |
|    2. Superior Court Subject Matter Jurisdiction | 3-3 |
|    3. Limited vs. Unlimited Civil Cases | 3-3 |
|      a. Actions not subject to classification as limited civil cases | 3-3 |
|    4. Limited Civil Cases | 3-4 |
|      a. Actions at law | 3-4 |
|        (1) Exception—legality of taxes, etc. | 3-4 |
|        (2) Forcible or unlawful detainer | 3-4 |
|        (3) Cases designated by statute | 3-4 |
|      b. Equitable relief | 3-4 |
|        (1) Limitations | 3-4 |
|          (a) No permanent injunctions | 3-4 |
|          (b) No determining title to real property | 3-5 |
|          (c) No enforcement or modification of child/spousal support orders | 3-5 |
|          (d) Limited declaratory relief | 3-5 |
|            1) Compare—unnecessary prayer for declaratory relief | 3-5 |
|        (2) Ancillary remedies | 3-5 |
|        (3) Proceedings in equity | 3-6 |
|        (4) "Actions based on equitable principles" | 3-7 |
|        (5) Equitable defenses | 3-7 |
|        (6) Cross-complaint for third party indemnification | 3-7 |
|        (7) Matters subject to contractual arbitration | 3-8 |
|          (a) Attorney-client fee disputes | 3-8 |
|        (8) Equitable relief from judgment | 3-8 |
|        (9) Class actions | 3-8 |
|      c. Small claims divisions | 3-9 |
|        (1) Types of claims | 3-10 |
|        (2) Joinder of individual actions | 3-10 |
|        (3) Annual limitation—no more than two actions exceeding $2,500 | 3-10 |

(a) Exception—actions by local public
entities ................................................................3-11
(4) No assigned claims ............................................3-11
(5) No splitting of claims .........................................3-11
(6) Equitable relief ..................................................3-11
(7) Defendant may counterclaim............................3-11
(a) Counterclaim in excess of small
claims jurisdiction .......................................3-11
(8) Disadvantages of small claims actions.............3-12
(a) No jury ........................................................3-12
(b) Limited right to appeal ..............................3-12
1) Appeal allowing trial de novo on all
claims? ....................................................3-12
2) Other considerations re appeal .............3-13
(c) No representation at hearing ......................3-14
(d) Limited appearances through
representatives ............................................3-14
1) Corporations .........................................3-14
2) Partnerships and other entities..............3-15
3) Sole proprietors ....................................3-15
4) Spouses ...............................................3-15
5) Nonresidents sued on claims relating
to their local property..............................3-15
(e) No collateral estoppel ................................3-15
1) Includes trial de novo in superior
court .......................................................3-16
(f) No discovery in small claims court or on
appeal ..........................................................3-16
(g) Use of hearsay evidence in small claims
court and on appeal .....................................3-16
(h) Plaintiff cannot obtain reclassification for
increased damages .....................................3-16
(i) No involuntary transfers to small claims
court ............................................................3-16
(9) No subsequent action for malicious
prosecution ......................................................3-17
5. Determining Amount in Controversy ......................3-17
a. Prayer of complaint determinative .....................3-17
(1) Demand "in excess of $25,000" precludes
limited civil case .............................................3-18
(2) Property actions—value of property in
controversy .....................................................3-18
(3) Actions for rent ...................................................3-18
(a) Effect of rent accruing ................................3-18
(4) Personal injury and death actions ......................3-18
(5) Punitive damages claims ...................................3-19
b. Deterrents to exaggerated demands ..................3-19
(1) Costs penalty .......................................................3-19
(2) Court procedures as deterrents .........................3-19
(3) Court's power to reclassify as limited civil
case .................................................................3-19

Rev. #1 2004

    c. Matters excluded in determining amount in
       controversy ...................................................................3-19
       (1) Interest excluded .....................................................3-19
       (2) Costs excluded ........................................................3-20
       (3) Attorney fees excluded ...........................................3-20
          (a) Example ...........................................................3-20
          (b) Fees exceeding $25,000 ................................3-20
    d. Waiver of excess demand to retain limited civil
       case classification ......................................................3-20
       (1) Procedure for waiving excess.................................3-21
       (2) Waiver after judgment ............................................3-21
    e. Joinder of claims as affecting amount in
       controversy ...................................................................3-21
       (1) Single plaintiff vs. single defendant ......................3-21
          (a) Example ...........................................................3-21
          (b) Class actions ...................................................3-21
       (2) Single plaintiff vs. several defendants .................3-22
          (a) Example ...........................................................3-22
          (b) Compare—one claim exceeding $25,000 .....3-22
       (3) Several plaintiffs vs. one or more defendants......3-22
          (a) Joint claim .......................................................3-22
          (b) Separate claims ..............................................3-22
          (c) Compare—one claim exceeds $25,000 ........3-22
    f. Amendment of complaint affecting jurisdictional
       classification ...............................................................3-23
       (1) Amendment may require leave of court ..............3-23
          (a) Limitation—no amendment after verdict in
             limited civil case ...............................................3-23
       (2) Caption must indicate reclassification .................3-23
    g. Cross-complaint affecting jurisdictional
       classification ...............................................................3-23
       (1) Cross-complaint for more than $25,000 in
          action filed as limited civil case .............................3-24
          (a) Caption of cross-complaint ............................3-24
          (b) Fees payable by cross-complainant .............3-24
       (2) Cross-complaint for less than $25,000 in action
          filed as unlimited civil case ...................................3-24
    h. Reclassification by stipulation.....................................3-24
  6. Motion to Reclassify Action ...............................................3-25
    a. Time limit for motion ...................................................3-25
       (1) Limitation—no reclassification after verdict .........3-25
       (2) Compare—no extension of time to plead ...........3-25
    c. Procedural safeguards ................................................3-25
       (1) Notice and hearing required ..................................3-26
       (2) Adequate record required .....................................3-26
    d. Determining whether case correctly classified ..........3-26
       (1) Test—whether case *necessarily involves* less
          than $25,000 ...........................................................3-27
          (a) No determination on merits ............................3-27
          (b) Settlement negotiations protected ...............3-27

        (c) Compare—evaluation based on conducting settlement conference ...................................3-27
- e. Fee considerations ....................................................3-28
- f. Appellate review .......................................................3-28
- g. Procedures following reclassification ........................3-28
    (1) No effect on jurisdiction ......................................3-28
    (2) Motion for further reclassification .......................3-29
7. Limitations on Subject Matter Jurisdiction ......................3-29
- a. Exclusive federal jurisdiction ...............................3-29
- b. Jurisdiction vested in other tribunals .......................3-29
- c. Disputes interfering with PUC regulations ...............3-29
    (1) Effect..............................................................3-29
    (2) Application ......................................................3-30
    (3) Compare—"primary jurisdiction" doctrine...........3-31
- d. Religious disputes ..................................................3-31
- e. Abstention re membership disputes in private organizations .......................................................3-32
- f. Cases lacking justiciable controversy ......................3-33
- g. Foreign sovereign immunity....................................3-34
    (1) "Commercial activity" exception .........................3-34
    (2) Effect of federal removal jurisdiction ..................3-34
- h. Indian tribal immunity .............................................3-34
- i. Abatement based on related case in another superior court ......................................................3-35
    (1) Cases need not be identical ...............................3-35
    (2) Abatement mandatory.......................................3-35
    (3) Rule *not* jurisdictional ....................................3-35
       (a) May be waived .............................................3-36
    (4) Procedure for abatement .................................3-36
- j. Related cases in different states ............................3-36
    (1) Grounds for stay..............................................3-37
    (2) Effect of sister state's refusal to stay proceedings .....................................................3-37
8. Effect of Lack of Subject Matter Jurisdiction ..................3-37
- a. Defect cannot be waived ......................................3-38
    (1) Compare—lack of personal jurisdiction ..............3-38
9. Procedure for Challenging Subject Matter Jurisdiction..........................................................................3-38
- a. Who may challenge .............................................3-38
    (1) Losing plaintiff may challenge jurisdiction which it invoked .....................................................3-38
- b. Time for raising defect .........................................3-39
    (1) On appeal .....................................................3-39
    (2) After judgment final .........................................3-39
**B. JURISDICTION OVER PARTIES—PERSONAL JURISDICTION** ........................................................3-39
1. Bases for Personal Jurisdiction—General Considerations .....................................................3-40
- a. When required ......................................................3-40
- b. Effect of lack of personal jurisdiction .....................3-40

        (1) Defect can be waived ............................... 3-40
  2. "Traditional" Bases for In Personam Jurisdiction .............. 3-40
    a. Service on persons physically present .................... 3-40
       (1) Effect—"gotcha" jurisdiction ............................ 3-41
         (a) Application ..................................... 3-41
         (b) Immunity for nonresident parties or
             witnesses? ................................... 3-41
       (2) Limitations ................................... 3-41
         (a) Personal service required ............... 3-41
         (b) States may reject in-state service as basis
             for jurisdiction ............................. 3-42
         (c) Forum non conveniens ............... 3-42
       (3) Unresolved issues ........................... 3-42
    b. Domicile .......................................... 3-43
       (1) Domicile vs. residence ..................... 3-43
       (2) Domicile at time action commenced ........ 3-43
         (a) Compare—jurisdiction based on other
             "contacts" ................................... 3-43
       (3) Proving domicile ........................... 3-44
       (4) Service of process requirements ........... 3-44
    c. Appearance or consent ........................... 3-44
       (1) Appearance ................................. 3-44
         (a) Comment ................................... 3-44.1
         (b) "Waiver" of objections to service ....... 3-44.1
         (c) Compare—acts constituting "appearance"
             *absent timely motion to quash or*
             *responsive pleading* ..................... 3-44.1
       (2) Commencement of suit as consent to related
         claims ...................................... 3-44.1
       (3) Contractual consent ("forum-selection
         clauses") .................................. 3-45
         (a) Rationale ................................... 3-45
         (b) Includes choice-of-law clauses ......... 3-45
           1) Application ............................. 3-45
           2) Even more liberal policy where
              California law chosen ............... 3-46
         (c) Claims covered ........................... 3-46
         (d) Parties who may enforce ............... 3-46
           1) Third party beneficiary ............... 3-46
           2) Nonsignatory "closely related" to
              contract ............................... 3-47
         (e) Limitation—consent must be clear ....... 3-47
           1) Designating agent for service of
              summons insufficient ............... 3-48
           2) Acknowledging receipt of summons
              insufficient ........................... 3-48
           3) Agreeing to be bound by result of
              litigation insufficient ............... 3-48
         (f) Limitation—lack of notice as ground for
            refusing enforcement ..................... 3-48

     (g) Limitation—unreasonableness ...................... 3-49
         1) Burden of proof ........................................ 3-49
         2) Adhesion contracts *not* unreasonable
            per se ..................................................... 3-49
         3) Forum selected need not be domicile
            of either party ...................................... 3-50
         4) Factors considered ............................... 3-50
     (h) Limitation—public policy ........................... 3-50.1
         1) Securities transactions violating
            California law ...................................... 3-50.1
         2) Insurance covering California risks ...... 3-50.1
         3) Construction subcontracts ................... 3-50.2
         4) Franchise agreements ......................... 3-50.2
         5) Actions under Consumers Legal
            Remedies Act ..................................... 3-50.2
         6) Actions within small claims
            jurisdiction ......................................... 3-50.2
         7) Compare—actions removed to federal
            court .................................................... 3-50.3
     (i) Limitation—forum non conveniens ............ 3-50.3
     (j) Limitation—defendant may seek transfer
        or removal .............................................. 3-50.3
3. "Minimum Contacts" Doctrine ...................................... 3-50.3
  a. "Long arm" statute analysis .................................. 3-50.4
    (1) California statute ................................... 3-50.4
      (a) Effect .......................................... 3-50.4
    (2) Due process determinations ................ 3-50.4
    (3) Other constitutional limitations ........... 3-50.4
  b. Factors considered ............................................... 3-50.5
    (1) Past vs. present relationship ............... 3-50.5
    (2) Size of claim ....................................... 3-50.5
      (a) Class actions .............................. 3-50.5
  c. Doctrine applies to each defendant individually ........ 3-50.6
    (1) Employer-employee ............................ 3-50.6
    (2) Parent-subsidiary ................................ 3-50.6
    (3) Foreign corporation vs. officers, employees,
        etc. ..................................................... 3-50.6
    (4) Foreign partnership vs. partners ........ 3-50.6
    (5) Conspirators ....................................... 3-50.7
    (6) Compare—claims against decedent's
        estate .................................................. 3-50.7
  d. Agency concepts applicable ................................. 3-50.7
    (1) No immunity for sister states ............... 3-50.7
  e. Effect of plaintiff's residence ................................ 3-50.7
    (1) Compare—inconvenient forum .......... 3-50.8
  f. Different standards for general vs. limited
  personal jurisdiction .............................................. 3-50.8
    (1) General (unlimited) personal jurisdiction
      based on "doing business" locally .................... 3-50.8
      (a) Nonresident persons or corporations ........ 3-50.8

      (b)  Higher level of "contacts" required ............3-50.8
      (c)  Application—activities held sufficient for
          general jurisdiction ......................................3-51
      (d)  Application—activities held NOT sufficient
          for general jurisdiction ..................................3-51
          1)  Local purchases ...............................3-52
          2)  Local advertising ..............................3-52
          3)  Local sales through independent sales
              representative .....................................3-52
          4)  Irregular local deliveries....................3-52
    (2) Limited ("specific") jurisdiction ............................3-53
      (a)  "Purposeful" requirement ..............................3-53
          1)  Rationale ...........................................3-53
          2)  Foreseeability of being sued locally ........3-54
          3)  Acts by plaintiff or others not sufficient ...3-54
          4)  "Substantial connection" resulting from
              defendant's own acts ..............................3-55
          5)  Nature and quality of acts (not quantity)
              determinative .........................................3-55
              a)  Single act may suffice ......................3-55
              b)  Mail, telephone, e-mail, etc. ............3-55
                  1/  Internet activity ..........................3-56
              c)  Limitation—acts creating only
                  "attenuated" contact ........................3-57
          6)  Causing "effects" subject to special
              regulation in forum state .........................3-57
      (b)  Relationship between plaintiff's claim
          and defendant's forum activities....................3-57
           1)  Claims may "arise" outside forum
              state .....................................................3-58
          2)  "Substantial connection" (nexus)
              sufficient ...............................................3-58
              a)  Causal relationship *not* required ......3-58
              b)  "Substantive relevance" *not*
                  required ...........................................3-59
              c)  Sliding scale utilized .......................3-59
      (c)  "Reasonableness" .........................................3-60
          1)  Effect .................................................3-60
          2)  Factors considered ............................3-60
          3)  Additional considerations with alien
              defendants ...........................................3-60
          4)  Application .........................................3-61
          5)  Burden of proof re
              unreasonableness .................................3-61
g.  Limited jurisdiction based on liability-producing acts ....3-62
    (1) Acts committed within California .........................3-62
      (a) Tort actions ................................................3-63
      (b) Contract actions .........................................3-63
    (2) Acts committed outside California "causing
      effect" within ...............................................3-64

    (a) Intentional torts ...........................................3-64
        1) Application ...............................................3-64
        2) Defamation actions ................................3-65
            a) No higher standard because of
               First Amendment concerns .............3-65
            b) Sufficiency of "contacts" ..................3-65
        3) Limitation—both act *and injury* outside
           state ......................................................3-66.1
        4) Limitation—"remoteness"? ....................3-67
    (b) Product liability cases; "stream of
       commerce" theory ........................................3-67
        1) Manufacturer or national distributor ........3-67
            a) Sale and injuries outside
               California ......................................3-68
            b) Compare—goods specifically sold
               for use in California ......................3-68
        2) Retailer or regional distributor ..............3-69
        3) Supplier of defective component ...........3-69
            a) Example ......................................3-70
            b) State cases ..................................3-71
        4) Designer, engineer, etc. ........................3-71
        5) Service and repair ................................3-72
    (c) False advertising, unfair competition ..........3-72
  (3) Contract cases ................................................3-72
    (a) Mechanical tests rejected ......................3-72.1
    (b) Relevant factors .....................................3-73
        1) Choice of law as factor ..........................3-73
        2) Lack of physical presence
           immaterial ..............................................3-73
        3) Effect of forum-selection clause .............3-73
    (c) Franchises ..............................................3-73
    (d) Local purchases ......................................3-74
        1) No general jurisdiction ...........................3-74
        2) Limited jurisdiction .................................3-75
            a) Isolated purchases insufficient .........3-75
            b) Compare—systematic purchases ....3-75
    (e) Employing local counsel .........................3-76
    (f) Loan and financing transactions ...............3-76
    (g) Consumer transactions ...........................3-76
    (h) Assignment ...........................................3-76.1
  (4) Family support and parentage .........................3-76.1
    (a) Constitutionality .....................................3-76.1
    (b) Compare—"palimony" actions....................3-76.2
  (5) Professional services ......................................3-77
    (a) Nonresident accountants .........................3-77
    (b) Nonresident attorneys ..............................3-77
        1) Effect of maintaining California
           license ....................................................3-77
        2) Effect of representing California
           clients ....................................................3-78

    (c)  Nonresident doctors ........................................3-78
        1)  Includes follow-up care ...........................3-79
        2)  Compare—effect of national
            marketing ...............................................3-79
        3)  Compare—nonresident consultants? .....3-79
        4)  Effect of maintaining California
            license? ...................................................3-79
  (6) Other activities subject to special regulation .......3-80
    (a)  Insurance ....................................................3-80
        1)  Local offices not required .......................3-80
        2)  Isolated transactions ..............................3-80
        3)  Automobile liability insurers ...................3-81
        4)  Liability insurer's refusal to defend
            local lawsuit ............................................3-81
        5)  Compare—"first party" actions...............3-82
        6)  Compare—actions *between*
            nonresident insurers ..............................3-82
        7)  Compare—insurance guaranty
            associations ...........................................3-83
    (b)  Issuance of securities ...............................3-83
    (c)  Parents' failure to supervise minor
        children ........................................................3-83
h.  Corporate defendants—special considerations .........3-84
  (1) California corporations ......................................3-84
    (a)  Service of process .....................................3-84
  (2) Out-of-state corporations ..................................3-84
    (a)  Effect of qualification .................................3-84
        1)  Designation of agent for service of
            summons ................................................3-84
        2)  Not a consent to jurisdiction ..................3-84
    (b)  Acts constituting appointment of local
        agent for service of process......................3-84.1
        1)  Nonadmitted insurers ............................3-84.1
        2)  Violations of Franchise Investment
            Law .........................................................3-85
    (c)  "Minimum contacts" more readily found ........3-85
        1)  General vs. limited personal
            jurisdiction .............................................3-85
        2)  Ownership or control of local
            subsidiary ...............................................3-85
            a)  Alter ego.........................................3-86
                1/  Factors considered ...................3-86
            b)  Agency ............................................3-86
            c)  "Representative services doctrine"...3-86
            d)  "Purposeful availment" .....................3-86
        3)  Successor liability ..................................3-87
    (d)  Compare—capacity to sue or defend ..........3-87
i.  Corporate officers, directors, agents and
employees—special considerations ..........................3-87
  (1) No automatic immunity for acts committed on
    behalf of corporation .........................................3-87

        (a) Same rule applies to partnerships ...............3-88
      (2) Nature of acts determinative of jurisdiction .........3-88
  j.  Claims involving property .......................................3-89
      (1) Example ................................................................3-89
      (2) Validity of nonresident attachment statutes? .......3-89
      (3) Local property as sufficient "contact" in certain
           actions.........................................................................3-89
         (a) Title actions .................................................3-90
            1) Marital property ....................................3-90
         (b) Liability claims relating to local property .......3-90
         (c) Assets in insurance solvency proceedings ...3-90
      (4) Property outside forum state .............................3-90
4.  Procedures to Challenge Personal Jurisdiction ..............3-91
  a.  Motion to quash service of summons ......................3-91
      (1) Forms ...................................................................3-91
      (2) Time of filing .......................................................3-91
         (a) May be filed simulataneously with
            responsive pleading ....................................3-91
         (b) May also be filed *before* responsive
            pleading .........................................................3-92
         (c) Compare—not after responsive pleading .....3-92
      (3) Jurisdictional objection preserved .......................3-92
      (4) Discovery ............................................................3-92
      (5) Notice and hearing date .....................................3-93
         (a) Adequacy of notice served by mail? ............3-93
      (6) Burden of proof on plaintiff .................................3-93
         (a) Preponderance required ...............................3-93
         (b) Timing of motion; continuance to conduct
            discovery.......................................................3-93
      (7) Evidence on motion ............................................3-94
         (a) Unverified pleadings .....................................3-94
         (b) Hearsay declarations insufficient ..................3-94
         (c) Commission of tort as basis for
            jurisdiction ....................................................3-95
         (d) Conflicts in evidence ....................................3-95
      (8) Time to plead extended.......................................3-95
      (9) Further extension if mandamus sought ...............3-95
      (10) Proceeding on merits waives jurisdictional
          defect ..........................................................................3-96
  b.  Affirmative defense and motion to dismiss in lieu of
      motion to quash?.......................................................3-96
  c.  Suffer default judgment, then attack on
      jurisdictional grounds................................................3-97
      (1) Motion to set aside default judgment
         coupled with motion to quash ...........................3-97
         (a) Time limits ....................................................3-97
      (2) Appeal................................................................3-97
         (a) Time limits ....................................................3-97
      (3) Independent action to set aside judgment
         ("collateral attack") ..............................................3-98

Rev. #1 2004

        (a) Limitation—collateral estoppel ....................3-98
        (b) Limitation—due diligence ...........................3-98

**C. FORUM NON CONVENIENS** ................................................3-98
  1. Nature of Challenge .......................................................3-98
    a. Difference between stay and dismissal ....................3-99
    b. Exception for "major contracts" ...............................3-99
  2. Who May Challenge ......................................................3-100
    a. Defendants ..............................................................3-100
    b. Plaintiffs...................................................................3-100
  3. Procedure ......................................................................3-100
    a. Timing .....................................................................3-100
       (1) Waived if not raised when filing demurrer or
          motion to strike.................................................3-100
    b. May be coupled with motion to quash ....................3-100
    c. Not a general appearance .......................................3-101
  4. Burden of Proof .............................................................3-101
  5. Requirement of "Suitable" Alternative Forum ................3-101
    a. Forum in which defendant subject to personal
       jurisdiction ................................................................3-101
       (1) Multiple defendants ...........................................3-102
    b. Forum in which statute of limitations no bar ...........3-102
    c. Forum law must provide remedy ............................3-102
       (1) "No remedy at all" exception very limited ..........3-102
    d. Compliance with conditions ....................................3-103
  6. Balancing of Private and Public Factors .......................3-103
    a. Private interest factors .............................................3-104
    b. Public interest factors ..............................................3-104
  7. Particular Factors ..........................................................3-106
    a. Plaintiff's choice of forum as factor .......................3-106
    b. Plaintiff's local residence as factor ........................3-106
       (1) Action *cannot* be *dismissed* ...........................3-106
         (a) Exceptional cases .......................................3-106
       (2) Stay may be ordered .......................................3-107
         (a) Factors justifying stay .................................3-107
    c. Defendant's local residence as factor .....................3-108
       (1) Presumption favoring local jurisdiction .............3-108
    d. Effect if all parties nonresidents .............................3-108
    e. Suability of third parties as factor ...........................3-108
    f. Effect of forum-selection contract ..........................3-109
       (1) Contracts requiring suit in California .................3-109
         (a) Compare—contracts requiring parties to
            submit to California jurisdiction ...................3-109
       (2) Contracts requiring suit outside California ........3-109
         (a) Application .................................................3-110
         (b) Limitation—public policy ...........................3-110
         (c) Effect of joinder of noncontracting
            parties.........................................................3-110
  8. No Findings Required ....................................................3-111
  9. Nature of Dismissal.......................................................3-111

**D. VENUE** ....................................................................3-111
  1. Nature of Requirement ............................................3-111
    a. Purpose of venue rules .......................................3-111
    b. May not be waived in advance .............................3-111
    c. Not jurisdictional ..............................................3-111
      (1) Exceptions ..................................................3-111
    d. Compare—"proper" judicial district for limited civil
      cases ..............................................................3-111
    e. Compare—"proper" branch of superior court...........3-112
  2. Venue Rules Depend on Whether Action "Transitory"
    or "Local"...............................................................3-112
    a. Classification of actions .....................................3-112
      (1) Transitory actions .....................................3-112.1
      (2) Local actions ...........................................3-112.1
      (3) Mixed actions ..........................................3-112.1
        (a) Several causes joined, one local,
          another transitory ...............................3-112.1
        (b) Single cause seeking both forms of relief ...3-113
    b. Determined at outset of action ............................3-113
  3. Venue in Local Actions .............................................3-113
    a. Not jurisdictional ..............................................3-114
      (1) Exception—condemnation actions; venue
        jurisdictional ................................................3-114
    b. Court at situs may transfer ................................3-114
      (1) Includes condemnation actions .....................3-114
    c. Local actions involving land ...............................3-114
    d. Other local actions...........................................3-115
      (1) Marriage dissolution proceedings ..................3-115
        (a) Compare—annulment, separation
          proceedings ......................................3-116
      (2) Child support proceedings ...........................3-116
        (a) Compare—parentage proceedings.............3-116
      (3) Corporate dissolution proceedings.................3-116
      (4) Against a fiduciary.....................................3-116
  4. Venue in Transitory Actions......................................3-116
    a. Actions triable at defendant's residence ...............3-116
      (1) The "general rule" of venue .........................3-116
        (a) Limitation—other counties may also be
          "proper" ...........................................3-116
        (b) Limitation—court's power to transfer..........3-117
      (2) "Residence" means domicile ........................3-117
        (a) Corporations .................................3-117
      (3) Residence of any defendant..........................3-117
        (a) Example ......................................3-117
        (b) Includes "Doe" defendants .....................3-118
        (c) Later dismissal of resident defendant .........3-118
          1) Compare—remaining defendants
            may choose dismissed defendant's
            residence ...................................3-118
        (d) Limitation—resident defendant must be
          properly joined .................................3-118

Rev. #1 2004

               1) Example ............................................. 3-119
               2) Sanctions may be imposed ................. 3-119
           (e) Limitation—individual and corporate
              defendants joined in same action .............. 3-119
       (4) Residence unknown or out-of-state ................... 3-119
   b. Actions triable EITHER at defendant's residence
     or other counties ........................................ 3-119
     (1) Actions for personal injury or death ................... 3-120
       (a) "Personal injury" narrowly construed ........... 3-120
     (2) Actions for injury to personal property ......... 3-120
       (a) Compare—injury to real property .............. 3-120
     (3) Actions for breach of contract (other than
       consumer obligations) ....................................... 3-120
       (a) "County where contract entered into" .......... 3-120
       (b) "County where obligation to be
         performed" .............................................. 3-120.1
         1) "Special contract in writing"
           requirement ...................................... 3-120.1
         2) Example ........................................... 3-120.1
         3) Compare—actions against
           corporations ...................................... 3-120.1
     (4) Actions on certain consumer obligations ........ 3-120.1
       (a) Special pleading requirement ................. 3-120.2
       (b) Defendant's consent to improper court .... 3-120.2
     (5) Other special venue statutes ......................... 3-120.3
   c. Causes of action with conflicting venue
     provisions—the "mixed action" rule ...................... 3-120.3
     (1) Rationale ................................................ 3-121
     (2) Public policy exceptions ........................... 3-121
 5. Venue in Actions Against Corporations or Other
   Entities ............................................................ 3-121
   a. Actions against corporations ........................... 3-121
     (1) Principal place of business; corporate
       designation governs .......................................... 3-122
     (2) Place of performance ................................. 3-122
     (3) Effect of suing in wrong county .................. 3-123
     (4) Out-of-state corporations ........................... 3-123
       (a) Not qualified to do business in California .... 3-123
       (b) Compare—jurisdiction problem ................. 3-123
     (5) Effect of joinder of individual codefendant
       ("residence" venue) ........................................ 3-123
       (a) "Residence" of either proper ..................... 3-123
         1) Compare—actions subject to special
           venue rules ...................................... 3-124
       (b) Suit filed elsewhere ................................ 3-124
       (c) Compare—individual sued as alter ego
         of corporation ......................................... 3-124
     (6) Multiple causes of action ........................... 3-125
   b. Actions against partnerships or unincorporated
     associations .................................................... 3-125

  (1)  Purpose ...........................................................3-125
  (2)  When filed .....................................................3-125
  (3)  Effect of joinder of individual partners ..............3-125
 c.  Actions against governmental entities ...................3-126
  (1)  Actions against State of California ..................3-126
  (2)  Actions against city, county or local districts .....3-127
  (3)  Compare—actions BY governmental entity ......3-128
   (a)  Supports removal, not original venue .........3-129
   (b)  Corporation as "resident" ..........................3-129
   (c)  Effect of joinder of other plaintiffs ..............3-129
   (d)  Compare—actions against State ................3-130
6. Procedure for Change of Venue—Motion to Transfer.....3-130
 a.  Grounds.................................................................3-130
  (1)  "Wrong court" ground (transfer mandatory) .......3-130
   (a)  Effect ......................................................3-130
   (b)  Where several venues would be proper ......3-130
   (c)  Compare—"wrong court" transfers on
    consumer obligations ...............................3-130
  (2)  "Convenience of witnesses and ends of
   justice" (transfer discretionary) .....................3-130.1
   (a)  Importance...............................................3-130.1
    1)  Applies to *any* action ..........................3-131
    2)  Limits defendant's right to compel
     transfer ...............................................3-131
   (b)  Whose "convenience" ...............................3-131
   (c)  Timeliness ...............................................3-132
  (3)  Other statutory grounds for transfer ...............3-132
 b.  Waiver of grounds ................................................3-132
 c.  Time for motion ....................................................3-132
  (1)  "Wrong court" motion must be made at
   outset ..........................................................3-132
   (a)  May be filed concurrently with answer or
    demurrer .................................................3-133
  (2)  Motion based on "convenience of
   witnesses" ground must be filed within
   "reasonable time" AFTER answer ...................3-133
   (a)  Reasonable time ......................................3-133
   (b)  Plaintiff may move for retransfer on this
    ground ....................................................3-133
 d.  Form and content of motion ..................................3-134
  (1)  Forms .........................................................3-134
  (2)  Notice must specify statutory ground ..............3-134
  (3)  Burden on moving party ................................3-134
   (a)  "Wrong court" ground requires showing
    of defendant's residence ..........................3-134
    1)  Must negate alternative grounds .........3-135
   (b)  "Convenience of witnesses" ground ...........3-135
    1)  Admissible evidence required.............3-135
  (4)  Costs and fees must be posted if motion
   made on "convenience of witnesses" ground ....3-136

    e.  Court's jurisdiction suspended while motion
        pending ......................................................................3-136
        (1) Exception—marital dissolution proceedings .....3-136
        (2) Exception—joinder of "Doe" defendant .............3-136
        (3) Effect on discovery ............................................3-136
    f.  Ruling on motion ..........................................................3-137
        (1) Sanctions against losing party .........................3-137
            (a) Where motion made on "wrong court"
                ground.............................................................3-137
                1) Losing party's attorney
                    *personally* liable ...................................3-137
                2) Factors considered ...............................3-137
                3) Findings required? ................................3-138
            (b) Where motion made on "convenience
                of witnesses" ground .................................3-138
        (2) If motion granted, transferor court loses
            jurisdiction .......................................................3-138
            (a) Jurisdictional "hiatus" until transfer
                complete? .....................................................3-138
        (3) Liability for fees and costs on transfer ..............3-139
        (4) Time to respond if motion denied ......................3-139
        (5) Time to respond if motion granted ....................3-139
    g.  Appellate review of ruling .........................................3-139
        (1) Unlimited civil cases .........................................3-139
        (2) Orders for change of venue in limited civil
            cases ................................................................3-140
  7.  Rules Designating "Proper" Court for Trial of Limited
    Civil Cases ..........................................................................3-140
  8.  Rules Designating "Proper" Branch or District of
    Superior Court .....................................................................3-140
    a.  Counties with branch courts ......................................3-140
        (1) Effect of filing at wrong location .......................3-140
    b.  Los Angeles County .................................................3-140
        (1) Mandatory filings ...............................................3-141
            (a) Not jurisdictional ........................................3-141
        (2) Optional filings .................................................3-142
        (3) Certificate required............................................3-142
        (4) Transfers between districts ................................3-142

**E. FEDERAL VS. STATE COURTS** ..............................3-143
  1.  "Exclusive" Federal Jurisdiction ....................................3-143
    a.  Impact of federal preemption .....................................3-144
        (1) Example ..............................................................3-144
        (2) State claims "recharacterized" as federal .........3-144
        (3) Effect on state court subject matter
            jurisdiction .......................................................3-144.1
  2.  "Concurrent" Federal-State Jurisdiction .......................3-145
    a.  "Federal question" cases ..........................................3-145
        (1) "Supplemental jurisdiction" for state law
            claims ...............................................................3-145
        (2) Effect of federal preemption of state law ..........3-145

  (3) Defendant's right to remove ..............................3-146
 b. "Diversity" cases exceeding $75,000 .....................3-146
  (1) Diversity of citizenship.......................................3-146
  (2) Other instances of diversity ..............................3-146
 c. Effect of dual filings ...............................................3-146
3. Removal Jurisdiction ......................................................3-146.1
 a. Exception .................................................................3-146.1
 b. Procedure ................................................................3-146.1
4. Considerations Affecting Choice of Federal vs.
 State Court .......................................................................3-147
 a. Territorial jurisdiction ...............................................3-147
  (1) Exceptions—nationwide personal
   jurisdiction ........................................................3-147
 b. Substantive law .......................................................3-147
  (1) Where state law uncertain ...............................3-147
 c. Procedural rules ......................................................3-148
  (1) "Outcome determinative" rules ..........................3-148
  (2) Pleading and practice rules ..............................3-148
   (a) Class actions ..............................................3-148
   (b) Mandatory disclosures ...............................3-148
   (c) Evidence rules ............................................3-149
   (d) Joinder problems ........................................3-149
   (e) "Doe" pleading and late amendments .........3-149
   (f) Change of venue .........................................3-149
    1) Multi-district transfers ...........................3-150
 d. Practical considerations...........................................3-150
  (1) Delay in getting to trial .....................................3-150
  (2) Geographic convenience ...................................3-150
  (3) "All purpose" assignment to single judge
   in federal court ..................................................3-150
   (a) Perception of impartiality ............................3-150
   (b) Perception that federal judges more
    likely to grant dispositive motions ..............3-151
   (c) Perception that federal judges more
    receptive to federal claim or defense ..........3-151
   (d) Perception that federal judges sterner
    taskmasters ................................................3-151
   (e) No peremptory challenge of federal
    judge ..........................................................3-151
  (4) Jury selection ....................................................3-152
  (5) Jury verdict requirements ..................................3-152
  (6) Lack of familiarity with federal
   procedures ........................................................3-152

**FORMS**
- Notice of Motion to Quash Service of Summons .................3-153
- Declaration in Support of Motion to Quash Service of
 Summons ..............................................................................3-155
- Notice of Motion to Stay or Dismiss Action (Inconvenient
 Forum) ..................................................................................3-157

- Declaration in Support of Motion to Stay or Dismiss Action (Inconvenient Forum) ................................................. 3-159
- Notice of Motion for Order Transferring Action (Change of Venue) ................................................................................ 3-161
- Declaration in Support of Motion for Order Transferring Action ("Wrong Court" Ground) ............................................. 3-163
- Declaration in Support of Motion for Order Transferring Action ("Convenience of Witnesses" Ground) ...................... 3-165
- Checklist: Motion to Quash Service ................................. 3-169
- Checklist: Motion to Change Venue ................................ 3-170
- Checklist: Forum Non Conveniens .................................. 3-171

**RESERVED**

# JURISDICTION AND VENUE

## [3:1] STRATEGY RE CHOOSING COURT

The first step in commencing a lawsuit is to choose the court in which to file the action. That choice will depend on the following essential considerations:

- **Subject Matter Jurisdiction:** Which state courts are *competent* under California law to adjudicate the type of action involved? (*See ¶3:2 ff.*)

  — If the claim is *based on federal law,* can state courts adjudicate at all, or must the case be heard in federal court? I.e., is federal jurisdiction "exclusive" or "concurrent" (*see ¶3:611*)? (The same issue arises where federal law *preempts* a state law claim, so that the only viable claim is a federal claim; *see ¶3:612.*)

- **Personal Jurisdiction:** Assuming the action is filed in a competent court, can that court exercise jurisdiction over the defendants? Is there a constitutionally-sufficient "contact" or relationship with the defendant to permit California courts to render a valid judgment? (*See ¶3:130 ff.*)

- **Venue:** Among the various state courts that would be competent to adjudicate the action, which is the "proper" court *geographically* for trial of the action? (*See ¶3:450 ff.*) (The choice is important because if venue is improper, *sanctions* may be imposed against *plaintiff's attorney personally! See ¶3:583 ff.*)

  In addition to choosing a proper county, should the case be filed in a particular branch or district of a county court having several branches or districts? Some local rules govern choice of districts (*see ¶3:599 ff.*) and the jury pool may vary widely from one district to another.

- **Federal vs. State Jurisdiction:** Claims subject to "exclusive" federal jurisdiction must of course be filed in federal court (*see ¶3:611*). But many "diversity" and "federal question" claims are within the "concurrent" jurisdiction of federal and state courts (*see ¶3:619*). In such cases, are there any *advantages* to suing in state court vs. federal? (*See ¶3:630 ff.*)

- **Tactical Considerations:** If defendant is a nonresident, it will almost always be advantageous for plaintiff to file suit in local courts, rather than at defendant's residence. It will be easier for plaintiff to deal with local counsel, to produce

---

**STRATEGY RE CHOOSING COURT**
**(Cont'd)**

witnesses and evidence in a local trial, and plaintiff may find a more sympathetic jury close to home. Conversely, it is often more difficult and expensive for a nonresident defendant to defend an action in local courts.

However, suing a nonresident in California courts often complicates the litigation:

— It may provoke jurisdictional challenges that will be costly and time-consuming to oppose. Writs and appeals on the jurisdictional issue will almost certainly delay getting to trial, and could jeopardize any judgment obtained by plaintiff on the merits (*see ¶3:201*).

— Even if jurisdiction is conceded, the nonresident may be entitled to *remove* the action to federal court if federal jurisdictional requirements are met (complete diversity, etc.; *see ¶3:627*).

— The fact that a nonresident is involved suggests possible *choice of law* issues (*see ¶1:509*); and therefore there is no certainty California courts will apply California law.

---

## A. SUBJECT MATTER JURISDICTION (COMPETENCY)

**[3:2]** The first prong in the jurisdiction analysis is which state courts have subject matter jurisdiction. The court in which the action is filed must be *competent* under California law to render a judgment; i.e., the state constitution or statutes must empower it to adjudicate the *type* of lawsuit involved and to render a judgment for the *amount in controversy.* [See *Marriage of Jensen* (2003) 114 CA4th 587, 593, 7 CR3d 701, 705 (citing text)]

1. **[3:2.1] Background—Trial Court Unification:** Until 1998, each county in California had a superior court and at least one municipal court with separate subject matter jurisdiction.

   The California Constitution was amended in 1998 to permit unification of the municipal and superior courts in each county into a single superior court upon approval by the judges of both courts (Const. Art. VI, §5; Gov.C. §70200 et seq.).

   Courts in all California counties are now unified; municipal courts have ceased to exist. [See *TrafficSchoolOnline, Inc. v. Sup.Ct. (Ohlrich)* (2001) 89 CA4th 222, 227, 107 CR2d 412, 415]

   a. **[3:2.2] Limited vs. unlimited civil cases:** Civil cases formerly within the jurisdiction of municipal courts are now classified as "limited civil cases" (CCP §85; *see ¶3:8 ff.*). All others are "unlimited civil cases" (CCP §88).

Existence of a statute relating to a court's authority in one type of case (limited or unlimited jurisdiction) does not itself imply that the same authority does or does not exist in the other. [CCP §89]

2. **[3:3] Superior Court Subject Matter Jurisdiction:** There is one superior court in each county in California. [Cal. Const. Art. VI, §4]

Each superior court has *general* subject matter jurisdiction, meaning that it can adjudicate any and all cases brought before it (subject to various exceptions and limitations discussed at ¶*3:123 ff.*).

3. **[3:4] Limited vs. Unlimited Civil Cases:** Superior courts have subject matter jurisdiction in both limited and unlimited civil cases. [See CCP §32.5—"limited civil case *or otherwise*" (emphasis added)]

Cases classified as "limited" civil cases, however, are subject to special rules and jurisdictional limitations, discussed below.

   a. **[3:5] Actions not subject to classification as limited civil cases:** By statute, certain actions are not subject to the special rules governing limited civil cases, regardless of the amount in controversy and regardless of cross-complaints. These include:

   - **Family law cases:** All proceedings under the Family Code (including marriage dissolution, legal separation and nullity; child custody/visitation; child, spousal and family support; paternity; and adoptions). [Fam.C. §200]

   - **Probate proceedings** [Prob.C. §201]

   - **Trust administration** [Prob.C. §17000; see *Saks v. Damon Raike & Co.* (1992) 7 CA4th 419, 429-430, 8 CR2d 869, 876, fn. 7—trial court that first obtains jurisdiction over a trust under petition brought pursuant to Probate Code has *exclusive* jurisdiction of proceedings concerning that trust's internal affairs]

   - **Guardianship and conservatorship proceedings** [Prob.C. §2200]

   - **Eminent domain proceedings** [CCP §1250.010]

   - **Corporate dissolution proceedings** [Corps.C. §§1800(a), 1904]

   - **Uninsured motorist arbitration proceedings** [CCP §86(a)(10)]

- **Good faith improvements:** Actions to recover the value of good faith improvements made on the land of another. [See CCP §871.3(a)]

    [3:6-7] *Reserved.*

4. **[3:8] Limited Civil Cases:** All cases are classified as unlimited civil cases, except the following actions which are designated as limited civil cases:

    a. **[3:9] Actions at law:** Cases at law in which the *demand*, exclusive of interest, or the *value of the property* in controversy, is $25,000 or less. [CCP §86(a)(1)]

        (1) **[3:10] Exception—legality of taxes, etc.:** The only exception is cases involving the *legality* of any "tax, impost, assessment, toll or fine." Such cases are *not* limited civil cases, even if less than $25,000 is involved. [CCP §86(a)(1); see *Cardellini v. Casey* (1986) 181 CA3d 389, 398, 226 CR 659, 664]

        (2) **[3:11] Forcible or unlawful detainer:** All actions in "forcible entry" or "forcible or unlawful detainer" where the total damages claimed is $25,000 or less. (The rental value of the property is immaterial.) [CCP §86(a)(4)]

        A landlord can sue in superior court for *ejectment*, but that will not provide the summary remedy available in unlawful detainer. [See *Stokus v. Marsh* (1990) 217 CA3d 647, 653, 266 CR 90, 93, fn. 2; and detailed discussion in Friedman, Garcia & Hagarty, *Cal. Prac. Guide: Landlord-Tenant* (TRG)]

        (3) **[3:11.1] Cases designated by statute:** Certain actions or proceedings are designated by statute as limited civil cases, some without regard to the amount of the demand or value of the subject matter. [See CCP §85(c)—enumerating 22 such statutes]

            - [3:11.2] For example, a petition to declare a mobilehome abandoned, *regardless of its value,* is classified as a limited civil case (see Civ.C. §798.61(c)). [CCP §85(c)(1)]

    b. **[3:12] Equitable relief:** Only certain types of equitable relief can be granted in connection with limited civil cases (i.e., amount in controversy $25,000 or less):

        (1) **[3:13] Limitations:** Courts cannot grant the following types of equitable relief in limited civil cases (see CCP §580(b)):

            (a) **[3:14] No permanent injunctions:** [See CCP §86(a)(8)—authorizing only TROs and PIs]

(b) [3:15] **No determining title to real property:** [See CCP §86(b)(1)—authorizing only determining title to personal property worth $25,000 or less]

(c) [3:16] **No enforcement or modification of child/ spousal support orders:** Such proceedings must be heard as superior court unlimited civil cases. [Fam.C. §200; see *Marriage of Lackey* (1983) 143 CA3d 698, 702, 191 CR 309, 312— municipal court had no jurisdiction in suit for arrearages under superior court order for child support]

(d) [3:17] **Limited declaratory relief:** Courts may not grant declaratory relief in a limited civil case *except:*
— when sought in a *cross-complaint for indemnity* as to the relief sought in the complaint in an action that is otherwise a limited civil case;
— in connection with a trial de novo after nonbinding fee arbitration between attorney and client where the amount in controversy is $25,000 or less. [See CCP §86(a)(7)]

1) [3:18] **Compare—unnecessary prayer for declaratory relief:** If a money judgment for $25,000 or less will fully resolve the dispute, so that there is *no need for a declaration* as to future conduct, a prayer "for declaratory relief" will not preclude classification of the action as a limited civil case. [See *Cardellini v. Casey* (1986) 181 CA3d 389, 396, 226 CR 659, 663— "the rights of the complaining party have crystallized into a cause of action for past wrongs"]

(2) [3:19] **Ancillary remedies:** However, as long as the relief sought qualifies the case as a limited civil case, the court may grant certain ancillary remedies in order to preserve the status quo pending trial. For example:

• *Temporary restraining orders* and *preliminary injunctions* (but, as stated above, no permanent injunctions);

• Orders for an *accounting*;

• Orders appointing a *receiver*, and any other order or act under the Code provisions relating to enforcement of judgments;

• Orders determining *title* to *personal property* (not real property) that has been seized or levied upon (by attachment, claim and delivery, etc.) in connection with a pending action. [CCP §86(a)(8)]

(3) [3:20] **Proceedings in equity:** In addition, suits seeking certain equitable relief involving money or property valued at $25,000 or less are limited civil cases. This includes:

- [3:21] **Rescission or cancellation of contracts,** if sought in connection with restitution of money paid or property delivered under such contract, worth $25,000 or less. [CCP §86(a)(3)]

- [3:22] **Reformation** of a written contract, if sought in connection with an action upon the contract, and where the money or property involved in the dispute is valued at $25,000 or less. [CCP §86(a)(3)]

- [3:23] **Dissolution of partnership,** where the partnership assets are worth $25,000 or less. [CCP §86(a)(2)]

- [3:24] **Interpleader,** where the amount of money or value of property involved is $25,000 or less. [CCP §86(a)(2)]

- [3:25] **Suit to determine title to personal property** worth $25,000 or less. [CCP §86(b)(1)] (If the property had been seized or levied upon, the court could also try title under CCP §86(a)(8), ¶3:19.)

- [3:26] **Suit to foreclose liens on personal property,** where the amount of the lien is $25,000 or less. [CCP §86(a)(5)]

- [3:27] **Suit to foreclose, enforce or release mechanic's lien on real property,** where the amount of the lien is $25,000 or less. [CCP §86(a)(6)] (This also covers materialmen, artisans, laborers and others entitled to liens under Civ.C. §3109 et seq.)

  *Limitation:* Such actions cannot be dealt with as limited civil cases if other mechanics' lien actions affecting the same property and exceeding $25,000 are pending, or where there are mechanics' lien actions affecting the same property where the aggregate liens exceed $25,000. [CCP §86(a)(6)]

- [3:28] **Suit to foreclose assessment lien on a "common interest development"** (condos, etc.) where the amount of the lien is $25,000 or less. [CCP §86(a)(6)]

  *Limitation:* Same limitation for aggregate liens as for mechanics' liens; *see* ¶3:27.

- [3:29] **Suit by judgment creditor against third person** to recover personal property belonging to the judgment debtor, or to enforce payment of a debt owing by the judgment debtor (see CCP §708.210), where the interest or debt is worth $25,000 or less. [CCP §86(a)(9)]

- [3:29.1] **Arbitration orders and awards:** Petitions to compel arbitration on claims of $25,000 or less; and to affirm, modify or vacate awards where the amount is $25,000 or less. [See CCP §86(a)(10)]

- [3:29.2] **Compare—abandonment of mobilehome:** Upon complying with requisite procedures, a mobilehome park owner may obtain a judicial declaration that a mobilehome has been abandoned. The proceeding is a limited civil case *regardless of the value* of the mobilehome. [See Civ.C. §798.61(c) (amended 2003); and detailed discussion in Friedman, Garcia & Hagarty, *Cal. Prac. Guide: Landlord-Tenant* (TRG), Ch. 11]

(4) [3:30] **"Actions based on equitable principles":** In addition, in any action where the amount of money or value of property involved does not exceed $25,000, "the court may impose liability whether the theory upon which liability is sought to be imposed involves legal or equitable principles." [CCP §580(a)]

(a) [3:31] **Example:** Suit for damages for breach of contract based on doctrine of promissory estoppel, an equitable doctrine. [See *C & K Engineering Contractors v. Amber Steel Co., Inc.* (1978) 23 C3d 1, 8, 151 CR 323, 326—dealing with right to jury trial in actions based on promissory estoppel]

(5) [3:32] **Equitable defenses:** Similarly, the court may hear and determine equitable defenses pleaded by the defendant in an action that otherwise qualifies as a limited civil case. [CCP §86(b)(2)]

(a) [3:33] **Examples:** In defense to one of the equitable proceedings above (¶3:20), a court hearing a limited civil case may hear and determine whatever equitable defenses are available—e.g., unclean hands, laches, equitable estoppel, etc. (Normally, such defenses are *not* available where the only claim is for money damages.)

(6) [3:34] **Cross-complaint for third party indemnification:** Normally, declaratory relief cannot be granted in a limited civil case (*see* ¶3:17). However, where an

action otherwise qualifies as a limited civil case, the court can grant declaratory relief as to defendant's right to indemnity from any third person as to the claim on which defendant is being sued. This enables the court to settle any indemnity claims in the same lawsuit that determines liability, rather than in a separate action. [CCP §86(a)(7); see ¶3:18]

(a) [3:35] **Example:** Plaintiff files property damage claim for $10,000 against Owner of vehicle which caused damage. Owner may cross-complain against Driver of vehicle for declaration of right to indemnification if Owner held liable to Plaintiff.

(7) [3:36] **Matters subject to contractual arbitration:** Petitions to compel contractual arbitration or to confirm or set aside an arbitration award, where the amount in controversy or value of the property does not exceed $25,000, are limited civil cases. (Exception: Uninsured motorist arbitration proceedings do not qualify as limited civil cases, regardless of the amount involved.) [CCP §86(a)(10)]

(a) [3:36.1] **Attorney-client fee disputes:** Actions to set aside binding arbitration awards up to $25,000 in fee disputes between attorney and client (under Bus. & Prof.C. §6200 et seq.) are also limited civil cases. [CCP §86(a)(10)(B)] (Such awards are binding, however, only if the parties so agree after the dispute arises or fail to request a trial de novo; see Bus. & Prof.C. §6203.)

(8) [3:37] **Equitable relief from judgment:** A proceeding to vacate a judgment or court order in a limited civil case obtained through "extrinsic fraud, mistake, inadvertence or excusable neglect" is itself treated as a limited civil case. [CCP §86(b)(3)]

[3:38] *Reserved.*

(9) [3:39] **Class actions:** Class actions may qualify as limited civil cases if the amount in controversy does not exceed $25,000. However, because the claims of individual class members are *aggregated* in determining the amount in controversy, class actions nearly always exceed these limits. [See *Archibald v. Cinerama Hotels* (1976) 15 C3d 853, 861, 126 CR 811, 817; *Little v. Sanchez* (1985) 166 CA3d 501, 507, 213 CR 297, 300; and discussion at ¶14:69]

[3:40-40.4] *Reserved.*

➡️[3:40.5] *PRACTICE POINTERS—Whether to File as Limited Civil Case:* On claims arguably worth more than $25,000, *practical* considerations may dictate whether to file as a limited civil case. The following matters may affect that decision:

- length of time to trial;
- "fast track" rules (*see* ¶ *12:4 ff.*);
- limits on discovery in limited civil cases (*see* ¶*8:1806 ff.*);
- in an *unlawful detainer* action filed as a limited civil case, the *public* (e.g., including newspapers) cannot access the court file for 60 days after filing; and if defendant prevails within that period, public access is forever barred (see CCP §1161.2 (added 2003));
- affidavits and declarations can be used instead of live testimony (including expert opinions) in limited civil cases if served on opposing parties at least 30 days before trial (CCP §98(a));
- deposition transcripts may be used in lieu of live testimony if the party against whom the transcripts are offered had an *opportunity* to participate in the deposition (CCP §98(b), *see* ¶*8:876*);
- judgments in limited civil cases are appealable only to the appellate division of the superior court (see CCP §904.2);
- judgments in limited civil cases are res judicata as between the parties or their successors in interest but *do not collaterally estop* a party in subsequent litigation with a nonparty (see CCP §99).

c. **[3:41] Small claims divisions:** Each trial court has a small claims division, in which special rules and procedures apply to provide an expedited and simplified adjudication (see CCP §116.110 et seq.). A limited civil case may be filed in the small claims division if the claim is within the jurisdictional limits noted below. Such claims are governed by the small claims rules and procedures rather than those applicable to limited civil cases generally. [CCP §87(a)]

Small claims divisions have subject matter jurisdiction in the following cases:

- Actions for *money damages* not exceeding $5,000. [CCP §116.220(a)(1)] (But *not* unlawful detainer actions; and there is a limit on the number of small claims actions a person can file each year, *see* ¶*3:44*.)
- Actions by hotelkeepers, etc. to enforce possessory liens on baggage or other property belonging to guests or boarders, after obtaining judgments for room charges

not exceeding $5,000. [CCP §116.220(a)(3); Civ.C. §1861.5]

- Actions to enforce payment of unsecured personal property taxes up to $5,000 if defendant does not contest the legality of the tax. [CCP §116.220(a)(2)]

- Actions involving arbitration awards under Bus. & Prof.C. §6200 involving fee disputes between attorney and client. If the award is *binding* (by agreement of the parties or by failure to request trial de novo), the court has jurisdiction to confirm, correct or vacate an award up to $5,000. If the award is *nonbinding*, the court may hear *de novo* a fee dispute of up to $5,000. [CCP §116.220(a)(4)]

- *Limitation—claims against guarantors:* Actions to enforce a guarantee cannot exceed $2,500 ($4,000 if guarantor charged a fee for its guarantee). [CCP §116.220(c)]

Note: If the demand exceeds small claims jurisdiction, plaintiff *may waive* the excess (effective upon entry of judgment in the small claims action). [CCP §116.220(d)]

(1) **[3:42]  Types of claims:**  Any type of claim for recovery of money up to $5,000 falls within small claims court jurisdiction. [CCP §116.220(a)]

This includes most contract and tort claims, as well as statutory actions for recovery of money. [See *Miller v. Mun.Ct.* (1943) 22 C2d 818, 852, 142 P2d 297, 316— consumer action under Emergency Price Control Act]

It also includes *civil rights actions* (including employment and housing discrimination) where the claim is $5,000 or less. [Civ.C. §52.2]

(2) **[3:43]  Joinder of individual actions:**  Numerous plaintiffs can file similar claims against a single defendant, and these can be consolidated for trial in a small claims court. It makes no difference that the actions are filed simultaneously as a coordinated effort. [*City & County of San Francisco v. Small Claims Division, Mun.Ct.* (1983) 141 CA3d 470, 473, 190 CR 340, 342— numerous homeowners filed separate small claims actions against S.F. Airport for damages from airport noise and pollution]

(3) **[3:44]  Annual limitation—no more than two actions exceeding $2,500:**  No one may file more than two small claims actions for more than $2,500 in the same calendar year anywhere in the state. Plaintiff must file a declaration stating compliance with this two-action limit whenever the demand exceeds $2,500. [CCP §116.231]

(a) [3:44a] **Exception—actions by local public entities:** There is no limitation on the number of small claims actions that may be filed by local public entities such as cities, counties, school districts, etc. But any such action involving between $2,500 and $5,000 must be transferred out of the small claims division if defendant advises the court in writing that he or she is represented by counsel. [CCP §116.231]

(4) [3:44.1] **No assigned claims:** Except as noted below, no action may be maintained in small claims court on an assigned claim by the assignee thereof. [CCP §116.420]

Exceptions: Small claims actions are allowed by a trustee in bankruptcy; or by the holder of a security agreement, retail installment contract or lien contract, if not an assignee for collection. Also, local governments that are self-insured for workers' compensation purposes may file subrogation claims against those responsible for their workers' injuries. [See CCP §116.420]

(5) [3:45] **No splitting of claims:** Nor may a plaintiff sue on only *part* of what is basically a *single claim*. Suit on any part bars later suit on the balance. For example, if a landlord sues for only *part* of the rent owed when the action was filed, no later suit can be brought for the balance. [*Lekse v. Mun.Ct.* (1982) 138 CA3d 188, 194, 187 CR 698, 702—second small claims judgment held void]

(6) [3:46] **Equitable relief:** A small claims court can grant equitable relief in the form of rescission, restitution, reformation or specific performance, in connection with any money damage claim otherwise within its jurisdiction. [CCP §116.220(b)]

(7) [3:47] **Defendant may counterclaim:** Counterclaims are never mandatory in small claims actions. But defendant has the option of filing a claim against plaintiff in the same proceeding. The claims need not relate to the same subject matter. [See CCP §116.360; *Universal City Nissan, Inc. v. Sup.Ct. (Magdamo)* (1998) 65 CA4th 203, 205, 75 CR2d 910, 911]

(a) [3:47.1] **Counterclaim in excess of small claims jurisdiction:** If defendant's claim is for more than $5,000 and arises out of the same transaction or event as plaintiff's claim, defendant must file a *separate action* in a court of competent jurisdiction and seek transfer of the small claims action. In ruling on a transfer motion, the small claims court may either:

> — render judgment on the small claims case prior to the transfer;
> — transfer without rendering judgment; or
> — refuse to transfer on the grounds that the "ends of justice" would not be served thereby. [CCP §116.390]

(8) [3:48] **Disadvantages of small claims actions:** There are a number of special considerations re filing a small claims action:

  (a) [3:48.1] **No jury:** There is no right to jury trial *at any point* in a small claims action, including on appeal of a small claims judgment to the superior court. [CCP §116.770(b); *Crouchman v. Sup.Ct. (El Dorado Investors)* (1988) 45 C3d 1167, 1173, 248 CR 626, 628]

  (b) [3:49] **Limited right of appeal:** A defendant may appeal from an adverse small claims court judgment and obtain a trial de novo in superior court. But a *plaintiff cannot;* having chosen the small claims forum, plaintiff must accept the result. [CCP §116.710(a); see *Linton v. Sup.Ct. (Obinna)* (1997) 53 CA4th 1097, 1105-1106, 62 CR2d 202, 203]

Similar rules apply where a small claims court defendant files a claim for affirmative relief against plaintiff: I.e., if defendant wins, *plaintiff* can appeal from the judgment. But defendant cannot appeal an adverse decision on its own affirmative claim; having chosen to assert its claim in small claims court, it must accept the result. [CCP §116.710(b); see *Linton v. Sup.Ct. (Obinna)*, supra, 53 CA4th at 1105-1106, 62 CR2d at 203]

A different judge must hear the appeal. [CCP §116.770(a); see *General Elec. Capital Auto. Fin'l Services, Inc. v. Appellate Division (Harris)* (2001) 88 CA4th 136, 142, 105 CR2d 552, 556-557]

  1) [3:49.1] **Appeal allowing trial de novo on all claims?** An appeal to the superior court "shall consist of a new hearing"; and "the scope of the hearing shall include the claims of all parties . . ." [CCP §116.770(a),(d)]

Even so, courts are split on whether an appellant can obtain *affirmative relief* in superior court. (E.g., where D appeals from a small claims judgment that awarded P $2,000 and D nothing, can the superior court award D $1,000?) [See *Linton v. Sup.Ct. (Obinna)*, su-

pra, 53 CA4th at 1105-1106, 62 CR2d at 203,
207-208—yes, superior court must retry all
claims; *Universal City Nissan, Inc. v. Sup.Ct.
(Magdamo)* (1998) 65 CA4th 203, 207, 75
CR2d 910, 912—same; compare *Township
Homes v. Sup.Ct. (Spehar)* (1994) 22 CA4th
1587, 1595, 27 CR2d 852, 857—no, defendant's claim can be asserted *only as an offset*
to plaintiff's claim]

2) **Other considerations re appeal**

- [3:50]   Note also that *defendant's insurer*
may appeal a judgment against defendant
exceeding $2,500 if it *stipulates that its
policy covers* the matter on which the judgment is based. [CCP §116.710(c)]

- [3:51]   *Reimbursement of expenses on
appeal:* The superior court may (discretionary) award either party up to $150 for reim-
bursement of attorney fees, plus up to $150
for lost earnings and transportation expenses in connection with the appeal,
"where necessary to achieve substantial
justice." [CCP §116.780(c)]

In addition, if the appeal was "without substantial merit" and *not in good faith*, but was
intended to harass or delay, the court may
—after notice and hearing—award up to
$1,000 for reimbursement of attorney fees,
plus up to $1,000 for lost earnings and
transportation expenses. [CCP §116.790]

- [3:51.1]   *No consolidation with related
case:* An appeal from a judgment rendered
in a small claims action may *not* be consolidated with a related case pending in the
superior court because this would violate
the prohibitions against pretrial discovery,
jury trial and plaintiff's appeal in small
claims actions. [*Acuna v. Gunderson Chevrolet, Inc.* (1993) 19 CA4th 1467, 1472-
1473, 24 CR2d 62, 65]

- [3:51.2]   *No dismissal of small claims action:* The superior court has power to dismiss defendant's appeal from the small
claims judgment. But it cannot dismiss the
small claims action, even on plaintiff's request. [*Acuna v. Gunderson Chevrolet, Inc.*,
supra, 19 CA4th at 1473, 24 CR2d at 66]

• [3:51.3] *Judgment on a small claims appeal is final and not appealable:* The judgment of the superior court following trial de novo on a small claims appeal is "final and nonappealable." [CCP §116.780(a)]

[3:51.4] This renders a small claims appeal judgment *immune from virtually any postjudgment attack,* including motions:
— for new trial (CCP §659) or to vacate the judgment (CCP §663) (*Eloby v. Sup.Ct. (Candelieri)* (1978) 78 CA3d 972, 976, 144 CR 597, 598-599); or
— for relief from the judgment (CCP §473(b)) (*ERA-Trotter Girouard Assoc. v. Sup.Ct. (Miller)* (1996) 50 CA4th 1851, 1857, 58 CR2d 381, 384).

[3:51.5] There is a split of authority, however, on whether a petition for *rehearing* can be granted. [See *Adamson v. Sup.Ct. (M. M. Bitker)* (1980) 113 CA3d 505, 508-509, 169 CR 866, 868—yes; *ERA-Trotter Girouard Assoc. v. Sup.Ct. (Miller),* supra, 50 CA4th at 1857, 58 CR2d at 384—no]

[3:51.6] Appellate review may be had by superior court certification of issues to the court of appeal, to secure uniformity of decision or settle important questions of law. [CRC 63]

Also, if there is a need for statewide precedent on an issue, a court of appeal may entertain a petition for extraordinary writ. [*ERA-Trotter Girouard Assoc. v. Sup.Ct. (Miller),* supra, 50 CA4th at 1857, 58 CR2d at 384, fn. 4]

(c) [3:52] **No representation at hearing:** An attorney, or an insurer or other expert in the matter, may assist a party before or after the hearing, but *not* during the conduct of the hearing. [CCP §§116.530-116.531]

(d) [3:52.1] **Limited appearances through representatives:** No one other than the plaintiff or defendant may take part in a small claims action except in the following cases: [CCP §116.540(a)]

1) [3:52.2] **Corporations:** Corporations may appear through a regular employee or officer or

director appointed for purposes other than appearance in small claims court. [CCP §116.540(b); see *Nebel v. Sulak* (1999) 73 CA4th 1363, 1368, 87 CR2d 385, 388-389]

2) [3:52.3] **Partnerships and other entities:** Similarly, partnerships and other entities may appear through a regular employee or partner, officer or director engaged for purposes other than representing the party in small claims court. [CCP §116.540(c); see *Nebel v. Sulak,* supra, 73 CA4th at 1368, 87 CR2d at 388-389]

3) [3:52.4] **Sole proprietors:** A representative may appear for a party doing business as a sole proprietorship if:
   — the party's claim can be proved or disputed by *admissible business records* and there is no other issue of fact in the case; and
   — the representative is a regular employee of the party for purposes other than representing the party in small claims court and is qualified to testify to the identity and mode of preparation of the business records. [CCP §116.540(d)]

4) [3:52.5] **Spouses:** Where both spouses are named as parties, either may appear on behalf of both if:
   — the claim involved is a joint claim;
   — the other spouse consents; and
   — the court determines that the "interests of justice" would be served. [CCP §116.540(j)]

5) [3:52.6] **Nonresidents sued on claims relating to their local property:** A nonresident owner of real property may defend against a claim relating to that property without a personal appearance by (i) submitting written declarations and/or (ii) allowing another person to appear on his or her behalf (provided that person is not compensated and has not appeared on behalf of others in small claims actions more than four times during the calendar year). [CCP §116.540(g)]

(e) [3:53] **No collateral estoppel:** Recognizing that the parties may not have fully litigated all issues because of the small amounts involved, a small claims judgment will not be given collateral estoppel effect in other proceedings. [*Vandenberg v. Sup.Ct. (Centennial Ins. Co.)* (1999) 21 C4th 815, 829, 88 CR2d 366, 375]

1) **[3:53.1] Includes trial de novo in superior court:** If a small claims judgment is appealed to the superior court, the matter is tried *de novo*. But the hearing is "conducted informally," just as in the small claims court (see CCP §116.770(b)), and it is generally impossible to know precisely what issues were actually litigated and decided. Therefore, the superior court judgment is *not* entitled to collateral estoppel effect in later litigation. [*Rosse v. DeSoto Cab Co.* (1995) 34 CA4th 1047, 1052-1053, 40 CR2d 680, 683]

(f) **[3:54] No discovery in small claims court or on appeal:** There is no right of discovery in a small claims action, nor in de novo proceedings on appeal to the superior court. [CCP §116.310(b); *Rosenberg v. Sup.Ct. (Cantu)* (1998) 67 CA4th 860, 865, 79 CR2d 365, 368]

(g) **[3:54.1] Use of hearsay evidence in small claims court and on appeal:** Because small claims courts are designed for unsophisticated litigants with no knowledge of the rules of evidence, relevant hearsay evidence is admissible ... subject only to the law of privileges and to Ev.C. §352 (discretionary exclusion where evidentiary burdens outweigh benefits). [*Houghtaling v. Sup.Ct. (Rossi)* (1993) 17 CA4th 1128, 1139, 21 CR2d 855, 861 — affidavit by out-of-state witness admissible in small claims hearing]

The same rule applies on a trial *de novo* in superior court following defendant's appeal from a small claims judgment because the parties usually appear in propria persona in such proceedings. [*Houghtaling v. Sup.Ct. (Rossi)*, supra, 17 CA4th at 1139, 21 CR2d at 861]

(h) **[3:54.2] Plaintiff cannot obtain reclassification for increased damages:** Filing a small claims action *waives* damages over $5,000. If the damages exceed that sum, plaintiff must dismiss the small claims action and file an independent action in superior court. [*Jellinek v. Sup.Ct. (Duvall)* (1991) 228 CA3d 652, 656, 279 CR 6, 8]

Rules applicable to reclassifying limited civil cases (¶3:108) do not appear applicable to small claims actions (CCP §87(a)).

(i) **[3:54.3] No involuntary transfers to small claims court:** Conversely, if a claimant chooses to file a limited civil case, it cannot be transferred to the small claims division without the claimant's consent. Claims for $5,000 or less are within the *concurrent jurisdiction* of the small claims division and the superior court. [*Rosenberg v. Sup.Ct. (Cantu)* (1998) 67 CA4th 860, 867, 79 CR2d 365, 368]

(9) [3:55] **No subsequent action for malicious prosecution:** Defendants who win a small claims action, either in the original trial or after de novo review, *cannot* turn around and sue the plaintiff for malicious prosecution. Rationale: Small claims proceedings are not designed to provide a springboard for further litigation. [*Pace v. Hillcrest Motor Co.* (1980) 101 CA3d 476, 479, 161 CR 662, 664; see *Cooper v. Pirelli Cable Corp.* (1984) 160 CA3d 294, 299, 206 CR 581, 584]

⇨[3:56] *PRACTICE POINTER:* If you are asked to file suit on a claim where the net recovery to the client (after your fees) is likely to be less than $5,000, don't hesitate to recommend that the client file in small claims court.

For this reason, you need to be familiar with small claims court rules and procedures. Keep on hand copies of the official *Small Claims Forms* that you can give to the client.

5. [3:57] **Determining Amount in Controversy:** As seen above, whether an action is classified as a limited or unlimited civil case usually depends on whether the demand or value of the property in controversy exceeds $25,000.

"Amount in controversy" means the amount of the demand, or the recovery sought, or the value of the property, or the amount of the lien, which is in controversy in the action—exclusive of attorney fees, interest and costs. [CCP §85(a)]

a. [3:58] **Prayer of complaint determinative:** Whether an action qualifies as a limited civil case is determined initially from the prayer for relief (demand) in plaintiff's complaint . . . *not* from the evidence at trial or the amount of the ultimate judgment. Thus, unless the prayer is fraudulent or fictitious *on its face,* a demand for more than $25,000 establishes jurisdiction in an unlimited civil case. [CCP §§85, 88; *Engebretson & Co., Inc. v. Harrison* (1981) 125 CA3d 436, 444-445, 178 CR 77, 82 (involving superior vs. municipal court jurisdiction)]

Once a case is classified as a limited civil case, that classification normally continues throughout the case. On the other hand, the failure to classify it as limited civil case does not affect the court's power to award a lesser amount; i.e., a judgment for less than $25,000 is not invalid for lack of jurisdiction. [*Rodley v. Curry* (1898) 120 C 541, 543, 52 P 999, 1000]

But there are deterrents to exaggerated claims; and the court can *reclassify* a case that "necessarily" involves less than $25,000 as a limited civil case. *See ¶3:112 ff.*

(1) [3:59] **Demand "in excess of $25,000" precludes limited civil case:** The exact amount of damages is not required to be specified in the complaint. A complaint seeking damages "in excess of $25,000" is all that is required to establish that the action is not a limited civil case. [*Engebretson & Co., Inc. v. Harrison*, supra]

(2) [3:60] **Property actions—value of property in controversy:** Plaintiff's simple allegation that the value of the property in controversy exceeds $25,000 is all that is required to establish that the action is not a limited civil case—even if it turns out at trial that the property was not worth so much.

(3) [3:61] **Actions for rent:** Where the total rent owed at the time of filing suit is $25,000 or less, the action is a limited civil case. [CCP §86(a)(4); *see ¶3:11*]

(a) [3:62] **Effect of rent accruing:** If the complaint also seeks rent accruing during the pendency of the action, there is always a *potential* that if the trial is delayed long enough, the damages may exceed $25,000. (Example: Prayer for back rent of $20,500 plus rent accruing at the rate of $800 per month; damages will exceed $25,000 within 6 months.) But this potential is not enough to prevent the action from being a limited civil case at the outset of the action. Such status attaches at the outset and continues until it appears that the damages have *in fact* exceeded $25,000. [*Babcock v. Antis* (1979) 94 CA3d 823, 830, 156 CR 673, 676 (disapproved on other grounds in *Snukal v. Flightways Mfg., Inc.* (2000) 23 C4th 754, 775, 98 CR2d 1, 19-20, fn. 6)]

[3:63] *Reserved.*

(4) [3:64] **Personal injury and death actions:** The amount of damages sought must not be alleged. [CCP §425.10(b), *discussed at ¶6:279 ff.*]

➪[3:65] *PRACTICE POINTER:* To qualify the case as an unlimited civil case, the complaint should allege, "The total amount of damages sought exceeds $25,000." Conversely, to qualify it as a limited civil case, the allegation should be,

"The total amount of damages sought in this action does not exceed $25,000."

(5) [3:66] **Punitive damages claims:** A complaint seeking punitive damages may *not* allege the amount of punitives sought. [Civ.C. §3295(e), *discussed at ¶6:291 ff.*]

[3:67] *Reserved.*

b. [3:68] **Deterrents to exaggerated demands:** Although plaintiff can avoid an action being classified as a limited civil case simply by claiming damages in excess of $25,000 (*see ¶3:58*), there are several deterrents to exaggerating the amount of a claim to avoid such classification:

(1) [3:69] **Costs penalty:** If plaintiff fails to recover more than $25,000, plaintiff loses the *right* to court costs (filing fees, witness fees, jury fees, etc.). However, the trial judge has *discretion* to award such costs nonetheless. [CCP §1033(a)]

(2) [3:70] **Court procedures as deterrents:** As a practical matter, procedures applicable to cases not classified as limited civil cases may deter inflating claims in order to avoid that classification: e.g., greater delay in getting to trial in many courts; more expensive discovery (*see ¶8:1806 ff.*); and mandatory judicial arbitration of smaller claims (*see ¶13:21 ff.*).

(3) [3:71] **Court's power to reclassify as limited civil case:** In addition, the court has the power to reclassify as a limited civil case cases that *necessarily involve* less than $25,000. Such reclassification may be granted at any time—i.e., even at the time of trial. [See CCP §403.040(a), *discussed at ¶3:112 ff.*]

[3:72-83] *Reserved.*

c. [3:84] **Matters excluded in determining amount in controversy:** Attorney fees, interest and costs are excluded in determining the amount in controversy for purposes of determining whether an action is a limited civil case. This allows a court handling a limited civil case to award up to $25,000 *plus* applicable interest, attorney fees and court costs. [CCP §85(a)]

(1) [3:85] **Interest excluded:** Interest on the principal sum demanded is not counted in determining the amount in controversy. [CCP §85(a)]

This applies both to interest accrued *before* the action was filed and interest accruing after filing up to the date of judgment. [*Christian v. Sup.Ct.* (1898) 122 C 117, 120, 54 P 518, 519]

    (a) [3:86] **Example:** Claim for $25,000 principal due under promissory note, *plus* $3,000 interest accrued before action filed, *plus* additional interest accruing to date of judgment is a limited civil case.

  (2) [3:87] **Costs excluded:** The amount of court costs that may be awarded plaintiff at the end of the case is also not counted in determining the amount in controversy. [See CCP §85(a)]

    (a) [3:88] **Example:** Claim for $25,000 damages "plus costs of suit" is still a limited civil case.

  (3) [3:89] **Attorney fees excluded:** A demand for attorney fees is not counted in determining the "amount in controversy." [CCP §85(a)]

Whether recoverable under statute or by contract, fee awards are generally treated *as costs incidental to the judgment*, not as part of the damages. [See *Stokus v. Marsh* (1990) 217 CA3d 647, 651, 266 CR 90, 92]

    (a) [3:90] **Example:** A claim for $25,000 due under a promissory note plus $1,000 attorney fees as authorized by said note is a limited civil case.

    (b) [3:91] **Fees exceeding $25,000:** The law is unclear whether attorney fees in excess of $25,000 may be awarded in a limited civil case:

      • [3:91.1] One case holds "the award for attorney fees *cannot in itself* exceed the jurisdictional limit." [*Bakkebo v. Mun.Ct. (Indian Hill Investment Co.)* (1981) 124 CA3d 229, 236, 177 CR 239, 242 (emphasis added)]

      • [3:91.2] But a later case is contra. [See *Stokus v. Marsh*, supra, 217 CA3d at 653, 266 CR at 94 — upholding *$75,000* fee award in hotly-contested municipal court unlawful detainer action]

  d. [3:92] **Waiver of excess demand to retain limited civil case classification:** If a complaint is captioned as a limited civil case but the alleged damages or demand exceeds $25,000, the excess may be waived and the action may continue as a limited civil case. [CCP §403.040(f)]

    ⇨[3:93] *PRACTICE POINTER:* In deciding whether to waive excess damages, plaintiff's attorney should consider the factors listed at ¶*3:40.5* (re whether to file as a limited civil case initially).

(1) **[3:94]  Procedure for waiving excess:**  The simplest procedure is to amend the prayer and limit the demand to $25,000.

Absent such amendment, a waiver may not be implied. [See *Williams v. Rosinksy Motor Co.* (1955) 133 CA2d Supp. 798, 803, 284 P2d 979, 981] (Comment: This case may be questioned in light of *Babcock v. Antis*, discussed at ¶*3:62*.)

⇨ **[3:95]  *PRACTICE POINTER:***  To avoid any doubt, consider inserting the following clause in any complaint in which you wish to protect the limited civil case classification:
— "Plaintiff hereby waives and remits any amount or relief in excess of that available in a limited civil case."

(2) **[3:96]  Waiver after judgment:**  If a judgment has been rendered in a limited civil case, it will not be set aside merely because the complaint prayed for damages accruing daily that *potentially* could have exceeded $25,000. As long as this did not materialize, the action retains its limited civil case classification. And, in any event, the trial or appellate court can order the complaint amended to limit damages to the court's jurisdiction . . . even after the judgment was rendered. [See *Babcock v. Antis* (1979) 94 CA3d 823, 829-831, 156 CR 673, 676-677; *see also* ¶*3:62*]

e.  **Joinder of claims as affecting amount in controversy**

(1) **[3:97]  Single plaintiff vs. single defendant:**  If there is only one plaintiff suing one defendant, all of plaintiff's claims are *aggregated* in determining the amount in controversy to determine if the action is a limited civil case. [*Hammell v. Sup.Ct.* (1932) 217 C 5, 7, 17 P2d 101, 102]

(a) **[3:98]  Example:**  P sues D for $10,000 on a promissory note and for $18,000 property damage. The amount in controversy is $28,000, so the action should *not* be filed as a limited civil case.

**[3:99]**  *Reserved.*

(b) **[3:100]  Class actions:**  Claims of class members are aggregated in determining the amount in controversy; *see* ¶*3:39*.

(2) **[3:101]  Single plaintiff vs. several defendants:**
If plaintiff sues several defendants on a *joint* obligation (i.e., a single demand against all defendants), that is the amount in controversy.

But where *separate* claims are asserted against each defendant, each demand is treated separately in determining the amount in controversy.

(a) **[3:102]  Example:**  P has three separate $10,000 insurance policies covering his $30,000 sports car. If the car is stolen, and P sues the three carriers in a single action, the amount in controversy is $10,000 as to each defendant; so that the case qualifies as a limited civil case. [*Heavilin v. Westchester Fire Ins. Co.* (1936) 12 CA2d 695, 56 P2d 252, 253]

[3:103]  *Reserved.*

(b) **[3:104]  Compare—one claim exceeding $25,000:**  If any of several claims joined in the complaint exceeds $25,000, no part of the case is subject to the rules governing limited civil cases . . . provided the rules on joinder of claims are complied with (¶*6:262 ff.*).

(3) **Several plaintiffs vs. one or more defendants**

(a) **[3:105]  Joint claim:**  If the plaintiffs have a common interest in the claim sued upon (e.g., as partners, cotenants, joint obligees), their total claim is the amount in controversy—even though each plaintiff's share is a lesser amount. Example: Husband and Wife sue for $30,000 damage to their community property; the amount in controversy is $30,000, although each spouse's interest is only half that sum. [*Frost v. Mighetto* (1937) 22 CA2d 612, 614-615, 71 P2d 932, 934]

(b) **[3:106]  Separate claims:**  However, if each plaintiff's claim is separate from the others, the amounts are *not* aggregated. Example: P-1, P-2 and P-3 each claim $10,000 property damage as the result of D's acts; these claims are separate (not joint), and therefore they cannot be aggregated. The action must be filed as a limited civil case. [See *Hammell v. Sup.Ct.* (1932) 217 C 5, 7, 17 P2d 101, 102]

(c) **[3:107]  Compare—one claim exceeds $25,000:**  Again, however, if any of the claims joined exceeds $25,000, the action does not qualify as a limited civil case and therefore all properly joined claims for lesser sums will be adjudicated under the procedures governing cases not so classified. [See *Emery v. Pacific Employers Ins. Co.* (1937) 8 C2d 663, 667, 67 P2d 1046, 1049]

f.  [3:108] **Amendment of complaint affecting jurisdictional classification:**  The plaintiff (or cross-complainant) has the right to change the jurisdictional classification of the case by amending the complaint; i.e., by increasing the demand to more than $25,000 and changing the caption to show that it is *not* a limited civil case. Upon the *filing* of the amended complaint and "simultaneous" payment of reclassification fees (*see ¶3:121 ff.*), the clerk will promptly reclassify the case. [CCP §403.020]

*Compare:* No reclassification fee is required where the amendment lowers the demand, changing the jurisdictional classification from unlimited to limited; the clerk will promptly reclassify the case accordingly. [CCP §§403.020(a), 403.060(c)]

(1)  [3:109] **Amendment may require leave of court:**  Plaintiff has the right to amend the complaint once, without leave of court, *before* defendant answers or its demurrer is heard (CCP §472, *see ¶6:602*). Thereafter, however, plaintiff must obtain leave of court to file an amended complaint (CCP §473(a)). *See discussion of procedure at ¶6:611 ff.*

[3:109.1-109.2]  *Reserved.*

(a)  [3:109.3] **Limitation—no amendment after verdict in limited civil case:**  The complaint may not be amended to reclassify the case as unlimited after a verdict for more than $25,000 has been rendered. The defendant may have taken actions and adopted trial strategy in reliance upon the limited amount of damages alleged in the complaint. [*Wozniak v. Lucutz* (2002) 102 CA4th 1031, 1045, 126 CR2d 310, 320]

[3:109.4]  *Reserved.*

(2)  [3:109.5] **Caption must indicate reclassification:**  Where a case is reclassified as the result of an amended complaint, amended cross-complaint or other amended pleading, the pleading's caption must so indicate and state both the former and current classification (e.g., "LIMITED CIVIL CASE RECLASSIFIED BY THIS PLEADING AS AN UNLIMITED CIVIL CASE" or other words to this effect). [CRC 201(f)(11)]

g.  [3:110] **Cross-complaint affecting jurisdictional classification:**  Classification as a limited or unlimited civil case may also be affected by a cross-complaint filed in the action.

(1) **[3:111]** **Cross-complaint for more than $25,000 in action filed as limited civil case:** Where a complaint is filed as a limited civil case but the cross-complaint seeks more than $25,000 (or other relief unavailable in a limited civil case), the clerk will reclassify the case as an unlimited civil case upon compliance with the following procedures (CCP §403.030):

    (a) **[3:111.1]** **Caption of cross-complaint:** The caption of the cross-complaint must state words to the following effect: "LIMITED CIVIL CASE RECLASSIFIED BY THIS PLEADING AS AN UNLIMITED CIVIL CASE." [CCP §403.030; CRC 201(f)(11)]

    (b) **[3:111.2]** **Fees payable by cross-complainant:** The reclassification fees (*see ¶3:121*) are payable by the party who files the cross-complaint. [CCP §403.030]

    [3:111.3-111.4] *Reserved.*

(2) **[3:111.5]** **Cross-complaint for less than $25,000 in action filed as unlimited civil case:** If the action is filed as an unlimited civil case, the court has jurisdiction to render judgment on a cross-complaint in *any* amount. [See *Sullivan v. California Realty Co.* (1904) 142 C 201, 206-208, 75 P 767, 769-770—plaintiff lost on complaint and defendant awarded $180 on cross-complaint]

But the action's classification as an unlimited civil case may be affected by *dismissal* of the complaint. I.e., if the amount demanded in the cross-complaint is *less than $25,000*, the court may on its own motion or on defendant's motion *reclassify* the action as a limited civil case. [See CCP §403.040, *discussed at ¶3:123*]

[3:111.6-111.9] *Reserved.*

h. **[3:111.10]** **Reclassification by stipulation:** The parties may stipulate to reclassify the case within the time allowed for the initial responsive pleading. [CCP §403.050]

As with reclassifications resulting from amended pleading, the caption of the stipulation must state that the action is reclassified and the former and current classifications (*see ¶3:109.5*). [CRC 201(f)(11)]

If the case is being reclassified as an *unlimited* civil case, a *reclassification fee* must be paid when the stipulation is filed; otherwise the clerk will not reclassify it. (No fee is required where the case is being reclassified as a limited civil case.) [CCP §§403.050(b), 403.060(c)]

6. [3:112] **Motion to Reclassify Action:** Where a case has been misclassified by failure to properly label the pleadings (e.g., plaintiff fails to caption the case as a limited civil case or to check the appropriate box on the civil case cover sheet, *see Form 6:Q.1*), any party may file a motion to have the case reclassified, or the court may do so on its own motion. [CCP §403.040(a)]

Reclassification, however, is not essential to subject matter jurisdiction. The court is not required to reclassify an action in order to render a valid judgment; i.e., the fact that the judgment to be rendered is one that might have been rendered in a limited civil case does *not* affect the court's power to render judgment in an unlimited civil case. [See CCP §403.040(e)]

a. [3:113] **Time limit for motion:** A motion to reclassify may be made at any time. If made by a plaintiff (or cross-complainant or petitioner), the motion *must* be granted if made within the time allowed for amending the initial complaint as a matter of right (i.e., before an answer is filed or the demurrer hearing; *see ¶6:303*). If the motion is made by a defendant (or cross-defendant), the motion must be granted if made within the time allowed for filing a responsive pleading. [CCP §403.040(a)]

If the motion is made later, the moving party must demonstrate *good cause* for not seeking reclassification earlier. [CCP §403.040(b)]

However, the court may reclassify the case on its own motion at any time. [CCP §403.040(a)]

(1) [3:114] **Limitation—no reclassification after verdict:** A limited civil case may *not* be reclassified after a verdict for more than $25,000 has been rendered. [*Wozniak v. Lucutz* (2002) 102 CA4th 1031, 1044, 126 CR2d 310, 319; *see ¶3:109.3*]

(2) [3:114.1] **Compare—no extension of time to plead:** A motion to reclassify does not extend the moving party's time to amend or answer or otherwise respond. [CCP §403.040(a)]

c. [3:115] **Procedural safeguards:** To assure that reclassifications to the limited civil case category are not used simply to clear court calendars, adequate procedural safeguards must be provided: i.e., adequate notice, an opportunity to be heard and an adequate record. [See *Kent v. Sup.Ct. (Kramer Motors, Inc.)* (1992) 2 CA4th 1392, 1394, 4 CR2d 21, 23—reversing sua sponte transfer to municipal court without hearing or record]

(1) [3:116] **Notice and hearing required:** Reclassification may be granted on either a party's motion or the court's own motion. [CCP §403.040(a)]

Thus, the usual motion procedures apply, including adequate notice and opportunity to be heard. [*Stern v. Sup.Ct. (Getz, Krycler & Jakubovits)* (2003) 105 CA4th 223, 129 CR2d 275, 279—error to reclassify on court's own motion at status conference where parties had no prior notice of court's intent to do so and no opportunity to present evidence contesting reclassification]

*Compare—waiver:* The opposing party's failure to request a continuance to file opposition may constitute a waiver of lack of notice. [See *Campisi v. Sup.Ct. (Broadway Motors Ford)* (1993) 17 CA4th 1833, 1839, 22 CR2d 335, 338-339]

(2) [3:117] **Adequate record required:** An adequate record must be made of the hearing on the motion to reclassify the action, to enable appellate courts to determine whether the trial judge was fully informed of the facts and whether those facts support the exercise of the court's discretion. [*Walker v. Sup.Ct. (Residential Construction Enterprises)* (1991) 53 C3d 257, 271, 279 CR 576, 585; *Andre v. Sup.Ct. (Cheatham)* (1991) 2 CA4th 11, 19, 2 CR2d 815, 819, fn. 7]

That record may contain such matters as:

— CCP §425.11 statements of damages;
— Deposition testimony and discovery documents;
— Results of *arbitration* (where the case has been arbitrated); and
— The judge's own personal familiarity with the facts and circumstances of the case (e.g., through unsuccessful settlement conferences). [See *Campbell v. Sup.Ct. (Cala Foods)* (1989) 213 CA3d 147, 150, 261 CR 509, 512; *Williams v. Sup.Ct. (RD Instruments)* (1989) 216 CA3d 378, 386, 264 CR 677, 680]

d. [3:118] **Determining whether case correctly classified:** A motion for reclassification must be granted "regardless of any fault or lack of fault" (CCP §403.040(a)). But the statute does not state *how* the court is to determine whether the case is classified incorrectly. Instead, the Judicial Council is granted authority to prescribe rules governing the procedure for reclassification. [CCP §403.090]

No such rules have as yet been adopted. It is anticipated, however, that the Judicial Council may look to case law decided prior to trial court unification which determined when a superior court case was transferable to municipal court:

(1) [3:119]  **Test—whether case *necessarily involves less than $25,000*:**  It is not enough that recovery of more than $25,000 is improbable or highly unlikely. Rather, it must be shown that the claim *necessarily involves less than $25,000*; i.e., that a greater recovery "could not be obtained" or is "virtually unobtainable." [See *Walker v. Sup.Ct. (Residential Construction Enterprises)* (1991) 53 C3d 257, 269-270, 279 CR 576, 583-584]

   (a) [3:119.1]  **No determination of merits:**  The trial court must assume the existence of facts supporting the complaint. It must not evaluate the case based on its own determination of the merits. [See *Walker v. Sup.Ct. (Residential Construction Enterprises)*, supra, 53 C3d at 269, 279 CR at 584; see also *Chahal v. Sup.Ct. (Greyhound Lines, Inc.)* (1999) 73 CA4th 399, 402, 86 CR2d 428, 430]

   (b) [3:119.2]  **Settlement negotiations protected:**  Settlement negotiations should not be improperly divulged in connection with a motion to reclassify the action as a limited civil case: "The policy reason behind this concern is plain: inappropriate disclosure might discourage plaintiffs from offering to settle below the . . . jurisdictional amount." [See *Walker v. Sup.Ct. (Residential Construction Enterprises)*, supra, 53 C3d at 271, 279 CR at 584]

   (c) [3:119.3]  **Compare—evaluation based on conducting settlement conference:**  But it is not improper for a judge to reclassify a case using the judge's *personal evaluation* based on the parties' settlement conference disclosures. Indeed, this may be the best way of valuing the case. [*Campisi v. Sup.Ct. (Broadway Motors)* (1993) 17 CA4th 1833, 1838, 22 CR2d 335, 339—judge also discussed case with other judges assigned to early disposition program]

(2) [3:120]  **Application:**  Courts proceed with caution in determining whether a verdict will necessarily involve less than $25,000 because improper classification could impair plaintiff's right of recovery. [See *Walker v. Sup.Ct. (Residential Construction Enterprises)*, supra, 53 C3d at 270-271, 279 CR at 584-585]

   • [3:120.1]  P's superior court complaint alleged no physical injury, medical expenses or wage loss, but claimed general damages exceeding $500,000. An arbitrator awarded $1,400. Based on the low arbitration award and the trial court's own familiarity with the facts of the case, a transfer to municipal court was upheld. [*Campbell v. Sup.Ct. (Cala Foods)* (1989) 213 CA3d 147, 153-154, 261 CR 509, 514, cited with approval in *Walker v. Sup.Ct. (Residential Construction Enterprises)*, supra, 53 C3d at 273, 279 CR at 586]

- **[3:120.2]** P's complaint alleged physical injury, $6,000 medical expenses and $40,000 wage loss. An arbitrator awarded only $17,000. But that did not "necessarily" establish a jury would award $25,000 or less. Hence, an order transferring the case to municipal court was an abuse of discretion. [*Williams v. Sup.Ct. (Gemco/Lucky Stores, Inc.)* (1990) 219 CA3d 171, 179-180, 268 CR 61, 66, cited with approval in *Walker v. Sup.Ct. (Residential Construction Enterprises)*, supra, 53 C3d at 273, 279 CR at 586]

e. **[3:121]** **Fee considerations:** Where a limited civil case is reclassified as an unlimited civil case, a reclassification fee ($125) must be paid to the court clerk. [CCP §403.060(a)]

If the reclassification fee is not paid at the time the amended complaint or other pleading is filed, the case will remain classified as a limited civil action. [CCP §403.060(b)]

No fee is due where a case is reclassified as a *limited* civil case. Nor is there a right to refund for the filing and appearance fees paid before reclassification. [CCP §403.060(c)]

f. **[3:122]** **Appellate review:** No immediate appeal lies from an order granting or denying a motion to reclassify the action. But an aggrieved party may file a petition for writ of mandamus in the court of appeal within 20 days after being served with notice of the order (the trial court may extend this time limit for up to an additional 10 days). A copy of the petition must be filed "immediately" with the superior court. [CCP §403.080; see *Yousafzai v. Hyundai Motor America* (1994) 22 CA4th 920, 925, 27 CR2d 569, 572]

[3:122.1-122.4] *Reserved.*

g. **[3:122.5]** **Procedures following reclassification:** The court may allow or require whatever amendment of pleadings, or supplemental pleadings, or other procedures as it determines may be necessary for the determination of the action or proceeding as reclassified. [CCP §403.070(b)]

(1) **[3:122.6]** **No effect on jurisdiction:** Reclassification does *not* affect the court's jurisdiction or any prior proceedings in the action. The action is deemed

commenced when the complaint was initially filed, not at the time of reclassification. [CCP §403.070]

(2) [3:122.7] **Motion for further reclassification:** After reclassification of an action as a limited civil case, plaintiff may move for reclassification as an unlimited civil case if able to later show a likelihood of a larger verdict. [*Williams v. Sup.Ct. (RD Instruments)* (1989) 216 CA3d 378, 386, 264 CR 677, 682, fn. 6]

7. [3:123] **Limitations on Subject Matter Jurisdiction:** The following are recognized exceptions and limitations on superior court subject matter jurisdiction:

a. [3:123.1] **Exclusive federal jurisdiction:** Superior courts lack subject matter jurisdiction in cases within the *exclusive* jurisdiction of federal courts (*see ¶3:611*).

b. [3:123.2] **Jurisdiction vested in other tribunals:** Superior courts lack subject matter jurisdiction in controversies which, by statute, are to be heard by other tribunals (e.g., workers' compensation claims must be heard by the Workers' Compensation Appeals Board; licensing matters by various state licensing authorities, etc.). [See *Greener v. Workers' Comp. Appeals Bd.* (1993) 6 C4th 1028, 1043, 25 CR2d 539, 548—no subject matter jurisdiction to enjoin enforcement of Workers' Compensation Act; *Smith v. California State Bar* (1989) 212 CA3d 971, 976, 261 CR 24, 27—no subject matter jurisdiction to hear challenges to State Bar admissions]

c. [3:123.3] **Disputes interfering with PUC regulations:** A superior court has no jurisdiction "to review, reverse, correct, or annul any order or decision of the (Public Utilities Commission) . . . *or interfere with* the commission in the performance of its official duties . . ." [Pub.Util.C. §1759(a) (emphasis and parentheses added)]

(1) [3:123.4] **Effect:** Actions against a public utility are barred in superior court wherever an award of damages "would simply have the effect of undermining a general supervisory or regulatory policy of the commission, i.e., when it would 'hinder' or 'frustrate' or 'interfere with' or 'obstruct' that policy." [*San Diego Gas & Elec. Co. v. Sup.Ct. (Covalt)* (1996) 13 C4th 893, 919, 55 CR2d 724, 738]

"The PUC has exclusive jurisdiction over the regulation and control of utilities, and once it has assumed jurisdiction, it cannot be hampered, interfered with, or second-guessed by a concurrent superior court action addressing the same issue." [*Hartwell Corp. v. Sup.Ct. (Santamaria)* (2002) 27 C4th 256, 275, 115 CR2d 874, 890 (internal quotes omitted)]

On the other hand, where the PUC does *not* possess *exclusive* regulatory authority over a matter, the district attorney may sue public utilities for violations of law. [*People ex rel. Orloff v. Pacific Bell* (2003) 31 C4th 1132, 1150-1151, 7 CR3d 315, 328-329]

**Caution:** These issues are presently before the California Supreme Court in *Pacific Gas & Elec. Co. v. Sup.Ct. (Emery)*, Case No. S104412.

(2) **Application**

- [3:123.5]   A court cannot adjudicate claims that magnetic fields from public utility power lines damaged plaintiff's property. Such adjudication would impermissibly interfere with the PUC's broad regulatory policy on this subject. [*San Diego Gas & Elec. Co. v. Sup.Ct. (Covalt)*, supra, 13 C4th at 915, 55 CR2d at 737]

- [3:123.6]   Likewise, a court may not adjudicate claims against a telephone company for failure to furnish adequate service where the PUC had approved the company's use of a tariff provision limiting its liability for ordinary negligence to credit allowance and had taken this provision into account in setting rates. [*Waters v. Pacific Tel. Co.* (1974) 12 C3d 1, 4, 114 CR 753, 754]

- [3:123.7]   Similarly, because the PUC's role is to ensure that water utilities comply with state and federal water quality standards, a superior court has no jurisdiction to issue injunctive relief for current water quality violations. A court injunction, predicated on a finding of utility noncompliance, would clearly conflict with the PUC's regulatory functions in determining the need to establish prospective remedial programs. [*Hartwell Corp. v. Sup.Ct. (Santamaria)*, supra, 27 C4th at 278, 115 CR2d at 892-893]

  [3:123.8-123.9]   *Reserved.*

- [3:123.10]   *Compare:* But damage claims that *would not hinder or frustrate* the commission's declared supervisory and regulatory policies are within the superior court's jurisdiction. [*Pink Dot, Inc. v. Teleport Communications Group* (2001) 89 CA4th 407, 417-418, 107 CR2d 392, 399—tariff filed with PUC cannot restrict utility's liability for *fraud and intentional misconduct; Cundiff v. GTE Calif., Inc.* (2002) 101 CA4th 1395, 1409, 125 CR2d 445, 454 —class action to recover rental charges for obsolete or nonexistent telephones does not challenge rates and are within superior court jurisdiction]

[3:123.11]   *Reserved.*

- [3:123.12]   *Compare:* Similarly, consumer fraud claims against a public utility are not within the PUC's exclusive regulatory authority. Therefore, district attorneys may prosecute such actions against a public utility as long as it will not jeopardize the PUC's own investigations or authority. [*People ex rel. Orloff v. Pacific Bell* (2003) 31 C4th 1132, 1151, 7 CR3d 315, 328-329]

[3:123.13-123.14]   *Reserved.*

(3) [3:123.15]   **Compare—"primary jurisdiction" doctrine:**   Where a superior court case involves issues that could be affected by the PUC's potential adoption of a policy or regulatory scheme, the court may (discretionary) invoke the "primary jurisdiction doctrine" and stay proceedings to allow the PUC to act first should it desire to do so. [*Wise v. Pacific Gas & Elec. Co.* (1999) 77 CA4th 287, 295, 91 CR2d 479, 485]

*Cross-refer:* The "primary jurisdiction doctrine" is discussed further at ¶*1:907 ff.*

[3:123.16-123.19]   *Reserved.*

d.   [3:123.20]   **Religious disputes:**   The First Amendment's freedom of religion clauses bar civil courts from exercising jurisdiction in cases involving a church's governance of "religious" or "ecclesiastical" matters. "These constitutional concepts of religious autonomy which assure both free exercise and nonestablishment apply to state as well as federal action through the incorporation of their principles into the Fourteenth Amendment due process clause." [*Schmoll v. Chapman Univ.* (1999) 70 CA4th 1434, 1438, 83 CR2d 426, 429, fn. 3]

Thus, a superior court cannot adjudicate a theological controversy, or questions of church discipline, ecclesiastical government or the conformity of church members to standards of morality. But a superior court *can* adjudicate disputes involving church *property rights* or *torts or criminal conduct* by members of the clergy. [*Jones v. Wolf* (1979) 443 US 595, 599-605, 99 S.Ct. 3020, 3023; *Molko v. Holy Spirit Ass'n* (1988) 46 C3d 1092, 1116-1117, 252 CR 122, 136; *Vukovich v. Radulovich* (1991) 235 CA3d 281, 292, 286 CR 547, 554]

- [3:123.21]   A superior court may not exercise jurisdiction in claims related to the *hiring, firing, discipline or administration* of clergy or other employees whose primary responsibility is dissemination of church doctrine. [*Higgins v. Maher* (1989) 210 CA3d 1168, 1175, 258 CR 757, 760-761 — no jurisdiction in Priest's action against Bishop for alleged defamation and wrongful removal from his position where acts taken were part of Bishop's administration of his ecclesiastical functions; *Schmoll v. Chapman Univ.*, supra, 70 CA4th at 1438, 83 CR2d at 429 — no FEHA claim by campus chaplain against church-affiliated university]

- [3:123.22] A court cannot adjudicate property disputes between competing factions in a church who are involved in an *ecclesiastical dispute.* [See *Metropolitan Philip v. Steiger* (2000) 82 CA4th 923, 930, 98 CR2d 605, 609-610 — civil courts ill-equipped to determine which faction represents the "true church"]

But a court may adjudicate a dispute that can be determined *by applying neutral principles of law* and *without reference to any ecclesiastical controversy.* [See *Singh v. Singh* (2004) 114 CA4th 1264, 1280-1281, 9 CR3d 4, 16-17 — based on evidence presented, court determined that church bylaws and religious traditions did *not* confer life term on directors]

[3:123.23] *Reserved.*

- [3:123.24] The First Amendment does not necessarily bar a church member's tort claims against a church or pastor for sexual abuse by the pastor. But a court cannot adjudicate such claims where the injurious conduct was allegedly "*dictated by a sincerely held religious belief* or carried out in accordance with established beliefs and practices of the religion to which the pastor belongs." [*Richelle L. v. Roman Catholic Archbishop of San Francisco* (2003) 106 CA4th 257, 279, 130 CR2d 601, 616 (emphasis added)]

- [3:123.24a] Nor are First Amendment rights impaired by enjoining an expelled church member from engaging in disruptive conduct during church services. [*Church of Christ in Hollywood v. Sup.Ct. (Lady Cage-Barile)* (2002) 99 CA4th 1244, 1257, 121 CR2d 810, 819 — church had right to treat her as trespasser]

e. [3:123.25] **Abstention re membership disputes in private organizations:** Courts *may* (discretionary) *decline* to exercise jurisdiction in disputes involving the rights and duties of membership in a private voluntary association: "(J)udicial attempts to construe ritual or obscure rules and laws of private organizations may lead the courts into what Professor Chafee called the 'dismal swamp.'" [*California Dental Ass'n v. American Dental Ass'n* (1979) 23 C3d 346, 353, 152 CR 546, 550]

(1) [3:123.26] **Test:** Courts may abstain where either:
- the challenged action "does not *plainly contravene*" the association's charter or bylaws; or
- if it does, where the interest in protecting the organization's autonomy *outweighs* the interest in protecting the aggrieved party's rights. [*California Dental Ass'n v. American Dental Ass'n,* supra, 23 C3d at 350, 152 CR at 548]

(2) **Application**

- [3:123.27] Because the National Football League's (NFL) operation of a European football league *did not "plainly contravene"* the NFL constitution, courts would *abstain* from interceding in a member club's dispute with the NFL regarding compelled participation in the European league. [*Oakland Raiders v. National Football League* (2001) 93 CA4th 572, 582, 113 CR2d 255, 262]

- [3:123.28] But judicial intervention is proper where the organization has adopted an *unreasonable* construction of a *plain and unambiguous provision* of its constitution or bylaws. In such cases, a judicial remedy does not seriously impair any interest of the members or the organization's interest in autonomy. [*California Dental Ass'n v. American Dental Ass'n,* supra, 23 C3d at 355, 152 CR at 552 — court directed organization's adjudicatory body to utilize standards required by organization's bylaws in deciding member's appeal]

[3:123.29-123.34] *Reserved.*

f. [3:123.35] **Cases lacking justiciable controversy:** To invoke a court's jurisdiction, there must be presented to the court "a *genuine and existing controversy,* calling for present adjudication as involving present rights." [*Housing Group v. United Nat'l Ins. Co.* (2001) 90 CA4th 1106, 1111, 109 CR2d 497, 501 (internal quotes omitted)]

- [3:123.36] Thus, a court may not exercise jurisdiction where the parties come to court with a *negotiated settlement* (no remaining issues to be determined) and ask only that the court appoint a judicial officer of their choosing to ratify it. [*Housing Group v. United Nat'l Ins. Co.,* supra, 90 CA4th at 1111, 109 CR2d at 501]

- [3:123.37] Likewise, courts should decline to exercise jurisdiction over a "sham" or "moot" action involving no actual controversy. [*Housing Group v. United Nat'l Ins. Co.,* supra, 90 CA4th at 1111, 109 CR2d at 501]

[3:123.38-123.39] *Reserved.*

g. [3:123.40] **Foreign sovereign immunity:** A foreign state (or any "agency" or "instrumentality" thereof) is immune from both federal and state court jurisdiction *except* as provided by federal law. [See 28 USC §1604]

(1) [3:123.41] **"Commercial activity" exception:** Foreign states may be sued in actions "based upon a commercial activity carried on in the United States . . . or upon an act outside the . . . United States in connection with a commercial activity of the foreign state that causes a direct effect in the United States." [28 USC §1606(a)(2)]

(2) [3:123.42] **Effect of federal removal jurisdiction:** Where there is no sovereign immunity, a foreign state can be sued in either federal or state courts. If sued in a state court, however, the foreign state may (and almost inevitably will) *remove* the action to federal court. [28 USC §1441(d)]

[3:123.43-123.44] *Reserved.*

*Cross-refer:* See detailed discussion in Schwarzer, Tashima & Wagstaffe, *Cal. Prac. Guide: Federal Civ. Pro. Before Trial* (TRG), Ch. 2B.

h. [3:123.45] **Indian tribal immunity:** An aboriginal American tribe is a sovereign nation and is subject to suit only where Congress has authorized the suit or the tribe has waived its immunity. [*Kiowa Tribe of Oklahoma v. Manufacturing Technologies, Inc.* (1998) 523 US 751, 754, 118 S.Ct. 1700, 1702; *Redding Rancheria v. Sup.Ct. (Hansard)* (2001) 88 CA4th 384, 387, 105 CR2d 773, 775]

Unlike foreign sovereign immunity, the immunity for aboriginal Indian tribes extends to activities both on and off the tribe's reservation; and no distinction is drawn between "governmental" and "commercial" activities. [*Kiowa Tribe of Oklahoma v. Manufacturing Technologies, Inc.*, supra, 523 US at 754, 118 S.Ct. at 1703; *Redding Rancheria v. Sup.Ct. (Hansard)*, supra, 88 CA4th at 387-388, 105 CR2d at 775-776]

The tribe's sovereign immunity does not, however, prevent plaintiff from suing *individual members* of the tribe. [*Redding Rancheria v. Sup.Ct. (Hansard)*, supra, 88 CA4th at 390, 105 CR2d at 777]

Nor does a tribe's sovereign immunity preclude a court from ordering discovery relating to the claimed immunity. [*Warburton/Buttner v. Sup.Ct. (Tunica-Biloxi Tribe of Louisiana)* (2002) 103 CA4th 1170, 1189, 127 CR2d 706, 721]

[3:123.46-123.49] *Reserved.*

i. **[3:123.50]** **Abatement based on related case in another superior court:** Sometimes, parties will file suits against each other in different superior courts, both suits relating to the same subject matter. (Example: P sues D for personal injuries in the county where the accident occurred; D sues P for injuries suffered in the same accident, but files suit in the county where both parties reside.)

In such cases, the established rule of "exclusive concurrent jurisdiction" applies: i.e., the first court to assert subject matter jurisdiction assumes it to the exclusion of all others, and has the power to enjoin the later proceedings in other courts. [See *Franklin & Franklin v. 7-Eleven Owners for Fair Franchising* (2000) 85 CA4th 1168, 1175, 102 CR2d 770, 774-775]

The rule is designed to avoid the spectacle of the same parties litigating the same issues in two different courts at the same time, "including the real possibility of unseemly conflict between courts that might arise if they were free to make contradictory decisions or awards." [*Franklin & Franklin v. 7-Eleven Owners for Fair Franchising*, supra, 85 CA4th at 1175, 102 CR2d at 775]

(1) **[3:123.51]** **Cases need not be identical:** This rule does *not* require absolute identity of parties, causes of action or remedies sought in the two actions. It is sufficient that both actions deal with the same *subject matter* and the court in the first action has the power to grant complete relief. It need *not* be shown that its judgment would be res judicata in the second action. [*Plant Insulation Co. v. Fibreboard Corp.* (1990) 224 CA3d 781, 788, 274 CR 147, 152]

• **[3:123.52]** It is sufficient that the *attorney fee issue* in both suits is the same and arises out of the same transaction or events. [See *Franklin & Franklin v. 7-Eleven Owners for Fair Franchising*, supra, 85 CA4th at 1175, 102 CR2d at 775]

**[3:123.53-123.54]** *Reserved.*

(2) **[3:123.55]** **Abatement mandatory:** Where the requisite conditions are shown, abatement is mandatory, not merely discretionary. (But erroneous failure to abate does *not* affect the court's jurisdiction; see below.) [*Lawyers Title Ins. Corp. v. Sup.Ct.* (1984) 151 CA3d 455, 460, 199 CR 1, 4]

(3) **[3:123.56]** **Rule *not* jurisdictional:** The rule of "exclusive concurrent jurisdiction" is *not* jurisdictional in the sense that failure to comply renders further proceedings void. Thus, the second court's erroneous refusal to stay

proceedings does not void relief granted by that court. [*County of San Diego v. State of Calif.* (1997) 15 C4th 68, 88-89, 61 CR2d 134, 145-146]

(a) [3:123.57]  **May be waived:**  The "exclusive concurrent jurisdiction" rule may be waived by a party's delay in raising the objection. [*People ex rel. Garamendi v. American Autoplan, Inc.* (1993) 20 CA4th 760, 774, 25 CR2d 192, 200—court in second proceedings did not err in granting preliminary injunction where objection had not been properly raised]

[3:123.58-123.59]  *Reserved.*

(4) [3:123.60]  **Procedure for abatement:**  The rule of "exclusive concurrent jurisdiction" must be raised:
— by demurrer where the defect appears on the face of the complaint or from matters judicially noticed (demurrer on the ground of "another action pending between the same parties on the same cause"; CCP §430.10(c), *see* ¶*7:74*); or
— as an affirmative defense in the answer where factual issues must be resolved (CCP §597, *see* ¶*6:475*).

• [3:123.61]  If not so raised, grounds for abatement of an action are *waived.* [CCP §430.80(a); *see* ¶*7:32*]

• [3:123.62]  If the ground for abatement is timely raised, defendant may move to *dismiss or abate* the action, or may file a motion for summary judgment. [*People ex rel. Garamendi v. American Autoplan, Inc.,* supra, 20 CA4th at 771, 25 CR2d at 199—raising issue in papers opposing summary judgment *not* sufficient]

• [3:123.63]  Upon sustaining a plea in abatement, the court may enter an *interlocutory judgment* in defendant's favor staying trial or other issues until final determination of the action in the other court. [CCP §597]

[3:123.64-123.69]  *Reserved.*

j. [3:123.70]  **Related cases in different states:**  The rules are the same where parallel proceedings involving the same dispute are pending in two courts in different states. But the analysis is framed in terms of comity and judicial discretion rather than abatement. [*Thomson v. Continental Ins. Co.* (1967) 66 C2d 738, 746-747, 59 CR 101, 107; see *Simmons v. Sup.Ct. (Simmons)* (1950) 96 CA2d 119, 123-124, 214

P2d 844, 848—California action ordered stayed under principles of comity where defendant had previously filed an action in Texas]

(1) **[3:123.71]** **Grounds for stay:** In deciding whether to stay the action, the court must consider:

- the importance of discouraging litigation designed solely to harass the adverse party;

- the importance of avoiding unseemly conflicts with the courts of other jurisdictions; and

- whether the parties' rights can best be determined by the other court because of:
  - the nature of the subject matter,
  - the availability of witnesses, or
  - the stage to which the proceedings in the other court have advanced. [*Thomson v. Continental Ins. Co.*, supra, 66 C2d at 746-747, 59 CR at 107]

(2) **[3:123.72]** **Effect of sister state's refusal to stay proceedings:** Even though the case is first filed in California, California courts may enjoin a party from pursuing parallel litigation in a sister state only under "an exceptional circumstance that outweighs the threat to judicial restraint and comity principles." [*Advanced Bionics Corp. v. Medtronic, Inc.* (2002) 29 C4th 697, 708, 128 CR2d 172, 180]

Thus, parallel actions generally proceed simultaneously in both states until a final judgment that is binding on the parties is rendered in one of the actions. [*Advanced Bionics Corp. v. Medtronic, Inc.*, supra, 29 C4th at 708, 128 CR2d at 180]

8. **[3:124]** **Effect of Lack of Subject Matter Jurisdiction:** If the court in which the action is filed does not have the power to adjudicate the action, the proceedings are void. [*Marlow v. Campbell* (1992) 7 CA4th 921, 928, 9 CR2d 516, 520]

The parties *cannot* by stipulation or agreement confer subject matter jurisdiction on a court that otherwise lacks it. [See *Crowell v. Downey Comm. Hosp. Found.* (2002) 95 CA4th 730, 739, 115 CR2d 810, 817]

This issue may arise in those few types of cases in which superior courts lack subject matter jurisdiction: e.g., claims within exclusive federal jurisdiction or within the primary jurisdiction of another tribunal, claims involving religious doctrine or discipline, etc. *See discussion at ¶3:123 ff.*

a. **[3:125]** **Defect cannot be waived:** Lack of subject matter jurisdiction is such a fundamental defect that it is not waived by delay or failure to object. [*People v. National Auto. & Cas. Ins. Co.* (2000) 82 CA4th 120, 125, 97 CR2d 858, 862—subject matter jurisdiction *cannot* be conferred by consent, waiver or estoppel]

The defect can be raised at any time and by any available procedure: "A judgment rendered by a court that does not have subject matter jurisdiction is void and unenforceable and may be attacked anywhere, directly or collaterally, by parties or by strangers." [*Marlow v. Campbell*, supra, 7 CA4th at 928, 9 CR2d at 520 (internal quotes omitted)]

(1) **[3:125.1]** **Compare—lack of personal jurisdiction:** The requirements as to territorial jurisdiction ("minimum contacts," etc.) are for the protection of defendant, and therefore *can* be waived by him or her (¶*3:134*). But subject matter jurisdiction requirements go to the very power of the court to act at all, and hence cannot be waived.

9. **[3:126]** **Procedure for Challenging Subject Matter Jurisdiction:** Lack of subject matter jurisdiction is such a fundamental defect that it can be raised at any time (even for the first time on appeal). It can be raised:
— by demurrer to the complaint where the defect appears on the face of the complaint or from matters judicially noticeable (CCP §430.10(a); see ¶7:63 ff.);
— by motion to strike (CCP §§435, 437);
— by motion for judgment on the pleadings;
— by motion for summary judgment (CCP §437c); or
— as an affirmative defense in the answer. [*Greener v. Workers' Comp. Appeals Bd.* (1993) 6 C4th 1028, 1036-1037, 25 CR2d 539, 543; see *Parrott v. Mooring Townhomes Ass'n, Inc.* (2003) 112 CA4th 873, 876, 6 CR3d 116, 118, fn. 1 (citing text)]

Compare: The challenge may *not*, however, be made in a "special appearance" by a motion to quash service of summons (which lies to challenge the court's *personal* jurisdiction over the moving party; see ¶3:376). [*Greener v. Workers' Comp. Appeals Bd.*, supra, 6 C4th at 1036, 25 CR2d at 543]

a. **[3:127]** **Who may challenge:** Lack of subject matter jurisdiction may be raised by either of the parties; or by the court on its own motion. [*Chromy v. Lawrance* (1991) 233 CA3d 1521, 1527, 285 CR 400, 403—appellate court raised *sua sponte*]

(1) **[3:127.1]** **Losing plaintiff may challenge jurisdiction which it invoked:** Plaintiff who has lost on the merits may obtain reversal on appeal by proving the

court in which he or she filed the action lacked subject matter jurisdiction. [*Chromy v. Lawrance*, supra, 233 CA3d at 1528, 285 CR at 403—plaintiff filed death-on-high-seas claim in state court; after losing at trial, plaintiff obtained reversal by proving claim was within exclusive federal jurisdiction]

b. [3:128] **Time for raising defect:** Since lack of subject matter jurisdiction renders the proceedings *void*, the defect can be raised at any time. Failure to raise it in the pleadings does *not* waive the defect. [CCP §430.80; see *Parrott v. Mooring Townhomes Ass'n, Inc.*, supra, 112 CA4th at 876, 6 CR3d at 118, fn. 1 (citing text)]

(1) [3:128.1] **On appeal:** Moreover, the policy against courts acting in excess of their power is so strong that lack of subject matter jurisdiction can even be raised for the first time on appeal. [*Ash v. Hertz Corp.* (1997) 53 CA4th 1107, 1112, 62 CR2d 192, 195—immaterial that earlier writ petition had been denied]

(2) [3:128.2] **After judgment final:** Once a judgment becomes final, it is normally res judicata as to any errors or defects in the proceedings. But the policy against courts acting in excess of their subject matter jurisdiction is so strong that later attack may be permitted where:

• The jurisdictional issue was *not* actually litigated; and

• The issue is one of *law,* rather than of fact; and

• The court's lack of jurisdiction is "clear," and the policy against permitting the court to act beyond its jurisdiction is "strong." [See Rest.2d Conflict of Laws §97, comment "d"]

[3:129] *Reserved.*

B. **JURISDICTION OVER PARTIES—PERSONAL JURISDICTION**

[3:130] Assuming the action will be filed in a court having subject matter jurisdiction, the next step is to determine whether that court will have the power to render an effective judgment against the defendants involved in the action.

The question is whether the intended defendants are subject to *personal jurisdiction* in the forum state, which depends on two factors:

• Existence of a constitutionally-sufficient *basis* for personal jurisdiction over each defendant (below); *and*

• *Acquisition* of jurisdiction by *service of process* in accordance with statutory and due process requirements. [*Ziller Electronics*

*Lab GmbH v. Sup.Ct. (Grosh Scenic Studios)* (1988) 206 CA3d 1222, 1229, 254 CR 410, 413; see *Dill v. Berquist Const. Co., Inc.* (1994) 24 CA4th 1426, 1439, 29 CR2d 746, 753, fn. 13 (citing text)]

This Chapter deals primarily with the first requirement—*bases* for personal jurisdiction. *Service of process requirements are discussed in Ch. 4.*

## 1. Bases for Personal Jurisdiction—General Considerations

a. **[3:131] When required:** In personam jurisdiction over defendant is required whenever a personal judgment against him is sought; e.g., a judgment for money damages, or an injunction. This covers the vast majority of lawsuits, and hence personal jurisdiction is a major factor in most litigation.

**[3:132]** *Reserved.*

b. **[3:133] Effect of lack of personal jurisdiction:** Without personal jurisdiction over defendant, the court cannot impose any personal liability upon him or affect his personal rights.

(1) **[3:134] Defect can be waived:** The rules as to personal jurisdiction are for the protection of the defendant, and hence can be waived by defendant. Indeed, jurisdictional defects are *deemed* waived unless defendant objects thereto promptly and by the proper procedure (¶3:375 ff.).

## 2. [3:135] "Traditional" Bases for In Personam Jurisdiction: It has been recognized since common law times that state courts may exercise personal jurisdiction over nonresidents where certain "traditional" bases for personal jurisdiction exist. [*Burnham v. Sup.Ct. (Burnham)* (1990) 495 US 604, 609, 110 S.Ct. 2105, 2110]

The three "traditional" bases for personal jurisdiction are:
— service on persons *physically present* in forum state (¶3:136);
— *domicile* within the state (¶3:153); and
— *consent* or *appearance* in the action (¶3:161). [See *Pennoyer v. Neff* (1877) 95 US 714, 733]

a. **[3:136] Service on persons physically present:** For due process purposes, service of summons upon a person voluntarily present in the forum state "suffice(s) to confer jurisdiction without regard to whether the defendant was only briefly in the State or whether the cause of action was related to his activities there." [*Burnham v. Sup.Ct. (Burnham)*, supra, 495 US at 612, 110 S.Ct. at 2111; see also *Marriage of Fitzgerald & King* (1995) 39 CA4th 1419, 1426, 46 CR2d 558, 562-563]

[3:137-138]   *Reserved.*

(1) [3:139]   **Effect—"gotcha" jurisdiction:**   There is no constitutional barrier to state courts exercising personal jurisdiction over nonresidents who are served while present in the forum state . . . *no matter how transient their presence* . . . and even if the lawsuit is completely *unrelated* to their presence.

Thus, plaintiffs can follow nonresident defendants into any state in which they travel on business or pleasure, file a lawsuit and serve summons—so-called "gotcha" jurisdiction.

(a)  **Application**

- [3:140]   New Jersey Husband made a 3-day trip to California, partly for business and partly to visit Daughter who was living with Estranged Wife in California. While in California, he was served with process in a marriage dissolution action. California courts had personal jurisdiction. [*Burnham v. Sup.Ct. (Burnham)*, supra]

[3:141]   *Reserved.*

(b) [3:142]   **Immunity for nonresident parties or witnesses?**   Under former law, nonresidents entering the state to participate in litigation were immune from service while attending court and for a reasonable time in coming and going. But the immunity rule was *rejected* in at least one case. [*Silverman v. Sup.Ct. (Galper)* (1988) 203 CA3d 145, 149, 249 CR2d 724, 727]

1) [3:143]   **Comment:** *Silverman* may not be definitive on this issue. It relied on an earlier case, *Severn v. Adidas* (1973) 33 CA3d 754, 109 CR 328, upholding *service of process* on a nonresident appearing in another state (Florida) for depositions. However, in *Severn*, the nonresident *had* "minimum contacts" with California, so that service of process was *not* being relied upon as the *basis for jurisdiction*. *Silverman* fails to note or discuss this distinction.

(2)  **Limitations**

(a) [3:144]   **Personal service required:**   Although substitute service may be effective for other purposes, only *personal service* of process supports personal jurisdiction over nonresidents temporarily present in the state.

*Cross-refer:* Service of process requirements are discussed in *Ch. 4.*

(b) [3:145] **States may reject in-state service as basis for jurisdiction:** State courts do not have to exercise jurisdiction in such cases. I.e., nothing prevents states from abandoning in-state service as a basis for jurisdiction. [*Burnham v. Sup.Ct. (Burnham)*, supra, 495 US at 627, 110 S.Ct. at 2119]

However, most states—including California—*uphold* personal jurisdiction in such cases. [See *Silverman v. Sup.Ct. (Galper)*, supra, 203 CA3d at 149, 249 CR at 727]

(c) [3:146] **Forum non conveniens:** In addition, state courts have *discretion* to *decline to exercise* their jurisdiction in particular cases (i.e., to stay or dismiss the action) on the ground of *inconvenient forum.* [CCP §418.10(a); *see discussion at ¶3:407 ff.*]

(3) [3:147] **Unresolved issues:** Basing jurisdiction on in-state service alone raises a number of issues that will have to be resolved in future cases, including:

• [3:148] *Voluntary vs. involuntary presence:* Whether exercise of jurisdiction is permitted over nonresidents whose presence in the forum state was *involuntary*: e.g., persons extradited or entering as a result of force or fraud.

• [3:149] *Immunities from service:* Whether any immunity from service will be recognized, as a matter of due process or otherwise.

[3:150] Under former law, an immunity was recognized for persons entering as *parties and witnesses* in unrelated litigation. This immunity was *rejected* in a recent case, but its analysis is debatable (*see ¶3:142-143*).

• [3:151] *"Attenuated" presence:* Whether exercise of personal jurisdiction is permitted where the nonresident's presence in the forum state is so "attenuated" as to be deemed "unreasonable" under a "minimum contacts" analysis: e.g., service effected during airport stopovers, or while flying overhead, or while attending trade show, etc. (see Brennan opn. in *Burnham v. Sup.Ct. (Burnham)*, supra, 495 US at 630, 110 S.Ct. at 2121).

- [3:152] *"Vicarious presence":* Whether in-state service on an *officer or agent* subjects a nonresident corporation or partnership to personal jurisdiction if the agent's presence is *unrelated* to corporate business (e.g., he or she was served while on vacation).

b. [3:153] **Domicile:** State courts can exercise personal jurisdiction over persons domiciled within the state at the time the lawsuit is commenced even if they are not actually present here. [*Milliken v. Meyer* (1940) 311 US 457, 462, 61 S.Ct. 339, 342; *Allen v. Sup.Ct.* (1953) 41 C2d 306, 310-311, 259 P2d 905, 907]

Domicile is one of the "traditional" bases for personal jurisdiction and thus *satisfies due process (see ¶3:135)*. Therefore, no other "contacts" with defendant need be shown; and it is immaterial whether the cause of action involved relates to defendant's local domicile.

(1) [3:154] **Domicile vs. residence:** "Residence" is simply the place where one lives, even temporarily, regardless of intent to remain. "Domicile," on the other hand, is the place one resides with the *intent to remain* indefinitely. [*DeYoung v. DeYoung* (1946) 27 C2d 521, 524, 165 P2d 457, 458]

(a) [3:155] A person can have several residences concurrently; but because of the intent requirement, only one domicile at a time. [*Marriage of Tucker* (1991) 226 CA3d 1249, 277 CR 403, 408]

(b) [3:156] Once established, domicile continues although the person is absent from the state. It continues until the person takes up residence elsewhere *with the requisite intent* to remain at the new residence indefinitely. [*DeYoung v. DeYoung*, supra; *Marriage of Tucker*, supra, 226 CA3d at 1258, 277 CR at 408]

(2) [3:157] **Domicile at time action commenced:** Personal jurisdiction cannot be based solely on the fact that defendant had been domiciled in California at some earlier time. Defendant's domicile "contact" with California must be intact when the action is filed, for due process purposes. [*Hoerler v. Sup.Ct. (Hoerler)* (1978) 85 CA3d 533, 538, 149 CR 569, 570]

(a) [3:158] **Compare—jurisdiction based on other "contacts":** But jurisdiction may be asserted against a former California domiciliary based on some other "contact" with the state: e.g., commission of some tortious act while domiciled here (*see* ¶3:264).

(3) **[3:159]** **Proving domicile:** Actions speak louder than words in determining where a person is domiciled. Thus, for example, a person may file documents stating that he is a Nevada resident (e.g., for tax reasons), but still be found to be a California domiciliary if he spends most of his time here, has most of his property here, etc. [See *Briggs v. Sup.Ct.* (1947) 81 CA2d 240, 250, 183 P2d 758, 765]

(4) **[3:160]** **Service of process requirements:** Domicile serves only as the *basis* for personal jurisdiction. Defendant must also receive adequate notice of the action through service of summons.

*Cross-refer:* Service of process requirements are discussed in *Ch. 4.*

c. **[3:161]** **Appearance or consent:** Personal jurisdiction over a nonresident defendant may be upheld if he or she *appears* in the action, or otherwise has *consented* to the court's exercise of such jurisdiction.

This is another of the "traditional" bases for personal jurisdiction that defines due process (¶3:135). Thus, jurisdiction may be upheld even in the absence of "minimum contacts" between the nonresident and the forum state.

(1) **[3:162]** **Appearance:** A nonresident defendant or cross-defendant who appears in an action submits to the court's exercise of personal jurisdiction in that action: "A general appearance operates as a consent to jurisdiction of the person, dispensing with the requirement of service of process, and curing defects in service . . . A general appearance can make up for a complete failure to serve a summons." [*Fireman's Fund Ins. Co. v. Sparks Const., Inc.* (2004) 114 CA4th 1135, 1145, 8 CR3d 446, 453]

An appearance is "general" if it contests the merits of the case or raises other than jurisdictional objections. [*Fireman's Fund Ins. Co. v. Sparks Const., Inc.*, supra, 114 CA4th at 1145, 8 CR3d at 453]

Thus, a defendant or cross-defendant "appears generally" in an action by:

- *Failure to make a CCP §418.10 motion to quash service of summons simultaneously* with its answer, demurrer or motion to strike (*see* ¶3:376 ff.); or

- If a CCP §418.10 motion to quash service of summons is made and *denied* (and any writ proceeding concluded), *thereafter filing an answer, demurrer or motion to strike.* [CCP §418.10(e); *see discussion at* ¶*3:393.1*]

(a) [3:163] **Comment:** The former distinction between "general" and "special" appearances has been abolished. Once a motion to quash is *denied* (by order of the superior court and denial of any petition for writ of mandate), a later answer, demurrer or motion to strike constitutes a "general appearance" by the defendant or cross-defendant, *waiving* any challenge to the court's personal jurisdiction.

(b) [3:164] **"Waiver" of objections to service:** Although the rule is often phrased in terms of waiver, it is more accurately a matter of *forfeiture:* "A defendant who makes a general appearance forfeits any objection to defective service even when the defendant does not know at the time that such an objection is available." [*Fireman's Fund Ins. Co. v. Sparks Const., Inc.*, supra, 114 CA4th at 1148, 8 CR3d at 456]

(c) [3:165] **Compare—acts constituting "appearance"** *absent timely motion to quash or responsive pleading:* A nonresident defendant who has filed neither a motion to quash nor a responsive pleading within the time allowed (*see* ¶*3:376*) may nevertheless be held to have "appeared" in an action by *acts recognizing the court's authority to proceed;* e.g., by seeking a change of venue, initiating discovery, etc. [See *Mansour v. Sup.Ct. (Eidem)* (1995) 38 CA4th 1750, 1756, 46 CR2d 191, 194 (decided under former version of CCP §418.10 but holding presumably still valid)]

[3:166-169] *Reserved.*

(2) [3:170] **Commencement of suit as consent to related claims:** When nonresident plaintiffs commence suit in California, they consent to local personal jurisdiction on any cross-complaint in that action, *or in any related action*: "This is the price which the state may exact as the condition of opening its courts to the plaintiff." [*Nobel Floral, Inc. v. Pasero* (2003) 106 CA4th 654, 659, 130 CR2d 881, 885 (internal quotes omitted)]

- [3:171] Mexican Attorney filed suit in California for fees owed by California clients for work done in Mexico. They filed a separate suit against him for malpractice. Although Mexican Attorney had no "contacts" with California, he was subject to personal jurisdiction in the malpractice action because

**RESERVED**

he had commenced suit here on a related claim. [*Nobel Floral, Inc. v. Pasero, supra,* 106 CA4th at 659-660, 130 CR2d at 886]

[3:172-176]   *Reserved.*

(3) [3:177]   **Contractual consent ("forum-selection clauses"):**   California courts may also exercise personal jurisdiction over a nonresident who has consented in advance to such jurisdiction, even in the absence of other "contacts" with such person. (Example: Contract providing that "in event of dispute, parties will be subject to the jurisdiction of the courts of the State of California, regardless of their residence.") [See *National Equip. Rental Ltd. v. Szukhent* (1964) 375 US 311, 315-316, 84 S.Ct. 411, 414]

The validity and effect of a forum-selection clause may depend on whether federal or state claims are being asserted. Federal standards apply where only *federal* claims are involved. [*Carnival Cruise Lines, Inc. v. Shute* (1991) 499 US 585, 590, 111 S.Ct. 1522, 1525—federal law governs validity and effect of forum-selection clause in passenger ticket for ocean voyage]

(a) [3:177.1]   **Rationale:**   Personal jurisdiction requirements can be waived. Thus, where such forum-selection clauses have been "freely negotiated" and are not "unreasonable and unjust," their enforcement does not offend due process. [*The Bremen v. Zapata Off-Shore Co.* (1972) 407 US 1, 15, 92 S.Ct. 1907, 1916; *Smith, Valentino & Smith, Inc. v. Sup.Ct. (Life Assur. Co. of Penn.)* (1976) 17 C3d 491, 497, 131 CR 374, 377]

(b) [3:177.2]   **Includes choice-of-law clauses:** California courts follow the same liberal approach in upholding contractual choice-of-law clauses (e.g., "this agreement shall be *governed by* the law of Hong Kong").

The law of the state or country chosen by the parties will be applied in California *unless:*
— there is "no reasonable basis" for the parties' selection; *or*
— the law is contrary to a "fundamental policy" of California. [*Nedlloyd Lines, B.V. v. Sup.Ct. (Seawinds)* (1992) 3 C4th 459, 464-465, 11 CR2d 330, 334]

1) [3:177.2a]   **Application:**   Texas Lender loaned money to Texas Borrower secured by California real estate. A provision calling for

application of Texas law was enforceable in California even though Texas law allows *deficiency judgments* following foreclosure and California has a "fundamental policy" *against* such judgments (see CCP §580b). California's policy was not implicated because the transaction involved Texas parties and Texas had a legitimate interest in ensuring their justified expectations were met. [*Guardian Sav. & Loan Ass'n v. MD Assocs.* (1998) 64 CA4th 309, 315-316, 75 CR2d 151, 155]

2) **[3:177.3] Even more liberal policy where California law chosen:** In certain contracts involving $250,000 or more, a choice-of-law clause designating California law will be upheld "whether or not the contract . . . bears a reasonable relation" to California. [See Civ.C. §1646.5]

[3:177.4] *Reserved.*

(c) **[3:177.5] Claims covered:** What disputes are covered by a forum-selection clause is a matter of contract interpretation. Unless the language used compels a contrary conclusion, the clause may apply to *tort* as well as contract claims. [*Cal-State Business Products & Services, Inc. v. Ricoh* (1993) 12 CA4th 1666, 1677, 16 CR2d 417, 423—"all causes of action arising directly or indirectly from the business relationship evidenced by the contract"]

- [3:177.6] A clause requiring litigation in Mexico of any dispute arising "regarding the *interpretation* or *fulfillment* of this contract" did *not* apply to claims of fraudulent inducement to enter into the contract. [*Bancomer v. Sup.Ct. (Reilly)* (1996) 44 CA4th 1450, 1461, 52 CR2d 435, 442]

[3:177.7-177.9] *Reserved.*

(d) **[3:177.10] Parties who may enforce:** In addition to the parties to the contract, certain nonsignatories may be entitled to enforce a forum-selection clause:

1) **[3:177.11] Third party beneficiary:** A forum-selection clause may be enforced by a nonsignatory who was the *intended beneficiary* of the underlying agreement. [See Civ.C. §1559; *Bancomer v. Sup.Ct. (Reilly)*, supra, 44 CA4th at 1458-1459, 52 CR2d at 440]

[3:177.12-177.13] *Reserved.*

2) **[3:177.14]** **Nonsignatory "closely related" to contract:** A forum-selection clause may also be enforced by nonsignatories who are "closely related" to the contractual relationship involved. [*Bancomer v. Sup.Ct. (Reilly)*, supra, 44 CA4th at 1459, 52 CR2d at 441; *Bugna v. Fike* (2000) 80 CA4th 229, 233, 95 CR2d 161, 164-165]

- **[3:177.15]** A franchise agreement between California parties (Franchisee and Franchiser) required that all disputes be litigated in Florida, where Franchiser's *corporate parent* was headquartered. Franchisee sued Franchiser and its corporate parent for fraud. The forum-selection clause was enforced even though the corporate parent *had not signed* the franchise agreement. The corporate parent was alleged to be the alter ego of Franchiser and was alleged to have participated in the fraud. Therefore, its conduct was "closely related" to the franchise in question. [*Lu v. Dryclean-U.S.A. of Calif., Inc.* (1992) 11 CA4th 1490, 1494, 14 CR2d 906, 908]

- **[3:177.16]** But Corporation A's purchase of Corporation B's stock was not enough by itself to allow Corporation A to enforce a forum-selection clause in an agreement entered into years previously by Corporation B: "There is nothing unfair about requiring a nonparty to a contract who had no close relationship to the contractual transaction to litigate an action in an otherwise proper forum." [*Berclain America Latina v. Baan Co. N.V.* (1999) 74 CA4th 401, 408, 87 CR2d 745, 750]

(e) **[3:178]** **Limitation—consent must be clear:** Whatever form or agreement is relied upon must show the nonresident's awareness of the consequences of consent: i.e., that he or she was *submitting to the power of a California court* to order payment of money (on pain of fine or imprisonment where nonpayment is punishable as a contempt). Moreover, the form should advise nonresidents they will *not* be subject to that power if they choose *not* to sign the form! [*Marriage of Merideth* (1982) 129 CA3d 356, 362, 180 CR 909, 912—signature of nonresident defendant on an acknowledgment of service *merely acknowledged service* outside California; it did not confer personal jurisdiction absent notice of type stated above; *Hunt v. Sup.Ct. (Commercial Money Ctr.)* (2000) 81 CA4th 901, 907, 97 CR2d 215, 219—consent to personal jurisdiction "of the applicable jurisdiction" not sufficient]

1) **[3:179] Designating agent for service of summons insufficient:** Designating a local agent for service of summons does not necessarily constitute submission to the personal jurisdiction of local courts. It merely reflects the nonresident's agreement *to facilitate service* of process (*see ¶4:53*).

This is particularly true where the appointment of a local agent is involuntary or mandated by statute (e.g., foreign corporations qualifying to do business in California; see Corps.C. §2105).

In such cases, personal jurisdiction over the nonresident *cannot* be based solely on service on the local agent; other "contacts" must be shown. [See *Gray Line Tours of Southern Nevada v. Reynolds Electrical & Engineering Co., Inc.* (1987) 193 CA3d 190, 193-194, 238 CR 419, 421; *and ¶3:349*]

2) **[3:180] Acknowledging receipt of summons insufficient:** Merely signing an *acknowledgment of receipt of summons* does *not* constitute consent by a nonresident to California jurisdiction. The acknowledgment of receipt does not imply acknowledgment of the consequences or legal effect of the documents served upon him. [*Marriage of Merideth*, supra]

3) **[3:180.1] Agreeing to be bound by result of litigation insufficient:** A nonparty's agreement to be bound by the result of litigation between other parties does not confer jurisdiction on the court to enter a judgment binding on the nonparty. [*Tokio Marine & Fire Ins. Corp. v. Western Pac. Roofing Corp.* (1999) 75 CA4th 110, 119, 89 CR2d 1, 7]

(f) **[3:181] Limitation—lack of notice as ground for refusing enforcement:** A forum-selection clause may be unenforceable if the contesting party did not have sufficient notice of its existence: "Absent such notice, the requisite mutual consent to that contractual term is lacking ..." [*Carnival Cruise Lines, Inc. v. Sup.Ct. (Williams)* (1991) 234 CA3d 1019, 1027, 286 CR 323, 328]

1) [3:181.1] **Comment:** What constitutes sufficient notice is unclear, but *actual* notice is probably *not* required. For example, under federal law, limitations printed conspicuously on a ticket issued by a common carrier (e.g., airline) are enforceable even if not read by the passengers. It is enough that the passengers had an *opportunity* to read the limitations before embarking on the journey. [See *Deiro v. American Airlines, Inc.* (9th Cir. 1987) 816 F2d 1360, 1364]

(g) [3:182] **Limitation—unreasonableness:** The agreement must designate a forum bearing some legitimate relationship to the parties or their dispute: "Forum selection clauses . . . may be given effect . . . in the absence of a showing that enforcement of such a clause would be *unreasonable.*" [*Smith, Valentino & Smith, Inc. v. Sup.Ct. (Life Assur. Co. of Penn.)* (1976) 17 C3d 491, 497, 131 CR 374, 377]

Thus, forum-selection clauses in standard form contracts are subject to judicial scrutiny for "fundamental fairness." [*Carnival Cruise Lines, Inc. v. Shute* (1991) 499 US 585, 595, 111 S.Ct. 1522, 1528—upholding clause in passenger ticket designating cruise line's principal place of business]

1) [3:182.1] **Burden of proof:** A forum-selection clause is *prima facie valid* and will be enforced unless the resisting party meets the "heavy burden" of proving enforcement would be *unreasonable* under the circumstances of the case. [*Bancomer v. Sup.Ct. (Reilly)* (1996) 44 CA4th 1450, 1457, 52 CR2d 435, 439]

This requires plaintiffs to prove that litigating in the designated forum would be so *gravely inconvenient* that it would effectively deny them their day in court. [*The Bremen v. Zapata Off-Shore Co.* (1972) 407 US 1, 18, 92 S.Ct. 1907, 1917—a "heavy burden of proof"; *CQL Original Products, Inc. v. National Hockey League Players Ass'n* (1995) 39 CA4th 1347, 1354, 46 CR2d 412, 416—plaintiff must show the forum selected "would be unavailable or *unable to accomplish* substantial justice" (emphasis added)]

[3:182.2-182.9] *Reserved.*

2) [3:182.10] **Adhesion contracts *not* unreasonable per se:** The test is not whether the

provision was negotiated but whether it is fundamentally unfair:

— "The fact that a forum-selection clause is contained in a contract of adhesion and was not the subject of bargaining does not defeat enforcement as a matter of law, *where there is no evidence of unfair use of superior power* to impose the contract upon the other party and where the covenant is within the reasonable expectations of the party against whom it is being enforced." [*Cal-State Business Products & Services, Inc. v. Ricoh* (1993) 12 CA4th 1666, 1679, 16 CR2d 417, 425 (emphasis added)]

3) **[3:182.11] Forum selected need not be domicile of either party:** The chosen forum need bear only a "reasonable" relationship to the parties or their dispute. It need not be related to the parties' domicile or their dispute. Indeed, the parties may choose a neutral forum with expertise in the subject matter. [*The Bremen v. Zapata Off-Shore Co.*, supra, 407 US at 17, 92 S.Ct. at 1917]

• **[3:182.12]** For example, a New Jersey corporation may, in dealing with a California resident, insist on a forum-selection clause designating New York as the forum. Although New York is not the domicile of either party and has no relation to their dispute, "it is a major commercial center" and New York courts presumably have "a great deal of expertise in commercial litigation." [*Cal-State Business Products & Services, Inc. v. Ricoh* (1993) 12 CA4th 1666, 1682, 16 CR2d 417, 426]

**[3:182.13-182.14]** *Reserved.*

4) **[3:182.15] Factors considered:** Relevant factors include:

— whether the forum was chosen by one party to *discourage claims* by the other (i.e., a "remote, alien forum");

— whether the contesting party's consent was obtained by *fraud or overreaching;*

— whether the dispute is an essentially local one inherently more suitable to resolution in one state than any other; and

— whether the contesting party had *adequate notice* of the provision. [*Carnival Cruise*

Lines, Inc. v. Shute, supra, 499 US at 590,
111 S.Ct. at 1528]

5) **Application**

- [3:182.16] A licensing agreement required Licensee to litigate any claims
against Licensor in Toronto, Canada, where
Licensor had its principal office. The choice
of forum provision was reasonable because
it protected Licensor from being confronted
by a myriad of different state and national
forums. It was immaterial that Licensee
could not negotiate to alter this provision;
the forum-selection clause was part of the
price to be paid for dealing with Licensor.
[CQL Original Products, Inc. v. National
Hockey League Players Ass'n (1995) 39
CA4th 1347, 1355, 46 CR2d 412, 417]

[3:183]  *Reserved.*

(h) [3:184]  **Limitation—public policy:**  Even a
knowledgeable, voluntary forum-selection agreement may be unenforceable if it would violate a
strong California public policy or result in evasion of
statutes enacted for the protection of California citizens. Rationale: *Only California courts* can be relied
upon to interpret and enforce California public
policy (courts in other states might apply their own
laws). [Hall v. Sup.Ct. (Imperial Petroleum, Inc.)
(1983) 150 CA3d 411, 416-418, 197 CR 757, 761-
762]

1) [3:185]  **Securities transactions violating
California law:**  California residents went to
Nevada to consummate stock deal violating
California law. Their agreement stated that only
Nevada law should apply to the transaction and
that any litigation had to be in Nevada courts. In
a suit brought in California, the agreement to
litigate in Nevada was held unenforceable because it violated statutes enacted for protection
of California citizens. [Hall v. Sup.Ct. (Imperial
Petroleum, Inc.), supra]

2) [3:186]  **Insurance covering California risks:**
Oil companies formed Bermuda-based mutual
insurance company to cover risks worldwide. It
structured its affairs so that most contacts with
its insureds took place outside of the U.S. And,
its insurance contracts expressly stated that the
only means for resolving disputes thereunder is

by arbitration in London, applying New York law. This did not prevent California courts from exercising personal jurisdiction in an action filed by a *non*insured claimant (and presumably by its insureds as well) for losses suffered in California. [*A.I.U. Ins. Co. v. Sup.Ct. (Oil Ins. Ltd.)* (1986) 177 CA3d 281, 291, 222 CR 880, 886]

[3:187]    *Reserved.*

3) **[3:187.1]    Construction subcontracts:**  By statute, contracts between a contractor and a subcontractor with principal offices in California for construction here *may not require* that disputes be litigated or arbitrated elsewhere; nor may they prohibit the subcontractor from seeking relief in local courts. [CCP §410.42]

4) **[3:187.2]    Franchise agreements:**  A forum-selection clause in a franchise agreement involving a franchisee doing business in California is *void* if it attempts to "restrict venue" to a forum outside the State. [Bus. & Prof.C. §20040.5—applicable to post-1994 franchises and renewals]

Under agreements entered into *before 1995*, the burden is on franchisors to show that enforcement of a forum-selection clause will not subvert substantive rights of California citizens under California law. [See *Wimsatt v. Beverly Hills Weight Loss Clinics Int'l, Inc.* (1995) 32 CA4th 1511, 1522, 38 CR2d 612, 618]

5) **[3:187.3]    Actions under Consumers Legal Remedies Act:**  In an action under the Consumers Legal Remedies Act (Civ.C. §1750 et seq.), the party relying on a forum-selection clause has the burden of proving that enforcement of the clause *would not diminish substantive rights* of California consumers under the Act. [*America Online, Inc. v. Sup.Ct. (Mendoza)* (2001) 90 CA4th 1, 9-10, 108 CR2d 699, 705-706—forum-selection clause unenforceable because designated forum did not allow class actions in consumer protection cases]

6) **[3:187.4]    Actions within small claims jurisdiction:**  An agreement (entered into or renewed after 1/1/03) designating a forum outside California is void and unenforceable in actions within small claims court jurisdiction that arise from the sale of goods, services or

property, or the extension of credit primarily for family or household purposes. [CCP §116.225]

7) **[3:187.5] Compare—actions removed to federal court:** State public policy is *not* controlling in actions commenced in or *removed* to federal court. Even in diversity cases, enforceability of forum-selection clauses is determined by *federal*, not state, law. (Federal law generally favors enforcement of such clauses.) [See *Stewart Organization, Inc. v. Ricoh Corp.* (1988) 487 US 22, 30-32, 108 S.Ct. 2239, 2245]

(i) **[3:188] Limitation—forum non conveniens:** The existence of a valid forum-selection clause under which California courts *could* exercise jurisdiction does not necessarily obligate them to do so. If neither the litigants nor the public have any real interest in having the matter litigated in California, local courts may *dismiss* the action under the doctrine of *forum non conveniens* (CCP §410.30, *see* ¶3:407). [*Appalachian Ins. Co. v. Sup.Ct. (Union Carbide Corp.)* (1984) 162 CA3d 427, 437-438, 208 CR 627, 633-634]

*Forum non conveniens is discussed at ¶3:407 ff.*

[3:189-192] *Reserved.*

(j) **[3:193] Limitation—defendant may seek transfer or removal:** A nonresident's consent to jurisdiction of a particular court ("the Superior Court for Los Angeles shall have jurisdiction over the parties . . .") does not waive its right to seek a change of venue to another state court or to remove the action to federal court. (And, following removal to federal court, the action conceivably could be transferred to any other federal court in the country under 28 USC §1404(a); *see* ¶3:645.) [*Hunt Wesson Foods, Inc. v. Supreme Oil Co.* (9th Cir. 1987) 817 F2d 75, 77]

Of course, the clause may be drafted to limit jurisdiction *exclusively* to a designated court ("any such dispute shall be litigated *only* in the Superior Court for Los Angeles, *and no other*"). Any ambiguity as to the matter, however, will be resolved against the party drafting the provision. [*Hunt Wesson Foods, Inc. v. Supreme Oil Co.*, supra, 817 F2d at 77-78]

[3:194] *Reserved.*

3. **[3:195] "Minimum Contacts" Doctrine:** Due process also permits state courts to exercise personal jurisdiction over

nonresidents where "minimum contacts" exist between the non-resident and the forum state. "Minimum contacts" means the relationship is such that the exercise of jurisdiction over the nonresident does not offend "*traditional notions of fair play and substantial justice.*" [*International Shoe Co. v. Washington* (1945) 326 US 310, 316, 66 S.Ct. 154, 158]

a. [3:196] **"Long arm" statute analysis:** "Minimum contacts" with a nonresident vest constitutional power in the *forum state* to adjudicate claims against the nonresident. It is up to each state to decide *to what extent* its jurisdictional power is conferred upon its courts.

Thus, the starting point in personal jurisdiction analysis is to examine state law—so-called "long arm" statutes.

(1) [3:197] **California statute:** California has the broadest kind of "long arm" statute. Local courts are authorized to exercise jurisdiction over parties "... *on any basis not inconsistent with the Constitution* of this state or the United States." [CCP §410.10 (emphasis added)]

(a) [3:198] **Effect:** The full power of the state is vested in the state courts. The only limitations on exercise of personal jurisdiction are constitutional in nature. California courts therefore can assert power over residents and nonresidents alike, to the outer limits of constitutional due process. [*Sanders v. CEG Corp.* (1979) 95 CA3d 779, 783, 157 CR 252, 255]

(2) [3:199] **Due process determinations:** Because 14th Amendment due process is involved, the U.S. Supreme Court is the ultimate authority in this area. However, its decisions in this area are few and far between. Therefore, it is often necessary to rely on lower federal and state court decisions.

(3) [3:200] **Other constitutional limitations:** State jurisdictional power may also be limited by *federal statutes and treaties* which are the "supreme Law of the Land" (U.S. Const., Art. VI, cl. 2).

Thus, California courts cannot exercise jurisdiction over foreign nationals where to do so would violate an international treaty to which the United States is a party. [*Shoei Kako Co., Ltd. v. Sup.Ct. (MacIsaac)* (1973) 33 CA3d 808, 819, 109 CR 402, 410]

⇨[3:201] *PRACTICE POINTER:* Be careful about stretching "long arm" jurisdiction too far. Any case in which local jurisdiction is asserted over nonresidents could end up before the U.S. Supreme Court!

Rev. #1 2003

Moreover, even if the case never makes it to the Supreme Court, the defendant's jurisdictional challenges are likely to run up the litigation costs and delay trial on the merits.

Thus, if "long arm" jurisdiction is in doubt, it may be better for your client to file suit in the state or country where the defendant is located.

b. [3:202] **Factors considered:** The "minimum contacts" doctrine provides no mechanical yardstick. Rather, personal jurisdiction depends on the facts of each case . . . the test being whether, under those facts, California has a sufficient *relationship with the defendant and the litigation* to make it *reasonable* ("fair play") to require him or her to defend the action in California courts. The following factors will be considered:

- The *extent to which the lawsuit relates to defendant's activities* or contacts with California;

- The availability of evidence, and the location of witnesses;

- The availability of an alternative forum in which the claim could be litigated (defendant's amenability to suit elsewhere);

- The relative costs and burdens to the litigants of bringing or defending the action in California rather than elsewhere; and

- Any state policy in providing a forum for this particular litigation (e.g., protection of California resident, or assuring applicability of California law). [See *World-Wide Volkswagen Corp. v. Woodson* (1980) 444 US 286, 292, 100 S.Ct. 559, 564; and *Fisher Governor Co. v. Sup.Ct. (Prestwich)* (1959) 53 C2d 222, 225-226, 1 CR 1, 3-4]

(1) [3:202.1] **Past vs. present relationship:** The relevant period during which "minimum contacts" must have existed is apparently *when the cause of action arose* rather than when the complaint was filed or served. [See *Boaz v. Boyle & Co., Inc.* (1995) 40 CA4th 700, 717, 46 CR2d 888, 899]

[3:202.2-202.4] *Reserved.*

(2) [3:202.5] **Size of claim:** Where the amount at issue is relatively small, a California court may be the only one available as a practical matter to a California resident. If required to litigate at the defendant's residence, plaintiff may be unable to afford the opportunity to seek redress: "The due process clause must be applied flexibly so as to ensure that commercial actors are not effec-

tively judgment proof for the consequences of obligations they voluntarily assume in other States." [*West Corp. v. Sup.Ct. (Stanford)* (2004) 116 CA4th 1167, , 11 CR3d 145, 158]

(a) [3:202.6] **Class actions:** The class action nature of a lawsuit does not itself make local jurisdiction "unfair." Indeed, where the individual claims are in small amounts, a class action may be the only practical approach. [*West Corp. v. Sup.Ct. (Stanford)*, supra, 116 CA4th at , 11 CR3d at 158]

c. [3:203] **Doctrine applies to each defendant individually:** Each defendant's contacts with the forum state must be assessed individually. [*Calder v. Jones* (1984) 465 US 783, 790, 104 S.Ct. 1482, 1487]

But corporate veils may be pierced and agents' activities may be attributed to their principals in appropriate cases. [See *Calder v. Jones*, supra, 465 US at 789-790, 104 S.Ct. at 1486-1487; and *Vons Cos., Inc. v. Seabest Foods, Inc.* (1996) 14 C4th 434, 458, 58 CR2d 899, 915, fn. 7]

(1) [3:204] **Employer-employee:** Jurisdiction over a nonresident employer does not automatically confer personal jurisdiction over its nonresident employees and agents. [*Keeton v. Hustler Magazine, Inc.* (1984) 465 US 770, 781, 104 S.Ct. 1473, 1482, fn. 13; *see* ¶*3:357*]

(2) [3:205] **Parent-subsidiary:** A parent corporation's "contacts" with the forum do *not* create personal jurisdiction over its subsidiaries; and vice versa. *See further discussion at* ¶*3:352 ff.*

(3) [3:205.1] **Foreign corporation vs. officers, employees, etc.:** An out-of-state corporation may be subject to personal jurisdiction in California although its officers and employees individually are not. *See detailed discussion at* ¶*3:357 ff.*

(4) [3:205.2] **Foreign partnership vs. partners:** Although general partners may be *liable* individually for partnership debts, jurisdiction over the partnership does *not* automatically establish jurisdiction over the partners individually. Each defendant's "contacts" with California must be evaluated individually. [*Goehring v. Sup.Ct. (Bernier)* (1998) 62 CA4th 894, 904, 73 CR2d 105, 111—Texas partners who signed documents in Texas that furthered partnership's activities in California did *not* thereby establish "minimum contacts" with California]

[3:205.3-205.4] *Reserved.*

(5) [3:205.5] **Conspirators:** California does *not* recognize conspiracy as a basis for acquiring personal jurisdiction over a party. I.e., jurisdiction over one alleged conspirator does *not* establish jurisdiction over other, nonresident conspirators. In deciding whether personal jurisdiction exists, the focus is on *each individual's* forum-related activities. [*Mansour v. Sup.Ct. (Eidem)* (1995) 38 CA4th 1750, 1758, 46 CR2d 191, 197]

(6) [3:206] **Compare—claims against decedent's estate:** If the decedent had sufficient "contacts" with California to be subject to jurisdiction here, the administrator or executor of his or her estate is also subject to California jurisdiction in an action against the decedent's estate. It is irrelevant that the administrator or executor personally has no "contacts" with California. [*Mitsui Manufacturers Bank v. Tucker* (1984) 152 CA3d 428, 430-432, 199 CR 517, 519-520]

d. [3:207] **Agency concepts applicable:** "Minimum contacts" by a nonresident's agents or employees are imputed to the nonresident. (E.g., foreign corporations are consistently held subject to local personal jurisdiction based upon their agents' activities within the forum state.) However, the existence of the agency relationship is a question of fact that must be proved in each case. [*Magnecomp Corp. v. Athene Co., Ltd.* (1989) 209 CA3d 526, 536-537, 257 CR 278, 283-284]

(1) [3:207.1] **No immunity for sister states:** Sister states who engage in activities within California (through agents or employees) are subject to suit in California courts with respect to those activities. [*Hall v. University of Nevada* (1972) 8 C3d 522, 525, 105 CR 355, 358—State of Nevada suable in California for injuries to California resident on local roads caused by Nevada employee driving within scope of employment; see also *State of Oregon v. Sup.Ct. (Lillard)* (1994) 24 CA4th 1550, 1558-1559, 29 CR2d 909, 913-914 (disapproved on other grounds in *Vons Cos., Inc. v. Seabest Foods, Inc.* (1996) 14 C4th 434, 465, 58 CR2d 899, 919)—upholding Calif. jurisdiction over sister state which had recruited Calif. athlete in Calif. in action for his wrongful death while playing basketball in Calif.]

e. [3:208] **Effect of plaintiff's residence:** There is *no* requirement that plaintiff reside in the forum state for local courts to exercise jurisdiction over a nonresident defendant. But if plaintiff *is* a local resident, the forum state may have more of an interest in the matter, making it easier to justify such exercise of jurisdiction. [See *Keeton v. Hustler Magazine, Inc.* (1984) 465 US 770, 780, 104 S.Ct. 1473, 1481;

*Ford Motor Co. v. Insurance Co. of No. America* (1995) 35 CA4th 604, 610-611, 41 CR2d 342, 346]

(1) [3:209] **Compare—inconvenient forum:** Notwithstanding sufficient "contacts" with the defendant for jurisdiction purposes, a court has discretion to *decline* jurisdiction under the doctrine of forum non conveniens (CCP §418.10(a)(2); *see* ¶*3:407*). The court is more likely to do so where both the plaintiff and defendant are nonresidents of the forum state (*see* ¶*3:432*).

f. [3:210] **Different standards for general vs. limited personal jurisdiction:** The extent to which a California court can exercise personal jurisdiction over a defendant depends on the nature and quality of defendant's "contacts" with the state.

(1) [3:211] **General (unlimited) personal jurisdiction based on "doing business" locally:** Nonresidents whose commercial activities impact California on a "substantial, continuous and systematic" basis are subject to general (unlimited) jurisdiction here. I.e., they may be sued on *any* cause of action, even on causes of action *unrelated* to their activities within the state. [*Perkins v. Benguet Consolidated Mining Co.* (1952) 342 US 437, 446-447, 72 S.Ct. 413, 418-419; *Cornelison v. Chaney* (1976) 16 C3d 143, 147, 127 CR 352, 354]

"Such a defendant's contacts with the forum are so wide-ranging that *they take the place of physical presence* in the forum state as a basis for jurisdiction." [*Vons Cos., Inc. v. Seabest Foods, Inc.* (1996) 14 C4th 434, 446, 58 CR2d 899, 906 (emphasis added)]

When the nonresident ceases to do business in the state, it is no longer subject to general jurisdiction on causes of action independent of that business. [See *Serafini v. Sup.Ct. (Khadir)* (1998) 68 CA4th 70, 79, 80 CR2d 159, 165]

(a) [3:211.1] **Nonresident persons or corporations:** Although this basis for jurisdiction can be asserted against nonresident individuals as well as business entities, "there is a dearth of case law on general jurisdiction over natural persons." [*Serafini v. Sup.Ct. (Khadir)*, supra, 68 CA4th at 79, 80 CR2d at 165]

(b) [3:212] **Higher level of "contacts" required:** Where the cause of action is *unrelated* to the nonresident defendant's local activities, a higher level of "contacts" with the forum state is required to support local jurisdiction. This is implicit in the requirement of "fair play and substantial justice." [See *Fisher Governor Co. v. Sup.Ct. (Prestwich)* (1959) 53 C2d 222, 224, 1 CR 1, 3]

(c) [3:213] **Application—activities held sufficient for general jurisdiction:** The following are examples of cases in which a nonresident has been held subject to personal jurisdiction in California on a cause of action *unrelated* to its activities here:

- [3:213.1] KLM Airlines was sued in California for wrongful death of a California resident, killed in a plane crash in England. KLM had no flights into or out of California, but did have a reservations office here, and an office for purchasing airplane parts and supplies. These activities were "substantial, continuous and systematic," and thus KLM was subject to general personal jurisdiction in California—even on causes of action completely *unrelated* to its local activities. [*Koninklijke Luchtvaart Maatschappij v. Sup.Ct.* (1951) 107 CA2d 495, 500-501, 237 P2d 297, 300-301]

- [3:213.2] Hotel Chain was authorized to do business in California, licensed hundreds of hotels here to use its name, maintained a business office here, advertised collectively for in-state member hotels, and maintained a cooperative reservation system. These continuous and purposeful activities subjected it to *general* personal jurisdiction in California in an action for injuries suffered at a licensee hotel in Mexico that had *no connection with its activities in California.* [*Hesse v. Best Western International, Inc.* (1995) 32 CA4th 404, 410, 38 CR2d 74, 77]

- [3:213.3] Mail Order Company sold millions of dollars in goods (6% of its total sales) in California through its catalog, toll-free number *and an Internet Web site* that served as a "virtual store." Such "continuous and systematic" contacts sufficed to subject Mail Order Company to general jurisdiction in California courts. [*Gator.Com Corp. v. L.L. Bean, Inc.* (9th Cir. 2003) 341 F3d 1072, 1074]

(d) [3:214] **Application—activities held NOT sufficient for general jurisdiction:** There are more cases in which general jurisdiction against a nonresident is declined than in which it is upheld. The following are typical:

1) **[3:215] Local purchases:** Purchasing (as opposed to selling) goods and services in the forum state, even at regular intervals, is *not* enough by itself to subject a nonresident to general jurisdiction. Thus, absent other "contacts," it cannot be sued locally on causes of action *unrelated* to those purchase transactions. [*Helicopteros Nacionales de Colombia, S.A. v. Hall* (1984) 466 US 408, 416, 104 S.Ct. 1868, 1873]

   [3:216] *Reserved.*

2) **[3:217] Local advertising:** A Las Vegas hotel's advertising and maintaining an "800" telephone number in California were *not* sufficiently "pervasive" and "substantial" activities to subject it to general personal jurisdiction in California. Hence, it was not subject to suit here for property loss suffered by a hotel guest. [*Circus Circus Hotels, Inc. v. Sup.Ct. (Haynie)* (1981) 120 CA3d 546, 567, 174 CR 885, 897 (disapproved on other grounds in *Vons Cos., Inc. v. Seabest Foods, Inc.* (1996) 14 C4th 434, 461, 58 CR2d 899, 916)]

3) **[3:218] Local sales through independent sales representative:** Sales and sales promotion activities through *independent*, nonexclusive sales representatives are not enough by themselves to subject an out-of-state company to California jurisdiction in actions *unrelated* to those sales activities. [*Fisher Governor Co. v. Sup.Ct. (Prestwich)*, supra, 53 C2d at 224-225, 1 CR at 3; *Congoleum Corp. v. DLW Aktiengesellschaft* (9th Cir. 1984) 729 F2d 1240, 1242— German corporation not subject to jurisdiction in California on a claim arising out of its activities in France]

   [3:219-220] *Reserved.*

4) **[3:221] Irregular local deliveries:** An out-of-state trucker who was licensed by the California Public Utilities Commission, and who made *irregular* deliveries into California (20 trips a year), was not subject to general personal jurisdiction in California (but it was subject to limited jurisdiction in suits based on its trucking activities; *see ¶3:242*). [*Cornelison v.*

*Chaney* (1976) 16 C3d 143, 147, 127 CR 352, 354]

[3:222-224] *Reserved.*

(2) [3:225] **Limited ("specific") jurisdiction:** Even if a nonresident defendant's "contacts" with California are not sufficiently "continuous and systematic" for general jurisdiction, it may still be subject to jurisdiction *on claims related to its activities* on contacts here. Such "limited" or "specific" personal jurisdiction requires a showing that:

- The out-of-state defendant *purposefully* established contacts with the forum state;

- Plaintiff's cause of action "arises out of" or is "related to" defendant's contacts with the forum state; and

- The forum's exercise of personal jurisdiction in the particular case comports with "*fair play and substantial justice.*" [*Burger King Corp. v. Rudzewicz* (1985) 471 US 462, 477-478, 105 S.Ct. 2174, 2184-2185; see *Data Disc, Inc. v. Systems Technology Associates, Inc.* (9th Cir. 1977) 557 F2d 1280, 1287; and *Vons Cos., Inc. v. Seabest Foods, Inc.* (1996) 14 C4th 434, 446, 58 CR2d 899, 906]

(a) [3:226] **"Purposeful" requirement:** First of all, the nonresident defendant must have *purposefully directed* its activities at forum residents, or *purposefully availed itself* of the privilege of conducting activities within the forum state, thus invoking the benefits and protections of local law. [*Hanson v. Denckla* (1958) 357 US 235, 253, 78 S.Ct. 1228, 1239-1240; see *Vons Cos., Inc. v. Seabest Foods, Inc.*, supra, 14 C4th at 446, 58 CR2d at 906; *Bridgestone Corp. v. Sup.Ct. (T & T Truck & Crane Service, Inc.)* (2002) 99 CA4th 767, 773, 121 CR2d 673, 677]

"Parties who *reach out* beyond one state and create *continuing relationships and obligations* with citizens of another are subject to regulation and sanctions in the other State for the consequences of their activities." [*Burger King Corp. v. Rudzewicz*, supra, 471 US at 473, 105 S.Ct. at 2182 (emphasis added; internal quotes omitted)]

1) [3:227] **Rationale:** The "purposeful availment" requirement assures that a nonresident will be aware that it is subject to suit in the forum state. It can then protect against the costs

of litigating there by purchasing insurance; or, if the costs and risks are too great, by severing its connections with the forum state. [*World-Wide Volkswagen Corp. v. Woodson* (1980) 444 US 286, 297, 100 S.Ct. 559, 567]

2) **[3:228] Foreseeability of being sued locally:** Foreseeability of causing injury in the forum state is *not* enough by itself to subject a nonresident to jurisdiction there. [*World-Wide Volkswagen Corp. v. Woodson*, supra, 444 US at 295, 100 S.Ct. at 566; *see ¶3:287*]

Rather, "the foreseeability that is critical to due process analysis . . . is that the defendant's conduct and connection with the forum State are such that he should *reasonably anticipate being haled into court there.*" [*World-Wide Volkswagen Corp. v. Woodson*, supra, 444 US at 297, 100 S.Ct. at 567 (emphasis added)]

3) **[3:229] Acts by plaintiff or others not sufficient:** Unilateral activity by plaintiff or other persons over whom the nonresident defendant has no control do not themselves satisfy the "purposeful availment" requirement. [*Helicopteros Nacionales de Colombia, S.A. v. Hall* (1984) 466 US 408, 417, 104 S.Ct. 1868, 1873]

For example, due process forbids the exercise of jurisdiction where:

- [3:230] An out-of state car dealer, who otherwise has no contacts with the forum state, is sued for injuries resulting from a customer's decision to drive a car there. [*World-Wide Volkswagen Corp. v. Woodson*, supra, 444 US at 289, 100 S.Ct. at 563; *see ¶3:287*]

- [3:231] A divorced husband is sued for child support in a state with which he has no connection other than the fact that his ex-wife has settled there, and his daughter has chosen to live with the ex-wife. [*Kulko v. Sup.Ct. (Horn)* (1978) 436 US 84, 96-98, 98 S.Ct. 1690, 1699-1700; *see ¶3:328*]

- [3:232] A trustee is sued for an accounting in a state with which its only connection resulted from the settlor's decision to move there. [*Hanson v. Denckla* (1958) 357 US 235, 253-254, 78 S.Ct. 1228, 1239-1240]

4) **[3:233]** **"Substantial connection" resulting from defendant's own acts:** The "purposeful availment" requirement is satisfied "where the (forum-related) contacts proximately result from actions by the defendant *himself* that create a 'substantial connection' with the forum State." [*Burger King Corp. v. Rudzewicz*, supra, 471 US at 475, 105 S.Ct. at 2184 (emphasis in original)]

   a) **[3:234]** **Application:** Particular liability-producing acts or omissions by nonresidents that have been held to establish a "substantial connection" to the forum state are discussed at ¶*3:263 ff.*

   **[3:235-237]** *Reserved.*

5) **[3:238]** **Nature and quality of acts (not quantity) determinative:** For limited jurisdiction, courts focus on the nature and quality of defendant's activity in the forum state, not the quantity. Reason: "Otherwise, states would be unable to provide their injured citizens with redress against large companies because the sales in any one state would represent a small fraction of the company's total revenue." [*As You Sow v. Crawford Laboratories, Inc.* (1996) 50 CA4th 1859, 1870, 58 CR2d 654, 659—limited jurisdiction upheld based on 16 sales to California residents over 6-year period, amounting to less than 1% of defendant's total sales]

   a) **[3:239]** **Single act may suffice:** Provided a "substantial connection" with the forum is created thereby, even a single act may support limited personal jurisdiction over a nonresident. [*McGee v. International Life Ins. Co.* (1957) 355 US 220, 223, 78 S.Ct. 199, 201]

      • **[3:239.1]** Issuance of a single life insurance policy to a California resident and collecting premiums thereon was enough to support a California court's jurisdiction over a Texas insurer. [*McGee v. International Life Ins. Co.*, supra]

      **[3:239.2-239.4]** *Reserved.*

   b) **[3:239.5]** **Mail, telephone, e-mail, etc.:** The means of communication is not determinative. "Minimum contacts" may be created by a nonresident's use of mail, telephone or electronic mail (e-mail) through the Internet. [See *Hall v. LaRonde* (1997) 56 CA4th 1342, 1344, 66 CR2d 399, 400—nonresident contracted with Calif. resident via e-mail and telephone; *see ¶3:312.5*]

1/ [3:239.6] **Internet activity:** Whether personal jurisdiction can be based on Internet activity depends on the *nature and quality* of the acts involved:

[3:239.7] A nonresident defendant who enters into contracts with local residents through *knowing and repeated transmission* of computer files over the Internet, is subject to local personal jurisdiction (the same as if by mail or telephone). [See *Jewish Defense Organization, Inc. v. Sup.Ct. (Rambam)* (1999) 72 CA4th 1045, 1060, 85 CR2d 611, 620; see also *Gator.Com Corp. v. L.L. Bean, Inc.* (9th Cir. 2003) 341 F3d 1072, 1078-1079 (*discussed at ¶3:213.7*)]

[3:239.8] But a nonresident's posting information on a *passive* Internet Web site that is accessible to forum residents is *not* an act "directed at the forum state," and thus not enough for the exercise of local personal jurisdiction. Express aiming or intentional targeting toward the forum state is required. [*Pavlovich v. Sup.Ct. (DVD Copy Control Ass'n, Inc.)* (2002) 29 C4th 262, 277, 127 CR2d 329, 341—no personal jurisdiction over nonresident Web site owner who posted illegal DVD decryption program that might harm California entertainment industries (mere foreseeability not enough); see also *Nam Tai Electronics, Inc. v. Titzer* (2001) 93 CA4th 1301, 1311, 113 CR2d 769, 776 —no personal jurisdiction over Colorado author based on messages posted on Internet Web server located in California and defaming Hong Kong corporation]

[3:239.9]   If the Web site is *interactive* (user can exchange information with the host computer), the exercise of jurisdiction must be determined "by examining the level of interactivity and commercial nature of the exchange of information that occurs on the Web site." [*Jewish Defense Organization, Inc. v. Sup.Ct. (Rambam)*, supra, 72 CA4th at 1060, 85 CR2d at 620]

*(Text cont'd on p. 3-57)*

**RESERVED**

*Cross-refer:* See further discussion and out-of-state cites in Schwarzer, Tashima & Wagstaffe, *Cal. Prac. Guide: Federal Civ. Pro. Before Trial* (TRG), Ch. 3.

c) **[3:240]** **Limitation—acts creating only "attenuated" contact:** The more "isolated" the act, the less foreseeable it may be that the nonresident would be "haled into court locally" (the rationale for the "purposeful" requirement). Thus, some "single or occasional acts" may create only an *"attenuated"* affiliation with the forum that will *not* support exercise of personal jurisdiction. [See *Burger King Corp. v. Rudzewicz*, supra, 471 US at 475, 105 S.Ct. at 2184, fn. 13; *Vons Cos., Inc. v. Seabest Foods, Inc.* (1996) 14 C4th 434, 448, 58 CR2d 899, 907-908]

6) **[3:240.1]** **Causing "effects" subject to special regulation in forum state:** Limited jurisdiction may also be upheld where a nonresident intentionally causes injurious "effects" in the state "of a nature that the State treats as exceptional and subjects to special regulation." Indeed, according to some cases, such jurisdiction exists even if the nonresident *has not otherwise invoked the benefits and protections* of local law. [*Jamshid-Negad v. Kessler* (1993) 15 CA4th 1704, 1708-1709, 19 CR2d 621, 623-624; *see further discussion at ¶3:333 ff.*]

• **[3:240.2]** By financing their minor son's education in California while negligently failing to supervise his activities, nonresident parents caused injurious "effects" subject to special regulations in California, including Civ.C. §1714.1 (imputing liability to parents for minor's willful misconduct). Hence, nonresidents were suable here for injuries caused by their son. [*Jamshid-Negad v. Kessler*, supra, 15 CA4th at 1709, 19 CR2d at 624; *see further discussion at ¶3:327*]

(b) **[3:241]** **Relationship between plaintiff's claim and defendant's forum activities:** The U.S. Supreme Court requires for specific jurisdiction that plaintiff's claim *"arise out of"* or be *"related to"* defendant's forum activities. [See *Burger King Corp.*

*v. Rudzewicz* (1985) 471 US 462, 477-478, 105 S.Ct. 2174, 2184-2185]

1) [3:242] **Claims may "arise" outside forum state:** The cause of action, however, need not arise within California. *It can arise outside the state*, as long as a sufficient "nexus" (connection) with defendant's California-related activities is shown. [*Cornelison v. Chaney* (1976) 16 C3d 143, 149-150, 127 CR 352, 355-356]

- [3:242.1] Trucker made irregular deliveries to and from California (too irregular for general jurisdiction). While *en route* to California, he caused accident and injuries in Nevada. California jurisdiction upheld. He was engaged in a California-related activity (heading for California to deliver goods) at time of accident . . . even though the cause of action itself arose in Nevada. [*Cornelison v. Chaney*, supra]

2) [3:243] **"Substantial connection" (nexus) sufficient:** The U.S. Supreme Court has not yet provided criteria for determining how connected plaintiff's claim must be to defendant's forum-related activity. But the California Supreme Court has:

"A claim need not arise directly from the defendant's forum contacts in order to be sufficiently related to the contact to warrant the exercise of specific jurisdiction. Rather, as long as the claim bears a *substantial connection* to the nonresident's forum contacts, the exercise of specific jurisdiction is appropriate." [*Vons Cos., Inc. v. Seabest Foods, Inc.* (1996) 14 C4th 434, 452, 58 CR2d 899, 910 (emphasis added)]

a) [3:243.1] **Causal relationship *not* required:** Thus, defendant's forum-related activity *need not be* the "immediate preceding legal cause" (proximate cause) of the occurrence giving rise to plaintiff's claim. [*Vons Cos., Inc. v. Seabest Foods, Inc.*, supra, 14 C4th at 460-462, 58 CR2d at 916-917]

Nor need it be a "but for" cause (direct cause) of plaintiff's claim. [*Vons Cos., Inc. v. Seabest Foods, Inc.*, supra, 14 C4th at 464-465, 58 CR2d at 918-919]

Rev. #1 2003

b) [3:243.2] **"Substantive relevance"** *not* **required:** Nor need defendant's forum-related activity provide an essential element of plaintiff's cause of action (as required for pleading purposes). All that need be shown is a "substantial connection" between them. [*Vons Cos., Inc. v. Seabest Foods, Inc.*, supra, 14 C4th at 469-470, 58 CR2d at 922-923]

c) [3:243.3] **Sliding scale utilized:** The greater the intensity of defendant's forum-related contacts, the lesser the relationship required between those contacts and plaintiff's claim. [*Vons Cos., Inc. v. Seabest Foods, Inc.,* supra, 14 C4th at 453, 58 CR2d at 911]

3) **Application**

- [3:244] Washington Franchisees enter into franchise contracts with California Franchiser to operate Jack-in-the-Box restaurants in Washington. Franchisees initiated the relationship in order to benefit from Franchiser's nationwide advertising and goodwill. The franchise contracts require that all disputes be litigated in California.

  If Franchiser were to sue Washington Franchisees for breach of contract, California courts "would have no difficulty finding specific jurisdiction" in such a case. [*Vons Cos., Inc. v. Seabest Foods, Inc.,* supra, 14 C4th at 451, 58 CR2d at 909]

- [3:244.1] Specific jurisdiction may also be asserted as to *tort* claims—by Franchiser *or others*—having a "substantial connection" to the franchise contract.

  Thus, under the facts above, Washington Franchisees serving contaminated hamburgers at their restaurant in Washington were subject to personal jurisdiction in California on resulting tort claims having a "substantial connection" with their dealings with California Franchiser. This included an indemnification claim by a California meat supplier for negligent preparation of the hamburgers because the meat had been sold to Franchiser who supplied it to Franchisees. [*Vons Cos., Inc. v. Seabest Foods,*

*Inc.,* supra, 14 C4th at 456, 58 CR2d at 913]

[3:245-246] *Reserved.*

(c) [3:247] **"Reasonableness":** Finally, it must appear that the exercise of jurisdiction by local courts in the particular case would "comport with fair play and substantial justice." [*Burger King Corp. v. Rudzewicz,* supra, 471 US at 476-477, 105 S.Ct. at 2184]

   1) [3:247.1] **Effect:** The "reasonableness" requirement—the requirement of "fair play and substantial justice"—may defeat local jurisdiction *even if defendant has purposefully engaged in forum-related activities.* [See *Asahi Metal Industry Co., Ltd. v. Sup.Ct. (Cheng Shin Rubber Industrial Co., Ltd.)* (1987) 480 US 102, 115, 107 S.Ct. 1026, 1034-1035; and *Burger King Corp. v. Rudzewicz,* supra, 471 US at 477-478, 105 S.Ct. at 2185]

   2) [3:248] **Factors considered:** This is determined by the factors previously listed at ¶3:202.

   3) [3:249] **Additional considerations with alien defendants:** The "unique burdens" placed upon a foreign national defending itself locally "should have significant weight" in assessing the "reasonableness" of a local court's exercise of personal jurisdiction. [*Asahi Metal Industry Co., Ltd. v. Sup.Ct. (Cheng Shin Rubber Industrial Co., Ltd.),* supra, 480 US at 114, 107 S.Ct. at 1034]

This does not mean that local courts can never exercise jurisdiction over foreign nationals. The interests of the plaintiff and forum often will justify even the serious burdens placed on a foreign defendant with whom minimum contacts have been established. [*Asahi Metal Industry Co., Ltd. v. Sup.Ct. (Cheng Shin Rubber Industrial Co., Ltd.),* supra, 480 US at 114, 107 S.Ct. at 1034]

   — "In this area of fax machines and discount air travel," requiring a German citizen to defend an action in California did not constitute so great an inconvenience as to violate due process. [*Integral Develop. Corp. v. Weissenbach* (2002) 99 CA4th 576, 592, 122 CR2d 24, 37]

Not so, however, where *plaintiff also is an alien* and the litigation relates to claims arising overseas. In such cases, the plaintiff's and forum's interests are "slight" and the exercise of local jurisdiction would be "unreasonable and unfair." [*Asahi Metal Industry Co., Ltd. v. Sup.Ct. (Cheng Shin Rubber Industrial Co., Ltd.),* supra, 480 US at 116, 107 S.Ct. at 1035]

[3:250] *Reserved.*

4) [3:251] **Application:** The burdens on the nonresident must *clearly outweigh* the plaintiff's and forum's interests. For example:

- [3:252] It was "unreasonable" for California courts to assert jurisdiction over Japanese Manufacturer on an indemnity claim by Taiwanese Manufacturer for defective parts shipped to Taiwan, which allegedly caused injury to a California purchaser. [*Asahi Metal Industry Co., Ltd. v. Sup.Ct. (Cheng Shin Rubber Industrial Co., Ltd.),* supra, 480 US at 116, 107 S.Ct. at 1035]

- [3:253] It was "unreasonable" for California courts to exercise jurisdiction over an English insurer on a claim by an insured who: a) was a British subject; b) was an attorney; and c) spent half his time in England. The burden on the English insurer in having to defend here was great, whereas there was little burden in forcing the insured to litigate in England; and California had no strong interest in providing redress. [*Fields v. Sedgwick Associated Risks, Ltd.* (9th Cir. 1986) 796 F2d 299, 302-303]

- [3:254] It was "unreasonable" for California courts to exercise jurisdiction in a suit against a Utah car dealer in an action arising out of injuries suffered in Arizona by an Arizona purchaser. Although the chain of title from the Utah dealer to the Arizona purchaser led through an auto auction in Los Angeles, California had no real interest in providing a forum and the burdens of defending here were substantial. [*Brand v. Menlove Dodge* (9th Cir. 1986) 796 F2d 1070, 1076]

5) [3:255] **Burden of proof re unreasonableness:** If plaintiff shows that the nonresident

defendant has "purposefully availed" itself of benefits and protections of forum law, that defendant bears the burden of proving it would be unreasonable for local courts to exercise jurisdiction. [*Burger King Corp. v. Rudzewicz*, supra, 471 US at 476, 105 S.Ct. at 2184]

6) [3:256] **Comment:** As a practical matter, jurisdiction is *rarely* declined on "reasonableness" grounds—especially in cases involving *commercial* activities impacting the forum state. [*Asahi Metal Industry Co., Ltd. v. Sup.Ct. (Cheng Shin Rubber Industrial Co., Ltd.)*, supra]

Courts recognize that a nonresident can alleviate the risk of being sued locally by buying insurance, passing the potential litigation costs on to its customers, or simply curtailing its activities in the forum state. [*World-Wide Volkswagen Corp. v. Woodson* (1980) 444 US 286, 297, 100 S.Ct. 559, 567]

Also, any undue burden in defending locally can be alleviated through change of venue or forum non conveniens (*see* ¶3:407). And, choice-of-law rules can be utilized to avoid policy conflicts with other states. [See *Burger King Corp. v. Rudzewicz*, supra, 471 US at 477, 105 S.Ct. at 2185]

[3:257-262] *Reserved.*

g. [3:263] **Limited jurisdiction based on liability-producing acts:** The most common examples of limited jurisdiction are cases in which a nonresident is sought to be held liable in California for acts causing loss or damage to a California resident. In such cases, jurisdiction is *limited* to causes of action that bear a *substantial connection* to the nonresident's forum-related contacts or activities. [*Vons Cos., Inc. v. Seabest Foods, Inc.* (1996) 14 C4th 434, 452, 58 CR2d 899, 910]

In addition, the nature of the acts and defendant's relationship to California must make the exercise of such jurisdiction "reasonable" under the circumstances (again, "fair play and substantial justice"). [*Burger King Corp. v. Rudzewicz* (1985) 471 US 462, 472-473, 105 S.Ct. 2174, 2182]

(1) [3:264] **Acts committed within California:** If the nonresident committed the liability-producing acts while physically present in California, the exercise of jurisdiction by state courts will almost always be held "reason-

able." His or her presence here while committing such acts will almost always constitute a sufficient "contact" to satisfy due process in lawsuits arising from those acts. [*Lundgren v. Sup.Ct. (Kahne)* (1980) 111 CA3d 477, 484, 168 CR 717, 720]

(a) [3:265] **Tort actions:** This principle is most frequently encountered in cases involving torts committed by nonresidents while temporarily in the state. For example:

- [3:266] A nonresident motorist who causes injury while driving on California highways is subject to personal jurisdiction here in a damages action for such injury. His or her tortious conduct while within the state is a sufficient "minimum contact" to support local jurisdiction in such action. [*Hess v. Pawloski* (1927) 274 US 352, 356, 47 S.Ct. 632, 633; see Veh.C. §17451]

- [3:267] Jurisdiction may also be asserted over the nonresident motorist's *employer or principal*. Rationale: The authority given to drive the car into California is a sufficient "contact" with California to support jurisdiction in actions against the employer or principal for injuries caused by the motorist. [See *Indiana Ins. Co. v. Pettigrew* (1981) 115 CA3d 862, 865, 171 CR 770, 771]

- [3:268] Oregon accountant came to California to assist client in fraud upon California resident. Although his stay was short, the accountant's tortious act while here was a sufficient "minimum contact" for due process purposes to support California jurisdiction in the fraud action. [*Lundgren v. Sup.Ct. (Kahne),* supra]

(b) [3:269] **Contract actions:** The fact that a nonresident enters California to execute or perform a contract with a California resident does not *per se* establish "minimum contacts." The Supreme Court requires a "highly realistic" approach that considers all factors affecting negotiation, execution and performance of the contract in determining whether defendant purposefully established minimum contacts with the forum. [*Burger King Corp. v. Rudzewicz* (1985) 471 US 462, 479, 105 S.Ct. 2174, 2184-2185; see ¶3:309]

But the fact that the nonresident enters California to negotiate or perform a contract is no doubt an important *factor* in the jurisdictional equation. [See *Safe-Lab, Inc. v. Weinberger* (1987) 193 CA3d 1050, 1053-1054, 238 CR 712, 714]

[3:270]   *Reserved.*

(2) **[3:271]   Acts committed outside California "causing effect" within:**   If the nonresident defendant operates entirely outside California, the mere fact that its acts "cause an effect" within the state, or even that such effect was "foreseeable," is *not* enough by itself to support local personal jurisdiction.

Rather, it must be shown that the act was *"purposeful"* (¶*3:226*), that the lawsuit *arises* from such acts, and that the exercise of California jurisdiction "comports with *fair play and substantial justice.*" [*Burger King Corp. v. Rudzewicz* (1985) 471 US 462, 476, 105 S.Ct. 2174, 2184; see *Sibley v. Sup.Ct. (Carlsberg Mobile Home Properties, Ltd.)* (1976) 16 C3d 442, 446-447, 128 CR 34, 37; *and* ¶*3:225*]

(a) **[3:272]   Intentional torts:**   If a nonresident, acting outside the state, intentionally causes injuries *within* the state, local jurisdiction is *presumptively not unreasonable:* "Where a defendant who purposefully has directed his activities at forum residents seeks to defeat jurisdiction, he must present a compelling case that . . . would render jurisdiction unreasonable." [See *Burger King Corp. v. Rudzewicz*, supra, 471 US at 475-476, 105 S.Ct. at 2184]

1) **[3:273]   Application:**   The following cases are illustrative:

• [3:274]   Pennsylvania resident prepared false financial statements for use in connection with corporate stock issuance in California. The nonresident was held subject to California jurisdiction in a fraud action filed by persons who had relied on the false financials. [*Quattrone v. Sup.Ct. (Whittaker Corp.)* (1975) 44 CA3d 296, 306, 118 CR 548, 554]

• [3:275]   New York woman made obscene and threatening phone calls to her ex-husband and his new wife, living in California. She was held subject to California jurisdiction in an action for intentional infliction of emotional distress resulting from her phone calls. [*Schlussel v. Schlussel* (1983) 141 CA3d 194, 198-199, 190 CR 95, 97]

- **[3:275.1]** German Employee, who misappropriated trade secrets of his employer, a California corporation, and used this information to injure the employer, had requisite minimum contacts with California for exercise of personal jurisdiction. [*Integral Develop. Corp. v. Weissenbach* (2002) 99 CA4th 576, 587, 122 CR2d 24, 33]

- **[3:275.2]** Transferring a known pedophile priest to a California diocese of the Catholic church supported a California court's jurisdiction over an out-of-state diocese: "By sending a known pedophile into California, the Milwaukee Archdiocese aimed its intentional conduct directly at this state." [*Archdiocese of Milwaukee v. Sup.Ct. (Paino)* (2003) 112 CA4th 423, 438, 5 CR3d 154, 167]

2) **[3:276] Defamation actions:** Similarly, nonresident publishers, editors, etc. may be sued locally for defamations published outside California.

   For example, Reporter and Editor, both Florida residents, wrote defamatory stories regarding Actress, a California resident, for publication in a national magazine. They were subject to personal jurisdiction in a California defamation action: "An individual injured in California need not go to Florida to seek redress from persons who, though remaining in Florida, *knowingly cause the injury in California.*" [*Calder v. Jones* (1984) 465 US 783, 789, 104 S.Ct. 1482, 1486-1487 (emphasis added)]

   a) **[3:277] No higher standard because of First Amendment concerns:** No higher standard of "contacts" is required in defamation actions against nonresident publishers. Any potential "chill" on free speech is already taken into account in the constitutional limitations on the substantive law governing defamation actions. [*Calder v. Jones,* supra, 465 US at 790, 104 S.Ct. at 1487]

   b) **[3:278] Sufficiency of "contacts":** However, the mere fact that a defamatory publication enters California is not enough by itself to subject the out-of-state publisher to local jurisdiction.

- [3:279] Jurisdiction will be upheld, of course, where the defamation appears in a national magazine having a large publication in California, and involves a California resident, so that the brunt of the harm is suffered in California (the "effects" test). [*Calder v. Jones*, supra, 465 US at 789, 104 S.Ct. at 1487]

- [3:280] Jurisdiction may also be upheld where the out-of-state publisher has "*continuously and deliberately exploited* the local market"—even if the plaintiff is *not* a resident of the forum state and the bulk of the harm done by the defamatory publication occurred elsewhere. I.e., the victim of a libel may sue in any forum with which the defendant has the requisite "minimum contacts." [*Keeton v. Hustler Magazine, Inc.* (1984) 465 US 770, 780, 104 S.Ct. 1473, 1481—New York resident sued Ohio publisher in New Hampshire to take advantage of its longer statute of limitations]

  (Note: California and most other states have adopted the "single publication rule." This requires that all damages from a multistate libel be recovered in a single action, and protects the defendant from multiple suits. See Civ.C. §3425.1.)

- [3:281] *Compare:* But where an out-of-state magazine or newspaper has only "incidental" or "insignificant" readership locally, and the story has no particular local appeal or interest (so that it would not be expected to receive particular attention here), the risk of injury from its circulation in California may be too remote to sustain personal jurisdiction. [*Sipple v. Des Moines Register & Tribune* (1978) 82 CA3d 143, 151-152, 147 CR 59, 64—less than 1% of Iowa publication sent to California subscribers; *Evangelize China Fellowship, Inc. v. Evangelize China Fellowship* (1983) 146 CA3d 440, 448-449,

194 CR 240, 245—7% of Hong Kong
publication sent to California readers]

- [3:281.1] *Compare—defamations
and intentional torts on Internet: See
discussion at ¶3:239.6 ff.*

3) [3:282] **Limitation—both act *and injury*
outside state:** But where both act *and injury*
occur *outside* California, there may not be sufficient "contacts" to support local jurisdiction

*(Text cont'd on p. 3-67)*

**RESERVED**

over a nonresident. [See *Scott v. Breeland* (9th Cir. 1986) 792 F2d 925, 928—Tennessee passenger assaulted Stewardess while plane on ground in Nevada; fact that Stewardess resided in California and plane en route here did *not* support California jurisdiction over passenger who had no other contacts here]

The fact a California resident is *affected* is not enough. [*Beckman v. Thompson* (1992) 4 CA4th 481, 486, 6 CR2d 60, 62—California resident sued New York Corporation for inducing breach of contract to be performed in Tennessee: jurisdiction denied because inducement occurred in New York and Corporation had no "contacts" with California]

4) **[3:283] Limitation—"remoteness"?** A nonresident intentional tortfeasor may not be subject to California jurisdiction if the tortious conduct is "too remote in time and causal connection" to the injuries suffered in California. [*Farris v. Capt. J.B. Fronapfel Co.* (1986) 182 CA3d 982, 990, 227 CR 619, 624]

- **[3:284]** Florida boat inspector fraudulently misrepresented condition of boat in Florida to California resident (P), who relied thereon in purchasing boat from Florida seller. Boat sank en route to California. California courts could *not* exercise jurisdiction over Florida boat inspector. The only "effect" in California of his alleged fraud was P's loss of money; and this was "*too remote in time and causal connection* to *fairly and justly* require" the Florida boat inspector to defend the action here. [*Farris v. Capt. J.B. Fronapfel Co.*, supra]

[3:285-286] *Reserved.*

(b) **[3:287] Product liability cases; "stream of commerce" theory:** Numerous cases deal with whether local courts may exercise personal jurisdiction against nonresidents in product liability actions. The issue is whether the mere fact that the "stream of commerce" brings the nonresident's product into the forum state is enough "contact" to support personal jurisdiction over the nonresident.

1) **[3:288] Manufacturer or national distributor:** A manufacturer or national distributor (as distinguished from a retailer or local distributor)

may be subject to personal jurisdiction wherever the product causes injury. It is enough that the manufacturer or distributor *"purposefully" attempts to serve* a market in the forum state. Where this is shown, local courts may properly "assert personal jurisdiction over a corporation that *delivers its products into the stream of commerce* with the expectation that they will be purchased by consumers in the forum State." [*World-Wide Volkswagen Corp. v. Woodson* (1980) 444 US 286, 297-298, 100 S.Ct. 559, 567 (emphasis added)]

[3:289-290]   *Reserved.*

a) [3:291]   **Sale and injuries outside California:**   Specific personal jurisdiction *cannot* be established where the allegedly defective goods were manufactured and sold outside the forum and caused injury outside the forum, and the manufacturer or supplier has no other "contacts" with the forum. In such cases, the nonresident defendant's acts *cannot* be said to have been "purposefully directed" at residents of the forum state. [*Boaz v. Boyle & Co., Inc.* (1995) 40 CA4th 700, 717, 46 CR2d 888, 899—allegedly defective drug sold in New York to New York and New Jersey residents causing injuries there; no basis for jurisdiction in California]

b) [3:292]   **Compare—goods specifically sold for use in California:**   But jurisdiction has been upheld where an out-of-state seller *knowingly* sold its product *for use within California*. [*Secrest Machine Corp. v. Sup.Ct. (Ramos)* (1983) 33 C3d 664, 671-672, 190 CR 175, 180; *Cassiar Mining Corp. v. Sup.Ct. (Anderson)* (1998) 66 CA4th 550, 555, 78 CR2d 167, 170— Canadian mine sold raw asbestos to California purchasers for over 30 years]

Even *isolated or sporadic sales* are sufficient where the manufacturer makes a direct effort to serve the market for its product in the forum state. [*As You Sow v. Crawford Laboratories, Inc.* (1996) 50 CA4th 1859, 1870, 58 CR2d 654, 659—limited jurisdiction based on 16 sales to California residents over 6-year period, amounting to less than 1% of defendant's total sales]

- **[3:293]** California employer went to Virginia to purchase machine from manufacturer (which had no office or sales force in California). Employer took delivery in Virginia and brought the machine to California, where it caused injury to Employee. Virginia manufacturer was subject to California jurisdiction because it *knew* the machine was being sold for use in California. It was an *effort by the manufacturer to develop a market for its product in California*, and "should have caused (the manufacturer) to anticipate being haled into a California court to defend an action arising from alleged defects in its product." [*Secrest Machine Corp. v. Sup.Ct. (Ramos)* (1983) 33 C3d 664, 671, 190 CR 175, 180]

2) **[3:294] Retailer or regional distributor:** An out-of-state retailer or regional distributor that does *not* regularly sell its products in the forum state and has no "contacts" there, is *not* subject to local jurisdiction in product liability actions. This is true even if it was foreseeable that the goods it sells (e.g., automobiles) might be brought into the forum state. I.e., the *purchaser's unilateral activity* of bringing such goods into the forum state *does not constitute "purposeful availment"* by the out-of-state retailer or distributor. [*World-Wide Volkswagen Corp. v. Woodson* (1980) 444 US 286, 297, 100 S.Ct. 559, 567]

- **[3:295]** East Coast Volkswagen distributor sold allegedly defective car to New York retailer who sold it to New York purchaser. Car was being driven through Oklahoma when it went out of control and injured plaintiff. Oklahoma courts would not exercise personal jurisdiction over the distributor or retailer. [*World-Wide Volkswagen Corp. v. Woodson*, supra]

**[3:296]** *Reserved.*

3) **[3:297] Supplier of defective component:** It is unclear whether the "stream of commerce" rationale extends to a nonresident parts supplier that otherwise has no "contacts" with California. I.e., does a nonresident's *mere aware-*

*ness* that the component it manufactures or sells *outside* the forum state will reach the forum in the "stream of commerce" constitute "minimum contacts" with the forum state for due process purposes?

a) **[3:298]** **Example:** Japanese Supplier sells tire valves to Taiwanese Manufacturer, knowing the valves will be assembled there into tires shipped by Manufacturer to California. P suffers injury from a defective tire valve and files suit against Manufacturer in California. Manufacturer seeks to cross-complain against Supplier for equitable indemnity. Is Japanese Supplier subject to personal jurisdiction here, absent any other "contact" with California?

**[3:299]** The U.S. Supreme Court was faced with these facts in *Asahi Metal Industry Co., Ltd. v. Sup.Ct. (Cheng Shin Rubber Industrial Co., Ltd.)* (1987) 480 US 102, 107 S.Ct. 1026, but was unable to agree on an opinion on this issue. (It found the exercise of California jurisdiction "unreasonable" in any event; *see ¶3:249.*)

- **[3:300]** Four justices were of the view that placing a product in the "stream of commerce" with awareness of its ultimate destination is *not* enough. The nonresident must have *purposefully directed* its activities toward the forum state by *additional conduct*; e.g., by designing its product for a market in that state, or by advertising there, or by marketing through a distributor there. [*Asahi Metal Industry Co., Ltd. v. Sup.Ct. (Cheng Shin Rubber Industrial Co., Ltd.)*, supra, 480 US at 112, 107 S.Ct. at 1033]

- **[3:301]** But four other justices would apply the "stream of commerce" theory without any additional requirement. Jurisdiction may be upheld as against any participant in the manufacture and distribution process who is *aware* that the final product is being marketed in the forum state. No further "purposeful availment" is required. [*Asahi Metal Industry Co., Ltd. v. Sup.Ct. (Cheng Shin*

*Rubber Industrial Co., Ltd.),* supra, 480 US at 116, 107 S.Ct. at 1035 (Brennan opn.)]

b) **[3:302]** **State cases:** California cases have rejected the "stream of commerce" argument where the foreign defendant, though aware its products might reach this state, made no specific efforts to accomplish this result: "Merely knowing the product will enter California, *without having some control over its ultimate destination,* does not satisfy the due process clause." [*Carretti v. Italpast* (2002) 101 CA4th 1236, 1246, 125 CR2d 126, 132-133 (emphasis added; internal quotes omitted); *Felix v. Bomoro Kommanditgesellschaft* (1987) 196 CA3d 106, 117, 241 CR 670, 676— foreign manufacturer of door latch supplied to Volkswagen not subject to suit in California for injuries suffered when latch failed and passenger thrown from car]

4) **[3:303]** **Designer, engineer, etc.:** It is unclear whether a nonresident designer, engineer, etc. is subject to local jurisdiction in actions for injuries suffered here, caused by faulty design work done elsewhere:

a) **[3:304]** One case upholds jurisdiction despite no direct contacts between the designer and the forum state: "It is sufficient that . . . the defendant purposefully set his product or designs into the stream of commerce, *knowing or having reason to know that they will reach the forum state* and that they create a potential of injury." [*Rice Growers Ass'n v. First National Bank of Minneapolis* (1985) 167 CA3d 559, 580-581, 214 CR 468, 483 (emphasis added)— tug-barge designed in Louisiana for use in California]

b) **[3:305]** But other courts reach the opposite result, on the ground that the mere expectation that a product or equipment will be *used* within the forum state is not sufficient to subject the nonresident to local jurisdiction. The "stream of commerce" rationale is not applicable because it applies only to products manufactured or distributed with expectation of *sale* to consumers in the forum. [*Sousa v. Ocean Sunflower Shipping Co.* (ND CA 1984) 608 F.Supp. 1309, 1314-1315—Japanese company designed and built ship for use in transporting steel from Japan to California]

5) [3:306] **Service and repair:** Nonresidents who service or repair products destined for California are not *by that fact alone* subject to suit here for injuries caused by their work. [See *Alexander v. Heater* (1987) 193 CA3d 1241, 1246-1247, 238 CR 795, 798]

- [3:307] Oregon residents negligently installed a lift gate on a truck in Oregon. The gate malfunctioned in California, causing injury to California residents. Based on the minimal nature of their acts, it would not be fair or reasonable for California courts to exercise personal jurisdiction over the Oregon residents. [*Alexander v. Heater,* supra, 193 CA3d at 1246, 238 CR at 798]

[3:307.1-307.4] *Reserved.*

(c) [3:307.5] **False advertising, unfair competition:** A foreign corporation has been held subject to California jurisdiction based on activities purposefully directed at California residents in an action for false advertising and unfair competition under Bus. & Prof.C. §17200 and related claims. [*Snowney v. Harrah's Entertainment, Inc.* (2004) 116 CA4th 996, 1004-1005, 11 CR3d 35, 41-42—Nevada hotels advertised in California, maintained interactive Web site and toll-free telephone number used by California residents for hotel reservations]

- [3:307.6] An *out-of-state telemarketer* may be subject to California jurisdiction in an action for false advertising and related claims based on calls *to* a California resident, or *in an "upsell"* (a sales pitch for an additional product or service) during calls initiated *by* California residents. [*West Corp. v. Sup.Ct. (Stanford)* (2004) 116 CA4th 1167,      , 11 CR3d 145, 157]

[3:307.7-307.9] *Reserved.*

(3) [3:308] **Contract cases:** A *"highly realistic"* approach is required in determining whether a nonresident contracting party is subject to local jurisdiction. It must be recognized that a "contract is ordinarily but an *intermediate step* serving to tie up prior business negotia-

tions with future consequences which themselves are the real object of the business transaction." [*Burger King Corp. v. Rudzewicz* (1985) 471 US 462, 479, 105 S.Ct. 2174, 2185 (emphasis added)]

(a) [3:309] **Mechanical tests rejected:** Thus, the mere fact that a nonresident enters into a contract with a forum resident does *not* establish "minimum contacts" between the nonresident and the forum state.

Nor is jurisdiction established automatically because the forum was the "place of contracting" or "place of performance"; nor because breach has "caused an effect" (financial loss) in California. [*Burger King Corp. v. Rudzewicz*, supra; see *Sibley v. Sup.Ct. (Carlsberg Mobile Home Properties, Ltd.)* (1976) 16 C3d 442, 446-447, 128 CR 34, 37]

The place where a contract is executed "is of far less importance than where the consequences of performing that contract come to be felt." [*Stone v. State of Texas* (1999) 76 CA4th 1043, 1048, 90 CR2d 657, 660—hiring California resident did not subject

*(Text cont'd on p. 3-73)*

**RESERVED**

nonresident employer to California jurisdiction where services were rendered outside California]

[3:310] *Reserved.*

(b) [3:311] **Relevant factors:** Instead, recognizing the contract as merely an "intermediate step" (see above), courts must evaluate the following factors in determining whether the defendant "purposefully" established minimum contacts within the forum:

- *Prior negotiations;*

- *Contemplated future consequences;*

- The *terms of the contract;* and

- The parties' *actual course of dealings.* [*Burger King Corp. v. Rudzewicz*, supra, 471 US at 482, 105 S.Ct. at 2185]

1) [3:312] **Choice of law as factor:** The fact that contracting parties stipulate local law shall apply to their transaction does not *by itself* subject them to local jurisdiction. But it may be a relevant "contact" for jurisdictional purposes; i.e., agreement to be bound by forum law shows "purposeful availment" of the benefits and protections of local law. [*Burger King Corp. v. Rudzewicz*, supra, 471 US at 482, 105 S.Ct. at 2187; *Safe-Lab, Inc. v. Weinberger* (1987) 193 CA3d 1050, 1053-1054, 238 CR 712, 714]

2) [3:312.1] **Lack of physical presence immaterial:** Lack of physical presence in the forum state is usually immaterial: "(I)n this age of telecommunications, FAX machines, and rapid mail services it is possible to perform these functions without face-to-face meetings in any jurisdiction." [*Checker Motors Corp. v. Sup.Ct. (Garamendi)* (1993) 13 CA4th 1007, 1018, 17 CR2d 618, 624, 625]

[3:312.2-312.4] *Reserved.*

3) [3:312.5] **Effect of forum-selection clause:** Due process requirements can be waived. Thus, parties may expressly *consent* to personal jurisdiction in a forum with which they otherwise have no "contacts." But such consent must be clear and the forum designated must not be "unreasonable or unjust" (*see ¶3:177*).

(c) [3:313] **Franchises:** A Michigan franchisee was held subject to personal jurisdiction in Florida, where the franchisor had its principal office, because:

- The franchisee was a sophisticated businessman who had *initiated* the franchise transaction ("reaching out beyond" Michigan);

- The agreement called for a long-term, close business relationship with the franchisor in Florida; and

- The agreement expressly stated that the franchise was established in Florida and governed by Florida law. (It did *not*, however, contain a forum-selection clause consenting to jurisdiction in Florida; *see ¶3:177.*)

These factors established the franchisee's *"purposeful affiliation"* with Florida and the *reasonable foreseeability of litigation there*, so that—absent any showing of "fundamental unfairness"—Florida's exercise of jurisdiction was not unconstitutional. [*Burger King Corp. v. Rudzewicz*, supra, 471 US at 487, 105 S.Ct. at 2190; see also *Vons Cos., Inc. v. Seabest Foods, Inc.* (1996) 14 C4th 434, 448-450, 58 CR2d 899, 907-909]

1) [3:314] **Limitations:** This does *not* mean that every franchisee is subject to personal jurisdiction at its franchisor's place of business. The quality and nature of the "contacts" have to be decided on a case-by-case basis. Factors such as great inconvenience, disparity of bargaining power, or a smaller amount in controversy, may lead to different results in other cases. [*Burger King Corp. v. Rudzewicz*, supra, 471 US at 485, 105 S.Ct. at 2189, fn. 28]

(d) [3:315] **Local purchases:** The extent to which a nonresident subjects itself to local jurisdiction by making purchases within the state is somewhat unclear:

1) [3:316] **No general jurisdiction:** Purchasing (as opposed to selling) goods and services within the forum state, even at regular intervals, is *not a sufficiently "substantial, continuous and systematic" activity to support general* (unlimited) personal jurisdiction. Thus, absent other contacts, a nonresident purchaser cannot be sued on causes of action *unrelated* to its local purchases. [*Helicopteros Nacionales de Colombia, S.A. v. Hall* (1984) 466 US 408, 418, 104 S.Ct. 1868, 1874; *see ¶3:215*]

2) [3:317] **Limited jurisdiction:** Where the action *is* related to the local purchases, courts must weigh the factors enumerated at ¶*3:311* in deciding whether the nonresident purchaser has "purposefully" established a *business* relationship in the forum state: "Jurisdiction over an out-of-state buyer must be premised on a substantial basis such as an *ongoing relationship or course of dealings* with the plaintiff." [*Futuresat Industries, Inc. v. Sup.Ct. (Bay Area Interconnect)* (1992) 3 CA4th 155, 159, 4 CR2d 74, 76 (emphasis added)]

a) [3:318] **Isolated purchases insufficient:** Nonresident buyers who make isolated purchases from a California seller do *not* thereby subject themselves to the jurisdiction of California courts. It is immaterial that the nonresident buyer *initiated* the transaction and the purchase price was made payable in California. [*Futuresat Industries, Inc. v. Sup.Ct. (Bay Area Interconnect)*, supra—Texas buyer heard California seller had videos for sale; all negotiations were by phone and letter; buyer's stating it was "looking forward to doing more business with you" did *not* establish ongoing business activity in California]

[3:318.1] Rationale: To sustain personal jurisdiction in such cases would discourage interstate commerce. [*Futuresat Industries, Inc. v. Sup.Ct. (Bay Area Interconnect)*, supra, 3 CA4th at 161, 4 CR2d at 77]

b) [3:319] **Compare—systematic purchases:** On the other hand, purchasing activity in California that is *regular and recurrent* may subject the nonresident purchaser to California jurisdiction. The test is whether the nonresident has *purposefully established* a *business relationship* in California. [*Rocklin De Mexico v. Sup.Ct. (Rocklin Forest Products)* (1984) 157 CA3d 91, 98, 203 CR 547, 551; *Futuresat Industries, Inc. v. Sup.Ct. (Bay Area Interconnect)* (1992) 3 CA4th 155, 159, 4 CR2d 74, 76—same]

[3:319.1] Example: Mexican corporation initiated lumber purchases in California; the purchases were regular and recurrent; title to the goods was taken in California; the goods were for business rather than personal use; and the value of the purchases was "substantial." Such purchases should have caused the purchaser to anticipate the possibility of having to defend suit in California and hence exercise of California jurisdiction was proper. [*Rocklin De Mexico v. Sup.Ct. (Rocklin Forest Products)*, supra, 157 CA3d at 98, 203 CR at 551]

(e) **[3:320] Employing local counsel:** A nonresident client's employing local counsel may be a sufficient "purposeful availment" to subject the client to local personal jurisdiction in an action by the attorney to collect his or her fees. [*Dunne v. Florida* (1992) 6 CA4th 1340, 1345-1346, 8 CR2d 483, 486—State of Florida subject to personal jurisdiction in California in fee dispute with attorneys it hired to represent it in California]

(f) **[3:321] Loan and financing transactions:** Nonresidents who *borrow* from California creditors are not automatically subject to personal jurisdiction here in an action to enforce payment of the loan. [See *Hunt v. Sup.Ct. (Commercial Money Ctr.)* (2000) 81 CA4th 901, 906, 97 CR2d 215, 218—California lender provided financing for equipment lease negotiated and executed in Maryland involving equipment located there]

*Compare:* California creditors may include forum-selection clauses in their loan agreements in order to obtain personal jurisdiction over nonresident debtors; *see ¶3:177 ff.*

1) **[3:322]** Similarly, nonresidents who *lend* money to California residents do not automatically subject themselves to personal jurisdiction in California. The mere receipt of payments from a California resident does not itself constitute "purposeful availment" of benefits under California law. [See *Thomas J. Palmer, Inc. v. Turkiye Is Bankasi A.S.* (1980) 105 CA3d 135, 154, 164 CR 181, 192—nonresident was beneficiary under letter of credit receiving funds from Calif. bank]

[3:323-324.4] *Reserved.*

(g) **[3:324.5] Consumer transactions:** Jurisdictional rules may not be employed against small consumers so as to "cripple their defenses" by suing them in distant forums. Thus, unsophisticated local residents who *respond to solicitations* from out-of-state lenders or sellers are generally *not* subject to personal jurisdiction in other states. [See *Yu v. Signet Bank/Virginia* (1999) 69 CA4th 1377, 1388-1389, 82 CR2d 304, 311-312—Californians using credit card offered by Virginia Bank to purchase family and household goods were not thereby subject to personal jurisdiction in Virginia; default judgment obtained in Virginia held void ("distant forum abuse"); see also *Yu v. Signet Bank/Virginia ("Yu II")* (2002) 103 CA4th 298, 319, 126 CR2d 516, 530]

[3:325] *Reserved.*

(h) [3:326] **Assignment:** A nonresident who accepts assignment of a California-related contract may thereby become subject to California jurisdiction. I.e., if the assignor would have been subject to personal jurisdiction here, so is the assignee . . . because *one cannot assume the benefits of a contract without assuming its burdens* (Civ.C. §1589). Moreover, the assumption shows the nonresident's "purposeful availment" of California-related dealings; and California has a strong interest in providing a forum for local residents. [*Bruns v. DeSoto Operating Co.* (1988) 204 CA3d 876, 882-883, 251 CR 462, 465-466]

(4) [3:327] **Family support and parentage:** The Family Code provides that in interstate actions to determine parentage or for spousal or child support, a nonresident may be subject to California on various grounds, including:

— the nonresident *resided with the child* in California;

— the child resides here *as a result of the nonresident's acts* or directives;

— the nonresident engaged in *sexual intercourse* here and the child "may have been conceived by that act of intercourse";

— "any other basis consistent with the constitutions of this state and the United States for the exercise of personal jurisdiction." [Fam.C. §4905]

(a) [3:328] **Constitutionality:** "It is reasonable that a state should exercise judicial jurisdiction over the defendant as to causes of action arising from an act done, or caused to be done, by him in the state *which the state subjects to special regulation.*" [*County of Humboldt v. Harris* (1988) 206 CA3d

857, 864, 254 CR 49, 54 (emphasis added), quoting Rest.2d, Conflict of Laws, §36, comm. "e"]

- **[3:328.1]** A man whose only "contact" with California was a single act of sexual intercourse here may be subject to local personal jurisdiction in actions for support of a child conceived thereby. [*County of Humboldt v. Harris*, supra, 206 CA3d at 864, 254 CR at 54]

  **[3:328.2-328.4]** *Reserved.*

- **[3:328.5]** *Compare:* New York Father's only "contact" with California was that he *acquiesced* in his daughter moving to California to live with his ex-wife. The ex-wife then sued in California for additional support. The fact the daughter might derive benefits from California (education, etc.) did *not* show "purposeful availment" by Father of such benefits, and hence he was *not* subject to California personal jurisdiction. [See *Kulko v. Sup.Ct. (Horn)* (1978) 436 US 84, 96-98, 98 S.Ct. 1690, 1699-1700]

*Cross-refer:* See further discussion of personal jurisdiction in support actions in Hogoboom & King, *Cal. Prac. Guide: Family Law* (TRG), Ch. 3.

(b) **[3:329] Compare—"palimony" actions:** Similar concepts have been applied in actions arising

*(Text cont'd on p. 3-77)*

out of a *nonmarital* relationship. [See *Kroopf v. Guffey* (1986) 183 CA3d 1351, 1357-1358, 228 CR 807, 810—man gave up job to live with other man pursuant to agreement to share earnings; California jurisdiction upheld because they had lived in California during a *portion* of the time they were together]

(5) **[3:330]** **Professional services:** Nonresident professional persons who "purposefully avail" themselves of local laws or business may be subject to local jurisdiction in actions arising out of their activities. [*Hylwa v. Palka* (9th Cir. 1987) 823 F2d 310, 314]

(a) **[3:331]** **Nonresident accountants:** A Kansas accountant continued to serve a business client who moved to California. Although the accountant rarely came to California, local courts could exercise personal jurisdiction in the client's malpractice suit against the accountant. [*Hylwa v. Palka*, supra]

(b) **[3:332]** **Nonresident attorneys:** It is not entirely clear whether lawyers in other states are suable here for malpractice occurring outside of California. The issue is one of *federal* due process of law. [See *Sher v. Johnson* (9th Cir. 1990) 911 F2d 1357, 1363]

1) **[3:332.1]** **Effect of maintaining California license:** Maintaining a license to practice law in California is *not enough by itself* to subject a nonresident lawyer to personal jurisdiction here. [*Crea v. Busby* (1996) 48 CA4th 509, 515, 55 CR2d 513, 516]

• **[3:332.2]** Oregon Attorney was retained in Oregon to represent an Oregon corporation in a breach of contract action in Oregon court. After the Oregon suit was settled, a California shareholder of the Oregon corporation sued Attorney for breach of fiduciary duty. Attorney's sole contact with California was that he was licensed to practice here (but had not done so for many years). His California law license was not enough by itself to subject him to local jurisdiction. [*Crea v. Busby*, supra, 48 CA4th at 515, 55 CR2d at 516]

• **[3:332.3]** *Compare:* Lawyer, who was licensed in California, resided in New York and was employed by a New York Law Firm. He performed legal services there *relating to California law for a California resident.* Lawyer and the New York Law Firm were subject to personal jurisdiction of the California courts in a malpractice action based on the services rendered. [*Simons v. Steverson* (2001) 88 CA4th 693, 697, 106 CR2d 193, 196]

[3:332.4] *Reserved.*

2) [3:332.5] **Effect of representing California clients:** Under appropriate circumstances, nonresident attorneys who represent California clients may be found to have "purposefully availed" themselves of the benefits and protections of California law:

- [3:332.6] One case upheld personal jurisdiction over Texas lawyers who had been retained through plaintiff's California counsel to prosecute a personal injury action in Texas. The Texas lawyers' communications and *fee-splitting arrangement* with the California lawyers constituted "purposeful availment" of the privilege of doing business here. [*Brown v. Watson* (1989) 207 CA3d 1306, 1314, 255 CR 507, 512]

- [3:332.7] But other cases hold out-of-state legal representation of a California resident (which necessarily involves fee payments from California and communications with the client) by itself does *not* establish "purposeful availment" of the privilege of conducting activities in California. [*Edmunds v. Sup.Ct. (Ronson)* (1994) 24 CA4th 221, 236, 29 CR2d 281, 291—Hawaii attorney represented Calif. partnership in Hawaii litigation, although deposition taken in Calif.; see also *Sher v. Johnson,* supra, 911 F2d at 1362-1363]

[3:332.8-332.9] *Reserved.*

(c) [3:332.10] **Nonresident doctors:** Where a prospective patient travels out of state to a doctor and there receives negligent treatment, the patient's home state courts *cannot* exercise personal jurisdiction over the nonresident doctor in a malpractice action . . . even though the effects of the doctor's negligence are felt in the patient's home state. [See *Prince v. Urban* (1996) 49 CA4th 1056, 1058, 57 CR2d 181, 182]

Rationale: Doctor's services are personal in nature and therefore the focus must be on the *place where such services are rendered.* [*Prince v. Urban,* supra, 49 CA4th at 1059, 57 CR2d at 182]

1) **[3:332.11] Includes follow-up care:** Nor is the nonresident doctor subject to local jurisdiction because the doctor consulted with the patient by telephone after the patient returned home, *charged a fee* for such consultation, and supplied the patient with additional medication and prescriptions: "A treating physician cannot ethically abandon his or her patient just because the patient is returning home to another state." [*Prince v. Urban,* supra, 49 CA4th at 1067, 57 CR2d at 187]

    [3:332.12-332.14] *Reserved.*

2) **[3:332.15] Compare—effect of national marketing:** Nonresident doctors who attain national prominence and *invite* out-of-state patients to come under their care may be sued in their patients' home states for malpractice. Such doctors have purposefully directed their activities at the forum state. [*Prince v. Urban,* supra, 49 CA4th at 1060, 57 CR2d at 184]

3) **[3:332.16] Compare—nonresident consultants?** Under appropriate circumstances, nonresident doctors who are consulted by local physicians and who misdiagnose the patient's conditions (e.g., misanalyze tissue samples) *may* also be subject to local jurisdiction. [See *Prince v. Urban,* supra, 49 CA4th at 1061, 57 CR2d at 184—"The diagnosis—which was, after all, *the* critical service provided by the (nonresident) doctor—was made 'through the mail'" (parentheses added)]

    [3:332.17-332.19] *Reserved.*

4) **[3:332.20] Effect of maintaining California license?** It is not clear whether a nonresident physician is suable in California for malpractice committed elsewhere solely because he or she also maintains a license to practice medicine in California. By analogy, however, the same rule should be applied as in the case of lawyers (*see ¶3:332.1*).

(6) [3:333] **Other activities subject to special regulation:** Nonresidents may also be subject to local personal jurisdiction if they intentionally engage in local activities that the forum state treats as "exceptional and subjects to special regulation." [*Bresler v. Stavros* (1983) 141 CA3d 365, 369, 189 CR 58, 61—practice of medicine is such an activity]

Because of the state's regulatory interest in such activities, exercise of jurisdiction may be appropriate even where the nonresident's activities are *not* closely connected to state-conferred benefits or privileges. [*Bresler v. Stavros*, supra, 141 CA3d at 369, 189 CR at 61]

[3:334] *Reserved.*

(a) [3:335] **Insurance:** California has a strong interest in providing its residents with effective redress against out-of-state or foreign insurers who refuse to pay claims. California policy is to protect local policyholders against the cost and inconvenience of having to sue the insurance company in its home state. [See *Haisten v. Grass Valley Medical Reimbursement Fund, Ltd.* (9th Cir. 1986) 784 F2d 1392, 1400—insurance company set up in Cayman Islands to provide malpractice coverage for California doctors held subject to local jurisdiction]

1) [3:336] **Local offices not required:** Foreign insurance companies may be subject to California jurisdiction even if they have no office or sales force here; and even though its policies were negotiated and delivered elsewhere. If they *derive significant economic benefits* from insuring California assets and activities, they should anticipate being "haled into court here." [*A.I.U. Ins. Co. v. Sup.Ct. (Oil Ins. Ltd.)* (1986) 177 CA3d 281, 291, 222 CR 880, 886— Bermuda insurance company formed by oil companies to insure risks worldwide held subject to California jurisdiction on claims for risks located here]

2) [3:337] **Isolated transactions:** *Soliciting* and issuing a policy to a forum resident and collecting premiums thereon may support local jurisdiction over a nonresident insurer in an action to enforce the policy even if it has no other contacts with the forum state. [See *McGee v. International Life Ins. Co.* (1957) 355 US 220, 223, 78 S.Ct. 199, 201, *discussed at* ¶3:239]

a) **[3:337.1]** **Compare:** But the result may be different where the foreign insurer *did not solicit* the forum resident. [See *Malone v. Equitas Reinsurance Ltd.* (2000) 84 CA4th 1430, 1440, 101 CR2d 524, 531 — Calif. resident obtained insurance through agent in England from English insurer covering business risks there; no substantial connection existed between English insurer and Calif.]

3) **[3:338]** **Automobile liability insurers:** Out-of-state automobile liability insurers may be subject to local jurisdiction in actions by injured parties to enforce a judgment covered by the insurance policy where the underlying loss occurred in the forum state. [See *Southeastern Express Systems v. Southern Guar. Ins. Co. of Georgia* (1995) 34 CA4th 1, 9, 40 CR2d 216, 221]

- **[3:338.1]** Alabama Insurer issued an auto liability policy covering accidents anywhere in the country. Insured negligently caused injuries in California. Injured Party obtained judgment here against Insured and then sued Insurer to enforce that judgment. Insurer was subject to California jurisdiction in Injured Party's action. It was immaterial that Insurer, Insured and Injured Party were *all nonresidents.* The very nature of Insurer's business contemplated appearances *anywhere* a covered accident occurred. [*McClanahan v. Trans-America Ins. Co.* (1957) 149 CA2d 171, 173, 307 P2d 1023, 1025]

  **[3:338.2-338.4]** *Reserved.*

4) **[3:339]** **Liability insurer's refusal to defend local lawsuit:** Similarly, a nonresident general liability insurance company may be subject to local jurisdiction in a "bad faith" action *by its insured* based on the insurer's wrongful refusal to defend a local lawsuit filed against the insured: "California has a significant interest in assuring that injuries and losses suffered in this state are afforded insurance coverage." [*Southeastern Express Systems v. Southern Guar. Ins. Co. of Georgia* (1995) 34 CA4th 1, 7, 40 CR2d 216, 220]

- [3:339.1] Georgia insurer provided nationwide liability coverage to Georgia residents (insureds) who sold and serviced computers in California. They were sued in California by a third party but Insurer refused to defend the action. Insureds then sued Insurer locally for damages resulting from its refusal to defend. Insurer was subject to local jurisdiction although it had no physical presence or "contacts" in California. Reason: Insurers of nationwide businesses derive economic benefits from their insureds' activities in California and should reasonably anticipate being sued here for refusal to provide policy benefits (defense of third party claims). [*Southeastern Express Systems v. Southern Guar. Ins. Co. of Georgia*, supra, 34 CA4th at 6-7, 40 CR2d at 219]

    [3:339.2-339.4] *Reserved.*

5) [3:339.5] **Compare—"first party" actions:** A nonresident insurer is also apparently suable locally in actions *by its insured* for policy benefits (e.g., repairs to car, medical coverages, etc.). I.e., as long as the insurer "purposefully availed" itself of the benefits of an economic market in the forum state, it should make no difference whether the local action is by an injured party or its own insured. [See *Southeastern Express Systems v. Southern Guar. Ins. Co. of Georgia*, supra, 34 CA4th at 9-10, 40 CR2d at 221-222 (dictum) (contrary authority rejected)]

    - [3:339.6] But a Mississippi medical insurer was *not* subject to limited jurisdiction in California simply because one of its insureds (*not* a California resident) became ill while traveling in California. The insurer had *not* "purposefully availed" itself of an economic market in California. [*Benefit Ass'n Int'l, Inc. v. Sup.Ct. (Drach)* (1996) 46 CA4th 827, 54 CR2d 165, 169]

    [3:340] *Reserved.*

6) [3:341] **Compare—actions *between* nonresident insurers:** Jurisdiction is less likely to be upheld in an action by one foreign insurer against another for indemnity. It is *not* enough

that the claim for which indemnity is sought had been made by a California resident (the claim having been paid); or that some of the premiums paid for the indemnity agreement related to insurance written in California. [*Great-West Life Assurance Co. v. Guarantee Co. of North America* (1988) 205 CA3d 199, 209, 252 CR 363, 369—*Guarantee* showed a "substantial burden" in having to defend in California. Moreover, "California has little interest in adjudicating a contractual dispute between two Canadian insurance companies . . . where the underlying claims of California residents already have been disposed of . . ."]

7) **[3:341.1] Compare—insurance guaranty associations:** But jurisdiction over an out-of-state insurer does not extend to an out-of-state insurance guaranty association that has assumed its obligations upon that insurer's insolvency. [*Pennsylvania Life & Health Ins. Guar. Ass'n v. Sup.Ct. (Laughlin)* (1994) 22 CA4th 477, 487-488, 27 CR2d 507, 514]

[3:341.2-341.4] *Reserved.*

(b) **[3:341.5] Issuance of securities:** Nonresidents who cause issuance of securities by a California corporation may be subject to local jurisdiction because of the State's special regulation of securities transactions through the Corporate Securities Law. [*Quattrone v. Sup.Ct. (Whittaker Corp.)* (1975) 44 CA3d 296, 306-307, 118 CR 548, 554—Pennsylvania defendant, who had no "contacts" with California, fraudulently induced issuance of shares by California corporation]

[3:341.6-341.8] *Reserved.*

(c) **[3:341.9] Parents' failure to supervise minor children:** California law imposes special regulations on parents' negligent failure to supervise minors—including Civ.C. §1714.1, which imputes civil liability to the parents. Thus, nonresident parents are suable in California for injuries caused by their minor child's willful misconduct here. By financing the child's education in California, they have caused "effects" which the State treats as "exceptional and subject to special regulation." [*Jamshid-Negad v. Kessler* (1993) 15 CA4th 1704, 1709, 19 CR2d 621, 624]

h. **[3:342] Corporate defendants—special considerations:** Special considerations apply where the defendant is a corporation:

(1) **[3:343] California corporations:** Incorporation within California is equivalent to domicile here for jurisdiction purposes; i.e., the corporation is subject to the *general personal jurisdiction* of California courts, even if the corporation's head office or plant is located outside the state.

(a) **[3:344] Service of process:** California corporations are required to designate and maintain a local agent for service of process in any action against the corporation. [Corps.C. §§202, 1502(b)] Alternatively, service may be made on certain officers of the corporation or on the Secretary of State; *see* ¶4:49-62.

(2) **[3:345] Out-of-state corporations:** Whether or not the corporation has "qualified" to do business in California, it is subject to personal jurisdiction here if "minimum contacts" exist between it and California. [CCP §410.10; *International Shoe Co. v. Washington* (1945) 326 US 310, 316, 66 S.Ct. 154, 158; *see ¶3:210 ff.*]

**[3:346]** *Reserved.*

(a) **[3:347] Effect of qualification:** An out-of-state corporation can "qualify" to do business in California by filing a prescribed form with the Secretary of State and paying statutory fees. [See Corps.C. §2105]

But merely qualifying to do business in California, without more, does not subject a foreign corporation to personal jurisdiction of California courts. [*Snowney v. Harrah's Entertainment, Inc.* (2004) 116 CA4th 996, 1008, 11 CR3d 35, 44—Nevada hotel company had qualified to do business in California but had no other "contacts" with California]

1) **[3:348] Designation of agent for service of summons:** As part of the "qualification" process, a foreign corporation must appoint a local agent for service of process (or consent to service on the Secretary of State). [See Corps.C. §2105(a)(5); and Ins.C. §1600 for similar provision as to out-of-state insurance companies]

2) **[3:349] Not a consent to jurisdiction:** However, designating an agent for service of process in California is *not* a submission to personal jurisdiction here. I.e., although service of

summons may be made, the action cannot be maintained against a foreign corporation absent "minimum contacts" with California. [*Gray Line Tours of Southern Nevada v. Reynolds Electrical & Engineering Co., Inc.* (1987) 193 CA3d 190, 193-194, 238 CR 419, 421]

[3:349.1-349.4]  *Reserved.*

(b) [3:349.5]  **Acts constituting appointment of local agent for service of process:**  By statute, specified acts by an out-of-state or foreign corporation may subject the corporation to service of process here, even if it has *not qualified to do business* in California. Again, however, service of process does not equate to personal jurisdiction absent "minimum contacts" between the corporation and California. [See *Tri-West Ins. Services, Inc. v. Seguros Monterrey Aetna, S.A.* (2000) 78 CA4th 672, 676-677, 93 CR2d 78, 80]

1) [3:349.6]  **Nonadmitted insurers:**  For example, Ins.C. §§1610-1611 provide that specified acts by a nonadmitted insurer (e.g., collecting insurance premiums from or delivering an insurance policy to a California resident) *constitute the appointment* of the California Insurance Commissioner as its agent for service of process in actions relating to the policy. Such appointment, however, does *not* subject the insurer to personal jurisdiction in California in the

*(Text cont'd on p. 3-85)*

**RESERVED**

absence of "minimum contacts." [*Tri-West Ins. Services, Inc. v. Seguros Monterrey Aetna, S.A.*, supra, 78 CA4th at 676-677, 93 CR2d at 80; *Martin v. Martin* (1989) 207 CA3d 1426, 1433, 255 CR 720, 723]

[3:349.7-349.9] *Reserved.*

2) **[3:349.10] Violations of Franchise Investment Law:** Corps.C. §31420 provides that a nonresident who engages in conduct violating the Franchise Investment Law appoints the Commissioner of Corporations as its attorney to receive *service of process.* This is a service of process statute and does *not* create an independent basis for personal jurisdiction. [*Thomson v. Anderson* (2003) 113 CA4th 258, 270, 6 CR3d 262, 270]

(c) **[3:350] "Minimum contacts" more readily found:** As a practical matter, courts are usually more willing to find the requisite "contacts" in an action against a foreign corporation than in an action against a nonresident individual. Corporations often have more interstate activities, greater resources, and better ability to defend in a distant forum, making the exercise of jurisdiction "reasonable." [See *Ruger v. Sup.Ct. (Houghton)* (1981) 118 CA3d 427, 433-434, 173 CR 302, 306—court had jurisdiction over nonresident corporation, but not its president]

1) **[3:351] General vs. limited personal jurisdiction:** Whether the foreign corporation is subject to jurisdiction on a cause of action *unrelated* to its California activities depends on whether such activities are "substantial, continuous and systematic"; *see ¶3:211.*

2) **[3:352] Ownership or control of local subsidiary:** Neither ownership nor control of a California subsidiary is itself sufficient to subject a foreign corporation to personal jurisdiction in California (*see ¶3:203*). [*DVI, Inc. v. Sup.Ct. (Papworth)* (2002) 104 CA4th 1080, 1092, 128 CR2d 683, 691]

Nor does ownership or control of a foreign subsidiary that is doing business in California subject its parent corporation to California jurisdiction. [*Snowney v. Harrah's Entertainment, Inc.* (2004) 116 CA4th 996, 1008, 11 CR3d 35, 44]

However, the result may be different in the following cases:

a) [3:352.1] **Alter ego:** The parent is subject to local jurisdiction where the subsidiary is merely the *alter ego* of the parent. [*Sonora Diamond Corp. v. Sup.Ct. (Sonora Union High School Dist.)* (2000) 83 CA4th 523, 538, 99 CR2d 824, 837]

   1/ [3:352.2] **Factors considered:** Courts focus on the same factors as in "alter ego" liability cases generally:
—whether the parent and subsidiary *in reality* maintained separate identities (particularly in dealings with each other); and
—whether treating the subsidiary as a separate entity would lead to an "inequitable result." [*Sonora Diamond Corp. v. Sup.Ct. (Sonora Union High School Dist.)*, supra, 83 CA4th at 538, 99 CR2d at 837]

*Cross-refer:* "Alter ego" liability is discussed in detail in Friedman, *Cal. Prac. Guide: Corporations* (TRG), Ch. 2.

b) [3:352.3] **Agency:** Where the degree of control exercised by the parent over the subsidiary is *pervasive and continual*, the parent may be deemed subject to local jurisdiction for acts of its subsidiary under agency principles. [*Rollins Burdick Hunter of So. Calif., Inc. v. Alexander & Alexander Services, Inc.* (1988) 206 CA3d 1, 9, 253 CR 338, 342]

c) [3:352.4] **"Representative services doctrine":** As a variant of the agency doctrine, the foreign parent may be subject to local personal jurisdiction where its subsidiary performs functions that the parent *would otherwise have had to perform itself* as part of its business operations. [*Sonora Diamond Corp. v. Sup.Ct. (Sonora Union High School Dist.)*, supra, 83 CA4th at 542, 99 CR2d at 839]

d) [3:352.5] **"Purposeful availment":** The parent corporation may also be subject to local personal jurisdiction where it purposefully avails itself of protections and benefits of the forum state *through* a subsidiary (e.g., forming local subsidiary to expand market for parent's product or services). [*Sonora Diamond Corp. v. Sup.Ct. (Sonora Union High School Dist.)*, supra, 83 CA4th at 551, 99 CR2d at 846]

[3:353]   *Reserved.*

3) [3:354] **Successor liability:** California courts may exercise jurisdiction over a foreign corporation which itself has absolutely *no* "contacts" with California ... if it has *assumed the liabilities* of a predecessor corporation that was subject to California jurisdiction on the cause of action sued upon. [*Sanders v. CEG Corp.* (1979) 95 CA3d 779, 786, 157 CR 252, 257]

*Cross-refer:* Successor liability is discussed in detail in Flahavan, Rea & Kelly, *Cal. Prac. Guide: Personal Injury* (TRG), Ch. 2.

[3:355-356.4]   *Reserved.*

(d) [3:356.5] **Compare—capacity to sue or defend:** Regardless of whether an out-of-state corporation has "minimum contacts" with California or has "qualified" to do intrastate business here, it *has* the capacity to *sue and defend* actions in California courts. But it cannot "maintain" actions here until it qualifies. [Corps.C. §2203(c); *see discussion at* ¶2:105 ff.]

i. [3:357] **Corporate officers, directors, agents and employees—special considerations:** As discussed earlier, each defendant's contacts with the forum state must be assessed individually (¶3:203). Thus, the mere fact that a nonresident employer is subject to California jurisdiction does not necessarily mean that all its officers, directors, agents and employees are subject to jurisdiction here as well. [See *Calder v. Jones* (1984) 465 US 783, 790, 104 S.Ct. 1482, 1487; and *Mihlon v. Sup.Ct. (Murkey)* (1985) 169 CA3d 703, 713, 215 CR 442, 447; *People v. Cole* (2003) 113 CA4th 955, 994, 7 CR3d 333, 365—mere status as officer or director will not subject individual to personal jurisdiction for wrongs committed by corporation]

(1) [3:358] **No automatic immunity for acts committed on behalf of corporation:** There is no "fiduciary shield" or jurisdictional immunity for nonresident corporate officers and directors who act on behalf of a corporation *if their acts otherwise* would subject them to local personal jurisdiction (see below). [*Keeton v. Hustler*

*Magazine, Inc.* (1984) 465 US 770, 787, 104 S.Ct. 1473, 1482, fn. 13; *Taylor-Rush v. Multitech Corp.* (1990) 217 CA3d 103, 116-117, 265 CR 672, 679-680]

(a) **[3:359]** **Same rule applies to partnerships:** Similarly, a nonresident general partner who commits tortious acts on behalf of his or her partnership is not immune from local personal jurisdiction because he or she acted on behalf of a partnership. [See *Goehring v. Sup.Ct. (Bernier)* (1998) 62 CA4th 894, 906, 73 CR2d 105, 112]

**[3:360]** *Reserved.*

(2) **[3:361]** **Nature of acts determinative of jurisdiction:** Nonresident employees are generally *not* suable for "mere untargeted negligence" performed outside the state. For example, a welder employed in Florida, who works on a boiler that later explodes in California, may not be sued here for injuries caused by his negligent welding . . . since he has no control over and *derives no direct benefit* from his employer's sales in California. [See *Calder v. Jones*, supra, 465 US at 789-790, 104 S.Ct. at 1487]

On the other hand, *intentional* tortfeasors must be prepared to defend themselves *wherever* their acts cause injury (*see* ¶3:272). Thus, corporate agents or employees who are *primary* participants in *intentional* wrongdoing causing injury locally are suable here along with their employer. [*Calder v. Jones*, supra, 465 US at 789-790, 104 S.Ct. at 1487; *see* ¶3:276]

(3) **Application**

- **[3:362]** Florida reporter and editor who wrote article defaming California actress were subject to local personal jurisdiction (along with magazine publisher) in defamation action. Although they acted in Florida, their intentional acts were directed at a California resident and caused injury here. [*Calder v. Jones*, supra]

- **[3:363]** New York officers and directors of New York corporation who defrauded California resident in business transaction were subject to local personal jurisdiction in fraud action (along with their corporation). Even if the fraud took place in New York, their acts were directed at a California resident and had a tortious effect here. [*Taylor-Rush v. Multitech Corp.* (1990) 217 CA3d 103, 117-118, 265 CR 672, 680]

- **[3:364]** Japanese Shareholder guaranteed Corporation's debt *and fraudulently misrepresented* its ability to pay California Supplier. Corporation went bankrupt. Japanese Shareholder was *not* suable on his guarantee because he had insufficient "contacts" with California. But he was subject to personal jurisdiction on the *fraud* claim because his acts in Japan caused a *tortious effect* in California (inducing Supplier to extend credit to Corporation). [*Seagate Technology v. A.J. Kogyo Co., Ltd.* (1990) 219 CA3d 696, 705, 268 CR 586, 591]

[3:365]   *Reserved.*

j.   [3:366]   **Claims involving property:**   Earlier cases held a court could exercise jurisdiction over property or other "things" located in the state, although it lacked personal jurisdiction over its owner. That view is now obsolete. The "minimum contacts" doctrine (¶3:211) applies to every exercise of judicial power. Actions involving property affect the rights of the property owners. Therefore, the question in each case is whether constitutionally sufficient "contacts" exist between the forum state and the *owners* of the property. [*Shaffer v. Heitner* (1977) 433 US 186, 207, 97 S.Ct. 2569, 2581]

[3:367]   *Reserved.*

(1)  [3:368]   **Example:**   Shareholders sued corporate officers for breach of fiduciary duty occurring outside the forum state, and levied on their shares of stock in a local corporation. Defendants were nonresidents of the forum state and not subject to personal jurisdiction locally. Local courts could not grant relief. The levy on defendants' shares did not establish "minimum contacts" in an action unrelated to those shares. [*Shaffer v. Heitner, supra,* 433 US at 213-214, 97 S.Ct. at 2584-2585]

(2)  [3:369]   **Validity of nonresident attachment statutes?**   CCP §492.010 et seq. authorizes attachment of property in actions against nonresidents for recovery of money. However, these statutes must be read in light of *Shaffer v. Heitner, supra,* and the dictates of 14th Amendment Due Process. I.e., attachment of a nonresident's property does *not* empower local courts to render money judgments against persons who otherwise lack "minimum contacts" with California.

(3)  [3:370]   **Local property as sufficient "contact" in certain actions:**   As to certain types of actions, the most significant "contact" for jurisdictional purposes will be the location of the property itself. In such action, the fact that the property that is the subject of the dispute is within the state *may* empower local courts to adjudicate, even if the owners are nonresidents: "The pres-

ence of property in a state may bear on the existence of jurisdiction by providing contacts among the forum State, the defendant and the litigation." [*Shaffer v. Heitner*, supra, 433 US at 207, 97 S.Ct. at 2581; and see *Rush v. Savchuk* (1980) 444 US 320, 327-328, 100 S.Ct. 571, 577]

(a) **[3:371] Title actions:** Presence of the property itself is usually the most significant "contact" in actions to determine title to real property located within the state: "The State's strong interests in assuring the marketability of property within its borders and in providing a procedure for peaceful resolution of disputes about the possession of that property would also support jurisdiction." [*Shaffer v. Heitner*, supra, 433 US at 208, 97 S.Ct. at 2581]

    1) **[3:372] Marital property:** Location of marital property (real estate, bank accounts, etc.) in California is a "contact" with a nonresident spouse, and suggests existence of other ties sufficient to allow California courts to adjudicate the spouses' respective interests in such property. [See *Khan v. Sup.Ct. (Khan)* (1988) 204 CA3d 1168, 1179, 251 CR 815, 822]

(b) **[3:373] Liability claims relating to local property:** Arguably, presence of property in the forum state may also favor jurisdiction in suits for injury suffered on the land of an absentee owner where the defendant's ownership of the land is conceded but the cause of action is otherwise related to rights and duties growing out of that ownership. [*Shaffer v. Heitner*, supra, 433 US at 208, 97 S.Ct. at 2581-2582]

    [3:373.1-373.4] *Reserved.*

(c) **[3:373.5] Assets in insurance insolvency proceedings:** State courts overseeing insurance insolvency proceedings may exercise in rem jurisdiction over assets of *other entities* having an "identity of interest" with the insolvent insurer, if necessary to preserve its assets. [*Garamendi v. Executive Life Ins. Co. (Morgan Stanley Mortgage Capital, Inc.)* (1993) 17 CA4th 504, 520-521, 21 CR2d 578, 588 — court could assert jurisdiction over assets of partnership in which insolvent insurer held 92% interest in order to promote insurer's reorganization]

(4) **[3:374] Property outside forum state:** If *all property owners are before the court*, California courts may determine rights in property outside the state. I.e., the

court's jurisdiction over the parties may give it power to order them to convey title to land located anywhere. Courts at the situs of the land may be relied upon to enforce the decree on principles of res judicata or comity. [See *Fall v. Eastin* (1909) 215 US 1, 7, 30 S.Ct. 3, 6; *Tomaier v. Tomaier* (1944) 23 C2d 754, 760, 146 P2d 905, 908]

4. [3:375] **Procedures to Challenge Personal Jurisdiction:** Defendant may challenge the court's personal jurisdiction in several ways:
   — by a *motion to quash service of summons* at the outset of the action (¶*3:376*);
   — (possibly) by raising it as an *affirmative defense* in the answer (*see* ¶*3:395.5*); or
   — by not appearing in the action, and then *attacking the default judgment* on appeal or in collateral proceedings (*see* ¶*3:401*).

   a. [3:376] **Motion to quash service of summons:** The defendant's first line of attack normally is a motion to quash service for lack of personal jurisdiction under CCP §418.10(a)(1). (Note: The same motion is used to attack defects in the manner in which summons was *issued* or *served*; ¶*4:169-173*.)

   If the motion is granted, the court may dismiss the action without prejudice as to the particular defendant involved. [See CCP §581(h)]

   (1) *FORMS*

   • Notice of Motion to Quash Service of Summons, *see Form 3:A.*

   • Declaration in Support of Motion to Quash Service of Summons, *see Form 3:B.*

   • Checklist for Motion to Quash Service of Summons, *see Form 3:I.*

   (2) [3:377] **Time of filing:** Defendant must serve and file the motion to quash within the time permitted to plead, unless the court extends the time for good cause shown. [CCP §418.10(a)]

   (a) [3:378] **May be filed simultaneously with responsive pleading:** The defendant (or cross-defendant) need not file the motion before responding to the complaint. A motion to quash service of summons may be filed *simultaneously* with a responsive pleading—i.e., answer, demurrer or motion to strike. [CCP §418.10(e)]

   Although a responsive pleading is filed simultaneously, defendant is not deemed to have made a general appearance in the action unless and until its motion to quash is denied. [CCP §418.10(e)(1)]

(b) **[3:378.1]** **May also be filed** *before* **responsive pleading:** Defendant may also choose to file a motion to quash *before* filing an answer, demurrer or motion to strike. The motion to quash *extends* defendant's time to plead. [CCP §418.10(b); *see* ¶*3:392*]

➡ **[3:378.2]** *PRACTICE POINTER:* Defense counsel often choose to wait until their motion to quash is denied before filing responsive pleadings. This provides more time to investigate and obviates the need for such pleadings if the motion is successful.

**[3:378.3-378.4]** *Reserved.*

(c) **[3:378.5]** **Compare—not after responsive pleading:** On the other hand, if defendant has previously answered, demurred or moved to strike, it is too late to file a motion to quash. The previous pleading or motion constitutes a general appearance, *waiving* any objection to personal jurisdiction (or to service of process, inconvenient forum or delay in prosecution). [CCP §418.10(e)(3); *see* ¶*3:162*]

(3) **[3:379]** **Jurisdictional objection preserved:** Neither the motion to quash itself nor relief sought incidental thereto (e.g., for extension of time to plead or to set aside default) is deemed a general appearance by defendant. [CCP §418.10(d)]

The motion to quash preserves the jurisdictional objection so that defendant may file whatever motions and take whatever action it chooses (e.g., discovery) without waiving the objection. [CCP §418.10(e)(1)]

(4) **[3:380]** **Discovery:** In order to meet its burden of proof (below), plaintiff is entitled to conduct discovery with regard to the issue of jurisdiction before the hearing on the motion to quash; e.g., to establish the nature and extent of the defendant's "contacts" in California. (The hearing date is often continued to facilitate such discovery.) [*Mihlon v. Sup.Ct. (Murkey)* (1985) 169 CA3d 703, 711, 215 CR 442, 446]

But a continuance may be denied if there is no showing that discovery would likely produce evidence of additional "contacts." [*Beckman v. Thompson* (1992) 4 CA4th 481, 486-487, 6 CR2d 60, 63]

(5) [3:381] **Notice and hearing date:** The notice of motion must set a hearing date *within 30 days* after the notice is filed. The service requirements are those on motions generally (CCP §1005 requires at least 21 calendar days' notice, increased for service by mail, see below). [CCP §418.10(b)]

*Effect of scheduling hearing date beyond 30 days?* Although the matter is unclear, scheduling a hearing date *beyond* 30 days should not invalidate a motion to quash. Nothing in CCP §418.10 suggests the court must overlook lack of personal jurisdiction or proper service because of a defendant's failure to schedule a hearing date within 30 days.

(a) [3:382] **Adequacy of notice served by mail?** The requirement that the matter be heard within 30 days may require the moving party to obtain an order shortening time where service is made by mail to an address outside California. (CCP §1005 requires 26 days' notice for service by mail in California to an address in the state, *31 days* if either the place of mailing or the address is in another state, and *41 days* if the place of mailing or the address is in another country.) [CCP §1005(b); *see* ¶9:87]

⇨[3:383] *PRACTICE POINTER:* If planning to serve your motion by mail to an address outside California, ask for a court *order shortening notice* when filing your motion. Doing so may eliminate notice problems and last-minute continuances.

(6) [3:384] **Burden of proof on plaintiff:** Although defendant is the moving party, the burden of proof is on the *plaintiff:* "Where jurisdiction is challenged by a nonresident defendant, the burden of proof is upon the plaintiff to demonstrate that 'minimum contacts' exist between defendant and the forum state to justify imposition of personal jurisdiction." [*Mihlon v. Sup.Ct. (Murkey)* (1985) 169 CA3d 703, 710, 215 CR 442, 445; *Floveyor Int'l, Ltd. v. Sup.Ct. (Shick Tube-Veyor Corp.)* (1997) 59 CA4th 789, 793, 69 CR2d 457, 459-460]

(a) [3:385] **Preponderance required:** The burden is on the plaintiff to demonstrate by a *preponderance* of the evidence that all jurisdictional criteria are met. [*Ziller Electronics Lab GmbH v. Sup.Ct. (Grosh Scenic Studios)* (1988) 206 CA3d 1222, 1232, 254 CR 410, 416]

(b) [3:386] **Timing of motion; continuance to conduct discovery:** Plaintiff is entitled to conduct discovery on the jurisdictional issues presented by the motion to quash and, if unable to complete such discovery before the hearing on the motion, is entitled to a continuance for this purpose. [*Ziller Electronics Lab GmbH v. Sup.Ct. (Grosh Scenic Studios)*, supra, 206 CA3d at 1232, 254 CR at 416; *School Dist. of Okaloosa County v. Sup.Ct. (City of Orange)* (1997) 58 CA4th 1126, 1131, 68 CR2d 612, 615 (citing text)]

(7) **[3:387]** **Evidence on motion:** Jurisdictional facts must be proved by competent evidence at the hearing on the motion to quash. This generally requires affidavits or declarations by competent witnesses. A properly verified complaint may be treated as a declaration for this purpose. [See *Evangelize China Fellowship, Inc. v. Evangelize China Fellowship* (1983) 146 CA3d 440, 444, 194 CR 240, 242]

(a) **[3:388]** **Unverified pleadings:** An unverified pleading has *no* evidentiary value in determining personal jurisdiction. [*Mihlon v. Sup.Ct. (Murkey)*, supra]

Even so, such pleadings are relevant in defining the cause of action asserted, and whether it arises out of the nonresident's alleged local activities. (Of course, plaintiff need not prove the cause of action pleaded to justify the court's exercise of jurisdiction.) [*Mihlon v. Sup.Ct. (Murkey)*, supra]

(b) **[3:389]** **Hearsay declarations insufficient:** Except as otherwise provided by statute, hearsay declarations are *not* competent proof of facts alleged. [*Floveyor Int'l, Ltd. v. Sup.Ct. (Shick Tube-Veyor Corp.)* (1997) 59 CA4th 789, 796, 69 CR2d 457, 462—declaration by plaintiff's *attorney* stating "discovery in this case revealed . . ." was "nothing more than inadmissible hearsay"]

⇨ **[3:389.1]** *PRACTICE POINTERS FOR PLAINTIFF:* If you represent the plaintiff, obtain declarations from persons (your client or others) with *personal knowledge* of defendant's activities in California.

Also, be sure to draft those declarations to show the *source* of the declarant's knowledge (e.g., "I saw . . ."; "I was present when Defendant said . . . ," etc.). Allegations claiming "personal knowledge" may not suffice if the source of such knowledge is unclear.

➡️ **[3:389.2]** **_PRACTICE POINTER FOR DE-
FENDANT:_** If you represent the defendant,
be on the lookout for declarations containing
statements "_on information and belief._" They
should be challenged as hearsay!

(c) [3:390] **Commission of tort as basis for jurisdiction:** Normally, liability issues are irrelevant on
a motion to quash. But where jurisdiction is asserted on the basis of defendant's having caused
_tortious effects_ in California, defendant may _defeat
jurisdiction_ by unequivocal proof that it did not
cause plaintiff's injury: Plaintiff "cannot demand that
we judge the question of jurisdiction in the light of
a claim he apparently does not have." [_J.M. Sahlein
Music Co., Inc. v. Nippon Gakki Co., Ltd._ (1987) 197
CA3d 539, 545, 243 CR 4, 7]

(d) [3:391] **Conflicts in evidence:** Where the parties' declarations conflict on the jurisdictional facts,
it is up to the trial court to decide which to believe.
As long as supported by substantial evidence, its
decision will not be disturbed on appeal. [_Evange-
lize China Fellowship, Inc. v. Evangelize China
Fellowship,_ supra]

(8) [3:392] **Time to plead extended:** Filing a motion to
quash automatically extends defendant's time to plead
until _15 days after service of notice_ that the motion has
been denied. (And, the court can grant up to 20 days'
additional time for good cause shown.) [CCP
§418.10(b)]

No default may be entered against defendant before expiration of its time to plead. [CCP §418.10(d)]

(a) [3:393] Again, shorter time limits apply in _unlaw-
ful detainer_ or forcible detainer actions: Defendant
must plead within _5 days_ after service of notice that
the motion to quash has been denied. (And, the
court can grant only 15 days additional time for
good cause.) [CCP §1167.4(b)]

(b) [3:393.1] The motion to quash is not deemed denied until entry of the order denying the motion; and
if a timely petition for writ of mandamus is filed (_see_
¶3:394), not until the writ proceedings are completed. [CCP §418.10(e)(2)]

(9) [3:394] **Further extension if mandamus sought:** If
the motion to quash is denied, defendant may seek
appellate review by filing a petition for writ of mandamus
in the court of appeal within 10 days after being served

with notice of the denial. This time limit can be extended by the trial court for up to an additional 20 days. [CCP §418.10(c)] (The time limit is also extended for service by mail under CCP §1013. See *Shearer v. Sup.Ct. (Thundervolt)* (1977) 70 CA3d 424, 426, 138 CR 824, 827, cited with approval in *Camper v. WCAB* (1992) 3 C4th 679, 687, 12 CR2d 101, 105.)

Defendant may then file and serve on plaintiff a written notice that a petition for writ of mandamus has been filed in the appellate court. If this is served and filed before expiration of its time to plead (above), defendant's time to plead is extended until 10 days after it is served with written notice of final judgment in the mandate proceeding. (This time limit can also be extended by the trial court for up to an additional 20 days.) [CCP §418.10(c)]

(10) [3:395] **Proceeding on merits waives jurisdictional defect:** If the motion to quash is denied, and so is mandamus, defendant faces a tough choice: either to answer the complaint and go to trial on the merits (thereby *waiving* the jurisdiction objection); or default to the complaint and later appeal from the default judgment (see below). [*McCorkle v. City of Los Angeles* (1969) 70 C2d 252, 257-258, 74 CR 389, 394—if mandamus is not sought or is denied, defending on merits waives jurisdictional challenge; not ground for later appeal from judgment]

[3:395.1-395.4]  *Reserved.*

b. [3:395.5] **Affirmative defense and motion to dismiss in lieu of motion to quash?** Although the statute is unclear, it is arguable that a defendant can preserve its jurisdictional objection by first raising it as an affirmative defense in the answer, without making a motion to quash. CCP §418.10(e)(3) states the jurisdictional objection is waived if a motion to quash is not made "at the time of filing a demurrer or motion to strike," which implicitly suggests the objection is *not* waived if first raised in the *answer* as an alternative to the motion. (This result is also consistent with legislative history stating the intent to conform California practice to federal rules; see Stats. 2002, Ch. 69, §2.)

⇨ [3:395.6] *PRACTICE POINTER:* Don't gamble on this interpretation. Judges may disagree and hold you have waived the objection by omitting a motion to quash. Moreover, as a practical matter, it is usually better to resolve the jurisdictional issue before undertaking the expense of discovery and preparing for trial.

c. **[3:396]** **Suffer default judgment, then attack on jurisdictional grounds:** The other alternative open to defendant is to default to the complaint, allow entry of default judgment, and then attack that judgment for lack of jurisdiction. Several procedures are available for such attack.

(1) **[3:397]** **Motion to set aside default judgment coupled with motion to quash:** If defendant did not get actual notice of the proceedings in time to file a motion to quash, he may move the court to set aside the default and any judgment entered thereon. [CCP §473.5, *discussed at* ¶*5:420*] (Or, the motion to set aside may be based on "mistake, inadvertence, surprise or excusable neglect" under CCP §473(b); ¶*5:282*.)

**[3:398]** Setting aside the default judgment will not, of course, resolve any jurisdictional objections. Hence, defendant will have to file a motion to quash concurrently with his or her motion to set aside the default judgment. If the court finds ground to set aside the judgment, it can proceed directly to rule on the jurisdictional issues raised by the motion to quash. [CCP §418.10(d)]

**[3:399]** *Reserved.*

(a) **[3:400]** **Time limits:** But there are time limits on moving to set aside a judgment. If based on lack of notice, such motion must be made *within 2 years* after entry of the default judgment (¶*5:428*). If based on "mistake, inadvertence, surprise or excusable neglect," *within 6 months* after entry of the *default* (not the default judgment). (*See* ¶*5:365*.)

(2) **[3:401]** **Appeal:** Alternatively, defendant may simply appeal the default judgment. But such appeal will be limited to *jurisdictional* grounds. Defendant cannot attack plaintiff's case on the merits, because by defaulting he has conceded the allegations of the complaint. (Where defendant has received adequate notice of the proceedings, an appeal will be the most likely procedure to attack the judgment.)

(a) **[3:402]** **Time limits:** An appeal must be timely: In general, notice of appeal must be filed in the appropriate appellate court within 180 days after entry of the default judgment, or 60 days after notice of entry, whichever is earlier. [CRC 2(a)]

**[3:403]** *PRACTICE POINTER:* The decision to suffer a default judgment and then appeal it on jurisdictional grounds is *very risky:* If the appellate court rules against you on the jurisdictional issue, that ends the case because your default waives any right to defend on the merits. And, since the jurisdictional issue has now been litigated (in the appellate court), the judgment will be immune from collateral attack on jurisdictional grounds (see below).

(3) **[3:404]** **Independent action to set aside judgment ("collateral attack"):** Even after all other time limits have expired, defendant may sue to set aside the default judgment (*or defend* an action to enforce the judgment) for lack of personal jurisdiction . . . *provided* the jurisdiction issue was not litigated at all in the original proceedings: "(A) defendant is always free to ignore the judicial proceedings, risk a default judgment, and then challenge that judgment on jurisdictional grounds in a collateral proceeding." [*Yu v. Signet Bank/Virginia* (1999) 69 CA4th 1377, 1386, 82 CR2d 304, 309 (internal quotes omitted)]

(a) **[3:405]** **Limitation—collateral estoppel:** If defendant litigated the jurisdiction issue in the original proceedings (e.g., by motion to quash or appeal), he will be barred from raising the same arguments again. The earlier judgment serves as a collateral estoppel on all issues litigated. [See *Sabek, Inc. v. Englehard Corp.* (1998) 65 CA4th 992, 998, 76 CR2d 882, 885—direct estoppel where same jurisdictional issue raised in subsequent lawsuit on same claim]

(b) **[3:406]** **Limitation—due diligence:** A proceeding to set aside a default judgment is equitable in nature, and equity demands due diligence. Therefore, if defendant *knew* about the proceedings against him or her in time to raise the jurisdictional defect in the trial court, or on appeal, and simply failed to do so, collateral attack may *not* be permitted. *See discussion at ¶5:435 ff.*

## C. FORUM NON CONVENIENS

**[3:407]** Even if the court has subject matter and personal jurisdiction, it may *stay* or *dismiss* the action on the ground of inconvenient forum. [CCP §418.10(a)]

1. **[3:408]** **Nature of Challenge:** If the court finds that "in the interest of substantial justice" an action filed in California should be adjudicated elsewhere, it may stay or dismiss the action on such conditions as may be just. [CCP §410.30(a)]

The statute codifies the common law doctrine of *forum non conveniens.* This is *not* a jurisdictional doctrine. Rather, it is "an equitable doctrine invoking the *discretionary* power of a court to *decline* the exercise of jurisdiction (to stay or dismiss) it has over a transitory cause of action when it believes that the action may be more appropriately and justly tried elsewhere." [*Stangvik v. Shiley, Inc.* (1991) 54 C3d 744, 751, 1 CR2d 556, 559 (emphasis and parentheses added); *In re Christopher B.* (1996) 43 CA4th 551, 559, 51 CR2d 43, 47 — because forum non conveniens doctrine not jurisdictional, objection cannot be raised for first time on appeal]

The inquiry is not whether some other state or country provides a *better* forum than does California, but whether California is a *seriously inconvenient* forum. [*Ford Motor Co. v. Insurance Co. of No. America* (1995) 35 CA4th 604, 611, 41 CR2d 342, 346]

*Cross-refer—child custody cases:* Special rules govern application of this doctrine in child custody cases. See Fam.C. §3427; and detailed discussion in Hogoboom & King, *Cal. Prac. Guide: Family Law* (TRG), Ch. 7.

a. **[3:409] Difference between stay and dismissal:** The court's ruling on a forum non conveniens motion may turn on whether dismissal, or only a stay, is sought. If a *stay* is granted, the California court retains jurisdiction, so that if for any reason plaintiff is denied a prompt trial in the alternative forum, the California court can order the action resumed in California. On the other hand, once a *dismissal* is ordered, the California court loses jurisdiction and there is nothing left to resume. For this reason, the court's power to dismiss an action for inconvenient forum is more limited than its power to stay. [*Archibald v. Cinerama Hotels* (1976) 15 C3d 853, 858-859, 126 CR 811, 815]

b. **[3:410] Exception for "major contracts":** An action *cannot* be dismissed under forum non conveniens if it involves a contract that:

- Designates California Law as governing (in whole or in part); and

- Relates to a transaction involving at least $1,000,000 or more (contingent or otherwise); and

- Contains an agreement by the nonresident parties to submit to the jurisdiction of California courts. [CCP §410.40]

(1) **[3:411] Purpose:** Legislative history discloses these provisions are designated to promote California as an international commercial trade center. They enable foreign and out-of state businesses to look to California to provide a neutral forum for resolution of their disputes, either through arbitration or judicial proceedings. There

is little chance for overreaching because parties to such large contracts are usually represented by counsel.

2. **[3:412] Who May Challenge:** Theoretically, any party may challenge convenience of the forum.

   a. **[3:413] Defendants:** The fact the defendant may have consented or submitted to California jurisdiction does not prevent it from moving to stay or dismiss the action on forum non conveniens grounds. [*Appalachian Ins. Co. v. Sup.Ct. (Union Carbide Corp.)* (1984) 162 CA3d 427, 440, 208 CR 627, 635; *see ¶3:188*]

   b. **[3:414] Plaintiffs:** Plaintiff is usually in no position to claim the forum is inconvenient because it initiated the action. But even plaintiffs may raise the challenge where suit was filed locally in good faith response to a perceived emergency. [See *Lifeco Services Corp. v. Sup.Ct. (Robison)* (1990) 222 CA3d 331, 337, 271 CR 385, 388]

      (1) **[3:415] Example:** Texas Employer sought injunctive relief against California Employee. A TRO was granted but a preliminary injunction was denied. Employee then cross-complained. The fact Employer had sued first, obtained a TRO, and had sought a preliminary injunction did *not* bar its later motion to stay the action on the ground that Employee's contract contained a forum-selection clause requiring suit in Texas. [*Lifeco Services Corp. v. Sup.Ct. (Robison)*, supra]

3. **[3:416] Procedure:** The usual noticed motion procedure (*see ¶9:28 ff.*) applies to a motion to stay or dismiss under CCP §418.10.

**FORMS**

- Notice of Motion to Stay or Dismiss Action, *see Form 3:C.*
- Declaration in Support of Motion to Stay or Dismiss, *see Form 3:D.*
- Checklist for Inconvenient Forum, *see Form 3:I.*

   a. **[3:417] Timing:** The defendant may make a motion to stay or dismiss on ground of inconvenient forum simultaneously with filing an answer, demurrer or motion to strike. [CCP §418.10(e)]

      (1) **[3:417.1] Waived if not raised when filing demurrer or motion to strike:** Failure to make the inconvenient forum motion when filing a demurrer or motion to strike waives the objection. [CCP §418.10(e)(3)]

      **[3:417.2-417.4]** *Reserved.*

   b. **[3:417.5] May be coupled with motion to quash:** If personal jurisdiction is also contested, a motion to quash service (¶*3:376 ff.*) may be made *concurrently* with the motion to stay or dismiss on grounds of inconvenient forum. [CCP §418.10(a)]

In such event, even if the nonresident loses on the jurisdiction point, the court can still exercise its *discretion* as to allowing the action to proceed in California.

➡ **[3:417.6]** ***PRACTICE POINTER:*** If you represent a nonresident defendant, you may have better luck with a motion to stay or dismiss for inconvenient forum than you will with your motion to quash service for lack of personal jurisdiction. Reason: The court *must* deny a motion to quash if there are "minimum contacts" with the nonresident defendant; and many opinions broadly construe what constitutes "minimum contacts"! On the other hand, courts have considerable *discretion* in ruling on a motion to stay or dismiss for inconvenient forum. For this reason, it is generally wise to couple any motion to quash with a motion to stay or dismiss.

 c. [3:418] **Not a general appearance:** The motion to stay or dismiss the action is not a general appearance by defendant, and thus preserves any objection to personal jurisdiction raised in the accompanying motion to quash. [CCP §418.10(d)]

4. [3:419] **Burden of Proof:** As the moving party, defendant bears the burden of proof that the action should be tried elsewhere. Plaintiff's choice of forum will not be disturbed unless the court is convinced:

- a *"suitable" alternative forum* exists (*see* ¶*3:420*); *and*

- the balance of *private and public interest factors* makes it "just" that the litigation proceed in the alternative forum (*see* ¶*3:424*). [*Stangvik v. Shiley, Inc.* (1991) 54 C3d 744, 751, 1 CR2d 556, 559]

5. [3:420] **Requirement of "Suitable" Alternative Forum:** There must be a "suitable" alternative forum available, meaning one in which a *valid judgment may be obtained* against defendant. [See *Stangvik v. Shiley, Inc.*, supra, 54 C3d at 752, 1 CR2d at 560, fn. 3]

 a. [3:421] **Forum in which defendant subject to personal jurisdiction:** Defendant must be subject to service of process in the alternative forum. Alternatively, defendant must be willing to *submit* to jurisdiction there *as a condition* of the California court granting its motion to stay or dismiss the California action. [See *Stangvik v. Shiley, Inc.*, supra, 54 C3d at 752, 1 CR2d at 560]

(1) [3:421.1] **Multiple defendants:** Where there are multiple defendants, they must *all* be subject to personal jurisdiction in the alternative forum (not just the "primary" defendants). [*American Cemwood Corp. v. American Home Assur. Co.* (2001) 87 CA4th 431, 440, 104 CR2d 670, 676-677]

- [3:421.2] Where the defendants are so *numerous* that it cannot be determined whether *all* are subject to suit in the other forum, the California court may *stay* (rather than dismiss) the action. Plaintiffs can seek to have the stay lifted if, after filing suit in the other forum, they can show that some of the defendants are not subject to personal jurisdiction there. [*Hansen v. Owens-Corning Fiberglas Corp.* (1996) 51 CA4th 753, 759, 59 CR2d 229, 233-asbestos liability case against 200 named manufacturers and distributors]

b. [3:422] **Forum in which statute of limitations no bar:** The statute of limitations in the other forum must not have run on plaintiff's claim; or, alternatively, defendant must be willing to *waive* the statute as a condition of the court's granting his or her motion. [*Stangvik v. Shiley, Inc.*, supra, 54 C3d at 752, 1 CR2d at 560; *Delfosse v. C.A.C.I., Inc.-Federal* (1990) 218 CA3d 683, 691, 267 CR 224, 228-229]

c. [3:423] **Forum law must provide remedy:** The alternative forum is "suitable" if its law provides a remedy for the claim sued upon. "A forum is suitable if there is *jurisdiction* and *no statute of limitations bar* to hearing the case on the merits." [*Chong v. Sup.Ct. (HBZ Finance Ltd.)* (1997) 58 CA4th 1032, 1036-1037, 68 CR2d 427, 430 (emphasis added)]

The other forum's law *need not be as favorable to plaintiff* as local law. (If that were required, most forum non conveniens motions would be denied!) [*Stangvik v. Shiley, Inc.*, supra, 54 C3d at 754, 1 CR2d at 562—advantages of Calif. procedural or substantive law "*cannot be considered as a factor*"]

Indeed, the alternative forum's law is *irrelevant* unless the remedy provided is so clearly inadequate or unsatisfactory that it is *no remedy at all.* [*Stangvik v. Shiley, Inc.*, supra, 54 C3d at 764, 1 CR2d at 568; *Piper Aircraft Co. v. Reyno* (1981) 454 US 235, 254, 102 S.Ct. 252, 265—fact Scotland does not recognize products liability claim did not constitute deprivation of "any" remedy, since negligence recovery possible]

(1) [3:423.1] **"No remedy at all" exception very limited:** The "no remedy at all" exception applies only in

*rare* circumstances, "such as where the alternative forum is a foreign country whose courts are ruled by a dictatorship, so that there is no independent judiciary or due process of law." [*Shiley, Inc. v. Sup.Ct. (Alsup)* (1992) 4 CA4th 126, 133-134, 6 CR2d 38, 43]

The fact that a plaintiff will be disadvantaged by the law of the alternative forum or that the plaintiff will *probably or even certainly lose* does not render the forum "unsuitable." [*Boaz v. Boyle & Co., Inc.* (1995) 40 CA4th 700, 711, 46 CR2d 888, 895—fact that courts in other forum had already *rejected* the claim did not make that forum "unsuitable"]

- [3:423.2] A concern that Hong Kong courts would not provide due process after return to Chinese rule did *not* justify denial of a forum non conveniens motion. But because the matter could not be determined with certainty, the California proceedings were *stayed* pending trial in Hong Kong; the stay could be lifted if the party was unable to receive a fair trial there. [*Chong v. Sup.Ct. (HBZ Finance Ltd.)* (1997) 58 CA4th 1032, 1039-1040, 68 CR2d 427, 431-432]

[3:423.3-423.4]  *Reserved.*

d.  [3:423.5]  **Compliance with conditions:**  Questions as to the "suitability" of the alternative forum may be avoided by defendant's agreement to comply with such conditions as:
— *submission to jurisdiction* there;
— *tolling the statute of limitations* for the time the action was pending in California;
— agreeing to comply with *discovery* orders of the foreign court;
— agreeing to produce *physical evidence* and documents in its possession at defendant's expense available for inspection as required in the foreign proceedings;
— agreement to make past and present employees available to testify in the foreign court at defendant's cost, if so ordered by courts there. [*Stangvik v. Shiley, Inc.*, supra, 54 C3d at 750, 1 CR2d at 559, fn. 2]

6.  [3:424]  **Balancing of Private and Public Factors:**  Assuming a "suitable" alternative forum exists, the weight of recognized private and public interest factors must be determined. The jurisdiction with the greater interest in the litigation normally should bear the burden of entertaining it. [*Stangvik v. Shiley, Inc.*, supra, 54 C3d at 758, 1 CR2d at 564]

All of the following factors must be weighed in each case. [*Shiley, Inc. v. Sup.Ct. (Alsup)* (1992) 4 CA4th 126, 133-134, 6 CR2d 38, 43]

a. [3:424.1] **Private interest factors:** Private interest factors relate to where the trial and enforcement of any judgment will be the most expeditious and least expensive. Included are such matters as:

- Access to sources of proof (residence of parties, witnesses, location of physical evidence);

- Cost of obtaining attendance of witnesses;

- Availability of compulsory process for attendance of unwilling witnesses. [*Stangvik v. Shiley, Inc.*, supra, 54 C3d at 751, 1 CR2d at 559; see also *Great Northern Railway Co. v. Sup.Ct. (Curtin)* (1970) 12 CA3d 105, 113-114, 90 CR 461, 466-467]

b. [3:424.2] **Public interest factors:** The public interest factors include:

- Avoiding overburdening local courts with congested calendars, particularly where numerous actions and parties are involved; [See *Stangvik v. Shiley, Inc.*, supra, 54 C3d at 758, 1 CR2d at 564—court congestion posed by 235 separate actions; *Campbell v. Parker-Hannifin Corp.* (1999) 69 CA4th 1534, 1542, 82 CR2d 202, 207—same where 20 separate plaintiffs involved; compare *Roulier v. Cannondale* (2002) 101 CA4th 1180, 1190, 124 CR2d 877, 884—court congestion not a factor where single plaintiff involved]

- Protecting the interests of potential jurors so that they are not called upon to decide cases in which the local community has little concern; and

- Weighing the competing interests of California and the alternative jurisdiction in the litigation, which may include such matters as:

  — California's interest in regulating the transaction or activities involved (e.g., affecting property located here or products manufactured here);

  — The foreign state's concerns in making technology and products available to its citizens that might be impeded if American liability laws were applied to actions brought by foreign residents;

  — The competitive disadvantage to California business if resident corporations are required to defend lawsuits here based on injuries incurred elsewhere. [*Stangvik v. Shiley, Inc.*, supra, 54 C3d at 751, 1 CR2d at 559-560; see also *Great Northern Railway Co. v. Sup.Ct. (Curtin)*, supra, 12 CA3d at 113-114, 90 CR at 466-467; and *Ford Motor Co. v. Insurance Co. of No. America* (1995) 35 CA4th 604, 612-618, 41 CR2d 342, 347-351]

c. **Application**

- [3:425] Norwegian families sued California heart-valve manufacturer in California for deaths resulting from defective valves implanted in Norway. Public interest factors favored litigation in Norway because (1) the valves were sold worldwide and more than 235 similar suits were already pending, burdening California courts; and (2) California's interest in deterring negligent conduct by local manufacturers could be vindicated in similar suits *by California residents.* [*Stangvik v. Shiley, Inc.*, supra, 54 C3d at 753-755, 1 CR2d at 559-560; see also *Campbell v. Parker-Hannifin Corp.* (1999) 69 CA4th 1534, 1542-1543, 82 CR2d 202, 206-207—forum non convenience stay granted in wrongful death suit by Australians based on airplane crash in Australia]

- [3:425.1] Nevada residents filed product liability action in California against Japanese car manufacturer and wholly-owned subsidiaries doing business in California. The action was properly *dismissed* under forum non conveniens. Nevada was a more "suitable" forum because:
  — plaintiffs lived in Nevada, bought the allegedly defective vehicle there, and the accident occurred there;
  — the California corporate defendants did not manufacture or design the subject vehicle;
  — witnesses would be inconvenienced by trial in California; and
  — the lawsuit would be a burden on California courts, taxpayers and jurors. [*Rinauro v. Honda Motor Co.* (1995) 31 CA4th 506, 510, 37 CR2d 181, 183]

  [3:425.2] *Reserved.*

- [3:425.3] Worker and family sued Fiberglass Manufacturer and 199 other defendants for personal injury and wrongful death of Worker's wife, allegedly caused by asbestos exposure. The action was properly stayed and plaintiff directed to file suit in Montana because:
  — Worker and wife had lived in Montana since 1945 and never lived in California;
  — most of the asbestos exposure occurred in Montana, and none in California;
  — most of the medical treatment took place in Montana and all of the treating physicians lived there; and
  — the vast majority of defendants had contacts in both California and Montana. [*Hansen v. Owens-Corning Fiberglas Corp.* (1996) 51 CA4th 753, 759-760, 59 CR2d 229, 233-234]

  [3:425.4-425.5] *Reserved.*

- **[3:425.6]** Swiss bicyclist, injured in Switzerland, filed product liability action in California against Delaware Manufacturer and California Dealer. Although Switzerland was a "suitable forum," the public and private interest factors did *not* support a stay or dismissal because:

  — (*private interest factors*) only one percipient witness lived in Switzerland; relevant witness and documents were available in California; defendants had the opportunity to have plaintiff medically examined in California, to depose him here, and were provided with plaintiff's medical records;

  — (*public interest factors*) this is a single, simple case which will not impact court congestion; the product continues to be sold in California; California has an interest in the safety of products sold in the state; *defendant delayed nine months and conducted discovery* before making the motion. [*Roulier v. Cannondale,* supra, 101 CA4th at 1187-1190, 124 CR2d at 882-884]

  **[3:425.7-425.9]** *Reserved.*

7. **Particular Factors**

   a. **[3:425.10]** **Plaintiff's choice of forum as factor:** Plaintiff's choice of where to sue is entitled to great weight in this analysis, even if plaintiff is a *nonresident*: "Unless the balance is strongly in favor of the defendant, the plaintiff's choice of forum should rarely be disturbed." [*Ford Motor Co. v. Insurance Co. of No. America* (1995) 35 CA4th 604, 610-611, 41 CR2d 342, 346 (internal quotes omitted)]

   b. **[3:426]** **Plaintiff's local residence as factor:** Plaintiff's decision to sue here is entitled to considerable deference if plaintiff is a California resident. [*Northrop Corp. v. American Motorists Ins. Co.* (1990) 220 CA3d 1553, 1562, 270 CR 233, 237]

      (1) **[3:426a]** **Action *cannot* be *dismissed:*** California's interest in assuring a forum for litigation by California residents *precludes dismissal* of such actions on forum non conveniens grounds: "Except in extraordinary cases a trial court has no discretion to dismiss an action brought by a California resident on grounds of forum non conveniens." [*Archibald v. Cinerama Hotels* (1976) 15 C3d 853, 858, 126 CR 811, 814; *Beckman v. Thompson* (1992) 4 CA4th 481, 487, 6 CR2d 60, 64; see *Berg v. MTC Electronic Technologies* (1998) 61 CA4th 349, 356, 71 CR2d 523, 527 (citing text)]

         (a) **[3:426.1]** **Exceptional cases:** The only cases which would justify dismissal on forum non conveniens grounds are those in which California cannot provide an adequate forum (e.g., because indispensable parties not suable here) or has no interest in doing so (e.g., nominal plaintiff suing on behalf of foreign parties). [*Archibald v. Cinerama Hotels*, supra, 15 C3d at 859, 126 CR at 815]

(2) [3:427] **Stay may be ordered:** Although an action filed by a California resident may not be dismissed, the trial court may *stay* the action when "substantial justice" requires trial elsewhere (e.g., for witness inconvenience, cost of trial, etc.). [See *Archibald v. Cinerama Hotels*, supra, 15 C3d at 860, 126 CR at 816]

(a) [3:428] **Factors justifying stay:** Where there is no real hardship in litigating in an alternative forum, "convenience" factors may justify staying a local action, although *all plaintiffs are California residents! [Klein v. Sup.Ct. (Thomas)* (1988) 198 CA3d 894, 901, 244 CR 226, 229]

(b) **Application**

- [3:429] Sister and Brother sued Other Brother and his business entities for misappropriating family assets in Switzerland. *Sister, Brother and Other Brother all resided in California.* But California was an "inconvenient" forum because similar litigation was already pending in Switzerland; the assets were located there; the alleged malfeasance occurred there (so Swiss law would apply to the dispute); and difficult 5th Amendment problems would be encountered if the action were to proceed in California. [*Klein v. Sup.Ct. (Thomas)*, supra, 198 CA3d at 901, 244 CR at 229]

- [3:430] California Insurance Co.'s suit against Policyholder for declaratory relief was properly stayed because (i) litigation on the same issue was already pending between the same parties (and others) in Hawaii; (ii) Hawaii had a strong interest in interpreting the insurance policy because it was issued there; and (iii) there was no strong countervailing justification for proceeding in California. [*Century Indemn. Co. v. Bank of America, FSB* (1997) 58 CA4th 408, 413, 68 CR2d 132, 134-135]

- [3:430.1] A California shareholder's fraud action against the issuer was properly stayed because (i) similar claims had been pending in class actions in New York for several years; (ii) extensive depositions and other discovery had been completed in the New York proceedings;

and (iii) California was clearly *not* the "center of gravity" (most events occurred elsewhere). [*Berg v. MTC Electronic Technologies* (1998) 61 CA4th 349, 362-363, 71 CR2d 523, 531-532]

c. **[3:431] Defendant's local residence as factor:** The fact that one or more defendants lives here does not affect the court's power to stay or dismiss the action for forum non conveniens. [CCP §410.30]

Indeed, the doctrine is particularly valuable in multiparty, multiaction litigation arising out of a single occurrence, where some defendants are local and others nonresidents. [See *Dendy v. MGM Grand Hotels* (1982) 137 CA3d 457, 461, 187 CR 95, 97—suit for injuries suffered in Nevada hotel fire; court suggested that California plaintiff sue in Nevada so that all actions could be consolidated; stay granted on condition that plaintiff's deposition and medical exam be taken there]

(1) **[3:431.1] Presumption favoring local jurisdiction:** A presumption of convenience to defendants arises from the fact they are incorporated in California and have their principal place of business here. [*Stangvik v. Shiley, Inc.* (1991) 54 C3d 744, 760, 1 CR2d 556, 566]

d. **[3:432] Effect if all parties nonresidents:** Where all parties live outside California, and the action arises elsewhere, forum non conveniens may *compel dismissal.* California has no interest in providing a forum for disputes between nonresidents involving claims about which California has no interest: "Under these circumstances, even if general jurisdiction is assumed, it would be an *abuse of discretion* for a trial court to do anything but dismiss the actions." [See *Baltimore Football Club, Inc. v. Sup.Ct. (Ramco, Inc.)* (1985) 171 CA3d 352, 365, 215 CR 323, 330-331 (emphasis added)]

e. **[3:433] Suability of third parties as factor:** If defendant has a cross-complaint against third parties who are *suable only in the foreign forum,* "substantial justice" to defendant may require stay or dismissal of the California action (to avoid multiplicity of suits and possibly inconsistent judgments).

However, a mere *potential* cause of action against a foreign third party cannot be considered. "(I)t is inappropriate to shift the forum based upon the fact that (defendant) *may* join others when it has not taken any steps to do so." [*Corrigan v. Bjork Shiley Corp.* (1986) 182 CA3d 166, 183, 227 CR 247, 257 (emphasis in original) (disapproved on other grounds in *Stangvik v. Shiley, Inc.* (1991) 54 C3d 744, 764, 1 CR2d 556, 569)]

[3:434-443]  *Reserved.*

f.  [3:444]  **Effect of forum-selection contract:**  The parties' knowing and voluntary agreement to litigate their dispute in a particular state or country (with which they have *reasonable* contacts) is normally given effect (*see ¶3:177 ff.*). [See *Berg v. MTC Electronic Technologies* (1998) 61 CA4th 349, 358-359, 71 CR2d 523, 529 (citing text)]

Under some contracts, one party may agree to submit to jurisdiction in a forum chosen by the other. (E.g., insurance policies often contain a "service of suit" clause in which the insurer agrees to submit to any court of competent jurisdiction chosen by the insured.) In such cases, "the parties' convenience normally weighs in favor of suit in the forum chosen by the plaintiff *although transfer could be warranted by the remaining factors.*" [*Ford Motor Co. v. Insurance Co. of No. America* (1995) 35 CA4th 604, 611, 41 CR2d 342, 347 (emphasis added)]

(1)  [3:445]  **Contracts requiring suit in California:**  Thus, a *valid* forum-selection clause that *requires* litigation in California (e.g., "only in courts of the State of California and not elsewhere") is usually given effect. Having agreed to California in advance, there is little room for claiming litigation here is "inconvenient." [See *Appalachian Ins. Co. v. Sup.Ct. (Union Carbide Corp.)* (1984) 162 CA3d 427, 439, 208 CR 627, 634]

(a)  [3:445.1]  **Compare—contracts requiring parties to submit to California jurisdiction:**  The result is different where the contract merely requires defendants to submit to the jurisdiction of local courts and *does not expressly mandate* litigation here. (E.g., "In the event of litigation arising under this agreement, the parties agree to submit to the jurisdiction of California courts.") Such clauses are "permissive" and are "only one factor in the forum non conveniens mix." [*Berg v. MTC Electronic Technologies, supra,* 61 CA4th at 359, 71 CR2d at 529 (citing text); see also *Hunt Wesson Foods, Inc. v. Supreme Oil Co.* (9th Cir. 1987) 817 F2d 75, 77—clause stating "courts of California shall have jurisdiction over the parties" did *not* make California jurisdiction exclusive]

(2)  [3:446]  **Contracts requiring suit outside California:**  Conversely, if a valid forum-selection contract requires the dispute to be litigated in a different state or country, and the choice is reasonable, a California court

normally will stay or dismiss a local action without analyzing the "convenience" factors. [*Furda v. Sup.Ct. (Serological Biopsy)* (1984) 161 CA3d 418, 426, 207 CR 646, 651 —abuse of discretion to deny stay]

"[A] party which has contracted away its right to choose its home forum . . . has presumably done so because the value it receives from the negotiated deal is worth the chance the party may be required to litigate disputes elsewhere. To apply the general ("convenience") factors in this context would in essence be rewriting the bargain struck between the parties . . ." [*Cal-State Products & Services, Inc. v. Ricoh* (1993) 12 CA4th 1666, 1683, 16 CR2d 417, 426 (parentheses added)]

(a) **Application**

- [3:446.1]   Contract between Michigan researcher and California corporation required disputes to be resolved in Michigan, where much of the work was performed. Litigation in California was stayed on forum non conveniens grounds. [*Furda v. Sup.Ct. (Serological Biopsy)*, supra, 161 CA3d at 425-426, 207 CR at 650]

- [3:446.2]   Employee's stock option agreement with Employer, a German corporation, designated Hamburg, Germany, as "the place of jurisdiction." The forum-selection clause was enforceable absent a showing that substantial justice could not be obtained in a German court. [*Intershop Communications, AG v. Sup.Ct. (Martinez)* (2002) 104 CA4th 191, 200, 127 CR2d 847, 854]

  [3:446.3-446.4]   *Reserved.*

(b) [3:446.5]   **Limitation—public policy:**   But a forum-selection contract requiring litigation outside California may be *void* where a strong public policy requires that the dispute be heard here. See ¶3:184 ff.

(c) [3:447]   **Effect of joinder of noncontracting parties:**   If other parties are joined in the action (persons who were not parties to the forum-selection contract), the action may be severed or the stay lifted as to them. [*Cal-State Business Products & Systems, Inc. v. Ricoh* (1993) 12 CA4th 1666, 1674, 16 CR2d 417, 421]

*Cross-refer:* Forum-selection clauses are discussed further at ¶3:177 ff.

8. [3:448] **No Findings Required:** The court is not required to make findings of fact in ruling on a motion to stay or dismiss on inconvenient forum grounds. [See *Cal-State Business Products & Services, Inc. v. Ricoh*, supra, 12 CA4th at 1676, 16 CR2d at 422]

9. [3:449] **Nature of Dismissal:** If the court decides to dismiss rather than stay the action, it may dismiss without prejudice, or it may dismiss only as to particular defendants. [CCP §581(h)]

## D. VENUE

1. [3:450] **Nature of Requirement:** Venue rules designate a particular *county* (or counties) within California as the "proper" place for trial of the action. Since jurisdiction is statewide, the venue rules serve to narrow geographically the place for trial.

   a. [3:451] **Purpose of venue rules:** To give defendant some control in the choice of the forum. Otherwise, plaintiff might file the action in some remote county where it would be difficult or impractical for defendant to defend. [*Smith v. Smith* (1891) 88 C 572, 576, 26 P 356, 358; *Alexander v. Sup.Ct. (Brix Group, Inc.)* (2003) 114 CA4th 723, 731, 8 CR3d 111, 117]

   b. [3:452] **May not be waived in advance:** The venue statutes declare the public policy of this state with respect to the proper court for an action. Therefore, agreements fixing venue in some location other than that allowed by statute are contrary to public policy: "(I)t is not for the parties or the courts to set venue. That is the role of the legislature." [*General Accept. Corp. of Calif. v. Robinson* (1929) 207 C 285, 288, 277 P 1039, 1040; *Alexander v. Sup.Ct. (Brix Group, Inc.)* (2003) 114 CA4th 723, 731, 8 CR3d 111, 117; see also CCP §395(c)—waivers of statutory venue requirements in contracts involving consumer transactions "void and unenforceable"]

   c. [3:453] **Not jurisdictional:** Generally, venue rules are *not* jurisdictional. This means that if the action is filed in an "improper" court, and no objection is raised, that court can render an enforceable judgment. [*Barquis v. Merchants Collection Ass'n* (1972) 7 C3d 94, 121-122, 101 CR 745, 765]

      (1) [3:454] **Exceptions:** By statute, a few actions *must* be commenced in a designated county. This requirement is deemed jurisdictional, so that courts in other counties could *not* render an enforceable judgment if the action was commenced there. *See ¶3:469.*

   d. [3:455] **Compare—"proper" judicial district for limited civil cases:** Venue rules designate the proper *county* for trial of the action. Local rules usually designate in which judicial district within the county a limited civil case should be filed; *see ¶3:595, 3:601.2a.*

e.  [3:456]  **Compare—"proper" branch of superior court:** Some superior courts have several branches or districts within the same county. Court rules designate in which district or branch the action is triable; *see ¶3:599-606.*

---

### DETERMINING PROPER VENUE

[3:456.1]   Venue choices can be costly. First of all, if plaintiff files suit where venue is improper, sanctions can be imposed against plaintiff's attorney *personally* (*see ¶3:583*); and unnecessary delay and expense will be encountered in transferring the action to proper venue. In addition, plaintiff forfeits the right to choose among various counties in which venue would be proper, which allows defendant to force transfer to a county that is seriously inconvenient to plaintiff.

The following analytical approach may be helpful in choosing the county in which to commence a lawsuit:

☐  Does the *main relief* relate to rights in land or other res? (If so, venue is "proper" only where the res is located; *see ¶3:467.*)

☐  If not, is the action governed by a *special venue rule*, permitting suit to be filed *either* where the defendant resides *or elsewhere*? (E.g., actions for personal injury or death, breach of contract, etc.; *see ¶3:496 ff.*)

  ☐  What is the effect of joining causes of action with *conflicting* venue provisions? (The "mixed action" rule; *see ¶3:515.*)

☐  *If no special venue rule applies*, where does defendant(s) "reside"? (If there are several defendants, venue is proper where *any* defendant resides; *see ¶3:487.*)

  ☐  Is the *only* defendant a corporation, partnership, or governmental entity? (If so, a wider choice of venue may be available than defendant's residence; *see ¶3:519 ff.*)

  ☐  What is the effect of naming an *individual* and a corporation or partnership as *codefendants*? (Venue may be proper at the "residence" of either; *see ¶3:528.*)

---

2.  **Venue Rules Depend on Whether Action "Transitory" or "Local"**

a.  [3:457]  **Classification of actions:**   For venue purposes, actions are classified as "local" or "transitory." To determine whether an action is local or transitory, the court looks to the "main relief" sought. Where the main relief sought is personal, the action is transitory. Where the main relief relates to rights in real property, the action is local. [*Brown v. Sup.Ct. (C.C. Myers, Inc.)* (1984) 37 C3d 477, 482, 208 CR 724, 726, fn. 5]

(1) **[3:458]** **Transitory actions:** "Transitory" actions are those in which the claim may have arisen anywhere. Such actions are subject to the "general rule" of venue that the action be tried in the county of *defendant's residence*; *see ¶3:480.*

(2) **[3:459]** **Local actions:** "Local" actions are those dealing with *land* or certain other local relationships that are deemed to require local adjudication, regardless where the defendant resides; *see ¶3:467.*

(3) **[3:460]** **Mixed actions:** Some actions do not fit neatly into either category.

    (a) **[3:461]** **Several causes joined, one local, another transitory:** If the plaintiff's complaint joins several separate causes of action, one of which is local and another transitory, the *transitory action controls* as to venue. "Plaintiff cannot deprive a defendant of his normal right to have a transitory ac-

*(Text cont'd on p. 3-113)*

**RESERVED**

tion tried in the county of his residence by joining a local cause of action." [*Central Bank v. Sup.Ct. (R.P. Richards, Inc.)* (1973) 30 CA3d 913, 917-918, 106 CR 696, 699]

    (b) **[3:462]** **Single cause seeking both forms of relief:** If plaintiff asserts only a single cause of action, but seeks different forms of relief, one local and the other transitory, venue is determined by the "*main relief*" sought . . . although guidelines for identifying the "main" relief are difficult to find!

        **[3:462.1]** **Example:** P sued for specific performance of a land sale contract, plus damages for delay in conveying title. The "main" relief related to rights in land, hence a local action; the incidental demand for damages is disregarded for venue purposes. [*Grocers' Fruit Growing Union v. Kern County Land Co.* (1907) 150 C 466, 472, 89 P 120, 122]

        **[3:463]** **Example:** P sued to recover for the value of labor and materials rendered, plus foreclosure of a mechanic's lien on land improved thereby. The "main" relief sought was money damages, hence a transitory action; the demand for lien foreclosure was only incidental thereto, and hence was disregarded for venue purposes. [*Central Bank v. Sup.Ct. (R.P. Richards, Inc.)*, supra]

  b. **[3:464]** **Determined at outset of action:** The classification of the action as "local" or "transitory" is determined at the outset of the action from the allegations of plaintiff's *original* complaint. If venue is proper under the complaint as it stands at the time a motion for change is made, it remains proper notwithstanding any later amendment to the complaint. [*Brown v. Sup.Ct. (C.C. Myers, Inc.)* (1984) 37 C3d 477, 482, 208 CR 724, 726; *Armstrong Petroleum Corp. v. Sup.Ct. (Oil Leases)* (1981) 114 CA3d 732, 737, 170 CR 767, 769]

    (1) **[3:465]** This is true even if the only cause of action in the original complaint which made venue proper is subsequently dismissed! [*Armstrong Petroleum Corp. v. Sup.Ct. (Oil Leases)*, supra]

    (2) **[3:466]** Conversely, if venue is *not* proper under the original complaint, plaintiff cannot prevent transfer of the action by amending the complaint to include a cause of action under which venue would have been proper.

  3. **[3:467]** **Venue in Local Actions:** As seen, local actions are triable in the county where the land (or other res or relationship)

is located—regardless of defendant's residence. If the action involves land extending into several counties, then venue is proper in any of those counties. [CCP §392(1)]

a. **[3:468]** **Not jurisdictional:** But in most cases the local venue rule is not jurisdictional, so that courts in other counties can adjudicate if the defendant fails to raise any objection to venue there.

   (1) **[3:469]** **Exception—condemnation actions; venue jurisdictional:** The one exception to the above is condemnation actions. A special statute requires that eminent domain proceedings *be commenced* in the county where the land is located. [CCP §1250.020] This is a *jurisdictional* requirement, so that if the complaint were to be filed in any other county, any judgment rendered in the action would be void (even if subsequently transferred to the "proper" county)!

b. **[3:470]** **Court at situs may transfer:** Although venue is "proper" only in the county where the land (or other res or relationship) is located, the court there has discretion to transfer the action to any other county "for the convenience of witnesses and the ends of justice." [CCP §397(c); *see* ¶*3:553-555*]

   (1) **[3:471]** **Includes condemnation actions:** As long as *commenced* in the proper county, an eminent domain action can be transferred to another county for trial on the ground stated above. [CCP §1250.040, *and* ¶*3:553*]

   In addition, the defendant (landowner) has a statutory right to have the action transferred to a county other than the one in which the condemning agency is located. [See CCP §394(a), *discussed at* ¶*3:546*; *Clayton v. Sup.Ct. (City of San Diego)* (1998) 67 CA4th 28, 31, 78 CR2d 750, 751—right to transfer may be exercised even when landowner has withdrawn deposit of probable compensation]

c. **[3:472]** **Local actions involving land:** The following are the most commonly encountered local actions:

   • For *recovery of possession* of land (e.g., unlawful detainer, ejectment) [CCP §392(a)(1)] (Where there are *branch courts*, an unlawful detainer action should be filed at the location where the court tries such proceedings that is "nearest or most accessible" to the property; CCP §392(b).)

   • For "injury to real property" (e.g., trespass, slander of title; or damage to building *affixed* to real property, *see* ¶*3:473.2*) [CCP §392(a)(1)]

(Comment: Note that such actions are local although the relief sought is *money damages*, which in any other case would make the action transitory!)

- For *partition* of land [CCP §872.110(b)(1)]
- For *foreclosure of lien or mortgage* on land [CCP §392(a)(2)]
- For *determination of any other right or interest in* land (e.g., quiet title, set aside deed, specific performance of land contract) [CCP §392(a)(2)]

### (1) Application

- [3:473]   An action to *reform* a trust deed, to delete the power of sale, is a "local" action for venue purposes, because the relief sought would have a direct impact on the *lender's security interest* in the land. [*Massae v. Sup.Ct. (LeClerc)* (1981) 118 CA3d 527, 539, 173 CR 527, 537]

- [3:473.1]   An action for damages to *growing crops* is a local action: "(G)rowing crops are a part of the realty as long as unsevered." [*Stauffer Chem. Co. v. Sup.Ct. (Arthur)* (1968) 265 CA2d 1, 3, 71 CR 202, 203]

- [3:473.2]   A suit for damages for *negligent design and construction* of a building is an action "for injury to real property" so that venue is proper at the location of the building. [*Foundation Engineers, Inc. v. Sup.Ct. (Olivewood I Prof. Offices Owners Ass'n)* (1993) 19 CA4th 104, 110, 23 CR2d 469, 471, 472-473]

  [3:473.3]   Compare: The result would be different if a cause of action for *breach of contract* or *personal injuries* were alleged (*see* ¶3:497, 3:501), or defendant is a corporation with a different principal place of business (*see* ¶3:520). [*Foundation Engineers, Inc. v. Sup.Ct. (Olivewood I Prof. Offices Owners Ass'n)*, supra, 19 CA4th at 112, 23 CR2d at 474]

d. [3:474]   **Other local actions:**   Each of the following involves some res or relationship that is so "localized" that only one county is the "proper" place for trial. (Keep in mind, however, that these rules are *not* jurisdictional; and that the court at the situs retains discretionary power to transfer; ¶3:470.)

(1) [3:475]   **Marriage dissolution proceedings:**   Marriage dissolution proceedings are triable in the county

in which *either spouse* resided during the 3-month period prior to filing. [CCP §395(a)]

   (a) [3:475.1] **Compare—annulment, separation proceedings:** Proceedings for nullity of marriage or legal separation are triable in the county in which either spouse resides *at the commencement* of the proceeding (no 3-month residence requirement). [CCP §395(a)]

  (2) [3:476] **Child support proceedings:** Proceedings for child support are triable in the county where the child resides. [CCP §395(a)]

   (a) [3:476.1] **Compare—parentage proceedings:** Proceedings to determine a child's parentage can be brought either where the child resides "or is found"; or if the father is deceased, where his estate has been or could be probated. [See Fam.C. §7620(b)]

   [3:477] *Reserved.*

  (3) [3:478] **Corporate dissolution proceedings:** The "proper county" for voluntary dissolution proceedings (Corps.C. §1904) or involuntary dissolution proceedings (Corps.C. §1800) is the county where the corporation's principal office is located; or if the principal office is not in California, or if the corporation has no such office, the County of Sacramento. [Corps.C. §177]

  (4) [3:479] **Against a fiduciary:** Actions against an executor, administrator, guardian or trustee are triable in the county having jurisdiction of the estate. [CCP §395.1]

4. [3:480] **Venue in Transitory Actions:** "Except as otherwise provided by law, and subject to the power of the court to transfer . . . *the county in which the defendants or some of them reside* at the commencement of the action is the proper county for the trial of the action." [CCP §395(a); see *Brown v. Sup.Ct. (C.C. Myers, Inc.)* (1984) 37 C3d 477, 483, 208 CR 724, 727]

  a. **Actions triable at defendant's residence**

   (1) [3:481] **The "general rule" of venue:** The defendant has the *right* to have a transitory action against him or her tried in the county where he or she resides. As stated earlier, the purpose of the venue rules is to protect defendants from being forced to trial at some remote location; ¶3:451.

   (a) [3:482] **Limitation—other counties may also be "proper":** Defendant's right to have the action tried at his residence is subject to the qualification "Except as otherwise provided by law . . . " (see above). By statute, many important types of actions are triable *either* at defendant's residence *or* in certain other counties; *see ¶3:496 ff.* In such cases, plaintiff can pick whichever of these counties he or she wants, and defendant cannot compel transfer.

    1) [3:483] **Effect:** The "general rule" of venue has effect *only when no other venue provision applies.* Wherever there is a more specific venue statute, the "general rule" is subordinated. [*Brown v. Sup.Ct. (C.C. Myers, Inc.),* supra, 37 C3d at 483, 208 CR at 727]

   (b) [3:484] **Limitation—court's power to transfer:** Likewise, the statute provides that defendant's right to have the action tried at his residence is "subject to the power of the court to transfer . . ." (see above). Thus, even though defendant asserts his right to compel transfer to the county of his residence, the court there may, in its discretion, order the action *retransferred* to the same county in which plaintiff filed (or some other county) "for the convenience of witnesses and the ends of justice." [CCP §397(c), *¶3:553-555*]

 (2) [3:485] **"Residence" means domicile:** For venue purposes, a person's residence is interpreted as domicile; i.e., the place he or she resides with the intent to remain indefinitely. [*Enter v. Crutcher* (1958) 159 CA2d Supp. 841, 844-845, 323 P2d 586, 589; *and see ¶3:154*]

   (a) [3:486] **Corporations:** As to the "residence" of corporations and other entities, *see ¶3:520.*

 (3) [3:487] **Residence of any defendant:** The Code provides that venue is proper in the county where defendant *or some of them* reside. [CCP §395(a), above] Thus, in an action against several properly-joined defendants, residing in different counties, plaintiff may pick whichever of the counties he or she likes best. The other defendants have *no* right to compel transfer to their residence—even if the resident defendant joins in their motion. [*Monogram Co. v. Kingsley* (1951) 38 C2d 28, 34, 237 P2d 265, 269]

   (a) [3:488] **Example:** A multiple cause of action lawsuit was filed in Alameda County against ten defendants, only one of whom lived there. The other nine lived in Los Angeles, and filed a motion to transfer the case to Los Angeles for trial; the

Alameda defendant joined in their motion. Motion denied. It made no difference that most of the causes of action in the complaint did not affect the Alameda defendant; it was sufficient that one did. [*Monogram Co. v. Kingsley*, supra]

(b) [3:488.1] **Includes "Doe" defendants:** The court is required to consider the residence of a party sued as a "Doe" and whose true name is substituted (and residence ascertained) before the hearing on the motion to change venue. [*Gutierrez v. Sup.Ct. (Ojai Valley Inn)* (1966) 243 CA2d 710, 724, 52 CR 592, 602]

(c) [3:489] **Later dismissal of resident defendant:** Venue is determined at the outset of the action from the *original* complaint (¶*3:464*). Therefore, venue based on the residence of a bona fide defendant remains proper, even though that defendant is later dismissed from the action. I.e., the other defendants *cannot* then compel transfer to their residences. [*Ferguson v. Koerber* (1924) 69 CA 47, 230 P 476, 477]

1) [3:489.1] **Compare—remaining defendants may choose dismissed defendant's residence:** On the other hand, plaintiff cannot object if the remaining defendants *want* the action tried at the dismissed defendant's residence. Their willingness to waive trial at their own residence does *not* waive their objection to trial at plaintiff's residence. [*Lyons v. Brunswick-Balke-Collender Co.* (1942) 20 C2d 579, 584, 127 P2d 924, 928]

[3:489.2] **Example:** P sued D1 and D2 in Los Angeles County. D1 resided in San Francisco County and D2 resided in San Mateo County. They demurred and D1 moved to change venue to San Francisco. D2 consented to San Francisco. However, P then dismissed D1. D2 promptly moved to change venue to San Francisco. D2's motion must be granted: "His residence being near the city and county of San Francisco, there was no reason for him to insist on a trial in San Mateo County. He did not at any time consent to trial in ... Los Angeles County." [*Lyons v. Brunswick-Balke-Collender Co.*, supra, 20 C2d at 584, 127 P2d at 927-928]

(d) [3:490] **Limitation—resident defendant must be properly joined:** If the resident defendant has been "improperly joined" or "has been made a defendant *solely* for the purpose of having the action tried at his residence," his residence will be disregarded in determining venue. [CCP §395(a)]

1) [3:491] **Example:** P filed breach of contract actions against D1 and D2 in Sacramento County, residence of D2. D1 moved for change of venue to his residence, San Francisco, with affidavit showing that D2 was not a party to the contract sued upon. Hence, no valid cause of action existed against D2. Court concluded that D2 had been "improperly joined" and therefore venue could *not* be based on his residence in Sacramento. [*Heringer v. Schumacher* (1928) 88 CA 349, 263 P 550, 552]

2) [3:492] **Sanctions may be imposed:** The court hearing the motion to transfer may order plaintiff's *attorney* to pay defendant's expenses and attorney's fees in such cases. [CCP §396b(b), ¶*3:583-585*]

3) [3:492.1] **Comment:** However, apparently not much is required to overcome claims of sham joinder: "If the allegations in question did no more than *shadow forth the semblance* of a cause of action, they would be proof against assault upon the ground they were sham and frivolous." [*McClung v. Watt* (1922) 190 C 155, 160, 211 P 17, 20 (emphasis added)]

(e) [3:493] **Limitation—individual and corporate defendants joined in same action:** If a corporation is joined as a codefendant, venue is proper *either* in the county where the individual defendant resides *or* at the corporation's headquarters (its "residence" for venue purposes). *See discussion at* ¶*3:527 ff.*

1) [3:494] But note: *Other* counties may *also* be proper in actions subject to special venue rules (e.g., actions for personal injury, wrongful death, breach of contract, etc.; *see* ¶*3:496 ff.*).

(4) [3:495] **Residence unknown or out-of-state:** "If none of the defendants reside in the state, or if the county in which they reside is unknown to the plaintiff, the action may be tried in *any county* designated by plaintiff . . ." [CCP §395(a)]

b. [3:496] **Actions triable EITHER at defendant's residence or other counties:** Defendant's right to have a transitory action against him or her tried where he or she lives is subject to the important limitation that in the most common actions, venue may be proper in *several* counties: i.e., either in the county in which defendant resides or elsewhere. In such cases, plaintiff obviously has greater latitude in choosing where to file, and defendant cannot force a transfer to the county where he or she lives. (Remember, however, that the court always has *discretionary* power to order a transfer "for convenience of witnesses and the interests of justice"; *see ¶3:553-555.*)

(1) [3:497] **Actions for personal injury or death:** Such actions are triable either in the county where defendant resides OR in the county *where the injury occurred* (including the injury causing the death). [CCP §395(a)]

The choice is up to plaintiff; defendants have no right to have the action tried at their residence.

   (a) [3:498] **"Personal injury" narrowly construed:** This venue rule applies only to actions for *physical* injury. Actions for injury to reputation, or even for mental or emotional distress, are triable only at defendant's residence. [*Carruth v. Sup.Ct. (Stoike)* (1978) 80 CA3d 215, 219-220, 145 CR 344, 346; and *Cubic Corp. v. Sup.Ct. (Warren)* (1986) 186 CA3d 622, 625, 231 CR 18, 19—emotional distress, shock, etc. may be bodily injury for *pleading* purposes, but not for venue purposes]

(2) [3:499] **Actions for injury to personal property:** The same venue rule applies here as well. I.e., such actions are triable either where defendant resides OR in the county *where the injury occurred.* [CCP §395(a)]

   (a) [3:500] **Compare—injury to real property:** Trespass or other injury to real property is a *local* action, triable *only* at the situs (and *not* at defendant's residence); *see ¶3:467 ff.*

(3) [3:501] **Actions for breach of contract (other than consumer obligations):** Such actions are triable in the county where defendant resides OR *where the contract was entered into* OR *where it was to be performed* (if specified in writing). [CCP §395(a)]

   (a) [3:502] **"County where contract entered into":** This means the place where the *acceptance* occurred (e.g., where it was mailed, or where words of acceptance spoken). [See *Wilson v. Scannavino* (1958) 159 CA2d 369, 370-371, 324 P2d 350, 351—contract negotiated by telephone "entered into" where acceptor spoke]

Rev. #1 2003

(b) [3:503] **"County where obligation to be performed"**: The place of making is deemed to be the place of performance unless a different place is specified in a "special contract in writing." [CCP §395(a)]

    1) [3:504] **"Special contract in writing" requirement:** The "special contract in writing" may either be the contract sued upon or a separate writing between the parties. But it must be *specific* as to the place of performance. I.e., for venue to be proper there, it must *expressly* state the *geographic location* where payment or other performance is due. [*Caffrey v. Tilton* (1952) 38 C2d 371, 373-374, 240 P2d 273, 274]

    This may *not* be shown by parol evidence or implication. [*Mitchell v. Sup.Ct. (Nat'l Union Fire Ins. Co.)* (1986) 186 CA3d 1040, 1047, 231 CR 176, 180]

    Absent such express provision, venue is proper only where the contract was entered into (or at defendant's residence). [*Mitchell v. Sup.Ct. (Nat'l Union Fire Ins. Co.)*, supra]

    2) [3:505] **Example:** Contractor sued for balance due under written contract to build house in Alameda County. The contract did not specifically state that Owner was to make *payments* in Alameda County; and this could not be shown by parol. Venue therefore was proper only in the county where the contract had been entered into (or at defendant's residence). [*Armstrong v. Smith* (1942) 49 CA2d 528, 122 P2d 115, 120]

    3) [3:506] **Compare—actions against corporations:** The writing requirement applies only in actions against individual, as opposed to corporate, defendants. In actions against corporations, venue is proper "where *the contract is made or to be performed*" (no requirement of writing specifying place of performance). [CCP §395.5, ¶3:520]

(4) [3:507] **Actions on certain consumer obligations:** There are a number of special venue rules scattered throughout the Codes dealing with actions based on consumer obligations:

- **[3:508]** Actions to enforce obligations for *goods or services intended primarily for personal, family or household use*; venue proper *either* in county where defendant (consumer) signed the contract, or resided at that time, or resided at commencement of action. [CCP §395(b)]

  The same rule applies to actions arising out of consumer transactions resulting from *unsolicited telephone calls* by the seller or electronic transmissions (*e-mail*) by a buyer or lessee in response to solicitation by the seller. [CCP §395(b)]

  Where there are *branch courts*, such actions should be filed at the location where the court tries that type of case that is "nearest or most accessible" to the place specified above. [CCP §395(b)]

- **[3:509]** Actions to enforce *installment sales of motor vehicles*; same as above, plus venue also proper in county where car permanently garaged. [Civ.C. §2984.4]

  Where there are *branch courts*, the action should be filed at the location where the court tries that type of case that is "nearest or most accessible" to the place specified above. [Civ.C. §2984.4(b)]

- **[3:510]** Actions to enforce other *retail installment sales contracts*; same as above, plus venue also proper in county where goods permanently affixed to real property if such is the case. [Civ.C. §1812.10]

  Where there are *branch courts*, the action should be filed at the location where the court tries that type of case that is "nearest or most accessible" to the place specified above. [Civ.C. §1812.10(b)]

(a) **[3:511]** **Special pleading requirement:** In most civil actions, venue need not be pleaded; it is presumptively proper (*see "pleadings," ¶6:98*). However, in the actions noted above (and in unlawful detainer actions), the *facts* upon which venue is based must be *specially pleaded* in the complaint, or in a separate affidavit served and filed along with the complaint. Otherwise, the complaint is subject to dismissal. (*See ¶6:101.*)

(b) **[3:512]** **Defendant's consent to improper court:** As with other venue rules, they are for the protection of defendant, and hence can be waived. But with consumer obligations under CCP §395(b), no consent to improper venue is allowed unless defendant was represented by counsel. [CCP §396a]

(5) **[3:513] Other special venue statutes:** Numerous other statutes have venue provisions which alter normal venue requirements. Typically, such provisions give the plaintiff a broader choice of where to sue, by *enlarging* the number of counties in which venue is proper:

- [3:514] For example, an action for violation of the Fair Employment and Housing Act (Gov.C. §12900 et seq.) may be brought "in any county in the state in which the unlawful practice is alleged to have been committed, in the county in which the records relevant to such practice are maintained ... or in the county in which the aggrieved person would have worked ..." [Gov.C. §12965(b)]

  This broad choice of venue makes it easier for financially stressed litigants to bring FEHA actions in locations where travel and other costs will be minimized. [*Richfield Hotel Management, Inc. v. Sup.Ct. (Riddell)* (1994) 22 CA4th 222, 225, 27 CR2d 161, 163; see also *Ford Motor Credit Co. v. Sup.Ct. (Danford)* (1996) 50 CA4th 306, 310, 57 CR2d 682, 684—venue *cannot* be based solely on plaintiff's residence]

- [3:514.1] Holocaust victims, their heirs or beneficiaries, who reside in California, may sue in the county in which they reside for unpaid benefits under designated insurance policies issued by insurers subject to jurisdiction in California. [CCP §354.5]

c. **[3:515] Causes of action with conflicting venue provisions—the "mixed action" rule:** It sometimes happens that plaintiff alleges two or more causes of action, each governed by a different venue provision; or joins two or more defendants who are subject to different venue standards.

In such cases, venue must be proper as to *all* causes of action and defendants joined. If not, any defendant is entitled to seek a change of venue (usually, of course, to the county where any defendant resides): "In cases with mixed causes of action, a motion for change of venue must be granted on the entire complaint if the defendant is entitled to a change of venue on any one cause of action." [*Brown v. Sup.Ct. (C.C. Myers, Inc.)* (1984) 37 C3d 477, 488, 208

*(Text cont'd on p. 3-121)*

**RESERVED**

CR 724, 730; see *Capp Care, Inc. v. Sup.Ct. (Proffitt)* (1987) 195 CA3d 504, 508, 241 CR 741, 744]

(1) [3:516] **Rationale:** Were the rule otherwise, it would be too easy for plaintiff to "manufacture" proper venue by joining a cause of action which might not be genuine. [*Ah Fong v. Sternes* (1889) 79 C 30, 33, 21 P 381, 382]

(2) [3:517] **Public policy exceptions:** There are some cases, however, in which the "mixed action" rule is not followed. Rather, for *public policy reasons*, plaintiff's right to choose the place of trial is preferred over defendant's right to have the action tried at its residence. [*Brown v. Sup.Ct. (C.C. Myers, Inc.)*, supra]

  (a) [3:518] **Example:** P sued for intentional infliction of emotional distress, wrongful discharge and violation of the Fair Employment and Housing Act (Gov.C. §12900), all arising out of the *same facts*. Venue was proper under the FEHA which allows suits in the county where the "unlawful practice is alleged to have been committed." Defendants were *not* entitled to a change of venue to the county of their residence: "Although the mixed action rule recognizes a preference for trial in the county of defendant's residence, *that preference is outweighed by the strong countervailing policies* of the FEHA which favors a plaintiff's choice of venue." [*Brown v. Sup.Ct. (C.C. Myers, Inc.)*, supra, 37 C3d at 488, 208 CR at 731]

  (b) [3:518.1] **Compare:** But there is no policy favoring plaintiff's residence in suits under the Consumer Legal Remedies Act (Civ.C. §§1750 ff.). It creates no right to sue at the consumer's residence (authorizing only suit at the county of *defendant's* residence, principal place of business, any county where defendant is doing business, or in the county where the transaction or any substantial portion thereof occurred; see Civ.C. §1780). Nor does suit elsewhere necessarily disadvantage the consumer. [*Gallin v. Sup.Ct. (Jeffrey)* (1991) 230 CA3d 541, 545-546, 281 CR 304, 306]

5. [3:519] **Venue in Actions Against Corporations or Other Entities:** A wider choice of venue is permitted in actions against corporations or other entities than is permitted in actions against individual defendants.

  a. [3:520] **Actions against corporations:** Actions against a corporation are triable *either* in the county:

- Where it has its *principal place of business* (its "residence" for venue purposes); OR

- Where the *contract was made or to be performed* (whether specified in writing or not); OR

- Where the *obligation or liability arose* or the breach occurred. [CCP §395.5] (In tort cases, "liability arises" wherever *injury* occurs; see *Mission Imports, Inc. v. Sup.Ct. (Monterey Bay Co., Inc.)* (1982) 31 C3d 921, 931, 184 CR 296, 302—beer distributor allegedly lost profits in each county its beer was sold, and therefore could sue in any of these counties; see also *Black Diamond Asphalt, Inc. v. Sup.Ct. (CIGA)* (2003) 109 CA4th 166, 172, 134 CR2d 510, 514-515—declaratory relief action to determine insurer's duty to defend may be commenced in county where a third party *claimant* sues because that is where the *insurer's liability* arises.)

[3:521] *Limitation—special rule for involuntary dissolution:* Suits for involuntary dissolution are triable only in the county in which the corporation has its principal executive office (or, if no such office in California, in Sacramento County). [Corps.C. §§177, 1800; *Capp Care, Inc. v. Sup.Ct. (Proffitt)* (1987) 195 CA3d 504, 508, 241 CR 741, 744 (citing text); see ¶3:478]

(1) [3:521.1] **Principal place of business; corporate designation governs:** A corporation is *bound* for venue purposes by its designation of its "principal place of business" in corporate documents filed with the Secretary of State (e.g., articles of incorporation and "Statement by Domestic Stock Corporation" filed annually with the Secretary of State). The corporation cannot claim its principal office is actually somewhere else. [*Rosas v. Sup.Ct. (Mercury Cas. Co.)* (1994) 25 CA4th 671, 677, 30 CR2d 609, 613]

(2) [3:522] **Place of performance:** Unlike venue in actions against individuals, in actions against corporations venue is proper in the "place of performance" whether or not specified in writing (¶3:506).

- [3:523] Where the corporation's breach is failure to pay for goods sold and delivered, the "place of performance" is the place *where payment was due*—rather than where the goods were delivered. [*Anaheim Extrusion Co. v. Sup.Ct. (Classic Molding Co.)* (1985) 170 CA3d 1201, 1203, 216 CR 815, 816]

[3:523.1-523.4] *Reserved.*

(3) [3:523.5] **Effect of suing in wrong county:** If plaintiff sues in a county other than one of the above, the defendant corporation may move to change venue to its *residence* (principal place of business). But it *cannot* have venue changed to some other county in which plaintiff could have brought the action initially: "The provision allowing suit against a corporation in certain counties other than its residence is for the benefit of the plaintiff and does not give the defendant corporation the same rights." [*Beutke v. American Securities Co.* (1955) 132 CA2d 354, 361, 282 P2d 201, 206]

(4) [3:524] **Out-of-state corporations:** If a foreign corporation has "qualified" to do business in California, it will have filed a statement designating the county in which it maintains its principal local office. [See Corps.C. §2105(a)(3)] In such event, the foreign corporation can be sued only in a county in which venue would be proper in an action against a California corporation, under CCP §395.5, above.

    (a) [3:525] **Not qualified to do business in California:** However, if the corporate defendant has *not* filed such statement designating a principal office in California, venue is proper in *any county* in the State. Plaintiff's motives for filing in some remote county are immaterial (although transfers for convenience may still be available). [*Easton v. Sup.Ct. (Schneider Bros., Inc.)* (1970) 12 CA3d 243, 246-247, 90 CR 642, 644]

    (b) [3:526] **Compare—jurisdiction problem:** The fact that a foreign corporation has not "qualified" to do business in California does not mean, of course, that it is not subject to personal jurisdiction here. California courts can exercise jurisdiction if the corporate defendant has "minimum contacts" with the state; ¶3:349-356. Thus, once jurisdiction is established, there is *no* venue problem; because, as stated above, venue is proper in *any* county in the state.

(5) [3:527] **Effect of joinder of individual codefendant ("residence" venue):** The wide choice of venue permitted in actions against a corporation (CCP §395.5, above) is limited where an individual is joined as codefendant. Such suits may be commenced in the county in which the "defendants *or some of them reside.*" [CCP §395(a)]

    (a) [3:528] **"Residence" of either proper:** Where an action is brought against both corporate and individual defendants, venue is proper *either* where any individual defendant resides *or* where the corporation has its principal office (its "residence" for venue purposes). Plaintiff thus has a choice of where to sue. If suit is filed where the corporation has its principal office, the individual defendants *cannot* compel transfer to the counties where they reside. [*Hale v. Bohannon* (1952) 38 C2d 458, 472, 241 P2d 4, 12; *see* ¶3:493]

1) **[3:528.1] Compare—actions subject to special venue rules:** In actions subject to special venue rules (actions for personal injury, wrongful death, breach of contract, etc.; *see* ¶3:496 ff.), *other counties may also be proper:* e.g., where the injury occurred, where the contract was executed, etc.

(b) **[3:529] Suit filed elsewhere:** But venue is *not* proper in any of the other counties in which the corporation alone might be sued under CCP §395.5 (e.g., place where contract made or performed; or where obligation or liability arose). Joinder of an individual defendant restricts plaintiff to *residence* of one of the defendants. If plaintiff sues elsewhere, the individual defendant can compel transfer to the county in which he or she resides; or if that defendant prefers, to the county in which the corporate defendant has its principal office. [*Brown v. Sup.Ct. (C.C. Myers, Inc.)* (1984) 37 C3d 477, 482, 208 CR 724, 726, fn. 6; *Walker v. Wells Fargo Bank* (1937) 24 CA2d 220, 74 P2d 849, 850]

- **[3:529.1]** P filed suit in Alameda County against D Corp. and two individuals, D1 and D2. Venue was conceded to be proper as to D Corp. in Alameda because the obligation apparently arose there. But D1 resided in San Diego and D2 resided in San Mateo. D1 was entitled to a change of venue to San Diego. (The court could not transfer to San Mateo where D2 resided—although venue would have been proper had P chosen to file there originally!) [*Cubic Corp. v. Sup.Ct. (Warren)* (1986) 186 CA3d 622, 625, 231 CR 18, 20]

[3:529.2-529.4] *Reserved.*

(c) **[3:529.5] Compare—individual sued as alter ego of corporation:** Where the individual defendant is sued as the *alter ego* of the corporation, the effect is to make the individual a co-obligor on the claim against the corporation. Venue is thus proper where the action could be commenced for breach of contract against an individual or corporate defendant (e.g., where the breach occurred). [*Lebastchi v. Sup.Ct. (Poway Wal-Mart Plaza)* (1995) 33 CA4th 1465, 1470, 39 CR2d 787, 790]

(6) **[3:530] Multiple causes of action:** The same rule applies as in actions against individual defendants: i.e., venue must be proper on *all* causes of action joined, or the corporate defendant is entitled to a transfer of the action. (Usually, of course, it will seek transfer to the county in which it has its principal office.) [*Capp Care, Inc. v. Sup.Ct. (Proffitt)* (1987) 195 CA3d 504, 508, 241 CR 741, 744; *and see ¶3:515-518*]

b. **[3:531] Actions against partnerships or unincorporated associations:** The same venue rules apply as in actions against corporations (above), *provided* the partnership or association has filed a statement with the Secretary of State designating the county in which it maintains its principal office (as required by Corps.C. §24003). [CCP §395.2]

If the partnership or association has failed to file the required statement, venue in any action against it is proper in the county in which *any* partner or member *resides*. [See *Juneau Spruce Corp. v. International Longshoremen's & Warehousemen's Union* (1951) 37 C2d 760, 763-764, 235 P2d 607, 608-609]

(1) **[3:532] Purpose:** The main purpose of CCP §395.2 is to enable unincorporated associations, by filing a designation of principal office address, to protect themselves from exposure to suit in some remote county where one of its members may reside. [*San Francisco Foundation v. Sup.Ct. (County of Marin)* (1984) 37 C3d 285, 297, 208 CR 31, 36]

(2) **[3:533] When filed:** To protect this right, the unincorporated association may file the statement even *after* suit against it is commenced. [*San Francisco Foundation v. Sup.Ct. (County of Marin)*, supra]

(3) **[3:534] Effect of joinder of individual partners:** Where individual partners are joined as defendants in the action (as is usually the case), venue is *also* proper where *any* joined partner *resides*. [*Mosby v. Sup.Ct. (Lucas)* (1974) 43 CA3d 219, 226, 117 CR 588, 593]

Plaintiff thus has a choice of where to sue. If suit is filed where one of the joined partners resides, the partnership cannot compel transfer to a different county where its principal office is located (and vice versa). [*Buran Equipment Co., Inc. v. Sup.Ct. (Brobeck, Phleger et al.)* (1987) 190 CA3d 1662, 1666, 236 CR 171, 173]

Note: It is immaterial whether the partners joined are those involved in the transaction sued upon. It is enough that they are responsible for the debts of the partnership. [*Buran Equipment Co., Inc. v. Sup.Ct. (Brobeck, Phleger et al.)*, supra]

## c. Actions against governmental entities

### (1) Actions against State of California

(a) [3:535]   Certain tort actions against the State for *personal injury* or *death*, or injury to personal property, are triable where the cause of action arose (i.e., where the injury occurred). [Gov.C. §955.2]

(There are some statutory exceptions; see, e.g., *Hatcher v. California State Univ.* (1983) 146 CA3d Supp. 1, 4-5, 194 CR 756, 758.)

1) [3:536]   The statute (Gov.C. §955.2) says "the court" may change the place of trial for convenience of witnesses and ends of justice. But this refers to the *court where venue is proper* (i.e., place of injury). In actions filed elsewhere, the court cannot consider "convenience" grounds to deny the State's motion to transfer. [*State of Calif. v. Sup.Ct. (Clark)* (1987) 193 CA3d 328, 330, 238 CR 315, 316]

(b) [3:537]   Actions against state officers for acts done by virtue of their office, are triable where the cause of action arose. [CCP §393(b)]

1) [3:538]   This covers *writ proceedings* against state officials and agencies; e.g., mandamus, prohibition or injunction. [*Tharp v. Sup.Ct. (Jennings)* (1982) 32 C3d 496, 498, 186 CR 335, 336]

2) [3:539]   The cause of action normally "arises" wherever the plaintiff would be injured by the state action complained of; e.g., where the plaintiff resides or does business: "A cause arises in the county where the effects of the administrative action are felt, not where the

agency signs the challenged order or takes the challenged action." [*Lipari v. Department of Motor Vehicles* (1993) 16 CA4th 667, 670, 20 CR2d 246, 248, fn. 2]

(c) [3:540] Actions for *inverse condemnation* (taking or damaging private property for public use) are triable where the *property* is located. [Gov.C. §955]

(d) [3:541] In actions based on express *contracts* or for *negligence*, the Attorney General has the right,

*(Text cont'd on p. 3-127)*

**RESERVED**

by written demand at or before answering, to a *change* of venue to Sacramento County. [Gov.C. §955; see *Tharp v. Sup.Ct. (Jennings)*, supra]

Alternatively, any action triable in or removable to Sacramento County can be commenced or tried in any other county in which the *Attorney General has an office* (i.e., San Francisco, Los Angeles, or San Diego). [CCP §401(1)]

## (2) **Actions against city, county or local districts**

(a) **[3:542]** Actions by a private plaintiff for *negligent* injury to persons or property occurring in the city or county are triable locally (so called "home county" rule). [CCP §394; *County of Orange v. Sup.Ct. (Barrie)* (1999) 73 CA4th 1189, 1192, 86 CR2d 923, 925]

### 1) **Application**

- **[3:542.1]** Plaintiff was arrested in San Francisco and later imprisoned in Orange County on an invalid arrest warrant issued by Orange County (thus claiming injury in *both* counties). She filed a personal injury action in San Francisco against Orange County only. Orange County was entitled to a change of venue to Orange County Superior Court because at least some of plaintiff's injuries occurred there. [*County of Orange v. Sup.Ct. (Barrie)* (1999) 73 CA4th 1189, 1192, 86 CR2d 923, 925]

- **[3:542.2]** Where an action was commenced against two public entities from different counties, suit could be commenced in either county. But after settlement and dismissal of the entity in whose county the suit was commenced, the remaining entity had an absolute right to have the case transferred to its county. [*Ventura Unified School v. Sup.Ct. (Lopez)* (2001) 92 CA4th 811, 815, 112 CR2d 260, 262]

### 2) **[3:543] Transfer discretionary:** Although the action must be commenced locally, either party may later seek transfer to a different county on discretionary grounds ("impartial trial cannot be had"; "convenience of witnesses," etc.; see CCP §397, ¶*3:553 ff.*). [*Paesano v. Sup.Ct. (Mono Co.)* (1988) 204 CA3d 17, 20-21, 250 CR 842, 844; *County of Orange v.*

Sup.Ct. (Barrie), supra, 73 CA4th at 1192-1193, 86 CR2d at 926]

(b) [3:544]   In any other kind of action against a city or county or local district, it has the right to a transfer to a "neutral" county, in order to avoid any local prejudice. [CCP §394] (But note: This is *not* really a venue statute; and, hence, *plaintiff cannot choose* to file in the neutral county; see *Dorame v. Sup.Ct. (County of Orange)* (1978) 81 CA3d 70, 72, 146 CR 162, 163-164.)

(c) [3:545]   If venue is proper in a transitory action against local officials in the county where the cause of action arose, *public entities in other counties may be joined* as defendants based on common issues of law or fact. [*Colusa Air Pollution Control Dist. v. Sup.Ct. (Dunn-Edwards Corp.)* (1991) 226 CA3d 880, 890, 277 CR 110, 115—manufacturer filed suit in Los Angeles against Los Angeles district and two Northern California air pollution control districts, challenging pollution control regulations adopted by all districts]

(3) [3:546]   **Compare—actions BY governmental entity:**   In suits by a city, county or public agency (as plaintiff) against a resident of another county, *either* party has the right to transfer to a "neutral" county. Or, where a jury trial has been waived or there is no right to a jury trial (e.g., injunction or probate proceedings), the local court may, in lieu of transferring, request assignment of a "neutral" judge (from a "neutral" county) to hear the case. [CCP §394(a)]

(The purpose is to protect against possible bias against the out-of-county defendant. See *Westinghouse Elec. Corp. v. Sup.Ct. (San Francisco Bay Area Rapid Transit Dist.)* (1976) 17 C3d 259, 266, 131 CR 231, 236.)

There is a split of authority whether this also applies to *cross-complaints* by local governments. [See *Kennedy/ Jenks Consultants, Inc. v. Sup.Ct. (City of Richmond)* (2000) 80 CA4th 948, 956, 95 CR2d 817, 823—yes; *City of Chico v. Sup.Ct. (Williams)* (1979) 89 CA3d 187, 191, 152 CR 380, 382—no]

*Compare—actions by State:* CCP §394(a) does not apply to actions commenced by the State of California. [*Nguyen v. Sup.Ct. (People)* (1996) 49 CA4th 1781, 57 CR2d 611, 616—not applicable to "red light abatement" action filed by district attorney acting on behalf of State]

*Compare—actions by public guardian:* Although the public guardian is a county agency, CCP §394(a) does not apply to actions filed by the public guardian on behalf of a private ward. Such actions are not "brought by" a public entity within the meaning of the statute because the economic interests of the county's citizens are not affected thereby. [*Transamerica Homefirst, Inc. v. Sup.Ct. (San Mateo Public Guardian)* (1999) 69 CA4th 577, 579-580, 81 CR2d 705, 706-707]

(a) [3:547] **Supports removal, not original venue:** CCP §394(a) is a removal statute. It does not allow a local government plaintiff to commence the action in a "neutral" county of its choosing if venue is not otherwise proper there. [*County of San Bernardino v. Sup.Ct. (Redevelopment Agency of City of Adelanto)* (1994) 30 CA4th 378, 384-385, 35 CR2d 760, 763]

(b) [3:548] **Corporation as "resident":** A corporation sued by a local governmental entity is not entitled to a transfer if it is a "resident" of the same county. The rationale is local businesses are not likely to be subject to prejudice in local courts. [See *San Francisco Foundation v. Sup.Ct. (County of Marin)* (1984) 37 C3d 285, 298, 208 CR 31, 37]

- [3:548.1] For purposes of this statute, a corporation is a "resident" only if its activities in the county are substantial enough that it can reasonably be viewed as being intimately identified with the affairs or closely associated with the people of the community. [*Westinghouse Elec. Corp. v. Sup.Ct. (San Francisco Bay Area Rapid Transit Dist.)* (1976) 17 C3d 259, 272-273, 131 CR 231, 240-241]

- [3:548.2] Additionally, if any defendant is not "doing business" in the county under this expanded definition, the case must be transferred to a "neutral" county even though all other defendants are "doing business" in the county. [*Westinghouse Elec. Corp. v. Sup.Ct. (San Francisco Bay Area Rapid Transit Dist.)*, supra, 17 C3d at 275-276, 131 CR at 242-243]

[3:548.3-548.4] *Reserved.*

(c) [3:548.5] **Effect of joinder of other plaintiffs:** It is the local government's right to an impartial jury trial that is protected. The fact coplaintiffs joined in the action want a local jury trial on their causes of action does *not* defeat the court's power to transfer to a disinterested judge. [*Brennan v. Sup.Ct. (County of Sutter)* (1994) 30 CA4th 454, 461, 35 CR2d 693, 697]

(d) [3:548.6] **Compare—actions against State:** Actions by a local public agency against the State of California may be tried in the county where the local agency is situated. But the Attorney General may, before answering, move to change the place of trial to Sacramento County under CCP §397 (*see* ¶3:549 ff.*). [Gov.C. §955.3]

6. **Procedure for Change of Venue—Motion to Transfer**

   a. [3:549] **Grounds:** The grounds upon which a court may transfer the action are entirely statutory.

   (1) [3:550] **"Wrong court" ground (transfer mandatory):** On timely motion, the court *must* order a transfer of an action "whenever the court designated in the complaint is *not the proper court*." [CCP §§396b, 397(a)]

   (a) [3:551] **Effect:** If plaintiff has failed to heed the venue rules above, and defendant makes timely objection, the court *must* order the action transferred to any "proper" county requested by defendant. (This is true even if grounds exist for retransferring the action back to the county where filed, on grounds of "convenience of witnesses"; see below.)

   (b) [3:552] **Where several venues would be proper:** Where codefendants reside in different counties, they usually decide among themselves who will move to change venue. The court must transfer to the county selected by the *moving defendant,* although the other defendants' residences would also be proper venues. [See *Cubic Corp. v. Sup.Ct. (Warren)* (1986) 186 CA3d 622, 625, 231 CR 18, 20; *and* ¶3:529.1]

   Effect: Had plaintiff sued at any other defendant's residence originally, no transfer could be ordered on "wrong court" grounds. But since plaintiff chose a "wrong" court, venue selection is in the hands of whichever defendant moves for transfer!

   [3:552.1-552.4] *Reserved.*

   (c) [3:552.5] **Compare—"wrong court" transfers on consumer obligations:** Special venue rules specify the "proper court" and the "proper court location" for actions based on certain consumer obligations (*see* ¶3:507 ff.*). If an action on a consumer obligation is commenced elsewhere, the court must transfer it to the "proper court" or "proper court location" unless defendant *consents*—in writing or in open court—to keeping the action where filed. [CCP §396a(b)]

If a defendant had been served but had not yet appeared when the transfer was ordered, that defendant's time to respond to the complaint is measured from the date defendant is *notified* that the action has been filed in the proper court. [CCP §396a(c)]

If a motion is made to transfer such an action to a branch court of the same superior court, "proceedings shall be had as provided by local rules of the superior court." [CCP §396a(f)]

(2) [3:553] **"Convenience of witnesses and ends of justice" (transfer discretionary):** Even if filed in a "proper" county, on appropriate motion, the court has *discretionary* power to transfer the case to any other county "when the convenience of witnesses and the ends of justice would be promoted by the change." [CCP §397(c)]

(a) [3:554] **Importance:** This is an extremely important provision. It gives the court inherent power to moderate the parties' choices as to where the action should be tried. Plaintiff may have the right

*(Text cont'd on p. 3-131)*

**RESERVED**

to file wherever venue is "proper" under the rules stated above, but the court still has discretion to transfer if trial locally would be seriously inconvenient to the witnesses and defeat the ends of justice.

1) [3:554.1] **Applies to *any* action:** Section 397 applies to *any action or proceeding* within its terms . . . even actions under statutes (e.g., FEHA) giving plaintiff the broadest possible choice of venue. [*Richfield Hotel Management, Inc. v. Sup.Ct. (Riddell)* (1994) 22 CA4th 222, 225, 27 CR2d 161, 163]

2) [3:554.2] **Limits defendant's right to compel transfer:** Moreover, the court's discretionary power to transfer tempers defendant's right to compel transfer of an action filed in an "improper" county . . . because even though defendant is entitled to such transfer (¶*3:550*), the transferee-court has discretion to *retransfer* the case either to the court in which it was originally filed, or some third court altogether!

(b) [3:555] **Whose "convenience":** It is only the convenience of the *nonparty witnesses* that is important. Absent extraordinary circumstances (below), the *parties' conveniences are not considered*—even if they are to testify. [*Wrin v. Ohlandt* (1931) 213 C 158, 160, 1 P2d 991]

(Thus, for example, defendant cannot obtain a transfer solely on the ground it will be more difficult or expensive for him to defend the action in the county chosen by plaintiff.)

1) [3:556] Convenience of *counsel* is not a permissible consideration on a change of venue motion. [*Lieppman v. Lieber* (1986) 180 CA3d 914, 920, 225 CR 845, 848]

2) [3:557] Nor is the convenience of *expert witnesses* who may be called to testify, but who have no personal knowledge of any facts in the case. [See *Wrin v. Ohlandt*, supra]

3) [3:558] Nor is consideration given to the convenience of witnesses who are *employees* of the litigants. [*Stute v. Burinda* (1981) 123 CA3d Supp. 11, 17, 177 CR 102, 105-106]

(This does not apply, however, where the employee is being called to testify by the *opposing party*. See *J.C. Millett Co. v. Latchford-Marble*

*Glass Co.* (1959) 167 CA2d 218, 227, 334 P2d 72, 77.)

4) [3:559]   Under *extraordinary circumstances*, the court *may* consider the conveniences of a party. But this is usually limited to cases where a party is extremely ill or feeble so that travel to a distant county would endanger his or her health. [See *Simonian v. Simonian* (1950) 97 CA2d 68, 69, 217 P2d 157, 158]

[3:559.1-559.4]   *Reserved.*

(c) [3:559.5]   **Timeliness:**   Although CCP §397 contains no express time limitation, a motion for change of venue based on convenience of witnesses must be made within a *reasonable* time after the answer is filed. What constitutes a "reasonable" time rests largely in the trial court's discretion. [*Cooney v. Cooney* (1944) 25 C2d 202, 208, 153 P2d 334, 338]

### (3) Other statutory grounds for transfer

(a) [3:560]   "There is reason to believe that an *impartial trial cannot be had*" (in the county where action filed). [CCP §397(b)]

(b) [3:561]   "There is *no judge* qualified to act." [CCP 397(d)]

(c) [3:562]   In *marital dissolution* proceedings, or proceedings for annulment or legal separation, if *both spouses have moved* from the county, "the ends of justice and convenience of the parties" may be promoted by transfer to the county in which *either* spouse presently resides. [CCP §397.5]

(d) [3:562.1]   If *both spouses have moved* from the county in which a family law judgment was rendered, *modification or enforcement proceedings* may be transferred to the county in which *either* party now resides if "the ends of justice and the convenience of the parties would be promoted by the change." [CCP §397.5]

b.   [3:563]   **Waiver of grounds:**   The grounds for change of venue may be deemed waived unless presented by a *timely* motion for transfer in *proper form*. (Each of these requirements is discussed below.)

c.   **Time for motion**

(1) [3:564]   **"Wrong court" motion must be made at outset:**   A motion for transfer on the ground that the action was filed in an "improper" court (mandatory trans-

fer) must be made within the time permitted to plead; i.e., 30 days after service, unless extended by stipulation or court order. [CCP §396b]

(a) **[3:565]** **May be filed concurrently with answer or demurrer:** Defendant's motion for transfer can be filed by itself (i.e., without answering or demurring); or, it can be filed concurrently with an answer or demurrer. [CCP §396b]

➪**[3:566]** *PRACTICE POINTER:* Do *not* file an answer or demurrer when you make a motion for change of venue. There is no need to do so, because no default can be taken against you while your motion is pending. [CCP §585] If your motion is denied, the court must grant you time within which to plead. [CCP §396b(e); *see* ¶*3:590*]

Moreover, there is a big *disadvantage* to filing an *answer* concurrently with a motion to transfer. Your answer puts the case "at issue" . . . so that the court *may* consider opposition to the motion on grounds of "convenience of witnesses and ends of justice" (see below). [CCP §396b(d)] Thus, by answering, you may *waive* defendant's otherwise absolute right to compel transfer on "wrong court" grounds!

(2) **[3:567]** **Motion based on "convenience of witnesses" ground must be filed within "reasonable time" AFTER answer:** Until defendant answers, the court cannot ascertain the issues which may be involved at trial. Therefore, it cannot tell which witnesses' testimony at trial will be necessary, and cannot rule effectively on a motion for transfer based on "convenience of witnesses." [See *Buran Equipment Co., Inc. v. Sup.Ct.* (*Brobeck, Phleger et al.*) (1987) 190 CA3d 1662, 1665, 236 CR 171, 172]

(a) **[3:568]** **Reasonable time:** What constitutes a "reasonable" time depends on the facts of each case, and the court's determination as to whether delay in making the motion bars relief will usually be upheld. [See *Willingham v. Pecora* (1941) 44 CA2d 289, 112 P2d 328, 332]

(b) **[3:569]** **Plaintiff may move for retransfer on this ground:** If P has filed suit in the "wrong" county, and D moves for transfer to the proper county, P *cannot* ask the original court to retain the action on "convenience of witnesses" ground . . . because until D answers, such motion would be premature (see above). However, once D's motion for change is granted, and D's answer then filed, P may move the transferee-court to transfer the case *back* to the original court for "convenience of witnesses and ends of justice." [See *Scribner v. Sup.Ct. (People)* (1971) 19 CA3d 764, 766, 97 CR 217, 218]

d. **[3:570]** **Form and content of motion:** The requirements for motions generally (¶*9:28 ff.*) apply to motions for transfer; i.e., proper notice of motion, points and authorities, and declarations containing the requisite factual showing.

(1) *FORMS*

- Notice of Motion for Transfer of Action, *see Form 3:E.*

- Declaration in Support of Motion for Transfer of Action, *see Forms 3:F & 3:G.*

- Checklist for Motion for Transfer of Action, *see Form 3:J.*

(2) **[3:571]** **Notice must specify statutory ground:** Since the grounds upon which a court may order transfer are entirely statutory, the notice of motion must be based on one or more of these grounds (CCP §397, ¶*3:549 ff.*). The court may refuse to consider grounds not specified in the notice of motion. [See *McDonald v. California Timber Co.* (1907) 151 C 159, 161, 90 P 548, 549]

(a) **[3:572]** The notice should follow the statutory language. For example, a notice based solely on the ground of "convenience of witnesses" may be held defective . . . because the statutory ground is "convenience of witnesses *and* the ends of justice, etc." (CCP §397(c), ¶*3:553*). [See *Willingham v. Pecora* (1941) 44 CA2d 289, 112 P2d 328, 332]

(3) **[3:573]** **Burden on moving party:** The burden is on the moving party to establish whatever facts are needed to justify transfer. Normally this requires affidavits or declarations containing admissible evidence. But the court may also consider facts alleged in the moving party's *verified complaint* if *uncontroverted* by opposing affidavits. [*Mission Imports, Inc. v. Sup.Ct. (Monterey Bay Co., Inc.)* (1982) 31 C3d 921, 929, 184 CR 296, 300, fn. 7]

(a) **[3:574]** **"Wrong court" ground requires showing of defendant's residence:** Where defendant is seeking transfer to the county of his or her residence, he or she must establish that at the time the action was commenced, he or she resided in the county to which transfer is sought. And, if there are *several codefendants, he or she must establish that no defendant resided in the county in which plaintiff filed suit.* [*Sequoia Pine Mills v. Sup.Ct. (Avram)* (1968) 258 CA2d 65, 68, 65 CR 353, 355]

1) [3:575] **Must negate alternative grounds:** If venue is proper in either of several counties (i.e., actions triable at defendant's residence or elsewhere; ¶3:496), defendant must do more than merely show residence in another county. Rather, defendant has the burden of "*negating the propriety of venue as laid on all possible grounds*": i.e., it must show that the county selected by plaintiff was *not* the place of injury or contracting, etc. [*Karson Industries, Inc. v. Sup.Ct. (Triangle Auto Sales, Inc.)* (1969) 273 CA2d 7, 8-9, 77 CR 714, 715]

   • **FORM:** Declaration in Support of Motion for Transfer of Action (Improper Court), *see Form 3:F.*

(b) [3:576] **"Convenience of witnesses" ground:** A much more extensive factual showing is required for motions based on the "convenience of witnesses and the ends of justice." [CCP §397(c)] Affidavits or declarations must show [*Juneau v. Juneau* (1941) 45 CA2d 14, 113 P2d 463, 464]:

   • The *names* of each witness expected to testify for *both* parties;

   • The *substance of their expected testimony*;

   • Whether the witness has been deposed or has given a statement regarding the facts of the case (and if so, the date of the deposition or statement);

   • The *reasons* why it would be "inconvenient" for the witnesses to appear locally; and

   • The *reasons* why the "ends of justice" would be promoted by transfer to a different county (e.g., to permit view of the scene or make other material evidence available).

1) [3:576.1] **Admissible evidence required:** The declarations must be competent evidence. A change of venue cannot be based on affidavits consisting of hearsay and conclusions. [*Lieppman v. Lieber* (1986) 180 CA3d 914, 919,

225 CR 845, 847; *Tutor-Saliba-Perini Joint Venture v. Sup.Ct. (San Diego Unified Port Dist.)* (1991) 233 CA3d 736, 744, 285 CR 1, 5 (citing text)]

⇨[3:577] ***PRACTICE POINTER:*** Get affidavits or declarations from each witness, if possible. *Do not rely on declarations by counsel alone.* (Declarations by the moving party's counsel as to where the witnesses reside, and their "conveniences," are usually hearsay or conclusions.)

• ***FORM:*** Declaration in Support of Motion for Transfer of Action (Convenience of Witnesses), *see Form 3:G.*

(4) [3:578] **Costs and fees must be posted if motion made on "convenience of witnesses" ground:** To avoid any delay if the motion is granted, defendant is required to post in advance (when filing motion) the clerk's costs and fees for transferring the action. [CCP §399; same requirement also applies to motions based on the other statutory grounds enumerated at ¶*3:560 ff.*]

[3:579] *Reserved.*

e. [3:580] **Court's jurisdiction suspended while motion pending:** A motion for transfer operates as a stay of any other motion or proceeding then pending or thereafter filed; e.g., demurrers, discovery orders, etc. [*Pickwick Stages v. Sup.Ct.* (1934) 138 CA 448, 32 P2d 433] (This can be a real problem if a preliminary injunction is sought and no temporary restraining order is outstanding.)

(1) [3:581] **Exception—marital dissolution proceedings:** The Code provides, however, that even though a motion for transfer is pending, the court in a marital dissolution proceeding can issue restraining orders, and can also provide for temporary support, attorney fees and costs. [CCP §§396b, 397(e)]

(2) [3:581.1] **Exception—joinder of "Doe" defendant:** A defendant's true name may be substituted for a "Doe" after the motion is filed and before the hearing (in which event, the court is required to consider the "Doe" defendant's residence). [*Gutierrez v. Sup.Ct. (Ojai Valley Inn)* (1966) 243 CA2d 710, 724, 52 CR 592, 602]

(3) [3:582] **Effect on discovery:** Although the court's jurisdiction is suspended while a motion to transfer is pending, this should not affect a party's right to conduct *discovery*—so long as the discovery proceedings are

self-executing (all are, except motions for medical examinations; *see Ch. 8*).

Of course, if the opposing party resists the discovery, a motion to compel could not be obtained until the court's jurisdiction is restored. (Likewise, if the opposing party wants to limit or prevent discovery, it could not obtain a protective order until the transfer motion is resolved.)

f.  **Ruling on motion**

(1)  **Sanctions against losing party**

(a)  [3:583]  **Where motion made on "wrong court" ground:**  If the motion is made upon the ground that the action was filed in an "improper" county, the court may order the losing party to pay the prevailing party's reasonable expenses and attorney fees in making or resisting the motion. [CCP §396b]

However, such sanctions cannot be imposed without adequate notice and opportunity to be heard. Notice may be given in the prevailing party's papers or in the court's own noticed motion. [CCP §396b(b); see *Cacciaguidi v. Sup.Ct. (Sec. Pac. Corp.)* (1990) 226 CA3d 181, 187, 276 CR 465, 469—notice sufficient where fee request included in Memorandum of Points and Authorities instead of Notice of Motion]

1)  [3:584]  **Losing party's attorney *personally* liable:**  The attorney, rather than client, is charged with knowledge of the venue rules. Hence, the attorney is made *personally* liable for payment of such sanctions to the other party ... and "as between the attorney and client, such expenses and fees shall be the personal liability of the attorney *not chargeable to the party* ... " [CCP §396b(b)]

2)  [3:585]  **Factors considered:**  In deciding on fees, the court considers (1) whether an *offer to stipulate* to change of venue was reasonably made and rejected; and (2) the party's "good faith"—*given the facts and law known* to such party—in making the motion or selecting the venue originally. [CCP §396b(b); *Mission Imports, Inc. v. Sup.Ct. (Monterey Bay Co., Inc.)* (1982) 31 C3d 921, 931-932, 184 CR 296, 302]

▭▷[3:585.1]  ***PRACTICE POINTER:***  If you are seeking attorney fees, be sure to support your motion with declarations showing: (1) your request to plaintiff's attorney to have venue changed to the correct county; and (2) the time spent in making the motion.

3) **[3:586] Findings required?** CCP §396b does not expressly require the court to make specific findings as to the conduct justifying the award. Arguably, however, such findings should be required in any case where sanctions are imposed. Otherwise, arbitrary imposition of sanctions "could imperil the independence of the bar and undermine the adversary system." [See *Fegles v. Kraft* (1985) 168 CA3d 812, 817, 214 CR 380, 382—sanctions for improper venue motion granted under CCP §128.5 ("frivolous actions and delaying tactics"), rather than under CCP §396b; CCP §128.5 expressly requires findings] (CCP §128.5 applies only to cases commenced before 1995; see ¶9:1010 ff.)

(b) **[3:587] Where motion made on "convenience of witnesses" ground:** By its terms, CCP §396b does not seem to apply to motions under CCP §397(c) ("convenience of witnesses"). But the point is unresolved. [See *Lieppman v. Lieber* (1986) 180 CA3d 914, 919, 225 CR 845, 847]

*Cross-refer:* See further discussion of possible sanctions in *Ch. 9(III).*

(2) **[3:588] If motion granted, transferor court loses jurisdiction:** Cases hold that an order granting transfer divests the transferor court of jurisdiction (except to dismiss if the transfer fees are not paid, see below). Further proceedings must take place in the transferee court *after* it receives the file. [*London v. Morrison* (1950) 99 CA2d 876, 879, 222 P2d 941, 944—voluntary dismissal "an idle act" where filed in transferor court after transfer ordered]

(a) **[3:588.1] Jurisdictional "hiatus" until transfer complete?** This apparently creates a jurisdictional "hiatus" during the inevitable delay between the time a transfer is ordered and the time the case file is actually received by the transferee court (often weeks or even months). If so, neither court could grant temporary restraining orders, hear emergency ex parte matters, etc., in the interim.

Comment: Arguably, in the interest of justice, the transferor court should have the power to set aside its transfer order for purposes of ruling on such matters. But there is no known authority so holding.

(3) [3:589] **Liability for fees and costs on transfer:** If transfer is ordered on the ground that plaintiff filed in the "wrong court," plaintiff is responsible for paying the costs and fees of transferring the action to whichever county the court orders, within 30 days after service of notice of the transfer order. If plaintiff fails to do so *within 5 days* after service of notice of the order, any other interested party, whether named in the complaint or not, may pay such costs and fees in order to expedite the transfer. (If the fees and costs are not paid within 30 days, the action is subject to dismissal.) [CCP §399; *and see* ¶*11:280*]

If transfer was ordered on "convenience of witnesses" or other statutory grounds, defendant is required to post the costs and fees for transfer in advance (¶*3:578*).

(4) [3:590] **Time to respond if motion denied:** If a motion to transfer on "wrong court" grounds is *denied*, and no response has previously been filed, defendant has *30 days* to answer, demur, move to strike or otherwise plead (unless the court specifies a different time). [CCP §396b(e); CRC 326]

(5) [3:591] **Time to respond if motion granted:** On the other hand, if a motion to transfer on "wrong court" grounds is *granted*, and no response has previously been filed, defendant has only *30 days* to respond after the transferee court *mails notice* that the case has been received, and of its new case number. [CCP §586(a)(6)(B); see CRC 326]

g. [3:592] **Appellate review of ruling:** An order granting or denying a motion for transfer, together with any award of fees and costs in connection therewith (above), is subject to appellate review as follows:

(1) [3:593] **Unlimited civil cases:** No appeal lies from orders in unlimited civil cases granting or denying a motion to transfer. Such orders are reviewable only by petition for extraordinary writ (mandamus). [*Calhoun v. Vallejo City Unified School Dist.* (1993) 20 CA4th 39, 41, 24 CR2d 337, 338]

The party seeking appellate review must petition the appropriate appellate court for such writ *within 20 days* after service of the superior court order. (For "good cause" and before expiration of the 20-day period, the superior court may extend this for an additional period of not more than 10 days.) [CCP §400]

Immediately after filing the petition with the appellate court, a copy must be filed with the trial court. Such filing does *not* automatically stay proceedings in the trial court; but the appellate court has discretionary power to stay such proceedings until it acts upon the petition. [CCP §400]

(2) **[3:594]** **Orders for change of venue in limited civil cases:** Orders granting or denying motions for change of venue in a limited civil case are reviewable by *appeal* to the appellate division of the local superior court. [CCP §904.2(c)] The appeal does *not* automatically stay proceedings in the trial court, but the reviewing court may grant such a stay pending determination of the appeal on the venue issue.

7. **[3:595]** **Rules Designating "Proper" Court for Trial of Limited Civil Cases:** The venue rules discussed above designate which *county* in the state is the proper place for trial of an action.

Local rules usually govern the place *within the county* where limited civil cases are to be filed; *see ¶3:601.2a.*

The procedure for transfer within the county under these local rules is generally the same as on a motion for change of venue; *see ¶3:549 ff.*

**[3:596-598]** *Reserved.*

8. **Rules Designating "Proper" Branch or District of Superior Court**

a. **[3:599]** **Counties with branch courts:** In larger counties, the superior court has branches or departments located elsewhere than at the county seat. Each court may specify by local rule the location at which certain types of actions may be filed, heard or tried. [CCP §402]

Typically, however, civil cases are filed and run from the county seat; they are merely assigned for trial to branch courts for convenience of the parties and counsel. The court may for any reason transfer an action or proceeding in one location to another location of the same court. [CCP §402(b)]

(1) **[3:599.1]** **Effect of filing at wrong location:** The court clerk may not reject (nor may the court dismiss) a case filed at a court location other than the one designated by local rule. Instead, the court may transfer the case on its own motion to the proper court location. [CCP §402(a)]

b. **[3:600]** **Los Angeles County:** Los Angeles County, however, has an unique system. The L.A. Superior Court is divided into 11 geographic districts, including one "Central District" located at the county seat. Under local rules, certain actions *must*, and others *may*, be filed in the various districts. (Again, these rules are distinct from venue requirements, which merely fix a "proper" county.)

(1) **[3:601]** **Mandatory filings:** Actions for "*bodily injury, wrongful death or tortious damage to property*" must be filed in the district in which the injury or damage occurred. [L.A. Sup.Ct. Rule 2.0(b)]

- **[3:601.1]** "Bodily injury" is defined as "actual physical damage to a person." [L.A. Sup.Ct. Rule 2.0(b)]

  Claims for emotional distress, defamation, discrimination and malpractice (other than medical malpractice) are *not* forms of "bodily injury." Such claims may therefore be filed in the Central District or in the district where the claim arose. [L.A. Sup.Ct. Rule 2.0(b),(c)]

- **[3:601.2]** "Damage to real property" means "actual physical damage to land, buildings or other items affixed to the land including vegetation." [L.A. Sup.Ct. Rule 2.0(b)]

  Actions to *quiet title* or for breach of real estate or construction contracts are *not* actions for "damage to real property." Such claims may therefore be filed in either the Central District or the district where the real property is located; or if a contract is involved, where performance is required or where the defendant resides. [L.A. Sup.Ct. Rule 2.0(b),(c)]

- **[3:601.2a]** *Limited civil and small claims cases* are filed by determining in which district the case would otherwise be assigned under local rules (defendant's residence, location of property, etc.); and then by reference to the courthouse serving the particular zip codes involved. [See chart in L.A. Sup.Ct. Rule 2.0(b)]

  **[3:601.3]** There are also some other "mandatory" filing rules: e.g., *class actions* and petitions for writs of prohibition or mandate (with some exceptions) must be filed in the Central District. [L.A. Sup.Ct. Rule 2.0(b)]

(a) **[3:601.4]** **Not jurisdictional:** Although "mandatory," these requirements are not jurisdictional. Misfilings do not affect the court's power to render an enforceable judgment.

➪ **[3:602]** *PRACTICE POINTER:* Even so, it's risky to file in the wrong district! Your case may be denied trial setting. Also, Central District judges follow the policy of transferring *sua sponte* cases improperly filed in the Central District, and ordering counsel to show cause why sanctions should not be imposed under CCP §177.5 for violation of court orders (*see ¶9:1270 ff.*).

(2) **[3:603]** **Optional filings:** Other specified types of cases may be filed in *either* the Central District or another specified district, including: *inverse condemnation* (where the property is located); *unlawful detainer* (where the property is located); *receivership* (where "the defendant functions wholly therein"). [See L.A. Sup.Ct. Rule 2.0(c)]

(3) **[3:604]** **Certificate required:** The Los Angeles Superior Court requires that a four-page "Civil Case Cover Sheet Addendum" be filed with the complaint. The form requires counsel to specify, under penalty of perjury, the grounds for filing the action in the district where the action is filed. Additionally, the form requires counsel to provide a trial estimate and state whether a jury is demanded. The form must be served with the summons and complaint. [L.A. Sup.Ct. Rule 2.0; *see discussion at ¶6:41.2*]

*Rule not preempted:* CRC 201.8 expressly authorizes the use of a local civil cover sheet in addition to the mandatory statewide cover sheet and is therefore not preempted under CRC 981.1 (*see ¶9:13.2*).

*Sanctions:* If a party fails to file a required statewide or local civil cover sheet or submits a defectively completed cover sheet, *the clerk must nevertheless file* the papers. The party and counsel, however, are subject to sanctions (*see ¶9:1279 ff.*).

- **FORM:** Civil Case Cover Sheet Addendum and Statement of Location (Los Angeles Superior Court), *see Form 6:Q.2.*

(4) **[3:605]** **Transfers between districts:** Motions to transfer a case due to filing in an improper district are heard in Department One of the Central District. [L.A. Sup.Ct. Rule 2.0(e)]

Cases may also be transferred between districts to ease congestion and distribute the court's workload, or for the convenience of witnesses or "to promote the ends of justice." [L.A. Sup.Ct. Rule 2.0(e)]

⇨**[3:606]** ***PRACTICE POINTER:*** If a case is filed in the wrong district, transfer to a correct district cannot be accomplished by stipulation alone. A court order transferring the case is still required.

[3:607-609]   *Reserved.*

## E.  FEDERAL VS. STATE COURTS

[3:610]   A final consideration in choosing the court in which to file the action is whether the action may, or must, be filed in the local federal district court. Detailed treatment of federal court jurisdiction is beyond the scope of this Guide. But the following are some of the factors that California lawyers must consider with respect to federal vs. state court jurisdiction.

1.   [3:611]   **"Exclusive" Federal Jurisdiction:**   There are a *few* cases which *must* be filed in federal court. By virtue of federal law, state courts have no power to adjudicate (no subject matter jurisdiction).

**Examples**

- [3:611.1]   *Patent and copyright claims.* [28 USC §1338(a)]

- [3:611.2]   *Admiralty and maritime claims.* [28 USC §1333]

  ***Caution:***   Whether state courts have jurisdiction to adjudicate claims under the Jones Act (46 USC §688) for injuries to or death of a sailor in U.S. territorial waters is presently before the California Supreme Court in *Donaldson v. National Marine, Inc.*, Case No. S110301.

- [3:611.3]   *Claims arising out of bankruptcy proceedings.* [28 USC §1334; *Pauletto v. Reliance Ins. Co.* (1998) 64 CA4th 597, 602, 75 CR2d 334, 337—state courts lack jurisdiction in action for malicious prosecution based on defendant's having filed adversary proceeding in bankruptcy court: "it is for Congress and the federal courts, not state courts, to decide what incentives and penalties shall be utilized in the bankruptcy process"; *Choy v. Redland Ins. Co.* (2002) 103 CA4th 789, 798, 127 CR2d 94, 100—state courts lack jurisdiction of malicious prosecution action based on alleged bad faith filing of voluntary bankruptcy petition]

- [3:611.4]   *Claims under Sherman Antitrust Act.* [15 USC §4]

- [3:611.5]   *Claims under Securities Exchange Act of 1934* (including Rule 10b-5 actions). [15 USC §78aa]

- [3:611.6]   *Claims involving activities regulated by federal labor laws.* E.g., the Labor Management Reporting and Disclosure Act (29 USC §401 et seq.) preempts state power to adjudicate claims based on union contracts or union activities, unless of "merely peripheral concern" to the Act. [*San Diego Bldg. Trades Council, etc. v. Garmon* (1959) 359 US 236, 247-248, 79 S.Ct. 773, 781-782; *Bassett v. Attebery* (1986) 180 CA3d 288, 294-295, 225 CR 399, 402—NLRB (rather than federal court) has exclusive jurisdiction over wrongful discharge claim alleging violation of federal labor laws]

- [3:611.7] *Certain ERISA actions:* Suits for injunctive or other equitable relief against an employer or insurer under the Employee Retirement Income Security Act (ERISA). (But federal and state courts have *concurrent* jurisdiction of claims for *benefits* due.) [29 USC §1132(e)(1)]

*Cross-refer:* See detailed discussion of which claims fall within exclusive federal jurisdiction in Schwarzer, Tashima & Wagstaffe, *Cal. Prac. Guide: Federal Civ. Pro. Before Trial* (TRG), Ch. 2B.

a. [3:612] **Impact of federal preemption:** Normally, federal preemption of state law is merely a defense to application of the state law. However, in a few instances (notably ERISA and federal labor laws), state law is "completely preempted" and *replaced by a federal claim, creating a basis for removal* to federal court.

(1) [3:613] **Example:** For example, the Employee Retirement Income Security Act of 1974 (ERISA; 29 USC §1144) contains broad "exclusive remedy" provisions. These provisions have been held to preempt:

- [3:614] State law actions against ERISA group insurers for mishandling claims (e.g., common law or statutory "bad faith" actions) are preempted. [*Pilot Life Ins. Co. v. Dedeaux* (1987) 481 US 41, 56-57, 107 S.Ct. 1549, 1558—common law tort action; *Commercial Life Ins. Co. v. Sup.Ct. (Juliano)* (1988) 47 C3d 473, 484-485, 253 CR 682, 689—statutory action under Ins.C. §790.03(h); *Kanne v. Connecticut Gen. Life Ins. Co.* (9th Cir. 1989) 867 F2d 489, 494]

- [3:615] Fraud claims by retirees against their former employer for inducing them to retire before certain retirement benefits became effective. [*Lembo v. Texaco, Inc.* (1987) 194 CA3d 531, 537, 239 CR 596, 598]

[3:616] *Reserved.*

(2) [3:617] **State claims "recharacterized" as federal:** Plaintiff may have *pleaded* only common law (state law) claims. However, because ERISA "completely preempts" state regulation, there can be no state law claim. Thus, even if the complaint makes no mention of federal

law, the claim before the court *is* a *federal* claim. In effect, the state law claim is "recharacterized" as a federal claim. [*Metropolitan Life Ins. Co. v. Taylor* (1987) 481 US 58, 67, 107 S.Ct. 1542, 1548—common law tort claim against ERISA group insurer "recharacterized" as an ERISA claim]

(3) **[3:618]** **Effect on state court subject matter jurisdiction:** The fact that a federal claim is involved does not necessarily mean state courts lack power to adjudicate. I.e., some federal claims are within the "*concurrent jurisdiction*" of state and federal courts (see below). But if the federal law preempting state regulation *also vests jurisdiction* of claims arising under that law *exclusively* in federal courts (see above), state courts have *no subject matter jurisdiction.* [*De Tomaso v. Pan Ameri-*

*(Text cont'd on p. 3-145)*

**RESERVED**

Rev. #1 2003

can *World Airways, Inc.* (1987) 43 C3d 517, 520, 235 CR 292, 293, fn. 1; see *United Airlines, Inc. v. Sup.Ct. (Terry)* (1991) 234 CA3d 1085, 1087-1088, 286 CR 159, 160—Employee's claims against employer for tortious investigation of sexual harassment complaints against employee preempted by federal law because governed by collective bargaining agreement and Railway Labor Act]

*Cross-refer:* See further discussion in Schwarzer, Tashima & Wagstaffe, *Cal. Prac. Guide: Federal Civ. Pro. Before Trial* (TRG), Ch. 2D.

2. [3:619] **"Concurrent" Federal-State Jurisdiction:** Many other cases can be filed *either* in federal or state court. These are cases which fall within the limited subject matter jurisdiction of federal courts, but which are *not* "exclusive" to the federal courts (above). Indeed, there is a "deeply rooted *presumption* in favor of concurrent state jurisdiction." [*Tafflin v. Levitt* (1990) 493 US 455, 458-459, 110 S.Ct. 792, 795]

a. [3:620] **"Federal question" cases:** Certain claims arising under the Constitution, laws or treaties of the U.S. can be filed either in federal or state court. (Examples: claims based on federal civil rights acts, federal securities laws.) [28 USC §1331; 42 USC §1983; *Ochoa v. Sup.Ct. (County of Santa Clara)* (1985) 39 C3d 159, 173, 216 CR 661, 670, fn. 10; *Tafflin v. Levitt,* supra; *Robbins v. Foothill Nissan* (1994) 22 CA4th 1769, 1780, 28 CR2d 190, 197—claims against FDIC as receiver of insolvent financial institution]

(1) [3:620.1] **"Supplemental jurisdiction" for state law claims:** Where at least one federal claim is involved, federal courts have supplemental jurisdiction over state law claims that are so related to the federal claim that they form part of the same case or controversy. [See 28 USC §1367(a)]

But federal courts may *decline* to exercise supplemental jurisdiction where the state law claim predominates over the federal claim or raises novel or complex issues of state law, or the federal claim is dismissed. [See 28 USC §1367(c)]

Where a state law claim is thus dismissed, the statute of limitations on that claim is tolled for a period of 30 days after the dismissal, unless state law provides a longer tolling period. [See 28 USC §1367(d)]

*Cross-refer:* See further discussion in Schwarzer, Tashima & Wagstaffe, *Cal. Prac. Guide: Federal Civ. Pro. Before Trial* (TRG), Ch. 2B.

(2) [3:621] **Effect of federal preemption of state law:** As mentioned above, the fact that federal law preempts

state law does not necessarily mean state courts are ousted of jurisdiction. If the federal law allows state courts to exercise *concurrent jurisdiction* over the federal claim (e.g., for benefits due under ERISA), the state court has power to continue the action and grant whatever relief is available under the federal law.

(3) [3:622] **Defendant's right to remove:** As a practical matter, federal claims usually end up in federal court. If filed in state court, defendants have the right to remove to federal court (*¶3:627 ff.*) and usually do so.

Comment: Some defendants may prefer a state court forum with which they are more familiar.

b. [3:623] **"Diversity" cases exceeding $75,000:** Claims between citizens of different states where the claim or value of the property in controversy *exceeds $75,000* (exclusive of interest or costs) may be filed in federal court as well as state court. [28 USC §1332]

(1) [3:624] **Diversity of citizenship:** "Citizenship" means domicile (*see discussion of domicile, ¶3:153 ff.*). If there are several plaintiffs and defendants, none of the plaintiffs can reside in the same state as any of the defendants (*complete* diversity required). Plaintiff can "create" diversity of citizenship with defendant by moving to another state before filing suit; but the change of domicile must be bona fide (intent to remain indefinitely). If there is diversity when the action is filed, federal court jurisdiction is proper, even if a subsequent change of domicile destroys diversity.

For diversity purposes, a corporation is deemed a citizen of *both* the state in which it was incorporated *and* the state in which it has its principal place of business (28 USC §1332(c)(1)). Thus, a corporation is deemed a California citizen if *either* incorporated here or its principal place of business is here.

*Cross-refer:* See detailed discussion in Schwarzer, Tashima & Wagstaffe, *Cal. Prac. Guide: Federal Civ. Pro. Before Trial* (TRG), Ch. 2C.

(2) [3:625] **Other instances of diversity:** Federal court jurisdiction also exists in actions between citizens and aliens, and in suits by foreign nations against U.S. citizens. [See 28 USC §1332(a)(2),(4)]

c. [3:626] **Effect of dual filings:** Where jurisdiction is concurrent, the same action can be filed in either or *both* federal and state courts. If filed in both, each court acquires jurisdiction . . . but neither acquires exclusive jurisdiction. Each may proceed at its own pace until one or the other reaches final judgment and becomes res judicata on the claim. Neither will interfere with or try to restrain each other's proceedings. [*Donovan v. City of Dallas* (1964) 377 US 408, 412, 84 S.Ct. 1579, 1582; *Fowler v. Ross* (1983) 142 CA3d 472, 476-477, 191 CR 183, 186]

Note: The rule that the first of two courts having concurrent jurisdiction retains it to the exclusion of all others applies only to courts in the same state. It *does not apply* where one tribunal is a state and the other a federal court. [*Fowler v. Ross*, supra]

3. [3:627] **Removal Jurisdiction:** If the case falls within the concurrent jurisdiction of federal and state courts (*above*), but plaintiff chose to file in state court, defendant generally has the right to remove (transfer) the action to federal court. Compliance with statutory procedures automatically ousts the state court of jurisdiction. [28 USC §1441]

   a. [3:628] **Exception:** A case cannot be removed to federal court on the basis of diversity of citizenship if *any* defendant served in the action is a citizen of the state in which the state court action is pending. [28 USC §1441(b)]

     The reason, of course, is that removal jurisdiction in diversity cases is intended to protect against possible prejudice to "outsiders" that may exist in state courts. Where one or more defendants is a local resident, such prejudice is unlikely; and therefore removal to federal court is not allowed.

     Joining a local party as a codefendant, therefore, is an effective way of preventing removal of an action to federal court (provided the joinder is in good faith).

     However, "Doe" defendants are *disregarded* in determining existence of diversity. [28 USC §1441(a)]

   b. [3:629] **Procedure:** Defendant simply files a Notice of Removal in the local federal court (with copies of the state court pleadings) *within 30 days* after receipt of process in the

*(Text cont'd on p. 3-147)*

# RESERVED

state court action (by service or otherwise). Filing the Notice automatically suspends all further proceedings in the state court. If the removal is claimed to be improper, plaintiff must file a motion in the federal court to remand the action to the state court. [28 USC §§1446, 1447]

(1) **Forms:** See Schwarzer, Tashima & Wagstaffe, *Cal. Prac. Guide: Federal Civ. Pro. Before Trial* (TRG), Ch. 2D, "Removal Checklist" and Forms.

4. **[3:630]** **Considerations Affecting Choice of Federal vs. State Court:** Except where federal court jurisdiction is "exclusive" (¶*3:611*), filing or removing a case to federal court is always optional. The following considerations may affect that choice:

a. **[3:631]** **Territorial jurisdiction:** In most cases, federal courts have *no broader power* over persons or property outside the state than do the local state courts. [FRCP 4(k)(1)] Thus, a plaintiff who is unable to obtain jurisdiction over a nonresident defendant in a state court action, will not be any better off suing in a federal court. [*Omni Capital International v. Rudolph Wolff & Co., Ltd.* (1987) 484 US 97, 101, 108 S.Ct. 404, 408]

(1) **[3:632]** **Exceptions—nationwide personal jurisdiction:** But there are a *few* cases in which federal statutes authorize nationwide personal service. Example: statutory interpleader actions (28 USC §2361); also, actions under the 1934 Securities Exchange Act (15 USC §78aa).

b. **[3:633]** **Substantive law:** There will be no difference in the substantive law applied in federal or state court. On all "federal" issues, state courts are bound to apply the same rules as federal courts (under U.S. Const. Art. VI—the "supremacy clause"). And, on all nonfederal issues, federal courts are bound to apply the same rules as the courts of the state in which they are located. [*Erie R.R. Co. v. Tompkins* (1938) 304 US 64, 78, 58 S.Ct. 817, 822]

(1) **[3:634]** **Where state law uncertain:** If there is no state law on point, a federal court *may* make a "guess" at what the state supreme court would decide. Alternatively, if the matter is of great public importance, a federal court may *abstain* (stay or dismiss the action) until the state courts can decide.

⇨**[3:635]** *PRACTICE POINTER:* If state law appears *unfavorable*, plaintiff will be better off in state court rather than federal. Federal courts are bound to follow the state rule even if they disagree with it. But plaintiff can appeal the matter up to the state supreme court, if necessary, in an effort to get the state law changed.

c. **[3:636] Procedural rules:** Procedural rules may differ somewhat, depending on the type of rule involved.

(1) **[3:637] "Outcome determinative" rules:** Rules that may have a significant effect on the outcome of the case (e.g., statute of limitations, choice of law, burden of proof, etc.) will be the same whether the action is filed in federal or state court. Such rules are "substantive" for *Erie* doctrine purposes, and therefore federal courts are bound to follow the state rules. [See *Hanna v. Plumer* (1965) 380 US 460, 465-467, 85 S.Ct. 1136, 1141-1142]

(2) **[3:638] Pleading and practice rules:** Rules of pleading and practice are rarely outcome determinative, and therefore federal courts apply their own rules.

Most of the differences between federal and state rules are minor; e.g., notice pleading in federal courts vs. code pleading in state courts. (Even so, lack of familiarity with federal rules often discourages attorneys from litigating in federal court; see below.)

However, certain differences between federal and state rules may impact the choice of court in certain types of cases:

(a) **[3:639] Class actions:** This is one area in which the federal rules are much more restrictive than state rules (*see ¶ 14:5*), and as a result, filing in state court is often dictated.

[3:640] *Reserved.*

(b) **[3:641] Mandatory disclosures:** Shortly after a federal action is filed, the parties must disclose (without awaiting a discovery request) the names of all witnesses and copies of documentary evidence which support their positions, as well as a computation of damages and insurance policies. [FRCP 26(a)(1)]

In addition, at least 90 days before trial, the parties must disclose the identity of their expert witnesses, together with a report signed by the expert setting forth all matters on which he or she is expected to testify. [FRCP 26(a)(2)]

Finally, detailed disclosures are required at the time of the final pretrial conference regarding the evidence to be presented at trial, except for impeachment evidence. [FRCP 26(a)(3)]

*Cross-refer:* See detailed discussion in Schwarzer, Tashima & Wagstaffe, *Cal. Prac. Guide: Federal Civ. Pro. Before Trial* (TRG), Ch. 8.

(c) [3:642] **Evidence rules:** There are some differences. For example:

- In federal question cases, federal courts may not recognize witness privileges provided by state law (see FR Ev. 501).

- Prior inconsistent statements can be used for substantive purposes in federal court only if given under oath, but that is not required in state court (see Cal.Ev.C. §1235 and FR Ev. 801(d)).

- Federal judges have greater power to exclude expert testimony that the judge determines is unreliable (see FR Ev. 702).

- Federal judges have greater power to admit hearsay that does not fit within recognized exceptions to the hearsay rule under a so-called "catch-all" exception (FR Ev. 807).

(d) [3:643] **Joinder problems:** State courts have unlimited subject matter jurisdiction and can usually adjudicate any kind of claim as to any party before the court. (The only exception is claims within the exclusive jurisdiction of federal courts; *see ¶3:611.*) On the other hand, federal courts have only *limited* subject matter jurisdiction, and therefore may not be able to adjudicate *all* claims against *all* parties whom plaintiff may wish to sue in the action. Even if federal "pendent" jurisdiction is available, it is *discretionary* with the federal judge.

(e) [3:644] **"Doe" pleading and late amendments:** California law permits plaintiffs to name "Doe" defendants and (in a proper case) to serve a party as a "Doe" even after the statute of limitations has run. This is *not* permissible in federal practice, at least in diversity cases. Thus, if plaintiff is uncertain as to the names or identities of important potential defendants, it will be better to file in state rather than federal court.

(f) [3:645] **Change of venue:** A state court action can be transferred to another county on "convenience" grounds (*see ¶3:553*). But a federal action can be transferred *outside* California "for the convenience of *parties* and witnesses, in the interest of justice" to any other district in which it could have been filed originally (i.e., in which both jurisdiction and venue requirements are satisfied). [28 USC §1404(a)] (Note that federal courts can consider the convenience of the parties as well as the witnesses, whereas party convenience is generally irrelevant under state venue rules; see ¶3:555.)

1) [3:646] **Multi-district transfers:** Where *related* cases are pending in *several* districts, they can all be transferred for pretrial purposes to *any* federal district ... even to one in which venue or jurisdiction would otherwise *not* be proper! [See 28 USC §1407] (Plaintiff thus faces a risk of having the action transferred to a distant forum and losing control of the lawsuit.)

d. [3:647] **Practical considerations:** Ultimately, plaintiff's decision re filing in federal vs. state court (and defendant's decision to remove to federal court if he can) is usually based on practical considerations, including the following:

(1) [3:648] **Delay in getting to trial:** Delays in getting to trial are substantial in many federal district courts. In most California counties, parties may expect a trial date within 12 to 18 months after filing the complaint. Counsel should check on local conditions when speedy trial is a consideration.

[3:649] *Reserved.*

(2) [3:650] **Geographic convenience:** If the action is filed in state court, venue rules may result in the trial being held outside a metropolitan area (e.g., where defendant resides, or where the injury occured). But federal actions are triable only at the federal courthouses, which are all in metropolitan areas: Los Angeles, San Francisco, Sacramento, San Diego, Fresno, San Jose and Santa Ana. Litigating in these cities may be deemed advantageous to one side or the other.

(3) [3:651] **"All purpose" assignment to single judge in federal court:** In federal courts, cases are assigned at the time of filing to a particular judge. That judge will handle the case from start to finish, unlike state practice where different judges may hear law and motion matters, settlement conferences and trial.

(Note: The "all purpose" assignment to a single judge is becoming more common in state practice as well. See discussion of "fast track" rules at ¶12:4 ff.)

(a) [3:652] **Perception of impartiality:** Out-of-state parties are sometimes concerned about local judges and juries being biased in favor of local residents. This concern can be lessened by an out-of-state plaintiff suing in the federal court, which is perceived to be impartial to state citizenship.

(b) **[3:653]** **Perception that federal judges more likely to grant dispositive motions:** Federal judges are commonly perceived as being more willing to grant summary judgments and dismissals than their state counterparts. (This may be because the "all purpose" assignment system enables the federal judge to become familiar with the case at an earlier stage.)

(c) **[3:654]** **Perception that federal judges more receptive to federal claim or defense:** Federal judges are likely to be more familiar with federal claims and defenses, which may help whichever party is relying thereon. E.g., federal judges may be more responsive than state judges to claims that federal law *preempts* or supersedes a state law cause of action.

(d) **[3:655]** **Perception that federal judges sterner taskmasters:** Federal judges often require lawyers to work harder. Court hearings are scheduled regularly, requiring counsel to report on the status of the case. Dismissal for lack of prosecution is a real threat in federal court. A signed order is required even for routine matters (e.g., extensions of time to plead or answer discovery) and despite the fact that all parties have so stipulated. Continuances are usually hard to obtain. And, some federal judges are notorious for imposing *sanctions* against counsel who fail to "dot the i's and cross the t's!"

(e) **[3:656]** **No peremptory challenge of federal judge:** The peremptory challenge allowed under CCP §170.6 to remove state court judges has no counterpart in federal practice. Therefore, a litigator in federal court is usually stuck with the judge assigned to the case!

▷**[3:657]** *PRACTICE POINTER:* The "all purpose" assignment to a single judge is often the most important factor in the choice of federal vs. state court. The caliber and attitude of the judge to whom the case is assigned can mean the difference between winning and losing the case. Therefore, it is essential that you learn as much as possible about your local federal judges. And, do so *before* filing or removing the case, because you get no peremptory challenge in federal court (see above).

If dissatisfied with the federal judge assigned, you can voluntarily dismiss the federal action and sue in state court. But you *cannot* refile in federal court in hopes of getting a different judge.

(4) **[3:658]** **Jury selection:** Most federal courts now use *6-member* juries in civil actions; and the federal judge does all or most of the questioning of prospective jurors. In state courts, juries are still generally composed of 12 members; and the attorneys are allowed a much more active role in interrogating prospective jurors (see CRC 228). Also, more peremptory challenges may be available in state court actions (if single party on each side, 6 in state court, 3 in federal). [See 28 USC §1870; and CCP §231(c)]

(5) **[3:659]** **Jury verdict requirements:** A *unanimous* verdict is required in federal civil trials, whereas a 3/4 verdict of the jurors is authorized in California state court trials. In close liability cases, therefore, plaintiff may be better off filing in state court; and defendant may wish to remove to federal court (if he or she can, *see ¶3:627*).

(6) **[3:660]** **Lack of familiarity with federal procedures:** Many lawyers practice in federal court infrequently and are uncomfortable with the more formal federal court environment and the differences in procedure. Such lawyers may be hesitant to file suit in federal court. Conversely, if defense counsel are more experienced in federal practice, they may be anxious to remove to federal court if they can.

➡**[3:661]** *PRACTICE POINTER:* Another problem for inexperienced litigators in federal court is the sheer number of federal rules to learn: It is *not* enough simply to know the FRCP. There are local district rules in each federal district (published by the Los Angeles Daily Journal and other "Rules of Court" publishers). In addition, each federal judge has the power to adopt rules for his or her own court (which may not be published anywhere but can be obtained by asking the court clerk).

*Cross-refer:* For more detailed discussion of federal vs. state court jurisdiction and removal procedures, see Schwarzer, Tashima & Wagstaffe, *Cal. Prac. Guide: Federal Civ. Pro. Before Trial* (TRG).

# NOTICE OF MOTION TO QUASH SERVICE OF SUMMONS

1  *Attorney name*
   State Bar No.:.................
2  ...*law office address*.........
   ...*st....cia*............
3  ....*phone #., fax #. email*.

4

5  Attorney for ...*Client's name*....

6

7

8              SUPERIOR COURT OF THE STATE OF CALIFORNIA

9                     COUNTY OF .........                    *incorrect*

10 ........................., ) CASE NO. ............
                              )
11              Plaintiff,    ) HEARING DATE/TIME: ..........
                              ) DEPT. NO. ...................
12 vs.                        ) HEARING JUDGE: ...... *(if known)*
                              )
13 ........................., ) NOTICE OF MOTION TO QUASH
                              ) SERVICE OF SUMMONS; DECLARATION
14              Defendant.    ) OF .....; POINTS AND
                              ) AUTHORITIES; PROPOSED ORDER
15                            )
                              ) DATE ACTION FILED: ..........
16 _____) DATE SET FOR TRIAL: ... *(if set)*

17     TO EACH PARTY AND THE ATTORNEY OF RECORD FOR EACH PARTY:

18     YOU ARE HEREBY NOTIFIED THAT on ...... *(date)* ...... at ......

19 .... *(time)* .... in Department No.: ..... of this Court, located at

20 ......... *(address)* .........., defendant ..... *(name)* ..... will

21 move the court for an order quashing the service of summons in this

22 action on said defendant. Said motion will be made upon the ground

23 that ........... *(e.g., "summons was not properly served upon said*

24 *defendant"; or "this court lacks power to exercise personal juris-*

25 *diction as to said defendant as no constitutionally-sufficient*

26 *basis for jurisdiction exists between said defendant and the State*

27 /////

28 /////

                              1

                 MOTION TO QUASH SERVICE OF SUMMONS

```
 1  of California") ........................... Said motion will
 2  be based on this Notice, the points and authorities set forth
 3  herein-below, the attached declaration of .............., and the
 4  complete files and records of this action.
 5                        /s/
                          ─────────────────────────────
 6                        Attorney for Defendant ................
 7
 8              POINTS AND AUTHORITIES IN SUPPORT OF MOTION
 9      (Follow suggestions in Law and Motion Practice Chapter, ¶9:64-81)
10
11
12
13
14
15
16
17
18
19
20
21
22
23
24
25
26
27
28
                                    2
        ─────────────────────────────────────────────────────────
                    MOTION TO QUASH SERVICE OF SUMMONS
```

# DECLARATION IN SUPPORT OF
# MOTION TO QUASH SERVICE OF SUMMONS

```
1  ..............................
   State Bar No. ...............
2  ..............................
3  ..............................
   ..............................
4
5  Attorney for: ...............
6
7
8            SUPERIOR COURT OF THE STATE OF CALIFORNIA
9                     COUNTY OF .........
10
11 ............................,  ) CASE NO. ............
                                  )
12            Plaintiff,          ) HEARING DATE/TIME: ...........
                                  ) DEPT. NO. ...................
13 vs.                            ) HEARING JUDGE: ...... (if known)
                                  )
14 ............................,  ) DECLARATION OF ......... IN
                                  ) SUPPORT OF MOTION TO QUASH
15            Defendant.          ) SERVICE OF SUMMONS
                                  )
16                                ) DATE ACTION FILED: ...........
                                  ) DATE SET FOR TRIAL: ... (if set)
17 _____  )
```

18      I, the undersigned, declare as follows: *(for motion based on*

19 *lack of personal jurisdiction)*

20      1.   I am the defendant *(or one of the defendants)* in this

21 action and have personal knowledge of each fact stated herein.

22      2.   I reside and am domiciled outside the State of

23 California. My residence is located at ........ *(address outside*

24 *California)* ...... My occupation *(or employment)* is as follows

25 ...................; my office *(or employment)* address is ......

26 ..........................

27 ///

28 ///

                              1
_____

1     3.   I was served with copies of the summons and complaint in

2 this action in the following manner and on the following date .....

3 .............. (e.g., "by certified mail, return receipt requested,

4 postmarked ................, received by me at my residence address

5 above, on ........." ) ...... .

6     4.   I maintain no residence or place of business within the

7 State of California now or at the time this action was filed.  My

8 only contacts or relationship with, or activities within, the State

9 of California prior to the institution of this action were as

10 follows: ...........................................................

11 ...................... .  I own no property within California other

12 than ...................................... .

13     5.   This action is not related in any way to the contacts,

14 relationship, activities or property specified in the preceding

15 paragraph.  The complaint in this action is based on a cause of

16 action for ......................., arising out of alleged acts or

17 events that took place, if at all, in the State of ..............,

18 and not in California.

19     6.   I have not consented to the exercise of jurisdiction over

20 me by the courts of the State of California, and make this declara-

21 tion only as a special appearance in support of the motion to quash

22 service of summons.

23     I declare under penalty of perjury under the laws of the State

24 of California that the foregoing is true and correct.

25 DATED: ............. at ...................................

26

27                  /s/

28                  Defendant

2

DECL'N OF ........ IN SUPPORT OF
MOTION TO QUASH SERVICE OF SUMMONS

# NOTICE OF MOTION TO STAY OR DISMISS ACTION
## (INCONVENIENT FORUM)

```
 1  ...............................
    State Bar No.:................
 2  ...............................
    ...............................
 3  ...............................

 4

 5  Attorney for ................

 6

 7

 8           SUPERIOR COURT OF THE STATE OF CALIFORNIA

 9                    COUNTY OF .........

10  ........................., ) CASE NO. ...........
                               )
11           Plaintiff,        ) HEARING DATE/TIME: ..........
                               ) DEPT. NO. ...................
12  vs.                        ) HEARING JUDGE: ...... (if known)
                               )
13  ........................., ) NOTICE OF MOTION TO STAY OR
                               ) DISMISS ACTION; DECLARATION OF
14           Defendant.        ) ..........; POINTS AND
                               ) AUTHORITIES; PROPOSED ORDER
15                             )
                               ) DATE ACTION FILED: ..........
16  _____) DATE SET FOR TRIAL: ... (if set)

17       TO EACH PARTY AND TO THE ATTORNEY OF RECORD FOR EACH PARTY:

18       YOU ARE HEREBY NOTIFIED THAT on ....... (date) ....... at

19  ..... (time) ...... in Department No.: ..... of this Court, located

20  at ...... (address) ...... defendant ......... will move the court

21  for an order dismissing this action, or in the alternative staying

22  all further proceedings herein. Said motion will be made upon the

23  ground that California is a seriously inconvenient forum for the

24  trial of this action. Said motion will be based upon this Notice,

25  the points and authorities set forth hereinbelow, the attached

26  /////

27  /////

28  /////
```

1

MOTION TO STAY OR DISMISS

1 | declaration of ......... and the complete files and records of
2 | this action.
3 | DATED: .........., ......

4 | /s/
Attorney for Defendant

5 |

6 | POINTS AND AUTHORITIES IN SUPPORT OF MOTION
7 | *(Follow suggestions in Law and Motion Practice Chapter, ¶9:64-81)*

8 |
9 |
10 |
11 |
12 |
13 |
14 |
15 |
16 |
17 |
18 |
19 |
20 |
21 |
22 |
23 |
24 |
25 |
26 |
27 |
28 |

2

MOTION TO STAY OR DISMISS

Rev. #1 2001

# DECLARATION IN SUPPORT OF MOTION
# TO STAY OR DISMISS ACTION
# (INCONVENIENT FORUM)

```
 1  .............................
    State Bar No.:................
 2  .............................
    .............................
 3  .............................
 4
 5  Attorney for Defendant ................
 6
 7
 8              SUPERIOR COURT OF THE STATE OF CALIFORNIA
 9                     COUNTY OF .........
10  ..........................., ) CASE NO. ............
                                 )
11              Plaintiff,       ) HEARING DATE/TIME: ..........
                                 ) DEPT. NO. ...................
12  vs.                          ) HEARING JUDGE: ...... (if known)
                                 )
13  ..........................., ) DECLARATION OF ........ IN
                                 ) SUPPORT OF MOTION TO STAY OR
14              Defendant.       ) DISMISS ACTION
                                 )
15                               ) DATE ACTION FILED: ...........
    _____) DATE SET FOR TRIAL: ... (if set)
16
```

17    I, the undersigned, declare as follows:

18    1.  I am the Defendant *(or one of the Defendants)* in this

19 action, and have personal knowledge of each of the facts stated

20 herein.

21    2.  I reside and am domiciled outside the State of

22 California. My residence is located at ......... *(address outside*

23 *California)* ....... . My occupation *(or employment)* is as follows:

24 ..............................................................

25 My office *(or employment)* address is ............ *(address outside*

26 *California)* ..... .

27    3.  I maintain no residence or place of business within the

28 State of California.

1

---

DECL'N OF ........ IN SUPPORT OF MOTION<br>TO STAY OR DISMISS

1    4.   It would be unfair and seriously inconvenient to me to
2    have to defend this action in the courts of the State of California
3    for the following reasons: ........... *(address factors enumerated*
4    *in ¶3:107 of the text)* ............................. .
5    5.   An alternative forum for the maintenance of this action
6    is available.  I am subject to personal jurisdiction in the follow-
7    ing states *(or countries)*: ....................... . No statute of
8    limitations bars action against me on the cause of action sued upon
9    herein in any of said states *(or countries)*.
10   6.   I hereby consent and agree to submit to the jurisdiction
11   of the courts of the State of ...................... in any action
12   instituted by plaintiff on the cause of action sued upon herein.
13   I certify and declare under penalty of perjury under the laws
14   of the State of California that the foregoing is true and correct.
15   DATED: ................. at ................................... .
16
17                           _/s/_____
18                           Declarant
19
20
21
22
23
24
25
26
27
28

2

DECL'N OF ........ IN SUPPORT OF MOTION
TO STAY OR DISMISS

# NOTICE OF MOTION FOR ORDER TRANSFERRING ACTION
## (CHANGE OF VENUE)

```
 1  ...............................
    State Bar No.:..................
 2  ...............................
 3  ...............................
    ...............................
 4
 5  Attorney for Defendant ..................
 6
 7
 8           SUPERIOR COURT OF THE STATE OF CALIFORNIA
 9                    COUNTY OF ..........
10
11  ........................,  ) CASE NO. .............
                               )
12         Plaintiff,          ) HEARING DATE/TIME: ..........
                               ) DEPT. NO. ..................
13  vs.                        ) HEARING JUDGE: ...... (if known)
                               )
14  ........................,  ) NOTICE OF MOTION FOR ORDER
                               ) TRANSFERRING ACTION;
15         Defendant.          ) DECLARATION OF ........;POINTS
                               ) AND AUTHORITIES; PROPOSED ORDER
16                             )
                               ) DATE ACTION FILED: ..........
17  _____    ) DATE SET FOR TRIAL: ... (if set)
18      TO EACH PARTY AND TO THE ATTORNEY OF RECORD FOR EACH PARTY:
19      YOU ARE HEREBY NOTIFIED THAT on ...... (date) ...... at ......
20  (time) ....... in Department No. ....... of this Court, located at
21  ......... (address) ..........., Defendant ..... (name) ..... will
22  move the court for an order transferring this action for trial to
23  the ................. Court of the State of California, County of
24  .................. Said motion will be made upon the ground that
25  .......................................................................
26  ... (one or more of the grounds enumerated in CCP §397; e.g., "this
27  court is not a proper court for trial, and the court to which
28  transfer is sought is a proper court"; or "the convenience of wit-
```

1

MOTION FOR ORDER TO TRANSFER

1 *nesses and the ends of justice would be promoted by such transfer,"*

2 *etc.)* . . . . . . . . . . . . . . . . . . . . . . . . . . . . . . . . . . . . . . . . . . . . . . . . . . . . .

3      *(Where motion made on "wrong court" ground)* Moving party will

4 also seek an order imposing sanctions against *(counsel for*

5 *plaintiff)* in the sum of $. . . . . . . . . for its reasonable expenses and

6 attorneys' fees incurred in making this motion pursuant to Code of

7 Civil Procedure Section 396b.

8      Said motion will be based upon this Notice, the points and

9 authorities set forth below, the attached declaration of . . . . . . . . .

10 . . . . . . . . . . . . . . ., and the complete files and records of this action.

11

12 DATED: . . . . . . . . . . . .

13

14                   By: . . . . . . . . . . . . . . . . . . . . . . . . . . . . . . . .

15                     Attorney for Defendant. . . . . . . . .

16         POINTS AND AUTHORITIES IN SUPPORT OF MOTION

17 *(Follow suggestions in Law and Motion Practice Chapter, ¶9:64-81)*

18

19

20

21

22

23

24

25

26

27

28

2

MOTION FOR ORDER TO TRANSFER

# DECLARATION IN SUPPORT OF MOTION
# FOR ORDER TRANSFERRING ACTION
# (CHANGE OF VENUE ON "WRONG COURT" GROUND)

```
 1  ..............................
    State Bar No.:.................
 2  ..............................
    ..............................
 3  ..............................

 4

 5  Attorney for .................

 6

 7

 8            SUPERIOR COURT OF THE STATE OF CALIFORNIA

 9                  COUNTY OF .........

10  ........................., ) CASE NO. ............
                               )
11            Plaintiff,       ) HEARING DATE/TIME: ..........
                               ) DEPT. NO. ...................
12  vs.                        ) HEARING JUDGE: ...... (if known)
                               )
13  ........................., ) DECLARATION OF ....... IN
                               ) SUPPORT OF MOTION TO TRANSFER
14            Defendant.       ) ACTION
                               )
15                             ) DATE ACTION FILED: ..........
                               ) DATE SET FOR TRIAL: ... (if set)
16  _____)

17      I, the undersigned, declare as follows:

18      1.  I am the ...... (defendant/attorney for defendant) ......

19  in this action.

20      2.  None of the defendants named in this action resided in

21  the county in which this court is located at time this action was

22  commenced. Defendant ...................... resided then and now

23  at ........................ in the County of ...................

24  (Add similar statement for each other named defendant. If state-

25  ment is made on "information and belief," add the facts upon which

26  such statement is based.)

27      3.  The alleged injury (or death) that is the subject of

28  plaintiff's action did not occur in the county in which this court
```

1

1 is located. Rather, said alleged injury occurred, if at all, in
2 the County of ..................

OR

4    The alleged contract that is the subject of plaintiff's action
5 was neither entered into nor to be performed in the county in which
6 this court is located. Rather, said contract was entered into, if
7 at all, and was to be performed, if at all, in the County of
8 ........................

9    4.    *(Where motion made on "wrong court" ground)* Defendant has
10 incurred reasonable expenses including attorney's fees in making
11 this motion aggregating $..........., consisting of the following:
12 *(detail attorneys' services and other expenses)*.

13         Prior to making this motion, I offered to stipulate to a
14 change of venue to .............. County in order to eliminate the
15 necessity for the motion, but plaintiff's counsel, ...............
16 rejected my offer.

17         Moving party contends that plaintiff's selection of venue
18 in this action was not made in good faith given the facts and law
19 plaintiff either knew or should have known. Said contention is
20 based on the following facts: *(detail whatever facts would estab-*
21 *lish proper venue elsewhere and plaintiff's knowledge thereof)*.

22         I declare under penalty of perjury under the laws of the State
23 of California that the foregoing is true and correct.
24 DATED:.............       ...................................
25                          Declarant

26

27

28

2

DECL'N OF ........ IN SUPPORT<br>OF MOTION TO TRANSFER

# DECLARATION IN SUPPORT OF MOTION
# FOR ORDER TRANSFERRING ACTION
# (CHANGE OF VENUE ON
# "CONVENIENCE OF WITNESSES" GROUND)

```
 1   ...................................
     State Bar No.:...................
 2   ...................................
     ...................................
 3   ...................................

 4

 5   Attorney for .................

 6

 7

 8              SUPERIOR COURT OF THE STATE OF CALIFORNIA

 9                      COUNTY OF .........

10   ..........................,  ) CASE NO. ...........
                                  )
11              Plaintiff,        ) HEARING DATE/TIME: ...........
                                  ) DEPT. NO. ..................
12   vs.                          ) HEARING JUDGE: ...... (if known)
                                  )
13   ..........................,  ) DECLARATION OF ....... IN
                                  ) SUPPORT OF MOTION TO TRANSFER
14              Defendant.        ) ACTION
                                  )
15                                ) DATE ACTION FILED: ...........
                                  ) DATE SET FOR TRIAL: ... (if set)
16   ─────────────────────────────
```

17        I am the ...... (defendant/attorney for defendant) ........ in

18   this action.

19        1.   The following is the name of each witness who is expected

20   to testify at the trial of this action, and the substance of his or

21   her expected testimony:

22            (a)  .................................... is expected to

23   testify that ...................................................

24   ...............................................................

25            (b)  .................................... is expected to

26   testify that ...................................................

27   ...............................................................

28            (continue for each witness, including <u>opposing</u> witnesses)

1

1   It would be seriously inconvenient for the witnesses
2   identified in paragraphs .................... above to appear and
3   give their testimony in the county in which this court is located
4   for the reason that ..... *(detail specific reasons; e.g., inability*
5   *to travel, loss of time off work, cost of attending, etc.)* ........
6   ......................................................
7   The ends of justice would be promoted by transferring
8   this action for trial to the .............. Court of the State of
9   California, County of ............... for the reason that .......
10  *(state relevance of witnesses' testimony, likely to impact on jury,*
11  *reasons why deposition testimony not satisfactory, etc.)* .........
12  *(See detailed discussion as to required factual showing,*
13  *¶3:289-289.1)*
14  2.   Concurrently with filing the Notice of Motion to which
15  this Declaration is attached, I paid or caused to be paid to the
16  clerk of this court, the costs and fees demanded by said clerk for
17  transferring this action to the ..................... Court of the
18  State of California, County of ........................, and of
19  filing the papers in the said court to which transfer is sought, in
20  compliance with Code of Civil Procedure Section 399.
21  I declare under penalty of perjury under the laws of the State
22  of California that the foregoing is true and correct.
23  DATED: .............        ....................................
24                                       Declarant
25
26
27
28

2

DECL'N OF ........ IN SUPPORT
OF MOTION TO TRANSFER

**RESERVED**

**RESERVED**

# CHECKLIST
# MOTION TO QUASH SERVICE

*[Ed. Note: This form or similar forms are used by many courts. Counsel should use this as a checklist when preparing a motion or opposition because it may raise factors of concern to the court. Declarations or points and authorities should be prepared to address each of the points on the checklist.]*

Discovery Cut-off: _____

Motion Cut-off: _____

Trial Date: _____

Calendar: _____

Date: _____

Notice: _____

**MOTION TO QUASH SERVICE**
**Lack of Jurisdiction/**
**Defective Service**
**(CCP § 418.10(a)(1))**
**(CONFIDENTIAL COURT DOCUMENT WHEN COMPLETED)**

NAME OF MOVING PARTY: _____

NAME OF RESPONDING PARTY: _____

CORRECT ADDRESS IN PROOF OF SERVICE (CCP §§ 1013, 1013a): _____

NO MORE THAN 30-DAY LAPSE UNDER § 418.10(b): _____

21- DAY LAPSE UNDER CCP § 1005(a)(4)): _____

❏ Previous or concurrent <u>GENERAL APPEARANCE</u> by moving party:

❏ <u>WAIVER</u> by addressing merits:

❏ STATUTORILY DEFECTIVE SERVICE:

    <u>DATE OF SERVICE</u> of summons:

    <u>TYPE</u> of service:    ❏ Personal    ❏ Substituted    ❏ Mail    ❏ Publication

    ❏ Sufficient <u>DECLARATION OF DILIGENCE</u>:

    ❏ Proof of Service properly <u>VERIFIED</u>: _____

    ❏ No authorization of <u>AGENT</u>: _____

    ❏ Other service defect: _____

DECLARATION OF MOVING PARTY (CCP § 2015.5; CRC 315(a)):

DECLARATION OF OPPOSING PARTY OR PROCESS SERVER:
    (Registered server has presumption (Evid. Code, § 647) and complainant has burden to show valid service. (<u>Dill</u> vs. <u>Berquist Const. Co.</u> (1994) 24 Cal.App.4th 1426, 1439))

TENTATIVE RULING:

    ❏ Grant and quash service

    ❏ Deny

    ❏ OSC re failure to show service (L.R. 7.7(c))

    ❏ Dismiss moving party without prejudice (CCP §581(h))

**[FORM 3:J]**

# CHECKLIST
# MOTION TO CHANGE VENUE

*[Ed. Note: This form or similar forms are used by many courts. Counsel should use this as a checklist when preparing a motion or opposition because it may raise factors of concern to the court. Declarations or points and authorities should be prepared to address each of the points on the checklist.]*

Discovery Cut-off: _____        Calendar: _____

Motion Cut-off: _____           Date: _____

Trial Date: _____               Notice: _____

**MOTION TO CHANGE VENUE**
**(CCP § 392 et seq.)**
**PROPER COURT FOR TRIAL**
**(CCP § 397)**
**(CONFIDENTIAL COURT DOCUMENT WHEN COMPLETED)**

NAME OF MOVING PARTY: _____

NAME OF RESPONDING PARTY: _____

CORRECT ADDRESS IN PROOF OF SERVICE (CCP §§ 1013, 1013a): _____

21- DAY LAPSE UNDER CCP § 1005: _____

❑ PRIOR TO OR CONCURRENT WITH ANSWER, DEMURRER OR MOTION TO STRIKE WITHIN TIME TO RESPOND TO COMPLAINT. (CCP § 396b(a))

❑ ANSWER FILED (L.R. 2.0(e)).

❑ COMPETENT DECLARATIONS WITH MINIMUM INFORMATION (L.R. 2.0(e); Weil & Brown, Civ. Pro. Bef. Trial (TRG 2002) ¶3:576).

CHANGE VENUE TO: _____

CO-DEFENDANTS PROPERLY SERVED:

CAUSE OF ACTION SOUNDS     ❑ IN CONTRACT          ❑ IN TORT       ❑ MIXED ACTION
(Complaint nature ascertained based on allegations at outset of action. Weil & Brown, Civ. Pro. Bef. Trial (TRG 2002) ¶3:464).

RESIDENCE OF M/P AT COMMENCEMENT OF ACTION: _____

PLACE CAUSE OF ACTION AROSE: _____

DEFENDANT IS: ❑ CORPORATION   ❑ INDIVIDUAL   ❑ PARTNERSHIP/UNINCORPORATED ASSOCIATION
❑ GOVERNMENT

DECLARATION OF MOVING PARTY (CCP § 2015.5; CRC 315(a)):

OPPOSITION:

IF MOTION IS BASED ON CCP § 397(c) THESE FACTORS ARE CONSIDERED:

Requirements: (Juneau v. Juneau (1941) 45 Cal.App.2d 14).
❑ Motion filed with or after answer
❑ Names of witnesses listed
❑ Testimony to be elicited -- relevant
❑ Reasons why attendance inconvenient
❑ Showing convenience in desired court
❑ Reasonable time (Cooney v. Cooney, 25 Cal.2d 202, 208 (1944))

Convenience of following not considered:
Parties to Action: Wrin v. Ohlandt, 213 Cal. 158, 160 (1931)
Employees of Parties: Barnett v. United Oil Co., 5 Cal.App.2d 175, 179 (1935)
Non-eyewitness Experts: Wrin at 160; Barnett at 181

Convenience motion made in reasonable time. Weil & Brown, Civ. Pro. Bef. Trial (TRG 2002) ¶3:559.5.

RECOMMENDED RULING:

❑ Grant, change venue to _____

❑ Deny (without prejudice)

Plead within _____ days

Rev. #1 2003

# CHECKLIST
# FORUM NON CONVENIENS

*[Ed. Note: This form or similar forms are used by many courts. Counsel should use this as a checklist when preparing a motion or opposition because it may raise factors of concern to the court. Declarations or points and authorities should be prepared to address each of the points on the checklist.]*

Discovery Cut-off: _____

Motion Cut-off: _____

Trial Date: _____

Calendar: _____

Date: _____

Notice: _____

### FORUM NON CONVENIENS
### (CCP § 418.10(a)(2))
### (CONFIDENTIAL COURT DOCUMENT WHEN COMPLETED)

NAME OF MOVING PARTY: _____

NAME OF RESPONDING PARTY: _____

RELIEF REQUESTED:  ❏ Stay Action
❏ Dismiss Action, without prejudice to file in jurisdiction _____

21-DAY LAPSE (CCP § 1005):

CORRECT ADDRESS IN PROOF OF SERVICE (CCP §§ 1013, 1013a):

FACTORS  (Great N.Ry. Co. vs. Sup.Ct. (1970) 12 Cal.App.3d 105, 112)

| For Grant + | Neu- Tral 0 | For Deny - | | |
|---|---|---|---|---|
| ❏ | ❏ | ❏ | 1. | Amenability of D to personal jurisdiction in other forum |
| ❏ | ❏ | ❏ | 2. | Relative convenience to parties and witnesses |
| ❏ | ❏ | ❏ | 3. | Prejudice due to difference of conflict-of-law rules |
| ❏ | ❏ | ❏ | 4. | Principal place and extent of business of D in either state |
| ❏ | ❏ | ❏ | 5. | Transaction occurred in or substantially related to California |
| ❏ | ❏ | ❏ | 6. | Any party substantial disadvantage trying case in California or other forum |
| ❏ | ❏ | ❏ | 7. | Enforceability of judgment by California process or proceedings |
| ❏ | ❏ | ❏ | 8. | Inconvenience of witnesses in California or in other forum |
| ❏ | ❏ | ❏ | 9. | Relative expense to parties in trying case in California or other forum |
| ❏ | ❏ | ❏ | 10. | View of scene by trier of fact necessary or helpful |
| ❏ | ❏ | ❏ | 11. | Unfair burden on California in view of relation of parties or action to California |
| ❏ | ❏ | ❏ | 12. | Relation of parties to California obliging court participation in California |
| ❏ | ❏ | ❏ | 13. | Interest of California in providing forum for any parties |
| ❏ | ❏ | ❏ | 14. | Interest of California in regulating situation or conduct involved |
| ❏ | ❏ | ❏ | 15. | Avoidance of multiplicity of actions/inconsistent adjudication |
| ❏ | ❏ | ❏ | 16. | Relative ease of access to sources of proof |
| ❏ | ❏ | ❏ | 17. | Availability of compulsory process for witnesses |
| ❏ | ❏ | ❏ | 18. | Relative advantages and obstacles of fair trial |
| ❏ | ❏ | ❏ | 19. | Public interest in case |
| ❏ | ❏ | ❏ | 20. | Admin. difficulties/court congestion more probable in California |
| ❏ | ❏ | ❏ | 21. | Imposition of jury duty on community having no relation to case |
| ❏ | ❏ | ❏ | 22. | Injustice to and burden on local courts and taxpayers |
| ❏ | ❏ | ❏ | 23. | Difficulty to D, ct, jurors re presentation of testimony by depo |
| ❏ | ❏ | ❏ | 24. | Availability of forum claimed to be more appropriate |
| ❏ | ❏ | ❏ | 25. | Other considerations making trial convenient, fast, inexpensive |

FORUM SELECTION CLAUSE (Weil & Brown, §3:444 (normally given effect)) _____

DECLARATION OF MOVING PARTY (CCP § 2015.5; CRC 315(a)):

OPPOSITION:

RECOMMENDED RULING:

❏ Grant

❏ Deny

❏ Stay (Weil & Brown, §3:427)

❏ Dismiss

**RESERVED**

# CHAPTER 4

# SUMMONS

# CONTENTS

Page

**STRATEGY CONSIDERATIONS RE SERVICE OF
SUMMONS** .................................................................. 4-1

**A. REQUIREMENTS—IN GENERAL** ..................................... 4-2
   1.  Constitutional Requirement re Summons ......................... 4-2
      a.  Applies to all civil actions .................................... 4-2
      b.  "Best" method not constitutionally required .............. 4-2
      c.  Notice by MAIL as constitutional minimum
          where defendant's whereabouts ascertainable .......... 4-3
         (1) Ascertaining defendant's whereabouts .............. 4-3
         (2) Sufficiency of address ..................................... 4-3
      d.  Compare—statutory requirements ......................... 4-4
   2.  Statutory Requirements re Summons ............................ 4-4
      a.  Jurisdiction and Service of Process Act .................... 4-4
      b.  Statutes liberally construed .................................. 4-4
         (1) Application ..................................................... 4-5
         (2) Compare—total failure to comply ...................... 4-5
      c.  Effect of delay in service .................................... 4-5
         (1) Dismissal statutes .......................................... 4-5
         (2) "Fast track" rules ........................................... 4-6
            (a) No dismissal when counsel is to blame ........ 4-6
   3.  Compare—Federal Rules ........................................... 4-6
      a.  Effect of delay in service .................................... 4-6
      b.  No nationwide service ......................................... 4-6
   4.  Papers to be Served on Defendant Together With
      Summons and Complaint .......................................... 4-6
   5.  Requirements May be Waived by Defendant .................... 4-7
      a.  General appearance ........................................... 4-7
      b.  Appointing agent for service of process .................... 4-7
         (1) Compare—jurisdiction requirements ................... 4-7
      c.  Confession of judgment ....................................... 4-8
         (1) Procedural requirements ................................... 4-8
         (2) Strictly construed ........................................... 4-8

**B. ISSUANCE OF SUMMONS** .............................................. 4-9
   1.  General Procedure ................................................... 4-9
   2.  Amended Summons ................................................. 4-10

      a.   Not required for defendants named in original
          summons ........................................................................4-10
   3.  Replacement Summons ................................................4-10

**C.  CONTENT OF SUMMONS** .......................................................4-10
   1.  Civil Actions Generally ......................................................4-10
      a.   Use of Official Forms satisfies these requirements ...4-11
      b.   Date on summons not important .............................4-11
   2.  Actions With Special Summons Requirements................4-11
      a.   Unlawful detainer proceedings ......................................4-11
      b.   Joint debtor proceedings .......................................4-12
      c.   Family law proceedings .........................................4-12
      d.   Probate revocation and will contests .......................4-12
      e.   Eminent domain proceedings .................................4-12
      f.   Suits to establish title ...........................................4-12
      g.   Forfeiture proceedings...........................................4-12
      h.   Challenging acts of public agency ...........................4-12
   3.  Notice re Capacity in Which Person Served ...................4-12
      a.   Actions against corporations, partnerships or
          limited liability companies .....................................4-13
         (1) Notice must appear on summons itself ..............4-13
         (2) Substantial compliance sufficient ......................4-14
            (a) Example.......................................................4-14
            (b) Compare—summons incomplete..................4-14
            (c) Compare—failure to serve authorized
                person ........................................................4-14
      b.   Actions against "Doe" defendants ...........................4-15
         (1) Corporation served as "Doe" .............................4-15

**D.  SERVICE OF SUMMONS** ......................................................4-16
   1.  Who May Serve Summons ...............................................4-16
      a.   Peace officers.......................................................4-16
      b.   Private individuals .................................................4-16
         (1) Plaintiff's lawyer may serve ...............................4-16
         (2) Persons protected by TRO deemed "party" ........4-16
         (3) Compare—effect of process server registration
            requirement .......................................................4-16
   2.  Fees for Serving Summons .............................................4-16
      a.   Recoverability as court costs .................................4-16
   3.  Upon Whom Service May be Made ...............................4-17
      a.   Individuals ...........................................................4-17
         (1) Minors ...............................................................4-17
         (2) Wards and conservatees....................................4-17
            (a) Compare—persons not adjudicated
                incompetent ...............................................4-17
         (3) Political candidates ...........................................4-18
         (4) Agents to accept service of process ..................4-18
         (5) Prisoners ...........................................................4-19
         (6) Decedent's liability covered by insurance ...........4-19
         (7) Compare—service on "Doe" defendants .............4-19
      b.   Corporations .........................................................4-20

        (1) Officers of the corporation ................................. 4-20
           (a) Bank officers ............................................ 4-20
           (b) "General manager" ................................. 4-20
        (2) Agents for service of process ......................... 4-21
           (a) Designated agents ................................... 4-21
           (b) Implied authority ..................................... 4-21
           (c) Compare—agency cannot be proved by
               agent's statements alone ......................... 4-21
        (3) Secretary of State .......................................... 4-22
           (a) Procedure as to California corporations ........ 4-22
             1) Showing required .............................. 4-22
             2) When service effective ...................... 4-22
           (b) Procedure as to out-of-state
               corporations ............................................. 4-22
           (c) Out-of-state insurance companies ............. 4-23
        (4) Compare—defunct corporation ...................... 4-23
        (5) Compare—suspended corporation .................. 4-23
        (6) Compare—joint stock company ...................... 4-24
    c. Partnerships and other unincorporated
      associations .......................................................... 4-24
      (1) Partner or officer ........................................... 4-24
      (2) Designated agent .......................................... 4-24
           (a) When required ......................................... 4-24
           (b) Effect of failure to designate .................... 4-24
    d. Limited liability companies .................................... 4-25
      (1) Designated agent .......................................... 4-25
           (a) Method of service .................................... 4-25
      (2) Secretary of State .......................................... 4-25
    e. Public entities ..................................................... 4-25
      (1) Actions against State ...................................... 4-25
      (2) Against local agencies .................................... 4-25
  4. Manner of Service ...................................................... 4-26
    a. Personal delivery to defendant or authorized
      agent ("personal service") ...................................... 4-27
      (1) Advantages ................................................... 4-27
      (2) Effect of defendant's refusal to accept ............. 4-27
           (a) Effect of third party helping to evade
               service ...................................................... 4-28
           (b) Service in gated communities .................... 4-28
      (3) Original summons not necessary ..................... 4-28
      (4) Date of service to be shown on copy ................ 4-28
    b. "Substitute service"—delivery to someone else
      coupled with mailing ............................................. 4-29
      (1) Applies both to individual and entity
          defendants ..................................................... 4-29
      (2) Limitation—not available for individual
          defendants unless personal service first
          attempted ...................................................... 4-30
           (a) Burden on plaintiff .................................... 4-30
           (b) "Reasonable diligence" ............................. 4-30

                1)  Different standard for high public
                    officials? ................................................4-30
            (c) Application .................................................4-30
            (d) Compare—small claims actions...................4-31
        (3) Procedure for substitute service .........................4-31
            (a) On individual defendant .............................4-31
                1)  "Dwelling house or usual place of
                    abode" ..............................................4-32
                2)  "Usual mailing address" ........................4-32
                3)  "Competent member of household" ........4-32
                4)  "Person apparently in charge of office
                    or place of business" ...........................4-33
                5)  Substitute service attempt may result
                    in personal service ..............................4-33
            (b) On entity defendant ..................................4-33
                1)  Physical address known ......................4-34
                2)  Physical address unknown ...................4-34
                3)  "Physical address"? ............................4-34
            (c) On "business organization, form
                unknown" .................................................4-34
                1)  Sole proprietorships? ..........................4-35
        (4) When service effective ....................................4-35
            (a) Compare—personal service ......................4-35
            (b) Compare—dismissal for delay in service
                of summons ............................................4-35
    c.  Service by mail and acknowledgment of receipt........4-35
        (1) What must be mailed .......................................4-36
        (2) How mailed ....................................................4-36
            (a) Compare—service outside the state...........4-36
        (3) Mailing address may include post office box .......4-36
            (a) Compare—substitute service....................4-36
        (4) Notice and acknowledgment form ......................4-37
        (5) Effect of acknowledgment ...............................4-37
            (a) When service effective .............................4-37
            (b) No extension of time for other acts .............4-37
            (c) Not a submission to jurisdiction ..................4-37
        (6) Effect of refusing acknowledgment .....................4-38
            (a) Compare—service on persons outside
                California ...............................................4-38
            (b) Liability for costs of service ......................4-38
                1)  Procedure .........................................4-38
    d.  Service by publication .............................................4-39
        (1) Constitutional limitation ....................................4-39
        (2) Procedure for obtaining court order ...................4-39
        (3) Affidavit requirements .....................................4-39
            (a) Reasonable diligence to serve by other
                methods................................................4-40
                1)  Includes service by mail .....................4-40
                2)  Probative facts required .....................4-40
                3)  "Reasonable diligence" .......................4-40
                    a)  Particular searches .....................4-40

    b) Limitation—restricted data bases ..... 4-41
   4) Application ............................................. 4-42
   5) Effect of too many defendants to
     serve individually? .................................. 4-42
  (b) Existence of cause of action OR
    interest in property .................................. 4-43
  (c) Effect of defects or inaccuracies in
    affidavit ................................................. 4-43
  (d) Procedure to challenge affidavit ........... 4-44
 (4) Content of court order .................................. 4-44
  (a) Publication ............................................. 4-44
   1) Nonresident defendants ................... 4-44
   2) Duration and frequency of
     publication ....................................... 4-44.1
  (b) Mailing .................................................. 4-44.1
 (5) When service complete .................................. 4-44.1
  (a) Compare—publication under different
    statutes ................................................. 4-44.1
 (6) Other service during publication period ........... 4-44.2
 (7) No extension of deadline for service of
   summons ....................................................... 4-44.2
 e. Compare—unlawful detainer actions where
  defendant's whereabouts unknown ......................... 4-45
5. Service on Defendants Outside California ..................... 4-45
 a. Defendant in another state ..................................... 4-45
  (1) Certified or registered mail with return-
   receipt-requested ........................................... 4-46
   (a) Mailing to person to be served ................ 4-46
    1) Out-of-state corporations ................... 4-46
   (b) Service complete 10 days after mailing ........ 4-47
    1) Compare—when service complete
     for dismissal purposes ......................... 4-47
   (c) Proof of service requires proof of actual
    receipt .................................................... 4-47
   (d) Compare—service by mail coupled with
    acknowledgment of receipt ...................... 4-47
  (2) Statutory actions authorizing service on
   designated state officials ................................. 4-48
   (a) Example—nonresident motorist statute ........ 4-48
   (b) Other examples ...................................... 4-48
   (c) CCP methods also available ...................... 4-49
 b. Defendant in foreign country .................................. 4-49
  (1) Hague Convention as limitation on manner
   of service ..................................................... 4-50
   (a) Preempts California methods ...................... 4-50
    1) Exception—service by publication .......... 4-50
    2) Exception—serving domestic
     subsidiary as "involuntary agent" of
     foreign corporation ............................. 4-51
    3) Exception—foreign corporations
     qualified to do business in California ...... 4-51

4) Exception—foreign corporation *not*
qualified to do business ........................4-51
(b) Service methods authorized by Hague
Convention ...........................................4-51
(c) Failure to comply voids service ...............4-53
(2) Inter-American Convention as limitation on
manner of service ......................................4-54
(a) Methods of service authorized .................4-54
(b) Effect of failure to comply ......................4-55
6. Service on Foreign State .......................................4-55
a. Governing family compared ...........................4-55
7. Service Deadline ..................................................4-55
a. Longer if authorized by local rule .................4-55
b. Longer if due diligence shown ......................4-55
c. Service on later-named defendants ...............4-56
d. Fictitiously-named defendants? ....................4-56
e. Application for extension of time ..................4-56
(1) Diligence depending on amount involved? .........4-56
f. Effect of delay in service of summons .............4-56
(1) Response .................................................4-57
(2) Sanctions ................................................4-57
(a) Dismissal as sanction? ...........................4-57

E. **RETURN OF SUMMONS** ......................................4-57
1. Necessity for Return of Summons; Proof of Service ........4-57
a. Summons lost after service ...........................4-57
b. Creates presumption of valid service .............4-58
(1) Preemption of local rules requiring additional
documents .................................................4-58
2. Proof of Service Requirements ...............................4-58
a. Separate form required ................................4-58
b. Service made within California .......................4-58
(1) Personal service ........................................4-58
(a) Process server's registration .....................4-58
(b) Special requirement for service on "Doe" .......4-59
(2) Substitute service ......................................4-59
(3) Service by mail with acknowledgment of
receipt .....................................................4-59
(4) Service by publication .................................4-59
(5) Service by posting (unlawful detainer actions) ....4-59
(6) Service pursuant to alternative statutory
methods .....................................................4-59
(7) Defendant's written admission of service ...........4-59
c. Service made outside California .......................4-60
(1) Methods authorized for service within state ........4-60
(2) Service by certified or registered mail with
return-receipt-requested ................................4-60
(a) Strict compliance ...................................4-60
(b) Application ...........................................4-60
(c) Compare—mail refused ...............................4-60.1
(3) Service per foreign law or court order ...............4-61

        (4)  Defendant's written admission of service ............ 4-61
           (a)  Compare—knowledge of action not
               enough ................................................................. 4-61
   3.  Deadline for Return of Summons .................................. 4-61
      a.  Compare—return of summons served on
          nonresidents .......................................................... 4-62
**F.  PROCEDURES FOR CHALLENGING SERVICE OF
    SUMMONS** ........................................................................ 4-62
   1.  Motion to Quash Service of Summons [CCP §418.10] .... 4-62
      a.  Grounds ................................................................. 4-63
          (1)  Lack of proper service ................................... 4-63
          (2)  Compare—lack of personal jurisdiction .............. 4-63
          (3)  Compare—challenging sufficiency of
              unlawful detainer complaint ............................ 4-63
             (a)  General demurrer improper ........................ 4-64
             (b)  Compare—special demurrer ........................ 4-64
      b.  Time for filing ........................................................ 4-64
      c.  Hearing on motion to quash .................................... 4-64
      d.  Review of ruling on motion to quash ...................... 4-64
   2.  Motion to Dismiss for Delay in Service of Summons ....... 4-64
      a.  Rationale ............................................................... 4-65
      b.  Burden of proving valid service .............................. 4-65
   3.  Motion to Set Aside Default Judgment ......................... 4-65
      a.  Time limit for motion ............................................. 4-65
      b.  Not a general appearance ....................................... 4-66
      c.  Procedure on motion and hearing ........................... 4-66
   4.  Default and Appeal .................................................... 4-66
   5.  Motion to Vacate Renewal of Judgment ........................ 4-66
      a.  Effect .................................................................... 4-66
   6.  Collateral Attack ........................................................ 4-66
   7.  Compare—Tort Action for False Proof of Service ............ 4-67
      a.  Privilege? ............................................................... 4-67

**FORMS**
•  Summons ...................................................................... 4-69
•  Additional Parties Attachment ......................................... 4-71
•  Notice and Acknowledgment of Receipt ............................ 4-72
•  Declaration of Lost Summons After Service ....................... 4-73
•  Ex Parte Application for Order for Publication of
   Summons ...................................................................... 4-75
•  Declaration in Support of Application for Order for
   Publication of Summons ................................................. 4-77
•  Order for Publication of Summons ................................... 4-80
•  Checklist: Motion to Quash Service (Defective Service) ........ 4-82
•  Request for Service Abroad of Judicial or Extrajudicial
   Documents ................................................................... 4-84
•  Proof of Service ............................................................. 4-87
•  Ex Parte Application for Extension of Time to Serve
   Pleading ....................................................................... 4-89

**RESERVED**

# SUMMONS

**[4:1] Nature of "Summons":** A "summons" is a form of court process issued in the course of a judicial proceeding. [CCP §17(6)]

Its function is to *notify* defendants that a lawsuit is pending against them, that they have a limited period of time within which to file a response, and of the consequences if they fail to do so (*see ¶4:75*).

**[4:2] Service of summons as notice AND as basis for jurisdiction:** If the defendant is served with summons *within the state*, such service accomplishes two separate functions: It provides notice of the lawsuit, *and* generally establishes personal jurisdiction over such defendant (*¶3:136 ff.*).

However, if the defendant is *outside* the state when served, such service may be effective only as notice of the proceedings. For service outside the state to create personal jurisdiction, defendant must also have sufficient "minimum contacts" with the state (*see ¶3:195 ff.*).

---

### STRATEGY CONSIDERATIONS RE
### SERVICE OF SUMMONS
#### [4:3]

Under modern rules, discussed below, *any* defendant *anywhere* can be served with summons—one way or another. Whether such service will subject the defendant to personal jurisdiction is another question (as stated above, it depends on the defendant's "contacts" with California). But effecting service of summons by itself is usually *not* a major problem.

This being so, whether you represent plaintiffs or defendants, it makes sense to take a *practical* approach to serving summons:

(1) **If you represent the plaintiff**, and are having trouble locating or serving the defendant, call the defendant's lawyers or insurance carrier and see if they are willing to accept service on defendant's behalf. In many cases, they will have authority and be willing to do so.

   This is also a good idea where the defendant is a nonresident or out-of-state corporation who could raise *jurisdictional* objections. You may find that defense counsel, or the insurance carrier representing said defendant, have the same interest in litigating the case locally that you have, and are willing to accept service and make a general appearance on defendant's behalf—waiving any jurisdictional objection!

   If you do not know the names or whereabouts of defendants, also consider seeking leave of court for an *early deposition* pursuant to CCP §2025(b)(2). *See ¶8:444.*

---

---

**STRATEGY CONSIDERATIONS RE
SERVICE OF SUMMONS (Cont'd)**

(2) **If you represent the defendant**, and are asked to accept service on behalf of the defendant, make sure you have your client's authority (in writing, if possible) before agreeing to anything.

Obviously, you won't make a general appearance if there is any issue as to the court's jurisdiction, or if the 3-year statute on service of summons (CCP §583.210) has already run. But in other cases there is usually no valid reason to refuse to accept service. Authority from the client should be forthcoming if you explain that there is no way to prevent service, and that resisting service will merely run up the costs for which he or she ultimately may be held liable.

(One possible exception: Defense counsel often will *not* recommend accepting service where the defendant is a *foreign* national, living abroad. Plaintiffs' counsel often have trouble effecting valid service in such cases because of special treaty requirements; *see ¶4:316*.)

(3) **Moving to quash summons** rarely makes sense where based on defects in the *manner* of service (e.g., papers left with someone not authorized to receive service on defendant's behalf). Except perhaps where the statutes authorizing dismissal for delay in service have run (*see ¶11:51*), there is little to gain by a motion to quash.

---

## A. REQUIREMENTS—IN GENERAL

1. **[4:4] Constitutional Requirement re Summons:** A summons must provide notice and opportunity to be heard in compliance with the 14th Amendment due process clause. Basically, this requires a *reasonable effort* to notify the defendant of the proceedings pending against him and of his right to appear and defend the action. " ... (T)he means employed must be such as one desirous of actually informing the defendant might reasonably adopt to accomplish it." [*Mullane v. Central Hanover Bank & Trust Co.* (1950) 339 US 306, 314, 70 S.Ct. 652, 657]

   a. **[4:5] Applies to all civil actions:** The nature of the claim sued upon (e.g., personal claims vs. property claims) is not controlling as to the method of service constitutionally required. Rather, the sufficiency of any particular method of service depends on its ability to inform the defendant of the *potential adverse consequences* of the lawsuit. [*Greene v. Lindsey* (1982) 456 US 444, 450-451, 102 S.Ct. 1874, 1878-1879]

   b. **[4:6] "Best" method not constitutionally required:** The Constitution does not require personal service of summons in every case. Nor does it require, as a substitute for personal service, the method which is "most likely" to reach the defendant. All that is required is a method *reasonably* likely to provide notice. [See *Greene v. Lindsey*, supra, 456 US at 455, 102 S.Ct. at 1881]

If such a method is followed, due process is satisfied even if defendant did not receive *actual* notice of the proceedings. [*Evans v. Department of Motor Vehicles* (1994) 21 CA4th 958, 971, 26 CR2d 460, 468—administrative proceedings; *In re Emily R.* (2000) 80 CA4th 1344, 1353, 96 CR2d 285, 290—notice by publication satisfies due process in dependency proceedings where alleged father's address is unknown and cannot be determined with due diligence]

c. **[4:7]  Notice by MAIL as constitutional minimum where defendant's whereabouts ascertainable:**  The Supreme Court has refrained from passing on the constitutionality of particular methods of service. But it has held that where a defendant's name and address are reasonably ascertainable, "*notice by mail or other means as certain to ensure actual notice*" is the minimum the Constitution requires. Notice by publication in a newspaper (¶4:245) or posting on defendant's property is not sufficient when defendant's address is known or can be obtained. [*Mennonite Board of Missions v. Adams* (1983) 462 US 791, 800, 103 S.Ct. 2706, 2712 (emphasis added); see also *Tulsa Professional Collection Services, Inc. v. Pope* (1988) 485 US 478, 490-491, 108 S.Ct. 1340, 1347-1348]

(1) **[4:8]  Ascertaining defendant's whereabouts:**  A defendant's whereabouts are "reasonably ascertainable" if shown in a public record in the locality in which the proceeding is pending. [*Mennonite Board of Missions v. Adams*, supra, 462 US at 798, 103 S.Ct. at 2711, fn. 4]

If public records do not disclose defendant's whereabouts, plaintiff must make *some* effort to locate defendant. The Supreme Court has not set any standards for such efforts except to state that "extraordinary efforts" (e.g., hiring a private investigator) are *not* required. [*Mennonite Board of Missions v. Adams*, supra]

(2) **[4:9]  Sufficiency of address:**  If the *city* or *county* in which the defendant is located is ascertainable, service by mail must be attempted, even if defendant's street address is unknown. "Simply mailing a letter to (defendant in the county) quite likely would have provided actual notice, given the well-known skill of postal officials and employees in making proper delivery of letters defectively addressed." [*Mennonite Board of Missions*

*v. Adams,* supra, 462 US at 798, 103 S.Ct. at 2711, fn. 4 (internal quotes omitted)]

- **[4:10] Comment:** The practicality of this requirement in urban areas remains to be seen!

d. **[4:11] Compare—statutory requirements:** The Constitution may permit methods of service *not* permissible under state law. For example, notice by mail alone may satisfy due process requirements; but it does *not* constitute valid service on local residents under California law, unless accompanied by defendant's acknowledgment of receipt (¶*4:225*). Since our statutory standards are more demanding than required by due process, constitutional issues re service of summons are rarely reached in California actions.

**[4:12-14]** *Reserved.*

2. **[4:15] Statutory Requirements re Summons:** Even though the constitutional "notice" requirement is satisfied, service of summons is not effective to confer jurisdiction over a defendant unless applicable statutory requirements are also met. I.e., even if the defendant has actual notice of the lawsuit, he or she must still be served in compliance with the statutes discussed in this chapter. [*Ruttenberg v. Ruttenberg* (1997) 53 CA4th 801, 808, 62 CR2d 78, 82]

a. **[4:16] Jurisdiction and Service of Process Act:** The applicable statutory requirements are contained in the Jurisdiction and Service of Process Act, CCP §§410.10-418.11, covering:

- The *contents* of summons (¶*4:75 ff.*);

- Who may *issue* summons (¶*4:65-73*);

- Who may *serve* summons (¶*4:110-116*);

- *Upon whom* summons may be served (¶*4:65-73 ff.*);

- The *manner* in which summons may be served within California, outside the state, and abroad (¶*4:180 ff.*);

- The *return* of summons (¶*4:360 ff.*);

- The procedures for *challenging* service of summons (¶*4:411 ff.*).

b. **[4:17] Statutes liberally construed:** The statutory requirements are construed to uphold jurisdiction, rather than defeat it. As long as the defendant receives actual notice of the lawsuit, *substantial compliance* with the Code provisions governing service of summons will generally be held sufficient. [*Pasadena Medi-Center Associates v. Sup.Ct. (Houts)* (1973) 9 C3d 773, 778, 108 CR 828, 832; *County of Riverside v. Sup.Ct. (Hill)* (1997) 54 CA4th 443, 450, 62 CR2d 747, 751]

An exception to liberal statutory construction exists when courts interpret the service by publication statute (*see* ¶4:245).

Strict compliance is also required when interpreting the service periods for actions challenging decisions of legislative bodies. [See *Wagner v. City of South Pasadena* (2000) 78 CA4th 943, 950, 93 CR2d 91, 96—need for timeliness and certainty in determining compliance with Gov.C. §65009(c)]

(1) **Application**

- [4:18] P served Parthenon Computers, Inc. on behalf of "Ironsides Computer Corporation." Parthenon was doing business under the fictitious name "Ironsides Computers," but there was no separate corporation by that name. Service on Parthenon was upheld. It clearly had notice of the proceedings and was not prejudiced by the technical error in how it was served. [*Hammer Collections Co., Inc. v. Ironsides Computer Corp.* (1985) 172 CA3d 899, 902, 218 CR 627, 629; see *Pinkerton's, Inc. v. Sup.Ct. (Schrieber)* (1996) 49 CA4th 1342, 1349, 57 CR2d 356, 360-361—same]

    [4:19-24] *Reserved.*

(2) [4:25] **Compare—total failure to comply:** The purpose of the statutory requirements is to assure adequate notice. Therefore, "(w)hile partial compliance may sometimes be determined to be substantial and therefore sufficient, liberal construction cannot cure a plaintiff's *complete failure to comply* with statutory requirements when attempting to serve a defendant." [*Dill v. Berquist Const. Co., Inc.* (1994) 24 CA4th 1426, 1439, 29 CR 746, 753, fn. 12 (emphasis added)]

- [4:26] The persons who may be served on behalf of a corporation are designated by statute (CCP §416.10(b); *see* ¶4:137 ff.). Serving someone else *cannot* be considered "substantial" compliance. [*Dill v. Berquist Const. Co., Inc.*, supra, 24 CA4th at 1439, 29 CR at 753; *see* ¶4:99 ff.]

    [4:27-29] *Reserved.*

c. [4:30] **Effect of delay in service:** Delay in service may be ground for dismissal of the action.

(1) [4:31] **Dismissal statutes:** Dismissal is *discretionary* if summons and complaint are not served within *2 years* after commencement of the action (CCP §583.420(a)(1), *see* ¶11:111.5). If not served within *3*

*years,* dismissal is *mandatory* (CCP §§583.210, 583.250; *see ¶11:51).*

(2) [4:32] **"Fast track" rules:** Local "fast track" rules may require service of summons within a short period of time (e.g., 60 days) after commencement of the action (*see ¶12:53, 12:71).* Violation of these rules may result in sanctions, including dismissal of the action if lesser sanctions are ineffective. [See Gov.C. §68608(b), *discussed at ¶12:92 ff.*; and *Tliche v. Van Quathem* (1998) 66 CA4th 1054, 1055, 78 CR2d 458, 459]

(a) [4:33] **No dismissal when counsel is to blame:** However, dismissal is *not* a permitted sanction if the delay was the fault of plaintiff's counsel rather than plaintiff. [*Garcia v. McCutchen* (1997) 16 C4th 469, 476, 66 CR2d 319, 324; *see ¶9:1277.3*]

[4:34-39] *Reserved.*

3. [4:40] **Compare—Federal Rules:** The methods of service under the Federal Rules are substantially the same as California law. In addition, the Federal Rules authorize service by any means allowable under state law (see FRCP 4(e)(1)). Thus, practitioners familiar with California service rules can utilize the same procedures in federal court.

a. [4:41] **Effect of delay in service:** The Federal Rules require prompt service of summons. The action is subject to dismissal (without prejudice) if summons is not served within 120 days after filing the suit unless "good cause" for the delay is shown. [FRCP 4(m)]

b. [4:42] **No nationwide service:** In most cases, federal courts do *not* have nationwide jurisdiction. Service on persons outside the state in which the federal court is located is subject to the same limitations as in state court actions. [FRCP 4(e); *and see discussion at ¶3:631-632*]

[4:43-44] *Reserved.*

4. [4:45] **Papers to be Served on Defendant Together With Summons and Complaint:** Various papers must be served on the defendant together with copies of the summons and complaint:

- [4:46] **"ADR information package":** The court will make an "ADR information package" available to the plaintiff when suit is filed, which plaintiff must serve on each defendant together with the summons and complaint. [CRC 201.9(c); *see ¶1:479 ff.*]

- [4:47] **Case cover sheet in complex cases:** Plaintiff must file a case cover sheet describing the type of case involved (see ¶6:40). If plaintiff indicates on the cover sheet that the case is "complex" under CRC 1800 et seq., a copy of the cover sheet must be served together with the summons and complaint. [CRC 201.8(a); see ¶6:40.2]

- [4:48] **Certificate of grounds for assignment to court location (Los Angeles):** The Los Angeles Superior Court requires a "Civil Case Cover Sheet Addendum and Certificate of Grounds for Assignment to Court Location" (see ¶6:41.2). A copy must be served together with the summons and complaint. [L.A.Sup.Ct. Rule 2.0(d)]

- [4:49] **(Optional) Statement of damages in personal injury, wrongful death cases:** Because the complaint may not allege the amount of damages claimed in personal injury and wrongful death cases (see ¶6:279), a separate statement of damages must be filed before a default judgment can be entered (see ¶5:82 ff.). Thus, if there is a likelihood of default, it may be good practice to serve the statement of damages on defendant along with the summons and complaint (see ¶5:93).

5. [4:50] **Requirements May be Waived by Defendant:** The constitutional and statutory requirements re summons exist for defendant's protection, and therefore are subject to waiver by him or her . . . provided the waiver is knowledgeable and voluntary. [See *D.H. Overmyer Co. v. Frick Co.* (1972) 405 US 174, 185-186, 92 S.Ct. 775, 782]

   a. [4:51] **General appearance:** By making a general appearance in the action, defendant submits to the court's personal jurisdiction (¶3:163) and no further service of summons is required.

   b. [4:52] **Appointing agent for service of process:** A party may, by contract, appoint someone as agent to receive service of process on his or her behalf in actions arising from the contract (¶3:179, 4:46). Also, such designation may be required by statute in order for the defendant to engage in regulated activities or businesses (see ¶4:141).

      Such provisions effectively waive the requirement that summons be served personally. Service on the designated agent satisfies due process even if the party does not know the agent personally, as long as the agent in fact forwards the summons upon receipt. [*National Equip. Rental, Ltd. v. Szukhent* (1964) 375 US 311, 316, 84 S.Ct. 411, 414]

      (1) [4:53] **Compare—jurisdiction requirements:** But service on a designated agent does not necessarily subject a nonresident to local personal jurisdiction in

actions unrelated to its local activities (*see ¶3:179, 3:349*).

⇨[4:54] **PRACTICE POINTER:** This procedure can facilitate enforcement of debts in several ways:

The agent *need not be a disinterested person,* because the agent's only obligation is to forward summons to the debtor. [See *National Equip. Rental, Ltd. v. Szukhent,* supra, 375 US at 317, 84 S.Ct. at 415—designated agent was related to officer of plaintiff corporation] This greatly facilitates personal service, particularly where defendant is a nonresident.

In addition, defendant's *time to respond* to the complaint runs from personal service on the agent, not from when the papers are actually received by defendant. Again, this is a particular advantage where the debtor is a nonresident.

c. [4:55] **Confession of judgment:** Similarly, contract provisions whereby a party appoints another as his or her attorney with power to "confess judgment" effectively waive service of summons. [*D.H. Overmyer Co. v. Frick Co.*, supra, 405 US at 185-186, 92 S.Ct. at 782]

"A confession of judgment is in effect a private admission to liability for a debt without trial, upon which a court places its imprimatur when submitted to the clerk for entry." [*Efstratis v. First Northern Bank of Dixon* (1997) 59 CA4th 667, 672, 69 CR2d 445, 448]

(1) [4:56] **Procedural requirements:** There are various procedural safeguards to prevent abuse of this mechanism, including:

- [4:57] An attorney "*independently representing* the defendant" must sign a *certificate* that he or she has advised the defendant with respect to the waiver of rights and defenses under the confession of judgment procedure and had advised defendant to utilize the procedure. [See CCP §1132(b)]

- [4:58] Defendant must sign an *affidavit* authorizing the entry of judgment for a specific sum, stating concisely the facts showing that the sum confessed is "justly due." [See CCP §1133]

(2) [4:59] **Strictly construed:** These requirements are strictly construed; failure to comply invalidates a judgment entered by confession. [*Rivercourt Co., Ltd. v. Dyna-Tel, Inc.* (1996) 41 CA4th 1477, 1482, 49 CR2d

279, 282—attorney with conflict of interest could not be considered "independent counsel" and therefore could not supply certificate required by §1132(b); *Efstratis v. First Northern Bank of Dixon* (1997) 59 CA4th 667, 674, 69 CR2d 445, 449—certificate by attorney who was also the defendant rendered confessed judgment invalid]

⮕[4:60] *PRACTICE POINTER:* Attorneys often have problems obtaining a judgment based solely on a confessed judgment. Because the procedure is not widely used, court clerks are usually not familiar with their power to enter judgment (see CCP §1134). If the matter is referred to the court, many judges regard a confessed judgment as an "extreme procedure" and look upon it with disfavor.

[4:61-64] *Reserved.*

## B. ISSUANCE OF SUMMONS

1. [4:65] **General Procedure:** Blank summons forms are available from the clerk of each court or on the court's Web site. The summons is usually a Judicial Council form; *see* ¶4:76.

   • [4:66] Plaintiff's counsel fills in the blanks showing counsel's name and address, and the names of each party plaintiff and defendant named in the complaint. Then, any time after commencing the action (and paying the requisite filing fees), the court clerk will "issue" summons at the request of plaintiff's counsel. [CCP §412.10; *Maginn v. City of Glendale* (1999) 72 CA4th 1102, 1107, 85 CR2d 639, 643 (citing text)]

   • [4:67] The clerk "issues" summons simply by affixing a signature or stamp to the form prepared by plaintiff's counsel, and returning it to counsel. (The court's seal will also be affixed at time of issuance, although most courts today supply blank forms upon which facsimile seals are imprinted in advance.)

   If local rules permit electronic filings, the court may electronically transmit to the party filing the complaint a summons with the court seal and case number. [See CCP §1010.6(a)(5), *discussed at* ¶9:90.56]

   • [4:68] Copies of the summons are then conformed to show the clerk's signature and date of issuance. The copies are then available for service on the defendants (¶4:110 ff.); the original is normally returned to the court with proof of service of such copies (¶4:360 ff.).

   [4:69] *Reserved.*

2. **[4:70] Amended Summons:** An amended summons is necessary only when the complaint is amended to add a *new party* defendant (as distinguished from amendments substituting the defendant's true name for a "Doe"). In such a case, a new summons is required because the new party is not named in the original; hence service of the original would not confer jurisdiction. [CCP §412.10, comment]

   a. **[4:71] Not required for defendants named in original summons:** But there is no need for an amended summons against a defendant named in the original summons (as a "Doe" or otherwise) . . . even if the complaint is amended before service. I.e., the summons issued on the *original* complaint can be served together with the *amended* complaint. [*Gillette v. Burbank Comm. Hosp.* (1976) 56 CA3d 430, 433-434, 128 CR 636, 637-638]

   ➪**[4:72] *PRACTICE POINTER:*** According to the Judicial Council, the preferred practice in such a case is to obtain issuance of a "summons on amended complaint." [See CCP §412.10, "comment—amendment" of summons] However, this is not actually required according to the *Gillette* case, supra.

3. **[4:73] Replacement Summons:** If the original summons is lost or destroyed, the clerk of the court will simply issue another to replace it, at the request of plaintiff's counsel. No court order or showing of any kind is required. [CCP §412.10, comment—"alias" summons eliminated]

   **[4:74]** *Reserved.*

## C. CONTENT OF SUMMONS

1. **[4:75] Civil Actions Generally:** The following information is required in a summons issued in civil actions generally, under CCP §412.20(a):

   • **Warning to defendant:** In boldface print at the *top* of the summons, in both English and Spanish: "Notice! You have been sued. The court may decide against you without your being heard unless you respond within 30 days. Read information below." [CCP §412.20(a)(6)]

      **Other languages:** The above warning must appear in both English and Spanish. In addition, each county, by ordinance, may require such warning in any other foreign language. [CCP §412.20(b)] (So far as is known, however, none have done so.)

   • **Title of the court** in which the action is pending. [CCP §412.20(a)(1)]

Rev. #1 2003

- **Names of all parties** (each plaintiff, and each defendant named in the complaint; i.e., *no* "et al."). [CCP §412.20(a)(2)]

  If there is not enough room for all names on the summons form, an "additional parties attachment" form must be used. *See Form 4:A.1.*

- **Notice that responsive pleading must be filed:** The summons must notify defendant that he or she has 30 days after service within which to file a written pleading; that his or her default may be taken if he or she fails to do so; that he or she may may seek an attorney's advice, and this should be done promptly so that a pleading may be filed within the time required. [See CCP §412.20(a)(3)-(5) for required wording]

a. [4:76] **Use of Official Forms satisfies these requirements:** Use of the Official Form Summons approved by the Judicial Council, with the proper information inserted in the blanks, automatically satisfies the above requirements. [See CCP §412.20(c); and *Form 4:A*]

   (1) [4:77] *Caution:* Make sure you use the *most current* version of the Official forms. Use of outdated Summons forms may result in defective service.

   ⇨[4:78] *PRACTICE POINTER:* All Official forms are available online at: http://www.courtinfo.ca.gov/forms.

b. [4:79] **Date on summons not important:** All summons forms have a place for insertion of the date they are issued. But the date is *not* required by CCP §412.20(a), above. Thus, failure to include the date, or even *misdating* a summons, does not affect its validity. [*Hibernia Sav. & Loan v. Churchill* (1900) 128 C 633, 635, 61 P 278, 279; *Ystrom v. Handel* (1988) 205 CA3d 144, 152, 252 CR 110, 114]

2. [4:80] **Actions With Special Summons Requirements:** There are a few actions in which there are special summons requirements, including:

a. [4:81] **Unlawful detainer proceedings:** Unlawful detainer defendants have 5 days to respond (instead of 30). [CCP §1167; see ¶6:386]

   There is no due process violation in a shortened time for response. [See *Deal v. Mun.Ct.* (1984) 157 CA3d 991, 997, 204 CR 79, 82]

   A *different summons form* is used in unlawful detainer proceedings. See Friedman, Garcia & Hagarty, *Cal. Prac. Guide: Landlord Tenant* (TRG), Ch. 8.

b. [4:82] **Joint debtor proceedings.** [CCP §§989-991]

A *different summons form* is used in joint debtor proceedings. See Ahart, *Cal. Prac. Guide: Enforcing Judgments and Debts* (TRG), Ch. 6G.

c. [4:83] **Family law proceedings:** *Different summons forms* are used in family law proceedings. See Hogoboom & King, *Cal. Prac. Guide: Family Law* (TRG), Ch. 3.

d. [4:84] **Probate revocation and will contests:** A *different summons form* is used in probate revocation and will contest proceedings. See Ross, *Cal. Prac. Guide: Probate* (TRG), Chs. 3 & 15.

e. [4:85] **Eminent domain proceedings:** A description of the property is required if the summons is to be served by publication. [CCP §1250.120(b)]

f. [4:86] **Suits to establish title:** Where land records are destroyed, there are distinct summons requirements for actions to prove title. [See CCP §751.05]

Actions to determine adverse interests in real property arising out of public improvement assessments and bonds also have specific statutory summons requirements. [See CCP §801.6]

g. [4:87] **Forfeiture proceedings:** No summons is required in proceedings for forfeiture of property involved in criminal activities. Instead, notice must be given as provided in Health & Saf.C. §11488.4. [*People v. Mendocino County Assessor's Parcel No. 056-500-09* (1997) 58 CA4th 120, 126, 68 CR2d 51, 53]

h. [4:88] **Challenging acts of public agency:** In proceedings challenging official action by a public agency (so-called "reverse validation actions"), the form and manner of service of summons is governed by CCP §861.1. A shorter time for response is authorized (minimum 10 days). [See *County of Riverside v. Sup.Ct. (Hill)* (1997) 54 CA4th 443, 445, 62 CR2d 747, 748—challenges to redevelopment project]

[4:89] *Reserved.*

3. [4:90] **Notice re Capacity in Which Person Served:** The summons itself must notify the person to whom it is delivered of the capacity in which he or she is being served, if not named as a defendant therein or if he or she is being served on behalf of another.

The Official Form Summons (*see Form 4:A*) contains the following provision for such notice:

NOTICE TO THE PERSON SERVED: You are served
1. ❏ As an individual defendant.
2. ❏ As the person sued under the fictitious name of:

.................................................................................
3. ❏ On behalf of ......................................................

Under: ❏ CCP 416.10 (Corporation)
❏ CCP 416.20 (Defunct Corporation)
❏ CCP 416.40 (Association or Partnership)
❏ CCP 416.60 (Minor)
❏ CCP 416.70 (Conservatee)
❏ CCP 416.90 (Individual)
❏ Other:
4. ❏ By personal delivery on (Date): .......................

➭[4:91] **PRACTICE POINTER:** This provision is usually left blank when the summons is issued, because the contents may vary for each defendant. Therefore, when a copy of the summons is sent out for service, it is up to plaintiff's counsel to *make sure that this provision is filled in correctly before service.* Failure to do so leads to problems as noted in the cases below.

a. **[4:92] Actions against corporations, partnerships or limited liability companies:** In an action against a corporation, partnership, limited liability company (see Corps.C. §17000 et seq.) or other unincorporated association, the summons form itself must notify the person to whom it is delivered that he or she is being served *on behalf of* a specific entity-defendant (and also individually, if such is the case). [CCP §412.30]

➭[4:93] **PRACTICE POINTER re serving limited liability companies:** Until the summons forms are revised to include limited liability companies, use the "other" block on the summons form (see above) and *write in* "Corps.C. §17061 (service on Limited Liability Company)" in the space provided when serving such an entity.

(1) **[4:94] Notice must appear on summons itself:** It is not enough that the corporation or partnership is named as a defendant in the action.

Nor is it material that the process server *told* the person served that he or she was being sued on behalf of the entity-defendant. "It is the summons, not the process server, which asserts judicial power." [*MJS Enterprises, Inc. v. Sup.Ct. (Serpa)* (1984) 153 CA3d 555, 558, 200 CR 286, 288—default judgment against corporation void for lack of jurisdiction]

(2) [4:95]  **Substantial compliance sufficient:**  However, substantial compliance with CCP §412.30 is all that is necessary. Slight defects may be overlooked if the entity-defendant had actual notice of the lawsuit, and the summons itself was such that the entity must *reasonably* have known that the summons was being directed to it. [*Cory v. Crocker Nat'l Bk.* (1981) 123 CA3d 665, 669, 177 CR 150, 153; *Dill v. Berquist Const. Co., Inc.* (1994) 24 CA4th 1426, 1436-1437, 29 CR2d 746, 751-752]

  (a) [4:96]  **Example:**  Bank was the only defendant named in a summons served on one of its officers. The notice paragraph read:

> "NOTICE TO THE PERSON SERVED:   You are served ....
> "1.......
> "2.......
> "3. ❑ On behalf of ... (blank) ......"
> "Under ☒ CCP 416.10 (Corporation)."

  The summons was technically defective because Bank's name was omitted from the notice paragraph. However, since Bank was the only corporation named in the summons, it could not have been misled by the omission. [*Cory v. Crocker Nat'l Bk.,* supra]

  (b) [4:97]  **Compare—summons incomplete:**  P amended his complaint to name Mannesmann, Inc. as a "Doe" defendant. P then delivered the amended complaint and summons to a corporate officer of Mannesmann, Inc. But the summons *did not name the corporation* and *none of the notice boxes were checked* (so that the person served would not know he was being served on behalf of a corporation). The summons was so incomplete that there was no valid service. [*Mannesmann Demag, Ltd. v. Sup.Ct. (Welch)* (1985) 172 CA3d 1118, 1124, 218 CR 632, 636]

  • [4:98]  It was irrelevant that Mannesmann, Inc. had actual notice of the action (by reason of correspondence between its lawyer and P's lawyer): "Notice of the litigation does not confer personal jurisdiction absent substantial compliance with the statutory requirements for service of summons." [*Mannesmann Demag, Ltd. v. Sup.Ct. (Welch)*, supra, 172 CA3d at 1124, 218 CR at 636]

  (c) [4:99]  **Compare—failure to serve authorized person:**  There is no "substantial compliance" where plaintiff fails to direct the summons toward a person who can be served on the corporation's behalf under CCP §416.10(b). [*Dill v. Berquist Const. Co., Inc.* (1994) 24 CA4th 1426, 1439, 29 CR2d 746, 753, fn. 12]

- **[4:100]** It was *not* "substantial compliance" to deliver summons to a corporate employee where there was no evidence that he or she was an officer or authorized to receive service on the corporation's behalf. It was immaterial that the employee had "acknowledged receipt" by the corporation. [*Dill v. Berquist Const. Co., Inc.*, supra, 24 CA4th at 1438-1439, 29 CR2d at 753]

b.  **[4:101]** **Actions against "Doe" defendants:** Where the summons and complaint name "Doe" defendants, the summons itself must notify the person served that he or she is being served as "Doe 1" or "Doe 2," etc. [CCP §474]

(1) **[4:102]** **Corporation served as "Doe":** A corporation may be served as a "Doe" ... but in such event, the summons must notify the person served *both* that he or she is being served on behalf of a specific corporation, *and* that the corporation is being served as a specific "Doe." [*Schering Corp. v. Sup.Ct. (Ingraham)* (1975) 52 CA3d 737, 742, 125 CR 337, 340]

(a) **[4:103]** **Example:** Summons in a product liability action named Supplier and several "Doe" defendants. Later, plaintiff attempted to join Manufacturer as "Doe 1" by serving summons on its local agent. The notice paragraph read:

> "NOTICE TO THE PERSON SERVED: You are served ....
> "1.......
> "2. ❑ As the person sued under the fictitious name of ... DOE 1 .......
> "3. ❑ On behalf of ...(blank) ...
> Under ☒ CCP 416.10 (Corporation)."

The summons was defective because it failed to name Manufacturer as the party to whom it was directed (Manufacturer's name should have been inserted in paragraph "3"). It was *immaterial* that the process server *told* the person served that he was being served on behalf of Manufacturer. [*Schering Corp. v. Sup.Ct. (Ingraham)*, supra]

**[4:104-109]** *Reserved.*

## D. SERVICE OF SUMMONS

1. **[4:110] Who May Serve Summons:** "Any person who is at least 18 years of age, and not a party to the action" may serve a summons. [CCP §414.10]

   a. **[4:111] Peace officers:** Certain public officers are specially authorized by law to serve process in civil actions; e.g., sheriffs and marshals. [Gov.C. §26665]

   b. **[4:112] Private individuals:** Anyone over 18 years old who is not a party may serve summons. They need *not* be a professional process server.

      (1) **[4:113] Plaintiff's lawyer may serve:** It follows that summons can be served upon the defendant by plaintiff's counsel. [*Sheehan v. All Persons, etc.* (1926) 80 CA 393, 398, 252 P 337, 339]

      ➪**[4:114] PRACTICE POINTER:** However, it is *not* a good practice for plaintiff's lawyer to serve summons. If any factual issue arises as to the service, the lawyer would have to testify as a witness; and by so doing, limit his or her effectiveness in arguing the issue.

      (2) **[4:115] Persons protected by TRO deemed "party":** A named person protected by a temporary restraining order may be *deemed a party* to the action and thus incapable of service of process. Reason: This supports public policy of separating persons who may be involved in violence toward each other. [*Caldwell v. Coppola* (1990) 219 CA3d 859, 865, 268 CR 453, 456— D enjoined from harassing P or *Sister* living with her: Sister could not serve D]

      (3) **[4:116] Compare—effect of process server registration requirement:** Persons who frequently serve process are required to file a registration certificate and bond with the State. [See Bus. & Prof.C. §22350 for requirements and exemptions for attorneys, private investigators, etc.] In any event, the process server's failure to register *does not invalidate* an otherwise proper service. [CCP §413.40]

2. **[4:117] Fees for Serving Summons:** The fee payable to a sheriff or marshal for serving summons is set by law (Gov.C. §26721). Private process servers frequently charge more.

   a. **[4:118] Recoverability as court costs:** Service fees are recoverable as court costs if plaintiff obtains judgment.

- [4:119]   If service is by a *sheriff or marshal*, the amount recoverable is that officer's statutory fee at the time of service. [CCP §1033.5(a)(4)(A)]

- [4:120]   If service is by a *registered process server*, plaintiff can recover whatever fees were actually incurred to effect service—including, but not limited to, costs of a stake-out or other means employed in locating the person to be served. (But the defendant may challenge such costs as not "reasonably necessary.") [CCP §1033.5(a)(4)(B) & (c)]

3. [4:121]   **Upon Whom Service May be Made:**   The Code specifies the various methods by which service may be made upon individuals, corporations and other entities.

   a. [4:122]   **Individuals:**   Individual defendants are served by delivering copies of the summons and complaint to them personally or to someone else authorized by law to accept summons on their behalf.

      (1) [4:123]   **Minors:**   If the defendant is a child, service must be made on the parent or guardian; or if none can be located after reasonable efforts, on any other person having care or control of the child, or with whom the child resides or by whom the child is employed. [CCP §416.60; see *Dill v. Berquist Const. Co., Inc.* (1994) 24 CA4th 1426, 1436, 29 CR2d 746, 751, fn. 7]

      And, if the child is age *12 years* or older, *an additional copy* must be served on the child. [CCP §416.60]

      (2) [4:124]   **Wards and conservatees:**   If a person (other than a minor) has been *adjudicated* incompetent or in need of a conservator, and a guardian or conservator appointed, summons must be served on *both* the ward or conservatee and upon his or her guardian or conservator. [CCP §416.70; see *Dill v. Berquist Const. Co., Inc.* (1994) 24 CA4th 1426, 1436, 29 CR2d 746, 751, fn. 7]

      The court may dispense with the requirement for service on the ward or conservatee if it finds that person so incompetent as to be unable to understand the nature of the documents served; or that the service might be harmful to his or her mental state. [See CCP §416.70, comment]

         (a) [4:125]   **Compare—persons not adjudicated incompetent:**   Until a defendant has been *adjudicated* incompetent or in need of a conservator, he or she can be served as any other individual, by delivery of summons.

⇨[4:126] ***PRACTICE POINTER:*** However, *it may be difficult to sustain a default* taken against a person with mental disorders. Judges are likely to set aside defaults where it is shown that at the time of service, the defendant was incapable of managing his or her own affairs, even if no formal adjudication of incompetency had been made.

Consequently in such cases, plaintiff's counsel should make sure that copies of the summons and complaint (or other notice of the lawsuit) are also given to *other persons* likely to be concerned with the defendant's interests: e.g., attorneys, insurance carriers, family members, etc.

(3) [4:127] **Political candidates:** A special statute applies in actions against a political candidate relating to his or her candidacy or the election laws. If the candidate cannot be served after reasonable diligence, plaintiff's counsel may obtain a *court order* authorizing service of summons on the Secretary of State or a county clerk. [CCP §416.80; see Elec.C. §12]

(4) [4:128] **Agents to accept service of process:** An individual may also be served by delivering summons and complaint to someone authorized to accept service on his or her behalf. [See CCP §416.90]

Such authority may be *actual* (by appointment) or *implied* (ostensible), as where defendant causes it to appear that another has been authorized to accept service on his or her behalf. [See *Warner Bros. Records, Inc. v. Golden West Music Sales* (1974) 36 CA3d 1012, 1018, 112 CR 71, 75]

*Compare—substitute service:* By contrast, substitute service on *entity defendants* may be effected by leaving summons with secretaries, receptionists, doorkeepers, or other persons "apparently in charge" of the premises (*see ¶4:193*). They need not be authorized to accept summons on defendant's behalf.

⇨[4:129] ***PRACTICE POINTER:*** When such a person bars access to premises of an entity defendant, the best course is to *serve that person* with a summons completed for substitute service and follow this with the required mailing (*¶4:218*).

(a) [4:130] The mere fact that a person is another's agent for *business matters* is generally *not* enough to establish actual or implied authority to accept service of process ... even if the lawsuit is related to the business matters. [*Warner Bros. Records, Inc. v. Golden West Music Sales*, supra]

(b) [4:131]   Nor is service on a person's *lawyer* sufficient if that lawyer is not specifically authorized to accept service in the action. The fact the defendant *knows* the lawsuit is pending does not excuse service of summons requirements. [See *Zirbes v. Stratton* (1986) 187 CA3d 1407, 1416-1417, 232 CR 653, 659]

(5) [4:132]   **Prisoners:**   Summons directed to a prisoner may be served on the sheriff or jailer having custody of the prisoner. The sheriff or jailer must "forthwith" deliver such papers to the prisoner. [See Pen.C. §4013; CCP §416.90]

(6) [4:133]   **Decedent's liability covered by insurance:** In actions filed against a decedent's estate to establish the decedent's liability on a claim covered by liability insurance (e.g., personal injury claims against decedent), the decedent's executor or administrator need not be joined as a party (*see ¶2:127*). Summons may be served on a *person designated in writing by the decedent's liability insurer;* or if none is designated, on the insurer itself. Plaintiff's recovery is limited, however, to the amount of the insurance. [Prob.C. §552(a)]

*Cross-refer:* For further discussion of such proceedings, see Ross, *Cal. Prac. Guide: Probate* (TRG), Ch. 8.

(7) [4:134]   **Compare—service on "Doe" defendants:** Special rules apply where the complaint names "Doe" defendants (*see ¶6:86 ff.*) and plaintiff wants to serve someone as a "Doe":

- *Notice requirement:* The summons (or first pleading) served on that person must contain a notice stating substantially as follows:

  "TO THE PERSON SERVED; YOU ARE HEREBY SERVED IN THE WITHIN ACTION AS THE PERSON SUED UNDER THE FICTITIOUS NAME OF (DOE)." [CCP §474; *see ¶6:88*]

- *Return of service requirement:* The affidavit of service must state the name under which the person was served and the fact that the above notice was endorsed upon the summons. [CCP §474; *see ¶4:369*]

Failure to comply with these requirements prevents entry of default or default judgment against the person served. [CCP §474]

b. [4:135] **Corporations:** Effecting service upon a corporation requires delivery of summons and complaint to some person *on behalf of* the corporation. [*Dill v. Berquist Const. Co., Inc.* (1994) 24 CA4th 1426, 1437, 29 CR2d 746, 752]

It must appear from the allegations of the complaint or summons that the defendant is in fact a corporation. Otherwise, no one can be served on its behalf (i.e., as a representative of the corporation). [*Earl W. Schott, Inc. v. Kalar* (1993) 20 CA4th 943, 946, 24 CR2d 580, 582]

It must also appear that the person served is *in fact* a person who may be served on behalf of the corporation, as discussed below. [*Dill v. Berquist Const. Co., Inc.*, supra, 24 CA4th at 1437, 29 CR2d at 752]

🢭[4:136] *PRACTICE POINTER—Serving Foreign Corporations:* Many foreign corporations do business in California and, if so, can be served in the state by serving a "general manager" located in the state (*see* ¶4:139). If there is no such manager, check whether an agent for service of process has been appointed (*see* ¶4:140 ff.). If no such agent has been appointed and the corporation is doing business in California, service on the Secretary of State may be appropriate (*see* ¶4:147 ff.).

(1) [4:137] **Officers of the corporation:** Service may be made upon "the president, or other head of the corporation, a vice president, a secretary or assistant secretary, a treasurer or assistant treasurer, a general manager . . ." [CCP §416.10(b)]

For out-of-state or foreign corporations, service may be made on "any officer of the corporation or its general manager in this state." [Corps.C. §2110; see *In re Title U.S.A. Ins. Corp.* (1995) 36 CA4th 363, 368, 42 CR2d 498, 500-501—officer served need not be authorized to appear in court on corporation's behalf]

(a) [4:138] **Bank officers:** And, if the corporation is a bank, service may *also* be made on " . . . a cashier or assistant cashier . . ." [CCP §416.10(c); Corps.C. §2110—foreign corporations]

(b) [4:139] **"General manager":** Service is valid if the person served as "general manager" is *apparently in charge* of the corporation's office or headquarters, as long as the person served is of such rank to make it reasonably certain that the corporation will be apprised of service. [See *Roehl v. Texas Co.* (1930) 107 CA 691, 291 P 255, 261; *Gibble v. Car-Lene Research, Inc.* (1998) 67 CA4th 295, 302-303, 78 CR2d 892, 896—manager of regional office]

(2) **[4:140]** **Agents for service of process:** Service may *also* be made upon " . . . any person authorized by the corporation to receive service of process." [CCP §416.10(b); Corps.C. §2110—foreign corporations]

(a) **[4:141]** **Designated agents:** This includes persons who are designated as the corporation's agent for service of process in various statements which a domestic or foreign corporation is required to file with the Secretary of State under various provisions of the Corporations Code. [See CCP §416.10(a)]

California corporations are required to appoint a local agent for service of process in their articles of incorporation and biennial information statement filed with the Secretary of State (see Corps.C. §§202(c), 1502). Foreign corporations must do likewise in order to "qualify" to do business here (see Corps.C. §§2105, 1505).

Similar requirements exist for out-of-state insurance companies. [See Ins.C. §§1600, 1602, 1603]

(b) **[4:142]** **Implied authority:** Again, the authority to accept service may be actual or implied (ostensible). Thus, where the corporation holds a certain person out as one of its principal officers, that person may be held to have *ostensible* authority to receive service of summons on the corporation's behalf . . . even if such person actually held no office at the time. [*Pasadena Medi-Center Associates v. Sup.Ct. (Houts)* (1973) 9 C3d 773, 777, 108 CR 828, 831]

• **[4:143]** The fact a person is authorized *to receive mail* on behalf of a corporation and to sign postal receipts acknowledging delivery does *not* mean he or she is authorized *to receive process* on behalf of the corporation that is served by mail. [*Dill v. Berquist Const. Co., Inc.* (1994) 24 CA4th 1426, 1437, 29 CR2d 746, 752]

**[4:144]** *Reserved.*

(c) **[4:145]** **Compare—agency cannot be proved by agent's statements alone:** Actual or ostensible agency cannot be based exclusively on statements or conduct by the purported agent in the absence of the purported principal. [*Dill v. Berquist Const. Co., Inc.* (1994) 24 CA4th 1426, 1437, 29 CR2d 746, 752]

- **[4:146]** Summons was sought to be served on an out-of-state corporation by certified mail addressed to the corporation (under CCP §415.40, *see* ¶4:292). The service was invalid because not addressed to a *person* upon whom service could be made on the corporation's behalf. The fact someone signed the postal receipt as "agent" for the corporation did *not* establish that person as the corporation's agent for service of process. [*Dill v. Berquist Const. Co., Inc.*, supra, 24 CA4th at 1437-1438, 29 CR2d at 752]

(3) **[4:147]** **Secretary of State:** If, despite reasonable diligence, *summons cannot be served* on any of the foregoing, service may be made on the Secretary of State as provided herein (see CCP §416.10(d)):

(a) **[4:148]** **Procedure as to California corporations:** Plaintiff's counsel must first obtain a court *order* authorizing hand delivery to the Secretary of State or the Secretary's assistant or deputy. (The order may be that of a federal court or the court of another state in which the action or proceeding has been filed.) [Corps.C. §1702(a),(d)]

1) **[4:149]** **Showing required:** The court order must be based upon a factual showing (affidavits or declarations) that the corporate defendant either (a) has failed to file with the Secretary of State the annual statement of names and addresses of corporate officers and agents for service of process required by Corporations Code §1502; or (b) that the designated officers or agents cannot be found after diligent search. [Corps.C. §1702(a)]

2) **[4:150]** **When service effective:** Service upon the corporation is deemed complete *10 days after* delivery to the Secretary of State (so that the corporation has until 40 days thereafter to respond). [Corps.C. §1702(a)]

(b) **[4:151]** **Procedure as to out-of-state corporations:** In addition to the procedure outlined above, plaintiff's counsel must make a factual showing (affidavits or declarations) that the corporation is "doing business" in California, or otherwise has sufficient "contacts" with California to be subject to personal jurisdiction. [Corps.C. §2111(a)] (Foreign corporations doing business in California are required to file biennial statements designating a local agent for service of process; see Corps.C. §§2105(a), 1502(a),(b).)

(c) [4:152] **Out-of-state insurance companies:** Foreign insurers doing business in California must stipulate to service on the Insurance Commissioner under certain circumstances. [See Ins.C. §§1604, 12931]

Foreign insurers are also required to designate a local agent for service of process. *See ¶4:141.*

⇨[4:153] *PRACTICE POINTER:* The above procedures are rarely necessary. First of all, if the corporation is represented by local counsel or an insurance company, it's a good idea to call and ask if the corporation will authorize them to accept service on its behalf. The corporation may agree ... in which event, you will save yourself the effort and expense of getting a court order and serving the Secretary of State.

Moreover, you can serve a *nonresident* by certified or registered mail with return receipt requested. [CCP §415.40; *see ¶4:293-304*] So, in an action against an out-of-state corporation, service on the Secretary of State is rarely required.

(4) [4:154] **Compare—defunct corporation:** If the corporation's charter or right to do business has been revoked, or the corporation dissolved, summons can be served either on:

(a) The person who is *trustee* of the corporation and of its stockholders or members (CCP §416.20(a)); or

(b) Any officer, director or other person having custody or control of its assets; or

(c) If no such person can be found, then upon "any agent upon whom process could have been served at the time of dissolution"; or if none can be found, upon proper showing of diligence, a court order may be obtained authorizing service on the Secretary of State. [CCP §416.20(b)]

[4:155-159] *Reserved.*

(5) [4:160] **Compare—suspended corporation:** A corporation that has been suspended but continues to

operate as an ongoing business may be served under CCP §416.10, like any other corporation (*see ¶4:135 ff.*). [*Gibble v. Car-Lene Research, Inc.* (1998) 67 CA4th 295, 302, 78 CR2d 892, 896; *Schwab v. Southern Calif. Gas Co.* (2004) 114 CA4th 1308, 1320, 8 CR3d 627, 635, fn. 9]

(6) [4:161] **Compare—joint stock company:** Service is made in the same way and on the same persons as a corporation (both existing corporations and defunct corporations; see above). [CCP §416.30]

c. [4:162] **Partnerships and other unincorporated associations:** Service can be made upon such entities by delivering copies of the summons and complaint to:

(1) [4:163] **Partner or officer:** If the defendant is a partnership, summons may be delivered to any *general* partner, or to the *general manager* of the partnership business. [CCP §416.40(a)]

If the defendant is any other unincorporated association (union, homeowners' association, etc.), summons may be delivered to the president or other head of the association; a vice president; a secretary or assistant secretary; treasurer or assistant treasurer; or general manager. [CCP §416.40(b)]

(2) [4:164] **Designated agent:** Alternatively, summons may be delivered to any person designated as its agent for service of process. [CCP §416.40(a),(b); Corps.C. §24003]

(a) [4:165] **When required:** A *California* partnership or unincorporated association *may* file a statement with the Secretary of State designating its agent for service of process; but such filing is *not* required. [See CCP §416.40(a),(b); Corps.C. §24003]

However, an *out-of-state partnership or association* doing business in California is *required* to file with the Secretary of State a statement designating a local agent for service of process. [Corps.C. §15800]

(b) [4:166] **Effect of failure to designate:** If the out-of-state partnership fails to do so, summons may be served on the Secretary of State (no court order required). [CCP §416.40(c); Corps.C. §15800]

But the rule is different as to California partnerships or associations: If they fail to designate an agent for service of process (under Corps.C. §24003), *and* if delivery to other authorized persons *cannot be effected* despite "reasonable diligence," plaintiff's counsel may, based on a showing of these facts, obtain a *court order* authorizing service on *any one* of the members of the partnership or association, *plus mailing* to its last known business address. [CCP §416.40(c); Corps.C. §24007]

[4:167-169]  *Reserved.*

d.  [4:170]  **Limited liability companies:**  Like a corporation, a limited liability company is required to designate an agent for service of process on the information form filed biennially with the Secretary of State. [Corps.C. §17060(a)(2)]

(1) [4:171]  **Designated agent:**  Service on a limited liability company is effected by serving the person designated as its agent for service of process. (If its designated agent is a corporation, service must be made on the person listed as the corporation's agent for service of process on its information return filed with the Secretary of State.) [Corps.C. §17061(b)]

(a) [4:172]  **Method of service:**  The designated agent may be served either by personal service (CCP §415.10, ¶*4:184 ff.*); substitute service (CCP §415.20(a), ¶*4:193 ff.*); or service by mail with acknowledgment of receipt (CCP §415.30(a), ¶*4:225 ff.*).

(2) [4:173]  **Secretary of State:**  If an affidavit shows that the designated agent has resigned or cannot be located or that service cannot be effected by any of the methods stated above, the court may order service on a limited liability company made by delivery to the Secretary of State, together with a copy of the order authorizing such service. [Corps.C. §17061(c)(1)]

e.  **Public entities**

(1) [4:174]  **Actions against State:**  In an action against the State, service of summons must be made upon the Attorney General. [Gov.C. §955.4] (There are a few exceptions in which service may be made on the Attorney General *or* some other specified state official; see Gov.C. §§955.6 and 955.8; and Gov.C. §8880.72 for actions against State Lottery Commission.)

(2) [4:175]  **Against local agencies:**  In suits against any other public authority or agency, service may be made by delivering copies of the summons and complaint to "the clerk, secretary, president, presiding officer or other head of its governing body." [CCP §416.50(a);

see *Wagner v. City of South Pasadena* (2000) 78 CA4th 943, 951, 93 CR2d 91, 96-97—service on associate in law firm representing city insufficient]

⇨[4:176]  ***PRACTICE POINTER:***  The Secretary of State maintains a *Roster of Public Agencies*, and every public entity is required to submit the names and addresses of its governing board members and officers for inclusion in said roster. [Gov.C. §§53050, 53051]

In addition, the county clerk of each county is required to maintain a similar roster for those public agencies having offices within the county. [Gov.C. §53051(c)]

Consequently, always consult one of these rosters before attempting service on a public entity defendant. This will assure valid service on the defendant. (Also, the roster listing will give you the exact name of the agency, so that you can make sure you are suing it by its correct name.)

[4:177-179]  *Reserved.*

4.  [4:180]  **Manner of Service:**  The manner in which summons must be served depends on the following:

- [4:181]  **Service within California:**  CCP §415.10 et seq. prescribes four basic methods:

    (1)  Personal delivery to defendant (¶*4:184 ff.*);

    (2)  Delivery to someone else at defendant's usual residence or place of business (¶*4:193 ff.*);

    (3)  Service by mail coupled with acknowledgment of receipt (¶*4:225 ff.*);

    (4)  Service by publication (¶*4:245 ff.*).

- [4:182]  **Service elsewhere in U.S.:**  Summons may be delivered by any of the four methods listed above; *or* by registered or certified mail with return receipt requested (¶*4:293-299*); *or* any other method prescribed by the law of the place where the person is served. [CCP §413.10(b), ¶*4:292*]

- [4:183]  **Service outside the U.S.:**  In countries which have signed the Hague Convention on Service of Process, summons must be served in the manner provided by that Convention (*see* ¶*4:316 ff.*). Service may also be possible under the Inter-American Convention on Letters Rogatory (*see* ¶*4:334 ff.*).

Rev. #1 2004

Otherwise, summons may be delivered by any of the methods listed in the preceding paragraph; but "any other method" prescribed by the foreign country is valid only if the court finds (before or after such service) that the method was "reasonably calculated to give actual notice." [CCP §413.10(c), ¶4:315]

a. **[4:184]** **Personal delivery to defendant or authorized agent ("personal service"):** Delivering copies of the summons and complaint to defendant personally constitutes "personal service" of summons. [CCP §415.10]

Delivery to agents authorized to accept service on defendants' behalf also constitutes "personal service" of the summons and complaint.

(1) **[4:185]** **Advantages:** Personal service is the simplest method because service is complete at the time of delivery. [CCP §415.10]

- Since defendant's time to respond is measured from the date service is complete (¶5:22 ff.), personal service puts defendant under more time pressure than other methods of service. (As discussed below, other forms of service are not complete until some period of time after mailing or publication, so that defendant has 30 days from this later date to respond.)

- Personal service gives defendant less opportunity to claim lack of notice of the action.

- Also, the 10-day "hold" on plaintiff commencing discovery (20 days for noticing depositions) is measured from "service" of summons; *see* ¶8:39.6. Personal service thus puts plaintiff in a position to commence discovery sooner.

[4:186] *Reserved.*

(2) **[4:187]** **Effect of defendant's refusal to accept:** As long as the process server identifies himself or herself and tells the reluctant defendant that he or she is being served with process, and leaves the papers as close as possible to the defendant, service is valid notwithstanding the defendant's refusal to accept. [*Trujillo v. Trujillo* (1945) 71 CA2d 257, 260, 162 P2d 640, 641]

In fact, *personal* service may occur in these circumstances even when the process server is attempting *substituted* service (*see* ¶4:193 ff.). [See *Stafford v. Mach* (1998) 64 CA4th 1174, 1183, 75 CR2d 809, 814—defendant denied identity, but process server noted in proof of service description matching defendant]

*Compare:* The result is different, of course, where defendant did not refuse to accept the papers and was not attempting to flee or otherwise evade service. In such cases, dropping the papers nearby or delivering them to someone else is not sufficient. [See *Sternbeck v. Buck* (1957) 148 CA2d 829, 833, 307 P2d 970, 972— no valid service on Husband where process server delivered papers to Wife instead of to Husband, who was working 100 feet away out of process server's sight]

(a) **[4:188]** **Effect of third party helping to evade service:** One who intentionally aids another to evade service of process may apparently be punished for contempt for "interference with the process or proceedings of a court." [CCP §1209(a)(8); see *In re Holmes* (1983) 145 CA3d 934, 944, 193 CR 790, 797—helping spouse to evade service of *subpoena* held punishable contempt]

(b) **[4:189]** **Service in gated communities:** Guards at gated communities must allow peace officers and licensed process servers access for the purpose of serving process, upon proper identification. [See CCP §415.21]

If access is refused, *substitute service* may be made upon the gate guard. [*Bein v. Brechtel-Jochim Group, Inc.* (1992) 6 CA4th 1387, 1393, 8 CR2d 351, 354; see ¶*4:213*]

(3) **[4:190]** **Original summons not necessary:** Service is effected by delivering a *copy* of the summons issued by the court. The original summons (bearing the clerk's signature and court seal) does *not* have to be shown to the defendant, nor even be in the process server's possession. [*Torgersen v. Smith* (1979) 98 CA3d 948, 952, 159 CR 781, 783 (disapproved on other grounds in *Johnson & Johnson v. Sup.Ct. (Lawton)* (1985) 38 C3d 243, 254-255, 211 CR 517, 524, fn. 7)— upholding service where original summons had inadvertently been returned to court *before* service; *Ystrom v. Handel* (1988) 205 CA3d 144, 151-152, 252 CR 110, 114—upholding service of *copy* of conformed copy of summons accompanied by "Declaration of Lost Original Summons"]

(4) **[4:191]** **Date of service to be shown on copy:** The process server is required to place the date of service on the copy served at the time of its delivery. (The purpose is to assist the person served in determining when

his or her responsive pleading is due.) However, failure to include the date does *not* affect the validity of service. [CCP §415.10]

☞[4:192]   **PRACTICE POINTER:**   Use your process server to obtain information you may need to prove validity of the service or to prove up a default. Instruct the process server to get the following information from the person served (or someone else if the person served refuses to cooperate):

- *The full name of the person served;* and, if such person is being served on behalf of a corporation or other entity, his or her *office or capacity.* This equips the process server to testify in the event defendant later challenges the service. Also, it alerts you to amend the complaint, if necessary, to correct errors in defendant's name, so that any judgment you obtain will be enforceable against assets held in that name.

- *Whether in military service:* Federal law requires an affidavit or declaration that the defendant is not in military service, before any *default judgment* can be rendered (Servicemembers Civil Relief Act, 50 USC App. §521 et seq.). If you have no other way of obtaining this information, the process server can be instructed to verify that the defendant is not in military service, so that in event of default you can obtain a judgment. Otherwise, although a default may be entered, no default judgment may be obtained. [See *Interinsurance Exch. of Auto. Club of So. Calif. v. Collins* (1994) 30 CA4th 1445, 1447-1448, 37 CR2d 126, 127]

b.   [4:193]   **"Substitute service"—delivery to someone else coupled with mailing:**   Under certain circumstances, service is authorized by delivering copies of the summons and complaint to someone other than defendant; and thereafter mailing additional copies to defendant. [CCP §415.20]

(1) [4:194]   **Applies both to individual and entity defendants:**   Substitute service is authorized both for individual defendants, and for entity defendants (corporations, partnerships, public entities, etc.). [CCP §415.20(a),(b)]

(a) [4:195]   **Example:**   Process Server attempted to serve Corporation during business hours. Its doors were locked and the woman who responded refused to unlock the door or accept the papers. Service was effected by leaving summons and complaint outside the door and mailing a copy of the summons and complaint to Corporation. [*Khourie, Crew & Jaeger v. Sabek, Inc.* (1990) 220 CA3d 1009, 1015, 269 CR 687, 690]

(2) [4:196] **Limitation—not available for individual defendants unless personal service first attempted:** The big difference in using substitute service for individual, as opposed to entity, defendants is that a good faith effort at personal service must first be attempted. I.e., there must be a showing that summons "*cannot with reasonable diligence be personally delivered*" to the individual defendant. [CCP §415.20(b)] (No such showing is necessary for substitute service on entity defendants; see CCP §415.20(a).)

(a) [4:197] **Burden on plaintiff:** If defendant challenges this method of service, the burden is on plaintiff to show that *reasonable attempts were made* to serve defendant personally before resorting to substitute service. If defendant establishes that he or she was available for personal service, plaintiff will have to show why such personal service could not be effected. [*Evartt v. Sup.Ct. (Kellett)* (1979) 89 CA3d 795, 801, 152 CR 836, 839]

(b) [4:198] **"Reasonable diligence":** Two or three attempts to personally serve defendant at a "proper place" (*see ¶4:206*) ordinarily qualifies as "reasonable diligence." [*Espindola v. Nunez* (1988) 199 CA3d 1389, 1392, 245 CR 596, 598; *Stafford v. Mach* (1998) 64 CA4th 1174, 1182, 75 CR2d 809, 814]

1) [4:199] **Different standard for high public officials?** Repeated efforts to serve high public officials may not be required. For example, a process server attempting to serve the President of the United States need not be repeatedly thrown off the White House property by the Secret Service. In such cases, "we rather imagine one (attempt at service) would constitute due diligence." [See *Burchett v. City of Newport Beach* (1995) 33 CA4th 1472, 1478, 40 CR2d 1, 4, fn. 4 (parentheses added)]

(c) **Application**

• [4:200] "Reasonable diligence" was shown where Process Server attempted three times to serve defendants at their residence but was barred each time by a gate guard at the residential community. [*Bein v. Brechtel-Jochim Group, Inc.* (1992) 6 CA4th 1387, 1392, 8 CR2d 351, 353]

- [4:201]   But *no* "diligence" at all was shown where instead of attempting to serve defendant city officials personally, plaintiff simply left the papers with a deputy clerk. [*Burchett v. City of Newport Beach* (1995) 33 CA4th 1472, 1478, 40 CR2d 1, 3]

- [4:202]   P delayed attempts to serve D until just before expiration of the 3-year period for service of summons (CCP §583.210). At this point, D was out of town on vacation, so P utilized substitute service, leaving papers with D's son, and mailing a copy to D. Held: Service ineffective because D was available for service during most of the statutory period; P's unexplained delay in attempting personal service did *not* constitute "reasonable diligence" so as to justify substitute service. [*Evartt v. Sup.Ct. (Kellett)*, supra, 89 CA3d at 801, 152 CR at 839]

[4:203-204]   *Reserved.*

(d) [4:205]   **Compare—small claims actions:**  Substitute service can be used in small claims actions without first attempting personal service on the defendant. Service can be made by delivering the claim to the sheriff's or marshal's office. The sheriff or marshal is then responsible for delivering it to anyone (over age 18) whom the defendant has authorized to receive service and thereafter mailing a copy to defendant's usual mailing address. [CCP §116.340]

### (3) Procedure for substitute service

(a) [4:206]   **On individual defendant:**  A three-step process is required:

- Leave a copy of the summons and complaint either at the individual's:
  — dwelling house ("usual place of abode"),
  — usual place of business, or
  — usual mailing address (other than a U.S. Postal Service post office box);

- Leave it with a "competent member of the household" or person "apparently in charge of his office or place of business," *at least 18 years old*, who *must be told what the papers are;*

- Thereafter, *mail other copies* of the summons and complaint (first class mail, postage prepaid) to the defendant at the place where the copies were left. [CCP §415.20(b)]

1) [4:207] **"Dwelling house or usual place of abode"**: This means the place which the defendant holds out as his or her principal residence, and where he or she is most likely to receive actual notice. [*Zirbes v. Stratton* (1986) 187 CA3d 1407, 1415-1417, 232 CR 653, 658-659; see *Corcoran v. Arouh* (1994) 24 CA4th 310, 315, 29 CR2d 326, 329—service invalid where defendant was not shown to have had any connection with address at which substitute service attempted]

   a) [4:208] **Example:** Creditor left copies of summons and complaint against Wife (1) at the restaurant she owned with estranged Husband (but she did not work there); and (2) at her mother's home (listed as her residence on her driver's license). Service was ineffective. Her "dwelling house or usual place of abode" was where she lived with her children and where she received her mail. [*Zirbes v. Stratton*, supra, 187 CA3d at 1417, 232 CR at 659]

   [4:209] *Reserved.*

2) [4:210] **"Usual mailing address"**: This permits service at a place that may be *neither* the defendant's home nor place of business. "Usual mailing address" as used in CCP §415.20 includes *commercial "letter drop" facilities*—i.e., private businesses providing "post office boxes." [*Ellard v. Conway* (2001) 94 CA4th 540, 545, 114 CR2d 399, 402-403 (citing text)] (But a U.S. post office box is expressly excluded; see CCP §415.20.)

   [4:211] *Reserved.*

3) [4:212] **"Competent member of household"**: The person with whom the papers are left *need not* be a member of the family. [*Bein v. Brechtel-Jochim Group, Inc.* (1992) 6 CA4th 1387, 1393, 8 CR2d 351, 354, fn. 4]

   - [4:213] A *gate guard* at a gated community or a *doorman* in an apartment building is considered a "competent member of the household" (and a person "apparently in charge" of a corporate office; see below) where they *control access* to the residence. [*Bein v. Brechtel-Jochim Group, Inc.*, supra, 6 CA4th at 1393, 8 CR2d at 354]

The guard gate or front door of the apartment house constitutes part of the dwelling for service of process purposes: "The outer bounds of the actual dwelling place must be deemed to extend to the location at which the process server's progress is arrested." [*Bein v. Brechtel-Jochim Group, Inc.*, supra, 6 CA4th at 1394, 8 CR2d at 354, fn. 7]

4) [4:214] **"Person apparently in charge of office or place of business":** A "close connection" is required between defendant and the person receiving the summons. [See Judicial Council Comment to CCP §415.20]

Where defendant's "usual mailing address" was a private/commercial post office box facility, leaving the summons with the manager who knew the defendant showed a sufficient connection. [*Ellard v. Conway*, supra, 94 CA4th at 546, 114 CR2d at 403, fn. 3]

[4:215] *Reserved.*

5) [4:216] **Substitute service attempt may result in personal service:** An attempt at substituted service may result in personal service. [See *Stafford v. Mach* (1998) 64 CA4th 1174, 1183, 75 CR2d 809, 814]

• [4:217] On a process server's sixth attempt at personal service at defendant's residence, a person (the defendant) answered the door, but denied knowing defendant, refused to show ID and threatened to call the police. The process server "announced drop service," left the papers and later mailed the summons and complaint to defendant. [*Stafford v. Mach*, supra, 64 CA4th at 1183, 75 CR2d at 814—plaintiffs' declaration of "substitute service" was actually *personal* service on defendant]

(b) [4:218] **On entity defendant:** Slightly different procedures apply depending upon whether the entity's "physical address" is known:

1) **[4:218.1]** **Physical address known:** If the entity defendant's "physical address" is known, the following steps are required:

- Leave a copy of the summons and complaint in the office of the person authorized to be served on behalf of the entity (¶4:137-142) during usual office hours;

- Leave it with the person "apparently in charge thereof"; and

- Thereafter, mail other copies (prepaid by first class mail) to such person at the place where the copies were left. [CCP §415.20 (a)]

2) **[4:218.2]** **Physical address unknown:** If the entity defendant's "physical address" is unknown, service may be made at its *usual mailing address*, other than a U.S. post office box. Under this method of service, the following steps are required:

- Leave a copy of the summons and complaint with the person apparently in charge of the mailing establishment, *provided* this person is *at least 18 years old;*

- The person served must be informed (presumably orally) of the contents of the served documents; and

- Thereafter, mail other copies (prepaid by first class mail) to the defendant at the mailing address. [CCP §415.20(a) (amended 2003)]

3) **[4:218.3]** **"Physical address"?** The term "physical address" may cause problems. For example, a corporation may have its factory, equipment and inventory at one place, and its headquarters elsewhere. Or, it may have several factories, etc., in different places. Whether service at one place or the other constitutes service at the defendant's "physical address" is presently unclear.

[4:218.4-218.9] *Reserved.*

(c) **[4:218.10]** **On "business organization, form unknown":** Except where a corporation has a registered agent for service of process on file with the Secretary of State, a summons may be served on a "business organization" whose form is unknown (e.g., "XYZ Co., a business organization whose form is unknown") as follows:

- Leave a copy of the summons and complaint during usual office hours with the person who is apparently in charge of office; and

- Thereafter, mail other copies (prepaid by first class mail) "to the person to be served" at the place where the summons and complaint were left. [CCP §415.95 (added 2003)]

1) **[4:218.11]** **Sole proprietorships?** It is presently unclear whether this statute applies to individuals. Where individuals do business under a fictitious name and have not filed a Fictitious Business Name Statement (see Bus. & Prof.C. §17913), they may well qualify as a "business organization, form unknown" within the meaning of the statute.

(4) **[4:219]** **When service effective:** Substitute service is deemed *complete* on the *10th day after the mailing* . . . so that a defendant served in this manner has *40 days* after the mailing to respond. [CCP §§415.20(a),(b), 415.95(a); see *Tsakos Shipping & Trading, S.A. v. Juniper Garden Town Homes, Ltd.* (1993) 12 CA4th 74, 85, 15 CR2d 585, 590—service ineffective without mailing]

(a) **[4:220]** **Compare—personal service:** Personal service is complete upon delivery of the summons and complaint, so that the defendant has only 30 days to respond (¶4:184).

(b) **[4:221]** **Compare—dismissal for delay in service of summons:** A complaint is subject to dismissal if the summons and complaint are not served on the defendant within the time limits specified in the dismissal statutes (CCP §§583.210, 583.250(b) and 583.420(a)(1), *see* ¶11:51 *ff.*) or "fast track" rules, where applicable (*see* ¶4:32).

For dismissal purposes (only), when substitute service is utilized, the defendant is deemed "served" when the physical delivery and mailing requirements are completed—rather than 10 days later. (This avoids mandatory dismissal where the 3-year statute runs just after mailing.) [*Ginns v. Shumate* (1977) 65 CA3d 802, 805, 135 CR 604, 606]

[4:222-224] *Reserved.*

c. **[4:225]** **Service by mail and acknowledgment of receipt:** Another method of service authorized by the Code is simply to mail the defendant copies of the summons and complaint, with a request to acknowledge receipt thereof (*see Form 4:B*). If defendant signs the acknowledgment, it waives further service of process. If defendant *refuses*, some other method of service must be utilized (but defendant is liable for the costs incurred). [CCP §415.30]

☞[4:226] *PRACTICE POINTER:* In cases where prompt service is not essential, it's generally a good idea to try service by mail. This is particularly so if there are numerous defendants, as it may enable you to avoid some of the many separate process-serving charges that you'll otherwise have to pay. It's also a good idea when dealing with an *evasive* defendant: It may put you in a better position to recover the extra expenses you're likely to incur in effecting service upon such a defendant (*see ¶4:240*).

(1) [4:227] **What must be mailed:** The following must be mailed to defendant:

(a) A copy of the summons and complaint;

(b) *Two* copies of the *notice* and *acknowledgment* form (below);

(c) A return envelope, postage prepaid, addressed to the sender. [CCP §415.30(a)]

(2) [4:228] **How mailed:** Ordinary, first class mail is sufficient (need not be certified or registered or return-receipt-requested). [CCP §415.30(a)]

(a) [4:229] **Compare—service outside the state:** Service by mail on persons outside California is effective *without* an acknowledgment; but process must be sent by certified or registered mail with return-receipt-requested. [CCP §415.40, ¶4:293]

(3) [4:230] **Mailing address may include post office box:** As long as accompanied by an acknowledgment of receipt, service under §415.30 may be effective even if the mail was addressed to a post office box at which defendant is known to receive mail. [*Transamerica Title Ins. Co. v. Hendrix* (1995) 34 CA4th 740, 745, 40 CR2d 614, 617]

(a) [4:231] **Compare—substitute service:** Mailing to a post office box is *not* effective for purposes of "substitute service" under CCP §415.20 (*see ¶4:210*).

But the mailing address is less important under §415.30 because service is effective only if the mailing is coupled with defendant's *acknowledgment of receipt.*

(4) [4:232] **Notice and acknowledgment form:** The notice must apprise defendant that unless he or she signs and returns the acknowledgment within 20 days, service will be made in some other manner, and defendant held liable for the extra expenses so incurred. The acknowledgment must simply evidence receipt of a copy of the summons and complaint. [CCP §415.30(b)]

An Official Form for Notice and Acknowledgment of Receipt has been prepared by the Judicial Council. Use of the Official Form automatically satisfies the above requirements. [CCP §415.30(e)]

- *FORM:* Official Form Notice and Acknowledgment of Receipt, *see Form 4:B.*

(a) [4:233] Signing a *postal service return receipt* is *not* an acknowledgment of receipt of summons. [*Tandy Corp. v. Sup.Ct. (Lekoff)* (1981) 117 CA3d 911, 913, 173 CR 81, 82—pleadings and acknowledgment form sent by certified mail, return-receipt-requested; D signed the return-receipt, but refused the acknowledgment; no valid service obtained]

(5) [4:234] **Effect of acknowledgment:** Defendant need only sign and return one copy of the acknowledgment form to the sender. (It need not be witnessed or notarized.) Doing so effectively consents to this method of service.

(a) [4:235] **When service effective:** Service of summons is deemed complete on the date the defendant *signs* the acknowledgment (rather than the date it is mailed back). Defendant therefore has 30 days from the date of signing within which to respond to the complaint. [CCP §415.30(c); see *Wagner v. City of South Pasadena* (2000) 78 CA4th 943, 948-950, 93 CR2d 91, 95-96—service of initial pleadings challenging decision of legislative body under Gov.C. §65009(c)]

(b) [4:236] **No extension of time for other acts:** Where other kinds of process are served by mail, the recipient normally gets an additional 5 days within which to exercise any right or do any act. [See CCP §1013] However, such extension of time does *not* apply to service of summons by mail. [CCP §413.20]

(c) [4:237] **Not a submission to jurisdiction:** A *nonresident's* signing and returning the acknowledgment satisfies service of process requirements, but it does *not* constitute a submission to the court's jurisdiction. There would have to be *other* contacts to support exercise of personal jurisdiction over the nonresident. [*Marriage of Merideth* (1982) 129 CA3d 356, 362, 180 CR 909, 912; *see ¶3:180*]

(6) **[4:238]** **Effect of refusing acknowledgment:** If defendant fails to sign and return the acknowledgment, service is not complete and will have to be made in some other manner. I.e., service by mail *alone* is not effective.

(a) **[4:239]** **Compare—service on persons outside California:** Service by registered or certified mail with return-receipt-requested is sufficient for defendants outside the state (i.e., no separate acknowledgment of receipt). [CCP §415.40, *¶4:293-304*] But, in such cases, jurisdiction cannot be exercised unless the nonresident has had "minimum contacts" with California (*see ¶3:195 ff.*).

(b) **[4:240]** **Liability for costs of service:** The notice form, above, gives defendants the chance to avoid the costs involved in effecting service by some other method. Therefore, if they fail to sign and return the acknowledgment within *20 days* after it is mailed, they become liable for whatever costs plaintiff incurs in effecting service by some other method—*regardless of the outcome of the lawsuit.* I.e., even if defendants win the case, they will have to reimburse plaintiff for the costs incurred in serving the summons and complaint. [CCP §415.30(d)]

⇨**[4:241]** *PRACTICE POINTER:* Nothing in the statute requires plaintiff to wait until the end of the case to obtain reimbursement of service costs. In fact, it is a good idea to seek reimbursement *immediately.* Otherwise, if the case settles (as most cases do), plaintiff may have to waive such costs as part of the settlement.

1) **[4:242]** **Procedure:** The statute says plaintiff may obtain reimbursement on motion "with or without notice" to the defendant; and the court shall order such reimbursement "*except for good cause shown.*" [See CCP §415.30(d)]

2) **[4:243]** **Comment:** The statute is inherently contradictory: How can defendant show "good

cause" to avoid service costs if plaintiff seeks reimbursement "without notice" (i.e., ex parte)?

Of course, ex parte applications have their own brand of notice requirement (*see ¶9:352*). But it is doubtful that is what the Legislature was intending.

[4:244] *Reserved.*

d. [4:245] **Service by publication:** The final method of service authorized by the Code is by publication of summons in a newspaper of general circulation. Unlike the other methods discussed above, plaintiff must obtain a *court order* before attempting service by this method. [CCP §415.50]

This statute is *strictly* construed: "If there is any situation in which strict compliance can reasonably be required, it is that of service by publication." [*County of Riverside v. Sup.Ct. (Hill)* (1997) 54 CA4th 443, 450, 62 CR2d 747, 751]

(1) [4:246] **Constitutional limitation:** Service by publication is not adequate notice for due process purposes for defendants whose *whereabouts are known, and* who therefore could be notified by means such as personal service or mail. [*Mennonite Board of Missions v. Adams* (1983) 462 US 791, 795, 103 S.Ct. 2706, 2710; see also *Tulsa Professional Collection Services, Inc. v. Pope* (1988) 485 US 478, 491, 108 S.Ct. 1340, 1348; *and ¶4:7*]

(2) [4:247] **Procedure for obtaining court order:** Plaintiff's attorney must prepare an affidavit containing certain essential facts (below), and must submit same to the court in an *ex parte* hearing (defendant not present). If the judge is satisfied with the contents of the affidavit, it will order the defendant served by publication and mailing as described below.

**FORMS**

- Ex Parte Application for Order for Publication of Summons, *see Form 4:D.*

- Declaration in Support of Application for Order for Publication of Summons, *see Form 4:E.*

- Order for Publication of Summons, *see Form 4:F.*

(3) [4:248] **Affidavit requirements:** The affidavit for publication of summons must be by a person who is a *competent* witness to the following *facts* [CCP §415.50(a); *see Form 4:E*]:

(a) [4:249] **Reasonable diligence to serve by other methods:** The first requirement is a showing that reasonable attempts have been made to serve the defendant in some other authorized manner. [CCP §415.50(a)]

If defendant's address is *ascertainable*, some other method of service *must* be employed "because constitutional principles of due process of law, as well as the authorizing statute, require that service by publication be *utilized only as a last resort.*" [*Watts v. Crawford* (1995) 10 C4th 743, 749, 42 CR2d 81, 85, fn. 5 (emphasis added)]

1) [4:250] **Includes service by mail:** Service by mail under CCP §415.30 (coupled with acknowledgment of receipt, see above) is "another manner of service" within the meaning of §415.50. Therefore, if defendant's mailing address in California is known—even if it is only a *post office box*—reasonable attempts must be made to serve defendant by mail pursuant to §415.30 before seeking an order for publication of summons. [*Transamerica Title Ins. Co. v. Hendrix* (1995) 34 CA4th 740, 745, 40 CR2d 614, 617—post office box is sufficient address for service under §415.30]

2) [4:251] **Probative facts required:** The affidavit must establish reasonable diligence by "probative facts based on personal knowledge." [*Olvera v. Olvera* (1991) 232 CA3d 32, 42, 283 CR 271, 278]

3) [4:252] **"Reasonable diligence":** The term "reasonable diligence" denotes "a thorough, systematic investigation and inquiry conducted in good faith by the party or his agent or attorney." [*Watts v. Crawford* (1995) 10 C4th 743, 749, 42 CR2d 81, 85, fn. 5]

The basic test is whether the affidavit shows plaintiff took "those steps a reasonable person *who truly desired to give notice* would have taken under the circumstances." [*Donel, Inc. v. Badalian* (1978) 87 CA3d 327, 333, 150 CR 855, 859 (emphasis added)]

a) [4:253] **Particular searches:** "Reasonable diligence" requires a number of honest attempts to learn defendant's whereabouts or his or her address by:
— inquiry of relatives; and

— investigation of appropriate city and telephone directories, and assessor's office property indices situated near defendant's last known location.

"These are the likely sources of information, and consequently must be searched before resorting to service by publication." [*Watts v. Crawford,* supra, 10 C4th at 749, 42 CR2d at 85, fn. 5]

b) **[4:254] Limitation—restricted data bases:** To establish that a defendant cannot with reasonable diligence be served in another manner, the court may not require search of data bases for residential addresses if such searches by registered process servers are prohibited by law or by published agency policy, such as *voter registration rolls and DMV records.* [CCP §415.50(e)]

➡️ **[4:255] *PRACTICE POINTER:*** Here are some guidelines for preparing the requisite affidavits:

— First, the affidavit must be by someone with *personal knowledge* of the efforts made to locate and serve defendant. This usually means an investigator or process server (although, in some cases, plaintiff's counsel may have the requisite personal knowledge).

— If defendant's whereabouts are *known* but defendant has successfully evaded service by other means (e.g., personal service, or by mail or by substitute service), the affidavit should *describe those efforts* in detail.

— If defendant's whereabouts are *unknown*, the affidavit should *specify the efforts made to locate* him or her. E.g., that mail sent to defendant's last known address was returned undelivered showing "no forwarding address"; that appropriate directories have been checked with negative results (phone books, etc.); that defendant's family and neighbors state they do not know his or her address; that defendant's last known employer and co-workers state they do not know defendant's whereabouts, etc.

4) **Application**

- [4:256] P knew D was residing in the vicinity of Pismo Beach; P sent mail to D in care of D's mother's restaurant in Pismo Beach; and received a letter from D "with no personal return address" (suggesting some return address given). P's affidavit that D "cannot be found" was insufficient because there was no indication P employed "any of the usual means" to find D in Pismo Beach (e.g., contacting D's mother and other relatives, search of city directories, phone books, etc.). [*Olvera v. Olvera*, supra, 232 CA3d at 42, 283 CR at 278]

- [4:257] Although aware that D was a Canadian citizen, P applied for an order for publication of summons stating D's address was unknown, relying on an investigator's affidavit describing unsuccessful attempts to locate D in Los Angeles County. P made no effort to locate D in Canada. The order for publication was invalid because the affidavit did not show "reasonable diligence" to locate D's Canadian address. [*Kott v. Sup.Ct. (Beachport Entertainment Corp.)* (1996) 45 CA4th 1126, 1138-1139, 53 CR2d 215, 221-222]

  [4:258-259] *Reserved.*

5) [4:260] **Effect of too many defendants to serve individually?** The Supreme Court (by dictum) has suggested that service by publication *might* be proper where there are *too many* defendants to serve individually. The sheer number of defendants may make it impossible to serve them "with reasonable diligence" in any other manner. E.g., in an action against 252 trust deed beneficiaries, plaintiff "might have . . . request(ed) permission from the trial court to serve a summons on the beneficiaries by publication under CCP §415.50 . . ." [*Monterey S.P. Partnership v. W.L. Bangham, Inc.* (1989) 49 C3d 454, 461, 261 CR 587, 591, fn. 4, *discussed at* ¶2:233]

(b) [4:261] **Existence of cause of action OR interest in property:** The affidavit must also allege *either:*

- A cause of action exists against the defendant (or he is a necessary party to such action); *OR*

- Defendant claims an interest in real or personal property subject to the court's jurisdiction, and/or plaintiff seeks to exclude defendant from such property. [CCP §415.50(a)]

1) [4:262] A verified complaint is *no substitute* for the required affidavit establishing the existence of a cause of action. [*Olvera v. Olvera*, supra, 232 CA3d at 42, 283 CR at 278, fn. 9— a "jurisdictional prerequisite"]

2) [4:263] Again, the affidavit must be by someone with personal knowledge of the essential facts . . . usually, the plaintiff personally is required to sign. (This is often a separate affidavit from the affidavit of the lawyer or process server showing "reasonable diligence" to serve defendant, above.)

  - [4:264] Affidavits containing only hearsay and conclusory allegations are insufficient to state a cause of action, and hence do not support jurisdiction based on service by publication. [*Islamic Republic of Iran v. Pahlavi* (1984) 160 CA3d 620, 627, 206 CR 752, 756—allegations based on the "common knowledge of the Iranian people" were a "medley of conclusions and political declamation" and "failed to formulate a comprehensible cause of action"; hence court lacked jurisdiction based on service by publication]

3) [4:265] Plaintiff's lawyer can execute such affidavit only if he or she has the requisite *personal* knowledge of the facts comprising the cause of action. [*Harris v. Cavasso* (1977) 68 CA3d 723, 726, 137 CR 410, 411—verification of complaint by plaintiff's counsel on information and belief held *not* sufficient as sworn statement of facts for publication of summons]

(c) [4:266] **Effect of defects or inaccuracies in affidavit:** The affidavit requirements above are *jurisdictional* in nature. Unless the affidavit contains the requisite *factual* allegations by a person *competent* to testify thereto, the court has no power to order publication of summons. If it were to do so, service would be ineffective, and any default judgment based thereon would be *void.* [*Olvera v. Olvera* (1991) 232 CA3d 32, 41, 283 CR 271, 278]

Similarly, if the factual allegations are *proved false,* an order for publication based thereon must be set aside, invalidating any default judgment obtained against the defendant. [*Transamerica Title Ins. Co. v. Hendrix* (1995) 34 CA4th 740, 746, 40 CR2d 614, 618—affidavit stated defendant's address was "unknown" but plaintiff admittedly knew defendant had a post office box in Calif. at which it could be served by mail; *see* ¶4:250]

(d) **[4:267] Procedure to challenge affidavit:** Errors or defects in the affidavit can be challenged by motion to set aside the default judgment based on service by publication. [See *Transamerica Title Ins. Co. v. Hendrix, supra,* 34 CA4th at 742, 40 CR2d at 615]

Defects on the face of the affidavit can also be challenged by appeal from the default judgment or alternatively by collateral attack on the judgment when it is sought to be enforced. [See *Donel, Inc. v. Badalian* (1978) 87 CA3d 327, 333-334, 150 CR 855, 859]

(4) **[4:268] Content of court order** [CCP §415.50(b); *see Form 4:F*]

(a) **[4:269] Publication:** The court will order the summons published in a designated newspaper that is "most likely to give actual notice" to the defendant. [CCP §415.50(b)] Any California newspaper of general circulation is acceptable, although most lawyers request the court to designate one of the legal newspapers.

The requirement of publication in a newspaper "most likely to give actual notice" (CCP §415.50(b)) is not met if plaintiffs *know* defendant is not in the locale where the newspaper is published. [*Olvera v. Olvera, supra,* 232 CA3d at 43, 283 CR at 278—publication in Riverside newspaper insufficient because P knew D had left Riverside and was living in vicinity of Pismo Beach]

1) **[4:269.1] Nonresident defendants:** If the party to be served resides or is located outside California, "the court may *also* order the summons to be published" in an out-of-state news-

paper that is "most likely to give actual notice." [CCP §415.50(b) (emphasis added) (amended 2003)]

*Comment:* Because §415.50(b) uses the term "also," it seems to require publication in an out-of-state newspaper *in addition to* a California newspaper. Arguably, however, a California publication should not be required where defendant is located outside the state because *no* California newspaper is "most likely to give actual notice" in such a case.

➪[4:269.2] **PRACTICE POINTER:** Until this issue is resolved, the safest course is to publish both in a California newspaper *and* in a newspaper in the state where the party to be served is located.

2) [4:270] **Duration and frequency of publication:** The order will direct publication once a week for four successive weeks (unless a special statute provides otherwise, or the court in its discretion orders longer publication). [CCP §415.50(b); Gov.C. §6064]

(b) [4:271] **Mailing:** In addition, the order will provide that *if defendant's address is ascertained* before expiration of the time prescribed for publication of summons, copies of the summons, complaint and order for publication must be "mailed forthwith" to defendant (ordinary mail, no return-receipt required). [CCP §415.50(b)]

(5) [4:272] **When service complete:** Service is complete on the 28th day following the first day of publication. [CCP §415.50(c); Gov.C. §6064; see *Watts v. Crawford* (1995) 10 C4th 743, 747, 42 CR2d 81, 84, fn. 4]

Defendant then has 30 days within which to respond—i.e., a total of *58 days* from the first date of publication.

(a) [4:273] **Compare—publication under different statutes:** This rule does not apply, however, where service of summons is governed by a different statute. [See *County of Riverside v. Sup.Ct. (Hill)* (1997) 54 CA4th 443, 449, 62 CR2d 747, 751, fn. 11—"reverse validation proceedings" (¶4:88) governed by Gov.C. §6063, which provides *21-day* notice period]

- [4:274] Where a special statute requires the summons to *specify the date for defendant's response* (see CCP §861.1 governing "reverse validation proceedings"), failure to include such date in the published summons *invalidates* the service. [*County of Riverside v. Sup.Ct. (Hill)*, supra, 54 CA4th at 451, 62 CR2d at 752]

➡️[4:275] ***PRACTICE POINTER:*** Service and filing of proof of service must be completed within a limited period of time (60 days for the original complaint; 30 days for amended complaint or cross-complaint; *see* ¶*4:345 ff.*). Therefore, be sure to ask for a time extension, *before the time has run*, if the service by publication cannot be completed within this period.

(6) [4:276] **Other service during publication period:** Plaintiff is not precluded from other methods of service during the period of publication. Thus, if defendant's address is discovered, plaintiff can use personal or substitute service. Such service will *supersede* the published summons, and thus speed up the effective date of service. [CCP §415.50(d)]

➡️[4:277] ***PRACTICE POINTER:*** It's generally a good idea to abandon an ongoing service by publication in favor of personal service wherever possible. Not only will it speed up the effective date of service, but it also provides a *more reliable* form of service. Service by publication, and default judgments based thereon, are subject to rigid scrutiny because there is less assurance that the defendant has received actual notice. Accordingly, courts tend to be supertechnical and set aside such judgments wherever possible.

(7) [4:278] **No extension of deadline for service of summons:** An action is subject to dismissal if defendant is not served within 3 years (CCP §583.210(a); *see* ¶*11:51*). That 3-year period is tolled, however, where defendant is "not amenable to the process of the court"

*(Text cont'd on p. 4-45)*

(CCP §583.240(a); *see ¶11:97*) . . . which means defendant is not subject to *personal jurisdiction*. [*Watts v. Crawford* (1995) 10 C4th 743, 755, 42 CR2d 81, 89]

An order for publication of summons under CCP §415.50 requires a finding that defendant "cannot with reasonable diligence be served" in a manner other than by publication of summons (*see ¶4:249*). That is *not* the same as a finding that defendant is "not amenable to the process of the court" (not subject to personal jurisdiction), and hence does *not* toll the 3-year deadline for service of summons. [*Watts v. Crawford*, supra, 10 C4th at 761, 42 CR2d at 93]

[4:279]   *Reserved.*

e.   [4:280]   **Compare—unlawful detainer actions where defendant's whereabouts unknown:**   An unlawful detainer summons may be served by "posting" the property where the tenant has moved away from the rented premises and his or her whereabouts are unknown. Special procedural requirements apply (affidavit and order for posting and mailing). [See CCP §415.45]

*Cross-refer:* See Friedman, Garcia & Hagarty, *Cal. Prac. Guide: Landlord-Tenant* (TRG), Ch. 8.

[4:281-290]   *Reserved.*

5.   [4:291]   **Service on Defendants Outside California:**   The methods for service of summons on defendants outside the state are even more liberal than those discussed above. *But remember:* There have to be "minimum contacts" between the nonresident defendant and California for local courts to exercise jurisdiction (*see ¶3:195 ff.*). The broader methods for service of summons, therefore, are *not* being relied upon for jurisdictional purposes. Rather, their function is simply to provide *notice* of the lawsuit.

a.   [4:292]   **Defendant in another state:**   Service on a defendant residing in another state may be accomplished in any of the following ways:

- *Any of the four methods for serving persons within California* (e.g., personal delivery; substitute service; service by mail coupled with acknowledgment of receipt; or by publication); *or*

- *Certified* or registered mail with *return-receipt-requested (below); or*

- *Any other method* permissible under the law of the state where the service is made (although this does not add much because few states have methods for service of summons more liberal than California's). [CCP §413.10(b)]

(1) [4:293]  **Certified or registered mail with return-receipt-requested:**  This is the most liberal method for service of summons allowed under California law: A nonresident defendant can be served anywhere in the world simply by mailing him or her copies of the summons and complaint "by first-class mail, postage prepaid, requiring a return receipt" (i.e., certified or registered mail). [CCP §415.40]

   (a) [4:294]  **Mailing to person to be served:**  The summons must be mailed "to the person to be served." [CCP §415.40]

      1) [4:295]  **Out-of-state corporations:**  Where the defendant is a corporation, the "person to be served" is *one of the individuals* specified by statute (CCP §416.10(b)) *to be served on its behalf*: i.e., its president, vice president, secretary or assistant secretary, general manager, etc. (*see ¶4:137*). [*Dill v. Berquist Const. Co., Inc.* (1994) 24 CA4th 1426, 1436, 29 CR2d 746, 751]

        • [4:296]  Thus, mailing a summons to the corporation itself is *not* valid service. Rather, the summons must be mailed to an *individual* who may be served on its behalf. [*Dill v. Berquist Const. Co., Inc.*, supra, 24 CA4th at 1436, 29 CR2d at 751]

        *Comment:* Although the statute is not entirely clear, it is probably sufficient to mail the summons to an *unnamed* officer (e.g., "President of XYZ, Inc.").

        • [4:297]  In addition, the summons form must *notify* that person that he or she is being served *on behalf of* the corporation. (The "NOTICE TO THE PERSON SERVED" box on the reverse side of the form should be marked "on behalf of (name of corporation) under CCP §416.10.") [CCP §412.30; *see ¶4:92*]

     [4:298]  *Comment:* The above seems correct. But an earlier case reached the opposite result without really discussing the issue (upholding service where envelope was addressed to corporation rather than to any officer, etc.). [See *Shoei Kako Co. v. Sup.Ct. (MacIsaac)* (1973) 33 CA3d 808, 818, 109 CR 402, 409, *discussed at ¶4:384*]

(b) [4:299]   **Service complete 10 days after mailing:**   Service is deemed effective 10 days after the mailing ... even if the defendant has not yet signed or mailed back the return receipt. [CCP §415.40]

This 10-day grace period extends defendant's time to *plead*; i.e., no default can be entered for an additional 10 days beyond the normal time a responsive pleading is due. (But this provision does not determine when service was made; see below.)

1) [4:300]   **Compare—when service complete for dismissal purposes:**   An action is subject to dismissal for delay in service of summons (CCP §583.210; *see ¶11:51*). For dismissal purposes, "service" is effected by *mailing alone*; the 10-day grace period does not delay effective service. [*Johnson & Johnson v. Sup.Ct. (Lawton)* (1985) 38 C3d 243, 248, 211 CR 517, 520]

(c) [4:301]   **Proof of service requires proof of actual receipt:**   To prove service by mail on a nonresident pursuant to CCP §415.40, there must be hard evidence of actual delivery—either a signed receipt or other proof that the defendant (or someone authorized by defendant) *actually received* the mail (*see ¶4:379*).

(d) [4:302]   **Compare—service by mail coupled with acknowledgment of receipt:**   The provision for serving nonresidents as above is *in addition to* the CCP §415.30 provision for service by (ordinary) mail, which may also be used. The big difference is that *no separate acknowledgment* of receipt is necessary under CCP §415.40; i.e., the "return-receipt-requested" procedure assures receipt.

▷[4:303]   *PRACTICE POINTER:*   Although either method can be used to serve a nonresident, the certified or registered mail with return-receipt-requested is far more practical: Once defendant (or someone authorized on his or her behalf) signs for the letter, service is complete. You're not depending on the defendant's willingness to sign a separate acknowledgment of receipt, after having read through the papers!

▷[4:304]   *PRACTICE POINTER:*   If dealing with a defendant who is evasive and likely to refuse to sign for a letter from your office (knowing it may contain a summons), use an envelope *without your letterhead.* The sender's name and address can be that of your secretary or an associate or anyone else whose name won't arouse defendant's suspicion as to the content of the envelope.

(2) [4:305] **Statutory actions authorizing service on designated state officials:** In addition, there are some statutory actions which authorize service on a designated state official (e.g., the Secretary of State) *in lieu of* service on the nonresident defendant; but coupled with some notice or mailing of process to the nonresident.

 (a) [4:306] **Example—nonresident motorist statute:** A nonresident motorist who drives (or permits another to drive) his or her car into California "impliedly consents" to the appointment of the Director of Motor Vehicles as his or her *agent for service* of process in any action for injuries caused by operation of his or her car. [Veh.C. §§17451-17453]

 Therefore, in lieu of serving the nonresident defendant in such action, plaintiff can serve the Director of Motor Vehicles—by personal delivery, or by certified or registered mail with return-receipt-requested. [Veh.C. §17454]

 *In addition*, plaintiff must also send *notice* of such service to the nonresident, along with other copies of the summons and complaint; and these must be sent by *registered* mail with return-receipt-requested (or hand-delivery to the nonresident wherever he or she is located). [See Veh.C. §§17455, 17456]

 - [4:307] This method is also permitted in small claims actions arising from the accident, without regard to whether the defendant was a nonresident at the time of the accident. [See CCP §116.340(f)]

 (b) [4:308] **Other examples:** Similar procedures (appointing a state officer for service in lieu of serving the nonresident) are authorized in actions against nonresidents arising from business activities within the state, including:
 — selling insurance to California residents (Ins.C. §1610);
 — subdividing land in California (Bus. & Prof.C. §11007); and
 — becoming licensed as a real estate salesperson (Bus. & Prof.C. §10151.5).

(c) [4:309] **CCP methods also available:** Serving a designated state official in lieu of the nonresident defendant is *not* required. It is simply an *alternative* method of service in the statutory actions above. Plaintiff may still utilize the procedures set forth in CCP §§413.10(b) and 415.40, and thus serve the nonresident directly. [*Anderson v. Sherman* (1981) 125 CA3d 228, 237, 178 CR 38, 42-43; and CCP §415.40, comment]

(d) [4:310] **Comment:** The alternative statutory procedures were originally enacted when California's general service of summons statute was far more restrictive than it is today. They remain in the Codes, but the current general service of summons statute has reduced their importance.

⇨ [4:311] *PRACTICE POINTER:* The CCP §415.40 certified-mail-with-return-receipt-requested procedure will almost always be faster and simpler than serving a state official and mailing notice, as in the alternative procedures above. Consequently, the only time when it may be necessary to utilize any of the alternative methods is when you're dealing with a knowledgeable, *recalcitrant defendant who knows what's coming* and refuses to sign the certified or registered mail receipt!

[4:312-314] *Reserved.*

b. [4:315] **Defendant in foreign country:** Defendants living in another country can be served with summons in the same way as persons living in other states:

- Any of the four methods by which summons can be served on persons within California (i.e., personal delivery, substitute service, mail coupled with acknowledgment of receipt, publication); *or*

- Certified or registered mail with return-receipt-requested (¶4:293); *or*

- Any other method permitted under the law of the country where the service was made, *provided* the California court determines (before or after the service was made) that the method used was "reasonably calculated to give actual notice." [CCP §413.10(c)] (But this latter provision does not mean much because few foreign countries have more liberal methods for service than does California.)

However, international treaties may limit the manner of service on persons located in signatory countries:

(1) [4:316] **Hague Convention as limitation on manner of service:** The rules for serving persons in foreign countries are expressly subject to the Hague Service Convention (20 U.S.T. 361-367). [CCP §413.10(c), last sent.]

The Hague Service Convention is an international treaty governing service of process in countries that are parties to the treaty. Copies of the Convention and a list of the signatory countries are an "Appendix" to Rule 4 of the Federal Rules of Civil Procedure. [See "Treaties and Conventions" following Rule 4 in 28 USCA, vol. Rules 1-11]

California courts may not exercise jurisdiction in violation of an international treaty. [*Volkswagenwerk Aktiengesellschaft v. Schlunk* (1988) 486 US 694, 699, 108 S.Ct. 2104, 2107-2108; *Kott v. Sup.Ct. (Beachport Entertainment Corp.)* (1996) 45 CA4th 1126, 1136, 53 CR2d 215, 220 (citing text); *Floveyor Int'l, Ltd. v. Sup.Ct. (Shick Tube-Veyor Corp.)* (1997) 59 CA4th 789, 795, 69 CR2d 457, 461]

(a) [4:317] **Preempts California methods:** The methods enumerated in CCP §413.10(c) for serving defendants abroad all require transmission of documents abroad, and therefore are subject to the Hague Convention. [*Kott v. Sup.Ct. (Beachport Entertainment Corp.)*, supra, 45 CA4th at 1136, 53 CR2d at 220]

1) [4:318] **Exception—service by publication:** Service by publication under CCP §415.50 (parties' whereabouts unknown) is the only method of service under California law that does not require transmission of documents abroad, and consequently is not subject to the Hague Convention. (Article 1 of the Hague Convention states that it does not apply where the address of the person to be served with the document is not known.) [*Kott v. Sup.Ct. (Beachport Entertainment Corp.)*, supra, 45 CA4th at 1136, 53 CR2d at 220; see *People v. Mendocino County Assessor's Parcel No. 056-500-09* (1997) 58 CA4th 120, 125, 68 CR2d 51, 53—Hague Convention not applicable to civil forfeiture proceedings where defendant's whereabouts were unknown]

2) **[4:319] Exception—serving domestic subsidiary as "involuntary agent" of foreign corporation:** Nor does the Convention apply when a foreign corporation has a wholly-owned domestic subsidiary that is the foreign corporation's "involuntary agent" for service of process under applicable state law. In such event, service can be effected in this country by serving the subsidiary. [See *Volkswagenwerk Aktiengesellschaft v. Schlunk* (1988) 486 US 694, 707-708, 108 S.Ct. 2104, 2112]

- **[4:320]** *Caution: Schlunk*, supra, involved an Illinois long-arm statute and the validity of serving the subsidiary as "involuntary agent" was not contested. California law does *not* generally authorize serving domestic subsidiaries as agents of foreign corporations; *see* ¶3:205.

3) **[4:321] Exception—foreign corporations qualified to do business in California:** A foreign corporation that has qualified to do business in California (see Corps.C. §2105(a)) must appoint a local agent for service of process or the Secretary of State if the designated agent cannot be found (*see* ¶4:151). Service on either avoids service abroad, so that the Hague Convention does not apply.

4) **[4:322] Exception—foreign corporation *not* qualified to do business:** The same rule apparently applies where a non-USA corporation does business in California *without* having qualified to do so (under Corps.C. §2105) or designating an agent for service of process. Service of process is authorized on the Secretary of State in such cases (see Corps.C. §2111), thus avoiding service under the Hague Convention.

Comment: However, failure to comply with the Hague Convention may be ground for foreign courts to refuse enforcement of the judgment against local assets.

[4:323-324] *Reserved.*

(b) **[4:325] Service methods authorized by Hague Convention:** The Hague Convention authorizes the following methods of serving documents in foreign countries:

- **[4:326]** Articles 2 through 6 require each signatory country to create and designate a "Central Authority" to receive, and to reject or execute, requests from abroad for service on its citizens. (*See discussion of procedure in Practice Pointers at ¶4:333.*)

- **[4:327]** Alternatively, Article 8 permits service to be effected through diplomatic or consular agents of the country in which the process originated . . . *unless* the country in which the service is to be made has declared its opposition to such service on persons other than nationals of the originating country.

- **[4:328]** Or, under Article 9, the papers may be forwarded through consular or diplomatic channels to whatever authorities in the host country are designated by it for the purpose of service.

- **[4:329]** Article 10(a) permits the "*sending*" of judicial documents by mail to persons abroad "provided the State of destination does not object."

  Courts disagree whether the term "sending of judicial documents" in Article 10(a) includes *service of process by mail:*
  — See *Denlinger v. Chinadotcom Corp.* (2003) 110 CA4th 1396, 1399-1400, 2 CR3d 530, 533-534 (collecting cases)— "better and more modern view" is that Hague Convention authorizes service of process by mail unless receiving nation has *objected* to Article 10(a).
  — Contra, *In re Alyssa F.* (2003) 112 CA4th 846, 853, 6 CR3d 1, 5—"send" does *not* include service of process by mail; *Honda Motor Co. v. Sup.Ct. (Opperwall)* (1992) 10 CA4th 1043, 1046-1047, 12 CR2d 861, 862-863 (same).

  *Comment:* Interpretation of the Hague Convention is a question of *federal law.* Unfortunately, federal courts are also split on whether the Convention permits mail service. [See Schwarzer, Tashima & Wagstaffe, *Cal. Prac. Guide: Federal Civ. Pro. Before Trial* (TRG), Ch. 5]

- **[4:330]** Article 10(b)-(c) allows *service* through judicial officers, officials, or other competent persons of the receiving state "provided the State of destination does not object." [*Balcom v. Hiller* (1996) 46 CA4th 1758, 1765, 54 CR2d 536, 540—British process server was a "competent person" to effect service in United Kingdom]

⇨[4:331] ***PRACTICE POINTER:*** Service and filing of proof of service must be completed within a limited period of time (60 days for the original complaint; 30 days for amended complaint or cross-complaint; *see ¶4:345 ff.*). Therefore, be sure to ask for a time extension, *before the time has run*, if the service by publication cannot be completed within this period.

(c) [4:332] **Failure to comply voids service:** Failure to comply with the Hague Convention procedures *voids* the service . . . even though it was made in compliance with California law, and even though the defendant had actual notice of the lawsuit. [*Kott v. Sup.Ct. (Beachport Entertainment Corp.)* (1996) 45 CA4th 1126, 1136, 53 CR2d 215, 220 (citing text); *Dr. Ing. H.C.F. Porsche A.G. v. Sup.Ct. (Schilling)* (1981) 123 CA3d 755, 762, 177 CR 155, 159—since West Germany objected to service by mail and through diplomatic channels, attempts to serve German corporation in this manner were void]

Moreover, even if service is ultimately obtained by some other method, failure to comply with the Hague Convention may be ground for foreign courts to refuse enforcement of the judgment against local assets.

⇨[4:333] ***PRACTICE POINTERS:*** If you plan to serve someone living in another country, you need to determine (1) whether that country is a signatory to the Hague Convention; and (2) if it is, whether that country has registered *objection* to service by mail or through diplomatic channels. (If it has, you will have to go through whatever "Central Authority" it has designated.)

- To determine which countries have adopted the Convention, check the list of signatories (*see ¶4:316*). Great Britain, France, West Germany, Israel, Japan and the U.S. are among the original signatories.

To determine whether any other nations have subsequently adopted the Convention, contact the Department of State, Treaty Affairs Section, Washington, D.C.; Attn: Office of Legal Adviser.

- To determine whether a signatory country opposes service of process under Articles 8 and 10 (service by mail, etc.), you have to check the declarations and reservations of that country when it adopted the Convention. (These can also be found in "Treaties and Conventions" following Rule 4, at 28 USCA, vol. Rules 1-11.)

- If the country opposes service by mail or through diplomatic channels, you will have to invoke the aid of that country's "Central Authority." (The addresses of each country's "Central Authority" are attached to the Convention; see "Treaties and Conventions" following Rule 4, at 28 USCA, vol. Rules 1-11.)

You will need to send a "Request for Service Abroad" form, describing each document to be served.

*FORM:* Request for Service Abroad of Judicial or Extrajudicial Documents, *see Form 4:H.*

These forms are available at the U.S. Marshal's office in each federal courthouse. (The forms contain a blank certificate to be filled in by the foreign authority upon effecting service.)

To avoid problems, fill out the forms *both* in English and in the language of the place where service is to be made. Hire a translator, if necessary!

(2) [4:334] **Inter-American Convention as limitation on manner of service:** The U.S. has also ratified the "Inter-American Convention on Letters Rogatory" (which follows 28 USC §1781).

"Letters rogatory" by definition are requests by one country to another for assistance in the administration of justice, and may be used to seek assistance in serving or deposing foreign residents. [*Kreimerman v. Casa Veerkamp, S.A.* (5th Cir. 1994) 22 F3d 634, 640, fn. 27]

Other original signatories include Mexico, Argentina, Chile, Ecuador, Guatemala, Uruguay, Venezuela and Spain.

(a) [4:335] **Methods of service authorized:** The Convention provides the methods for service similar to those provided in the Hague Convention (¶4:317).

(b) [4:336] **Effect of failure to comply:** The Inter-American Convention does *not* preempt other methods of service on a defendant residing in a signatory country. Unlike the Hague Convention, it does not expressly or impliedly prohibit other methods of service. [*Kreimerman v. Casa Veerkamp, S.A.* (5th Cir. 1994) 22 F3d 634, 639—Mexican defendants subject to service under Texas long-arm statute]

[4:337-339] *Reserved.*

6. [4:340] **Service on Foreign State:** Service of process on a foreign state or its political subdivisions must comply with the Foreign Sovereign Immunities Act. [28 USC §1608(a)]

a. [4:341] **Governing family compared:** Individual members of a governing family holding no governmental position are *not* subject to the requirements of 28 USC §1608(a). [*Bolkiah v. Sup.Ct.* (*Bijan Fragrances, Inc.*) (1999) 74 CA4th 984, 996-997, 88 CR2d 540, 548-549—normal service procedures vested California court with jurisdiction]

*Cross-refer:* Service requirements pursuant to the Foreign Sovereign Immunities Act are discussed in detail in Schwarzer, Tashima & Wagstaffe, *Cal. Prac. Guide: Federal Civ. Pro. Before Trial* (TRG), Ch. 5.

[4:342-344] *Reserved.*

7. [4:345] **Service Deadline:** Except as provided below, the complaint must be *served on all named defendants, and proof of service filed with the court, within 60 days* after filing the complaint. [CRC 201.7(b)]

If the last day falls on a weekend or court holiday, the time is extended to the next day that is not a holiday. [CCP §12a(a); see *Ystrom v. Handel* (1988) 205 CA3d 144, 148, 252 CR 110, 112]

a. [4:345.1] **Longer if authorized by local rule:** Exceptions for longer periods of time may be granted as authorized by local rule. [Gov.C. §68616(a)]

[4:345.2-345.5] *Reserved.*

b. [4:345.6] **Longer if due diligence shown:** A longer period of time for service of the complaint "*shall be granted on a showing that service could not reasonably be achieved within the time required with the exercise of due diligence consistent with the amount in controversy.*" [Gov.C. §68616(a)]

The procedure for obtaining such extension is discussed at ¶4:348.

c. **[4:346] Service on later-named defendants:** If the complaint is amended to *add* a defendant, the added defendant must be served and proof of service filed *within 30 days* after filing of the amended complaint. [CRC 201.7(b)]

(Comment: By its terms, this rule seems applicable only to amendments adding *new* defendants, rather than amendments substituting the real names of persons designated as "Doe" defendants in the original complaint; see below.)

Similarly, where a cross-complaint adds new parties, the cross-complaint must be served on all parties and proof of service on the new parties filed within 30 days of filing the cross-complaint. [CRC 201.7(c)]

d. **[4:347] Fictitiously-named defendants?** The requirement that the complaint be served on all "*named* defendants" within 60 days probably does not apply to defendants sued under *fictitious* names ("Doe" defendants). To require that "Doe" defendants be served within 60 days would appear to be inconsistent with CCP §474, which allows plaintiffs to *amend* the complaint *upon discovery* of a "Doe" defendant's true name (*see ¶6:86*).

e. **[4:348] Application for extension of time:** The court may extend the time for service above *sua sponte* or on application of any party. Such application, however, *must be filed before* the time for service has elapsed. In addition, the application must be accompanied by a declaration:
— *showing why* service has not been effected;
— *documenting the efforts* that have been made to effect service; and
— *specifying a date* by which service is proposed to be effected. [CRC 201.7(e)]

[4:348.1] ***FORM:*** The application for an extension of time for service may be made on optional Judicial Council form CM-020: Ex Parte Application for Extension of Time to Serve Pleading, *see Form 4:J.*

(1) **[4:349] Diligence depending on amount involved?** Although not mentioned in Rule 201.7(e), above, plaintiff is entitled to an extension of time for service of the complaint "on a showing that service could not be achieved within the time required with the exercise of due diligence *consistent with the amount in controversy.*"[Gov.C. §68616(a) (emphasis added)]

f. **[4:350] Effect of delay in service of summons:** Failure to serve and file pleadings as required by the above rules may result in the court's issuing an "Order to Show Cause" why *sanctions* shall not be imposed. [CRC 201.7(f)]

(1) **[4:351] Response:** Responsive papers to such an Order to Show Cause must be filed at least five calendar days before the hearing. [CRC 201.7(i)]

(2) **[4:352] Sanctions:** The sanctions a court may impose for violation of Rule 201.7 presumably are limited to monetary or disciplinary sanctions against counsel.

(a) **[4:353] Dismissal as sanction?** Involuntary dismissal for delay in prosecution is authorized only if an action has not been brought to trial or conditionally settled *within two years* after filing. [CCP §583.410; *see ¶11:127*] (Dismissal is mandatory if summons and complaint have not been served *within three years*; CCP §583.210, *see ¶11:51*.)

Therefore, even in the simplest cases, plaintiff may not be penalized for complete inaction during that period; i.e., the court may sanction plaintiff's attorney but has no inherent power to dismiss the case for delay of less than two years (*see ¶11:127*) or for violation of court rules that are the attorney's responsibility (*see ¶11:127.1*).

**[4:354-359]** *Reserved.*

**E. RETURN OF SUMMONS**

1. **[4:360] Necessity for Return of Summons; Proof of Service:** Unless defendant makes a general appearance in the action (*see ¶3:163 ff.*), the summons must be returned to the court with *proof of service* on the defendant, for the court to exercise jurisdiction. [CCP §417.30(a)]

All proofs of service must be on official forms adopted by the Judicial Council, and filed with the clerk of the court. [CCP §§417.10(f), 417.30(a); see *Johnson & Johnson v. Sup.Ct. (Lawton)* (1985) 38 C3d 243, 254, 211 CR 517, 523-524]

Most of the Official Form Summons contain blank spaces for the proof of service, showing the time, place and manner in which defendant was served. The process server normally fills in these blanks at the time of service, signs the declaration at the bottom of the page, and returns the completed summons form to plaintiff's counsel.

a. **[4:361] Summons lost after service:** If the summons form is lost after service, the process server can provide the same information on a separate affidavit or declaration stating the time, place and manner of service. That affidavit or declaration can be filed with the court with the same effect as if the original summons had been returned. [CCP

§417.30(b); *Bishop v. Silva* (1991) 234 CA3d 1317, 1321, 285 CR 910, 913]

- **FORM:** Declaration of Lost Summons After Service, *see Form 4:C.*

b. **[4:362] Creates presumption of valid service:** Filing a proof of service that complies with statutory standards (below) creates a *rebuttable* presumption that service was proper. [See *Dill v. Berquist Const. Co., Inc.* (1994) 24 CA4th 1426, 1441-1442, 29 CR2d 746, 755—no presumption of proper service where proof of service showed service on unauthorized person; see also *Floveyor Int'l, Ltd. v. Sup.Ct. (Shick Tube-Veyor Corp.)* (1997) 59 CA4th 789, 795, 69 CR2d 457, 461 (citing text)]

   (1) **[4:363] Preemption of local rules requiring additional documents:** Local rules requiring the filing of additional documents along with the summons and proof of service are preempted. [CRC 981.1(a)]

   **[4:364]** *Reserved.*

2. **[4:365] Proof of Service Requirements:** After the summons is served, the original summons must be returned to the court together with proof of service. [CCP §417.30]

   a. **[4:365.1] Separate form required:** The proof of service must be made on a separate Judicial Council form. (The official form Summons does not contain space for proof of service.) [See CCP §417.10(f)]

   - **[4:365.2] FORM:** The Proof of Service form adopted by the Judicial Council (POS-010) must be used for this purpose; *see Form 4:I.*

     A computer-generated or typewritten form may be substituted if certain requirements are met. [See CRC Rule 982.9 (eff. 2004)]

   **[4:365.3]** The proof of service must show service by one of the methods discussed below.

   b. **[4:366] Service made within California:** If the defendant was served within California, the proof of service must show either:

      (1) **[4:367] Personal service:** The process server's declaration must show the time and place where the summons and complaint were delivered to defendant; and, if to a corporation or entity, the name and capacity of the person served on its behalf. [CCP §417.10(a)]

         (a) **[4:368] Process server's registration:** If the process server is registered as such (Bus. & Prof.C. §22350), the proof of service must also state the *county* in which he or she is registered and his or her *registration number.* [CCP §417.40; Bus. & Prof.C. §22360]

(b) [4:369] **Special requirement for service on "Doe":** Where the complaint names "Doe" defendants, the summons must contain a special *notice* to whomever is served as a "Doe" of the identity in which he or she is being served. [CCP §474; *see* ¶*4:135*]

The return of service must state the fictitious name under which such person was served (e.g., "Doe One") and certify that the summons served contained the requisite notice of identity (above). [CCP §474; *see* ¶*4:135*]

(2) [4:370] **Substitute service:** The same requirements apply as for personal service. In addition, there must be an affidavit showing *mailing* of an additional copy of the summons and complaint, as required by CCP §415.20 (¶*4:193*).

(3) [4:371] **Service by mail with acknowledgment of receipt:** The proof of service must include an acknowledgment of receipt, in the form provided by CCP §415.30 (¶*4:232*).

(4) [4:372] **Service by publication:** The proof of service must contain an affidavit by the "publisher or printer, or his foreman or principal clerk" showing the dates and place of publication. And, if copies of the summons and complaint were mailed to the defendant (where defendant's whereabouts were ascertained), another affidavit showing the date and place of mailing is required. [CCP §417.10(b)]

(5) [4:373] **Service by posting (unlawful detainer actions):** Two affidavits are required: one from the person who posted the summons on the property, showing when and where it was posted; and another showing when and where copies of the complaint were mailed to the defendant. [CCP §417.10(e)]

(6) [4:374] **Service pursuant to alternative statutory methods:** The proof of service must conform to the special statutory methods discussed at ¶*4:305-308* (e.g., delivery to Secretary of State, etc.). [CCP §417.10(c)]

(7) [4:375] **Defendant's written admission of service:** In lieu of any of the foregoing, proof of service may be made by defendant's signed admission of service (or by his or her attorney, if authorized). [CCP §417.10(d)]

[4:376] *Reserved.*

c. **[4:377]** **Service made outside California:** If the defendant was served in another state or country, the proof of service must show an authorized method of service was used.

(1) **[4:378]** **Methods authorized for service within state:** If service was made by personal delivery, substitute service, mail and acknowledgment, or publication, the proof of service requirements are the same as discussed above. [CCP §417.20(a)]

(2) **[4:379]** **Service by certified or registered mail with return-receipt-requested:** If service on the nonresident was made pursuant to CCP §415.40 (¶*4:293*), the proof of service must show evidence of *actual delivery* . . . either the signed return receipt, or "other evidence of receipt" satisfactory to the court. [CCP §417.20(a)]

(a) **[4:380]** **Strict compliance:** Service by mail on a nonresident requires *strict* compliance with CCP §417.20(a). [*Bolkiah v. Sup.Ct. (Bijan Fragrances, Inc.)* (1999) 74 CA4th 984, 1001, 88 CR2d 540, 551]

(b) **Application**

1) **[4:381]** A return receipt signed by someone *authorized* by the nonresident defendant to sign for his or her mail is sufficient. But in such a case, plaintiff will have to provide *separate evidence establishing the authority* of the person who signed the return receipt on defendant's behalf (e.g., affidavit by third person stating D's office manager was authorized to sign for D's mail). [*Neadeau v. Foster* (1982) 129 CA3d 234, 237-238, 180 CR 806, 807; and see *Taylor-Rush v. Multitech Corp.* (1990) 217 CA3d 103, 110, 265 CR 672, 675—service invalid where neighbors signed return receipt but no evidence they were authorized to do so]

2) **[4:382]** A return receipt signed by the defendant's mother is insufficient (unless she was D's designated agent for service of process). But *other evidence of actual receipt* may validate the service: e.g., defendant's lawyer acknowledges D's receipt of the papers. [*Marriage of Tusinger* (1985) 170 CA3d 80, 82-83, 215 CR 838, 839—"I am writing with reference to the divorce petition which Gary Tusinger received a few days ago"]

3) **[4:383]** "Other evidence" of receipt has also been found where plaintiff served nonresident

defendants at addresses defendants used in correspondence. Moreover, defendants had directed plaintiff to use one address to ensure that mail and merchandise would reach them. [*Bolkiah v. Sup.Ct. (Bijan Fragrances, Inc.)*, supra, 74 CA4th at 1001, 88 CR2d at 551]

4) [4:384] An international mail receipt, written in both English and French and signed by defendant's employee, has been held sufficient . . . even though the defendant (a Japanese company) may not have understood the language in which it was written. [*Shoei Kako Co., Ltd. v. Sup.Ct. (MacIsaac)* (1973) 33 CA3d 808, 823-824, 109 CR 402, 412-413]

a) [4:385] **Caution:** There is a split of authority whether service of process by mail may be effected under the Hague Convention. *See ¶4:329.*

(c) [4:386] **Compare—mail refused:** But mail refused, or returned to the sender "unclaimed," with-

*(Text cont'd on p. 4-61)*

**RESERVED**

out a signed receipt, is *not* sufficient to establish service under CCP §415.40. [*Stamps v. Sup.Ct. (Wellington)* (1971) 14 CA3d 108, 110, 92 CR 151, 152]

[4:387-389] *Reserved.*

(3) [4:390] **Service per foreign law or court order:** Either of these requires proof that service was made in accordance with the foreign law, or otherwise as directed by the California court. [CCP §417.20(b),(c); see *Floveyor Int'l, Ltd. v. Sup.Ct. (Shick Tube-Veyor Corp.)* (1997) 59 CA4th 789, 795, 69 CR2d 457, 461 (citing text)—certificate of service in England signed and sealed by designated "Central Authority" created prima facie showing that service was valid pursuant to Hague Convention]

(4) [4:391] **Defendant's written admission of service:** Again, this is sufficient in lieu of any other proof of service. [CCP §417.20(d)]

(a) [4:392] **Compare—knowledge of action not enough:** Declarations and pleadings by a defendant showing its awareness of the lawsuit are *not* sufficient as admissions of service. [See *Tsakos Shipping & Trading, S.A. v. Juniper Garden Town Homes, Ltd.* (1993) 12 CA4th 74, 85, 15 CR2d 585, 590]

[4:393-399] *Reserved.*

3. [4:400] **Deadline for Return of Summons:** To avoid mandatory dismissal of the action, "return of summons or other proof of service" must be made no later than 3 years and 60 days after commencement of the action. [CCP §583.210(b); *see* ¶11:53]

Thus, even if the complaint is timely served, delay in filing the proof of service may result in *mandatory dismissal* of the action! (Comment: The reason for such a highly technical rule is unclear; *see discussion at* ¶11:55.)

*Compare—"fast track" rules:* Local case management rules often require earlier filing of proof of service and authorize dismissal for unexcused delay. [See L.A. Sup.Ct. Rule 7.7(a)(1)—proof of service to be filed within 90 days after complaint filed unless defendant has appeared; Orange Sup.Ct. Rule 438—within 60 days after complaint filed unless a certificate of progress filed explaining why service has not been made; S.F. Unif. Rule 3.3(A)—within 60 days after filing unless extension has been obtained from Presiding Judge (requires written application showing why service has not been effected, steps taken to effect service, and proposed date by which service is expected to be effected); *see also* ¶12:71.1]

⇨[4:401]   ***PRACTICE POINTER:***   Another reason not to delay filing proof of service is to *avoid disputes as to validity* of service. If the defendant denies service, plaintiff's delay in return of service may raise "serious doubt as to the veracity of the alleged service of process." [*Graf v. Gaslight* (1990) 225 CA3d 291, 296, 274 CR 759, 761 (disapproved on other grounds in *Watts v. Crawford* (1995) 10 C4th 743, 758, 42 CR2d 81, 92, fn. 13)]

a.   [4:402]   **Compare—return of summons served on nonresidents:**   Where a nonresident is served by certified mail with return-receipt-requested pursuant to CCP §415.40, proof of service requires the signed return receipt or other proof of actual receipt by the defendant (¶4:379). Without such "hard evidence of actual delivery," no default can be entered against the nonresident. [See *Johnson & Johnson v. Sup.Ct. (Lawton)* (1985) 38 C3d 243, 254, 211 CR 517, 524]

But such proof is *not* required to prevent dismissal of the action. The "return of summons" requirement in the *dismissal* statute (CCP §583.210) is satisfied "when the plaintiff provides the court with *notice* that he or she has *completed all acts necessary to effect service*" within the statutory period . . . i.e., regardless of actual receipt by the defendant. [*Johnson & Johnson v. Sup.Ct. (Lawton)*, supra, 38 C3d at 254, 211 CR at 524; *see discussion at ¶11:65*]

[4:403]   **Example:**   P returned summons with an affidavit stating that summons and complaint had been mailed to nonresident D pursuant to CCP §415.40, before expiration of the 3-year dismissal period. P's return did *not* include the signed certified mail receipt or other proof of actual receipt by D, which is required to complete service under §415.40 (¶4:161). Even so, P's affidavit prevented dismissal because it showed that *all acts required of P* had been completed before expiration of the statutory period. [*Johnson & Johnson v. Sup.Ct. (Lawton)*, supra, 38 C3d at 255, 211 CR at 524; *see ¶11:65*]

[4:404-409]   *Reserved.*

## F.   PROCEDURES FOR CHALLENGING SERVICE OF SUMMONS

[4:410]   Various procedures may be utilized to attack a summons that has been improperly issued or served, or in which the proof of service is defective.

1.   [4:411]   **Motion to Quash Service of Summons [CCP §418.10]:**   This is the first line of defense against an improper summons or service. It is the *only* procedure which can be utilized at the outset of the action without waiving the objection,

because filing an answer or demurrer or other motion constitutes a general appearance (¶*3:163 ff.*).

🖐>[4:412]  *PRACTICE POINTER:*  But unless the time for service has expired (¶*4:345*), the motion is rarely worthwhile where improper service is the *only* objection. Plaintiff will merely reserve the papers and nothing will be accomplished except some delay and unnecessary expense for the parties; *see* ¶*4:3.*

*FORM:*  Checklist for Motion to Quash Service (Defective Service), *see Form 4:G.*

a.  [4:413]  **Grounds:**  Without valid service of summons, the court never acquires jurisdiction over defendant. Hence, the statutory ground for the motion to quash is that the court *lacks jurisdiction* over the defendant. [CCP §418.10(a)(1)]

(1) [4:414]  **Lack of proper service:**  A defendant is under no duty to respond in any way to a defectively served summons. It makes no difference that defendant had actual knowledge of the action. Such knowledge does not dispense with statutory requirements for service of summons. [*Kappel v. Bartlett* (1988) 200 CA3d 1457, 1466, 246 CR 815, 821; *Ruttenberg v. Ruttenberg* (1997) 53 CA4th 801, 808, 62 CR2d 78, 82]

🖐>[4:415]  *PRACTICE POINTER:*  If defendant denies service, plaintiff's counsel should simply re-serve the summons! It could be a big waste of time and money to proceed in an action where jurisdiction is not clearly established. Moreover, if it turns out that the defendant is right and your process server made a false declaration of service, there is a risk of *tort liability* (abuse of process)! [See *Kappel v. Bartlett*, supra, 200 CA3d at 1464, 246 CR at 818; *and* ¶*4:437*]

(2) [4:416]  **Compare—lack of personal jurisdiction:**  The same statutory ground is utilized to challenge the constitutional sufficiency of a nonresident defendant's "contacts" with California (*see* ¶*3:375-395*).

(3) [4:417]  **Compare—challenging sufficiency of unlawful detainer complaint:**  Ordinarily, of course, a demurrer is the proper procedure for challenging the sufficiency of the complaint. However, where the special *5-day summons* for unlawful detainer actions has been served, a motion to quash service is the proper method to challenge the sufficiency of the complaint. Reason: If the complaint fails to state a cause of action for unlawful detainer, service of the 5-day summons is

improper! [*Delta Imports, Inc. v. Mun.Ct. (Missimer)* (1983) 146 CA3d 1033, 1036, 194 CR 685, 687—complaint failed to allege written notice to tenant]

(a) **[4:418] General demurrer improper:** The motion to quash is the *only* procedure to test whether a complaint states a cause of action for *unlawful detainer*, and thereby supports a 5-day summons. [*Delta Imports, Inc. v. Mun.Ct. (Missimer)*, supra, 146 CA3d at 1036, 194 CR at 687]

Reason: A general demurrer would be overruled if the complaint states *any* cause of action, even if other than unlawful detainer (e.g., nonpayment of rent as breach of contract). Moreover, a demurrer constitutes a general appearance (¶*3:165.1*), and therefore would waive the very point sought to be raised (improper use of the 5-day summons). [*Delta Imports, Inc. v. Mun.Ct. (Missimer)*, supra]

Caution: *Delta Imports* may not be reliable. *See discussion at* ¶7:7a.

(b) **[4:419] Compare—special demurrer:** But *special* demurrers can still be used in unlawful detainer actions (even in "limited civil cases," and despite economic litigation reforms). [CCP §91(b); *see* ¶7:38.1] (But a special demurrer also constitutes a general appearance and therefore cannot be used to attack jurisdiction.)

Comment: Allowing special demurrers in unlawful detainer actions seems to be a legislative oversight. It makes little sense to allow *more* pleadings in what is supposed to be a summary proceeding!

b. **[4:420] Time for filing:** The motion to quash must be made as the defendant's initial appearance in the action, on or before the last day to plead. (Again, defendant's filing an answer or demurrer or other motion waives any defect in jurisdiction or service.)

(1) **[4:421]** Filing the motion extends the defendant's time to answer or demur. [CCP §418.10(b); *see* ¶3:392] And, a further extension is available if defendant seeks appellate review of denial of his or her motion. [CCP §418.10(b),(c); ¶3:394]

c. **[4:422] Hearing on motion to quash:** *See* ¶3:381-383.

d. **[4:423] Review of ruling on motion to quash:** *See* ¶3:394.

2. **[4:424] Motion to Dismiss for Delay in Service of Summons:** Failure to serve summons within 3 years after com-

mencement of the action is ground for mandatory dismissal. [CCP §583.210; for detailed discussion, see ¶11:51 ff.]

A motion to dismiss for delay in service of summons is *not* a general appearance, even if joined with a motion to quash service of summons or to set aside a default judgment. [CCP §583.220(b); see ¶11:82.3]

Where the alleged service occurs just before expiration of the 3-year period, a motion to dismiss lies to challenge defective service, because the requirement that the summons be "served" within 3 years "necessarily raises the issue of the *validity* of the service." [*Mannesmann Demag, Ltd. v. Sup.Ct. (Welch)* (1985) 172 CA3d 1118, 1124-1125, 218 CR 632, 636; *Dill v. Berquist Const. Co., Inc.* (1994) 24 CA4th 1426, 1433, 29 CR2d 746, 749]

    a.  **[4:425]**  **Rationale:**  A motion to quash would also lie, but it would serve no purpose where it is too late for plaintiff to cure the defect. In such cases, a motion to dismiss under the 3-year statute is proper. [*Mannesmann Demag, Ltd. v. Sup.Ct. (Welch)*, supra, 172 CA3d at 1125, 218 CR at 636]

⇨**[4:426]**  **PRACTICE POINTER:**  If you represent defendant, wait until *after* expiration of the 3-year dismissal period before filing either a motion to quash or dismiss. If you file either motion before then, the plaintiff may get a chance to perfect service . . . because the dismissal period is *tolled* while the "validity of service was the subject of litigation" (see CCP §583.240(c), ¶11:108).

    **[4:427]**  *Caution:*  If you obtain extensions of time to respond in order to get beyond the 3-year dismissal period, you may be *estopped* from asserting the statutory bar. [*Tresway Aero, Inc. v. Sup.Ct. (Dent)* (1971) 5 C3d 431, 441-442, 96 CR 571, 578-579; see ¶11:89, 11:92 ff.]

    b.  **[4:428]**  **Burden of proving valid service:**  Proving the existence of jurisdiction is always plaintiff's burden. Therefore, even though defendant is the moving party on a motion to dismiss, the burden is on plaintiff to show valid service within the statutory period. [*Dill v. Berquist Const. Co., Inc.* (1994) 24 CA4th 1426, 1439-1440, 29 CR2d 746, 753-754]

  3.  **[4:429]**  **Motion to Set Aside Default Judgment:**  If the defectively-served summons deprived defendant of *actual* notice of the proceedings in time to raise the defect before his or her default was taken, he or she may move the court to set aside the default and any judgment thereon, so as to permit consideration of a motion to quash service of the summons. [CCP §473.5(a)]

    a.  **[4:430]**  **Time limit for motion:**  This method of challenging service of summons requires a motion to be made within a "reasonable time," and in no event later than *2 years* after the entry of the default judgment, or *180 days after notice* of entry of the *default,* whichever is earlier. [CCP §473.5(a); see *Gibble v. Car-Lene Research, Inc.* (1998) 67 CA4th 295, 300, 78 CR2d 892, 895, fn. 3]

    b.  **[4:431] Not a general appearance:** Like the motion to quash itself, the motion to set aside the default under §473.5 is protected as a special appearance, and thus will not waive whatever objection defendant has to the summons or the service. [CCP §418.10(d)]

    c.  **[4:432] Procedure on motion and hearing:** *See discussion at ¶5:430 ff.*

  4.  **[4:433] Default and Appeal:** Alternatively, defendant may avoid any appearance in the trial court and simply appeal from the default judgment on ground of improper service of summons. To challenge service of summons by this method, the appeal must be *timely* (no later than 180 days after entry of the judgment, or 60 days after notice thereof). And, it is also risky, because if defendant loses on the summons issue, he or she has waived any right to contest the merits (¶3:401-403).

  5.  **[4:434] Motion to Vacate Renewal of Judgment:** The judgment creditor may seek to extend the 10-year period for enforcement of a judgment by filing an "Application for Renewal" before expiration of the 10-year period and serving notice of such renewal on the judgment debtor (see CCP §683.130 et seq.). The judgment debtor then has 30 days within which to move to *vacate the renewal* on any ground that would be a defense to an action on the judgment (see CCP §683.170). One such ground is failure to serve summons in the original action on which the judgment was based. [*Fidelity Creditor Service, Inc. v. Browne* (2001) 89 CA4th 195, 207, 106 CR2d 854, 863]

    a.  **[4:435] Effect:** Although the judgment debtor has only two years within which to move to set aside a default judgment for lack of service (CCP §473.5(a), *see ¶4:147*), if the judgment remains in effect for *10 years,* the judgment debtor may raise lack of service as ground to *oppose its renewal.* [*Fidelity Creditor Service, Inc. v. Browne,* supra, 89 CA4th at 203, 106 CR2d at 860]

  6.  **[4:436] Collateral Attack:** Finally, if all other time limits have expired, defendant may be able to raise the improper service of summons by collateral attack: i.e., a separate suit in equity to have the judgment set aside for lack of jurisdiction; or defendant may wait until the judgment is sought to be enforced and then raise the lack of jurisdiction as a defense to its enforcement. [*Donel, Inc. v. Badalian* (1978) 87 CA3d 327, 333-334, 150 CR 855, 859]

*Caution: A collateral attack is not allowed if defendant appeared* in the original action—even if his or her appearance was limited to litigating the jurisdiction issue. Once the jurisdiction issue is raised, defendant's remedy is limited to appeal; defendant is barred from relitigating the issue in a later suit (*see ¶3:404-406*).

7. **[4:437] Compare—Tort Action for False Proof of Service:** A process server who knowingly executes a false proof of service is subject to liability for the tort of abuse of process; so also is the process server's employer, under respondeat superior. [*Kappel v. Bartlett* (1988) 200 CA3d 1457, 1465, 246 CR 815, 820]

⇨**[4:438]** *PRACTICE POINTER:* This is good reason to use *independent* process serving companies to serve summons, rather than your employees! (Care still must be taken in selection of the process serving company to avoid claims of negligence.)

a. **[4:439] Privilege?** It is an *open question* whether a false proof of service is protected as a "publication . . . in a judicial proceeding" under Civ.C. §47(b). [*Kappel v. Bartlett, supra,* 200 CA3d at 1469, 246 CR at 822-823, fn. 2]

**RESERVED**

# SUMMONS

## SUMMONS
### (CITACION JUDICIAL)

**NOTICE TO DEFENDANT:**
*(AVISO AL DEMANDADO):*

**SUM-100**

FOR COURT USE ONLY
*(SOLO PARA USO DE LA CORTE)*

**YOU ARE BEING SUED BY PLAINTIFF:**
*(LO ESTÁ DEMANDANDO EL DEMANDANTE):*

You have 30 CALENDAR DAYS after this summons and legal papers are served on you to file a written response at this court and have a copy served on the plaintiff.   A letter or phone call will not protect you.   Your written response must be in proper legal form if you want the court to hear your case.   There may be a court form that you can use for  your response. You can find these court forms and more information at the California Courts Online Self-Help Center (www.courtinfo.ca.gov/selfhelp), your county law library, or the courthouse nearest you.   If you cannot pay the filing fee, ask the court clerk for a fee waiver form.   If you do not file your response on time, you may lose the case by default, and your wages, money, and property may be taken without further warning from the court.
There are other legal requirements. You may want to call an attorney right away. If you do not know an attorney, you may want to call an attorney referral service. If you cannot afford an attorney, you may be eligible for free legal services from a nonprofit legal services program. You can locate these nonprofit groups at the California Legal Services Web site (www.lawhelpcalifornia.org), the California Courts Online Self-Help Center (www.courtinfo.ca.gov/selfhelp), or by contacting your local court or county bar association.

*Tiene 30 DÍAS DE CALENDARIO después de que le entreguen esta citación y papeles legales para presentar una respuesta por escrito en esta corte y hacer que se entregue una copia al demandante. Una carta o una llamada telefónica no lo protegen. Su respuesta por escrito tiene que estar en formato legal correcto si desea que procesen su caso en la corte. Es posible que haya un formulario que usted pueda usar para su respuesta. Puede encontrar estos formularios de la corte y más información en el Centro de Ayuda de las Cortes de California (www.courtinfo.ca.gov/selfhelp/espanol), en la biblioteca de leyes de su condado o en la corte que le quede más cerca. Si no puede pagar la cuota de presentación, pida al secretario de la corte que le dé un formulario de exención de pago de cuotas. Si no presenta su respuesta a tiempo, puede perder el caso por incumplimiento y la corte le podrá quitar su sueldo, dinero y bienes sin más advertencia.*
*Hay otros requisitos legales. Es recomendable que llame a un abogado inmediatamente. Si no conoce a un abogado, puede llamar a un servicio de remisión a abogados. Si no puede pagar a un abogado, es posible que cumpla con los requisitos para obtener servicios legales gratuitos de un programa de servicios legales sin fines de lucro. Puede encontrar estos grupos sin fines de lucro en el sitio web de California Legal Services, (www.lawhelpcalifornia.org), en el Centro de Ayuda de las Cortes de California, (www.courtinfo.ca.gov/selfhelp/espanol) o poniéndose en contacto con la corte o el colegio de abogados locales.*

The name and address of the court is:
*(El nombre y dirección de la corte es):*

CASE NUMBER:
*(Número del Caso):*

The name, address, and telephone number of plaintiff's attorney, or plaintiff without an attorney, is:
*(El nombre, la dirección y el número de teléfono del abogado del demandante, o del demandante que no tiene abogado, es):*

DATE: _____  Clerk, by _____ , Deputy
*(Fecha)* *(Secretario)* *(Adjunto)*

*(For proof of service of this summons, use Proof of Service of Summons (form POS-010).)*
*(Para prueba de entrega de esta citatión use el formulario Proof of Service of Summons, (POS-010)).*

**NOTICE TO THE PERSON SERVED:** You are served

[SEAL]

1. ☐  as an individual defendant.
2. ☐  as the person sued under the fictitious name of *(specify):*

3. ☐  on behalf of *(specify):*

    under: ☐  CCP 416.10 (corporation)          ☐  CCP 416.60 (minor)
           ☐  CCP 416.20 (defunct corporation)  ☐  CCP 416.70 (conservatee)
           ☐  CCP 416.40 (association or partnership) ☐  CCP 416.90 (authorized person)
           ☐  other *(specify):*
4. ☐  by personal delivery on *(date):*

Page 1 of 1

Form Adopted for Mandatory Use
Judicial Council of California
SUM-100 [Rev. January 1, 2004]

**SUMMONS**

Code of Civil Procedure §§ 412.20, 465

**RESERVED**

# ADDITIONAL PARTIES ATTACHMENT

| SHORT TITLE: | CASE NUMBER: |
|---|---|
|  |  |

## INSTRUCTIONS FOR USE

► This form may be used as an attachment to any summons if space does not permit the listing of all parties on the summons.

► If this attachment is used, insert the following statement in the plaintiff or defendant box on the summons: "Additional Parties Attachment form is attached."

List additional parties *(Check only one box. Use a separate page for each type of party.)*:

☐ Plaintiff    ☐ Defendant    ☐ Cross-Complainant    ☐ Cross-Defendant

Page _____ of _____

Form Adopted by Rule 982(a)(9)(A)
Judicial Council of California
982(a)(9)(A) (New January 1, 1993)

**ADDITIONAL PARTIES ATTACHMENT**
**Attachment to Summons**

**[FORM 4:B]**

# NOTICE AND ACKNOWLEDGMENT OF RECEIPT

982(a)(4)

| NAME AND ADDRESS OF SENDER:      TELEPHONE NO.: | For Court Use Only: |
|---|---|
| Insert name of court, judicial district or branch court, if any, and Post Office and Street Address: | |
| PLAINTIFF: | |
| DEFENDANT: | |
| **NOTICE AND ACKNOWLEDGMENT OF RECEIPT** | Case Number: |

TO:. . . . . . . . . . . . . . . . . . . . . . . . . . . . . . . . . . . . . . . . . . . . . . . . . . . . . . . . . . . . . . . . . . . . . . . . . .

(insert name of individual being served)

This summons and other document(s) indicated below are being served pursuant to Section 415.30 of the California Code of Civil Procedure. Your failure to complete this form and return it to me within 20 days may subject you (or the party on whose behalf you are being served) to liability for the payment of any expenses incurred in serving a summons on you in any other manner permitted by law.

If you are being served on behalf of a corporation, unincorporated association (including a partnership), or other entity, this form must be signed by you in the name of such entity or by a person authorized to receive service of process on behalf of such entity. In all other cases, this form must be signed by you personally or by a person authorized by you to acknowledge receipt of summons. Section 415.30 provides that this summons and other document(s) are deemed served on the date you sign the Acknowledgment of Receipt below, if you return this form to me.

Dated:. . . . . . . . . . . . . . . . . . . . . . . .     _____

(Signature of sender)

**ACKNOWLEDGMENT OF RECEIPT**

This acknowledges receipt of: (To be completed by sender before mailing)

1. ☐ A copy of the summons and of the complaint.
2. ☐ A copy of the summons and of the Petition (Marriage) and:
   - ☐ Blank Confidential Counseling Statement (Marriage)
   - ☐ Order to Show Cause (Marriage)
   - ☐ Blank Responsive Declaration
   - ☐ Blank Financial Declaration
   - ☐ Other: (Specify)

**(To be completed by recipient)**

Date of receipt:. . . . . . . . . . . . . . . . . . . . . . . . . . . . . _____

(Signature of person acknowledging receipt, with title if<br>acknowledgment is made on behalf of another person)

Date this form is signed:. . . . . . . . . . . . . . . . . . _____

(Type or print your name and name of entity, if any,<br>on whose behalf this form is signed)

| Form Adopted by the<br>Judicial Council of California<br>Revised Effective January 1, 1975<br>[982(a)(4)]<br>Mandatory Form | **NOTICE AND ACKNOWLEDGMENT OF RECEIPT** |  WEST<br>GROUP | CCP 415.30, 417.10;<br>Cal. Rules of Court,<br>Rule 1216 |

# DECLARATION OF LOST SUMMONS AFTER SERVICE

982(a)(12)

| ATTORNEY OR PARTY WITHOUT ATTORNEY *(Name, state bar number, and address):* | FOR COURT USE ONLY |
|---|---|
| TELEPHONE NO.:                    FAX NO.: | |
| ATTORNEY FOR *(Name):* | |
| NAME OF COURT: | |
| STREET ADDRESS: | |
| MAILING ADDRESS: | |
| CITY AND ZIP CODE: | |
| BRANCH NAME: | |
| PLAINTIFF/ PETITIONER: | |
| DEFENDANT/ RESPONDENT: | |

| DECLARATION OF LOST SUMMONS AFTER SERVICE | CASE NUMBER: |
|---|---|

1. At the time of service, I was at least eighteen (18) years of age and not a party to this action.

2. On *(date):* _____ , I served a copy of a *Summons* together with *(specify documents):*

   on defendant/cross-defendant/respondent in this proceeding, in the manner described below.

3. Name of party served and title, if any:

4. Person with whom a copy of the *Summons* was left, and title or relationship to party served:

5. Mailing date and type of mail:

6. Address, city, and state *(when required, indicate whether address is home or business):*

7. Manner of service:
   a. ☐ **Personal service.** By personally delivering copies to person served. (Code Civ. Proc., § 415.10.)
   b. ☐ **Substituted service on a corporation or unincorporated association (including partnership or public entity).** By leaving, during usual office hours, copies in the office of the person served, with the person who apparently was in charge and thereafter mailing (by first-class mail, postage prepaid) copies to the person served at the place where the copies were left. (Code Civ. Proc., § 415.20(a).)
      Place of mailing *(specify):*
   c. ☐ **Substituted service on natural person, minor, or incompetent.** By leaving copies at the dwelling house, usual place of abode, or usual place of business of the person served with or in the presence of a competent member of the household or a person apparently in charge of the office or place of business, at least 18 years of age, who was informed of the general nature of the papers, and thereafter mailing (by first-class mail, postage prepaid) copies to the person served at the place where the copies were left. (Code Civ. Proc., § 415.20(b).) Attached is a separate declaration or affidavit stating acts relied on to establish reasonable diligence in first attempting personal service.
      Place of mailing *(specify):*
   d. ☐ **Mail and acknowledgment of service.** By mailing (by first-class mail, postage prepaid) copies to the person served, together with two copies of the notice and acknowledgment provided for in Code of Civil Procedure section 415.30(b) and a return envelope, postage prepaid, addressed to the sender. (Code Civ. Proc., § 415.30.) Attached is a completed copy of the notice and acknowledgment of receipt mailed to the sender.
      Place of mailing *(specify):*

(Continued on reverse)

Form Adopted for Mandatory Use
Judicial Council of California
982(a)(12) [New July 1, 2000]

**DECLARATION OF LOST SUMMONS
AFTER SERVICE**

Code of Civil Procedure,
§§ 417.30(b), 2015.5

| PLAINTIFF/PETITIONER: | CASE NUMBER: |
|---|---|
| DEFENDANT/RESPONDENT: | |

e. ☐ **Certified or registered mail service.** By mailing to an address outside California (by registered or certified mail with return receipt requested) copies to the person served. (Code Civ. Proc., § 415.40.) Attached is a signed return receipt or other evidence of actual delivery to the person served.
   Place of mailing *(specify)*:

f. ☐ **Other.** Specify other manner of service and authorizing code sections:

   ☐ Continued on Attachment 7f.

8. The following notice appeared on the copy of the *Summons* served (Code Civ. Proc., § 412.30, 415.10, or 474):
   a. ☐ You are served as an individual defendant.
   b. ☐ You are served as (or on behalf of) the person sued under the fictitious name of *(specify)*:
   c. ☐ You are served on behalf of *(specify)*:
   under: (1) ☐ Code Civ. Proc., § 416.10 (corporation)     (5) ☐ Code Civ. Proc., § 416.60 (minor)
   (2) ☐ Code Civ. Proc., § 416.20 (defunct corporation)     (6) ☐ Code Civ. Proc., § 416.70 (conservatee)
   (3) ☐ Code Civ. Proc., § 416.40 (association/partnership)     (7) ☐ Code Civ. Proc., § 416.90 (individual)
   (4) ☐ By personal delivery on *(date)*:

9. This declaration is returned in lieu of the original *Summons*.

10. Declarant's current address and telephone number are as follows:
    a. Address:

    b. Telephone number:

I declare under penalty of perjury under the laws of the State of California that the foregoing is true and correct.

Date:

_____          ► _____
(TYPE OR PRINT NAME)                              (SIGNATURE OF DECLARANT)

# EX PARTE APPLICATION FOR
# ORDER FOR PUBLICATION OF SUMMONS

```
1   ............................
    State Bar No...................
2   ............................
    ............................
3   ............................

4

5   Attorney for ................

6

7

8           SUPERIOR COURT OF THE STATE OF CALIFORNIA

9                   COUNTY OF .........

10

11  ........................... )    CASE NO. .....................
                                 )
12          Plaintiff,           )
                                 )    EX PARTE APPLICATION FOR ORDER
13  vs.                          )    FOR PUBLICATION OF SUMMONS
                                 )    [CCP §415.50]; DECLARATION AND
14  ........................... )    POINTS AND AUTHORITIES IN
                                 )    SUPPORT
15                               )
            Defendant.           )
16  _____)
```

17      Plaintiff, through his attorney of record, hereby applies for

18  an order directing services of summons on the defendant ..........

19  ........................ by publication in a newspaper of general

20  circulation, pursuant to Code of Civil Procedure Section 415.50.

21      Such application is made upon the ground that said defendant

22  cannot with reasonable diligence be located and served in any other

23  manner specified in Code of Civil Procedure Sections 415.10 through

24  415.30, and that as shown by the complaint on file herein, a cause

25  of action for damages exists against said defendant.

26  /////

27  /////

28  /////

---

1

APPL. FOR ORDER
FOR PUBLICATION OF SUMMONS

1     Such application is based on the attached declaration of .....
2     .............., the points and authorities set forth below, and the
3     complete files and records of this action.
4     DATED: ........., ......        /s/_____
                                      Attorney for Plaintiff
5
6          POINTS AND AUTHORITIES IN SUPPORT OF MOTION
7     *(Follow suggestions in Law and Motion Practice Chapter, ¶9:64-81)*
8
9
10
11
12
13
14
15
16
17
18
19
20
21
22
23
24
25
26
27
28

_____

APPL. FOR ORDER
FOR PUBLICATION OF SUMMONS

# DECLARATION IN SUPPORT OF APPLICATION FOR ORDER FOR PUBLICATION OF SUMMONS

```
 1   ............................
     State Bar No..................
 2   ............................
     ............................
 3   ............................

 4

 5   Attorney for  ................

 6

 7

 8            SUPERIOR COURT OF THE STATE OF CALIFORNIA

 9                   COUNTY OF .........

10

11   ...........................  )    CASE NO. .....................
                                  )
12            Plaintiff,          )
                                  )    DECLARATION IN SUPPORT OF
13   vs.                          )    APPLICATION FOR ORDER FOR
                                  )    PUBLICATION OF SUMMONS
14   ...........................  )
                                  )
15            Defendant.          )
                                  )
16   _____     )

17       I, the undersigned, declare as follows:

18       1.   I am the ...................... in this action and have

19   personal knowledge of each of the facts set forth in this Declara-

20   tion, and can testify competently thereto, except as to the matters

21   stated on information and belief, and as to such matters I believe

22   them to be true.

23       2.   This declaration is being submitted in support of Plain-

24   tiff's Application for an order directing publication of summons

25   against defendant ............. pursuant to the provisions of CCP

26   §415.50.

27   /////

28   /////
```

1

1     3.   Plaintiff's complaint in this action was filed on ......,

2 and contains a cause of action against defendant ................

3 as follows: ......................................................

4     *(ALTERNATIVE: "said defendant claims an interest in the*

5 *real or personal property that is the subject matter of this*

6 *action, as follows:...............................................)*

7     4.   The ....................... is a newspaper of general

8 circulation, published in California. I am informed and believe

9 that publication of summons in said newspaper is most likely to

10 give actual notice to defendant ............................... of

11 the pendency of this action, because said defendant's last known

12 address was within the city and county in which said newspaper is

13 published, and said defendant has friends, relatives and coworkers

14 residing and employed in said city, county and state, as more fully

15 stated in the paragraphs below.

16     5.   I have made the following attempts to deliver copies of

17 the said summons and complaint to defendant personally, all of

18 which attempts have been unsuccessful: .........................

19 ................................................................

20 ................................................................

21     6.   I have made the following attempts to serve copies of the

22 summons and complaint on said defendant by substitute service,

23 pursuant to the provisions of CCP §415.20, all of which attempts

24 have been unsuccessful: .........................................

25 ................................................................

26 ................................................................

27     7.   I have made the following attempts to serve copies of the

28 summons and complaint on said defendant by mail with acknowledgment

2

DECL'N OF ........ IN SUPPORT OF
APPL'N FOR ORDER FOR PUBLICATION OF SUMMONS

                                   Rev. #1 2003

```
1   of receipt, and pursuant to the provisions of CCP §415.30, all of
2   which attempts have been unsuccessful, and said mail returned
3   marked "undeliverable" (or "moved--left no forwarding address"):
4   ............................................................
5   ............................................................
6   .............................................
7        8.   I have been unable to locate said defendant, within or
8   outside the State of California, despite reasonable efforts and
9   diligence.  The following is a description of the records that I
10  have checked, the persons whom I have asked, and the other investi-
11  gations I have made, in the effort to locate said defendant, all of
12  which have been unsuccessful: ..................................
13  ............................................................
14  ..........................................................
15       9.   To the best of my knowledge, no person, firm, or entity
16  other than as mentioned above knows, or is likely to know, the
17  whereabouts of said defendant, and I know of no other source from
18  which the defendant's whereabouts can be ascertained.
19       I declare under penalty of perjury under the laws of the State
20  of California that the foregoing is true and correct.
21       Executed on ............... at ...........................
22                                  /s/
                                    ─────────────────────────────
                                    Declarant
23
24
25
26
27
28
```

DECL'N OF ........ IN SUPPORT OF
APPL'N FOR ORDER FOR PUBLICATION OF SUMMONS

# ORDER FOR PUBLICATION OF SUMMONS

SUPERIOR COURT OF THE STATE OF CALIFORNIA

COUNTY OF .........

| | |
|---|---|
| ........................... )<br>                                )<br>         Plaintiff,   )<br>                                )<br>vs.                         )<br>                                )<br>........................... )<br>                                )<br>        Defendant.   ) | CASE NO. ..................... <br><br>ORDER FOR PUBLICATION OF SUMMONS<br>[CCP §415.50] |

Upon reading and considering the Application of Plaintiff ....
................ for an order directing the publication of summons
against Defendant ............................., and the evidence
presented in support thereof, and it satisfactorily appearing to
the Court that said defendant cannot be served with reasonable
diligence in any other manner provided in Sections 415.10 through
415.30 of the Code of Civil Procedure, and it also appearing that
a good cause of action exists against said Defendant, or that he is
a necessary or proper party to this action, or that he has or
claims an interest in the property which is the subject of this
action and which is subject to the jurisdiction of this Court, and
being fully advised,

1

ORDER FOR PUBLICATION OF SUMMONS

Rev. #1 2003

1    IT IS HEREBY ORDERED THAT

2        (1)  Service of summons in this action be made on Defendant

3    ................... by publication in the .......................

4    newspaper of general circulation published in ...................,

5    which is hereby designated as the newspaper most likely to give

6    actual notice to said Defendant; and that said publication be made

7    at least once a week for four successive weeks; and

8        (2)  A copy of the summons and of the complaint and of the

9    order for publication be mailed to Defendant .....................

10   forthwith, in the event his address is ascertained before the expi-

11   ration of the time herein prescribed for publication of summons.

12   DATED:  .............., .....        /s/ _____
                                             Judge

13

14

15

16

17

18

19

20

21

22

23

24

25

26

27

28

2

ORDER FOR PUBLICATION OF SUMMONS

# CHECKLIST
# MOTION TO QUASH SERVICE
# (DEFECTIVE SERVICE)

*[Ed. Note: This form or similar forms are used by many courts. Counsel should use this as a checklist when preparing a motion or opposition because it may raise factors of concern to the court. Declarations or points and authorities should be prepared to address each of the points on the checklist.]*

Discovery Cut-off: _____          Calendar: _____

Motion Cut-off: _____          Date: _____

Trial Date: _____          Notice: _____

**MOTION TO QUASH SERVICE**
**Lack of Jurisdiction**
**Defective Service**
**(CCP § 418.10(a)(1))**

NAME OF MOVING PARTY: _____

NAME OF RESPONDING PARTY: _____

CORRECT ADDRESS IN PROOF OF SERVICE (CCP §§ 1013, 1013a): _____

NO MORE THAN 30-DAY LAPSE UNDER § 418.10(b): _____

21- DAY LAPSE UNDER CCP § 1005(a)(4)): _____

Previous or concurrent GENERAL APPEARANCE by moving party:

WAIVER by addressing merits:

DATE OF SERVICE of summons:

TYPE of service:          Personal          Substituted          Mail          Publication

Sufficient DECLARATION OF DILIGENCE:

Proof of Service properly VERIFIED: _____

No authorization of AGENT: _____

DECLARATION OF MOVING PARTY (CCP § 2015.5; CRC 315(a)):

PROCESS SERVER DECLARATION:
   (Registered server has presumption (Evid. Code, § 647) and complainant has burden to show valid service.
   (Dill vs. Berquist Const. Co. (1994) 24 Cal.App.4th 1426, 1439))

OPPOSITION:

TENTATIVE RULING:

    ❑ Grant

    ❑ Deny

    ❑ OSC re failure to show service (L.R. 7.7(c))

WTLM0897.021.wpd

**[FORM 4:H]**

# REQUEST FOR SERVICE ABROAD OF JUDICIAL OR EXTRAJUDICIAL DOCUMENTS

### REQUEST

#### FOR SERVICE ABROAD OF JUDICIAL OR EXTRAJUDICIAL DOCUMENTS

*DEMANDE*
*AUX FINS DE SIGNIFICATION OU DE NOTIFICATION A L'ÉTRANGER*
*D'UN ACTE JUDICIAIRE OU EXTRAJUDICIAIRE*

Convention on the service abroad of judicial and extrajudicial documents in civil or commercial matters, signed at the The Hague, November 15, 1965.

*Convention relative à la signification et à la notification à l'étranger des actes judiciaires ou extrajudiciaires en matière civile ou commerciale, signée à La Haye, le 15 Novembre 1965.*

| Identity and address of the applicant<br>*Identité et adresse du requérant* | Address of receiving authority<br>*Adresse de l'autorité destinataire* |
|---|---|
| | |

The undersigned applicant has the honour to transmit - in duplicate - the documents listed below and, in conformity with article 5 of the above-mentioned Convention, requests prompt service of one copy thereof on the addressee, i.e.,
(identity and address)

*Le requérant soussigné a l'honneur de faire parvenir - en double exemplaire - a l'autorité destinataire les documents ci-dessous énumérés, en la priant conformément à l'article 5 de la Convention précitée, d'en faire remettre sans retard un exemplaire au destinataire, savoir:*
*(identité et adresse)* _____

_____

☐ (a) in accordance with the provisions of sub-paragraph (a) of the first paragraph of article 5 of the Convention.*
*a) selon les formes légales (article 5, alinéa premier, lettre a).*

☐ (b) in accordance with the following particular method (sub-paragraph (b) of the first paragraph of article 5)*:
*b) selon la forme particulière suivante (article 5, alinéa premier, lettre b):* _____

_____

_____

☐ (c) by delivery to the addressee, if he accepts it voluntarily (second paragraph of article 5)*.
*c) le cas échéant, par remise simple (article 5, alinéa 2).*

The authority is requested to return or to have returned to the applicant a copy of the documents - and of the annexes* - with a certificate as provided on the reverse side

*Cette autorité est priée de renvoyer ou de faire renvoyer au requérant un exemplaire de l'acte - et de ses annexes - avec l'attestation figurant au verso.*

**List of documents**
*Enumération des pièces*

_____
_____
_____
_____
_____
_____
_____

Done at _____ , the _____
*Fait à _____ , le _____*

Signature and/or stamp.
*Signature et/ou cachet.*

*Delete if inappropriate.*
*Rayer les mentions inutiles.*

1 (Formerly OBD-116 which was formerly LAA-116, both of which may still be used)

USM-94
(Est. 11/22/77

4-84

Rev. #1 2003

CERTIFICATE

*ATTESTATION*

The undersigned authority has the honour to certify, in conformity with article 6 of the Convention,
*L'autorité soussignée a l'honneur d'attester conformément à l'article 6 de ladite Convention,*

1) that the document has been served*
*1. que to demande a été exécutée*

-the (date)
*-te (date)* _____

-at (place, street, number)
*-à (localité, rue numéro)* _____
_____

-in one of the following methods authorised by article 5-

*-dans une des formes suivantes prévues à l'article 5:*

☐ **(a) in accordance with the provisions of sub-paragraph (a) of the first paragraph of article 5 of the Convention*.**
   *a) selon les formes légales (article 5, alinéa premier, lettre a).*

☐ **(b) in accordance with the following particular method*:**
   *b) selon la forme particulière suivante:* _____
   _____

☐ **(c) by delivery to the addressee, who accepted it voluntarily.***
   *c) par remise simple*

The documents referred to in the request have been delivered to:
*Les documents mentionnés dans la demande ont été remis à:*

-(identity and description of person)
*-(identité et qualité de la personne)* _____
_____

-relationship to the addressee (family, business or other):
*-liens de parenté, de subordination ou autres, avec le destinataire de l'acte:* _____
_____

2) that the document has not been served, by reason of the following facts*:
*2. que la demande n'a pas été exécutée, en raison des faits suivants:*
_____
_____
_____

In conformity with the second paragraph of article 12 of the Convention, the applicant is requested to pay or reimburse the expenses detailed in the attached statement*.

*Conformément à l'article 12, alinéa 2, de ladite Convention, le requérant est prié de payer ou de rembourser les frais dont le détail figure au mémoire ci-joint.*

Annexes
*Annexes*
Documents returned:
*Pièces renvoyées:*
_____
_____

Done at _____ , the _____
*Fait à _____ , le _____*

In appropriate cases, documents establishing the service:
*Le cas échéant, les documents justificatifs de l'exécution:*
_____
_____
_____

Signature and/or stamp.
*Signature et/ou cachet.*

_____

*Delete if inappropriate.
*Rayer les mentions inutiles.*

2

2

# SUMMARY OF THE DOCUMENT TO BE SERVED
## *ELEMENTS ESSENTIELS DE L'ACTE*

Convention on the service abroad of judicial and extrajudicial documents in civil or commercial matters, signed at The Hague, November 15, 1965.

*Convention relative à la signification et à la notification à l'étranger des actes judiciaires ou extrajudiciaires en matière civile ou commerciale, signée à La Haye, le 15 Novembré 1965.*

**(article 5, fourth paragraph)**
*(Article 5, alinéa 4)*

**Name and address of the requesting authority:**
*Nom et adresse de l'autorité requérante:* _____
_____
_____

**Particulars of the parties*:**
*Identité des parties:* _____
_____
_____

### JUDICIAL DOCUMENT**
### *ACTE JUDICIAIRE*

**Nature and purpose of the document:**
*Nature et object de l'acte:* _____
_____
_____

**Nature and purpose of the proceedings and, where appropriate, the amount in dispute:**
*Nature et object de l'instance, le cas échéant, le montant du litige:* _____
_____
_____

**Date and place for entering appearance**:**
*Date et lieu de la comparution:* _____
_____
_____

**Court which has given judgment**:**
*Juridiction qui a rendu la décision:* _____
_____

**Time limits stated in the document**:**
*Indication des délias figurant dans l'acte:* _____
_____

### EXTRAJUDICIAL DOCUMENT**
### *ACTE EXTRAJUDICIAIRE*

**Nature and purpose of the document:**
*Nature et objet de l'acte:* _____
_____
_____

**Time limits stated in the document**:**
*Indication des délias figurant dans l'acte:* _____
_____
_____

\* If appropriate, identity and address of the person interested in the transmission of the document
*S'd a lieu, identité et adresse de la personne intéressée à la transmission de l'acte.*

\*\* Delete is inappropriate.
*Raver les mentions hutiles*

✿ U.S. GOVERNMENT PRINTING OFFICE: 1988 - 202-041/86121

# PROOF OF SERVICE

POS-010

| ATTORNEY OR PARTY WITHOUT ATTORNEY (Name, State Bar number, and address): | FOR COURT USE ONLY |
|---|---|
| | |

TELEPHONE NO.:         FAX NO. (Optional):
E-MAIL ADDRESS (Optional):
ATTORNEY FOR (Name):

**SUPERIOR COURT OF CALIFORNIA, COUNTY OF**
  STREET ADDRESS:
  MAILING ADDRESS:
  CITY AND ZIP CODE:
  BRANCH NAME:

| | |
|---|---|
| PLAINTIFF/PETITIONER: | CASE NUMBER: |
| DEFENDANT/RESPONDENT: | |

| | |
|---|---|
| **PROOF OF SERVICE OF SUMMONS** | Ref. No. or File No.: |

*(Separate proof of service is required for each party served.)*

1. At the time of service I was at least 18 years of age and not a party to this action.

2. I served copies of the summons and

    a. ☐ complaint

    b. ☐ Alternative Dispute Resolution (ADR) package

    c. ☐ Civil Case Cover Sheet *(served in complex cases only)*

    d. ☐ cross-complaint

    e. ☐ other *(specify documents):*

3. a. Party served *(specify name of party as shown on documents served):*

    b. Person served: ☐ party in item 3a ☐ other *(specify name and relationship to the party named in item 3a):*

4. Address where the party was served:

5. I served the party *(check proper box)*

    a. ☐ **by personal service.** I personally delivered the documents listed in item 2 to the party or person authorized to receive service of process for the party (1) on *(date):*      (2) at *(time):*

    b. ☐ **by substituted service.** On *(date):*     at *(time):*     I left the documents listed in item 2 with or in the presence of *(name and title or relationship to person indicated in item 3b):*

        (1) ☐ **(business)** a person at least 18 years of age apparently in charge at the office or usual place of business of the person to be served. I informed him or her of the general nature of the papers.

        (2) ☐ **(home)** a competent member of the household (at least 18 years of age) at the dwelling house or usual place of abode of the party. I informed him or her of the general nature of the papers.

        (3) ☐ **(physical address unknown)** a person at least 18 years of age apparently in charge at the usual mailing address of the person to be served, other than a United States Postal Service post office box. I informed him or her of the general nature of the papers.

        (4) ☐ I thereafter mailed (by first-class, postage prepaid) copies of the documents to the person to be served at the place where the copies were left (Code Civ. Proc., § 415.20). I mailed the documents on *(date):*    from *(city):*    or ☐ a declaration of mailing is attached.

        (5) ☐ I attach a **declaration of diligence** stating actions taken first to attempt personal service.

Page 1 of 2

| | |
|---|---|
| Form Adopted for Mandatory Use<br>Judicial Council of California POS-010<br>[Rev. January 1, 2004] | Code of Civil Procedure, § 417.10 |

c. ☐ **by mail and acknowledgment of receipt of service.** I mailed the documents listed in item 2 to the party, to the address shown in item 4, by first-class mail, postage prepaid,

    (1) on *(date):*                       (2) from *(city):*

    (3) ☐ with two copies of the *Notice and Acknowledgment of Receipt* (form 982(a)(4)) and a postage-paid return envelope addressed to me. *(Attach completed* Notice and Acknowledgement of Receipt *(form 982(a)(4).)* (Code Civ. Proc., § 415.30.)

    (4) ☐ to an address outside California with return receipt requested. (Code Civ. Proc., § 415.40.)

d. ☐ **by other means** *(specify means of service and authorizing code section):*

    ☐ Additional page describing service is attached.

6. The "Notice to the Person Served" (on the summons) was completed as follows:
  a. ☐ as an individual defendant.
  b. ☐ as the person sued under the fictitious name of *(specify):*
  c. ☐ On behalf of *(specify):*

    under the following Code of Civil Procedure section:

| | |
|---|---|
| ☐ 416.10 (corporation) | ☐ 415.95 (business organization, form unknown) |
| ☐ 416.20 (defunct corporation) | ☐ 416.60 (minor) |
| ☐ 416.30 (joint stock company/association) | ☐ 416.70 (ward or conservatee) |
| ☐ 416.40 (association or partnership) | ☐ 416.90 (authorized person) |
| ☐ 416.50 (public entity) | ☐ 415.46 (occupant) |
| | ☐ other: |

7. **Person who served papers**
  a. Name:
  b. Address:
  c. Telephone number:
  d. **The fee** for service was: $
  e. I am:
    (1) ☐ not a registered California process server.
    (2) ☐ exempt from registration under Business and Professions Code section 22350(b).
    (3) ☐ registered California process server:
      (i) ☐ Employee or independent contractor.
      (ii) Registration No.:
      (iii) County:

8. ☐ **I declare** under penalty of perjury under the laws of the State of California that the foregoing is true and correct.

    or

9. ☐ **I am a California sheriff or marshal and** I certify that the foregoing is true and correct.

Date:

_____      ▶      _____
(NAME OF PERSON WHO SERVED PAPERS/SHERIFF OR MARSHAL)           (SIGNATURE )

# EX PARTE APPLICATION FOR
# EXTENSION OF TIME TO SERVE PLEADING

CM-020

| ATTORNEY OR PARTY WITHOUT ATTORNEY *(Name, State Bar number, and address):* | FOR COURT USE ONLY |
|---|---|
| TELEPHONE NO.: FAX NO. *(Optional):* <br> E-MAIL ADDRESS *(Optional):* <br> ATTORNEY FOR *(Name):* | |

**SUPERIOR COURT OF CALIFORNIA, COUNTY OF**
STREET ADDRESS:
MAILING ADDRESS:
CITY AND ZIP CODE:
BRANCH NAME:

PLAINTIFF/PETITIONER:

DEFENDANT/RESPONDENT:

| EX PARTE APPLICATION FOR EXTENSION OF TIME TO SERVE PLEADING AND ORDER ☐ EXTENDING TIME TO SERVE AND ☐ ORDER CONTINUING CASE MANAGEMENT CONFERENCE | CASE NUMBER: |
|---|---|

**APPLICATION**

| | HEARING DATE: |
|---|---|
| | DEPT.: TIME: |

1. Applicant *(name):*
   is
   a. ☐ plaintiff
   b. ☐ cross-complainant
   c. ☐ petitioner
   d. ☐ defendant
   e. ☐ cross-defendant
   f. ☐ respondent
   g. ☐ other *(describe):*

2. The complaint or other initial pleading in this action was filed on *(date):*

3. Applicant requests that the court grant an order extending time for service of the following pleading:
   a. ☐ Complaint
   b. ☐ Cross-complaint
   c. ☐ Petition
   d. ☐ Answer or other responsive pleading
   e. ☐ Other *(describe):*

4. Service of the pleading listed in item 3 is presently required to be completed by *(date):*

5. Previous applications, orders, or stipulations for an extension of time to serve in this action are:
   a. ☐ None
   b. ☐ The following *(describe all, including the length of any previous extensions):*

6. Applicant requests an extension of time to serve the pleading listed in item 3 on the following parties *(name each):*

Form Approved for Optional Use
Judicial Council of California
CM-020 [New January 1, 2004]

**EX PARTE APPLICATION FOR EXTENSION OF TIME
TO SERVE PLEADING AND ORDERS**

Cal. Rules of Court,
rules 201.7 and 379

| CASE NAME: | CASE NUMBER: |
|---|---|

7. The pleading has not yet been served on the parties listed in item 6 for the following reasons *(describe the efforts that have been made to serve the pleading and why service has not been completed):*

☐ Continued on Attachment 7.

8. An extension of time to serve the pleading should be granted for the following reasons:

☐ Continued on Attachment 8.

9. If an extension of time is granted, service on the parties listed in item 6 will be completed by *(date):*

10. Notice of this application under rule 379 ☐ has been provided as required *(describe all parties or counsel to whom notice was given; the date, time, and manner of giving notice; what the parties or counsel were told and their responses; and whether opposition is expected)* or ☐ is not required *(state reasons):*

☐ Continued on Attachment 10.

11. Number of pages attached: ____

I declare under penalty of perjury under the laws of the State of California that the foregoing is true and correct.

Date:

_____
(TYPE OR PRINT NAME OF APPLICANT OR ATTORNEY FOR APPLICANT)

▶

_____
(SIGNATURE OF APPLICANT OR ATTORNEY FOR APPLICANT)

Order on Application is ☐ below ☐ on a separate document.

## ORDER

1. The application for an order extending time to serve the pleading is ☐ granted ☐ denied.
2. The pleading must be served no later than *(date):*
3. ☐ The case management conference is rescheduled to *(date):*
4. Other orders:

5. A copy of this application and order must be served on all parties or their counsel that have appeared in the case.

Date:

_____
JUDICIAL OFFICER

**EX PARTE APPLICATION FOR EXTENSION OF TIME
TO SERVE PLEADING AND ORDERS**

# CHAPTER 5

# DEFAULTS:

# HOW TO OBTAIN THEM AND HOW TO CURE THEM

## CONTENTS

Page

A. GENERAL ................................................................. 5-1
  1. Defendant "In Default" ........................................ 5-1
    a. Late pleadings by defendant ........................... 5-1
  2. Entry of Default by Court Clerk ........................... 5-1
    a. Mandatory duty ............................................ 5-2
    b. Effect of default entry .................................... 5-2
      (1) Jurisdictional ........................................... 5-2
        (a) Compare—motion to dismiss as motion
           for relief from default? ......................... 5-2
      (2) Admissions ............................................. 5-3
    c. Date of entry ................................................ 5-3
      (1) Backdating register of actions .................. 5-3
    d. Compare—amended complaint may "open up"
      default ........................................................ 5-3
  3. Default Judgments—General Considerations .......... 5-4
    a. Judgment by clerk vs. judgment by court ......... 5-4
      (1) Compare—default judgment as discovery
        sanction ................................................. 5-4
    b. Time limit to obtain default judgment ............... 5-4
    c. Limitations on default judgments .................... 5-4
    d. Res judicata effect of default judgment ........... 5-4
      (1) Collateral estoppel as to issues adjudicated ........ 5-5
  4. Case Management Standards ............................. 5-5
    a. Grounds for extension of time? ...................... 5-5
    b. Effect of delay ............................................. 5-5
    c. Sanctions ................................................... 5-5
      (1) Refusing default or default judgment? ......... 5-6

B. ENTRY OF DEFAULT ................................................ 5-6
  1. Conditions for Entry of Default ........................... 5-6
    a. Manner of service permitting entry of default ......... 5-6
      (1) Includes service by publication ................. 5-6
    b. Expiration of time to respond ......................... 5-6
      (1) Time to respond ..................................... 5-7
        (a) When service deemed complete ......... 5-7

       (2)  Where time extended ........................................... 5-7

  c.  Defendant's failure to respond ................................ 5-8.1

      (1)  Responses to original complaint preventing
          entry of default ........................................ 5-8

         (a)  Late pleading immaterial .............................. 5-9

         (b)  Title of response determinative ..................... 5-9

         (c)  Sufficiency of response immaterial ............... 5-9

            1)  Compare—"moribund" demurrers ...........5-10

         (d)  Response must be filed, not merely
            served ....................................................5-10

         (e)  Compare—cases removed to federal
            court, then remanded ................................5-11

            1)  Where no prior general appearance .......5-11

            2)  Where no answer filed before removal ...5-11

      (2)  Default based on failure to provide further
          response ......................................................5-11

         (a)  After motion to quash or stay ......................5-12

            1)  Extension of time if motion denied .........5-12

            2)  Further extension if mandamus
               sought.....................................................5-12

         (b)  After motion to change venue ......................5-12

            1)  Extension of time if motion granted ........5-12

            2)  Court will grant extension if motion
               denied.....................................................5-12

               a)  If appellate review sought ...............5-12

         (c)  After motion to dismiss for delay in serving
            summons .................................................5-13

         (d)  After demurrer...........................................5-13

            1)  If demurrer sustained ............................5-13

            2)  If demurrer overruled .............................5-13

              a)  Defendant ordered to answer ...........5-14

              b)  No order to answer ...........................5-14

              c)  Time to answer runs from notice
                 of ruling ...........................................5-14

         (e)  After motion to strike ..................................5-14

            1)  If motion granted ..................................5-14

            2)  If motion denied.....................................5-15

              a)  Time runs from notice of ruling ........5-15

         (f)  Compare—after plaintiff amends
            complaint .................................................5-15

            1)  Amendments making substantive
               changes ................................................5-15

            2)  No substantive changes .........................5-16

  d.  Compare—defaults ordered by court despite
     responsive pleading.............................................5-16

      (1)  Compare—no default for failure to appear at
          trial .............................................................5-16

2.  Ethical Obligation to Warn Opposing Counsel .................5-16

  a.  No legal obligation .................................................5-17

  b.  Effect of failure to warn..........................................5-17

3. Dealing With Pro Per Defendants ...................................... 5-18
   a. Corporate defendants ............................................... 5-18
4. Procedure for Entry of Default ...................................... 5-18
   a. Time requirement .................................................... 5-18
   b. Documentation required ........................................ 5-19
   c. "Request for Entry of Default" form ..................... 5-20
      (1) Request to clerk ................................................ 5-20
      (2) Venue declaration .......................................... 5-20
      (3) Mailing declaration ........................................ 5-21
         (a) Length of notice required? ..................... 5-21
         (b) Nonreceipt of notice not ground for
            setting aside default ............................... 5-21
         (c) Effect of notice ...................................... 5-21
         (d) Effect of defective declaration ............ 5-22
      (4) Other portions of form not required for
         default entry ..................................................... 5-22
5. Additional Procedures Required in Particular
  Actions ............................................................................. 5-22
   a. Statement of damages in injury and death
     actions (CCP §425.11) ........................................... 5-22
     (1) Due process requirement ............................. 5-22
        (a) Notice from other sources insufficient ......... 5-23
        (b) Effect of improper allegations in complaint ... 5-23
     (2) Also required where default ordered as
        discovery sanction ......................................... 5-23
     (3) Actions in which statement required ............. 5-23
        (a) Application ............................................. 5-24
        (b) Cross-complaints for indemnity and
           contribution ............................................. 5-24
           1) Where amount unknown ..................... 5-24
        (c) Compare—"incidental" claim for
           emotional distress ................................... 5-24
     (4) Sufficiency of notice .................................... 5-25
        (a) Both special and general damages ............. 5-25
           1) Definitions ...................................... 5-25
           2) General damages alone insufficient ....... 5-26
           3) Unsegregated demand insufficient ......... 5-26
        (b) Constructive notice by failing to designate
           action as limited civil case? .................... 5-26
        (c) Constructive notice from other documents
           filed in action? ....................................... 5-26
           1) Settlement demands ......................... 5-26
     (5) Method of service ........................................ 5-26
        (a) Effect—"double service" required in
           default cases ......................................... 5-27
        (b) Service excused where defendant served
           by publication? ...................................... 5-27
     (6) Defendant's time to respond? ..................... 5-28
        (a) 30 days required .................................... 5-28
        (b) "Reasonable time" sufficient ................. 5-28

      (c) Compare—time for requesting entry of
          default ..........................................................5-28
    (7) Damages statement must accompany
      request for entry of default ...........................5-28.1
  b. Notice of amount of punitive damages claimed ...... 5-28.1
    (1) Due process requires notice ..........................5-28.1
      (a) Effect of improper allegations in
          complaint .....................................................5-28.1
    (2) Statutory notice requirement ...........................5-28.1
      (a) Form .........................................................5-28.1
      (b) Manner of service ....................................5-29
      (c) Time for service? ....................................5-29
      (d) Not a limit on recovery if defendant
          appears....................................................5-30
  c. Accounting actions ...............................................5-30
    (1) Form, content and service ...............................5-30
6. Clerk's Entry of Default ..............................................5-31
  a. "Entry of default"...................................................5-31
  b. Clerk's authority limited ........................................5-31
7. Effect of Default Entry.................................................5-31

**C. DEFAULT JUDGMENT BY CLERK** .....................................5-31
1. When Authorized .......................................................5-32
  a. Comment...............................................................5-32
  b. Other cases ...........................................................5-32
  c. Special rule in unlawful detainer cases ...................5-32
2. Requirement That Action be Based on Contract or
  Judgment ...................................................................5-32
  a. "Contract" actions .................................................5-32
  b. "Judgment" actions ...............................................5-32
3. Requirement That Action be for Fixed or Determinable
  Amount ......................................................................5-32
  a. Amount due fixed or determinable from contract.......5-32
  b. Amount due NOT fixed or determinable ..................5-33
  c. Demand for attorney fees ......................................5-34
    (1) Contract provision for fixed amount.....................5-34
    (2) Contract provision for "reasonable" fee................5-34
      (a) If fee schedule in effect.............................5-34
      (b) Plaintiff may insist on court judgment ...........5-35
4. Effect of Joinder of Other Causes of Action.....................5-35
  a. Separate and distinct causes ................................5-35
  b. "Contract" claim as alternative legal theory .............5-35
5. Effect of Joining Several Defendants .............................5-36
  a. Effect....................................................................5-36
  b. Example ................................................................5-36
  c. Rationale ...............................................................5-36
  d. Compare—all defendants in default ........................5-36
6. Procedure ..................................................................5-36
  a. Filling out "Request for Entry of Default" form ..........5-36
    (1) Request to clerk ..............................................5-37
      (a) Attorney fees............................................5-37

        (2)  Amount of judgment sought .................................. 5-37
        (3)  Venue declaration ............................................... 5-37
        (4)  Mailing declaration ............................................. 5-37
        (5)  Memorandum of costs declaration ..................... 5-37
        (6)  Declaration re nonmilitary status ....................... 5-38
            (a)  Current information required ....................... 5-38
            (b)  If no declaration obtainable ........................ 5-38
    b.  Other documentation required for clerk's default
       judgment ................................................................... 5-38
       (1)  A promissory note or other written obligation
          to pay money ..................................................... 5-38
       (2)  Certified copy of the judgment .......................... 5-39
       (3)  Request for dismissal with prejudice as to
          unserved defendants .......................................... 5-39
       (4)  Any additional documentation required ............. 5-39
       (5)  Clerk's judgment ............................................... 5-39
            (a)  Compare—unlawful detainers ...................... 5-39

**D.  DEFAULT JUDGMENT BY COURT** ................................. 5-40
  1.  When Required .................................................... 5-40
  2.  Preparing Case for Court Judgment ..................... 5-40
    a.  Documentation and evidence required from
       plaintiff ..................................................................... 5-40
       (1)  Request for "Entry of Default" form .................. 5-41
            (a)  Optional—multi-purpose judgment form ....... 5-41
       (2)  Supporting documentation ................................. 5-41
            (a)  Case summary ............................................. 5-41
            (b)  Declarations ................................................. 5-42
            (c)  Interest computations ................................... 5-42
            (d)  Costs memo ................................................. 5-42
            (e)  Affidavit re military service .......................... 5-42
            (f)  Proposed judgment ...................................... 5-42
            (g)  Memorandum of costs .................................. 5-42
            (h)  Dismissals ................................................... 5-42
            (i)  Exhibits ....................................................... 5-43
               1)  Photocopies ........................................... 5-43
               2)  Originals ................................................. 5-43
            (j)  Attorney fees ............................................... 5-43
               1)  Fee schedules ........................................ 5-43
               2)  Declarations ........................................... 5-43
       (3)  Additional requirements where summons
          served by publication ......................................... 5-44
            (a)  Proof of publication ...................................... 5-44
            (b)  Notice to defendant of application for
                judgment .................................................... 5-44
       (4)  Additional evidentiary requirements in actions
          affecting land ..................................................... 5-44
    b.  Checklist ................................................................. 5-45
    c.  Hearing date set by clerk ....................................... 5-45
    d.  Special procedures if defendant in military service ... 5-46
       (1)  Court must appoint counsel ............................... 5-46

      (2) Judgments subject to set-aside .............................5-46
      (3) Statutes of limitations tolled ...............................5-46
         (a) Effect ................................................................5-46
   3. Prove-Up Procedure ......................................................5-47
     a. Court may permit affidavits instead of live
       testimony .........................................................................5-47
      (1) Exceptions—live testimony required ...................5-47
         (a) Quiet title actions ............................................5-47
         (b) Nonresident defendant served by
            publication ...................................................5-47
      (2) Affidavit requirements .........................................5-47
      (3) No formal hearing necessary ..............................5-48
      (4) Local practices ....................................................5-48
     b. Court may require live testimony ...............................5-48
      (1) Hearsay testimony may be considered ..............5-48
     c. Court may refer issues to jury or order
       accounting .......................................................................5-48
      (1) Ultimate decision rests with court .......................5-48
     d. Standard of proof........................................................5-49
     e. Evidence limited to claims pleaded ...........................5-49

**E. LIMITATIONS ON DEFAULT JUDGMENTS** ........................5-49
   1. No Default Judgment Against Certain Defendants .........5-49
     a. Defendants in military service ...................................5-49
     b. Involuntary plaintiffs...................................................5-49
     c. "Doe" defendants ......................................................5-49
      (1) Summons requirement .........................................5-49
      (2) Proof of service requirement ...............................5-50
      (3) Amendment of complaint .....................................5-50
         (a) No effect on default............................................5-50
   2. Must be Based on Claims Well Pleaded ........................5-50
     a. Compare—no basis for collateral attack ..................5-50
     b. Effect of variance between pleadings and prove-
       up .....................................................................................5-50
   3. Cannot Exceed Relief Demanded in Complaint..............5-51
     a. As limit on *type* of relief ...........................................5-52
      (1) Application .............................................................5-52
      (2) If proper *type* of relief prayed, need *amount*
         be demanded? .......................................................5-52
         (a) Marital dissolution actions................................5-52
         (b) Other types of actions .......................................5-53
            1) Exception for accountings? ...................5-53
     b. As limit on damages .................................................5-54
      (1) Determining demand.............................................5-54
      (2) General demands insufficient...............................5-54
      (3) Specific damage allegations may cure
         defective prayer .....................................................5-55
         (a) Application ..........................................................5-55
         (b) Compare—fact allegations vs. damage
            allegations .....................................................5-55

        (4)  Effect of inconsistency between damage allegation and prayer ........................................... 5-56

        (5)  Demands in limited civil cases ........................... 5-56

    c.  Excessive default judgment "void" ........................... 5-57

        (1)  Application ......................................................... 5-57

        (2)  Procedures to challenge excessive judgment ......................................................... 5-57

            (a)  Compare—CCP §473(b) motion ................... 5-58

            (b)  Compare—sufficiency of evidence to support judgment ...................................... 5-58

            (c)  Compare—inadequate damage award ........ 5-58

        (3)  Vacating judgment not ground for "opening" default ............................................................... 5-58

            (a)  Excessive damages as "de facto" amendment of complaint? .......................... 5-58

            (b)  Should plaintiff be given option to amend complaint? ...................................... 5-58

        (4)  Remedying excessive judgment ...................... 5-58.1

        (5)  Compare—effect of proving *different* cause of action than pled ........................................... 5-58.1

    d.  Compare—personal injury and death cases .......... 5-58.2

    e.  Compare—claims for punitive damages ................. 5-58.2

    f.  Compare—accounting actions ............................. 5-58.2

  4.  Default Judgment Improper Where Codefendant Raises Exonerating Defense ................................... 5-58.3

    a.  Defaulting defendant only liable if answering defendant liable ................................................. 5-58.3

    b.  Defaulting defendant jointly liable with answering defendant ............................................ 5-58.3

        (1)  Example ............................................................ 5-58.3

        (2)  Compare—defendants jointly and severally liable .................................................................. 5-59

            (a)  Judgment before trial discretionary .............. 5-59

  5.  Default Judgment on Cross-Complaint Discretionary ...... 5-59

  6.  Quiet Title Actions? .................................................. 5-59

  7.  No Default Against "DBA" of Party Appearing in Corporate Name ................................................... 5-59

**F.  CHALLENGING DEFAULT JUDGMENT ON APPEAL** ......... 5-60

  1.  Either Party May Appeal ........................................... 5-60

    a.  Time limit for appeal ........................................... 5-60

    b.  Effect of reversal on appeal ................................. 5-60

        (1)  Motion for new trial? ........................................ 5-60

  2.  Compare—Collateral Attack ..................................... 5-60

**G.  RELIEF FROM DEFAULT** ............................................... 5-61

  1.  Time Limits Depend on Ground for Relief .................. 5-61

    a.  Within 6 months after entry of default .................. 5-61

    b.  Within 6 months after default judgment ............... 5-62

    c.  Within 2 years of default judgment ...................... 5-62

    d.  Within 60 days after execution ............................ 5-62

    e.   At any time ................................................5-62
2.  Relief for "Mistake, Inadvertence, Surprise or
Excusable Neglect" (CCP §473(b)) ........................5-62
    a.   Who may seek relief under CCP §473(b) ...............5-62
         (1) Defendant or plaintiff ..............................5-63
         (2) Legal representative ..............................5-63
             (a) Assignee ......................................5-63
             (b) Grantee .......................................5-63
             (c) Liability insurer ..............................5-64
    b.   Showing required for relief ................................5-64
         (1) Attorney affidavit of fault .........................5-64
             (a) Relief *mandatory* ......................5-65
                 1)   Neglect need not be "excusable" ...........5-66
                 2)   Attorney fault need not be only cause ....5-66
                    a)  Client partially at fault? .....................5-66
                    b)  Fault of co-counsel ..........................5-67
                    c)  Declaration by nonattorney
                        insufficient .................................5-67
                 3)   Immaterial that client also an attorney ......5-67
             (b) Relief from both default and default
                judgment ......................................5-67
                 1)   Includes defaults entered by court ..........5-67
             (c) Relief from dismissals ...................5-68
                 1)   Which dismissals ...........................5-68
                      a)  Dismissals *equivalent to default* .......5-68
                    b)  Relief from other dismissals not
                      mandatory .................................5-68
             (d) No relief after contested judgment or order .....5-69
            (e) Compare—judgment or order not based
                on hearing on merits .....................5-69
            (f) No relief from statutes authorizing
                dismissal for prior conduct ...............5-70
            (g) No relief for late filings ....................5-70.1
            (h) Limitation—no relief where attorney not at
                fault ..............................................5-71
                 1)   Client solely at fault ........................5-71
                      a)  Compare—client and attorney both
                      at fault .....................................5-72
                 2)   Attorney fault in connection with
                    default judgment not enough ..................5-72
            (i) Procedural requirements ...................5-72
                 1)   Motion specifying mandatory ground
                   for relief ....................................5-72
                 2)   Declaration or affidavit ......................5-72
                 3)   Application must be timely ...................5-72
                      a)  Time runs from entry of judgment ....5-73
                      b)  No deadline if no judgment
                      entered? .................................5-73
                    c)  Diligence required? ....................5-73
                 4)   Copy of proposed pleading attached ......5-74

Rev. #1 2004

    (j)  Compensation to nonmoving party ..............5-74
        1)  Fees and costs mandatory .....................5-74
        2)  Sanctions discretionary ........................5-74
        3)  Relief not conditioned on payment .........5-74
           a)  Applicable to dismissals? .................5-74
  (2) *Without* attorney affidavit of fault .........................5-75
    (a)  "Mistake" ..............................................5-75
        1)  Mistake of fact ....................................5-75
        2)  Mistake of law ....................................5-76
           a)  Test for excusable "mistake" .............5-76
           b)  Application .....................................5-76
        3)  Fraud ..................................................5-77
           a)  Intrinsic or extrinsic .........................5-77
           b)  Fraud on court................................5-78
    (b)  "Surprise" ..............................................5-78
    (c)  "Excusable neglect" ..............................5-78
        1)  Reasonable diligence as test................5-78
           a)  Neglect by party ........................5-78.1
           b)  Neglect by third person ...................5-79
           c)  Neglect by defendant's insurer? .......5-80
        2)  Inexcusable attorney neglect—no
           "attorney affidavit of fault" filed ..............5-80
           a)  Test .............................................5-80
           b)  Incompetent representation .............5-81
           c)  "Press of business" alone no
               excuse ......................................5-81
           d)  Other inexcusable neglect...............5-81
        3)  Excusable attorney neglect—no
           "attorney affidavit of fault" filed ..............5-82
        4)  "Positive misconduct" by attorney ..........5-83
           a)  Court must weigh competing
               policies .............................................5-84
           b)  Application .....................................5-84
           c)  Compare—court's inherent equity
               power as ground for relief.................5-85
           d)  CCP §286 as alternative ground
               for relief ........................................5-85
        5)  Compare—lack of prejudice to
           opposing party as affecting excuse ........5-86
  c.  Time within which relief must be sought ....................5-86
  (1) Jurisdictional limit—6 months...............................5-87
    (a)  Runs from entry of default (not judgment) ....5-87
        1)  Rationale .............................................5-87
        2)  Compare—relief may be granted
           from judgment only ................................5-87
        3)  Compare—relief based on attorney
           affidavit of fault .....................................5-87
    (b)  Filing of motion within 6 months
        sufficient ...............................................5-87
    (c)  Compare—relief from procedural time
        limits ....................................................5-87

   (d) Time may be shortened in property
     actions ..................................................5-88
  (2) Discretionary limit—"reasonable time" ...............5-88
   (a) Compare—relief based on attorney
     affidavit of fault.............................................5-89
   (b) Effect of delay ...............................................5-89
   (c) Application .....................................................5-89
   (d) Prejudice from delay? ....................................5-90
  (3) Compare—equitable relief from judgment ..........5-90
 d. Procedure ......................................................................5-90
  (1) Notice of motion ...................................................5-90
   (a) Hearing judge ................................................5-91
  (2) Proposed pleading required .................................5-91
   (a) "Substantial compliance" ...............................5-91
    1) Effect of filing proposed answer after
     expiration of 6-month period ...................5-91
  (3) Other supporting papers ......................................5-92
   (a) Attorney affidavit of fault—relief
     mandatory......................................................5-92
   (b) Without attorney affidavit of fault—relief
     discretionary .................................................5-92
  (4) Proposed order .....................................................5-92
  (5) Checklist ...............................................................5-93
 e. Burden of proof.............................................................5-93
  (1) Competent evidence .............................................5-93
 f. Ruling on motion ...........................................................5-94
  (1) Where "attorney affidavit of fault" filed.................5-94
  (2) Where no "attorney affidavit of fault" filed............5-94
   (a) Policy favoring relief .....................................5-94
    1) "Weak showing" may suffice ...................5-94
   (b) Relief from default vs. relief from default
     judgment .......................................................5-94
  (3) Imposition of conditions .......................................5-94
   (a) Fees and cost awards ....................................5-95
    1) Where "attorney affidavit of fault"
     filed..........................................................5-95
    2) Where no "attorney affidavit of fault"
     filed..........................................................5-95
   (b) Nonmonetary conditions ...............................5-95
   (c) Security for judgment as condition .................5-95
   (d) Sanctions ......................................................5-96
    1) Statement of reasons required where
     sanctions imposed ...................................5-96
    2) No relief until sanctions paid ...................5-96
  (4) Relief from judgment but not default ....................5-96
 g. Appellate review ...........................................................5-97
  (1) Orders granting relief ...........................................5-97
  (2) Orders denying relief ............................................5-97
   (a) Where "attorney affidavit of fault" filed ..........5-97
   (b) Where no "attorney affidavit of fault" filed .....5-97

       (c) Default judgments for punitive damages
           disfavored ................................................... 5-98
3.  Relief Under CCP §473.5 for "Lack of Actual
    Notice" .................................................................. 5-98
    a.  Ground for relief ....................................... 5-98
       (1) Application ......................................... 5-98
       (2) Compare—invalid service of summons ............... 5-99
       (3) Compare—*in rem* proceedings (service of
           summons not required) ......................... 5-99
    b.  Defendant not responsible for lack of notice ............ 5-99
       (1) Attorney's neglect imputed to client ................... 5-99
    c.  Time limit on application for relief ........................... 5-99
       (1) Compare—time limit for relief under CCP
           §473(b) ............................................. 5-100
    d.  Procedure ................................................... 5-100
       (1) Declarations must establish lack of notice ........ 5-100
       (2) Proposed pleading ............................... 5-100
    e.  Ruling on motion ......................................... 5-100
       (1) Conditions may be imposed ...................... 5-100
4.  Relief From Default in Consumer Actions Filed in
    Improper Court .................................................. 5-100
    a.  Time within which relief sought .............................. 5-101
    b.  Procedure ................................................... 5-101
    c.  Relief ........................................................ 5-101
       (1) Fee awards ........................................ 5-101
5.  Equitable Relief From Judgment ............................. 5-101
    a.  Diligence in seeking relief .................................. 5-101
       (1) Public policy as limitation ........................... 5-102
       (2) Laches as defense ................................. 5-102
           (a) Compare—where relief sought before
              judgment entered .......................... 5-102
    b.  Grounds for relief ......................................... 5-102
       (1) "Extrinsic" vs. "intrinsic" ........................... 5-103
           (a) Representation by counsel significant ........ 5-103
       (2) Application ........................................ 5-103
           (a) "Extrinsic fraud" ............................ 5-103
              1) Relief likely where violation of
                 confidential relationship shown ............. 5-104
                 a) "Confidential relationship" ............. 5-104
              2) Fraud inducing default ......................... 5-104
              3) Fraud preventing continuance ............. 5-105
              4) Compare—intrinsic fraud ..................... 5-105
           (b) "Extrinsic mistake" ....................... 5-105
              1) Relying on another to defend .............. 5-105
              2) Disability ....................................... 5-106
              3) Attorney's "positive misconduct" ........... 5-106
              4) Attorney's conflict of interest ................ 5-107
              5) Clerical error in entering default .......... 5-107
              6) Compare—ignorance of law NOT
                 ground for relief ................................. 5-108

　　　　　7)　Attorney's mistake as ground for
　　　　　　　relief ...................................................5-109
　　　　　8)　Lack of notice of *in rem* proceeding ......5-109
　　c.　Procedure ...............................................................5-109
　　　(1)　Alternative procedures available ....................5-109
　　　　(a)　Remedies cumulative..................................5-109
　　　　(b)　Compare—collateral estoppel if issues
　　　　　　fully tried in main action .............................5-110
　　　　　1)　What constitutes "full opportunity" to
　　　　　　　litigate ..............................................5-110
　　　(2)　Compare—limited civil cases ....................5-111
　　　(3)　Moving papers.......................................5-111
　　　(4)　Meritorious defense ...............................5-111
　　d.　Appeal ...................................................................5-112
6.　Relief From Judicial Error in Rendering Default
　Judgment ...........................................................................5-112
　　a.　Motion for new trial .............................................5-112
　　　(1)　Rationale ...............................................5-112
　　　(2)　Compare .................................................5-112
　　　(3)　Time limit ...............................................5-113
　　b.　Appeal ...................................................................5-113
　　　(1)　Time limit ...............................................5-113
　　c.　Compare—clerical error .....................................5-113
7.　Relief From VOID Judgment .............................................5-113
　　a.　Application.............................................................5-113
　　b.　Alternative procedures available .........................5-114
　　　(1)　Direct attack ..........................................5-114
　　　(2)　Collateral attack .....................................5-114
　　　　(a)　Motion to vacate renewal of judgment ........5-114
　　c.　Timeliness ............................................................5-115
　　　(1)　Exception—judgment void for *improper
　　　　　service;* 2-year limit .................................5-115
　　d.　Not necessary to show meritorious defense...........5-116
　　　(1)　Compare—voidable judgments .......................5-116
　　e.　Prejudice not required .........................................5-116.1

**FORMS**
・　Request for Entry of Default...............................................5-117
・　Default/Clerk's Judgment Rejection Notice .........................5-121
・　Judgment ..........................................................................5-123
・　Memorandum of Costs (Summary) .......................................5-128
・　Memorandum of Costs (Worksheet) .....................................5-130
・　Reasons for Rejection of Prove-Up Documents ..................5-135
・　Checklist: Motion for Relief ("Mistake, Inadvertence,
　Surprise or Neglect")........................................................5-137
・　Attorney Affidavit of Fault (CCP §473(b)) .............................5-139

Rev. #1 2004

# DEFAULTS:

## HOW TO OBTAIN THEM AND HOW TO CURE THEM

### A. GENERAL

[5:1]   This Chapter deals with the procedures by which a default judgment may be obtained . . . and the procedures by which it may be later set aside.

It is important to understand the terminology used in connection with default judgments: i.e., "defendant in default," clerk's "entry of default," plaintiff's "proving up the default," etc.

Although the rules below are stated in terms of "plaintiff," "defendant" and "complaint," in each instance "plaintiff" includes cross-complainant, "defendant" includes cross-defendants and "complaint" includes cross-complaint. Thus, cross-complainants may obtain defaults on cross-complaints under the same conditions as plaintiffs may obtain defaults on complaints. Similarly, the remedies available to defendants to set aside defaults are also available to cross-defendants.

1. [5:2] **Defendant "In Default":**   Technically, defendants are "in default" if they fail to file an answer, demurrer or other permitted response (¶5:31) within the time allowed by law (¶5:21 ff.) and without a court order excusing such filing.

   By itself, being "in default" has no legal consequences because defendant can still appear in the action until the clerk has *entered* his or her default (below).

   a. [5:3]  **Late pleadings by defendant:**   Thus, even though the time to respond has expired, if no default yet has been entered, defendant can file a pleading or motion. The court clerk *cannot refuse* to accept it for filing merely because the time to respond has expired. [*Goddard v. Pollock* (1974) 37 CA3d 137, 141, 112 CR 215, 218]

   But a pleading or motion filed after expiration of the time to respond is *subject to a motion to strike.* Although discretionary with the court, if the motion is granted, the defendant's default can then be entered. [*Buck v. Morrossis* (1952) 114 CA2d 461, 464-465, 250 P2d 270, 273]

2. [5:4]  **Entry of Default by Court Clerk:**   This is the procedure that establishes defendant's default: a formal entry by the court clerk. Such entry does not happen automatically. Rather, plaintiff must *request* the court clerk to make such entry *within 10 days* after expiration of the time to respond, and the request must be supported by proper documentation (¶5:72 ff.).

If all is in order, the court clerk "enters" the default by signing the appropriate box on the request form (*see Form 5:A*).

The clerk is also required to make an appropriate notation in the register of actions (see Gov.C. §§69845-69845.5). However, the "entry" of default is deemed complete when signed by the court clerk (*see ¶5:9*).

a. **[5:5] Mandatory duty:** The court clerk has no discretion to refuse a proper request for entry of default. [*W.A. Rose Co. v. Mun.Ct. (FitzSimmons)* (1959) 176 CA2d 67, 71, 1 CR 49, 52; *and see ¶5:113*]

b. **[5:6] Effect of default entry:** Entry of defendant's default instantaneously cuts off its right to appear in the action. The defendant is "out of court." It has no right to participate in the proceedings until either (a) its default is set aside (in which event, it may respond to the complaint), or (b) a default judgment is entered (in which event, it may appeal). [*Devlin v. Kearny Mesa AMC/Jeep/Renault, Inc.* (1984) 155 CA3d 381, 385-386, 202 CR 204, 207]

For example, a defaulting defendant has no right to take depositions of plaintiff's witnesses, or to appear in court at the "prove up" hearing in an attempt to block entry of a default judgment (*see ¶5:171*). [*Devlin v. Kearny Mesa AMC/Jeep/Renault, Inc.,* supra; see *People v. One 1986 Toyota Pickup* (1995) 31 CA4th 254, 259, 37 CR2d 29, 32— because no default had been entered, defendant had right to appear and be heard at prove-up proceedings]

(1) **[5:7] Jurisdictional:** Entry of default ousts the court of jurisdiction to consider any motion other than a motion for relief from default. [*W.A. Rose Co. v. Mun.Ct. (FitzSimmons),* supra—court clerk improperly refused to enter default; prohibition granted to prevent court from considering defendant's late-filed motion for change of venue]

(a) **[5:7.1] Compare—motion to dismiss as motion for relief from default?** One case holds that a motion to dismiss on jurisdictional grounds (e.g., improper service of summons, etc.) may be treated as a motion for relief from default . . . because the court cannot dismiss an action without first setting aside the default judgment. [*Dill v. Berquist Const. Co., Inc.* (1994) 24 CA4th 1426, 1443, 29 CR2d 746, 756—involving motion to vacate judgment after 6-month period for CCP §473 relief had expired]

➡️ **[5:7.2] PRACTICE POINTER:** Don't count on it! Other courts are likely to take the technically correct position that a defendant in default is "out of court" on any motion other than for relief from default.

(2) **[5:8]** **Admissions:** By defaulting, defendant is deemed to *admit* the material allegations of the complaint for purposes of the action. [See *Vasey v. California Dance Co., Inc.* (1977) 70 CA3d 742, 749, 139 CR 72, 76; *Molen v. Friedman* (1998) 64 CA4th 1149, 1156, 75 CR2d 651, 655]

c. **[5:9]** **Date of entry:** In busy courts, there is often a delay of several days between the date plaintiff files a request for entry of default and the date of formal entry in the register of actions. The default is deemed "entered" when the clerk *signs* the appropriate box on the request form (*see Form 5:A*) although it may not show up in the register of actions until several days thereafter.

(1) **[5:9.1]** **Backdating register of actions:** The current policy in many courts is to *backdate* the entry in the register of actions to the *filing date* on plaintiff's request . . . so that any delay by the clerk in signing the request form or entry in the register of actions does not extend defendant's time to plead.

⇨**[5:9.2]** *PRACTICE POINTER FOR DEFENDANT:* If the time to file a responsive pleading has expired, do *not* rely solely on the fact no default appears in the register of actions, especially if a request for entry of default has been served on you or your client (*see* ¶5:77*). (Otherwise, you may next hear of the case after a writ of execution on a default judgment is levied on your client's assets; and maybe after the time to set aside your client's default has expired!)

The safest practice is to seek a stipulation or court order permitting late filing. Alternatively, if you file without such stipulation or order, be sure to *check the register of actions again* 3 or 4 weeks later to make sure the clerk has not backdated an entry of default. (If this has occurred, you will need to seek relief promptly under CCP §473(b).)

If a default was entered *after* a responsive pleading was filed, the default is invalid. Many courts will vacate such defaults *sua sponte* upon the matter being called to their attention. Others still require motions.

**[5:9.3-9.4]** *Reserved.*

d. **[5:9.5]** **Compare—amended complaint may "open up" default:** An amended complaint making *substantive* changes in the cause of action asserted against a defaulting defendant *supersedes* the original complaint. In effect, it "opens the default" because plaintiff is required to *serve the amended complaint on the defendant*; and the defendant is then entitled to answer, demur or otherwise respond to the amended complaint. The purpose is to allow the defendant to reassess whether to contest the action in light of the changes made in the complaint. [*Ostling v. Loring* (1994) 27 CA4th 1731, 1734, 33 CR2d 391, 398; *Engebretson & Co., Inc. v. Harrison* (1981) 125 CA3d 436, 442-443, 178 CR 77, 81; *and see* ¶6:698-701]

3.   [5:10]   **Default Judgments—General Considerations:**   After defendant's default has been entered, plaintiff may apply for a judgment based on such default.

   a.   [5:11]   **Judgment by clerk vs. judgment by court:**   In certain kinds of cases (typically, collection cases for fixed amounts), the court clerk is empowered to enter default judgment directly—without any judicial action or hearing (¶*5:120 ff.*).

   In all other cases, however, plaintiff is required to "prove up" the default to the court in order to obtain judgment (¶*5:171 ff.*).

      (1)   [5:12]   **Compare—default judgment as discovery sanction:**   Even though defendant has *appeared* in the action, the court has power to *strike* defendant's answer and *render a default judgment* as the ultimate sanction for refusal to obey discovery orders. [CCP §2023(b)(4)(D); *see Ch. 8*]

   b.   [5:13]   **Time limit to obtain default judgment:**   The party who obtained the default must obtain a default judgment *within 45 days* after entry of default, unless an extension of time is obtained. [CRC 201.7(h)]

   Failure to do so may result in the court issuing an Order to Show Cause why sanctions should not be imposed (CRC 201.7(h)). Plaintiff then has *5 calendar days within* which to file and serve responsive papers. [CRC 201.7(i)]

   In addition, the court has power at any time to *dismiss* an action for unreasonable delay in prosecution, which includes unreasonable delay in obtaining a default judgment. [See CCP §583.310 (mandatory 5-year dismissal) and §583.420 (a)(2) (discretionary dismissal), *discussed at* ¶*11:124 ff.*]

   c.   [5:14]   **Limitations on default judgments:**   Important limitations on default judgments are discussed at ¶*5:219 ff.*

   d.   [5:15]   **Res judicata effect of default judgment:**   A default judgment is treated as a judgment "on the merits" and res judicata as to the claim involved. Thus, defendant is not permitted to relitigate his or her liability on the claim. [See *Martin v. General Finance Co.* (1966) 239 CA2d 438, 443, 48 CR 773, 776]

(1) **[5:16]** **Collateral estoppel as to issues adjudicated:** A default judgment collaterally estops the defendant from raising *issues* in a later lawsuit that were *necessarily adjudicated* against defendant in the earlier action. [*English v. English* (1937) 9 C2d 358, 363-364, 70 P2d 625, 628]

The collateral estoppel is limited, however, to *material issues well pleaded* in the complaint in the former action. It does not apply to immaterial allegations or issues not raised in the pleadings. [*Burtnett v. King* (1949) 33 C2d 805, 810, 205 P2d 657, 660; *Four Star Elec., Inc. v. F & H Const.* (1992) 7 CA4th 1375, 1380, 10 CR2d 1, 3—immaterial allegations did not give rise to collateral estoppel]

[5:16.1-16.4] *Reserved.*

4. **[5:16.5]** **Case Management Standards:** Plaintiff's request for entry of default must be filed *within 10 days* after expiration of defendant's time to respond unless the court grants an extension of time. [CRC 201.7(g)]

In addition, *within 45 days* after entry of default, plaintiff must *obtain a default judgment* against the defendant unless the court grants an extension of time. [CRC 201.7(h)]

a. **[5:16.6]** **Grounds for extension of time?** CRC 201.7 does not specify the grounds or procedure for obtaining extension of time for requesting entry of default or entry of default judgment. (The detailed requirements for obtaining an extension of time to *serve or respond* to the complaint do *not* apply; see CRC 201.7(e).)

[5:16.7-16.9] *Reserved.*

b. **[5:16.10]** **Effect of delay:** Failure to file a request for entry of default within 10-day period or to obtain a default judgment within the 45-day period, may result in issuance of an "Order to Show Cause" why sanctions shall not be imposed. [See CRC 201.7(g),(h)]

[5:16.11-16.14] *Reserved.*

c. **[5:16.15]** **Sanctions:** The sanctions a court may impose for violation of Rule 201.7(g) or (h) are apparently limited to monetary or disciplinary sanctions against counsel. A court *cannot dismiss* an action for violation of court rules that are the attorney's responsibility (*see ¶11:127.1*).

(1) **[5:16.16]** **Refusing default or default judgment?** It is *unclear* whether the court clerk may refuse entry of default because the request for entry of default was filed beyond the 10-day period. It is also unclear whether a court has discretion to refuse to grant a default judgment sought after the 45-day period.

## B. ENTRY OF DEFAULT

1. **[5:17]** **Conditions for Entry of Default:** The following conditions must be shown to exist before plaintiff may apply for entry of defendant's default:

   • Defendant has been *served* with summons and complaint in a *manner* permitting entry of default (*see ¶5:18 ff.*);

   • The *time* allowed by law for responding to the complaint (*see ¶5:21 ff.*) has expired; *and*

   • Defendant has *failed to file* a pleading or motion permitted by law or otherwise appear in the action (*see ¶5:30 ff.*).

   a. **[5:18]** **Manner of service permitting entry of default:** First of all, the court clerk will examine the *proof of service* (*¶4:360 ff.*) to determine the date and manner in which the summons and complaint were served. (If the proof of service has not been previously filed, it must be filed together with the "Request for Entry of Default" form.) (Since papers may be lost or filed, it is better practice not to file the proof of service separately.)

      (1) **[5:19]** **Includes service by publication:** The clerk is authorized to enter default upon proof of service by any manner, *including* service by publication. [See CCP §585(c); see *Taylor v. Varga* (1995) 37 CA4th 750, 756, 43 CR2d 904, 907-908, fn. 4 (citing text)—same rule under local practice in some courts prior to statute]

      ➪ **[5:20]** **PRACTICE POINTER:** Make sure your service on the defendant is *letter-perfect* before seeking entry of default. Judges and court clerks are likely to "nit pick" your proof of service. More important, defects in service can be raised by appeal or *collateral attack* on your default judgment. You could be forced to start all over again years later (perhaps facing time limits on service of summons; *see ¶11:106.4*).

   b. **[5:21]** **Expiration of time to respond:** Next, it must appear that the time allowed by law for defendant's response to the complaint has expired. The court clerk determines this from the *proof of service* (above), showing the manner and date upon which service was made.

Rev. #1 2003

(1) [5:22]  **Time to respond:**  In the usual case, defendant has *30 days* after *service is complete* within which to respond to the complaint. [CCP §412.20(a)(3)] (Exception: In unlawful detainer or forcible detainer cases, only *5 days*. See CCP §§1167, 1167.3; *and* ¶6:386.)

  (a) [5:23]  **When service deemed complete:**  This depends on the *manner* in which summons and complaint were served.

    1)  [5:24]  If by *personal service*, service is complete when made. [CCP §415.10, ¶4:185]

    2)  [5:25]  If by *substitute service*, on the 10th day after other copies are mailed. [CCP §415.20(a), ¶4:219]

    3)  [5:26]  If by *mail with acknowledgment of receipt*, on the date defendant *signs* the acknowledgment, if the acknowledgment is returned to the sender. [CCP §415.30(c), ¶4:235]

    [5:26.1-26.4]  *Reserved.*

    4)  [5:26.5]  If by *publication*, on the 28th day after the first publication. [Gov.C. §6064; *see* ¶4:272]

  (b)  **Examples**

    1)  [5:27]  In a personal injury action, if summons is served by substitute service, D's response is not due until *40 days* after copies of the summons and complaint were *mailed* to the defendant (10 days after the mailing, plus 30 days to respond) . . . whereas if D had been served personally, he or she would have had only 30 days to respond.

    2)  [5:28]  In an unlawful detainer action, if the summons and complaint are served personally, D has only 5 days within which to file a responsive pleading . . . but if substitute service is used, D would have *15 days* after other copies are *mailed.*

(2) [5:29]  **Where time extended:**  Defendant's time to respond to the complaint may be extended, either by stipulation with plaintiff's counsel (limited to 15 days—Gov.C. §68616), or by court order on a showing of "good cause" (limited to 30 days without adverse party's consent—CCP §1054).

  (a) [5:29.1]  *Duty to extend:* Unless time is of the essence, judges expect counsel to grant a request for extension within the 15-day limitation imposed by Gov.C. §68616, so as to obviate the need for defendant making an ex parte application which the court is likely to grant routinely.

Some local rules require that consideration be given to an opponent's "schedule of professional and personal engagements" and that no unfair and extraneous conditions be attached to a stipulated extension of time to plead. [See L.A. Sup.Ct. Rule 7.12(a)]

(b) [5:29.2] *Duty to warn?* On expiration of the extension, plaintiff's counsel may request entry of defendant's default. *However*, where the time to respond was extended by stipulation, plaintiff's *duty to warn* before entry of default is *particularly strong*. Entry of default immediately upon expiration of the extension, without prior warning to defense counsel, is a professional discourtesy and would almost certainly be set aside. *See* ¶5:68-71.

(c) [5:29.3] *Limitation:* Under "fast-track" rules, parties may not stipulate to more than one 15-day extension of time to plead without court order. [Gov.C. §68616, *see* ¶12:55; see also CRC 201.7(d); and L.A. Sup.Ct. Rule 7.7(a)(3); S.F. Unif. Rule 3.3B; San Diego Sup.Ct. Rule 2.6; Orange Sup.Ct. Rule 439] (Even though these local rules "relate" to pleadings, they are *not* preempted by CRC 981.1(a) because they are expressly authorized by Gov.C. §68616.)

(d) [5:29.4] *Application for further extension:* The court may extend the time to respond *sua sponte* or on application by any party. Such application, however, *must be filed before* the time for filing a responsive pleading has elapsed. In addition, the application must be accompanied by a declaration:
— *showing why* a responsive pleading has not been filed;
— *documenting the efforts* that have been made to effect such filing; and
— *specifying a date* by which it is proposed to be filed. [CRC 201.7(e)]

**FORM:** The application for further extension may be made on optional Judicial Council form CM-020, Application for Ex Parte Extension of Time to Serve Pleading; *see Form 4:J.*

c. [5:30] **Defendant's failure to respond:** Next, it must be shown that defendant has failed to file an answer, demurrer or other permitted response when the application for default is filed.

(1) [5:31] **Responses to original complaint preventing entry of default:** Defendant's filing any of the following pleadings or motions prevents entry of default (CCP §585(a)-(c)):

- Answer

- Demurrer (even if to only one of several causes of action; *see ¶7:34.1*)

- Motion to strike (if filed within the time allowed by law; CCP §435(b), *¶7:159*)

- Motion to transfer action to *proper* court (i.e., where action filed in improper court) (CCP §396b, *¶3:564-566*)

- Motion to quash service of summons (CCP §418.10, *¶3:376-395, 4:169-173*)

- Motion to stay or dismiss action for inconvenient forum (CCP §418.10, *¶3:407 ff.*)

- Motion to dismiss for failure to serve summons or for delay in bringing action to trial (CCP §418.10(a)(3); *see ¶11:50 ff.*)

- Comparable motions or pleadings *on removal to federal court* (*see ¶5:43*)

➪[5:32] *PRACTICE POINTER:* Other motions or pleadings may not prevent entry of default. For example, a *motion for extension of time* to plead does *not* prevent entry of default. (Consequently, be sure to request your extension early.)

Nor will a *motion for summary judgment* extend defendant's time to plead or prevent entry of default (*see ¶10:62*). (Defendants should ask plaintiff for a stipulation not to seek entry of default; if plaintiff refuses, defendants should file a "protective" demurrer or answer before or concurrently with a motion for summary judgment.)

Nor does a motion to reclassify an action as a "limited civil case" extend the moving party's time to answer or respond. [CCP §403.040(a)]

*(Text cont'd on p. 5-9)*

**RESERVED**

(a) **[5:33]** **Late pleading immaterial:** Any of the above responses prevents entry of default even if the filing is late. I.e., defendant may prevent default by filing a pleading or motion any time until its default is actually entered.

(b) **[5:34]** **Title of response determinative:** The court clerk is entitled to rely on a document's title in determining whether it is one of the permitted responses. Defendant cannot claim it has filed an answer if the document filed is labelled otherwise! [*Wisdom v. Ramirez* (1985) 177 CA3d Supp. 1, 8, 222 CR 923, 926 (disapproved on other grounds in *Janssen v. Luu* (1997) 57 CA4th 272, 276, 66 CR2d 838, 841)]

- **[5:35]** **Example:** D filed a "Declaration in Opposition to Preliminary Injunction" but no answer or other responsive pleading. D's "Declaration" did not prevent entry of default although it contained denials of the complaint: "The clerk . . . was not authorized to peruse the document in question to determine whether or not it constituted an answer or should be construed as one." [*Wisdom v. Ramirez*, supra, 177 CA3d Supp. at 8, 222 CR at 926]

⇨ **[5:36]** *PRACTICE POINTER:* Avoid this problem! If you represent defendant, make sure your answer, demurrer or other responsive pleading is *properly labelled* . . . so the clerk won't be misled!

(c) **[5:37]** **Sufficiency of response immaterial:** The court clerk has no authority to determine the legal sufficiency of the pleading or motion filed by the defendant. Thus, as long as it *appears* to be one of the permissible responses (answer, demurrer, etc.), the clerk *must* refuse a request for default; and any default actually entered by the clerk would be void. [*Stevens v. Torregano* (1961) 192 CA2d 105, 112-113, 13 CR 604, 610]

⇨ **[5:37.1]** *PRACTICE POINTER:* If the document filed bears a title that would preclude entry of default, although insufficient, plaintiff's remedy is a *motion to strike* (*see* ¶7:156 ff.*) concurrently with a motion to enter default.

1) **[5:38] Compare—"moribund" demurrers:** The fact that a demurrer has been filed may not always prevent entry of default. If the demurrer is off calendar and otherwise "moribund," the clerk may enter the default: "We would like to think that in spite of bureaucracy, a clerk entering a default is permitted to exercise his or her common sense and ignore a demurrer that is more than moribund." [*Barragan v. Banco BCH* (1986) 188 CA3d 283, 298, 232 CR 758, 767]

   a) **[5:39] Example:** D demurred on ground that another action was pending between the same parties on the same cause of action (CCP §430.10(c)). The demurrer went off calendar pending outcome of the other action. After final judgment in the other action, the demurrer was moot. But D failed to notice a hearing on the demurrer or otherwise plead. The clerk properly entered default. [*Barragan v. Banco BCH*, supra]

   b) **[5:40] Comment:** It is debatable whether entry of default should depend on a court clerk's "exercise of common sense" as to mootness of a demurrer. The result in *Barragan* seems inconsistent with the rule that a court clerk is *not* authorized to review *contents* of a document to determine whether it is one of the permitted responses (*see ¶5:35*).

   ➡**[5:41] *PRACTICE POINTER:*** Plaintiff can avoid the problem by *asking the court* for an ex parte order directing the clerk to enter default in such cases.

   (However, to obtain an ex parte order, advance notification to the defendant will be required; *see ¶9:352 ff.* And, to avoid any misunderstanding, the court might give defendant additional time within which to respond.)

(d) **[5:42] Response must be filed, not merely served:** It is not enough that defendant has served copies of a responsive pleading on plaintiff's lawyer before entry of default. If the response has not yet been *filed* with the court clerk, it would be the clerk's duty to enter defendant's default on request by plaintiff's lawyer. [See *Fletcher v. Maginnis* (1902) 136 C 362, 363, 68 P 1015, 1016] (Of course, a court would probably be inclined to set aside such a default; *see ¶5:276 ff.*)

(e) **[5:43]** **Compare—cases removed to federal court, then remanded:** If, before making any appearance in the state court action, defendant *removes* the case to federal court, his or her pleadings there may constitute a sufficient "appearance" to prevent entry of default should the case later be remanded to state court. [*Laguna Village, Inc. v. Laborers Int'l Union* (1983) 35 C3d 174, 182, 197 CR 99, 104]

1) **[5:43.1]** **Where no prior general appearance:** If defendants have not generally appeared in *either* state or federal court, they have *30 days* from the date the state court receives the case on remand to move to stay or dismiss the action, or to quash service of summons for:
   — lack of jurisdiction (*see ¶3:375 ff.*); or
   — inconvenient forum (*see ¶3:407 ff.*); or
   — delay in service of summons (*see ¶11:51 ff.*) . . .
   *provided* the state court had not ruled on a similar motion before the action was removed to federal court. [CCP §430.90(a)(1)]

2) **[5:43.2]** **Where no answer filed before removal:** If defendants had not filed *an answer* in state court before removing the action to federal court, they have *30 days* from the date the state court receives the case on remand to:
   — answer the complaint; or
   — demur or move to strike the complaint *provided* no answer was filed in federal court *and* no demurrer and/or motion to strike raising the same or similar issues had been ruled on by the state court before removal or by the federal court before remand; and if the demurrer or motion to strike is denied, 30 days to answer the complaint. [CCP §430.90(a)(2)]

(2) **[5:44]** **Default based on failure to provide further response:** Notwithstanding a timely response to the original complaint, a default may be entered for defendant's failure to file some further response in the action:

(a) [5:45]  **After motion to quash or stay:**  If defendant's original responsive pleading is a motion to quash summons (¶3:376-395, 4:169-173), or stay the action for inconvenient forum (¶3:407 ff.), a further pleading may be due from defendant if these motions are denied. A default may be entered if defendant fails to respond within the time provided by law. [CCP §586(a)(4)]

    1) [5:46]  **Extension of time if motion denied:** If a motion to quash or stay is denied, defendant has *15 days* after a written *notice* of such denial is served on him or her within which to respond to the complaint (by answer, demurrer, or motion to strike). For "good cause," however, the court can extend this time for up to an additional 20 days. [CCP §418.10(b), ¶3:392]

    2) [5:47]  **Further extension if mandamus sought:**  If defendant seeks appellate review of the denial by writ of mandamus, and gives proper notice of such application, he or she is entitled to a further extension of time to plead until 10 days after service on him or her of notice of the appellate court's refusal to grant the writ. [CCP §418.10(c), ¶3:394]

(b) [5:48]  **After motion to change venue:**  Similarly, if defendant's original response to the complaint was a motion to transfer the action on "wrong court" grounds (CCP §§396a, 396b, ¶3:550 ff.), further responses may be due after the court's ruling on the motion.

    1) [5:49]  **Extension of time if motion granted:** If defendant's motion to transfer the action is granted, his or her time to plead is extended until the case has been transferred to the proper court. Defendant has until *30 days* after the *mailing* to him or her of notice from the clerk of the court to which the action has been transferred that the transfer has been completed and a new case number assigned. [CCP §586(a)(6) (B),(C)]

    2) [5:50]  **Court will grant extension if motion denied:**  The court's order denying the motion to transfer will fix the time within which defendant must answer the complaint. [CCP §586(a)(6)(A)]

        a) [5:51]  **If appellate review sought:**  An order granting, or denying, a motion to change venue is reviewable by appeal to the appellate division of the superior court in limited civil cases (CCP §904.2); and by writ of *mandamus* in other actions (CCP §400). If such review is sought, the trial court will extend defendant's time to answer the complaint for a "reasonable time" after the appeals court has ruled. [CCP §586(a)(6)(C)]

[5:51.1-51.4] *Reserved.*

(c) [5:51.5] **After motion to dismiss for delay in serving summons:** Similarly, if defendant's original response is a motion to dismiss for delay in service of summons (CCP §583.250; *see* ¶11:51 *ff.*), and that motion is denied, the court will fix a time within which defendant must further respond to the complaint by answer, demurrer or motion to strike. A default may be entered if defendant fails to respond within the time allowed. [CCP §586(a)(8),(b)] (For purposes of CCP §586(b), "respond" means *only* to answer, demur or move to strike.)

(d) [5:52] **After demurrer:** If defendant's original response was a demurrer, a further responsive pleading may be due after the court's ruling on the demurrer.

1) [5:53] **If demurrer sustained:** Plaintiff will normally be given leave to amend (*see* ¶7:129-132a). Defendant need do nothing further until plaintiff's amended complaint is served and filed. Defendant must then respond to the *amended* complaint within the same time permitted by law to respond to the original (i.e., 30 days), unless the court orders otherwise. If defendant fails to do so, his default may be entered as in any other case. [CCP §471.5]

Defendant may respond to the amended complaint by any of the responses permitted to the original complaint (except a motion to quash or stay the action or to change venue will no longer lie).

2) [5:54] **If demurrer overruled:** Defendant must *answer* the complaint within *10 days* (5 days in an unlawful detainer action) or such longer period of time as the court may allow. If defendant fails to do so, default may be entered. [CCP §§472a, 586(a)(2); and see CRC 325(e)]

a) **[5:55]** **Defendant ordered to answer:**
If a demurrer is overruled and defendant *ordered to answer*, no other motion or pleading will prevent entry of default.

b) **[5:56]** **No order to answer:** However, if the court simply overrules the demurrer—i.e., *without ordering defendant to answer*—an answer is not the only response that will prevent default. Defendant apparently can *demur again* or move to strike or otherwise plead! [CRC 325(g); *Skrbina v. Fleming Cos., Inc.* (1996) 45 CA4th 1353, 1365, 53 CR2d 481, 488 (citing text); and see discussion of "piecemeal demurrers" at ¶7:34.1 ff.]

c) **[5:57]** **Time to answer runs from notice of ruling:** Unless notice of the court's ruling is waived in open court, defendant's time to answer the complaint is measured from the date of service of *written notice* of the court's overruling his or her demurrer. [CCP §472b]

➡**[5:58]** *PRACTICE POINTER:* If you're representing the defendant, and plaintiff (or the judge hearing the matter) asks you whether you will "waive notice" of the court's ruling on demurrer, do not hesitate to ask for more than 10 days to answer if you need it. Otherwise, refusing to waive merely causes additional work for opposing counsel and may lead to antagonism that impairs settlement opportunities.

(e) **[5:59]** **After motion to strike:** Similar rules apply where defendant's original response was a motion to strike all or part of the complaint.

1) **[5:60]** **If motion granted:** If defendant's motion to strike is granted as to the entire complaint, plaintiff will normally be granted leave to file an amended complaint (*see* ¶7:202-204). If so, defendant need do nothing until the amended complaint is served and filed; and defendant will then have 30 days within which to respond to the amended complaint—by answer, demurrer or further motion to strike. [CCP §471.5]

If defendant's motion to strike was granted only *in part*, defendant must *answer* the *unstricken* portion of the complaint within the time allowed by the court (unless a demurrer was filed concurrently therewith and is still pending). [CCP §586(a)(3)]

⇨ [5:60.1] ***PRACTICE POINTER:*** If plaintiff has been granted *leave to amend*, the court may not want a response until the amendment has been filed. Defense counsel should clarify this at the hearing.

2) [5:61] **If motion denied:** Similarly, if defendant's motion to strike is denied, defendant must answer the complaint within whatever time is ordered by the court (again, unless a demurrer was filed concurrently therewith and is still pending). [See CCP §586(a)(3)]

   a) [5:62] **Time runs from notice of ruling:** Unless notice is waived, plaintiff is required to give written notice of the court's ruling; and defendant's time to answer is measured from service of such notice. [See CCP §1019.5, *discussed at ¶9:320 ff.*]

(f) [5:63] **Compare—after plaintiff amends complaint:** If plaintiff amends the complaint, it may set off a new round of pleadings, and defendant may answer, demur or move to strike the amended complaint just as the original (*see ¶6:688*).

However, *failure* to respond to an amended complaint does *not* automatically justify entry of defendant's default (as would failure to respond to the original). Rather, it depends upon the nature of the amendment.

1) [5:64] **Amendments making substantive changes:** If the amended complaint changes the basic cause of action, or adds a new one, it constitutes an *abandonment* of the original issues (¶6:704). A response thereto is required, and therefore—even if defendant has answered the original—failure to respond to the amended complaint properly results in entry of default and a default judgment. [See *Carrasco v. Craft* (1985) 164 CA3d 796, 808-809, 210 CR 599, 607]

   a) [5:65] **Cross-refer:** An amendment making substantive changes also has the effect of "opening" any default earlier taken, giving the defendant whose default had been entered another chance to plead; *see* ¶*6:698.*

2) [5:66] **No substantive changes:** However, if the amended complaint does not change the cause of action originally pleaded or add any substantive new allegations against the defendant, no default can be entered for failure to respond: *The original answer stands as the answer to the amended complaint except as to matters therein not placed in issue by the answer to the original complaint.* [*Carrasco v. Craft*, supra, 164 CA3d at 808-809, 210 CR at 607-608; *and see* ¶*6:691*]

- [5:67] **Example:** P amended his complaint to increase damage allegations and correct ambiguities, etc., but stated no new causes of action against D. It was error to enter default and default judgment against D for failure to answer the amended complaint. [*Carrasco v. Craft*, supra]

[5:67.1-67.4] *Reserved.*

d. [5:67.5] **Compare—defaults ordered by court despite responsive pleading:** The court has the power to order a defendant's answer *stricken* and its default entered as a *sanction* for certain improper litigation conduct:

- [5:67.6] Discovery abuses. [See CCP §2023(b)(4); ¶*8:1231*]

- [5:67.7] Filing pleadings or other papers violating CCP §128.7 certificate of merit. [See CCP §128.7(d); ¶*9:1215*]

- [5:67.8] Conduct violating local court rules. [See CCP §575.2(a); ¶*9:1275*]

[5:67.9-67.14] *Reserved.*

(1) [5:67.15] **Compare—no default for failure to appear at trial:** The court may *not* enter a default for defendant's failure to appear at trial. The appropriate procedure is to proceed with the trial in defendant's absence. [*Heidary v. Yadollahi* (2002) 99 CA4th 857, 864, 121 CR2d 695, 699]

2. [5:68] **Ethical Obligation to Warn Opposing Counsel:** If plaintiff's counsel knows the identity of the lawyer representing defendant, he or she owes an ethical obligation to warn before requesting entry of defendant's default. Failure to do so is a *professional discourtesy* to opposing counsel that will not be con-

doned by the courts: "The quiet speed of plaintiffs' attorney in seeking a default judgment without the knowledge of defendants' counsel is not to be commended." [*Smith v. Los Angeles Bookbinders' Union No. 63* (1955) 133 CA2d 486, 500, 284 P2d 194, 201 (disapproved on other grounds in *MacLeod v. Tribune Pub. Co., Inc.* (1959) 52 C2d 536, 551, 343 P2d 36, 44)]

"Even legitimate tactics must sometimes yield to the only goal that justifies the very existence of our judicial system; i.e., the resolution of our citizens' disputes and the administration of justice." [*Brown v. Presley of So. Calif.* (1989) 213 CA3d 612, 620, 261 CR 779, 784, fn. 3—the notion that ours is a "dog-eat-dog business" governed by the "law of the jungle" should be curtailed, not rewarded]

a. [5:69] **No legal obligation:**  The duty to warn opposing counsel is an ethical rather than a legal requirement. As noted by one court, "While as a matter of professional courtesy counsel should have given notice of the impending default, and we decry this lack of professional courtesy . . . counsel was *under no legal obligation* to do so." [*Bellm v. Bellia* (1984) 150 CA3d 1036, 1038, 198 CR 389, 390 (emphasis added)]

b. [5:70] **Effect of failure to warn:**  In the absence of a prior warning of default, courts are inclined to grant CCP §473(b) motions to set aside defaults. [See *Smith v. Los Angeles Bookbinders' Union No. 63*, supra, 133 CA2d at 500, 284 P2d at 201; and *Pearson v. Continental Airlines* (1970) 11 CA3d 613, 619, 89 CR 853, 857]

But, in the absence of an "attorney affidavit of fault" (*see ¶5:292 ff.*), such relief is not mandatory; and denial of relief is not necessarily an abuse of discretion. I.e., the failure to warn *does not require* the court to grant relief. [*Bellm v. Bellia* (1984) 150 CA3d 1036, 1038, 198 CR 389, 390]

⇨ [5:71] **PRACTICE POINTER:**  If you're representing plaintiff, and have had *any* contact with a lawyer representing defendant, don't even *attempt* to get a default entered without first giving such lawyer *written* notice of your intent to request entry of default, and a *reasonable time* within which defendant's pleading must be filed to prevent your doing so.

If you give such warning, courts may be less sympathetic to claims by defendant's lawyer of "mistake, inadvertence, surprise or excusable neglect" in failing to plead on time, and thus less willing to grant discretionary relief under CCP §473(b), *¶5:310 ff.* It will also make it more difficult for opposing counsel to file an "affidavit of fault," which mandates relief from default (*see ¶5:292*).

On the other hand, if you fail to give such notice, courts will usually set aside the default, so that the net result may be a waste of your time and your client's money. In addition, taking a "secret" default is a sure way of antagonizing opposing counsel, and thereby complicating future handling of the case!

[5:71.1-71.4]   *Reserved.*

3.   **[5:71.5]   Dealing With Pro Per Defendants:**   Defendants appearing in pro per are not entitled to special treatment. But where one party is represented by counsel and the other is not, the trial judge must monitor the proceedings to make sure the pro per defendant is "*not misled* either by the represented party or by the court." [See *Gamet v. Blanchard* (2001) 91 CA4th 1276, 1284, 111 CR2d 439, 445 (emphasis added)]

a.   **[5:71.6]   Corporate defendants:**   This may include advising a *corporation* that attempts to appear in propria persona that it cannot represent itself: "It is the duty of the trial judge to advise the representative of the corporation of the necessity to be represented by an attorney." [See *Gamet v. Blanchard*, supra, 91 CA4th at 1284, 111 CR2d at 445, fn. 5]

[5:71.7-71.9]   *Reserved.*

⇨[5:71.10]   **PRACTICE POINTER:**   When a pro per party is involved, *avoid* verbal communications wherever possible. Make sure your written communications are *absolutely clear and unambiguous*, particularly as to deadlines, times and dates. Confusing or misleading use of legal jargon or shorthand (by counsel or the court) may be ground to set aside any default or judgment against the pro per. [*Gamet v. Blanchard*, supra, 91 CA4th at 1285, 111 CR2d at 445]

4.   **[5:72]   Procedure for Entry of Default:**   The court will not enter a defendant's default automatically. Plaintiff must apply to the court clerk to have the default entered in accordance with the following procedures:

a.   **[5:72.1]   Time requirement:**   The request for entry of default must be filed within 10 days after expiration of the time for service of a responsive pleading unless an extension of time has been granted. [CRC 201.7(g); *see* ¶5:16.5]

Failure to do so may result in the court issuing an Order to Show Cause why sanctions should not be imposed (CRC 201.7(g)). Plaintiff then has 5 calendar days within which to file and serve responsive papers. [CRC 201.7(i)]

b. [5:73] **Documentation required:** The application for entry of default normally consists of the following documents:

- "Request to Enter Default" form, including a *declaration of mailing* copies to defendant and defendant's counsel if known (*see ¶5:74*);

- Proof of service of summons (if the original summons has not already been returned with proof of service) or of notice of order fixing time for further response (e.g., after demurrer overruled);

- In superior court *injury* or *death* actions, where the damage amount is not alleged in the complaint, a CCP §425.11 statement of damages and proof of service thereof (*see ¶5:82*).

  Similar statements of damages may also be necessary in:
  — *limited civil* injury or death cases if the complaint does not allege the amount of damages sought (*see ¶5:259*);
  — actions seeking *punitive* damages (*see ¶5:102*); and
  — *accounting* actions (*see ¶5:108*).

  ⇨[5:73a] *PRACTICE POINTER:* It is a good idea to include a statement of damages with *every* application for a default judgment (or at least *check* to be sure the complaint specifically alleges the amount of damages sought). Including the separate statement avoids uncertainty as to whether the complaint falls in one of the above categories requiring a separate statement of damages.

(1) [5:73.1] *Compare:* A *declaration of nonmilitary status* is required before entry of a default *judgment* (CRC 388(a); *see ¶5:159, 5:175.1*). But it is *not* required for entry of default. [*Interinsurance Exchange of Auto. Club of So. Calif. v. Collins* (1994) 30 CA4th 1445, 1447, 37 CR2d 126, 127]

**FORMS**

- Request for Entry of Default, *see Form 5:A.*

- Proof of Service (Return on Original Summons), *see Form 4:A.*

- Default/Clerk's Judgment Rejection Notice, *see Form 5:C.*

(2) [5:73.2] *Compare—family law cases:* Different forms are used in family law cases. See Hogoboom & King, *Cal. Prac. Guide: Family Law* (TRG), Ch. 12.

c. [5:74] **"Request for Entry of Default" form:** The "Request for Entry of Default" (*Form 5:A*) is a multi-purpose form. It can be used simply to request entry of defendant's default (see below). It can also be used to obtain a clerk's default judgment (¶5:120 ff.); or to request a default judgment hearing by the court (¶5:175).

Where the form is used *solely* to obtain entry of a clerk's default, the following requirements apply:

(1) [5:74.1] **Request to clerk:** Paragraph "1.a.-c." of the form asks the clerk to enter the default of the defendant(s) named therein to the complaint or cross-complaint of the plaintiff(s) named therein. In addition, the box in the caption labeled "Entry of Default" should be checked. This constitutes "written application" for entry of default. [CCP §585(a),(b),(c)]

➡[5:75] *PRACTICE POINTER:* Make sure that you insert defendant's name in paragraph "1.c." *exactly* as it appears in the summons and complaint. Otherwise, the court will refuse to enter default.

- *If defendant is named incorrectly* in the complaint, you should correct the complaint before seeking entry of default. (Otherwise, you may end up with an unenforceable default judgment against a nonexistent defendant.) You may file an ex parte application for leave to *amend the complaint* to correct defendant's name. [CCP §473(a)(1); *see* ¶6:618 ff.] After the amendment, proceed with the default.

- *Similarly, if defendant was served as a "Doe,"* you should amend the complaint to show the true name of the person served *before* applying for a default. (This may not be strictly necessary to obtain a default, but it is required before a default *judgment* can be entered; *see* ¶5:226.)

(2) [5:76] **Venue declaration (paragraph "5"):** No default may be entered without a declaration showing whether the action is based on certain consumer contracts having special venue provisions. (*See* ¶3:507-512.) These contracts are identified in paragraph "5" of the Request for Entry of Default (*Form 5:A*). [CCP §585.5]

*Cross-refer:* A default judgment in a consumer action filed in an improper court will be set aside on timely application; *see ¶5:434.1.*

➡️ **[5:76.1]** ***PRACTICE POINTER:*** If you check any of the three boxes in paragraph "5" showing that the action is on one of the three types of consumer contracts, the court clerk will then check the venue allegations of your complaint to make sure that the local court is a "proper" one under the applicable statute. If not, the clerk will decline to enter default.

(3) **[5:77]** **Mailing declaration (paragraph "6"):** No default may be entered without a declaration stating that a copy of the "application . . . for entry of default" (i.e., the Request form) was mailed to defendant's attorney of record; or if none, to defendant at his or her last known address. If defendant's address is unknown, check box "a." under paragraph "6" and list defendant's name. [CCP §587]

➡️ **[5:77.1]** ***PRACTICE POINTER:*** Although not legally required, if you are aware of the identity of counsel representing defendant, you may be *ethically* obligated to warn such counsel *before* requesting entry of default (*see ¶5:68*).

(a) **[5:78]** **Length of notice required?** There is no statutory requirement as to how long before filing the request the copy must be mailed to defendant. Presumably, the notice is sufficient if mailed the instant before the request was filed with the clerk.

(b) **[5:79]** **Nonreceipt of notice not ground for setting aside default:** Defendant's allegation that he or she did not receive a copy of the mailed request is not enough, by itself, to set aside the default or any judgment based thereon. (Other grounds of "mistake, inadvertence, surprise, or excusable neglect" would have to be shown.) [See CCP §587; *Jackson v. Bank of America* (1983) 141 CA3d 55, 59, 190 CR 78, 80]

(c) **[5:79.1]** **Effect of notice:** If defendant is represented by counsel or defendant's address is known, such notice makes it difficult to justify any delay by defendant in seeking immediate relief from default under CCP §473(b) (*¶5:276*). It also tends to prevent any claim of lack of actual notice of the proceedings (ground for delayed relief under CCP §473.5; ¶5:420).

[5:79.2-79.4]   *Reserved.*

(d) [5:79.5]   **Effect of defective declaration:**   Defects in the mailing declaration are not ground to set aside a resulting default judgment, at least where defendant had *actual* notice of all relevant proceedings. [*Taylor v. Varga* (1995) 37 CA4th 750, 760, 43 CR2d 904, 910 (dictum)—mailing declaration contained wrong date and was ambiguous as to defendant's address, but defendant's insurer had actual notice]

(4) [5:80]   **Other portions of form not required for default entry:**   Paragraph "2" (judgment to be entered), Paragraph "7" (memorandum of costs) and Paragraph "8" (declaration of nonmilitary status) are *not* required to be completed for entry of defendant's default. They are required, however, for entry of default *judgment.* [See CCP §1033.5 (specifying allowable costs); 50 USC App. §520; *and* ¶5:158-162] (Some court clerks continue to require a declaration of nonmilitary service for *entry* of default despite case law stating it is not necessary; *see* ¶5:73.1.)

5.   [5:81]   **Additional Procedures Required in Particular Actions:**   In addition to the general default procedures, above, special notice to defendant may be required in the following types of actions:

a.   [5:82]   **Statement of damages in injury and death actions (CCP §425.11):**   In personal injury and wrongful death actions, the complaint must not state the amount of damages sought (CCP §425.10; *see* ¶6:279). Therefore, *before a default may be entered,* plaintiff must serve defendant with a "statement of the nature and amount of damages sought." [CCP §425.11(b),(c); see *Hamm v. Elkin* (1987) 196 CA3d 1343, 1345-1346, 242 CR 545, 546—service *after* default entry but before prove-up not sufficient; *see also* ¶6:283 ff.]

Proof of service of a §425.11 statement must accompany any request for entry of default to assure that defendants received actual notice of their potential liability. But the §425.11 statement itself *need not be filed with the court;* and failure to do so is not ground for setting aside a default. [*Scognamillo v. Herrick* (2003) 106 CA4th 1139, 1150, 131 CR2d 393, 401]

(1) [5:83]   **Due process requirement:**   The purpose is to give defendant "one last chance" to respond, knowing exactly what judgment may be entered if he or she

fails to appear. Absent such statement, defendant lacks notice of the actual liability threatened, so that any default judgment is void. [*Stevenson v. Turner* (1979) 94 CA3d 315, 319, 156 CR 499, 502; *Janssen v. Luu* (1997) 57 CA4th 272, 275, 66 CR2d 838, 840]

(a) [5:84]  **Notice from other sources insufficient:** The fact that defendant knows the amount of plaintiff's claim from other sources (e.g., through settlement negotiations) does *not* excuse a CCP §425.11 statement: "The possibility that defendant could divine the amount of damages claimed through collateral sources does not satisfy due process." [*Morgan v. Southern Calif. Rapid Transit Dist.* (1987) 192 CA3d 976, 986, 237 CR 756, 763 (disapproved on other grounds in *Schwab v. Rondel Homes, Inc.* (1991) 53 C3d 428, 434, 280 CR 83, 87)]

Even plaintiff's *sworn answers to interrogatories* regarding damages are no substitute for the unsworn statement of damages required by CCP §425.11! [*Morgan v. Southern Calif. Rapid Transit Dist.*, supra]

(b) [5:84.1]  **Effect of improper allegations in complaint:**  It is improper to allege the amount of damages in superior court personal injury and wrongful death complaints (CCP §425.10(b)). Even so, improper allegations of damages in the complaint may satisfy due process requirements. [*Uva v. Evans* (1978) 83 CA3d 356, 360-361, 147 CR 795, 798]

Rationale: "Right or wrong," the complaint *provides notice*. Defendant has various remedies (e.g., a motion to strike) to challenge improper pleadings. Failing to pursue such remedies waives the objection. [*Uva v. Evans*, supra, 83 CA3d at 361, 147 CR at 798]

(2) [5:85]  **Also required where default ordered as discovery sanction:**  A CCP §425.11 statement is required for entry of default where an answer has been filed but is later ordered stricken as a *discovery sanction*. I.e., due process requires such notice "whether (defendants) default by inaction or by wilful obstruction" of discovery. [*Greenup v. Rodman* (1986) 42 C3d 822, 826, 231 CR 220, 222; *Morgan v. Southern Calif. Rapid Transit Dist.*, supra, 192 CA3d at 985, 237 CR at 762 (parentheses added)]

(3) [5:86]  **Actions in which statement required:**  The statement is required in an "action . . . for personal injury

or wrongful death" (CCP §425.11). This is interpreted broadly to include actions in which injury or death claims are *closely tied* to whatever other relief is requested. [See *Jones v. Interstate Recovery Service* (1984) 160 CA3d 925, 930, 206 CR 924, 927]

(a) **[5:86.1]** **Application:** The following actions were held to require service of a CCP §425.11 statement before entry of default:

- **[5:86.2]** A complaint for trespass and conversion of personal property with "closely tied" claims for assault and intentional infliction of emotional distress. [*Jones v. Interstate Recovery Service* (1984) 160 CA3d 925, 930, 206 CR 924, 927]

- **[5:86.3]** A complaint for unlawful housing discrimination (Civ.C. §54.1) seeking both statutory damages and damages for mental and emotional distress. [*Schwab v. Rondel Homes, Inc.* (1991) 53 C3d 428, 433, 280 CR 83, 85]

  **[5:86.4-86.9]** *Reserved.*

(b) **[5:86.10]** **Cross-complaints for indemnity and contribution:** Plaintiff's service of a §425.11 statement of damages does *not* satisfy the statute as to a codefendant's indemnity or contribution claim against the defaulting defendant. (Example: P sues D1 and D2 for personal injuries; P notifies defaulting D1 that she is claiming $100,000 damages and then settles with D2 for $50,000; D2 must serve defaulting D1 with a §425.11 statement as to the amount of money it is seeking.) [*Schwab v. Southern Calif. Gas Co.* (2004) 114 CA4th 1308, 1326, 8 CR3d 627, 640]

1) **[5:86.11]** **Where amount unknown:** A CCP §425.11 notice is required even where there has been no settlement and the cross-complainants therefore do not know the precise amount of damages for which indemnity is sought against the defaulting defendant. In such a case, the CCP §425.11 notice should *estimate* the amount of damages that P may recover. [See *Schwab v. Southern Calif. Gas Co.*, supra, 114 CA4th at 1326, 8 CR3d at 640—CCP §§585 and 425.10 do not require notice of a precise amount of damages]

(c) **[5:87]** **Compare—"incidental" claim for emotional distress:** No CCP §425.11 statement is required where an emotional distress claim is merely "incidental" to the cause of action. [*Schwab v. Rondel Homes, Inc.* (1991) 53 C3d 428, 432, 280 CR 83, 85]

1) [5:87.1] **Example:** Husband's and Wife's main claim against Bank was for fraud and conversion of property. Husband's separate claim for false imprisonment was "*not* closely tied" thereto. Therefore, failure to serve a CCP §425.11 statement of damages for emotional distress on the false imprisonment claim did not void the default judgment in favor of both spouses (at least where their economic loss on the fraud claim supported the entire judgment). [*Barragan v. Banco BCH* (1986) 188 CA3d 283, 304-305, 232 CR 758, 770-771]

[5:88] *Reserved.*

(4) [5:89] **Sufficiency of notice:** The statement must provide *actual* notice of the *nature and amount* of damages being sought by plaintiff—i.e., the potential liability defendant faces. [*Schwab v. Rondel Homes, Inc.* (1991) 53 C3d 428, 433, 280 CR 83, 86]

**FORM:** Statement of Damages (Personal Injury or Wrongful Death), *see Form 6:T.*

(a) [5:89.1] **Both special and general damages:** The statement should include the amount of special and general damages sought to be recovered. [See *Schwab v. Rondel Homes, Inc.*, supra, 53 C3d at 435, 280 CR at 87; *and Form 6:T*]

1) [5:89.2] **Definitions:** "Special damages" means out-of-pocket losses that can be documented (e.g., medical and related expenses, loss of income, costs of services). [*Beeman v. Burling* (1990) 216 CA3d 1586, 1599, 265 CR 719, 727]

"General damages" includes pain and suffering, emotional distress, loss of privacy and other "subjective" detriment that is not directly quantifiable. [*Beeman v. Burling*, supra, 216 CA3d at 1599, 265 CR at 727]

- [5:89.3] *Future losses* that cannot be fixed with certainty (e.g., loss of future earnings, or future possessory interests in land) are "general damages." [*Beeman v. Burling*, supra, 216 CA3d at 1600, 265 CR at 727]

[5:89.4] *Reserved.*

2) [5:89.5] **General damages alone insufficient:** A statement as to general damages alone is insufficient, because the amount of generals recovered is usually based on the amount of special damages proved. [*Jones v. Interstate Recovery Service* (1984) 160 CA3d 925, 929-930, 206 CR 924, 926]

3) [5:89.6] **Unsegregated demand insufficient:** Similarly, a statement of plaintiff's "total demand," without a breakdown between general and special damages, is insufficient. [*Plotitsa v. Sup.Ct. (Kadri)* (1983) 140 CA3d 755, 761-762, 189 CR 769, 772]

(b) [5:90] **Constructive notice by failing to designate action as limited civil case?** Failing to designate the action as a limited civil case does *not necessarily* impart notice that plaintiff is claiming more than $25,000 in general and special damages. [See *Schwab v. Rondel Homes, Inc.* (1991) 53 C3d 428, 434, 280 CR 83, 86—because complaint also sought $500,000 punitive damages, it could not be assumed general damages exceeded $25,000]

[5:90.1] Likewise, the fact the complaint alleges the "relief sought . . . is within the jurisdiction of this court" is not notice of the actual amount of general and special damages sought. [*Parish v. Peters* (1991) 1 CA4th 202, 216, 1 CR2d 836, 845]

[5:90.2-90.4] *Reserved.*

(c) [5:90.5] **Constructive notice from other documents filed in action?** Other documents served and filed in the action generally do *not* serve the function of a CCP §425.11 notice stating the general and special damages sought. [*Debbie S. v. Ray* (1993) 16 CA4th 193, 199, 19 CR2d 814, 817]

1) [5:90.6] **Settlement demands:** CCP §998 settlement demands (*see ¶12:590 ff.*) and settlement conference statements do *not* constitute actual notice of general and special damages. They are designed to facilitate settlement rather than to fix the potential judgment at trial. [*Debbie S. v. Ray*, supra, 16 CA4th at 199, 19 CR2d at 817-818]

(5) [5:91] **Method of service:** If defendant has not appeared in the action, the CCP §425.11 statement of damages must be served "in the same manner as a summons" (i.e., personal service). [CCP §425.11(d)(1)]

If defendant *has* appeared, the notice may be served by mail on defendant's attorney of record or on defendant if in pro per. [CCP §425.11(d)(2)]

(a) [5:92] **Effect—"double service" required in default cases:** Thus, in most personal injury and wrongful death actions, defendant may have to be served personally *twice*: first, with summons and complaint, and then (if he or she fails to appear) a second time with a CCP §425.11 notice.

 • [5:92.1] *Caution* **re earlier case law:** Before the 1993 amendment to CCP §425.11, some courts allowed service by mail on defendants who had not appeared (*California Novelties, Inc. v. Sokoloff* (1992) 6 CA4th 936, 945, 7 CR2d 795, 800). These cases should no longer be relied upon.

 ➡[5:93] *PRACTICE POINTER:* If you represent plaintiffs, it makes sense to serve a CCP §425.11 statement *along with the summons and complaint.* That way, if defendant fails to respond, you won't have to serve him or her a second time!

 [5:94] *Reserved.*

(b) [5:95] **Service excused where defendant served by publication?** Cases are split on whether a CCP §425.11 statement is required where the summons and complaint are served by publication because defendant's whereabouts are unknown:

 • [5:95.1] One case holds service may be *excused* as futile where the defendant's whereabouts are unknown: "The law neither does nor requires idle acts." [Civ.C. §3532; *Candelaria v. Avitia* (1990) 219 CA3d 1436, 1441, 269 CR 32, 34]

 • [5:95.2] Another case is contra, holding due process mandates service of a statement of damages *in the same manner* as the summons and complaint (i.e., by publication, if necessary). [*Parish v. Peters* (1991) 1 CA4th 202, 212, 1 CR2d 836, 842]

 ➡[5:96] *PRACTICE POINTER:* Defaults are *likely* when summons is served by publication. Therefore, when obtaining an order for publication of summons, consider asking for an order authorizing publication of a CCP §425.11 statement of damages *at the same time*. This should facilitate obtaining a default judgment. (*Also see Practice Pointer at* ¶5:93.)

(6) [5:97] **Defendant's time to respond?** CCP §425.11 does not state how long before entry of default the damages statement must be served. Courts are split:

    (a) [5:98] **30 days required:** Several cases treat a §425.11 statement as an *amendment to the complaint*, thus giving defendant the same time to respond as to an amended complaint. Under this approach, no default can be entered until at least *30 days* after service of the CCP §425.11 statement. [*Plotitsa v. Sup.Ct. (Kadri)* (1983) 140 CA3d 755, 761, 189 CR 769, 772; *Twine v. Compton Supermarket* (1986) 179 CA3d 514, 517, 224 CR 562, 563—default judgment entered 3 days after service of damages statement held *void*, thus subject to collateral attack after time for appeal expired]

    (b) [5:99] **"Reasonable time" sufficient:** However, the Supreme Court has stated (in dictum) that "a defendant is entitled to actual notice of the liability to which he or she may be subjected, *a reasonable period of time* before default may be entered." [*Schwab v. Rondel Homes, Inc.* (1991) 53 C3d 428, 435, 280 CR 83, 87 (emphasis added) (dictum)]

    Accordingly, several cases hold only "reasonable" notice prior to entry of default is required. [*California Novelties, Inc. v. Sokoloff* (1992) 6 CA4th 936, 945, 7 CR2d 795, 800—case-by-case approach required to determine if applicable statutes and due process satisfied (17 days' notice held "reasonable"); *Schwab v. Southern Calif. Gas Co.* (2004) 114 CA4th 1308, 1321, 8 CR3d 627, 636 (same)]

    (c) [5:100] **Compare—time for requesting entry of default:** Plaintiff must file an application for entry of default within 10 days after expiration of the time for service of a responsive pleading, or face *sanctions* for failing to do so. [See CRC 201.7(g)]

    Comment: Service of a CCP §425.11 statement apparently does *not* extend the time for requesting entry of default because no "responsive pleading" is required to a §425.11 statement.

☞[5:100.1] *PRACTICE POINTER:* It is better to avoid this problem altogether. If there is even a possibility the matter may go by default, serve the CCP §425.11 statement *together with the summons and complaint.*

(7) [5:101] **Damages statement must accompany request for entry of default:** A request for entry of default in a personal injury or wrongful death case must be accompanied by plaintiff's statement of damages with proof of service on defendant. [See CCP §425.11(c)]

b. [5:102] **Notice of amount of punitive damages claimed:** It is not proper to allege in the complaint the *amount or amounts* of punitive damages sought. [Civ.C. §3295(e), ¶*5:261*]

(1) [5:103] **Due process requires notice:** Notice of the amount of plaintiff's claim is an essential element of due process. A general allegation in the complaint of entitlement to punitive damages "is not reasonably calculated to apprise the defendant of potential financial liability for punitive damages if judgment is taken by default." [*Wiley v. Rhodes* (1990) 223 CA3d 1470, 1473, 273 CR 279, 280 (citing text)]

(a) [5:103.1] **Effect of improper allegations in complaint:** Although it is improper to allege the amount of punitive damages in the complaint, such allegations may satisfy due process ... despite the violation of Civ.C. §3295! [*Cummings Med. Corp. v. Occupational Med. Corp. of America, Inc.* (1992) 10 CA4th 1291, 1297-1298, 13 CR2d 585, 589]

(2) [5:104] **Statutory notice requirement:** To preserve the right to seek punitive damages as part of a default judgment, plaintiffs must serve defendants with a statement in the form provided below. [CCP §425.115(b),(f)]

This notice must be *separate from the complaint* because Civ.C. §3295(e) bars such allegations in the complaint. [See *Wiley v. Rhodes,* supra, 223 CA3d at 1474, 273 CR at 281, fn. 4 (citing text)]

But it may be *part of a CCP §425.11 statement* of damages in injury and death cases. [CCP §425.115(e)]

(a) [5:104.1] **Form:** The following statement or "its substantial equivalent" is required:

*(Text cont'd on p. 5-29)*

**RESERVED**

"NOTICE TO .....(*defendant's or cross-defendant's name*).......

"(*Plaintiff's or cross-complainant's name*) ............. .................... reserves the right to seek $.......(*dollar amount*) in punitive damages when ................... .....................(*plaintiff's or cross-complainant's name*) seeks a judgment in the suit filed against you.

"Dated: ..............

" .......................................(*name of attorney or party appearing in propria persona*)" [CCP §425.115(b)]

(b) **[5:105]** **Manner of service:** As stated above, this notice may be served as part of a CCP §425.11 statement in cases involving death or bodily injury. Otherwise, it may be served in the same manner as a §425.11 statement (¶*5:91 ff.*); i.e., for defendants who have not yet appeared in the action, it must be served in the same manner as a summons. [CCP §425.115(g)]

⇨**[5:105.1]** *PRACTICE POINTER:* The statute neither authorizes nor prohibits serving the §425.115 statement *concurrently* with the summons and complaint. Doing so may be a good tactic where defendant is likely to default because it will avoid the necessity of duplicate personal service.

*Caution:* However, there is no authority approving such concurrent service and it *may* be contrary to the purpose of Civ.C. §3295; *see* ¶*6:292.*

(c) **[5:106]** **Time for service?** The statute requires rather enigmatically that the statement be served "before a default may be taken, *where the motion for default judgment* includes a request for punitive damages." [CCP §425.115(f) (emphasis added)]

Comment: Although the meaning is not entirely clear, the statute probably does *not* require that "the motion for default judgment" be *pending* before a default may be entered. That would prevent entry of default in most cases because the application for default judgment normally *follows* entry of the default (*see* ¶*5:10*).

(d) [5:107]  **Not a limit on recovery if defendant appears:**  Where defendant appears in the action, the amount of punitive damages stated in the §425.115 statement is not a limit on the amount plaintiff may recover at trial. [CCP §425.115(c)]

c.  [5:108]  **Accounting actions:**  Where the complaint seeks only an accounting (e.g., on dissolution of a partnership), it has been held that no default judgment for a specific amount may be entered unless a *separate notice* is first provided to a defaulting defendant as to its potential liability. [*Ely v. Gray* (1990) 224 CA3d 1257, 1263-1264, 274 CR 536, 539-540]

However, no special notice may be necessary if the complaint contains an *estimate of the amount due* and plaintiff is willing to be bound by that amount. [*Ely v. Gray*, supra, 224 CA3d at 1262, 274 CR at 539 (dictum)]

Also, notice of the specific amount sought may not be required where the defaulting defendant possesses the information upon which the accounting is based. "We foresee no danger that defaulting defendants will be taken by surprise . . ." [*Cassel v. Sullivan, Roche & Johnson* (1999) 76 CA4th 1157, 1163-1164, 90 CR2d 899, 904—complaint for accounting, valuation and payment of former partner's interest need only specify type of relief sought]

(1) [5:109]  **Form, content and service:**  The form, content and service of the required notice should be governed "by analogy to the statutes on wrongful death and personal injury damages" (CCP §425.11; *see ¶5:82 ff.*). [*Ely v. Gray*, supra, 224 CA3d at 1263, 274 CR at 540] (*See ¶5:108* for possible exceptions to separate notice requirement.)

(2) [5:110]  **Comment:**  *Ely* was decided before the Supreme Court decision in *Marriage of Lippel* (dealing with child support awards on marital dissolution, *see ¶5:234-235*). Whether *Ely* is consistent with the rationale of *Lippel* is not entirely clear; *see ¶5:239.*

*Cassel v. Sullivan, Roche & Johnson*, supra (*¶5:108*), decided after *Marriage of Lippel*, does not specifically state that *Ely* was erroneously decided. Whether the special notice is required probably depends on whether the records upon which the accounting is based are in defendants' possession.

⇨[5:111]  *PRACTICE POINTER:*  Avoid the problem! If you are representing the plaintiff in an accounting action, *include a high estimate of the amount due* in the complaint. Even under *Ely*, above, a default judgment for that amount may be upheld.

6. [5:112] **Clerk's Entry of Default:** Upon receipt of the documentation above from plaintiff, showing the statutory requirements for entry of default exist, the court clerk is under a mandatory duty to enter defendant's default. [CCP §585(a),(b),(c)]

   a. [5:112.1] **"Entry of default":** This means the clerk's checking the appropriate box on plaintiff's request for entry of default ("Default entered as requested on (*date*) . . ."; *see Form 5:A*), and signing and filing the form (*see ¶5:4*).

   b. [5:113] **Clerk's authority limited:** The clerk may reject an application for entry of default if it is incomplete or fails to show the statutory requirements for entry of default: i.e., service of summons in a manner permitting entry of default (*¶5:18 ff.*); expiration of time to respond (*¶5:21 ff.*); defendant's failure to respond (*¶5:30 ff.*); and copies of the application mailed to defendant and counsel (*¶5:77 ff.*).

   But the clerk has *no* authority to determine the accuracy of plaintiff's declarations or legal sufficiency of claimed service upon defendant, or the sufficiency of an answer or other pleading on file. [See *W.A. Rose Co. v. Mun. Ct. (FitzSimmons)* (1959) 176 CA2d 67, 71, 1 CR 49, 52—clerk must look at record to see if answer or other permitted response has been filed, but if none, *must* enter the default]

   [5:114] *Reserved.*

   ➪[5:115] *PRACTICE POINTER:* Entry of default is the first step toward a default judgment. Where the court clerk is authorized to enter a default judgment, you will have to follow up with the court clerk (*see ¶5:120*). Where a default judgment must be entered by the court, you will have to apply to the court for such a judgment (*see ¶5:173 ff.*).

7. [5:116] **Effect of Default Entry:** Once default is entered by the clerk, defendant's right to appear in the action thereafter is cut off. The only motion that defendant can file is a motion to be relieved from default under CCP §473. The court has no authority to consider any other pleading or motion (*see ¶5:6-8*).

   [5:117-119] *Reserved.*

## C. DEFAULT JUDGMENT BY CLERK

[5:120] In certain cases, after entry of defendant's default, the court clerk is authorized (upon request by plaintiff) to enter judgment against the defendant *without* a court hearing or judicial action of any kind.

1. **[5:121]** **When Authorized:** Entry of default judgment by the court clerk is authorized only if:

   - The action is one "*arising upon a contract or judgment*"; and

   - Seeks recovery of "money or damages only" in a *fixed or determinable amount*; and

   - Defendant was *not served* by publication. [CCP §585(a)]

   a. **[5:122]** **Comment:** Allowing the court clerk to enter an immediate default judgment against the defendant is akin to a grant of judicial power. Hence, the requirements above are *very strictly construed* (see below).

   b. **[5:123]** **Other cases:** In all other cases, a default judgment can be granted only by the court upon an *evidentiary showing*.

      This showing may be made by live testimony (CCP §585(b),(c); ¶5:171 ff.); or, in the court's discretion, by affidavits or declarations (CCP §585(d); ¶5:202).

   c. **[5:124]** **Special rule in unlawful detainer cases:** In unlawful detainer cases, the clerk will enter judgment for possession of the premises "immediately" upon proper request therefor (see CCP §1169). However, plaintiff must apply to the court for damages or any other relief sought in the complaint (including costs of suit). [CCP §1169]

2. **[5:125]** **Requirement That Action be Based on Contract or Judgment:** The first requirement for a clerk's judgment is that the action be one "arising upon a contract or judgment ..." [CCP §585(a)]

   a. **[5:126]** **"Contract" actions:** This includes implied, as well as express, contracts: e.g., actions in quasi-contract (for a fixed and determinable amount, see below).

   b. **[5:127]** **"Judgment" actions:** The clerk is authorized to enter default judgment in an action based on a judgment rendered in *any* previous court action (not limited to California judgments). [CCP §585(a)]

3. **[5:128]** **Requirement That Action be for Fixed or Determinable Amount:** The recovery sought must be of "money or damages only." Courts have construed this language narrowly. As a result, in an action based on contract, the amount due must either be *fixed* in the contract itself, or be *determinable by calculation* from its terms. If there is any uncertainty as to the amount due, the court clerk has no power to resolve it. Instead, a court judgment will be required. [*Liberty Loan Corp. of North Park v. Petersen* (1972) 24 CA3d 915, 919, 101 CR 395, 397]

   a. **[5:129]** **Amount due fixed or determinable from contract:** The court clerk is authorized to enter default judgment where the amount due can be *computed* from the contract itself. *Examples:*

(1) [5:130]  Action on *open book account* (e.g., running charge account balances). [*Diamond National Corp. v. Golden Empire Builders, Inc.* (1963) 213 CA2d 283, 288-289, 28 CR 616, 620]

(2) [5:131]  Action on *account stated* (statements received and accepted by defendant showing charges and credits to date). [*Fallon & Co. v. United States Overseas Airlines, Inc.* (1961) 194 CA2d 546, 551-552, 15 CR 354, 357]

b. [5:132]  **Amount due NOT fixed or determinable:**  But the court clerk cannot adjudicate the amount due by taking evidence or exercising discretion. Thus, where the amount claimed by plaintiff cannot be computed from the contract itself, the court clerk has no power to enter judgment. A judgment by the court is required. *Examples*:

(1) [5:133]  Action for an *accounting*. [*Crossman v. Vivienda Water Co.* (1902) 136 C 571, 574, 69 P 220, 222]

(2) [5:134]  Action for "*reasonable value*" of property or services conferred; or "*net profits*" of a business. [See *Gray v. Laufenberger* (1961) 195 CA2d Supp. 875, 878, 15 CR 813, 815]

(3) [5:135]  Action on secured promissory note claiming that security has become "worthless" (testimony necessary to determine whether this is so). [*Ford v. Sup.Ct. (Orton)* (1973) 34 CA3d 338, 342, 109 CR 844, 847]

(4) [5:136]  Action on secured promissory note for $500, where demand was only $253, without any explanation as to how reduction occurred (complaint failed to negate possibility that the collateral securing the note had not been dealt with or sold). [*Liberty Loan Corp. of North Park v. Petersen* (1972) 24 CA3d 915, 919-920, 101 CR 395, 397]

[5:136.1-136.4]  *Reserved.*

(5) [5:136.5]  **Compare—injury, death, punitive damages actions?**  CCP §585(a) states that "the clerk . . . shall enter the default of the defendant . . . and *immediately thereafter enter judgment* for the principal amount demanded . . . in the statement required by Section 425.11, or in the statement provided for in Section 425.115 . . ." [CCP §585(a) (emphasis added)]

Comment: This *seems* to allow the court clerk to enter judgment in actions for wrongful death, personal injury or punitive damages. But that is clearly not intended. The statute deals with default "in an action arising *upon a contract or judgment* . . ." (CCP §585(a)); and should have no application to wrongful death, personal injury and punitive damages cases.

Instead, these cases should be handled as "other actions" (see CCP §585(b), which also refers to CCP §§425.11 and 425.115). In these cases, plaintiff should be required to present evidence to a judge and obtain a default judgment authorized by the *judge, not* a court clerk (*see ¶5:171 ff.*).

c.  [5:137]  **Demand for attorney fees:**  If plaintiff's complaint includes a demand for attorney fees, this may affect the clerk's power to enter default judgment.

(1)  [5:138]  **Contract provision for fixed amount:**  If the contract sued upon stipulates the amount of attorney fees recoverable in such action, the clerk is authorized to enter judgment accordingly. Example: Promissory note providing for attorney's fee in an amount equal to 10% of principal and interest due; court clerk can compute and enter amount. [*Alexander v. McDow* (1895) 108 C 25, 30-31, 41 P 24, 25] (Some courts, however, may require a "prove-up" hearing and court judgment in any event.)

(2)  [5:139]  **Contract provision for "reasonable" fee:**  But where the contract merely calls for an "attorney's fee as fixed by the court," or a "reasonable attorney's fee," the court clerk has no power to determine the amount. [*Landwehr v. Gillette* (1917) 174 C 654, 657-658, 163 P 1018, 1020]

(a)  [5:140]  **If fee schedule in effect:**  Courts are authorized to adopt schedules of attorney fees allowable in default cases where a *statute or contract authorizes* fee awards (e.g., actions on a promissory note containing an attorney fee provision). [CRC 388(b)]

Where such fee schedules are in effect, and plaintiff is willing to accept the scheduled fee, the court clerk may include that amount in the default judgment. [CCP §585(a)]

1)  [5:141]  **Examples:**  Attorney fee schedules are contained in L.A. Sup.Ct. Rule 3.2(a); Orange Sup.Ct. Rule 366; San Diego Sup.Ct. Rule 2.53; and S.F. Unif. Rule 10.3 (applicable to limited civil cases only).

For most courts, a complete list of such fees can be found on the court's Web site. These local court Web sites may be accessed through the California Judicial Council home page (www.courtinfo.ca.gov).

(b) [5:142] **Plaintiff may insist on court judgment:** Plaintiff is not required to accept the scheduled fee. But the court clerk has no authority to enter default judgment for any different amount. Consequently, if plaintiff is unwilling to accept the scheduled fee, he or she will have to request a court judgment. The court can award attorney fees in whatever amount it determines to be reasonable. [CCP §585(a)]

4. [5:143] **Effect of Joinder of Other Causes of Action:** Problems may arise where the complaint pleads several causes of action, one of which would be proper for a clerk's default judgment (i.e., a "contract" or "judgment" claim), and the others which would not:

a. [5:144] **Separate and distinct causes:** If the causes of action joined are in fact separate and distinct, the clerk can enter default judgment on the "contract" or "judgment" cause of action only. Plaintiffs who want judgment on the other cause of action as well will have to obtain a default judgment from the court. [*Norman v. Berney* (1965) 235 CA2d 424, 431-432, 45 CR 467, 472-473]

(1) [5:145] **Example:** P's complaint joins cause of action for breach of construction contract with cause of action to foreclose mechanic's lien for work done. The clerk can enter default judgment only on the "contract" cause of action. If P wants his mechanic's lien foreclosed, he will have to obtain a court judgment. [*Norman v. Berney,* supra]

b. [5:146] **"Contract" claim as alternative legal theory:** But the clerk *cannot* enter a valid default judgment where the "contract" cause of action is merely an alternative theory for recovery on a *claim that otherwise does not qualify* for a clerk's default judgment. [*Brown v. Sup.Ct. (Stewart)* (1966) 242 CA2d 519, 525, 51 CR 633, 636-637]

(1) [5:147] **Example:** P's complaint joins cause of action for "reasonable value" of services rendered with cause of action for "account stated" based on billings for same services. Since the clerk could not enter a default judgment on the "reasonable value" count (no fixed or determinable amount; ¶5:134), and the "account stated" claim is merely an *alternative theory* for recovery, the clerk has no authority to enter default judgment on *either* count. A court judgment is required. [*Brown v. Sup.Ct. (Stewart),* supra]

5. **[5:148] Effect of Joining Several Defendants:** CCP §579 provides that: "In an action against several defendants, the court may, in its discretion, render judgment against one or more of them, leaving the action to proceed against the others, whenever a *several judgment* is proper."

   a. **[5:149] Effect:** It is *discretionary* with the *court* whether to enter a judgment against one of several defendants before trial (*see ¶5:269*). Thus, where one of several contracting defendants defaults, and the others answer, a court judgment is required. [*Kooper v. King* (1961) 195 CA2d 621, 628, 15 CR 848, 851]

   b. **[5:150] Example:** P sues D1 and D2 for $4,000 due by them under contract. D1 answers; D2 defaults. The clerk is *not* authorized to enter default judgment against D2. A court judgment is required. [*Kooper v. King,* supra]

   c. **[5:151] Rationale:** Where the defenses raised by the answering defendant (D1) affect plaintiff's right to recover *at all* (as distinguished from his right to recover against only that defendant), the court should decide whether to render judgment against the defaulting defendant. In effect, the answering defendant's defenses may inure to his benefit. [*Kooper v. King,* supra, 195 CA2d at 629, 15 CR at 852]

   d. **[5:152] Compare—all defendants in default:** But where all the contracting defendants are in default, there is no judicial discretion to be exercised, and thus a clerk's default judgment is proper. [*Diamond National Corp. v. Golden Empire Builders, Inc.* (1963) 213 CA2d 283, 288, 28 CR 616, 620—also emphasizing that defendants' liability was "presumptively joint and several, possibly joint, but not exclusively several"]

6. **[5:153] Procedure:** The procedural requirements for obtaining a default judgment by the court clerk involve filling out the "Request for Entry of Default" form and providing other documentation.

   a. **[5:154] Filling out "Request for Entry of Default" form:** The same multi-purpose form used for requesting the clerk's entry of default (*¶5:74 ff., Form 5:A*) is also used to request entry of default judgment by the court clerk.

   If a "Request for Entry of Default" has already been filed solely to obtain entry of defendant's default, another form will have to be filed to obtain entry of the default judgment by the clerk. In this event, check box "1.e.(3)" on the second form and insert the date on which the default was previously entered.

(1) **[5:155]** **Request to clerk:** Paragraph "1.a.-c." requests the clerk to enter default of the named defendant (*see detailed discussion at ¶5:74.1-75*).

Paragraph "1.e.(2)" must *also* be checked, requesting a clerk's default judgment. (Despite the apparent mandatory language of CCP §585(a) that "judgment shall be entered" immediately after entry of default, most court clerks will not do so unless "1.e.(2)" is checked!)

   (a) **[5:156]** **Attorney fees:** A special box "2.e." is provided where the contract authorizes attorney fees, and the court has adopted a schedule of attorney fees (*¶5:140-141*). If plaintiff is willing to accept the scheduled fee, plaintiff should write in the amount opposite "2.e." If plaintiff wants greater fees (or the court has no approved fee schedule), a judgment by the court will be required . . . in which event, box "1.d." should be checked.

(2) **[5:157]** **Amount of judgment sought (paragraph "2"):** Paragraph "2.a.-g." of the form should be filled out to show the amount of judgment to be entered:

   • the dollars demanded in the *complaint*, including the amount of *special and general damages* set forth in the *statement of damages*, if required (*see ¶5:82*);

   • plus *interest* (as provided for in the contract, or allowable by law);

   • plus *costs* (as enumerated in paragraph "7" of the form; *see ¶5:158*);

   • plus the amount of *attorney fees* (if fixed by the contract, or by statute, or by court's schedule of fees; *see ¶5:156*);

   • plus computation of *daily damages* for those actions demanding daily damages—e.g., unlawful detainer, breach of contract, etc.

Deductions for any credits or payments are required to be shown under the "credits acknowledged" column of the form.

(3) **Venue declaration (paragraph "5"):** *See ¶5:76-76.1.*

(4) **Mailing declaration (paragraph "6"):** *See ¶5:77-79.*

(5) **[5:158]** **Memorandum of costs declaration (paragraph "7"):** This paragraph must be filled in at the

time judgment is sought, showing plaintiff's recoverable costs and disbursements to date; e.g., filing fees, process server fees, notary fees, etc. [CCP §1033.5] A declaration is required from plaintiff's attorney as to the correctness of the costs claimed.

(6) **[5:159] Declaration re nonmilitary status (paragraph "8"):** Federal law provides that no default judgment may be rendered without proof that the defendant is not in military service. [50 USC App. §521(b), *discussed at ¶5:198 ff.*]

(Note: Such declaration is *not* required when only requesting *entry of default; see ¶5:73.1.*)

(a) **[5:160] Current information required:** The declaration may be completed by anyone with personal knowledge that defendant is not in the armed services at the present time and should be *current*.

(b) **[5:161] If no declaration obtainable:** If plaintiff cannot provide such declaration, he must file an affidavit stating either that defendant is in military service, or that his military status cannot be ascertained. In either event, the court will have to *appoint an attorney to represent defendant* before a valid default judgment can be entered. [50 USC App. §520(1), *¶5:199*]

➥**[5:162]** *PRACTICE POINTER:* If you are suing a defendant whom the plaintiff does not know personally, *ask the process server* to inquire at the time summons is served whether defendant is in military service. Then, you may be able to use the process server's declaration.

**[5:162.1]** *CHECKLIST:* Some court clerks use forms listing reasons for their refusal to enter a default or default judgment. See Los Angeles Superior Court Default/Clerk's Judgment Rejection Notice, *Form 5:C.*

b. **Other documentation required for clerk's default judgment .**

(1) **[5:163] A promissory note or other written obligation to pay money** (e.g., negotiable instrument), if any, upon which the action is brought. The court clerk is required to note across the face of the writing, over his official signature, the date and fact that judgment has been rendered on such contract. [CRC 234] (After such

notation, the contract is treated as an exhibit, and may be returned to the plaintiff on ex parte application to the court.) [See *Kahn v. Lasorda's Dugout, Inc.* (2003) 109 CA4th 1118, 1124, 135 CR2d 790, 795 (citing text)]

If the original has been lost or destroyed, the court has discretion to accept a copy. [*Kahn v. Lasorda's Dugout, Inc.*, supra, 109 CA4th at 1124, 135 CR2d at 795]

[5:164]   ***PRACTICE POINTER:***   If the original writing has been *lost or destroyed*, obtain a declaration to that effect from the plaintiff; and apply

*(Text cont'd on p. 5-39)*

**RESERVED**

for an ex parte court order directing the court clerk to accept a *copy* in lieu of the original.

(2) [5:165] **Certified copy of the judgment,** if the action is one to enforce an earlier judgment.

(3) [5:166] **Request for dismissal with prejudice as to unserved defendants:** If the claim is one on which defendants are jointly liable, some courts require a request for dismissal with prejudice as to all unserved defendants (to prevent obtaining a second judgment on the same obligation). Rules containing such a requirement probably violate CRC 981.1(a). However, the judge may impose such a requirement before permitting a judgment to be entered.

If the defendants are *severally* liable, the court has discretion to enter the default judgment against one and permit the action to proceed against the others. [CCP §579]

However, the court may also choose to defer entry of the default judgment until a single judgment can be entered against all defendants.

(4) [5:167] **Any additional documentation required:** For example, where the action is on an open book account, the court clerk may require copies of the bills or invoices, and a declaration negating the existence of any written agreement with the defendant.

(5) [5:168] **Clerk's judgment:** The optional Judicial Council form (JUD-100) may be used for a clerk's default judgment by checking the box marked "Clerk's Judgment." (This multi-purpose form may also be used for a default judgment by the court, a stipulated judgment or judgment after trial.)

*Comment:* The report to the Judicial Council recommending adoption of this form indicated its use was to be limited to "simple civil cases." This limitation, however, does not appear on the form itself.

***FORM:*** Judgment, *see Form 5:D.*

(a) [5:168.1] **Compare—unlawful detainers:** Different forms are used in unlawful detainer cases. See Friedman, Garcia & Hagerty, *Cal. Prac. Guide: Landlord-Tenant* (TRG), Ch. 8.

[5:169] *Reserved.*

☞[5:170] ***PRACTICE POINTER:*** Find out in advance how long it generally takes to obtain a clerk's default judgment in the court in which your case is pending. In view of the long delays encountered in some courts (and the penchant of some clerks to "bounce" requests for even minor irregularities), you *may* be better off asking for a default judgment by the court! (In any event, you are not *required* to obtain a clerk's default judgment, even in cases in which it is available.)

## D. DEFAULT JUDGMENT BY COURT

1. **[5:171] When Required:** Plaintiff is required to "prove up" the default (i.e., present evidence to a judge) to obtain a default judgment in any case other than those in which a clerk's default judgment is allowed (see above). Thus, a court judgment is required in the following kinds of cases:

   • Cases *not* "arising upon contract or judgment";

   • "Contract or judgment" cases where the relief sought is *not* a fixed or determinable amount of money or damages; and

   • Cases in which defendant was *served by publication.* [CCP §585(b),(c)]

   (A court judgment is also required where plaintiff seeks "reasonable" *attorney fees,* and there is either no court-approved schedule of fees in effect, or plaintiff wants more than the scheduled fee; *see ¶5:139-142.*)

   ⇨ **[5:172]** *PRACTICE POINTER:* As shown below, there may be a lot of work involved in preparing a case for default "prove-up." That time and effort will be wasted if the court later grants relief from default, and a motion for such relief is likely where defendant is represented by counsel. Therefore, consider *asking* counsel whether he or she intends to file a CCP §473 motion *before* preparing for the default hearing. Doing so is also a good tactic . . . because the longer counsel delays in taking steps to have the default set aside, the less likely the court will be to grant such relief! [See *Beeman v. Burling* (1990) 216 CA3d 1586, 1602-1603, 265 CR 719, 729-730]

2. **[5:173] Preparing Case for Court Judgment:** Plaintiffs seeking a default judgment based on declarations must comply with CRC 388 (*see ¶5:176 ff.*).

   Local court rules and policies may regulate the time and place in which default judgments may be sought from the court. [See L.A. Sup.Ct. Rule 9.10(a),(b)]

   But local rules may *not* regulate the "form and format of papers" required to be filed with the court (CRC 981.1(a); *see ¶9:7.1*).

   a. **[5:174] Documentation and evidence required from plaintiff:** Before a case is ready for submission to the court for a default judgment, plaintiff must file the following:

(1) [5:175] **Request for "Entry of Default" form:** The same multi-purpose form used to obtain entry of default and clerk's default judgment must be used (see CRC 388(a)), except that:
— the "Court Judgment" box is checked on the title line; and
— paragraph "1.d." is checked ("I request a court judgment").

**FORM:** Request for Entry of Default, *see Form 5:A.*

(a) [5:175.1] **Optional—multi-purpose judgment form:** An optional Judicial Council form (JUD-100) may be used for a default judgment by the court. This multi-purpose judgment form may also be used for a clerk's default judgment (¶*5:168.1*), a stipulated judgment, or judgment after a court trial.

*Comment:* The report to the Judicial Council recommending adoption of this form indicated its use was to be limited to "simple civil cases." This limitation, however, does not appear on the form itself.

**FORM:** Judgment, *see Form 5:D.*

(2) [5:176] **Supporting documentation:** When seeking a default judgment from the court *based on declarations* (as distinguished from live testimony), plaintiff must include the following in the documents filed with the clerk: [CRC 388(a)]

▷ [5:176.1] **PRACTICE POINTER:** It is good practice to provide the same documentation when seeking a default judgment *based on live testimony.* Even if technically not required, it enables the court to handle the matter more efficiently and may avoid questions that could sidetrack your presentation.

Some judges *prefer* evidence in the form of declarations, others permit it on request, and still others wish to hear live testimony (*see* ¶*5:209*). Counsel should check with the clerk of the department where the prove-up will take place to determine the judge's preferences in this regard. (Live testimony is *required* as a matter of law in certain cases; *see* ¶*5:203 ff.*)

(a) [5:177] **Case summary:** A *brief* summary of the case identifying the parties and the nature of plaintiff's claims. (Exception: This requirement does not apply in unlawful detainer cases.) [CRC 388(a)(1)]

(b) [5:178] **Declarations:** *Declarations or other admissible evidence* in support of the judgment requested (*see ¶5:207*). [CRC 388(a)(2)]

(c) [5:179] **Interest computations:** Interest computations as necessary. [CRC 388(a)(3)]

☞[5:179.1] *PRACTICE POINTER:* Because most default prove-ups are handled without a hearing, counsel cannot accurately predict exactly when the court will sign the judgment. Therefore, your interest calculation should include a *per diem* amount (e.g., "$77.50 per day from June 15, 20 . . to date of entry of judgment herein"). This allows the court to include interest up to the date the judgment is signed.

(d) [5:180] **Costs memo:** A memorandum of costs and disbursements. [CRC 388(a)(4)]

Paragraph 7 of the multipurpose form (*Form 5:A*) should be used for this purpose (*see ¶5:158*).

(e) [5:180.1] **Affidavit re military service:** A *declaration of nonmilitary status* for each defendant against whom judgment is sought. [CRC 388(a)(5)]

Paragraph 8 of the multipurpose form (*Form 5:A*) should be used for this purpose (*see ¶5:159-162*).

(f) [5:180.2] **Proposed judgment:** A proposed form of judgment (*see Form 5:G*). [CRC 388(a)(6)]

(g) [5:180.3] **Memorandum of costs:** Also, a memorandum of costs to be added to the judgment (*see Forms 5:H and 5:H.1*).

(h) [5:180.4] **Dismissals:** Dismissal of all parties against whom judgment is not sought or an application for separate judgment against specified parties under CCP §579, supported by a showing of grounds for each defendant (*see ¶5:148-152*). [CRC 388(a)(7)]

☞[5:180.5] *PRACTICE POINTER:* Instruct the court clerk *not to file any dismissals* until after the court orders entry of a default judgment. If for any reason a default judgment is refused, you may want to continue the action against the other defendants.

(i) [5:181] **Exhibits:** Exhibits as necessary. [CRC 388(a)(8)]

1) [5:181.1] **Photocopies:** Legible photocopies of documents or records are usually acceptable if properly authenticated (e.g., by declarations stating declarant has original in his or her possession and attached is a true and correct copy). [See Ev.C. §1521—secondary evidence rule; Ev.C. §1550—photocopies and other types of reproductions of business records; and CCP §1045—court may authorize use of copies where original papers or pleadings lost]

*Cross-refer:* Documentary evidence and the secondary evidence rule are discussed in detail in Wegner, Fairbank, Epstein & Chernow, *Cal. Prac. Guide: Civil Trials & Evidence* (TRG), Ch. 8C.

2) [5:181.2] **Originals:** Remember, however, that if the suit is on a promissory note or other written obligation to pay money, the original must be submitted to the court clerk for cancellation. [CRC 234; *see* ¶5:163-164]

(j) [5:182] **Attorney fees:** A *request for attorney fees* if allowed by statute or the parties' agreement. [CRC 388(a)(9)]

⇨[5:182.1] *PRACTICE POINTER:* Although not required, it is a good idea to state the basis for your attorney fees request in the case summary (above). Attach the contract or other document with an attorney fees provision to a declaration authenticating the contract or other document.

1) [5:182.2] **Fee schedules:** Many courts have established schedules of reasonable attorney fees for use in default judgment cases where a fee award is authorized by statute or contract; *see* ¶5:140.

2) [5:182.3] **Declarations:** Declarations by plaintiff's counsel are required where the court has not adopted a fee schedule or where counsel seeks more than the scheduled fee (*see* ¶5:142). Such declarations must be competent evidence—i.e., describing the services rendered, the hours involved, the billing rate, etc.

(3) [5:183] **Additional requirements where summons served by publication:** In addition to the foregoing, where defendant was served only by publication, plaintiff must provide:

(a) [5:184] **Proof of publication:** An affidavit by the newspaper publisher showing the dates on which summons was published (*see ¶4:372*).

[5:185-186] *Reserved.*

(b) [5:187] **Notice to defendant of application for judgment:** As in all defaults, an affidavit must be filed before the hearing stating that a copy of the "Request for Entry of Default" form, and accompanying documentation (above) has been mailed to defendant's attorney of record or, if none, to defendant. [CCP §587; *see ¶5:77*]

1) [5:188] Although this is a mandatory requirement, its purpose is only to assure actual notice to defendant. Hence, if it is shown that defendant *had* actual notice that a default judgment would be taken, the failure to mail such notice will not invalidate the judgment. [*Marriage of Harris* (1977) 74 CA3d 98, 102, 141 CR 333, 336]

2) [5:189] Moreover, one case held the failure to mail "harmless error" where evidence showed defendant was *unlikely to have received* the mail. [*Candelaria v. Avitia* (1990) 219 CA3d 1436, 1444, 269 CR 32, 36—defendant's whereabouts unknown and prior mailings to defendant's last known address had been returned undelivered]

a) [5:189.1] *Comment: Candelaria*, supra, has been strongly criticized as disregarding both the requirements of due process and statutory language. [*Parish v. Peters* (1991) 1 CA4th 202, 211-214, 1 CR2d 836, 841-844]

(4) [5:190] **Additional evidentiary requirements in actions affecting land:** A higher standard of evidence is required to obtain a default judgment affecting title to or possession of land.

(a) [5:191] A "paper title" to real property (title of record) is not sufficient to support a default judgment affecting title or possession. Evidence that plaintiff has an *equitable right* to the relief sought is also required. [CCP §585(c)]

(b) [5:192]   If defendant was served by publication, proof of plaintiff's *occupancy* of the land is *not* enough to establish plaintiff's title or right to possession (unless such occupancy continued for so long a period as to establish title by adverse possession, or prescriptive rights). [CCP §585(c)]

(c) [5:193]   Nor is mere occupancy sufficient to support a default judgment for *possession* of land— *unless* coupled with proof of ouster by defendant, and the complaint is verified and alleges that no other party to the action claims title. [CCP §585(c)]

(d) [5:194]   Live testimony, instead of affidavits, may be required at the prove-up hearing of a quiet title action. [CCP §764.010, ¶*5:204*]

⟹[5:195]   ***PRACTICE POINTER:***   The rules and procedures for "proving up a default" vary widely from court to court. Therefore, before even *starting* to prepare the documentation above, it is good practice to find out in which department "prove-up" hearings are held, and *ask the court clerk* of that department for guidance as to local policies and procedures. Doing so will save a lot of time and effort!

b.   [5:196]   **Checklist:**   Before submitting papers for a default "prove-up," it is good practice to use a checklist covering the various requirements above. A checklist of the matters that may delay entry of judgment has been prepared by the Clerk of the Los Angeles Superior Court; similar checklists are in use in other courts as well.

- ***FORM:***   Reasons for Rejection of Default Prove-Up Documents, *see Form 5:I.*

c.   [5:197]   **Hearing date set by clerk:**   Upon receipt of proper documentation from plaintiff's counsel, the court clerk may set the matter for hearing before a judge (or court commissioner in counties where such officers are appointed). In some courts (e.g., San Francisco), it is up to plaintiff's counsel to telephone the Department of the Presiding Judge for a hearing date. [S.F. Unif. Rule 6.6(A)(2) (but defaults in limited civil cases are heard on declarations only; see S.F. Unif. Rule 6.6(B) *and* ¶*5:209*)]

- In many courts, the clerk simply transmits the papers to the appointed judge or commissioner for review. In direct calendar courts (cases assigned to individual judges from the outset), the assigned judge usually handles his or her own default prove-ups.

- The judge or commissioner then decides whether judgment can be rendered on the papers presented or whether a live hearing is required. Hearings are usually ordered only when intangible damages (i.e., extent of personal injury) are involved.

d. **[5:198] Special procedures if defendant in military service:** As discussed earlier, federal law prohibits entry of a default judgment against any individual defendant without an affidavit showing that said defendant is *not* in military service. [50 USC App. §521(b)]

(1) **[5:199] Court must appoint counsel:** If defendant *is* in military service, the court *must appoint an attorney* to represent the defendant's interest before a judgment can be entered against such defendant. [50 USC App. §521(b)]

(2) **[5:200] Judgments subject to set-aside:** Defendants whose *ability to defend was prejudiced* by being in military service may move to vacate any judgment—default or otherwise—obtained against them while they were in military service, provided:
— such motion is filed *within 90 days after leaving* military service; and
— a "*meritorious or legal* defense to the action or some part thereof" is shown. [50 USC App. §521(g) (emphasis added)]

(3) **[5:200.1] Statutes of limitations tolled:** Any deadline for "bringing any action *or proceeding*" by *or against* a person in military service (or by or against his or her heirs) is tolled for the length of the military service. [50 USC App. §526 (emphasis added)]

It need *not* be shown the person's military service prevented him or her from bringing the action on time: "The statutory command . . . is unambiguous, unequivocal and unlimited." [See *Conroy v. Aniskoff* (1993) 507 US 511, 514, 113 S.Ct. 1562, 1564—Army officer could redeem property from tax sale after statutory redemption period without showing military service prejudiced his ability to redeem earlier]

(a) **[5:200.2] Effect:** *Military service can be a time bomb!* A person retiring from military service at the end of 30 years can sue—and apparently *be* sued—on obligations arising at any time during that 30-year period. The statute of limitations is tolled *without regard* to whether military service prejudiced the person's ability to sue (or be sued) earlier!

➡ **[5:200.3] *PRACTICE POINTER:*** This could play havoc with any statute of limitations defense. Therefore, if your client has *ever* served in the military, order copies of his or her *service records* to make sure you know the exact length of tolling involved. Also, *ask each opposing party* by deposition or interrogatory whether he or she has had military service and obtain copies of his or her service records as well.

3. [5:201] **Prove-Up Procedure:** The court is required to render default judgment only "for such sum . . . as appears to be just." [CCP §585(b)] Therefore, it is up to plaintiff to "prove-up" the right to relief, by introducing sufficient evidence to support his or her claim. Without such evidence, the court may refuse to grant a default judgment for any amount, notwithstanding defendant's default. [*Taliaferro v. Hoogs* (1963) 219 CA2d 559, 560, 33 CR 415, 416]

It is the court's responsibility to act as a "gatekeeper," ensuring that only the appropriate claims get through and that the judgment is not inconsistent with or in excess of the complaint. [*Heidary v. Yadollahi* (2002) 99 CA4th 857, 868, 121 CR2d 695, 703]

a. [5:202] **Court may permit affidavits instead of live testimony:** The court has *discretion* to allow affidavits or declarations in lieu of personal testimony at the default "prove-up" hearing. [CCP §585(d)]

(1) [5:203] **Exceptions—live testimony required:** In a few cases, special statutes apparently require live testimony at the "prove-up" hearing:

(a) [5:204] **Quiet title actions:** The court must "examine into and determine" the validity of plaintiff's claims to title, and "hear" such evidence as may be offered regarding defendant's claims. [CCP §764.010; see *Winter v. Rice* (1986) 176 CA3d 679, 683, 222 CR 340, 342]

(b) [5:205] **Nonresident defendant served by publication:** In any case in which a nonresident defendant was served by publication, plaintiff or his or her agent must be "examined on oath" as to any payments made on the claim. [CCP §585(c)]

(c) [5:206] **Comment:** Arguably, CCP §585(d) would permit affidavits in lieu of live testimony even in such cases. But there is no authority in point.

(2) [5:207] **Affidavit requirements:** Where affidavits or declarations are used, they must state facts "with particularity" and be based on the *personal knowledge* of the affiant or declarant, and affirmatively show that such person is *competent to testify* to such facts. [CCP §585(d)]

(3) [5:208]  **No formal hearing necessary:**  Where plaintiff's whole case is supported by affidavits or declarations, no formal hearing may be necessary; and some courts dispense with the need for any appearance by counsel. Instead, the court clerk merely submits the matter to the judge or commissioner.

(4) [5:209]  **Local practices:**  Many courts *encourage* the use of affidavits in lieu of live testimony to "prove up" defaults. [See L.A. Sup.Ct. Rule 9.11(a),(b)—determination on the basis of affidavits "is the preferred procedure"; oral hearings normally scheduled only in quiet title actions or pursuant to special court order]

Others, however, generally insist upon live testimony. [See S.F. Unif. Rule 6.6(A)(3)] (On the other hand, declarations are *required*—no live testimony permitted—for default prove-ups in *limited civil cases* and in Health & Saf.C. §11488.4 *forfeiture* actions; see S.F. Unif. Rules 6.6(B), 8.13(A).)

b.   [5:210]  **Court may require live testimony:**  Live testimony is required in a few cases (*see ¶5:203-206*). In addition, even where proof by affidavit is the norm, the court always has discretion to require live testimony . . . and often does so in cases involving a large element of credibility. Typically, cases involving proof of fraud, malice, alter ego; or claims to large damages for personal injury or wrongful death.

(1) [5:211]  **Hearsay testimony may be considered:**  The court has discretion to consider hearsay testimony given by a live witness at a default "prove-up" hearing. Hearsay received without objection is competent to support a judgment (and defendant is not present to object). [*City Bank of San Diego v. Ramage* (1968) 266 CA2d 570, 584, 72 CR 273, 283]

*Compare—declarations:* But where the default prove-up is done on declarations, courts usually refuse to consider hearsay testimony; *see ¶5:207.*

c.   [5:212]  **Court may refer issues to jury or order accounting:**  The court has power to impanel a jury to determine any question of fact (e.g., the amount of damages to which plaintiff is entitled). Similarly, if a detailed accounting is required, it can appoint a referee to assist the court. [CCP §§585(b), 639]

(1) [5:213]  **Ultimate decision rests with court:**  But any such reference is *not binding* on the court because CCP §585(b) requires the *court* to render judgment. Thus, the judge or commissioner may modify or reject any determination made by the jury or referee. [*Cyrus v. Haveson* (1976) 65 CA3d 306, 318, 135 CR 246, 254]

d. [5:213.1] **Standard of proof:** Where a cause of action is stated in the complaint, plaintiff merely needs to introduce evidence establishing a prima facie case for damages. [*Johnson v. Stanhiser* (1999) 72 CA4th 357, 361, 85 CR2d 82, 84—trial court erroneously applied preponderance of evidence standard]

Thus, the defaulting defendant confesses the material allegations of the complaint.

e. [5:214] **Evidence limited to claims pleaded:** Plaintiff may not introduce evidence on claims not pleaded in the complaint. I.e., defendant may not be subjected to liability in a greater amount or on different claims than those pleaded in the complaint to which he or she has defaulted. Proof of other claims would operate as a "de facto amendment" of the complaint, opening the default and entitling defendant to another chance to plead! [*Jackson v. Bank of America* (1986) 188 CA3d 375, 387, 233 CR 162, 169, *discussed at ¶5:228-232.1, 5:256-256.2*]

[5:215-218] *Reserved.*

## E. LIMITATIONS ON DEFAULT JUDGMENTS

[5:219] The following rules serve to limit the parties against whom a default judgment may be taken and the amount of relief that may be awarded:

1. [5:220] **No Default Judgment Against Certain Defendants:** Special rules bar entry of default judgments against the following types of defendants:

   a. [5:221] **Defendants in military service:** By federal law, no default judgment may be taken against persons in military service, unless special procedural requirements are met. [50 USC App. §521(b)—Servicemembers Civil Relief Act, *see ¶5:198-200*] (For this reason, a *declaration of nonmilitary status* is required before a default judgment may be granted; *see ¶5:159-162.*)

   b. [5:222] **Involuntary plaintiffs:** If a person aligned in interest with plaintiff refuses to join in the lawsuit, he or she may be sued as a defendant therein (the reason therefor being stated in the complaint). [See CCP §382, *¶2:158*] But a default judgment *cannot* be taken against such a defendant . . . because his or her interest is really that of a *plaintiff.* [*Watkins v. Nutting* (1941) 17 C2d 490, 498-499, 110 P2d 384, 389]

   c. [5:223] **"Doe" defendants:** No default or default judgment may be entered against someone served as a "Doe" *unless* the following additional requirements are met:

      (1) [5:224] **Summons requirement:** The summons served must bear the *special notice* required by CCP

§474 ("To the person served: You are hereby served in the within action as the person sued under the fictitious name of ('Doe')"). [CCP §474; *see* ¶*4:134*]

(2) **[5:225]** **Proof of service requirement:** The proof of service must state the fictitious name under which the defendant was served and that the summons bore the requisite notice (above). [CCP §474; *see* ¶*4:369 & 6:612 ff.*]

(3) **[5:226]** **Amendment of complaint:** Plaintiff must also amend the complaint to show the defendant's true name: "(W)hen his true name is discovered, the pleading or proceeding *must be amended* accordingly." [CCP §474 (emphasis added)]

This has been interpreted to mean that no *default judgment* may be entered until the complaint is amended: "A complaint which has not been amended in conformity with CCP §474 will not support a default judgment against a party served as a fictitious defendant." [*Jonson v. Weinstein* (1967) 249 CA2d 954, 957, 58 CR 32, 34]

(a) **[5:227]** **No effect on default:** But failure to amend does not prevent entry of defendant's default: "Failure to amend in conformity with section 474 causes no failure of jurisdiction over the person served as a fictitious defendant." [*Jonson v. Weinstein*, supra, 249 CA2d at 958, 58 CR at 35]

*Cross-refer:* The procedure to amend a complaint to show a "Doe" defendant's real name is discussed at ¶*6:612 ff.*

2. **[5:228]** **Must be Based on Claims Well Pleaded:** A defendant who defaults admits only facts well pleaded in the complaint. Thus, if the complaint fails to state a cause of action, a default judgment is erroneous and will be set aside on appeal. [*Molen v. Friedman* (1998) 64 CA4th 1149, 1153-1154, 75 CR2d 651, 653-654]

a. **[5:228.1]** **Compare—no basis for collateral attack:** However, the complaint's failure to state a cause of action is not a basis for a *collateral* attack on a default judgment (e.g., separate lawsuit to set aside void judgment) as long as the complaint was sufficient to apprise defendant of the *nature of plaintiffs' demand.* [*Molen v. Friedman*, supra, 64 CA4th at 1156-1157, 75 CR2d at 655—collateral attack lies only for defects in personal jurisdiction or subject matter jurisdiction or granting relief beyond court's power (e.g., default judgment exceeding amount demanded in complaint)]

b. **[5:229]** **Effect of variance between pleadings and prove-up:** If plaintiff proves claims at the default hearing different from those pleaded in the complaint, it *may* operate as a "de facto amendment" that "opens up" the default and *entitles defendant to be served anew* with an amended pleading and to respond thereto. [*Jackson v. Bank of America* (1986) 188 CA3d 375, 387, 233 CR 162, 169; *see* ¶*6:698*]

(1) [5:230] **Application:** P sued to prevent Bank from selling bonds pledged as security for a loan. Bank defaulted. By the time of the "prove up" hearing, the bonds had been sold, so P proved damages from the allegedly wrongful sale of the bonds. This was improper because the sale occurred *after the complaint had been filed.* Use of such evidence operated as a *de facto amendment* to the complaint, "opening up" Bank's default and entitling it to plead anew. [*Jackson v. Bank of America,* supra—$2,500,000 default judgment set aside; *but see* ¶*5:256.2*]

(a) [5:231] **Comment:** *Jackson* takes an extremely critical view of the role of *pleadings* in default judgments. P had alleged damage claims, but the court held them insufficient to support the default judgment because they were "conclusory" and lacking in "causal connection" between Bank's conduct and the monetary loss (188 CA3d at 387, 233 CR at 169).

*Jackson* has also been criticized for depicting the default hearing proceedings as a "de facto amendment" of the complaint because it implies that "immaterial evidence" and "inappropriate argument" at the hearing require setting aside the default. [*Ostling v. Loring* (1994) 27 CA4th 1731, 1743-1744, 33 CR2d 391, 397-398—only actual amendment opens default; *see* ¶*5:256-256.2*]

(2) [5:232] **Compare:** D defaulted to complaint for wrongful eviction, fraud and punitive damages. Testimony at the default "prove-up" re *other* wrongful evictions *by D's partners* in the same building was *not* a "de facto amendment" of the complaint. It showed a *course of conduct* relative to the punitives claim. [*Beeman v. Burling* (1990) 216 CA3d 1586, 1595, 265 CR 719, 724]

3. [5:233] **Cannot Exceed Relief Demanded in Complaint:** Relief not demanded in the complaint cannot be granted by default judgment even though such relief otherwise would have been proper. [CCP §580—"The relief granted to the plaintiff, if there is no answer, cannot exceed that which he or she shall have demanded in his or her complaint, in the statement required by Section 425.11 (personal injury or death actions), or in the statement provided for by Section 425.115 (punitive damages actions) . . ." (parentheses added)]

*Limitation—limited civil cases:* Default judgments in limited civil cases are restricted to the types of relief formerly available in municipal court: i.e., monetary damages up to $25,000; but no permanent injunction, no determination of title to real property and only limited declaratory relief (*see ¶3:8 ff.*). [CCP §§580, 586]

a. **[5:234]** **As limit on *type* of relief:** "It is fundamental to the concept of due process that a defendant be given notice of the existence of a lawsuit and notice of the *specific relief* which is sought in the complaint served upon him." [*Marriage of Lippel* (1990) 51 C3d 1160, 1166, 276 CR 290, 292 (emphasis added)]

(1) **Application**

- **[5:235]** Where a box labeled "child support" was not checked in the official form marriage dissolution petition served on Husband, none could be awarded on default. [*Marriage of Lippel*, supra, 51 C3d at 1166, 1171, 276 CR at 292, 296]

- **[5:236]** Similarly, where the petition requested only that Husband be restrained from entering the family home, a default judgment could not award Wife title to the property. [*Burtnett v. King* (1949) 33 C2d 805, 807, 205 P2d 657, 658]

- **[5:236.1]** Where the complaint does not request attorney fees, the court cannot award fees against a defaulting defendant. It makes no difference that the fees are awardable by statute. [*Feminist Women's Health Center v. Blythe* (1995) 32 CA4th 1641, 1675, 39 CR2d 189, 208—no right to CCP §1021.5 fees against defaulting defendants]

(2) **[5:237]** **If proper *type* of relief prayed, need *amount* be demanded?** In actions for *money damages* a default judgment is limited to the amount demanded in the complaint (see below). Whether a similar rule applies in actions for *other than money damages* is presently unclear ... although the Supreme Court has noted that CCP §580 "does not distinguish between the type and amount of relief sought." [*Becker v. S.P.V. Const. Co.* (1980) 27 C3d 489, 493, 165 CR 825, 827]

(a) **[5:238]** **Marital dissolution actions:** In *Marriage of Lippel*, supra, the Supreme Court stated (dictum) that *checking or not checking boxes* on the standard form marriage dissolution petition—
❑ spousal support
❑ child support
❑ property division

"informs and *puts the respondent on notice* of what specific relief the petitioner is, or is not, seeking." [*Marriage of Lippel* (1990) 51 C3d 1160, 1169-1170, 276 CR 290, 295 (emphasis added)]

This suggests a default judgment would be upheld if the proper *type of relief* was checked even if *no specific amount* was demanded.

1) [5:238.1] In a later case, Wife checked the box indicating she was seeking division of community property. An attached declaration listed the community assets and liabilities but *no values* were assigned. A default judgment ordering Husband to pay $10,000 as an "equalizing payment" was upheld: "If he desired to be heard on the subject of the valuation and division of the listed items, he should have appeared." [*Marriage of Andresen* (1994) 28 CA4th 873, 879-880, 34 CR2d 147, 150-151]

(b) [5:239] **Other types of actions:** *Lippel*, supra, was decided in the special context of a marriage dissolution action. Read broadly, it allows a default judgment to exceed the amount demanded in the complaint *when the type of relief is specified* on a *statutorily-mandated form that does not provide* for a monetary demand in a specific amount.

It is doubtful, however, that such a procedure provides sufficient notice in other cases. Due process requires notice to the defaulting defendant both as to the type *and amount* of relief sought. [*Finney v. Gomez* (2003) 111 CA4th 527, 538, 3 CR3d 604, 610—court lacked jurisdiction to render default judgment in *partition action* for damages exceeding amount demanded in complaint]

1) [5:239.1] **Exception for accountings?** One court holds that a default judgment in an accounting action may exceed the amount requested in the complaint *where defendant possesses the information* upon which the accounting is to be based and therefore can calculate its exposure. In such a case, "the complaint need only specify the type of relief requested, and not the specific dollar amount sought." [*Cassel v. Sullivan, Roche & Johnson* (1999) 76 CA4th 1157, 1163-1164, 90 CR2d 899, 904—accounting sought in partnership dissolution where defendant partnership had control of partnership finances and records]

But another court is contra: "An extension of the reasoning in *Lippel* beyond the unique circumstances of marital dissolution actions entails a departure from the fundamental fairness section 580 was intended to protect." [*Finney v. Gomez*, supra, 111 CA4th at 541-542, 3 CR3d at 614—accounting sought in connection with partition action: "(U)nlike a marital dissolution action in which the court must value and divide the community estate of the parties equally, the ordering of an accounting under the partition statute falls under the wide range of discretion accorded a court in equity . . . (S)uch discretion at equity does not include the awarding of judgments where there has not been adequate notice, no matter how reasonable it may appear in the instant case"]

➡️**[5:239.2]** ***PRACTICE POINTER:*** Where plaintiffs do not know the exact amount owing, they can either:

— *allege an estimate* of the amount due, and receive a default judgment *limited* to that amount; or

— similar to the procedure outlined for personal injury suits (*see ¶5:82*), serve defendant with a precise statement of damages at a reasonable time *before the default* is entered. [See *Finney v. Gomez*, supra, 111 CA4th at 543-544, 3 CR3d at 615-616]

b.  **[5:240]  As limit on damages:** Similar due process considerations limit the amount of damages awardable on default: "In all default judgments, the demand sets a ceiling on recovery." [*Greenup v. Rodman* (1986) 42 C3d 822, 824, 231 CR 220, 222]

(1) **[5:241]  Determining demand:** The amount demanded in the complaint is determined both from the *prayer* and from the *damage allegations* of the complaint. [*National Diversified Services, Inc. v. Bernstein* (1985) 168 CA3d 410, 417-418, 214 CR 113, 118]

*Exceptions:* Damages allegations are prohibited in superior court *injury* and *death* actions (except in limited civil cases); and where *punitive damages* are sought. Other procedures are utilized to determine the amount demanded in such cases (*see ¶5:81 ff.*).

(2) **[5:242]  General demands insufficient:** General demands in the prayer do not provide adequate notice

of the relief sought to support a default judgment. For example:

- [5:243] If no specific damages are alleged in the complaint, a prayer *"for such other and further relief as the court deems just"* will not support a default judgment for any specific sum.

- [5:244] A prayer for *"damages in excess of $20,000"* will not support a default judgment for more than that amount. [*Becker v. S.P.V. Const. Co., Inc.* (1980) 27 C3d 489, 494-495, 165 CR 825, 828—but default judgment void only as to excess]

(3) [5:245] **Specific damage allegations may cure defective prayer:** However, specific damage allegations in the complaint may provide notice to the defendant of the amounts being sought and thus cure a defective prayer. [*National Diversified Services, Inc. v. Bernstein* (1985) 168 CA3d 410, 418, 214 CR 113, 118; *Greenup v. Rodman*, supra, 42 C3d at 829-830, 231 CR at 224-225]

(a) **Application**

- [5:246] A prayer for *"damages according to proof"* passes muster if a specific amount of damages is alleged in the body of the claim (or in a separate statement of damages served under CCP §425.11). [*Becker v. S.P.V. Const. Co., Inc.*, supra, 27 C3d at 494, 165 CR at 828]

- [5:247] P's complaint alleged D breached agreement to sell two Ferrari cars for $75,284, payable by P's "conveying a boat with a trade-in value of $22,500 and owing $52,784." P alleged his delivery of the boat and prayed for recovery of the boat plus "damages for deterioration and loss of its use amounting to in excess of $10,000."

  The maximum default judgment recoverable under these allegations was $32,500 ($22,500 as the value of the boat, plus $10,000 damages). [*National Diversified Services, Inc. v. Bernstein*, supra]

(b) [5:248] **Compare—fact allegations vs. damage allegations:** Allegations of fact that include monetary amounts are not necessarily allegations of damages. [*Heidary v. Yadollahi* (2002) 99 CA4th 857, 866, 121 CR2d 695, 701—allegation that defendant transferred sums of money from account jointly-owned with plaintiff did not show damages, absent any allegation of misappropriation]

(4) **[5:249] Effect of inconsistency between damage allegation and prayer:** Where the damage allegations in the body of the complaint *exceed* the amount demanded in the prayer, "the prayer controls." [*Barragan v. Banco BCH* (1986) 188 CA3d 283, 305, 232 CR 758, 771—various causes of action alleged compensatory damages of $1,000,000, but prayer requested only $500,000: default judgment limited to $500,000]

    (a) **[5:250] Rationale:** Defaulting parties have a constitutional right to adequate notice of the maximum judgment that may be assessed against them (¶5:240). The prayer provides such notice by setting "the ceiling" on default judgments. [*Barragan v. Banco BCH*, supra, 188 CA3d at 305, 232 CR at 771]

    (b) **[5:251] Comment:** It is unclear whether "the prayer controls" when the damages alleged in the body of the complaint are *less* than those set forth in the prayer. Arguably, damages should be limited to the lower amount to prevent confusion and protect defendant's right to adequate notice.

(5) **[5:252] Demands in limited civil cases:** Except in actions for personal injury or wrongful death (*see* ¶5:258), complaints in limited civil cases should state the amount of damages sought (CCP §425.10; *see* ¶6:273). Problems may arise where the complaint simply prays for "damages according to proof" and states "all amounts in excess of the court's jurisdiction are hereby *waived*." (A judgment in a limited civil case cannot exceed $25,000; *see* ¶3:9.)

Such waiver of relief in excess of the court's jurisdiction *does not satisfy due process*. A default judgment is *void* to the extent it exceeds the amounts alleged in the complaint. Defendant's awareness of the limited civil case jurisdictional limit ($25,000) is *immaterial*. [See *Janssen v. Luu* (1997) 57 CA4th 272, 279, 66 CR2d 838, 843 (*rejecting* contrary position taken by Los Angeles Superior Court Appellate Department in *Wisdom v. Ramirez* (1985) 177 CA3d Supp. 1, 9, 222 CR 923, 927; and *Brown v. McAdoo* (1987) 196 CA3d Supp. 20, 23, 242 CR 473, 474)]

➪**[5:253] *PRACTICE POINTER:*** Proper pleading of the amount of damages will avoid this problem. If your complaint (improperly) leaves the amount of damages open, serve a statement of damages before requesting entry of default (*see* ¶*5:89 ff.*).

c. **[5:254] Excessive default judgment "void":** A default judgment for greater relief or a different form of relief than demanded in the complaint is beyond the court's jurisdiction. [*Marriage of Lippel* (1990) 51 C3d 1160, 1167, 276 CR 290, 293]

A default judgment for an amount in excess of the prima facie evidence produced at the default hearing is likewise beyond the court's jurisdiction. [See *Johnson v. Stanhiser* (1999) 72 CA4th 357, 361-362, 85 CR2d 82, 84]

(1) **Application**

- **[5:254.1]** P's complaint sought damages "in excess of $20,000" *plus punitive* damages and costs. A default judgment for $26,000 compensatory damages and $2,500 attorney fees was vacated on appeal. It was immaterial that the award was less than the total of compensatory and punitives combined. A demand for one is not a demand for the other. [*Becker v. S.P.V. Const. Co.* (1980) 27 C3d 489, 492, 165 CR 825, 827]

- **[5:254.2]** P's complaint sought $50,000 damages for trespass "and treble said amount pursuant to statute" (Civ.C. §3346 for "wrongful injury" to trees). A default judgment for $150,000 *actual* damages, without regard to multiplication under Civ.C. §3346, was vacated on appeal. [*Ostling v. Loring* (1994) 27 CA4th 1731, 1742, 33 CR2d 391, 397]

(2) **[5:255] Procedures to challenge excessive judgment:** If the default judgment is promptly discovered, the claim that the judgment exceeds the prayer may be raised by:
— *motion to vacate* the judgment; or
— *motion for new trial* (new judgment hearing) in the trial court; or
— *appeal* from the judgment. [*Ostling v. Loring* (1994) 27 CA4th 1731, 1745, 33 CR2d 391, 398]

If the time for a new trial motion or appeal has expired, the default judgment is subject to collateral attack by a *separate lawsuit* to set aside (or vacate) the judgment. [*Marriage of Lippel* (1990) 51 C3d 1160, 1168-1169, 276 CR 290, 293-294—collateral attack allowed *16 years later*]

(a) [5:255.1]  **Compare—CCP §473(b) motion:** Damages exceeding the prayer is not by itself ground for relief under CCP §473(b). (Relief under CCP §473(b) requires a showing of "mistake, inadvertence, surprise or excusable neglect"; *see* ¶*5:276 ff.*)

(b) [5:255.2]  **Compare—sufficiency of evidence to support judgment:**  The motion to vacate can be used to challenge the judgment for exceeding the prayer, but *not* to challenge the sufficiency of the evidence introduced at the default hearing to support the judgment. [*Ostling v. Loring*, supra, 27 CA4th at 1749, 33 CR2d at 401]

Nor can the motion to vacate challenge the credibility of the evidence submitted in support of the judgment. [See *Johnson v. Stanhiser* (1999) 72 CA4th 357, 361-362, 85 CR2d 82, 84]

(c) [5:255.3]  **Compare—inadequate damage award:**  Where the amount of damages awarded after the default prove-up is less than the prima facie proof, plaintiff may appeal. [*Johnson v. Stanhiser* (1999) 72 CA4th 357, 361-362, 85 CR2d 82, 84; *see* ¶*5:272 ff.*]

(3) [5:256]  **Vacating judgment not ground for "opening" default:**  Vacating a default judgment because it exceeds the prayer does *not* affect the underlying default. It simply returns the case to the default status it had before the erroneous judgment was entered. [*Ostling v. Loring*, supra, 27 CA4th at 1743, 33 CR2d at 397]

(a) [5:256.1]  **Excessive damages as "de facto" amendment of complaint?**  One case holds that plaintiff's arguing and proving more damages than pled "constituted a *de facto* amendment of his complaint which relieved (the defendant) of its default *and entitled it to be served anew* and then to answer." [*Jackson v. Bank of America* (1986) 188 CA3d 375, 387, 233 CR 162, 169 (parentheses and emphasis added)]

- [5:256.2]  **Comment:**  This seems incorrect because plaintiff has *not* sought to amend the complaint. The excessive judgment may be error but it does not reopen the pleadings. [See *Ostling v. Loring*, supra, 27 CA4th at 1744, 33 CR2d at 398; *and* ¶*5:228-232.1*]

(b) [5:256.3]  **Should plaintiff be given option to amend complaint?**  In some cases, plaintiff may be given the *option* either to accept a reduced judgment (the amount of the prayer) or *amend* the complaint to allege the damages or relief sought. By amending, however, the default will be "opened" and defendant entitled to respond to all issues, including liability. [*Greenup v. Rodman* (1986) 42 C3d 822, 830, 231 CR 220, 225]

- **[5:256.4] Comment:** *Greenup* allowed such amendment because the default judgment was held excessive on an issue of first impression (whether the rule limiting a default judgment to the relief demanded in the complaint applies where the answer is stricken as a discovery sanction). Whether such amendment would be permitted in other cases is not clear.

(4) **[5:257] Remedying excessive judgment:** "Ordinarily when a judgment is vacated on the ground the damages awarded exceeded those pled, the appropriate action is to *modify the judgment* to the maximum amount warranted by the complaint." [*Ostling v. Loring*, supra, 27 CA4th at 1743, 33 CR2d at 397 (emphasis added); see also *Becker v. S.P.V. Const. Co.* (1980) 27 C3d 489, 493, 165 CR 825, 827]

(a) **Application**

- **[5:257.1]** P's complaint prayed for $50,000 damages for trespass, plus treble damages pursuant to Civ.C. §3346 for "wrongful injury" to another's trees. A judgment for $150,000 actual damages was excessive. But, because Civ.C. §3346 *mandates doubling* actual damages (trebling is discretionary), the appellate court ordered judgment entered for $100,000. [*Ostling v. Loring*, supra, 27 CA4th at 1750, 33 CR2d at 402]

[5:257.2-257.4] *Reserved.*

(5) **[5:257.5] Compare—effect of proving *different* cause of action than pled:** The result is different where plaintiff "wholly departs from the existing complaint" at the prove-up hearing. I.e., if plaintiff's evidence proves a *different* cause of action than pled, there is no room to modify the judgment. Rather, the judgment must be *reversed* for *failure of proof (see ¶6:9)*: "This procedure protects the defaulting defendant from the prospect of damages that are insupportable under the complaint with which he has been served." [*Ostling v. Loring*, supra, 27 CA4th at 1746-1747, 33 CR2d at 399]

d. **[5:258] Compare—personal injury and death cases:** No amount of damages may be alleged or demanded in a superior court complaint for personal injury or wrongful death. [CCP §425.10; see ¶6:279 ff.]

Since the complaint is silent as to damages, no default can be entered, and no default judgment taken, until plaintiff furnishes the defaulting defendant with notice as to the *nature* and *extent* of damages being claimed. [CCP §425.11; *Plotitsa v. Sup.Ct. (Kadri)* (1983) 140 CA3d 755, 761-762, 189 CR 769, 772-773; *Schwab v. Southern Calif. Gas Co.* (2004) 114 CA4th 1308, 1320, 8 CR2d 627, 635; *see ¶5:82, 6:283 ff.*]

This gives defendant "one last chance" to respond, knowing exactly what he or she stands to lose, satisfying the requirements of procedural due process. [*Stevenson v. Turner* (1979) 94 CA3d 315, 319-320, 156 CR 499, 502; *Twine v. Compton Supermarket* (1986) 179 CA3d 514, 517, 224 CR 562, 563—default void where entered only 3 days after service of CCP §425.11 statement]

Where such notice has been given, a default judgment may not exceed the amount stated in the CCP §425.11 notice. [CCP §§580, 585(b),(c)]

*Cross-refer:* See detailed discussion of CCP §425.11 statement of damages at ¶5:82 ff.

[5:259-260] *Reserved.*

e. **[5:261] Compare—claims for punitive damages:** Claims for punitive damages may not state the *amount* sought, either in the body of the complaint or in the prayer. [Civ.C. §3295(e); see ¶6:175 ff.]

Like personal injury and death actions, the statute specifies how notice is to be provided to defendant where a default judgment is sought. [CCP §425.115; see ¶5:104 ff.]

f. **[5:262] Compare—accounting actions:** Similar considerations are held to apply in actions for an accounting (e.g., on dissolution of partnership). Defendant is entitled to *special notice* of the *amount sought* before a default judgment for that amount is proper, unless:
— plaintiff includes an *estimate* of the amount due in the *complaint;* or
— the accounting is based on *information* in *defendant's possession.* [See *Ely v. Gray* (1990) 224 CA3d 1257, 1263, 274 CR 536, 539; *Cassel v. Sullivan, Roche & Johnson* (1999) 76 CA4th 1157, 1163-1164, 90 CR2d 899, 904; *and ¶5:108 ff.*]

4. **[5:263]** **Default Judgment Improper Where Codefendant Raises Exonerating Defense:** A default judgment may be improper against one of several codefendants if the other has raised *defenses which, if proven, would establish the nonliability of the defaulting defendant.*

   a. **[5:264]** **Defaulting defendant only liable if answering defendant liable:** If it appears that the defaulting defendant's liability is *dependent* upon the answering defendant being held liable, no default judgment is proper. [*Adams Mfg. & Eng. Co. v. Coast Centerless Grind. Co.* (1960) 184 CA2d 649, 655, 7 CR 761, 765]

      (1) **[5:265]** **Example:** P sues Employee and Employer (on respondeat superior theory) for Employee's tort. Employee answers, denying liability. No default judgment can be taken against Employer . . . because if Employee wins, Employer has no liability. [See *Adams Mfg. & Eng. Co. v. Coast Centerless Grind. Co.*, supra]

   b. **[5:266]** **Defaulting defendant jointly liable with answering defendant:** Similarly, no default judgment can be taken where several defendants are sued on a *joint* liability, and one of them answers asserting defenses which would *exonerate the defaulting defendant* from such liability. [*Mirabile v. Smith* (1953) 119 CA2d 685, 689, 260 P2d 179, 181]

      (1) **[5:267]** **Example:** P sues Partner A and Partner B on a partnership debt for which they are jointly liable.

*(Text cont'd on p. 5-59)*

**RESERVED**

Partner A answers, asserting defenses which would exonerate B as well. No default judgment can be taken against B. [*Mirabile v. Smith*, supra]

(2) [5:268] **Compare—defendants jointly and severally liable:** However, a default judgment may be rendered against one of several defendants where their liability is joint *and several* (or exclusively several). In such cases, if the answering defendant raises *defenses not involving the defaulting defendant*, there is no reason to delay entry of a default judgment. [See *Mirabile v. Smith*, supra]

(a) [5:269] **Judgment before trial discretionary:** However, whenever a several judgment is sought against codefendants, it is *discretionary* with the trial court whether to grant a default judgment against one of them before trial. The court may, if it chooses, defer such judgment until after trial of the other defendants. [CCP §579]

5. [5:270] **Default Judgment on Cross-Complaint Discretionary:** The court has *discretion* to grant a default judgment on a cross-complaint although the main action is still pending. The court must determine that a separate judgment on the cross-complaint will "not substantially delay" trial of the main action. [See CCP §585(e); *Saum v. Reppert* (1995) 35 CA4th 1766, 1768, 42 CR2d 454, 455—without mentioning CCP §585(e), court upheld default judgment on cross-complaint]

6. [5:271] **Quiet Title Actions?** It is provided by statute that, in quiet title actions, ". . . The court *shall not enter judgment by default* but shall in all cases require evidence of plaintiff's title and hear such evidence as may be offered respecting claims of any of the defendants . . ." [CCP §764.010]

Comment: However, the provision against default judgments appears to be a misnomer; i.e., it seems only to require a higher standard of evidence at the "prove-up" hearing (*see* ¶5:204).

[5:271.1-271.4] *Reserved.*

7. [5:271.5] **No Default Against "DBA" of Party Appearing in Corporate Name:** Where plaintiff sues a corporation by both its corporate name and a fictitious business name ("DBA"—doing business as), and the corporation *appears under its corporate name*, plaintiff cannot obtain a default judgment against the fictitious business name as a legally distinct entity from the corporation. [*Pinkerton's, Inc. v. Sup.Ct. (Schrieber)* (1996) 49 CA4th 1342, 1347-1349, 57 CR2d 356, 359-360]

• [5:271.6] P sued "Pinkerton's Inc., DBA Pinkerton Security and Investigation Services." D demurred under its corporate name "Pinkerton's Inc." and obtained a dismissal from the case. Nevertheless, P requested and the clerk entered a default against "Pinkerton's Inc., DBA Pinkerton Security and Investigation Services." The default was set aside as improperly entered. [*Pinkerton's, Inc. v. Sup.Ct. (Schrieber)*, supra, 49 CA4th at 1347-1349, 57 CR2d at 359-360]

## F. CHALLENGING DEFAULT JUDGMENT ON APPEAL

1. **[5:272] Either Party May Appeal:** A default judgment is reviewable on appeal the same as any other civil judgment. The fact that defendant defaulted in the trial court does not bar its right to appeal the judgment entered. [*Misic v. Segars* (1995) 37 CA4th 1149, 1153-1154, 44 CR2d 100, 102 (citing text)]

   Likewise, a plaintiff dissatisfied with the default judgment or, more typically, the amount of damages awarded, may appeal. [*Johnson v. Stanhiser* (1999) 72 CA4th 357, 361-362, 85 CR2d 82, 84]

   a. **[5:273] Time limit for appeal:** But in order to appeal, the defaulting defendant will have to find out about the judgment in time to file a notice of appeal within the applicable time limits (60 days after service of notice of entry of judgment, 60 days after mailing by the clerk of a "notice of entry of judgment," or 180 days after entry, whichever is earliest; see CRC 2).

   b. **[5:274] Effect of reversal on appeal:** If a default judgment is vacated for lack of personal jurisdiction, plaintiff will have to obtain service on the defendant before the action can proceed.

   But if the default judgment is vacated on other grounds (e.g., because damages excessive), the defaulting defendant is still "out of court." I.e., it still has no right to appear or interpose a defense. The trial court will proceed in its absence to conduct a new "prove-up" hearing and enter a new judgment. [*Devlin v. Kearny Mesa AMC/Jeep/Renault, Inc.* (1984) 155 CA3d 381, 386, 202 CR 204, 207]

   (1) **[5:274.1] Motion for new trial?** The defaulting defendant, however, may be able to move for a new trial on such issues as excessive damages. [See *Devlin v. Kearny Mesa AMC/Jeep/Renault, Inc.*, supra, 155 CA3d at 385-386, 202 CR at 207—*cannot* move for new trial (dictum); *Misic v. Segars* (1995) 37 CA4th 1149, 1154, 44 CR2d 100, 103 (citing text)—*can* move for new trial (questioning *Devlin* dictum); see ¶5:477 ff.]

2. **[5:275] Compare—Collateral Attack:** If no appeal is timely filed, a defaulting defendant may be able to collaterally attack the judgment on *jurisdictional* grounds (*see* ¶3:120, 3:404).

No collateral attack will lie, however, for failure of the complaint to state a cause of action. [*Molen v. Friedman* (1998) 64 CA4th 1149, 1156-1157, 75 CR2d 651, 655; *see ¶5:228.1*]

## G. RELIEF FROM DEFAULT

**[5:276]** **In General:** The trial court has broad discretion to vacate the judgment and/or the clerk's entry of default that preceded it. However, that discretion can be exercised only if the moving party (defendant) establishes a proper *ground* for relief, by the proper *procedure,* and within the *time limits* below.

**[5:277]** **Compare—void judgments:** The discussion below assumes there has been *valid service of summons.* If not, the judgment violates due process of law; it is void and can be set aside *at any time* (*see ¶5:484*). [*Peralta v. Heights Med. Ctr.* (1988) 485 US 80, 84-85, 108 S.Ct. 896, 899]

**[5:277.1]** **Compare—judgments after trial:** The discussion below focuses upon relief from default judgments under CCP §473(b). The same statute, however, also applies to judgments rendered after trial. (Post-trial relief may also be available under other procedures: e.g., motion for new trial, judgment notwithstanding verdict, etc.) Post-trial motions are beyond the scope of this Practice Guide.

*Cross-refer:* See discussion in Wegner, Fairbank, Epstein & Chernow, *Cal. Prac. Guide: Civ. Trials & Evidence* (TRG), Ch. 18.

1. **[5:278]** **Time Limits Depend on Ground for Relief:** Different time limits apply depending upon the ground asserted for relief from default:

   a. **[5:279]** **Within 6 months after entry of default:** Defendant may seek discretionary relief from default under CCP §473(b) on grounds of "*mistake, inadvertence, surprise or excusable neglect*" (*¶5:282 ff.*).

   The motion for discretionary relief must be filed within 6 months after the clerk's entry of default. The motion is ineffective if filed thereafter, even if it is within 6 months after entry of the default *judgment* (these are separate procedures; see below).

   Where relief is sought from a court order enforcing a procedural time limit, the six-month period starts to run from the date the court enters the order (rather than from an earlier date on which the deadline is raised in opposition papers). [*Lee v. Wells Fargo Bank, N.A.* (2001) 88 CA4th 1187, 1199-1200, 106 CR2d 726, 736]

   - **[5:279.1]** But a motion for *mandatory* relief from default based on an "*attorney affidavit of fault*" (*¶5:292 ff.*)

is timely if filed within 6 months after entry of judgment (*¶5:305 ff.*).

[5:279.2-279.4]   *Reserved.*

b.  [5:279.5]   **Within 6 months after default judgment:**   A separate 6-month period runs from entry of the default judgment, during which the court may grant relief under CCP §473(b) on the grounds stated above. (If the 6-month period after entry of default has expired, the court may set aside the judgment without disturbing the default; *see ¶5:413.*)

c.  [5:280]   **Within 2 years of default judgment:**   After expiration of the 6-month period, defendant may obtain relief by showing "lack of notice" of the proceedings (CCP §473.5, *¶5:420 ff.*). Relief must be sought within 2 years of the default judgment *or 180 days after* service of a written notice that the default judgment has been entered, whichever is earlier. [CCP §473.5(a); *see ¶5:428*]

d.  [5:280.1]   **Within 60 days after execution:**   Relief from default in certain consumer actions must be sought within 60 days after defendant first receives notice of any procedure to enforce the judgment. [CCP §585.5; *see ¶5:434.2*]

e.  [5:281]   **At any time:**   Equitable relief from a default judgment can be sought at any time on the ground of "extrinsic fraud or mistake"; *see ¶5:435 ff.*

- [5:281.1]   *Compare—marriage dissolution actions:* Other grounds are available for relief from default judgments in marital dissolution actions, including duress, mental incapacity, perjury; *see ¶5:438.*

2.  [5:282]   **Relief for "Mistake, Inadvertence, Surprise or Excusable Neglect" (CCP §473(b)):**   The court is empowered to relieve a party "upon such terms as may be just . . . from a judgment, dismissal, order or other proceeding taken against him or her through his or her mistake, inadvertence, surprise or excusable neglect." [CCP §473(b)]

The reference to "judgment . . . order or other proceedings" allows relief both from default judgments and from the entry of default that preceded it. It also includes *any step taken in a case*, whether by the court or by one of the parties: "Anything done from the commencement to the termination is a proceeding." [*Zellerino v. Brown* (1991) 235 CA3d 1097, 1105, 1 CR2d 222, 227—relief from untimely demand for exchange of expert witness lists]

a.  [5:283]   **Who may seek relief under CCP §473(b):**   Any party to the action, or his or her legal representative, may seek relief under CCP §473(b).

(1) [5:284] **Defendant or plaintiff:** Typically, of course, defendant is the moving party, seeking to have a default or default judgment set aside.

But relief under CCP §473(b) is also available to *plaintiffs*. Examples:

- From an order of *dismissal* for failure to make discovery, because such dismissal is the "practical equivalent of a default judgment." [*Aldrich v. San Fernando Valley Lumber Co.* (1985) 170 CA3d 725, 736, 216 CR 300, 306; *but see* ¶5:299.3 ff., discussing limitations on court's power to grant plaintiff relief from dismissals under §473(b)]

- From *admissions* resulting from failure to respond to discovery requests. [*Elston v. City of Turlock* (1985) 38 C3d 227, 234, 211 CR 416, 420; *see Ch. 8*]

(2) [5:285] **Legal representative:** A nonparty who is the "legal representative" of a party may move for relief from a default taken against that party. [CCP §473(b)]

The term "legal representative" has been interpreted with considerable liberality to permit one who would not normally be considered a party's "representative" but has a *sufficient interest in the action* to maintain the motion. [*Clemmer v. Hartford Ins. Co.* (1978) 22 C3d 865, 885, 151 CR 285, 296]

(a) [5:286] **Assignee:** An assignee may seek relief from a default taken against the assignor. [*Credit Managers Ass'n of So. Calif. v. National Independent Business Alliance* (1984) 162 CA3d 1166, 1172-1173, 209 CR 119, 123]

- [5:287] **Example:** Debtor made an assignment for benefit of creditors to Credit Managers. Credit Managers sued NIBA for monies owed Debtor. NIBA cross-complained against Debtor and took a default judgment (prejudicing the claim assigned to Credit Managers). Credit Managers had standing as the "legal representative" of Debtor to have the default set aside. [*Credit Managers Ass'n of So. Calif. v. National Independent Business Alliance, supra*]

(b) [5:288] **Grantee:** Where a grantee purchases property which is the subject of litigation by a third party, the grantee becomes the "legal representative" of the grantor in that litigation, and has standing to seek relief from a default judgment previously taken against the grantor. [See *Credit Managers Ass'n of So. Calif. v. National Independent Business Alliance,* supra, citing *Plummer v. Brown* (1884) 64 C 429, 1 P 703]

(c) **[5:289]** **Liability insurer:** The defendant's liability insurer has standing to move to set aside a default judgment against its insured because it would be obliged to pay the judgment. [*Clemmer v. Hartford Ins. Co.* (1978) 22 C3d 865, 885, 151 CR 285, 296; see *Eigner v. Worthington* (1997) 57 CA4th 188, 196, 66 CR2d 808, 814, fn. 5; compare *Tomassi v. Scarff* (2000) 85 CA4th 1053, 1058, 102 CR2d 750, 753—insurer that has denied coverage and refused to defend is not an "aggrieved party" within meaning of statute allowing motion to vacate judgment]

*Cross-refer:* See further discussion in Croskey, Kaufman et al., *Cal. Prac. Guide: Insurance Litigation* (TRG), Ch. 7B.

b. **[5:290]** **Showing required for relief:** Relief under CCP §473(b) may be based *either* on:

- An "attorney affidavit of fault", in which event, relief is *mandatory* (¶5:292 ff.); or

- Declarations or other evidence showing "mistake, inadvertence, surprise or excusable neglect," in which event relief is *discretionary* (¶5:310 ff.).

➡**[5:291]** *PRACTICE POINTER:* These are *alternative* procedures for relief. You do not have to file an "attorney affidavit of fault." If you feel certain the "mistake," etc. is *excusable*, you may seek discretionary relief and avoid paying the costs involved (see below). On the other hand, in close cases where relief might otherwise be denied and an attorney affidavit of fault is factually available, you will probably want to file an attorney affidavit in order to assure relief (and avoid possible malpractice claims).

It *may* be possible to seek discretionary relief first and, if that is denied, then file an attorney affidavit of fault to obtain mandatory relief. (Whether this is proper under CCP §473(b) will have to be determined by future case law.)

(1) **[5:292]** **Attorney affidavit of fault:** "(W)henever an application for relief is timely, in proper form, and accompanied by an attorney's *sworn affidavit* attesting to his or her mistake, inadvertence, surprise or neglect, (the

court shall) vacate any (1) resulting *default* entered by the clerk . . . or (2) resulting *default judgment or dismissal* entered against his or her client . . ." [CCP §473(b) (emphasis and parentheses added)]

The only limitation is that the court may deny relief if it finds the default or dismissal "was *not* in fact caused by the attorney's mistake, inadvertence, surprise or neglect" (e.g., where attorney is attempting to "cover up" for client). [CCP §473(b) (emphasis added); *see* ¶*5:301 ff.*]

⇨[5:293] ***PRACTICE POINTER FOR DEFEN-DANT:*** Since relief is *mandatory* when an "attorney affidavit of fault" is filed (see below), most of these cases should be handled *outside* of court. Before filing your motion, contact opposing counsel and attempt to resolve the matter. If this fails, you can inform the court of your good faith efforts to settle the matter, which should minimize any exposure to sanctions (*see* ¶*5:307*).

⇨[5:293.1] ***PRACTICE POINTER FOR PLAIN-TIFF:*** You should negotiate for two things before stipulating to set aside the default:

1) Adequate compensatory fees and costs (to which you are entitled; *see* ¶*5:306*).

2) A waiver of the 5-year mandatory dismissal statute for the period of time the default has been in effect. If defendant refuses to so stipulate and the matter goes to hearing, ask the court to order the 5-year period extended as a "condition" to relief from default.

(Note: CCP §473(b) does *not* lengthen the 5-year period within which to bring an action to trial. However, tolling may be possible under CCP §583.340 ("*impossible, impracticable or futile*"). See *Howard v. Thrifty Drug & Discount Stores* (1995) 10 C4th 424, 438-439, 41 CR2d 362, 371; *and* ¶*11:257 ff.*)

(a) [5:294] **Relief *mandatory*:** If the attorney is willing to take the blame—and pay the costs (below)—the court *must* set aside the default judgment (unless a "cover-up," etc. is found). The client's interests are protected and the culpable attorney avoids a potential malpractice action or disciplinary proceeding. [See *Beeman v. Burling* (1990) 216 CA3d 1586, 1604, 265 CR 719, 730-731; *Lorenz v. Commercial*

*Accept. Ins. Co.* (1995) 40 CA4th 981, 989, 47 CR2d 362, 366 (citing text)]

1) **[5:295] Neglect need not be "excusable":** Where an "attorney affidavit of fault" is filed, there is no requirement that the attorney's mistake, inadvertence, etc. be excusable. I.e., relief *must* be granted even where the default resulted from *inexcusable* neglect by the defendant's attorney! [See *Beeman v. Burling,* supra; *Graham v. Beers* (1994) 30 CA4th 1656, 1660, 36 CR2d 765, 767—same rule applies to dismissals resulting from plaintiffs' inexcusable neglect; see also *Vaccaro v. Kaiman* (1998) 63 CA4th 761, 770, 73 CR2d 829, 834-835]

The court is not concerned with the reasons for the attorney's mistake. [*Billings v. Health Plan of America* (1990) 225 CA3d 250, 256, 275 CR 80, 84 (citing text)]

- **[5:295.1]** *"Fault" of attorney's employee:* An attorney is responsible for supervising the work of legal assistants. Therefore, a paralegal employee's scheduling error that resulted in default was the "fault" of the attorney for purposes of CCP §473(b), and relief was mandatory. [*Hu v. Fang* (2002) 104 CA4th 61, 64, 127 CR2d 756, 758]

  **[5:295.2-295.4]** *Reserved.*

2) **[5:295.5] Attorney fault need not be only cause:** The lawyer's negligence need not be the exclusive or sole cause of the client's loss, so long as it was in fact a proximate cause. [*Milton v. Perceptual Develop. Corp.* (1997) 53 CA4th 861, 867, 62 CR2d 98, 101]

   a) **[5:295.5a] Client partially at fault?** One case states mandatory relief under CCP §473 is available "only if the party is *totally innocent* of any wrongdoing and the attorney was the *sole* cause of the default or dismissal." [*Lang v. Hochman* (2000) 77 CA4th 1225, 1248, 92 CR2d 322, 336 (emphasis added)]

   Other courts, however, distinguish between *negligence* and *intentional misconduct,* and hold relief mandatory where the default was caused in part by the client's negligence. [*Benedict v. Danner Press* (2001) 87 CA4th 923, 930-932, 104 CR2d 896, 901-

902—default resulted both from client's mistake regarding whether he had been personally served and counsel's negligence in failing to challenge process server's declaration of service]

b) **[5:295.6]** **Fault of co-counsel:** Defendants represented by *several* attorneys may obtain relief without affidavits of fault from each co-counsel. An affidavit by the attorney whose negligence was the *proximate cause* of the default is sufficient. [*Milton v. Perceptual Develop. Corp.*, supra, 53 CA4th at 867, 62 CR2d at 101, fn. 5]

c) **[5:295.7]** **Declaration by nonattorney insufficient:** On the other hand, a nonattorney's declaration of fault does not trigger the right to mandatory §473(b) relief. [*Stafford v. Mach* (1998) 64 CA4th 1174, 1187-1189, 75 CR2d 809, 817-818—declaration of fault by claims representative of defendant's liability insurer]

3) **[5:295.8]** **Immaterial that client also an attorney:** The mandatory relief provision applies even though the client is also an attorney. Section 473's policy that a client not suffer from the admitted errors of his or her attorney does not disappear merely because the client is a lawyer. [*Vaccaro v. Kaiman* (1998) 63 CA4th 761, 770-771, 73 CR2d 829, 834-835—only exception to mandatory provision is if error was "not in fact caused by the attorney's mistake"]

(b) **[5:296]** **Relief from both default and default judgment:** As long as the *default* resulted from attorney neglect, the attorney's "affidavit of fault" compels relief from both the default *and* any resulting default judgment. [See *Cisneros v. Vueve* (1995) 37 CA4th 906, 909, 44 CR2d 682, 684, fn. 2]

1) **[5:297]** **Includes defaults entered by court:** Although the statute refers to relief from "default entered by the clerk," these words merely describe the usual process. An attorney "affidavit of fault" also compels relief from defaults entered by court order. [*Lorenz v. Commercial Accept. Ins. Co.* (1995) 40 CA4th 981, 991, 47 CR2d 362, 367—court entered default after defendant failed to post bond ordered by court;

attorney neglected to advise client of bond requirement]

[5:298]   *Reserved.*

(c) [5:299]   **Relief from dismissals:**   The statute also requires the court to set aside a *dismissal* based on an "attorney affidavit of fault" . . . but this does *not* lengthen the 5-year period for bringing the action to trial. [CCP §473(b) (last sent.); *but see* ¶5:293.1, 11:257 ff.]

1) [5:299.1]   **Which dismissals:**   The court must vacate dismissals "resulting" from the attorney's "mistake, inadvertence, surprise or neglect." [CCP §473(b)]

a) [5:299.2]   **Dismissals *equivalent* to *default:***   Relief is mandatory only from those dismissals which are the "procedural equivalent of a default"; i.e., those which deprive *plaintiffs* of their day in court. [See *Leader v. Health Industries of America, Inc.* (2001) 89 CA4th 603, 618, 107 CR2d 489, 501]

For example, this may include dismissals based on plaintiffs':

— *failure to amend or file pleadings* within the time ordered by the court (*see* ¶5:300.25*)*; or

— *failure to oppose* a dismissal motion. [See *Bernasconi Comm'l Real Estate v. St. Joseph's Regional Healthcare System* (1997) 57 CA4th 1078, 1082, 67 CR2d 475, 477; see *J.A.T. Entertainment, Inc. v. Reed* (1998) 62 CA4th 1485, 1492-1494, 73 CR2d 365, 369-372]

[5:299.3-299.4]   *Reserved.*

b) [5:299.5]   **Relief from other dismissals not mandatory:**   CCP §473(b) was never intended to be a "catch-all remedy for every case of poor judgment on the part of counsel which results in dismissal." [*Gotschall v. Daley* (2002) 96 CA4th 479, 483-484, 116 CR2d 882, 885-886]

Thus, the mandatory provision is inapplicable to a dismissal:

    — for delay in service of summons;
    — after demurrer sustained with leave to amend;
    — based on lapse of the statute of limitations; or
    — for discovery violations. [See *Gotschall v. Daley,* supra, 96 CA4th at 483-484, 116 CR2d at 885-886 (collecting cases)]

[5:299.6-299.9] *Reserved.*

c) [5:299.10] **Comment:** The distinction is whether CCP §473(b) relief is sought based on *conduct or matters preceding* the motion or on *failure to oppose* the motion. In the latter case, relief is mandatory; in the former, it is not.

(d) [5:300] **No relief after contested judgment or order:** An attorney affidavit of fault does not warrant relief from judgments or orders based on a determination of the merits (i.e., after plaintiff has "had his or her day in court"). [*English v. IKON Business Solutions, Inc.* (2001) 94 CA4th 130, 137-138, 114 CR2d 93, 99—summary judgment not a "default," "default judgment" or "dismissal" within meaning of CCP §473(b)]

- [5:300.1] Late filing of a request for trial de novo after arbitration was not ground for setting aside the judgment based on the arbitration award. [*Brown v. Williams* (2000) 78 CA4th 182, 188-189, 92 CR2d 634, 639]

- [5:300.2] Failure to adequately oppose a motion for summary judgment was not ground for relief from the judgment. [*Garcia v. Hejmadi* (1997) 58 CA4th 674, 681, 68 CR2d 228, 232]

- [5:300.3] Failure to meet the burden of proof was not ground for relief from the judgment. [*Generale Bank Nederland, N.V. v. Eyes of the Beholder Ltd.* (1998) 61 CA4th 1384, 1397, 72 CR2d 188, 196; *Gotschall v. Daley,* supra, 96 CA4th at 484, 116 CR2d at 885—no relief from dismissal due to attorney's failure to disclose expert witness whose testimony was necessary to establish plaintiff's claim]

[5:300.4-300.9] *Reserved.*

(e) [5:300.10] **Compare—judgment or order not based on hearing on merits:** Some cases (questioned by others) have extended the application of CCP §473(b) "mandatory relief" to situations where the attorney's neglect prevented plaintiff from "having his or her day in court"—i.e., cases in which the judgment or order was *not* based on a hearing on the merits:

- **[5:300.11]** Attorney's affidavit of fault mandated relief where Party failed to appear at trial because former counsel (substituted out one week prior to the trial date) failed to advise Attorney of trial date; hence judgment was "more in the nature of a default." [*Marriage of Hock & Gordon-Hock* (2000) 80 CA4th 1438, 1446-1447, 96 CR2d 546, 552]

- **[5:300.12]** Attorney's affidavit of fault mandated relief where Party lost the opportunity to participate in judicial arbitration due to Attorney's negligence, and the award became final also due to Attorney's misfeasance. [*Yeap v. Leake* (1997) 60 CA4th 591, 601-602, 70 CR2d 680, 686-687]

- **[5:300.13]** Attorney's affidavit of fault mandated relief where court granted summary judgment *without considering* opposition due to Attorney's late filing of papers; hence it was "analogous to a default judgment." [*Avila v. Chua* (1997) 57 CA4th 860, 868, 67 CR2d 373, 377]

1) **[5:300.14] Comment:** The above cases may not be reliable authority. CCP §473(b) limits mandatory relief to a "default" or "default judgment" or "dismissal" entered against the client. A judgment entered after a trial or hearing, even if unopposed, simply does not fall in this category. [See *English v. IKON Business Solutions, Inc.*, supra, 94 CA4th at 139, 114 CR2d at 100; see also *Leader v. Health Industries of America, Inc.* (2001) 89 CA4th 603, 619, 107 CR2d 489, 502—"The mandatory relief provision does *not* allow relief from 'orders' or 'other proceedings' taken against a party or counsel"]

[5:300.15-300.19] *Reserved.*

(f) **[5:300.20] No relief from statutes authorizing dismissal for prior conduct:** Mandatory relief is available only where the attorney *failed adequately* *to oppose* a motion to dismiss, not where the dismissal results from the attorney's *conduct preceding* the motion to dismiss. Section 473(b) is "not the perfect escape hatch from the dismissal statutes." [*Graham v. Beers* (1994) 30 CA4th 1656, 1661, 36 CR2d 765, 768]

- **[5:300.21]** Where Attorney's delay in service of summons or other negligent failure to prosecute an action results in dismissal under CCP §583.410 (discretionary dismissal for delay of more than 2 years; *see* ¶*11:124*), Attorney's mea culpa affidavit does *not* compel relief from the dismissal. [*Graham v. Beers*, supra, 30 CA4th at 1661, 36 CR2d at 768]

  [5:300.22-300.24]  *Reserved.*

(g) **[5:300.25]** **No relief for late filings:** Nor does an Attorney's affidavit of fault prevent dismissal of an action based on running of the statute of limita-

*(Text cont'd on p. 5-71)*

**RESERVED**

tions or entitle a party to relief from other time limitations on filing claims. [*Life Sav. Bank v. Wilhelm* (2000) 84 CA4th 174, 178, 100 CR2d 657, 660]

- [5:300.26]  Attorney's affidavit of fault does not entitle party to relief from claim-filing requirement under the Government Tort Claims Act or excuse late filing of a claim. [*Tackett v. City of Huntington Beach* (1994) 22 CA4th 60, 64-65, 27 CR2d 133, 135-136]

- [5:300.27]  Attorney's affidavit of fault does not entitle a party to relief from the time limit on filing a costs bill after judgment. [*Douglas v. Willis* (1994) 27 CA4th 287, 291, 32 CR2d 408, 410]

- [5:300.28]  Nor does an attorney affidavit of fault prevent a discretionary dismissal based on plaintiff's failure to file an amended complaint within the time allowed by the court. [*Leader v. Health Industries of America, Inc.* (2001) 89 CA4th 603, 619, 107 CR2d 489, 502]

(h) [5:301]  **Limitation—no relief where attorney not at fault:**  The major limitation on use of an attorney "affidavit of fault" is that the court may deny relief if it finds "the *default or dismissal* was *not in fact* caused by the attorney's mistake, inadvertence, surprise or neglect." [CCP §473(b) (emphasis added)]

This provision tests both the *credibility* of the declaration and the *causation* of the default. [*Milton v. Perceptual Develop. Corp.* (1997) 53 CA4th 861, 866-867, 62 CR2d 98, 101]

1) [5:302]  **Client solely at fault:**  Thus, relief may be denied where the court determines the *client* was at fault in causing the default or dismissal. For example, the attorney's "affidavit of fault" may be ineffective where the court finds:

- [5:302.1]  Attorney is attempting to "cover up" for client. [See *Todd v. Thrifty Corp.* (1995) 34 CA4th 986, 991, 40 CR2d 727, 730—having previously attributed the delay to client's health problems, attorney could not thereafter take personal blame; see also *Rogalski v. Nabers Cadillac* (1992) 11 CA4th 816, 821, 14 CR2d 286, 289, fn. 5]

- [5:302.2]  Attorney did not represent client *at time of default.* [*Rogalski v. Nabers Cadillac,* supra, 11 CA4th at 821, 14 CR2d at 289, fn. 5; see also *Cisneros v. Vueve* (1995) 37 CA4th 906, 912, 44 CR2d 682, 686, fn. 4 (citing text)]

[5:302.3-302.9]  *Reserved.*

a)  [5:302.10]  **Compare—client and attorney both at fault:**  *See discussion at ¶5:295.5a.*

2)  [5:303]  **Attorney fault in connection with default judgment not enough:**  Where the default (i.e., the failure to respond) was *not* the attorney's fault, an attorney "affidavit of fault" relating to the subsequent default judgment does not compel relief. There is no policy favoring "neglectful clients who allow their default to be entered simply because that neglect is compounded by attorney neglect in permitting the judgment to be perfected." [*Cisneros v. Vueve* (1995) 37 CA4th 906, 911, 44 CR2d 682, 685]

- [5:303.1]  Attorney was hired to represent Defendant whose default had already been entered. Attorney forgot about the matter and did nothing for over 6 months. By the time Attorney moved to set aside the default, a default judgment had been entered. Attorney's affidavit of fault did not compel relief from the judgment (or the default). [*Cisneros v. Vueve*, supra, 37 CA4th at 908, 44 CR2d at 683]

(i)  **Procedural requirements**

1)  [5:304]  **Motion specifying mandatory ground for relief:**  The motion must state that it seeks *mandatory relief* under CCP §473. If it refers only to discretionary relief, the court need not set aside the default even if the motion is *accompanied by* an affidavit indicating the attorney was at fault. [*Luri v. Greenwald* (2003) 107 CA4th 1119, 1125, 132 CR2d 680, 685]

[5:304.1-304.4]  *Reserved.*

2)  [5:304.5]  **Declaration or affidavit:**  Ordinarily, a declaration under penalty of perjury may be used whenever an affidavit is required. [CCP §2015.5]

3)  [5:305]  **Application must be timely:**  The application for mandatory relief based on an attorney affidavit of fault must be made "*no more than six months* after entry of judgment." [CCP §473(b) (emphasis added)]

a) **[5:305.1]** **Time runs from entry of judgment:** The wording of the statute makes clear that the 6-month period runs from entry of the default judgment, not the original default. [*Sugasawara v. Newland* (1994) 27 CA4th 294, 297, 32 CR2d 484, 486]

A motion made within that period is timely although the attorney neglect *predated* the entry of default. [See *Sugasawara v. Newland,* supra, 27 CA4th at 296, 32 CR2d at 485]

b) **[5:305.2]** **No deadline if no judgment entered?** If no default judgment has been entered, there appears to be no time limit on a motion for relief based on an attorney affidavit of fault.

c) **[5:305.3]** **Diligence required?** It is not clear whether an attorney can safely wait until the last day of the 6-month period to seek relief:

- **[5:305.4]** One case states that diligence is required: "(T)he provision for mandatory relief for attorney error, did not alter the diligence requirement . . . (D)elays of three months or more routinely result in denial of relief where there is no explanation for the delay." [*Caldwell v. Methodist Hosp.* (1994) 24 CA4th 1521, 1525, 29 CR2d 894, 896 (dictum because relief not based on attorney affidavit of fault)]

- **[5:305.5]** But other cases hold the statute has *eliminated* the timeliness/ diligence requirement: "(T)he mandatory provisions . . . do not require a showing that the attorney's neglect was excusable nor a showing of diligence short of the six-month time limit." [*Metropolitan Service Corp. v. Casa de Palms, Ltd.* (1995) 31 CA4th 1481, 1488, 37 CR2d 575, 579; *Douglas v. Willis* (1994) 27 CA4th 287, 292, 32 CR2d 408, 410; *Milton v. Perceptual Develop. Corp.* (1997) 53 CA4th 861, 868, 62 CR2d 98, 102]

- **[5:305.6]** *Comment:* Former wording of CCP §473(b) required that the application for mandatory relief be "timely." Based on the elimination of "timely" from the statute, the better reasoned rule only applies the 6-month deadline.

[5:305.7-305.9]   *Reserved.*

4)  [5:305.10]  **Copy of proposed pleading attached:**   Another precondition for obtaining relief is that the application "shall be accompanied by a copy of the answer or other pleading proposed to be filed therein, otherwise the application shall not be granted." [See CCP §473(b) (second sent.); *and ¶5:385*]

(j)  **Compensation to nonmoving party**

1)  [5:306]  **Fees and costs mandatory:**   In granting relief based on an "attorney affidavit of fault," the court *must* "direct the attorney to pay reasonable compensatory legal fees and costs" to the opposing counsel or parties. [CCP §473(b)]

2)  [5:307]  **Sanctions discretionary:**   In *addition* to the award of fees and costs, the court *may* impose sanctions against the culpable attorney as follows:

- An offending attorney may be ordered to pay monetary sanctions up to $1,000 to opposing parties; or

- An offending attorney may be ordered to pay up to $1,000 to the State Bar Client Security Fund; or

- The court may "grant other relief as is appropriate." [CCP §473(c)(1)(A),(B) & (C)]

3)  [5:308]  **Relief not conditioned on payment:** Relief granted on the basis of an attorney affidavit of fault *may not be made conditional* on the attorney's payment of any fees, costs or sanctions ordered by the court. [CCP §473(c) (2)]

a)  [5:309]  **Applicable to dismissals?**   By its terms, the statute precludes conditional relief from "a default or default judgment"

*(Text cont'd on p. 5-75)*

but there is no mention of dismissals. (Comment: However, this appears to be a legislative "glitch"; there is no apparent reason not to bar conditional relief from dismissals as well.)

**FORM:** Attorney Affidavit of Fault, *see Form 5:K.*

(2) **[5:310]** ***Without* attorney affidavit of fault:** Unless the application is accompanied by an "attorney affidavit of fault" (¶*5:292 ff.*), relief is *discretionary* and must be based on a showing of "mistake, inadvertence, surprise or excusable neglect." [CCP §473(b); see *Lorenz v. Commercial Accept. Ins. Co.* (1995) 40 CA4th 981, 989, 47 CR2d 362, 365-366 (citing text)]

---

Attorney affidavits of fault are normally used whenever appropriate because relief is *mandatory* and the costs are predictable. Discretionary relief under §473(b) is usually sought only where:

— the default was entered before defendant retained counsel; or

— the defendant was solely at fault (¶*5:302*) (or has been "defrauded" or "surprised"; *see* ¶*5:322 ff.*); or

— the attorney is unwilling to accept the blame and *pay* for it!

---

⇨ **[5:310.1]** ***PRACTICE POINTER:*** Consider seeking relief *in the alternative*. For example:

— "for relief on the grounds of the attached affidavit of fault (mandatory grounds) or, if for any reason the court finds that the requirements for mandatory relief have not been met, then on grounds of mistake, inadvertence, surprise, or excusable neglect (discretionary grounds)."

(a) **[5:311]** **"Mistake":** Relief may be granted on a showing of mistake by a party or attorney. Such mistake may be one of fact or law, but in either case, it must be *material*.

1) **[5:312]** **Mistake of fact:** Relief under §473(b) is proper where defendant (or a lawyer unwilling to sign an "attorney affidavit of fault"; *see* ¶*5:292 ff.*) was mistaken as to some fact material to the defendant's duty to respond, by reason of which defendant failed to make a timely response. E.g., defendant's lawyer mistakenly thought only one of two defendants he was employed to defend had been served. [See

*Lieberman v. Aetna Ins. Co.* (1967) 249 CA2d 515, 523-524, 57 CR 453, 458]

2) [5:313] **Mistake of law:** Absent an "attorney affidavit of fault" (*see ¶5:292 ff.*), an attorney's mistake of law is charged to the client, and mere ignorance of the law or negligence in conducting legal research is *not* excusable neglect. [*Anderson v. Sherman* (1981) 125 CA3d 228, 237-238, 178 CR 38, 43]

But where the legal problem posed "*is complex and debatable,*" an honest mistake of law is a valid ground for relief, even absent the "attorney affidavit of fault." [*State Farm Fire & Cas. Co. v. Pietak* (2001) 90 CA4th 600, 611, 109 CR2d 256, 263; *McCormick v. Board of Supervisors* (1988) 198 CA3d 352, 360, 243 CR 617, 621]

[5:314] *Reserved.*

a) [5:315] **Test for excusable "mistake":** The controlling factors in determining whether an attorney's mistake was reasonable are:

- the *reasonableness* of the misconception; and

- the justifiability of the failure to determine the correct law. [*Anderson v. Sherman,* supra; *McCormick v. Board of Supervisors* (1988) 198 CA3d 352, 360, 243 CR 617, 621]

b) [5:316] **Application:** Thus, without an "attorney affidavit of fault" (*¶5:292 ff.*), it is difficult to obtain relief from the court for a "mistake of law." After all, it is a lawyer's duty to look up the law if he or she does not know it. Judicial disfavor for this ground is reflected as follows:

- [5:317] Defense lawyer's erroneous belief that summons had to be served in a particular manner did not justify relief from default. It was "a simple and obvious point of law . . . and elementary legal research would have cleared it up." [*Anderson v. Sherman,* supra]

- [5:318] But defense counsel's mistake as to whether certain unique statutory requirements re publication of summons applied to a taxpayer's action to test the validity of a city's constructing a stadium, has been held ground for relief. The issue was one of first impression, and "complex and debatable." [*City of Ontario v. Sup.Ct. (Duck)* (1970) 2 C3d 335, 345-346, 85 CR 149, 156-157]

- **[5:319]** Counsel erroneously believed he could verify answers to RFAs for out-of-county defendants (and that a codefendant with power of attorney could verify for others). *Because the law on the subject was then unsettled*, counsel's erroneous belief was an "honest mistake of law" that *mandated reversal* of summary judgment based on admissions resulting from the defective verifications. [*Brochtrup v. Intep* (1987) 190 CA3d 323, 332, 235 CR 390, 395]

  **[5:320]** *Reserved.*

- **[5:321]** An attorney's mistaken assumption that a CCP §998 offer to compromise (*see ¶12:590 ff.*) included attorney fees is *not* the type of reasonable mistake that a court can remedy under CCP §473(b). [*Pazderka v. Caballeros Dimas Alang, Inc.* (1998) 62 CA4th 658, 671-672, 73 CR2d 242, 248-249; see also *Premium Comm'l Services Corp. v. National Bank of Calif.* (1999) 72 CA4th 1493, 1496, 86 CR2d 65, 67]

3) **[5:322] Fraud:** Fraud is not specifically mentioned as a ground for discretionary relief under CCP §473(b). However, such relief can certainly be granted where fraud is shown . . . on the theory that the fraud caused a *mistake* by the party seeking relief. [*Rice v. Rice* (1949) 93 CA2d 646, 651, 209 P2d 662, 665]

   a) **[5:323] Intrinsic or extrinsic:** Where the motion is made under §473(b), relief may be granted whether the fraud is "intrinsic or extrinsic." [*Rice v. Rice*, supra] (Compare: Only *extrinsic* fraud is ground for equitable relief from a judgment; ¶5:438.)

b) [5:324] **Fraud on court:** If the fraud has deceived the *court*, rather than the defendant (e.g., perjured testimony by plaintiff at prove-up hearing), the court has *inherent power* to set aside the default judgment. Since the relief is not based on CCP §473(b), the 6-month limitation of that section does not apply. Even so, the same time limitation is recognized as a "judicially established rule of procedure." [*Don v. Cruz* (1982) 131 CA3d 695, 702, 182 CR 581, 586, fn. 2]

(b) [5:325] **"Surprise":** This term refers to "some condition or situation in which a party . . . is unexpectedly placed to his injury, *without* any default or *negligence* of his own, which ordinary prudence could not have guarded against." [*Credit Managers Ass'n of So. Calif. v. National Independent Business Alliance* (1984) 162 CA3d 1166, 1173, 209 CR 119, 123]

1) [5:326] **Example:** Credit Managers sued as assignee for benefit of creditors on Debtor's claim against NIBA. NIBA cross-complained against Debtor, and obtained a default judgment (which prejudiced the assigned claim Credit Managers was suing on). Credit Managers had not been told of NIBA's service of process on Debtor, or of Debtor's default, or of the default judgment. It was entitled to have Debtor's default set aside on the ground of surprise, so that it could be substituted in place of Debtor and defend the cross-complaint. [*Credit Managers Ass'n of So. Calif. v. National Independent Business Alliance*, supra]

(c) [5:327] **"Excusable neglect":** This is by far the most common ground for obtaining *discretionary* relief from default. The issue boils down to whether the moving party has shown a *reasonable excuse* for the default. [*Davis v. Thayer* (1980) 113 CA3d 892, 905, 170 CR 328, 334]

[5:328] *Compare—attorney affidavit of fault:* Where an attorney "affidavit of fault" is filed (¶5:292 *ff.*), relief is mandatory, even if the attorney's neglect was *inexcusable!*

1) [5:329] **Reasonable diligence as test:** In the absence of an "attorney affidavit of fault," the burden is on the moving party to show that the neglect was *excusable:* i.e., that the default

could not have been avoided through the exercise of ordinary care. [*Jackson v. Bank of America* (1983) 141 CA3d 55, 58, 190 CR 78, 80—"the acts which brought about the default must have been the acts of a reasonably prudent person under the same circumstances"]

The following cases illustrate application of this reasonable diligence approach:

a) **Neglect by party**

- [5:330]   Evidence that the defendant was seriously *ill*, or *feeble*, or *unable to*

*(Text cont'd on p. 5-79)*

**RESERVED**

*understand* that he was being served with process, is sufficient to justify discretionary relief under §473(b). Such evidence shows "excusable neglect" in allowing default to occur. [See *Kesselman v. Kesselman* (1963) 212 CA2d 196, 207-208, 27 CR 769, 776-777]

- [5:331]   Similarly, evidence that the defendant *mislaid or misfiled* the papers, and as a result failed to contact a lawyer in time, *may* show "excusable" neglect. [*Bernards v. Grey* (1950) 97 CA2d 679, 683-686, 218 P2d 597, 599-601]

- [5:332]   But it is *not* enough simply to show that the client was "busy" and "forgot" about the lawsuit; i.e., such neglect is *inexcusable*. [*Andrews v. Jacoby* (1919) 39 CA 382, 383-384, 178 P 969, 970]

[5:333]   *Reserved.*

- [5:334]   Likewise, it is *not* ground for relief that defendant failed to answer the complaint because he was *indigent* and couldn't afford a lawyer; or that he was preoccupied with *criminal proceedings* pending against him. Defendant could have obtained help from legal aid offices, or appeared in forma pauperis. And, defending a criminal case does not prevent a person from defending a civil suit as well. [*Davis v. Thayer* (1980) 113 CA3d 892, 905-906, 170 CR 328, 335]

[5:335-336]   *Reserved.*

b) [5:337]   **Neglect by third person:**   Entrusting the matter to a friend, or relative who promises to "take care of the matter," is *not by itself* ground for relief under §473(b). [*Davis v. Thayer* (1980) 113 CA3d 892, 909-910, 170 CR 328, 337-338—elderly defendant was ill and also preoccupied with caring for her dying husband; turned papers over to her son who promised "to take care of the problem," but never did; this was *insufficient as a matter of law* to give trial court discretion to set aside default under §473]

c) [5:338] **Neglect by defendant's insurer?** Courts disagree on whether a defendant's reliance on its liability insurer's promise to defend the action establishes ground for relief under CCP §473(b):

- [5:339] One view is that a liability insurer's failure to defend its insured is "analogous to positive misconduct" by an attorney hired to defend the case, entitling the defendant to relief from default. [*Rogalski v. Nabers Cadillac* (1992) 11 CA4th 816, 821, 14 CR2d 286, 289]

- [5:340] Other courts hold the liability insurer's inexcusable neglect is chargeable to its insured and therefore deny relief. Otherwise, the insurer could recklessly ignore filing deadlines. [*Don v. Cruz* (1982) 131 CA3d 695, 701, 182 CR 581, 585; *Scognamillo v. Herrick* (2003) 106 CA4th 1139, 1149, 131 CR2d 393, 400]

2) [5:341] **Inexcusable attorney neglect—no "attorney affidavit of fault" filed:** In the absence of an "attorney affidavit of fault" (¶5:292 ff.), attorney neglect is imputed to the client. If the neglect is "excusable," the party is excused. If "inexcusable," the client may have a malpractice action against the attorney, but there is no ground for relief under CCP §473(b). [See *Elston v. City of Turlock* (1985) 38 C3d 227, 236, 211 CR 416, 421, fn. 6]

(**Compare:** Acts by an attorney that are so grossly irresponsible they constitute "*positive misconduct,*" are not imputed to the client, so that discretionary relief may be available under CCP §473(b); *see* ¶5:355.)

a) [5:341.1] **Test:** The court inquires whether a *reasonably prudent* attorney might have made the same error under similar circumstances. [*Generale Bank Nederland, N.V. v. Eyes of the Beholder Ltd.* (1998) 61 CA4th 1384, 1399, 72 CR2d 188, 198]

b) **[5:341.2]** **Incompetent representation:** Counsel's failure to discharge *routine professional duties* is not excusable: "Conduct falling below the professional standard of care, such as *failure to timely object* or to properly advance an argument, is not therefore excusable." [*Generale Bank Nederland, N.V. v. Eyes of the Beholder Ltd.*, supra, 61 CA4th at 1400, 72 CR2d at 198 (emphasis added)]

"There is nothing in section 473 to suggest it was intended to be a catch-all remedy for every case of poor judgment on the part of counsel which results in dismissal." [*State Farm Fire & Cas. Co. v. Pietak* (2001) 90 CA4th 600, 611-612, 109 CR2d 256, 264]

c) **[5:342]** **"Press of business" alone no excuse:** The mere fact that a lawyer was busy and therefore allowed a default to be taken against D is *not enough by itself* to justify *discretionary* relief under CCP §473(b). [*Martin v. Taylor* (1968) 267 CA2d 112, 117-118, 72 CR 847, 850-851]

(But coupled with other extenuating circumstances, "press of business" may be a factor showing the neglect was excusable; see ¶5:347 ff.)

d) **Other inexcusable neglect**

- **[5:343]** Relief from default was properly denied where counsel failed to produce requested documents after having received four extensions of time and despite two court orders compelling production. Counsel also failed to appear at two court hearings, the last of which resulted in dismissal of the action. [*Elston v. City of Turlock* (1985) 38 C3d 227, 236, 211 CR 416, 421-422]

- **[5:344]** Nor is relief justified on the ground that defense counsel erroneously believed the case was moot, and that no answer was necessary (resulting in case being placed in "inactive" file). [*Jackson v. Bank of America* (1983) 141 CA3d 55, 58, 190 CR 78, 80]

- [5:345] Nor is *delay in the mails* by itself "good cause" for relief; it is counsel's duty to seek an extension of time. [See *Mannino v. Sup.Ct. (Southern Calif. Edison Co.)* (1983) 142 CA3d 776, 778, 191 CR 163, 164]

- [5:346] D's Liability Insurer failed to employ counsel to appear for D because it erroneously believed he had not been properly served. Relief from default was denied because Liability Insurer *undertook no investigation* regarding the propriety of service, relying entirely on D's statements, despite knowing that D was not particularly credible and had difficulty with the English language. (Also, the motion for relief was unreasonably delayed.) [*Stafford v. Mach* (1998) 64 CA4th 1174, 1186-1187, 75 CR2d 809, 816-817]

3) [5:347] **Excusable attorney neglect—no "attorney affidavit of fault" filed:** Even if an attorney is unwilling to file an "attorney affidavit of fault" (*see ¶5:292 ff.*), relief may still be justified where the attorney's neglect was *excusable*: e.g., where his or her "press of business," coupled with *additional, extenuating circumstances,* made the default unavoidable.

⇨ [5:348] *PRACTICE POINTER:* These are generally cases in which counsel was *unaware* of the duty to appear or respond on behalf of the client . . . *unlike* the "press of business" cases where the attorney was so busy he or she simply forgot! [See *Elston v. City of Turlock* (1985) 38 C3d 227, 234, 211 CR 416, 420]

Again, in the absence of an "attorney affidavit of fault" (¶5:292 ff.), relief is only *discretionary:* i.e., the battle will be won or lost on the strength of your declarations. So make sure you include *detailed, competent evidence* of the reasons you or defendant's former counsel were *unaware*

*(Text cont'd on p. 5-83)*

*or unable* to respond. *See "Practice Pointer" at ¶5:390.1.*

a) [5:349] **Examples:** The following are examples of cases in which attorney neglect has been held "excusable":

[5:350] *Reserved.*

- [5:351] Despite reasonable supervision, attorney's *secretary misfiled the papers* or *failed to enter the appearance date* in the office calendar: "Where an attorney states that he was unaware of his duty to appear or answer because his employees misplaced papers or misinformed him as to a relevant date, *relief is routinely granted.*" [See *Elston v. City of Turlock,* supra, 38 C3d at 234, 211 CR at 420]

- [5:352] Attorney was ill or absent from the office, and answer was due within a short period of time. [See *Robinson v. Varela* (1977) 67 CA3d 611, 616, 136 CR 783, 785—unlawful detainer complaint required answer during Christmas week]

[3:353] *Reserved.*

- [5:354] There was excusable neglect for failing to timely file an amended complaint where, among other factors, counsel's law firm disbanded shortly before filing deadline; counsel received appellate court opinion requiring her to prepare petition for hearing to Supreme Court; issues in case were complex; and counsel's mobility was impaired due to injury. [*Contreras v. Blue Cross of California* (1988) 199 CA3d 945, 951, 245 CR 258, 262]

4) [5:355] **"Positive misconduct" by attorney:** If the attorney's neglect amounts to "positive misconduct" toward the client, and the client is relatively free from negligence, then, even in the absence of an "attorney affidavit of fault" (¶5:292 ff.), the client may be entitled to relief under §473(b). The theory is that the "positive misconduct" *terminates* the attorney-client relationship, so that the attorney's neglect is *not*

imputed to the client. [*Daley v. County of Butte* (1964) 227 CA2d 380, 391, 38 CR 693, 700]

But "positive misconduct" is narrowly construed. It will be found only where there is a *total failure* on the part of counsel to represent the client, amounting to a "de facto severance of the attorney-client relationship." [*Carroll v. Abbott Laboratories* (1982) 32 C3d 892, 898, 187 CR 592, 595]

a) [5:355.1] **Court must weigh competing policies:** Even where the lawyer's conduct amounts to abandonment, the court must consider other equitable factors. [*Seacall Develop., Ltd. v. Santa Monica Rent Control Bd.* (1999) 73 CA4th 201, 205, 86 CR2d 229, 231]

Factors to be considered include:

- client's own conduct;

- prejudice to defendant;

- whether the dismissal was mandatory or discretionary;

- policy favoring a trial on the merits;

- policy favoring finality of judgments;

- policy disfavoring unreasonable delays in litigation;

- policy that innocent clients should not have to suffer from their attorneys' gross negligence; and

- policy that grossly incompetent attorneys should not be relieved from the consequences of their incompetence. [*Seacall Develop., Ltd. v. Santa Monica Rent Control Bd.,* supra, 73 CA4th at 205, 86 CR2d at 231]

*Cross-refer:* "Positive misconduct" is discussed further in connection with the court's inherent equitable power to set aside a judgment at ¶5:454 ff. and discretionary dismissals at ¶11:154.2.

b) **Application**

- [5:356] Positive misconduct was found where P's counsel failed to serve process, appear at pretrial conferences, and communicate with P, the court and other attorneys. Moreover, P's counsel held the substitution of attorneys for several months "while his client's cause ripened for disaster." P was entitled to relief under CCP §473 because legal representation existed only in a "nominal and technical sense." [*Daley v. County of Butte*, supra, 227 CA2d at 391-392, 38 CR at 700]

[5:357-358]   *Reserved.*

- [5:359]   But relief was held improper where P's complaint was dismissed for failure to produce certain documents in response to discovery requests. Although P's counsel had grossly mishandled the matter, he *had not abandoned the client* (the attorney had taken depositions, etc., and sought and obtained relief from the dismissal). Hence, there was *no* "positive misconduct," and granting relief under CCP §473 was reversible error. [*Carroll v. Abbott Laboratories*, supra]

c)  [5:360]   **Compare—court's inherent equity power as ground for relief:** Where discretionary relief for an attorney's positive misconduct would be untimely under CCP §473(b) (*see* ¶5:364 ff.), relief may still be possible based on the court's inherent equity power (*see* ¶5:435 ff., 5:454 ff.).

A client has the right to rely on the attorney's performance, and therefore is not barred from relief for failing to check on the status of the case . . . even over a protracted period of time! "A client should not be required to act as a 'hawklike inquisitor' of his own counsel." [*Aldrich v. San Fernando Valley Lumber Co.* (1985) 170 CA3d 725, 740, 216 CR 300, 308—P did not discover until 3 years later that his case had been dismissed due to attorney's "positive misconduct"]

d)  [5:361]   **CCP §286 as alternative ground for relief:**   When an attorney dies, or is removed or suspended, or otherwise "ceases to act as such," the *adverse party* must serve written notice on the party for whom the attorney had been acting, to appoint another attorney or appear in person. Until such notice is given, *no further proceedings* can be had against the now-unrepresented party. [CCP §286]

Failure to give such notice is an alternative ground for relief in cases where "positive misconduct" by the attorney is shown. [*Aldrich v. San Fernando Valley Lumber Co.,* supra, 170 CA3d at 741, 216 CR at 309]

5) **[5:362] Compare—lack of prejudice to opposing party as affecting excuse:** Lack of prejudice to the opposing party is not specifically required for discretionary relief under CCP §473(b). But it may lighten the moving party's burden: If granting the relief will not prejudice the opposing party (other than losing the advantage of the default), "the original negligence in allowing the default to be taken *will be excused on a weak showing.*" [*Aldrich v. San Fernando Valley Lumber Co.* (1985) 170 CA3d 725, 740, 216 CR 300, 308 (emphasis added); see ¶5:402]

**[5:363] *PRACTICE POINTER:*** The burden of showing prejudice is on the opposing party (*see* ¶5:380). But, in light of the above, it is a good idea for the moving party to show no prejudice to the opposing party if relief granted; e.g., declarations showing case not ready for trial, unserved parties, incomplete discovery, no trial date, etc. *See "Practice Pointer" at* ¶5:390.1.

c. **[5:364] Time within which relief must be sought:** The application for discretionary relief under CCP §473(b) must be made " . . . within a *reasonable time* . . . " and " . . . *in no case exceeding six months* . . . " after entry of the default except as stated below. [CCP §473(b)]

*Compare—relief based on attorney affidavit of fault:* The rule is different for mandatory relief based on an attorney affidavit of fault. Application for such relief must be made "no more than six months *after entry of judgment.*" [CCP §473(b); see *Sugasawara v. Newland* (1994) 27 CA4th 294, 297, 32 CR2d 484, 486, ¶5:305.1]

There are thus two time limits to consider:

(1) [5:365] **Jurisdictional limit—6 months:** The outside time limit for seeking relief under §473(b) is 6 months. This limit is jurisdictional in the sense that the court has no power to grant relief after this time . . . regardless of whether an "attorney affidavit of fault" (¶5:292 ff.) is filed or how reasonable the excuse for the delay. [CCP §473(b); *Davis v. Thayer* (1980) 113 CA3d 892, 901, 170 CR 328, 332—as used in §473(b), "six months" means *182 days*]

(a) [5:366] **Runs from entry of default (not judgment):** The 6-month limit for discretionary relief under §473(b) runs from the date the clerk entered the original default . . . and *not* the date on which default judgment is entered. Thus, any delay between entry of the default and obtaining the default judgment will not extend the defendant's time to seek relief under §473(b). [*Rutan v. Summit Sports, Inc.* (1985) 173 CA3d 965, 970, 219 CR 381, 383]

   1) [5:367] **Rationale:** Otherwise, setting aside the judgment could be an idle act; i.e., the default would still be in effect and would permit immediate entry of another default judgment. [*Rutan v. Summit Sports, Inc.*, supra, 173 CA3d at 970, 219 CR at 383]

   2) [5:368] **Compare—relief may be granted from judgment only:** Nonetheless, the default and default judgment are separate procedures, and relief may be granted from the judgment only—leaving the default in effect. [*Rutan v. Summit Sports, Inc.*, supra]

   3) [5:368.1] **Compare—relief based on attorney affidavit of fault:** The time limit for mandatory relief based on an attorney affidavit of fault does not begin to run until "*entry of judgment*" (CCP §473(b); see ¶5:305).

(b) [5:369] **Filing of motion within 6 months sufficient:** It is sufficient if defendant *applies* for relief from default within the 6-month period; i.e., by serving and filing notice of motion for relief (*see* ¶5:383). The hearing and ruling on the motion may take place after expiration of the 6-month period. [See *Northridge Fin. Corp. v. Hamblin* (1975) 48 CA3d 819, 826, 122 CR 109, 113]

(c) [5:370] **Compare—relief from procedural time limits:** CCP §473(b) empowers courts to relieve parties from consequences of failure to meet procedural time limits (e.g., time to file amended pleadings): "The 'default' sought to be excused is a failure to take, within time, one of the requisite steps in the prosecution of the proceeding." [*Estate of Simmons* (1914) 168 C 390, 395-396, 143 P 697, 699]

The 6-month period for relief in such cases does not commence *until the opposing party takes some action* based on the missed time limit (e.g., motion to dismiss) or a court order is made as a result thereof. [*Save Our Forest & Ranchlands v. County of San Diego* (1996) 50 CA4th 1757, 1770, 58 CR2d 708, 714-715]

- [5:370.1] P filed a motion for attorney fees after recovering judgment. The motion was untimely under applicable court rules. The 6-month period for relief under §473(b) did not commence *until D raised the time limit* in opposition to the fee motion (i.e., it did not run from when the time limit was missed). [*Save Our Forest & Ranchlands v. County of San Diego,* supra, 50 CA4th at 1770, 58 CR2d at 714-715]

  [5:371-372]  *Reserved.*

(d) [5:373]  **Time may be shortened in property actions:**  To reduce uncertainty regarding ownership of property, a special procedure is authorized where a default judgment affects title to or possession of real or personal property:
  — Plaintiff may serve notice on defendant and defendant's attorney that a default judgment has been entered and that defendant's time to seek relief pursuant to CCP §473(b) will expire 90 days after service of the notice.
  — If such notice is served, defendant's application for relief must be made within 90 days thereafter. [CCP §473(b)]

(2) [5:374]  **Discretionary limit—"reasonable time":** Defendant's motion for relief under §473(b) must also be made within a "reasonable time" after discovery of the default: i.e., defendant must act diligently in seeking relief. This is, in effect, a separate, *discretionary* time limitation on granting relief.

"In order to qualify for relief under section 473, the moving party *must act diligently* in seeking relief . . ." [*Elston v. City of Turlock* (1985) 38 C3d 227, 234, 211 CR 416, 420]

(a) **[5:375] Compare—relief based on attorney affidavit of fault:** It is unclear whether an attorney can safely wait until the last day of the 6-month period after entry of the default judgment to seek relief. *See ¶5:305.3 ff.*

(b) **[5:376] Effect of delay:** If there is any substantial delay between discovery of the default and defendant's filing a motion for relief under §473(b), defendant must show a *reasonable excuse* for the delay. Otherwise, regardless of the "mistake" or "neglect" causing entry of the default originally, defendant's application for relief will be denied. [*Ludka v. Memory Magnetics, Int'l* (1972) 25 CA3d 316, 321, 101 CR 615, 618]

(c) **Application**

- **[5:377]** An *unexplained 3-month delay* between defendant's discovery of default and the filing of his motion under §473 shows *lack* of diligence, which by itself justifies denial of the motion. [*Ludka v. Memory Magnetics, Int'l,* supra; see also *Kendall v. Barker* (1988) 197 CA3d 619, 625, 243 CR 42, 45]

- **[5:378]** But a motion for relief filed *45 days* after discovery of the default was held timely, where there was a satisfactory showing of *diligence* during this period (defendant's lawyer couldn't reach defendant who was travelling abroad; notified plaintiff's lawyer that a motion for relief from default would be made; and finally did so on his own when still unable to reach defendant). [*Romer, O'Connor & Co. v. Huffman* (1959) 171 CA2d 342, 349, 341 P2d 62, 66-67]

- **[5:379]** In determining whether relief was sought within a "reasonable" time, the court may properly take into consideration *defendant's lack of funds to obtain counsel.* However, granting or denial of relief is still discretionary: i.e., defendant's lack of money to employ counsel does *not,* as a matter of law, require setting aside of the default. [*Carrasco v. Craft* (1985) 164 CA3d 796, 805-806, 210 CR 599, 605-606—delay of 5 months held inexcusable where D had conferred with counsel shortly after service and was aware of the significance of default being entered, but lacked money to employ counsel until months later]

(d) [5:380] **Prejudice from delay?** Prejudice is one of the factors the trial court may properly consider in determining whether the moving party acted diligently.

The *burden of proof* is on the opposing party to show such prejudice (e.g., by declarations setting forth substantial evidence of missing witnesses, evidence destroyed, etc.). [*Aldrich v. San Fernando Valley Lumber Co.* (1985) 170 CA3d 725, 740, 216 CR 300, 309]

(3) [5:381] **Compare—equitable relief from judgment:** The 6-month limit does not apply where relief is sought on equitable grounds; e.g., extrinsic fraud or mistake, judgment void, etc. (*see* ¶5:484 ff.). Moreover, a court *may* treat a motion under CCP §473(b) as a motion for equitable relief. [*Rappleyea v. Campbell* (1994) 8 C4th 975, 981, 35 CR2d 669, 672]

d. [5:382] **Procedure:** The regular noticed motion procedure is used to apply for relief under CCP §473(b).

(1) [5:383] **Notice of motion:** The moving party's notice of motion should state the usual calendaring information (time, date, place, etc.), the *relief* sought (setting aside default and default judgment), and one or more of the statutory *grounds* for relief ("mistake, inadvertence, surprise or excusable neglect").

⇨[5:384] *PRACTICE POINTER:* If a default judgment has been entered against your client, be sure that your motion seeks relief *both* from the default judgment *and the clerk's entry of default.* Otherwise, even if your motion is granted, the clerk's default would still be on the record . . . so that the opposing party could obtain another judgment! [See *Howard Greer Custom Originals v. Capritti* (1950) 35 C2d 886, 888-889, 221 P2d 937, 938] (But an order "vacating judgment by default" *may* be *interpreted* as applying to the clerk's entry of default as well, provided the motion is timely (¶5:364) and relief from default had not previously been denied; see *Airline Trans. Carriers v. Batchelor* (1951) 102 CA2d 241, 245-246, 227 P2d 480, 482-483.)

Also, wherever possible, move for relief on both discretionary and mandatory grounds, *in the alternative (see* ¶5:310-310.1). For example:
— "for relief on the grounds of the attached affidavit of fault (mandatory grounds) or, if for any

reason the court finds that the requirements for mandatory relief have not been met, then on grounds of mistake, inadvertence, surprise, or excusable neglect (discretionary grounds)."

[5:384.1-384.4]  *Reserved.*

(a) [5:384.5]  **Hearing judge:**  Where relief is sought from a judgment, sound judicial policy requires that the motion be heard by the same judge who rendered the challenged judgment. [*Walker v. San Francisco Housing Auth.* (2002) 100 CA4th 685, 693, 122 CR2d 758, 764]

(2) [5:385]  **Proposed pleading required:**  The statute specifies that the application for relief "shall be *accompanied* by a copy of the answer or other pleading proposed to be filed . . . otherwise, the application shall not be granted." [CCP §473(b)]

(a) [5:386]  **"Substantial compliance":**  The term "accompanied" is interpreted liberally. Relief from default may be granted even where the proposed answer is served and filed *separately* from the notice of motion (but before the motion hearing). This may be deemed "substantial compliance" with the CCP §473(b) requirements. [See *Puryear v. Stanley* (1985) 172 CA3d 291, 294, 218 CR 196, 197-198]

1) [5:387]  **Effect of filing proposed answer after expiration of 6-month period:**  CCP §473(b) requires that the motion be "accompanied" by the proposed answer or other responsive pleading (*see* ¶5:385). Cases are split on whether relief can be granted where the proposed answer is not filed until after expiration of the 6-month period:

• [5:387.1]  One court denied relief on the ground that untimely filing of the proposed answer is "*not* substantial compliance" with CCP §473(b). [*Puryear v. Stanley* (1985) 172 CA3d 291, 294-295, 218 CR 196, 198]

• [5:387.2]  But other courts uphold relief on the rationale that §473(b) should be construed "liberally with a view to substantial compliance." The only purpose of the proposed answer is to require defendant to show good faith and a readiness to respond if the motion is granted. [*Job v. Farrington*

(1989) 209 CA3d 338, 340-341, 257 CR 210, 211 (internal quotes omitted); *County of Stanislaus v. Johnson* (1996) 43 CA4th 832, 836-838, 51 CR2d 73, 76-77]

(3) **[5:388]** **Other supporting papers:** The notice of motion for relief under §473(b) should also be accompanied by (1) an "attorney affidavit of fault" (see below), in which case relief is *mandatory*; or (2) declarations establishing the "mistake" or "excusable neglect," in which case relief is *discretionary*; and relevant points and authorities.

(a) **[5:389]** **Attorney affidavit of fault—relief mandatory:** See detailed discussion at ¶5:292 ff.

(b) **[5:390]** **Without attorney affidavit of fault—relief discretionary:** Where the moving party is responsible for the default, or where his or her attorney is unwilling to file an "attorney affidavit of fault," declarations must be filed establishing that the "mistake," "neglect," etc. was *excusable.*

⇨**[5:390.1]** *PRACTICE POINTER:* Be meticulous in drafting an "attorney affidavit of fault" or declarations in support of a motion under §473(b). First of all, make sure they are made on the basis of *personal knowledge* by one who is *competent to testify* to the facts involved.

Next, include *detailed factual explanations* as to how the claimed "mistake" or "neglect" occurred. Avoid generalizations or conclusions. Be very specific as to exactly what happened.

Where discretionary relief is sought, it is sometimes wise to give judges something "to hang their hat on." Make a point, therefore, of showing that there will be *no prejudice* to the opposing party from setting aside the default. Or, if there have been some costs or expenses (e.g., attorney fees) incurred, *offer to compensate* your opponent as a condition of setting aside the default.

[5:391] *Reserved.*

(4) **[5:392]** **Proposed order:** The party prevailing on a motion must prepare and serve a proposed order within 5 days after the court's ruling unless the parties waive

notice or the court orders otherwise. [CRC 391; *see Ch. 9(I)*]

➡️[5:392.1] ***PRACTICE POINTER:*** Including the proposed order in the moving papers speeds up the process and allows earlier entry of the order granting relief. This may not be feasible, however, with complicated motions or in which complex rulings are anticipated.

*(Text cont'd on p. 5-93)*

**RESERVED**

Also, some judges prefer to prepare a minute order specifying the ground for ruling. It is always a good idea to check with the court clerk in advance on the judge's policy in this regard. You may be able to save yourself the time and trouble of preparing a formal order.

(5) [5:393] **Checklist:** It is good practice to use a checklist of the various requirements for relief under CCP §473(b) *before* filing the motion.

- *FORM:* Checklist for Relief From Default ("Mistake, Inadvertence, Surprise or Neglect"), *see Form 5:J.*

e. [5:394] **Burden of proof:** The moving party bears the burden of proving that he or she is entitled to relief under CCP §473(b). If an "attorney affidavit of fault" is filed, this burden is met since relief is *mandatory (see ¶5:292 ff.).* However, absent such affidavit, the moving party's evidence must *preponderate* as to the claimed "mistake, surprise, inadvertence or excusable neglect." Also, the moving party must show due diligence in seeking *discretionary* relief after discovering the default. [*Luz v. Lopes* (1960) 55 C2d 54, 62, 10 CR 161, 165-166; *see also ¶5:374 ff.*]

It is unclear whether the moving party must show due diligence when seeking *mandatory* relief based on an attorney affidavit of fault. *See ¶5:305.3 ff.*

(1) [5:395] **Competent evidence:** Evidence is usually presented in the form of declarations by the moving party and/or his or her counsel. These declarations must contain competent evidence—i.e., facts stated on the basis of personal knowledge rather than hearsay. Opinions and statements made on the basis of "information and belief" do not satisfy the moving party's burden. [*Kendall v. Barker* (1988) 197 CA3d 619, 624, 243 CR 42, 44]

*Cross-refer:* Declarations as evidence are discussed further at *¶9:46 ff.*

- [5:396] D's new attorney moved for relief from default entered after D's former attorney ignored warnings from P's counsel. The only supporting evidence was a declaration from D's new attorney stating D's former attorney had "excusably neglected" to answer the complaint. This conclusory and hearsay statement was not competent evidence and could not support an order granting relief. [*Kendall v. Barker,* supra, 197 CA3d at 624, 243 CR at 44]

[5:397-398]   *Reserved.*

f.   **Ruling on motion**

(1) [5:399]   **Where "attorney affidavit of fault" filed:**   If an "attorney affidavit of fault" accompanies a timely, proper application for relief, and the court finds the alleged attorney fault to be true, the court *must* grant the motion (CCP §473(b); *see detailed discussion at ¶5:292 ff.*).

(2) [5:400]   **Where no "attorney affidavit of fault" filed:**   In the absence of such affidavit, granting or denial of the motion rests within the sound discretion of the trial court.

(a) [5:401]   **Policy favoring relief:**   However, doubtful cases are usually resolved in favor of *granting* relief: "Because the law strongly favors trial and disposition on the merits, any doubts in applying section 473 *must* be resolved in favor of the party seeking relief from default." [*Elston v. City of Turlock* (1985) 38 C3d 227, 233, 211 CR 416, 419 (emphasis added)]

1) [5:402]   **"Weak showing" may suffice:**   Where the party in default moves promptly to seek relief, and *no prejudice* to the opposing party will result from setting aside the default and letting the case go to trial on the merits, *"very slight evidence* will be required to justify a court in setting aside the default." [*Elston v. City of Turlock* (1985) 38 C3d 227, 233, 211 CR 416, 419; *Miller v. City of Hermosa Beach* (1993) 13 CA4th 1118, 1136, 17 CR2d 408, 419]

(b) [5:403]   **Relief from default vs. relief from default judgment:**   The default and default judgment are separate procedures. The latter may be set aside without disturbing the former. [*Rutan v. Summit Sports, Inc.* (1985) 173 CA3d 965, 970, 219 CR 381, 384—relief sought more than 6 months after default entered but within 6 months after judgment; *Jonson v. Weinstein* (1967) 249 CA2d 954, 958, 58 CR 32, 35—default judgment void for award of excess relief did not affect validity of default]

(3) [5:404]   **Imposition of conditions:**   Relief is authorized "upon any terms as may be just" (CCP §473(b)).

Thus, the court has authority, under appropriate circumstances, to condition relief from default as follows:

(a) **Fees and cost awards**

1) [5:405] **Where "attorney affidavit of fault" filed:** Payment of the other side's attorney fees and costs is *mandatory* where relief from default is based on an "attorney affidavit of fault": "The court shall direct the attorney to pay reasonable compensatory legal fees and costs to opposing counsel or parties." [CCP §473(b)]

But relief shall *not* be made conditional on the attorney paying such fees and costs. [CCP §473(c)(2); *see* ¶5:308]

2) [5:406] **Where no "attorney affidavit of fault" filed:** If relief from default is based on evidence other than an "attorney affidavit of fault," the court *may in its discretion* order the defendant to pay the *costs*, including *attorney fees*, incurred by the plaintiff in obtaining the default judgment. [*Rogalski v. Nabers Cadillac* (1992) 11 CA4th 816, 823, 14 CR2d 286, 290]

(b) [5:407] **Nonmonetary conditions:** Nonmonetary conditions may be imposed where appropriate (e.g., inspection of books or a restraint on transfer of defendant's property). [See *Reeves v. Hutson* (1956) 144 CA2d 445, 453, 301 P2d 264, 270]

(c) [5:408] **Security for judgment as condition:** Where appropriate, the court may condition default relief on the moving party's providing security (e.g., cash deposit or surety bond) for any judgment that may ultimately be returned against that party. Imposition of such a condition is not *per se* unreasonable or unjust. [*Goodson v. Bogerts, Inc.* (1967) 252 CA2d 32, 42, 60 CR 146, 152-153]

1) [5:409] **Limitations:** However, the amount must be "reasonably proportionate" to the *other party's prejudice or expense* resulting from the default. And, in cases where no surety bond is available or the cost is excessive, consideration must be given to whether the bond requirement would effectively put defendant out of court. [*Kirkwood v. Sup.Ct. (Chaussee)* (1967) 253 CA2d 198, 201-202, 61 CR 316, 318—requirement that D post $50,000 bond as condition of relief held *abuse of discretion* where only prejudice to P was slight delay and legal fees in connection with the default]

2) **[5:410] Comment:** A "protective deposit" is more likely to be upheld where the facts warrant *unconditional denial* of relief. In such cases, the reasonableness of the conditions imposed on granting relief is less important. [*Goodson v. Bogerts, Inc.*, supra]

(d) **[5:411] Sanctions:** Whenever the court grants relief from default judgment under §473, it may:

- impose a maximum penalty of $1,000 on the offending attorney or defaulting party;

- direct an offending attorney to pay a maximum of $1,000 to the State Bar Client Security Fund; or

- grant "any other relief as is appropriate." [CCP §473(c)(1)(A),(B) & (C)]

1) **[5:412] Statement of reasons required where sanctions imposed:** Due process requires the court to provide a written statement of its reasons for imposition of monetary sanctions against a party or counsel. This rule applies where, as a condition of granting relief from default, the court orders the moving party to pay the attorney fees incurred by the party who had obtained the default. [*Hearst v. Ferrante* (1987) 189 CA3d 201, 204, 234 CR 385, 387; *see ¶9:1108 ff.*]

2) **[5:412.1] No relief until sanctions paid:** Where the court conditions relief on the defaulting party's payment of sanctions, the default or default judgment remains in effect until the sanctions are *paid.* [*Howard v. Thrifty Drug & Discount Stores* (1995) 10 C4th 424, 439, 41 CR2d 362, 371, fn. 5]

(4) **[5:413] Relief from judgment but not default:** The default and default judgment are separate procedures (¶5:4, 5:10). The latter may be set aside without disturbing the former. [*Jonson v. Weinstein* (1967) 249 CA2d 954, 958, 58 CR 32, 35]

- **[5:414]** Such relief is appropriate where defendant has failed to prove "excusable neglect" or other ground for relief from default, but the default judgment as entered is erroneous (e.g., in excess of amount demanded in the complaint). [*Jonson v. Weinstein*, supra; and see *Rutan v. Summit Sports, Inc.* (1985) 173 CA3d 965, 970-971, 219 CR 381, 383-384—improper notice re sale of collateral rendered deficiency judgment improper but provided no ground for vacating earlier default]

g. **Appellate review**

(1) [5:415] **Orders granting relief:** Appellate courts are inclined to *affirm* orders granting relief from default because the law favors trial on the merits, whenever possible. Thus, even where relief is not mandatory—i.e., where no "attorney affidavit of fault" is filed (*see ¶5:292 ff.*)—minimal evidence of excuse is enough to support the order on appeal: "When a party in default moves promptly to seek relief, *very slight evidence* is required to justify a trial court's order setting aside a default." [*Shamblin v. Brattain* (1988) 44 C3d 474, 478, 243 CR 902, 905; *Misic v. Segars* (1995) 37 CA4th 1149, 1154, 44 CR2d 100, 102-103 (citing text); *Uriarte v. United States Pipe & Foundry Co.* (1996) 51 CA4th 780, 789-790, 59 CR2d 332, 338]

(2) [5:416] **Orders denying relief:** On the other hand, orders *denying* relief under CCP §473 are more carefully scrutinized. [*Elston v. City of Turlock* (1985) 38 C3d 227, 234, 211 CR 416, 420]

(Technically, the appeal lies from the default *judgment* rather than from the order denying relief; see *Velicescu v. Pauna* (1991) 231 CA3d 1521, 1522-1523, 282 CR 832, 833.)

(a) [5:417] **Where "attorney affidavit of fault" filed:** It is *reversible error* to deny relief from default where an application is timely, in proper form, *and accompanied by an "attorney affidavit of fault"* (unless the attorney was *not* in fact to blame; *see ¶5:292 ff.*).

(b) [5:418] **Where no "attorney affidavit of fault" filed:** Even in the absence of an "attorney affidavit of fault"—i.e., where relief is discretionary—the trial court's decision will not be overturned absent a clear abuse of discretion. [*Elston v. City of Turlock, supra*]

In such cases, the general rule of deference to the trial court's discretion may be outweighed by the strong policy of the law favoring trial on the merits (*¶5:401*). Appellate courts are inclined to reverse if *some* reasonable excuse was shown (even if disputed) and no *prejudice* to the opposing party will result from setting aside the default.

Even so, the denial of relief may be upheld where there is *clear* evidence of *inexcusable* neglect. [See

*Elston v. City of Turlock, supra,* 38 C3d at 236, 211 CR at 421; and *Border v. Kuznetz* (1980) 103 CA3d Supp. 14, 18, 162 CR 881, 884]

(c) **[5:419]** **Default judgments for punitive damages disfavored:** Default judgments awarding punitive damages are looked upon with particular disfavor. Such judgments may be reversed on appeal even though the trial court is *not* shown to have abused its discretion in denying relief from default. [*Nicholson v. Rose* (1980) 106 CA3d 457, 462-463, 165 CR 156, 160]

3. **[5:420]** **Relief Under CCP §473.5 for "Lack of Actual Notice":** Where service of summons has not resulted in actual notice to a party in time to defend the action, the court is empowered to grant relief from a default or default judgment. [CCP §473.5]

This section is designed to provide relief where there has been *proper* service of summons but defendant nevertheless did not find out about the action in time to defend. Typically, these are cases in which *service was made by publication.* [See *Randall v. Randall* (1928) 203 C 462, 464-465, 264 P 751, 752]

a. **[5:421]** **Ground for relief:** A defendant is entitled to relief under CCP §473.5 if he or she has not received *actual* notice of the proceedings. Imputed or constructive notice is *not* "actual" notice (see Civ.C. §18). [*Rosenthal v. Garner* (1983) 142 CA3d 891, 895, 191 CR 300, 302]

(1) **Application**

- **[5:421.1]** When P was unable to locate D, he sent copies of the summons and complaint to the attorney who had represented D in a *previous lawsuit* (out of which the present litigation arose), and then proceeded to publish summons. D's former attorney never told her of the action. Held: D was entitled to relief under CCP §473.5 since she had no actual notice; constructive or imputed notice is *not* sufficient. [*Rosenthal v. Garner, supra*]

**[5:421.2]** *Reserved.*

- **[5:421.3]** P sued D for breach of contract, fraud and specific performance. Summons served by publication did not result in actual notice to D. However, D learned about the lawsuit *from another source* (a recorded lis pendens). D was still entitled to relief under CCP §473.5. She did not have "actual knowledge" of the various matters which service of summons would impart (nature of claims, amount in controversy, time to respond, etc.). [*Olvera v. Olvera* (1991) 232 CA3d 32, 41, 283 CR 271, 277]

(2) [5:422] **Compare—invalid service of summons:** If the summons was not properly served, the judgment would be *void*, and can be set aside at *any* time; *see* ¶*5:485.*

(3) [5:423] **Compare—*in rem* proceedings (service of summons not required):** Defendant's failure to receive actual notice of the proceedings is *not* ground for §473.5 relief in *in rem* proceedings (probate or other proceedings to determine interests in property). Service of summons is not required in such proceedings; due process is satisfied by constructive notice (*see* ¶*4:86*).

Nor is lack of notice in such proceedings ground for relief under CCP §473. [*Estate of Leonis* (1902) 138 C 194, 200, 71 P 171, 174—probate proceedings; *Parage v. Couedel* (1997) 60 CA4th 1037, 1042-1043, 70 CR2d 671, 675—escheat proceedings]

[5:424-425] *Reserved.*

b. [5:426] **Defendant not responsible for lack of notice:** A defendant seeking relief under CCP §473.5 must show that his or her lack of actual notice in time to defend was not caused by inexcusable neglect or avoidance of service. [*Tunis v. Barrow* (1986) 184 CA3d 1069, 1077-1078, 229 CR 389, 394]

(1) [5:427] **Attorney's neglect imputed to client:** Ordinarily, an attorney's neglect is imputed to the client and may not be offered by the client as the basis for relief under §473.5. [*Buckert v. Briggs* (1971) 15 CA3d 296, 301, 93 CR 61, 64]

However, if the attorney's neglect is so extreme as to amount to abandonment or "*positive misconduct*" (*see* ¶*5:355*), the client is not charged with knowledge of facts known to the attorney. [*Tunis v. Barrow,* supra— Lawyer continually reassured D that P's claim had been taken care of and concealed fact that P had filed suit]

c. [5:428] **Time limit on application for relief:** Relief under CCP §473.5 must be sought " . . . within a reasonable time . . ." (discretionary time limit; *see* ¶*5:374-379*); and ". . . in no event later than *2 years after entry of default judgment* or *180 days after service of written notice* that such default or default judgment has been entered," whichever comes first. [CCP §473.5]

(1) **[5:429] Compare—time limit for relief under CCP §473(b):** Under CCP §473(b), the 6-month limit is measured from entry of the clerk's default. Here, the 2-year period is measured from entry of the *judgment*. Thus, delay in obtaining judgment after clerk's default serves to extend the period within which relief may be sought (unless notice of default is served on the defendant).

d. **[5:430] Procedure:** The procedure on a motion for relief under CCP §473.5 is substantially the same as a motion for *discretionary* relief under CCP §473(b) (*see ¶5:382 ff.*). [CCP §473.5(b)]

(1) **[5:431] Declarations must establish lack of notice:** The notice of motion must be accompanied by an affidavit or declaration showing (a) defendant's lack of notice of the action in time to defend; and (b) that such lack "was not caused by his or her avoidance of service or *inexcusable* neglect." [CCP §473.5(b)]

(2) **[5:432] Proposed pleading:** Defendant must also file with the notice of motion a copy of the answer, motion or other pleading proposed to be filed in the action. [CCP §473.5(b)]

e. **[5:433] Ruling on motion:** If the court finds that the motion was timely made and that defendant's lack of notice was *not* due to his or her avoiding service or inexcusable neglect, it may set aside the default judgment and permit trial on the merits. [CCP §473.5(c)]

(1) **[5:434] Conditions may be imposed:** The court is empowered to grant such relief "on such terms as may be just" . . . i.e., it may impose costs, attorney fees, or other conditions to remedy any unfairness to the plaintiff in setting aside the default judgment. [CCP §473.5(c)]

However, it is an abuse of discretion to impose such conditions where it was *more plaintiff's fault* than defendant's that service did not provide actual notice, and nothing more is at issue than plaintiff's legal expenses in opposing relief. [See *Kodiak Films, Inc. v. Jensen* (1991) 230 CA3d 1260, 1264-1265, 281 CR 728, 731]

4. **[5:434.1] Relief From Default in Consumer Actions Filed in Improper Court:** The request for entry of default form (*Form 5:A*) includes a venue declaration stating the action is not subject to certain consumer obligation statutes with special venue

requirements (CCP §395(b); Civ.C. §§1812.10, 2984.4; *see* ¶*3:507 ff.*). [See CCP §585.5]

Defaults and default judgments obtained in violation of these special venue statutes may be set aside as provided below:

a. [5:434.2] **Time within which relief sought:** A motion to set aside the default or default judgment must be served and filed *within 60 days* after defendant first receives notice of *any procedure to enforce* the judgment (e.g., levy of writ of execution). [CCP §585.5(b)]

b. [5:434.3] **Procedure:** Normal rules for filing and serving motions apply. An affidavit is required, showing the action was not commenced in the proper court under the special venue statutes above. A copy of the proposed answer or other responsive pleading must be included.

c. [5:434.4] **Relief:** If the court finds the motion is timely and the special venue statutes above were violated, it *must* set aside the default judgment "on such terms as may be just" and allow defendant to defend in the proper court. [CCP §585.5(d)]

(The action must thereafter be transferred to the proper court. CCP §397(a); *see* ¶*3:550.*)

(1) [5:434.5] **Fee awards:** Unless plaintiff can show it used reasonable diligence to avoid filing in an improper court, the court "shall" award defendant "actual damages and costs including reasonable attorney's fees." [CCP §585.5(e)] (Presumably, this means damages and costs in moving to set aside any levy under execution, as well as to set aside the default.)

5. [5:435] **Equitable Relief From Judgment:** Apart from any statutory authority, a court has inherent, equitable power to set aside a judgment on the ground of "*extrinsic* fraud or mistake." [*Olivera v. Grace* (1942) 19 C2d 570, 576, 122 P2d 564, 568]

There are three essential requirements to obtain relief. The party in default must show:
— a *meritorious* defense;
— a *satisfactory excuse* for not presenting a defense to the original action; and
— *diligence* in seeking to set aside the default once it was discovered. [*Rappleyea v. Campbell* (1994) 8 C4th 975, 982, 35 CR2d 669, 672-673—leaving open, however, whether the same test applies where a default but *no judgment* has been entered]

a. [5:436] **Diligence in seeking relief:** The statutory time limits on relief under CCP §473(b) or §473.5, supra, do *not* apply. The court may be asked to grant equitable relief from a default judgment *whenever* the "extrinsic fraud or mistake" is discovered. But once discovered, a party is expected to proceed *diligently* to seek relief (below). This requirement is "inextricably intertwined with prejudice" to the plaintiff. [*Rappleyea v. Campbell*, supra, 8 C4th at 983-984, 35 CR2d at 674]

(1) [5:436.1] **Public policy as limitation:** Beyond the 6-month period in which relief can be obtained under CCP §473(b), "there is a strong public policy in favor of the finality of judgments and only in *exceptional cases* should relief be granted." [*Rappleyea v. Campbell*, supra, 8 C4th at 982, 35 CR2d at 672 (emphasis added; internal quotes omitted)]

(2) [5:437] **Laches as defense:** Since the equitable power of the court is being invoked, the relief sought is subject to equitable defenses, including *laches.* Thus, relief may be denied if it is shown that the moving party has been guilty of *unreasonable delay* in seeking relief, causing *prejudice* to the opposing party. [*McCreadie v. Arques* (1967) 248 CA2d 39, 46-47, 56 CR 188, 194—plaintiff would be prejudiced by having to prove matters 5 years old if judgment set aside]

"The greater the prejudice to the responding party, the more likely it is that the court will determine that equitable defenses such as laches or estoppel apply to the request to vacate a valid judgment." [*Rappleyea v. Campbell*, supra, 8 C4th at 983, 35 CR2d at 674]

(a) [5:437.1] **Compare—where relief sought before judgment entered:** Prejudice to the plaintiff is less of a problem where defendant seeks equitable relief before a judgment has been entered, and correspondingly lowers the burden on defendants of showing diligence. [*Rappleyea v. Campbell*, supra, 8 C4th at 984, 35 CR2d at 674]

b. [5:438] **Grounds for relief:** Relief is generally available only for "extrinsic fraud or mistake." But these terms are given a broad interpretation and cover almost any circumstance by which a party has been *deprived of a fair hearing.* There need be no actual "fraud" or "mistake" in the strict sense. [*Marriage of Park* (1980) 27 C3d 337, 342, 165 CR 792, 796]

*Exception—marital dissolution judgments:* Much broader grounds for relief are available from judgments in marital dissolution actions (including duress, mental incapacity and perjury in declarations or evidence) . . . but subject to statutory time limits. [See Fam.C. §2120 et seq.; and detailed discussion in Hogoboom & King, *Cal. Prac. Guide: Family Law* (TRG), Ch. 16]

(1) [5:439] **"Extrinsic" vs. "intrinsic":** Equitable relief is available only where the fraud or mistake was "extrinsic"—meaning the party was denied the opportunity to be heard. If the fraud or mistake goes to the merits of the action, or occurred at trial, it is deemed "intrinsic" and *not* ground for relief. (Examples of "intrinsic" fraud: forgery, bribery, perjury.) The theory is that "intrinsic" fraud or mistake can be guarded against through diligence during the proceedings. [*Marriage of Stevenot* (1984) 154 CA3d 1051, 1069, 202 CR 116, 129]

  (a) [5:440] **Representation by counsel significant:** The usual case in which "extrinsic" fraud is found is where a party was *not* represented by counsel. If the defendant had a lawyer and the opportunity to litigate, any fraud or mistake will usually be classified as "intrinsic" (hence, not ground for equitable relief). [*Marriage of Stevenot,* supra]

  The result is otherwise where the attorney has *totally* failed to represent the client. Such "positive misconduct" may be ground for equitable relief from the judgment. [*People v. One Parcel of Land* (1991) 235 CA3d 579, 584, 286 CR 739, 742; *see* ¶5:454]

(2) **Application**

  (a) [5:441] **"Extrinsic fraud":** Extrinsic fraud is a broad concept that "tends to encompass *almost any set of extrinsic circumstances which deprive a party of a fair adversary hearing.*" [*Estate of Sanders v. Sutton* (1985) 40 C3d 607, 614, 221 CR 432, 436]

  Extrinsic fraud has been found:

  - "(W)here the unsuccessful party has been prevented from exhibiting fully his case by fraud or deception practiced on him by his opponent, as by keeping him away from court by a false promise of a compromise; or

  - "(W)here the defendant never had knowledge of the suit, being kept in ignorance by the acts of the plaintiff; or

  - "(W)here an attorney fraudulently or without authority assumes to represent a party and connives at his defeat; or

  - "(W)here the attorney regularly employed corruptly sells out his client's interest to the other side . . ." [*Estate of Sanders v. Sutton*, supra, 40 C3d at 614, 221 CR at 436, quoting *United*

*States v. Throckmorton* (1878) 98 US 61, 65-66]

1) [5:442] **Relief likely where violation of confidential relationship shown:** The breach of a fiduciary duty, arising out of a confidential relationship between the parties, may warrant setting aside the judgment even though the same conduct in a nonfiduciary relationship would not be considered extrinsic fraud. [*Estate of Sanders v. Sutton*, supra, 40 C3d at 615, 221 CR at 436]

   a) [5:443] **"Confidential relationship":** A "confidential relationship" may exist although there is no fiduciary relationship between the parties. It is enough that one person has gained the trust or confidence of the other, as is typically the case among *family members* and *friends*. [*Estate of Sanders v. Sutton*, supra, 40 C3d at 615, 221 CR at 436-437]

2) [5:444] **Fraud inducing default:** Equitable relief is appropriate where a party has been *induced* not to appear or contest the action by misrepresentations of fact or false promises to dismiss or to compromise the claim. [*Aheroni v. Maxwell* (1988) 205 CA3d 284, 292, 252 CR 369, 373—defaulting party must have *relied* on opponent's false assurances before relief can be granted based on extrinsic fraud]

   These cases often involve prior dissolution proceedings between the parties:

   [5:445] *Reserved.*

   • [5:446] Husband (in pro per), an unsophisticated person of limited education, relied on misstatements by Wife's Attorney in defaulting. (Attorney told Husband he did not need a lawyer; that hiring a lawyer would just cost him more money; and that if Husband didn't sign property settlement, he would have to go to court which would also end up costing him more.) [*Marriage of Adkins* (1982) 137 CA3d 68, 76-77, 186 CR 818, 822-823]

   • [5:447] *Compare:* But where there was no deception, Wife is not entitled to relief based on claims that Husband was "intimidating and overbearing" and had told her there was no use going to a lawyer since they charge more than the value of the property Husband was offering her in settlement. [*Marriage of Stevenot*, supra, 154 CA3d at 1069, 202 CR at 129]

3) [5:448] **Fraud preventing continuance:** Similarly, Husband's *concealment* from the court of the fact that Wife had been deported, constituted "extrinsic" fraud . . . since such facts would have justified a postponement or continuance of the hearing. [*Marriage of Park,* supra, 27 C3d at 342, 165 CR at 796—Wife's attorney was new to the case and did not know reason for her absence]

4) [5:448.1] **Compare—intrinsic fraud:** "Fraud is intrinsic and not a valid ground for setting aside a judgment when the party has . . . had an opportunity to present his case and to protect himself from any mistake or fraud of his adversary, but has unreasonably neglected to do so." [*Marriage of Melton* (1994) 28 CA4th 931, 937-938, 33 CR2d 761, 765]

[5:448.2] *Reserved.*

- [5:448.3] Deliberate concealment of material evidence during discovery or at trial is held to be intrinsic fraud. [See *Los Angeles Airways, Inc. v. Hughes Tool Co.* (1979) 95 CA3d 1, 8, 156 CR 805, 809; *Kachig v. Boothe* (1971) 22 CA3d 626, 634, 99 CR 393, 398]

(b) [5:449] **"Extrinsic mistake":** This term is broadly applied to cover situations in which circumstances extrinsic to the litigation have cost a party a hearing on the merits. [*Rappleyea v. Campbell* (1994) 8 C4th 975, 981, 35 CR2d 669, 672]

These are usually cases of *excusable neglect* by defendant or defendant's attorney in failing to appear and present a defense: "If such neglect results in an unjust judgment without a fair adversary hearing the basis for equitable relief is present and is often called 'extrinsic mistake.'" [*Kulchar v. Kulchar* (1969) 1 C3d 467, 471, 82 CR 489, 491]

The following cases are illustrative:

1) [5:450] **Relying on another to defend:** Extrinsic mistake may be found where one

party *reasonably relies* on another to defend the action, but the other fails to do so through unforeseen circumstances constituting *excusable neglect.* [*Weitz v. Yankosky* (1966) 63 C2d 849, 855-856, 48 CR 620, 624-625]

- **[5:451] Example:** Defendant sent papers served on him to his insurance carrier, but the papers were *lost in the mail,* so that no answer was ever filed on defendant's behalf. [*Weitz v. Yankosky,* supra]

2) **[5:452] Disability:** Extrinsic mistake may be found where the party seeking relief was *mentally incompetent* when judgment was entered, and no guardian was appointed; or where the party's *attorney was incapacitated* and unable to act. [See *Kulchar v. Kulchar* (1969) 1 C3d 467, 471-472, 82 CR 489, 491]

- **[5:453] Imprisonment:** A party's imprisonment at the time of the hearing is treated as a disability justifying relief from an adverse judgment on the ground of "extrinsic mistake." [*Humes v. Margil Ventures, Inc.* (1985) 174 CA3d 486, 499-500, 220 CR 186, 193-194—relief from Labor Commissioner's decision]

  **Compare:** But imprisonment does not justify such relief where the incarcerated defendant is *able* to appear by filing a timely written response. [*Aheroni v. Maxwell* (1988) 205 CA3d 284, 293, 252 CR 369, 373-374—no excusable neglect where imprisoned pro per litigant obtained extension to respond, had access to prison law library and other pro per privileges, yet failed to file answer to complaint]

3) **[5:454] Attorney's "positive misconduct":** "Extrinsic mistake" may be found where the moving party was deprived of a hearing by reason of his or her lawyer's "*positive misconduct.*" [*Aldrich v. San Fernando Valley Lumber Co.* (1985) 170 CA3d 725, 739, 216 CR 300, 308]

(Compare: "Positive misconduct" of counsel as ground for discretionary relief under CCP §473(b) is discussed at ¶5:355.)

- **[5:455]** P's lawyer failed to respond to discovery requests or to oppose a motion to dismiss for failure to make discovery, and was *suspended by the State Bar* shortly before the dismissal was granted, all unbeknownst to P until several years later. Relief from the dismissal was properly granted on ground of "extrinsic mistake." [*Aldrich v. San Fernando Valley Lumber Co.*, supra]

- [5:455.1] Landowner hired Attorney to defend forfeiture proceedings (for drug trafficking on the property). A default judgment was entered against Landowner as a result of Attorney's failure to oppose a motion. Attorney's failure "suggests positive misconduct through a total failure to represent the client." [*People v. One Parcel of Land* (1991) 235 CA3d 579, 584, 286 CR 739, 742]

- [5:455.2] D's lawyer did not keep his promise to file an answer raising defenses on D's behalf. The lawyer also failed to appear at the trial or to seek relief from the judgment, despite assuring D he would do so. D was entitled to relief under the court's inherent equity power because the lawyer had de facto substituted himself out of the case. [*Orange Empire Nat'l Bank v. Kirk* (1968) 259 CA2d 347, 352-353, 66 CR 240, 244]

    [5:456-458.4] *Reserved.*

4) [5:458.5] **Attorney's conflict of interest:** An attorney who purports to represent clients whose interests actually conflict deprives one or both of a fair trial. This is sufficient "extrinsic fraud or mistake" for relief from a judgment (default or otherwise). [See *Tsakos Shipping & Trading, S.A. v. Juniper Garden Town Homes, Ltd.* (1993) 12 CA4th 74, 97, 15 CR2d 585, 598—sister state judgment held unenforceable because rendered in an action in which defense counsel purported to represent both a partnership and a partner individually with conflicting interests]

5) [5:459] **Clerical error in entering default:** "Extrinsic mistake" also may be found where a default judgment was entered as the result of clerical error. [*Rappleyea v. Campbell* (1994) 8 C4th 975, 981-983, 35 CR2d 669, 672-673;

*Baske v. Burke* (1981) 125 CA3d 38, 43-44, 177 CR 794, 798]

- **[5:460]** Defendant, a 90-year old woman, wrote letters to the court that were in effect an answer to the complaint, and offered to pay filing fees; but court clerk failed to place her letters in the court file or to seek instructions from the court. Entry of default held to be clerical error, and equitable relief from default judgment granted for "extrinsic mistake." [*Baske v. Burke*, supra]

- **[5:460.1]** A court clerk misinformed pro per defendants as to the filing fee for their answer (quoting the fee for a sole defendant). The underpayment delayed getting their answer on file, resulting in a default judgment. It was an abuse of discretion to deny equitable relief for "extrinsic mistake." [*Rappleyea v. Campbell*, supra, 8 C4th at 983, 35 CR2d at 673]

- **[5:460.2]** A complaint was sent to the clerk's office for filing several days before the statute of limitations ran. Deputy County Clerk called plaintiff's lawyer to state a balance was owing on the filing fee (due to a recent increase) but assured him the complaint would be timely filed. The balance was promptly paid but the complaint was not filed until after the statute had run. Clerk's assurance that the complaint would be timely filed despite the incorrect filing fee constituted an extrinsic mistake (plaintiff could have arranged payment the same day). The complaint was deemed filed within the limitations period. [*Mirvis v. Crowder* (1995) 32 CA4th 1684, 1687-1688, 38 CR2d 644, 646]

- **[5:460.3]** Where the clerk improperly refuses to file a pleading and, as a result, the pleading is filed late, it will be deemed filed as of the day it was presented for filing. [*Rojas v. Cutsforth* (1998) 67 CA4th 774, 778, 79 CR2d 292, 294; *see discussion at* ¶6:46]

6) **[5:461] Compare—ignorance of law NOT ground for relief:** "Extrinsic mistake" does

not extend to situations where defendant was simply *ignorant* of the law and therefore failed to file a timely answer. [*Stiles v. Wallis* (1983) 147 CA3d 1143, 1148-1149, 195 CR 377, 380—Australian citizen claimed lack of familiarity with California law; not sufficient for relief]

7) [5:462] **Attorney's mistake as ground for relief:** An attorney's mistake is not ground for relief unless caused by the adversary. Where an attorney knows the facts but mistakenly interprets their legal significance, that mistake is intrinsic and will *not* warrant equitable relief from a default judgment. [*Janetsky v. Avis* (1986) 176 CA3d 799, 811, 222 CR 342, 349]

[5:462.1-462.4] *Reserved.*

8) [5:462.5] **Lack of notice of *in rem* proceeding:** Because constructive notice is sufficient in *in rem* proceedings (e.g., probate proceedings; *see ¶4:86*), lack of personal notice does *not* amount to extrinsic fraud or mistake justifying relief from a judgment in such proceedings. [*Parage v. Couedel* (1997) 60 CA4th 1037, 1042-1043, 70 CR2d 671, 675]

c. **Procedure**

(1) [5:463] **Alternative procedures available:** Equitable relief from a default judgment may be sought *either* by a noticed motion in the main action; *or* by an independent lawsuit to set aside the judgment in the original action. [*Olivera v. Grace* (1942) 19 C2d 570, 575-576, 122 P2d 564, 567-568]

(a) [5:464] **Remedies cumulative:** A judgment procured by extrinsic fraud or mistake may be attacked either by a motion in the same action or by an independent suit to set aside the judgment. The remedies are distinct and cumulative . . . so that denial of the motion is *not res judicata or collateral estoppel* as to a later, independent suit on the same grounds. [*Rohrbasser v. Lederer* (1986) 179 CA3d 290, 297, 224 CR 791, 794; *Groves v. Peterson* (2002) 100 CA4th 659, 668, 123 CR2d 164, 170— no collateral estoppel because of limitations of motion procedure]

1) [5:465] **Rationale:** The type of proof that can be used in support of a motion is usually limited to affidavits from willing witnesses. Different proof may be available in a separate suit

(e.g., unwilling witnesses can be subpoenaed into court, their depositions can be taken, etc.).

Therefore, the latter remedy should not be barred by reason of having attempted the former. Indeed, as one court has observed, it is "*better practice* to seek a summary disposition of the issue upon motion and 'if defeated in that proceeding to commence a separate action for relief . . .'" [*Rohrbasser v. Lederer*, supra, 179 CA3d at 298, 224 CR at 795 (emphasis added)]

(b) **[5:466]** **Compare—collateral estoppel if issues fully tried in main action:** The result is different, however, "where the person attacking the judgment has made a *full presentation* of the issues of fraud or mistake, or was given a *full opportunity* at the time of the motion hearing to develop the issues by *oral testimony*." In such a case, issues adjudicated are binding on the parties under the doctrine of *collateral estoppel*. [*Rohrbasser v. Lederer*, supra, 179 CA3d at 298, 224 CR at 795 (emphasis added); see *Darlington v. Basalt Rock Co.* (1961) 188 CA2d 706, 710, 10 CR 556, 559—motion hearing took one day, included oral testimony, and judge urged counsel to produce whatever evidence they felt necessary]

1) **[5:467]** **What constitutes "full opportunity" to litigate:** The party claiming collateral estoppel has the burden of proving that the issue was actually litigated in the prior action. Merely showing that *affidavits* raising the issue were submitted may not suffice. On the other hand, a full adversarial hearing is *not* required in every case: "Rather, we think the appropriate principle is that while the party urging the estoppel must prove that the issue was actually litigated and that *evidence was not restricted,* he need not establish that any particular type of evidence, such as oral testimony, was presented." [*Barker v. Hull* (1987) 191 CA3d 221, 227, 236 CR 285, 289 (emphasis in original)—court took *judicial notice* of file in prior action in determining parties had full opportunity to litigate the issue in prior action]

(c) **[5:468]** **Comment:** The same principles apply whether the motion is made for discretionary relief under CCP §473 or is addressed to the inherent equity power of the court. [*Rohrbasser v. Lederer*, supra, 179 CA3d at 299, 224 CR at 795]

⇨[5:469]  **PRACTICE POINTER:**  A motion for relief in the main action is swifter and less expensive. But it will usually be heard on a law and motion calendar, and the judge may be unwilling to allow subpoenaed witnesses and live testimony.

On the other hand, if the judge *does* allow live testimony, you run the risk of collateral estoppel if you lose the motion (see above).

If the case turns on credibility, you may be better off *not* filing a motion for relief in the main action. Filing an independent action gives you an opportunity to take depositions, subpoena independent witnesses, etc., that you may not have on a motion hearing. It will also avoid any claim of collateral estoppel that might otherwise arise.

(2)  [5:470]  **Compare—limited civil cases:**  Motions for equitable relief from a judgment or order obtained on grounds of "extrinsic fraud, mistake, inadvertence or excusable neglect" may be made in limited civil cases. [CCP §86(b)(3); *see* ¶3:37-38]

But an *independent* action to set aside a judgment in a limited civil case is not a limited civil case. (This is not one of the types of equitable relief available in limited civil cases; *see* ¶3:12.)

(3)  [5:471]  **Moving papers:**  If proceeding by *noticed motion*, defendant must accompany his motion with declarations based on personal knowledge of competent witnesses stating *facts* sufficient to constitute "extrinsic fraud or mistake." Also, points and authorities, and a copy of the proposed answer or other pleading must accompany the motion. (*See detailed discussion of procedure for discretionary relief under CCP §473(b),* ¶5:382 *ff.*)

If proceeding by *independent lawsuit*, defendant will have to serve and file a complaint seeking relief from the judgment. The complaint should allege ultimate facts constituting "extrinsic fraud or mistake" and showing the pleader entitled to relief from the judgment.

(4)  [5:472]  **Meritorious defense:**  A default judgment that is merely *voidable* (rather than void, *see* ¶5:494) will not be set aside unless it is likely that the result would be different if the case went to trial. Therefore, whether defendant proceeds by noticed motion in the main action or independent lawsuit to set aside the judgment, he must show a meritorious defense. [*Smith v.*

*Busniewski* (1952) 115 CA2d 124, 129-130, 251 P2d 697, 700-701]

(a) **[5:473]** If defendant proceeds by noticed motion in the main action, his or her moving papers should contain a *copy of a proposed answer showing a valid defense, and declarations* showing facts to support such defense. [*Shields v. Siegel* (1966) 246 CA2d 334, 337, 54 CR 577, 578]

(b) **[5:474]** If defendant files an independent lawsuit to set aside the judgment, he or she must plead and prove a meritorious defense to the original action in order to prevail. [*Smith v. Busniewski,* supra]

d. **[5:475]** **Appeal:** An order denying a motion to vacate a judgment is appealable under CCP §904.1(a)(2) as an order made after judgment. But such appeal lies only where the moving party lacked effective opportunity to appeal from the judgment itself (i.e., because of extrinsic fraud or mistake, etc.). [See *Estate of Baker* (1915) 170 C 578, 582, 150 P 989, 991; *Daley v. County of Butte* (1964) 227 CA2d 380, 389, 38 CR 693, 698-699]

6. **[5:476]** **Relief From Judicial Error in Rendering Default Judgment:** Judicial error in rendering a default judgment (e.g., awarding excessive damages) is *not* ground for relief under CCP §473. That section, by its terms, applies only to "mistakes" by the moving party—not to mistakes by the court. [*Don v. Cruz* (1982) 131 CA3d 695, 702, 182 CR 581, 586]

However, relief from judicial error in rendering a default judgment can be obtained in the same manner as for judgments following a contested trial. [*Misic v. Segars* (1995) 37 CA4th 1149, 1153-1154, 44 CR2d 100, 103 (citing text)]

a. **[5:477]** **Motion for new trial:** Although in default, defendant can attack the default judgment in the trial court by motion for new trial on the ground of "excessive or inadequate" damages or "because the verdict or decision is against the law" (CCP §657(5),(6)). [*Misic v. Segars,* supra, 37 CA4th at 1154, 44 CR2d at 103 (citing text)]

(1) **[5:478]** **Rationale:** Since defendant can raise such grounds by appeal (see below), it should be allowed to raise such grounds in the trial court by motion for new trial, and thus avoid wasteful appeals. [*Don v. Cruz,* supra]

(2) **[5:479]** **Compare:** A more recent case contains dictum to the contrary: "A defendant against whom a default has been entered ... *cannot* thereafter ... move for a new trial ..." [See *Devlin v. Kearny Mesa AMC/ Jeep/Renault, Inc.* (1984) 155 CA3d 381, 385-386, 202

CR 204, 207] But this dictum is unsupported by any recent authority, and is believed to be incorrect. [See *Misic v. Segars*, supra, 37 CA4th at 1154, 44 CR2d at 103 (citing text)]

(3) **[5:480]** **Time limit:** To file a motion for new trial, the defaulting defendant will have to find out about the default judgment in time to do so. A motion for new trial must be filed either within 15 days after the clerk mails notice of entry of judgment, or a party serves such notice, or within 180 days after entry of judgment, whichever is sooner, and supporting papers within 10 days thereafter. [See CCP §659; CRC 236.5]

b. **[5:481]** **Appeal:** Alternatively, a defendant may appeal from a default judgment for judicial error. The default entered in the trial court does not affect defendant's right to appeal. [*Uva v. Evans* (1978) 83 CA3d 356, 360, 147 CR 795, 797; *see ¶5:272*]

(1) **[5:482]** **Time limit:** Again, however, the appeal must be filed within the time limit applicable to appeals generally (*see ¶5:273*).

c. **[5:483]** **Compare—clerical error:** But error by the court clerk in entering a default judgment is considered "extrinsic mistake" and can be corrected even after expiration of the time limits for motion for new trial or appeal. [*Baske v. Burke* (1981) 125 CA3d 38, 43-44, 177 CR 794, 798; *see ¶5:459*]

7. **[5:484]** **Relief From VOID Judgment:** In addition to any other ground for vacating a default judgment, the court has power to set aside a judgment that is void as a matter of law. [CCP §473(d)]

a. **[5:485]** **Application:** A judgment may be void as a matter of law for many reasons, including:

- Lack of subject matter jurisdiction (*¶3:2 ff.*).

- Lack of personal jurisdiction (*¶3:130 ff.*).

- Lack of actual or constructive notice of proceedings (e.g., because papers served on defendant's attorney who had been suspended by State Bar and thus had no authority to represent defendant). [*Lovato v. Santa Fe Int'l Corp.* (1984) 151 CA3d 549, 553, 198 CR 838, 840]

- *Lack of or improper service* of summons (*¶4:110 ff.*). However, substantial compliance with the service of summons statutes is sufficient to defeat a motion under CCP §473(d). [*Gibble v. Car-Lene Research, Inc.* (1998) 67 CA4th 295, 313, 78 CR2d 892, 903; *Ellard v. Conway* (2001) 94 CA4th 540, 544, 114 CR2d 399, 401—court may set aside default judgment valid on its face, but void as a matter of law due to improper service]

- Default improperly entered—e.g., without service on defendant of CCP §425.11 statement of damages required in personal injury and death actions. [*Heidary v. Yadollahi* (2002) 99 CA4th 857, 862, 121 CR2d 695, 698—default improperly entered for failure to appear at trial, *see ¶5:82*]

- Default judgment exceeding amount demanded in complaint (*¶5:233 ff.*).

(1) [5:486] **Compare:** *Failure to return summons* with proof of service within 3 years (plus 60 days) is ground for *dismissal* (CCP §§583.210(a),(b), 583.250; *see ¶11:54*). But if no answer is filed, the ensuing default judgment is *not void*. The delay in returning summons would be ground for direct attack (appeal) or relief from default within 6 months. But it is *not* ground for collateral attack after the judgment has become final. [*National Diversified Services, Inc. v. Bernstein* (1985) 168 CA3d 410, 416, 214 CR 113, 117]

b. [5:487] **Alternative procedures available:** The party attacking a void judgment has the choice of either direct or collateral attack. However, use of one may bar the other because issues adjudicated in the first proceeding may be entitled to collateral estoppel effect in the second proceeding.

(1) [5:488] **Direct attack:** If defendant finds out about the judgment in time, he or she may *appeal* therefrom. Or, he or she may file a motion for relief under CCP §473(d), and then appeal from any adverse determination of his or her motion. [CCP §904.1(a)(2); *Wilkinson v. Wilkinson* (1970) 12 CA3d 1164, 1166, 91 CR 372, 373]

(2) [5:489] **Collateral attack:** Alternatively, a void judgment is subject to collateral attack—either by separate lawsuit to set aside the judgment; or by raising it as a defense to separate action by the judgment creditor to enforce the judgment. (*See ¶3:404.*)

(a) [5:489.1] **Motion to vacate renewal of judgment:** Any defense to an action on the judgment is also ground for a motion to vacate *renewal* of the judgment after the 10-year period allowed by law for enforcement of the judgment (CCP §683.120). (The motion to vacate the renewal must be filed within 30 days after the judgment debtor is served with "Notice of Renewal.") [CCP §683.170; see *Fidelity Creditor Service, Inc. v. Browne* (2001) 89 CA4th

195, 207, 106 CR2d 854, 863—lack of service of summons on original judgment ground for vacating renewal of judgment]

c. [5:490] **Timeliness:** There is no time limit on a *collateral attack* on a void judgment (other than possibly the equitable defense of laches): "A judgment void on its face . . . is subject to collateral attack at any time." [*Rochin v. Pat Johnson Mfg. Co.* (1998) 67 CA4th 1228, 1239, 79 CR2d 719, 725—amended judgment entered without notice to plaintiff violated due process]

Nor is there any time limit on a motion for relief under CCP §473 where it is clear from the *face of the record* that the judgment should not have been entered: "(A) default that is void on the face of the record when entered is subject to challenge *at any time* irrespective of lack of diligence in seeking to set it aside within the six-month period of section 473." [*Plotitsa v. Sup.Ct. (Kadri)* (1983) 140 CA3d 755, 761, 189 CR 769, 772 (emphasis added)—CCP §425.11 statement of damages not personally served on defendant]

(1) [5:491] **Exception—judgment void for *improper service;* 2-year limit:** However, a motion for relief from a judgment *valid* on its face but void for improper service, is governed *by analogy to CCP §473.5* (relief for lack of actual notice where summons served by publication; *see ¶5:428*). Thus, relief must be sought no later than 2 years after entry of the default judgment (sooner if notice given). [*Rogers v. Silverman* (1989) 216 CA3d 1114, 1121-1122, 265 CR 286, 293—process server served wrong person; and see *Thorson v. Western Development Corp.* (1967) 251 CA2d 206, 210-211, 59 CR 299, 301-302; *Gibble v. Car-Lene Research, Inc.* (1998) 67 CA4th 295, 300, 78 CR2d 892, 895, fn. 3]

(a) [5:492] **Rationale:** Earlier versions of §473 expressly made challenges for improper service subject to the time limit now appearing in CCP §473.5. [*Rogers v. Silverman*, supra, 216 CA3d at 1121, 265 CR at 289-290]

☞[5:493] *PRACTICE POINTER:* The 2-year limit applies only to challenges in the main action under CCP §473. You can still file an *independent action* to set aside the judgment for lack of personal jurisdiction. There is *no time limit* on a collateral attack on the judgment. [*Dill v. Berquist Const. Co.*, Inc. (1994) 24 CA4th 1426, 1444, 29 CR2d 746, 757]

*Caution:* If you make the motion under CCP §473 and *lose,* collateral estoppel may bar relitigation in any later independent action of issues adjudicated on the §473 motion hearing; *see ¶5:466.*

d. **[5:494] Not necessary to show meritorious defense:** A void judgment must be set aside regardless of the merits of the underlying case.

Thus, for example, where there was never valid service of summons, the court cannot insist that defendant show a meritorious defense before setting aside the judgment: "Where a person has been deprived of property in a manner contrary to the most basic tenets of due process, it is no answer to say that in his particular case due process of law would have led to the same result because he had no adequate defense upon the merits." [*Peralta v. Heights Medical Center, Inc.* (1988) 485 US 80, 86-87, 108 S.Ct. 896, 900 (internal quotes omitted)]

(1) **[5:495] Compare—voidable judgments:** The result is different where the judgment is merely voidable because of "extrinsic fraud or mistake." In such cases, a meritorious defense must be shown; *see ¶5:472.*

e. **[5:496] Prejudice not required:** Prejudice is not a factor in setting aside a void judgment or order. [See *Sindler v. Brennan* (2003) 105 CA4th 1350, 1354, 129 CR2d 888, 891—dismissal order entered in violation of bankruptcy stay]

Rev. #1 2004

# REQUEST FOR ENTRY OF DEFAULT

982(a)(6)

| ATTORNEY OR PARTY WITHOUT ATTORNEY *(Name, state bar number, and address)*: | FOR COURT USE ONLY |
|---|---|
| TELEPHONE NO.:  FAX NO.: | |
| ATTORNEY FOR *(Name)*: | |
| Insert name of court and name of judicial district and branch court, if any: | |
| PLAINTIFF: | |
| DEFENDANT: | |

| REQUEST FOR (Application) | ☐ ENTRY OF DEFAULT  ☐ CLERK'S JUDGMENT  ☐ COURT JUDGMENT | CASE NUMBER: |
|---|---|---|

1. **TO THE CLERK:** On the complaint or cross-complaint filed
   a. on *(date)*:
   b. by *(name)*:
   c. ☐ Enter default of defendant *(names)*:

   d. ☐ I request a court judgment under Code of Civil Procedure sections 585(b), (c), 989, etc., against defendant *(names)*:

   *(Testimony required. Apply to the clerk for a hearing date, unless the court will enter a judgment on an affidavit under Code of Civil Procedure section 585(d).)*

   e. ☐ Enter clerk's judgment
      (1) ☐ for restitution of the premises only and issue a writ of execution on the judgment. Code of Civil Procedure section 1174(c) does not apply. (Code Civ. Proc., § 1169.)

      ☐ Include in the judgment all tenants, subtenants, named claimants, and other occupants of the premises. The *Prejudgment Claim of Right to Possession* was served in compliance with Code of Civil Procedure section 415.46.

      (2) ☐ under Code of Civil Procedure section 585(a). *(Complete the declaration under Code Civ. Proc., § 585.5 on the reverse (item 5).)*
      (3) ☐ for default previously entered on *(date)*:

2. **Judgment to be entered**

| | Amount | Credits acknowledged | Balance |
|---|---|---|---|
| a. Demand of complaint . . . . . . . . . . . $ | $ | $ | |
| b. Statement of damages * | | | |
| (1) Special  . . . . . . . . . . . . . . . . . $ | $ | $ | |
| (2) General . . . . . . . . . . . . . . . . $ | $ | $ | |
| c. Interest . . . . . . . . . . . . . . . . . . . . . $ | $ | $ | |
| d. Costs *(see reverse)* . . . . . . . . . . . $ | $ | $ | |
| e. Attorney fees . . . . . . . . . . . . . . . . $ | $ | $ | |
| f. **TOTALS** . . . . . . . . . . . . . . . . $ | $ | $ | |

   g. **Daily damages** were demanded in complaint at the rate of: $               per day beginning *(date)*:
   (* *Personal injury or wrongful death actions; Code Civ. Proc., § 425.11)*

3. ☐ *(Check if filed in an unlawful detainer case)* **LEGAL DOCUMENT ASSISTANT OR UNLAWFUL DETAINER ASSISTANT** information is on the reverse *(complete item 4)*.

Date:

▶

_____
(TYPE OR PRINT NAME)

_____
(SIGNATURE OF PLAINTIFF OR ATTORNEY FOR PLAINTIFF)

| FOR COURT USE ONLY | (1) ☐ Default entered as requested on *(date)*:  (2) ☐ Default NOT entered as requested *(state reason)*: |
|---|---|
| | Clerk, by _____ , Deputy |

Page 1 of 2

Form Adopted for Mandatory Use
Judicial Council of California
982(a)(6) [Rev. July 1, 2003]

**REQUEST FOR ENTRY OF DEFAULT**
(Application to Enter Default)

Code of Civil Procedure,
§§ 585-587, 1169
www.courtinfo.ca.gov
American LegalNet, Inc.
www.USCourtForms.com

4. **LEGAL DOCUMENT ASSISTANT OR UNLAWFUL DETAINER ASSISTANT (Bus. & Prof. Code, § 6400 et seq.)** A **legal document assistant or unlawful detainer assistant** ☐ did ☐ did **not** for compensation give advice or assistance with this form. *(If declarant has received any help or advice for pay from a legal document assistant or unlawful detainer assistant, state):*

   a. Assistant's name:

   c. Street address, city, and ZIP:

                                                                b. Telephone No.:

   d. County of registration:

   e. Registration No.:                                    e. Expires on *(date)*

5. ☐ **DECLARATION UNDER CODE OF CIVIL PROCEDURE SECTION 585.5** *(Required for entry of default under Code Civ. Proc., § 585(a))* This action

   a. ☐ is ☐ is not   on a contract or installment sale for goods or services subject to Civ. Code, § 1801 et seq. (Unruh Act).

   b. ☐ is ☐ is not   on a conditional sales contract subject to Civ. Code, § 2981 et seq. (Rees-Levering Motor Vehicle Sales and Finance Act).

   c. ☐ is ☐ is not   on an obligation for goods, services, loans, or extensions of credit subject to Code Civ. Proc., § 395(b).

6. **DECLARATION OF MAILING (Code Civ. Proc., § 587)** A copy of this *Request for Entry of Default* was

   a. ☐ **not mailed** to the following defendants whose addresses are **unknown** to plaintiff or plaintiff's attorney *(names):*

   b. ☐ **mailed** first-class, postage prepaid, in a sealed envelope addressed to each defendant's attorney of record or, if none, to each defendant's last known address as follows:

      (1) Mailed on *(date):*                   (2) To *(specify names and addresses shown on the envelopes):*

I declare under penalty of perjury under the laws of the State of California that the foregoing items 4, 5, and 6 are true and correct.

Date:

▶

_____        _____
      (TYPE OR PRINT NAME)                (SIGNATURE OF DECLARANT)

7. **MEMORANDUM OF COSTS** *(Required if judgment requested)* **Costs and disbursements** are as follows (Code Civ. Proc., § 1033.5):

   a. Clerk's filing fees  . . . . . . . . . . . . . . . . . $

   b. Process server's fees  . . . . . . . . . . . . . $

   c. Other *(specify):* . . . . . . . . . . . . . . . . . . $

   d. . . . . . . . . . . . . . . . . . . . . . . . . . . . . . . $

   e. **TOTAL** . . . . . . . . . . . . . . . . . . . . . . . $_____

   f. ☐ Costs and disbursements are waived.

   g. I am the attorney, agent, or party who claims these costs. To the best of my knowledge and belief this memorandum of costs is correct and these costs were necessarily incurred in this case.

I declare under penalty of perjury under the laws of the State of California that the foregoing is true and correct.

Date:

▶

_____        _____
      (TYPE OR PRINT NAME)                (SIGNATURE OF DECLARANT)

8. ☐ **DECLARATION OF NONMILITARY STATUS** *(Required for a judgment)* No defendant named in item 1c of the application is in the military service so as to be entitled to the benefits of the Soldiers' and Sailors' Civil Relief Act of 1940 (50 U.S.C. Appen. § 501 et seq.).

I declare under penalty of perjury under the laws of the State of California that the foregoing is true and correct.

Date:

▶

_____        _____
      (TYPE OR PRINT NAME)                (SIGNATURE OF DECLARANT)

**RESERVED**

**RESERVED**

**[FORM 5:C]**

# DEFAULT/CLERK'S JUDGMENT REJECTION NOTICE

| | |
|---|---|
| **SUPERIOR COURT OF CALIFORNIA** <br><br> **COUNTY OF LOS ANGELES** | Reserved for Clerk's File Stamp |
| COURTHOUSE ADDRESS: | |
| PLAINTIFF: | |
| DEFENDANT: | |
| **DEFAULT / CLERK'S JUDGMENT REJECTION NOTICE** | CASE NUMBER: |

Your request to enter default and/or clerk's judgment submitted on _____ is rejected for the following reason(s):

☐ 1. _____ form is obsolete; please submit current form.

☐ 2. Answer/demurrer/motion of a nature preventing entry of default filed on _____ by _____ . (CCP 585)

☐ 3. Original/amended Summons or Declaration re: Lost Summons required. (CCP 417.30)

☐ 4. The original Summons must be returned within 3 years and 60 days subject to CCP 583.210 and CCP 583.250.

☐ 5. File Substitution of Attorney/ Change of Address/ Association of Attorney.

**Request to Enter Default**

☐ 6. Date that Request to Enter Default filed is omitted.

☐ 7. Date that complaint was filed is omitted / incorrect.

☐ 8. Requesting party is omitted / listed incorrectly.

☐ 9. Name(s) of defendant(s) not corresponding to complaint or summons.

☐ 10. Applicable box(es) not marked/completed under item(s) number.

☐ 11. Date / printed name / signature of plaintiff / attorney of record / declarant required on item number.

☐ 12. Separate address for each defendant / attorney of record on CCP 587 Declaration required.

☐ 13. Mailing date on CCP 587 Declaration (item 4a) cannot precede date of request to enter default.

☐ 14. ☐ a. Mailing date on CCP 587 Declaration (4a) cannot precede date of CCP 585.5 Declaration.
       ☐ b. Dates under CCP 587 Declaration cannot precede date of mailing.

☐ 15. Names of defendants to whom the default request was "not mailed" must be listed under item 4a.

☐ 16. Request is premature. Default may be entered no sooner than _____ .

☐ 17. Declaration of non-military status is not completed.

☐ 18. Default entered as to _____
       ☐ Complete and submit a new default request as to _____

☐ 19. _____

**Proof of Service**

☐ 20. Original proof of service not filed pursuant to CCP 471.10 and/or CCP 417.30.

☐ 21. The document(s) served are not indicated. / Proof of service does not indicate that summons and complaint were served.

☐ 22. **Separate** proof of service required for each defendant.

DEFAULT/CLERK'S JUDG. REJECTION NOTICE

CIV 098 12-01                                    Page 1 of 2

Rev. #1 2003                                                              5-121

| | 23. | Defendant not served as sued. Name of defendant must correspond to the name on the complaint. Submit a new proof of service as to _____. |
|---|---|---|
| ☐ | 24. | No indication of service on corporate officer or authorized agent pursuant to CCP 412.30 and 416.10. |
| ☐ | 25. | Date (month/day/year) / time (hour/AM-PM) / complete address where service was performed required. Specify home or business. |
| ☐ | 26. | Date (month/day/year) / place of mailing (city & state) for substitute service required pursuant to CCP 415.20. |
| ☐ | 27. | Manner of service not specified / in error. (CP 417.10) |
| ☐ | 28. | Original acknowledgment of receipt required as to _____ pursuant to CCP 415.30. |
| ☐ | 29. | Notice to Person Served is incomplete / in error due to _____. |
| ☐ | 30. | Status of person performing the service is not specified pursuant to CCP 417.40. |
| ☐ | 31. | Name / Address / Phone number of person performing the service is required. |
| ☐ | 32. | If person is registered process server, county of registration and registration number are required pursuant to CCP 417.40. |
| ☐ | 33. | Original signature of process server is missing. / Date of signature is missing. |
| ☐ | 34. | Declaration of due diligence for substitute service was not submitted. |
| ☐ | 35. | Date of declaration / signature of declarant is missing on declaration of due diligence. |
| ☐ | 36. | Proof of service by publication pursuant to CCP 415.50 and GC 6064 and declaration of mailing or inability to ascertain address must be submitted. |

**Others**

| | 37. | **A Court Judgment is required** for the following reasons: |
|---|---|---|

| | ☐ | a. | Obligation is based on secured agreement; there is no allegation in complaint that security has not been resorted to. [**Petersen v. Green** (1972) 24 Cal. App. 3d 915] |
|---|---|---|---|
| | ☐ | b. | Complaint is for reasonable value of legal services rendered. [**Lewis v. LeBaron** (1967) 254 Cal. App. 2d 270] |
| | ☐ | c. | There is a doubtful contractual liability of non-signing defendant(s). [CCP 585(a)] [**Petersen v. Green** (1972) 24 Cal. App. 3d 915] |
| | ☐ | d. | Attorney fees exceed those prescribed in the Attorney Fee schedule. |

| ☐ | 38. | Submit written testimony [CCP 585(d) declaration], Request for Default Judgment by Court and a stamped, self-addressed envelope. |
|---|---|---|
| ☐ | 39. | Submit copy of note, contract or other written obligation signed by the defendant(s) pursuant to CRC 522. |
| ☐ | 40. | Entry of default judgment is stayed, depending on the outcome of trial of the issues raised by the answering parties. At the time of trial, the judicial officer will render judgment with respect to the defendant in default. |
| ☐ | 41. | Pursuant to CCP 579, a court order is required for a several judgment. |
| ☐ | 42. | A corporation/trust/partnership/association must be represented by an attorney. |
| ☐ | 43. | Statement of damages and proof of service of statement pursuant to CCP 425.11 are required. All dollar amounts must be complete. |
| ☐ | 44. | _____ |

Please return corrected forms and/or additional document(s) required to process your request to the address shown on the front of this notice.

John A. Clarke, Executive Officer/ Clerk

_____     By     _____, Deputy
                    Date

**DEFAULT/CLERK'S JUDG. REJECTION NOTICE**

# JUDGMENT

**JUD-100**

| ATTORNEY OR PARTY WITHOUT ATTORNEY *(Name, state bar number, and address):* | FOR COURT USE ONLY |
|---|---|
| | |

TELEPHONE NO.:      FAX NO. *(Optional):*

E-MAIL ADDRESS *(Optional):*

ATTORNEY FOR *(Name):*

**SUPERIOR COURT OF CALIFORNIA, COUNTY OF**

STREET ADDRESS:

MAILING ADDRESS:

CITY AND ZIP CODE:

BRANCH NAME:

PLAINTIFF:

DEFENDANT:

| **JUDGMENT** | CASE NUMBER: |
|---|---|
| ☐ By Clerk    ☐ By Default    ☐ After Court Trial<br>☐ By Court    ☐ On Stipulation    ☐ Defendant Did Not Appear at Trial | |

**JUDGMENT**

1. ☐ **BY DEFAULT**
   - a. Defendant was properly served with a copy of the summons and complaint.
   - b. Defendant failed to answer the complaint or appear and defend the action within the time allowed by law.
   - c. Defendant's default was entered by the clerk upon plaintiff's application.
   - d. ☐ **Clerk's Judgment** (Code Civ. Proc., § 585(a)). Defendant was sued only on a contract or judgment of a court of this state for the recovery of money.
   - e. ☐ **Court Judgment** (Code Civ. Proc., § 585(b)). The court considered
     - (1) ☐ plaintiff's testimony and other evidence.
     - (2) ☐ plaintiff's written declaration (Code Civ. Proc., § 585(d)).

2. ☐ **ON STIPULATION**
   - a. Plaintiff and defendant agreed (stipulated) that a judgment be entered in this case. The court approved the stipulated judgment and
   - b. ☐ the signed written stipulation was filed in the case.
   - c. ☐ the stipulation was stated in open court    ☐ the stipulation was stated on the record.

3. ☐ **AFTER COURT TRIAL.** The jury was waived. The court considered the evidence.
   - a. The case was tried on *(date and time):*
     before *(name of judicial officer):*
   - b. Appearances by:
     - ☐ Plaintiff *(name each):*          ☐ Plaintiff's attorney *(name each):*
       - (1)                                    (1)
       - (2)                                    (2)
     - ☐ Continued on Attachment 3b.
     - ☐ Defendant *(name each):*          ☐ Defendant 's attorney *(name each):*
       - (1)                                    (1)
       - (2)                                    (2)
     - ☐ Continued on Attachment 3b.
   - c. ☐ Defendant did not appear at trial. Defendant was properly served with notice of trial.
   - d. ☐ A statement of decision (Code Civ. Proc., § 632) ☐ was not ☐ was   requested.

Page 1 of 2

| PLAINTIFF: | CASE NUMBER: |
|---|---|
| DEFENDANT: | |

**JUDGMENT IS ENTERED AS FOLLOWS BY:** ☐ **THE COURT** ☐ **THE CLERK**

4. ☐ **Stipulated Judgment.** Judgment is entered according to the stipulation of the parties.

5. **Parties.** Judgment is

   a. ☐ for plaintiff *(name each):*

     and against defendant *(names):*

     ☐ Continued on Attachment 5a.

   b. ☐ for defendant *(name each):*

   c. ☐ for cross-complainant *(name each):*

     and against cross-defendant *(name each):*

     ☐ Continued on Attachment 5c.

   d. ☐ for cross-defendant *(name each):*

6. **Amount.**

   a. ☐ Defendant named in item 5a above must pay plaintiff on the complaint:

| (1) ☐ | Damages | $ |
|---|---|---|
| (2) ☐ | Prejudgment interest at the annual rate of    % | $ |
| (3) ☐ | Attorney fees | $ |
| (4) ☐ | Costs | $ |
| (5) ☐ | Other *(specify):* | $ |
| (6) | **TOTAL** | $ |

   c. ☐ Cross-defendant named in item 5c above must pay cross-complainant on the cross-complaint:

| (1) ☐ | Damages | $ |
|---|---|---|
| (2) ☐ | Prejudgment interest at the annual rate of    % | $ |
| (3) ☐ | Attorney fees | $ |
| (4) ☐ | Costs | $ |
| (5) ☐ | Other *(specify):* | $ |
| (6) | **TOTAL** | $ |

   b. ☐ Plaintiff to receive nothing from defendant named in item 5b.
     ☐ Defendant named in item 5b to recover costs $
       ☐ and attorney fees $

   d. ☐ Cross-complainant to receive nothing from cross-defendant named in item 5d.
     ☐ Cross-defendant named in item 5d to recover costs $
       ☐ and attorney fees $

7. ☐ Other *(specify):*

Date:        ☐ _____
                                JUDICIAL OFFICER

Date:        ☐ Clerk, by _____ , Deputy

| (SEAL) | **CLERK'S CERTIFICATE** *(Optional)* |
|---|---|
| | I certify that this is a true copy of the original judgment on file in the court. |
| | Date: |
| | Clerk, by _____ , Deputy |

**RESERVED**

## RESERVED

**RESERVED**

**[FORM 5:H]**

# MEMORANDUM OF COSTS (SUMMARY)

**MC-010**

| ATTORNEY OR PARTY WITHOUT ATTORNEY *(Name, state bar number, and address)*: | FOR COURT USE ONLY |
|---|---|

TELEPHONE NO.: FAX NO.:

ATTORNEY FOR *(Name)*:

INSERT NAME OF COURT, JUDICIAL DISTRICT, AND BRANCH COURT, IF ANY:

PLAINTIFF:

DEFENDANT:

| MEMORANDUM OF COSTS (SUMMARY) | CASE NUMBER: |
|---|---|

**The following costs are requested:**

**TOTALS**

1. Filing and motion fees ........................................................ 1. $ _____

2. Jury fees ........................................................ 2. $ _____

3. Jury food and lodging ........................................................ 3. $ _____

4. Deposition costs ........................................................ 4. $ _____

5. Service of process ........................................................ 5. $ _____

6. Attachment expenses ........................................................ 6. $ _____

7. Surety bond premiums ........................................................ 7. $ _____

8. Witness fees ........................................................ 8. $ _____

9. Court-ordered transcripts ........................................................ 9. $ _____

10. Attorney fees *(enter here if contractual or statutory fees are fixed without necessity of a court determination; otherwise a noticed motion is required)* ........................................................ 10. $ _____

11. Models, blowups, and photocopies of exhibits ........................................................ 11. $ _____

12. Court reporter fees as established by statute ........................................................ 12. $ _____

13. Other ........................................................ 13. $ _____

**TOTAL COSTS** ........................................................ $ _____

I am the attorney, agent, or party who claims these costs. To the best of my knowledge and belief this memorandum of costs is correct and these costs were necessarily incurred in this case.

Date:

▶

................ (TYPE OR PRINT NAME) ................ (SIGNATURE)

(Proof of service on reverse)

Form Approved for Optional Use
Judicial Council of California
MC-010 [Rev. July 1, 1999]

**MEMORANDUM OF COSTS (SUMMARY)**

WEST GROUP
Official Publisher

Code of Civil Procedure,
§§ 1032, 1033.5

## PROOF OF ☐ MAILING ☐ PERSONAL DELIVERY

1. At the time of mailing or personal delivery, I was at least 18 years of age and **not a party** to this legal action.
2. My residence or business address is *(specify)*:

3. I mailed or personally delivered a copy of the *Memorandum of Costs (Summary)* as follows *(complete either a or b)*:
   a. ☐ **Mail.** I am a resident of or employed in the county where the mailing occurred.
      (1) I enclosed a copy in an envelope AND
         (a) ☐ **deposited** the sealed envelope with the United States Postal Service with the postage fully prepaid.
         (b) ☐ **placed** the envelope for collection and mailing on the date and at the place shown in items below following our ordinary business practices. I am readily familiar with this business' practice for collecting and processing correspondence for mailing. On the same day that correspondence is placed for collection and mailing, it is deposited in the ordinary course of business with the United States Postal Service in a sealed envelope with postage fully prepaid.
      (2) The envelope was addressed and mailed as follows:
         (a) Name of person served:
         (b) Address on envelope:

         (c) Date of mailing:
         (d) Place of mailing *(city and state)*:

   b. ☐ **Personal delivery.** I personally delivered a copy as follows:
      (1) Name of person served:
      (2) Address where delivered:

      (3) Date delivered:
      (4) Time delivered:

I declare under penalty of perjury under the laws of the State of California that the foregoing is true and correct.

Date:

▶

. . . . . . . . . . . . . . . . . . . . . . . .
(TYPE OR PRINT NAME)

_____
(SIGNATURE OF DECLARANT)

Rev. #1 2003                                                    5-129

**[FORM 5:H.1]**

# MEMORANDUM OF COSTS (WORKSHEET)

MC-011

| SHORT TITLE: | CASE NUMBER: |
|---|---|

**MEMORANDUM OF COSTS (WORKSHEET)**

1. **Filing and motion fees**

                Paper filed                 Filing fee

  a. _____ $ _____

  b. _____ $ _____

  c. _____ $ _____

  d. _____ $ _____

  e. _____ $ _____

  f. _____ $ _____

  g. ☐ Information about additional filing and motion fees is contained in Attachment 1g.

                                  TOTAL   1.   $

2. **Jury fees**

              Date                 Fee & mileage

  a. _____ $ _____

  b. _____ $ _____

  c. _____ $ _____

  d. _____ $ _____

  e. ☐ Information about additional jury fees is contained in Attachment 2e.

                                  TOTAL   2.   $

3. **Juror food: $** _____ **and lodging: $** _____     TOTAL   3.   $

4. **Deposition costs**

| Name of deponent | Taking | Transcribing | Travel | Video-taping | Subtotals |
|---|---|---|---|---|---|
| a. _____ | $ _____ | $ _____ | $ _____ | $ _____ | $ _____ |
| b. _____ | $ _____ | $ _____ | $ _____ | $ _____ | $ _____ |
| c. _____ | $ _____ | $ _____ | $ _____ | $ _____ | $ _____ |
| d. _____ | $ _____ | $ _____ | $ _____ | $ _____ | $ _____ |

  e. ☐ Information about additional deposition costs is contained in Attachment 4e.

                                  TOTAL   4.   $

(Continued on reverse)

Form Approved for Optional Use
Judicial Council of California
MC-011 [Rev. July 1, 1999]

**MEMORANDUM OF COSTS (WORKSHEET)**

WEST GROUP
Official Publisher

Code of Civil Procedure,
§§ 1032, 1033 5

Page _____ of _____

                                                Rev. #1 2003

| SHORT TITLE: | CASE NUMBER: |
|---|---|

5. **Service of process**

| | Name of person served | Public officer | Registered process | Publication | Other (specify) |
|---|---|---|---|---|---|
| a. | _____ | $ ____ | $ ____ | $ ____ | $ _____ |
| b. | _____ | $ ____ | $ ____ | $ ____ | $ _____ |
| c. | _____ | $ ____ | $ ____ | $ ____ | $ _____ |

d. ☐ Information about additional costs for service of process is contained in Attachment 5d.

TOTAL   5. | $ |

6. **Attachment expenses** (specify): ........................................................   6. | $ |

7. **Surety bond premiums** (itemize bonds and amounts): ...................................   7. | $ |

8. a. **Ordinary witness fees**

| | Name of witness | Daily fee | Mileage | Total |
|---|---|---|---|---|
| (1) | _____ | ____ days at ____ $/day | ____ miles at ____ ¢/mile .... | $ _____ |
| (2) | _____ | ____ days at ____ $/day | ____ miles at ____ ¢/mile .... | $ _____ |
| (3) | _____ | ____ days at ____ $/day | ____ miles at ____ ¢/mile .... | $ _____ |
| (4) | _____ | ____ days at ____ $/day | ____ miles at ____ ¢/mile .... | $ _____ |
| (5) | _____ | ____ days at ____ $/day | ____ miles at ____ ¢/mile .... | $ _____ |

(6) ☐ Information about additional ordinary witness fees is contained in Attachment 8a(6).

SUBTOTAL 8a. | $ |

(Continued on next page)

Page ____ of ____

**MEMORANDUM OF COSTS (WORKSHEET)**

WEST GROUP
Official Publisher

**MEMORANDUM OF COSTS (WORKSHEET)** *(Continued)*

8. b. **Expert fees** *(per Code of Civil Procedure section 998)*

        <u>Name of witness</u>          <u>Fee</u>

    (1) _____ _____ hours at $ _____ /hr ... $ _____

    (2) _____ _____ hours at $ _____ /hr ... $ _____

    (3) _____ _____ hours at $ _____ /hr ... $ _____

    (4) _____ _____ hours at $ _____ /hr ... $ _____

    (5) ☐ Information about additional expert witness fees is contained in Attachment 8b(5).

                                         SUBTOTAL 8b. | $ |

  c. **Court-ordered expert fees**

        <u>Name of witness</u>          <u>Fee</u>

    (1) _____ _____ hours at $ _____ /hr ... $ _____

    (2) _____ _____ hours at $ _____ /hr ... $ _____

    (3) ☐ Information about additional court-ordered expert witness fees is contained in Attachment 8c(3).

                                         SUBTOTAL 8c. | $ |

                                TOTAL (8a, 8b, & 8c)   8. | $ |

9. **Court-ordered transcripts** *(specify):* . . . . . . . . . . . . . . . . . . . . . . . . . . . . . . . . . . . . . . . . . . . 9. | $ |

10. **Attorney fees** *(enter here if contractual or statutory fees are fixed without necessity of a court determination; otherwise a noticed motion is required):* . . . . . . . . . . . . . . . . . . . . . . . . . . . . . 10. | $ |

11. **Models, blowups, and photocopies of exhibits** *(specify):* . . . . . . . . . . . . . . . . . . . . . . . . . 11. | $ |

12. **Court reporter fees** *(as established by statute)*

  a. *(Name of reporter):* _____ Fees: $ _____

  b. *(Name of reporter):* _____ Fees: $ _____

  c. ☐ Information about additional court reporter fees is contained in Attachment 12c.

                                         TOTAL  12. | $ |

13. **Other** *(specify):* . . . . . . . . . . . . . . . . . . . . . . . . . . . . . . . . . . . . . . . . . . . . . . . . . . . . 13. | $ |

**TOTAL COSTS** . . . . . . . . . . . . . . . . . . . . . . . . . . . . . . . . . . . . . . . . . . . . . . . . . . . . . . . $ _____

*(Additional information may be supplied on the reverse)*      Page _____ of _____

**MEMORANDUM OF COSTS (WORKSHEET)** *(Continued)*

1
2
3
4
5
6
7
8
9
10
11
12
13
14
15
16
17
18
19
20
21
22
23
24
25
26
27

Page _____ of _____

**RESERVED**

# REASONS FOR REJECTION OF
# PROVE-UP DOCUMENTS

## The Superior Court

JOHN A. CLARKE    I  I  I    NORTH HILL STREET ● LOS ANGELES ● CALIFORNIA 90012
EXECUTIVE OFFICER/CLERK

(213) 974-6271

Case No. _____

The Default Judgment Prove-up documents submitted to this office  on _____
are being returned for the following reason(s):

____ 1.　　Default(s) against Defendant(s) _____  _____
　　　　　　are not entered.  Contact Default Section Room 426, Courthouse at
　　　　　　(213) 974-7923 for information re:  entry of default.

____ 2.　　Additional Defendant(s) are named in Complaint and have timely
　　　　　　answered.  Resubmit with declaration(s) and/or Points and Authorities
　　　　　　for separate default judgment pursuant to Section 579 CCP or with
　　　　　　properly executed Request for Dismissal (clerk's Form 3) as to each
　　　　　　named defendant.

____ 3.　　Request for Dismissal (Form 3) has not been submitted as to fictitious
　　　　　　("Doe") defendants/unserved or non-answering defendants.

____ 4.　　Memorandum of Costs and Disbursements (Cost Bill) has not been
　　　　　　submitted/is incomplete/is not properly executed as follows:

　　　　　　_____.
　　　　　　Resubmit with properly executed cost bill.

____ 5.　　A cross-complaint has been filed in this action.  Resubmit with
　　　　　　declarations and/or points and authorities re:  propriety of separate
　　　　　　default judgment on complaint/cross-complaint.

____ 6.　　A brief summary of the case identifying the parties and the nature of
　　　　　　plaintiff's claim has not been submitted (See 388 CRC).

____ 7.　　Declarations in lieu of oral testimony pursuant to Section 585(d) CCP
　　　　　　have not been submitted/are not properly executed pursuant to
　　　　　　Section 2015.5 CCP/do not show: _____.
　　　　　　Resubmit with properly executed declarations(s).  (No hearing is
　　　　　　required).

(over)

_____ 8.   Exhibits have not been submitted/are unreadable/are not properly authenticated/original written obligation to pay money not submitted for cancellation per CRC 234/are voluminous and not properly indexed for use by the Court/other: _____.

_____ 9.   Proposed Judgment by Court After Default has not been submitted/is not the proper form/is not in triplicate/does not contain the following information: _____.
Forms may be obtained through www.lasuperiorcourt.org.

_____ 10.  Precise clause of contract allowing attorney's fees not stated per LASCR 9.15(f).   Basis for claiming attorney's fees not stated.

_____ 11.  Declaration Non-Military Status has not been submitted/is more than six months old.

_____ 12.  Documents submitted do not meet requirements.  Resubmit with documents properly captioned and containing pre-punched holes.  Each document is to have a Footer per CRC 201.

_____ 13.  Indicate how interest was computed.

_____ 14.  Submit Default Request form with the judgment to be entered portion completed.

After the above corrections have been made, please resubmit the file and all documents to Room 542.  If a hearing date is ordered by the Court, written notice will be mailed.  You will be notified when judgment has been granted or denied.

Please include stamped, addressed return envelopes for return of hearing notices and conformed copies of documents.  Be certain that the envelopes are large enough to contain the copies requested.  DO NOT include more than one copy of any document or pleading to be conformed or copies of documents already included (filed) in the court file.

OTHER:


Documents returned:   ___ via attorney service       ___ via U.S. Mail


_____              _____
     Date                                      Deputy Clerk

# CHECKLIST
# MOTION FOR RELIEF
# ("MISTAKE, INADVERTENCE, SURPRISE OR NEGLECT")

[*Ed. Note: This form or similar forms are used by many courts. Counsel should use this as a checklist in preparing a motion or opposition because it may raise factors of concern to the court. Declarations or points and authorities should be prepared to address each of the points on the checklist.*]

Discovery Cut-off: _____          Calendar: _____

Motion Cut-off: _____          Date: _____

Trial Date: _____          Notice: _____

**MOTION TO VACATE DEFAULT/DEFAULT JUDGMENT**
**(CCP § 473; 473.5; equity)**
**(CONFIDENTIAL COURT DOCUMENT WHEN COMPLETED)**

NAME OF MOVING PARTY: _____

NAME OF RESPONDING PARTY: _____

CORRECT ADDRESS IN PROOF OF SERVICE (CCP §§ 1013, 1013a) _____

21-DAY LAPSE (CCP § 1005): _____

RELIEF REQUESTED:   Vacate default jdm.   Vacate default entry   Permit pleading

| **CHRONOLOGY** | **TYPE OF SERVICE** |
|---|---|

Date SUMMONS served: _____          ❑ personal    ❑ substituted    ❑ other

Date ANSWER filed: _____          **PLACE OF SERVICE**

Date DEFAULT entered: _____          ❑ home ❑ business    ❑ _____

Date JUDGMENT entered: _____          ❑ Sufficient Declaration of Diligence
(at least 3 unsuccessful attempts)

Date MOTION herein filed: _____          ❑ Yes          ❑ No

Time from default to motion: _____

Judgment rendered by:          ❑ Court          ❑ Clerk

Judgment PROPER:          (Clerk judgment proper if liquidated damages in contract action and no security interest (Liberty Loan Corp. etc. v. Petersen (1972) 24 Cal.App.3d 915, 919))

Moving DECLARATIONS verified: _____

Is there CCP § 473.5 DECLARATION: _____          Verified: _____

Date when moving party first learned of case _____          Time elapsed _____

❑ Relief mandatory for attorney admission of fault _____
(The mandatory relief provision of Section 473, based upon an attorney affidavit of fault, applies to a dismissal that is akin to a default. Gotschall v. Daley (2002) 96 Cal.App.4th 479, 484 (inapplicable where attorney failed to follow statute on expert witness disclosure); Leader v. Health Industries of America, Inc. (2001) 89 Cal.App.4th 603, 618 (inapplicable where attorney failed to amend complaint within time ordered); Yeap v. Leake (1997) 60 Cal.App.4th 591, 601 (lawyer's failure to act timely); In re Marriage of Hock & Gordon-Hock (2000) 80 Cal.App.4th 1438, 1444 (counsel's failure to appear at trial). Section 473 does not permit an escape hatch from a discretionary dismissal based upon evaluations of factors. Graham v. Beers (1994) 30 Cal.App.4th 1656, 1661, modified 94 C.D.O.S. 9792 (summary judgment or judgment after trial); English v. IKON Business Solutions, Inc. (2001) 94 Cal. App. 4th 130, 138 (summary judgment); Ayala v. Southwest Leasing & Rental, Inc. (1992) 7 Cal.App.4th 40, 44).

❑ Reasons in declarations as to why moving party failed to timely answer or otherwise act, or received default sanction?

(Attorney negligence is not a basis for discretionary relief under Code of Civil Procedure Section 473. Pazderka v. Caballeros Dimas Alang, Inc. (1998) 62 Cal.App.4th 658, 672; Garcia v. Hejmadi (1997) 58 Cal.App.4th 674, 682.).

OPPOSITION:

| Re CCP § 473.5 | Equity | CCP § 473 |
|---|---|---|
| --Decl of no avoidance of serv. or inexcusable neglect | --Adeq. show of excuse, etc. | --Reasonable time |
| --Motion filed within reasonable time | --No laches | (6 months max.) |
|     (within 180 days of default or judgment | --Meritorious defense | --Proposed    pleading |
|     served or 2 years after judgment entered) | --Extrinsic fraud/mistake | --Attorney decl. re fault |
| --Proposed Pleading | --Lack of jurisdiction | --Excusable neglect etc. |
| --No actual notice until after default | --Improper summons service | |

RECOMMENDED RULING:

    ❏ GRANT

    ❏ DENY
        ❏ without PREJUDICE

    ❏ CONDITIONS _____

Rev. #1 2003

# ATTORNEY AFFIDAVIT OF FAULT
## (CCP §473(b))

```
 1   ....................................
     State Bar No. .................
 2   ...............................
     ...............................
 3   ...............................

 4

 5   Attorney for .................

 6

 7

 8          ........... COURT OF THE STATE OF CALIFORNIA

 9              COUNTY OF .........

10

11   ..........................  )    CASE NO. ....................
                                 )
12          Plaintiff,           )    Hearing: ...... (date) .......
                                 )    Dept. No. ...................
13   vs.                         )    Time: .......................
                                 )
14   ..........................  )    ATTORNEY DECLARATION
                                 )    (AFFIDAVIT) OF FAULT IN
15                               )    SUPPORT OF MOTION TO SET ASIDE
            Defendant.           )    DEFAULT JUDGMENT [CCP §473(b)]
16   _____)
```

17       I, the undersigned, declare as follows:

18       1.   I am the attorney for defendant ................ in this

19   action, and have personal knowledge of each fact stated herein.

20       2.   On ............, ....., a default judgment was entered in

21   this action against defendant ................................. .

22   Entry of said judgment was the result of my *(mistake, inadvertence,*

23   *surprise and/or neglect)* as more fully set forth below.

24       3.   Summons and complaint in this action were served on

25   defendant ................... on or about ..............., ...... .

26   A response was due on or before ..................., ...... .

27       4.   On ..........., ....., defendant retained me to represent

28   *(his/her)* interest in this action.

1

ATTORNEY AFFIDAVIT OF FAULT

1      5.    Notwithstanding the foregoing, I failed to file a respon-

2 sive pleading on behalf of defendant as follows: ............ *(set*

3 *forth facts supporting attorney mistake, inadvertence, surprise or*

4 *neglect)* ........... .

5      On ................, ......, I contacted plaintiff's attorney

6 and offered to pay the sum of $............, as and for reasonable

7 attorney fees and costs incurred by plaintiff in connection with

8 entry of the above default judgment. I also requested counsel to

9 stipulate to set aside said default judgment. However, plaintiff's

10 attorney refused such offer.

11      I declare under penalty of perjury under the laws of the State

12 of California that the foregoing is true and correct.

13 DATED: ................., ......

14                /s/_____

                     Declarant

15

16

17

18

19

20

21

22

23

24

25

26

27

28

2

ATTORNEY AFFIDAVIT OF FAULT

# CHAPTER 6

# PLEADINGS

## CONTENTS

Page

A. **INTRODUCTION** ....................................................... 6-1
  1. Single Form of Action ......................................... 6-1
  2. Limited Number of Pleadings ............................... 6-1
  3. Fact Pleading ..................................................... 6-1
  4. Official Forms .................................................... 6-1
    a. Complaints, answers and cross-complaints .............. 6-2
    b. Optional only ................................................. 6-2
  5. Role of Pleadings at Trial .................................... 6-2
    a. What constitutes "failure of proof" ...................... 6-2
    b. What constitutes "immaterial variance" ................ 6-3
    c. Policy to construe pleadings liberally .................... 6-3

B. **COMPLAINTS** ....................................................... 6-4
  1. Format Requirements—In General ....................... 6-4
    a. Official Form complaints .................................. 6-4
      (1) Multi-page forms .................................... 6-4
      (2) Hole punching ...................................... 6-4
    b. All other complaints ...................................... 6-4
      (1) Type size, paper size, pagination .............. 6-4
      (2) Line spacing and numbering ..................... 6-4
      (3) Page numbering and hole punching ............ 6-4
      (4) Footers ............................................... 6-4
      (5) First page layout ................................... 6-5
        (a) Attorney ...................................... 6-5
          1) Optional information .............. 6-5
        (b) Court ......................................... 6-6
        (c) Title of case ................................. 6-6
          1) Compare—other pleadings may use
            "short caption" ........................ 6-6
          2) Compare—motions, pleadings directed
            to cross-complaints ................... 6-7
        (d) Case number .............................. 6-7
        (e) Nature of pleading and action .......... 6-7
          1) Example ............................... 6-7
          2) Purpose ............................... 6-7
          3) Where Official Forms used ........ 6-7

         (f)  Limited civil cases .......................................... 6-7

            1)  Example ................................................. 6-8

            2)  Effect of failure to designate ................... 6-8

            3)  Reclassification by later pleading or stipulation ............................................... 6-8

         (g)  Causes of action numbered and identified ..... 6-9

         (h)  Footer ............................................................ 6-9

      (6)  Other format guidelines......................................... 6-9

      (7)  Additional papers required for filing .................... 6-10

         (a)  Civil case cover sheet .................................. 6-10

            1)  Purpose ................................................ 6-10

            2)  Service not required (except in complex cases) ................................................... 6-10

            3)  Not a substitute for local cover sheets .... 6-10

            4)  Effect of failure to comply ...................... 6-10

         (b)  Local rules requiring other papers generally preempted ................................................... 6-10

            1)  Compare—local civil cover sheets .......... 6-11

               a)  Certificate re district filing (Los Angeles Superior Court) ................. 6-11

            2)  Format requirements ............................. 6-11

    c.  Changes on face of complaint .................................. 6-11

    d.  Effect of format defects ............................................ 6-11

      (1)  Compare—violation of local rules ...................... 6-11

      (2)  Papers improperly rejected deemed filed ........... 6-12

2.  Designating Parties ......................................................... 6-12

    a.  Corporations .............................................................. 6-12

      (1)  Corporate plaintiffs—alleging "qualified to do business"............................................................. 6-12

         (a)  Official Forms ............................................... 6-12

         (b)  Purpose ....................................................... 6-12

         (c)  Application ................................................... 6-12.1

         (d)  Compare—element of plaintiff's case ........ 6-12.1

      (2)  Corporate defendants ....................................... 6-13

         (a)  Status uncertain or unknown ....................... 6-13

         (b)  Pleading corporate status waives right to challenge .................................................... 6-14

         (c)  Necessity of correct name and capacity ...................................................... 6-14

            1)  "DBA" not separate entity ...................... 6-14

         (d)  Recommended procedure ............................ 6-14

            1)  Caption ................................................. 6-15

            2)  Allegations in body of complaint ............. 6-15

               a)  *Caution—constructive knowledge* ......................................... 6-15

            3)  Amend complaint when status ascertained ........................................... 6-15

    b.  Partnerships ............................................................. 6-16

      (1)  Partnership (or other unincorporated association) as plaintiff....................................... 6-16

        (a) Caption ...................................................... 6-16

        (b) Allegations in body of complaint ................... 6-16

        (c) Fictitious name statute ................................. 6-17

            1) Not applicable to tort claims ................... 6-17

     (2) Partnership (or other unincorporated

        association) as defendant ................................ 6-17

        (a) Caption ...................................................... 6-18

        (b) Status uncertain or unknown ........................ 6-18

  c. Sole proprietor ("d.b.a.") ........................................... 6-18

     (1) As plaintiff .................................................... 6-18

        (a) Caption ...................................................... 6-18

        (b) Fictitious name statute ................................. 6-18

        (c) License status ............................................. 6-18

     (2) As defendant ................................................ 6-19

        (a) Status unknown or uncertain ........................ 6-19

  d. Persons acting in representative capacity ................. 6-19

     (1) Executor, administrator, trustee, receiver ........... 6-19

        (a) Compare—estate is nonentity and

           cannot sue ............................................... 6-19

     (2) Compare—guardian or guardian ad litem .......... 6-19

  e. "Doe" defendants ...................................................... 6-20

     (1) Plaintiff must be genuinely ignorant of

        defendant's identity or liability ........................... 6-20

        (a) Effect on statute of limitations ...................... 6-21

            1) Compare—ignorance of defendant's

                identity does not toll statute ................... 6-21

     (2) Caption ......................................................... 6-21

     (3) Allegations required in body of complaint .......... 6-21

        (a) Examples ................................................... 6-21

        (b) Compare ..................................................... 6-22

        (c) Charging allegations must run against

           "Doe" defendants ..................................... 6-22

     (4) Amend when identity ascertained ..................... 6-22

     (5) Service of process ......................................... 6-22

        (a) "Doe" status indicated on summons ............. 6-22

        (b) Proof of service requirements ...................... 6-23

        (c) Serving "Doe" defendant after statute

           of limitations has run ................................ 6-23

     (6) Limitation—no "sham" complaints ..................... 6-23

  f. Incomplete or erroneous designation ........................ 6-23

     (1) "Idem sonans" doctrine .................................... 6-23

     (2) Allegations in body of complaint may cure

        errors in caption ............................................. 6-23

  g. List of parties ........................................................... 6-24

3. Allegations re Venue ...................................................... 6-24

  a. Generally not required ............................................... 6-24

  b. Statutory exceptions ................................................. 6-24.1

     (1) Verified complaint or affidavit required .............. 6-24.1

  c. Official Forms .......................................................... 6-24.1

4. Alleging the Cause of Action ........................................... 6-24.2

a. Format rules ...........................................................6-24.2
   (1) Each cause of action numbered and labeled,
      and affected parties identified ..........................6-24.2
      (a) "Cause of action" vs. "count" ......................6-24.2
      (b) Comment ...................................................6-24.3
      (c) Definitions .................................................6-24.3
   (2) Nature of claim and parties affected ...............6-24.4
      (a) Remedy for noncompliance? ......................6-24.4
   (3) Paragraph numbering .....................................6-24.5
      (a) Compare—Official Forms ..........................6-24.5
b. Fact pleading required ...............................................6-24.5
   (1) Facts to be pleaded determined by
      substantive law.................................................6-24.5
   (2) Form of allegations—"ultimate facts"
      required .............................................................6-24.6
      (a) Distinguishing "ultimate facts" from
         "evidence" or "conclusions" ......................6-24.6
      (b) Exception—"common counts" ...................6-24.6
         1) Limitation ............................................6-24.7
         2) Complaint on "open book account".........6-25
            a) Not for balance due under express
               contracts ...........................................6-25
         3) Complaint "on account stated"...............6-25
            a) Statute of limitations.........................6-25
         4) Complaint "for money had and
            received".................................................6-25
         5) Complaint "for work and labor done" ......6-26
   (3) Consequence of improper fact pleading.............6-26
   (4) Fair notice as test ..........................................6-26
      (a) Negligence, product liability ..........................6-27
         1) Negligence per se ...............................6-27
         2) Causation ............................................6-27
            a) Limitation—where causation not
               readily inferred ...............................6-27
            b) Consider "Doe" defendants .............6-28
            c) Which of several defendants
               caused injury ...................................6-28
            d) Ethical limitation against joining
               every potential defendant .................6-29
      (b) Ownership....................................................6-29
      (c) Intent, malice ...............................................6-29
      (d) Contract provisions ......................................6-30
      (e) Contract conditions ......................................6-30
      (f) Statutory conditions ......................................6-31
   (5) Special pleading requirements .........................6-31
      (a) Fraud ...........................................................6-31
         1) Effect ...................................................6-32
            a) Application .......................................6-32
            b) Fraud by corporation .......................6-33
         2) Impact of Official Form complaint ..........6-33

3) Exception—defendant fully informed ......6-34
   a) Compare—matters unknown to
     either side .........................................6-34
4) Practical considerations...........................6-34
   a) Multiple misrepresentations .............6-35
(b) Negligent misrepresentation? ......................6-35
  1) Compare—stockholder wrongfully
    induced to refrain from selling stock .......6-35
(c) Agency or employment ...............................6-35
(d) Conspiracy .........................................6-36
  1) Limitation—illegal acts specially
    pleaded.............................................6-36
  2) Limitation—prior court order required
    for attorney-client conspiracy claim ........6-37
(e) Punitive damages claims .............................6-37
  1) Limited to tort actions ......................6-37
  2) Specific pleading required? ..................6-37
    a) Language approved .........................6-38
    b) Language disapproved .....................6-39
    c) Procedure for challenging
      punitives allegations .........................6-40
  3) Allegations required on punitives
    claim against employer .........................6-40
    a) Corporate employers .......................6-41
    b) Language approved .........................6-41
    c) Language disapproved .....................6-41
  4) Limitation—amount of punitives
    claim must not be alleged......................6-41
  5) Limitation—prior court order required
    for certain punitive damages claims .......6-42
(f) "Pleading around" defense disclosed on
   face of complaint....................................6-42
(g) Defendant's duty to control third persons to
   prevent injury to plaintiff .............................6-43
  1) Added requirements in suit against
    governmental entity ...............................6-43
  2) Claims against public entity common
    carrier ...............................................6-44
(h) Declaratory relief ...................................6-44
  1) Present controversy required..................6-45
  2) Pleading requirement ...........................6-45
  3) Need not be separately stated................6-45
  4) Limitation—relief unnecessary or
    improper .............................................6-45
(i) Compare—nonfraud tort claims .................6-46.1
(j) Compare—litigation expenses that are
   not recoverable as "costs" or "fees" ...........6-46.1
(k) Claims against public officers .................6-46.1
  1) Breach of official duty .......................6-46.2
(l) Governmental tort claims .....................6-46.2

c. Fact pleading under the Official Forms ................. 6-46.2
  (1) Unlawful detainer complaint complete in
     itself ................................................................ 6-46.2
  (2) Tort and contract complaints require
     attachments ..................................................... 6-46.2
    (a) Attachments approved by Judicial
       Council ........................................................ 6-46.2
      1) For personal injury, property damage,
         wrongful death complaints ................... 6-46.3
      2) For breach of contract complaints ....... 6-46.3
    (b) Attachments prepared by plaintiff's
       attorney ...................................................... 6-47
  (3) Attachments containing required ultimate
     facts ................................................................ 6-47
    (a) Cause of Action—Motor Vehicle .................. 6-47
    (b) Cause of Action—Product Liability .............. 6-47
  (4) Attachments requiring plaintiff to insert
     ultimate facts .................................................. 6-48
    (a) Cause of Action—Premises Liability ............ 6-48
      1) Insufficient without more ....................... 6-48
    (b) Cause of Action—Intentional Tort ............... 6-49
    (c) Cause of Action—General Negligence ......... 6-49
    (d) Exemplary Damages Attachment ................. 6-49
  (5) How to attack improperly executed Official
     Forms ............................................................... 6-50
    (a) Omitting facts essential to cause of action ... 6-50
    (b) Omitting facts NOT essential to state
       cause of action ........................................... 6-50
    (c) Checking too many boxes ........................... 6-50
d. Form of allegations ............................................. 6-50
  (1) Direct allegations required .............................. 6-50
  (2) Allegations on information and belief ............... 6-51
    (a) Traditional form ........................................... 6-51
    (b) Official Forms ............................................. 6-51
    (c) Important where pleading verified ................ 6-51
    (d) Limitations—presumptive or constructive
       knowledge ................................................... 6-51
    (e) *Caution—impact of CCP §128.7?* .............. 6-52
  (3) Incorporation by reference .............................. 6-52
    (a) Exhibits ...................................................... 6-52
      1) Effect of ambiguous terms ..................... 6-53
    (b) Allegations in other causes of action ........... 6-53
      1) Incorporating whole causes of action
        as creating uncertainty? ........................ 6-53
    (c) Other pleadings in same lawsuit .................. 6-54
    (d) Pleadings in different lawsuit ....................... 6-54
  (4) "On or about" allegations ................................ 6-54
e. Right to plead inconsistently or in the alternative ...... 6-54
  (1) Example ........................................................ 6-55
  (2) Limitation against pleading alternatively or
     inconsistently in same cause of action ............. 6-55

|  |  | (a) | How to attack | 6-55 |
| | (3) | | Limitation against pleading inconsistent FACTS in verified complaint | 6-55 |
| | | (a) | How to attack | 6-56 |
| f. | | | Limitation—election of remedies | 6-56 |
| g. | | | Limitation—rule against "splitting" single cause of action into separate lawsuits | 6-57 |
| | (1) | | What constitutes "same" cause of action | 6-57 |
| | (2) | | Application—same cause of action | 6-58 |
| | (3) | | Application—different causes of action | 6-59 |
| | (4) | | Construction defects? | 6-59 |
| | (5) | | Effect of prior declaratory relief judgment | 6-60 |
| | (6) | | How to attack "splitting" | 6-60 |

5. Joinder of Causes of Action ............................................................ 6-60
   a. No compulsory joinder ................................................................ 6-60
      (1) Risk of violating rule against "splitting" cause of
          action ...................................................................................... 6-61
      (2) Risk of collateral estoppel ................................................... 6-61
      (3) Court may order consolidation or coordination .... 6-61
   b. Permissive joinder of causes of action ................................... 6-62
      (1) Limitation where several defendants ................................ 6-62
      (2) Power of court to sever ......................................................... 6-62
6. Prayer for Relief ................................................................................. 6-62
   a. Amount must be stated ................................................................ 6-62
      (1) Attorney fees .......................................................................... 6-63
      (2) Prejudgment interest ............................................................. 6-63
          (a) Court's power to award without prayer .......... 6-63
      (3) Exception—no damages allegations in injury
          or death actions ....................................................................... 6-63
          (a) Purpose ............................................................................ 6-64
          (b) Application .................................................................... 6-64
          (c) Challenge by motion to strike ............................... 6-64
          (d) Procedure for notice to defendant .................... 6-64
              1) Time for furnishing statement .................. 6-64
              2) Content of statement ................................... 6-65
              3) Not filed ............................................................... 6-65
              4) Enforcing response ....................................... 6-65
          (e) Special requirements upon default ............... 6-65
          (f) Not a limit on recovery in nondefault
              cases ....................................................................... 6-65
      (4) Exception—no allegations as to amount of
          punitive damages ................................................................... 6-66
          (a) Purpose ............................................................................ 6-66
          (b) Procedure for notice to defendant ................... 6-66
   b. Effect of prayer in contested cases ......................................... 6-66
      (1) Determines subject matter jurisdiction ................ 6-66
      (2) Determines right to jury trial ............................................. 6-66
      (3) Not a limit on judgment ....................................................... 6-66
          (a) Court may grant any relief "embraced
              within the issue" .......................................................... 6-66

          (b)  Damage allegations no limit on judgment ..... 6-67
              1)   Compare—where defendant *fails to
                   appear* at trial .......................................... 6-67
          (c)  Compare—complaint containing remission
               clause (limited civil cases) ........................... 6-67
    c.   Effect of prayer in default cases ........................... 6-67
    d.   Effect of improper prayer ..................................... 6-68
       (1)  Not ground for demurrer ..................................... 6-68
       (2)  Ground for motion to strike ................................ 6-68
  7.  Subscription ...................................................... 6-68
    a.   Effect of omission .............................................. 6-68
    b.   Signature as certification of merits .......................... 6-68
       (1)  Effective 1995 ............................................... 6-68.1
       (2)  Sanctions .................................................... 6-68.1
  8.  Verification ...................................................... 6-68.1
    a.   Required in a few cases ....................................... 6-68.1
       (1)  Effect of failure to verify ................................... 6-68.1
          (a)  Compare ................................................ 6-68.1
          (b)  Curing by amendment ................................. 6-68.2
       (2)  Defects in verification ....................................... 6-68.2
       (3)  Public entities exempt ....................................... 6-68.2
    b.   Optional in other cases ....................................... 6-68.2
       (1)  Advantages .................................................. 6-68.2
       (2)  Disadvantages .............................................. 6-68.3
    c.   Persons who may verify complaint .......................... 6-68.4
       (1)  Information and belief ....................................... 6-68.4
       (2)  Attorney verification discouraged ...................... 6-68.4
    d.   Verification may be executed anywhere ................. 6-68.5
  9.  Prior Court Order Required for Certain Claims ............ 6-68.5
    a.   Punitive damages claims against health care
       providers ....................................................... 6-68.5
       (1)  "Health care provider" ..................................... 6-68.5
          (a)  Application ............................................. 6-68.6
          (b)  Compare—elder care custodian ................. 6-68.6
       (2)  Actions "arising out of professional
          negligence" ................................................ 6-68.6
          (a)  Application ............................................. 6-68.7
          (b)  Includes claims by nonpatients ................. 6-70
       (3)  Procedure to add punitives claim ...................... 6-70
          (a)  Evidentiary showing ................................ 6-70
       (4)  Time limit on motion to amend ......................... 6-70
          (a)  "Date matter first set for trial" ...................... 6-70
          (b)  Effect of trial continuance ......................... 6-70.1
          (c)  Exception for priority cases ....................... 6-70.1
          (d)  Exception where trial set within 9 months
             after filing ............................................ 6-70.1
          (e)  Court's discretion to permit untimely
             amendment ........................................... 6-70.1
              1)   Showing required ............................... 6-70.1
       (5)  "Substantial probability" of success
          required ...................................................... 6-70.2

Rev. #1 2004

        (a) How determined ........................................ 6-70.2
        (b) No weighing of evidence ........................... 6-70.2
    (6) Effect ................................................................ 6-70.3
        (a) Opportunity to amend? ............................. 6-70.3
    (7) Challenging defect ......................................... 6-70.3
        (a) Waiver ....................................................... 6-70.3
b.  Punitive damages claims against religious
    corporation ............................................................. 6-70.4
    (1) Claims of any type ......................................... 6-70.4
    (2) Procedure to add punitives claim ..................... 6-70.4
        (a) Earlier denial no bar to renewed motion .... 6-70.4
    (3) Requirement that plaintiff "substantiate"
        claim............................................................. 6-70.4
        (a) "Substantiates".......................................... 6-70.4
        (b) No weighing of evidence ........................... 6-70.5
c.  Claim against attorney for conspiracy with client .... 6-70.5
    (1) Purpose ......................................................... 6-70.5
    (2) Effect .............................................................. 6-70.5
    (3) Complaints affected ....................................... 6-70.5
        (a) Application ................................................. 6-70.6
        (b) Exceptions ................................................ 6-70.6
            1) Independent legal duty owed to
                plaintiff ..................................................... 6-70.7
            2) Acts beyond legal representation for
                attorney's own financial gain ................. 6-71
    (4) Procedure ...................................................... 6-71
        (a) "Verified petition" ........................................ 6-71
        (b) Timeliness ................................................. 6-72
            1) Laches as limitation ............................... 6-72
        (c) Service and response ............................... 6-72
        (d) Compare—statute of limitations tolled ......... 6-72
    (5) Requirement that plaintiff establish
        "reasonable probability" of success ..................... 6-72
        (a) "Reasonable probability" ............................. 6-72
        (b) No weighing of evidence ............................. 6-73
    (6) Order permissive or mandatory?...................... 6-73
    (7) Effect of failure to obtain order ....................... 6-73
        (a) Preanswer challenge by attorney charged
            with conspiracy ........................................... 6-73
        (b) Waiver of defense .................................... 6-74
    (8) Appellate review............................................. 6-74
        (a) Effect of failure to appeal denial ................. 6-74
d.  Negligence claims against officers, directors of
    nonprofit corporations............................................. 6-74
    (1) Complaints affected ....................................... 6-75
        (a) Exceptions and limitations ......................... 6-75
    (2) Procedure ...................................................... 6-75
    (3) Requirement that evidence "substantiate"
        claim............................................................. 6-75
    (4) Statute of limitations tolled ............................. 6-75
    (5) Effect on discovery? ....................................... 6-76

10. Filing Fee Considerations .............................................6-76

**C. ANSWER** ................................................................6-76
  1. Function ...........................................................6-76
  2. Time for Filing Answer ....................................6-76
    a. Petition to compel arbitration in lieu of answer .......6-76.1
    b. Filing fee for each defendant ..................................6-76.1
  3. Format ............................................................6-76.1
    a. Official Form answers satisfy format rules .............6-76.1
    b. Other answers must comply with the following
      rules ...........................................................6-77
      (1) Type size, paper size, pagination, etc. ...............6-77
      (2) First page requirements ...................................6-77
      (3) Footers ...................................................6-77
      (4) Body of answer .............................................6-77
        (a) Response to each cause of action of
          complaint ...............................................6-77
        (b) Defenses or objections to entire
          complaint ...............................................6-78
        (c) Incorporating by reference ...........................6-78
  4. Effective Denials ............................................6-79
    a. Failure to deny constitutes admission ......................6-79
      (1) Material vs. immaterial allegations .....................6-79
      (2) Effect of admission ........................................6-79
    b. General vs. specific denials .................................6-80
      (1) General denial .............................................6-80
        (a) Permitted if complaint unverified ...................6-80
          1) "Material" vs. "immaterial" allegations .....6-80
          2) Ineffective to raise negotiable
            instrument forgery defense ....................6-80
          3) Impact of CCP §128.7? ...........................6-80
        (b) Not permitted if complaint verified ...............6-80
          1) Exception—limited civil cases ...............6-81
          2) Special rule for third party collection
            cases .....................................................6-81
          3) Special rule in actions involving
            $1,000 or less ...............................6-81
      (2) Specific denial .............................................6-82
        (a) Denial by parts ....................................6-82
        (b) Factual denials ....................................6-82
    c. "Negative pregnants"—and how to avoid them .......6-82.1
      (1) Examples .................................................6-83
        (a) Denials in the conjunctive ...........................6-83
        (b) Denials of specifics ................................6-83
        (c) Denials of amounts, damages .....................6-83
      (2) No "negative pregnant" where general
        denial or denial by parts used ...........................6-83
    d. Positive vs. nonpositive denials (information and
      belief) ...........................................................6-84
      (1) Denial based on information and belief .............6-84
      (2) Denial for lack of information or belief .................6-85

Rev. #1 2004

(3) Limitations—presumptive or constructive knowledge .................................................6-85

5. "New Matter" ................................................................6-85
   a. Affirmative defenses ...............................................6-86
     (1) Determined by substantive law .........................6-86
     (2) Application ........................................................6-86
       (a) Tort actions ...............................................6-86
         1) Compare—matters negating essential allegation of complaint ...........................6-87
         2) Workers' compensation as exclusive remedy for work-related injury ...............6-87
       (b) Contract actions ........................................6-87
         1) Compare—failure of conditions ..............6-88
         2) Promissory note actions .........................6-88
         3) Compare—illegality ...............................6-88
         4) Compare—causation ..............................6-89
       (c) Unlawful detainer cases .............................6-89
       (d) Set-offs .......................................................6-89
         1) Cross-demands for money ....................6-90
         2) Exception where complaint based on common counts .......................................6-90
         3) Compare—unrelated debts ...................6-91
         4) Special rule on comparative fault defense to action by condo owners' association ..............................................6-91
           a) Association need not be party ..........6-92
       (e) Res judicata ...............................................6-92
         1) Compare—collateral estoppel ...............6-92
       (f) Judicial estoppel ........................................6-92
       (g) Privilege ....................................................6-93
       (h) Agreement to arbitrate dispute ...................6-93
       (i) Facts constituting both defense and ground for affirmative relief .......................6-94
     (3) Statute of limitations no bar to affirmative defenses.................................................................6-94
     (4) Pleading requirements .....................................6-94
       (a) Fact pleading required ................................6-94
         1) Official Forms .........................................6-95
           a) Unlawful detainer ............................6-95
           b) Contract and tort actions .................6-95
         2) Exception—statute of limitations ...........6-95
           a) Narrowly interpreted.......................6-96
       (b) Right to plead inconsistent defenses ...........6-96
       (c) Separately stated......................................6-97
     (5) Challenging inadequate pleading ......................6-97
       (a) Waiver ......................................................6-97
     (6) Effect of failure to plead ..................................6-97
       (a) Exception—lack of subject matter jurisdiction.................................................6-97
       (b) Objection may be waived ...........................6-97

    b.  Pleas in abatement............................................6-98
    c.  New matter deemed controverted by plaintiff ...........6-98
        (1) Effect.................................................6-98
        (2) Examples ............................................6-98
        (3) Exception—replication permitted in mandamus
            or prohibition .......................................6-99
  6.  Prayer .............................................................6-99
    a.  Official Forms ............................................6-99
    b.  No affirmative relief ....................................6-99
    c.  Attorney fees ............................................6-99
  7.  Subscription ...................................................6-100
  8.  Verification ....................................................6-100
    a.  Exceptions ...............................................6-100
        (1) Limited civil cases ...............................6-100
        (2) Actions against public entity or official .............6-100
        (3) Compare—defendant sued by public entity
            must verify answer, even though complaint not
            verified .............................................6-100
    b.  Who may verify ..........................................6-100.1
        (1) Caution—attorney verification ......................6-100.1
    c.  How to attack failure to verify ...............6-100.1
        (1) Objection waived by delay until trial .................6-101
    d.  Verification and self-incrimination ...........6-101
    e.  Verification and attorney-client privilege .................6-101
  9.  Filing and Service .............................................6-101

**D. CROSS-COMPLAINT** .............................................6-101
  1.  General Considerations .....................................6-101
    a.  Function .................................................6-101
    b.  Who may file............................................6-102
    c.  Cross-complaint as independent action .................6-102
        (1) Not affected by dismissal of complaint .............6-102
        (2) Discovery admissions ...............................6-102
        (3) Compare—collateral estoppel .........................6-102
  2.  Cross-Complaint Against Plaintiff—Permissive vs.
    Compulsory ..................................................6-103
    a.  Always permissive—no subject matter relationship
       required .................................................6-103
        (1) Exceptions .........................................6-103
        (2) Court may sever ....................................6-103
    b.  Compulsory if related to plaintiff's complaint ...........6-103
        (1) "Related cause of action" ..........................6-103
            (a) Test ...........................................6-104
        (2) Existing at time answer filed.......................6-104
        (3) Effect of failure to plead .........................6-105
            (a) Relief granted ................................6-105
                1) Discretion to refuse? ...........................6-105
            (b) After judgment, recovery on unpleaded
                "related" claim barred .............................6-105
        (4) Exceptions .........................................6-105

Rev. #1 2004

(5) Special rule limits cross-complaints for
    indemnity against condo owners' association ...6-107
Tactical Considerations ...............................................6-107
3. Cross-Complaints Against Other Parties—When
   Permitted .................................................................6-108
   a. Subject matter relationship required ......................6-108
     (1) Application .....................................................6-109
       (a) Same transaction or series of
          transactions ......................................6-109
       (b) Property .....................................................6-109
     (2) Equitable indemnity cross-complaints ..............6-109
       (a) Limitation—attorney sued for malpractice
          may not cross-complain against
          successor...................................................6-110
          1) Rationale .............................................6-110
          2) Compare—malpractice indemnity
            from co-counsel ...................................6-110
       (b) Unfairness as limitation..............................6-111
          1) Apportionment of liability not
            necessarily unfair...............................6-111
       (c) Limitation on indemnity claims against
          condo owners' association ........................6-111
       (d) Limitation on indemnity claims against
          plaintiff's employer .................................6-111
   b. Joinder of other claims permitted ...........................6-112
   c. Joinder of other parties permitted .........................6-112
   d. Court may sever ...................................................6-112
   e. Compare—no mandatory third-party cross-
     complaints ...........................................................6-112
4. Drafting the Cross-Complaint .....................................6-113
   a. Separate pleading ...............................................6-113
   b. Format................................................................6-113
     (1) Caption.............................................................6-113
     (2) Footers .............................................................6-113
   c. Official Forms .......................................................6-113
     (1) Contract actions ...............................................6-114
     (2) Personal injury, property damage, wrongful
       death .............................................................6-114
5. Filing the Cross-Complaint ..........................................6-114
   a. Right to file against plaintiff or cross-
     complainant at time of answer ..............................6-114
   b. Right to file against third parties until first trial
     date ....................................................................6-114
     (1) Trial date vacated .............................................6-114
   c. When leave of court required ................................6-114
     (1) Limitations .......................................................6-115
       (a) No cross-complaint after entry of
          judgment ..................................................6-115
       (b) No cross-complaint *by plaintiff*
          whose complaint dismissed for failure
          to prosecute .............................................6-115

        (c) No cross-complaint for malicious
            prosecution of main action ........................ 6-115
    (2) Noticed motion procedure ............................ 6-116
        (a) Moving papers ...................................... 6-116
    (3) Showing required .......................................... 6-116
    (4) Judicial policy ............................................... 6-116
        (a) Leave to file compulsory cross-
            complaint ........................................... 6-116
        (b) Leave to file permissive cross-
            complaint against plaintiff ................. 6-116
        (c) Greater showing required for cross-
            complaints against others .......................... 6-116
        (d) Effect of trial setting ......................... 6-116.1
        (e) Conditions imposed on granting leave ..... 6-116.1
  6. Service of Cross-Complaint ................................. 6-116.1
    a. Existing parties served by mail ............................. 6-116.1
    b. New parties must be served with summons
       and prior pleadings ............................................. 6-116.1
    c. Proof of service requirements ............................ 6-116.2
    (1) Court may extend time .................................... 6-116.2
  7. Responsive Pleading Required .................................... 6-116.2
    a. "Special answer" permitted ................................... 6-116.2
    b. Cross-complaint to cross-complaint ......................... 6-117
    (1) Against new parties; subject matter
        relationship required ...................................... 6-117
    (2) Against cross-complainant; may be
        compulsory .................................................... 6-117
    (3) "Daisy-chain" pleading? ................................. 6-118
  8. Cross-Complaint Requiring Reclassification or
    Transfer ............................................................... 6-118
  9. Effect of Statute of Limitations ................................ 6-118
    a. Claim already time-barred before action filed .......... 6-118
    (1) Example ....................................................... 6-118
    (2) Money demands "deemed compensated" ......... 6-118
        (a) May be asserted by answer ...................... 6-118
        (b) Example ............................................... 6-118
        (c) Equitable limitations? .............................. 6-119
    b. Claim alive when action filed .............................. 6-119
    (1) Compulsory cross-complaint against
        plaintiff; "relation back" doctrine ...................... 6-119
        (a) Rationale ............................................. 6-119
        (b) Example ............................................... 6-119
        (c) Limited to compulsory cross-complaints ..... 6-120
           1) No tolling for independent action .......... 6-120
        (d) May be amended to allege different
           injuries ............................................... 6-120
    (2) Cross-complaint against other parties ............. 6-120
    (3) Special rule—contractor vs. subcontractor ........ 6-121
**E. AMENDED AND SUPPLEMENTAL PLEADINGS** ............. 6-121
  1. Amendments as a Matter of Right ................................ 6-121

a.  Amendment of complaint or cross-complaint ..........6-121
    (1) May add new parties .........................................6-122
    (2) Procedure .........................................................6-122
    (3) Service of amendment .......................................6-122
        (a) Personal service required if defendant
            has not appeared .........................................6-122
b.  Amendment of answer.............................................6-123
2.  Amendments Requiring Leave of Court.........................6-123
a.  Amendments to substitute defendant's true
    name for "Doe" ........................................................6-123
    (1) Procedure .........................................................6-123
        (a) Application to amend .................................6-123
        (b) Leave routinely granted ex parte ...............6-123
        (c) Service of amendment not required............6-123
    (2) Effect of failure to comply ................................6-124
        (a) Cured by amendment prior to judgment .....6-124
    (3) Compare—special procedures in childhood
        sexual abuse actions .........................................6-124
    (4) Identity unknown when complaint filed? ............6-124
b.  Ex parte amendments to add or delete parties .......6-125
    (1) Nature of mistakes correctable..........................6-125
    (2) Caution—effect of statute of limitations ...........6-125
    (3) Procedure for ex parte amendments .................6-125
        (a) Amendment to pleading vs. amended
            pleading ......................................................6-125
            1) Amendment on face of pleading ...........6-125
            2) Amendment to pleading .......................6-125
            3) Amended pleading ...............................6-126
                a) Strong judicial preference .............6-126
                b) Caption.............................................6-126
        (b) Application for court order............................6-126
        (c) Ex parte order ............................................6-127
        (d) Service of copies ........................................6-127
c.  Amendments after demurrer sustained or motion
    to strike granted......................................................6-127
    (1) Procedure .........................................................6-127
    (2) Amended pleading rather than amendment ......6-127
    (3) Service of amended or new pleading.................6-128
    (4) Scope of permissible amendment......................6-128
d.  Amendments on noticed motion ..............................6-128
    (1) Discretion of court ............................................6-129
    (2) Factors affecting court's exercise of
        discretion ...........................................................6-129
        (a) Policy favoring amendment.........................6-129
            1) Denial rarely justified ...........................6-129
        (b) Nature of proposed amendment .................6-129
            1) Caution—statute of limitations
               problems...............................................6-130
            2) Caution—actions against public
               entities .................................................6-130
            3) Compare—amended answers .............6-130

(c) Validity of proposed amendment ...............6-130
   1) Failure to state cause of action or
      defense ................................................6-130
   2) Sham amendments .............................6-131
(d) Proximity to trial or during trial ...................6-132
   1) Loss of "at issue" status if leave
      granted ................................................6-132
   2) P's willingness to postpone trial............6-132
   3) Same policy under "fast track"
      rules .....................................................6-133
(e) Effect of prejudicial delay in seeking
   amendment.................................................6-133
   1) What constitutes "prejudice" to
      opposing party .....................................6-133
   2) Absent prejudice, delay alone not
      ground for denial..................................6-134
(f) Court may impose conditions .....................6-135
(3) Limitation—court order required for
amendments adding punitive damage
claims in medical malpractice actions ...............6-135
(4) Limitation—no amendment of SLAPP
complaint if free speech connection shown........6-135
(5) Procedure—noticed motion for leave to
amend .................................................................6-135
Moving papers required ....................................6-136
(a) Notice of motion.............................................6-136
(b) Copy of proposed amended pleading .........6-137
   1) Amended pleading vs. amendments
      to pleadings .........................................6-137
(c) Memorandum of points and authorities ......6-137
(d) Declaration....................................................6-137
(e) Proposed order granting leave to
amend............................................................6-138
(6) Filing of amended pleading ...............................6-138
(7) Service of amended pleading ............................6-138
(a) Personal service on defendants who
have not appeared .........................................6-139
e. Amendments to conform to proof at trial ................6-139
(1) Factors considered ..............................................6-139
(2) Extent to which issues tried ...............................6-139
3. New Round of Pleadings ...........................................6-140
a. Effect of failure to respond to amended
complaint ...................................................................6-140
(1) Answer required where substantive changes
made ......................................................................6-140
(2) No answer required where no substantive
changes .................................................................6-140
(a) "Immaterial" corrections ...............................6-140
(b) Changes affecting other defendants ..........6-141
(c) Changes in damage allegations ................6-141

          1)  Compare—as ground for "opening up" default ................................................. 6-141
  b.  Stipulations excusing answer ................................. 6-141
  c.  Defaults "opened" ...................................................... 6-141
     (1)  Personal service required on defendants in default ......................................................... 6-142
     (2)  What constitutes "substantive changes" ............ 6-142
  d.  Effect on trial setting ................................................ 6-142
4.  Amended Pleading Supersedes Original ....................... 6-142
  a.  Limitation—former pleading as evidence at trial ................................................................................ 6-142.1
  b.  Limitation—effect of contradicting former pleading ...................................................................... 6-142.1
  c.  Limitation—effect of omitting harmful facts alleged in former pleading ..................................... 6-142.1
     (1)  Example ......................................................... 6-142.1
     (2)  Verified vs. unverified complaints ................... 6-142.2
     (3)  Compare—omissions immaterial to amended claim or defense ............................. 6-142.2
     (4)  Compare—inconsistent legal theories .......... 6-142.2
  d.  Effect of dropping defendant ................................. 6-142.3
     (1)  Rejoining dropped defendant ....................... 6-142.3
5.  "Relation Back" Doctrine ............................................... 6-142.3
  a.  How issue arises ...................................................... 6-142.3
  b.  Requirements for "relation back" effect ................ 6-142.3
     (1)  "Same general set of facts" ........................... 6-142.4
     (2)  "Same injury" .................................................. 6-143
        (a)  Application .............................................. 6-143
        (b)  Compare—different rule as to compulsory cross-complaints against plaintiff ............... 6-144
     (3)  "Same accident" (same offending instrumentality) ......................................... 6-144
        (a)  Application .............................................. 6-145
        (b)  Compare—same "chain of causation" ......... 6-145
     (4)  Compare—new defendants ............................. 6-146
     (5)  Compare—substitution of plaintiffs ................. 6-146
  c.  Additional requirements in amending to include "Doe" defendants after statute has run ........ 6-146
     (1)  Statute of limitations extended by commencing action against "Doe" ................... 6-147
        (a)  Impact .................................................... 6-147
        (b)  Broad application ................................... 6-147
        (c)  Court's discretion to deny leave .................. 6-148
     (2)  Statute also tolled as to amended claims ......... 6-148
        (a)  Example .................................................. 6-148
        (b)  Impact .................................................... 6-148
     (3)  Requirement that original complaint state claim against "Doe" defendants ..................... 6-148
        (a)  Effect of failure to include "Doe" defendants .............................................. 6-149

        (b) Defective "Doe" allegations ........................ 6-149
        (c) Defective substitution of "Doe" .................. 6-149
    (4) Requirement that plaintiff be "genuinely
        ignorant" .................................................................. 6-149
        (a) Test is "actual knowledge" .......................... 6-150
            1) Negligence in discovering facts
                immaterial .............................................. 6-150
            2) No constructive notice .......................... 6-150
            3) Impact on statute of limitations ............. 6-151
        (b) Cases where relation-back effect given ...... 6-151
            1) Ignorance of identity ............................. 6-151
            2) Ignorance of existence ......................... 6-151
            3) Ignorance of facts creating liability ....... 6-152
                a) Dismissed defendant brought back
                    into suit ............................................ 6-152
            4) Developments in the law creating
                basis for recovery .............................. 6-152.1
            5) Delay not prejudicial to defendant ........ 6-153
        (c) Cases where relation-back effect denied .... 6-153
            1) Plaintiff knew identity of "Doe"
                when original complaint filed ................ 6-153
    (5) Laches as limitation ......................................... 6-154
        (a) Delay alone insufficient ............................... 6-154
    (6) Exception—claims against public entities ......... 6-155
        (a) Claims against public employees ................ 6-155
    (7) Cross-refer—dismissal for delay in service of
        summons ........................................................... 6-155
  d. Adding NEW defendant after statute has run ......... 6-155
    (1) Example ............................................................ 6-156
    (2) Defendant previously dismissed ....................... 6-156
    (3) Compare—correcting misnomers ...................... 6-156
    (4) Estoppel exception—entities with similar
        names ................................................................ 6-157
  e. Adding new PLAINTIFFS after statute has run? ..... 6-157
    (1) Application—permissible amendments ............. 6-158
    (2) Application—impermissible amendments ......... 6-158
    (3) Adding professional corporation after statute
        has run ............................................................. 6-159
6. Supplemental Pleadings ................................................. 6-159
  a. Function ................................................................... 6-159
    (1) Compare—amended pleadings ........................ 6-159
        (a) Example ....................................................... 6-159
        (b) Title not controlling ..................................... 6-159
    (2) Does not replace original pleading ................... 6-160
        (a) Compare—second pleading filed
            without leave of court .................................. 6-160
    (3) Cannot allege "new" cause of action or
        defense ............................................................. 6-160
        (a) Comment ..................................................... 6-160
        (b) Cannot "cure" premature lawsuit ................ 6-161

    (4) "Relation back" for statute of limitation
       purposes? ..........................................................6-161
       (a) View denying "relation back" .......................6-161
       (b) View allowing "relation back" ......................6-162
  b. Procedure ................................................................6-163
    (1) Exception—paternity and child support
       claims ..............................................................6-163
    (2) Caption................................................................6-163
    (3) Filing, summons and service? .........................6-163
    (4) Responsive pleadings .....................................6-164
  c. Discretion of court ...................................................6-164

## FORMS

- Official Form Complaint: Personal Injury, Property
  Damage, Wrongful Death Actions .........................................6-165
- Official Form Cause of Action: Motor Vehicle .......................6-168
- Official Form Cause of Action: General Negligence .............6-169
- Official Form Cause of Action: Intentional Tort ....................6-170
- Official Form Cause of Action: Premises Liability ................6-171
- Official Form Cause of Action: Products Liability .................6-172
- Official Form: Exemplary Damages Attachment ...................6-173
- Official Form Cross-Complaint: Personal Injury, Property
  Damage, Wrongful Death Actions .........................................6-174
- Official Form Answer: Personal Injury, Property Damage,
  Wrongful Death Actions .........................................................6-177
- Official Form Complaint and Cross-Complaint: Contract
  Actions ...................................................................................6-179
- Official Form Cause of Action: Breach of Contract..............6-181
- Official Form Cause of Action: Common Counts..................6-182
- Official Form Cause of Action: Fraud ...................................6-183
- Official Form Answer: Contract .............................................6-185
- Official Form Complaint: Unlawful Detainer .........................6-187
- Official Form Answer: Unlawful Detainer..............................6-189
- Attachment to Judicial Council Form.....................................6-191
- Complaint: First Page Format ...............................................6-192
- Civil Case Cover Sheet .......................................................6-192.1
- Civil Case Cover Sheet Addendum and Statement of
  Location (Los Angeles Superior Court) ...............................6-192.3
- Sample Cause of Action Not Covered by Official Forms ......6-193
- Request for Statement of Damages .....................................6-195
- Statement of Damages .........................................................6-196
- Verification ............................................................................6-198
- General Denial ......................................................................6-199
- Notice of Motion for Leave to File Cross-Complaint;
  Declaration and Points and Authorities in Support..............6-201
- Amendment to Complaint to Substitute True Name of
  "Doe" Defendant (Los Angeles Superior Court) ..................6-207
- Application and Order for Amendment to Complaint............6-209
- Amendment to Complaint ......................................................6-212
- Notice of Motion for Leave to File Amended Complaint;
  Declaration and Points and Authorities in Support..............6-213

**RESERVED**

# PLEADINGS

## A. INTRODUCTION

[6:1] California is a code pleading state. Originally, the code rules were rather restrictive because the parties had to rely on the pleadings alone to prepare for trial. There were rigid limits on how various claims had to be pleaded, what claims could be joined in the same lawsuit, what amendments would be permitted, etc.

Today, pleadings occupy a far lesser role in civil litigation. Indeed, the California Supreme Court has stated: "Any rule that penalizes a plaintiff for the mere form in which the pleadings are cast is inherently unfair and *deserves to be discarded.*" [*Barrington v. A.H. Robins Co.* (1985) 39 C3d 146, 157, 216 CR 405, 412 (emphasis added)]

As a result, California's pleading rules today are quite liberal, and have the following unique characteristics:

1.  [6:2] **Single Form of Action:** "There is in this state but one form of civil action for the enforcement or protection of private rights and the redress or prevention of private wrongs." [CCP §307]

    This is one of the basic characteristics of code pleading: The complaint may join causes of action of any kind—tort, contract, property, etc.—in a single lawsuit. And, it may pursue both legal and equitable remedies at the same time.

2.  [6:3] **Limited Number of Pleadings:** The pleadings allowed in superior court civil actions are "complaints, demurrers, answers and cross-complaints." [CCP §422.10] (The pleadings in limited civil cases are the same except that no special demurrers are allowed; CCP §92, ¶7:38.)

3.  [6:4] **Fact Pleading:** "A complaint or cross-complaint shall contain . . . a statement of the *facts* constituting the *cause of action* in ordinary and concise language." [CCP §425.10]

    This requirement is discussed in detail, ¶6:120 ff. Suffice it to note at this point that fact pleading is unique to code pleading. It requires more precision and detail than is required in "notice pleading" jurisdictions—the federal courts, for example. (As a practical matter, however, lawyers usually plead a case the same way in federal or California courts, except for special allegations required in federal court—e.g., federal jurisdiction.)

4.  [6:5] **Official Forms:** To further simplify the pleading process, the Legislature directed the Judicial Council to draft offi-

cial forms "in nontechnical language" for use in the most common civil actions:

- Personal Injury;
- Property Damage;
- Wrongful Death;
- Breach of Contract;
- Fraud; and
- Unlawful Detainer. [CCP §425.12]

a. **[6:6]** **Complaints, answers and cross-complaints:** Official Forms are now available for complaints, answers and cross-complaints in the above actions; and for various causes of action to be attached to the complaint or cross-complaint (*see ¶6:200 ff.*).

(1) **FORMS:** Official Form Complaints, Answers, Cross-Complaints and Attachments, *see Forms 6:A through 6:P.*

b. **[6:7]** **Optional only:** Use of the Official Forms is optional, not mandatory. [CCP §425.12]

5. **[6:8]** **Role of Pleadings at Trial:** The pleadings are supposed to define the issues to be tried. Therefore, if a party offers evidence on an issue not pleaded, the opposing party may object for lack of *relevance* (Ev.C. §350). The court, however, may grant leave to amend the pleadings, even at trial (*see ¶6:685*).

Moreover, even if no objection is raised, recovery may be barred for *failure of proof* (see below). On the other hand, "immaterial variances" between the pleadings and proof can be disregarded; or the court may order the pleadings amended to conform to the proof at trial. [See CCP §§469-471]

a. **[6:9]** **What constitutes "failure of proof":** "Where a party alleges facts amounting to a certain cause of action and the evidence (at trial) sets forth an entirely separate set of facts constituting an *entirely different cause of action* from the one pled, the result is not an immaterial variance but a failure of proof." [*Fineberg v. Niekerk* (1985) 175 CA3d 935, 939, 221 CR 106, 107-108]

"If the action be for a libel or personal tort, the court cannot order in the case specific performance of a contract. If the action be for the possession of real property, the court is powerless to admit in the case the probate of a will . . . The judgments mentioned, given in the cases supposed, would not be merely erroneous, they would be absolutely void; because the court in rendering them would transcend the limits of its authority in those cases." [*Tokio Marine & Fire Ins. Corp. v. Western Pac. Roofing Corp.* (1999) 75 CA4th 110, 122, 89 CR2d 1, 9 (internal quotes omitted)]

b. **[6:10]** **What constitutes "immaterial variance":** However, "no variance between the allegation in a pleading and the proof is deemed to be material, unless it has *actually misled the adverse party to his prejudice* in maintaining his action or defense upon the merits . . ." [CCP §469 (emphasis added)]

"It has long been settled law that where (1) a case is tried on the merits and (2) the issues are thoroughly explored during the course of the trial, and (3) the theory of the trial is well known to court and counsel, the fact that some of the issues were not pleaded does not preclude an adjudication of those issues . . ." [*Frank Pisano & Assocs. v. Taggart* (1972) 29 CA3d 1, 16, 105 CR 414, 424]

In determining the issues raised by the pleadings, the pleadings of *both* parties must be considered. Issues raised in the answer may support relief on theories not specifically raised in the complaint. [See *Estrin v. Sup.Ct.* (1939) 14 C2d 670, 676, 96 P2d 340, 343]

Moreover, a variance between pleadings and proof is harmless error where it is clear that a retrial on amended pleadings would result in the same judgment. [*Appel v. Burman* (1984) 159 CA3d 1209, 1214, 206 CR 259, 262]

c. **[6:11]** **Policy to construe pleadings liberally:** In determining whether a failure of proof has occurred, the policy is to construe the complaint liberally in favor of the plaintiff, in order to uphold the judgment . . . at least where no prejudice to defendant is shown. [*Fineberg v. Niekerk*, supra, 175 CA3d at 939, 221 CR at 108; see also *White v. Western Title Ins. Co.* (1985) 40 C3d 870, 889-890, 221 CR 509, 519-520]

d. **Examples**

- **[6:12]** P pled an oral contract. D's answer alleged the contract was in writing. At trial, the court found for P on the basis of the written contract alleged by D. There was no failure of proof. The terms of the oral contract and the written contract, although not identical, covered the same subject matter; and D clearly was not prejudiced because it had pleaded the written contract. [*Johnson v. DeWaard* (1931) 113 CA 417, 298 P 92, 95; see also *Fredericks v. Filbert Co.* (1987) 189 CA3d 272, 277, 234 CR 395, 397]

- **[6:13]** P sued for breach of a film distribution contract calling for certain payments within 2 years. At trial, D produced a contract similar to the one alleged by P but payments were not due for 5 years. The court granted relief based on the contract produced by D. The variance between the pleadings and proof was "immaterial" and, since D produced the contract in question, it was not prejudiced thereby. [*Fineberg v. Niekerk,* supra]

## B. COMPLAINTS

1. **[6:14] Format Requirements—In General:** To be acceptable for filing, a complaint must be drafted in accordance with rules applicable to pleadings generally; see CRC 201.

   All complaints filed must be on *recycled paper* (CRC 201(b), 201.1(k)) (attorney filing complaint certifies document was produced on paper purchased as required).

   *Caution re local rules:* Local court rules governing "form or format" of pleadings are *preempted* and voided by CRC 981.1(a); *see discussion at ¶9:13.2.*

   a. **[6:15] Official Form complaints:** The Judicial Council Official Form complaints have been designed to comply with all applicable statewide format rules; *see ¶6:5.*

      (1) **[6:16] Multi-page forms:** If a multiple-page Official Form complaint is used, it may be filed either on:

      — pages *printed on one side only* (even if the original form has two printed sides); *or*

      — a *"tumbled" two-sided* sheet (reverse of form rotated 180 degrees and printed head to foot). [CRC 201(g)]

      (2) **[6:16.1] Hole punching:** See CRC 201.1(*l*).

   b. **[6:17] All other complaints:** Complaints other than Official Form complaints must also meet the following format requirements:

      (1) **[6:18] Type size, paper size, pagination:** See CRC 201(c). (Note: Type size may be *no smaller than 12 point.*)

      (2) **[6:19] Line spacing and numbering:** See CRC 201(d).

      (3) **[6:20] Page numbering and hole punching:** See CRC 201(e).

      (4) **[6:20.1] Footers:** Each page of each filed paper (except exhibits) must bear a footer in the bottom margin, below the page number and divided from the rest of the document by a printed line. The footer must con-

tain the title of the document (e.g., "Complaint" or "Motion for Summary Judgment") or some clear and concise abbreviation, in at least 10-point type. [CRC 201(g)]

Although not required, the title of the document is usually shown centered in the footer in capital letters.

_- 7 -_

FIRST AMENDED COMPLAINT

(5) **[6:21]** **First page layout:** The following information must be included on designated lines of the first page of the complaint:

**FORM:** Complaint (First Page Format), *see Form 6:Q.*

(a) **[6:22]** **Attorney:** Commencing on Line 1, at the left margin, the following information regarding the attorney filing the pleading:
— name;
— office address (or if none, a residence address . . . but *not* a P.O. Box number);
— telephone number; and
— *State Bar number.* [CRC 201(f)]

The name, office address, telephone number and State Bar number can be printed in advance on each page. [CRC 201(f)]

1) **[6:23]** **Optional information:** Although not required by the CRC, it is common practice to include certain additional information:

• *Name of law firm and member handling case:* Where plaintiff is represented by a law firm, the caption should show both the name of the firm *and* one or more of its members, to facilitate communicating with the lawyer handling the case.

• *Attorney's fax number and e-mail address:* Inclusion of this information is optional, and "does not constitute consent to service by fax or e-mail unless otherwise provided by law." [CRC 201(f)(1); *see* ¶9:86.11]

• *Names of parties represented:* If the attorney represents less than all of the named plaintiffs, the full name of each plaintiff on whose behalf the complaint is filed should be stated (on line 5 immediately below the attorney's name). Where the complaint is filed on behalf of *all* plaintiffs, the attorney can simply state "Attorney for Plaintiffs" instead of listing each plaintiff's name.

2) [6:24] **Example:** The following form is recommended:

| | |
|---|---|
| 1 | BARBARA JONES, State Bar No. 26607 |
| | BROWN, BLACK & JONES, Attorneys at Law |
| 2 | 245 Center Street, Suite 300 |
| | Centerville, CA 99022-7675 |
| 3 | (602) 757-2928 |
| 4 | |
| 5 | Attorneys for Plaintiffs MARY GREEN |
| | and SAMUEL GREEN |
| 6 | |
| 7 | |

[6:25] *Reserved.*

(b) [6:26] **Court:** Commencing on line 8, the name of the court. [CCP §422.30; CRC 201(f)]

➡️[6:27] *PRACTICE POINTER:* The Official Form complaints also require the *mailing address* and *street address* of the courthouse (e.g., *see Form 6:A*). Although not presently required for other complaints, it may be a good idea to include this information.

(c) [6:28] **Title of case:** The original complaint or cross-complaint must contain the *full* names of *all* parties on the left of the page. [CCP §422.40]

Each party's name must appear on a *separate line* beginning at the left margin. [CRC 201(f)(4)] For example:

"John Smith and
"Mary Smith,

   Plaintiffs,

"vs.

"Betty Jones and
"Harold Jones,

   Defendants."

1) [6:28.1] **Compare—other pleadings may use "short caption":** After the original complaint or cross-complaint, any pleading, motion or demurrer may use as a "short caption" the name of the first party on each side; and, if cross-complaints have been filed, a collective reference thereto at the bottom of the "short

caption." [CCP §422.40; CRC 312(h), 201(f)] For example:

"John Smith et al.,
Plaintiffs,
"vs.
"Betty Jones et al.,
Defendants,
"And Related Cross-Actions."

2) [6:28.2] **Compare—motions, pleadings directed to cross-complaints:** The full title of the case is *not* used in a pleading or motion pertaining to a particular cross-complaint. Such pleadings or motions shall identify the cross-complaint by its "short caption"; i.e., the names of the first-named cross-complainant and first-named cross-defendant in the original cross-complaint. [CRC 312(h)]

For example:

"Demurrer to Cross-Complaint of Rachel Black et al. vs. Robert Brown et al."

(d) [6:29] **Case number:** On the right side of the page, opposite the title of the case. The case number will be inserted on the original by the clerk at the time of filing. Copies will be conformed by the clerk, if requested. [CRC 201(f)]

(e) [6:30] **Nature of pleading and action:** Just below the case number, the type of pleading (complaint) and brief indication of the nature of the action. [CRC 201(f)]

1) [6:31] **Example:** "COMPLAINT FOR DEFAMATION"

2) [6:32] **Purpose:** Designation of the nature of the action is primarily for the court's use for calendar control and statistical purposes. It does *not* affect or limit the claims pleaded or the relief that may be awarded.

☞ [6:33] ***PRACTICE POINTER:*** Although not required, it is good practice to list *all causes of action* ("counts"). This helps the court and can facilitate discussion between the court and counsel.

3) [6:34] **Where Official Forms used:** Greater specificity as to the nature of the action may

be required where Official Forms are used. For example, the Official Form Complaint for Personal Injury, Property Damage, Wrongful Death (*Form 6:A*) requires designation of the action as:

❑ MOTOR VEHICLE    ❑ OTHER
    ❑ Property Damage    ❑ Wrongful Death
    ❑ Personal Injury    ❑ Other Damages
                               (specify)

[6:34.1-34.4]   *Reserved.*

(f)  [6:34.5]  **Limited civil cases:**  Where the relief sought is of a type that may be granted in a limited civil case (e.g., $25,000 or less), the caption of the complaint must state "Limited Civil Case." [CCP §422.30(b); CRC 201(f)(10)]

In addition (to enable the court clerk to ascertain the appropriate filing fee), the complaint in a limited civil case must also state, *immediately below the character of the action or proceeding*, either:
— "Amount demanded exceeds $10,000"; or
— "Amount demanded does not exceed $10,000." [Gov.C. §72055; CRC 201(f)(9)]

1)  [6:34.6]  **Example**

SUPERIOR COURT OF CALIFORNIA

COUNTY OF ...............

Case No. .....

LIMITED CIVIL CASE

COMPLAINT ON
PROMISSORY NOTE
AMOUNT DEMANDED
EXCEEDS $10,000

2)  [6:34.7]  **Effect of failure to designate:** Where the caption incorrectly designates or erroneously fails to designate a limited civil case as such, the court may (on defendant's motion or sua sponte) *reclassify* it as a limited civil case and order plaintiff to pay the costs and fees of the reclassification proceedings. [CCP §403.040(a); *see ¶3:112 ff.*]

3)  [6:34.8]  **Reclassification by later pleading or stipulation:**  If a subsequent pleading (e.g., amended complaint, cross-complaint) or a stipulation causes the case to be reclassified

(e.g., limited civil reclassified as unlimited civil), the caption of that pleading or stipulation must specifically note the reclassification. [CRC 201(f)(11); *see further discussion at ¶3:109.5*]

(g) [6:35] **Causes of action numbered and identified:** Each cause of action (or affirmative defense) should be separately stated (*see ¶6:104*), must be separately numbered, and must identify the parties asserting the claim and against whom it is asserted. [CRC 201(i), 312(g); *see ¶6:104*]

1) [6:35.1] **Example:** Thus, each separately stated cause of action should state:
— its number (e.g., "FIRST CAUSE OF ACTION");
— the party asserting it if the complaint is filed on behalf of more than one plaintiff (e.g., "BY PLAINTIFF JONES"); and
— the party or parties against whom it is directed (e.g., "AGAINST DEFENDANT SMITH"). *See further discussion at ¶6:104.*

[6:35.2-35.4] *Reserved.*

(h) [6:35.5] **Footer:** *See ¶6:20.1.*

(6) [6:36] **Other format guidelines:** Although not dictated by statute or the CRC, certain additional information and format guidelines may be required under local practice:

• [6:37] *Name of assigned judge and department number:* In some courts, the clerk stamps the complaint with the name of the judge assigned for all purposes at the time of filing. All subsequent documents filed in the case must have this name typed on the face page, under the nature of the paper or character of the action or proceeding (see CRC 201(f)(7)), as follows:

"ASSIGNED FOR ALL PURPOSES TO JUDGE: *(insert name)*
"DEPARTMENT: *(insert number)."*

*Referee:* In a case pending before a referee appointed pursuant to CCP §§638 or 639 (*see ¶8:1803 ff.*), the word "Referee" followed by the name of the referee must be inserted below the nature of the paper or character of the action or proceeding. [CRC 201(f)(8)]

• [6:38] *Paragraph numbering:* Many lawyers number paragraphs *consecutively throughout the com-*

*plaint* (rather than within each cause of action), using Arabic numerals (rather than Roman numerals).

*See further discussion at ¶6:114 ff.*

- [6:39] *Venue allegations:* In some courts, it is customary to state in the *first paragraph* of the complaint the factual basis for the choice of venue; e.g., if venue is based on a party's residence, the party's name and city of residence.

  *See further discussion at ¶6:98 ff.*

(7) **Additional papers required for filing**

(a) [6:40] **Civil case cover sheet:** The complaint (or other first paper filed in an action or proceeding) must be accompanied by a civil case cover sheet (Judicial Council form CM-010). [CRC 201.8(a)]

**FORM:** Civil Case Cover Sheet, *see Form 6:Q.1.*

1) [6:40.1] **Purpose:** The cover sheet is used for statistical purposes only. It does *not* affect case assignment except for cases designated as "complex." [CRC 201.8(a)]

2) [6:40.2] **Service not required (except in complex cases):** The case cover sheet need not be served on opposing parties unless plaintiff checks the box indicating the case is "complex," in which event a copy of the cover sheet must be served with the complaint. [CRC 201.8(a)]

3) [6:40.3] **Not a substitute for local cover sheets:** The case cover sheet required by CRC 201.8 must be filed *in addition to* any cover sheet required by local rule (below). [CRC 201.8(a)]

4) [6:40.4] **Effect of failure to comply:** If a party fails to file a civil case cover sheet (or other form required by the CRC), or files an incorrect or incomplete cover sheet, the court may impose sanctions. [CRC 201.8(c); *see also* ¶9:1279 ff.] (But the court clerk may *not refuse* to file the papers; *see* ¶6:44.)

(b) [6:41] **Local rules requiring other papers generally preempted:** Any local court rules requiring additional papers to be filed along with the complaint are apparently *preempted* by CRC 981.1; *see* discussion at ¶9:13.2 ff.

1) **[6:41.1] Compare—local civil cover sheets:** An exception to preemption is provided for local rules requiring a local civil cover sheet *in addition to* the mandatory statewide cover sheet *(Form 6:Q.1).* [CRC 201.8(a)]

    a) **[6:41.2] Certificate re district filing (Los Angeles Superior Court):** The Los Angeles Superior Court requires that a four-page "Civil Case Cover Sheet Addendum" be filed and served with the summons and complaint. The form requires counsel to specify, under penalty of perjury, the grounds for filing the action in the district where the action is filed; and to provide a trial estimate and state whether a jury is demanded. [L.A. Sup.Ct. Rule 2.0(b),(d)]

    *FORM:* Civil Case Cover Sheet Addendum and Statement of Location (Los Angeles Superior Court), *see Form 6:Q.2.*

2) **[6:42] Format requirements:** Where local court forms are permitted, they must conform to the same format rules governing Official Form complaints *(see ¶6:14 ff.).* [CRC 201.3]

c. **[6:43] Changes on face of complaint:** The complaint filed with the court should be error-free. If there are any changes or interlineations on the original complaint, they *must be initialed by the court clerk,* and all copies conformed to show the corrections and the clerk's initials. [CRC 201(h)]

d. **[6:44] Effect of format defects:** Absent a court order based on good cause shown, the court clerk "shall not accept for filing or file" papers that do not comply with the CRC. [CRC 201(j)]

*Exception—handwritten pleadings:* The clerk may *not* reject papers solely on the ground they are handwritten or handprinted or that the writing is in a color other than blue-black or black. [CRC 201(j)(1)]

(1) **[6:45] Compare—violation of local rules:** The court clerk may *not* refuse to file a complaint for noncompliance with a local rule. As long as the pleading presented for filing complies with CRC 201, and appropriate fees are paid, the clerk must file it. [*Carlson v. State of Calif. Dept. of Fish & Game* (1998) 68 CA4th 1268, 1272, 80 CR2d 601, 603-604—complaint improperly rejected because not accompanied by certificate of assignment as required by Los Angeles Superior Court rule]

(2) [6:46] **Papers improperly rejected deemed filed:** The court clerk has no discretion to refuse filing a pleading that *substantially conforms* to the CRC. (The clerk must file the complaint and then notify the attorney or party to correct the defect.) If the clerk refuses to file papers for insignificant defects, the papers are deemed filed—for statute of limitations purposes—on the date they were first presented for filing. [*Rojas v. Cutsforth* (1998) 67 CA4th 774, 778, 79 CR2d 292, 294—complaint rejected because declaration of court assignment was unsigned deemed filed when first presented (before expiration of statute of limitations)]

[6:47] *Reserved.*

2. [6:48] **Designating Parties:** The full name of each plaintiff and each defendant must be shown on the first page of the complaint. For parties other than natural persons, their status or capacity should be alleged in the body of the complaint. The following are the most common examples:

a. [6:49] **Corporations:** The corporation's name generally is followed by the words "a corporation" in the caption on the first page. In addition, the corporation's status is generally alleged in the opening paragraphs of the complaint.

(1) [6:50] **Corporate plaintiffs—alleging "qualified to do business":** It is common practice, although not required, for a corporate plaintiff to allege in the opening paragraphs of the complaint as follows:

"Plaintiff_____is a corporation organized and existing under the laws of the State of _____, and is and was at all times mentioned herein qualified to do business in California."

(a) [6:51] **Official Forms:** The Official Form complaints simplify this allegation as follows:

"2. Each plaintiff is a competent adult ☐ except plaintiff (name): ...........................................................

☐ *a corporation qualified to do business* in California . . ."

[*See Form 6:A, para. 2.a.; and Form 6:J, para. 2.a.*]

(b) [6:52] **Purpose:** The above allegation is *not* usually necessary to state a cause of action on the corporation's behalf. Rather, it is used to *negate* possible defenses as to the corporation's capacity to sue, by *forcing admission* thereof in defendant's answer (or establishing the matter without the necessity of proof if defendant defaults).

(c) [6:53] **Application:** If defendant *admits* the above allegation in the complaint, it avoids the following possible defenses:

- An out-of-state corporation doing business in California that has not "qualified" with the Secretary of State (by filing certain forms and paying certain fees) cannot sue in local courts. [Corps.C. §2203]

- A domestic corporation that has been suspended for nonpayment of the franchise tax, can *neither sue nor defend itself* in California courts until it is revived. [Rev. & Tax.C. §23301]

(d) [6:54] **Compare—element of plaintiff's case:** There are a few cases in which the corporation's status or capacity to sue is an essential element of its case.

For example, a corporation suing on a debt on which the interest payable exceeds the usury rate, must *allege and prove* that it is *exempt* from the usury limitations (Calif. Const. Art. XV). But if defendant *admits* the corporation's allegation that it is ex-

*(Text cont'd on p. 6-13)*

**RESERVED**

empt, or defaults on the complaint (which is common in collection cases), plaintiff's *exempt status* is established. It can recover the excessive interest without proof of the exemption.

(2) [6:55] **Corporate defendants:** A corporate defendant *may* be identified as "a corporation" in the caption and body of the complaint. But identifying its status is not essential unless a default judgment is likely, or unless the status is somehow relevant to the cause of action pleaded (e.g., a shareholder's derivative suit). [*Earl W. Schott, Inc. v. Kalar* (1993) 20 CA4th 943, 945-946, 24 CR2d 580, 581 (citing text)]

➪ [6:56] *PRACTICE POINTER:* Do *not* allege that a corporate *defendant* is "organized and existing under the laws of California" . . . or that it is "qualified to do business in California." Doing so may stipulate away a possible ground for preventing the corporation from defending itself! (As pointed out above, a domestic corporation cannot defend itself in state courts if it has been suspended for nonpayment of the franchise tax; Rev. & Tax.C. §23301.)

(a) [6:57] **Status uncertain or unknown:** Sometimes, plaintiff will not know for sure whether a business entity defendant *is* a corporation. For example, a business operating as "Greenthumb Co." could conceivably be a corporation, *or* a partnership, *or* a sole proprietorship (individual doing business under fictitious name).

➪ [6:57.1] *PRACTICE POINTER:* You can find out whether the entity is a California corporation by calling or writing to the Secretary of State, Corporate Filings Section, 1230 J Street, Sacramento, CA 95814; telephone (916) 445-2900.

But you have to know the exact name of the corporation (a problem where it is doing business under a fictitious name). Also, an out-of-state corporation won't be on file with the Secretary of State unless it has qualified to do business here.

Another possibility is to check with the County Clerk in the county in which the business operates to see if it has filed a "Fictitious Business Name Statement" as required by Bus. & Prof.C. §17900 et seq. (commonly called "dba" statements). If filed, the statement will disclose the entity's status.

(b) **[6:58]** **Pleading corporate status waives right to challenge:** One who sues an alleged corporation as such thereby necessarily admits that *it is* a corporation, and may be *estopped to deny* its corporate existence in that action. [*Wynn v. Treasure Co.* (1956) 146 CA2d 69, 76-77, 303 P2d 1067, 1072—having sued the entity without alleging it was anyone's alter ego, plaintiff was estopped in later action to claim corporation was alter ego of one of its officers]

(c) **[6:59]** **Necessity of correct name and capacity:** To obtain an enforceable judgment, the complaint must name the business entity in its *right* capacity. That is usually no problem in a contested case, because plaintiff can find out through discovery whether defendant is a corporation, partnership, etc., and *amend* the complaint, if necessary. But if defendant *defaults* (e.g., in a collection case), any judgment entered will be enforceable only against the entity named in the complaint. The sheriff or marshal may refuse to levy execution on assets held in any different name. [*Earl W. Schott, Inc. v. Kalar* (1993) 20 CA4th 943, 945-946, 24 CR2d 580, 581 (citing text)]

   1) **[6:59.1]** **"DBA" not separate entity:** Complaints often name defendants both individually *and* under a fictitious business name (e.g., "XYZ, Inc., a corporation, doing business as Susan's Flowers"). A fictitious business name is *not a separate entity*, however; therefore, no default judgment can be rendered against it *apart from* the named defendant. [*Pinkerton's, Inc. v. Sup.Ct. (Schrieber)* (1996) 49 CA4th 1342, 1347-1349, 57 CR2d 356, 359-360—after dismissing corporate defendant, plaintiff could not obtain default judgment against corporation's fictitious business name; *see* ¶5:271.5-271.6]

(d) **[6:60]** **Recommended procedure:** The safest procedure in such cases is to sue the business entity under whatever name is known (together with any known partners or proprietors) *in every plausible capacity,* and to include plenty of "Doe" defendants, as well. For example:

1) [6:61] **Caption**

"JEAN JONES,

Plaintiff,

vs.

GREENTHUMB CO.; GREENTHUMB CO., INC., a corporation; GREENTHUMB CO., a partnership; JAY GREEN, individually and as a partner of GREEN-THUMB CO. partnership; TOM THUMB, individually and as a partner of GREENTHUMB CO. partnership; DOES ONE through TEN inclusive,

Defendants."

2) [6:62] **Allegations in body of complaint:** In the opening paragraphs of the complaint, plaintiff (being unsure of the defendant's actual status or capacity) should allege as follows:

"Defendant GREENTHUMB CO. is a *business organization form unknown.*" (*See Official Form Complaint, Form 6:A, para. 3.a.*)

"Plaintiff is *informed and believes* and thereupon alleges that defendant GREENTHUMB CO., INC. is a corporation; that defendant GREENTHUMB CO. is a partnership; that defendant JAY GREEN is a partner of GREENTHUMB CO. partnership; that defendant TOM THUMB is a partner of GREENTHUMB CO. partnership; that defendant JAY GREEN is engaged in business as a sole proprietor doing business as GREENTHUMB CO.; that defendant TOM THUMB is engaged in business as a sole proprietor doing business as GREENTHUMB CO."

"The true names and capacities of defendants DOES ONE through TEN are unknown to plaintiff, and plaintiff will seek leave of court to amend this complaint to allege such names and capacities as soon as they are ascertained."

  a) [6:62.1] *Caution—constructive knowledge:* Such allegations "on information and belief" may not be proper where the facts are *ascertainable from public records* (*see ¶6:232*). Consequently, be sure to check available public records *(see ¶6:57.1)* before including such allegations.

3) [6:63] **Amend complaint when status ascertained:** After the true name and capacity of the business entity is determined, it may be necessary to amend the complaint accordingly. (*See procedure on amendment of complaint, ¶6:602 ff.*) If the firm name is slightly different than any of the names in the caption (e.g.,

"GREENTHUMB, LTD." instead of "GREEN-THUMB CO."), it may be necessary to serve the defendant as a "DOE."

⇨[6:64]   ***PRACTICE POINTER:***   As a matter of routine in every case against a business entity defendant, *verify its status* as soon as possible. Your opening *discovery* should ask the defendant to disclose its status, and the names of all proprietors, partners, corporate officers, etc. Also, ask whether it acknowledges that it is the person, firm or entity whose acts or omissions are alleged in the complaint (to save rude surprises at the time of trial!).

b.  **Partnerships**

(1) [6:65]   **Partnership (or other unincorporated association) as plaintiff:**   A partnership (or other unincorporated association) may sue in the firm name. [CCP §369.5(a)] Indeed, the partnership is the real party in interest on any claim belonging to the entity. Thus, the action *must* be filed in the partnership name, rather than in the name of the partners individually (*see ¶2:1 ff.*). [*Dickson, Carlson & Campillo v. Pole* (2000) 83 CA4th 436, 441, 99 CR2d 678, 682, fn. 1]

*Limited liability companies* (see Corps.C. §17000 et seq.), like other unincorporated associations, have capacity to sue and be sued in the entity name; *see ¶2:123.*

(a) [6:66]   **Caption**

"GREENTHUMB COMPANY, a partnership, Plaintiff"

(b) [6:67]   **Allegations in body of complaint:**   Although not required to state a cause of action, it is customary to allege the partnership status in the opening paragraphs of the complaint. For example:

"Plaintiff GREENTHUMB COMPANY is a partnership consisting of Jay Green and Alan Ames . . . "

**Official Form Complaints,** *Forms 6:A and 6:J,* para. 2.a., have a box for inserting the partnership status:

"Each plaintiff . . . is a competent adult . . . except plaintiff (name): _____

. . .

☐   an unincorporated entity (describe): _____
_____ "

(c) [6:68]  **Fictitious name statute:**  If the partnership does not disclose the surname of each partner, the complaint should also allege compliance with the fictitious name statute (Bus. & Prof.C. §17918).

Although not necessary to state a cause of action, noncompliance would be ground for abatement of an action based on "any contract made, or transaction had" until the required statement is filed and published. [Bus. & Prof.C. §17918; see *Kadota Fig Ass'n of Producers v. Case-Swayne Co.* (1946) 73 CA2d 796, 804-805, 167 P2d 518, 523]

The following allegation may be used:

> "Plaintiff GREENTHUMB COMPANY is a partnership consisting of Jay Green and Alan Ames, and has filed the statement and published the notice required by California Business and Professions Code Section 17918."

➡[6:68a]  *PRACTICE POINTER:*  Make sure that your clients *have* complied with the fictitious name statute *before* filing your lawsuit. Ask to see copies of the requisite statement and published notice. (Sometimes, clients mistakenly think that obtaining a business license in a fictitious name is sufficient.) Unless there is a statute of limitations problem, hold off filing suit until you can confidently allege compliance with the fictitious name statute.

1) [6:68b]  **Not applicable to tort claims:**  By its terms, Bus. & Prof.C. §17918 applies only to actions "on account of any contract made or transaction had in the fictitious business name." Therefore, failure to file a fictitious business name statement does not bar commencement or maintenance of a *tort* action by a party doing business under a fictitious name. [*American Alternative Energy Partners II, 1985 v. Windridge, Inc.* (1996) 42 CA4th 551, 562, 49 CR2d 686, 692]

(2) [6:68.1]  **Partnership (or other unincorporated association) as defendant:**  A partnership or other unincorporated association (including a limited liability company) can also be sued in the firm name. But if a judgment is sought against the members individually, they must be separately named in the complaint. [CCP §369.5(a),(b); see *American Alternative Energy Partners II, 1985 v. Windridge, Inc.*, supra, 42 CA4th at 559, 49 CR2d at 692]

(a) [6:68.2] **Caption**

"JOHN JONES,

Plaintiff,

vs.

GREENTHUMB COMPANY,
a partnership, Jay Green
and Alan Ames,

Defendants."

(b) [6:68.3] **Status uncertain or unknown:** In claims against a business entity defendant, the plaintiff often does not know for sure whether the entity *is* a partnership. In such cases, the best procedure is to follow the suggestion at ¶6:60-64.

c. [6:68.4] **Sole proprietor ("d.b.a."):** A person doing business under a fictitious name should sue, or be sued, in his individual name, rather than solely in the business name.

(1) [6:68.5] **As plaintiff:** Although not required, it is common practice to show the business name following the individual name.

(a) [6:69] **Caption**

"JEAN SMITH, doing business as The Locker Room,

Plaintiff"

(b) [6:70] **Fictitious name statute:** Where the business name does not show the owner's surname, the complaint should allege compliance with the fictitious name statute (Bus. & Prof.C. §17918). Lack of compliance would be grounds for abating the action; *see* ¶6:68.

Therefore, the complaint should allege:

"Jean Smith is now and at all times herein mentioned was engaged in business under the fictitious name, 'The Locker Room', and has filed the statement and published the notice required by California Business and Professions Code §17918."

⇨[6:71] *PRACTICE POINTER:* Again, make sure that your client *has* complied before filing suit. See ¶6:68a.

(c) [6:72] **License status:** If plaintiff is required by law to be licensed in order to enforce the obligation in question, his or her license status should be alleged. Doing so forces the defendant to admit or deny such status (and denial *cannot* be on information and belief because it is a matter of public record; *see ¶6:427-429*). If admitted by defendant, there is no need to prove the license at trial.

Therefore, the complaint should allege:

> "Plaintiff (name) has complied with all applicable licensing requirements as a licensed (e.g., architect, general contractor, etc.)."

(*See Official Form Complaint, Form 6:J, para. 2.b.*)

(2) **[6:73]** **As defendant:** A sole proprietor should be sued in his individual name; the business name can be disregarded.

    (a) **[6:74]** **Status unknown or uncertain:** If there is any doubt about the ownership of the business, follow the suggestions at *¶6:60-64*.

d. **Persons acting in representative capacity**

(1) **[6:75]** **Executor, administrator, trustee, receiver:** Parties acting in these capacities should be described as such—either as plaintiffs or defendants. For example:

> "ALAN AMES, as Executor of the
> Will of Amy Ames, deceased,
>
>                       Plaintiff,
>
> vs.
>
> BEA BAKER, as Trustee of
> the Baker Family Trust No. 12,
>
>                    Defendant."

    (a) **[6:76]** **Compare—estate is nonentity and cannot sue:** A decedent's estate is *not* a legal entity. It is simply a collection of the decedent's assets. It, therefore, has no capacity to sue, or to be sued. Any suit must be brought by, or against, the executors or administrators. [See CCP §369; and *Estate of Bright v. Western Air Lines* (1951) 104 CA2d 827, 828-829, 232 P2d 523, 524]

(2) **[6:77]** **Compare—guardian or guardian ad litem:** Causes of action belonging to a minor or incompetent are prosecuted by or *through* a guardian. But the right to sue belongs to the minor or incompetent. [CCP §372] Hence, the correct designation in the complaint is:

> "CARY CRAIG, a minor, by
> Celia Craig, his guardian ad
> litem,
>
> Plaintiff,
>
> vs.
>
> DONNA DUNN, an incompetent
> by David Dunn, her conservator of the estate,
>
> Defendant."

   (a) **[6:78] Note:** The parents may also have their own cause of action for injuries to an unmarried minor child (see CCP §376). They can sue for their damages (medical expenses, loss of services, etc.) in their own name. (Caution: There may be a conflict of interest in the parent acting as guardian ad litem in such cases; *see ¶2:40.1a.*)

e. **[6:79] "Doe" defendants:** If ignorant of any defendant's true name or liability, plaintiff may include fictitious names as defendants in the complaint (e.g., "Does 1 through 10 inclusive") and allege that the identities and capacities in which they acted are unknown. [CCP §474]

   **[6:79.1] *PRACTICE POINTER:*** Naming "Doe" defendants can be useful in several situations:

- Where plaintiff does not know the names of the persons who injured him or her (or knows them only by nicknames or incorrect names).

- Where plaintiff knows the names of the persons who injured him or her, but has reason to believe they were not acting alone; i.e., that others, whose names plaintiff does not know, may be liable on theories of respondeat superior, agency, conspiracy, etc.

- Where plaintiff does not know all the *facts* upon which liability depends, and therefore is ignorant of the defendants' liability (even if plaintiff knew their names all along; *see ¶6:735*).

   (1) **[6:80] Plaintiff must be genuinely ignorant of defendant's identity or liability:** Designating a defendant by a fictitious name is proper only if plaintiff is genuinely ignorant of the defendant's true name *or the facts rendering defendant liable* when the complaint was filed. [*Woo v. Sup.Ct. (Zarabi)* (1999) 75 CA4th 169, 177, 89 CR2d 20, 27; *Taito v. Owens Corning* (1992) 7 CA4th 798, 802, 9 CR2d 687, 689, fn. 4 (citing text); *and ¶6:748 ff.*]

(a) **[6:80.1]** **Effect on statute of limitations:** Because plaintiffs have up to 3 years in which to serve summons (CCP §583.210, see ¶11:51), naming Doe defendants *effectively enlarges* the statute of limitations period as to unknown defendants for the 3-year period. [*Bernson v. Browning-Ferris Industries, Inc.* (1994) 7 C4th 926, 932, 30 CR2d 440, 443]

   1) **[6:80.2]** **Compare—ignorance of defendant's identity does not toll statute:** Ignorance of the defendant's identity does *not* excuse failure to commence suit within the statutory period. The statute begins to run when plaintiffs have reason to suspect they have been wronged *even if they do not know whom to sue.* [*Norgart v. Upjohn Co.* (1999) 21 C4th 383, 398-399, 87 CR2d 453, 464; see ¶6:751.5]

(2) **[6:81]** **Caption**

"JOHN JONES,

                                   Plaintiff,

vs.

JEAN SMITH, DOE ONE
through TEN inclusive,

                                   Defendants."

(3) **[6:82]** **Allegations required in body of complaint:** Plaintiff must state in the body of the complaint that he or she is ignorant of the true names of the defendants sued by fictitious names, *and* that such names are fictitious. In the absence of such allegations, plaintiff may not utilize CCP §474 later to substitute in a real person as a defendant. [*Kerr-McGee Chemical Corp. v. Sup.Ct. (Cubit)* (1984) 160 CA3d 594, 598, 206 CR 654, 656]

   (a) **[6:83]** **Examples:** Either of the following allegations is sufficient to invoke CCP §474:

      "Plaintiff is ignorant of the true names or capacities of the defendants sued herein under the fictitious names DOE ONE through TEN inclusive."

    *OR*

      "Defendants DOES ONE through TEN inclusive are sued herein pursuant to CCP §474."

    [See *Motor City Sales v. Sup.Ct. (Proulx)* (1973) 31 CA3d 342, 347-348, 107 CR 280, 283]

(b) [6:84] **Compare:** But "Kerr-McGee Chemical Corp." *cannot* be substituted as defendant for "Trona Medical Clinic" under CCP §474 where the complaint did not allege that "Trona Medical Clinic" was a fictitious name and that plaintiff was ignorant of its true name. [*Kerr-McGee Chemical Corp. v. Sup.Ct. (Cubit)*, supra]

(c) [6:85] **Charging allegations must run against "Doe" defendants:** It is not enough, of course, simply to name "Doe" defendants. Rather, the complaint must allege that they were *responsible* for the acts complained of. [*Winding Creek v. McGlashan* (1996) 44 CA4th 933, 941, 52 CR2d 236, 240 (citing text)]

Usually, this is accomplished by alleging that the wrongful acts were committed by "defendants and each of them." (Where separate wrongs were committed by several defendants, the "Doe" defendants can be split into groups; e.g., alleging a named defendant and DOES ONE through FIVE committed certain acts; and another named defendant and DOES SIX through TEN committed others.) [*Winding Creek v. McGlashan*, supra, 44 CA4th at 941-942, 52 CR2d at 240—allegation that " . . . each of the fictitiously named Defendants *is responsible in some manner* for the occurances [sic] herein alleged . . . " and "proximately caused" plaintiff's damages, coupled with allegation that each was acting as agent for the others, was sufficient to charge "Doe" defendants (parentheses and brackets added)]

(4) [6:86] **Amend when identity ascertained:** After ascertaining the true identity of a defendant sued as a "Doe," plaintiff should seek leave of court to amend the complaint accordingly. (*See ¶6:612-615*.)

(5) [6:87] **Service of process:** Plaintiff should then serve the defendant with copies of the summons and complaint (and amendment showing his or her true name, if filed at time of service).

(a) [6:88] **"Doe" status indicated on summons:** The *summons* form should be filled out to show that the person is being served as one of the "Doe" defendants. [CCP §§412.20, 474; see ¶4:134]

"2.  NOTICE TO THE PERSON SERVED: You are served
. . .

      b.  ☐  As the person sued under the fictitious name of_____."

(b) [6:89] **Proof of service requirements:** In addition, the return of service must state the name of the person served, the fictitious name under which such person was served (e.g., "Doe One") and that the summons contained the notice of identity (above). [CCP §474; *see ¶4:152.1*]

(c) [6:90] **Serving "Doe" defendants after statute of limitations has run:** *See detailed discussion at ¶6:735 ff.*

[6:90.1-90.4] *Reserved.*

(6) [6:90.5] **Limitation—no "sham" complaints:** An action that names *only* "Doe" defendants may be dismissed as a sham after adequate opportunity for discovery of the fictitious defendants' real identities. [See *Pearlson v. Does 1 To 646* (1999) 76 CA4th 1005, 1010, 90 CR2d 787, 790—complaint for trespass and invasion of privacy named 646 "Doe" defendants but after several years not one defendant had been identified, and plaintiff failed to show any significant potential to determine the identity of a viable defendant]

f. [6:91] **Incomplete or erroneous designation:** Errors in parties' names are common, and are usually correctable by amendment.

(1) [6:92] **"Idem sonans" doctrine:** Absolute accuracy in spelling names is not required in legal proceedings. Under the doctrine of "idem sonans," if the defendant is served with summons and complaint and defendant's name is *pronounced* the same way it is written in the complaint, defendant must answer. For example, the names Eliot, Elliot and Elliott are idem sonans. [See *Orr v. Byers* (1988) 198 CA3d 666, 669, 244 CR 13, 14; see also *Earl W. Schott, Inc. v. Kalar* (1993) 20 CA4th 943, 947, 24 CR2d 580, 581, 582—"Seaver" and "Seavers" substantially the same, but "Gary Kalar dba Kalar Const. Co." *not* the same as "Kalar Construction, Inc."]

(a) [6:93] **Limitations:** This doctrine applies primarily for *identification* purposes. It does *not* apply where the opposing party has been *misled* to his or her prejudice. Nor does it apply where an innocent third party is involved (e.g., constructive notice from official records). [*Orr v. Byers*, supra—abstract of judgment in misspelled name not constructive notice to innocent purchaser of defendant's land]

(2) [6:94] **Allegations in body of complaint may cure errors in caption:** In determining whether a particular person or entity is adequately designated as a party

to the action, courts look to the body of the complaint as well as to the caption. If correctly designated in the body, so that a reasonable person would realize he or she is the party intended to be named defendant, errors in the caption can be cured by amendment . . . even after the statute of limitations has run. [*Plumlee v. Poag* (1984) 150 CA3d 541, 547, 198 CR 66, 70]

(a) **[6:95] Example:** P sued on a creditor's claim against a decedent's estate. The caption named D individually but the body of the complaint alleged D was being sued as executor of the decedent's estate, so D was not misled as to the capacity in which he was being sued. The caption could be amended to name D as executor after expiration of the statutory time limit for suing executors (the Probate Code requires suit within 3 months of claim rejection). [*Plumlee v. Poag*, supra]

(b) **[6:96] Example:** Allegations in the body of P's malpractice complaint stated a cause of action against Hospital and other defendants. However, Hospital's name was *omitted* in the caption. This was a "formal defect," curable by amendment although the statute of limitations had run. [See *Bell v. Tri-City Hospital Dist.* (1987) 196 CA3d 438, 448-449, 241 CR 796, 802-803]

g. **[6:97] List of parties:** If more than two parties have appeared in a case, and are represented by *different counsel*, the plaintiff first named in the complaint must maintain a current list of all parties and their addresses. The list is to be furnished on request to another party to the court; and to be served on any new party later joined. Every party is required to advise that plaintiff of any change of address, etc. [CRC 202.7]

3. **Allegations re Venue**

a. **[6:98] Generally not required:** Plaintiff's filing a complaint in the wrong county or judicial district does *not* affect the court's jurisdiction or power to grant relief in most cases. Rather, it is merely ground for a change of venue motion by the defendant; and if not raised by the defendant, the objection is waived. It follows, therefore, that plaintiff generally need *not* allege compliance with the various statutory venue requirements in his or her complaint; i.e., venue allegations are optional (*see* ¶6:39).

☞**[6:99] PRACTICE POINTER:** Even so, some practitioners include a venue allegation in every complaint, as a reminder to themselves to *check* the venue requirements. If a complaint is filed in the wrong court, and defendant objects, the court has discretionary power to *impose attorneys' fees and costs* against the *attorney* responsible for filing the action. [CCP §396b; *see ¶3:583 ff.*]

b. **[6:100] Statutory exceptions:** Several statutes require plaintiff to affirmatively allege the proper court and proper court location in actions to enforce consumer obligations. These include:

- Actions on *installment sale of motor vehicles* [Civ.C. §2984.4];

- Actions on *other retail installment sales* [Civ.C. §1812.10];

- Limited civil cases for *goods or services intended primarily for personal, family or household use* [CCP §§396a, 395(b)];

- Limited civil cases for *unlawful detainer* [CCP §396a].

(1) **[6:101] Verified complaint or affidavit required:** In such actions, plaintiff is required to plead *facts* in a verified complaint (or separate affidavit served and filed with the complaint) showing the action has been commenced in the "proper court" and "proper court location" for the claim involved. Otherwise, the action is subject to dismissal without prejudice. [CCP §396a(a)]

c. **[6:102] Official Forms:** Various of the Official Form Complaints contain allegations showing the action is filed in the "proper" court for venue purposes. Such allegations serve as a reminder to the pleader to *check* the statutory venue requirements; and (if true) negate any ground for defendant's challenging venue.

For example, the Official Form Complaint for tort actions (*see Form 6:A, para. 5.*) contains the following allegation re venue:

"5. The court is the proper court because

    a. ☐ at least one defendant now resides in its jurisdictional area.

    b. ☐ the principal place of business of a corporation or unincorporated association is in its jurisdictional area.

    c. ☐ injury to person or damage to personal property occurred in its jurisdictional area.

    d. ☐ other (specify): _____ ."

And the Official Form Complaint for contract actions (*see Form 6:J, para. 6.*) contains the following:

"6. This action is filed in this ☐ county
☐ judicial district because

   a. ☐ a defendant entered into the contract here.
   b. ☐ a defendant lived here when the contract was entered into.
   c. ☐ a defendant lives here now.
   d. ☐ the contract was to be performed here.
   e. ☐ a defendant is a corporation or unincorporated association and its principal place of business is here.
   f. ☐ real property that is the subject of this action is located here.
   g. ☐ other (specify): _____ ."

▷[6:103] **PRACTICE POINTER:** Although the Official Forms don't say so, you apparently can—and should—check *more* than one box, if appropriate. That way, if one of the grounds fails, you'll have some other to rely on.

## 4. Alleging the Cause of Action

### a. Format rules

(1) [6:104] **Each cause of action numbered and labeled, and affected parties identified:** Each cause of action must be numbered separately and its nature stated (e.g., "First Cause of Action for Fraud"). In addition, where there is more than one plaintiff or defendant, the names of the plaintiffs asserting the particular cause of action and the defendants against whom the cause of action is asserted must appear (e.g., "by Plaintiffs Jones and Smith against all Defendants"; or "by all Plaintiffs against Defendant Smith"). [CRC 201(i), 312(g); *see also ¶6:36*]

*Compare—separately stated?* Neither the Code nor the CRC specifically require that each "cause of action" be separately stated. (CRC 201(i) merely requires that each "separately stated cause of action" be separately numbered.) Even so, pleadings which jumble together several distinct "causes of action" may be subject to a demurrer for uncertainty.

(a) [6:105] **"Cause of action" vs. "count":** The terms "count" and "cause of action" may be used interchangeably in referring to the separately stated portions of the complaint. I.e., either of the following is technically acceptable:

"FIRST CAUSE OF ACTION FOR DEFAMATION"

*or*

"FIRST COUNT FOR DEFAMATION"

(b) [6:106] **Comment:** Few lawyers or judges use the term "count." Complaints are usually broken into "causes of action" and most lawyers and judges are accustomed to this usage.

(c) [6:107] **Definitions:** However, as noted by the Supreme Court, such usage is "imprecise" and "indiscriminate." [*Bay Cities Paving & Grading, Inc. v. Lawyers' Mut. Ins. Co.* (1993) 5 C4th 854, 860, 21 CR2d 691, 693, fn. 1 (dictum)]

- [6:108] *"Cause of action"* technically refers to the *invasion of a primary right*: e.g., injury to person, property, etc. *(see ¶6:250 ff.)*. It is based on the *harm suffered*, as opposed to the particular theory of recovery asserted by the litigant. [*Bay Cities Paving & Grading, Inc. v. Lawyers' Mut. Ins. Co.*, supra, 5 C4th at 860, 21 CR2d at 694]

  The most salient characteristic of a primary right is that it is *indivisible*: i.e., violation of a single primary right gives rise to but a single cause of action. A pleading stating two "causes of action" involving the same primary right contravenes the rule against "splitting" a cause of action (*see ¶6:250 ff.*). [*Crowley v. Katleman* (1994) 8 C4th 666, 681-682, 34 CR2d 386, 393; *Hamilton v. Asbestos Corp., Ltd.* (2000) 22 C4th 1127, 1145, 95 CR2d 701, 713]

  The fact plaintiff seeks several different *remedies* does *not* necessarily establish different causes of action. Alternative forms of relief are often available for enforcement of a single right (e.g., damages or rescission for fraud). [See *Bay Cities Paving & Grading, Inc. v. Lawyers' Mut. Ins. Co.*, supra, 5 C4th at 860, 21 CR2d at 694—"Both demands having arisen out of the same transaction, there is but one cause of action with two forms of relief"; *Olsen v. Breeze, Inc.* (1996) 48 CA4th 608, 625-626, 55 CR2d 818, 826]

- [6:109] *"Count"* means a group of related paragraphs in the complaint setting forth a legal theory of recovery. Counts "are merely ways of stating the same cause of action differently." [*Bay Cities Paving & Grading, Inc. v. Lawyers' Mut. Ins. Co.*, supra, 5 C4th at 860, 21 CR2d at 693, fn. 1; see also *Hayter Trucking, Inc. v. Shell Western E&P, Inc.* (1993) 18 CA4th 1, 12, 22 CR2d 229, 236 (citing text)]

(d) **Application**

- [6:110] Where a complaint seeks recovery for the same personal injury under *several different legal theories* (e.g., negligence, breach of implied warranty and strict liability), there is really only a *single* cause of action. [*Barrett v. Sup.Ct. (Paul Hubbs Const. Co.)* (1990) 222 CA3d 1176, 1182, 272 CR 304, 306, fn. 1; *Uhrich v. State Farm Fire & Cas. Co.* (2003) 109 CA4th 598, 605, 135 CR2d 131, 135-136—complaint improperly labeled emotional distress damages and civil conspiracy liability as separate causes of action]

- [6:111] An attorney committed several separate acts of malpractice in seeking to enforce a client's claim. Since the client suffered only a single injury, it had only one cause of action against the attorney. [*Bay Cities Paving & Grading, Inc. v. Lawyers' Mut. Ins. Co.*, supra, 5 C4th at 860, 21 CR2d at 693-694 (dictum)]

(2) [6:112] **Nature of claim and parties affected:** Each cause of action (or "count") should be headed so as to identify briefly the nature of the claim asserted; and, if there is more than one plaintiff or defendant, it should identify the plaintiff or plaintiffs who assert the cause of action (or "all plaintiffs") and the defendant or defendants against whom the cause of action is being asserted (or "all defendants"). [CRC 312(g); *see* ¶6:35, *6:104*]

Example:

"FIRST CAUSE OF ACTION FOR DEFAMATION BY PLAINTIFF ALAN AMES AGAINST DEFENDANTS BEN BAKER, BARBARA BAKER AND DOES ONE THROUGH FIVE"

"SECOND CAUSE OF ACTION FOR INVASION OF PRIVACY BY PLAINTIFF AMY AMES AGAINST DEFENDANTS BEN BAKER AND DOES SIX THROUGH TEN"

(a) [6:113] **Remedy for noncompliance?** Failure to comply with CRC 312(g) (above) presumably renders a complaint subject to *motion to strike* (CCP §436, ¶7:167) or a *special demurrer for uncertainty* (CCP §430.10(f), ¶7:84).

1) [6:113.1] **Comment:** Earlier cases held these remedies appropriate for noncompliance with *local rules* requiring identification of parties and causes of action in the complaint. [See

*Williams v. Beechnut Nutrition Corp.* (1986) 185 CA3d 135, 139, 229 CR 605, 606, fn. 2]

Although such local rules are now preempted by CRC 981.1(a) (*see ¶9:13.2*), these earlier cases suggest the same remedies would also be appropriate for failure to comply with CRC 312(g).

(3) [6:114] **Paragraph numbering:** There are no CRC requirements governing paragraph numbering. (Local rules governing this subject are clearly preempted by CRC 981.1(a).)

(a) [6:115] **Compare—Official Forms:** In several of the Official Form complaints, the paragraphs are numbered consecutively *within each cause of action* using Arabic numerals. (The cause of action attachment forms use an abbreviation derived from the title of the cause of action: "Prod.L.-1," "Prod.L.-2," etc.)

⇨[6:116] *PRACTICE POINTER:* In actions not covered by the Official Forms, it is good practice to number paragraphs *consecutively throughout the entire complaint* (rather than within each cause of action). E.g., Paragraphs 1 through 8 may be in the First Count; Paragraphs 9 through 17 in the Second Count, etc.

It is much easier for both the judge and lawyers to locate "Paragraph 21" than it is to locate "Paragraph 5 of the Third Count."

[6:117-119] *Reserved.*

b. [6:120] **Fact pleading required:** The complaint must contain "a statement of the *facts* constituting the *cause of action* in ordinary and concise language." [CCP §425.10]

(1) [6:121] **Facts to be pleaded determined by substantive law:** The essential elements to be pleaded to state a cause of action are determined by the substantive law.

⇨[6:122] *PRACTICE POINTER:* Use "BAJI" (Book of Approved Jury Instructions) as a *checklist* of the substantive law in the civil actions covered thereby. These instructions indicate the elements that plaintiff must *prove* at trial to recover, and these are usually the same elements plaintiff must *plead* to state a cause of action.

Also, check the Pleadings chapter in Witkin, California Procedure. Its table of contents can be used as a *checklist* of the elements of each cause of action to be pleaded.

(2) [6:123] **Form of allegations—"ultimate facts" required:** First of all, the "facts" to be pleaded are those upon which liability depends (i.e., "the facts constituting the cause of action"). These are commonly referred to as "ultimate facts."

(a) [6:124] **Distinguishing "ultimate facts" from "evidence" or "conclusions":** In the past, lawyers and judges struggled with these distinctions. "Ultimate facts" were those that raise the issues on which the *right to recover* depends: i.e., the essential elements of the cause of action. Allegations of unnecessary details were objectionable as "evidentiary" pleading; whereas generalized arguments were objectionable as "legal conclusions."

1) [6:125] **Example:** A complaint in a personal injury case alleges that: (1) defendant drove his car immediately after having consumed a fifth of vodka; (2) defendant drove while under the influence of alcohol; and (3) defendant drove in violation of California drunk driving law.

Allegation "(1)" is objectionable as "evidentiary" matter; "(3)" is a "legal conclusion"; while "(2)" is the ultimate fact.

(b) [6:126] **Exception—"common counts":** The most notable exceptions to the fact pleading requirement are the "common counts": e.g., that D is indebted to P in a particular amount:

- "For money had and received"; or
- "For goods sold and delivered"; or
- "For work and labor done"; or
- "For materials furnished"; or
- "On an open book account," etc.

These are conclusions of law rather than ultimate facts, but are good against both general and special demurrers. The only explanation is that lawyers were familiar with the common counts when our pleading rules were adopted, and their continued use is justified by their simplicity and convenience. (They are permissible under the federal rules, as well.) [*Farmers Ins. Exchange v. Zerin* (1997) 53 CA4th 445, 460, 61 CR2d 707, 715]

The only essential allegations of a common count are (1) the statement of indebtedness in a certain sum; (2) the consideration—i.e., goods sold, work done, etc.; and (3) nonpayment. [*Farmers Ins. Exchange v. Zerin*, supra, 53 CA4th at 460, 61 CR2d at 715]

1) [6:126.1] **Limitation:** A common count does not state a cause of action where it is *contradicted by other facts alleged* in the same cause of action. [*Farmers Ins. Exchange v. Zerin*, supra, 53 CA4th at 460, 61 CR2d at 715]

a) [6:126.2] P alleged that "D became indebted to P for money had and received," premised on the existence of an equitable lien claimed in a previous cause of action. If the court determines that the equitable lien is invalid, the common count also falls. [*Farmers Ins. Exchange v. Zerin*, supra, 53 CA4th at 460, 61 CR2d at 715]

[6:126.3-126.4]   *Reserved.*

*(Text cont'd on p. 6-25)*

**RESERVED**

2) [6:126.5] **Complaint on "open book account":** "Book account" means a detailed statement of transactions between creditor and debtor that constitutes the principal record of their dealings. [See CCP §337a]

a) [6:126.6] **Not for balance due under express contracts:** Monies due under an express contract, such as rent due under a lease, cannot be recovered in an action on an "open book account" in the absence of a contrary agreement between the parties. This prevents creditors from evading the statute of limitations as a bar to recovery of payments due more than 4 years earlier. [*Tsemetzin v. Coast Fed'l Sav. & Loan Ass'n* (1997) 57 CA4th 1334, 1343, 67 CR2d 726, 731]

[6:126.7-126.9] *Reserved.*

3) [6:126.10] **Complaint "on account stated":** A common count may also be pleaded "based upon an account stated based upon an account *in writing.*" [See CCP §337 subd. 2 (emphasis added); *Iverson, Yoakum, Papiano & Hatch v. Berwald* (1999) 76 CA4th 990, 997, 90 CR2d 665, 670]

a) [6:126.11] **Statute of limitations:** An action based on an "account stated in writing" is subject to the 4-year statute of limitations (CCP §337) governing obligations in writing. [See CCP §339 subd. 1]

But where the underlying written obligation is *unenforceable,* a 2-year statute of limitations (CCP §339) applies. [*Iverson, Yoakum, Papiano & Hatch v. Berwald*, supra, 76 CA4th at 997, 90 CR2d at 670— because underlying fee agreement and promissory note were *voidable* as a matter of law, action on account stated was subject to 2-year statute]

4) [6:126.12] **Complaint "for money had and received":** A common count can be utilized where defendant is indebted to plaintiff in a certain sum "for money had and received by the defendant for the use of the plaintiff." [*Schultz v. Harney* (1994) 27 CA4th 1611, 1623, 33 CR2d 276, 283]

This cause of action can be used to recover money paid pursuant to a contract, even if the contract is void for illegality. [*Schultz v. Harney*, supra, 27 CA4th at 1623, 33 CR2d at 283]

[6:126.13-126.14]   *Reserved.*

5)   [6:126.15]   **Complaint "for work and labor done":**   This common count can be utilized to recover the value of services rendered under a contract, even if the contract is unenforceable because not in writing: "(Q)uantum meruit is a theory which implies a promise to pay for services as a matter of law for reasons of justice." [*Iverson, Yoakum, Papiano & Hatch v. Berwald*, supra, 76 CA4th at 996, 90 CR2d at 669]

⇨[6:126.16]   *PRACTICE POINTER FOR DEFENDANTS:*   If plaintiff pleads a "common count," defendants may demand a "*bill of particulars*" (a document setting forth the details of the account sued upon; *see ¶8:1765*). This is more potent than an interrogatory or other discovery request because if plaintiffs fail to provide the details within 10 days, they may be precluded from proving the debt! [CCP §454; *see ¶8:1784*]

(3)   [6:127]   **Consequence of improper fact pleading:** Failure to plead ultimate facts subjects the complaint to *demurrer* for "failure to state facts constituting the *cause of action.*" [CCP §430.10(e); *see ¶7:39 ff.*]

"A complaint must allege the ultimate facts necessary to the statement of an actionable claim. It is both improper and insufficient for a plaintiff to simply plead the *evidence* by which he hopes to prove such ultimate facts." [*Careau & Co. v. Security Pac. Business Credit, Inc.* (1990) 222 CA3d 1371, 1390, 272 CR 387, 396-397 (emphasis in original)]

(But if sufficient ultimate facts are alleged, additional "evidentiary" matter or "legal conclusions" can be disregarded as surplusage; or, may be subject to motion to strike. *See ¶7:156 ff.*)

(4)   [6:128]   **Fair notice as test:**   The distinction between "ultimate facts" and "evidentiary" matters and "legal conclusions" is of diminishing importance. Our courts have become *increasingly liberal* in their attitude toward pleading—in some cases approximating the notice-pleading standards of federal courts. [*Perkins v. Sup.Ct. (General Tel. Directory Co.)* (1981) 117 CA3d 1, 6, 172 CR 427, 429—"The distinction is not at all clear and in-

volves at most a matter of degree . . . What is important is that the complaint as a whole contain *sufficient facts to apprise* the defendant of the basis upon which the plaintiff is seeking relief . . ."]

There is no need to require specificity in the pleadings "because *modern discovery procedures* necessarily affect the amount of detail that should be required in a pleading." [*Ludgate Ins. Co. v. Lockheed Martin Corp.* (2000) 82 CA4th 592, 608, 98 CR2d 277, 288 (emphasis added; internal quotes omitted)]

(a) [6:129] **Negligence, product liability:** Thus, for example, negligence and product liability claims can be pleaded *generally*, without specifying the particular breach or the particular manner in which the accident occurred. (*See Official Form Causes of Action, Forms 6:C and 6:F.*)

  1) [6:129.1] **Negligence per se:** To plead a cause of action for negligence per se, plaintiff must allege:
     — defendant violated a statute, ordinance or regulation;
     — the violation proximately caused death or injury to plaintiff;
     — such death or injury was of the kind that the statute, ordinance or regulation was designed to prevent; and
     — plaintiff belonged to the class of persons for whose protection the statute, ordinance or regulation was adopted. [See Ev.C. §669(a); *Randi W. v. Muroc Joint Unified School Dist.* (1997) 14 C4th 1066, 1087, 60 CR2d 263, 276]

     [6:129.2-129.4] *Reserved.*

  2) [6:129.5] **Causation:** Ordinarily, general allegations of causation are sufficient (e.g., "P suffered personal injuries and emotional distress as a direct and proximate result of the acts previously alleged").

     a) [6:129.6] **Limitation—where causation not readily inferred:** When the pleaded facts of negligence and injury *do not naturally give rise to an inference of causation*, plaintiff must plead specific facts "*explaining how* the conduct caused or contributed to the injury." [*Bockrath v. Aldrich Chem. Co., Inc.* (1999) 21 C4th 71, 78, 86 CR2d 846, 851 (emphasis added)—allegation

that plaintiff was exposed to "most and perhaps all" of products used by employer not
sufficient]

• [6:129.7]   Where plaintiff claims injury
from exposure to multiple toxic chemicals produced by several defendants,
he or she must allege facts showing
*each defendant's* product was a "substantial factor" in causing the injury.
Specifically, plaintiff must allege:
—he or she was *exposed* to each of the
toxic materials claimed to have caused
a specific illness;
—the identity of each product that allegedly caused injury;
—as a result of the exposure, toxins
entered his or her body;
—he or she suffers from a *specific illness* and that each toxin that entered
his or her body was a *substantial factor*
in causing, prolonging or aggravating
that illness; and
—each toxin so absorbed was manufactured or distributed by a named defendant (except where market share liability, below, is claimed). [*Bockrath v.
Aldrich Chem. Co., Inc.*, supra, 21 C4th
at 80, 86 CR2d at 852]

Such facts *may* be alleged in a *conclusory* fashion where plaintiff's knowledge of the precise cause of injury is
limited. [*Bockrath v. Aldrich Chem. Co.,
Inc.*, supra, 21 C4th at 80, 86 CR2d at
852-853]

[6:129.8-129.9]   *Reserved.*

b) [6:129.10]   **Consider "Doe" defendants:**
If plaintiffs lack sufficient information to
plead that a particular defendant was responsible for particular injuries, the complaint may name "Doe" defendants to protect against the statute of limitations until
the defendants can be identified and
named. [*Bockrath v. Aldrich Chem. Co.,
Inc.*, supra, 21 C4th at 81, 86 CR2d at 852]

[6:129.11-129.14]   *Reserved.*

c) [6:129.15]   **Which of several defendants
caused injury:**   Normally, plaintiff must

allege that *each* named defendant caused his or her injuries. But plaintiff may be able to proceed on either of the following theories *without* identifying which defendant caused the injury:

— *"Alternative liability"* (plaintiff unable to ascertain which of several defendants acting concurrently caused the injury). [See *Summers v. Tice* (1948) 33 C2d 80, 86, 199 P2d 1, 3]

— *"Market share liability"* (plaintiff unable to identify which of several defendants manufacturing the product sold the product causing his or her injury). [See *Sindell v. Abbott Laboratories* (1980) 26 C3d 588, 597, 163 CR 132, 135; *Bockrath v. Aldrich Chem. Co., Inc.,* supra, 21 C4th at 80, 86 CR2d at 852]

d) [6:129.16] **Ethical limitation against joining every potential defendant:** The California Supreme Court has cautioned that "it is sharp practice to implead defendants in a products liability suit alleging long-term exposure to multiple toxins *unless, after a reasonable inquiry,* the plaintiff actually believes that evidence has been or is likely to be found raising a reasonable medical probability that each defendant's product was a substantial factor in causing the harm." [*Bockrath v. Aldrich Chem. Co., Inc.,* supra, 21 C4th at 83, 86 CR2d at 853 (emphasis added)]

Such "shotgun pleading" may also result in *sanctions* under CCP §128.7, *discussed at ¶9:1135 ff.*

(b) [6:130] **Ownership:** Likewise, ownership of property can be pleaded generally although it is a conclusion of law. [*Moore v. Regents of Univ. of Calif.* (1990) 51 C3d 120, 136, 271 CR 146, 155, fn. 19—allegation that patient "owned" biological material taken from his body]

(c) [6:131] **Intent, malice:** Moreover, pleading certain conclusions ("willfully," "maliciously," "oppression, fraud and malice") is permissible where the complaint also contains sufficient facts to support these conclusions. [*Perkins v. Sup.Ct. (General Tel.*

*Directory Co.)* (1981) 117 CA3d 1, 6-7, 172 CR 427, 430]

(d) [6:132] **Contract provisions:** A *written* contract may be pleaded either *in haec verba* (word for word) or generally "according to its legal intendment and effect" (e.g., "Defendant agreed to sell the described property to Plaintiff for $100,000"). [*Construction Protective Services, Inc. v. TIG Specialty Ins. Co.* (2002) 29 C4th 189, 198-199, 126 CR2d 908, 914—plaintiff may plead the legal effect of the contract rather than its precise language]

An *oral* contract may be pleaded generally as to its effect because it is rarely possible to allege the exact words. [*Khoury v. Maly's of Calif., Inc.* (1993) 14 CA4th 612, 616, 17 CR2d 708, 710]

- [6:133] A complaint for breach of an oral distributorship agreement was sufficient although it did not allege the duration of the agreement. The law implies a reasonable term, and what constitutes a commercially reasonable time is presumptively within both parties knowledge. [*Khoury v. Maly's of Calif., Inc.,* supra, 14 CA4th at 616, 17 CR2d at 710]

⇨[6:133.1] *PRACTICE POINTER:* Where there is a written contract, plaintiff should simply attach it as an exhibit to the complaint and incorporate it by reference. Doing so may draw an admission from defendant that will obviate problems of proof. Conversely, failure to do so may raise questions as to which document is claimed to be the contract.

(e) [6:134] **Contract conditions:** Satisfaction of contract conditions may be pleaded generally (e.g., "plaintiff has duly performed all conditions on his part"). [*Careau & Co. v. Security Pac. Business Credit, Inc.* (1990) 222 CA3d 1371, 1390, 272 CR 387, 396]

But this is subject to several *limitations*:

- Where the condition is an *event*, as distinguished from an act to be performed by plaintiff, its happening must be specially alleged (allegation that "all conditions have been satisfied" is impermissible legal conclusion);

- Where plaintiff pleads facts showing *less* than complete performance, a general allegation that all conditions were "duly performed" does not suffice; and

- Where plaintiff claims the conditions were *excused or waived*, specific—not general—allegations are required. [*Careau & Co. v. Security Pac. Business Credit, Inc.* (1990) 222 CA3d 1371, 1390, 272 CR 387, 396]

(f) [6:135] **Statutory conditions:** The performance of conditions precedent to rights provided by statute or ordinance may be pleaded *generally*; e.g., "P duly performed all conditions on his part required under Government Code Section . . ." [CCP §459; see *Hata v. Los Angeles County Harbor/UCLA Med. Ctr.* (1995) 31 CA4th 1791, 1805-1806, 37 CR2d 630, 638]

⇨[6:136] *PRACTICE POINTER:* Even though modern rules lean toward notice pleading, there are still some cases where detailed, factual pleadings may be advantageous. For example:

- **Injunctions:** A verified complaint containing enough evidentiary facts will support issuance of a *temporary restraining order* or preliminary injunction without further affidavits or proof (*see* ¶9:579).

- **Defaults:** Detailed factual allegations may also be advantageous if defendant defaults. If the complaint is too "conclusory" or omits essential facts, evidence introduced at the default "prove up" hearing may be treated as a "de facto amendment" to the complaint, *opening up the default* (*see* ¶5:229 ff.).

(5) [6:137] **Special pleading requirements:** Notwithstanding this general policy of liberality, there are certain cases in which a stricter pleading standard is required:

(a) [6:138] **Fraud:** The traditional rule is that fraud actions are subject to a stricter pleading standard, because they involve a serious attack on defendant's character. Fairness requires that allegations of fraud be pleaded "*with particularity*" so that the court can weed out nonmeritorious actions before defendant is required to answer. This is said to be the "last remaining habitat" of common law pleading standards. [*Committee on Children's Television, Inc. v. General Foods Corp.* (1983) 35 C3d 197, 216,

197 CR 783, 795; *Small v. Fritz Cos., Inc.* (2003) 30 C4th 167, 183, 132 CR2d 490, 502]

1) **[6:139] Effect:** Every element of the cause of action for fraud must be alleged in full, factually and specifically. The policy of liberal construction of pleading will *not* be invoked to sustain a pleading defective in any material respect. [*Wilhelm v. Pray, Price, Williams & Russell* (1986) 186 CA3d 1324, 1332, 231 CR 355, 358]

The particularity requirement necessitates pleading *facts* that "show *how, when, where, to whom, and by what means* the representations were tendered." [*Lazar v. Sup.Ct. (Rykoff-Sexton, Inc.)* (1996) 12 C4th 631, 645, 49 CR2d 377, 385; *Stansfield v. Starkey* (1990) 220 CA3d 59, 73, 269 CR 337, 345 (emphasis added)]

Plaintiff must also specially plead the "detriment proximately caused" by defendant's tortious conduct (Civ.C. §3333). This requires factual allegations of both the injury or damage suffered and its causal connection with plaintiff's reliance on defendant's representations. [*Service By Medallion, Inc. v. Clorox Co.* (1996) 44 CA4th 1807, 1818, 52 CR2d 650, 656; see *Furia v. Helm* (2003) 111 CA4th 945, 956, 4 CR3d 357, 366—fraud complaint sufficient against demurrer if it alleges *type of damage* suffered although it fails to allege specific dollar amount]

a) **Application**

- **[6:139.1]** Investors alleged that Defendants prepared fraudulent financial statements intentionally overstating the value of Corporation's assets. Because the complaint contained *numerous specific misrepresentations supporting those allegations*, it provided enough information for respondents to know what purported falsehoods they must defend against. [*Murphy v. BDO Seidman, LLP* (2003) 113 CA4th 687, 692, 6 CR3d 770, 774]

- **[6:140]** *Compare:* Complaint against Lawyer alleged he "knew" the representations he was communicating to P on behalf of a client were false and untrue. But it was not alleged *how* Lawyer knew this. This was held insufficient to state a cause of action for fraud. [*Wilhelm v. Pray, Price, Williams & Russell,* supra]

- **[6:141]** P alleged that breast implant Manufacturer and other defendants "falsely and fraudulently represented" their product was safe for use and would not require frequent removal from her body. These conclusory terms "did not come close" to the required specificity for a fraud complaint; it cannot be determined *what* was said or *by whom* or in *what manner* (orally or in writing). [*Goldrich v. Natural Y Surgical Specialties* (1994) 25 CA4th 772, 783, 31 CR2d 162, 168-169]

  [6:142-144]  *Reserved.*

b) [6:145]  **Fraud by corporation:**  In fraud complaints against a corporation, plaintiff must allege:
— the *names of the persons* who made the misrepresentations;
— *their authority* to speak for the corporation;
— to whom they spoke;
— what they said or wrote; and
— when it was said or written. [*Lazar v. Sup.Ct. (Rykoff-Sexton, Inc.)* (1996) 12 C4th 631, 645, 49 CR2d 377, 385; *Tarmann v. State Farm Mut. Auto. Ins. Co.* (1991) 2 CA4th 153, 157, 2 CR2d 861, 862-863]

2) [6:146]  **Impact of Official Form complaint:** The Official Form cause of action for fraud (*Form 6:M*) does little to lighten the pleading burden. It contains only the skeleton of a fraud cause of action. The pleader must provide the details as to what representations were made, why they were false, in what way plaintiff was induced to act, etc. (*See allegations FR-2 through FR-5 on Form 6:M.*)

➡️ [6:146.1]  *PRACTICE POINTER:*  The Official Form complaint should be avoided in fraud actions. It is better to draft a complaint setting forth each of the essential allegations in the requisite detail.

3) **[6:147] Exception—defendant fully informed:** An exception to the strict pleading standard is recognized when it appears that the facts lie more within defendant's knowledge than plaintiff's: i.e., less specificity is required where "defendant must *necessarily possess full information* concerning the facts of the controversy." [*Committee on Children's Television, Inc. v. General Foods Corp.*, supra, 35 C3d at 216, 197 CR at 795]

This is especially true where defendant is alleged to be a fiduciary. [*Eldridge v. Tymshare, Inc.* (1986) 186 CA3d 767, 777, 230 CR 815, 821]

a) **[6:148] Compare—matters unknown to either side:** But the above exception does not apply where defendant has no more knowledge of the facts than does plaintiff. [*Tarmann v. State Farm Mut. Auto. Ins. Co.* (1991) 2 CA4th 153, 158, 2 CR2d 861, 863]

[6:149] For example, allegations of misrepresentations by "agents or employees" of a large corporate defendant are insufficient *where defendant has no more reason than plaintiff to know* which of its employees made the statements in question. [*Tarmann v. State Farm Mut. Auto. Ins. Co.*, supra, 2 CA4th at 158, 2 CR2d at 863—P claimed statements were made by D's "adjustors and/or claims supervisors/managers" but did not know their names]

4) **[6:150] Practical considerations:** Also, the requirement of "particularity" in pleading fraud should not be overdone. Complaints must be kept to a reasonable length. If they are too detailed (e.g., setting forth each statement verbatim, specifying the time, place and medium by which made), they may provide *less* effective notice, and be less useful in framing the issues, than would a shorter, more generalized version. [*Committee on Children's Television, Inc. v. General Foods Corp.*, supra, 35 C3d at 217, 197 CR at 796]

a) [6:151] **Multiple misrepresentations:**
Where the alleged misrepresentations are
numerous and made to many different
people (e.g., in public advertisements),
plaintiff may set forth or attach a *representative selection* thereof. "This method . . .
represents a reasonable accommodation
between defendant's right to a (specific)
pleading . . . and the importance of avoiding pleading requirements so burdensome
as to preclude relief . . ." [*Committee on
Children's Television, Inc. v. General Foods
Corp.*, supra, 35 C3d at 218, 197 CR at
796]

[6:151.1-151.4] *Reserved.*

(b) [6:151.5] **Negligent misrepresentation?** It is
unclear whether the same specificity required in
pleading fraud actions is required in pleading actions for negligent misrepresentation generally. [See
*Small v. Fritz Cos., Inc.* (2003) 30 C4th 167, 184,
132 CR2d 490, 503—"we express no view" on this
issue]

1) [6:151.6] **Compare—stockholder wrongfully induced to refrain from selling
stock:** But specific pleading *is required* in a
stockholder's complaint against a corporation
for fraudulent *or negligent* misrepresentations
in financial reports that cause the plaintiff to
forbear selling his or her shares. Because of the
risk of false claims, plaintiffs who rely on a for-
bearance theory must *specifically plead* how
many shares they would have sold and when
they would have sold them. [*Small v. Fritz Cos.,
Inc.*, supra, 30 C4th at 184, 132 CR2d at 502-
503; *Murphy v. BDO Seidman, LLP* (2003) 113
CA4th 687, 702, 6 CR3d 770, 781]

(c) [6:152] **Agency or employment:** In the past, at
least, plaintiffs often alleged agency and employment relationships in conclusory terms. For example:

"Each of the defendants was the agent, joint
venturer and employee of each of the remaining defendants . . . and in doing the things here-
inafter alleged, each was acting within the
course and scope of said agency, employment
and joint venture with the advance knowledge,
acquiescence or subsequent ratification of
each and every remaining defendant."

However, the Supreme Court has criticized such allegations as "egregious examples of generic boilerplate." [*Moore v. Regents of Univ. of Calif.* (1990) 51 C3d 120, 134, 271 CR 146, 153, fn. 12]

**[6:153]** **Comment:** "Boilerplate" or not, such allegations may be necessary! Particularly at the outset of a lawsuit, before discovery, plaintiffs may be unable to allege facts establishing the agent's authority. (Keep in mind, however, that joining a defendant party *without probable cause* may expose the client to liability for malicious prosecution or sanctions under CCP §128.7; *see* ¶9:1135 ff.)

(d) **[6:154]** **Conspiracy:** Conspiracy itself is *not a separate cause of action*. Rather, it is a theory of *vicarious liability* under which certain defendants may be held liable for torts committed by others. I.e., all parties to a conspiracy are jointly liable for tortious acts committed by any of them pursuant to the conspiracy. [*Okun v. Sup.Ct. (Maple Properties)* (1981) 29 C3d 442, 454, 175 CR 157, 164]

The complaint must allege acts that would have given rise to a tort cause of action *without* the conspiracy. Absent such allegations, the conspiracy allegations are meaningless. [*Manor Invest. Co., Inc. v. F.W. Woolworth* (1984) 159 CA3d 586, 595, 206 CR 37, 42-43 (disapproved on other grounds in *Applied Equip. Corp. v. Litton Saudi Arabia Ltd.* (1994) 7 C4th 503, 521, 28 CR2d 475, 485, fn. 10)]

The conspiracy must be properly pleaded. Conclusory allegations of a "conspiracy" will not withstand demurrer. To render defendant liable for wrongs committed by another, the complaint must allege (1) defendant had *knowledge* of and *agreed* to both the objective and course of action to injure the plaintiff; (2) the wrongful act pursuant to such agreement; and (3) resulting damage to plaintiff. [See *Quelimane Co., Inc. v. Stewart Title Guar. Co.* (1998) 19 C4th 26, 47, 77 CR2d 709, 721—conspiracy in restraint of trade]

"General allegations of agreement have been held sufficient . . . and the conspiracy averment has even been held unnecessary, providing the unlawful acts or civil wrongs are otherwise sufficiently alleged." [*Quelimane Co., Inc. v. Stewart Title Guar. Co.*, supra, 19 C4th at 47, 77 CR2d at 721]

1) **[6:154.1]** **Limitation—illegal acts specially pleaded:** Where the alleged conspiracy was

to commit illegal acts, "plaintiff must allege *certain facts* in addition to the elements of the alleged unlawful act so that the defendant can understand the nature of the alleged wrong and discovery is not merely a blind 'fishing expedition' for some unknown wrongful acts." [*Smith v. State Farm Mut. Auto. Ins. Co.* (2001) 93 CA4th 700, 722, 113 CR2d 399, 418 (emphasis in original)]

2) **[6:155] Limitation—prior court order required for attorney-client conspiracy claim:** No cause of action may be pleaded against an attorney for civil conspiracy with a client without a prior court order. [Civ.C. §1714.10; *see detailed discussion at ¶6:354 ff.*]

(e) **[6:156] Punitive damages claims:** In tort cases, plaintiff may seek punitive damages for "oppression, fraud or malice" by the defendant. [Civ.C. §3294(a)] (Recovery depends on plaintiff's producing "clear and convincing" evidence showing defendant guilty of such conduct.)

The statute contains its own definitions:

- "Malice" means conduct *intended* by the defendant *to cause injury* to the plaintiff or *despicable conduct* that is carried on by the defendant with a *willful and conscious disregard* for the rights or safety of others. [Civ.C. §3294(c)(1)]

- "Oppression" means despicable conduct that subjects a person to cruel and unjust hardship in conscious disregard of that person's rights. [Civ.C. §3294(c)(2)]

- "Fraud" means intentional misrepresentation, deceit or concealment of a material fact with the intention of depriving a person of property or legal rights or otherwise causing injury. [Civ.C. §3294(c)(3)]

1) **[6:157] Limited to tort actions:** Punitive damages are not recoverable in actions for breach of contract, even if defendant's conduct was "willful, oppressive or malicious." [See *Myers Bldg. Indus., Ltd. v. Interface Technology, Inc.* (1993) 13 CA4th 949, 960, 17 CR2d 242, 248]

2) **[6:158] Specific pleading required?** According to several older cases, punitive damages cannot be pleaded generally. I.e., allega-

tions that defendant acted "with oppression, fraud and malice" toward plaintiff are merely legal conclusions. Likewise, "despicable conduct" is a conclusion. Specific factual allegations are required to support a punitives claim. [*Brousseau v. Jarrett* (1977) 73 CA3d 864, 872, 141 CR 200, 205; and see *Perkins v. Sup.Ct. (General Tel. Directory Co.)* (1981) 117 CA3d 1, 6-7, 172 CR 427, 430]

Some courts are increasingly liberal as to what constitutes sufficient "fact-pleading" on a claim for punitive damages. The complaint will be read as a whole so that even conclusory allegations may suffice *when read in context* with facts alleged as to the defendant's wrongful conduct. [*Perkins v. Sup.Ct. (General Tel. Directory Co.)*, supra, 117 CA3d at 6-7, 172 CR at 430; *Clauson v. Sup.Ct. (Pedus Services, Inc.)* (1998) 67 CA4th 1253, 1255, 79 CR2d 747, 748]

*Comment:* Whether specific pleading is still required is unclear. The Supreme Court has stated that *fraud* complaints are the "last remaining habitat of the common law notion that a complaint should be sufficiently specific." (If so, this would exclude punitive damage claims.) [*Committee on Children's Television, Inc. v. General Foods Corp.* (1983) 35 C3d 197, 216, 197 CR 783, 795; *see ¶6:138*]

a) **Language approved**

- [6:159] Allegations that defendant "*knew* he was intoxicated and *knew* that he was driving at 65 mph in a 35 mph zone . . . with knowledge that serious injury would probably result to persons in the area" sufficiently allege "conscious disregard for the safety of others." [*Dawes v. Sup.Ct. (Mardian)* (1980) 111 CA3d 82, 88-89, 168 CR 319, 323]

- [6:160] Allegations that Farmer crop-dusted with a dangerous pesticide, disregarding the risk to others in the area, shows a "conscious disregard" for the probable consequences. [*SKF Farms v. Sup.Ct. (Hummingbird, Inc.)* (1984) 153 CA3d 902, 906-907, 200 CR 497, 499-500]

- [6:161] Allegations that defendant-landlords knew of the serious potential danger to female tenants in their building, but intentionally misled plaintiff regarding such risk in order to advance their own pecuniary interests by renting her an apartment, sufficiently allege conscious disregard for her safety. [*O'Hara v. Western Seven Trees Corp.* (1977) 75 CA3d 798, 806, 142 CR 487, 492]

[6:162] *Reserved.*

- [6:163] Allegation that defendant telephone company shut off plaintiff's home phone *in retaliation* to unrelated complaints by plaintiff, is a sufficient allegation of fact to sustain the conclusion that defendant was guilty of "oppression, fraud and malice." [*Perkins v. Sup.Ct. (General Tel. Directory Co.),* supra]

[6:164] *Reserved.*

- [6:165] A properly pleaded *fraud* claim will itself support recovery of punitive damages. No allegations of "malice" or intent to injure plaintiff are required, because fraud is an *alternative basis for recovery* ("oppression, fraud or malice"). [*Stevens v. Sup.Ct. (St. Francis Med. Ctr.)* (1986) 180 CA3d 605, 610, 225 CR 624, 627]

b) **Language disapproved**

- [6:166] Allegations that defendant was "aware" of a defective condition on rented premises that could cause injury to the tenants, and "refused" to repair same, are *not* enough. They do *not* support the conclusion that defendant either intended to injure plaintiffs or acted in reckless disregard for their safety. At the very most, the above allegations show negligence. [*McDonell v. American Trust Co.* (1955) 130 CA2d 296, 300, 279 P2d 138, 141]

- [6:167] Allegation that defendant-mortuary negligently substituted another body for that of plaintiff's decedent in a funeral service with "wanton disregard of the sensibilities of plaintiff" is *not* sufficient to support an award of punitive damages. The allegation of "wanton" or "willful disregard" is nothing more than a legal conclusion. [*Cohen v. Groman Mortuary, Inc.* (1964) 231 CA2d 1, 8, 41 CR 481, 486 (disapproved on other grounds in *Christensen v. Sup.Ct. (Pasadena Crematorium)* (1991) 54 C3d 868, 889, 2 CR2d 79, 91)]

- **[6:168]** Allegations that defendant-drug manufacturer knew that its product was of a *type* that *might* cause injury, and put it on the market notwithstanding, are *not* sufficient for punitive damages. They fail to allege that defendant intended to injure customers, or acted in conscious disregard for their safety. [*G.D. Searle & Co. v. Sup.Ct. (Seaton)* (1975) 49 CA3d 22, 32, 122 CR 218, 225]

c) **[6:169] Procedure for challenging punitives allegations:** A general demurrer cannot be used to test the adequacy of punitive damage allegations (because a demurrer must be overruled if any cause of action is stated). The proper procedure is a motion to strike (*see ¶7:185*). [*Grieves v. Sup.Ct. (Fox)* (1984) 157 CA3d 159, 163-164, 203 CR 556, 561, fn. 9; see *PH II, Inc. v. Sup.Ct. (Ibershof)* (1995) 33 CA4th 1680, 1682-1683, 40 CR2d 169, 171]

3) **[6:170] Allegations required on punitives claim against employer:** Punitive damages can be imposed against an employer for wrongful acts committed by employees, only if the employer either:

- *Authorized* or *ratified* the employee's wrongful acts; or

- Knew in advance that the employee was likely to commit such acts, and employed him or her "with *conscious disregard* of the rights or safety of others"; or

- Was itself guilty of "*oppression, fraud or malice.*" [Civ.C. §3294(b) (emphasis added); see

*United Western Med. Ctrs. v. Sup.Ct.
(Michelle Marie H.)* (1996) 42 CA4th 500,
49 CR2d 682]

a) **[6:171]** **Corporate employers:** In addition, if the employer is a corporation, it must be shown that the authorization, ratification, advance knowledge, malice, etc., was on the part of an *officer, director or managing agent* of the corporation. [Civ.C. §3294(b)]

b) **Language approved**

- **[6:172]** Various persons who threatened plaintiff were "agents and employees" of Union, "acting within the scope of their employment" and with Union's "permission and consent." [*Kiseskey v. Carpenters' Trust* (1983) 144 CA3d 222, 235, 192 CR 492, 500—"permission and consent" sufficiently alleges authorization]

- **[6:173]** Drunk driver who acted in conscious disregard of risk to plaintiff was the "*principal owner* of and was employed in a *managerial capacity* by (defendant corporation) and was acting within the course and scope of his employment and with the authorization of (defendant corporation)." [*Dawes v. Sup.Ct. (Mardian)* (1980) 111 CA3d 82, 85, 168 CR 319, 321—decided, however, before Civ.C. §3294(b) was amended to require authorization, etc., by "officer, director or managing agent" of corporate employer]

c) **Language disapproved**

- **[6:174]** Hospital undertook care and treatment of Plaintiff, but was careless in hiring Doctors who performed unauthorized surgery (battery) on Plaintiff. Insufficient for punitive damages against Hospital because no allegation of Hospital's advance knowledge, authorization or ratification of the battery. [*Grieves v. Sup.Ct. (Fox)* (1984) 157 CA3d 159, 167-168, 203 CR 556, 561]

4) **[6:175]** **Limitation—amount of punitives claim must not be alleged:** No claim for

punitive damages shall state the amount or amounts of damages sought. [Civ.C. §3295(e)]

a) [6:176] **Comment:** The purpose is to prevent punitive damage claims being used as a financial bludgeon. (Under earlier practice, plaintiffs could demand millions of dollars of punitives without regard to their compensatory damage claims.)

b) [6:177] **Remedy:** A complaint that improperly alleges an amount of punitive damages is apparently subject to motion to strike (¶7:156).

5) [6:178] **Limitation—prior court order required for certain punitive damages claims:** A punitive damages claim against a health care provider or a religious corporation may be asserted only in an *amended* complaint filed with leave of court and pursuant to statutory procedures. [See CCP §§425.13(a), 425.14, *discussed at ¶6:327 ff.*]

(f) [6:179] **"Pleading around" defense disclosed on face of complaint:** Occasionally, in alleging the cause of action, plaintiff will include facts indicating the existence of some affirmative defense— e.g., the dates alleged show the action is barred by the statute of limitations. In such cases, plaintiff must *"plead around"* the defense, by alleging *specific facts* that would avoid the apparent defense. Absent such allegations, the complaint is subject to demurrer for failure to state a cause of action (*see* ¶7:60). *Gentry v. eBay, Inc.* (2002) 99 CA4th 816, 825, 121 CR2d 703, 710 (citing text); *Lee v. Escrow Consultants, Inc.* (1989) 210 CA3d 915, 917, 921-922, 259 CR 117, 119, 121-122]

1) [6:180] **Example:** P alleges injury more than a year before the complaint was filed. If P's position is that the one-year statute of limitations was tolled because she was unaware of either her injury or its negligent cause, she must *specifically plead* facts that show (1) the time and manner of discovery, *and* (2) her inability to have made an earlier discovery despite reasonable diligence. [*Barrington v. A.H. Robins Co.* (1985) 39 C3d 146, 154, 216 CR 405, 409-410; see also *McKelvey v. Boeing North American, Inc.* (1999) 74 CA4th 151, 160, 86 CR2d 645, 651]

Conclusory allegations that the delay in discovery was "unavoidable" or "despite reasonable diligence" are insufficient to withstand a general demurrer. [*CAMSI IV v. Hunter Technology Corp.* (1991) 230 CA3d 1525, 1536-1538, 282 CR 80, 86-87]

2) [6:181] **Example:** P sued for breach of contract attached to the complaint. The contract was *ambiguous on its face.* Plaintiff must allege its own interpretation of the agreement to establish an enforceable contract claim. [*Aragon-Haas v. Family Security Ins. Services, Inc.* (1991) 231 CA3d 232, 239, 282 CR 233, 237-238]

(g) [6:182] **Defendant's duty to control third persons to prevent injury to plaintiff:** As a general rule, defendant owes no duty to control third persons to prevent their harming plaintiff. But such a duty may be owed under special circumstances. (E.g., cases involving landowners and their invitees; and cases in which defendant has *created or increased* the risk of harm to plaintiff from a third person.) [See *Lehto v. City of Oxnard* (1985) 171 CA3d 285, 291-292, 217 CR 450, 453-454]

In such cases, general allegations that defendant was "negligent" in allowing a third person to injure plaintiff are not enough. Rather, the *specific circumstances or relationship* creating a duty of care to plaintiff must be alleged in order to state a cause of action. [See *Lehto v. City of Oxnard*, supra]

1) [6:183] **Added requirements in suit against governmental entity:** There is an added requirement where the action is against a governmental body for a public officer's failure to prevent injury by a third person: A public entity is liable in such a case only if under a *mandatory duty*, imposed by statute, to protect against the particular kind of injury. [Gov.C. §815.6] (Otherwise, a public entity is *immune* from liability for injuries resulting from a public officer's failure to prevent such injury; see Gov.C. §820.2.)

Where plaintiff sues on the theory that the public entity owed a mandatory duty to prevent injury, plaintiff must allege the specific *statute or regulation* creating the duty. Reason: "Without this requirement of specificity in pleading, a court would be hard pressed to determine whether the enactment relied upon was intended to impose an obligatory duty to take official action to prevent foreseeable injuries or whether it was merely advisory in character." [*Lehto v. City of Oxnard*, supra, 171 CA3d at 293, 217 CR at 455]

Example: P sued City for injuries caused by drunk driver. The drunk driver had been stopped earlier by City Police Officer, and P claimed Police Officer owed a "mandatory duty" to prevent the drunk driver from further driving his car. However, no cause of action was stated because *P did not allege any particular statute or regulation mandating such action.* (Moreover, Gov.C. §846 provides immunity for injuries resulting from failure to make arrest.) [*Lehto v. City of Oxnard*, supra]

2) **[6:184]** **Claims against public entity common carrier:** Common carriers owe a duty to protect passengers from foreseeable assaults by fellow passengers. [*Lopez v. Southern Calif. Rapid Transit Dist.* (1985) 40 C3d 780, 785, 221 CR 840, 842]

However, if the carrier is a *public entity*, general allegations of negligence are not enough. Every fact material to the entity's statutory liability must be pleaded *with particularity.* [*Lopez v. Southern Calif. Rapid Transit Dist.*, supra, 40 C3d at 795, 221 CR at 849-850]

- **[6:185]** **Example:** The following are sufficient: D is a common carrier; P was a passenger on D's bus; D knew assaults regularly occurred on this route; and D's driver knew violence had erupted among the passengers and failed to protect P. [*Lopez v. Southern Calif. Rapid Transit Dist.*, supra]

(h) **[6:186]** **Declaratory relief:** Any person claiming rights under a contract (oral or written) or under a written instrument other than a will or trust, or with respect to property, may bring an action for a declaration of his or her rights or duties with respect to another. The action may be brought before any breach of the obligation regarding which the declaration is sought. [CCP §1060; see *Columbia Pictures Corp. v. De Toth* (1945) 26 C2d 753, 760, 161 P2d 217, 220-221—applies to oral employment contracts]

Rev. #1 2004

➡️[6:187]  **PRACTICE POINTER:**  A valid declaratory relief action is entitled to *priority in trial setting* (CCP §1062.3; *see ¶12:245*).

1) [6:188]  **Present controversy required:** The main requirement for declaratory relief is a present and actual controversy between the parties. [*City of Cotati v. Cashman* (2002) 29 C4th 69, 80, 124 CR2d 519, 528]

   • [6:189]  The parties need *not* have present rights to the property in dispute. Declaratory relief may be granted even though the rights claimed are in litigation and dependent on future adjudication. [*Parsons v. Tickner* (1995) 31 CA4th 1513, 1533, 37 CR2d 810, 821]

2) [6:190]  **Pleading requirement:**  "(A)n actual, present controversy must be pleaded *specifically* and the facts of the respective claims concerning the (underlying) subject must be given." [*City of Cotati v. Cashman*, supra, 29 C4th at 80, 124 CR2d at 528 (parentheses added; internal quotes omitted)]

   • [6:190.1]  A complaint for declaratory relief is sufficient "if it sets forth facts showing the existence of an actual controversy relating to the legal rights and duties of the respective parties under a written instrument and requests that these rights and duties be adjudged by the court." [*Wellenkamp v. Bank of America* (1978) 21 C3d 943, 947, 148 CR 379, 381; *Ludgate Ins. Co. v. Lockheed Martin Corp.* (2000) 82 CA4th 592, 605, 98 CR2d 277, 285-286]

   [6:190.2-190.4]  *Reserved.*

3) [6:190.5]  **Need not be separately stated:** Plaintiff need not allege a separate count seeking declaratory relief or label his or her complaint as one for declaratory relief. It is enough that the complaint alleges facts showing an "actual controversy" and asks the court to adjudicate the parties' rights and duties. [*Olszewski v. Scripps Health* (2003) 30 C4th 798, 807, 135 CR2d 1, 9—plaintiff did not think he was proceeding under CCP §1060]

4) [6:191]  **Limitation—relief unnecessary or improper:**  However, declaratory relief may

be refused where the court's declaration or determination "is not necessary or proper at the time under all the circumstances." [CCP §1061]

a) **[6:192]** The availability of another form of adequate relief justifies denial of declaratory relief. [*C.J.L. Const., Inc. v. Universal Plumbing* (1993) 18 CA4th 376, 390, 22 CR2d 360, 369]

b) **[6:193]** A declaratory relief action will not lie to determine issues raised in other causes of action before the court. [*California Ins. Guar. Ass'n v. Sup.Ct. (Jakes)* (1991) 231 CA3d 1617, 1623, 283 CR 104, 108]

- **[6:194]** For example, P sues for *breach of contract* and for "declaratory relief" as to the parties' rights and obligations thereunder. Because the contract claim has already accrued, declaratory relief is unnecessary; the only determination required is the ultimate liability of one party to another. [See *Hood v. Sup.Ct. (United Chambers Administrators, Inc.)* (1995) 33 CA4th 319, 323-324, 39 CR2d 296, 298-299]

c) **[6:195]** Similarly, *where an issue can be raised as an affirmative defense*, a declaratory relief complaint raising that issue should be dismissed. E.g., a separate declaratory relief action will not lie to determine the *validity of a release* because that matter can be asserted as a defense to any action on the underlying claim. [See *C.J.L. Const., Inc. v. Universal Plumbing* (1993) 18 CA4th 376, 391, 22 CR2d 360, 369, and cases cited therein]

d) **[6:196]** Where a statute provides the *exclusive remedy* to enforce a statutory right, that remedy may not be circumvented by a declaratory relief action. [*Filarsky v. Sup.Ct. (City of Manhattan Beach)* (2002) 28 C4th 419, 432, 121 CR2d 844, 852]

- **[6:196.1]** The California Public Records Act (Gov.C. §6259) provides the exclusive procedure to enforce a request to inspect and copy public records. If no such enforcement procedure is pending, a public agency may not file a preemptive declaratory relief suit to determine its obligation to disclose public records to the person seeking them. [*Filarsky v. Sup.Ct. (City of Manhattan Beach*), supra, 28 C4th at 432, 121 CR2d at 852]

[6:197]   *Reserved.*

(i) [6:198]   **Compare—nonfraud tort claims:**   Earlier cases required specific fact pleadings for various nonfraud torts (e.g., intentional infliction of emotional distress, interference with business relations, unfair competition, etc.). [See *Khoury v. Maly's of Calif., Inc.* (1993) 14 CA4th 612, 618, 17 CR2d 708, 712]

However, the California Supreme Court has held that "*fraud is the only remaining cause of action* in which specific pleading is required to enable the court to determine on the basis of the pleadings alone whether a foundation existed for the charge . . ." [*Quelimane Co., Inc. v. Stewart Title Guar. Co.* (1998) 19 C4th 26, 46-47, 77 CR2d 709, 720 (emphasis added)]

1) [6:198.1]   **Comment:**   *Khoury* has been implicitly overruled by *Quelimane* and should not be relied upon.

(j) [6:199]   **Compare—litigation expenses that are not recoverable as "costs" or "fees":**   A contract may authorize the prevailing party to recover litigation expenses *other than* those recoverable as statutory "costs" or "attorney fees." To be recoverable, however, such expenses must be *specially pleaded* and proven. [*Carwash of America-PO LLC v. Windswept Ventures No. 1* (2002) 97 CA4th 540, 541, 118 CR2d 536, 536—where contract authorized prevailing party to recover "expert witness fees," such fees could not be awarded as item of costs if not pleaded and proven separately]

[6:199.1-199.9]   *Reserved.*

(k) [6:199.10]   **Claims against public officers:**   Any complaint for damages in a civil action brought against a public official in his or her individual capacity must allege "*with particularity*" sufficient material facts to establish the individual liability of the public official and plaintiff's right to recover therefrom. [Gov.C. §951]

1) [6:199.10a] **Breach of official duty:** It is presumed that an official duty has been regularly performed (Ev.C. §664). Therefore, where the claim is that an official duty was not appropriately performed, plaintiff must specifically allege "how and in exactly what manner the alleged facts rebut the existing presumption of regularity." [*Lavine v. Jessup* (1958) 161 CA2d 59, 67, 326 P2d 238, 245]

(*l*) [6:199.11] **Governmental tort claims:** Government tort liability is dependent on the existence of an authorizing statute. To state a cause of action against a governmental entity, "every fact essential to the existence of statutory liability *must be pleaded with particularity*, including the existence of a statutory duty." [*Searcy v. Hemet Unified School Dist.* (1986) 177 CA3d 792, 802, 223 CR 206, 212 (emphasis added); *Susman v. City of Los Angeles* (1969) 269 CA2d 803, 809, 75 CR 240, 244]

c. [6:200] **Fact pleading under the Official Forms:** Adoption of Official Forms for the most common civil actions (*see* ¶6:5) has *not* changed the statutory requirement that the complaint contain "*facts* constituting the cause of action." [CCP §425.10(a)] Thus, to be demurrer-proof, an Official Form complaint must contain whatever *ultimate facts* are essential to state a cause of action under existing statutes or case law. [*People ex rel. Dept. of Transp. v. Sup.Ct. (Verdeja)* (1992) 5 CA4th 1480, 1484, 7 CR2d 498, 500 (citing text)]

(1) [6:201] **Unlawful detainer complaint complete in itself:** The Official Form complaint for unlawful detainer (*see Form 6:O*) contains all allegations essential to state a cause of action for such relief. (The form itself alleges: plaintiff's ownership interest; defendant in possession under rental agreement; breach of the rental agreement; service of appropriate notice, etc.) Plaintiff is merely required to check appropriate boxes, fill in names, dates, addresses, etc.

(2) [6:202] **Tort and contract complaints require attachments:** The other Official Form complaints, however, are *not* complete in themselves. Rather, they are basically shells that identify the parties, and allege proper venue, etc. *To state a cause of action, plaintiff must attach one or more cause-of-action pages.* These cause-of-action pages contain the charging allegations ("ultimate facts") relevant to the particular case.

(a) [6:203] **Attachments approved by Judicial Council:** Official Form cause-of-action pages are available for the most common causes of action.

1) [6:204] **For personal injury, property damage, wrongful death complaints:** One or more of the following cause-of-action pages must be attached to the Official Form complaint:

- Motor Vehicle (*Form 6:B*);

- Product Liability (*Form 6:F*);

- Premises Liability (*Form 6:E*);

- Intentional Tort (*Form 6:D*);

- General Negligence (*Form 6:C*).

2) [6:205] **For breach of contract complaints:** One or more of the following cause-of-action pages must be attached to the Official Form complaint:

- Breach of Contract (*Form 6:K*);

- Common Counts (*Form 6:L*);

- Fraud (*Form 6:M*).

➡️[6:206] *PRACTICE POINTER:* There may be cases in which one of the normal "contract" cause of action pages may be used in connection with a "tort" complaint; or vice versa. For example, landlord sued for fraudulent concealment of dangerous condition on rented premises which caused personal injury to tenant (see *O'Hara v. Western Seven Trees Corp.* (1977) 75 CA3d 798, 806, 142 CR 487, 492, ¶*6:161*); tenant may file a personal injury complaint with a *fraud* cause of action attachment!

*(Text cont'd on p. 6-47)*

**RESERVED**

(b) [6:207] **Attachments prepared by plaintiff's attorney:** There will doubtless be cases covered by one of the Official Form complaints for which *no* cause-of-action page has been prepared. (Example: Complaint for personal injury based on professional negligence—i.e., medical malpractice.) In such cases, the plaintiff's attorney is required to draft a cause-of-action page for attachment to the Official Form complaint.

- *FORM:* Sample Attorney-Prepared Attachment, *see Form 6:R.*

(3) [6:208] **Attachments containing required ultimate facts:** Some of the Official Form cause-of-action pages contain all of the allegations required to state a cause of action. Plaintiff need only check appropriate boxes, and fill in descriptions, dates, places, names, etc. Examples:

(a) [6:209] **Cause of Action—Motor Vehicle (*Form 6:B*)**

"MV-1 Plaintiffs allege the *acts of defendant were negligent*; the acts were the legal (proximate) cause of injuries and damages to plaintiff; the acts occurred on(date)_____at (place)_____."

(b) [6:210] **Cause of Action—Product Liability (*Form 6:F*)**

"PROD.L.-1 On or about (date) plaintiff was injured by the following product:

"PROD.L.-2 Each of the defendants knew the product would be purchased and used without inspection for defects. The *product was defective* when it left the control of each defendant. The product at time of injury was being

a. ☐ used in the manner intended by defendants.

b. ☐ used in a manner that was reasonably foreseeable by defendant as involving a substantial danger not readily apparent. Adequate warnings of the danger were not given.

"PROD.L.-3 Plaintiff was ☐ purchaser of the product; ☐ user of the product; ☐ bystander to the use of the product . . .

"PROD.L.-4 Plaintiff's injury was the legal (proximate) result of

☐ **Count One—Strict Liability** of the following defendants who:

☐ manufactured or assembled the product (names) . . .
☐ designed and manufactured component parts supplied to the manufacturer (names) . . .
☐ sold the product to the public (names) . . .

☐ **Count Two—Negligence** of defendants who owed a duty to plaintiff (names) . . .

☐ **Count Three—Breach of Warranty** by defendant (names) . . . . . . ."

(c) **[6:211] Comment:** The above cause-of-action pages will presumably be held demurrer-proof as long as plaintiff checks the appropriate boxes, and fills in the requested names, places, dates, etc. No further charging allegations or ultimate facts are apparently required to state a cause of action.

(4) **[6:212] Attachments requiring plaintiff to insert ultimate facts:** Most of the other cause-of-action pages approved by the Judicial Council contain blanks for the charging allegations. The circumstances upon which liability depends in such cases are simply too varied for standardization. For example:

(a) **[6:213] Cause of Action—Premises Liability (*Form 6:E*)**

"Prem.L-1 . . . On (date) plaintiff was injured on the following premises in the following fashion (*description of premises and circumstances of injury*): . . ."

1) **[6:214] Insufficient without more:** These allegations by themselves do *not* state a cause of action. They fail to state *in what manner* the premises were hazardous and the nature of the relationship between the allegedly hazardous condition and the injuries suffered by plaintiff: "It is up to the pleader to add the details that complete the picture." [See *People ex rel. Dept. of Transp. v. Sup.Ct. (Verdeja)* (1992) 5 CA4th 1480, 1484, 7 CR2d 498, 500 (citing text)]

(b) [6:215] **Cause of Action—Intentional Tort** (*Form 6:D*)

"IT-1 . . . By the following acts or omissions to act, defendant intentionally caused the damage to plaintiff on (date) at (place) (*description of reasons for liability*) . . ."

(c) [6:216] **Cause of Action—General Negligence** (*Form 6:C*)

"GN-1 . . . By the following acts or omissions to act, defendant negligently caused the damage to plaintiff on (date) at (place) (*description of reasons for liability*) . . ."

(d) [6:217] **Exemplary Damages Attachment** (*Form 6:G*)

"EX-1 . . . Plaintiff alleges that the defendant was guilty of (malice, fraud or oppression) as defined in Civil Code Section 3294 and plaintiff should recover, in addition to actual damages to make an example of and to punish defendant.

"EX-2 . . . The facts supporting plaintiff's claim are as follows: . . ."

(*See ¶6:156 ff. for allegations required for punitive damages.*)

(e) [6:218] **Comment:** It remains to be seen how much detail judges will require in determining the sufficiency of the "circumstances of injury" or "reasons for liability" or "facts supporting plaintiff's claim."

1) Some may conclude that since the statute authorizes the forms to be drafted in "non-technical language" (CCP §425.12), a lesser showing should be required . . . i.e., something roughly equivalent to "notice pleading" under the Federal Rules.

2) However, most judges apparently think otherwise: Since CCP §425.10 still requires a "statement of the *facts* constituting the *cause of action*" (¶6:120), *whatever ultimate facts were required before adoption of the Official Forms are still required.* Under this view, plaintiff's attorney will have to insert in the cause-of-action pages enough "ultimate facts" (¶6:123) to make the complaint demurrer-proof. (If so, the Forms will have little real impact on the *content* of the complaint—even though the format and appearance are drastically altered.)

(5) **[6:219]** **How to attack improperly executed Official Forms:** The Official Forms require a lot of box-checking and filling-in-blanks. (For example, there are 79 boxes that may be checked on a personal injury complaint with various attachments!)

What is the effect of *failing* to check an appropriate box . . . or checking *too many* (where only one is appropriate) . . . or *not filling in* all of the blanks on the Official Forms?

(a) **[6:220]** **Omitting facts essential to cause of action:** Failing to check a box or fill in a blank may render the complaint subject to a *general demurrer* if the information requested is essential to state a cause of action (*see* ¶7:39 ff.). [*People ex rel. Department of Transp. v. Sup.Ct. (Verdeja)* (1992) 5 CA4th 1480, 1486, 7 CR2d 498, 501]

(b) **[6:221]** **Omitting facts NOT essential to state cause of action:** Omissions of other information required on the Official Form (e.g., failing to fill in names, dates, places in a personal injury complaint) would at most subject the complaint to *demurrer for uncertainty* (*see* ¶7:84 ff.).

- **[6:222]** **Comment:** Omission of certain information requested in the Official Forms may not be ground for demurrer or motion of any kind. E.g., omitting the *place* of accident in a personal injury complaint does not render the complaint subject to general *or* special demurrer (the place of accident being relevant to venue rather than the cause of action).

(c) **[6:223]** **Checking too many boxes:** If only one of several statements in the Official Forms is appropriate (e.g., boxes in personal injury complaint identifying plaintiff as a corporation *or* unincorporated entity *or* public entity *or* minor, etc.), checking more than one may render the complaint subject to *demurrer for uncertainty* (¶7:84 ff.).

d. **Form of allegations**

(1) **[6:224]** **Direct allegations required:** Each ultimate fact should be alleged directly, rather than inferentially or by way of recital.

For example, if the fact to be alleged is that A executed a contract as agent for B, it should be alleged as:

- "At all times herein mentioned, A was the agent of B, and in executing the contract hereafter mentioned, was acting in the scope of his authority as such agent and with the permission and consent of B."

It should *not* be alleged as:

- *"While acting as B's agent,* A executed the contract hereafter mentioned . . . "

(2) **[6:225]** **Allegations on information and belief:** Where plaintiff is basing his or her allegations on hearsay or surmise, rather than personal knowledge, they should be pleaded "on information and belief."

(a) **[6:226]** **Traditional form:** The traditional language has been: "Plaintiff is informed and believes and *based on such information and belief alleges that . . .* "

(b) **[6:227]** **Official Forms:** The modern language used in the Official Forms is simply, "I am informed and believe that . . . " (Cross-Complaint, Personal Injury, para. 6.a., *see Form 6:H).* Or simply, "The following paragraphs of this complaint are alleged on information and belief." (Complaint, Personal Injury, para. 6., *see Form 6:A.)*

(c) **[6:228]** **Important where pleading verified:** If plaintiff verifies the complaint (*see* ¶6:309-325), it constitutes an *oath* that each allegation therein is true "... *except* as to matters alleged therein on information and belief . . ." [CCP §446; and see *City of Santa Cruz v. Mun.Ct. (Kennedy)* (1989) 49 C3d 74, 88, 260 CR 520, 528]

- [6:229] **Comment:** Pleading on information and belief gives plaintiff some leeway in making a verified claim. I.e., where the facts are difficult or impossible to establish on personal knowledge, plaintiff can state the claim broadly on "information and belief" without running the risk of perjury.

(d) **[6:230]** **Limitations—presumptive or constructive knowledge:** However, plaintiff may *not* allege facts "on information and belief" where he has reason to know them directly. For example:

- [6:231] Matters *presumptively* within plaintiff's knowledge; e.g., whether or not plaintiff owns the easement that is the subject of the litigation. [See *Thompson v. Sutton* (1942) 50 CA2d 272, 279, 122 P2d 975, 979]

- [6:232] Matters of which plaintiff has *constructive* knowledge; e.g., facts ascertainable from public records. [*Searcy v. Hemet Unified School Dist.* (1986) 177 CA3d 792, 802, 223 CR 206, 211]

(e) [6:232.1] ***Caution—impact of CCP §128.7?*** An attorney's signature on a pleading is deemed an implied certification that all factual contentions have evidentiary support . . . "or, *if specifically so identified*, are likely to have evidentiary support after reasonable opportunity for further investigation or discovery." [CCP §128.7 (emphasis added) (applies to cases filed after 1994); *see discussion at* ¶*9:1135 ff.*]

It remains to be seen whether the traditional qualification that facts are alleged "on information and belief" satisfies this requirement. Meanwhile, it is safer to use the language of §128.7. (E.g., "The following allegations are likely to have evidentiary support after a reasonable opportunity for further investigation or discovery: . . .")

[6:232.2-232.4] *Reserved.*

➡️[6:232.5] ***CAUTION—No protection against malicious prosecution:*** Making a statement "on information and belief" may insulate a declarant or affiant from criminal liability for perjury (for statements under oath); and it may avoid a judicial admission. But it does *not* insulate the pleader from liability for malicious prosecution: "(N)o one can obtain a license to maliciously prosecute a lawsuit simply by reciting 'on information and belief.'" [*Mabie v. Hyatt* (1998) 61 CA4th 581, 596, 71 CR2d 657, 667, fn. 9]

(3) **Incorporation by reference**

(a) [6:233] **Exhibits:** Plaintiff may attach a copy of a document to the complaint and incorporate it by reference. By so doing, the documents become part of the complaint as if set forth verbatim therein. Thus, the contents of the *exhibit may supply the ultimate facts* required to state the cause of action. [*Del Mar Beach Club Owners Assn., Inc. v. Imperial Contracting Co., Inc.* (1981) 123 CA3d 898, 908, 176 CR 886, 891]

Typically, the complaint alleges: "Plaintiff and defendant executed the written agreement, a copy of which is attached hereto as Exhibit A and incorporated herein by this reference."

1) [6:234] **Effect of ambiguous terms:** Usually, no further pleading of the terms and conditions of the agreement is required. But, if any part of the incorporated agreement is ambiguous, plaintiff must allege the meaning he or she ascribes to it. Otherwise, the matter may be dismissed: i.e., the complaint is subject to demurrer for failure to state a cause of action. [*Beck v. American Health Group Int'l, Inc.* (1989) 211 CA3d 1555, 1561, 260 CR 237, 241]

➡ [6:235] *PRACTICE POINTER:* Even where an agreement is *unambiguous* on its face, it is good practice to allege the essential terms. This will assist the court in determining exactly what provision of the agreement is in dispute, what breach is claimed, etc.

(b) [6:236] **Allegations in other causes of action:** It is common practice to incorporate by reference various allegations from previous causes of action in the complaint to save repetition (typically, allegations as to venue, party status, sequence of events, etc.). The latter cause of action will then be read as if it contained each allegation so incorporated. [*Kajima Eng. & Const., Inc. v. City of Los Angeles* (2002) 95 CA4th 921, 931-932, 116 CR2d 187, 195 (citing text)]

Example: "Plaintiff incorporates by this reference each and all of the allegations contained in Paragraphs 2, 3, 6 and 8 of the First Cause of Action of this complaint, as fully as though set forth at length herein."

➡ [6:237] *PRACTICE POINTER: Be careful not to incorporate too much from an earlier cause of action. Doing so may raise problems if the later cause of action contains inconsistent or conflicting facts or theories (see ¶6:242-249).*

1) [6:238] **Incorporating whole causes of action as creating uncertainty?** Some cases criticize incorporating *entire* causes of action ("chain letter" pleading), as creating ambiguity and redundancy. [See *International Billing Ser-*

*vices, Inc. v. Emigh* (2000) 84 CA4th 1175, 1179, 101 CR2d 532, 534; *Uhrich v. State Farm Fire & Cas. Co.* (2003) 109 CA4th 598, 605, 135 CR2d 131, 136]

Other courts find no problem with this practice: "It is axiomatic that a civil plaintiff may for the sake of convenience incorporate by reference previous portions of his pleading *for informational purposes only.*" [*Cal-West Nat'l Bank v. Sup.Ct. (Phillips)* (1986) 185 CA3d 96, 100-101, 229 CR 431, 434 (emphasis added)—24th cause of action incorporated by reference 2nd through 23rd causes of action; claim of uncertainty was "nonsense"]

(c) [6:239] **Other pleadings in same lawsuit:** Although there is no rule against it, it is generally *not* good practice to incorporate by reference parts of other pleadings in the same lawsuit. Doing so complicates, rather than simplifies, determining what is at issue. (E.g., Defendant #2 incorporates denials and defenses pleaded in answer filed by Defendant #1.)

One noteworthy exception: *Cross-complaints for indemnification* usually incorporate by reference the allegations of the complaint as a "shorthand" way of showing the existence of the claim for which indemnification is sought.

(d) [6:240] **Pleadings in different lawsuit:** A pleader *cannot* incorporate by reference all or part of some pleading in another lawsuit, even if pending in the same court. If necessary to state a cause of action, such other pleadings should be set forth verbatim in the present complaint, or a copy of those pleadings should be attached as an exhibit and incorporated by reference in the present complaint.

(4) [6:241] **"On or about" allegations:** Where the date is crucial (e.g., for statute of limitations purposes), an allegation that an event occurred "on or about" that date is sufficient to withstand demurrer. I.e., the complaint does not show on its face that it is time-barred (at most, it reveals only that it *may* be). [*Childs v. State of California* (1983) 144 CA3d 155, 160-161, 192 CR 526, 528-529; see ¶7:53.1]

e. [6:242] **Right to plead inconsistently or in the alternative:** In general, plaintiff may plead whatever version of facts, or whatever legal theory, would support recovery. And, if plaintiff is uncertain as to the facts or theory on which he or she can prevail, he or she is entitled to plead them in the *alternative*, or even *inconsistently*—subject to the limitations noted below. [*Rader Co. v. Stone* (1986) 178 CA3d 10, 29, 223 CR 806, 816; see *Jackson v. County of Los Angeles* (1997) 60 CA4th 171, 181, 70 CR2d 96, 102 (citing text)]

(1) [6:243] **Example:** A complaint seeking damages for fraud may properly allege:

- Defendant *intentionally* misrepresented material facts (deceit); and

- Defendant *negligently* misrepresented the facts (no deceit).

(2) [6:244] **Limitation against pleading alternatively or inconsistently in same cause of action:** Each version of the facts or each legal theory should be pleaded in a separate cause of action in the complaint. [*Campbell v. Rayburn* (1954) 129 CA2d 232, 276 P2d 671, 672]

(a) [6:245] **How to attack:** A complaint that jumbles together several inconsistent versions of the facts, or different legal theories, may be subject to a *demurrer for uncertainty* (CCP §430.10(f); *see* ¶7:84 *ff.*).

Further, in a proper case, the complaint could be subject to *general demurrer* for failure to state a cause of action. [*O'Hare v. Marine Elec. Co.* (1964) 229 CA2d 33, 36, 39 CR 799, 800—minority shareholder's complaint that each defendant was "an officer *and/or* director *and/or* shareholder" failed to state cause of action for breach of fiduciary duty . . . because no direct allegation that any defendant *was* a director or shareholder]

(b) [6:246] **Example:** In a breach of contract suit, P normally may allege his or her performance in general terms ("P duly performed all conditions on his part"). But "a general allegation of due performance will not suffice if plaintiff also sets forth what has actually occurred and such specific facts do *not* constitute due performance." [*Careau & Co. v. Security Pac. Business Credit, Inc.* (1990) 222 CA3d 1371, 1390, 272 CR 387, 396]

(3) [6:247] **Limitation against pleading inconsistent FACTS in verified complaint:** Inconsistent legal theories are permissible in any complaint—verified or not. But several appellate decisions hold that inconsistent *facts* are *not* permissible in a *verified* complaint . . . on the theory that the pleader "should not be permitted to blow hot and cold as to the facts" in a pleading that

is under oath. The rationale is that this would make a sham out of the oath (even if the inconsistent facts were pleaded on "information and belief"). [*Steiner v. Rowley* (1950) 35 C2d 713, 718-719, 221 P2d 9, 12] (The *Steiner* rule has been repeatedly criticized, but has not been overruled!)

The court is required to take as true those allegations which bear most strongly *against* the pleader. [*Manti v. Gunari* (1970) 5 CA3d 442, 449, 85 CR 366, 371— same rule applies to both verified and *unverified* pleadings (dictum)]

➡️[6:248]  **PRACTICE POINTER:**  Keep this in mind in deciding whether to have plaintiff verify the complaint. If plaintiff verifies, you can force a verified answer from the defendant (¶*6:317, 6:488*). But the trade-off is that you may have to plead more narrowly in order to avoid inconsistent factual allegations in the complaint.

(a) [6:249]  **How to attack:**  Demurrer for failure to state facts sufficient to constitute a cause of action (CCP §430.10(e); ¶*7:39 ff.*).

[6:249.1-249.4]  *Reserved.*

f.  [6:249.5]  **Limitation—election of remedies:**  Although plaintiff may proceed to trial on alternative theories with inconsistent remedies, an election of remedies may be required *before entry of judgment.* (E.g., P sues to rescind a contract for fraud or, in the alternative, for damages resulting from the fraud. P must elect one remedy—rescission or damages—before judgment.)

"The election of remedies doctrine states that accepting an actual benefit from an alternative theory that renders continued pursuit of the alternative unfair constitutes an election." [*Smith v. Golden Eagle Ins. Co.* (1999) 69 CA4th 1371, 1375, 82 CR2d 300, 303 (internal quotes omitted)]

•  [6:249.6]  P's complaint sought punitive damages for invasion of privacy (common law tort) and statutory penalties under Pen.C. §637.2(a) for unlawful wiretapping. Although P *could not recover* both punitive damages and statutory penalties for the same injury, it was permissible to proceed on both theories at the pleading stage: "Once the verdict is returned, plaintiffs, if they prevail, may then elect whether to accept the . . . statutory penalties or the punitive damage award." [*Clauson v. Sup.Ct. (Pedus Svcs., Inc.)* (1998) 67 CA4th 1253, 1256, 79 CR2d 747, 749]

g.  [6:250]  **Limitation—rule against "splitting" single cause of action into separate lawsuits:**  Full recovery for each cause of action (same "primary right") must be obtained in a single lawsuit. A plaintiff cannot "split" a cause of action into successive suits (*see ¶6:251*). [See *Hamilton v. Asbestos Corp., Ltd.* (2000) 22 C4th 1127, 1145, 95 CR2d 701, 713; *Craig v. County of Los Angeles* (1990) 221 CA3d 1294, 1301, 271 CR 82, 85-86; compare *Harris v. Grimes* (2002) 104 CA4th 180, 187, 127 CR2d 791, 796—"splitting" rule not applicable where *court*, not plaintiff, splits federal and state causes of action arising out of same injury]

The rule against splitting a single cause of action is in part a rule of *abatement:* i.e., if the first suit is still pending, defendant may raise as a defense to the second suit (by demurrer or answer) that "there is another action pending between the same parties on the same cause of action." [CCP §430.10(c); *Hamilton v. Asbestos Corp., Ltd.*, supra, 22 C4th at 1146, 95 CR2d at 713-714]

The rule against splitting is also in part an application of the doctrine of *res judicata:* i.e., a judgment on a "split" claim bars any later action for the balance. [*Hamilton v. Asbestos Corp., Ltd.*, supra, 22 C4th at 1146, 95 CR2d at 713-714; *Mycogen Corp. v. Monsanto Co.* (2002) 28 C4th 888, 899, 123 CR2d 432, 440]

(1)  [6:251]  **What constitutes "same" cause of action:** California courts follow the "primary rights" approach: i.e., there is a separate cause of action for invasion of each "primary right." Each different *type* of interest invaded is a separate primary right; e.g., bodily harm, property damage, harm to reputation, etc. [*Craig v. County of Los Angeles*, supra, 221 CA3d at 1301, 271 CR at 86]

"Even where there are multiple legal theories upon which recovery might be predicated, *one injury* gives rise to only one claim for relief." [*Slater v. Blackwood* (1975) 15 C3d 791, 795, 126 CR 225, 226-227 (emphasis added); *Bay Cities Paving & Grading, Inc. v. Lawyers' Mut. Ins. Co.* (1993) 5 C4th 854, 860, 21 CR2d 691, 695]

(a)  [6:251.1]  **Application:**  "Primary rights" include:
— the right to be free from personal injury;
— the right to possession of property;
— the right to performance of a contractual obligation. [*Olsen v. Breeze, Inc.* (1996) 48 CA4th 608, 625-626, 55 CR2d 818, 826]

*See further discussion at ¶6:107 ff.*

(2) **Application—same cause of action**

- **[6:252]** If plaintiff sues for personal injuries based on common law negligence, no subsequent lawsuit will lie for injury based on breach of statutory duty. The same "primary right" (to be free from bodily harm) is involved, and it cannot be split into successive lawsuits. Recovery in the earlier lawsuit bars the later suit. [See *Slater v. Blackwood* (1975) 15 C3d 791, 795, 126 CR 225, 226-227]

- **[6:252.1]** In a malpractice action against Lawyer, Client's "primary right" is the right to be free of the attorney's negligence in connection with the particular matter for which the attorney was retained. Thus, *separate acts* of negligence do *not* create separate causes of action. [*Bay Cities Paving & Grading, Inc. v. Lawyers' Mut. Ins. Co.* (1993) 5 C4th 854, 860, 21 CR2d 691, 695—Lawyer retained on debt collection matter allegedly negligently failed to file stop notice and also failed to foreclose upon previously-recorded mechanic's lien]

  **[6:253]** *Reserved.*

- **[6:254]** Insured recovered small claims judgment against Tortfeasor for portion of property damage not covered by her auto insurance. Insurer was barred from subsequently asserting its subrogation rights against Tortfeasor for the amount it had paid Insured: "(T)he rule against splitting a cause of action is violated where both the insurer and insured pursue separate actions." [*Allstate Ins. Co. v. Mel Rapton, Inc.* (2000) 77 CA4th 901, 908, 92 CR2d 151, 156]

  — **[6:254.1]** But there would be no impermissible splitting where the insured sues for *personal injuries* and the insurer later sues to recover the amount it paid the insured for *property damage* because these are not the same "cause of action." [See *Allstate Ins. Co. v. Mel Rapton, Inc.,* supra, 77 CA4th at 909, 92 CR2d at 157 (dictum)]

  — **[6:254.2]** A tortfeasor who is aware of the insurer's subrogation claim and nonetheless chooses to settle the insured's claim independent from the insurer's claim, *cannot* invoke the rule against splitting a cause of action to bar a later action by the insurer: "(S)uch a settlement, effected with knowledge, actual or constructive of the insurer's subrogation rights constitutes a 'fraud on the insurer.'" [See *Allstate Ins. Co. v.*

*Mel Rapton, Inc.,* supra, 77 CA4th at 912, 92 CR2d at 159 (dictum)]

*Cross-refer:* See further discussion of subrogation rights and duties in Croskey, Kaufman et al., *Cal. Prac. Guide: Insurance Litigation* (TRG), Ch. 9.

(3) **Application—different causes of action**

- [6:255]   P sued County to compel his employment as a Harbor Patrol Officer. Later, he filed a separate suit for fraud, emotional distress and civil rights violations based on County's initial refusal to employ him. These were different "primary rights" and thus there was no "splitting" of the same cause of action. [*Craig v. County of Los Angeles* (1990) 221 CA3d 1294, 1301-1302, 271 CR 82, 86]

   [6:256]   *Reserved.*

- [6:257]   A judgment against a corporation in a breach of contract action did not bar a separate action by the judgment creditor against the corporation and its shareholders for tortious conduct preventing collection of the judgment. A different primary right was involved in each suit; hence, res judicata did not apply. [*Brenelli Amedeo, S.P.A. v. Bakara Furn., Inc.* (1994) 29 CA4th 1828, 1837-1838, 35 CR2d 348, 352-353]

(4) [6:258]   **Construction defects?**   At least for *statute of limitations purposes*, defective construction gives rise to as many causes of action as there are *types* of property damage:

(a) **Application**

- [6:259]   Homeowners' Association sued Condo Developer for construction defects. Some were patent and others latent, and thus subject to different statutes of limitations. Because *separate areas of damage* were involved (water leaks, defective balconies, subsurface drainage, etc.), *separate causes of action* were recognized for statute of limitations purposes . . . although all had been pleaded as a single "cause of action" (breach of warranty). [*Winston Square Homeowner's Ass'n v. Centex West, Inc.* (1989) 213 CA3d 282, 289, 261 CR 605, 609; see *Chu v. Canadian Indem. Co.* (1990) 224 CA3d 86, 98, 274 CR 20, 27—similar result in "continuing damage" case where defects manifested over period of several years]

(b) [6:260] **Comment:** These cases dealing with the statute of limitations do not necessarily resolve the issue for *pleading* purposes: i.e., whether plaintiff can maintain *separate lawsuits* for each separate type of damage.

Arguably, if these are truly separate causes of action, successive lawsuits would *not* violate the rule against "splitting." But there is no known authority in point.

[6:260.1-260.4] *Reserved.*

(5) [6:260.5] **Effect of prior declaratory relief judgment:** A declaratory relief judgment is entitled to collateral estoppel effect (issue preclusive). But it is not necessarily res judicata (claim preclusive). [*Mycogen Corp. v. Monsanto Co.* (2002) 28 C4th 888, 898, 123 CR2d 432, 439]

Thus, a "pure" declaratory relief judgment does not bar a subsequent action to obtain damages or other relief. But if the action included a claim for *coercive* or other relief (e.g., for specific performance of contract), the judgment operates as res judicata, barring a later suit for damages. [CCP §1062; see *Mycogen Corp. v. Monsanto Co.*, supra, 28 C4th at 899, 123 CR2d at 440]

(6) [6:261] **How to attack "splitting":** Defendant may either:

- *Demur* to the complaint in the later action on the ground there is "another action pending between the same parties for the same cause of action." [CCP §430.10(c), ¶7:74-77]

- Or, raise a *plea in abatement* in his or her answer to the later complaint urging the same ground. (*See "pleas in abatement" at* ¶6:475.)

- If the first action has already proceeded to judgment, defendant may raise the defense of *res judicata* as a bar to the later action. I.e., whether plaintiff wins or loses, the judgment in the earlier action *extinguishes* the *cause of action*, so there is nothing left to sue on ... even if the second suit is based on a different theory or seeks a different remedy. [See CCP §1908; *Crowley v. Katleman* (1994) 8 C4th 666, 681-682, 34 CR2d 386, 393-394; *Weikel v. TCW Realty Fund II Holding Co.* (1997) 55 CA4th 1234, 1250, 65 CR2d 25, 34]

5. **Joinder of Causes of Action**

a. [6:262] **No compulsory joinder:** There is *no* requirement that plaintiffs join all related causes of action in a single lawsuit. Rather, plaintiffs may, if they choose, file as many separate lawsuits as they have separate claims.

Example: If plaintiff suffers both personal injuries and property damage in an auto accident, he or she could file two separate actions: i.e., an action for personal injuries; and a separate action for property damage.

➡ [6:263] **PRACTICE POINTER:** However, this is rarely a good idea! Separate lawsuits are costly and substantial *risks* are created thereby (below).

(1) [6:264] **Risk of violating rule against "splitting" cause of action:** Even if the pleader is convinced the related claims are separate, a judge might rule otherwise! If the various claims are held to be part of the *same* cause of action, they must be raised in the same lawsuit, or they are waived.

(2) [6:265] **Risk of collateral estoppel:** If plaintiff *loses* the first action, any *issues actually litigated* will be binding on him or her in the later action . . . even though a *separate* cause of action is involved. [See *Perez v. City of San Bruno* (1980) 27 C3d 875, 883, 168 CR 114, 118]

- [6:266] Thus, if plaintiff files a limited civil case for his or her car repairs and a jury finds defendant not negligent, the jury's finding may bar plaintiff's subsequent personal injury action! [See *Pratt v. Vaughan* (1934) 2 CA2d 722, 38 P2d 799, 800]

- [6:266.1] *Compare—small claims judgments:* Judgments in small claims actions, whether in small claims court or after appeal to the superior court, do not have collateral estoppel effect. [*Rosse v. DeSoto Cab Co.* (1995) 34 CA4th 1047, 1052-1053, 40 CR2d 680, 682-683]

  But a final small claims judgment is entitled to res judicata (claim preclusion) effect. [See *Allstate Ins. Co. v. Mel Rapton, Inc.* (2000) 77 CA4th 901, 907, 92 CR2d 151, 155]

(3) [6:267] **Court may order consolidation or coordination:** Even if separate causes of action are involved, the court has power to order consolidation of separate lawsuits pending in the same court involving "common questions of fact or law." [CCP §1048]

If the lawsuits are pending in different courts, either court may order "noncomplex" cases transferred to and consolidated with cases pending before the court; "complex" cases must be "coordinated" with each other. [CCP §§403, 404; *see ¶12:370 ff. & 12:405 ff.*]

*Cross-refer:* Consolidation and coordination are discussed in *Ch. 12 Part I.*

b. **[6:268] Permissive joinder of causes of action:** Modern practice permits "wide open" joinder of causes of action. There need be *no* subject matter relationship or "common question" between or among the various causes of action joined. [CCP §427.10(a)—"A plaintiff . . . may unite . . . any other causes which he has either alone or with any coplaintiffs . . ."]

(1) **[6:269] Limitation where several defendants:** The only limitation is that where there are several defendants, *at least one* of the causes of action joined must affect *all* of the defendants.

This results not from the rules on joinder of causes, but rather from the rules limiting joinder of parties-defendant, requiring that there be a "question of law or fact common to all." [CCP §379]

(2) **[6:270] Power of court to sever:** If plaintiff joins too many complex or unrelated claims in a single lawsuit, the court has discretionary power to order separate trials of some or all of the claims joined . . . "in furtherance of convenience or to avoid prejudice, or when conducive to expedition and economy." [CCP §1048(b)]

6. **[6:271] Prayer for Relief:** A complaint must contain a "demand for judgment for the relief to which the pleader claims to be entitled." [CCP §425.10(b)] This demand is usually called the "prayer," and is set forth in a separate paragraph at the end of the complaint. For example:

"WHEREFORE, plaintiff prays judgment against defendants and each of them as follows: . . . . . . . . . . . . "

⇨**[6:272] *PRACTICE POINTER:*** If you are seeking *different relief against different defendants*, you may find it helpful either to:

- Use multiple prayers (e.g., " . . . against Defendant A in the sum of $10,000, and against Defendant B in the sum of $50,000 . . ."); or

- Put a *separate prayer at the end of each cause of action* instead of at the end of the complaint.

a. **[6:273] Amount must be stated:** Except as stated below, if money damages are sought, the prayer must state the amount. [CCP §425.10(b)]

➪[6:274]   **PRACTICE POINTER:**   It is a good idea to plead *general* and *special* damages separately and specifically in the prayer in the event of a default judgment (*see ¶5:242 ff.* for detailed discussion regarding limitations on default judgments).

(1)  [6:275]   **Attorney fees:**   If plaintiff is entitled by statute or contract to attorney fees against the defendant (*see ¶1:224*), that fact should be pleaded in the complaint, and a demand included in the prayer. [*Wiley v. Rhodes* (1990) 223 CA3d 1470, 1474, 273 CR 279, 281 (citing text)—default judgment cannot include attorney fees not demanded in complaint]

- **Example:**   "And for an award of attorney's fees, in an amount the court determines to be reasonable, as authorized by the provisions of . . ." (the statute or contract authorizing the fee award).

(2)  [6:276]   **Prejudgment interest:**   If plaintiff is entitled by statute or contract to recover prejudgment interest on the obligation (e.g., Civ.C. §§3287(a), 3288, 3291, 3302), that fact should also be pleaded in the complaint, and a demand included in the prayer.

- **Example:**   "And for interest on the said sum at the rate of . . . percent per annum from . . . . . ., . . . to date of judgment herein."

(a)  [6:277]   **Court's power to award without prayer:** In a contested case, prejudgment interest may be awarded even though the complaint contains *no* prayer for interest. [*Newby v. Vroman* (1992) 11 CA4th 283, 286, 14 CR2d 44, 46]

Indeed, a request for "such other and further relief as the court deems proper" has been held sufficient to allow the court to award prejudgment interest that it deemed "just and equitable." The court had power to make the award on its own although plaintiff failed to request interest as an element of damages at trial. [*North Oakland Med. Clinic v. Rogers* (1998) 65 CA4th 824, 829, 76 CR2d 743, 746]

➪[6:278]   **PRACTICE POINTER:**   Even so, the more prudent practice is to plead the right to prejudgment interest in the complaint and to include a demand therefor in the prayer.

(3)  [6:279]   **Exception—no damages allegations in injury or death actions:**   In actions for personal injury

or wrongful death, the amount of plaintiff's damages claims "shall not be stated in the complaint." [CCP §425.10(b) (applies in both limited and unlimited civil cases)]

(a) [6:280] **Purpose:** The rule is designed to prevent exaggerated demands from being used as a financial bludgeon, and to avoid the potential harm to defendant's credit and reputation from publicity regarding such demands.

(b) [6:281] **Application:** Section 425.10(b) applies as well to *non*-personal injury claims that are *closely tied* to an injury or death cause of action. [See *Jones v. Interstate Recovery Service* (1984) 160 CA3d 925, 929, 206 CR 924, 927—cause of action for trespass and conversion of personal property held "closely tied" to claims for assault and intentional infliction of emotional distress]

(c) [6:282] **Challenge by motion to strike:** Improper allegations of the nature or amount of damages in a superior court injury or death action render the complaint vulnerable to a motion to strike (CCP §436; *see ¶7:167*).

(d) [6:283] **Procedure for notice to defendant:** Since the complaint is silent, a separate statutory procedure is provided to assure defendant notice of plaintiff's damage claims. Defendant may "at any time request a statement setting forth the nature and amount of damages being sought." [CCP §425.11(b); see *Argame v. Werasophon* (1997) 57 CA4th 616, 618, 67 CR2d 281, 282]

⇨[6:284] *PRACTICE POINTER:* The request for statement of damages is available *in addition to other forms of discovery* to which defendants are entitled. Thus, it makes sense for defendants to serve such demand at the outset of every case, and save their interrogatories for later!

*FORM:* Request for Statement re Damages, *see Form 6:S.*

1) [6:285] **Time for furnishing statement:** Plaintiff must furnish the damages statement within 15 days after defendant's request. [CCP §425.11(b)]

If no such request is made, plaintiff must nevertheless furnish the statement before a default may be taken. [CCP §425.11(c)]

2) **[6:286] Content of statement:** The damages statement must specify what amount is claimed for *special* damages, and what amount is claimed for *general* damages. If it states only the total damages claimed, without a breakdown as between special and general damages, it does not satisfy the statute. [*Plotitsa v. Sup.Ct. (Kadri)* (1983) 140 CA3d 755, 762, 189 CR 769, 772]

**FORM:** Statement of Damages, *see Form 6:T.*

3) **[6:287] Not filed:** Neither defendant's request for statement of damages, nor plaintiff's response, is filed with the court (unless in connection with default proceedings; see below). [CRC 201.5(a)(20)]

[6:287.1-287.4] *Reserved.*

4) **[6:287.5] Enforcing response:** If plaintiff fails to respond to a CCP §425.11 request, defendant's remedy is to move for an order compelling a response. The court may also require plaintiff (or plaintiff's counsel) to reimburse defendant for costs incurred in making the motion. [*Argame v. Werasophon,* supra, 57 CA4th at 618, 67 CR2d at 283, fn. 3]

If defendant fails to seek such order, however, defendant waives the right to object at trial to plaintiff's evidence of damages. [*Argame v. Werasophon,* supra, 57 CA4th at 618, 67 CR2d at 282]

(e) **[6:288] Special requirements upon default:** The statement of damages requirement makes entry of default more complicated: If defendant does not respond to the summons and complaint, plaintiff must go back and *re-serve* defendant with the statement of damages *before* seeking entry of default—i.e., double service may be required! *See ¶5:82 ff.*

➡ **[6:289] PRACTICE POINTER:** If there is a likelihood of default, it may be a good idea to attach the statement of damages to the summons and complaint and serve them all at the same time ... thus avoiding the delay and expense of double service.

(f) **[6:290] Not a limit on recovery in nondefault cases:** A CCP §425.11 statement replaces the prayer of the complaint. As such, it limits recovery in default cases but *not* in contested cases. The jury can award any amount supported by the evidence at trial. [*Damele v. Mack Trucks, Inc.* (1990) 219 CA3d 29, 42, 267 CR 197, 204; *see ¶6:296*]

(4) [6:291] **Exception—no allegations as to amount of punitive damages:** No claim for punitive damages shall state the amount or amounts demanded. [Civ.C. §3295(e)]

(a) [6:292] **Purpose:** The rule prevents plaintiff from using exaggerated demands for punitive damages as a financial bludgeon or for publicity purposes.

(b) [6:293] **Procedure for notice to defendant:** Notice of the amount of punitive damages claimed must be given to defendant in the form prescribed by CCP §425.115 prior to entry of default. [CCP §425.115; *see discussion at ¶5:104 ff.*]

b. **Effect of prayer in contested cases**

(1) [6:294] **Determines subject matter jurisdiction:** The type of relief sought and the amount in controversy is generally determined by the prayer of the complaint. This in turn determines whether the action is a limited or unlimited civil case (*see ¶3:2.2*).

(2) [6:295] **Determines right to jury trial:** The prayer of the complaint may also be determinative as to whether "legal" or "equitable" relief is being sought. There is no right to a jury trial where only "equitable" relief is sought. (*See ¶12:285 ff.*)

(3) [6:296] **Not a limit on judgment:** As long as defendant has appeared in the action, the prayer in the complaint does not control the judgment: ". . . (T)he Court may grant (plaintiff) any relief consistent with the case made by the complaint and embraced within the issue." [CCP §580; see *Furia v. Helm* (2003) 111 CA4th 945, 956, 4 CR3d 357, 366]

(a) [6:297] **Court may grant any relief "embraced within the issue":** The parameters of relief available in a contested case are established by the *substantive allegations* of the complaint; e.g., the damage claims. The prayer is not controlling: "When an answer is filed, the case becomes one in which the court is authorized regardless of the prayer to grant *any relief consistent with the plaintiff's averments.*" [*Wright v. Rogers* (1959) 172 CA2d 349, 367-368, 342 P2d 447, 458 (emphasis added)]

(b) [6:298] **Damage allegations no limit on judgment:** Damage allegations in the complaint are *not* controlling in a contested case. As long as there has been adequate opportunity for discovery and the damage issues have been fully tried, the court has power to render judgment for greater relief than demanded in the complaint: "It is lamentable that plaintiff counsel did not move to amend the pleadings to conform to proof but judicial economy would be ill served by requiring this case to be retried because of that technicality." [*Castaic Clay Mfg. Co. v. Dedes* (1987) 195 CA3d 444, 450, 240 CR 652, 655]

　　1) [6:298.1] **Compare—where defendant *fails to appear* at trial:** Where defendant files an answer and receives proper notice of trial but fails to appear, the court may enter judgment following an "uncontested" evidentiary hearing. [CCP §594(a)] (Note: This is *not* a default judgment because an answer is on file.)

　　Due process nevertheless applies. Therefore, the judgment may not exceed the amount that defendant had been given notice was at risk in the litigation (e.g., through discovery or settlement demands). [*Garamendi v. Golden Eagle Ins. Co.* (2004) 116 CA4th 694, 704, 10 CR3d 724, 734—voiding portions of judgment for personal injury damages and attorney fees because defendant had no notice that these were claimed]

(c) [6:299] **Compare—complaint containing remission clause (limited civil cases):** The result is different where the complaint contains a "clear, unambiguous and valid remission clause" to be treated as a "limited civil case" (i.e., maximum recovery $25,000). In that event, the defendant may have taken action and adopted a trial strategy in reliance upon the limitation and no amendment after trial is permitted to seek a greater amount. [*Wozniak v. Lucutz* (2002) 102 CA4th 1031, 1045, 126 CR2d 310, 320]

c. [6:300] **Effect of prayer in default cases:** Default judgments cannot exceed "the amount demanded in the complaint." [CCP §580]

The "amount demanded" is determined *both* from the prayer and from the damage allegations of the complaint (except for personal injury or wrongful death cases in which it is determined from the separate statement of damages required in such cases). [*National Diversified Services, Inc. v. Bernstein* (1985) 168 CA3d 410, 417-418, 214 CR 113, 117-118; *see ¶5:241*]

(1) [6:301] **Rationale:** Defaulting parties have a constitutional right to adequate notice of the maximum judgment that may be assessed against them. [*Becker v. S.P.V. Const. Co., Inc.* (1980) 27 C3d 489, 494, 165 CR 825, 828; *Greenup v. Rodman* (1986) 42 C3d 822, 829, 231 CR 220, 224]

*Cross-refer: See detailed discussion in Ch. 5 at ¶5:233 ff.*

d. [6:302] **Effect of improper prayer:** Sometimes, the prayer seeks a type of damages or form of relief not recoverable as a matter of law under the cause of action pleaded (e.g., punitive damages for a simple breach of contract).

(1) [6:303] **Not ground for demurrer:** A complaint is not demurrable because the prayer seeks a nonrecoverable form of relief: i.e., an improper prayer is irrelevant in determining the sufficiency of the cause of action pleaded. [*Gomez v. Volkswagen of America, Inc.* (1985) 169 CA3d 921, 925, 215 CR 507, 510—complaint found to contain valid cause of action for breach of warranty, notwithstanding prayer for "punitive damages for bad faith"]

(2) [6:304] **Ground for motion to strike:** An improper prayer is subject to a motion to strike. *See ¶7:182.*

7. [6:305] **Subscription:** Every pleading (and other court paper) must be signed by the attorney of record or by the party personally if not represented by counsel. [CCP §128.7]

Where the attorney of record is a law firm, the pleading must be signed by at least one member of the firm individually. [CCP §128.7]

a. [6:305.1] **Effect of omission:** An unsigned complaint "shall be stricken unless omission of the signature is corrected promptly after being called to the attention of the attorney or party." [CCP §128.7; *Vaccaro v. Kaiman* (1998) 63 CA4th 761, 768, 73 CR2d 829, 834 (citing text)—even if not corrected "promptly," striking complaint was abuse of discretion where plaintiff's counsel had in fact signed]

b. [6:306] **Signature as certification of merits:** By signing a court paper, the attorney (or party) certifies that to the best of his or her knowledge, information and belief "formed after an inquiry reasonable under the circumstances":
— the pleading is *not being presented primarily for an improper purpose*;

> — the claims and other legal contentions are *warranted under existing law* or by nonfrivolous argument for extension, modification or reversal of existing law; and

> — the allegations and other *factual contentions have evidentiary support*, or if specifically so identified, are likely to have evidentiary support after reasonable opportunity for discovery. [CCP §128.7(b)]

   (1) **[6:307] Effective 1995:** The above certification applies in actions commenced on or after January 1, 1995, and to all court papers filed in such actions. [CCP §128.7(i)]

   (2) **[6:308] Sanctions:** If the above certification proves incorrect, the court may impose sanctions against the attorney and/or party. [CCP §128.7(c)]

*Cross-refer:* CCP §128.7 is discussed in detail *at ¶9:1135 ff.*

8. **[6:309] Verification:** A verification is an affidavit or declaration under penalty of perjury that the complaint is true. It is usually made in the following language, derived from CCP §446: "...that the same is true of his own knowledge, except as to matters stated therein on information and belief, and as to those matters that he believes it to be true."

*FORM:* Verification, *see Form 6:U.*

  a. **[6:310] Required in a few cases:** The Code requires that complaints in certain cases be verified. These are basically situations in which there is a higher-than-normal risk of harm if the allegations in the complaint are untrue. Included in this category are:

    • Venue allegations in Unlawful Detainers (*see ¶6:100 ff.*) [CCP §1166]

    • Quiet Title [CCP §761.020]

    • All pleadings filed under the Family Code [Fam.C. §212]

    • Involuntary Dissolution of Corporation [Corps.C. §1800]

    • Venue allegations in actions to enforce consumer obligations (*see detailed discussion at ¶6:100 ff.*)

    • Petition for writ of mandate [CCP §1086]

   (1) **[6:311] Effect of failure to verify:** Where verification is required, lack of verification renders the complaint subject to *motion to strike (see ¶7:173).*

     (a) **[6:312] Compare:** In statutory actions to enforce consumer obligations and for unlawful detainer (*¶6:100*), failure to properly plead venue in a verified complaint (or separate affidavit) subjects the complaint to *dismissal; see ¶6:101.*

(b) [6:313] **Curing by amendment:** Failure to verify is generally curable by amendment. Indeed, a verification may be added even after the statute of limitations has run on the time to file the original complaint. [See *United Farm Workers v. Agricultural Labor Relations Board* (1985) 37 C3d 912, 915, 210 CR 453, 454]

(2) [6:314] **Defects in verification:** The verification must *substantially comply* with CCP §446. The test is whether it is sufficiently clear and certain to subject the party to perjury prosecution if material statements are false. [*Ancora-Citronelle Corp. v. Green* (1974) 41 CA3d 146, 150, 115 CR 879, 881]

But a mere "technical defect" in the verification does not render it insufficient. [*Sheeley v. City of Santa Clara* (1963) 215 CA2d 83, 86, 30 CR 121, 123—use of notarization and acknowledgment form instead of verification was "technical defect"]

Similarly, a verification may be upheld although signed by the party's *attorney*, rather than by the party. The mistake is a matter of "form" rather than "substance." [*Soltani-Rastegar v. Sup.Ct. (Brinzo)* (1989) 208 CA3d 424, 428, 256 CR 255, 258 (dealing with petition for relief from discovery order, but same principle presumably applies to complaints); *California State Univ. v. Sup.Ct. (McClatchy Co.)* (2001) 90 CA4th 810, 822 108 CR2d 870, 877, fn. 4 (petition for writ of mandate)]

(3) [6:315] **Public entities exempt:** CCP §446 (second paragraph) provides that when a public entity is the plaintiff, "the complaint need not be verified." This takes precedence over any of the above statutes requiring verification. [*Murrieta Valley Unified School Dist. v. County of Riverside* (1991) 228 CA3d 1212, 1223, 279 CR 421, 427]

b. [6:316] **Optional in other cases:** In any other case, the plaintiff *may* verify the complaint if he or she chooses. Doing so has some supposed advantages . . . but also some disadvantages:

(1) [6:317] **Advantages**

(a) If the complaint is verified, defendant's *answer also must be verified*; so that the defendant has to take the matter seriously, and runs the risk of impeachment, or even perjury, if he or she falsely denies plaintiff's allegations. [CCP §446, ¶6:488-491]

(b) The defendant's answer to a verified complaint *cannot* consist of a simple *general denial* (as it can if the complaint is unverified). [CCP §431.30(d); ¶*6:404*]

   (c)  A verified complaint *can be used as a substitute for an affidavit* in seeking a *preliminary injunction*, restraining order, etc. [CCP §527] (But this is *not* recommended; *see "Practice Pointer,"* ¶*6:319*.)

  (2)  **[6:318]**  **Disadvantages**

   (a)  The *rule against pleading inconsistent facts* in a verified complaint restricts how broadly plaintiffs can plead their claims (*see* ¶*6:247*);

   (b)  The risk of *impeachment*, or even perjury, if plaintiffs' proof at trial contradicts their verified complaint;

   (c)  The greater risk of drawing a malicious prosecution action from the defendant, if plaintiff loses the lawsuit;

   (d)  If verified by counsel, it *may* constitute a waiver of the *attorney-client privilege* as to matters alleged in the pleading (*see* ¶*6:497*); and

   (e)  If verified by the client, he or she is likely to be questioned at deposition or at trial about allegations in his or her verified complaint. Because complaints usually contain language with which the average lay person is not familiar, the client may be confused and give inappropriate responses.

**[6:319]**  ***PRACTICE POINTER:***  The disadvantages usually prevail, because the advantages of verifying (*above*) are more hypothetical than real:

- The possibility of impeaching a defendant for falsely denying the complaint is remote, because pleadings are increasingly general and form-like (e.g., Official Form complaints and answers). The allegations are usually broad enough to justify some sort of denial or contradiction and hence no basis for impeachment.

- Using a verified complaint as a substitute for a separate affidavit in *injunction* cases is a *bad* idea: To obtain an injunction, you need specific evidentiary allegations. A complaint containing such allegations would be an improper pleading ("ultimate facts" required; *see* ¶*6:123*). Further, it is risky to *plead* matters that specifically; if wrong, you're stuck with them. (A pleading constitutes a binding judicial admission; whereas affidavits are only evidence, and can be controverted if necessary at trial.)

c. **[6:320] Persons who may verify complaint**

- Any plaintiff (if there are several, any one of them may verify);

- Any *officer* of a corporate-plaintiff, or *partner* of a partnership-plaintiff;

- Plaintiff's *attorney* or any *other person* if the plaintiff is absent from the county where the attorney has his or her office or is otherwise *unable* to verify; "*or* the facts are within the *personal knowledge* of the attorney or other person verifying." In such cases, the verification must state the *reasons* why it is not made by the plaintiff. [CCP §446; see *League of Women Voters v. Eu* (1992) 7 CA4th 649, 656, 9 CR2d 416, 420]

  **FORM:** Verification, *see Form 6:U.*

(1) **[6:321] Information and belief:** If the complaint is verified by an officer of the corporate-plaintiff, it shall be made on information and belief. Likewise, as to verifications by an attorney or other person based on plaintiff's being absent from the county or otherwise unable to verify. [CCP §446; see *League of Women Voters v. Eu,* supra, 7 CA4th at 656, 9 CR2d at 420]

  (a) **[6:322] Effect:** A complaint so verified would be sufficient for pleading purposes . . . but *not* as an affidavit. Affidavits must be based on personal knowledge, rather than hearsay. A complaint verified "on information and belief" shows lack of personal knowledge (and thus, for example, it could *not* be used as an application for preliminary injunction or temporary restraining order).

(2) **[6:323] Attorney verification discouraged:** The courts have construed CCP §446 to permit attorney verification only where the client's absence from the county makes it impractical or *impossible* to obtain the client's signature. If the client can be reached by mail, no such impossibility exists . . . and attorney verification is not allowed! [*DeCamp v. First Kensington Corp.* (1978) 83 CA3d 268, 275, 147 CR 869, 873—verification of answer]

  **[6:324] PRACTICE POINTER:** Even if legally permissible for you to verify a pleading on behalf of a client, you should *avoid* doing so. In effect, it makes you a witness to the facts verified. Thus, you may properly be deposed by the other side, or even called to testify at time of trial, injuring your effectiveness as an advocate in a jury trial (see

CRPC 5-210). Indeed, if your testimony is crucial you may even be disqualified as trial counsel.

d. [6:325] **Verification may be executed anywhere:** If the proper language is used, the declaration can be executed by the client anywhere in the world. It need only state that the declaration under penalty of perjury is made "under the laws of the State of California." [CCP §2015.5]

9. [6:326] **Prior Court Order Required for Certain Claims:** "Gatekeeper" statutes limit the "pleadability" of certain claims by requiring court approval before such claims may be filed. This includes:

- Punitive damages claims against health care providers (CCP §425.13(a); ¶6:327 ff.).

- Punitive damages claims against religious corporations (CCP §425.14; ¶6:346 ff.).

- Negligence claims against volunteer directors or officers of nonprofit corporations (CCP §425.15; ¶6:377 ff.).

- Claims against attorneys for conspiracy with their clients (Civ.C. §1714.10(a); ¶6:354 ff.).

Although each statute has slightly different wording and procedures, they serve a similar purpose—i.e., to deter "frivolous" claims. In addition, as discussed below, the threshold question of "pleadability" under each statute is governed by the same legal standard (*see* ¶6:351). [*College Hosp., Inc. v. Sup.Ct. (Crowell)* (1994) 8 C4th 704, 717-718, 34 CR2d 898, 905-906]

a. [6:327] **Punitive damages claims against health care providers:** No claim for punitive damages may be included in an *original* complaint "(i)n any action for damages arising out of the *professional negligence* of a *health care provider.*" [CCP §425.13(a) (emphasis added)]

Any such claim may be raised only in an *amended* complaint, filed with leave of court pursuant to the procedures discussed below.

Section 425.13 was enacted amid concern over plaintiffs including sham intentional tort claims as a basis for punitive damages in medical malpractice actions. The statute alleviates this problem "by *shifting to the plaintiff the procedural burden* that would otherwise fall on the defendant to remove a 'frivolous' or 'unsubstantial' claim early in the suit." [*Covenant Care, Inc. v. Sup.Ct. (Inclan)* (2004)    C4th    , 11 CR3d 222, 233 (emphasis added)]

(1) [6:328] **"Health care provider":** "Health care provider" means any person *licensed or certified* pursuant to specified licensing provisions and any licensed clinic, health dispensary, or health facility and their legal rep-

resentatives (e.g., executors, administrators, etc.). [See CCP §425.13(b); *Covenant Care, Inc. v. Sup.Ct. (Inclan)*, supra,      C4th at      , 11 CR3d at 231]

(a) [6:328.1] **Application:** The term "health care provider" does *not* require a direct patient care relationship with the party seeking punitive damages. It has been held to include:

- a medical corporation providing utilization review for an HMO (*Palmer v. Sup.Ct. (Sharp Rees-Stealy Med. Group* (2002) 103 CA4th 953, 963, 127 CR2d 252, 259);

- a sperm bank and physicians providing genetic screening of potential sperm donors (*Johnson v. Sup.Ct. (California Cryobank, Inc.)* (2002) 101 CA4th 869, 882, 124 CR2d 650, 660);

- a tissue bank (*Cryolife, Inc. v. Sup.Ct. (Minvielle)* (2003) 110 CA4th 1145, 1157, 2 CR3d 396, 405).

[6:328.2-328.4] *Reserved.*

(b) [6:328.5] **Compare—elder care custodian:** A health care provider may assume responsibility for elderly and dependent adults. But a person or entity caring for elderly adults is *not* necessarily a "health care provider" within the meaning of §425.13: "Without question, health care provider and elder custodian 'capacities' are conceptually distinct." [*Covenant Care, Inc. v. Sup.Ct. (Inclan)*, supra,      C4th at      , 11 CR3d at 231]

(2) [6:329] **Actions "arising out of professional negligence":** CCP §425.13 is not limited to malpractice claims. It applies to any claim for injury—including intentional tort claims—"*directly related to the professional services provided*" by a health care provider. [*Central Pathology Service Med. Clinic, Inc. v. Sup.Ct. (Hull)* (1992) 3 C4th 181, 191, 10 CR2d 208, 215 (emphasis added); see also *Covenant Care, Inc. v. Sup.Ct. (Inclan)*, supra,      C4th at      , 11 CR3d at 229]

*Compare—other statutes:* This interpretation of "arising out of professional negligence" does *not* necessarily apply to other statutes using similar terminology (e.g., CCP §364 requires a prelawsuit notice of intent to sue in actions "based on professional negligence"; *see* ¶1:856). [See *Covenant Care, Inc. v. Sup.Ct. (Inclan)*, supra,      C4th at      , 11 CR3d at 233]

(a) [6:330] **Application:** Section 425.13 applies to a broad range of intentional torts typically pled in medical malpractice cases:

- [6:330.1] Thus, for example, a cause of action for *battery* based on treatment exceeding or different from that to which plaintiff consented is subject to the statute . . . because the injury arose out of the *manner* in which professional services were provided. [*Central Pathology Service Med. Clinic, Inc. v. Sup.Ct. (Hull)*, supra, 3 C4th at 192, 10 CR2d at 215]

*(Text cont'd on p. 6-69)*

**RESERVED**

- [6:331]   Likewise, claims for *fraud* relating to the manner in which defendants performed and communicated the results of medical tests are subject to the statute, as are claims for *intentional infliction* of emotional distress based on the same acts. [*Central Pathology Service Med. Clinic, Inc. v. Sup.Ct. (Hull)*, supra, 3 C4th at 192-193, 10 CR2d at 215; *Davis v. Sup.Ct. (Fuentes)* (1994) 27 CA4th 623, 629, 33 CR2d 6, 9-10—doctor allegedly lied about his qualifications and falsified his findings]

- [6:331.1]   A suit against a hospital for *negligence* in *failing to protect* patients from sexual assault by its employees by hiring and supervising competent staff, has been held subject to CCP §425.13. That claim arises out of the *manner* in which the hospital provided professional services. [*United Western Med. Ctrs. v. Sup.Ct. (Michelle Marie H.)* (1996) 42 CA4th 500, 49 CR2d 682, 684-685]

  [6:331.2-331.4]   *Reserved.*

- [6:331.5]   *Compare—elder abuse:* Claims against health care providers for elder abuse under Welf. & Inst.C. §15600 et seq. do *not* "arise out of professional negligence" where the neglect or other abuse *is reckless or done with "oppression, fraud or malice."* In such cases, the health care provider is not entitled to the special protections of CCP §425.13 and is subject to punitive damage claims. [*Covenant Care, Inc. v. Sup.Ct. (Inclan)*, supra,      C4th at    , 11 CR3d at 230 (emphasis added)]

- [6:332]   *Compare—sexual assault:* But a claim for sexual assault by the person providing the professional services would not "in most instances" be subject to the statute . . . because a sexual assault is *not* directly related to the manner in which professional care is furnished. [*Central Pathology Service Med. Clinic, Inc. v. Sup.Ct. (Hull)*, supra, 3 C4th at 192, 10 CR2d at 215]

  The result is different, however, where the services being rendered involve the patient's sex organs (e.g., a gynecologist touches plaintiff's sex organs improperly in the course of a gynecological examination). A sexual battery claim in such a case is necessarily "directly related to" the manner in which the gynecological services were rendered, and therefore subject to CCP §425.13. [*Cooper v. Sup.Ct. (Roberson)* (1997) 56 CA4th 744, 751, 65 CR2d 674, 678]

(b) **[6:333] Includes claims by nonpatients:** Plaintiff need not be a patient of the health care provider. The test is whether plaintiff's injury was *directly related to the manner* in which the provider was rendering professional services. [*Williams v. Sup.Ct. (San Diego Rehabilitation Institute)* (1994) 30 CA4th 318, 326, 36 CR2d 112, 116—business visitor claimed injuries resulting from Hospital's failure to control violent patient]

(3) **[6:334] Procedure to add punitives claim:** To assert a punitive damages claim against a health care provider, plaintiff must file a *motion to amend* the complaint to allow filing of such claim. [CCP §425.13(a)]

(a) **[6:334.1] Evidentiary showing:** The motion must be supported by *affidavits* (declarations) stating facts sufficient to support a finding that there is a "substantial probability" plaintiff will prevail on the punitive damages claim; *see ¶6:340.*

(4) **[6:335] Time limit on motion to amend:** Any motion to amend to add a punitives claim against a health care provider must be filed within 2 years after the original complaint was filed or 9 months before "the date the case is first set for trial," *whichever is earlier.* [CCP §425.13(a)]

The 9-month limit prevents the "last minute" insertion of a punitive damages claim into a case that has been prepared for trial without consideration of that issue. [*Goodstein v. Sup.Ct. (Pittman)* (1996) 42 CA4th 1635, 1642, 50 CR2d 459, 463]

The outside limit of 2 years prevents delayed assertion of a punitives claim where the issue and discovery requirements are likely to have become fixed. [*Goodstein v. Sup.Ct. (Pittman)*, supra, 42 CA4th at 1642, 50 CR2d at 463]

(a) **[6:336] "Date matter first set for trial":** This means the first trial date, not the date of the trial setting conference. [*Brown v. Sup.Ct. (Bengs)* (1990) 224 CA3d 989, 993, 274 CR 442, 445 (citing text)]

1) **[6:336.1] *Caution:*** Under fast track, many cases are now tried within a year or so from filing of complaint. This creates a narrow "window of opportunity"—perhaps only 3 or 4

months after filing—within which plaintiffs can seek leave to amend to allege punitive damages against a health care provider.

(b) [6:337] **Effect of trial continuance:** Because the 9-month period is measured from the *first* trial date, a continuance does not reopen the time for a motion to add a punitives claim. [*Brown v. Sup.Ct. (Bengs)*, supra, 224 CA3d at 994, 274 CR at 445]

(c) [6:338] **Exception for priority cases:** The 9-month time limit does not apply where plaintiff is entitled by statute to an early trial setting (e.g., because of age or illness; see CCP §36, *discussed at ¶12:246 ff.*). In such cases, the motion to amend may be made *less* than 9 months before the first trial date if necessary to preserve plaintiff's claim. [*Looney v. Sup.Ct. (Medical Center of No. Hollywood)* (1993) 16 CA4th 521, 536, 20 CR2d 182, 190]

(d) [6:339] **Exception where trial set within 9 months after filing:** Likewise, the 9-month limit should not bar amendments adding punitives in courts where cases are set for trial within 9 months after the action is filed . . . "arguably rendering compliance with section 425.13 impossible." [*Brown v. Sup.Ct. (Bengs)*, supra, 224 CA3d at 994, 274 CR at 445—court has flexibility at trial setting conference to accommodate plaintiff in such predicament]

(e) [6:339.1] **Court's discretion to permit untimely amendment:** Where necessary "in the interest of fairness and justice," the court has discretion to relieve plaintiff from an "impossible or impracticable" time limitation. [*Goodstein v. Sup.Ct. (Pittman)* (1996) 42 CA4th 1635, 1638, 50 CR2d 459, 460-461—trial set within 9 months although pleadings still at issue and discovery incomplete]

1) [6:339.2] **Showing required:** A "heavy burden" is required to obtain such relief. Plaintiff must show that:
— he or she was *unaware* of facts or evidence necessary to make a proper motion under §425.13 more than 9 months prior to the first assigned trial date;
— he or she made *reasonable, diligent and good faith efforts to discover* the necessary facts or evidence to support such a motion prior to the first assigned trial date;
— after assignment of the trial date, he or she made reasonable, diligent and good faith

efforts *to complete* the necessary discovery;
- he or she filed the §425.13 motion to amend as soon as reasonably practicable after completing such discovery (but in no event more than 2 years after commencement of the action); and
- defendant will suffer no surprise or prejudice by reason of any shortened time period and will be given reasonable opportunity to complete all necessary discovery to meet plaintiff's punitive damages allegations. [*Goodstein v. Sup.Ct. (Pittman),* supra, 42 CA4th at 1645, 50 CR2d at 465]

(5) **[6:340]** **"Substantial probability" of success required:** To obtain leave to amend to add a punitives claim against a health care provider, the statute requires plaintiff to establish a "substantial probability" that he or she will prevail on that claim. [CCP §425.13(a)]

"Substantial probability" requires plaintiff to show:
- a *legally sufficient* claim;
- that is *"substantiated"* by *competent, admissible* evidence (declarations, etc.). [*College Hosp., Inc. v. Sup.Ct. (Crowell)* (1994) 8 C4th 704, 719 , 34 CR2d 898, 907; *United Western Med. Ctrs. v. Sup.Ct. (Michelle Marie H.)* (1996) 42 CA4th 500, 49 CR2d 682, 685]

Stated slightly differently, the burden is on plaintiff to produce evidence that if accepted by the trier of fact would establish a *prima facie* showing of "malice, oppression or fraud" (bearing in mind the "clear and convincing" standard of proof required in such cases; see Civ.C. §3294(a)). [*Looney v. Sup.Ct. (Med. Ctr. of No. Hollywood)* (1993) 16 CA4th 521, 538, 20 CR2d 182, 193]

(a) **[6:341]** **How determined:** The court determines the motion on the basis of "supporting and opposing affidavits." [CCP §425.13]

"Substantiation" of a proposed punitive damages claim occurs where the factual recitals are made under penalty of perjury and set forth competent admissible evidence within the declarant's personal knowledge. [*College Hosp., Inc. v. Sup.Ct. (Crowell),* supra, 8 C4th at 719-720, 34 CR2d at 907-908, fn. 7 (citing text)—analogizing to rules governing summary judgments]

(b) **[6:342]** **No weighing of evidence:** However, the court may *not* weigh conflicting affidavits or predict the likely outcome at a trial: "(S)ection 425.13(a) does not authorize the trial court to reject a well pled and factually supported punitive damages claim simply because the court believes the evidence is not strong enough for probable success before a jury." [*College Hosp., Inc. v. Sup.Ct. (Crowell),* supra, 8 C4th at 709, 34 CR2d at 900]

(c) **Application**

- [6:343]   In action against Hospital, P's affidavit showed that while hospitalized for "panic disorders" she met Hospital Employee; that he was aware of her fragile emotional state although not responsible for her care; that she had a consensual off-premises sexual relationship with him; and that she suffered emotionally when he ended the relationship. This failed to "substantiate" a punitive damages claim *against Hospital* because there was no evidence that Employee was acting in the course and scope of his employment. [*College Hosp., Inc. v. Sup.Ct. (Crowell),* supra, 8 C4th at 723-724, 34 CR2d at 910]

(6) [6:344]   **Effect:**   The statutory procedure above operates much *like a demurrer and summary judgment in reverse*: i.e., instead of requiring the defendant to defeat a punitive damages claim by showing it is factually or legally meritless, the burden is on plaintiff to state and substantiate the merits of the claim. [*College Hosp., Inc. v. Sup.Ct. (Crowell),* supra, 8 C4th at 719, 34 CR2d at 907]

(a) [6:345]   **Opportunity to amend?**   Whether plaintiff is given an opportunity to improve its factual showing is discretionary with the court. But where the legal sufficiency of the proposed amended complaint is challenged, plaintiff must be allowed an opportunity to add whatever allegations are missing. [*College Hosp., Inc. v. Sup.Ct. (Crowell),* supra, 8 C4th at 719, 34 CR2d at 907, fn. 5]

[6:345.1-345.4]   *Reserved.*

(7) [6:345.5]   **Challenging defect:**   Failure to obtain the required order may be raised by demurrer or motion to strike plaintiff's punitive damages allegations. [*Vallbona v. Springer* (1996) 43 CA4th 1525, 1533-1535, 51 CR2d 311, 316-317]

(a) [6:345.6]   **Waiver:**   Waiting until the time of trial to challenge plaintiff's failure to comply with

§425.13 waives the defect. [*Vallbona v. Springer, supra,* 43 CA4th at 1533-1535, 51 CR2d at 316-317]

b. **[6:346] Punitive damages claims against religious corporation:** A separate statute limits "pleadability" of punitive damages claims against religious corporations: As with claims against health care providers (above), no punitive damages claim may be included in the original complaint; any such claim may be asserted only in an *amended* pleading, filed with leave of court. [CCP §425.14]

(1) **[6:347] Claims of any type:** CCP §425.14 applies to *any* complaint against a religious corporation. It erects a "pleading hurdle" to protect religious organizations from the expense of defending against punitive damage claims for which there is no likelihood of success. [See *Rowe v. Sup.Ct. (Church of Scientology of Orange Co.)* (1993) 15 CA4th 1711, 1723, 19 CR2d 625, 632, fn.13—suit against church for fraud, invasion of privacy, etc.]

(2) **[6:348] Procedure to add punitives claim:** The same motion for leave to amend procedure is required as for punitive damages claims against health care providers (*see* ¶6:334) . . . except that there is *no fixed time limit* on the motion. [See CCP §425.14]

(a) **[6:349] Earlier denial no bar to renewed motion:** A motion for leave to amend may be made whenever there is enough evidence to "substantiate" the punitive damages claim (below). Therefore, despite denial of an earlier motion for lack of sufficient evidence, plaintiff is free to renew the motion after timely discovery of more evidence. [*Rowe v. Sup.Ct. (Church of Scientology of Orange Co.),* supra, 15 CA4th at 1735, 19 CR2d at 641]

(3) **[6:350] Requirement that plaintiff "substantiate" claim:** The statute requires plaintiff to produce evidence that "substantiates" it will meet the "clear and convincing standard of proof" required for punitive damages under Civ.C. §3294. [CCP §425.14]

(a) **[6:351] "Substantiates":** This ambiguous term requires the same showing as the "substantial probability" standard applicable to punitive damages claims against health care providers (*see* ¶6:340): "It seems unlikely that (the) subtle difference in phraseology was intended to establish a completely different standard." [*College Hosp., Inc. v. Sup.Ct. (Crowell)* (1994) 8 C4th 704, 716, 34 CR2d 898, 905]

Thus, plaintiff must make the same showing as when seeking to plead a punitive damages claim against a health care provider (*see ¶6:340*).

- **[6:352]** Stated slightly differently, the statute requires only enough evidence to establish a *prima facie* case for punitive damages against the religious corporation; i.e., enough to avoid a summary judgment, nonsuit or directed verdict. [*Rowe v. Sup.Ct. (Church of Scientology of Orange Co.)*, supra, 15 CA4th at 1723, 19 CR2d at 632]

(b) **[6:353]** **No weighing of evidence:** Again, the court may *not* weigh conflicting affidavits or predict the likely outcome at a trial. [*Rowe v. Sup.Ct. (Church of Scientology of Orange Co.)*, supra, 15 CA4th at 1723, 19 CR2d at 632—amendment could not be refused on ground plaintiff's evidence was "unpersuasive"]

c. **[6:354]** **Claim against attorney for conspiracy with client:** A separate statute requires a prior court order before filing an action against an attorney that *includes* a claim for civil conspiracy with a client arising from any attempt to contest or settle a claim while representing the client. [Civ.C. §1714.10(a); see *Hung v. Wang* (1992) 8 CA4th 908, 924-925, 11 CR2d 113, 122—upholding constitutionality]

(1) **[6:355]** **Purpose:** The purpose of Civ.C. §1714.10 is to discourage frivolous claims that an attorney conspired with his or her client to harm another. [See *College Hosp., Inc. v. Sup.Ct. (Crowell)* (1994) 8 C4th 704, 718, 34 CR2d 898, 906—statute intended to weed out meritless claims against attorney "as a tactical ploy, particularly in actions against insurance companies"]

(2) **[6:355.1]** **Effect:** Rather than requiring the attorney-defendant to defeat plaintiff's pleading by showing it is legally or factually meritless, plaintiff is required to make a *prima facie* showing *before* being allowed to assert the claim (*see ¶6:364*). [*College Hosp., Inc. v. Sup.Ct. (Crowell)*, supra, 8 C4th at 719, 34 CR2d at 906-907]

(3) **[6:356]** **Complaints affected:** The statute directs that "No *cause of action* against an attorney for a civil conspiracy . . . shall be *included* in a complaint or other pleading unless the court enters an order allowing the pleading that includes the claim for civil conspiracy to be filed . . ." [Civ.C. §1714.10(a) (emphasis added)]

Where an attorney-client conspiracy cause of action is joined with other causes of action that do not require prefiling approval, only the conspiracy cause of action is subject to dismissal, not the entire complaint. [*Alden v. Hindin* (2003) 110 CA4th 1502, 1507, 2 CR3d 845, 849—failure to obtain prefiling approval as to conspiracy claim did not warrant dismissal of separate claim for malicious prosecution]

But where a *single* cause of action combines allegations of conspiracy against an attorney with similar allegations against a party not subject to the prefiling requirement, the entire cause of action is subject to the statute and must be dismissed in the absence of prefiling approval. [*Evans v. Pillsbury, Madison & Sutro* (1998) 65 CA4th 599, 605, 76 CR2d 679, 682]

[6:356.1]  *Reserved.*

(a) **Application**

- [6:356.2]  Attorneys representing real property buyers who drafted allegedly false documents were sued for "aiding and abetting" their clients' conduct; these allegations were the equivalent of a civil conspiracy. [*Howard v. Sup.Ct. (Simms)* (1992) 2 CA4th 745, 749, 3 CR2d 575, 576-577]

- [6:356.3]  But allegations that the client acted "by and through" an attorney do *not* state a cause of action for civil conspiracy between attorney and client to harm another. It is merely descriptive of the *client's* conduct. [See *Westamco Invest. Co. v. Lee* (1999) 69 CA4th 481, 487, 81 CR2d 634, 638]

- [6:356.4]  Civ.C. §1714.10 does not apply to a *malicious prosecution* action against an attorney based on representation of a client in former litigation with a third party. The attorney's alleged conduct (undertaking litigation against the third party without probable cause, etc.) is an independent tort, not merely a civil conspiracy with the client. [*Westamco Invest. Co. v. Lee,* supra, 69 CA4th at 487-488, 81 CR2d at 638-639; *Alden v. Hindin,* supra, 110 CA4th at 1507, 2 CR3d at 849]

(b) [6:357] **Exceptions:**  No such order is required for claims against an attorney for conspiring with his or her client where:
— the attorney had an *independent legal duty* to the party who is now the plaintiff in the instant case; or

Rev. #1 2004

— the attorney's acts go *beyond the performance of a professional duty to the client* and involve a conspiracy to violate a legal duty in further-ance of the attorney's *own financial gain.* [Civ.C. §1714.10(c); see *Shafer v. Berger, Kahn, Shafton, Moss, Figler, Simon & Gladstone* (2003) 107 CA4th 54, 85, 131 CR2d 777, 800 (citing text)]

1) **[6:357.1] Independent legal duty owed to plaintiff:** This exception "obviously speaks to

*(Text cont'd on p. 6-71)*

**RESERVED**

a relationship beyond that of attorney-client" (e.g., attorney as trustee). [*Evans v. Pillsbury, Madison & Sutro* (1998) 65 CA4th 599, 605, 76 CR2d 679, 682]

- [6:357.2] Attorneys owe an independent duty not to commit fraud. Thus, Civ.C. §1714.10 did not apply in an action against a corporation and its attorney for conspiring to conceal from potential investors threats of litigation by prior investors. [*Pavicich v. Santucci* (2000) 85 CA4th 382, 397, 102 CR2d 125, 137]

- [6:357.3] Similarly, Civ.C. §1714.10 did not apply to a claim against Attorney for conspiring with his client, Insurance Co., to defraud plaintiff by misrepresenting the scope of insurance coverage available. (Plaintiff was entitled to enforce the insurance as a third party judgment creditor of the insured.) Attorney owed a *duty to provide truthful information* to the plaintiff; i.e., a duty *not* to commit fraud. [*Safer v. Berger, Kahn, Shafton, Moss, Figler, Simon & Gladstone* (2003) 107 CA4th 54, 84, 131 CR2d 777, 800]

[6:357.4] *Reserved.*

2) [6:357.5] **Acts beyond legal representation for attorney's own financial gain:** The second exception applies where the alleged conspiracy is to violate a legal duty in furtherance of the attorney's own financial gain (e.g., where attorney-conspirator has a personal financial interest in the outcome of the litigation separate and apart from customary fees). [See *Evans v. Pillsbury, Madison & Sutro*, supra, 65 CA4th at 605-606, 76 CR2d at 683]

(4) [6:358] **Procedure:** To obtain a court order permitting the filing of such a complaint, the proposed plaintiff must file and present to the court:

- a *verified petition*;

- the proposed complaint; and

- supporting declarations stating *facts* upon which the conspiracy claim is based. [Civ.C. §1714.10(a)]

(a) [6:359] **"Verified petition":** A verified complaint accompanied by sworn declarations is the equivalent of a "verified petition" under Civ.C. §1714.10. [*Burtscher v. Burtscher* (1994) 26 CA4th 720, 727, 31 CR2d 682, 686]

(b) **[6:360] Timeliness:** There is no statutory time limit on filing a motion to add an attorney-client civil conspiracy cause of action. [*Burtscher v. Burtscher*, supra, 26 CA4th at 728, 31 CR2d at 687, fn. 7]

   1) **[6:361] Laches as limitation:** The motion may be denied on grounds of laches if the delay is unreasonable and has caused prejudice to the attorney. [See *Burtscher v. Burtscher*, supra, 26 CA4th at 728, 31 CR2d at 687—no clear showing of laches where motion to name attorney made within 5 months after filing complaint]

(c) **[6:362] Service and response:** Before deciding whether the proposed complaint may be filed, the court must order the above papers served on the attorney and permit the attorney to file opposing declarations. [Civ.C. §1714.10(a)]

(d) **[6:363] Compare—statute of limitations tolled:** Filing of the petition and supporting papers tolls any applicable statute of limitations until final determination of the matter. [Civ.C. §1714.10(a)]

(5) **[6:364] Requirement that plaintiff establish "reasonable probability" of success:** The statute requires plaintiff to demonstrate a "reasonable probability" of success on the conspiracy claim. [Civ.C. §1714.10(a)]

(a) **[6:365] "Reasonable probability":** This requires the same showing as the "substantial probability" standard applicable to punitive damages claims against health care providers (*see ¶6:340*): "It seems unlikely that (the) subtle difference in phraseology was intended to establish a completely different standard." [*College Hosp., Inc. v. Sup.Ct. (Crowell)* (1994) 8 C4th 704, 716, 34 CR2d 898, 905]

Thus, plaintiff must make the same showing as when seeking to plead a punitive damages claim against a health care provider (*see ¶6:340*) except that a legally sufficient claim of *conspiracy* must also be shown.

   • **[6:366]** Stated slightly differently, the statute requires plaintiff to establish a *prima facie* case—i.e., a cause of action subject to a civil conspiracy claim as a matter of law, and sufficient facts to avoid a summary judgment, non-suit or directed verdict. [*Hung v. Wang* (1992) 8 CA4th 908, 930, 11 CR2d 113, 127]

(b) [6:367] **No weighing of evidence:** "Reasonable probability" is a determination of law, not of fact. The court, therefore, may *not* weigh conflicting affidavits or predict the likely outcome at a trial. If plaintiff's declarations and proposed complaint meet the above standards, the court must grant the petition. [*Shafer v. Berger, Kahn, Shafton, Moss, Figler, Simon & Gladstone* (2003) 107 CA4th 54, 83, 131 CR2d 777, 799]

To do otherwise would violate plaintiff's right to trial by jury. [*Hung v. Wang*, supra, 8 CA4th at 930, 11 CR2d at 127]

(c) **Application**

- [6:368] A dispute arose over possession of a house in which P resided. Her verified complaint alleged that Attorney representing Defendant *resorted to "self-help"* to take possession; i.e., Attorney went to the house with her client in plaintiff's absence, called a locksmith to open the home, called a deputy sheriff to warn the occupant to leave, and arranged for removal and storage of plaintiff's belongings. These allegations established a *prima facie case* for civil conspiracy: "(Attorney) actively participated in conduct that went way beyond the role of legal representative; self-help is not the practice of law." [*Burtscher v. Burtscher* (1994) 26 CA4th 720, 727, 31 CR2d 682, 686]

(6) [6:369] **Order permissive or mandatory?** Civ.C. §1714.10 provides that the court "may" allow the filing of such complaint upon the requisite showing (above). However, an order in such cases is probably mandatory in order to protect plaintiff's right to access to the courts. [See *Hung v. Wang* (1992) 8 CA4th 908, 930, 11 CR2d 113, 127]

(7) [6:370] **Effect of failure to obtain order:** Failure to obtain the required court order is a *defense* to any such conspiracy action against an attorney. [Civ.C. §1714.10(b)]

Conspiracy allegations filed without a prior court order must be stricken *without leave to amend.* [See *Evans v. Pillsbury, Madison & Sutro* (1998) 65 CA4th 599, 607, 76 CR2d 679, 684]

(a) [6:371] **Preanswer challenge by attorney charged with conspiracy:** The defense of failure to obtain the required court order must be raised by the attorney charged with the conspiracy (rather than by another party). The defense must be raised in the attorney's *first appearance* "by demurrer, motion to strike, or such other motion or application as may be appropriate." [Civ.C. §1714.10(b) (amended 2000)]

- **[6:372]** Unlike most other defenses, this defense apparently *cannot* be raised for the first time in the answer. A preanswer motion of some kind is required.

- **[6:373]** Ordinarily, a demurrer or motion reaches only defects appearing on the face of the complaint (*see* ¶7:8). But a court may take *judicial notice* of its own files (*see* ¶7:12) to determine whether the requisite order was obtained.

(b) **[6:374] Waiver of defense:** The defense is waived if not timely raised. [Civ.C. §1714.10(b); see *Villa Pac. Building Co. v. Sup.Ct. (Himelstein)* (1991) 233 CA3d 8, 12, 284 CR 227, 230]

(8) **[6:375] Appellate review:** The court's ruling on a petition under Civ.C. §1714.10 is subject to immediate appellate review. [Civ.C. §1714.10(d); see *Hung v. Wang* (1992) 8 CA4th 908, 935, 11 CR2d 113, 129]

(a) **[6:376] Effect of failure to appeal denial:** If no appeal is taken from an order denying the petition, the order is entitled to *res judicata effect* in the subsequent trial on the merits; i.e., it is a binding determination that plaintiff has no prima facie case against the attorney. [*Castro v. Higaki* (1994) 31 CA4th 350, 359, 37 CR2d 84, 88]

This is true even if the court, in denying plaintiff's complaint, improperly weighed evidence. That error is reviewable only by appeal and cannot be raised after the time for appeal has expired. [*Castro v. Higaki*, supra, 31 CA4th at 359, 37 CR2d at 88]

d. **[6:377] Negligence claims against officers, directors of nonprofit corporations:** Another statute limits "pleadability" of negligence claims against volunteer officers and directors of certain nonprofit corporations.

A court order must be obtained before filing a complaint that *includes* a negligence claim against the officers or directors of certain nonprofit corporations who served without compensation of any kind (other than per diem mileage or other reimbursement of expenses). [CCP §425.15]

(1) [6:378] **Complaints affected:** As with conspiracy claims against an attorney (above), a court order is required for any complaint that "includes" such a negligence claim. Joinder of other causes of action against the officers and directors would not avoid the requirement.

    (a) [6:379] **Exceptions and limitations:** A prior court order is *not* required to file a complaint:
    — against the nonprofit corporation itself;
    — against officers or directors who *receive compensation* (other than reimbursement for expenses);
    — for negligent acts *outside the scope* of the officers' or directors' duties to the nonprofit corporation;
    — where the nonprofit corporation has not attained tax-exempt status, or unlawfully restricts membership, benefits or services on account of race, religion, sex, etc. [See CCP §425.15 (a)-(e)]

(2) [6:380] **Procedure:** The procedure to obtain the requisite order is the same as with conspiracy claims against an attorney: i.e., a *verified petition* accompanying the proposed pleading, supported by declarations stating the facts upon which the negligence claim is based (*see ¶6:358*). [CCP §425.15(a)]

(3) [6:381] **Requirement that evidence "substantiate" claim:** An order may be granted if plaintiff presents evidence that "substantiates" the claim against the officers and directors. [CCP §425.15(a)]

Although the wording is slightly different, it requires the same showing as the "substantial probability" standard applicable to punitive damages claims against health care providers (*see ¶6:340*): "It seems unlikely that (the) subtle difference in phraseology was intended to establish a completely different standard." [*College Hosp., Inc. v. Sup.Ct. (Crowell)* (1994) 8 C4th 704, 716, 34 CR2d 898, 905]

Thus, plaintiff must make the same showing as when seeking to plead a punitive damages claim against a health care provider (*see ¶6:340*) except that a legally sufficient claim of *negligence* must be shown.

(4) [6:382] **Statute of limitations tolled:** As with conspiracy claims against attorneys, filing of the petition and supporting papers tolls any applicable statute of limitations until final determination of the matter. [CCP §425.15(a)]

(5) **[6:383] Effect on discovery?** The statute says, rather enigmatically, "Nothing in this section shall affect the plaintiff's right to discover evidence on the issue of damages." [CCP §415.10(b)]

- **[6:383.1] Comment:** This apparently applies only where a complaint has been filed on *other claims* against the officers or directors and is sought to be *amended* to include a negligence claim, or where discovery takes place in a pending action against the nonprofit corporation. If no complaint has yet been filed, a proposed plaintiff would have no discovery rights. (The only way to obtain discovery would be to seek a court order to perpetuate evidence under CCP §2035; *see ¶8:422.*)

10. **[6:384] Filing Fee Considerations:** *See discussion at ¶1:950 ff.*

## C. ANSWER

1. **[6:385] Function:** An answer should contain whatever *denials* or *affirmative defenses* are necessary to controvert the material allegations of the complaint. Its function is to put the case "at issue" as to all important matters alleged in the complaint that defendant does not want to admit. (An answer *cannot* be used to claim affirmative relief; a cross-complaint must be filed.) [CCP §431.30]

2. **[6:386] Time for Filing Answer:** Unless extended by stipulation or court order, defendant's answer is due within 30 days after service of the complaint. [CCP §412.20(a)(3)]

The 30-day period is computed by excluding the first day and including the last (unless it is a weekend or holiday and then it is also excluded). [CCP §§12 ff.]

*Extension of time by stipulation:* The parties may stipulate without leave of court to *one 15-day extension* beyond the 30-day time period. [CRC 201.7(d); *see ¶12:71.3*]

*Extension of time by court order:* To obtain a court order extending time to plead, defendant must apply *before* the time to respond has expired and the application must be accompanied by a declaration:
— *showing why* a responsive pleading has not been filed;
— *documenting the efforts* that have been made to file such a pleading; and
— *specifying a date* by which the responsive pleading is proposed to be filed. [CRC 201.7(e); *see ¶12:73*]

- ***FORM:*** The application may be made on optional Judicial Council form CM-020, Ex Parte Application for Extension of Time to Serve Pleading; *see Form 4:J.*

*Special rule for unlawful detainer.* In unlawful detainer and forcible entry or detainer actions, defendant has only 5 days to respond, including Saturdays and Sundays (but excluding all other judicial holidays). If the last day falls on a Saturday or Sunday, the response is due the next court day. [CCP §§1167, 1167.3]

a. **[6:387]** **Petition to compel arbitration in lieu of answer:** Where the complaint is based on a contract providing for arbitration of disputes, defendant may file a petition to compel arbitration in lieu of an answer. [CCP §1281.7]

If the petition is granted, the action is stayed and the matter proceeds to arbitration. If the petition to compel arbitration is *denied*, defendant has 15 days after the denial to respond to the complaint. [CCP §1281.7]

[6:387.1-387.4] *Reserved.*

b. **[6:387.5]** **Filing fee for each defendant:** A filing fee is payable by *each* defendant, even if they file a joint pleading. [*Townzen v. County of El Dorado* (1998) 64 CA4th 1350, 1356, 76 CR2d 281, 284]

3. **[6:388]** **Format:** An answer must conform to the rules applicable to pleadings generally. [CRC 201 ff., 312(h) (governing paragraph numbering and captions); *see ¶6:14 ff.*]

a. **[6:389]** **Official Form answers satisfy format rules:** Official Form answers are available for use in the most common civil actions (personal injury, wrongful death, property damage, breach of contract, fraud and unlawful detainer). Their use is advantageous because they contain

*(Text cont'd on p. 6-77)*

**RESERVED**

effective denials and the most common defenses in such actions (with room for whatever additional defenses may be applicable). And they have been drafted in accordance with all applicable format rules.

- *FORMS:* Official Form Answers, *see Forms 6:I, 6:N, 6:P.*

b. **Other answers must comply with the following rules**

(1) [6:390] **Type size, paper size, pagination, etc.:** [CRC 201; *see ¶6:17 ff.*]

(2) [6:391] **First page requirements:** The same as for the complaint (*¶6:17 ff.*), *except that:*

(a) [6:392] The caption may contain just the name of the first party on each side, with appropriate indication of other parties ("et al."). [CCP §422.40]

(b) [6:393] Where there are *several defendants,* it is good practice (not required by CRC) to state the *name of each defendant* on whose behalf the answer is filed. For example:

"ALAN AMES, et al.,      NO. _____

                               ANSWER OF BEA BAKER

    Plaintiffs,

vs.

BRYAN BAKER, et al.,

    Defendants."

(3) [6:393.1] **Footers:** Each page of each filed paper (except exhibits) must bear a footer in the bottom margin, below the page number and divided from the rest of the document by a printed line. The footer must contain the title of the document (e.g. "Answer") or some clear and concise abbreviation, and must be in at least 10-point type. [CRC 201(g); *see ¶6:20.1*]

(4) [6:394] **Body of answer:** The answer must contain *effective* denials (*¶6:398 ff.*) and appropriate *defenses* or objections ("new matter," *¶6:430 ff.*).

(a) [6:395] **Response to each cause of action of complaint:** Except where a general denial is permissible (*¶6:404-409*), the customary approach is to start with denials of the material allegations of each cause of action of the complaint, followed by defenses applicable to that particular cause of action. Each should be separately stated and numbered (CRC 201(i)). For ease of reference, include the description of the cause of action given in the complaint. For example:

"ANSWER TO FIRST CAUSE OF ACTION FOR DEFAMATION

"1.  Defendant denies each allegation contained in paragraphs 3, 5 and 7 of (the first count of) the complaint.

"2.  Defendant lacks information or belief sufficient to answer the allegations in paragraphs 1, 4 and 10 of (the first count of) the complaint, and basing its denial on this ground, denies each allegation therein.

"3.  Defendant admits the allegations contained in paragraph 2 of (the first count of) the complaint, except it denies that . . .

"FIRST AFFIRMATIVE DEFENSE TO FIRST CAUSE OF ACTION

"4.  Plaintiff's First Cause of Action for Defamation is barred by the provisions of Code of Civil Procedure Section 340(c) (one-year statute of limitations for libel and slander).

"SECOND AFFIRMATIVE DEFENSE TO FIRST CAUSE OF ACTION

"5.  Before commencing this lawsuit, Plaintiff signed a written release of the claims alleged in the First Cause of Action.

"ANSWER TO SECOND CAUSE OF ACTION FOR INVASION OF PRIVACY" (etc.)

(b)  **[6:396]  Defenses or objections to entire complaint:**  Alternatively, if there are defenses or objections to the entire complaint (e.g., a plea in abatement, ¶6:475), they may be set forth following the denials and defenses to each cause of action. Each should be separately stated and numbered. [CRC 201(i)] And, for ease of reference, it is helpful to state briefly the nature of the defense or objection:

"FIRST AFFIRMATIVE DEFENSE TO ENTIRE COMPLAINT (ANOTHER ACTION PENDING)"

(c)  **[6:397]  Incorporating by reference:**  Denials or defenses to one count can be incorporated by reference into a later count, to save repetition. This is particularly helpful where plaintiff has incorporated parts of one count into another. For example, if the

Second Count of plaintiff's complaint incorporates various paragraphs from the First Count, the following wording effectively answers the parts so incorporated:

"ANSWER TO SECOND COUNT FOR INVASION OF PRIVACY

"1. Defendant incorporates by reference each and every denial, defense or objection contained in his answer to the First Count, *to the same extent that plaintiff has incorporated the allegations of the First Count into the Second Count of the complaint.*"

4. **[6:398] Effective Denials:** All material allegations of the complaint that the defendant does not intend to admit must be *effectively* denied.

   a. **[6:399] Failure to deny constitutes admission:** Any *material* allegation in the complaint that is not effectively denied is *deemed admitted.* [CCP §431.20(a); see *Hennefer v. Butcher* (1986) 182 CA3d 492, 504, 227 CR 318, 325]

     (1) **[6:400] Material vs. immaterial allegations:** Only *material* allegations are admitted by failure to deny. "Material" allegations are those so essential to the claim that they cannot be stricken without leaving the complaint insufficient as a matter of law (e.g., some element of the prima facie case). [CCP §431.10(a)]

An "immaterial" allegation is one that is not essential to the claim or irrelevant to the claim; or a demand for judgment requesting relief not supported by the claim pleaded. [See CCP §431.10(b)]

➯**[6:401] *PRACTICE POINTER:*** In drafting answers, do *not* base your decision on whether to deny something in the complaint on your judgment that it is an "immaterial" allegation, and hence need not be denied. A judge might disagree! The safe practice is to deny *all* allegations that you do not *intend* to *admit*.

     (2) **[6:402] Effect of admission:** Failure to deny has the effect of a stipulation to the truth of plaintiff's allegation. Plaintiff can wait until trial and use it in lieu of any evidence on the matter in question. Or, plaintiff may be able to use the admission as the basis for a motion for summary judgment or summary adjudication (CCP §437c; *see Ch. 10*).

b. **General vs. specific denials**

(1) [6:403] **General denial:** A general denial is a blanket denial of the whole complaint. E.g., "Defendant denies each and every allegation of plaintiff's complaint."

In the case of a complaint for breach of contract, a general denial denies that there is a contract, that plaintiff performed or had an excuse for nonperformance, that defendant did not perform, or that plaintiff was damaged. [*Walsh v. West Valley Mission Comm. College Dist.* (1998) 66 CA4th 1532, 1545, 78 CR2d 725, 733]

**FORM:** Official Form General Denial, *see Form 6:V.*

(a) [6:404] **Permitted if complaint unverified:** A general denial is effective to controvert all *material* allegations of an *unverified* complaint. [CCP §431.30(d)]

1) [6:405] **"Material" vs. "immaterial" allegations:** As to what allegations are "material," *see discussion at ¶6:400.*

2) [6:406] **Ineffective to raise negotiable instrument forgery defense:** But a general denial is ineffective to raise the defense of forgery on a negotiable instrument. [See Comm'l C. §3308(a)—signature on negotiable instrument stands admitted unless *specifically* denied]

3) [6:406.1] **Impact of CCP §128.7?** General denials may conflict with CCP §128.7(b)(3), which requires counsel to *certify* that every contention in a pleading has *evidentiary support (see ¶9:1162)*, . . . because there is usually *something* in the complaint that ought to be admitted.

Comment: In view of the long-standing use of general denials and, in the absence of any indication the Legislature intended to repeal §431.30(d)'s provision for general denials, it is unlikely courts will hold the procedure is no longer permitted.

(b) [6:407] **Not permitted if complaint verified:** Except as stated below, a general denial is *not* sufficient to controvert a *verified* complaint (even if the answer, containing such denial, is verified): i.e., a verified complaint must be denied positively or according to information and belief. [CCP §431.30(d)]

1) **[6:408] Exception—limited civil cases:** Under the economic litigation rules governing limited civil cases, a general denial puts in issue all material allegations of the complaint, *verified or not.* [CCP §431.30(d)]

   (Answers need not be verified in limited civil cases even if the complaint is verified; see CCP §92(b), *discussed at ¶6:489.*)

2) **[6:409] Special rule for third party collection cases:** This does not apply, however, to *verified* complaints on claims assigned for collection. Even in limited civil cases, the assignee's verified complaint must be denied positively or on information and belief. [CCP §431.30(d)]

3) **[6:410] Special rule in actions involving $1,000 or less:** Another special rule applies in actions involving $1,000 or less: "Any provision of law to the contrary notwithstanding . . . the defendant . . . in lieu of demurrer or other answer, may file a general denial and a brief statement of any new matter constituting a defense . . . in a form prescribed by the Judicial Council." [CCP §431.40(a) & (c)]

   - **Comment:** Presumably, a general denial may be filed in such cases even to a *verified* complaint in a *third party collection* case. I.e., CCP §431.40(a) prevails over §431.30(d) because it states "any provision of law to the contrary notwithstanding."

   - ***FORM:*** Official Form—General Denial, *see Form 6:V.*

     Note: Use of the Judicial Council form is *mandatory.* [CRC 201.1(b)]

⇨**[6:411]** ***PRACTICE POINTER:*** Most lawyers use general denials wherever possible. They prefer *not* to tie themselves down to admissions or denials of particular facts, because new facts often come to light as the case progresses.

On the other hand, some lawyers contend that general denials are improper in most cases because there is usually *something* in the complaint that is true and should be admitted. (This may be true, but as a practical matter, there is little plaintiff can do to capitalize on the fact that defendant has denied too much . . . i.e., it would probably *not* be effective impeachment at trial.)

(2) [6:412] **Specific denial:** Anything less than a general denial of the whole complaint is a "qualified" or "specific" denial. Several versions may be used:

(a) [6:413] **Denial by parts:** Defendant can direct his denials to specific sentences, paragraphs or parts of the complaint—controverting only those parts, while admitting all other *material* allegations. For example:

"Defendant DENIES each allegation of the following numbered paragraphs:_____"

*or*

"Defendant DENIES the following *portions* of paragraph _____: (beginning on page _____ at line _____ and ending on page _____ at line _____ )"

*or*

"Defendant ADMITS the following allegations and generally denies all others: _____"

(*See Official Form Answer (Personal Injury), Form 6:I, para. 3.*)

1) [6:414] **Effect:** Each of the above is effective to controvert the specific sentences, paragraphs or counts denied . . . and *only* those parts. All other *material* allegations of the complaint would be *deemed admitted.* [CCP §431.20(a)] (On "material" vs. "immaterial" allegations, *see ¶6:400.*)

(b) [6:415] **Factual denials:** Defendant can also effectively deny allegations in the complaint by alleging contrary or *inconsistent* facts. For example, if the complaint alleges, "Defendant was drunk . . . ," any of the following would be an effective denial:

• "Defendant denies he was drunk . . . "

• "Defendant was *not* drunk . . . "

• "Defendant was sober."

➡ [6:416] *PRACTICE POINTER:* This form of denial is generally *not* recommended. It usually takes more time to draft such denials than it does simply to deny specific parts of the complaint (¶*6:413*). Moreover, there's always the risk that your factual denials may not *exactly* controvert the allegations in the complaint . . . in which event, the allegations would stand admitted (¶*6:399*). Finally, factual denials are more likely to raise problems with "negative pregnants" (below).

c. **[6:417] "Negative pregnants"—and how to avoid them:** Certain factual denials may be "pregnant" with admission of the allegations supposedly denied, and thus fail to controvert the complaint.

*(Text cont'd on p. 6-83)*

**RESERVED**

(1) **Examples**

    (a) [6:418] **Denials in the conjunctive**

        Complaint alleges, "Defendant defamed plaintiff orally and in writing."

        Answer alleges, "Defendant *denies* he defamed plaintiff orally *and* in writing" (pregnant with an admission that defendant may have defamed plaintiff orally but not in writing; or vice versa.)

        **How to avoid:** Deny in the disjunctive ("Defendant denies that he defamed plaintiff orally *or* in writing, *or at all.*"). Or, even better, use denial by parts (*see ¶6:421*).

    (b) [6:419] **Denials of specifics**

        Complaint alleges, "Plaintiff delivered 14 carloads of coal to defendant in Wilmington in March, . . ."

        Answer alleges, "Plaintiff *did not* deliver 14 carloads of coal, etc." (pregnant with an admission that plaintiff may have delivered other amounts, or at other places, or at other times).

        **How to avoid:** Add "or any other amount, time or place" to the denial. Or better yet, use denial by parts (*see ¶6:421*).

    (c) [6:420] **Denials of amounts, damages**

        Complaint alleges, "Defendant owes plaintiff $100,000."

        Answer alleges, "Defendant denies that he owes plaintiff $100,000" (pregnant with an admission that some other sum is due, and will in fact support a judgment for $99,999).

        **How to avoid:** Add "or any other amount" to the denial. Or better yet, use denial by parts (see below).

(2) [6:421] **No "negative pregnant" where general denial or denial by parts used:** A general denial is effective to controvert all material allegations of the complaint (CCP §431.30(d)), but there are limits on its use (*see ¶6:404-407*).

The safe, simple and sure way to avoid a negative pregnant is to include a *denial of each paragraph* in question. "Defendant denies each and every allegation of paragraph _____ of the complaint" is sufficient to controvert *all material allegations* therein . . . even allegations as to damages, amounts due, etc. [*Conley v. Lieber* (1979) 97 CA3d 646, 655-656, 158 CR 770, 775-776]

➪[6:422]  ***PRACTICE POINTER:***  In view of the above, most lawyers use paragraph-by-paragraph denials throughout, rather than factual denials. (If portions of a paragraph have to be admitted, then the balance is denied.)

If you stray from this form and include factual denials, be sure to add an omnibus denial at the end of your answer, such as the following:

> "Except as otherwise admitted or denied herein, defendant denies each and every allegation contained in paragraphs _____ (number of each relevant paragraph of the complaint)."

This should be sufficient to insulate your answer against any claim of it being a "negative pregnant."

Keep in mind that paragraph-by-paragraph denials are proper only where *nothing* in the paragraph is true. If any part of it is true, a specific denial is required.

d.  [6:423]  **Positive vs. nonpositive denials (information and belief):**  If defendant knows or has *reason* to know the falsity of the matters alleged in the complaint, he should use a positive form of denial. ("Defendant denies . . .")

Where, however, he does not have positive knowledge that the matters alleged are false, he should base his denial either "upon information and belief, *or lack* of information or belief." [CCP §431.30(f)]

➪[6:424]  ***PRACTICE POINTER:***  Be careful in using positive denials. Plaintiff has the right, through discovery, to ask defendant to state the facts upon which his denial is based. Defendant may have difficulty if he lacked sufficient information. Also, it may constitute impeachment at trial. Therefore, whenever defendant lacks *positive* knowledge, use one of the following forms.

(1) [6:425]  **Denial based on information and belief**

> "Defendant DENIES, ON INFORMATION AND BELIEF, each allegation of the following numbered paragraphs: _____ "

(*See Official Form Answer (Personal Injury), Form 6:I, para. 3.*)

This is the form to use when defendant does not have positive knowledge of the facts, but has *hearsay* or other indirect knowledge that plaintiff's allegations are false.

(2) [6:426] **Denial for lack of information or belief**

"Defendant lacks information or belief sufficient to answer the allegations in paragraph _____, and basing his denial on this ground, denies each and every allegation thereof."

Or, even more simply:

"Defendant has no information or belief that the following statements are true, so defendant denies them: _____
_____ "

(*See Official Form Answers (Contract), Form 6:N, para. 3.b.(2), and (Unlawful Detainer), Form 6:P, para. 2.b.(2).*)

This is the form to use when defendant does not have any information as to the facts alleged, but still does not wish to admit the allegations.

(3) [6:427] **Limitations—presumptive or constructive knowledge:** Neither of the above forms may be used to place matters in issue if defendant is deemed to have sufficient knowledge to positively admit or deny. For example:

(a) [6:428] Matters of which defendant has *presumptive* knowledge (e.g., whether defendant is a nonprofit corporation as alleged in the complaint). [See *Oliver v. Swiss Club Tell* (1963) 222 CA2d 528, 540, 35 CR 324, 330-331]

(b) [6:429] Matters of public record (within California) of which defendant has *constructive knowledge.* [See, e.g., *Goldwater v. Oltman* (1930) 210 C 408, 424-425, 292 P 624, 631—whether plaintiff recorded fictitious name certificate as alleged in complaint; and *Transworld Systems, Inc. v. Rogan* (1989) 210 CA3d 731, 733-734, 258 CR 555, 556-557—whether plaintiff was a licensed collection agency as alleged in complaint]

5. [6:430] **"New Matter":** In addition to denials, the answer should contain whatever affirmative defenses or objections to the complaint that defendant may have, and that would otherwise *not be in issue under a simple denial.* Such defenses or objections are referred to as "new matter." [CCP §431.30(b)]

"New matter" is any ground urged in *avoidance* of the complaint; i.e., some independent reason why plaintiff should be barred from recovery, even if everything alleged in the complaint was true. Such grounds are not in issue under a denial, and, unless specially pleaded in the answer, evidence of such grounds is inadmissible at trial. [See *Walsh v. West Valley Mission Comm. College Dist.* (1998) 66 CA4th 1532, 1546, 78 CR2d 725, 733-734]

"What is put in issue by a denial is limited to the allegations of the complaint . . . A defense in the nature of 'yes, those allegations are true, but . . .' is not put in issue by the denial." [*FPI Development, Inc. v. Nakashima* (1991) 231 CA3d 367, 383-384, 282 CR 508, 517; compare *Walsh v. West Valley Mission Comm. College Dist.*, supra, 66 CA4th at 1545, 78 CR2d at 733—claim that plaintiff *failed to perform* contract *not* an affirmative defense, and is in issue under general denial]

a.  [6:431]  **Affirmative defenses:**  In general, whatever defendant bears the burden of proving at trial is "new matter," and thus must be specially pleaded in the answer. [*California Academy of Sciences v. County of Fresno* (1987) 192 CA3d 1436, 1442, 238 CR 154, 157]

(1)  [6:432]  **Determined by substantive law:**  Reference must be made to the substantive law to determine the matters on which each party bears the burden of proof in the particular action.

⇨[6:433]  *PRACTICE POINTER:*  Use BAJI (Book of Approved Jury Instructions) as a *checklist* of the substantive law in the civil actions covered thereby. These jury instructions indicate which party bears the burden of proof on which issues at trial. Also, check the Pleadings chapter in Witkin, California Procedure 3d. Its Table of Contents can be used as a checklist of the various issues raised by denial vs. those that must be pleaded as new matter.

⇨[6:434]  *PRACTICE POINTER:*  If at all in doubt, *plead* it as new matter. Do *not* rely on a denial alone. This will avoid any dispute as to whether the matter is in issue.

(2)  [6:435]  **Application:**  The following are the most common examples of affirmative defenses on which defendant bears the burden of proof . . . and pleading:

(a)  [6:436]  **Tort actions**

• Comparative fault of plaintiff in negligence action (*see Form 6:I, para. 4.*)

• Statute of limitations (*see Form 6:I, para. 5.*)

- Assumption of the risk (in personal injury or product liability actions)

- Release

1) **[6:437] Compare—matters negating essential allegation of complaint:** Facts showing some essential allegation of the complaint is not true are *not* "new matter" but only a traverse. Such matters are in issue under a general denial; i.e., they *need not* be specially pleaded in the answer. [*State Farm Mut. Auto. Ins. Co. v. Sup.Ct. (Johnson Kinsey, Inc.)* (1991) 228 CA3d 721, 725, 279 CR 116, 118]

   **[6:438] Example:** P sued Insurance Co. for "bad faith" refusal to provide coverage. Insurance Co. generally denied all allegations. At trial, Insurance Co. could introduce evidence of its *reliance on advice of counsel* although it was not pleaded in the answer. Advice of counsel was *not* new matter; it was relevant to *disprove* P's claim of "bad faith" (i.e., it tended to show Insurance Co. had proper cause for denying coverage). [*State Farm Mut. Auto. Ins. Co. v. Sup.Ct. (Johnson Kinsey, Inc.)*, supra, 228 CA3d at 725, 279 CR at 118]

   **[6:438.1-438.4]** *Reserved.*

2) **[6:438.5] Workers' compensation as exclusive remedy for work-related injury:** An employee's complaint against an employer for injury *within the course and scope of employment* is subject to demurrer because workers' compensation is the exclusive remedy for such injuries and the existence of workers' compensation insurance is *presumed.* [See *Gibbs v. American Airlines, Inc.* (1999) 74 CA4th 1, 12, 87 CR2d 554, 562—work-related claim for emotional distress]

   But, where the complaint *does not disclose* whether the injury occurred within the course and scope of employment, the defendant employer bears the burden of alleging and proving the "conditions of compensation" necessary for workers' compensation exclusivity. [*Gibbs v. American Airlines, Inc.*, supra, 74 CA4th at 13, 87 CR2d at 562]

(b) **[6:439] Contract actions**

- Statute of frauds

- Statute of limitations
- Fraud, mistake, duress
- Payment, release
- Waiver, estoppel [*California Academy of Sciences v. County of Fresno* (1987) 192 CA3d 1436, 1442, 238 CR 154, 157]

1) **[6:440] Compare—failure of conditions:** But failure of conditions (non-performance or defective performance) is *not* "new matter" . . . because *plaintiff* bears the burden of pleading and proving *performance* in a contract action. Hence, lack of performance is *in issue under a simple denial* of plaintiff's allegation of "performance" in the complaint. [*Eucalyptus Growers Ass'n v. Orange Co. Nursery & Land Co.* (1917) 174 C 330, 334, 163 P 45, 47]

   Thus, a general denial puts in issue the question whether there is a *failure of consideration* (failure to execute the bargained for promise). [*FPI Development, Inc. v. Nakashima* (1991) 231 CA3d 367, 383, 282 CR 508, 527]

2) **[6:441] Promissory note actions:** General denial of a complaint on a promissory note puts in issue such "defenses" as:
   — the note was never executed;
   — no consideration was given for the note;
   — the copy of the note is false;
   — the purported contract is wholly void;
   — the note has been paid in accordance with its terms. [*FPI Development, Inc. v. Nakashima* (1991) 231 CA3d 367, 383-384, 282 CR 508, 517]

3) **[6:442] Compare—illegality:** Public policy against enforcement of illegal contracts is so strong that illegality can be raised even if not pleaded in the answer. Indeed, the court can raise the matter on its own motion, even if neither party raises it. [*Kallen v. Delug* (1984) 157 CA3d 940, 948, 203 CR 879, 883, fn. 2; *Santoro v. Carbone* (1972) 22 CA3d 721, 732, 99 CR 488, 496 (disapproved on other grounds in *Tenzer v. Superscope, Inc.* (1985) 39 C3d 18, 30, 216 CR 130, 137)]

**[6:443] *PRACTICE POINTER:*** Even in these cases, it is better practice to plead them as affirmative defenses. Otherwise, a judge might disagree as to whether they are at issue, and you might end up having to fight the issue out on appeal.

4) **[6:444] Compare—causation:** Normally, causation (or lack thereof) is in issue under a simple denial of plaintiff's allegations of proximate causation.

**[6:445] Special rule in insurance cases:** However, more specific pleading may be required by an insurer defending a suit for policy benefits on the theory that the insured's loss was *caused at least in part by an excluded risk.* (Example: Insurer defends suit on homeowner's insurance policy on ground that damage resulted from earth movement, an excluded risk.)

In such cases, the insurer must *set forth and specify* in its answer:

- which peril was the proximate cause of the loss;

- in what manner the excluded peril contributed to the loss or itself caused the loss; and

- if the insurer claims that the excluded peril caused the loss, it must set forth and specify "upon what premises or at what place the peril excepted caused the peril insured against." [See CCP §431.50]

(c) **[6:446] Unlawful detainer cases:** Deficiencies in the 3-day notice to pay rent or quit must normally be pleaded as an affirmative defense to an unlawful detainer complaint. Not so, however, where the *defects appear on the face of the notice* which is attached to the complaint. In such event, defendants' denying the rent allegedly due places the sufficiency of the notice in issue. [*Bevill v. Zoura* (1994) 27 CA4th 694, 698, 32 CR2d 635, 638—notice defective because it stated part of rent was more than one year past due]

(d) **[6:447] Set-offs:** Generally, a set-off constitutes an affirmative defense, and therefore must be specially pleaded as new matter. [See CCP §431.70; *Interstate Group Administrators, Inc. v. Cravens,*

*Dargan & Co.* (1985) 174 CA3d 700, 706, 220 CR 250, 253]

The right to a set-off is founded on the *equitable* principle that when parties in litigation hold cross-demands for money, one should be applied against the other and only the balance recovered. [See *Granberry v. Islay Investments* (1995) 9 C4th 738, 744, 38 CR2d 650, 652]

Relief by way of setoff is limited to reducing or defeating plaintiff's claim. A defendant may not obtain affirmative relief against plaintiff by way of a setoff. [*Construction Protective Services, Inc. v. TIG Specialty Ins. Co.* (2002) 29 C4th 189, 195, 126 CR2d 908, 911]

[6:447.1-447.4]   *Reserved.*

1)  [6:447.5]   **Cross-demands for money:**   To constitute a valid set-off, each of the cross-demands must be legally enforceable and not barred by the statute of limitations. [CCP §431.70; see *Birman v. Loeb* (1998) 64 CA4th 502, 518, 75 CR2d 294, 305] (A time-barred claim, however, may be asserted as an offset to plaintiff's claim but not as the basis for affirmative relief; *see ¶6:587.*)

    •  [6:447.6]   Defendants foreclosed on a *purchase money mortgage* on Plaintiffs' property. More than $2 million remained unpaid on Plaintiffs' note, but it was *unenforceable* as a purchase money obligation (see CCP §580b). Plaintiffs then recovered $300,000 against Defendants on a fraud claim. The unenforceable $2 million balance on the note was *not* a valid offset to the $300,000 judgment on the fraud claim. [*Birman v. Loeb*, supra, 64 CA4th at 520, 75 CR2d at 306]

2)  [6:448]   **Exception where complaint based on common counts:**   However, a general denial may be sufficient where the complaint is in the form of common counts: In an action upon a common count, defendants may, under a general denial, prove set-offs *relating to the same account*; i.e., "any defense tending to show that the plaintiff has no right to recover or to recover to the extent he claims." [*Interstate Group Administrators, Inc. v. Cravens, Dargan*

*& Co.* (1985) 174 CA3d 700, 708, 220 CR 250, 255]

a) **[6:449] Rationale:** Because of the *uninformative character* of common count pleadings (¶*6:126*), a general denial is sufficient to raise defenses which otherwise must be specifically pled. [*Title Ins. Co. v. State Bd. of Equalization* (1992) 4 C4th 715, 731, 14 CR2d 822, 832]

b) **[6:450] Example:** P sued to recover a sum due on an open book account (one of the common counts). D's answer contained only a general denial. At trial, D offered proof of various overpayments it had made in the past relating to the same account. Such proof was admissible as a set-off although not specially pleaded. [*Interstate Group Administrators, Inc. v. Cravens, Dargan & Co.*, supra, 174 CA3d at 708, 220 CR at 504]

3) **[6:451] Compare—unrelated debts:** However, where the set-off arises out of a debt or obligation *not put in issue by the plaintiff*, it is "new matter" and must be specially pleaded in the answer. It makes no difference that the complaint is on a common count. [*Carranza v. Noroian* (1966) 240 CA2d 481, 485-486, 49 CR 629, 634]

a) **[6:452] Example:** P sued on common counts for farm labor provided in harvesting D's peach crop. D's answer contained only a general denial. At trial D sought to prove damages resulting from P's breach of a later contract to provide farm labor for D's fig crop, and for damage to his labor camp. These had nothing to do with the original contract for the peach crop. They constituted "new matter" and were not in issue under D's general denial. [*Carranza v. Noroian*, supra]

4) **[6:453] Special rule on comparative fault defense to action by condo owners' association:** In an action for damage sustained by a condo owners' association or its members, defendant must plead comparative fault of the association or its managing agents as an affir-

mative defense (no cross-complaint or separate action permitted). [CCP §383; *see* ¶*6:536*]

The association's or managing agents' comparative fault is a *set-off* to defendant's liability for damaging the association's or members' property. [CCP §383]

a) **[6:454]** **Association need not be party:** Indeed, it is a valid set-off even if the association is *not a party* to the action (or no longer a party because of settlement or dismissal). [CCP §383]

For example, the association's *insurer* sues as subrogee for damage by defendant to the condo common areas. Defendant can assert the association's comparative fault as a defense although the association is not a party to the action.

(e) **[6:455]** **Res judicata:** A defense that the action is barred by the judgment in a prior action must be specially pleaded or is waived. It is *not* in issue under a general denial. [See *Hulsey v. Koehler* (1990) 218 CA3d 1150, 1156, 267 CR 523, 526]

Example: The defense that plaintiff's claim in the present lawsuit is barred by his failure to assert it as a compulsory cross-complaint in the prior lawsuit is a "species" of res judicata; and thus waived by failure to plead it in the answer. [*Hulsey v. Koehler*, supra]

1) **[6:456]** **Compare—collateral estoppel:** But a party is *not* required to specially allege collateral estoppel as a defense, because "collateral estoppel merely involves conclusive *evidence* of a fact in issue." [See *Hulsey v. Koehler*, supra, 218 CA3d at 1158, 267 CR at 526 (emphasis added)]

(f) **[6:456.1]** **Judicial estoppel:** Judicial estoppel prevents a party from "playing fast and loose with the courts" by seeking to benefit through *totally inconsistent positions* in either the same or quasi-judicial proceedings. [*Jackson v. County of Los Angeles* (1997) 60 CA4th 171, 181, 70 CR2d 96, 101-102—plaintiff judicially estopped from suing employer for disability discrimination after having obtained workers' compensation award based on stipulation he could not perform work involved; see also *International Billing Services, Inc. v. Emigh* (2000) 84 CA4th 1175, 1190-1191, 101 CR2d 532, 542—after claiming contract authorized fee award to prevailing party, plaintiff was estopped from claiming contract did not authorize fee award to prevailing defendant; see also *Thomas v. Gordon* (2000) 85 CA4th 113, 117-118, 102 CR2d 28, 31-32]

The prior inconsistent statement need not be made to a court of law. Statements to administrative agencies or in arbitration proceedings may also give rise to judicial estoppel. [*People ex rel. Sneddon v. Torch Energy Services, Inc.* (2002) 102 CA4th 181, 189, 125 CR2d 365, 370]

*Comment:* Although there is no known authority in point, judicial estoppel apparently need not be pleaded as an affirmative defense because it is designed to *protect the judiciary*, rather than merely the rights of the litigants. [See *Cloud v. Northrop Grumman Corp.* (1998) 67 CA4th 995, 1016, 79 CR2d 544, 558]

[6:456.2-456.9]   *Reserved.*

(g) [6:456.10]   **Privilege:**   The general rule is that a privilege must be pled as an affirmative defense. [*Cruey v. Gannett Co., Inc.* (1998) 64 CA4th 356, 367, 76 CR2d 670, 676—privilege as defense to defamation action]

However, "recent California authority suggests an exception where the complaint alleges facts indicating applicability of a (privilege) defense." (I.e., in such cases, the privilege may be in issue under a general denial.) [See *Cruey v. Gannett Co., Inc.*, supra, 64 CA4th at 367, 76 CR2d at 676 (parentheses added) (dictum)]

(h) [6:456.11]   **Agreement to arbitrate dispute:** Where the parties have agreed to arbitrate the claims involved, defendant must raise the arbitration agreement as an affirmative defense (or promptly move to stay the lawsuit and compel arbitration). Failure to do so may result in a waiver of the right to arbitrate. [*Guess?, Inc. v. Sup.Ct. (Kirkland)* (2000) 79 CA4th 553, 558, 94 CR2d 201, 203]

*Cross-refer:* Waiver of contractual arbitration is discussed in detail in Knight, Fannin, Chernick & Haldeman, *Cal. Prac. Guide: Alternative Dispute Resolution* (TRG), Ch. 5.

(i) [6:457]   **Facts constituting both defense and ground for affirmative relief:**   Any claim for affirmative relief must be pleaded in a separate cross-complaint, not in the answer. [CCP §431.30(c)] Sometimes this requires pleading the same facts *both* as a defense in the answer, and as a cause of action in the cross-complaint. [See *Construction Protective Services, Inc. v. TIG Specialty Ins. Co.* (2002) 29 C4th 189, 195, 126 CR2d 908, 911]

    1) [6:458]   **Example:**   Plaintiff sues to enforce payment of a promissory note. Defendant claims he was fraudulently induced to sign the note, and is entitled to recover damages as the result of the fraud. Defendant must plead the fraud *both* as an affirmative defense in the answer, *and* as a cause of action in a separate cross-complaint. (Otherwise, defendant's claim for damages could be used only as an *offset* to the plaintiff's claim; *see ¶6:585-587.*)

    [6:458.1-458.4]   *Reserved.*

(3) [6:458.5]   **Statute of limitations no bar to affirmative defenses:**   The statute of limitations does not apply to defenses: "Under well-established authority, a defense may be raised at any time, even if the matter alleged would be barred by a statute of limitations if asserted as the basis for affirmative relief." [*Styne v. Stevens* (2001) 26 C4th 42, 51, 109 CR2d 14, 22]

The rule applies in particular to contract actions: "One may assert as defenses to a contract action matters that render the contract unenforceable, even if the same matters, alleged as grounds for restitution after rescission, would be untimely." [*Styne v. Stevens,* supra, 26 C4th at 51-52, 109 CR2d at 22]

• [6:458.6]   For example, when a contract is voidable on grounds of *fraud or illegality*, the innocent person whose performance is due under the contract need not seek rescission. Instead, he or she may wait until enforcement is sought and then assert the fraud or illegality as a defense. [*Styne v. Stevens,* supra, 26 C4th at 52, 109 CR2d at 22— Actress sued by Agent for sums allegedly due under agency contract could assert illegality of contract as defense]

(4) **Pleading requirements**

(a) [6:459]   **Fact pleading required:**   The same pleading of "ultimate facts" rather than "evidentiary" matter or "legal conclusions" is required as in pleading the complaint (¶6:123 ff.).

The answer must aver facts "as carefully and with as much detail as the facts which constitute the cause of action and which are alleged in the complaint." [*FPI Development, Inc. v. Nakashima* (1991) 231 CA3d 367, 384, 282 CR 508, 518—answer alleging "fraud in the inducement" and "failure of consideration" demurrable as mere conclusions]

### 1) Official Forms

a) **[6:460] Unlawful detainer:** The Official Form answer for *unlawful detainer* actions includes a wide variety of possible defenses, and sets them forth in some detail. Included are:

- Landlord's breach of rental agreement

- Landlord's breach of warranty to provide habitable premises

- Landlord's waiver of default

- Landlord waived, changed or cancelled notice to quit

- Retaliatory or discriminatory eviction

- Eviction violative of local rent control

**FORM:** Official Form Answer for Unlawful Detainer, *see Form 6:P.*

b) **[6:461] Contract and tort actions:** However, the Official Form answers for *contract* and *tort* (personal injury, wrongful death, property damage) actions do *not* set forth any defense in detail. It is up to the defendant in such actions to plead the ultimate facts constituting each defense.

**FORMS:** Official Form Answer for Tort Actions, *see Form 6:I;* for Contract Actions, *see Form 6:N.*

### 2) **[6:462] Exception—statute of limitations:** In pleading the statute of limitations, "it is *not* necessary to state the facts showing the defense, but it may be stated generally that the cause of action is barred by the provisions of Section ____ (giving the number of the section

and subdivision thereof, if it is so divided, relied upon) of the Code of Civil Procedure." [CCP §458]

➡ [6:463] *PRACTICE POINTER:* Be very careful that you specify the *right* Code section. Designating the wrong section may be treated as a *waiver* of the defense. If in doubt, specify every section that might apply.

a) [6:464] **Narrowly interpreted:** The statute applies *only* to pleading the statute of limitations. Such specificity is not required in pleading other statutory defenses (e.g., statutory immunity). [*Hata v. Los Angeles County Harbor/UCLA Med. Ctr.* (1995) 31 CA4th 1791, 1805-1806, 37 CR2d 630, 638—answer claiming immunity "under Gov.C. §§810-996.6" sufficient to raise immunity under §854.8]

(b) [6:465] **Right to plead inconsistent defenses:** Defendant can assert inconsistent defenses in the answer, similar to plaintiff's right to plead inconsistent causes of action in the complaint.

1) [6:466] For example, in answering a complaint for defamation, defendant can *deny* making the alleged defamatory statement; and at the same time assert *privilege* as a defense.

*Comment:* Such alternative pleading is designed to prevent a forced election of defenses early in the litigation. But it is proper only if defendant cannot *truthfully* adopt one position or the other at the time of the answer. It does *not* justify *evasive* pleadings.

2) [6:467] Moreover, defendant may *defend* on one theory and *cross-complain* against a third party on another. I.e., defendant is not compelled at the pleading stage to be consistent with his theories. [*Shepard & Morgan v. Lee & Daniel, Inc.* (1982) 31 C3d 256, 259-261, 182 CR 351, 352-353—defendant may *deny* existence of hazardous condition in its answer to plaintiff's complaint; and at same time file cross-complaint for indemnity against third person based on *existence* of such condition;

*Farmers Ins. Exch. v. Sup.Ct. (Han)* (2000) 79 CA4th 1400, 1404, 95 CR2d 51, 54, fn. 3— same]

(c) [6:468] **Separately stated:** The various affirmative defenses must be separately stated; and must refer to the causes of action to which they relate "in a manner by which they may be intelligently distinguished." [CCP §431.30(g); see *Hata v. Los Angeles County Harbor/UCLA Med. Ctr.* (1995) 31 CA4th 1791, 1805, 37 CR2d 630, 638]

   1) [6:469] For example:

   "FOURTH AFFIRMATIVE DEFENSE.

   "As a defense to Plaintiff's Second Cause of Action for Defamation, Defendant alleges as follows: . . ."

(5) [6:470] **Challenging inadequate pleading:** Plaintiff may *demur* to an answer on the ground of insufficient pleading of defenses (CCP §430.20, *see* ¶7:35). Alternatively, plaintiff may *object* on that ground to introduction of evidence at trial. [*Hata v. Los Angeles County Harbor/UCLA Med. Ctr.*, supra, 31 CA4th at 1804, 37 CR2d at 637]

   (a) [6:471] **Waiver:** Failure to demur or object at trial waives the right to challenge the pleading on appeal. Reason: Had plaintiff objected earlier, defendant probably would have been allowed to amend the answer. [*Hata v. Los Angeles County Harbor/UCLA Med. Ctr.*, supra, 31 CA4th at 1805, 37 CR2d at 637]

(6) [6:472] **Effect of failure to plead:** If not raised in the answer, matters constituting an affirmative defense are *irrelevant* at trial. [*Carranza v. Noroian* (1966) 240 CA2d 481, 488, 49 CR 629, 634]

   (a) [6:473] **Exception—lack of subject matter jurisdiction:** Lack of subject matter jurisdiction is not waived by failure to plead (CCP §430.80). Thus, for example, *federal preemption* may be a defense although never pleaded; if the federal law confers exclusive jurisdiction on federal courts, state courts have no subject matter jurisdiction. [*De Tomaso v. Pan American World Airways, Inc.* (1987) 43 C3d 517, 520, 235 CR 292, 293, fn. 1]

   (b) [6:474] **Objection may be waived:** Defendants' failure to plead new matter in the answer cannot be raised for the first time on appeal where plaintiff was aware of the affirmative defense and the case was tried as if it had been pleaded.

b. **[6:475]** **Pleas in abatement:** Any ground for demurrer (¶7:30) that does *not* appear on the face of the complaint can be raised as an objection in the answer. [CCP §430.30(b)] The most common such grounds are:

- Plaintiff *lacks capacity* to sue;

- Nonjoinder or misjoinder of *parties;*

- *Another action is already pending* between the same parties for the same cause. [CCP §430.10]

As seen, these are technical reasons why an action should not proceed. They are commonly referred to as "dilatory pleas" or "pleas in abatement" (reflecting their disfavored status). At any rate, like affirmative defenses, they are "new matter" and must be specially pleaded in the answer. Indeed, unless raised by demurrer or answer, such grounds are *waived* (CCP §430.80). Courts may deny leave to amend an answer to raise such matters for the first time, particularly late in the proceedings.

c. **[6:476]** **New matter deemed controverted by plaintiff:** No pleading by plaintiff is permitted in reply to defendant's answer in civil actions generally (¶6:3). Instead, whatever defenses and objections are raised by defendant in the answer are *deemed controverted* by plaintiff. [CCP §431.20(b)]

(1) **[6:477]** **Effect:** Plaintiff can assert whatever grounds he has for avoiding the defenses raised in the answer *without pleading* such grounds.

(2) **Examples**

- [6:478] P sued for personal injuries. D's answer pled settlement and release as an affirmative defense. At trial, P could introduce evidence to attack the release on ground of fraud, duress, etc. *without any prior pleading* of such grounds. [*Martin v. Sugarman* (1933) 218 C 17, 19, 21 P2d 428, 429]

- [6:479] P sued for personal injuries. D's answer pled the statute of limitations as an affirmative defense. At trial, P could introduce evidence of equitable tolling of the statute without any prior pleading. [*Aerojet General Corp. v. Sup.Ct. (Larson)* (1986) 177 CA3d 950, 953, 223 CR 249, 252]

⇨[6:480] *PRACTICE POINTER:* As a result, defense counsel must always be careful to *discover before trial* any ground plaintiff may have for avoidance of affirmative defenses pleaded in the answer.

The best procedure is to *use contention interrogatories.* For example, "Do you contend that the release agreement pleaded as an affirmative defense in the answer is unenforceable in whole or in part? If so, state the facts on which you base such contention, the names and addresses of each person who has personal knowledge of such facts; and describe each document that you contend is relevant to such contention."

(3) **[6:481]** **Exception—replication permitted in mandamus or prohibition:** In administrative mandamus or prohibition proceedings, the general rules of pleading apply. But there is one exception: Plaintiff is permitted to *reply* to matters raised in defendant's answer. This being so, plaintiff would be expected to plead whatever grounds there are for avoiding the defenses or objections pleaded by defendant.

6. **[6:482]** **Prayer:** Although not really necessary, it is customary to include the following wording at the end of the answer:

"WHEREFORE, defendant prays that plaintiff take nothing by the complaint, and that defendant be awarded judgment in this action (and attorney fees in the sum of $_____ ; see below), and costs of suit incurred herein."

a. **[6:483]** **Official Forms:** The prayer in the Official Form Answers is even more abbreviated:

"DEFENDANT REQUESTS

a. that plaintiff take nothing.
b. ☐ costs of suit.
c. ☐ other (specify)"

(*See Form 6:I.*)

b. **[6:484]** **No affirmative relief:** Remember that an answer cannot be used to obtain affirmative relief against the plaintiff. A separate cross-complaint must be filed. [CCP §431.30(c); see *Construction Protective Services, Inc. v. TIG Specialty Ins. Co.* (2002) 29 C4th 189, 195, 126 CR2d 908, 911, *discussed at ¶6:457*]

c. **[6:485]** **Attorney fees:** In an increasing number of cases, the court may have power to award reasonable attorney fees to a defendant who prevails in the action. No separate cross-complaint is normally required. But a request for such an award should be made in the prayer to bring the matter to the court's attention.

(1) **[6:486]** **Example:** Civil Code §1717 provides that in an action on a contract authorizing attorney fees to one party, whichever party prevails in the action is entitled to recover his or her fees. Since these fees are authorized by statute, they are taxable as costs; no separate cross-complaint is required. [*T.E.D. Bearing Co. v. Walter E. Heller & Co.* (1974) 38 CA3d 59, 64, 112 CR 910, 914]

⇨ **[6:486.1]** *PRACTICE POINTER FOR DEFEN-DANTS:* Where there is any question about the court's power to award fees, it may be better *not* to pray for attorney fees in your answer, even if the complaint seeks fees. Your prayer for fees might constitute an acquiescence that the prevailing party is, in fact, entitled to attorney fees, supporting an award against your client if you lose the case.

7. **[6:487]** **Subscription:** The answer is normally signed (subscribed) by the attorney, not the client. If the client signs, the *attorney must also sign* (see CCP §128.7(a) (applicable to post-1994 cases)).

By signing the answer, the attorney makes certain certifications regarding the merits, which, if untrue, may subject counsel to sanctions. [CCP §128.7(c); *see ¶6:305 ff., and 9:1157 ff.*]

8. **[6:488]** **Verification:** If the complaint is verified (*see ¶6:309*), defendant must verify the answer; i.e., attach a statement under oath or penalty of perjury ". . . that the same is true of his (or her) own knowledge, except as to matters stated therein on information and belief, and as to those matters that he (or she) believes it to be true." [CCP §446] (The attorney must still sign the answer; see above.)

a. **Exceptions**

(1) **[6:489]** **Limited civil cases:** Answers need not be verified in limited civil cases even if the complaint (or cross-complaint) was verified. [CCP §92(b)]

(2) **[6:490]** **Actions against public entity or official:** An answer by a governmental body or officer sued in his official capacity need not be verified—even if the complaint against them was verified. [CCP §446; *Trask v. Sup.Ct. (County of Los Angeles)* (1994) 22 CA4th 346, 350, 27 CR2d 425, 426, fn. 3]

(3) **[6:491]** **Compare—defendant sued by public entity must verify answer, even though complaint not verified:** Actions by a public agency need not be verified—even in actions where complaints by other

plaintiffs would have to be verified (¶*6:310*). But despite the unverified complaint of the public entity, the *defendant must verify* its answer thereto (unless admissions might subject defendant to criminal prosecution). [CCP §446; see *People v. $400 U.S. Currency* (1993) 17 CA4th 1615, 1619, 22 CR2d 161, 163-164]

   b.   **[6:492]** **Who may verify:** The same classes of persons authorized to verify a complaint (any of several coparties, authorized agent or attorney) may verify an answer. [CCP §446; *see ¶6:320*]

      (1)  **[6:493]** **Caution—attorney verification:** Attorney verification of answers is *particularly discouraged.* [See *DeCamp v. First Kensington Corp.* (1978) 83 CA3d 268, 275, 147 CR 869, 873]

   c.   **[6:494]** **How to attack failure to verify:** An answer that is required to be verified but is not, is subject to motion to strike, which provides for hearing and extension of time to answer. [CCP §435; *see ¶7:173 ff.*]

*(Text cont'd on p. 6-101)*

**RESERVED**

(1) [6:495] **Objection waived by delay until trial:** Defendant's failure to verify its answer is a pleading defect and is waived by plaintiff's delaying the objection until the time of trial. [*Zavala v. Board of Trustees* (1993) 16 CA4th 1755, 1761, 20 CR2d 768, 771]

d. [6:496] **Verification and self-incrimination:** A defendant cannot refuse to verify an answer on the ground that admissions therein may tend to incriminate him or her (except answers to complaints by public entities; *see ¶6:491*). However, since verification is statutorily required, immunity is provided against use of the defendant's answer in criminal proceedings. [See *DeCamp v. First Kensington Corp.* (1978) 83 CA3d 268, 280, 147 CR 869, 876]

Moreover, the fact that the defendant has verified his or her answer does not affect his or her right to claim the privilege against self-incrimination at trial. [*Alvarez v. Sanchez* (1984) 158 CA3d 709, 715, 204 CR 864, 868]

e. [6:497] **Verification and attorney-client privilege:** Like any other privilege, the attorney-client privilege may be waived by disclosure of a significant portion of the confidential communication (Ev.C. §912). However, defendant's verification of its answer does *not* waive the attorney-client privilege as to matters admitted or denied therein ... at least where the verification is on "information and belief," and the allegations in the answer are "vague, conclusional and lack factual depth." [*Alpha Beta Co. v. Sup.Ct. (Sundy)* (1984) 157 CA3d 818, 831, 203 CR 752, 758]

(1) [6:498] *Caution:* The above case seems to suggest that if the allegations in the answer are specific and factual, a positive verification (rather than one on lack of information and belief) *could* be construed as a waiver of the attorney-client privilege as to the matters alleged! (However, there is no known authority so holding.)

9. [6:499] **Filing and Service:** All pleadings subsequent to the complaint must be filed with the court, together with proof of service upon opposing parties or their counsel. [CCP §465]

## D. CROSS-COMPLAINT

### 1. General Considerations

a. [6:500] **Function:** A cross-complaint allows the defendant to assert claims for *affirmative relief* against the plaintiff, or a codefendant, or someone not yet a party to the action ... avoiding the necessity of filing separate lawsuits on such claims.

Claims against plaintiff can be asserted regardless of subject matter relationship (and may be compulsory if such relationship exists; see ¶6:508). Claims against anyone else, however, *must relate* to the subject matter or transaction alleged in plaintiff's complaint (¶6:525). [CCP §428.10(a),(b)]

b. [6:501] **Who may file:** A cross-complaint may be filed by the original defendant *or by anyone against whom a cross-complaint has been filed.* [CCP §428.10]

   (1) [6:502] **Example:** Plaintiff sues Defendant. Defendant cross-complains against Third Party (cross-defendant). Third Party may cross-complain against Defendant, or Plaintiff or nonparties.

   No subject matter relationship is required for Third Party's claims against Defendant (party who filed the cross-complaint against him). But it *is* required for claims against anyone else. [CCP §428.10(a), (b)]

c. [6:503] **Cross-complaint as independent action:** A cross-complaint is treated as an independent action. It is *not* dependent on plaintiff's action. The issues raised by the cross-complaint are treated as "completely severable" from the issues raised by the original complaint and answer. [*Security Pac. Nat'l Bank v. Adamo* (1983) 142 CA3d 492, 496, 191 CR 134, 137]

   (1) [6:504] **Not affected by dismissal of complaint:** Dismissal of plaintiff's complaint does not affect defendant's right to proceed to trial on his or her cross-complaint (against plaintiff or others). [See *Bertero v. National General Corp.* (1974) 13 C3d 43, 51, 118 CR 184, 191]

   (2) [6:505] **Discovery admissions:** Admissions made by defendant in response to discovery requests from plaintiff are not necessarily binding on defendant in proceedings on his or her cross-complaint against a third party. [*Shepard & Morgan v. Lee & Daniel, Inc.* (1982) 31 C3d 256, 259-260, 182 CR 351, 352-353; *see* ¶8:1394]

   (3) [6:506] **Compare—collateral estoppel:** If plaintiff's complaint goes to trial *before* defendant's cross-complaint, issues adjudicated in the earlier trial may bar later proceedings on the cross-complaint under res judicata or collateral estoppel principles. [*Wittman v. Chrysler Corp.* (1988) 199 CA3d 586, 591, 245 CR 20, 23]

       (a) [6:507] **Example:** P sued for judicial foreclosure of trust deed executed by D. D cross-complained for fraud in execution of underlying debt instruments.

Trial was bifurcated. A judgment was entered in P's favor in the foreclosure proceedings on findings that the underlying debt instruments were valid. This barred relitigation of these issues at trial of D's cross-complaint. [*Wittman v. Chrysler Corp.*, supra]

2. **Cross-Complaint Against Plaintiff—Permissive vs. Compulsory**

a. [6:508] **Always permissive—no subject matter relationship required:** Defendant always has the *option* of asserting *any* cause of action he or she has against the plaintiff in a cross-complaint. The cause of action *need not be related* to the subject matter of plaintiff's complaint in any way. The purpose is to allow plaintiff and defendant to settle all of their differences in a single lawsuit. [CCP §428.10(a)]

   (1) [6:509] **Exceptions:** Cross-complaints are not allowed in:

   - *Eminent domain* proceedings [CCP §428.10(a)]; or in

   - *Unlawful detainer* (to prevent delays in this summary proceeding) [*Superior Motels, Inc. v. Rinn Motor Hotels, Inc.* (1987) 195 CA3d 1032, 1066, 241 CR 487, 505-506]

   (2) [6:510] **Court may sever:** If the cross-complaint joins too many unrelated claims, the court has discretionary power to order separate trials on some or all of them. [CCP §1048(b)]

b. [6:511] **Compulsory if related to plaintiff's complaint:** If defendant's cause of action against plaintiff *is related* to the subject matter of the complaint, then it *must* be raised by cross-complaint . . . failure to plead it will *bar* defendant from asserting it in any later lawsuit. [CCP §426.30; see *AL Holding Co. v. O'Brien & Hicks, Inc.* (1999) 75 CA4th 1310, 1313-1314, 89 CR2d 918, 920]

The same rule applies where the defendant *raised* the same claim as a cross-complaint in a prior action but voluntarily dismissed it before it was adjudicated. [See *Hill v. City of Clovis* (1998) 63 CA4th 434, 445, 73 CR2d 638, 645; *Carroll v. Import Motors, Inc.* (1995) 33 CA4th 1429, 1436, 39 CR2d 791, 795]

   (1) [6:512] **"Related cause of action":** Defendant's cross-complaint is compulsory if the cause of action "arises out of the *same transaction* or *series* of transactions or occurrences as the cause of action in the complaint." [CCP §§426.10, 426.50]

(a) **[6:513] Test:** Causes of action arise out of the "same transaction or occurrence" if the factual or legal issues are *logically related.* They need not be absolutely identical. The basic approach is to avoid duplication of time and effort. [*Currie Medical Specialties, Inc. v. Bowen* (1982) 136 CA3d 774, 777, 186 CR 543, 544]

(b) **Application**

- **[6:514]** Action #1: A sued B, a former distributor, for unfair competition and trademark infringement for having usurped A's customers following termination of their distributorship agreement. The action was dismissed with prejudice.

  Action #2: B sues A for breach of the distributorship agreement.

  Held: Both lawsuits involve common issues of law and fact (i.e., the terms of the contract, who was in breach, etc.). B's action therefore is barred because not raised as a cross-complaint in A's earlier action. [*Currie Medical Specialties, Inc. v. Bowen,* supra]

- **[6:515]** Faced with conflicting demands for insurance proceeds, Insurance Co. filed an interpleader action naming Beneficiary as one of the defendants. (That action was ultimately settled by disbursing the proceeds to Beneficiary.) Beneficiary could not later sue Insurance Co. for wrongful delay in payment. Any such claim was related to the interpleader, and thus barred by failing to raise it as a cross-complaint in the interpleader action. Interpleader is not excluded from the compulsory cross-complaint statute. [*Cheiker v. Prudential Ins. Co.* (9th Cir. 1987) 820 F2d 334, 337—applying Calif. law]

(2) **[6:516] Existing at time answer filed:** To be considered a compulsory cross-complaint, the related cause of action must have existed at the time defendant served its answer to the complaint. [CCP §426.30(a); see *AL Holding Co. v. O'Brien & Hicks, Inc.,* supra, 75 CA4th at 1313-1314, 89 CR2d at 920]

Claims arising *thereafter* are *permissive*, not compulsory . . . even if subject-matter related to the complaint. [*Crocker Nat'l Bank v. Emerald* (1990) 221 CA3d 852, 864, 270 CR 699, 706]

(a) **[6:517] Example:** Creditor sued on a promissory note. After Debtor's answer was filed, Creditor disposed of collateral securing the note. Debtor sought leave to cross-complain on the ground the disposition was commercially unreasonable. Because Creditor's action took place *after* Debtor's answer was filed, the cross-complaint was *not* compulsory. [*Crocker Nat'l Bank v. Emerald*, supra]

(3) **Effect of failure to plead**

(a) [6:518] **Relief granted:** At any time during the course of the lawsuit, the court retains power to permit defendant to file or amend a cross-complaint to avoid forfeiture of defendant's "related" claim. Indeed, the court "shall grant" leave as long as defendant is acting in good faith. [CCP §426.50; see *Silver Organizations Ltd. v. Frank* (1990) 217 CA3d 94, 98-99, 265 CR 681, 683—even on "eve of trial," leave to file compulsory cross-complaint mandatory absent bad faith]

1) [6:519] **Discretion to refuse?** There is a split of authority as to whether trial courts have *any* discretion to deny:

- One view is that the requirement of "good faith" gives courts a "modicum of discretion" but the law strongly favors *granting leave.* [See *Sidney v. Sup.Ct. (Kinoshita)* (1988) 198 CA3d 710, 718, 244 CR 31, 36]

- The other view is that courts have no discretion to deny absent findings of bad faith based on substantial evidence. [See *Silver Organizations Ltd. v. Frank*, supra]

(b) [6:520] **After judgment, recovery on unpleaded "related" claim barred:** If the claim has still not been pleaded by the time the case goes to trial, *judgment* in the action will *bar* later recovery by defendant on the "related" claim. [CCP §426.30; *City of Hanford v. Sup.Ct. (GWF Power Systems, Inc.)* (1989) 208 CA3d 580, 587, 256 CR 274, 278 (citing text)]

Once judgment is entered, defendant cannot assert his or her unpleaded claim either affirmatively (in a separate lawsuit) or defensively (as an offset to some other claim by plaintiff). I.e., the rule that "cross-demands are deemed compensated" (¶6:587) does *not* apply to demands barred by CCP §426.30. [CCP §431.70]

(4) [6:521] **Exceptions:** But there is no bar from failure to assert a cross-complaint where:

- [6:521.1] Defendant's claim was *already pending* in a separate lawsuit when plaintiff filed the first action. [CCP §426.40(c); see *Morris v. Blank* (2001) 94 CA4th 823, 831, 114 CR2d 672, 677]

- [6:521.2] Defendant *defaulted* to the complaint in the first action. [CCP §426.30(b); see *Morris v. Blank*, supra, 94 CA4th at 831, 114 CR2d at 677]

  Nor does a judgment in the first action automatically bar prosecution of the later action under doctrines of *res judicata* or *collateral estoppel* unless the claim is the same or the issues are identical. [See *Morris v. Blank*, supra, 94 CA4th at 831, 114 CR2d at 677]

- [6:521.3] Both actions are filed in the *small claims* court. [CCP §426.60(b)]

  *Compare:* But failure to assert a compulsory cross-complaint in a superior court action would apparently bar a later small claims action. (E.g., A sues B for personal injury in the superior court and obtains judgment. No cross-complaint was filed although B suffered $3,000 property damage in the same accident. If B later sues A for the $3,000 property damage in small claims court, the small claims action would be barred.)

- [6:521.4] Plaintiff sought only *declaratory relief* in the first action. [CCP §426.60(c); see *E.L. White, Inc. v. Huntington Beach* (1978) 21 C3d 497, 505, 146 CR 614, 618, fn. 4]

  (Note: This does not affect the right to cross-complain in a declaratory relief action if parties *choose* to do so. See *California State Auto. Ass'n v. Sup.Ct. (Sousa)* (1986) 184 CA3d 1428, 1433, 229 CR 409, 412, fn. 6.)

- [6:521.5] Defendant was not subject to the court's *personal jurisdiction* in the first action. [CCP §426.30(b)]

- [6:521.6] Defendant's claim required for its adjudication the joinder of *additional parties* over whom the court could not obtain personal jurisdiction. [CCP §426.40(a)]

- [6:521.7] The court in the first action is *prohibited* by federal or state law from adjudicating the defendant's claim. [CCP §426.40(b)]

  For example, if defendant's claim falls within the exclusive subject matter jurisdiction of federal courts (e.g., patent, copyright, antitrust), it is not waived by failure to assert it in an earlier state court action.

- • **[6:521.8]** The first action is an *interpleader* under CCP §386 (stakeholder depositing funds to which conflicting claims are being made by others; *see* ¶*2:470*). Because *cross-complaints do not lie* against the stakeholder in an interpleader action (*see* ¶*2:491.1*), "(a)t the very least, it is arguable that §386 is an exception to the compulsory cross-complaint rule of CCP §426.30." [*State Farm Fire & Cas. Co. v. Pietak* (2001) 90 CA4th 600, 615, 109 CR2d 256, 266-267—Insurance Company interpleaded fire insurance proceeds claimed by both Insured and Lender; Insured's later bad faith action against Insurance Co. not barred by CCP §426.30]

(5) **[6:522]** **Special rule limits cross-complaints for indemnity against condo owners' association:** No cross-complaint for indemnity on comparative fault principles is permitted against a condo owners' association suing for damage to it or its members. (The defendant can only raise comparative fault as an affirmative defense; see CCP §383.) Hence, there is no compulsory cross-complaint in such cases. *See further discussion at* ¶*6:536.*

---

**TACTICAL CONSIDERATIONS**
**[6:523]**

Assuming the cross-complaint is *not* compulsory, defendant has to decide *whether* to cross-complain: i.e., whether it is more advantageous to join the claim in the original action, or to assert it instead in a separate lawsuit. This requires consideration of the advantages and disadvantages of these alternatives:

(1) **Advantages of cross-complaint over separate lawsuit**

- • If the claim is relatively simple, filing a cross-complaint in the original action will be less expensive than filing and serving a new lawsuit.

- • Defendant usually can get to trial faster (if he or she wants to) by cross-complaining in the original action.

- • If defendant files a separate lawsuit, there is always a risk that the judge in that action might rule that the claim was "related" to the original action, and hence waived because not pleaded therein (i.e., a compulsory cross-complaint, ¶*6:511 ff.*).

---

---

**TACTICAL CONSIDERATIONS (Cont'd)**

- Or, the judge might rule that some issue *adjudicated* unfavorably in the original action is binding on defendant under the doctrine of collateral estoppel.

(2) **Advantages of separate lawsuit over cross-complaint**

- A cross-complaint involving numerous new issues or parties may unduly complicate and delay the original action and confuse the jury; there is a better chance of a fair trial in a separate lawsuit.

- Plaintiff's evidence in the original action might make the jury unsympathetic to *any* cross-complaint; defendant can avoid this risk by filing a separate lawsuit.

- A new lawsuit can be filed wherever venue is proper; whereas, a cross-complaint is subject to the venue in the original action.

(3) **Compare—plaintiff's remedies to prevent separate trials:** If plaintiff opposes the idea of separate trials and wants the claims to be litigated concurrently, the proper remedy is a *motion to consolidate* (if separate suit filed in same court, *see ¶12:340 ff.*) or to *coordinate* (if filed in a different county, *see ¶12:370 ff.*).

---

3. **[6:524] Cross-Complaints Against Other Parties—When Permitted:** There are no compulsory cross-complaints against parties other than plaintiff. Rather, the issue usually is whether a cross-complaint against such parties will be permissible.

   a. **[6:525] Subject matter relationship required:** A defendant can cross-complain against a codefendant or third person not yet a party to the action only if the cause of action asserted " . . . (1) arises out of the *same transaction*, occurrence or *series* of transactions or occurrences (set forth in the complaint) . . . or (2) asserts a claim, right or interest in the *property* or *controversy* which is the subject of the cause of action brought against him." [CCP §428.10(b)]

      Note that this is somewhat *broader* than the "same-transaction-or-series" rule governing *compulsory* cross-complaints against plaintiff (*¶6:512-514*). Here, it is sufficient that the claims refer to the same property or controversy—even if not arising at the same time or out of the same series of events.

(1) [6:526] **Application:** The following illustrate proper cross-complaints:

  (a) [6:527] **Same transaction or series or transactions:** A frequent example in auto accident cases is where defendant claims that some third person was entirely or partially at fault in causing the accident in which plaintiff was injured. Example:

   • P sues D for personal injuries;

   • D cross-complains against Third Person, alleging that Third Person was wholly or partially at fault. (Such cross-complaint is basically for declaratory relief, urging a right of implied indemnity upon payment of any judgment or settlement in the case; see *American Motorcycle Ass'n v. Sup.Ct. (Viking Motorcycle Club)* (1978) 20 C3d 578, 607, 146 CR 182, 200-201; and *E.L. White, Inc. v. Huntington Beach* (1978) 21 C3d 497, 506, 146 CR 614, 619.)

   Another frequent example arises in construction defect cases. Example:

   • Property Owner sues General Contractor for construction defects;

   • General Contractor cross-complains against various Subcontractors, alleging the loss resulted from their negligence and seeking indemnification for General Contractor's liability to Property Owner;

   • Subcontractors in turn cross-complain against each other or against others (engineers, suppliers, etc.), seeking indemnification for the loss. [See *Newhall Land & Farming Co. v. McCarthy Const.* (2001) 88 CA4th 769, 774, 106 CR2d 10, 13]

  (b) [6:528] **Property:** Example: P sues D1 and D2 to quiet title to real property. D1 cross complains against D2 for damages for breach of contract to deliver marketable title. [See *Hanes v. Coffee* (1931) 212 C 777, 782, 300 P 963, 965]

(2) [6:529] **Equitable indemnity cross-complaints:** Except as noted below, defendants may cross-complain against any person from whom they seek equitable indemnity. Defendants need only allege that the harm for which they are being sued is attributable, at least in part, to the cross-defendant. [*Platt v. Coldwell Banker Residential Real Estate Services* (1990) 217 CA3d 1439, 1445, 266 CR 601, 604, fn. 7]

"Cross complaints for comparative equitable indemnity would appear virtually always transactionally related to the main action." [*Time for Living, Inc. v. Guy Hatfield Homes* (1991) 230 CA3d 30, 38, 280 CR 904, 909]

However, there are several public policy limitations on equitable indemnity cross-complaints:

(a) [6:530] **Limitation—attorney sued for malpractice may not cross-complain against successor:** Public policy prohibits an attorney sued for malpractice from cross-complaining for equitable indemnity against a successor attorney hired to remedy the problem. [*Holland v. Thacher* (1988) 199 CA3d 924, 929-930, 245 CR 247, 250; *Austin v. Sup.Ct. (Chambers, Noronha & Lowry)* (1999) 72 CA4th 1126, 1128-1129, 85 CR2d 644, 646]

1) [6:531] **Rationale:** Such cross-complaints can undermine the relationship between the client and the successor attorney. Moreover, they can discourage successor attorneys from attempting to assist clients harmed by the original attorney's negligence. [*Holland v. Thacher,* supra, 199 CA3d at 930, 245 CR at 250; *Austin v. Sup.Ct. (Chambers, Noronha & Lowry)*, supra, 72 CA4th at 1128-1129, 85 CR2d at 646]

2) [6:532] **Compare—malpractice indemnity from co-counsel:** There is no public policy, however, against concurrent counsel or co-counsel suing each other for indemnification of legal malpractice damages arising from joint representation of a client. Whether such a claim is allowed depends on the facts of the individual case . . . in particular, whether it may *endanger client confidences* or create a *potential conflict of interest* between the attorney and client. [*Musser v. Provencher* (2002) 28 C4th 274, 283-284, 121 CR2d 373, 380]

• [6:532.1] Family Law Lawyer, who was sued for malpractice resulting from reliance on advice given by Bankruptcy Lawyer, could seek indemnity from the latter. No client confidences were involved (the client had waived the attorney-client privilege with respect to Bankruptcy Lawyer's representation), and his self-interest in defending against the indemnity claim did not endanger any duty of loyalty owed to the client. [*Musser v. Provencher*, supra, 28 C4th at 283-284, 121 CR2d at 380]

[6:533] *Reserved.*

(b) [6:534] **Unfairness as limitation:** Equitable indemnification cross-complaints are also improper "where under the particular facts alleged, the cross-complaint would operate inequitably." [See *Platt v. Coldwell Banker Residential Real Estate Services* (1990) 217 CA3d 1439, 1450, 266 CR 601, 607]

Unfairness may exist where (i) defendant can obtain the same relief by *affirmative defense* to the complaint; and (ii) the cross-complaint would "jeopardize or entangle a *special relationship* which strong policies dictate be preserved." [*Jaffe v. Huxley Architecture* (1988) 200 CA3d 1188, 1193, 246 CR 432, 434]

1) [6:535] **Apportionment of liability not necessarily unfair:** The mere fact a cross-complaint seeks to apportion liability in the underlying action—thus tending to pit cross-defendants against each other—does *not* by itself make it "unfair" or "inequitable." [*Platt v. Coldwell Banker Residential Real Estate Services,* supra, 217 CA3d at 1450, 266 CR at 608]

(c) [6:536] **Limitation on indemnity claims against condo owners' association:** A common interest development association has standing to sue on behalf of its members for certain types of damage sustained by the association or its members (*see* ¶2:59*).

The defendant in such action may raise the comparative fault of the association or its members as an affirmative defense in its answer . . . but may *not* file a cross-complaint (or separate action) for contribution or indemnity against the association or its managing agents where the *only* damages claimed are to the association or its members. [CCP §383(b); *see* ¶2:59]

This prevents the defendant from dragging each individual owner into the litigation as a cross-defendant . . . greatly running up the costs to the association and its members.

(d) [6:537] **Limitation on indemnity claims against plaintiff's employer:** When an employee is injured on the job and sues a third party tortfeasor for causing those injuries, the defendant is entitled to an *offset* for any concurring negligence by the plaintiff's employer. The purpose is to defeat the negligent employer's lien for workers' compensation benefits paid to the injured employee. [See *Witt v. Jackson* (1961) 57 C2d 57, 71, 17 CR 369, 377]

This offset can be raised in the third party defendant's answer as an affirmative defense. It is not clear, however, whether a *cross-complaint* against the employer for indemnity and contribution is permissible *because the employer is exempt from liability* to the third party tortfeasor (see Lab.C. §3864). Courts are split on this issue. [See *Del Monte Corp. v. Sup.Ct. (Rockwell Int'l Corp.)* (1982) 127 CA3d 1049, 1053, 179 CR 855, 858—allowing cross-complaint; *C.J.L. Const., Inc. v. Universal Plumbing* (1993) 18 CA4th 376, 391, 22 CR2d 360, 370—rejecting cross-complaint; *State of Calif. v. Sup.Ct. (Glovsky)* (1997) 60 CA4th 659, 664-665, 71 CR2d 256, 259-260—same]

b.  [6:538]  **Joinder of other claims permitted:**  As long as there is one permissible "related" cause of action in the cross-complaint (¶*6:524 ff.*), defendant can join with it *any other* claims he has against any of the cross-defendants (i.e., need not be related to plaintiff's complaint). [CCP §428.30]

   (1)  [6:539]  **Example:**  P sues D for negligence. D cross-complains against Third Person, alleging that Third Person was partially at fault in causing P's injuries. D may join a separate cause of action against Third Person for property damage to D's car.

c.  [6:540]  **Joinder of other parties permitted:**  Again, as long as there is one permissible "related" cause of action in the cross-complaint, defendant can join all persons as cross-defendants *or cross-complainants* whose joinder would be permissible under the rules governing joinder of parties. [CCP §§378, 379, 428.20; *see ¶2:150 ff.*]

d.  [6:541]  **Court may sever:**  To prevent defendant from complicating the case too much, the court has discretionary power to order separate trial of any of the claims or issues asserted in the cross-complaint. [CCP §1048(b)]

[6:542-543]  *Reserved.*

e.  [6:544]  **Compare—no mandatory third-party cross-complaints:**  Cross-complaints against third parties are *permissive*, not mandatory. While it may be "more orderly and expeditious" to resolve all claims in a single lawsuit, this is not required. Defendants may wait and pursue their rights against third parties in subsequent, independent proceedings. [See *Insurance Co. of North America v. Liberty Mut. Ins. Co.* (1982) 128 CA3d 297, 303, 180 CR 244, 248]

### 4. Drafting the Cross-Complaint

a. **[6:545] Separate pleading:** A cross-complaint is a separate pleading—not a part of the answer. [CCP §428.40]

b. **[6:546] Format:** A cross-complaint must conform to the rules applicable to pleadings generally. [CRC 201 ff., 312(h); *see discussion at ¶6:14 ff.*]

(1) **[6:547] Caption:** The caption of a cross-complaint must identify *both* the original parties (plaintiff v. defendant) *and* the parties to the cross-complaint. However, the parties to the original action can be identified by an abbreviated title, showing the first name on each side. [CCP §422.40; CRC 312(h); *and see ¶6:35*]

Example:

"ALAN AMES, et al.,          NO. _____

      Plaintiffs,          CROSS-COMPLAINT
                         FOR INDEMNIFICATION
vs.

BEA BAKER, et al.,

      Defendants.

---

BEA BAKER and BEN BAKER,

      Cross-complainants
      and Defendants,

vs.

ALAN AMES and CARY CRAIG,

      Cross-defendants."

(2) **[6:547.1] Footers:** Each page of each filed paper, except exhibits, must bear a footer in the bottom margin, below the page number and divided from the rest of the document by a printed line. The footer must contain the title of the document (e.g. "Cross-complaint") or some clear and concise abbreviation, and must be in at least 10-point type. [CRC 201(g); *see discussion at ¶6:20.1*]

c. **[6:548] Official Forms:** Official Forms are now available for cross-complaints in breach of contract actions, and in personal injury, property damage or wrongful death actions. (There are no cross-complaints allowed in unlawful detainer actions; *see ¶6:509.*)

(1) [6:549] **Contract actions:** The same form is used for both the complaint and cross-complaint in contract actions (*see Form 6:J*). The basic form is completed by ·attaching either of several "cause of action attachments": contract, common counts (*see Forms 6:K and 6:L*).

(2) [6:550] **Personal injury, property damage, wrongful death:** A separate form cross-complaint is available for use in these actions. It contains detailed statements of the most common grounds for cross-complaints in such actions:

- Indemnification

- Apportionment of fault

- Declaratory relief

5. [6:551] **Filing the Cross-Complaint:** The first issue is whether leave of court is required to file the cross-complaint. The answer depends on when, and against whom, the cross-complaint is sought to be filed:

a. [6:552] **Right to file against plaintiff or cross-complainant at time of answer:** If the cross-complaint is filed *before* or at the *same time* as the answer, it may be filed as a matter of right—i.e., without leave of court. [CCP §428.50(a)]

b. [6:553] **Right to file against third parties until first trial date:** Cross-complaints against third party cross-defendants (e.g., for equitable indemnity) may be filed without leave of court any time before the court sets the *first* trial date. [CCP §428.50(b)]

(1) [6:554] **Trial date vacated:** Once a trial date has been set, leave of court is required to file a cross-complaint—even if the trial date is later vacated. "If every time a case was dropped from the trial calendar, the door was open to a new round of pleadings as a matter of right, trials would be further delayed..." [*Loney v. Sup.Ct. (Moneta)* (1984) 160 CA3d 719, 723, 206 CR 769, 771]

(Remember also that cross-complaints against third persons require *subject matter relationship* to plaintiff's complaint; *see ¶6:525*.)

c. [6:555] **When leave of court required:** Except as allowed by the preceding paragraphs, leave of court must be obtained to file a cross-complaint (most commonly, when defendant seeks to cross-complain against plaintiff *after* having previously filed an answer).

If the proposed cross-complaint is permissive (¶6:508, 6:524), leave of court may be granted "in the interests of justice" at any time during the course of the action (CCP §428.50(c)). On the other hand, if the proposed cross-complaint is compulsory (¶6:511 ff.), leave *must* be granted so long as defendant is acting in good faith (CCP §426.50; *and see ¶6:518 ff.*).

(1) [6:556] **Limitations:** However, there are a number of situations in which courts may properly refuse leave to file cross-complaints (even those that are "compulsory"):

    (a) [6:557] **No cross-complaint after entry of judgment:** The liberal policy re filing cross-complaints "at any time during the course of the action" (above) does not apply after entry of judgment. It is immaterial that the action remains pending for other purposes (e.g., appeal). [*City of Hanford v. Sup.Ct. (GWF Power Systems, Inc.)* (1989) 208 CA3d 580, 587, 256 CR 274, 278 (citing text)]

    (b) [6:558] **No cross-complaint *by plaintiff* whose complaint dismissed for failure to prosecute:** Where defendant cross-complains against plaintiff, plaintiff may assert new claims by way of cross-complaint. Indeed, such cross-complaint may be *compulsory* where plaintiff's claims arose out of the "same transaction" etc. set forth in defendant's cross-complaint. [See CCP §426.10, *discussed at ¶6:512*]

    However, this does not entitle plaintiff to assert the *same* cause of action previously asserted in a complaint that has been dismissed for failure to bring it to trial within 5 years (CCP §583.310, *see ¶11:191*). In such a case, the court has discretion to deny plaintiff leave to cross-complain. [*Flynn v. Page* (1990) 218 CA3d 342, 347, 266 CR 830, 832]

    (c) [6:559] **No cross-complaint for malicious prosecution of main action:** The tort of malicious prosecution requires a showing that the litigation in question was *terminated* in favor of the party claiming malicious prosecution. It follows that no cross-complaint for malicious prosecution may be filed in the *same action* which defendant claims is being maliciously prosecuted ... even after plaintiff drops one of several claims (if the action proceeds on the others). [See *Babb v. Sup.Ct. (Huntington)* (1971) 3 C3d 841, 846, 92 CR 179, 181; *Jenkins v. Pope* (1990) 217 CA3d 1292, 1299-1300, 266 CR 557, 561]

The result is different where the complaint is *ordered dismissed.* Such dismissal constitutes a "favorable termination" for malicious prosecution purposes . . . so that a cross-complaint may be filed if the action remains pending for other purposes. [*Loomis v. Murphy* (1990) 217 CA3d 589, 593-594, 266 CR 82, 84-85—court ordered dismissal after court of appeal directed summary judgment in favor of defendants]

(2) **[6:560]** **Noticed motion procedure:** In the absence of stipulation, the defendant seeking leave to file a cross-complaint must file a noticed motion.

    (a) **[6:561]** **Moving papers:** The moving papers must contain:

- Notice

- Declaration of counsel

- Points and authorities

- Copy of proposed cross-complaint

      **FORM:** Notice of Motion for Leave to File Cross-Complaint; Declaration and Points and Authorities in Support, *see Form 6:W.*

(3) **[6:562]** **Showing required:** The declarations of defendant's counsel should show that it would be "in the interest of justice" to grant leave to file; and some reasonable excuse why the cross-complaint was not filed earlier (mistake, inadvertence, excusable neglect . . . or most commonly, *recent discovery of new facts*).

(4) **Judicial policy**

    (a) **[6:563]** **Leave to file compulsory cross-complaint:** Where the proposed cross-complaint arises out of the same transaction as plaintiff's claim, leave to file *must* be granted as long as defendant is acting in good faith. [CCP §426.50; *and see ¶6:518, 6:555*]

    (b) **[6:564]** **Leave to file permissive cross-complaint against plaintiff:** Unless it would interfere with the trial date or otherwise prejudice the action, courts are inclined to grant leave to file any other cross-complaint *against the plaintiff.* This again reflects the judicial policy of settling all disputes between plaintiff and defendant in the same lawsuit if possible (*see ¶6:508*).

    (c) **[6:565]** **Greater showing required for cross-complaints against others:** A greater showing of "interest of justice" is required to obtain leave to file a cross-complaint against a *codefendant or some third person not yet a party to the action*. Here, the court will be concerned that the cross-complaint not unreasonably burden and complicate plaintiff's lawsuit with crossactions and third parties.

[6:566] *Reserved.*

(d) [6:567] **Effect of trial setting:** Once a trial setting conference is scheduled, courts are inclined to *deny* motions to file cross-complaints either against plaintiff or against third parties—except for *compulsory* cross-complaints (in which case CCP §426.50, above, applies). [See *Crocker Nat'l Bank v. Emerald* (1990) 221 CA3d 852, 864, 270 CR 699, 706—no abuse of discretion in denying leave to file *permissive* cross-complaint against plaintiff 5 months before trial and several years after action commenced]

(e) [6:568] **Conditions imposed on granting leave:** If leave to file is granted, the case usually loses its "place in line" for a trial date. The reason is simple: A case cannot be at issue and ready for trial when some party now has the right to demur, or move to strike, or otherwise respond to a newly-filed cross-complaint (*see ¶6:652*).

1) [6:569] Since plaintiff is not responsible for the delay, he or she may *request an early trial setting* as soon as the case is again at issue (i.e., after an answer to the cross-complaint is filed). Such request may be made at the next status conference or by formal motion (*see ¶12:86*).

6. [6:570] **Service of Cross-Complaint:** A cross-complaint must be served on *all* parties to the action—regardless of whether the cross-complaint is directed against them or they are affected thereby. [CCP §428.60]

a. [6:571] **Existing parties served by mail:** The cross-complaint can be served by mail upon the attorney for any party who has already appeared in the action (e.g., plaintiff or any codefendant). [CCP §§428.60, 1010]

b. [6:572] **New parties must be served with summons and prior pleadings:** Any person named as cross-defendant who is not already a party to the action (or who has not appeared therein) must be personally served with a summons on the cross-complaint. (The procedure for issuance and service of such summons is the same as for summons on the complaint; *see Ch. 4*.) [CCP §428.60]

In addition, such new parties must be served with copies of the most recently amended complaint and any answers thereto. [CRC 202]

c. **[6:573]** **Proof of service requirements:** A cross-complaint against an existing party must be accompanied by proof of service at the time it is filed. If the cross-complaint adds *new parties*, proofs of service on the new parties must be filed *within 30 days after* the cross-complaint is filed. [CRC 201.7(c)]

Failure to comply with these requirements may result in issuance of an Order to Show Cause why sanctions should not be imposed. (If an OSC is issued, any responsive papers must be filed at least 5 days before the hearing.) [CRC 201.7(f),(i)]

(1) **[6:573.1]** **Court may extend time:** The court may extend or modify the time for serving the cross-complaint. An application for such extension, however, must be filed *before* the time for service has elapsed and must be accompanied by a declaration indicating why service has not been effected, the efforts made, and the date by which service will be made. [CRC 201.7(e)]

**FORM:** The application may be made on optional Judicial Council form CM-020, Ex Parte Application for Extension of Time to Serve Pleading; *see Form 4:J.*

7. **[6:574]** **Responsive Pleading Required:** A person served as cross-defendant must file a responsive pleading thereto (if not, a default may be taken on the cross-complaint). The cross-defendant may either answer, demur, move to strike or otherwise plead to the cross-complaint, as to the original complaint. [CCP §432.10]

The responsive pleading is due within 30 days after service (see CCP §432.1). But the parties may stipulate, without leave of court, to one extension not to exceed 15 days. [CRC 201.7(d)]

a. **[6:575]** **"Special answer" permitted:** In addition to a regular answer to the cross-complaint, a cross-defendant may file a *separate document* called a "special answer." This is used primarily where the cross-complaint is for *indemnification.* It allows the cross-defendant to assert *defenses to the original complaint* which the defendant (cross-complainant) *failed* to raise. [CCP §428.70]

(1) **[6:576]** **Purpose:** To protect against D's failure or neglect to assert proper defenses; or to foreclose any collusion between P and D on the underlying cause of action (e.g., D agreeing not to raise certain defenses in exchange for an agreement not to execute on any judgment obtained against D, in order to saddle the cross-defendant with the liability). [*Administrative Manage-*

*ment Services, Inc. v. Fidelity & Dep.Co. of Maryland* (1982) 129 CA3d 484, 488, 181 CR 141, 143]

(2) [6:577] **Example:** P sues D on a claim barred by the statute of limitations. D answers but does *not* raise the limitations period as a defense; and at the same time sues Third Party for indemnification. Third Party should answer the cross-complaint; *and also file* a *separate* "special answer" raising the defense that P's complaint against D is barred by the statute of limitations. [*Administrative Management Services, Inc. v. Fidelity & Dep.Co. of Maryland*, supra]

(3) [6:578] **Procedure:** The "special answer" has to be filed *at the same time* as the answer to the cross-complaint. And, it has to be served both on the third party plaintiff (cross-complainant) and on the person who asserted the cause of action against the third party plaintiff (original plaintiff). [CCP §428.70]

b. [6:579] **Cross-complaint to cross-complaint:** In addition to answering, the cross-defendant may in turn file a cross-complaint . . . against any existing party, or even against a new party. [CCP §428.10]

(1) [6:580] **Against new parties; subject matter relationship required:** However, as to any *new party*, the cross-defendant's cross-complaint must be subject-matter related to that which is pending against him or her (which, in turn, must be subject-matter related to the facts pleaded in the original complaint). [CCP §428.10(b)]

("Subject-matter related" means that it arises out of the "same transaction or series of transactions" or claims an "interest in the same property or controversy"; *see* ¶6:525.)

(2) [6:581] **Against cross-complainant; may be compulsory:** As with a defendant's claims against plaintiff (*see* ¶6:511), if the cross-defendant has a claim for affirmative relief *against the cross-complainant* arising out of the "same transaction or series of transactions" set forth in the cross-complaint, that claim must be asserted (by cross-complaint to the cross-complaint), or it is waived. [CCP §426.30; ¶6:511]

(a) [6:582] **Example:** P sues D for personal injuries sustained in an auto accident. D files a cross-complaint against Third Person for damages sustained in the same accident. If Third Person has a claim for damages *against D* arising out of the same accident, he must file a cross-complaint against D or it will be waived.

(3) [6:582.1] **"Daisy-chain" pleading?** Nothing in the statutes or rules prohibits a plaintiff who is served with a cross-complaint, from filing a cross-complaint in turn. However, such an unending "daisy chain" of pleadings should be discouraged. Each party should assert all of its claims in a single complaint or cross-complaint.

8. [6:583] **Cross-Complaint Requiring Reclassification or Transfer:** The court must *reclassify* an action previously classified as a limited civil case when a cross-complaint demanding more than $25,000 is filed, upon payment of a reclassification fee. [CCP §403.030; *see discussion at ¶3:108 ff.*]

[6:584] *Reserved.*

9. **Effect of Statute of Limitations**

a. [6:585] **Claim already time-barred before action filed:** Defendant cannot cross-complain on a cause of action that was already barred by the statute of limitations even before plaintiff filed the lawsuit. The cross-complaint would be subject to the defense of the statute just as would any independent action on the claim. [*Liberty Mut. Ins. Co. v. Fales* (1973) 8 C3d 712, 715, 106 CR 21, 23, fn. 4]

(1) [6:586] **Example:** P sues for $25,000 damages for breach of *written* contract 3 years ago (4-year statute applies; CCP §337(1)). D's cross-complaint for $50,000 for breach of *oral* contract 3 years ago would be time-barred (because 2-year statute applies; CCP §339(1)).

(2) [6:587] **Money demands "deemed compensated":** But this does not deprive defendant of the right of *offset*: i.e., when cross-demands for *money* exist between two persons at a time when neither is barred by the statute of limitations, they are deemed compensated to the extent they equal each other. [CCP §431.70; *Safine v. Sinnott* (1993) 15 CA4th 614, 618, 19 CR2d 52, 55]

(a) [6:588] **May be asserted by answer:** Therefore, defendant can raise his claim as a *defense* in his *answer*, even though the claim would otherwise be time-barred. (It is already paid and discharged by operation of law, so there is nothing to be barred by the statute.) *But* no affirmative relief can be obtained; the claim can be asserted *only as an offset* to the plaintiff's complaint.

(b) [6:589] **Example:** Attorney sued former Client for more than $4,000 in legal fees and costs advanced. Client raised Attorney's malpractice as an affirmative defense in the answer and in a cross-complaint for $36,000 damages. The statute of limitations barred the legal malpractice cross-complaint. But since there was a time when each was indebted to the other, Client's time-barred malpractice claim could still be proved as an offset to Attorney's fee claim, reducing it to zero. [*Safine v. Sinnott*, supra, 15 CA4th at 618, 19 CR2d at 55]

(c) [6:590] **Equitable limitations?** According to several cases, this statutory set-off does not apply "when assertion of the right would defeat public policy protecting the debtor." [*Jess v. Herrmann* (1979) 26 C3d 131, 142-143, 161 CR 87, 93—no automatic set-off in comparative fault cases because it would defeat purposes of financial responsibility law; *Park Place Estates Homeowners Ass'n, Inc. v. Naber* (1994) 29 CA4th 427, 432, 35 CR2d 51, 54—condo owner cannot withhold homeowners' association dues by offsetting his damage claims against the association]

- [6:591] **Comment:** These cases seem to misinterpret CCP §431.70. It does not purport to provide an "absolute" right of offset (so that there is no need to discuss "equitable limitations"). Rather, CCP §431.70's function is to prevent one party from depriving the other of a statute of limitations defense on a cross-demand.

b. **Claim alive when action filed**

(1) [6:592] **Compulsory cross-complaint against plaintiff; "relation back" doctrine:** A cross-complaint that is *subject-matter related* to the plaintiff's complaint (i.e., a compulsory cross-complaint) "relates back" to when the action was commenced for statute of limitations purposes. [*Trindade v. Sup.Ct. (Jacolick)* (1973) 29 CA3d 857, 859-860, 106 CR 48, 50; *Sidney v. Sup.Ct. (Kinoshita)* (1988) 198 CA3d 710, 714, 244 CR 31, 33 (citing text)]

(a) [6:593] **Rationale:** Plaintiff's commencing an action *tolls the statute of limitations* on defendant's causes of action against plaintiff that are "relating to or dependent upon the contract, transaction, or accident upon which the complaint is brought." In effect, plaintiff's action *waives* any limitations statute that would prevent defendant from making a proper defense. [*Trindade v. Sup.Ct. (Jacolick)*, supra, 29 CA3d at 860, 106 CR at 49; *Luna Records Corp. v. Alvarado* (1991) 232 CA3d 1023, 1028, 283 CR 865, 868 (citing text)]

(b) [6:594] **Example:** P files a timely personal injury action against D. After expiration of the 1-year statute, D files a cross-complaint against P for injuries suffered in the same accident. D's cross-complaint "relates back" to the date P's action was filed, and hence avoids the statute of limitations. [*Trindade v. Sup.Ct. (Jacolick)*, supra]

(c) **[6:595] Limited to compulsory cross-complaints:** Such "relation back" applies only to compulsory cross-complaints—i.e., those *related* to the transaction, etc. set forth in plaintiff's complaint. No "waiver" of the statute of limitations can be inferred as to *unrelated* cross-complaints. [*Trindade v. Sup.Ct. (Jacolick)*, supra]

1) **[6:596] No tolling for independent action:** The "relation back" rule does not apply merely because defendant's claim *could have been* asserted as a cross-complaint. Thus, an independent action on the claim is subject to the statute of limitations. [*Luna Records Corp. v. Alvarado* (1991) 232 CA3d 1023, 1029-1030, 283 CR 865, 869]

(Comment: Note that an independent action on a subject-matter related claim would also be subject to the *compulsory counterclaim bar*, CCP §426.30, *see ¶6:511*.)

(d) **[6:597] May be amended to allege different injuries:** This "relation back" effect allows cross-complaints to be *amended* in ways that a complaint may not: i.e., a *complaint* may *not* be amended after the statute of limitations has run to allege *injuries different* from those alleged in the original complaint (*see ¶6:715 ff.*). But this does not restrict amendments to a compulsory cross-complaint. Since the statute of limitations is *suspended*, D may assert his or her claims either in the original cross-complaint or an amendment thereto. [*Sidney v. Sup.Ct. (Kinoshita)* (1988) 198 CA3d 710, 715, 244 CR 31, 34—original cross-complaint alleged only property damage resulting from accident set forth in P's complaint; amended cross-complaint alleged personal injuries as well]

(2) **[6:598] Cross-complaint against other parties:** There is no tolling or "relation back" to save cross-complaints against co-defendants or third persons. Such cross-complaints must be timely on the date they are filed. [See *Trindade v. Sup.Ct. (Jacolick)*, supra, 29 CA3d at 859-860, 106 CR at 49]

(a) [6:599] **Example:** P files a timely personal injury suit against D. After expiration of the 1-year statute of limitations, D files a cross-complaint against Third Person for injuries suffered in the same action on which P sued. D's cross-complaint is *not* timely as to Third Person. No "waiver" of the statute of limitations can be inferred as to Third Person. [*Sidney v. Sup.Ct. (Kinoshita)*, supra, 198 CA3d at 717, 244 CR at 35-36, fn. 4 (citing text)]

(3) [6:600] **Special rule—contractor vs. subcontractor:** Actions for property damage against a contractor or subcontractor are subject to a 10-year statute of limitations (CCP §337.15). But if the owner files a timely action against the contractor, a special statute permits a *cross-complaint* for *equitable indemnity* against the *subcontractor* responsible for the defects, even *after* expiration of the 10-year period. The statute assures the contractor of full recourse against his or her subs. [CCP §337.15(c); *Valley Circle Estates v. VTN Consolidated, Inc.* (1983) 33 C3d 604, 609, 189 CR 871, 874]

- [6:601] This extension applies only where the owner's complaint is filed *within* the 10-year period. Thus, although the owner may sue beyond the 10-year period under exceptional circumstances (see CCP §337.15(e)), no cross-complaint against subcontractors lies in such cases. [*Grange Debris Box & Wrecking Co., Inc. v. Sup.Ct. (San Rafael)* (1993) 16 CA4th 1349, 1357, 20 CR2d 515, 520]

## E. AMENDED AND SUPPLEMENTAL PLEADINGS

1. [6:602] **Amendments as a Matter of Right:** Each party has the *right* to amend its pleadings *once*—without leave of court—within a brief time after its original pleading is filed. The purpose is to facilitate prompt correction of errors or deficiencies in the original pleading.

a. [6:603] **Amendment of complaint or cross-complaint:** Plaintiffs can amend their complaint once "of course" (without leave of court) *before defendant's* answer is filed; or, if defendant demurs, *before the hearing on the demurrer.* (The same rule applies to amendment of cross-complaints.) [CCP §472; see *Woo v. Sup.Ct. (Zarabi)* (1999) 75 CA4th 169, 175, 89 CR2d 20, 24 (citing text)]

This enables plaintiff to concede any error or objection to the complaint raised by the defendant, or otherwise discovered, and immediately draft and file an amended complaint.

Because CCP §472 applies to "any pleading," where a demurrer has been sustained with leave to amend and plaintiff files an amended complaint, that pleading presumably can also be amended once "of course" (without leave of court) *before* defendant answers or demurs.

⇨ **[6:604]** *PRACTICE POINTER:* If the opposing party demurs to your pleading, and the demurrer appears to have some merit, it is usually smarter to *amend* than to spend the time and effort to oppose the demurrer. Not only will this save legal fees on the demurrer (i.e., money), but it also will speed up getting the case at issue: The opposing party will be required to answer the amended pleading without the delay which the hearing on the demurrer would entail!

⇨ **[6:605]** *PRACTICE POINTER:* If you decide to amend, be sure to let opposing counsel *and the court* know several days before the date set for the hearing on the demurrer ... to save their wasting time preparing for the hearing. Rushing in and filing your amended pleading just before the hearing may be legally permissible, but is extremely discourteous to opposing counsel *and* to the judge.

(1) **[6:606]** **May add new parties:** CCP §472 does not limit what types of amendments may be made of course and without leave of court. Thus, any part of the complaint may be changed without leave ... including the addition of new parties plaintiff or defendant. [*Ryan G. v. Department of Transportation* (1986) 180 CA3d 1102, 1105, 226 CR 49, 50—where applicable, CCP §472 prevails over CCP §473(a) (requiring leave of court to add new parties; *see* ¶6:618)]

(2) **[6:607]** **Procedure:** Plaintiff simply files a "First Amended Complaint"; or if the changes are minor an "Amendment to Complaint" (*see* ¶6:621-625).

(3) **[6:608]** **Service of amendment:** A copy of the amendment must be served on each defendant affected thereby. The defendant then has the statutory period (30 days) to answer, move to strike, etc.; *see* ¶6:688 ff.

(a) **[6:609]** **Personal service required if defendant has not appeared:** An amendment making *substantive changes* in the complaint must be *personally* served on any defendant who has not appeared in the action. And, if that defendant's default has already been entered, service of the amended complaint "opens" the default—entitling him to plead to the amended complaint; *see* ¶6:698. [*Engebretson*

& *Co., Inc. v. Harrison* (1981) 125 CA3d 436, 442-443, 178 CR 77, 81]

b. **[6:610] Amendment of answer:** Similarly, defendant can amend his answer once "of course" (without leave of court). If plaintiff has demurred to the answer, such amendment can be made *before the hearing on plaintiff's demurrer.* [CCP §472]

If not, the answer can be amended as a matter of right only during the time that a *demurrer could have been interposed* (i.e., within 10 days after the answer was filed). [CCP §430.40(b); *Bank of America v. Goldstein* (1938) 25 CA2d 37, 45, 76 P2d 545, 550]

2. **[6:611] Amendments Requiring Leave of Court:** In cases other than the above, amendment of any pleading requires prior order of court. However, as will be seen, permission usually is granted liberally. Various kinds of amendments may be allowed:

a. **[6:612] Amendments to substitute defendant's true name for "Doe":** As discussed earlier, it is common practice to include fictitious names as parties defendant (¶6:80). This permits a good deal of flexibility in pleading and service. Once the defendant's true name has been discovered, however, the complaint "must be amended accordingly." [CCP §474]

(1) **Procedure**

(a) **[6:613] Application to amend:** In some courts, plaintiff's attorney must prepare an application and order to amend the complaint. In other courts (e.g., Los Angeles), printed forms are available for amendments of this type; all the attorney has to do is fill in the name of the defendant who is being served as one of the "Does."

- **FORM:** Amendment to Complaint to Substitute True Name of "Doe" Defendant, *see Form 6:Y* (L.A. Superior Court).

(b) **[6:614] Leave routinely granted ex parte:** In most courts, leave to amend to substitute a defendant's true name for "Doe" is routinely granted without notice or hearing of any kind. The application for leave to amend (*see Form 6:Y*) is simply presented to a judge or commissioner for signature.

(Some judges insist on noticed hearings because CCP §473(a) does not specifically provide otherwise.)

(c) **[6:615] Service of amendment not required:** Defendant has notice from the summons served upon him that he is being sued under the fictitious name (¶*6:87-88*). Thus, the amendment form need not be served on defendant or other parties. [*Drotleff v. Renshaw* (1949) 34 C2d 176, 181, 208 P2d 969, 971-972]

(2) **[6:616]** **Effect of failure to comply:** If the complaint is not amended to substitute defendant's true identity, the court is without jurisdiction to render judgment against that defendant. [See *Meller & Snyder v. R & T Properties, Inc.* (1998) 62 CA4th 1303, 1311, 73 CR2d 740, 745—dealing with judgment in postjudgment joint debtor proceedings]

    (a) **[6:617]** **Cured by amendment prior to judgment:** Defective substitution of fictitious defendants is a procedural error and can be cured by amendment prior to trial. Indeed, absent prejudice to defendant, the court has no discretion to refuse such amendment. [*Streicher v. Tommy's Elec. Co.* (1985) 164 CA3d 876, 884-885, 211 CR 22, 27]

        • **[6:617.1]** P amended his complaint to name D as a defendant, but did not substitute D for any of the "Doe" defendants named in the original complaint. Such substitution was necessary to avoid the statute of limitations (¶*6:735*). The error was "procedural" and curable by amendment. [*Streicher v. Tommy's Elec. Co.*, supra]

        **[6:617.2-617.4]** *Reserved.*

(3) **[6:617.5]** **Compare—special procedures in childhood sexual abuse actions:** In a damages action for childhood sexual abuse, only "Doe" defendants may be named in the original complaint. A court order must be obtained to amend the complaint to substitute a named defendant for a "Doe." The application to amend the complaint must be accompanied by a "certificate of corroborative facts" executed by plaintiff's attorney. [CCP §340.1(n); *see* ¶*1:913.3*]

    **[6:617.6-617.9]** *Reserved.*

(4) **[6:617.10]** **Identity unknown when complaint filed?** *As long as the statute of limitations has not yet run,* the amendment cannot be challenged on the ground plaintiff was not "truly ignorant" of defendant's identity when the complaint was filed. Rationale: Plaintiff could have sought leave to amend the complaint to *add* that person as a defendant rather than serving him or her as a "Doe." To treat the "Doe" amendment differently "would elevate form over substance and would ignore

common sense." [*Davis v. Marin* (2000) 80 CA4th 380, 387, 94 CR2d 896, 901]

b. **[6:618]** **Ex parte amendments to add or delete parties:** The court may grant permission *ex parte* to amend a pleading "by adding or striking out the *name* of any party, or by correcting a mistake in the name of a party, or a mistake in any other respect . . ." [CCP §473(a)(1)]

(Of course, if no answer has yet been filed, plaintiff can amend the complaint once, *without* leave of court, in any way he or she chooses, under CCP §472; *see ¶6:603*.)

(1) **[6:619]** **Nature of mistakes correctable:** Only mistakes as to *form* or *party identity* are correctable through this *ex parte* procedure. (Changes in any of the essential facts, or nature of the claim, require a noticed motion and hearing; *see ¶6:636 ff.*) The following are examples of the kinds of "mistakes" that can be corrected *ex parte*:

- Correct misspellings of parties' names;
- Attach exhibits inadvertently left off at time of filing;
- Insert necessary phrases or words omitted in typing;
- Correct form of verification;
- Add or delete parties.

(2) **[6:620]** **Caution—effect of statute of limitations:** Amendments which seek to bring in *new parties*, or make *substantive changes* in the cause of action asserted after expiration of the statute of limitations raise special problems. *See ¶6:715 ff.*

(3) **Procedure for ex parte amendments**

(a) **Amendment to pleading vs. amended pleading**

1) **[6:621]** **Amendment on face of pleading:** The court has power to permit alterations on the face of the original pleading (which must then be initialed by the judge or clerk). [CRC 327(d); see *Smith v. Kessler* (1974) 43 CA3d 26, 31, 117 CR 470, 473]

But that is rarely done. Instead, the pleader is usually required to file a formal amendment— i.e., a *separate document* of either type discussed below.

2) **[6:622]** **Amendment to pleading:** If the changes are relatively simple, the pleader may be permitted to file an "Amendment to

Complaint"(or to an answer or cross-complaint)—listing each correction to be made, and the page, paragraph and line number of the prior pleading amended thereby. It is executed in the same manner as the prior pleading (i.e., verified, if the prior pleading was verified). [CCP §471.5]

The court may deem a motion to file an amendment to a pleading as a motion to file an amended pleading and require the filing of an amended pleading containing the approved amendments. [CRC 327(c)]

- **FORM:** Amendment to Complaint, *see Form 6:BB.*

3) **[6:623] Amended pleading:** Alternatively (and far more commonly), the court may require the pleader to redraft the entire pleading to incorporate the proposed amendments in a single new pleading. [CCP §471.5; CRC 327(c)]

   a) **[6:624] Strong judicial preference:** The greater the number of corrections, the more likely the court will require an amended pleading, rather than merely an amendment to the original pleading. (Judges dislike working with two separate pleadings, often separated in the court file.)

   b) **[6:625] Caption:** If an amended pleading is filed, it must be captioned as such. [CRC 327(a)(1)] For example:

      "FIRST AMENDED COMPLAINT FOR DEFAMATION"

(b) **[6:626] Application for court order:** The party seeking to amend should prepare a written application for leave to amend. Attached to the application should be:

- A *copy of the proposed amendment* or amended pleading [CRC 327(a)(1)];

- A *declaration by counsel* showing why the amendment is necessary (e.g., to correct misspellings, to add or delete party, to attach exhibit, etc.);

- A *proposed order* authorizing the amendments.

**FORM:** Application and Order for Amendment to Complaint, *see Form 6:AA.*

Rev. #1 2002

➪[6:626.1] *PRACTICE POINTER:* Although not required, it is good practice to fax or mail a copy of the application to opposing counsel *before* presenting it to the court; and to include a statement to this effect in your declaration (above).

(c) [6:627] **Ex parte order:** Because the changes being made are relatively minor, the court may grant the application without a formal hearing, provided the party seeking leave has complied with ex parte hearing procedures (notice to all parties no later than 10:00 a.m. one court day before the hearing; and a declaration of such notice to the court). [CRC 379(b); *see discussion at ¶9:345 ff.*]

(d) [6:628] **Service of copies:** An amendment or amended complaint must be served "on *all parties affected thereby.*" [CCP §471.5]

➪[6:629] *PRACTICE POINTER:* Even if not required, it is better practice to serve such amendments on *all* other parties (i.e., whether or not "affected thereby"). This avoids the confusion which results at trial where some lawyers have one set of pleadings and other lawyers have others.

c. [6:630] **Amendments after demurrer sustained or motion to strike granted:** Upon sustaining a demurrer or granting a motion to strike, the court normally grants leave to amend or file a new pleading (*see ¶7:129-132, 7:201-205*). The court will usually specify a time within which the amendment or new pleading is due (e.g., 20 days); if no time is specified, the amendment must be filed within 10 days after service of notice of ruling. [CCP §472a(c),(d); CRC 325(e)]

*Special rule in unlawful detainer:* In unlawful detainer and forcible entry or detainer actions, an amended answer must usually be filed within 5 days after a demurrer to the answer is sustained or a motion to strike is granted. [CCP §1167.3; CRC 325(e)]

(1) [6:631] **Procedure:** The pleader simply serves and files the amendment or new pleading. No further court order is required.

(2) [6:632] **Amended pleading rather than amendment:** Almost always, the court will order the pleader to serve and file an *amended pleading*, rather than simply an amendment to the prior pleading. The court has

discretion, however, to order either. [CCP §472a] (On "amended pleading" vs. "amendment to pleading," *see* ¶*6:621-633*.)

(3) **[6:633]** **Service of amended or new pleading:** Normally, when a demurrer is sustained, or motion to strike is granted, some material allegation of the prior pleading has to be changed. An amended pleading making *substantive* changes (changes in material allegations) is treated as a new pleading, and must be served on *all opposing parties*—not just those who objected to the prior pleading. [*Cohen v. Sup.Ct. (Southern Pacific Co.)* (1966) 244 CA2d 650, 656, 53 CR 378, 383]

(a) **[6:634]** **Rationale:** An amended pleading that makes *substantive* changes, as distinguished from mere changes in form, *supersedes* the prior pleading (*see* ¶*6:704*).

(b) **[6:635]** **Application:** Thus, after a demurrer is sustained, the amended complaint must be served not only on the defendants who demurred, but on *all other defendants as well.* They are then entitled to respond to or challenge the amended complaint as a new pleading. [*Leo v. Dunlap* (1968) 260 CA2d 24, 27, 66 CR 888, 891—change in amount of damages claimed held a "substantive" change, requiring service on all defendants]

[6:635.1-635.4] *Reserved.*

(4) **[6:635.5]** **Scope of permissible amendment:** Generally, where a court grants leave to amend after sustaining a demurrer, the scope of permissible amendment is limited to the cause(s) of action to which the demurrer has been sustained: "(S)uch granting of leave to amend must be construed as permission to the pleader *to amend the cause of action which he pleaded* in the pleading to which the demurrer has been sustained." [*People v. Clausen* (1967) 248 CA2d 770, 785-786, 57 CR 227, 238 (emphasis added)]

➡**[6:635.6]** *PRACTICE POINTER:* However, the court clearly has discretion to allow other amendments as well (*see* ¶*6:640*). Thus, if you propose to amend the complaint in a manner not apparent or consistent with your current cause of action (e.g., to add new parties and claims), *ask for leave of court* to do so when the demurrer is sustained.

d. **[6:636]** **Amendments on noticed motion:** The court may grant leave to amend the pleadings at any stage of the action. Typically, a party will discover the need to amend after all pleadings are completed (the case is "at issue"), and new information requires a *change in the nature of the claims or defenses* previously pleaded. Such changes cannot be made on ex parte procedure (¶6:619). Rather, a formal motion to amend must be served and filed.

(1) [6:637] **Discretion of court:** Motions for leave to amend the pleadings are directed to the sound discretion of the judge. "The court *may*, in *furtherance of justice*, and *on such terms as may be proper*, allow a party to amend any pleading . . ." [CCP §473(a)(1); and see CCP §576]

(2) **Factors affecting court's exercise of discretion**

(a) [6:638] **Policy favoring amendment:** First of all, judicial policy favors resolution of all disputed matters between the parties in the same lawsuit.

Thus, the court's discretion will usually be exercised *liberally* to *permit* amendment of the pleadings. [See *Nestle v. Santa Monica* (1972) 6 C3d 920, 939, 101 CR 568, 581; *Mabie v. Hyatt* (1998) 61 CA4th 581, 596, 71 CR2d 657, 666 (citing text)]

1) [6:639] **Denial rarely justified:** The policy favoring amendment is so strong that it is a rare case in which denial of leave to amend can be justified: "If the motion to amend is *timely* made and the granting of the motion will *not prejudice* the opposing party, it is *error to refuse* permission to amend; and, where the refusal also results in a party being deprived of the right to assert a meritorious cause of action or a meritorious defense, it is not only error but an abuse of discretion." [*Morgan v. Sup.Ct.* (1959) 172 CA2d 527, 530, 343 P2d 62, 64 (emphasis added); see *Mabie v. Hyatt*, supra, 61 CA4th at 596, 71 CR2d at 666 (citing text)]

(b) [6:640] **Nature of proposed amendment:** Subject to the limitations noted below, the court has discretion to permit *any* sort of amendment; i.e., the amendment need not relate to the claims or defenses originally pleaded. Thus, amended pleadings may set forth entirely different claims, add new parties, seek a different or greater remedy, etc.

Further, there is a right to amend "to correct inadvertent misstatements of facts or erroneous allegations of terms." [*Berman v. Bromberg* (1997) 56 CA4th 936, 945, 65 CR2d 777, 782]

1) **[6:641] Caution—statute of limitations problems:** If there is a statute of limitations problem, however, it must appear that the amendment is "based on the same general set of facts pleaded in the original complaint." [See *Hobson v. Raychem Corp.* (1999) 73 CA4th 614, 626, 86 CR2d 497, 505—court may be justified in denying leave to amend complaint that would apparently be barred by statute of limitations (dictum); *and detailed discussion at ¶6:715 ff.*]

2) **[6:642] Caution—actions against public entities:** Legal theories alleged in a damages action against a public entity may not vary from those set forth in the *claim* which preceded the action (Gov.C. §945.4).

3) **[6:643] Compare—amended answers:** Courts usually display great liberality in allowing amendments to answers because "a defendant denied leave to amend is permanently deprived of a defense." [*Hulsey v. Koehler* (1990) 218 CA3d 1150, 1159, 267 CR 523, 527—but matter still discretionary]

(c) **[6:644] Validity of proposed amendment:** Ordinarily, the judge will *not* consider the validity of the proposed amended pleading in deciding whether to grant leave to amend. Grounds for demurrer or motion to strike are premature. After leave to amend is granted, the opposing party will have the opportunity to attack the validity of the amended pleading; *¶6:688*. [See *Kittredge Sports Co. v. Sup.Ct. (Marker, U.S.A.)* (1989) 213 CA3d 1045, 1048, 261 CR 857, 859]

1) **[6:645] Failure to state cause of action or defense:** The judge undoubtedly has discretion to deny leave to amend where a proposed amendment fails to state a valid cause of action or defense. [See *California Casualty General Ins. Co. v. Sup.Ct. (Gorgei)* (1985) 173 CA3d 274, 280-281, 218 CR 817, 821(disapproved on other grounds in *Kransco v. American Empire Surplus Lines Ins. Co.* (2000) 23 C4th 390, 407, 97 CR2d 151, 164, fn. 11)]

a) **[6:646]** Such denial is "most appropriate" where the pleading is deficient as a matter of law *and the defect could not be cured by further appropriate amendment.* [*California*

Casualty General Ins. Co. v. Sup.Ct. (Gorgei), supra, 173 CA3d at 281, 218 CR at 821; Foxborough v. Van Atta (1994) 26 CA4th 217, 230, 31 CR2d 525, 532—proposed amendment barred by statute of limitations and no basis for "relation back"]

- **[6:646.1]** Leave to amend was properly rejected where proposed amendments were untimely and also subject to demurrer as being barred by res judicata and statute of limitations. [Yee v. Mobilehome Park Rental Review Bd. (1998) 62 CA4th 1409, 1429, 73 CR2d 227, 240]

b) **[6:647]** On the other hand, where the sufficiency of the proposed amendment is a novel question almost certain to be tested in an appellate court, the preferable practice is to permit the amendment and allow the parties to test its legal sufficiency by demurrer or other appropriate motion. That way, if the demurrer or other challenge is upheld, the appellate court will know on what ground the amendment was rejected. [California Casualty General Ins. Co. v. Sup.Ct. (Gorgei), supra, 173 CA3d at 281, 218 CR at 821]

2) **[6:648] Sham amendments:** The judge also has discretion to deny leave where the proposed amendment omits or contradicts harmful facts pleaded in the original pleading . . . unless a showing is made of mistake or other sufficient excuse for changing the facts. Absent such a showing, the amended pleading may be treated as a sham. [Vallejo Develop. Co. v. Beck Develop. Co. (1994) 24 CA4th 929, 946, 29 CR2d 669, 678-679; Amid v. Hawthorne Comm. Med. Grp., Inc. (1989) 212 CA3d 1383, 1390, 261 CR 240, 244; and ¶6:706]

a) **[6:649] Example:** Corp-A falsely alleged it was duly licensed, and thus entitled to enforce contract with D. When D obtained proof it was not licensed, Corp-A sought to amend to allege that the contract was actually with a wholly-owned subsidiary, Corp-B (which was licensed). Both corporations were owned and operated by the same individual. Held: Leave to amend properly denied. "Proposed amendments *contradicting* allegations in an earlier pleading will *not* be allowed in the absence of *very satisfactory evidence* upon which it is *clearly* shown that the earlier pleading was the result of *mistake* or inadvertence." [*American Adv. & Sales Co. v. Mid-Western Transport* (1984) 152 CA3d 875, 879, 199 CR 735, 738]

b) [6:650] **Example:** Insured sued Insurance Co. for disappearance of insured airplane. The plane had been leased to a third party who was apparently a drug smuggler. Insured sought to amend to allege he made the lease in reliance on Insurance Co.'s willingness to insure the lessee. But this *contradicted earlier declarations* (in opposition to summary judgment) as to the timing of the lease. Leave to amend was properly denied. [*Congleton v. National Union Fire Ins. Co.* (1987) 189 CA3d 51, 62, 234 CR 218, 225]

c) [6:651] **Compare:** But amending a complaint to delete allegations subject to federal preemption did not constitute sham pleading. [*Contreras v. Blue Cross of Calif.* (1988) 199 CA3d 945, 950, 245 CR 258, 261—P had right to amend wrongful termination complaint to state cause of action not barred by federal law: "ERISA does not preempt the entire state law of employment relationships"]

(d) [6:652] **Proximity to trial or during trial:** Courts are bound to apply a policy of great liberality in permitting amendments to the complaint "at any stage of the proceedings, up to and including trial," *absent prejudice* to the adverse party. [*Atkinson v. Elk Corp.* (2003) 109 CA4th 739, 761, 135 CR3d 433, 449 (internal quotes omitted)]

1) **Loss of "at issue" status if leave granted:** See ¶6:702.

2) [6:653] **P's willingness to postpone trial:** If P is the party seeking leave to amend (knowing the trial will be delayed), proximity to the trial date is not ground for denial. As long as no prejudice to the defendant is shown, the liberal policy re amendment prevails and it is an abuse of discretion to refuse the amendment. [*Mesler v. Bragg Mgt. Co.* (1985) 39 C3d 290, 297, 216

CR 443, 446—no surprise to defendant because parties had conducted discovery on the issues sought to be raised by amendment]

*Compare:* But the court abused its discretion when, on the day of trial, it permitted an amendment to the complaint based on a *different set of facts* and denied defendant's motion for a continuance. [*North 7th Street Associates v. Constante* (2001) 92 CA4th Supp. 7, 111 CR2d 815, 817]

3) [6:654] **Same policy under "fast track" rules:** An otherwise proper amendment should not be refused solely because the case is on fast track. This is true even where the amendment will require a *continuance* of the trial date. [*Honig v. Financial Corp. of America* (1992) 6 CA4th 960, 967, 7 CR2d 922, 926]

(e) [6:655] **Effect of prejudicial delay in seeking amendment:** If the party seeking the amendment has been dilatory, and the delay has *prejudiced* the opposing party, the judge has discretion to deny leave to amend. [See *Hirsa v. Sup.Ct. (Vickers)* (1981) 118 CA3d 486, 490, 173 CR 418, 420]

1) [6:656] **What constitutes "prejudice" to opposing party:** Prejudice exists where the amendment would require delaying the trial, resulting in loss of critical evidence or added costs of preparation, increased burden of discovery, etc. [*Magpali v. Farmers Group, Inc.* (1996) 48 CA4th 471, 486-488, 55 CR2d 225, 236-237]

But the fact that the amendment involves a change in legal theory which would make admissible evidence damaging to the opposing party is *not* the kind of "prejudice" the court will consider. [*Hirsa v. Sup.Ct. (Vickers)*, supra]

- [6:657] Defendant sought leave to amend answer on eve of trial to assert res judicata defense. Denial was not an abuse of discretion because of defendant's *lack of diligence* and the *prejudice to plaintiff* in incurring legal fees preparing for trial: "The plaintiff has a right to know his risk and weighs his exposure prior to trial." [*Hulsey v. Koehler* (1990) 218 CA3d 1150, 1159, 267 CR 523, 527]

- [6:658] Having lost the first trial on one defense, Defendant sought leave to amend to assert a different defense on the retrial. Denial was upheld because Defendant offered no excuse for failure to assert that defense originally. There was also evidence of "legal gamesmanship" (the defense contradicted Defendant's earlier position) and would have required additional discovery. [*Green v. Rancho Santa Margarita Mortgage Co.* (1994) 28 CA4th 686, 693-694, 33 CR2d 706, 709-710]

- [6:658.1] Leave to amend P's complaint on the eve of trial was properly denied where the proposed amendment would have *necessitated a continuance to allow D to depose* new witnesses. [*Magpali v. Farmers Group, Inc.* (1996) 48 CA4th 471, 488, 55 CR2d 225, 237]

2) [6:659] **Absent prejudice, delay alone not ground for denial:** If the delay in seeking the amendment has not misled or prejudiced the other side, the liberal policy of allowing amendments prevails. Indeed, it is an *abuse of discretion* to deny leave in such a case . . . even if sought as late as the time of trial! [*Higgins v. Del Faro* (1981) 123 CA3d 558, 564-565, 176 CR 704, 707-708]

[6:660] *Reserved.*

- [6:661] It was error to deny an amendment on the eve of trial to add a fraud count, where the delay was attributable to the opposing party's failure to comply with discovery requests, and no prejudice to that party was shown. [*Arthur L. Sachs, Inc. v. City of Oceanside* (1984) 151 CA3d 315, 319, 198 CR 483, 485]

- [6:662] Compare: But where plaintiff *knew* for over five months that certain claims had not been properly pleaded, and *took no action* to amend until after a summary judgment had been granted against it, it was not an abuse of discretion to deny leave to amend the complaint. [*Fisher v. Larsen* (1982) 138 CA3d 627, 649, 188 CR 216, 232]

(f) [6:663] **Court may impose conditions:** Even if some prejudice is shown, the judge may still permit the amendment, but impose conditions. The court is authorized to grant leave " . . . on such terms as may be proper . . . " [CCP §§473(a)(1), 576]

1) [6:664] **Example:** Thus, for example, the judge may continue the trial date (if requested by the opposing party); limit discovery; and/or order the party seeking the amendment to *pay the costs and fees* incurred by the opposing party in preparing for trial, etc. [See *Fuller v. Vista Del Arroyo Hotel* (1941) 42 CA2d 400, 404, 108 P2d 920, 922-923]

(Under master calendar systems, judges hearing law and motion matters usually do not order continuances of trial dates. That is left to the master calendar judge, which may necessitate an additional appearance.)

(3) [6:665] **Limitation—court order required for amendments adding punitive damage claims in medical malpractice actions:** See CCP §425.13, *discussed at ¶6:327 ff.*

[6:665.1-665.4] *Reserved.*

(4) [6:665.5] **Limitation—no amendment of SLAPP complaint if free speech connection shown:** A special procedure exists ("anti-SLAPP" motion) to challenge complaints that seek to inhibit a defendant's right of free speech in connection with public issues (see CCP §425.16, *discussed at ¶7:207 ff.*). If the court finds the requisite connection to First Amendment free speech, there is *no right to amend* such complaints:
— "Allowing a SLAPP plaintiff leave to amend the complaint once the court finds the prima facie showing has been met would completely undermine the statute by providing the pleader a ready escape from section 425.16's quick dismissal remedy." [*Simmons v. Allstate Ins. Co.* (2001) 92 CA4th 1068, 1073, 112 CR2d 397, 401]

(a) [6:665.6] **Comment:** CCP §473(a) authorizes a court "in furtherance of justice" to allow amendment of "*any* pleading." *Simmons* apparently concludes that it is *never* "in the interest of justice" to allow amendment of a SLAPP complaint once a free speech connection is shown.

(5) [6:666] **Procedure—noticed motion for leave to amend:** A regular noticed motion must be filed. An amendment making substantive changes *cannot* be

allowed ex parte (whereas an ex parte order is available to correct mere mistakes in form or party identity; ¶6:619). [CCP §473(a)(1)]

☞[6:667] ***PRACTICE POINTER:*** Before filing a motion for leave to amend, *ask opposing counsel to stipulate* to the amendment. If there is no statute of limitations problem, you may find there is no need for a formal motion.

☞[6:668] ***PRACTICE POINTER:*** If your opponent asks for such a stipulation, and there is no question of the statute of limitations or any real prejudice to your client, you may as well stipulate . . . because the court is almost certain to grant leave. You'll save your client the costs of fruitless opposition.

On the other hand, if the proposed amendment would delay the trial, or otherwise prejudice your client, you may want to oppose the request. But even here, don't count on the court denying leave to amend. As shown above, the court is going to be inclined to grant leave to amend (unless the pleading is obviously sham or bad). Instead, argue strongly for imposing *conditions* on the order. Focus on the prejudice to your client which may result from permitting the amendment. *Be prepared with declarations* showing in detail exactly what costs and expenses your client will suffer if the trial date is postponed, what additional discovery costs will be involved because of the amendment, etc.

### Moving papers required

(a) [6:669] **Notice of motion:** The form and content of a notice of motion for leave to amend are governed by the rules governing motions generally (CCP §1010; see ¶9:29 ff.).

The motion must:

- include a copy of the proposed amendment (*see ¶6:671*). [CRC 327(a)(1)]

- identify by page, paragraph, and line number any additions to and deletions from the prior pleading. [CRC 327(a)(2),(3)]

☞[6:670] ***PRACTICE POINTER:*** To speed up the process, the motion should include a request that the "proposed amended pleading *be deemed to be the amended pleading and that it be deemed filed and served as of the date of the granting of the motion."*

This will avoid the necessity of filing and serving the amended pleading; all you have to do is serve a notice of ruling (*see ¶9:320*) incorporating the above-quoted language.

(b) [6:671] **Copy of proposed amended pleading:** The motion must be accompanied by a copy of the proposed amendment or amended pleading, which must be serially numbered to distinguish it from the prior pleading (e.g., "Second Amended Cross-complaint"). [CRC 327(a)(1)]

⇨[6:672] *PRACTICE POINTER:* Although not required, it is a good idea to bring the executed original to the hearing and, when the motion is granted, ask the court clerk to mark the original "filed." This avoids having an unnecessary copy of the pleading in the court file. On the other hand, if a *filing fee* is required, the courtroom clerk cannot collect it and the document must be filed in the clerk's office.

1) [6:673] **Amended pleading vs. amendments to pleadings:** Except for amendments to change the name of a fictitiously-named defendant, courts generally require amended pleadings rather than amendments to pleadings. [CRC 327(c); *see ¶6:622*]

[6:674] *Reserved.*

(c) [6:675] **Memorandum of points and authorities** supporting the motion. [CRC 313(a); *see ¶9:64 ff.*]

⇨[6:676] *PRACTICE POINTER:* Although the notice of motion must state with particularity what allegations in the previous pleading are proposed to be deleted and what allegations are proposed to be added (*¶6:669*), it is a good idea to also include this detail in an introduction to the memorandum of points and authorities because many judges go to this document first to get a "feel" for the case.

(d) [6:677] **Declaration:** A declaration (usually by counsel for the moving party) must specify:

- the purpose and *effect* of the proposed amendments;

- why the proposed amendments are *necessary and proper*;

- when the facts giving rise to the proposed amendment were *discovered*; and

- the reasons why the request for amendment was not made earlier. [CRC 327(b)]

[6:678-679]   *Reserved.*

(e) [6:680] **Proposed order granting leave to amend:** Although statewide rules require attorney orders on motions generally (CRC 391, *see* ¶9:294), many courts still prefer to use minute orders for this kind of procedure (*see* ¶9:298).

Where attorney orders are used, it is prevailing counsel's responsibility to draft and submit an order granting the relief requested. [CRC 391; *see* ¶9:295]

(f) ***FORM:*** Notice of Motion for Leave to File Amended Complaint; Declaration and Points and Authorities in Support, *see Form 6:CC.*

(6) [6:681] **Filing of amended pleading:** If leave to amend is granted, the amended pleading is thereupon filed with the clerk of the court. (In courts where the original was attached to the motion, the clerk will do this automatically.)

Alternatively, the court may order that the *proposed* amended complaint *be deemed to be* the amended complaint, and that it be deemed filed and served as of the date the motion was granted (*see* ¶6:669.1).

(7) [6:682] **Service of amended pleading:** An amended pleading making substantive changes must be served on all parties affected thereby. [CCP §471.5] As discussed below, such amendment *supersedes* the original, and the opposing parties then have the same period to answer or demur as they did to the original; *see* ¶6:688.

⇨[6:683]   ***PRACTICE POINTER:*** It's good practice to serve an amended pleading on *all* opposing parties, whether or not it affects them; *see* ¶6:629.

Include in your notice of motion a request that the court order the proposed amended pleading *be deemed served* on opposing parties *as of the date the motion is granted.*

(a) [6:684] **Personal service on defendants who have not appeared:** Due process requires personal service of the amended pleading on any defendant who has not yet appeared in the action. Rationale: An amendment making substantive changes may affect such defendant's decision not to contest the action; therefore, it should be brought to his or her attention in the same way as the original complaint (i.e., personal service, rather than service by mail). [*Engebretson & Co., Inc. v. Harrison* (1981) 125 CA3d 436, 442-443, 178 CR 77, 81]

e. [6:685] **Amendments to conform to proof at trial:** Trial procedures are beyond the scope of this work. Suffice it to note that the trial judge has discretion to permit amendment of the pleadings even at or after the trial. Leave to amend is frequently granted to conform to proof offered at trial; i.e., where the evidence is technically outside the issues framed by the original pleadings. In such cases, the trial judge may order the pleadings amended to conform to the proof. [CCP §§473(a)(1), 576]

(1) [6:686] **Factors considered:** Trial courts are generally guided by:

- whether there is a *reasonable excuse* for the delay;

- whether the change relates to the *facts* or only legal theories; and

- whether the opposing party will be *prejudiced* by the amendment. [*City of Stanton v. Cox* (1989) 207 CA3d 1557, 1563, 255 CR 682, 685]

(2) [6:687] **Extent to which issues tried:** It is irrelevant that the opposing party had *opportunity* to present evidence on the issues sought to be added and failed to do so: "(F)ailure to contest an unexpected issue cannot be used by (moving party) to justify its tardy attempt to amend." [*City of Stanton v. Cox,* supra, 207 CA3d at 1564, 255 CR at 686 (parentheses added)—upholding denial of leave to amend during trial]

On the other hand, if those issues were in fact *fully* tried, it is difficult for the opposing party to claim prejudice. Under such circumstances, it may be an abuse of discretion to deny leave to amend to conform to proof. [See *South Bay Bldg. Enterprises, Inc. v. Riviera Lend-Lease, Inc.* (1999) 72 CA4th 1111, 1124, 85 CR2d 647, 654—

abuse of discretion to deny motion where opposing party supplied evidence that was basis for the motion]

3. [6:688] **New Round of Pleadings:** Once filed, an amended pleading *making substantive changes* supersedes the original. It constitutes an abandonment of the issues raised by the original pleading, and therefore a new round of pleadings is required: The amended pleading is subject to the same pleadings challenges (demurrer, motion to strike) as the original. And, the opposing party has the same opportunity to respond to the amended pleading as to the original.

   a. [6:689] **Effect of failure to respond to amended complaint:** The Code states that defendant must "answer" an amended complaint within 30 days after service or such other time as the court may order; and judgment by default may be entered for failure to "answer" (i.e., a response to the earlier complaint will not prevent entry of default). [CCP §471.5] (This rule is not applicable in family law cases where both parties have already filed pleadings; see CRC 5.108.)

   *Comment:* Although the statute says "answer," it probably should be construed to mean "respond," thus including demurrers or motions to strike amended complaints. [See CCP §472—allowing defendant to "respond" to amended complaint where amendment is "of course"; and CCP §435—allowing motion to strike "*any* pleading"]

   (1) [6:690] **Answer required where substantive changes made:** The Code provision requiring answers to amended complaints is interpreted as applying only to amendments making *substantive changes*— changing the basic cause of action, or adding a new one. [See *Carrasco v. Craft* (1985) 164 CA3d 796, 808-809, 210 CR 599, 607]

   (2) [6:691] **No answer required where no substantive changes:** Where the amended complaint does not change the basic cause of action pleaded in the original or add any new cause of action, defendants may answer de novo if they choose. But if they elect not to do so, they are not in default. Their original answer is effective to deny the original allegations that are repeated in the amended complaint. However, any *new matters* in the amended complaint, not effectively controverted by the original answer, stand admitted. [*Carrasco v. Craft,* supra]

      (a) [6:692] **"Immaterial" corrections:** P amended his complaint to clarify an ambiguity and to correct certain inaccuracies in the original pleading. However, these corrections were "immaterial" to the basic cause of action pleaded, and therefore D's failure to answer the amended complaint was not ground for entry of default. [*Carrasco v. Craft*, supra, 164 CA3d at 809, 210 CR at 608]

(b) **[6:693] Changes affecting other defendants:** Where the amended complaint makes new allegations concerning one of several codefendants, the others need not answer the amended pleading. Their answers to the original complaint prevent entry of default. [See *Carrasco v. Craft*, supra, 164 CA3d at 810, 210 CR at 608]

(c) **[6:694] Changes in damage allegations:** Changes in the amount of damages alleged do not change the basic cause of action and, therefore, do not require defendant to respond. [*Carrasco v. Craft*, supra—amended complaint sought $500,000, instead of $75,000, punitive damages]

   1) **[6:695] Compare—as ground for "opening up" default:** But where a defendant is *already in default*, an amendment increasing the damages sought has been held "substantive"—"opening up" the default, and giving defendant the right to respond to the amended pleading. [*Engebretson & Co., Inc. v. Harrison* (1981) 125 CA3d 436, 440, 178 CR 77, 80]

b. **[6:696] Stipulations excusing answer:** To avoid a new round of responsive pleadings, particularly where the changes are minor, the parties may stipulate that defendant's answer to the previous complaint be deemed its answer to the amended complaint.

➡ **[6:697]** *PRACTICE POINTER FOR DEFENDANT:* If you enter into such stipulation, be sure to include a provision that any new matter in the amended complaint is *deemed controverted*.

c. **[6:698] Defaults "opened":** Defendants who *defaulted* to the original complaint must be served with an amended complaint containing the substantive changes. In effect, plaintiff *waives* the right to obtain immediate judgment against defendants who have defaulted to the original complaint. Their defaults are "opened," and they are therefore entitled to demur, move to strike or answer the amended complaint—although they made no response to the original! [*Ostling v. Loring* (1994) 27 CA4th 1731, 1744, 33 CR2d 391, 398]

(1) **Personal service required on defendants in default:** *See ¶6:684.*

(2) [6:699] **What constitutes "substantive changes":** An amended complaint is held to "open" defaults only when it makes *substantive* changes in the claims asserted. Examples:

- Increasing the *damages* demanded. [*Leo v. Dunlap* (1968) 260 CA2d 24, 27, 66 CR 888, 890]

- Adding a *new cause of action* based on a *different* legal theory (e.g., amended complaint alleging negligent, instead of intentional, misrepresentation). [*Ford v. Sup.Ct. (Orton)* (1973) 34 CA3d 338, 343, 109 CR 844, 847]

(a) [6:700] **Compare:** On the other hand, mere typographical errors, or correction of names or places, usually can be made without waiving prior default entries.

(b) [6:701] **Comment:** Although there is no known case authority, the test for what is and is not a "substantive change" should focus on whether the correction or addition might give rise to any *different amount or form of liability, or indicate the existence of any defense or ground for avoiding liability, not reasonably disclosed in the original complaint.*

d. [6:702] **Effect on trial setting:** Where an amended complaint or cross-complaint is filed, responsive pleadings are normally required (*¶6:688*) so that the case is no longer "at issue" (unless defendant's answer to the prior complaint is stipulated to be its answer to the amended complaint, *see ¶6:696*).

Whether the new round of pleadings affects pending or future trial setting is normally resolved by the court at the next status conference (*see ¶12:77 ff.*).

- [6:703] Some independent calendar judges may intervene to avoid pleadings delays by ordering that "all allegations of the amended complaint are *deemed denied* and all *affirmative defenses* thereto are *deemed pled.*" The validity and effect of such orders is unclear.

4. [6:704] **Amended Pleading Supersedes Original:** As discussed earlier, an amendment to a pleading that merely corrects some minor mistake does not constitute a new pleading (*¶6:621*). But an amended pleading making substantive changes (*¶6:699*) *supersedes* the original.

a. **[6:705]** **Limitation—former pleading as evidence at trial:** Although superseded as a pleading, the original can still be used in evidence against the pleader at trial, where appropriate; e.g., as an admission or prior inconsistent statement by or on behalf of the party whose pleading is involved. That party, however, is entitled to *explain* that the allegations in question were unauthorized, or made inadvertently or under mistake of fact, etc. [*City of Pleasant Hill v. First Baptist Church* (1969) 1 CA3d 384, 419, 82 CR 1, 25]

b. **[6:706]** **Limitation—effect of contradicting former pleading:** Similarly, an amended pleading that contradicts facts alleged in an earlier pleading is subject to challenge. Unless the contradiction is satisfactorily explained (e.g., new information discovered), the rule requiring truthful pleading may result in denial of leave to amend (¶*6:648*); or, if the pleading has already been filed, render it subject to demurrer or motion to strike. (In ruling on such challenges, courts can take *judicial notice* of pleadings already on file; *see* ¶*7:16*.) [*Amid v. Hawthorne Comm. Med. Group* (1989) 212 CA3d 1383, 1390, 261 CR 240, 244]

- **[6:707]** **Example:** P's original complaint alleged the accident occurred on a public street adjacent to D's market. D demurred on the ground that City controlled the street in question. P's amended complaint alleged the accident occurred on D's premises. Absent satisfactory explanation for this change, it was properly disregarded. [*Owens v. Kings Supermarket* (1988) 198 CA3d 379, 384, 243 CR 627, 630; *see* ¶*7:48*]

c. **[6:708]** **Limitation—effect of omitting harmful facts alleged in former pleading:** Allegations in the original pleading that rendered it vulnerable to demurrer or other attack cannot simply be omitted without explanation in the amended pleading. The policy against sham pleadings requires the pleader to *explain* satisfactorily any such omission. Otherwise, the original defect "infects" the subsequent pleading as well. I.e., the self-destructive allegations of the original pleading will be "read into" the amended pleading as well. [*Wennerholm v. Stanford Univ. School of Medicine* (1942) 20 C2d 713, 716, 128 P2d 522, 524; *Vallejo Develop. Co. v. Beck Develop. Co.* (1994) 24 CA4th 929, 946, 29 CR2d 669, 679—court not bound to accept as true allegations contrary to *facts* alleged in former pleadings]

(1) **[6:709]** **Example:** Original complaint on its face discloses that claim is barred by the statute of limitations. Defendant demurs on this ground, and demurrer is sustained with leave to amend. Amended complaint

cannot simply omit all dates without explanation. The time allegations from the original complaint will be "read into" the amended complaint ... rendering it subject to demurrer on the same ground as the original. [See *Kenworthy v. Brown* (1967) 248 CA2d 298, 302, 56 CR 461, 463-464]

(2) **[6:710] Verified vs. unverified complaints:** Several cases state the rule in terms of *verified* complaints: E.g., "Where a *verified* complaint contains allegations destructive of a cause of action, the defect cannot be cured in subsequently filed pleadings by simply omitting such allegations without explanation." [*Hendy v. Losse* (1991) 54 C3d 723, 742, 1 CR2d 543, 555 (emphasis added); see also *McGee v. McNally* (1981) 119 CA3d 891, 896-897, 174 CR 253, 256; and *Appl v. Lee Swett Livestock Co.* (1987) 192 CA3d 466, 470, 237 CR 433, 436]

However, conceptually, there is no reason why unverified complaints should not be subject to the same rule. Several cases have so held. [See *Reichert v. General Ins. Co. of America* (1968) 68 C2d 822, 836, 837, 69 CR 321, 329; *Zappas v. King Williams Press, Inc.* (1970) 10 CA3d 768, 775, 89 CR 307, 311; *Pierce v. Lyman* (1991) 1 CA4th 1093, 1109, 3 CR2d 236, 245-246]

(3) **[6:711] Compare—omissions immaterial to amended claim or defense:** Omissions from a former pleading are not ground for challenge when the amended pleading asserts *different claims or defenses* to which the omitted allegations are immaterial. [See *Amarel v. Connell* (1988) 202 CA3d 137, 144, 248 CR 276, 280]

(a) **[6:712] Example:** The original complaint charged D with anticompetitive activities in both domestic and foreign markets in violation of state law. A demurrer was sustained because federal law preempts state law as to foreign trade. The amended complaint omitted the reference to foreign trade, focusing instead on local commerce. This was proper. P had merely "redefined" the claims asserted (and thereby avoided federal preemption). [*Amarel v. Connell*, supra, 202 CA3d at 144, 248 CR at 280]

[6:712.1-712.4] *Reserved.*

(4) **[6:712.5] Compare—inconsistent legal theories:** As long as the same facts are alleged in both complaints, there is no bar to alternative or inconsistent

pleading of the *legal effect* of those facts—i.e., inconsistent legal theories. [*Lim v. The.TV Corp. Int'l* (2002) 99 CA4th 684, 690, 121 CR2d 333, 337]

d. **[6:713] Effect of dropping defendant:** An amended complaint may add or omit parties (¶6:640). If it omits a defendant named in the original complaint, it serves as a *dismissal without prejudice* as to that defendant. [*Kuperman v. Great Republic Life Ins. Co.* (1987) 195 CA3d 943, 947, 241 CR 187, 189; *Fireman's Fund Ins. Co. v. Sparks Const., Inc.* (2004) 114 CA4th 1135, 1142, 8 CR3d 446, 451—omitting Doe defendants effectively dismissed them]

(1) **[6:714] Rejoining dropped defendant:** Since the dismissal is *without* prejudice, plaintiff may, by subsequent amended pleading, rejoin as a party the defendant dropped in the earlier amended pleading. (A new service of summons would be required.) [*Kuperman v. Great Republic Life Ins. Co.*, supra; see *Fireman's Fund Ins. Co. v. Sparks Const., Inc.*, supra, 114 CA4th at 1142, 8 CR3d at 451—cannot rejoin dropped defendants if statute of limitations has run]

5. **[6:715] "Relation Back" Doctrine:** A frequent problem with amended complaints is whether they "relate back" to the date the original complaint was filed.

a. **[6:716] How issue arises:** Typically, the issue arises when the statute of limitations has run between the date the action was filed and the time the amendment is sought. If the amended complaint "relates back" to a timely-filed original complaint, it escapes the bar of the statute of limitations. [*Austin v. Massachusetts Bonding & Ins. Co.* (1961) 56 C2d 596, 600, 15 CR 817, 819]

But the relation-back doctrine is not limited to statute of limitations problems. It also applies in determining whether an amended complaint is subject to dismissal for failure to serve summons within 3 years after commencement of the action under CCP §583.210 (¶11:51): i.e., if the amended complaint "relates back," summons must be served within 3 years after the original complaint was filed; but if the amendment does *not* "relate back," summons need only be served within 3 years after the amendment (*see discussion at* ¶11:61.1 ff.). [*Barrington v. A.H. Robins Co.* (1985) 39 C3d 146, 151-152, 216 CR 405, 408]

b. **[6:717] Requirements for "relation back" effect:** For an amended complaint to "relate back" to the original complaint, it must:

• Be based on the *"same general set of facts"* as the original; and

- Seek recovery for the "*same injuries*"; and

- Refer to the "*same incident*"—i.e., the "same accident" caused by the "same offending instrumentality." [*Barrington v. A.H. Robins Co.* (1985) 39 C3d 146, 150, 216 CR 405, 407; *Norgart v. Upjohn Co.* (1999) 21 C4th 383, 408-409, 87 CR2d 453, 471-472]

(There are additional requirements where "relation back" is sought against a "Doe" defendant; *see ¶6:735.*)

(1) [6:718] **"Same general set of facts":** First of all, the amended complaint must be based on the *same operative facts* alleged in the original. [*Barrington v. A.H. Robins Co.*, supra]

"Operative facts" are those creating a right to recovery. If these are the same in both pleadings, a *change in legal theory or cause of action* is permissible . . . even a change from a common law to a statutory cause of action. [*Goldman v. Wilsey Foods, Inc.* (1989) 216 CA3d 1085, 1094-1095, 265 CR 294, 299]

The doctrine "focuses on factual similarity rather than rights or obligations arising from the facts." [*Dudley v. Department of Transp.* (2001) 90 CA4th 255, 265, 108 CR2d 739, 748]

(a) **Application**

- [6:719] Plaintiff-widow sued City for wrongful death of her husband, claiming City policemen had *intentionally* killed him. After the statute of limitations had run, she sought leave to amend to allege that City had been *negligent* in employing these officers because it knew they were "trigger-happy." Although negligence was clearly a different cause of action from the intentional tort originally pleaded, the amendment was based on the same general set of facts (police killing husband). Hence, the amended complaint "related back" to the date the action was originally filed. [*Grudt v. City of Los Angeles* (1970) 2 C3d 575, 584-585, 86 CR 465, 468-469]

- [6:720] P's original complaint was for injuries resulting from defendant's failure to furnish him a safe workplace. His amended complaint added a products liability claim, alleging that his injuries were caused by a machine that was "defective, dangerous and unsafe for its intended use." Since the accident and injuries were the same, the products liability claim "related back" to the original complaint. [*Smeltzley v. Nicholson Mfg. Co.* (1977) 18 C3d 932, 939-940, 136 CR 269, 274]

- [6:721]   After her nonmarital relationship with D broke up, P sued for division of property held in D's name. Her complaint for breach of contract was held to be time-barred, so she sought to amend to seek equitable relief on a constructive trust theory (which was not time-barred). Held: P should be permitted to amend; there is no prejudice to D because the constructive trust theory is based on the same facts pleaded in the original complaint. [*Nelson v. Nevel* (1984) 154 CA3d 132, 142, 201 CR 93, 99]

- [6:721.1]   *Compare:* Employee's original complaint charged Employer with breach of contract and overtime pay violations. After the statute had run, she sought to add a claim for age dis-

*(Text cont'd on p. 6-143)*

**RESERVED**

crimination. The amendment was *not allowed* because the discrimination claim "did not arise out of the same set of facts" that supported the contractual and overtime claims. [*Kim v. Regents of Univ. of Calif.* (2000) 80 CA4th 160, 169, 95 CR2d 10, 16]

- [6:721.2]  Amendments are generally permitted *to substitute a plaintiff with standing to sue* for one who is not the real party in interest. The amendment relates back because the recovery is based on the same general facts so there is no prejudice to defendants. [*Haley v. Dow Lewis Motors, Inc.* (1999) 72 CA4th 497, 507, 85 CR2d 352, 359—plaintiffs who filed bankruptcy should be permitted to amend their complaint to substitute the bankruptcy trustee as plaintiff, even if they failed to list the claim as an asset in their bankruptcy proceedings]

  — [6:721.3]  But the "relation back" doctrine will *not* be applied to confer standing on a plaintiff who *knowingly lacked* it when the suit initially was filed. [See *Coats v. K-Mart Corp.* (1989) 215 CA3d 961, 968, 264 CR 12, 16—plaintiff sued as administratrix of decedent's estate *knowing* she had never been appointed as such; court had discretion to deny relation back effect to her appointment after statute of limitations had run]

  *Comment:* The continued viability of this holding is open to question; *see ¶6:789.3.*

(2) [6:722]  **"Same injury":**  The amended complaint must seek recovery for the "same injuries" as the original complaint. [*Barrington v. A.H. Robins Co.*, supra]

"Injury" is apparently defined in terms of *primary rights* (e.g., property rights; right to freedom from invasion of body, etc.). An amended complaint alleging invasion of the same primary right alleged in the original alleges the "same injury" . . . even if different damages are claimed. [See *Rowland v. Sup.Ct. (Zappia)* (1985) 171 CA3d 1214, 1217-1218, 217 CR 786, 788]

[6:723]  *Reserved.*

(a) **Application**

- [6:724]  Parents sued Doctor for emotional distress resulting from Doctor's failure to detect Down's syndrome in an unborn child, leading to its unwanted birth. After statute had run, Mother sought to amend to add cause of action for bodily injury resulting from Doctor's negligent medical treatment before, during and after childbirth. The amendment did not relate back: "... bodily injury by negligent medical treatment is distinct from ... emotional distress (resulting from) negligent failure to detect Down's syndrome *in utero.*" [*Andalon v. Sup.Ct. (Plowman)* (1984) 162 CA3d 600, 616, 208 CR 899, 909]

- [6:725]   P sued for wrongful death of his son who was electrocuted while swimming in a pool at D's motel. After the statute of limitations had run, P amended to add a cause of action for emotional distress from witnessing his son's death. The amendment "related back" because the "same injury"—loss of his son—was the basis for both the wrongful death and emotional distress causes of action. [*Rowland v. Sup.Ct. (Zappia)*, supra]

(b) [6:726]   **Compare—different rule as to compulsory cross-complaints against plaintiff:**   A cross-complaint may be amended to allege *different injuries* if it is a compulsory cross-complaint (arising out of same transaction as P's complaint; *see ¶6:511*). Reason: P's suing D *suspends the statute of limitations* as to all claims D has against P that are *related* to the accident or transaction set forth in P's complaint. *Any* cross-complaint based on such claims "relates back" to the commencement of P's action. It makes no difference whether the cross-complaint is the original or an amendment. [*Sidney v. Sup.Ct. (Kinoshita)* (1988) 198 CA3d 710, 714, 244 CR 31, 33 (citing text)—original cross-complaint alleged only property damage resulting from accident set forth in P's complaint; amended cross-complaint could allege personal injuries as well; *see ¶6:597*]

"We decline to restrict the 'relation-back rules' governing amendment of a compulsory cross-complaint to those governing amendment of a complaint. *Plaintiff and defendant are not in parallel positions.* Plaintiff chose to initiate the lawsuit. The defendant has no choice but to defend." [*Sidney v. Sup.Ct. (Kinoshita)*, supra, 198 CA3d at 717, 244 CR at 35 (emphasis added)]

(3) [6:727]   **"Same accident" (same offending instrumentality):**   No relation back is given where the amended complaint alleges a different instrumentality

as the *cause* of the plaintiff's injuries. Although the same injury at the same location may be involved, injury from a different "offending instrumentality" is *not* the "same accident." [*Coronet Mfg. Co. v. Sup.Ct. (McMahon)* (1979) 90 CA3d 342, 347, 153 CR 366, 369]

(a) **Application**

- [6:728]  P's original complaint charged "Doe" defendants with negligence in manufacture of a hair dryer, causing decedent's electrocution. After the statute of limitations had run, P amended the complaint to identify Coronet as a "Doe" and to allege that the electrocution was caused by a defective lamp socket and switch manufactured by Coronet.

  The amended complaint did *not* relate back to the filing of original, because it alleged injury from a *different instrumentality*: "The difference between being electrocuted by a hair dryer and by a table lamp is as great as (the difference between) being electrocuted . . . and being poisoned by some improperly processed food found on the kitchen shelf." [*Coronet Mfg. Co. v. Sup.Ct. (McMahon)*, supra, 90 CA3d at 347, 153 CR at 369]

- [6:729]  P's original complaint charged doctors and "Doe" defendants with negligent medical treatment and failure to warn of dangers involved in taking a certain drug (Darvon). P later amended her complaint to name Robins as a "Doe" and to allege that her injuries resulted from using a defective intrauterine device ("Dalkon Shield") manufactured by Robins. The amended complaint did *not* relate back because it involved a "different accident" caused by a separate and distinct "offending instrumentality." [*Barrington v. A.H. Robins Co.*, supra, 39 C3d at 151, 216 CR at 407—since no relation back, amended complaint not subject to dismissal for failure to serve summons within 3-years after commencement of action; see CCP §583.210, ¶11:61.1 ff.]

  [6:730]  *Reserved.*

(b) [6:731]  **Compare—same "chain of causation":** But an amended complaint relates back where the offending instrumentality is deemed to be in the "chain of causation." [*Olson v. Volkswagen of America* (1988) 201 CA3d 1437, 1443, 247 CR 719, 722]

- [6:732] Plaintiff sued steering wheel manufacturer and "Doe" defendants for injuries sustained in automobile accident. After statute ran, plaintiff discovered automobile itself was defectively designed. Plaintiff's amendment adding automobile manufacturer related back for statute of limitations purposes: "Appellant has shown defendants . . . to be in the chain of causation of the originally pleaded cause of action involving use of the steering wheel and its component parts." [*Olson v. Volkswagen of America*, supra, 201 CA3d at 1443, 247 CR at 722]

(4) [6:733] **Compare—new defendants:** Even if the facts, injuries and accident alleged are the same as in the original, an amended complaint that adds *new defendants* (defendants not named in the original complaint or served as "Does") does *not* "relate back." The statute of limitations as to such new defendants is determined by the date the *amended* complaint was filed, not the date of the original complaint. [*Woo v. Sup.Ct. (Zarabi)* (1999) 75 CA4th 169, 176, 89 CR2d 20, 24 (citing text); *McGee Street Productions v. Workers' Comp. App. Bd.* (2003) 108 CA4th 717, 724, 133 CR2d 813, 818 (citing text)]

- [6:734] P filed suit in 1984 against D-1, D-2 and D-3. An amended complaint was filed in 1986 naming D-4. (D-4 could not be served as a "Doe" because his identity was known in 1984.) The 1986 complaint naming D-4 *did not "relate back"* to 1984 for statute of limitations purposes. [*Liberty Transport, Inc. v. Harry W. Gorst Co., Inc.* (1991) 229 CA3d 417, 428, 280 CR 159, 164-165]

  [6:734.1-734.4] *Reserved.*

(5) [6:734.5] **Compare—substitution of plaintiffs:** As long as the facts, injuries and accident alleged are the same as in the original, an amendment substituting a plaintiff with *standing to sue* (real party in interest) for one who lacks standing is given "relation back" effect after the statute of limitations has expired. Such an amendment "is one of form rather than of substance and in the interests of justice is to be treated as such." [*Cloud v. Northrop Grumman Corp.* (1998) 67 CA4th 995, 1007, 79 CR2d 544, 551—amendment to substitute plaintiff's trustee in bankruptcy]

c. [6:735] **Additional requirements in amending to include "Doe" defendants after statute has run:** There are additional requirements where a complaint is amended after the statute of limitations to identify a "Doe" defendant, and to assert a cause of action against that defendant not included in the original complaint. (This often results from discovery proceedings against the named defendants.)

The amended complaint will be given "relation back" effect, so as to avoid the statute of limitations, provided:

- The original complaint stated a valid cause of action against now-identified "Doe" defendants; and

- Plaintiff was "genuinely ignorant" of the defendant's identity or the facts rendering defendant liable when the original complaint was filed; and

- The amended complaint, identifying the defendant, is based on the "same general set of facts" as the original and refers to the "same accident and same injuries" (discussed above). [*Austin v. Massachusetts Bonding & Ins. Co.* (1961) 56 C2d 596, 600-601, 15 CR 817, 819]

(1) **[6:736]** **Statute of limitations extended by commencing action against "Doe":** CCP §474 effectively extends the statute of limitations. A suit filed against a "Doe" defendant within the statutory period tolls the statute of limitations *until expiration of the time for service of summons*—i.e., until 3 years after the suit was filed (CCP §583.210(a))! [*Sobeck & Assocs., Inc. v. B & R Investments* (1989) 215 CA3d 861, 869-870, 264 CR 156, 160]

   (a) **[6:737]** **Impact:** It makes no difference that the person served had no notice of the action before the statute ran. The statutory scheme, above, "represents a satisfactory compromise between the harsh effect on a plaintiff of the statute of limitations and the unfairness to a defendant of attempting to litigate a stale claim." [*Sobeck & Assocs., Inc. v. B & R Investments*, supra, 215 CA3d at 869-870, 264 CR at 161]

   (b) **[6:738]** **Broad application:** Moreover, the rule is interpreted broadly to apply to various statutes of limitation.

   For example, *mechanic's lien foreclosure actions* must be commenced within 90 days after the lien is recorded (Civ.C. §3144). This is interpreted to require *joinder of all persons* to be bound by the judgment. But as long as suit is commenced against Owner and "Doe" defendants within the 90-day period, the complaint can be amended later under CCP §474 to substitute a named defendant for the

"Doe." [*Sobeck & Assocs., Inc. v. B & R Investments*, supra, 215 CA3d at 869-870, 264 CR at 160]

(c) [6:739] **Court's discretion to deny leave:** Even so, the court has discretion to deny leave to amend where there is evidence of laches: i.e., *unreasonable delay* by plaintiff causing *specific prejudice* to the defendant. [*Sobeck & Assocs., Inc. v. B & R Investments*, supra, 215 CA3d at 870, 264 CR at 161; *see ¶6:769*]

(2) [6:740] **Statute also tolled as to amended claims:** The rule extending the statute of limitations as to "Doe" defendants applies both to the claim set forth in the original complaint *and any amendment based on the "same general set of facts"* as the original. [*Austin v. Massachusetts Bonding & Ins. Co.* (1961) 56 C2d 596, 600, 15 CR 817, 819]

(a) [6:741] **Example:** Employee sued Employer and "Doe" defendants for injuries resulting from failure to provide a safe workplace. After the statute had run, Employee amended to name Manufacturer as "Doe 1" and to allege that it had manufactured the machine which caused his injury, and that the machine was dangerous, defective and unsafe for its intended use. The amendment related back to avoid the statute of limitations because it was based on the same accident and same injury; and Employee was genuinely ignorant of Manufacturer's identity and the facts rendering it liable when the original complaint was filed. [*Smeltzley v. Nicholson Mfg. Co.* (1977) 18 C3d 932, 936, 136 CR 269, 271-272]

(b) [6:742] **Impact:** It makes no difference that the person served had no notice of the action before the statute ran; nor that the lapse of time may have prejudiced his ability to defend the action (e.g., it may be more difficult for him to locate witnesses, obtain physical evidence, etc.). This is a consequence of plaintiff's statutory right to sue defendants under a fictitious name (CCP §474; *see ¶6:79 ff.*).

(3) [6:743] **Requirement that original complaint state claim against "Doe" defendants:** For the amendment to relate back, the original complaint must name "Doe" defendants in the caption, *and* the charging allegations must state a valid claim against the fictitiously-named defendants. (It is sufficient if the allegations run against "defendants" generally; or against "defendants

and each of them." *See ¶6:85.*) [See *Austin v. Massa-chusetts Bonding & Ins. Co.*, supra, 56 C2d at 600, 15 CR at 819; see also *Woo v. Sup.Ct. (Zarabi)* (1999) 75 CA4th 169, 176, 89 CR2d 20, 24 (citing text)]

(a) **[6:744]** **Effect of failure to include "Doe" defendants:** If no "Doe" defendants were included in the original complaint, there is no "relation back" when an individual is named for the first time in an amended complaint filed after the statute of limitations has run. [See *Kralow Co. v. Sully-Miller Contracting Co.* (1985) 168 CA3d 1029, 1035-1036, 214 CR 630, 634—cross-complaint]

(b) **[6:745]** **Defective "Doe" allegations:** The "Doe" paragraph should allege that plaintiff is *ignorant* of the "Doe" defendants' identity. But a complaint that simply states that the "Doe" defendants "are sued as fictitious persons," has been held sufficient to permit later amendment under CCP §473(a)(1). In effect, the "Doe" terminology communicates that plaintiff does not know their true names. [*Dieckmann v. Sup.Ct. (Int'l Harvester Corp.)* (1985) 175 CA3d 345, 357-358, 220 CR 602, 610]

(c) **[6:746]** **Defective substitution of "Doe":** As long as "Doe" defendants were included in the original complaint, defective substitution of a "Doe" in the amended complaint is a procedural error, and can be cured by later amendment. Indeed, absent prejudice to the defendant, it is an abuse of discretion to refuse such amendment. [*Streicher v. Tommy's Elec. Co.* (1985) 164 CA3d 876, 884-885, 211 CR 22, 27]

- **[6:747]** **Example:** After the statute of limitations had run, P amended his complaint to name D, without substituting him for one of the "Doe" defendants named in the original complaint. The error was "procedural" and curable by amendment. [*Streicher v. Tommy's Elec. Co.*, supra]

*Cross-refer:* For the procedure to amend to identify "Doe" defendants, *see ¶6:612.*

(4) **[6:748]** **Requirement that plaintiff be "genuinely ignorant":** Serving someone as a "Doe" defendant after the statute of limitations has run may seriously impair his or her ability to defend. Hence, relation-back effect will be given only when plaintiff was proceeding in *good faith*; i.e., only where plaintiff was *genuinely* ignorant of that person's identity or liability when the

action was commenced. [*Miller v. Thomas* (1981) 121 CA3d 440, 445-446, 175 CR 327, 330]

To defeat the amendment, the *burden* is on *defendant* to prove plaintiff's earlier awareness of defendant's identity and facts creating its liability. [See *Fara Estates Homeowners Ass'n v. Fara Estates, Ltd.* (9th Cir. 1998) 134 F3d 377, 377 (applying Calif. law); *Breceda v. Gamsby* (1968) 267 CA2d 167, 179, 72 CR 832, 841]

(a) **[6:749]** **Test is "actual knowledge":** Whether plaintiff was genuinely "ignorant" or had "actual knowledge" of defendant's identity and liability when the complaint was filed is a *good faith* test: i.e., the "ignorance" must be real, not feigned. [*Munoz v. Purdy* (1979) 91 CA3d 942, 947, 154 CR 472, 475]

   1) **[6:750]** **Negligence in discovering facts immaterial:** But if good faith is shown, it is immaterial that plaintiff was negligent in not discovering the defendant's identity and liability before the complaint was filed: i.e., there is *no* requirement that plaintiff exercise reasonable care to identify all possible defendants before filing a complaint. [*Munoz v. Purdy*, supra; *Joslin v. H.A.S. Ins. Brokerage* (1986) 184 CA3d 369, 376, 228 CR 878, 882; see also *Fuller v. Tucker* (2000) 84 CA4th 1163, 1170, 101 CR2d 776, 781—statute applies "when (plaintiff) is actually ignorant of a certain fact, not when (plaintiff) might by the use of reasonable diligence have discovered it" (parentheses added)]

   Thus, "plaintiff will not be refused the right to use a Doe pleading even where the plaintiff's lack of actual knowledge is *attributable to plaintiff's own negligence.*" [*Grinnell Fire Protection Systems Co., Inc. v. American Sav. & Loan Ass'n* (1986) 183 CA3d 352, 359, 228 CR 292, 297]

   2) **[6:751]** **No constructive notice:** The fact a reasonable person would have been aware of defendant's identity does not prevent plaintiff from claiming he or she was "genuinely" ignorant. [*Balon v. Drost* (1993) 20 CA4th 483, 488, 25 CR2d 12, 15]

   However, another court has held that where plaintiff *knew* defendant's identity but then forgot it, the relation back doctrine does not apply unless plaintiff at least *reviewed readily avail-*

*able information* likely to refresh memory at the time of the original filing. [*Woo v. Sup.Ct. (Zarabi)* (1999) 75 CA4th 169, 180, 89 CR2d 20, 27 (disapproving broad forgiveness of negligence in *Balon,* supra)]

[6:751.1-751.4] *Reserved.*

3) [6:751.5] **Impact on statute of limitations:** Where separate acts by different parties cause plaintiff's injury, the limitations period begins to run when plaintiff knows of the injury and suspects *someone's* wrongdoing caused it. The statute commences even though plaintiff may not know or suspect that a particular defendant wrongfully caused the injury. [*Norgart v. Upjohn Co.* (1999) 21 C4th 383, 399, 87 CR2d 453, 469]

⟹[6:751.6] *PRACTICE POINTER:* To avoid the statute running, it may be necessary for plaintiff to file a complaint naming one or more "Doe" defendants (*see* ¶6:80.1*).

**(b) Cases where relation-back effect given**

1) [6:752] **Ignorance of identity:** Plaintiff was ignorant of the defendant's true *name* when the action was filed; or the defendant's *capacity* (i.e., whether a corporation, partnership, association, etc.). [*Hoffman v. Keeton* (1901) 132 C 195, 196, 64 P 264, 265]

a) [6:753] **Example:** Although P knew D's name at the time of the accident, she *forgot* it by the time she filed the complaint. She was entitled to rely on CCP §474. Although negligent, she was "ignorant" of D's identity when filing the complaint. [*Balon v. Drost* (1993) 20 CA4th 483, 489, 25 CR2d 12, 15]

2) [6:754] **Ignorance of existence:** Plaintiff knew the name of one defendant, and had reason to believe that *other persons, then unknown, were responsible* in some way for the known defendant's acts. The "Doe" defendants can be used to "keep the door open" to allow serving such other persons *when, as and if* their identities and responsibilities are discovered. [*Hollister Canning Co. v. Sup.Ct. (Swett)* (1972) 26 CA3d 186, 198, 102 CR 713, 721]

a) [6:755] **Example:** Persons acting as undisclosed principal of known defendant; employer of known defendant; concurrent tortfeasors, etc.

3) [6:756] **Ignorance of facts creating liability:** Plaintiff was ignorant of the facts which made the defendant liable and thus is deemed ignorant of the defendant's identity (even if his name was at all times known). [*General Motors Corp. v. Sup.Ct. (Jeffrey)* (1996) 48 CA4th 580, 593-594, 55 CR2d 871, 879-880]

- [6:757] Plaintiff sued Surgeon and several "Doe" defendants for medical malpractice. After statute of limitations, plaintiff served Anesthesiologist as a "Doe." Even though plaintiff knew his name all along, plaintiff had not discovered the *facts* indicating Anesthesiologist was liable until long after the complaint was filed. Hence, plaintiff deemed genuinely ignorant of claim against this doctor for relation-back purposes. [*Mishalow v. Horwald* (1964) 231 CA2d 517, 520, 41 CR 895, 897; see also *Fuller v. Trucker* (2000) 84 CA4th 1163, 1170, 101 CR2d 776, 781]

- [6:758] P hit her head on the steering wheel of her car when she was rear-ended in an auto accident. Within a year, she sued the driver of the other car and several Doe defendants. After the statute of limitations ran, P served Auto Manufacturer as a "Doe" defendant for producing a defective seatbelt. Although P knew Auto Manufacturer had manufactured her car, she was *ignorant of the facts suggesting a defect* in the seatbelt until after the statute had run. [*General Motors Corp. v. Sup.Ct. (Jeffrey)*, supra, 48 CA4th at 597, 55 CR2d at 882]

- [6:758.1] *Caution:* This issue is presently before the California Supreme Court in *Fox v. Ethicon Endo-Surgical, Inc.*, Case No. S121173.

a) [6:759] **Dismissed defendant brought back into suit:** Even a defendant *named* in the original complaint and later dismissed may be served as a "Doe" if facts establishing that defendant's liability are first discovered after the statute of limitations has run. [*Parker v. Robert E. McKee, Inc.* (1992) 3 CA4th 512, 516-517, 4 CR2d 347, 350]

**[6:759.1] Example:** P sued D and several others whom he believed to be subcontractors on a construction site. After voluntarily dismissing D, P discovered that D had been the general contractor on the job. This created a new factual basis for liability (i.e., D's control over the job site, etc.). Despite having previously dismissed D, P could serve D as a "Doe" after the statute of limitations had run. [*Parker v. Robert E. McKee, Inc.*, supra, 3 CA4th at 514, 4 CR2d at 348]

**[6:760]** *Reserved.*

4) **[6:761] Developments in the law creating basis for recovery:** Plaintiff may have known defendant's identity and the relevant facts all along, but there was no reasonably known legal basis for recovery against the defendant when the complaint was filed. I.e., *developments in the law* since filing the action give plaintiff the cause of action which he seeks to assert in the amended complaint. [*Marasco v. Wadsworth* (1978) 21 C3d 82, 86, 145 CR 843, 845]

a) **[6:762] Example:** Plaintiff-passenger amends complaint to name Driver of car in

*(Text cont'd on p. 6-153)*

**RESERVED**

which she was injured as "Doe," after change in case law holding guest statute unconstitutional. Although she clearly knew Driver's identity at all times, relation-back effect was given because until the change in the case law, plaintiff had no reason to know that she had a valid cause of action against Driver. (General allegations of negligence against Doe defendants in original complaint were sufficient to establish "same general set of facts" in amended complaint.) [*Marasco v. Wadsworth*, supra]

5) **[6:763]** **Delay not prejudicial to defendant:** Even if plaintiff has been dilatory in identifying a "Doe" defendant, delay alone will not bar such amendment absent actual prejudice to the defendant. [*Barrows v. American Motors Corp.* (1983) 144 CA3d 1, 9, 192 CR 380, 384]

a) **[6:764]** **Example:** Heirs of passenger killed in Jeep accident sued Driver for negligent operation and "Doe" for negligence in manufacture of vehicle. After settling with Driver, plaintiffs moved to amend complaint to name Manufacturer as "Doe." Manufacturer objected on ground that plaintiffs had delayed for more than 1 year after they had actual knowledge of its identity, but showed no prejudice resulting from the delay. *Held*: Delay alone is not ground for refusing a "Doe" amendment or its relation-back effect. [*Barrows v. American Motors Corp.*, supra]

(c) **Cases where relation-back effect denied**

1) **[6:765]** **Plaintiff knew identity of "Doe" when original complaint filed:** Plaintiff can utilize fictitious names in the complaint only if "genuinely ignorant" of the defendant's true name at the time the complaint is filed (CCP §474). Therefore, if it appears that plaintiff knew both the person's identity *and the facts making him or her liable* when the complaint was filed, but did not name him or her as a defendant, that person cannot be served as a "Doe" after the statute of limitations has run. [*Scherer v. Mark* (1976) 64 CA3d 834, 841, 135 CR 90, 94; see also *Hazel v. Hewlett* (1988) 201 CA3d 1458, 1465, 247 CR 723, 727—tort claim against

dentist dismissed where P knew dentist's name and wrong he perpetrated at time complaint filed but did not name dentist as defendant until after statute ran; see also *Taito v. Owens Corning* (1992) 7 CA4th 798, 802, 9 CR2d 687, 689, fn. 4 (citing text)]

[6:766]  *Reserved.*

- [6:767]  D could not be joined as a "Doe" because P's prelawsuit demand showed he knew both D's identity and the facts making D liable *when the original complaint was filed.* D's denial of liability was immaterial; and so was *P's claim that he relied on* D's denial in not naming D originally. [*Optical Surplus, Inc. v. Sup.Ct. (Niskar)* (1991) 228 CA3d 776, 784, 279 CR 194, 198]

- [6:768]  P knew that Dr. D was one of several doctors who treated his deceased wife, but did not name him as a "Doe" until 19 months after the original complaint (for wrongful death) was filed. P admitted "We knew he was involved, but we had no idea Your Honor, *how deeply* . . .". The court denied leave to amend, and its finding that P had actual knowledge was sustained on appeal. [*Dover v. Sadowinski* (1983) 147 CA3d 113, 117-118, 194 CR 866, 869— "actual knowledge" does *not* require that plaintiff have known each and every detail of the defendant's involvement; see also *Snoke v. Bolen* (1991) 235 CA3d 1427, 1432, 1 CR2d 492, 495; *Woo v. Sup.Ct. (Zarabi)* (1999) 75 CA4th 169, 178, 89 CR2d 20, 26]

(5) [6:769]  **Laches as limitation:**  The court has discretion to deny leave to amend to name a person as a "Doe" defendant where there is evidence of laches—i.e., *unreasonable* delay by plaintiff in seeking leave to amend causing *specific prejudice* to the defendant. [See *Barrows v. American Motors Corp.* (1983) 144 CA3d 1, 8, 192 CR 380, 383]

(a) [6:770]  **Delay alone insufficient:**  The running of the statute of limitations is only one factor to consider in determining whether there has been unreasonable delay or prejudice. [*Sobeck & Assocs., Inc. v. B & R Investments* (1989) 215 CA3d 861, 869-870, 264 CR 156, 160]

Rev. #1 2001

(6) [6:771] **Exception—claims against public entities:**
Amendments naming a public entity as a "Doe" do *not*
"relate back" to the original complaint. Reason: Public
entities are *immune* from suit except as provided by
statute (Calif.Const. Art. 3, §5); and the Tort Claims Act
requires claims filing and suit within 6 months following
rejection (Gov.C. §945.6; *see ¶1:710 ff.*). [*Chase v. State
of Calif.* (1977) 67 CA3d 808, 812-813, 136 CR 833,
835-836]

   (a) [6:772] **Claims against public employees:** If
   suit against a public entity is barred because of
   plaintiff's failure to comply with the Tort Claims Act,
   so also is any action against the public employees
   (or former public employees) who are responsible
   for plaintiff's injuries. [Gov.C. §950.2]

   [6:773] However, if the action is *timely* filed
   against the public entity, plaintiff can serve a public employee as a "Doe" defendant *after* expiration
   of the 6-month limit. CCP §474 applies in this situation, and is given a liberal application, because it
   is often difficult for plaintiff to discover the true
   names of the responsible employees. [See *Olden v.
   Hatchell* (1984) 154 CA3d 1032, 1037, 201 CR 715,
   719; *¶1:745*]

(7) [6:774] **Cross-refer—dismissal for delay in service
of summons:** Although an amended complaint may
"relate back" to the original to avoid the statute of limitations, it may still be subject to dismissal for delay in
service of summons (CCP §583.210, *¶11:51*). Ordinarily, this means that a "Doe" defendant must be identified and summons served no later than 3-years from
the commencement of the action. [See *Lopa v. Sup.Ct.
(Lopa)* (1975) 46 CA3d 382, 387, 120 CR 445, 448]

[6:775] However, where the complaint has been
amended *within* the 3-year dismissal period, and the
amendment is *not* based on the "same general set of
facts," the dismissal period runs from the date of the
*amendment*, not the commencement of the action.
[*Barrington v. A.H. Robins Co.* (1985) 39 C3d 146, 151-
152, 216 CR 405, 408]

[6:776] *Reserved.*

d. [6:777] **Adding NEW defendant after statute has run:**
Due process forbids "relation back" where the amended
complaint is against a *new* defendant—i.e., one not named
in the original complaint and not served as a "Doe": "The
straightforward rule is that amendment after the statute of
limitations has run will not be permitted where the result is

the addition of a party who, up to the time of the proposed amendment, was neither a named nor a fictitiously designated party to the proceeding." [*Ingram v. Sup.Ct. (Slinkard)* (1979) 98 CA3d 483, 492, 159 CR 557, 561-562; *Woo v. Sup.Ct. (Zarabi)* (1999) 75 CA4th 169, 176, 89 CR2d 20, 24]

(1) **[6:778]** **Example:** P sued Owner for negligence of Driver, who died in the accident. P did not name Driver or his estate as defendants. After statute of limitations had run, P sought to amend complaint to name Driver's estate as a defendant. (Estate could not be served as "Doe" because Driver's identity known at all times.) Held: Amendment not allowed; new parties cannot be joined by amendment after statute has run. [*Ingram v. Sup.Ct.*, supra]

(2) **[6:779]** **Defendant previously dismissed:** The same rule applies where the defendant had been timely sued but *dismissed* without prejudice. If plaintiff seeks to rejoin that defendant in the action *after* the statute has run, the amendment does *not* "relate back" to the original complaint. [*Troche v. Daley* (1990) 217 CA3d 403, 412, 266 CR 34, 39]

Compare: "Relation back" is allowed when a dismissed defendant is properly brought back into the suit as a "Doe"; *see* ¶6:760.

(3) **[6:780]** **Compare—correcting misnomers:** However, the court clearly has power under CCP §473(a)(1) to correct a mistake in a party's name (typically, clerical or typographical errors). E.g., "Southern Pacific Company" can be substituted for "Southern Pacific Railroad Company," even after the statute of limitations has run. [See *Kerr-McGee Chemical Corp. v. Sup.Ct. (Cubit)* (1984) 160 CA3d 594, 599, 206 CR 654, 656]

But the power to correct misnomers does *not* permit a substitution or *change* of defendants after the statute has run. E.g., "Kerr-McGee Chemical Corp." *cannot* be substituted for "Trona Medical Clinic" (not a fictitious name) after the statute has run. [*Kerr-McGee Chemical Corp. v. Sup.Ct.*, supra]

• **[6:781]** **Comment:** As long as only a single party or entity is involved, it should be possible to correct errors in its name or status (corporate, partnership or individual). But where there are separate entities or individuals with similar names, courts are much more cautious, and will not permit joinder of a new defendant under the guise of a claim of misnomer!

☞[6:782]  **PRACTICE POINTER:**  This problem can generally be avoided by *joining the correctly-named defendant as a "Doe"*—rather than attempting to change the name shown in the complaint. To join it as a "Doe," however, plaintiff must allege and show that he or she was "ignorant" of the said defendant's identity when the complaint was filed (*see ¶6:748*).

(4) [6:783]  **Estoppel exception—entities with similar names:**  A different rule applies where plaintiff sued an intended defendant under an erroneous name, and the defendant *appeared* and *allowed the mistake to continue* until after the statute of limitations had run. To avoid a miscarriage of justice, the intended defendant may be *estopped* to oppose an amendment to show the intended defendant's correct name. [*Omega Video Inc. v. Sup.Ct. (Robert Bosch Corp.)* (1983) 146 CA3d 470, 480-481, 194 CR 574, 580-581]

- [6:784]  P sued "Jensen Motors, Ltd." for breach of warranty, whereas he should have sued a related entity, "Jensen Motors, Inc." Nonetheless, "Inc." *appeared* in the action, and simply denied liability. Later, P was permitted to amend the complaint to name "Inc." as a defendant even though the statute of limitations had run. [*Prince v. Jensen Motors, Inc.* (1983) 139 CA3d 653, 655-656, 188 CR 911, 913—fact that "Inc." had cross-complained against manufacturer for indemnity showed that it was aware that it was being sued as seller]

  [6:785]  *Reserved.*

- [6:786]  P mistakenly named Budget, Inc. and Budget Rent-A-Car of Santa Monica as defendants. These entities answered the complaint and participated in litigation over a three-year period without revealing the proper defendant was Budget Rent-A-Car of Westwood. They were estopped to oppose P's motion to amend to name the correct defendant after the statute of limitations had run. P's mistake was excusable because of the "strikingly similar" names involved; and the named defendants' conduct had "perpetuated the error beyond the point of repair." [*Cuadros v. Sup.Ct. (Budget)* (1992) 6 CA4th 671, 676, 8 CR2d 18, 21]

e. [6:787]  **Adding new PLAINTIFFS after statute has run?**  Amendments naming a new party plaintiff are permissible if there is no change in the claim being asserted: e.g., to reflect an assignment of the claim; or, on plaintiff's death, to substitute his executor or administrator. [*Burgos v. Tamulonis* (1994) 28 CA4th 757, 33 CR2d 728, 731]

But, a new plaintiff *cannot* be joined after the statute of limitations has run where he or she seeks to enforce an *independent right* or to impose greater liability upon the defendant. In such cases, the amended complaint does *not* "relate back" to the filing of the original. [*Bartalo v. Sup.Ct. (Rosman)* (1975) 51 CA3d 526, 533, 124 CR 370, 374]

### (1) Application—permissible amendments

- [6:788]   An amendment joining the real party in interest is permissible even after the statute of limitations has run. [*Jensen v. Royal Pools* (1975) 48 CA3d 717, 721, 121 CR 805, 807—condo owners substituted for owners' association]

  [6:789]   *Reserved.*

### (2) Application—impermissible amendments

- [6:789.1]   Widow sued originally for wrongful death of her husband. After statute of limitations ran, she amended complaint to include a claim in her capacity as *administratrix* of decedent's estate, for damage suffered by him before death. Held: This claim did not relate back and was barred by the statute of limitations . . . because it was an independent right asserted by an independent party (decedent's estate). [*Dominguez v. City of Alhambra* (1981) 118 CA3d 237, 243, 173 CR 345, 348]

- [6:789.2]   P falsely alleged in survivor action she had standing to sue as administratrix of decedent's estate. P was appointed administratrix after statute of limitations ran. P contended her post-limitations appointment "related back" to filing of original complaint. Held: Action was time-barred. The "relation-back" doctrine does not confer standing on a plaintiff who knowingly lacked standing when suit was initially filed. [*Coats v. K-Mart Corporation* (1989) 215 CA3d 961, 968, 264 CR 12, 16]

  [6:789.3]   *Comment:* This seems contrary to a Supreme Court decision in *Klopstock v. Sup.Ct.* (1941) 17 C2d 13, 19-22, 108 P2d 906, 909-911, holding an amendment may substitute the real party in interest as long as the cause of action is not changed. (See also *Cloud v. Northrop Grumman Corp.* (1998) 67 CA4th 995, 1008-1009, 79 CR2d 544, 553-554, questioning validity of *Coats.*)

- [6:789.4] Complaint named Francine as plaintiff, whereas injuries were sustained by her sister, Mary Jo. It could not be amended after the statute of limitations had run to substitute Mary Jo as plaintiff because the original complaint *made no mention* of her. [*Diliberti v. Stage Call Corp.* (1992) 4 CA4th 1468, 1470-1471, 6 CR2d 563, 564-565]

(3) [6:790] **Adding professional corporation after statute has run:** Individual plaintiffs may be able to amend their complaints to add their professional corporations as coplaintiffs *even though the statute of limitations has run.* [*Pasadena Hospital Ass'n, Ltd. v. Sup.Ct. (Bienarz)* (1988) 204 CA3d 1031, 1036-1037, 251 CR 686, 688-689—where claims of doctor and his professional corporation were identical, doctor could add his professional corporation as coplaintiff after running of statute of limitations]

6. **Supplemental Pleadings**

a. [6:791] **Function:** A supplemental pleading is used to allege relevant facts *occurring after* the original pleading was filed. [CCP §464(a)]

(1) [6:792] **Compare—amended pleadings:** An amended pleading relates to matters *existing* when the original pleading was filed. (Some courts ignore this distinction, however, and treat supplemental complaints as "amended" pleadings; see *Honig v. Financial Corp. of America* (1992) 6 CA4th 960, 967, 7 CR2d 922, 926.)

(a) [6:793] **Example:** P filed defamation action against D several months ago, seeking $50,000 damages. He now discovers that (a) the damage to his reputation was more widespread than he realized when the action was filed; and (b) that since the action was filed, D has republished the defamation, causing additional harm.

P should seek leave of court to *amend* his complaint to allege (a); and to *supplement* his complaint to allege (b).

(b) [6:794] **Title not controlling:** Of course, the title of the pleading is not determinative: i.e., that which is labelled an "amended" complaint will be treated as a supplemental complaint, if the new facts pleaded occurred *after* the original complaint was filed. [*Hutnick v. United States Fid. & Guar. Co.* (1988) 47 C3d 456, 253 CR 236, 240, fn. 4]

Conversely, a pleading titled "supplemental complaint" will be treated as an *amended* complaint where it deals with matters occurring before commencement of the action. The erroneous designation of the pleading is immaterial. [*Jarchow v. Transamerica Title Ins. Co.* (1975) 48 CA3d 917, 948, 122 CR 470, 492 (overruled on another point in *Soto v. Royal Globe Ins. Corp.* (1986) 184 CA3d 420, 434, 229 CR 192, 200)—"supplemental complaint" alleged emotional distress after commencement of action from D's acts prior to that date]

(2) **[6:795]** **Does not replace original pleading:** Unlike an amended pleading, a supplemental pleading does *not* supersede the original. Rather, it simply adds new allegations to be considered in conjunction with the original.

(a) **[6:796]** **Compare—second pleading filed without leave of court:** The result may be different where the later complaint is filed *without leave of court* before any answer by the defendant. Such a pleading must be treated as an *amended* complaint. (Reason: Leave of court is required to "supplement" a complaint but plaintiff has the *right* to *amend* without leave of court before defendant answers; see CCP §472, *discussed at* ¶6:603). As an amended complaint, the second complaint *supersedes the original* complaint (*see* ¶6:704). [*Lee v. Bank of America NTSA* (1994) 27 CA4th 197, 215, 32 CR2d 388, 398—original complaint had never been served]

The result may be to deny relief on claims asserted *only* in the original complaint and not repeated in the second complaint. [*Lee v. Bank of America NTSA*, supra, 27 CA4th at 217, 32 CR2d at 400—original complaint sought relief for wrongful "demotion"; second complaint (filed without leave of court) claimed wrongful "termination"; court could not grant relief on "demotion" claim]

(3) **[6:797]** **Cannot allege "new" cause of action or defense:** It follows that a supplemental pleading cannot be used to allege facts constituting an entirely new cause of action or defense. I.e., the "occuring-after" facts must *supplement* the cause of action or defense originally pleaded. [*Flood v. Simpson* (1975) 45 CA3d 644, 647, 119 CR 675, 677]

(a) **[6:798]** **Comment:** Some cases apparently overlook this limitation and permit "amendments" that set forth new claims *arising after* commencement of the action. [See *Honig v. Financial Corp. of America* (1992) 6 CA4th 960, 966, 7 CR2d 922, 936—Employee's defamation claim against Employer arose after harassment action filed; *see* ¶*6:792*]

But these seem incorrect; *see* ¶*6:793*.

(b) [6:799] **Cannot "cure" premature lawsuit:** It follows that "(a) supplemental complaint cannot aid an original complaint which was filed *before the cause of action had arisen*." [*Radar v. Rogers* (1957) 49 C2d 243, 247, 317 P2d 17, 20 (emphasis added)]

- [6:800] Possible examples: suit for breach of contract before any breach or repudiation has occurred; suit for declaratory relief before any dispute has arisen. [See *Lee v. Bank of America NTSA* (1994) 27 CA4th 197, 207, 32 CR2d 388, 393]

- [6:801] Compare: But a "procedural" defect existing when the complaint was filed does not bar relief if it has since been remedied. [*Virgin v. State Farm Fire & Cas. Co.* (1990) 218 CA3d 1372, 1377, 267 CR 704, 707—insured had commenced bad faith action before insurer formally denied his claim; this "procedural defect" was not ground for summary judgment because claim had in fact been denied by time of summary judgment hearing]

(4) [6:802] **"Relation back" for statute of limitation purposes?** It is unsettled whether claims asserted by supplemental complaint "relate back" to the original complaint so as to avoid a statute of limitations defense.

(a) [6:803] **View denying "relation back":** Some cases hold that supplemental complaints do *not* relate back. A supplemental complaint does not supersede the original complaint (see above) and, therefore, claims asserted by supplemental complaint must stand on their own as far as the statute of limitations is concerned. [*ITT Gilfillan, Inc. v. Los Angeles* (1982) 136 CA3d 581, 589, 185 CR 848, 852]

- [6:804] Taxpayer sued City for tax refunds for 1963 and 1964. In 1980, Taxpayer filed an "amended and supplemental complaint" claiming additional refunds for 1969 through 1975, based on same facts as the original complaint except as to dates and amounts. Held: The later refund claims did *not* "relate back" to the original complaint, and hence were time-barred. [*ITT Gilfillan, Inc. v. Los Angeles*, supra]

- • [6:805]  Employee sued originally for wrongful *demotion*. She was fired shortly thereafter. More than 2 years later (after the statute had run on an independent action), she filed a "first amended complaint" for wrongful *termination*. The "amended" complaint did *not* "relate back" to the original complaint because it alleged *different wrongful conduct* by the employer than alleged in the original complaint. [*Lee v. Bank of America NTSA* (1994) 27 CA4th 197, 214, 32 CR2d 388, 398; but see contra, *Honig v. Financial Corp. of America* (1992) 6 CA4th 960, 966, 7 CR2d 922, 936, *discussed at* ¶6:798]

(b) [6:806]  **View allowing "relation back":**  But there are other cases contra, holding that where the original complaint gives notice that alleged wrongful conduct is of a continuing nature, a supplemental complaint based on the same conduct *does* relate back to the original pleading for statute of limitations purposes. [*Bendix Corp. v. Los Angeles* (1984) 150 CA3d 921, 926, 198 CR 370, 373]

- • [6:807]  P sued City for tax refunds for years prior to 1976. Case was delayed pending clarification of law. P was then permitted to file "supplemental and amended complaint" to join claim for 1976 and 1977 refunds, although limitations period had run. The original pleadings gave City notice of the subject of the dispute, and City was not prejudiced by the "relation back." [*Bendix Corp. v. Los Angeles*, supra]

- • [6:808]  Wife sued doctors for alleged medical malpractice, and Husband joined cause of action for loss of consortium. Wife died. More than 1 year later, Husband "amended" complaint to add cause of action for her wrongful death (in his new capacity as Wife's heir). The wrongful death claim was held to "relate back" to the original complaint, and thus escaped the 1-year statute of limitations (CCP §340.5). [*Lamont v. Wolfe* (1983) 142 CA3d 375, 381-382, 190 CR 874, 877-878]

  The court treated this as an amended, not supplemental, complaint—even though the wrongful death cause of action was not in existence when the original complaint was filed. It was enough that the wrongful death claim was for the *same kind of loss* as Husband's original claim (loss of consortium).

[6:809-811]   *Reserved.*

b.   [6:812]   **Procedure:**   The same notice motion procedure is followed, as when seeking leave to file amended pleadings (CCP §464(a); CRC 313(a), 327; *see ¶6:666 ff.*):

It is *unclear* whether recent (2002) amendments to CRC 327 governing motions for leave to amend pleadings also apply to motions for leave to file supplemental complaints. However, using the CRC 327 format is a good idea!

- Notice of motion

- Copy of proposed supplemental pleading

- Declaration by counsel

- Points and authorities

(1)  [6:813]  **Exception—paternity and child support claims:**   In child support proceedings, either parent may file a supplemental complaint for an order regarding paternity or support of the child in question *without* leave of court. [See CCP §464(b)]

(2)  [6:814]  **Caption:**   The supplemental pleading should be captioned accordingly. For example:

> "(FIRST) SUPPLEMENTAL COMPLAINT FOR DEFAMATION"

(3)  [6:815]  **Filing, summons and service?**   Traditionally, supplemental complaints were filed and served in the same manner as amended complaints; i.e., upon obtaining leave of court, the supplemental complaint was filed and served by mail upon counsel for opposing parties.

However, the statute now states that, upon filing a supplemental complaint, the court clerk will issue a "supplemental summons" that then must be served "*in the manner provided for the initial service of a summons* by this code." [CCP §464(c) (emphasis added)]

- [6:816]  **Comment:**   Legislative history suggests this summons and service provision was intended to apply only to *paternity and child support* supplemental complaints (because these are often filed years after the initial support and custody orders and the ex-spouses may no longer be represented by counsel). A parallel provision in the Family Code is so limited (see Fam.C. §2330.1).

Nonetheless, the summons and service provision is drafted in such a way that it appears to apply to *all* supplemental complaints. (It is set forth in a different paragraph than the provision dealing with paternity and child support.)

(4) **[6:817]** **Responsive pleadings:** The opposing parties may challenge or respond to the supplemental pleading as to the original. New matters alleged in a supplemental complaint must be controverted, or they are deemed admitted.

c. **[6:818]** **Discretion of court:** As with amended pleadings, a motion to file supplemental pleadings is addressed to the sound discretion of the court. And, the same policy favoring liberality in amending pleadings applies . . . so that all matters in dispute between the parties can be resolved in a single lawsuit if reasonably possible. [*Louie Queriolo Trucking, Inc. v. Sup.Ct. (Tumblin Co.)* (1967) 252 CA2d 194, 197, 60 CR 389]

(1) **[6:819]** **Comment:** Ordinarily, leave to file supplemental pleadings is granted even more readily than amended pleadings. There is far less chance that granting leave will prejudice the opposing parties, or delay the trial, because of the rule that supplemental pleadings cannot allege "new" causes of action or defenses (¶*6:797*).

# OFFICIAL FORM COMPLAINT
## PERSONAL INJURY, PROPERTY DAMAGE, WRONGFUL DEATH ACTIONS

982.1(1)

| ATTORNEY OR PARTY WITHOUT ATTORNEY *(Name, state bar number, and address):* | FOR COURT USE ONLY |
|---|---|

TELEPHONE NO:        FAX NO. *(Optional):*

E-MAIL ADDRESS *(Optional):*

ATTORNEY FOR *(Name):*

NAME OF COURT:

STREET ADDRESS:

MAILING ADDRESS:

CITY AND ZIP CODE:

BRANCH NAME:

PLAINTIFF:

. DEFENDANT:

☐ DOES 1 TO _____

**COMPLAINT—Personal Injury, Property Damage, Wrongful Death**
☐ **AMENDED** *(Number):*

**Type** *(check all that apply):*
☐ **MOTOR VEHICLE**  ☐ **OTHER** *(specify):*
  ☐ **Property Damage**  ☐ **Wrongful Death**
  ☐ **Personal Injury**  ☐ **Other Damages** *(specify):*

**Jurisdiction** *(check all that apply):*
☐ **ACTION IS A LIMITED CIVIL CASE**
  **Amount demanded**  ☐ **does not exceed $10,000**
        ☐ **exceeds $10,000, but does not exceed $25,000**
☐ **ACTION IS AN UNLIMITED CIVIL CASE (exceeds $25,000)**
☐ **ACTION IS RECLASSIFIED by this amended complaint**
  ☐ **from limited to unlimited**
  ☐ **from unlimited to limited**

CASE NUMBER:

1. PLAINTIFF *(name):*

   alleges causes of action against DEFENDANT *(name):*
2. This pleading, including attachments and exhibits, consists of the following number of pages: _____
3. Each plaintiff named above is a competent adult
   a. ☐ **except** plaintiff *(name):*
      (1) ☐ a corporation qualified to do business in California
      (2) ☐ an unincorporated entity *(describe):*
      (3) ☐ a public entity *(describe):*
      (4) ☐ a minor  ☐ an adult
         (a) ☐ for whom a guardian or conservator of the estate or a guardian ad litem has been appointed
         (b) ☐ other *(specify):*
      (5) ☐ other *(specify):*

   b. ☐ **except** plaintiff *(name):*
      (1) ☐ a corporation qualified to do business in California
      (2) ☐ an unincorporated entity *(describe):*
      (3) ☐ a public entity *(describe):*
      (4) ☐ a minor  ☐ an adult
         (a) ☐ for whom a guardian or conservator of the estate or a guardian ad litem has been appointed
         (b) ☐ other *(specify):*
      (5) ☐ other *(specify):*

   ☐ Information about additional plaintiffs who are not competent adults is shown in Complaint—Attachment 3.

Page 1 of 3

Form Approved for Optional Use
Judicial Council of California
982.1(1) [Rev. July 1, 2002]

**COMPLAINT—Personal Injury, Property Damage, Wrongful Death**

Code of Civil Procedure, § 425.12

4. ☐ Plaintiff *(name):*
   is doing business under the fictitious name *(specify):*

   and has complied with the fictitious business name laws.

5. Each defendant named above is a natural person
   a. ☐ **except** defendant *(name):*
      (1) ☐ a business organization, form unknown
      (2) ☐ a corporation
      (3) ☐ an unincorporated entity *(describe):*

      (4) ☐ a public entity *(describe):*

      (5) ☐ other *(specify):*

   c. ☐ **except** defendant *(name):*
      (1) ☐ a business organization, form unknown
      (2) ☐ a corporation
      (3) ☐ an unincorporated entity *(describe):*

      (4) ☐ a public entity *(describe):*

      (5) ☐ other *(specify):*

   b. ☐ **except** defendant *(name):*
      (1) ☐ a business organization, form unknown
      (2) ☐ a corporation
      (3) ☐ an unincorporated entity *(describe):*

      (4) ☐ a public entity *(describe):*

      (5) ☐ other *(specify):*

   d. ☐ **except** defendant *(name):*
      (1) ☐ a business organization, form unknown
      (2) ☐ a corporation
      (3) ☐ an unincorporated entity *(describe):*

      (4) ☐ a public entity *(describe):*

      (5) ☐ other *(specify):*

   ☐ Information about additional defendants who are not natural persons is contained in Complaint—Attachment 5.

6. The true names and capacities of defendants sued as Does are unknown to plaintiff.

7. ☐ Defendants who are joined pursuant to Code of Civil Procedure section 382 are *(names):*

8. This court is the proper court because
   a. ☐ at least one defendant now resides in its jurisdictional area.
   b. ☐ the principal place of business of a defendant corporation or unincorporated association is in its jurisdictional area.
   c. ☐ injury to person or damage to personal property occurred in its jurisdictional area.
   d. ☐ other *(specify):*

9. ☐ Plaintiff is required to comply with a claims statute, **and**
   a. ☐ plaintiff has complied with applicable claims statutes, **or**
   b. ☐ plaintiff is excused from complying because *(specify):*

10. The following causes of action are attached and the statements above apply to each *(each complaint must have one or more causes of action attached)*:
    a. ☐ Motor Vehicle
    b. ☐ General Negligence
    c. ☐ Intentional Tort
    d. ☐ Products Liability
    e. ☐ Premises Liability
    f. ☐ Other *(specify)*:

11. Plaintiff has suffered
    a. ☐ wage loss
    b. ☐ loss of use of property
    c. ☐ hospital and medical expenses
    d. ☐ general damage
    e. ☐ property damage
    f. ☐ loss of earning capacity
    g. ☐ other damage *(specify)*:

12. ☐ The damages claimed for wrongful death and the relationships of plaintiff to the deceased are
    a. ☐ listed in Complaint—Attachment 12.
    b. ☐ as follows:

13. The relief sought in this complaint is within the jurisdiction of this court.

14. **PLAINTIFF PRAYS** for judgment for costs of suit; for such relief as is fair, just, and equitable; and for
    a. (1) ☐ compensatory damages
       (2) ☐ punitive damages
    b. The amount of damages is *(you must check (1) in cases for personal injury or wrongful death)*:
       (1) ☐ according to proof
       (2) ☐ in the amount of: $ _____

       *? special damages*

15. ☐ The paragraphs of this complaint alleged on information and belief are as follows *(specify paragraph numbers)*:

Date:

▶

_____       _____
(TYPE OR PRINT NAME)       (SIGNATURE OF PLAINTIFF OR ATTORNEY)

982.1(1) [Rev. July 1, 2002]    **COMPLAINT—Personal Injury, Property Damage, Wrongful Death**    Page 3 of 3

**[FORM 6:B]**

# OFFICIAL FORM CAUSE OF ACTION
# MOTOR VEHICLE

| SHORT TITLE | CASE NUMBER |
|---|---|
| | |

_____ **CAUSE OF ACTION—**Motor Vehicle          Page _____
    (number)

ATTACHMENT TO ☐ Complaint  ☐ Cross-Complaint

*(Use a separate cause of action form for each cause of action.)*

Plaintiff *(name)*:

MV-1  Plaintiff alleges the acts of defendants were negligent; the acts were the legal (proximate) cause of injuries
and damages to plaintiff; the acts occurred
on *(date)*:
at *(place)*:

MV-2. DEFENDANTS
a. ☐ The defendants who operated a motor vehicle are *(names)*:

☐ Does _____ to _____
b. ☐ The defendants who employed the persons who operated a motor vehicle in the course of their employment
are *(names)*:

☐ Does _____ to _____
c. ☐ The defendants who owned the motor vehicle which was operated with their permission are *(names)*:

☐ Does _____ to _____
d. ☐ The defendants who entrusted the motor vehicle are *(names)*:

☐ Does _____ to _____
e. ☐ The defendants who were the agents and employees of the other defendants and acted within the scope
of the agency were *(names)*:

☐ Does _____ to _____
f. ☐ The defendants who are liable to plaintiffs for other reasons and the reasons for the liability are
☐ listed in Attachment MV-2f ☐ as follows:

☐ Does _____ to _____

Form Approved by the
Judicial Council of California
Effective January 1, 1982
Rule 982 1(2)
**CAUSE OF ACTION—**Motor Vehicle          CCP 425.12

# OFFICIAL FORM CAUSE OF ACTION
## GENERAL NEGLIGENCE

| SHORT TITLE | CASE NUMBER |
|---|---|
| | |

_____ **CAUSE OF ACTION**—General Negligence    Page _____
  (number)

ATTACHMENT TO ☐ Complaint    ☐ Cross-Complaint

*(Use a separate cause of action form for each cause of action.)*

GN-1  Plaintiff *(name)*:

alleges that defendant *(name)*:

☐ Does _____ to _____

was the legal (proximate) cause of damages to plaintiff. By the following acts or omissions to act, defendant negligently caused the damage to plaintiff
on *(date)*:
at *(place)*:

*(description of reasons for liability)*:

Form Approved by the
Judicial Council of California
Effective January 1, 1982
Rule 982.1(3)        **CAUSE OF ACTION**—General Negligence        CCP 425.12

**[FORM 6:D]**

# OFFICIAL FORM CAUSE OF ACTION
# INTENTIONAL TORT

| SHORT TITLE | CASE NUMBER |
|---|---|
|  |  |

_____ CAUSE OF ACTION—Intentional Tort          Page _____
(number)

ATTACHMENT TO ☐ Complaint   ☐ Cross-Complaint

(Use a separate cause of action form for each cause of action.)

IT-1   Plaintiff (name):

alleges that defendant (name):

☐ Does _____ to _____

was the legal (proximate) cause of damages to plaintiff. By the following acts or omissions to act, defendant intentionally caused the damage to plaintiff
on (date):
at (place):

(description of reasons for liability):

Form Approved by the
Judicial Council of California
Effective January 1, 1982
Rule 982.1(4)

**CAUSE OF ACTION—Intentional Tort**          CCP 425.12

# OFFICIAL FORM CAUSE OF ACTION
# PREMISES LIABILITY

| SHORT TITLE | CASE NUMBER |
|---|---|
| | |

_____ **CAUSE OF ACTION—Premises Liability**     **Page** _____
(number)

ATTACHMENT TO ☐ Complaint     ☐ Cross-Complaint

*(Use a separate cause of action form for each cause of action.)*

Prem.L-1.  Plaintiff *(name)*:
alleges the acts of defendants were the legal (proximate) cause of damages to plaintiff.
On *(date)*:                                     plaintiff was injured on the following premises in the following

fashion *(description of premises and circumstances of injury)*:

Prem.L-2.  ☐ **Count One—Negligence** The defendants who negligently owned, maintained, managed and operated
the described premises were *(names)*:

☐ Does _____ to _____

Prem.L-3.  ☐ **Count Two—Willful Failure to Warn** [Civil Code section 846] The defendant owners who willfully
or maliciously failed to guard or warn against a dangerous condition, use, structure, or activity were
*(names)*:

☐ Does _____ to _____
Plaintiff, a recreational user, was ☐ an invited guest ☐ a paying guest.

Prem.L-4.  ☐ **Count Three—Dangerous Condition of Public Property** The defendants who owned public property
on which a dangerous condition existed were *(names)*:

☐ Does _____ to _____
a. ☐ The defendant public entity had ☐ actual ☐ constructive notice of the existence of the
dangerous condition in sufficient time prior to the injury to have corrected it.
b. ☐ The condition was created by employees of the defendant public entity.

Prem.L-5.  a. ☐ **Allegations about Other Defendants** The defendants who were the agents and employees of the
other defendants and acted within the scope of the agency were *(names)*:

☐ Does _____ to _____
b. ☐ The defendants who are liable to plaintiffs for other reasons and the reasons for their liability are
☐ described in attachment Prem.L-5.b ☐ as follows *(names)*:

Form Approved by the
Judicial Council of California
Effective January 1, 1982
Rule 982.1(5)                **CAUSE OF ACTION—Premises Liability**                CCP 425.12

Rev. #1 1995                                                                      **6-171**

**[FORM 6:F]**

# OFFICIAL FORM CAUSE OF ACTION
# PRODUCTS LIABILITY

| SHORT TITLE | CASE NUMBER |
|---|---|
| | |

_____ **CAUSE OF ACTION**—Products Liability     **Page** _____
(number)

ATTACHMENT TO ☐ Complaint ☐ Cross-Complaint

*(Use a separate cause of action form for each cause of action.)*

Plaintiff *(name):*

Prod.L-1. On or about *(date):*            plaintiff was injured by the following product:

Prod L-2. Each of the defendants knew the product would be purchased and used without inspection for defects. The product was defective when it left the control of each defendant. The product at the time of injury was being
     ☐ used in the manner intended by the defendants.
     ☐ used in a manner that was reasonably foreseeable by defendants as involving a substantial danger not readily apparent. Adequate warnings of the danger were not given.

Prod L-3. Plaintiff was a
     ☐ purchaser of the product.           ☐ user of the product.
     ☐ bystander to the use of the product.     ☐ other *(specify):*

PLAINTIFF'S INJURY WAS THE LEGAL (PROXIMATE) RESULT OF THE FOLLOWING:
Prod L-4. ☐ **Count One—Strict liability** of the following defendants who
     a. ☐ manufactured or assembled the product *(names):*

         ☐ Does _____ to _____
     b. ☐ designed and manufactured component parts supplied to the manufacturer *(names):*

         ☐ Does _____ to _____
     c. ☐ sold the product to the public *(names):*

         ☐ Does _____ to _____
Prod L-5. ☐ **Count Two—Negligence** of the following defendants who owed a duty to plaintiff *(names):*

         ☐ Does _____ to _____
Prod L-6. ☐ **Count Three—Breach of warranty** by the following defendants *(names):*

         ☐ Does _____ to _____
     a. ☐ who breached an implied warranty
     b. ☐ who breached an express warranty which was
         ☐ written ☐ oral
Prod.L-7. ☐ The defendants who are liable to plaintiffs for other reasons and the reasons for the liability are
     ☐ listed in Attachment—Prod.L-7 ☐ as follows:

Form Approved by the
Judicial Council of California
Effective January 1, 1982
Rule 982 1(6)
         **CAUSE OF ACTION**—Products Liability          CCP 425 12

# OFFICIAL FORM
## EXEMPLARY DAMAGES ATTACHMENT

| SHORT TITLE | CASE NUMBER |
|---|---|
| | |

### Exemplary Damages Attachment          Page _____

ATTACHMENT TO ☐ Complaint ☐ Cross-Complaint

EX-1. As additional damages against defendant *(name):*

Plaintiff alleges defendant was guilty of
☐ malice
☐ fraud
☐ oppression
as defined in Civil Code section 3294, and plaintiff should recover, in addition to actual damages, damages to make an example of and to punish defendant.

EX-2. The facts supporting plaintiff's claim are as follows:

EX-3. The amount of exemplary damages sought is
a. ☐ not shown, pursuant to Code of Civil Procedure section 425.10.
b. ☐ $

Form Approved by the
Judicial Council of California
Effective January 1, 1982
Rule 982.1(13)          **Exemplary Damages Attachment**          CCP 425.12

**[FORM 6:H]**

# OFFICIAL FORM CROSS-COMPLAINT
## PERSONAL INJURY, PROPERTY DAMAGE, WRONGFUL DEATH ACTIONS

982.1(14)

| ATTORNEY OR PARTY WITHOUT ATTORNEY (Name, state bar number, and address): | FOR COURT USE ONLY |
|---|---|

TELEPHONE NO.        FAX NO. (Optional):
E-MAIL ADDRESS (Optional):
ATTORNEY FOR (Name):

NAME OF COURT:
STREET ADDRESS:
MAILING ADDRESS:
CITY AND ZIP CODE:
BRANCH NAME:

SHORT TITLE:

CROSS-COMPLAINANT:

CROSS-DEFENDANT:

☐ DOES 1 TO _____

**CROSS-COMPLAINT—Personal Injury, Property Damage, Wrongful Death**
☐ AMENDED (Number):
**Causes of Action** (check all that apply):
☐ **Apportionment of Fault**    ☐ **Declaratory Relief**
☐ **Indemnification**    ☐ **Other** (specify):
**Jurisdiction** (check all that apply):
☐ **ACTION IS A LIMITED CIVIL CASE ($25,000 or less)**
☐ **ACTION IS AN UNLIMITED CIVIL CASE (exceeds $25,000)**
☐ **It ☐ is ☐ is not reclassified as unlimited by this cross-complaint**

CASE NUMBER:

1. CROSS-COMPLAINANT (name):

   alleges causes of action against CROSS-DEFENDANT (name):

2. This pleading, including exhibits and attachments, consists of the following number of pages: _____

3. Each cross-complainant named above is a competent adult
   a. ☐ **except** cross-complainant (name):
      (1) ☐ a corporation qualified to do business in California
      (2) ☐ an unincorporated entity (describe):
      (3) ☐ a public entity (describe):
      (4) ☐ a minor ☐ an adult
         (a) ☐ for whom a guardian or conservator of the estate or a guardian ad litem has been appointed
         (b) ☐ other (specify):
      (5) ☐ other (specify):

☐ Information about additional cross-complainants who are not competent adults is contained in
   Cross-Complaint—Attachment 3.

(Continued on reverse)

Page one of three

Form Approved for Optional Use
Judicial Council of California
982.1(14) [Rev. January 1, 2001]

**CROSS-COMPLAINT—Personal Injury,
Property Damage, Wrongful Death**

 WEST GROUP

Code of Civil Procedure, § 425.12

4. Each cross-defendant named above is a natural person
   a. ☐ **except** cross-defendant *(name):*
   - (1) ☐ a business organization, form unknown
   - (2) ☐ a corporation
   - (3) ☐ an unincorporated entity *(describe):*

   - (4) ☐ a public entity *(describe):*

   - (5) ☐ other *(specify):*

   b. ☐ **except** cross-defendant *(name):*
   - (1) ☐ a business organization, form unknown
   - (2) ☐ a corporation
   - (3) ☐ an unincorporated entity *(describe):*

   - (4) ☐ a public entity *(describe):*

   - (5) ☐ other *(specify):*

   ☐ Information about additional cross-defendants who are not natural persons is contained in Cross-Complaint—
   Attachment 4.

5. The true names and capacities of cross-defendants sued as Does are unknown to cross-complainant.

6. ☐ Cross-complainant is required to comply with a claims statute, **and**
   a. ☐ has complied with applicable claims statutes, **or**
   b. ☐ is excused from complying because *(specify):*

7. ☐ _____ **Cause of Action—Indemnification**
   (NUMBER)

   a. Cross-defendants were the agents, employees, co-venturers, partners, or in some manner agents or principals, or both, for each other and were acting within the course and scope of their agency or employment.
   b. The principal action alleges, among other things, conduct entitling plaintiff to compensatory damages against me. I contend that I am not liable for events and occurrences described in plaintiff's complaint.
   c. If I am found in some manner responsible to plaintiff or to anyone else as a result of the incidents and occurrences described in plaintiff's complaint, my liability would be based solely upon a derivative form of liability not resulting from my conduct, but only from an obligation imposed upon me by law; therefore, I would be entitled to complete indemnity from each cross-defendant.

8. ☐ _____ **Cause of Action—Apportionment of Fault**
   (NUMBER)

   a. _____ ble, in whole or in part, for the injuries, if any, suffered by plaintiff.
   b. If I am judged liable to plaintiff, each cross-defendant should be required: (1) to pay a share of plaintiff's judgment which is in proportion to the comparative negligence of that cross-defendant in causing plaintiff's damages; and (2) to reimburse me for any payments I make to plaintiff in excess of my proportional share of all cross-defendants' negligence.

(Continued on page three)

**CROSS-COMPLAINT—Personal Injury,
Property Damage, Wrongful Death**

9. ☐ _____ **Cause of Action—Declaratory Relief**
(NUMBER)

An actual controversy exists between the parties concerning their respective rights and duties because cross-complainant contends and cross-defendant disputes ☐ as specified in Cross-Complaint—Attachment 9
☐ as follows:

10. ☐ _____ **Cause of Action—*(specify)*:**

11. ☐ The following additional causes of action are attached and the statements below apply to each *(in each of the attachments, "plaintiff" means "cross-complainant" and "defendant" means "cross-defendant")*:

a. ☐ Motor Vehicle
b. ☐ General Negligence
c. ☐ Intentional Tort
d. ☐ Products Liability
e. ☐ Premises Liability
f. ☐ Other *(specify)*:

12. **CROSS-COMPLAINANT PRAYS** for judgment for costs of suit; for such relief as is fair, just, and equitable; and for

a. ☐ total and complete indemnity for any judgments rendered against me.
b. ☐ judgment in a proportionate share from each cross-defendant.
c. ☐ a judicial determination that cross-defendants were the legal cause of any injuries and damages sustained by plaintiff and that cross-defendants indemnify me, either completely or partially, for any sums of money which may be recovered against me by plaintiff.
d. ☐ compensatory damages
   (1) ☐ (unlimited civil cases) according to proof.
   (2) ☐ (limited civil cases) in the amount of: $
e. ☐ other *(specify)*:

13. ☐ The paragraphs of this cross-complaint alleged on information and belief are as follows *(specify paragraph numbers)*:

Date:

▶

_____  _____
(TYPE OR PRINT NAME)  (SIGNATURE OF CROSS-COMPLAINANT OR ATTORNEY)

982.1(14) [Rev. January 1, 2001]      **CROSS-COMPLAINT—Personal Injury,**      Page three of three
**Property Damage, Wrongful Death**

6-176                                                              Rev. #1 2001

# OFFICIAL FORM ANSWER
## PERSONAL INJURY, PROPERTY DAMAGE,
## WRONGFUL DEATH ACTIONS

| ATTORNEY OR PARTY WITHOUT ATTORNEY (NAME AND ADDRESS) | TELEPHONE | FOR COURT USE ONLY |
|---|---|---|
| | | |
| ATTORNEY FOR (NAME) | | |
| Insert name of court, judicial district or branch court, if any, and post office and street address: | | |
| PLAINTIFF | | |
| DEFENDANT | | |

| ANSWER—Personal Injury, Property Damage, Wrongful Death <br> ☐ COMPLAINT OF *(name):* <br> ☐ CROSS-COMPLAINT OF *(name):* | CASE NUMBER: |
|---|---|

1. This pleading, including attachments and exhibits, consists of the following number of pages: _____

**DEFENDANT OR CROSS-DEFENDANT** *(name):*

2. ☐ Generally **denies** each allegation of the **unverified** complaint or cross-complaint.

3. a. ☐ DENIES each allegation of the following numbered paragraphs:

   b. ☐ ADMITS each allegation of the following numbered paragraphs:

   c. ☐ DENIES, ON INFORMATION AND BELIEF, each allegation of the following numbered paragraphs:

   d. ☐ DENIES, BECAUSE OF LACK OF SUFFICIENT INFORMATION OR BELIEF TO ANSWER, each allegation of the following numbered paragraphs:

   e. ☐ ADMITS the following allegations and generally denies all other allegations:

(Continued)

Form Approved by the
Judicial Council of California
Effective January 1, 1982
Rule 982.1(15)
**ANSWER—Personal Injury, Property Damage,
Wrongful Death**
CCP 425.12

ANSWER—Personal Injury, Property Damage, Wrongful Death      Page two

f. ☐ DENIES the following allegations and admits all other allegations:

g. ☐ Other *(specify):*

**AFFIRMATIVELY ALLEGES AS A DEFENSE**

4. ☐ The comparative fault of plaintiff or cross-complainant *(name):*
   as follows:

5. ☐ The expiration of the Statute of Limitations as follows:

6. ☐ Other *(specify):*

7. DEFENDANT OR CROSS-DEFENDANT PRAYS
   For costs of suit and that plaintiff or cross-complainant take nothing.
   ☐ Other *(specify):*

. . . . . . . . . . . . . . . . . . . . . . . . . .         _____

        (Type or print name)                    (Signature of party or attorney)

# OFFICIAL FORM COMPLAINT AND CROSS-COMPLAINT CONTRACT ACTIONS

982.1(20)

| | |
|---|---|
| ATTORNEY OR PARTY WITHOUT ATTORNEY *(Name, state bar number, and address)*: | FOR COURT USE ONLY |

TELEPHONE NO:         FAX NO. *(Optional)*:

E-MAIL ADDRESS *(Optional)*:

ATTORNEY FOR *(Name)*:

**SUPERIOR COURT OF CALIFORNIA, COUNTY OF**

STREET ADDRESS:

MAILING ADDRESS:

CITY AND ZIP CODE:

BRANCH NAME:

PLAINTIFF:

DEFENDANT:

☐ DOES 1 TO _____

## CONTRACT

☐ **COMPLAINT**     ☐ **AMENDED COMPLAINT** *(Number):*

☐ **CROSS–COMPLAINT** ☐ **AMENDED CROSS–COMPLAINT** *(Number):*

**Jurisdiction** *(check all that apply)*:

☐ **ACTION IS A LIMITED CIVIL CASE**

    **Amount demanded** ☐ **does not exceed $10,000**

                ☐ **exceeds $10,000, but does not exceed $25,000**

☐ **ACTION IS AN UNLIMITED CIVIL CASE (exceeds $25,000)**

☐ **ACTION IS RECLASSIFIED by this amended complaint or cross-complaint**

    ☐ **from limited to unlimited**

    ☐ **from unlimited to limited**

CASE NUMBER:

1. PLAINTIFF* *(names)*:

  alleges causes of action against DEFENDANT* *(names)*:

2. This pleading, including attachments and exhibits, consists of the following number of pages:

3. a. Each plaintiff named above is a competent adult
   ☐ **except** plaintiff *(name)*:
       ☐ a corporation qualified to do business in California
       ☐ an unincorporated entity *(describe)*:
       ☐ other *(specify)*:

   b. ☐   Plaintiff *(name)*:
       ☐ has complied with the fictitious business name laws and is doing business under the fictitious name of *(specify)*:

       ☐ has complied with all licensing requirements as a licensed *(specify)*:
   c. ☐  Information about additional plaintiffs who are not competent adults is shown in Complaint—Attachment 3c.

4. a. Each defendant named above is a natural person
   ☐ **except** defendant *(name)*:         ☐ **except** defendant *(name)*:
       ☐ a business organization, form unknown   ☐ a business organization, form unknown
       ☐ a corporation                      ☐ a corporation
       ☐ an unincorporated entity *(describe)*:     ☐ an unincorporated entity *(describe)*:

       ☐ a public entity *(describe)*:        ☐ a public entity *(describe)*:

       ☐ other *(specify)*:              ☐ other *(specify)*:     **Page 1 of 2**

* If this form is used as a cross-complaint, plaintiff means cross-complainant and defendant means cross-defendant.

Form Approved for Optional Use
Judicial Council of California
982.1(20) [Rev. July 1, 2002]

**COMPLAINT—Contract**

Code of Civ. Proc., § 425.12

**COMPLAINT—Contract**

4. *(Continued)*
    b. The true names and capacities of defendants sued as Does are unknown to plaintiff.
    c. ☐ Information about additional defendants who are not natural persons is contained in Complaint—Attachment 4c.
    d. ☐ Defendants who are joined pursuant to Code of Civil Procedure section 382 are *(names):*

5. ☐ Plaintiff is required to comply with a claims statute, **and**
    a. ☐ plaintiff has complied with applicable claims statutes, or
    b. ☐ plaintiff is excused from complying because *(specify):*

6. ☐ This action is subject to ☐ Civil Code section 1812.10 ☐ Civil Code section 2984.4.

7. This court is the proper court because
    a. ☐ a defendant entered into the contract here.
    b. ☐ a defendant lived here when the contract was entered into.
    c. ☐ a defendant lives here now.
    d. ☐ the contract was to be performed here.
    e. ☐ a defendant is a corporation or unincorporated association and its principal place of business is here.
    f. ☐ real property that is the subject of this action is located here.
    g. ☐ other *(specify):*

8. The following causes of action are attached and the statements above apply to each *(each complaint must have one or more causes of action attached):*
    ☐ Breach of Contract               ☐ Common Counts
    ☐ Other *(specify):*

9. ☐ Other:

10. **PLAINTIFF PRAYS** for judgment for costs of suit; for such relief as is fair, just, and equitable; and for
    a. ☐ damages of: $
    b. ☐ interest on the damages
        (1) ☐ according to proof
        (2) ☐ at the rate of    percent per year from *(date):*
    c. ☐ attorney's fees
        (1) ☐ of: $
        (2) ☐ according to proof.
    d. ☐ other *(specify):*

11. ☐ The following paragraphs of this pleading are alleged on information and belief *(specify paragraph numbers):*

Date:

▶

_____
(TYPE OR PRINT NAME)

_____
(SIGNATURE OF PLAINTIFF OR ATTORNEY)

*(If you wish to verify this pleading, affix a verification.)*

982.1(20) [Rev. July 1, 2002]          **COMPLAINT—Contract**          Page 2 of 2

# OFFICIAL FORM CAUSE OF ACTION
# BREACH OF CONTRACT

| SHORT TITLE | CASE NUMBER |
|---|---|
| | |

**CAUSE OF ACTION**—Breach of Contract     Page _____

_(number)_

ATTACHMENT TO ☐ Complaint ☐ Cross-Complaint

_(Use a separate cause of action form for each cause of action.)_

BC-1   Plaintiff _(name)_

     alleges that on or about _(date)_
     a ☐ written ☐ oral ☐ other _(specify)_:
     agreement was made between _(name parties to agreement)_:

     ☐ A copy of the agreement is attached as Exhibit A, **or**
     ☐ The essential terms of the agreement ☐ are stated in Attachment BC-1 ☐ are as follows _(specify)_:

BC-2   On or about _(dates)_:
     defendant breached the agreement by ☐ the acts specified in Attachment BC-2 ☐ the following acts
     _(specify)_

BC-3   Plaintiff has performed all obligations to defendant except those obligations plaintiff was prevented or
     excused from performing.

BC-4   Plaintiff suffered damages legally (proximately) caused by defendant's breach of the agreement
     ☐ as stated in Attachment BC-4 ☐ as follows _(specify)_:

BC-5   ☐ Plaintiff is entitled to attorney fees by an agreement or a statute
       ☐ of $
       ☐ according to proof.

BC-6   ☐ Other:

Form Approved by the
Judicial Council of California
Effective January 1, 1982
Rule 982 1(21)
     **CAUSE OF ACTION**—Breach of Contract      CCP 425.12

**[FORM 6:L]**

# OFFICIAL FORM CAUSE OF ACTION
# COMMON COUNTS

| SHORT TITLE | CASE NUMBER |
|---|---|
| | |

_____ **CAUSE OF ACTION—**Common Counts     **Page** _____
    *(number)*

ATTACHMENT TO ☐ Complaint ☐ Cross-Complaint

*(Use a separate cause of action form for each cause of action.)*

CC-1. Plaintiff *(name)*:

    alleges that defendant *(name)*:

    became indebted to ☐ plaintiff ☐ other *(name)*:

    a. ☐ within the last four years
        (1) ☐ on an open book account for money due.
        (2) ☐ because an account was stated in writing by and between plaintiff and defendant in which it
             was agreed that defendant was indebted to plaintiff.

    b. ☐ within the last ☐ two years ☐ four years
        (1) ☐ for money had and received by defendant for the use and benefit of plaintiff.
        (2) ☐ for work, labor, services and materials rendered at the special instance and request of defendant
             and for which defendant promised to pay plaintiff
             ☐ the sum of $
             ☐ the reasonable value.
        (3) ☐ for goods, wares, and merchandise sold and delivered to defendant and for which defendant
             promised to pay plaintiff
             ☐ the sum of $
             ☐ the reasonable value.
        (4) ☐ for money lent by plaintiff to defendant at defendant's request.
        (5) ☐ for money paid, laid out, and expended to or for defendant at defendant's special instance and
             request.
        (6) ☐ other *(specify)*:

CC-2. **$** _____ , which is the reasonable value, is due and unpaid despite plaintiff's demand,
    plus prejudgment interest ☐ according to proof ☐ at the rate of _____ percent per year
    from *(date)*:

CC-3. ☐ Plaintiff is entitled to attorney fees by an agreement or a statute
         ☐ of $
         ☐ according to proof.

CC.4. ☐ Other:

Form Approved by the
Judicial Council of California
Effective January 1, 1982
    Rule 982.1(22)
         **CAUSE OF ACTION—**Common Counts          CCP 425.12

# OFFICIAL FORM CAUSE OF ACTION
# FRAUD

| SHORT TITLE | CASE NUMBER |
|---|---|
| | |

_____ **CAUSE OF ACTION—Fraud**                    Page _____
(number)

ATTACHMENT TO ☐ Complaint ☐ Cross-Complaint

*(Use a separate cause of action form for each cause of action.)*

FR-1.  Plaintiff *(name):*

alleges that defendant *(name):*

on or about *(date).*                              defrauded plaintiff as follows:

FR-2. ☐  **Intentional or Negligent Misrepresentation**
     a. Defendant made representations of material fact ☐ as stated in Attachment FR-2.a ☐ as follows:

     b. These representations were in fact false. The truth was ☐ as stated in Attachment FR-2.b ☐ as follows:

     c. When defendant made the representations,
        ☐ defendant knew they were false, or
        ☐ defendant had no reasonable ground for believing the representations were true

     d. Defendant made the representations with the intent to defraud and induce plaintiff to act as described
        in item FR-5. At the time plaintiff acted, plaintiff did not know the representations were false and believed
        they were true. Plaintiff acted in justifiable reliance upon the truth of the representations.

FR-3. ☐  **Concealment**
     a. Defendant concealed or suppressed material facts ☐ as stated in Attachment FR-3.a ☐ as follows:

     b. Defendant concealed or suppressed material facts
        ☐ defendant was bound to disclose.
        ☐ by telling plaintiff other facts to mislead plaintiff and prevent plaintiff from discovering the concealed
           or suppressed facts.

     c. Defendant concealed or suppressed these facts with the intent to defraud and induce plaintiff to act
        as described in item FR-5. At the time plaintiff acted, plaintiff was unaware of the concealed or suppressed
        facts and would not have taken the action if plaintiff had known the facts.

(Continued)

Form Approved by the
Judicial Council of California
Effective January 1, 1982        **CAUSE OF ACTION—Fraud**              CCP 425 12
Rule 982 1(23)

| SHORT TITLE | CASE NUMBER |
|---|---|
|  |  |

_____ **CAUSE OF ACTION**—Fraud (Continued)                    Page _____
    (number)

FR-4. ☐ **Promise Without Intent to Perform**

   a. Defendant made a promise about a material matter without any intention of performing it ☐ as stated in Attachment FR-4.a ☐ as follows:

   b. Defendant's promise without any intention of performance was made with the intent to defraud and induce plaintiff to rely upon it and to act as described in item FR-5. At the time plaintiff acted, plaintiff was unaware of defendant's intention not to perform the promise. Plaintiff acted in justifiable reliance upon the promise.

FR-5. In justifiable reliance upon defendant's conduct, plaintiff was induced to act ☐ as stated in Attachment FR-5 ☐ as follows:

FR-6. Because of plaintiff's reliance upon defendant's conduct, plaintiff has been damaged ☐ as stated in Attachment FR-6 ☐ as follows:

FR-7. Other:

                                    Rev. #1 1995

**[FORM 6:N]**

# OFFICIAL FORM ANSWER
# CONTRACT

| ATTORNEY OR PARTY WITHOUT ATTORNEY (NAME AND ADDRESS)   TELEPHONE | FOR COURT USE ONLY |
|---|---|
| ATTORNEY FOR (NAME) | |

Insert name of court, judicial district or branch court, if any, and post office and street address:

PLAINTIFF

DEFENDANT

| ANSWER—Contract | CASE NUMBER |
|---|---|
| ☐ TO COMPLAINT OF *(name):* <br> ☐ TO CROSS-COMPLAINT OF *(name):* | |

1. This pleading, including attachments and exhibits, consists of the following number of pages: _____
2. DEFENDANT *(name):*

   answers the complaint or cross-complaint as follows:
3. *Check ONLY ONE of the next two boxes:*
   a. ☐ Defendant generally denies each statement of the complaint or cross-complaint. *(Do not check this box if the verified complaint or cross-complaint demands more than $1,000.)*
   b. ☐ Defendant admits that all of the statements of the complaint or cross-complaint are true EXCEPT:
      (1) Defendant claims the following statements are false *(use paragraph numbers or explain):*

      ☐ Continued on Attachment 3.b.(1).
      (2) Defendant has no information or belief that the following statements are true, so defendant denies them *(use paragraph numbers or explain):*

      ☐ Continued on Attachment 3.b.(2).
                     (Continued)

If this form is used to answer a cross-complaint, plaintiff means cross-complainant and defendant means cross-defendant.
Form Approved by the
Judicial Council of California
Effective January 1, 1982
Rule 982 1(35)          **ANSWER—Contract**                    CCP 425.12

### ANSWER—Contract

4. ☐ AFFIRMATIVE DEFENSES
   Defendant alleges the following additional reasons that plaintiff is not entitled to recover anything:

☐ Continued on Attachment 4.

5. ☐ Other:

6. DEFENDANT PRAYS
   a. that plaintiff take nothing.
   b. ☐ for costs of suit.
   c. ☐ other *(specify):*

_____          _____
(Type or print name)                      (Signature of party or attorney)

Page two

6-186

# OFFICIAL FORM COMPLAINT
# UNLAWFUL DETAINER

982.1(90)

| ATTORNEY OR PARTY WITHOUT ATTORNEY (Name, state bar number, and address): | FOR COURT USE ONLY |
|---|---|
| TELEPHONE NO.:     FAX NO. (Optional): <br> E-MAIL ADDRESS (Optional): <br> ATTORNEY FOR (Name): | |

**SUPERIOR COURT OF CALIFORNIA, COUNTY OF**
STREET ADDRESS:
MAILING ADDRESS:
CITY AND ZIP CODE:
BRANCH NAME:

PLAINTIFF:

DEFENDANT:

☐ DOES 1 TO _____

| **COMPLAINT—Unlawful Detainer***<br>☐ COMPLAINT   ☐ AMENDED COMPLAINT (Number): | CASE NUMBER: |
|---|---|
| **Jurisdiction** (check all that apply):<br><br>☐ ACTION IS A LIMITED CIVIL CASE<br>    Amount Demanded    ☐ does not exceed $10,000<br>                          ☐ exceeds $10,000, but does not exceed $25,000<br>☐ ACTION IS AN UNLIMITED CIVIL CASE (exceeds $25,000)<br>☐ ACTION IS RECLASSIFIED by this amended complaint or cross–complaint<br>     ☐ from limited to unlimited<br>     ☐ from unlimited to limited | |

1. PLAINTIFF (names):

    alleges causes of action against DEFENDANT (names):

2. a. Plaintiff is    (1) ☐ an individual over the age of 18 years    (4) ☐ a partnership
                     (2) ☐ a public agency                          (5) ☐ a corporation
                     (3) ☐ other (specify):
   b. ☐ Plaintiff has complied with the fictitious business name laws and is doing business under the fictitious name of
       (specify):
3. Defendants named above are in possession of the premises located at (street address, apt. no., city, zip code, and county):

4. Plaintiff's interest in the premises is   ☐ as owner   ☐ other (specify):
5. The true names and capacities of defendants sued as Does are unknown to plaintiff.
6. a. On or about (date):          defendants (names):
     (1) agreed to rent the premises for a   ☐ month-to-month tenancy   ☐ other tenancy (specify):
     (2) agreed to pay rent of $         payable   ☐ monthly   ☐ other (specify frequency):
         The rent is due on the   ☐ first of the month   ☐ other day (specify):
   b. This ☐ written   ☐ oral agreement was made with
     (1) ☐ plaintiff                        (3) ☐ plaintiff's predecessor in interest
     (2) ☐ plaintiff's agent             (4) ☐ other (specify):
   c. ☐ The defendants not named in item 6a are
     (1) ☐ subtenants    (2) ☐ assignees    (3) ☐ other (specify):
   d. ☐ The agreement was later changed as follows (specify):

   e. ☐ A copy of the written agreement is attached and labeled Exhibit 1.

**\*NOTE:** Do not use this form for evictions after sale (Code Civ. Proc., § 1161a).

Page 1 of 3

Form Approved for Optional Use<br>Judicial Council of California<br>982.1(90) [Rev. July 1, 2002]

**COMPLAINT—Unlawful Detainer**

Civil Code, § 1940 et seq.;
Code of Civil Procedure, § 425.12

7. ☐ a. Defendants (names):

were served the following notice on the same date and in the same manner:

    (1) ☐ 3-day notice to pay rent or quit     (4) ☐ 3-day notice to quit

    (2) ☐ 3-day notice to perform covenants or quit     (5) ☐ 30-day notice to quit

    (3) ☐ other (specify):

  b. (1) On (date):     the period stated in the notice expired at the end of the day.

    (2) Defendants failed to comply with the requirements of the notice by that date.

  c. All facts stated in the notice are true.

  d. ☐ The notice included an election of forfeiture.

  e. ☐ A copy of the notice is attached and labeled Exhibit 2.

  f. ☐ One or more defendants was served (1) with a different notice, or (2) on a different date, or (3) in a different manner, as stated in attachment 7f. *(Check item 8c and attach a statement providing the information required by items 7a-e and 8 for each defendant.)*

8. a. ☐ The notice in item 7a was served on the defendants named in item 7a as follows:

    (1) ☐ by personally handing a copy to defendant on (date):

    (2) ☐ by leaving a copy with (name or description):     , a person of suitable age and discretion, on (date):     at defendant's ☐ residence ☐ business AND mailing a copy to defendant at defendant's place of residence on (date): because defendant cannot be found at defendant's residence or usual place of business.

    (3) ☐ by posting a copy on the premises on (date):   ( ☐ and giving a copy to a person found residing at the premises) AND mailing a copy to defendant at the premises on (date):

        (a) ☐ because defendant's residence and usual place of business cannot be ascertained OR

        (b) ☐ because no person of suitable age or discretion can be found there.

    (4) ☐ (not for 3-day notice; see Civil Code section 1946 before using) by sending a copy by certified or registered mail addressed to defendant on (date):

    (5) ☐ (not for residential tenancies; see Civil Code section 1953 before using) in the manner specified in a written commercial lease between the parties.

  b. ☐ (Name):     was served on behalf of all defendants who signed a joint written rental agreement.

  c. ☐ Information about service of notice on the defendants named in item 7f is stated in attachment 8c.

9. ☐ Plaintiff demands possession from each defendant because of expiration of a fixed-term lease.

10. ☐ At the time the 3-day notice to pay rent or quit was served, the amount of **rent due** was $

11. ☐ The fair rental value of the premises is $     per day.

12. ☐ Defendants' continued possession is malicious, and plaintiff is entitled to statutory damages under Code of Civil Procedure section 1174(b). *(State specific facts supporting a claim up to $600 in attachment 12.)*

13. ☐ A written agreement between the parties provides for attorney fees.

14. ☐ Defendants' tenancy is subject to the local rent control or eviction control ordinance of (city or county, title of ordinance, and date of passage):

    Plaintiff has met all applicable requirements of the ordinances.

15. ☐ Other allegations are stated in attachment 15.

16. Plaintiff remits to the jurisdictional limit, if any, of the court.

17. PLAINTIFF REQUESTS

  a. possession of the premises.     f. ☐ damages at the rate stated in item 11 from

  b. costs incurred in this proceeding.     (date):     for each day

  c. ☐ past due rent of $     defendants remain in possession through entry of judgment.

  d. ☐ reasonable attorney fees.     g. ☐ statutory damages up to $600 for the conduct alleged in item 12.

  e. ☐ forfeiture of the agreement.     h. ☐ other (specify):

18. ☐ Number of pages attached (specify):

| PLAINTIFF *(Name):* | CASE NUMBER: |
|---|---|
| DEFENDANT *(Name):* | |

UNLAWFUL DETAINER ASSISTANT (Business and Professions Code sections 6400-6415)

19. *This item must be answered in all cases.* An unlawful detainer assistant ☐ did **not** ☐ did for compensation give advice or
    assistance with this form. *(If plaintiff has received **any** help or advice for pay from an unlawful detainer assistant, state):*
    a. Assistant's name:                          b. Telephone No.:
    c. Street address, city, and ZIP:

    d. County of registration:          e. Registration No.:              f. Expires on *(date):*

▶

| _____ | _____ |
|---|---|
| (TYPE OR PRINT NAME) | (SIGNATURE OF PLAINTIFF OR ATTORNEY) |

**VERIFICATION**
*(Use a different verification form if the verification is by an attorney or for a corporation or partnership.)*
I am the plaintiff in this proceeding and have read this complaint. I declare under penalty of perjury under the laws of the State of
California that the foregoing is true and correct.
Date:

▶

| _____ | _____ |
|---|---|
| (TYPE OR PRINT NAME) | (SIGNATURE OF PLAINTIFF) |

Rev. #1 2003                                                                 **6-188.1**

**RESERVED**

# OFFICIAL FORM ANSWER
# UNLAWFUL DETAINER

| ATTORNEY OR PARTY WITHOUT ATTORNEY *(Name and Address)* | TELEPHONE NO | FOR COURT USE ONLY |
|---|---|---|
| | | |

ATTORNEY FOR *(Name)*

NAME OF COURT

STREET ADDRESS

MAILING ADDRESS

CITY AND ZIP CODE

BRANCH NAME

PLAINTIFF:

DEFENDANT:

| **ANSWER—Unlawful Detainer** | CASE NUMBER |
|---|---|

1. Defendant *(names)*:

    answers the complaint as follows:

2. **Check ONLY ONE of the next two boxes:**
    a. ☐ Defendant generally denies each statement of the complaint. *(Do not check this box if the complaint demands more than $1,000).*
    b. ☐ Defendant admits that all of the statements of the complaint are true EXCEPT
       (1) Defendant claims the following statements of the complaint are false *(use paragraph numbers from the complaint or explain)*:

       ☐ Continued on Attachment 2b(1).
       (2) Defendant has no information or belief that the following statements of the complaint are true, so defendant denies them *(use paragraph numbers from the complaint or explain)*:

       ☐ Continued on Attachment 2b(2).

3. AFFIRMATIVE DEFENSES    *(NOTE: For each box checked, you must state brief facts to support it in the space provided at the top of page two (item 3j).)*
    a. ☐ *(nonpayment of rent only)* Plaintiff has breached the warranty to provide habitable premises
    b. ☐ *(nonpayment of rent only)* Defendant made needed repairs and properly deducted the cost from the rent, and plaintiff did not give proper credit.
    c. ☐ *(nonpayment of rent only)* On *(date)*:                        , before the notice to pay or quit expired, defendant offered the rent due but plaintiff would not accept it
    d. ☐ Plaintiff waived, changed, or canceled the notice to quit.
    e. ☐ Plaintiff served defendant with the notice to quit or filed the complaint to retaliate against defendant.
    f. ☐ By serving defendant with the notice to quit or filing the complaint, plaintiff is arbitrarily discriminating against the defendant in violation of the Constitution or laws of the United States or California.
    g. ☐ Plaintiff's demand for possession violates the local rent control or eviction control ordinance of *(city or county, title of ordinance, and date of passage)*:

       *(Also, briefly state the facts showing violation of the ordinance in item 3j.)*
    h. ☐ Plaintiff accepted rent from defendant to cover a period of time after the date the notice to quit expired.
    i. ☐ Other affirmative defenses are stated in item 3j.

(Continued on reverse)

Form Approved by the
Judicial Council of California
982 1(95) [Rev. January 1 1997]
**ANSWER—Unlawful Detainer**
Civil Code § 1940 et seq.
Code of Civil Procedure § 425 12

| PLAINTIFF *(Name)* | CASE NUMBER |
|---|---|
| DEFENDANT *(Name)* | |

3. AFFIRMATIVE DEFENSES *(cont'd)*

    j. Facts supporting affirmative defenses checked above *(identify each item separately by its letter from page one)*:

    (1) ☐ All the facts are stated in Attachment 3j.    (2) ☐ Facts are continued in Attachment 3j.

4. OTHER STATEMENTS

    a. ☐ Defendant vacated the premises on *(date)*:

    b. ☐ The fair rental value of the premises alleged in the complaint is excessive *(explain)*:

    c. ☐ Other *(specify)*:

5. DEFENDANT REQUESTS

    a. that plaintiff take nothing requested in the complaint.

    b. costs incurred in this proceeding.

    c. ☐ reasonable attorney fees.

    d. ☐ that plaintiff be ordered to (1) make repairs and correct the conditions that constitute a breach of the warranty to provide habitable premises and (2) reduce the monthly rent to a reasonable rental value until the conditions are corrected.

    e. ☐ other *(specify)*:

6. ☐ Number of pages attached *(specify)*:

**UNLAWFUL DETAINER ASSISTANT (Business and Professions Code sections 6400-6415)**

7. *(Must be completed in all cases)* An **unlawful detainer assistant** ☐ did not ☐ did for compensation give advice or assistance with this form. *(If defendant has received any help or advice for pay from an unlawful detainer assistant, state)*:

    a. Assistant's name:            b. Telephone No.:

    c. Street address, city, and ZIP:

    d. County of registration:        e. Registration No.:        f. Expires on *(date)*

▶

_____    _____

(TYPE OR PRINT NAME)            (SIGNATURE OF DEFENDANT OR ATTORNEY)

▶

_____    _____

(TYPE OR PRINT NAME)            (SIGNATURE OF DEFENDANT OR ATTORNEY)

*(Each defendant for whom this answer is filed must be named in item 1 and must sign this answer unless his or her attorney signs.)*

**VERIFICATION**

*(Use a different verification form if the verification is by an attorney or for a corporation or partnership.)*

I am the defendant in this proceeding and have read this answer. I declare under penalty of perjury under the laws of the State of California that the foregoing is true and correct.

Date

▶

_____    _____

(TYPE OR PRINT NAME)            (SIGNATURE OF DEFENDANT)

982 1(95) [Rev. January 1 1997]    **ANSWER—Unlawful Detainer**    Page two

# ATTACHMENT TO JUDICIAL COUNSEL FORM

MC-025

| SHORT TITLE: | CASE NUMBER: |
|---|---|

**ATTACHMENT** *(Number):* _____     Page ____ of ____
*(This Attachment may be used with any Judicial Council form.)*     *(Add pages as required)*

1
2
3
4
5
6
7
8
9
10
11
12
13
14
15
16
17
18
19
20
21
22
23
24
25
26
27   *(If the item that this Attachment concerns is made under penalty of perjury, all statements in this Attachment are made under penalty of perjury.)*

Form Approved for Optional Use
Judicial Council of California
MC-025 [New July 1, 2002]

**ATTACHMENT**
**to Judicial Council Form**

Cal. Rules of Court, rule 982

# [FORM 6:Q]

## COMPLAINT
## FIRST PAGE FORMAT

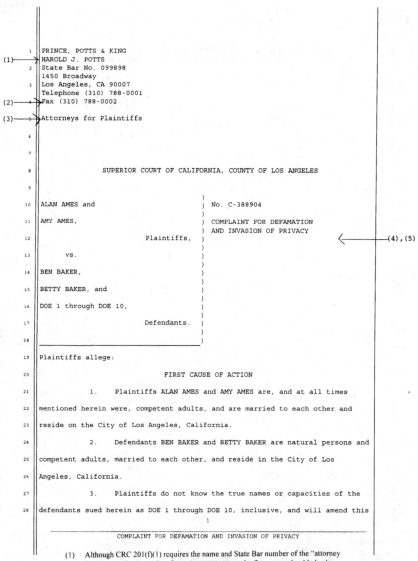

PRINCE, POTTS & KING
HAROLD J. POTTS
State Bar No. 099898
1450 Broadway
Los Angeles, CA 90007
Telephone (310) 788-0001
Fax (310) 788-0002

Attorneys for Plaintiffs

SUPERIOR COURT OF CALIFORNIA, COUNTY OF LOS ANGELES

ALAN AMES and ) No. C-388904
)
AMY AMES, ) COMPLAINT FOR DEFAMATION
) AND INVASION OF PRIVACY
Plaintiffs, )
)
vs. )
)
BEN BAKER, )
)
BETTY BAKER, and )
)
DOE 1 through DOE 10, )
)
Defendants. )
)

Plaintiffs allege:

FIRST CAUSE OF ACTION

1.  Plaintiffs ALAN AMES and AMY AMES are, and at all times mentioned herein were, competent adults, and are married to each other and reside on the City of Los Angeles, California.

2.  Defendants BEN BAKER and BETTY BAKER are natural persons and competent adults, married to each other, and reside in the City of Los Angeles, California.

3.  Plaintiffs do not know the true names or capacities of the defendants sued herein as DOE 1 through DOE 10, inclusive, and will amend this

1

COMPLAINT FOR DEFAMATION AND INVASION OF PRIVACY

(1)  Although CRC 201(f)(1) requires the name and State Bar number of the "attorney for the party," where a law firm represents a party the firm name should also be included.
(2)  Inclusion of fax number and e-mail address is optional; it does not itself constitute consent to service of responsive papers by fax or e-mail. [CRC 201(f), 2008(b)]
(3)  Sufficient only if all plaintiffs represented by these attorneys; if there are other plaintiffs, the name of each plaintiff represented should be given.
(4)  *If this is a limited civil case*, add the following: "This is a limited civil case."
"The amount demanded exceeds $10,000." *OR*
"The amount demanded does not exceed $10,000."
(5)  If case has been assigned to a particular judge, add name of judge and department number.

# CIVIL CASE COVER SHEET

CM-010

| ATTORNEY OR PARTY WITHOUT ATTORNEY *(Name, state bar number, and address)*: | FOR COURT USE ONLY |
|---|---|
| | |

TELEPHONE NO.:        FAX NO.:

ATTORNEY FOR *(Name)*:

SUPERIOR COURT OF CALIFORNIA, COUNTY OF
STREET ADDRESS:
MAILING ADDRESS:
CITY AND ZIP CODE:
BRANCH NAME:

CASE NAME:

| **CIVIL CASE COVER SHEET** | | **Complex Case Designation** | CASE NUMBER: |
|---|---|---|---|
| ☐ **Unlimited** (Amount demanded exceeds $25,000) | ☐ **Limited** (Amount demanded is $25,000 or less) | ☐ **Counter** ☐ **Joinder** Filed with first appearance by defendant (Cal. Rules of Court, rule 1811) | JUDGE: DEPT.: |

*All five (5) items below must be completed (see instructions on page 2).*

1. Check **one** box below for the case type that best describes this case:

| **Auto Tort** | **Contract** | **Provisionally Complex Civil Litigation** (Cal. Rules of Court, rules 1800–1812) |
|---|---|---|
| ☐ Auto (22) | ☐ Breach of contract/warranty (06) | ☐ Antitrust/Trade regulation (03) |
| ☐ Uninsured motorist (46) | ☐ Collections (09) | ☐ Construction defect (10) |
| **Other PI/PD/WD (Personal Injury/Property Damage/Wrongful Death) Tort** | ☐ Insurance coverage (18) | ☐ Mass tort (40) |
| | ☐ Other contract (37) | ☐ Securities litigation (28) |
| ☐ Asbestos (04) | **Real Property** | ☐ Environmental /Toxic tort (30) |
| ☐ Product liability (24) | ☐ Eminent domain/Inverse condemnation (14) | ☐ Insurance coverage claims arising from the above listed provisionally complex case types (41) |
| ☐ Medical malpractice (45) | | |
| ☐ Other PI/PD/WD (23) | ☐ Wrongful eviction (33) | **Enforcement of Judgment** |
| **Non-PI/PD/WD (Other) Tort** | ☐ Other real property (26) | ☐ Enforcement of judgment (20) |
| ☐ Business tort/unfair business practice (07) | **Unlawful Detainer** | **Miscellaneous Civil Complaint** |
| ☐ Civil rights (08) | ☐ Commercial (31) | ☐ RICO (27) |
| ☐ Defamation (13) | ☐ Residential (32) | ☐ Other complaint *(not specified above)* (42) |
| ☐ Fraud (16) | ☐ Drugs (38) | **Miscellaneous Civil Petition** |
| ☐ Intellectual property (19) | **Judicial Review** | ☐ Partnership and corporate governance (21) |
| ☐ Professional negligence (25) | ☐ Asset forfeiture (05) | ☐ Other petition *(not specified above)* (43) |
| ☐ Other non-PI/PD/WD tort (35) | ☐ Petition re: arbitration award (11) | |
| **Employment** | ☐ Writ of mandate (02) | |
| ☐ Wrongful termination (36) | ☐ Other judicial review (39) | |
| ☐ Other employment (15) | | |

2. This case ☐ is ☐ is not complex under rule 1800 of the California Rules of Court. If the case is complex, mark the factors requiring exceptional judicial management:
   a. ☐ Large number of separately represented parties    d. ☐ Large number of witnesses
   b. ☐ Extensive motion practice raising difficult or novel    e. ☐ Coordination with related actions pending in one or more courts issues that will be time-consuming to resolve      in other counties, states or countries, or in a federal court
   c. ☐ Substantial amount of documentary evidence    f. ☐ Substantial post-judgment judicial supervision
3. Type of remedies sought *(check all that apply)*:
   a. ☐ monetary   b. ☐ nonmonetary; declaratory or injunctive relief   c. ☐ punitive
4. Number of causes of action *(specify)*:
5. This case ☐ is ☐ is not a class action suit.
Date:      ▶

_____      _____
(TYPE OR PRINT NAME)        (SIGNATURE OF PARTY OR ATTORNEY FOR PARTY)

**NOTICE**
- Plaintiff must file this cover sheet with the first paper filed in the action or proceeding (except small claims cases or cases filed under the Probate, Family, or Welfare and Institutions Code). (Cal. Rules of Court, rule 201.8.) Failure to file may result in sanctions.
- File this cover sheet in addition to any cover sheet required by local court rule.
- If this case is complex under rule 1800 et seq. of the California Rules of Court, you must serve a copy of this cover sheet on **all** other parties to the action or proceeding.
- Unless this is a complex case, this cover sheet will be used for statistical purposes only.

Page 1 of 2

| Form Adopted for Mandatory Use Judicial Council of California CM-010 [Rev. July 1, 2003] | **CIVIL CASE COVER SHEET** | Cal. Rules of Court, rules 201.8, 1800–1812; Standards of Judicial Administration, § 19 www.courtinfo.ca.gov American LegalNet, Inc. www.USCourtForms.com |
|---|---|---|

# INSTRUCTIONS ON HOW TO COMPLETE THE COVER SHEET

**To Plaintiffs and Others Filing First Papers**

If you are filing a first paper (for example, a complaint) in a civil case, you **must** complete and file, along with your first paper, the *Civil Case Cover Sheet* contained on page 1. This information will be used to compile statistics about the types and numbers of cases filed. You must check **all five** items on the sheet. In item 1, you must check **one** box for the case type that best describes the case. If the case fits both a general and a more specific type of case listed in item 1, check the more specific one. If the case has multiple causes of action, check the box that best indicates the **primary** cause of action. To assist you in completing the sheet, examples of the cases that belong under each case type in item 1 are provided below. A cover sheet must be filed only with your initial paper. You do not need to submit a cover sheet with amended papers. Failure to file a cover sheet with the first paper filed in a civil case may subject a party, its counsel, or both to sanctions under rules 201.8(c) and 227 of the California Rules of Court.

**To Parties in Complex Cases**

In complex cases only, parties must also use the *Civil Case Cover Sheet* to designate whether the case is complex. If a plaintiff believes the case is complex under rule 1800 of the California Rules of Court, this must be indicated by completing the appropriate boxes in items 1 and 2. If a plaintiff designates a case as complex, the cover sheet must be served with the complaint on all parties to the action. A defendant may file and serve no later than the time of its first appearance a joinder in the plaintiff's designation, a counter-designation that the case is not complex, or, if the plaintiff has made no designation, a designation that the case is complex.

## CASE TYPES AND EXAMPLES

**Auto Tort**
Auto (22)–Personal Injury/Property Damage/Wrongful Death
Uninsured Motorist (46) *(if the case involves an uninsured motorist claim subject to arbitration, check this item instead of Auto)*

**Other PI/PD/WD (Personal Injury/ Property Damage/Wrongful Death) Tort**
Asbestos (04)
  Asbestos Property Damage
  Asbestos Personal Injury/ Wrongful Death
Product Liability *(not asbestos or toxic/environmental)* (24)
Medical Malpractice (45)
  Medical Malpractice– Physicians & Surgeons
  Other Professional Health Care Malpractice
Other PI/PD/WD (23)
  Premises Liability (e.g., slip and fall)
  Intentional Bodily Injury/PD/WD (e.g., assault, vandalism)
  Intentional Infliction of Emotional Distress
  Negligent Infliction of Emotional Distress
  Other PI/PD/WD

**Non-PI/PD/WD (Other) Tort**
Business Tort/Unfair Business Practice (07)
Civil Rights (e.g., discrimination, false arrest) *(not civil harassment)*(08)
Defamation (e.g., slander, libel) (13)
Fraud (16)
Intellectual Property (19)
Professional Negligence (25)
  Legal Malpractice
  Other Professional Malpractice *(not medical or legal)*
Other Non-PI/PD/WD Tort (35)

**Employment**
Wrongful Termination (36)
Other Employment (15)

**Contract**
Breach of Contract/Warranty (06)
  Breach of Rental/Lease Contract *(not unlawful detainer or wrongful eviction)*
  Contract/Warranty Breach–Seller Plaintiff *(not fraud or negligence)*
  Negligent Breach of Contract/ Warranty
  Other Breach of Contract/Warranty
Collections (e.g., money owed, open book accounts) (09)
  Collection Case–Seller Plaintiff
  Other Promissory Note/Collections Case
Insurance Coverage *(not provisionally complex)* (18)
  Auto Subrogation
  Other Coverage
Other Contract (37)
  Contractual Fraud
  Other Contract Dispute

**Real Property**
Eminent Domain/Inverse Condemnation(14)
Wrongful Eviction (33)
Other Real Property (e.g., quiet title) (26)
  Writ of Possession of Real Property
  Mortgage Foreclosure
  Quiet Title
  Other Real Property *(not eminent domain, landlord/tenant, or foreclosure)*

**Unlawful Detainer**
Commercial (31)
Residential (32)
Drugs (38) *(if the case involves illegal drugs, check this item; otherwise, report as Commercial or Residential.)*

**Judicial Review**
Asset Forfeiture (05)
Petition Re: Arbitration Award (11)
Writ of Mandate (02)
  Writ–Administrative Mandamus
  Writ–Mandamus on Limited Court Case Matter
  Writ–Other Limited Court Case Review
Other Judicial Review (39)
  Review of Health Officer Order
  Notice of Appeal–Labor Commissioner Appeals

**Provisionally Complex Civil Litigation (Cal. Rules of Court Rule 1800-1812)**
Antitrust/Trade Regulation (03)
Construction Defect (10)
Claims Involving Mass Tort (40)
Securities Litigation (28)
Toxic Tort/Environmental (30)
Insurance Coverage Claims *(arising from provisionally complex case type listed above)* (41)

**Enforcement of Judgment**
Enforcement of Judgment (20)
  Abstract of Judgment (Out of County)
  Confession of Judgment *(non-domestic relations)*
  Sister State Judgment
  Administrative Agency Award *(not unpaid taxes)*
  Petition/Certification of Entry of Judgment on Unpaid Tax
  Other Enforcement of Judgment Case

**Miscellaneous Civil Complaint**
RICO (27)
Other Complaint *(not specified above)* (42)
  Declaratory Relief Only
  Injunctive Relief Only *(non-harassment)*
  Mechanics Lien
  Other Commercial Complaint Case *(non-tort/non-complex)*
  Other Civil Complaint *(non-tort/non-complex)*

**Miscellaneous Civil Petition**
Partnership and Corporate Governance (21)
Other Petition *(not specified above)* (43)
  Civil Harassment
  Workplace Violence
  Elder/Dependent Adult Abuse
  Election Contest
  Petition for Name Change
  Petition for Relief from Late Claim
  Other Civil Petition

# CIVIL CASE COVER SHEET ADDENDUM
# AND STATEMENT OF LOCATION
## (Los Angeles Superior Court)

| SHORT TITLE: | CASE NUMBER |
|---|---|
| | |

### CIVIL CASE COVER SHEET ADDENDUM AND STATEMENT OF LOCATION
### (CERTIFICATE OF GROUNDS FOR ASSIGNMENT TO COURTHOUSE LOCATION)

**This form is required in all new civil case filings in the Los Angeles Superior Court**

I. Check the types of hearing and fill in the estimated length of hearing expected for this case:

JURY TRIAL? ☐ YES    CLASS ACTION? ☐YES    LIMITED CASE? ☐YES    TIME ESTIMATED FOR TRIAL_____ ☐ HOURS/ ☐ DAYS.

II. Select the correct district and courthouse location (4 steps – if you checked "Limited Case", skip to No. III, Pg. 4):

**1** After first completing the Civil Case Cover Sheet Form, find the main civil case cover sheet heading for your case in the left margin below, and, to the right in Column **1**, the Civil Case Cover Sheet case type you selected.

**2** Check **one** Superior Court type of action in Column **2** below which best describes the nature of this case.

**3** In Column **3**, circle the reason for the court location choice that applies to the type of action you have checked.

#### Applicable Reasons for Choosing Courthouse Location (See Column 3 below)

1. Class Actions must be filed in County Courthouse, Central District
2. May be filed in Central(Other county, or no Bodily Inj/Prop.Damage)
3. Location where cause of action arose.
4. Location where bodily injury, death or damage occurred.
5. Location where performance required or defendant resides.
6. Location of property or permanently garaged vehicle.
7. Location where petitioner resides.
8. Location wherein defendant/respondent functions wholly.
9. Location where one or more of the parties reside.
10. Location of Labor Commissioner Office.

**4** Fill in the information requested on page 4 in item III; complete item IV.  Sign the certificate.

| | -1-<br>Civil Case Cover Sheet<br>Category No. | -2-<br>Type of Action<br>(Check only one) | -3-<br>Applicable Reasons -<br>See Step 3 Above |
|---|---|---|---|
| **Auto Tort** | Auto (22) | ☐ A7100  Motor Veh. - Pers. Injury/Prop. Dam./Wrongful Death | 1., 2., 4. |
| | Uninsured Motorist (46) | ☐ A7110  Pers. Inj/Prop. Dam./Wrongful Death - Unins. Motorist | 1., 2., 4. |
| **Other PI/PD/WD Tort** | Asbestos (04) | ☐ A6070  Asbestos Property Damage | 2. |
| | | ☐ A7221  Asbestosis - Personal Injury/Wrongful Death | 2. |
| | Product Liability (24) | ☐ A7260  Product Liability (not asbestos or toxic/environmental) | 1., 2., 3., 4., 8. |
| | Medical Malpractice (45) | ☐ A7210  Medical Malpractice - Physicians & Surgeons | 1., 2., 4. |
| | | ☐ A7240  Other Professional Health Care Malpractice | 1., 2., 4. |
| | Other PI/PD/WD (23) | ☐ A7250  Premises Liability (e.g., slip and fall) | 1., 2., 4. |
| | | ☐ A7230  Intentional Bodily Injury/PD/WD (e.g., assault, vandalism, etc.) | 1., 2., 4. |
| | | ☐ A7270  Intentional Infliction of Emotional Distress | 1., 2., 3. |
| | | ☐ A7271  Negligent Infliction of Emotional Distress | 1., 2., 3. |
| | | ☐ A7220  Other Personal Injury/Property Dam./Wrongful Death | 1., 2., 4. |
| **Non-PI/PD/WD Tort** | Business Tort (07) | ☐ A6029  Other Commercial/Business Tort (not fraud/breach of contract) | 1., 2., 3. |
| | Civil Rights (08) | ☐ A6005  Civil Rights/Discrimination | 1., 2., 3. |
| | Defamation (13) | ☐ A6010  Defamation (slander/libel) | 1., 2., 3. |
| | Fraud (16) | ☐ A6013  Fraud (no contract) | 1., 2., 3. |
| | Intellectual Property (19) | ☐ A6016  Intellectual Property | 2., 3. |

**CIVIL CASE COVER SHEET ADDENDUM AND STATEMENT OF LOCATION**  LASC Rule 2.0

CIV 109  09-03

Page 1 of 4

| | -1-<br>Civil Case Cover Sheet<br>Category No. | -2-<br>Type of Action<br>(Check only one) | -3-<br>Applicable Reasons -<br>See Step 3 Above |
|---|---|---|---|
| **Non-PI/PD/WD Tort (Cont.)** | Prof. Negligence (25) | ☐ A6017  Legal Malpractice | 1., 2., 3. |
| | | ☐ A6050  Other Professional Malpractice (not medical or legal) | 1., 2., 3. |
| | Oth Non-PI/PD/WD Tort (35) | ☐ A6025  Other Non-PI/PD/WD Tort - Intentional | 2., 3. |
| | | ☐ A6026  Other Non-PI/PD/WD Tort - Negligence | 2., 3. |
| **Employment** | Wrongful Termination (36) | ☐ A6037  Wrongful Termination | 1., 2., 3. |
| | Other Employment<br>(15) | ☐ A6024  Other Employment Complaint Case | 1., 2., 3. |
| | | ☐ A6109  Labor Commissioner Appeals | 10. |
| **Contract** | Breach of Contract/<br>Warranty<br>(06)<br>(not insurance) | ☐ A6004  Breach of Rental/Lease Contract (not UD or wrongful eviction) | 2., 5. |
| | | ☐ A6008  Contract/Warranty Breach -Seller Plaintiff(no fraud/negligence) | 2., 5. |
| | | ☐ A6019  Negligent Breach of Contract/Warranty (no fraud) | 1., 2., 5. |
| | | ☐ A6028  Other Breach of Contract/Warranty (not fraud or negligence) | 1., 2., 5. |
| | Collections<br>(09) | ☐ A6002  Collections Case-Seller Plaintiff | 2., 5., 6. |
| | | ☐ A6012  Other Promissory Note/Collections Case | 2., 5. |
| | Insurance Coverage<br>(18) | ☐ A6015  Insurance Coverage (not complex) | 1., 2., 5., 8. |
| | Other Contract<br>(37) | ☐ A6009  Contractural Fraud | 1., 2., 3., 5. |
| | | ☐ A6031  Tortious Interference | 1., 2., 3., 5. |
| | | ☐ A6027  Other Contract Dispute(not breach/insurance/fraud/negligence) | 1., 2., 3., 8. |
| **Real Property** | Emnt Dom/Inv. Cond. (14) | ☐ A7300  Eminent Domain/Condemnation   Number of parcels_____ | 2. |
| | Wrongful Eviction (33) | ☐ A6023  Wrongful Eviction Case | 2., 6. |
| | Other Real Property<br>(26) | ☐ A6018  Mortgage Foreclosure | 2., 6. |
| | | ☐ A6032  Quiet Title | 2., 6. |
| | | ☐ A6060  Other Real Property(not em. domain, landlord/tenant, foreclosure) | 2., 6. |
| **Unlawful Detainer** | Unl. Det.-Commercial (31) | ☐ A6021  Unlawful Detainer-Commercial (not drugs or wrongful eviction) | 2., 6. |
| | Unl. Det.-Residential (32) | ☐ A6020  Unlawful Detainer-Residential (not drugs or wrongful eviction) | 2., 6. |
| | Unl. Det.-Drugs (38) | ☐ A6022  Unlawful Detainer-Drugs | 2., 6. |
| **Judicial Review** | Asset Forfeiture (05) | ☐ A6108  Asset Forfeiture Case | 2., 6. |

**CIVIL CASE COVER SHEET ADDENDUM AND STATEMENT OF LOCATION**  LASC Rule 2.0

CIV 109  09-03

Page 2 of 4

| -1-<br>Civil Case Cover Sheet<br>Category No. | -2-<br>Type of Action<br>(Check only one) | -3-<br>Applicable Reasons -<br>See Step 3 Above |
|---|---|---|
| Petition re Arbitration (11) | A6115 Petition to Compel/Confirm Arbitration | 2., 5. |
| Writ of Mandate<br><br>(02) | A6151 Writ - Administrative Mandamus | 2., 8. |
| | A6152 Writ - Mandamus on Limited Court Case Matter | 2. |
| | A6153 Writ - Other Limited Court Case Review | 2. |
| Oth. Jud. Review (39) | A6150 Other Writ /Judicial Review | 2., 8. |
| Antitrust/Trade Reg. (03) | A6003 Antitrust/Trade Regulation | 1., 2., 8. |
| Construction Defect (10) | A6007 Construction defect | 1., 2., 3. |
| Claims Inv. Mass Tort (40) | A6006 Claims Involving Mass Tort | 1., 2., 8. |
| Securities Litig. (28) | A6035 Securities Litigation Case | 1., 2., 8. |
| Tox. Tort/Envronm (30) | A6036 Toxic Tort/Environmental | 1., 2., 3., 8. |
| Ins Clms - Complx Case (41) | A6014 Insurance Coverage/Subrogation (complex case only) | 1., 2., 5., 8. |
| Enforcement<br>of Judgment<br><br>(20) | A6141 Sister State Judgment | 2., 9. |
| | A6160 Abstract of Judgment | 2., 6. |
| | A6107 Confession of Judgment (non-domestic relations) | 2., 9. |
| | A6140 Administrative Agency Award (not unpaid taxes) | 2., 8. |
| | A6114 Petition/Certificate for Entry of Judgment on Unpaid Tax | 2., 8. |
| | A6112 Other Enforcement of Judgment Case | 2., 8., 9. |
| RICO (27) | A6033 Racketeering (RICO) Case | 1., 2., 8. |
| Other Complaints<br>(Not Specified Above)<br><br>(42) | A6030 Declaratory Relief Only | 1., 2., 8. |
| | A6040 Injunctive Relief Only (not domestic/harassment) | 2., 8. |
| | A6011 Other Commercial Complaint Case (non-tort/non-complex) | 1., 2., 8. |
| | A6000 Other Civil Complaint (non-tort/non-complex) | 1., 2., 8. |
| Partnership/Corp.<br>Governance(21) | A6113 Partnership and Corporate Governance Case | 2., 8. |
| Other Petitions<br>(Not Specified Above)<br><br>(43) | A6121 Civil Harassment | 2., 3., 9. |
| | A6123 Workplace Harassment | 2., 3., 9 |
| | A6124 Elder/Dependent Adult Abuse Case | 2., 3., 9 |
| | A6190 Election Contest | 2. |
| | A6110 Petition for Change of Name | 2., 7. |
| | A6170 Petition for Relief from Late Claim Law | 2., 3., 4., 8. |
| | A6100 Other Civil Petition | 2., 9. |

Left margin (rotated): Judicial Review (Cont'd.) — Provisionally Complex Litig. — Enforcement of Judgment — Misc. Civil Petitions Misc. Civ. Cmplts

-4-

**CIVIL CASE COVER SHEET ADDENDUM AND STATEMENT OF LOCATION** LASC Rule 2.0

CIV 109 09-03

Page 3 of 4

| SHORT TITLE: | CASE NUMBER: |
|---|---|
| | |

III. Statement of Location: Enter the address of the accident, party residence or place of business, performance, or other circumstance indicated in No. II., item **3** on Page 1 as the proper reason for filing in the court location you selected.

| REASON: CHECK THE NUMBER UNDER ITEM -3- WHICH APPLIES IN THIS CASE | ADDRESS: |
|---|---|
| ☐1. ☐2. ☐3. ☐4. ☐5. ☐6. ☐7. ☐8. ☐9. ☐10. | |

| CITY: | STATE: | ZIP CODE: | |
|---|---|---|---|
| | | | |

IV. Certificate/Declaration of Assignment: The undersigned hereby certifies and declares that the above entitled matter is properly filed for assignment to the _____ courthouse in the _____ District of the Los Angeles Superior Court under Section 392 et seq., Code of Civil Procedure and Rule 2(b), (c) and (d) of this court for the reason checked above. I declare under penalty of perjury under the laws of the State of California that the foregoing is true and correct and this declaration was executed on_____at,_____California.

(date)          (city)

_____<br>(SIGNATURE OF ATTORNEY/FILING PARTY)

## New Civil Case Filing Instructions

This addendum form is required so that the court can assign your case to the correct courthouse location in the proper district for filing and hearing. It satisfies the requirement for a certificate as to reasons for authorizing filing in the courthouse location, as set forth in Los Angeles Superior Court Local Rule 2.0. It must be completed and submitted to the court along with the Civil Case Cover Sheet and the original Complaint or Petition in **ALL** civil cases filed in any district (including the Central District) of the Los Angeles County Superior Court. Copies of the cover sheet and this addendum must be served along with the summons and complaint, or other initiating pleading in the case.

> **PLEASE HAVE THE FOLLOWING DOCUMENTS COMPLETED AND READY TO BE FILED IN ORDER TO PROPERLY COMMENCE YOUR NEW COURT CASE:**

1. Original Complaint or Petition.

2. If filing a Complaint, a completed Summons form for issuance by the Clerk (Summons forms available at the Forms Counter.).

3. Civil Case Cover Sheet form required by California Rule of Court 982.2(b)(1), completely filled out (Cover Sheet forms available at the Forms Counter).

4. This "Addendum to Civil Case Cover Sheet" form [Superior Court Form Number CIV 109, revised 09-03], completely filled out (Item II. does not apply in limited civil cases) and submitted with the Civil Case Cover Sheet.*

5. Payment in full of the filing fee (unless filing on behalf of state or local government or no fee is due for the type of case being filed) or an Order of the Court waiving payment of filing fees in forma pauperis (fee waiver application forms available at the Filing Window)

6. In case of a plaintiff or petitioner who is a minor under 18 years of age, an Order of the Court appointing an adult as a guardian ad litem to act on behalf of the minor (Guardian ad Litem Application and Order forms available at the Forms Counter).

7. Additional copies of documents presented for endorsement by the Clerk and return to you.

* With the exception of unlimited civil cases concerning property damage, bodily injury or wrongful death occurring in this County, Labor Commissioner Appeals, and those types of actions required to be filed in the Central District by Local Court Rule 2(b), all unlimited jurisdiction civil actions may be optionally filed either in the Central District or in whichever other court location the rule would allow them to be filed. When a party elects to file an unlimited jurisdiction civil action in Central District that would also be eligible for filing in one or more of the other court locations, this form must still be submitted with location and assignment information completed.

---

**CIVIL CASE COVER SHEET ADDENDUM AND STATEMENT OF LOCATION**  LASC Rule 2.0
CIV 109  09-03                                                     Page 4 of 4

# SAMPLE CAUSE OF ACTION
# NOT COVERED BY OFFICIAL FORMS
## (To Be Attached to Official Form Complaint)

| Short Title: | Case Number: |
|---|---|
| ARTHUR ADAMS, et al. vs. MID-VALLEY HOSPITAL, et al. | C-3889700 |

FOURTH CAUSE OF ACTION FOR PROFESSIONAL NEGLIGENCE

AGAINST DEFENDANTS LANGDON M. SCHWARTZ, M.D., AND

DOES 6 THROUGH 10

Attachment to Complaint of Arthur Adams, et al.

PN-1.  Plaintiff ARTHUR ADAMS alleges that defendants LANGDON M. SCHWARTZ, M.D.
and DOES 6 through 10 were the legal and proximate cause of injuries and
damage to plaintiff, by the following acts or omissions to act on or about
September 30,....., at Los Angeles, California:

   a.  Said defendants were at all times mentioned herein physicians and
   surgeons licensed by the State of California to practice medicine
   and surgery, with offices in Los Angeles, California, and held
   themselves out as possessing the degree of skill and competence
   common to medical practitioners in said community.

   b.  In August,....., plaintiff ARTHUR ADAMS consulted said defendants
   for the purpose of obtaining diagnosis and treatment of an illness
   to his stomach.  Following such consultation, the said defendants
   recommended surgery, and plaintiffs employed said defendants to
   perform such surgery, and said defendants for valuable consideration
   accepted said employment and undertook and agreed to perform such
   surgery and otherwise to care for and treat plaintiff's illness as
   reasonably required.

   c.  In September,....., said defendants arranged to have plaintiff
   admitted to MID-VALLEY HOSPITAL for surgery on plaintiff's
   stomach.

- *(page)* -

_____

COMPLAINT FOR _____

FOURTH CAUSE OF ACTION FOR PROFESSIONAL NEGLIGENCE

AGAINST DEFENDANTS LANGDON M. SCHWARTZ, M.D., AND

DOES 6 THROUGH 10

    d.  On or about September 30,....., said defendants performed surgery on plaintiff's stomach at said hospital, but did so negligently and carelessly in that they allowed sponges and surgical instruments to remain in plaintiff's abdominal cavity after the surgery was completed and the incision closed, which acts or omissions are below the degree of skill and competence commonly exercised by medical practitioners in this community.

    e.  As a result of the acts and omissions alleged in the previous subparagraph, plaintiff's stomach illness was exacerbated, and plaintiff was compelled to undergo additional surgery for removal of the sponges and surgical instruments, causing him great mental and physical pain and suffering and the other damages, losses and expenses alleged in this complaint.

-(page)-

COMPLAINT FOR _____

# REQUEST FOR STATEMENT OF DAMAGES
## [CCP §425.11]

```
1   ................................
    State Bar No.:...................
2   ................................
    ................................
3   ................................
4
5   Attorney for ..................
6
7
8            SUPERIOR COURT OF THE STATE OF CALIFORNIA
9                     COUNTY OF .........
10
11  ........................... )      NO. ........................
                                 )
12            Plaintiffs,        )
                                 )      REQUEST FOR STATEMENT OF
13  vs.                          )      DAMAGES PURSUANT TO CCP §425.11
                                 )
14                               )
                                 )
15  ........................... )
                                 )
16 _____)
            Defendants.
17       TO: PLAINTIFFS .............................. AND TO THEIR
18  ATTORNEY OF RECORD:
19       Pursuant to Section 425.11 of the Code of Civil Procedure,
20  defendant ..........................................., through its
21  attorney of record, hereby requests that you furnish a statement
22  setting forth the nature and amount of damages being sought in this
23  action, within the time and in the manner required by law.
24  DATED: ............        .......................................
25                            Attorney for .......................
26
27
28
```

REQUEST FOR STATEMENT OF DAMAGES

**[FORM 6:T]**

# STATEMENT OF DAMAGES
## [CCP §425.11]

*— DO NOT FILE WITH THE COURT —*
*— UNLESS YOU ARE APPLYING FOR A DEFAULT JUDGMENT UNDER CODE OF CIVIL PROCEDURE § 585 —*

| ATTORNEY OR PARTY WITHOUT ATTORNEY *(Name and Address)*: | TELEPHONE NO.: | FOR COURT USE ONLY |
|---|---|---|
| ATTORNEY FOR *(name)*: | | |

**SUPERIOR COURT OF CALIFORNIA, COUNTY OF**
    STREET ADDRESS:
    MAILING ADDRESS:
    CITY AND ZIP CODE:
    BRANCH NAME:

    PLAINTIFF:
    DEFENDANT:

| STATEMENT OF DAMAGES (Personal Injury or Wrongful Death) | CASE NUMBER: |
|---|---|

To *(name of one defendant only)*:
Plaintiff *(name of one plaintiff only)*:
seeks damages in the above-entitled action, as follows:

1. **General damages**           **AMOUNT**
   - a. ☐ Pain, suffering, and inconvenience . . . . . . . . . . . . . . . . . . . . . . . . . . . . . . . . . $ _____
   - b. ☐ Emotional distress . . . . . . . . . . . . . . . . . . . . . . . . . . . . . . . . . . . . . . . . . . . . . . $ _____
   - c. ☐ Loss of consortium . . . . . . . . . . . . . . . . . . . . . . . . . . . . . . . . . . . . . . . . . . . . . . $ _____
   - d. ☐ Loss of society and companionship *(wrongful death actions only)* . . . . . . . . . . . . . . . . . . . $ _____
   - e. ☐ Other *(specify)* . . . . . . . . . . . . . . . . . . . . . . . . . . . . . . . . . . . . . . . . . . . . . . . . . . $ _____
   - f. ☐ Other *(specify)* . . . . . . . . . . . . . . . . . . . . . . . . . . . . . . . . . . . . . . . . . . . . . . . . . . $ _____
   - g. ☐ Continued on Attachment 1.g.

2. **Special damages**
   - a. ☐ Medical expenses *(to date)* . . . . . . . . . . . . . . . . . . . . . . . . . . . . . . . . . . . . . . . . . $ _____
   - b. ☐ Future medical expenses *(present value)* . . . . . . . . . . . . . . . . . . . . . . . . . . . . . . . . $ _____
   - c. ☐ Loss of earnings *(to date)* . . . . . . . . . . . . . . . . . . . . . . . . . . . . . . . . . . . . . . . . . . $ _____
   - d. ☐ Loss of future earning capacity *(present value)* . . . . . . . . . . . . . . . . . . . . . . . . . . . . $ _____
   - e. ☐ Property damage . . . . . . . . . . . . . . . . . . . . . . . . . . . . . . . . . . . . . . . . . . . . . . . . . $ _____
   - f. ☐ Funeral expenses *(wrongful death actions only)* . . . . . . . . . . . . . . . . . . . . . . . . . . . . $ _____
   - g. ☐ Future contributions *(present value) (wrongful death actions only)* . . . . . . . . . . . . . . . . $ _____
   - h. ☐ Value of personal service, advice, or training *(wrongful death actions only)* . . . . . . . . . . $ _____
   - i. ☐ Other *(specify)* . . . . . . . . . . . . . . . . . . . . . . . . . . . . . . . . . . . . . . . . . . . . . . . . . . $ _____
   - j. ☐ Other *(specify)* . . . . . . . . . . . . . . . . . . . . . . . . . . . . . . . . . . . . . . . . . . . . . . . . . . $ _____
   - k. ☐ Continued on Attachment 2.k.

3. ☐ **Punitive damages:** Plaintiff reserves the right to seek punitive damages in the amount of *(specify)* . . $ _____
   when pursuing a judgment in the suit filed against you.

Date:

                                  ▶

_____      _____
(TYPE OR PRINT NAME)                     (SIGNATURE OF PLAINTIFF OR ATTORNEY FOR PLAINTIFF)
(Proof of service on reverse)

Form Adopted by Rule 982
Judicial Council of California
982(a)(24) [New January 1, 1997]

**STATEMENT OF DAMAGES**
**(Personal Injury or Wrongful Death)**

Code of Civil Procedure, §§ 425.11, 425.115

Rev. #1 2001

| PLAINTIFF: | CASE NUMBER: |
|---|---|
| DEFENDANT: | |

## PROOF OF SERVICE

*(After having the other party served as described below, with any of the documents identified in item 1, have the person who served the documents complete this Proof of Service. Plaintiff cannot serve these papers.)*

1. I served the
   a. ☐ Statement of Damages   ☐ Other *(specify):*

   b. on *(name):*
   c. by serving   ☐ defendant   ☐ other *(name and title or relationship to person served):*

   d. ☐ by delivery   ☐ at home   ☐ at business
      (1) date:
      (2) time:
      (3) address:

   e. ☐ by mailing
      (1) date:
      (2) place:

2. Manner of service *(check proper box):*
   a. ☐ **Personal service.** By personally delivering copies. (CCP § 415.10)
   b. ☐ **Substituted service on corporation, unincorporated association (including partnership), or public entity.** By leaving, during usual office hours, copies in the office of the person served with the person who apparently was in charge and thereafter mailing (by first-class mail, postage prepaid) copies to the person served at the place where the copies were left. (CCP § 415.20(a))
   c. ☐ **Substituted service on natural person, minor, conservatee, or candidate.** By leaving copies at the dwelling house, usual place of abode, or usual place of business of the person served in the presence of a competent member of the household or a person apparently in charge of the office or place of business, at least 18 years of age, who was informed of the general nature of the papers, and thereafter mailing (by first-class mail, postage prepaid) copies to the person served at the place where the copies were left. (CCP § 415.20(b)) *(Attach separate declaration or affidavit stating acts relied on to establish reasonable diligence in first attempting personal service.)*
   d. ☐ **Mail and acknowledgment service.** By mailing (by first-class mail or airmail, postage prepaid) copies to the person served, together with two copies of the form of notice and acknowledgment and a return envelope, postage prepaid, addressed to the sender. (CCP § 415.30) *(Attach completed acknowledgment of receipt.)*
   e. ☐ **Certified or registered mail service.** By mailing to an address outside California (by first-class mail, postage prepaid, requiring a return receipt) copies to the person served. (CCP § 415.40) *(Attach signed return receipt or other evidence of actual delivery to the person served.)*
   f. ☐ Other *(specify code section):*
      ☐ additional page is attached.

3. At the time of service I was at least 18 years of age and not a party to this action.
4. Fee for service: **$**
5. Person serving:
   a. ☐ California sheriff, marshal, or constable
   b. ☐ Registered California process server
   c. ☐ Employee or independent contractor of a registered California process server
   d. ☐ Not a registered California process server
   e. ☐ Exempt from registration under Bus. & Prof. Code § 22350(b)

   f. Name, address and telephone number and, if applicable, county of registration and number:

I declare under penalty of perjury under the laws of the State of California that the foregoing is true and correct.

Date:

▶ _____
   (SIGNATURE)

*(For California sheriff, marshal, or constable use only)*
I certify that the foregoing is true and correct.

Date:

▶ _____
   (SIGNATURE)

982(a)(24) [New January 1 1997]

**PROOF OF SERVICE**
**(Statement of Damages)**

Page two
Code of Civil Procedure §§ 425 11, 425 115

# VERIFICATION

STATE OF CALIFORNIA )
                           )    SS.
COUNTY OF LOS ANGELES )

I, the undersigned, certify and declare that I have read the foregoing _____ *(complaint, answer or other document being verified)* _____ and know its contents. The statement following the box checked is applicable.

[ ]   I am a party to this action. The matters stated in the document described above are true of my own knowledge and belief except as to those matters stated on information and belief, and as to those matters I believe them to be true.

[ ]   I am [ ] an officer [ ] a partner [ ] a _____
of _____
a party to this action, and am authorized to make this verification for and on its behalf, and I make this verification for that reason. I am informed and believe and on that ground allege that the matters stated in the document described above are true.

[ ]   I am the attorney, or one of the attorneys for _____
_____, a party to this action. Such party is absent from the county where I or such attorneys have their offices and is unable to verify the document described above. For that reason, I am making this verification for and on behalf of that party. I am informed and believe and on that ground allege that the matters stated in said document are true.

Executed on _____, 19_____, at_____.

I declare under penalty of perjury under the laws of the State of California that the foregoing is true and correct.

_____

                                              

# GENERAL DENIAL

| ATTORNEY OR PARTY WITHOUT ATTORNEY *(Name and Address)* | TELEPHONE NO. | FOR COURT USE ONLY |
|---|---|---|
| ATTORNEY FOR *(Name)* | | |
| Insert name of court, name of judicial district, and branch court, if any: | | |
| PLAINTIFF: | | |
| DEFENDANT: | | |
| **GENERAL DENIAL** | | CASE NUMBER: |

You MUST use this form for your general denial if the amount asked for in the complaint or the value of the property involved is $1000 or less.

You MAY use this form if:
1. The complaint is not verified, OR
2. The complaint is verified, and the action is subject to the economic litigation procedures of the municipal and justice courts, EXCEPT

You MAY NOT use this form if the complaint is verified and involves a claim for more than $1000 that has been assigned to a third party for collection.

(See Code of Civil Procedure sections 90–100, 431.30, and 431.40.)

1. DEFENDANT *(name)*:
   generally denies each and every allegation of plaintiff's complaint.

2. ☐ DEFENDANT states the following FACTS as separate affirmative defenses to plaintiff's complaint *(attach additional pages if necessary)*:

Date:

▶

_____          _____
(TYPE OR PRINT NAME)                       (SIGNATURE OF DEFENDANT OR ATTORNEY)

If you have a claim for damages or other relief against the plaintiff, the law may require you to state your claim in a special pleading called a cross-complaint or you may lose your claim. (See Code of Civil Procedure sections 426.10–426.40.)

The original of this General Denial must be filed with the clerk of this court with proof that a copy was served on each plaintiff's attorney and on each plaintiff not represented by an attorney. *(See the other side for a proof of service.)*

Form Adopted by Rule 982
Judicial Council of California
982(a)(13) (Rev. January 1, 1987)

**GENERAL DENIAL**

CCP 431.30, 431.40

| PLAINTIFF (name): | CASE NUMBER |
|---|---|
| DEFENDANT (name): | |

## PROOF OF SERVICE
☐ Personal Service    ☐ Mail

A General Denial may be served by anyone at least 18 years of age EXCEPT you or any other party to this legal action. Service is made in one of the following ways:
(1) Personally delivering a copy to the attorney for the other party or, if no attorney, to the other party.
    **OR**
(2) Mailing a copy, postage prepaid, to the last known address of the attorney for the other party or, if no attorney, to the other party.
Be sure whoever serves the General Denial fills out and signs a proof of service. File the proof of service with the court as soon as the General Denial is served.

1. At the time of service I was at least 18 years of age and not a party to this legal action.

2. I served a copy of the General Denial as follows (check either a or b):

   a. ☐ **Personal service.** I personally delivered the General Denial as follows:
      (1) Name of person served:
      (2) Address where served:



      (3) Date served:
      (4) Time served:

   b. ☐ **Mail.** I deposited the General Denial in the United States mail, in a sealed envelope with postage fully prepaid. The envelope was addressed and mailed as follows:
      (1) Name of person served:
      (2) Address:



      (3) Date of mailing:
      (4) Place of mailing (city and state):
      (5) I am a resident of or employed in the county where the General Denial was mailed.

   c. My residence or business address is (specify):



   d. My phone number is (specify):


I declare under penalty of perjury under the laws of the State of California that the foregoing is true and correct.

Date:

▶

_____        _____
(TYPE OR PRINT NAME OF PERSON WHO SERVED THE GENERAL DENIAL)    (SIGNATURE OF PERSON WHO SERVED THE GENERAL DENIAL)

982(a-13) (Rev. January 1, 1987)          **GENERAL DENIAL**          Page two
                                          **(Proof of Service)**

# NOTICE OF MOTION FOR LEAVE TO FILE CROSS-COMPLAINT; DECLARATION AND POINTS AND AUTHORITIES IN SUPPORT

```
 1  ELIZABETH EAMES, State Bar No. 700000
    3044 Western Avenue
 2  Lynwood, California
    Telephone (213) 669-5540
 3

 4

 5  Attorney for Defendant
    BEN BAKER
 6

 7

 8          SUPERIOR COURT OF THE STATE OF CALIFORNIA

 9                  COUNTY OF LOS ANGELES

10

11  ALAN AMES, et al.,            ) CASE NO. 7765540
                                  )
12              Plaintiffs,       ) HEARING DATE/TIME: ...........
                                  ) DEPT. NO.: ..................
13  vs.                           ) HEARING JUDGE: ...... (if known)
                                  )
14  BEN BAKER, et al.,            ) NOTICE OF MOTION FOR LEAVE TO
                                  ) FILE CROSS-COMPLAINT;
15              Defendants.       ) DECLARATION OF .......; POINTS
                                  ) AND AUTHORITIES; PROPOSED ORDER
16                                )
                                  ) DATE ACTION FILED: ...........
17  _____) DATE SET FOR TRIAL: ... (if set)

18  TO EACH PARTY AND ATTORNEY OF RECORD:

19      PLEASE TAKE NOTICE THAT on May 15, ......., at 9:00 a.m. in

20  Dept. 81 of this Court, at the County Courthouse, 111 N. Hill

21  Street, Room 833, Los Angeles, California, defendant BEN BAKER will

22  move the Court for an order permitting the filing of a cross-

23  complaint, a copy of which is attached. This motion will be made

24  under CCP §426.50 on the ground that the proposed cross-complaint

25  arises out of the same transaction as the complaint and is a

26  "related cause of action" under CCP §426.10, but inadvertently was

27  not pleaded previously; and that allowing such filing at the

28  present time is in the interest of justice and will promote the
```

                                        1
                        _____

                        MOTION TO FILE CROSS-COMPLAINT;
                        SUPP. DECL'N; POINTS & AUTH.

1  efficient resolution of all claims between parties.  The motion
2  will be based on this notice, the attached declaration of defendant
3  BEN BAKER, the points and authorities attached hereto, and the
4  complete files and records of this action.
5  DATED:  April 18, .....

6                                      /s/ _____
                                       ELIZABETH EAMES
7                                      Attorney for Defendant BEN BAKER

8
9
10
11
12
13
14
15
16
17
18
19
20
21
22
23
24
25
26
27
28

                                    2

                    MOTION TO FILE CROSS-COMPLAINT;
                    SUPP. DECL'N; POINTS & AUTH.

1　　　　　　　MEMORANDUM OF POINTS AND AUTHORITIES

2　　　As long as the proposed cross-complaint arises out of the same

3　transaction as the plaintiff's complaint, leave to file the cross-

4　complaint after answering should be granted liberally to avoid

5　forfeiture of defendant's claim.　　CCP §426.50 authorizing such

6　leave, specifically provides that it shall be "construed liberally

7　to avoid forfeiture of causes of action."

8　　　In the present case, the damage to defendant's car is alleged

9　to have been caused by the same accident for which plaintiff seeks

10　to recover from defendant.　Hence, the cross-complaint would appear

11　to be compulsory under CCP §426.30.

12

13

14

15

16

17

18

19

20

21

22

23

24

25

26

27

28

3

MOTION TO FILE CROSS-COMPLAINT;<br>SUPP. DECL'N; POINTS & AUTH.

```
 1  ELIZABETH EAMES, State Bar No. 700000
    3044 Western Avenue
 2  Lynwood, California
    Telephone (213) 669-5540
 3

 4

 5  Attorney for Defendant
    BEN BAKER
 6

 7

 8            SUPERIOR COURT OF THE STATE OF CALIFORNIA

 9                    COUNTY OF LOS ANGELES

10

11  ALAN AMES, et al.,          ) CASE NO. 7765540
                                )
12              Plaintiffs,     ) HEARING DATE/TIME: ...........
                                ) DEPT. NO.: ..................
13  vs.                         ) HEARING JUDGE: ...... (if known)
                                )
14  BEN BAKER, et al.,          ) DECLARATION OF BEN BAKER IN
                                ) SUPPORT OF MOTION FOR LEAVE TO
15              Defendants.     ) FILE CROSS-COMPLAINT
                                )
16  _____ ) DATE ACTION FILED: ..........
                                ) DATE SET FOR TRIAL: ... (if set)
17
         I, the undersigned, certify and declare as follows:
18
         1.   I am the defendant, BEN BAKER, in this action, and have
19
    personal knowledge of each fact stated herein.
20
         2.   At the time I answered the complaint in this action, I
21
    was unaware that any injury or damage had been sustained by the
22
    vehicle I was driving at the time of the accident described in
23
    plaintiff's complaint.
24
         3.   However, on April 5, ......., my car became inoperative
25
    due the failure of a torsion bar linkage that had apparently been
26
    twisted in the accident with plaintiff's car.
27
    /////
28
                                4
```

---

MOTION TO FILE CROSS-COMPLAINT;
SUPP. DECL'N; POINTS & AUTH.

Rev. #1 2001

1   4. It is necessary to set up a claim for the repairs to my

2 car as a cross-complaint in this action, to avoid the risk of their

3 being barred by provisions of CCP §426.30.

4   5. The case had not yet been set for trial and discovery is

5 still proceeding. I have caused copies of the repair bills to my

6 car to be forwarded to plaintiff's attorney and have made the auto-

7 mobile parts in question available for his inspection.

8   I declare under penalty of perjury under the laws of the State

9 of California that the foregoing is true and correct.

10 DATED: .........., ......

11             /s/ _____

                Declarant

12

13

14

15

16

17

18

19

20

21

22

23

24

25

26

27

28

5

MOTION TO FILE CROSS-COMPLAINT;
SUPP. DECL'N; POINTS & AUTH.

# RESERVED

# AMENDMENT TO COMPLAINT
## TO SUBSTITUTE TRUE NAME OF "DOE" DEFENDANT
### (Los Angeles Superior Court)

| NAME, ADDRESS, AND TELEPHONE NUMBER OF ATTORNEY OR PARTY WITHOUT ATTORNEY: | STATE BAR NUMBER | Reserved for Clerk's File Stamp |
|---|---|---|
| | | |

ATTORNEY FOR (Name):

**SUPERIOR COURT OF CALIFORNIA, COUNTY OF LOS ANGELES**

COURTHOUSE ADDRESS:

PLAINTIFF:

DEFENDANT:

| **AMENDMENT TO COMPLAINT** (Fictitious /Incorrect Name) | CASE NUMBER: |
|---|---|

☐ **FICTITIOUS NAME** *(No order required)*

Upon the filing of the complaint, the plaintiff, being ignorant of the true name of the defendant and having designated the defendant in the complaint by the fictitious name of:

FICTITIOUS NAME

and having discovered the true name of the defendant to be:

TRUE NAME

amends the complaint by substituting the true name for the fictitious name wherever it appears in the complaint.

| DATE | TYPE OR PRINT NAME | SIGNATURE OF ATTORNEY |
|---|---|---|
| | | |

☐ **INCORRECT NAME** *(Order required)*

The plaintiff, having designated a defendant in the complaint by the incorrect name of:

INCORRECT NAME

and having discovered the true name of the defendant to be:

TRUE NAME

amends the complaint by substituting the true name for the incorrect name wherever it appears in the complaint.

| DATE | TYPE OR PRINT NAME | SIGNATURE OF ATTORNEY |
|---|---|---|
| | | |

## ORDER

THE COURT ORDERS the amendment approved and filed.

_____          _____
Date                                                              Judicial Officer

**AMENDMENT TO COMPLAINT**
(Fictitious / Incorrect Name)

CIV 105 07-02                                                       CCP 471.5, 472, 473, 474

**RESERVED**

# APPLICATION AND ORDER FOR
# AMENDMENT TO COMPLAINT

| | |
|---|---|
| 1 | COX, DUNN & EARLY |
| | ROBERT J. DUNN, State Bar No. 154899 |
| 2 | 1240 W. Temple Street |
| | Los Angeles, CA 90012 |
| 3 | Telephone (213) 677-8890 |
| 4 | |
| 5 | Attorneys for Plaintiffs |
| 6 | |
| 7 | |

8        SUPERIOR COURT OF CALIFORNIA, COUNTY OF LOS ANGELES

| | | |
|---|---|---|
| 9 | ALAN AMES, et al., | ) CASE NO. 7765540 |
| | | ) |
| 10 | Plaintiffs, | ) APPLICATION FOR ORDER ALLOWING |
| | | ) |
| 11 | vs. | ) AMENDMENT TO COMPLAINT; ORDER |
| | | ) |
| 12 | BEN BAKER, et al., | ) |
| | | ) |
| 13 | Defendants. | ) |

14        Plaintiffs ALAN AMES and AMY AMES hereby request that the Court allow

15    the filing of the attached Amendment to their Complaint originally filed

16    herein on April 21,........; and that such filing be allowed without hearing

17    or notice as provided by Code of Civil Procedure §473.

18        Said amendment is necessary to correct a mistake in the name of a party,

19    and other mistakes in the original complaint, as set forth in the attached

20    declaration of ROBERT J. DUNN

21    DATED: May 15, .........        COX, DUNN & EARLY

22                                    By /s/_____

23                                        ROBERT J. DUNN
                                          Attorney for Plaintiffs

24                                ORDER

25    Good cause appearing IT IS HEREBY ORDERED that plaintiff be allowed to file

26    the attached Amendment to Complaint.

27    DATED: May 15,.............        /s/_____
                                              JUDGE
28

1

APPLICATION AND ORDER FOR AMENDMENT TO COMPLAINT

```
1   COX, DUNN & EARLY
    ROBERT J. DUNN, State Bar No. 154899
2   1240 W. Temple Street
    Los Angeles, CA 90012
3   Telephone (213) 677-8890

4

5   Attorneys for Plaintiffs

6

7

8            SUPERIOR COURT OF CALIFORNIA, COUNTY OF LOS ANGELES

9   ALAN AMES, et al.,           )
                                 )   CASE NO. 7765540
10           Plaintiffs,         )
                                 )   DECLARATION OF ROBERT J. DUNN IN
11      vs.                      )
                                 )   SUPPORT OF PLAINTIFFS' APPLICATION TO
12  BEN BAKER, et al.,           )
                                 )   FILE AMENDMENT TO COMPLAINT
13           Defendants.         )
    _____ )
14  STATE OF CALIFORNIA      )
                             )   SS.
15  COUNTY OF LOS ANGELES    )

16  I, the undersigned, declare as follows:

17      1.    I am one of the attorneys of record herein for plaintiffs ALAN
18  AMES and AMY AMES;
19      2.    The present motion seeks to delete the name "Bertha Baker" on
20  page 1, line 12 of the complaint and replace it with the true name of
21  defendant, "Betty Baker."
22      3.    Also, the present motion seeks to delete on page 4, line 22 the
23  reference to "December 1" and replace it with "December 11."
24      4.    Finally, the present motion seeks to attach the promissory note
25  as an exhibit to the complaint.
26      5.    The effect of the amendments is to: correctly state the name of
27  defendant; accurately state the date the promissory note was executed; and
28  attach the promissory note, which is the basis of plaintiff's claims and
```

2

APPLICATION AND ORDER FOR AMENDMENT TO COMPLAINT

which is adverted to in the complaint at paragraphs three through nine at pages four through six.

 6. The amendments are necessary and proper so that the pleadings will accurately and completely allege the basis of plaintiff's claims.

 7. The errors were brought to my attention three days prior to execution of this declaration by defense counsel.

 8. The errors were not discovered earlier due to my inadvertence.

 9. I served a copy of the proposed amended complaint on defendants Ben Baker and Bertha Baker by mailing a copy thereof together with a copy of the attached application and this declaration to their attorney, Barbara Smith, at 1234 Center Street, Long Beach, CA 90802, on May 15, ...........

EXECUTED AT Los Angeles, California, on May 15, ..............

I declare under penalty of perjury under the laws of the State of California that the foregoing is true and correct.

/s/_____
    Robert J. Dunn

3

APPLICATION AND ORDER FOR AMENDMENT TO COMPLAINT

# AMENDMENT TO COMPLAINT

```
 1  COX, DUNN & EARLY
    ROBERT J. DUNN, State Bar No. 154899
 2  1240 W. Temple Street
    Los Angeles, California   90012
 3  Telephone (213) 677-8890

 4

 5  Attorneys for Plaintiffs

 6

 7

 8        SUPERIOR COURT OF CALIFORNIA, COUNTY OF LOS ANGELES

 9  ALAN AMES, et al.,            )   CASE NO.  7765540
                                  )
10             Plaintiffs,        )   AMENDMENT TO COMPLAINT
                                  )
11  vs.                           )
                                  )
12  BEN BAKER, et al.,            )
                                  )
13  _____Defendants.___)
```

Plaintiffs ALAN AMES and AMY AMES amend their complaint in this action in the following particulars:

   1.   The name of the defendant "BETTY BAKER" is amended and changed to "BERTHA BAKER" in the caption of the complaint, and wherever else it appears in the complaint (including without limitation page 1, line 20, and page 2, line 14).

   2.   On page 4, line 22, the date therein alleged is amended and changed from "December 1, 1981" to "December 11, .... ".

   3.   The copy of the promissory note which is attached hereto and which was referred to as "Exhibit A" in the complaint but which by inadvertence was not attached thereto at time of filing, is hereby made a part of said complaint as said "Exhibit A."

DATED:  May 15, .....          COX, DUNN & EARLY

                               By: /s/
                                  ROBERT J. DUNN
                                  Attorneys for Plaintiff

_____

                    AMENDMENT TO COMPLAINT

# NOTICE OF MOTION FOR LEAVE TO FILE AMENDED COMPLAINT; DECLARATION AND POINTS AND AUTHORITIES IN SUPPORT

```
1  EMILY P. BENNETT, ESQ. State Bar No. 500500
   FINE, GOOD & STRONG
2  3088 Wilshire Blvd., Suite 403
   Los Angeles, CA 90005
3  Telephone (213) 688-0201

4

5  Attorney for Plaintiff
   PATRICIA POTTS

6

7

8            SUPERIOR COURT OF CALIFORNIA, COUNTY OF LOS ANGELES
                                   )
9  PATRICIA POTTS,                 )  CASE NO. C-3799039
                                   )
10           Plaintiff,            )  HEARING DATE/TIME: ........
                                   )  DEPT. NO.: ...............
11 vs.                             )  HEARING JUDGE: ....... (if known)
                                   )
12 DOUGLAS DENTON et al.,          )  NOTICE OF MOTION FOR LEAVE TO FILE
                                   )  FIRST AMENDED COMPLAINT; DECLARATION
13           Defendants.           )  OF ......; POINTS AND AUTHORITIES
                                   )
14                                 )  DATE ACTION FILED: ........
                                   )  DATE SET FOR TRIAL: ....... (if set)
15 _____ )

16 TO EACH PARTY AND ATTORNEY OF RECORD IN THIS ACTION:

17 PLEASE TAKE NOTICE THAT on November 3, ...... at 9:00 A.M., or as

18 soon thereafter as counsel can be heard, plaintiff PATRICIA POTTS will move

19 this Court in Department 81 thereof, at the County Courthouse, 111 N. Hill

20 Street, Room 833, Los Angeles, California, for an order permitting plaintiff

21 to file an amended complaint, which is attached hereto and a copy of which

22 is served herewith. This motion will be made upon the ground that it is in

23 furtherance of justice to allow the filing of such amended complaint, and

24 will be based upon this notice, the attached points and authorities, and the

25 attached declaration of EMILY P. BENNETT.

26 DATED: October 2, ......     FINE, GOOD & STRONG

27                              BY: /s/_____

28                              Attorneys for Plaintiff PATRICIA POTTS

                                    1
   MOTION TO FILE AMENDED COMPLAINT; SUPP. DECL'N OF ........; POINTS & AUTH.
```

MEMORANDUM OF POINTS AND AUTHORITIES

    · "The court may, in furtherance of justice, and on such terms as may be proper, allow a party to amend any pleading or proceeding...The court may likewise, in its discretion, after notice to the adverse party, allow, upon such terms as may be just an amendment to any pleading or proceeding in other particulars..." [CCP §473]

    It is judicial policy to resolve all disputes between the parties on their merits, and to allow amendment of the pleadings to put all such disputes at issue at the time of trial.

> "While a motion to permit an amendment to a pleading to
> be filed is one addressed to the discretion of the
> court...it is a rare case in which a court will be
> justified in refusing a party leave to amend his
> pleadings so that he may properly present his case...
> If the motion to amend is timely made and the granting
> of the motion will not prejudice the opposing party, it
> is error to refuse permission to amend and where the
> refusal also results in a party being deprived of the
> right to assert a meritorious cause of action or a
> meritorious defense, it is not only error, but an abuse
> of discretion." [*Calif. Cas. Gen. Ins. Co. v. Sup.Ct.*
> *(Gorgei)* (1985) 173 CA3d 274, 278, 218 CR 817, 819
> (emphasis added)]

    "Trial courts are vested with the discretion to allow amendments to pleadings in furtherance of justice...That trial courts are to liberally permit such amendments, at _any_ stage of the proceeding, has been established policy in this state...resting on the fundamental policy that cases should be decided on their merits." [*Hirsa v. Superior Court (Vickers)* (1981) 118

---

2

MOTION TO FILE AMENDED COMPLAINT; SUPP. DECL'N OF .........; POINTS & AUTH.

Rev. #1 2002

1   CA3d 486, 488-489, 173 CR 418, 419 (emphasis in original)]

2        Where a change in law subsequent to filing the original

3   complaint demonstrates the possibility of recovery on a new legal theory,

4   but the same general set of facts, courts should permit amendment of the

5   complaint to set forth such theory. [*Marasco v. Wadsworth* (1978) 21 C3d 82,

6   145 CR 843]

7

8

9

10

11

12

13

14

15

16

17

18

19

20

21

22

23

24

25

26

27

28

```
 1 │ EMILY P. BENNETT, ESQ. State Bar No. 500500
   │ FINE, GOOD & STRONG
 2 │ 3088 Wilshire Blvd., Suite 403
   │ Los Angeles, CA 90005
 3 │ Telephone (213) 688-0201
   │
 4 │
   │
 5 │ Attorney for Plaintiff
   │ PATRICIA POTTS
 6 │
   │
 7 │
   │
 8 │           SUPERIOR COURT OF CALIFORNIA, COUNTY OF LOS ANGELES
   │
 9 │
   │                                  )
10 │ PATRICIA POTTS,                   )  CASE NO. C-3799039
   │                                   )
11 │           Plaintiff,             )  HEARING DATE/TIME:.........
   │                                   )  DEPT. NO.: ...............
12 │ vs.                               )  HEARING JUDGE: .......(if known)
   │                                   )
13 │ DOUGLAS DENTON et al.,            )  NOTICE OF MOTION FOR LEAVE TO FILE
   │                                   )  AMENDED COMPLAINT; DECLARATION OF
14 │           Defendants.            )  ......; POINTS AND AUTHORITIES
   │                                   )
15 │                                   )  DATE ACTION FILED: .........
   │                                   )  DATE SET FOR TRIAL: ....... (if set)
16 │ _____)
   │
17 │ STATE OF CALIFORNIA      )
   │                          )   SS.
18 │ COUNTY OF LOS ANGELES    )
   │
19 │ I, the undersigned, declare:
   │
20 │       1.    I am one of the attorneys of record herein for PATRICIA POTTS;
   │
21 │       2.    Plaintiff proposes to file a First Amended Complaint, which is
   │
22 │ attached to the Notice of Motion, served and filed concurrently with this
   │
23 │ Declaration;
   │
24 │       3.    Said amended complaint changes the original complaint in
   │
25 │ the following particulars only:
   │
26 │             a.    A "Fourth Cause of Action" is added thereto
   │
27 │ (commencing on page 6, at line 12 of the proposed First Amended Complaint).
   │
28 │ Said "Fourth Cause of Action" contains allegations of fact entitling
```

4

---

MOTION TO FILE AMENDED COMPLAINT; SUPP. DECL'N OF .........; POINTS & AUTH.

1 | plaintiff to an award of exemplary damages against defendant DOUGLAS DENTON
2 | not sought in the original complaint;

3          b.     The prayer of the complaint (commencing on page 8,
4 | at line 3) to include a demand against defendant DOUGLAS DENTON for
5 | $250,000.00 exemplary damage on the aforesaid Fourth Cause of Action.

6      4.     Said amendment is necessary and proper and allowing such
7 | amendment would be in furtherance of justice because at the time this action
8 | was originally filed, it did not appear possible to state a claim for
9 | punitive damages against defendant DOUGLAS DENTON for negligence in the
10 | operation of his vehicle at the time and place alleged in the complaint
11 | herein. However, DOUGLAS DENTON admitted in the course of his deposition on
12 | August 3, ......, that he had consumed two six-packs of beer immediately
13 | prior to getting into his car, and that he was purposefully hurrying to his
14 | destination. Discovery of these facts leads plaintiffs' attorney to the
15 | conclusion that a cause of action can be stated and proved against said
16 | defendant DOUGLAS DENTON for exemplary damages, based on conscious disregard
17 | for the safety of other drivers on the highway, within the meaning of *Taylor*
18 | *v. Superior Court* (1979) 34 C3d 890, 157 CR 893.

19      5.     I did not know of these additional facts until defendant was
20 | deposed. There was no police report prepared and plaintiff was too badly
21 | injured in the accident to have observed defendant's lack of sobriety.
22 | Defendant's deposition was noticed within 60 days of service of the
23 | complaint.

24      6.     No trial date has yet been set in this action, and to the best
25 | of my knowledge, allowing plaintiff to file the proposed First Amended
26 | Complaint would not prejudice defendant DOUGLAS DENTON or any other party to
27 | ///
28 | ///

---

1 this action in any way. Discovery is still continuing on both sides at the

2 present time.

3 I declare under penalty of perjury under the laws of the State of California

4 that the foregoing is true and correct.

5 DATED: ...............

6

/s/_____
Emily P. Bennett

7

8

9

10

11

12

13

14

15

16

17

18

19

20

21

22

23

24

25

26

27

28

MOTION TO FILE AMENDED COMPLAINT; SUPP. DECL'N OF .........; POINTS & AUTH.

# CHAPTER 7

# ATTACKING THE PLEADINGS

## CONTENTS

Page

**A. DEMURRERS** ............................................................................ 7-1
Strategy and Tactics Re Demurrers: Should You Demur? ....... 7-1
Strategy and Tactics for Opposing Party: Should You
Amend? ...................................................................................... 7-5
1. Function of Demurrer .......................................................... 7-5
   a. Demurrer as pleading .................................................... 7-5
     (1) Not permitted in family law cases ......................... 7-5
     (2) Unlawful detainer cases? .................................... 7-5
   b. Demurrer as motion ...................................................... 7-6
   c. Demurrer challenges only defects on face of
     pleading or judicially noticeable .................................. 7-6
     (1) Defects appearing on face of complaint ............... 7-7
     (2) Defects appearing from matters judicially
        noticeable ............................................................. 7-7
        (a) Matters judicially noticeable ........................... 7-8
          1) Court records and files ........................... 7-8
            a) Defense disclosed in other court
               records .............................................. 7-8
            b) Limitation—only matters
               indisputably true ............................... 7-8
               1/ No inadmissible hearsay ............. 7-8
               2/ Findings of fact .......................... 7-9
            c) Inconsistent statements in earlier
               pleadings ......................................... 7-9
            d) Contradictory discovery responses ... 7-9
          2) Matters of common knowledge .............. 7-10
          3) Indisputable facts ................................... 7-10
          4) Official acts ............................................ 7-11
            a) Example ........................................... 7-11
            b) Example ........................................... 7-11
            c) Limitation—official acts must be
               undisputed ....................................... 7-11
          5) Regulations and legislative
            enactments ............................................ 7-12
        (b) Procedure for invoking judicial notice ........... 7-12
          1) Of file in same court ............................... 7-12

        2) Of file in different court ...........................7-13
2.  Time to File Demurrer.......................................................7-13
    a.  Demurrer to complaint (or cross-complaint) ..............7-13
      (1) Demurrer filed in conjunction with motion to
         strike .................................................................7-13
      (2) Demurrer filed in conjunction with answer ...........7-13
    b.  Demurrer to answer (or answer to cross-
      complaint) .................................................................7-14
3.  Grounds for Demurrer .....................................................7-14
    a.  Demurrer to complaint (or cross-complaint) ..............7-14
      (1) Grounds can be raised in answer........................7-14
      (2) Waiver if not raised by demurrer or answer .........7-15
        (a) Exceptions ...............................................7-15
        (b) Rationale .................................................7-15
      (3) Demurrer to certain causes of action only ...........7-15
        (a) Defendant ordered to answer......................7-16
        (b) No order to answer—"piecemeal
           demurrers"? ...............................................7-16
    b.  Demurrer to answer .................................................7-16
      (1) Waiver of grounds .............................................7-17
    c.  "General" vs. "special" demurrers.............................7-17
      (1) No special demurrers in limited civil cases..........7-17
        (a) Exception for unlawful detainer actions? ......7-17
    d.  General demurrer—failure to state a cause of
      action .........................................................................7-17
      (1) Function ............................................................7-17
        (a) ANY valid cause of action overcomes
           demurrer ....................................................7-18
        (b) Improper remedy not ground for demurrer ....7-18
        (c) Defective part of claim not ground for
           general demurrer .........................................7-18
          1) Application .............................................7-19
          2) Compare—motion to strike .....................7-19
        (d) Ambiguous allegations not ground for
           general demurrer .........................................7-19
        (e) Declaratory relief—"actual controversy"
           allegation overcomes demurrer.....................7-19
      (2) Admits facts alleged in complaint ........................7-20
        (a) No matter how unlikely ..............................7-20
          1) Problems of proof irrelevant....................7-20
        (b) Limitation—allegations contradicted by
           judicial notice .............................................7-20
          1) Admissions and inconsistent
             statements in same case........................7-20
          2) Allegations contradicted by attached
             exhibit ...............................................7-21
             a) Example ...........................................7-21
             b) Compare—legal conclusions............7-21
          3) Plaintiff's duty to "plead around" earlier
             admissions .............................................7-21

Rev. #1 2003

　　　　　　　a) Verified or unverified pleadings ........7-22
　　　　　　4) Application .................................................7-22
　　　　　　　a) Deposition testimony? ......................7-22
　　　　　　5) Compare—right to plead inconsistent
　　　　　　　　theories ................................................7-23
　　　　　　6) Compare—right to explain contrary
　　　　　　　　pleading in different lawsuit? .................7-23
　　　　　　　a) Not conclusive ..................................7-23
　　　　　　　b) Conclusive .......................................7-23
　　　(3) Admits plaintiff's interpretation of ambiguous
　　　　　contract ....................................................7-24
　　　(4) Demurrer lies for defense disclosed on face of
　　　　　complaint....................................................7-24
　　　　　(a) Statute of limitations .................................7-25
　　　　　　1) Form of demurrer .................................7-25
　　　　　　2) Compare—dates not on face of
　　　　　　　　complaint ..............................................7-26
　　　　　　3) Compare—"on or about" allegations .......7-26
　　　　　　4) Compare—complaint fails to allege
　　　　　　　　whether contract sued upon is oral
　　　　　　　　or written ..............................................7-27
　　　　　　5) Compare—acts alleged before and
　　　　　　　　after statutory bar .................................7-27
　　　　　　6) Official Forms .......................................7-27
　　　　　(b) Statute of Frauds ....................................7-28
　　　　　　1) Compare—not on face of complaint .......7-28
　　　　　(c) Illegal contract ........................................7-28
　　　　　(d) Plaintiff's duty to "plead around" defense
　　　　　　　disclosed in complaint................................7-28
　　　(5) "Aider by demurrer"...........................................7-28
　　e. General demurrer—court lacks jurisdiction of
　　　subject matter....................................................7-29
　　　(1) Nature of objection.............................................7-29
　　　　　(a) Distinguish personal jurisdiction ..................7-29
　　　(2) Application ........................................................7-29
　　　　　(a) Exceptional cases in which superior court
　　　　　　　lacks subject matter jurisdiction ..................7-29
　　　(3) No waiver .........................................................7-30
　　f. Special demurrers .................................................7-30
　　　(1) Plaintiff lacks legal capacity to sue......................7-30
　　　　　(a) Rarely disclosed on face of pleading ............7-30
　　　　　(b) Compare—lack of standing to sue .................7-30
　　　(2) Another action pending .......................................7-30
　　　　　(a) Application .................................................7-31
　　　　　　1) "Pending" .................................................7-31
　　　　　　2) "Same parties" ..........................................7-31
　　　　　　3) "Same cause of action" ............................7-31
　　　　　　　a) Issue preclusion not enough ............7-31
　　　　　(b) How determined..........................................7-32
　　　　　(c) If demurrer sustained .................................7-32

(d) Compare—other action pending in federal or sister state court ..........................7-32
   1) Procedure ...............................................7-32
   2) Motion to stay distinguished from demurrer ................................................7-32
(3) Defect or misjoinder of parties ...........................7-33
  (a) Application .............................................7-33
   1) Defect (nonjoinder) of parties .................7-33
   2) Misjoinder of parties ..............................7-33
   3) Compare—plaintiff uncertain which defendant responsible ...........................7-33
  (b) Waiver................................................7-34
  (c) Prejudice from misjoinder required? ............7-34
(4) Uncertainty .............................................7-34
  (a) Disfavored ground .................................7-34
   1) Comment ...............................................7-34
   2) Example—failure to identify parties and claims ................................................7-35
  (b) Form of demurrer—"uncertainties" must be specified ......................................7-35
  (c) Waiver................................................7-36
(5) Failure to allege whether contract oral or written ................................................7-36
  (a) Application .............................................7-36
  (b) Limitation—action "upon a contract" ............7-36
  (c) Limitation—pleading common counts ...........7-37
(6) Failure to attach attorney certificate in certain malpractice actions .............................................7-37
  (a) Application .............................................7-37
  (b) Limitation—in pro per complaints .................7-37
  (c) Leave to amend .....................................7-37
(7) Failure to attach attorney certificate in actions by "common interest development" against contractor ....................................................7-37
(8) Failure to attach prelawsuit ADR certificate in certain actions involving "common interest developments"....................................................7-37
  (a) Application .............................................7-38
   1) Limitation—cross-complaints .................7-38
   2) Limitation—statute of limitations soon to expire .................................................7-38
4. Demurrers to Judicial Council Form Pleadings ................7-38
5. Procedure—Moving Papers .............................................7-38
  a. Demurrer ................................................7-39
  (1) Caption...............................................7-39
  (2) Grounds must be specified distinctly...................7-39
  (3) Each ground separately stated ........................7-39
   (a) Each ground in separate paragraph..............7-39
   1) Caution—demurrer "trap".......................7-39
   (b) Each ground directed to particular cause of action .........................................................7-39

Rev. #1 2004

          1)  Caution—demurrer "trap" ........................ 7-39
        (c)  Each paragraph consecutively numbered ..... 7-40
    (4)  Which of several defendants ............................. 7-40
        (a)  Caution—joint demurrer trap ...................... 7-40
    (5)  Suggested format ................................................ 7-40
    (6)  Signature ............................................................. 7-40
  b.  Notice of hearing ......................................................... 7-40
    (1)  Length of notice required ................................. 7-41
        (a)  Order shortening or extending time .............. 7-41
  c.  Points and authorities ................................................ 7-41
    (1)  Caption ................................................................ 7-42
    (2)  Content ................................................................ 7-42
        (a)  Reference to CCP §430.10 not enough ........ 7-42
        (b)  Grounds waived if not supported? ............... 7-42
        (c)  Effective arguments ..................................... 7-42
    (3)  Length limitation ................................................ 7-42
    (4)  Footers ................................................................ 7-42
  d.  Proof of service ........................................................... 7-43
  e.  Opposition papers ...................................................... 7-43
    (1)  Length limitation ................................................ 7-43
    (2)  Time requirement ............................................... 7-43
    (3)  Service requirement .......................................... 7-43
  f.  Reply papers ............................................................... 7-43
    (1)  Length limitation ................................................ 7-43
    (2)  Time requirement ............................................... 7-43
    (3)  Service requirement .......................................... 7-43
6.  Attending the Hearing ....................................................... 7-44
  a.  Parties' stipulation that demurrer go off calendar
    equivalent to order sustaining demurrer .................... 7-44
    (1)  Stipulation coupled with agreement to amend .... 7-44
    (2)  Stipulation coupled with agreement to abate
        action ................................................................. 7-44
  b.  Right to oral argument if requested ........................... 7-44
7.  Ruling on Demurrer ........................................................... 7-44
  a.  Policy to construe complaint liberally ........................ 7-44
    (1)  Impact ................................................................. 7-45
  b.  If demurrer sustained, judge must specify ground ..... 7-45
    (1)  Sufficiency of statement ................................... 7-45
    (2)  Waiver of specification ...................................... 7-46
    (3)  Effect of failure to specify ................................ 7-46
        (a)  Not reversible error ...................................... 7-46
        (b)  Special demurrers may be renewed ............. 7-46
  c.  Leave to amend routinely granted ............................. 7-46
    (1)  Error to deny leave if reasonable possibility
        exists to cure defect ......................................... 7-47
        (a)  Request for leave to amend *not* required ...... 7-47
        (b)  Burden on plaintiff to show reasonable
            possibility ...................................................... 7-47
    (2)  Compare—strictly legal issues; leave to
        amend may be denied ....................................... 7-48

         (3) Compare—failure to "plead around" earlier
             admission ................................................................7-48
     d.  Leave to amend may be granted conditionally .........7-48
     e.  Discovery may be stayed pending amendment ........7-49
     f.  Sanctions ................................................................7-49
     g.  Appellate review of order sustaining demurrer ..........7-49
  8. Time to Answer or Amend; Notice of Ruling ....................7-49
     a.  Runs from service of notice of ruling by
         prevailing party ......................................................7-50
         (1) Impact ..............................................................7-50
         (2) Clerk's notice sufficient? .................................7-50
         (3) File-stamped copy of order as service ...............7-51
         (4) Extension for service by mail ...........................7-51
     b.  Waiver of notice .....................................................7-51
     c.  Compare—after reversal on appeal .........................7-51
     d.  Effect of belated amendment .................................7-51
  9. Subsequent Pleadings and Procedures...........................7-52
     a.  Successive demurrers .............................................7-52
         (1) No demurrer on grounds previously overruled ....7-52
         (2) Contrary view ...................................................7-52
     b.  Answer to remaining causes of action ......................7-53
     c.  Dismissal of defendant whose demurrer sustained ...7-53
 10. Alternative Available to Losing Party ...............................7-53
     a.  Demurrer sustained with leave to amend ................7-53
         (1) Seek writ .........................................................7-53
             (a) Drawback ...................................................7-53
         (2) Amend the complaint .......................................7-53
             (a) Drawback ...................................................7-53
             (b) Scope of permissible amendment ...............7-54
         (3) Dismiss and refile.............................................7-54
             (a) Drawback ...................................................7-54
         (4) Refuse to amend; allow entry of judgment of
             dismissal .........................................................7-54
             (a) Drawback ...................................................7-54
             (b) Dismissal may be obtained ex parte ............7-55
                 1) Informal notice to opposing counsel
                     required ...............................................7-55
             (c) No statement of reasons required ...............7-55
     b.  Demurrer sustained *with* leave to amend as to *less
         than all* causes of action .......................................7-55
     c.  Demurrer sustained *without* leave to amend .............7-56
     d.  Demurrer sustained *without* leave to amend as to
         *less than all* causes of action ..................................7-56
         (1) New lawsuit improper .......................................7-56
         (2) Compare—multiparty lawsuit ............................7-56
     e.  Demurrer *overruled* as to all causes of action ..........7-57
         (1) Seek writ .........................................................7-57
             (a) Drawback ...................................................7-57
         (2) Answer .............................................................7-57
             (a) Drawback ...................................................7-57
     f.  Motion for reconsideration .....................................7-57

|  |  |  | (1) | Requirements | 7-57 |
|  |  |  | (2) | Comment | 7-58 |
|  |  |  | (3) | Proposed amended complaint as basis for motion to reconsider | 7-58 |
|  |  |  |  | (a) Court must allow | 7-58 |

**B. MOTIONS TO STRIKE** ........................................................ 7-58
   1. General Considerations ............................................ 7-58
      a. As defendant's initial pleading ........................... 7-58
         (1) Prevents entry of default ........................... 7-58.1
      b. Court may strike pleading on own motion .......... 7-58.1
      c. Improper motion to strike as motion for judgment on pleadings ................................... 7-58.1
      d. Limitations on use ........................................... 7-58.1
   2. Time to File Motion to Strike ................................. 7-58.1
      a. Motion to strike filed with demurrer ................. 7-58.2
         (1) Separate documents ................................. 7-58.2
         (2) Must be heard concurrently ..................... 7-58.2
         (3) Same notice requirements ........................ 7-59
         (4) No extension of time if filed separately from demurrer ........................................ 7-59
      b. Compare—motion used to attack opposing demurrer .......................................................... 7-59
      c. Motion to strike answer .................................... 7-59
   3. Grounds for Motion ................................................ 7-59
      a. Grounds must appear on face of pleading or by judicial notice ................................................ 7-59
         (1) Extrinsic evidence generally improper .......... 7-60
         (2) Compare—motion for summary judgment .......... 7-60
      b. Grounds for striking entire pleading ................. 7-60
         (1) Examples ................................................ 7-60
         (2) "False" pleadings .................................... 7-61
            (a) Limitation—no extrinsic evidence .......... 7-61
      c. Grounds for striking portions of pleading .......... 7-61
         (1) "Irrelevant matter" .................................. 7-61
         (2) Application ............................................. 7-61
            (a) Conclusionary allegations ................. 7-61
               1) Conclusory allegations permitted where supported by facts ........... 7-62
            (b) Improper demands or damage claims .......... 7-62
               1) Unauthorized attorney fees claims .......... 7-62
               2) Punitive damages claims ................. 7-62
               3) Improper rent claims in unlawful detainer actions ..................... 7-63
            (c) Substantive defects in portion of claim .......... 7-64
      d. Limitation in limited civil cases ..................... 7-64
   4. Moving Papers ....................................................... 7-64
      a. Notice of motion .............................................. 7-64
         (1) Notice required ....................................... 7-64
         (2) Portion to be stricken quoted verbatim .......... 7-65
      b. Declarations in support of motion ..................... 7-65

        (1) Not permitted ........................................... 7-65
        (2) Request for judicial notice ......................... 7-65
    c. Points and authorities in support ..................... 7-65
  5. Ruling on Motion ................................................. 7-65
    a. Policy to construe pleadings liberally ............. 7-65
    b. Allegations presumed true .............................. 7-65
    c. Motion to strike heard concurrently with demurrer ..... 7-65
    d. Motion to strike granted .................................. 7-66
        (1) If only a portion of pleading stricken ......... 7-66
        (2) If entire complaint stricken ....................... 7-66
           (a) Liberal policy re amendments ............... 7-66
           (b) Conditions imposed ................................ 7-66
           (c) Compare—noncorrectible defects ............ 7-66
        (3) If demurrer stricken ................................. 7-67
    e. Motion denied ............................................... 7-67
    f. Appellate review ............................................ 7-67

**C. SPECIAL MOTION TO STRIKE SLAPP SUITS ("ANTI-SLAPP MOTIONS")** .................................................... 7-67
  1. Interpretation and Limitations ............................. 7-68
  2. What Constitutes SLAPP Suit—In General ......... 7-68
    a. Differences .................................................... 7-68
  3. Exemptions (Actions Not Subject to SLAPP Statute) ...... 7-69
    a. Public enforcement actions ............................ 7-69
    b. Actions for public benefit ............................... 7-69
    c. Certain claims against business entities .......... 7-70
    d. Limitation—certain claims protected despite
       exemptions ..................................................... 7-70
    e. Limitation—certain parties protected despite
       exemptions ..................................................... 7-71
  4. "Persons" Protected by Anti-SLAPP Statute ......... 7-71
    a. Corporations ................................................. 7-71
    b. Nonprofits .................................................... 7-72
    c. Public entities and officials ............................. 7-72
    d. Political candidates ....................................... 7-72
    e. Attorney in earlier litigation? .......................... 7-72
  5. Activities Protected by Anti-SLAPP Statute ......... 7-72
    a. Statements or writings in official proceedings ....... 7-72
        (1) Need not concern public issue ................. 7-73
        (2) Constitutionally-protected activity ............. 7-73
        (3) No nexus required ................................... 7-73
        (4) Application—statements or writings in *judicial
           proceedings* ........................................... 7-73
           (a) Malicious prosecution action as SLAPP
              suit ..................................................... 7-74
           (b) Compare—attorney malpractice actions ...... 7-74
           (c) Compare—retaliatory lawsuits ............... 7-74
           (d) Compare—tort actions based on attorney
              conduct unrelated to judicial proceedings ..... 7-75
           (e) Protection extends to certain nonjudicial
              proceedings .......................................... 7-75

Rev. #1 2004

          1) Administrative proceedings ..................7-75
          2) Arbitration ................................7-75
     (5) Application—statements or writings in
        *legislative or executive proceedings* ..................7-75
  b. Statements or writings *in connection with issue*
     *under consideration* in official proceeding ..............7-76
     (1) Need not concern public issue ..........7-76
     (2) Constitutionally-protected activity ........7-76
     (3) Nexus required .............................7-76
  c. Statements or writings in public place or forum ........7-77
     (1) Must concern "issue of public interest" ..............7-78
     (2) Constitutionally-protected activity ........7-78
     (3) No nexus required .........................7-78
     (4) "Public forum" .............................7-78
  d. Other conduct in furtherance of free speech right .....7-79
     (1) Must concern "public issue or issue of public
        interest" ....................................7-79
     (2) Constitutionally-protected activity ........7-79
     (3) No nexus required .........................7-79
  e. What constitutes "public issue" or "issue of public
    interest" ......................................7-79
     (1) Broadly construed .........................7-80
     (2) Includes matters of interest to limited segment
        of public .....................................7-80
     (3) Application ................................7-80
     (4) Compare—purely commercial speech not
        protected ....................................7-82
        (a) Public interest in advertised product not
          sufficient .................................7-82
        (b) Compare—"educational" activities ..............7-82
6. Causes of Action Subject to Being Stricken ..................7-84
  a. "Arising from" ...................................7-84
     (1) Determined by "principal thrust" of plaintiff's
        claim ........................................7-84
     (2) Sequence not determinative ..............7-85
  b. Typical claims ....................................7-86
  c. Other actions subject to anti-SLAPP statute ............7-87
  d. Compare—oppressive litigation tactics not
    enough .........................................7-87
7. Effect of Joining Non-SLAPP Claims ..............................7-88
  a. Separate non-SLAPP causes of action ..................7-88
  b. Protected and nonprotected activities alleged in
    same cause of action ("mixed" cause of action) ........7-88
     (1) Contra authority ...........................7-88
8. Procedure ........................................................7-88
  a. Timing of motion ..................................7-88
     (1) Extension for service by mail ............7-88.1
     (2) After amended complaint ...............7-88.1
  b. Notice of motion ..................................7-88.1
  c. Declarations required ..............................7-88.1

d. Defendant's burden of proof .................................... 7-88.1
   (1) *Prima facie* showing sufficient ......................... 7-88.1
   (2) No "intent-to-chill" required ............................ 7-88.1
   (3) No actual "chilling" required ........................... 7-88.2
e. Plaintiff's burden of proof.................................... 7-88.2
   (1) What constitutes "probability" ......................... 7-88.2
      (a) Summary judgment standards ................... 7-88.2
   (2) Evidentiary considerations ............................. 7-88.3
      (a) Hearsay affidavits ................................. 7-88.3
      (b) Preliminary injunction shows "probability"
         of prevailing on merits ......................... 7-88.3
      (c) Denial of summary judgment in earlier
         lawsuit as bar to malicious prosecution
         claim ................................................ 7-88.3
         1) Compare—defense summary
            judgment *not* proof of lack of probable
            cause ......................................... 7-88.3
   (3) Application ............................................. 7-88.4
   (4) Where higher standard of proof required ......... 7-88.4
f. Ruling ......................................................... 7-88.4
   (1) Matters considered.................................... 7-88.5
      (a) Including opposing evidence ..................... 7-88.5
      (b) No weighing of evidence ......................... 7-88.5
   (2) Motion granted ....................................... 7-88.5
      (a) No leave to amend .............................. 7-88.5
   (3) Motion denied ........................................ 7-88.5
      (a) Limited effect .................................... 7-88.5
      (b) Later amendment disregarded for
         appellate review ................................. 7-88.6
g. Discovery stayed ............................................ 7-88.6
   (1) Procedure where discovery needed ................. 7-88.6
h. Fees and costs .............................................. 7-88.7
   (1) Recovery of fees and costs on dismissal ......... 7-88.7
      (a) Showing required? .............................. 7-88.7
      (b) Court-ordered dismissal before SLAPP
         motion heard ..................................... 7-88.8
      (c) Dismissal of appeal from order granting
         motion ............................................ 7-88.8
   (2) "Fees and costs" recoverable ....................... 7-88.8
      (a) Partially successful motion ...................... 7-88.8
      (b) Appellate fees and costs ......................... 7-88.9
   (3) Only reasonable fees ................................. 7-88.9
      (a) "Lodestar" approach ............................. 7-88.9
   (4) Pro bono representation .............................. 7-88.9
   (5) Procedure to obtain fees ............................. 7-88.9
i. Compare—sanctions for "frivolous" motion ............. 7-88.9
   (1) "Pursuant to §128.5" means standards of
      former statute ........................................ 7-88.10
   (2) "Frivolous" ........................................... 7-88.10
j. Appellate review ............................................ 7-88.10

Rev. #1 2004

       (1)  Automatic stay of action ..................................7-88.10

       (2)  Compare—other joined claims stayed? ........7-88.10

       (3)  Compare—stay of judgment awarding fees
           and costs ...............................................................7-88.11

  k.  Fax or e-mail copies to Judicial Council ..............7-88.11

**D.  MOTION FOR JUDGMENT ON THE PLEADINGS** ........7-88.11

  1.  In General ........................................................................7-88.11

    a.  Statutory basis ..........................................................7-88.11

    b.  Nonstatutory motion survives ...............................7-88.12

  2.  Motion by Party or Court...............................................7-88.12

  3.  Time for Motion ...............................................................7-88.12

    a.  Deadline .....................................................................7-88.12

    b.  Compare—nonstatutory motion ...........................7-88.12

    c.  Compare—other challenges ...................................7-89

  4.  Grounds .............................................................................7-89

    a.  Ground must appear on face of complaint or from
       facts judicially noticeable ........................................7-89

    b.  Matters set forth in answer not considered...............7-90

    c.  Limitation—*change in law* required where same
       ground raised by demurrer .....................................7-90

       (1)  Compare—nonstatutory motion .........................7-90

       (2)  Compare—demurrer on different ground ...........7-91

       (3)  Compare—same ground raised by other
           motions ...............................................................7-91

  5.  Procedure .........................................................................7-91

    a.  Notice directed to entire or part of pleading ..............7-91

    b.  Requesting judicial notice........................................7-92

    c.  Compare—*sua sponte* motion ...................................7-92

    d.  Compare—motion at time of trial..............................7-92

    e.  No extrinsic evidence ...............................................7-93

       (1)  Compare—summary judgment .........................7-93

       (2)  Summary judgment motion treated as motion
           for judgment on the pleadings .............................7-94

  6.  Ruling on Motion .............................................................7-94

    a.  Effect that general demurrer overruled ....................7-94

       (1)  Compare—nonstatutory motion .........................7-94

       (2)  Caution re judicial reaction .................................7-94

       (3)  Prior demurrer ruling should be disclosed in
           moving papers.....................................................7-94.1

          (a)  Sanctions for failure to disclose? .............7-94.1

    b.  Motion may be granted with or without leave to
       amend .........................................................................7-94.1

       (1)  Leave to amend routinely granted ....................7-94.1

    c.  Time to amend .........................................................7-94.2

       (1)  Effect ....................................................................7-94.2

       (2)  Compare—nonstatutory motion .........................7-94.2

       (3)  Computing time to amend ....................................7-94.3

  7.  Entry of Judgment ..........................................................7-94.3

    a.  Where leave to amend denied..................................7-94.3

b. Where leave granted but no amended pleading
filed ........................................................................ 7-94.3
c. Where leave granted but amended pleading *filed
late* ........................................................................ 7-94.3

**E. MOTION TO DISMISS** ...................................................... 7-94.4
   1. No Statutory Basis for Challenging Pleadings .............. 7-94.4
     a. Other applications .................................................. 7-94.4
     b. Compare—federal practice .................................... 7-94.4
   2. As Defendant's Initial Pleading .................................... 7-94.4
     a. Caution re entry of default ..................................... 7-94.4
     b. Bar to later demurrer? ........................................... 7-94.5
   3. No "Speaking" Motions ................................................ 7-94.5

**FORMS**
- Demurrer to Complaint; Notice of Hearing; Points and
Authorities in Support ............................................................. 7-95
- Checklist: Demurrer .................................................................. 7-100
- Notice of Ruling on Demurrer .................................................. 7-101
- Notice of Motion to Strike; Points and Authorities in
Support ...................................................................................... 7-103
- Notice of Motion for Judgment on the Pleadings; Request
to Take Judicial Notice; Points and Authorities in Support .... 7-107
- Checklist: Judgment on the Pleadings ................................... 7-113
- Checklist: Motion to Strike ...................................................... 7-114
- Checklist: Demurrer Dismissal ............................................... 7-115

# ATTACKING THE PLEADINGS

As discussed below, each party has several weapons to attack the other's pleadings:

— *demurrer (¶7:3 ff.)*;

— *motion to strike (¶7:156 ff.)*;

— *motion to dismiss (¶7:370 ff.); and*

— *motion for judgment on the pleadings (¶7:275 ff.)*.

**[7:1]** **Background:** In the past, these weapons were far more potent than they are today. Demurrers were usually the opening salvo in a battle to narrow the issues through the pleadings. However, in modern practice, demurrers and motions directed to the pleadings are of diminishing importance. In large part, this is due to our liberalized pleading rules *(see ¶6:1)*. But it also reflects judicial policy that, wherever possible, cases should be resolved on their merits rather than through technical challenges to the pleadings.

**[7:2]** **Impact of Official Forms:** With the adoption of Official Form complaints for the most common civil actions (¶6:5), the role of demurrers and motions directed to the pleadings may be even more limited.

**[7:2.1]** **Restrictions in limited civil cases:** The Legislature has further limited the procedures available to attack pleadings in limited civil cases. Special demurrers are not permitted; and motions to strike are allowed only on the ground that the relief sought is not recoverable as a matter of law under the allegations of the complaint. [CCP §92(d); see ¶7:38]

## A. DEMURRERS

### Strategy and Tactics Re Demurrers: Should You Demur?

(1) **[7:3]** **Considerations re special demurrers:** Most grounds for special demurrer ("uncertainty," "lack of capacity," "defect or misjoinder of parties," etc.) can be raised *either* by demurrer or answer. (They are waived only if not raised in either pleading; see CCP §430.80, ¶7:32.)

(a) **Advantages:** Loosely pleaded claims are difficult to deny or defend. A special demurrer can force plaintiffs to lay out their claims more clearly, possibly exposing grounds for defense and for summary judgment or summary adjudication later in the litigation.

---

### Strategy and Tactics Re Demurrers: Should You Demur? (Cont'd)

(b) **Disadvantages:** Special demurrers are rarely worth the time and money required to bring them. Almost invariably, the defect can be corrected and the court will grant leave to amend. Thus, little is gained beyond some delay . . . at considerable expense to your client!

⇨ *PRACTICE POINTER:* Before filing a special demurrer, always telephone plaintiff's counsel and point out what you perceive to be the defect in the complaint. Offer to stipulate to plaintiff's filing an amended complaint to eliminate the defect. Moreover, even if plaintiff declines your stipulation, it may be wiser to raise the defect in your answer than to spend the time and money on a special demurrer.

Also consider whether the uncertainties can be cured through interrogatories or other discovery devices.

(2) **[7:4] Considerations re general demurrers:** There is no problem of waiver with general demurrers (CCP §430.80, ¶7:33). You can attack the complaint for "failure to state facts sufficient to constitute a cause of action" even after the time for demurring; e.g., by motion for judgment on the pleadings (¶7:275; *but see* ¶7:285) or for a directed verdict at trial.

So, whether to demur is really a *tactical* decision.

(a) **Advantages:** A general demurrer makes sense in several situations:

— *Where plaintiff is asserting some novel cause of action:* A general demurrer is effective where there appears to be no legal authority for plaintiff's claim. The demurrer provides a prompt test of the claim's legal sufficiency, allowing the case to be disposed of more rapidly and at much less cost than going all the way through trial. (For example, claims for "palimony" and "wrongful life" were first adjudicated at the demurrer stage.)

— *Where it appears plaintiff cannot truthfully amend to allege omitted facts*: A general demurrer also makes sense where plaintiff appears to be *avoiding* allegations crucial to the

## Strategy and Tactics Re Demurrers: Should You Demur? (Cont'd)

cause of action he or she is attempting to plead (e.g., compliance with prelawsuit demand requirements, etc.). The demurrer may force plaintiff to realize there is a bar to recovery so that even if leave to amend is granted plaintiff will be unable (truthfully) to supply the missing allegations. In such event, settlement or dismissal may result forthwith.

— *Where a motion for summary judgment is contemplated:* It is incumbent upon a defendant moving for summary judgment to show there is no triable issue of fact as to any cause of action in the complaint (*see ¶10:240*). Vague or ambiguous pleadings by plaintiff make it difficult to ascertain exactly what claims are being asserted. A general demurrer can force plaintiff to clarify particular elements of the cause of action involved. Defendant may then be in a better position to satisfy its burden on the summary judgment motion.

— *Where case assigned to direct calendar judge:* Where the case has been assigned to a direct calendar judge, a demurrer can be used to signal fundamental weaknesses in plaintiff's case at an early stage of the litigation. Even if plaintiff is given leave to amend, the judge may insist on stricter pleadings of key elements, causing plaintiff to reevaluate the facts of the case, thus encouraging settlement.

(b) **Disadvantages:** There are also some distinct disadvantages to consider:

- **Judicial attitudes:** Judges (particularly under "fast track") are often unsympathetic to demurrers, preferring to move the case toward trial on the merits rather than to prolong the pleading process.

- **Cost:** If the defect in the complaint is correctable, the judge will simply grant leave to amend, and in all probability plaintiff will eventually correct the defect. In such event, all the demurrer will have accomplished is to run up the cost for all concerned . . . and some delay.

**Strategy and Tactics Re Demurrers: Should You Demur?**
**(Cont'd)**

- **Risk of "educating" plaintiff:** Moreover, the big disadvantage of a general demurrer is the risk that it may "educate" plaintiff's counsel: i.e., it may cause him or her to rethink the case, and come up with a stronger cause of action or legal theory. In such event, your demurrer will have backfired, as you end up having to defend against a much more difficult case! Therefore, in many cases it may be wiser to hold your fire until the time of trial. Trial judges may be far less lenient in allowing amendment to the pleadings, and may force plaintiff to "sink or swim" with the claims originally pleaded.

- **Risk of creating bad law on appeal:** If a general demurrer is sustained and the case ends up on appeal, the appellate court will reverse if the complaint was sufficient on any theory (*see ¶7:41*). Moreover, because of the policy favoring trial on the merits, the appellate court may stretch existing precedent, or even create new precedent, to uphold the complaint. If so, when the case is sent back for trial, the rules may be more favorable to the plaintiff than if no demurrer had been filed!

- **Risk of sanctions:** Finally, there is always a possibility the judge may disagree with you as to the merits of the demurrer! If the court concludes your demurrer is totally without merit, it may impose sanctions (*see ¶9:1026, 9:1177*).

➪ *PRACTICE POINTER:* Think long and hard before filing a general demurrer!

(3) **[7:4.1]** **Considerations re ALL demurrers:** Unless you're *certain* the defect in the opposing pleadings cannot be cured by amendment, *always* call opposing counsel, point out the defect and *offer to stipulate* to his or her amending the complaint accordingly. (Likewise, where a demurrer is filed against you and it appears to be well-taken, call opposing counsel and offer to stipulate to amending the complaint to address the defect.) This avoids the cost and delay of unnecessary demurrer hearings.

---

**Strategy and Tactics for Opposing Party:
Should You Amend?**

(1) [7:4.2]  If the demurrer appears to have *any* merit, it is usually smarter to *amend* than to spend the time and effort to oppose the demurrer. Not only does this save the legal fees in opposing the demurrer, it also speeds up getting the case at issue: Defendant will have to respond to the amended complaint without the delay the demurrer hearing would entail!

(2) [7:4.3]  If you decide to amend, be sure to let opposing counsel *and the court* know at least several days before the hearing date on the demurrer . . . to save their wasting time preparing for the hearing. Rushing in and filing an amended complaint just before the hearing may be legally permissible (*see ¶6:602 ff.*), but it is extremely discourteous to opposing counsel *and to the court.*

---

1. [7:5]  **Function of Demurrer:**  A demurrer is a pleading used to *test the legal sufficiency* of other pleadings. I.e., it raises issues of law, not fact, regarding the form or content of the opposing party's pleading (complaint, answer or cross-complaint). [CCP §§422.10, 589]

    It is *not* the function of the demurrer to challenge the truthfulness of the complaint; and for purposes of the ruling on the demurrer, all facts pleaded in the complaint are assumed to be true . . . however improbable they may be! (*See ¶7:43-48.*)

    a. [7:6]  **Demurrer as pleading:**  A demurrer may be the defendant's initial pleading. [CCP §422.10] If defendant has not previously appeared in the action, the demurrer constitutes a *general appearance*, subjecting defendant to the court's personal jurisdiction. [CCP §1014; see *Hamilton v. Asbestos Corp., Ltd.* (2000) 22 C4th 1127, 1147, 95 CR2d 701, 714]

        (1) [7:7]  **Not permitted in family law cases:**  By court rule, demurrers are not permitted in family law proceedings. [CRC 5.108]

        (2) [7:7a]  **Unlawful detainer cases?**  A defendant in an unlawful detainer action may "answer or demur." [CCP §1170]

            Nonetheless, it has been held that a motion to quash— and *not* a demurrer—is the "only" acceptable procedure to test whether a complaint states a cause of action for unlawful detainer supporting a five-day summons. [*Delta Imports, Inc. v. Mun.Ct. (Missimer)* (1983) 146 CA3d 1033, 1036, 194 CR 685, 687]

(a) [7:7b] **Rationale:** A general demurrer only tests whether the complaint states a cause of action for *something* . . . even if on a theory other than unlawful detainer (e.g., nonpayment of rent as breach of contract, recovery of possession from defaulting purchaser). Also, a demurrer constitutes a general appearance, thus waiving the very point defendant seeks to raise—namely, whether the court has personal jurisdiction over defendant served with a five-day summons. [*Delta Imports, Inc. v. Mun.Ct. (Missimer)*, supra, 146 CA3d at 1036, 194 CR at 687—no unlawful detainer cause of action stated because landlord failed to allege tenant had been given written notice of alleged breaches of lease]

(b) [7:7c] **Comment:** The *Delta* opinion does not even consider CCP §1170. Moreover, the California Supreme Court has not confirmed the *Delta* position.

However, the Supreme Court has by dictum acknowledged that "(t)he only situation in which a motion to quash service of summons has been approved as a procedure by which to challenge the sufficiency of the complaint is in unlawful detainer, where a demurrer is unavailable." [*Greener v. Workers' Comp. Appeals Bd.* (1993) 6 C4th 1028, 1036, 25 CR2d 539, 544 (citing *Delta*)]

The Supreme Court did not approve or disapprove the *Delta* holding since the issue was not before it. [See *Greener v. Workers' Comp. Appeals Bd.*, supra, 6 C4th at 1036, 25 CR2d at 544, fn. 5]

*Cross-refer:* For a detailed discussion, see Friedman, Garcia & Hagarty, *Cal. Prac. Guide: Landlord-Tenant* (TRG), Ch. 8.

b. [7:7.1] **Demurrer as motion:** For certain purposes, a demurrer is also treated as a motion—i.e., an application for a court order: For example, CCP §1008(a), authorizing the court to reconsider rulings on "motions," applies to demurrers. [*Rains v. Sup.Ct. (Center Foundation)* (1984) 150 CA3d 933, 943, 198 CR 249, 256; *see ¶9:324 ff.*]

Note also that the Civil Law & Motion Rules (CRC 301-391) apply generally to demurrers as well as to motions. [CRC 303(c); *see ¶9:6*]

c. [7:8] **Demurrer challenges only defects on face of pleading or judicially noticeable:** A demurrer can be used only to challenge defects that appear on the face of the pleading under attack; or from matters outside the pleading that are *judicially noticeable.* [*Blank v. Kirwan* (1985) 39 C3d 311, 318, 216 CR 718, 721; *Harboring Villas Homeowners Ass'n v. Sup.Ct. (Ce Mar Las Vegas IX, Inc.)* (1998) 63 CA4th 426, 429, 73 CR2d 646, 648—demurrer on ground of nonjoinder of trust deed holders as indispensable parties must be overruled where it did not appear from face of complaint that property was subject to deeds of trust]

No other extrinsic evidence can be considered (i.e., no "speaking demurrers"). [*Ion Equip. Corp. v. Nelson* (1980) 110 CA3d 868, 881, 168 CR 361, 367—error for court to consider facts asserted in memorandum supporting demurrer; *Afuso v. United States Fid. & Guar. Co., Inc.* (1985) 169 CA3d 859, 862, 215 CR 490, 492 (disapproved on other grounds in *Moradi-Shalal v. Firemen's Fund Ins. Cos.* (1988) 46 C3d 287, 250 CR 116)—error for court to consider contents of release which was not part of any court record]

(1) [7:9] **Defects appearing on face of complaint:** A demurrer can be utilized where the complaint itself is incomplete or *discloses some defense* that would bar recovery (e.g., dates pleaded in complaint show statute of limitations has run). [*Guardian North Bay, Inc. v. Sup.Ct. (Myers)* (2001) 94 CA4th 963, 971-972, 114 CR2d 748, 754]

"Face of the complaint" includes matters shown in *exhibits* attached to the complaint and incorporated by reference; or in a *superseded complaint* in the same action. [*Frantz v. Blackwell* (1987) 189 CA3d 91, 94, 234 CR 178, 179-180; *Barnett v. Fireman's Fund Ins. Co.* (2001) 90 CA4th 500, 505, 108 CR2d 657, 659—"(W)e rely on and accept as true the contents of the exhibits and treat as surplusage the pleader's allegations as to the legal effect of the exhibits"]

(a) [7:10] Some of the statutory grounds for demurrer rarely lie because they are not likely to be disclosed on the face of the complaint; e.g., plaintiff's lack of capacity to sue (¶7:70-71).

(b) [7:11] Also, plaintiff may be able to insulate his complaint from demurrer by artful pleading and use of form allegations; e.g., common counts. (Note, however, that even a common count is subject to demurrer where the complaint also alleges specific facts upon which the common counts are based, and those facts do not entitle plaintiff to recover.) [*Del E. Webb Corp. v. Structural Materials Co.* (1981) 123 CA3d 593, 601, 176 CR 824, 828]

(2) [7:12] **Defects appearing from matters judicially noticeable:** The Code specifically authorizes the

court to consider, as ground for demurrer, any matter which the court *must* or *may* judicially notice under Ev.C. §§451 or 452. [CCP §430.30(a)]

(a) [7:13]  **Matters judicially noticeable:**  Although not mentioned anywhere in the complaint, defendant can base a demurrer on the following matters:

   1)  [7:14]  **Court records and files:**  The court can take judicial notice of the records in the pending action, or in any other action pending in the same court or any other court of record in the U.S. [Ev.C. §452(d)]

      a)  [7:14.1]  **Defense disclosed in other court records:**  Thus, if such records disclose an absolute defense to the action or deficiency in the complaint, the matter can be adjudicated at the demurrer hearing. [*Bistawros v. Greenberg* (1987) 189 CA3d 189, 192, 234 CR 377, 378—court took judicial notice of its own files in sustaining demurrer on ground of another action pending between same parties on same cause (*see* ¶7:76); see also *Frommhagen v. Board of Supervisors of Santa Cruz County* (1987) 197 CA3d 1292, 1299, 243 CR 390, 393—court took judicial notice of complaint in prior action in determining whether to sustain demurrer based on res judicata; *Britz, Inc. v. Dow Chem. Co.* (1999) 73 CA4th 177, 180, 86 CR2d 188, 190-191—in ruling on demurrer, court could take judicial notice of prior order approving good faith settlement under CCP §877.6]

      b)  [7:15]  **Limitation—only matters indisputably true:**  Judicial notice of other court records and files is limited to matters that are *indisputably* true. This generally means judicial notice is limited to the orders and judgments in the other court file, as distinguished from the contents of documents filed therein.

         1/  [7:15.1]  **No inadmissible hearsay:** The court cannot accept as true the *contents* of pleadings or exhibits in the other action just because they are part of the court record or file. Such documents are inadmissible hearsay in the present case. [*Day v. Sharp* (1975) 50 CA3d 904, 914, 123 CR 918, 924]

[7:15.2] And, it is error for the court in ruling on a demurrer to take judicial notice of the *contents* of a sworn affidavit filed in a companion case. [See *Bach v. McNelis* (1989) 207 CA3d 852, 865, 255 CR 232, 238; *Lockley v. Law Office of Cantrell, Green, Pekich, Cruz & McCort* (2001) 91 CA4th 875, 882, 110 CR2d 877, 882]

[7:15.3-15.4] *Reserved.*

2/ [7:15.5] **Findings of fact:** The court may take notice of the *existence* of findings of fact made in the other action, but may *not* accept them as *true* on issues in dispute in the present case. I.e., the other court's findings are *not* indisputably true. Otherwise, the judge in the other case would be made "infallible" on all matters, usurping the doctrines of res judicata and collateral estoppel (which are limited to final *judgments*). [*Sosinsky v. Grant* (1992) 6 CA4th 1548, 1565, 8 CR2d 552, 561-562; see *Fowler v. Howell* (1996) 42 CA4th 1746, 1749, 50 CR2d 484, 486]

[7:15.6] *Caution re earlier cases:* Earlier cases suggest a court can take judicial notice of "factual findings" in other cases (see *Day v. Sharp,* supra) but fail to distinguish between the *existence* and *truth* of those findings.

c) [7:16] **Inconsistent statements in earlier pleadings:** The court may take judicial notice of *admissions* or inconsistent statements made by plaintiff in earlier pleadings. Unless plaintiff can "plead around" those earlier statements, contradictory allegations in the complaint may be disregarded and a demurrer sustained. *See discussion at ¶7:47 ff.*

[7:16.1-16.4] *Reserved.*

d) [7:16.5] **Contradictory discovery responses:** A complaint's allegations may be disregarded when they conflict with judicially-noticed discovery responses. [*Bockrath v. Aldrich Chem. Co., Inc.* (1999) 21 C4th 71, 83, 86 CR2d 846, 854—discovery responses binding, however, only as to matters within party's personal knowledge]

2) [7:17] **Matters of common knowledge:** The court may also take notice of facts outside the complaint if they are of such common knowledge in the community that they are beyond dispute; e.g., the existence of certain local landmarks, the character and direction of traffic on local streets, etc. [Ev.C. §452(g)]

- [7:17a] The court may take judicial notice of newspaper articles or transcripts of radio or television broadcasts as evidence of the *fact* of their *publication*, but *not* as to the truth of their content. [*McKelvey v. Boeing North American, Inc.* (1999) 74 CA4th 151, 162, 86 CR2d 645, 652-653—because of wide publicity, plaintiff had notice of facts reported regardless of their accuracy]

[7:17b-17d] *Reserved.*

3) [7:17e] **Indisputable facts:** The court may also take judicial notice of facts not reasonably subject to dispute and "capable of immediate and accurate verification by resort to sources of reasonably indisputable accuracy." [Ev.C. §452(h)]

This covers "facts which are widely accepted as established by experts and specialists in the natural, physical, and social sciences *which can be verified by reference to treatises, encyclopedias, almanacs* and the like . . ." [*Gould v. Maryland Sound Industries, Inc.* (1995) 31 CA4th 1137, 1145, 37 CR2d 718, 722 (emphasis added)]

[7:17f] *Reserved.*

- [7:17g] Thus, the court may take judicial notice of the ownership, easements and control over certain land. [*Bethman v. City of Ukiah* (1989) 216 CA3d 1395, 1399, 265 CR 539, 541, fn. 4]

- [7:17h] *Compare:* However, the court may *not* take judicial notice of the existence of a contract between private parties. [*Gould v. Maryland Sound Industries, Inc.,* supra, 31 CA4th at 1145, 37 CR2d at 722]

4) **[7:17.1]** **Official acts:** Further, the court may take notice of official acts of any state or federal legislative, executive or judicial department. [Ev.C. §452(c); see *Fowler v. Howell* (1996) 42 CA4th 1746, 1750, 50 CR2d 484, 486—court can take judicial notice of records and files of *state administrative agencies*]

   a) **[7:17.2]** **Example:** P sued to compel Reinsurance Co. to pay monies owed by insolvent insurer. In ruling on a demurrer, the court could take judicial notice of a *release* given by the State Insurance Commissioner, freeing Reinsurance Co. of liability for insolvent insurer's debts. [*Ascherman v. General Reinsurance Corp.* (1986) 183 CA3d 307, 310-311, 228 CR 1, 2-3]

   b) **[7:17.2a]** **Example:** In ruling on a demurrer to a complaint against a public hospital, the court properly took judicial notice of a statement of identity filed by the hospital with the Secretary of State and indexed in the "Roster of Public Agencies" (to determine whether P was excused from prelitigation claim filing requirements; *see* ¶1:668 ff.). [*Elmore v. Oak Valley Hosp. Dist.* (1988) 204 CA3d 716, 722, 251 CR 405, 409]

   c) **[7:17.3]** **Limitation—official acts must be undisputed:** Judicial notice cannot be taken where the official acts are themselves in dispute; e.g., a demurrer cannot be used to resolve a dispute as to whether the acts took place. [*Cruz v. County of Los Angeles* (1985) 173 CA3d 1131, 1134, 219 CR 661, 663]

      **Example:** County demurred to P's original complaint because not filed within 6 months following mailing of notice of rejection (¶1:734). P then amended his complaint to allege that the notice of rejection had never been received. County demurred again and requested judicial notice be taken of its method of preparing and mailing notices of rejection as an "official act" (under Ev.C. §452(c)). Judicial notice was *improper* because whether such practice had been followed was the very dispute which occasioned the request for judicial notice. [*Cruz v. County of Los Angeles*, supra, 173 CA3d at 1134, 219 CR at 663]

5) [7:17.4] **Regulations and legislative enactments:** Judicial notice may be taken of "regulations and legislative enactments" of the federal or state government or any political subdivision thereof (e.g., cities and counties). [Ev.C. §§452(b), 200]

a) [7:17.5] **Example:** A complaint was filed against San Mateo for failure to employ certain "required" bidding procedures. In sustaining a demurrer, the court took judicial notice of San Mateo's municipal code that indicated the bidding procedures were not mandatory. [*Beresford Neighborhood Ass'n v. City of San Mateo* (1989) 207 CA3d 1180, 1190, 255 CR 434, 440]

(b) [7:18] **Procedure for invoking judicial notice:** The demurring party must specify in the demurrer or attached points and authorities the particular matters which the court is requested to judicially notice. [CCP §430.70]

In addition, *copies* of the material to be so noticed *must* be furnished to the court and to each party. [CRC 323(c)] (The Rule does not state when such copies must be furnished, but may be interpreted to require that they accompany the moving papers.)

➡️[7:19] *PRACTICE POINTER:* File a *separate* "Request to Take Judicial Notice" with copies of the material to be noticed at the same time you file your demurrer. This is the surest way of bringing the matter to the court's attention. (A "Request to Take Judicial Notice" appears as part of *Form 7:F.*)

1) [7:20] **Of file in same court:** A party seeking to have judicial notice taken of material which is part of a file in the court in which the matter is being heard, must *also* (1) specify in writing the *part* of the file to be judicially noticed; and (2) make arrangements with the court clerk to *have the file in the courtroom* at the time of the hearing. [CRC 323(b)]

➡️[7:21] *PRACTICE POINTER:* Wherever feasible, *attach copies* of the material to be noticed to your moving papers. If the other file fails to arrive, you may be able to obtain a stipulation for the court to use the copies.

2) [7:22] **Of file in different court:** If the material to be judicially noticed is in a case file in a different court, the demurring party must either *subpoena* the file from the other court, or obtain *certified copies* of whatever portions of such file are to be noticed.

Note: Courts having more than one branch or district (e.g., Los Angeles Superior Court) may treat each district as a *different* court for purposes of judicial notice.

[7:23] *Reserved.*

## 2. Time to File Demurrer

a. [7:24] **Demurrer to complaint (or cross-complaint):** Defendant can demur within the same period of time it has to answer the complaint—i.e., *30 days* after service, unless extended by stipulation or court order. [CCP §430.40(a)]

A demurrer must be noticed for hearing not more than 35 days after filing or on the first available court date thereafter. [CRC 325(b); *see ¶7:110 ff.*]

(1) [7:24.1] **Demurrer filed in conjunction with motion to strike:** A demurrer may be filed in conjunction with a motion to strike (*see ¶7:162 ff.*).

*Compare:* But filing a motion to strike *by itself* does not extend the time to file a demurrer. [CCP §585(f)]

(2) [7:25] **Demurrer filed in conjunction with answer:** Usually, defendant will answer the complaint only after a demurrer has been overruled. But if defendant chooses to, it can answer and demur at the same time. [CCP §430.30(c)]

⇨[7:26] *PRACTICE POINTER:* Doing so would appear to make sense only if the demurrer was taken to some causes of action in the complaint and not to others. Defendant might choose to answer the remaining causes of action at the same time.

But there is *no particular advantage in doing this*. No default can be taken when a demurrer has been timely filed—whether it relates to one cause of action or the whole complaint. [CCP §585] And, the answer may be wasted . . . because if the demurrer is sustained and plaintiff files an amended complaint, defendant will probably have to file another answer (¶6:635, 6:688 ff.).

b. **[7:27]** **Demurrer to answer (or answer to cross-complaint):** Plaintiff can demur to defendant's answer, but has *only 10 days* following service of the answer within which to do so, unless extended by stipulation or court order. [CCP §430.40(b)]

(1) **[7:28]** **Comment:** The only apparent explanation for the shorter period of time allowed for demurring to an answer is that the demurring party (plaintiff) is already a party to the action. Whereas, with demurrers to the complaint, the demurrer may be the defendant's initial pleading, and defendant therefore may need a greater period of time to employ counsel and for counsel to become familiar with the case.

3. **[7:29]** **Grounds for Demurrer:** A demurrer can be taken only upon the grounds specified in the Code.

⇨**[7:29.1]** *PRACTICE POINTER:* Even so, some judges (particularly in direct calendar courts) are willing to consider other grounds by treating the demurrer as a *motion to strike*, in order to expedite resolution of challenges to the pleadings.

a. **[7:30]** **Demurrer to complaint (or cross-complaint):** The following are the possible grounds for objection to a complaint or cross-complaint under CCP §430.10:

- Court lacks subject matter jurisdiction (¶7:63 ff.);

- Plaintiff lacks capacity to sue (¶7:70 ff.);

- Nonjoinder or misjoinder of parties (¶7:78 ff.);

- Another action is pending between the same parties for the same cause of action (¶7:74 ff.);

- Failure to state facts sufficient to constitute a cause of action (¶7:39 ff.);

- Uncertainty (¶7:84 ff.);

- Failure to allege whether contract sued upon is written or oral or implied by conduct (¶7:90 ff.);

- Failure to attach attorney's certificate required in certain malpractice actions (¶7:95 ff.).

(1) **[7:31]** **Grounds can be raised in answer:** The statutory grounds above do *not* have to be raised by demurrer. The defendant may, if he or she chooses,

assert them instead as defenses or objections in his or her answer. [CCP §430.80(a)]

Also, as mentioned earlier, some of these objections (e.g., plaintiff's lack of capacity to sue) rarely appear on the face of the complaint. Thus, they *cannot* be raised by demurrer; they can only be raised as objections in the answer.

(2) [7:32] **Waiver if not raised by demurrer or answer:** Most of the statutory grounds for objection to a complaint, above, are automatically *waived* if not raised *either* by demurrer or in the answer. [CCP §430.80(a)]

   (a) [7:33] **Exceptions:** "Failure to state facts sufficient to constitute a cause of action," and the "court lacks subject matter jurisdiction," are *not* waived. These objections can be raised at any time, even if not asserted by demurrer or answer. [CCP §430.80(a); see *Sullivan v. Delta Air Lines, Inc.* (1997) 15 C4th 288, 307, 63 CR2d 74, 86 (subject matter jurisdiction); *Henry v. Associated Indem. Corp.* (1990) 217 CA3d 1405, 1413, 266 CR 578, 583, fn. 8 (failure to state cause of action)]

   (b) [7:34] **Rationale:** These latter two objections go to the court's *power* to grant relief; and hence, are never waived. But the other statutory grounds for demurrer are basically technical reasons why the complaint is defective, or the action should not proceed. They are "disfavored" objections, and therefore must be raised at the outset, if at all. After the answer is filed, it is too late to object for the first time on these grounds (although the court has power to permit amendment of the answer in proper cases).

(3) [7:34.1] **Demurrer to certain causes of action only:** A demurrer may be filed to one of several causes of action in the complaint, without answering the other causes of action. No default can be taken while the demurrer is pending. [CCP §585; CRC 325(g)]

If the demurrer is sustained, defendant has 10 days after the plaintiff amends the complaint within which to answer, move to strike, or demur again. [CRC 325(g)]

Likewise, if the demurrer is overruled, defendant has 10 days to answer, move to strike or demur again to the *remaining causes of action*—unless otherwise ordered by the court. [CRC 325(g)]

*Comment:* The validity of CRC 325(g) is questionable because the 10-day limit appears to conflict with CCP

§471.5, which allows defendants *30 days* to "answer" an amended complaint. (The word "answer" in §471.5 presumably means "respond" and thus includes the possibility for another demurrer; *see ¶6:689*.)

(a) **[7:34.2]** **Defendant ordered to answer:** Usually, when the court overrules a demurrer, it orders the defendant to answer within a certain number of days. In such cases, an answer is the only permissible response, and a default can be entered if, instead of answering, defendant files a motion to strike or another demurrer (¶*5:55*).

(b) **[7:34.3]** **No order to answer—"piecemeal demurrers"?** A demurrer may be directed to only one of several causes of action in the complaint. [CRC 325(g)] (However, this is *not* a good tactic if there are grounds for demurrer to the other causes of action as well; *see "Practice Pointer," below*.)

If, on overruling such demurrer, the court fails to order defendant to answer, defendant is free to challenge the remaining causes of action by demurrer or motion to strike. [CRC 325(g)]

Thus, "piecemeal demurrers" are theoretically possible: i.e., D could demur to the "First Cause of Action"; then, if that is overruled, demur to the "Second Cause of Action"; and so on, for each cause of action in the complaint! [*Skrbina v. Fleming Cos., Inc.* (1996) 45 CA4th 1353, 1365, 53 CR2d 481, 488 (citing text)]

🔾[7:34.4] *PRACTICE POINTER:* Don't expect a judge to permit such tactics!

The judge may order the defendant to answer after the first demurrer, in which event it would be too late to demur to the remaining causes of action. And, even if there was no order to answer, most judges would frown on "piecemeal demurrers" which would force them to review the same pleading time and again.

b. **[7:35]** **Demurrer to answer:** There are only three grounds for demurrer to an answer under CCP §430.20:

• Failure to state facts sufficient to constitute a defense;

• Uncertainty;

• Failure to state whether contract alleged in the answer is written or oral.

⇨[7:35.1]  **PRACTICE POINTER:**  A demurrer can be an effective tool for eliminating "boilerplate" affirmative defenses that often appear in answers (e.g., "waiver," "estoppel," "unclean hands," etc.). A demurrer may be on the ground of failure to plead sufficient facts to constitute a defense.

(1) [7:36]  **Waiver of grounds:**  An answer's "failure to state facts sufficient to constitute a defense" may be raised at any time (i.e., no waiver). But the other grounds for challenging the sufficiency of the answer *must* be raised by demurrer, or are automatically waived. [CCP §430.80(b)]

c.  [7:37]  **"General" vs. "special" demurrers:**  A demurrer for failure to state a cause of action (or defense) is commonly referred to as a "general demurrer." In addition, a demurrer to the complaint for lack of subject matter jurisdiction is treated as a "general demurrer," because the objection is never waived (¶*7:33, 7:69*). All other grounds for demurrer are "special" demurrers, and are waived unless timely raised (¶*7:34*).

(1) [7:38]  **No special demurrers in limited civil cases:**  Only general demurrers are allowed in limited civil cases. The grounds for special demurrer must be raised, if at all, as affirmative defenses in the answer. [CCP §92(c) (part of economic litigation rules governing limited civil cases)]

(a) [7:38.1]  **Exception for unlawful detainer actions?**  It is unclear whether demurrers are allowed at all in unlawful detainer actions (*see* ¶*7:7a*). If they are, then special demurrers may still be allowed in such actions (including unlawful detainers classified as limited civil cases) . . . because CCP §91(b) specifically *exempts* unlawful detainer actions from the economic litigation rules. (*Comment:* This appears to be a legislative oversight. There is no logic in allowing special demurrers in what is supposed to be a special proceeding!)

d.  [7:39]  **General demurrer—failure to state a cause of action:**  "The pleading does not state facts sufficient to constitute a cause of action." [CCP §430.10(e)]

(1) [7:40]  **Function:**  A demurrer for failure to state a cause of action provides a quick way of getting the case decided on assumed facts: Assuming the facts alleged in the complaint are true, do they state *any* valid cause of action? If they do, the general demurrer must be overruled. But if they do not, after leave to amend, the action may be dismissed.

(a) [7:41]  **ANY valid cause of action overcomes demurrer:**  It is not necessary that the cause of action be the one intended by plaintiff. The test is whether the complaint states *any* valid claim entitling plaintiff to relief. Thus, plaintiff may be mistaken as to the nature of the case, or the legal theory on which he or she can prevail. But if the essential facts of *some* valid cause of action are alleged, the complaint is good against a general demurrer. [*Quelimane Co., Inc. v. Stewart Title Guar. Co.* (1998) 19 C4th 26, 28, 77 CR2d 709, 715; *Adelman v. Associated Int'l Ins. Co.* (2001) 90 CA4th 352, 359, 108 CR2d 788, 792]

    1)  [7:42]  **Example:**  P sued his insurance agent for "fraud" for unauthorized signing of P's name to papers limiting his insurance coverage. A demurrer for failure to plead fraud properly must be overruled because the complaint stated a *malpractice* action against the insurance agent: "(E)rroneous or confusing labels attached by the inept pleader are to be ignored if the complaint pleads facts which would entitle the plaintiff to relief." [*Saunders v. Cariss* (1990) 224 CA3d 905, 908, 274 CR 186, 188]

(b) [7:42.1]  **Improper remedy not ground for demurrer:**  A motion to strike, not a general demurrer, is the procedure to attack an improper claim for punitive damages or other remedy demanded in the complaint. Reason: A general demurrer challenges only the sufficiency of the *cause of action* pleaded, and must be overruled if *any* valid cause of action is pleaded; a demand for improper relief does not vitiate an otherwise valid cause of action. [*Venice Town Council, Inc. v. City of Los Angeles* (1996) 47 CA4th 1547, 1561-1562, 55 CR2d 465, 475; *Grieves v. Sup.Ct. (Fox)* (1984) 157 CA3d 159, 164-165, 203 CR 556, 558]

*Compare:* Motion to strike improper damage claims; *see ¶7:182 ff.*

(c) [7:42.2]  **Defective part of claim not ground for general demurrer:**  A general demurrer does not lie to only *part* of a cause of action. If there are sufficient allegations to entitle plaintiff to relief, other allegations cannot be challenged by general demurrer. [*Kong v. City of Hawaiian Gardens Redevelop. Agency* (2003) 108 CA4th 1028, 1046, 134 CR2d 260, 272; *PH II, Inc. v. Sup.Ct. (Ibershof)* (1995) 33 CA4th 1680, 1682, 40 CR2d 169, 171]

1) **Application**

- [7:42.3] P sued D for legal malpractice, alleging several distinct acts of malpractice. One of these was not malpractice as a matter of law. This was *not* ground for demurrer to the complaint because the malpractice cause of action was supported by the other acts. [*PH II, Inc. v. Sup.Ct. (Ibershof)*, supra, 33 CA4th at 1682-1683, 40 CR2d at 170-171]

2) [7:42.4] **Compare—motion to strike:** Substantive defects in a portion of the complaint can be challenged by motion to strike; *see* ¶*7:188.1.*

(d) [7:42.5] **Ambiguous allegations not ground for general demurrer:** Clarity of pleading is not essential to overcome a general demurrer: "Objections that a complaint is ambiguous or uncertain, or that the essential facts appear only inferentially, or as conclusions of law, or by way of recitals, must be raised by *special demurrer*, and cannot be reached on general demurrer." [*Johnson v. Mead* (1987) 191 CA3d 156, 160, 236 CR 277, 280 (emphasis in original)]

- [7:42.6] The complaint alleged that P acceded to D's illegal demand in order to "secure" a contract from XYZ, Inc. If "secure" meant *bribe*, a general demurrer would lie because a defense (unclean hands) was disclosed on the face of the complaint (*see* ¶*7:49*). But "secure" was *ambiguous* because it could also mean merely to "protect or safeguard" the contract, which would not bar recovery. Courts cannot sustain demurrers without leave to amend based on such ambiguities. [*Crosstalk Productions, Inc. v. Jacobson* (1998) 65 CA4th 631, 635, 76 CR2d 615, 617]

[7:42.7-42.10] *Reserved.*

(e) [7:42.11] **Declaratory relief—"actual controversy" allegation overcomes demurrer:** A general demurrer to a cause of action for declaratory relief must be overruled as long as an actual controversy is alleged; the pleader need not establish it is also entitled to a favorable judgment. [See *Ludgate Ins. Co. v. Lockheed Martin Corp.* (2000) 82 CA4th 592, 606, 98 CR2d 277, 286-287—actual controversy allegation accepted as true] (*Ludgate* addressed a motion for judgment on the pleadings, but the same rules governing demurrers generally apply; *see ¶7:275 ff.*)

(2) [7:43] **Admits facts alleged in complaint:** For the purpose of testing the sufficiency of the cause of action, the demurrer admits the truth of all *material facts properly pleaded* (i.e., all ultimate facts alleged, but not contentions, deductions or conclusions of fact or law). [*Aubry v. Tri-City Hosp. Dist.* (1992) 2 C4th 962, 966-967, 9 CR2d 92, 95; *Serrano v. Priest* (1971) 5 C3d 584, 591, 96 CR 601, 605; *Adelman v. Associated Int'l Ins. Co.* (2001) 90 CA4th 352, 359, 108 CR2d 788, 792]

(a) [7:44] **No matter how unlikely:** The sole issue raised by a general demurrer is whether the facts pleaded state a valid cause of action—not whether they are true. Thus, no matter how unlikely or improbable, plaintiff's allegations must be accepted as true for the purpose of ruling on the demurrer. [*Del E. Webb Corp. v. Structural Materials Co.* (1981) 123 CA3d 593, 604, 176 CR 824, 829]

⇨ [7:44.1] **PRACTICE POINTER:** Even though highly improbable allegations must be accepted as true for purposes of a demurrer, making such allegations *without evidentiary support* could subject the pleader to sanctions (*¶9:1135 ff.*) or malicious prosecution liability (*¶1:514 ff.*)!

1) [7:45] **Problems of proof irrelevant:** The question of plaintiff's ability to prove these unlikely allegations, or possible difficulties in making such proof, is of no concern in ruling on a demurrer. [*Committee on Children's Television, Inc. v. General Foods Corp.* (1983) 35 C3d 197, 213-214, 197 CR 783, 793]

(b) [7:46] **Limitation—allegations contradicted by judicial notice:** The allegations of the complaint are *not* accepted as true if they contradict or are inconsistent with facts judicially noticed by the court. (As stated earlier, in ruling on a demurrer, the court may consider matters outside the complaint if they are judicially noticeable under Ev.C. §§452 or 453; *see ¶7:12-23.*)

1) [7:47] **Admissions and inconsistent statements in same case:** Thus, in ruling on a demurrer, a court may take judicial notice of admissions or inconsistent statements by plain-

tiff in discovery documents or earlier pleadings in the same lawsuit, and may *disregard conflicting factual allegations* in the complaint: "Thus, a pleading valid on its face may nevertheless be subject to demurrer *when matters judicially noticed render the complaint meritless*." [*Del E. Webb Corp. v. Structural Materials Co.* (1981) 123 CA3d 593, 604, 176 CR 824, 830 (emphasis added)]

2) **[7:47.1] Allegations contradicted by attached exhibit:** Similarly, facts appearing in exhibits attached to the complaint are given precedence over inconsistent allegations in the complaint. [*Holland v. Morse Diesel Int'l, Inc.* (2001) 86 CA4th 1443, 1447, 104 CR2d 239, 242]

   a) **[7:47.2] Example:** P's complaint alleged Bank had allowed improper withdrawals from his account. However, the account signature card, attached as an exhibit to the complaint, showed *P's corporation* (not P individually) was the customer. Demurrer was properly sustained. [*Dodd v. Citizens Bank* (1990) 222 CA3d 1624, 272 CR 623]

   b) **[7:47.3] Compare—legal conclusions:** But a complaint will not be rejected solely because attached documents contain *legal conclusions* contrary to the facts alleged in the complaint. [See *Herman v. Los Angeles County Metro. Transp. Auth.* (1999) 71 CA4th 819, 823, 84 CR2d 144, 147, fn. 5]

3) **[7:48] Plaintiff's duty to "plead around" earlier admissions:** Plaintiff can avoid the effect of earlier admissions by including in the complaint a satisfactory explanation why the earlier admissions are incorrect. Absent such explanation, however, the self-destructive allegations in the earlier pleading or discovery response are "read into" the complaint, and allegations inconsistent therewith treated as sham and disregarded. [*Owens v. Kings Supermarket* (1988) 198 CA3d 379, 384, 243 CR 627, 630; *see discussion at ¶6:705 ff.*]

"The general rule . . . is that *material factual* allegations in a *verified* pleading that are omitted in a subsequent amended pleading without adequate explanation will be considered by the court in ruling on a demurrer to the later plead-ing." [*Shoemaker v. Myers* (1990) 52 C3d 1, 13, 276 CR 303, 309 (emphasis added); *see* ¶7:48]

   a)  **[7:48a]**  **Verified or unverified plead-ings:**  Although *Shoemaker*, supra, dealt with a verified complaint, the principle has been held equally applicable to *unverified* complaints. [*Pierce v. Lyman* (1991) 1 CA4th 1093, 1109, 3 CR2d 236, 245-246]

4)  **[7:48.1]**  **Application:**  Thus, demurrers have been sustained because of admissions or inconsistent statements made by the pleader in:

-  **[7:48.2]**  An earlier complaint in the same lawsuit. [*Owens v. Kings Supermarket*, supra, 198 CA3d at 384, 243 CR at 630]

-  **[7:48.2a]**  Pleadings in a different lawsuit. [*Cantu v. Resolution Trust Corp.* (1992) 4 CA4th 857, 877-878, 6 CR2d 151, 162— "The principle is that of *truthful* pleading"]

-  **[7:48.3]**  Affidavits that are part of the court file and judicially noticed. [*Dwan v. Dixon* (1963) 216 CA2d 260, 264-265, 30 CR 749, 752]

-  **[7:48.4]**  Responses to requests for ad-mission. [*Stencel Aero Engr. Corp. v. Sup.Ct. (McCarthy)* (1976) 56 CA3d 978, 982, 128 CR 691, 692, fn. 6]

-  **[7:48.5]**  Declarations opposing earlier motion for summary judgment. [*Del E. Webb Corp. v. Structural Materials Co.,* supra, 123 CA3d at 604, 176 CR at 830]

   a)  **[7:48.6]**  **Deposition testimony?**  There is a split of authority on whether judicial notice may be taken of inconsistent state-ments made by the pleader in a deposition transcript filed as part of the court record:

One case holds the existence of the state-ments can be noticed but not the truth thereof . . . apparently on the rationale that deposition testimony is merely evidentiary. [See *Garcia v. Sterling* (1985) 176 CA3d 17, 22, 221 CR 349, 352]

But another case disagrees: "We are not prepared to say that a court on a demurrer can never accept the truth of statements in a deposition." [*Joslin v. H.A.S. Ins. Brokerage* (1986) 184 CA3d 369, 375, 228 CR 878, 882, fn. 1—refusing to take judicial notice of deposition testimony, however, where party opposing demurrer disputed truthfulness of the testimony; see also *Sosinksy v. Grant* (1992) 6 CA4th 1548, 1569, 8 CR2d 552, 564, fn. 9]

[7:48.7-48.10]   *Reserved.*

5)   [7:48.11]   **Compare—right to plead inconsistent *theories:***   Although a pleader may not "blow hot and cold" on the same evidentiary *facts* in the same lawsuit, he or she may properly allege different legal theories (i.e., different *ultimate facts*). *See* ¶6:242 ff.

a)   [7:48.12]   **Comment:**   This distinction is sometimes easier to state than to apply. E.g., where the original complaint alleged *negligence*, an amendment alleging D acted *intentionally* arguably should be disregarded unless the contradiction is satisfactorily explained. But most judges apparently *permit* such pleading as "inconsistent legal theories."

[7:48.13-48.15]   *Reserved.*

6)   [7:48.16]   **Compare—right to explain contrary pleading in different lawsuit?**   It is unclear whether facts pleaded (or admitted in discovery responses) in a *different* lawsuit are conclusive on the pleader in the present action:

a)   [7:48.17]   **Not conclusive:**   Several cases hold pleading admissions in a different lawsuit can be rebutted at trial (by showing mistake, lack of authority, etc.): i.e., they are *merely evidentiary* in nature. [See *Dolinar v. Pedone* (1944) 63 CA2d 169, 176, 146 P2d 237, 241]

From this, it follows that a pleader should *not* be bound by admissions in an earlier lawsuit and should be allowed to explain contradictions in the present pleadings. [*Magnolia Square Homeowners Ass'n v. Safeco Ins. Co.* (1990) 221 CA3d 1049, 1061, 271 CR 1, 7]

b)   [7:48.18]   **Conclusive:**   However, at least one case indicates to the contrary. [See *Dryden v. Tri-Valley Growers* (1977)

65 CA3d 990, 997, 135 CR 720, 725—letters attached to P's complaint in earlier lawsuit "conclusively demonstrate" facts contrary to allegations of present complaint, defeating P's complaint "as a matter of law"]

- [7:48.19] **Comment:** *Dryden* may not be reliable authority. First of all, it may be dictum (the court had other reasons for holding no cause of action stated). More important, there is no discernable reason why a pleader should be estopped from taking inconsistent positions in a different lawsuit involving a *different cause of action*.

  [7:48.20-48.24] *Reserved.*

(3) [7:48.25] **Admits plaintiff's interpretation of ambiguous contract:** If a contract set out in the complaint (or attached as an exhibit) is ambiguous, plaintiff's interpretation must be accepted as correct in testing the sufficiency of the complaint: "(A) general demurrer to the complaint admits not only the contents of the instrument but also *any pleaded meaning to which the instrument is reasonably susceptible*." [*Aragon-Haas v. Family Security Ins. Services, Inc.* (1991) 231 CA3d 232, 239, 282 CR 233, 238 (emphasis added)]

- [7:48.26] Employee's employment agreement was ambiguous on whether employer's right to terminate without cause continued after a one-year probationary period. Employee alleged she understood the agreement to mean she could not be so terminated after one year. Whether this was the correct interpretation could not be resolved on a demurrer hearing. [*Aragon-Haas v. Family Security Ins. Services, Inc.*, supra, 231 CA3d at 239, 282 CR at 238]

(4) [7:49] **Demurrer lies for defense disclosed on face of complaint:** A general demurrer may lie because the complaint alleges either too little, or too much: i.e., it can be used where the complaint is incomplete (plaintiff has failed to allege some "ultimate fact" required to state a cause of action). Or, it can be used where plaintiff has included allegations that *clearly* disclose some defense or bar to recovery (without "pleading around" the defense; ¶6:179). [*Cryolife, Inc. v. Sup.Ct. (Minvielle)* (2003) 110 CA4th 1145, 1152, 2 CR3d 396, 401 (citing text); *Casterson v. Sup.Ct. (Cardoso)* (2002) 101 CA4th 177, 183, 123 CR2d 637, 641 (citing text)]

Where plaintiff alleges a conclusion and *inconsistent* special facts from which the conclusion is drawn, the sufficiency of the complaint is determined from the special facts, *not* from the conclusion. [*Iverson, Yoakum, Papiano & Hatch v. Berwald* (1999) 76 CA4th 990, 995, 90 CR2d 665, 669]

(a) **[7:50] Statute of limitations:** Where the dates alleged in the complaint show the action is barred by the statute of limitations, a general demurrer lies. (It is not ground for special demurrer.) [See *Saliter v. Pierce Bros. Mortuaries* (1978) 81 CA3d 292, 300, 146 CR 271, 276, fn. 2; *Iverson, Yoakum, Papiano & Hatch v. Berwald*, supra, 76 CA4th at 995, 90 CR2d at 669]

The running of the statute must appear "clearly and affirmatively" from the dates alleged. It is not enough that the complaint *might* be barred. [*Marshall v. Gibson, Dunn & Crutcher* (1995) 37 CA4th 1397, 1403, 44 CR2d 339, 343; *Roman v. County of Los Angeles* (2000) 85 CA4th 316, 324-325, 102 CR2d 13, 19]

1) **[7:51] Form of demurrer:** According to the Code, the statute of limitations defense may be pleaded by stating "the cause of action is barred by the provisions of" the *appropriate statute, specifying the section and subdivision.* [CCP §458]

Presumably, this applies both to answers and demurrers (a demurrer is a pleading; see CCP §422.10). But courts are split on whether a demurrer that *fails to specify* the applicable statutory bar is sufficient:

- [7:51.1] Several cases hold a demurrer must specifically plead the applicable statutory bar. [*Zakaessian v. Zakaessian* (1945) 70 CA2d 721, 725, 161 P2d 677, 680; *Miller v. Parker* (1933) 128 CA 775, 777, 18 P2d 89, 90]

- [7:51.2] Other courts are contra: "(A) demurrer which merely states that the cause of action set forth in the complaint is on its face barred by the statute of limitations is sufficient to raise that defense." [*Williams v. International Longshoremen's & Warehousemen's Union* (1959) 172 CA2d 84, 87, 341 P2d 729, 731; see also

*Bainbridge v. Stoner* (1940) 16 C2d 423, 431, 106 P2d 423, 428; *Spreckels v. Spreckels* (1916) 172 C 775, 783, 158 P 537, 540]

➪[7:52] **PRACTICE POINTER:** Avoid the problem by *specifying* the applicable statute of limitations. The following form is recommended:
— "The complaint fails to state facts sufficient to constitute a cause of action because it shows on its face that the action is barred by CCP § . . ."

Be careful to allege the *correct* Code section. If several Code sections conceivably may apply, *specify them all!*

2) [7:53] **Compare—dates not on face of complaint:** The demurrer lies only where the dates in question are shown on the face of the complaint. If they are not, there is no ground for general or special demurrer (dates not being essential to the cause of action). [See *Union Carbide Corp. v. Sup.Ct. (Villmar Dental Labs, Inc.)* (1984) 36 C3d 15, 25, 201 CR 580, 586; *United Western Med. Ctrs. v. Sup.Ct. (Michelle Marie H.)* (1996) 42 CA4th 500, 49 CR2d 682, 685-686 (citing text)]

• Thus, a complaint alleging that defendant's conduct began "at a date unknown to P" is not subject to demurrer on statute of limitations grounds. Allegations as to *why* P did not discover D's conduct are generally not required (and, if included, defects therein can be disregarded as surplusage). [*Union Carbide Corp. v. Sup.Ct. (Villmar Dental Labs, Inc.),* supra]

The proper procedure in such cases is for defendant to answer the complaint and raise the statute of limitations as an *affirmative defense* therein (failing to plead it waives the defense). Once the answer is on file, defendant may follow with a motion for summary judgment on this ground.

3) [7:53.1] **Compare—"on or about" allegations:** Allegations that an event occurred "on or about" the crucial date for statute of limita-

tions purposes overcome a general demurrer. It is enough that the claim *may* be timely. (If it is not, defendant can move for summary judgment.) [*Childs v. State of California* (1983) 144 CA3d 155, 160, 192 CR 526, 528; ¶6:241]

4) **[7:54] Compare—complaint fails to allege whether contract sued upon is oral or written:** This is a statutory ground for *special* demurrer; *see* ¶7:90. It can be used to flush out a statute of frauds defense (i.e., if the contract was in fact oral, enforcement may be barred under the statute).

But it can also be used to flush out a *statute of limitations* defense. If plaintiff is forced to allege that the contract was oral, it will be subject to the shorter (2-year) statute of limitations— rather than the longer (4-year) statute governing actions on written contracts.

5) **[7:54.1] Compare—acts alleged before and after statutory bar:** If the complaint alleges wrongful conduct commencing at a time now barred by the statute of limitations, *but continuing* until a date not barred, there is no ground for a general demurrer based on the statute of limitations. I.e., the later acts support the cause of action. [See *Wyatt v. Union Mortg. Co.* (1979) 24 C3d 773, 786, 157 CR 392, 399—statute of limitations on continuing tort (conspiracy) cause of action does not begin to run until commission of last overt act]

6) **[7:55] Official Forms:** Each of the Official Form complaints has blank spaces for insertion of the date of the transaction sued upon. It is not yet clear what effect omission of the date will have.

a) **[7:56] Comment:** Since not essential to the cause of action, it would appear that such omission would *not* be ground for demurrer or any other pleadings motion. Instead, defendant's only apparent attack will be to raise the statute as an affirmative defense in the answer.

⇨ **[7:57]** ***PRACTICE POINTER:*** Sometimes the omission will be inadvertent. Telephone plaintiff's lawyer and point out the omission. In such cases, an amendment to the complaint may be appropriate

(¶*6:602 ff.*), and the matter effectively re-solved at the pleading stage.

(b) **[7:58]** **Statute of Frauds:** Where the complaint seeks to enforce an agreement required to be in writing under the statute of frauds, but nonetheless alleges the agreement was *oral*, a general demur-rer lies. The complaint on its face discloses a bar to recovery. [*Parker v. Solomon* (1959) 171 CA2d 125, 136, 340 P2d 353, 361]

   1) **[7:59]** **Compare—not on face of complaint:** If the complaint fails to allege whether the con-tract was oral or written, it is subject to special demurrer on this ground. [CCP §430.10(g), ¶*7:90*] (This ground applies to *all* contract causes of action, not just contracts falling within the statute of frauds.)

   If the complaint *falsely* alleges the agreement was written, defendant will have to file an an-swer denying this allegation; then move for summary judgment.

(c) **[7:59.1]** **Illegal contract:** A general demurrer also lies where the terms of the contract alleged are illegal and thus void. Again, the complaint discloses on its face a bar to recovery. [*Beck v. American Health Group Int'l, Inc.* (1989) 211 CA3d 1555, 1563, 260 CR 237, 242—contract between hospi-tal and psychiatrist for referral fees showed on its face violation of Bus. & Prof.C. §650]

(d) **[7:60]** **Plaintiff's duty to "plead around" de-fense disclosed in complaint:** Normally, plain-tiff is not required to anticipate in his or her com-plaint defenses that may be raised in the answer. But where the statute of limitations or some other defense is disclosed on the face of the complaint, plaintiff, in order to state a cause of action, is bound to "plead around" that defense . . . i.e., to allege facts in avoidance thereof. (*See* ¶*6:179*.)

(5) **[7:61]** **"Aider by demurrer":** Facts admitted in a de-murrer may plug gaps in the complaint. I.e., if the demur-rer (improperly) alleges matters not appearing on the face of the complaint (so-called "speaking demurrers"), such matters may be considered in determining whether the complaint states a cause of action! [*Mohlmann v. City of Burbank* (1986) 179 CA3d 1037, 1041, 225 CR 109, 110, fn. 2]

- [7:62] **Example:** P's complaint against City did not allege compliance with 100-day claims filing statute. But City's demurrer attached copies of correspondence showing such compliance. The defects in the complaint were cured by the (improper) "evidence" attached to the demurrer. [*Mohlmann v. City of Burbank*, supra]

e. [7:63] **General demurrer—court lacks jurisdiction of subject matter:** "The court has no jurisdiction of the subject of the cause of action alleged in the pleading." [CCP §430.10(a)]

(1) [7:64] **Nature of objection:** The challenge is to the court's *power* to grant relief. The demurrer lies only where it appears from the *face of the complaint* that the court is *not competent* to act. Since the ground is never waived (¶7:69), it is functionally similar to a demurrer for failure to state a cause of action, and therefore is deemed a "general demurrer." [*Buss v. J.O. Martin Co.* (1966) 241 CA2d 123, 133, 50 CR 206, 213]

(a) [7:65] **Distinguish personal jurisdiction:** Lack of personal jurisdiction over defendant is *not* ground for demurrer. It must be raised, if at all, by *motion to quash service of summons.* [CCP §418.10; *see* ¶3:376-395] If instead defendant demurs, the demurrer constitutes a general appearance, *waiving* any defect in personal jurisdiction! [CCP §1014]

(2) [7:66] **Application:** Keep in mind that the court's lack of subject matter jurisdiction must appear on the *face* of the complaint.

[7:67] *Reserved.*

(a) [7:68] **Exceptional cases in which superior court lacks subject matter jurisdiction:** Because trial courts are now unified, there are only a few cases where the superior court lacks subject matter jurisdiction, including:
— cases within *exclusive federal court jurisdiction* (e.g., patent and copyright claims);
— cases in which jurisdiction is vested in another tribunal (e.g., claims subject to workers' compensation exclusivity); and
— cases involving religious or ecclesiastical disputes. *See discussion at* ¶3:3.1 ff.

In such cases, if the lack of jurisdiction appears on the face of the complaint, a demurrer under CCP §430.10(a) is *one* of the ways in which this defect may be raised (*see* ¶3:126).

(3) **[7:69]** **No waiver:** The court's lack of subject matter jurisdiction is *not* waived by defendant's failure to raise it by demurrer or answer. The challenge is to the court's *power* and can be raised at any time. [CCP §430.80]

f. **[7:69.1]** **Special demurrers:** Except in limited civil cases (in which special demurrers are prohibited, *see* ¶7:38), special demurrers can be filed on any of the following grounds:

(1) **[7:70]** **Plaintiff lacks legal capacity to sue:** "The person who filed the pleading does not have the legal capacity to sue." [CCP §430.10(b)]

"Legal capacity to sue" usually refers to the party being a minor, deceased, or having been adjudicated incompetent or insane.

(a) **[7:71]** **Rarely disclosed on face of pleading:** Usually, this ground does *not* appear on the face of the pleading under attack; i.e., plaintiffs rarely allege their own incompetency. Hence, it is very rarely a proper ground for demurrer. Instead, defendant usually has to raise lack of capacity as an objection ("plea in abatement") in the answer; *see* ¶6:475.

(b) **[7:72]** **Compare—lack of standing to sue:** Sometimes, the plaintiff will be legally competent, but lack standing to sue (e.g., as where he is not the real party in interest). In such cases, the complaint may be subject to general demurrer (failure to state a cause of action in *this* plaintiff) if such lack of standing appears on the face of the complaint or from matters judicially noticeable.

1) **[7:73]** **Example:** Plaintiff, a bankrupt, files suit on a cause of action belonging to the bankruptcy estate. The plaintiff debtor lacks standing to sue; the court may take judicial notice of the bankruptcy proceedings and permit the trustee to be substituted in as the plaintiff. [*Cloud v. Northrop Grumman Corp.* (1998) 67 CA4th 995, 1002, 79 CR2d 544, 548]

(2) **[7:74]** **Another action pending:** "There is another action pending between the same parties on the same cause of action." [CCP §430.10(c)]

This is a plea in abatement: "A plea in abatement pursuant to section 430.10, subdivision (c), may be made by demurrer or answer when there is another action pending between the *same parties* on the *same cause of action*." [*Plant Insulation Co. v. Fibreboard Corp.*

(1990) 224 CA3d 781, 789, 274 CR 147, 151 (emphasis in original)]

*Compare—exclusive concurrent jurisdiction rule:* This statutory plea in abatement is similar in effect to the "exclusive concurrent jurisdiction rule" (which requires courts to abate a later-filed suit in favor of an earlier suit in a different court; *see ¶3:123.50*). The exclusive concurrent jurisdiction rule is *broader,* however, than the statutory plea of abatement because it *does not require absolute identity* of parties, causes of action or remedies sought in the initial and subsequent action. [*Plant Insulation Co. v. Fibreboard Corp.,* supra, 224 CA3d at 789, 274 CR at 151; *see ¶3:123.51*]

## (a) **Application**

1) [7:75] **"Pending":** This special demurrer lies only where the action is also pending *in California* (for out-of-state actions, see below). [*Leadford v. Leadford* (1992) 6 CA4th 571, 575, 8 CR2d 9, 12]

2) [7:75.1] **"Same parties":** The parties must stand in the same relationship (i.e., as plaintiff or defendant) in both suits. [See *Plant Insulation Co. v. Fibreboard Corp.,* supra, 224 CA3d at 789, 274 CR at 151—"absolute identity of parties" required in statutory plea of abatement]

3) [7:75.2] **"Same cause of action":** The identical cause of action must be involved in both suits, so that a judgment in the first action would be *res judicata* on the claim in the present lawsuit (claim preclusion). [*Bush v. Sup.Ct. (Rains)* (1992) 10 CA4th 1374, 1384, 13 CR2d 382, 388]

The identity of the "causes of action" is determined by a comparison of the *facts* alleged in each complaint. To be the same "cause of action," each complaint must allege invasion of the *same* "primary right." [*Bush v. Sup.Ct. (Rains),* supra, 10 CA4th at 1384, 13 CR2d at 387]

*Cross-refer:* The "primary rights" doctrine and the meaning of "cause of action" are discussed at *¶6:105 ff.*

a) [7:75.3] **Issue preclusion not enough:** The fact some of the same issues are involved so that a finding in either case would give rise to collateral estoppel (issue preclusion) in the other is not enough if in fact two different "causes of action" are involved. [*Bush v. Sup.Ct. (Rains)*, supra, 10 CA4th at 1384, 13 CR2d at 388]

(b) **[7:76]** **How determined:** The existence of the other lawsuit may not appear on the face of the complaint. But the court can take judicial notice of the court files in the same court, or in other courts. [Ev.C. §452] Matters so noticed can be considered as ground for demurrer. [CCP §430.30(a), ¶7:12; see *Bistawros v. Greenberg* (1987) 189 CA3d 189, 191-192, 234 CR 377, 378]

(c) **[7:77]** **If demurrer sustained:** The present action will normally be *stayed* pending disposition of the earlier lawsuit. If the first action goes to judgment, that will be res judicata as to the claim in the present lawsuit. If for any reason the first action is *not* decided on the merits, the present action can then proceed. [See *Branson v. SunDiamond Growers* (1994) 24 CA4th 327, 335, 29 CR2d 314, 317, fn. 2]

(d) **[7:77.1]** **Compare—other action pending in federal or sister state court:** This ground for demurrer does not lie where the other action is pending in a federal court or in a court of a sister state. [*Gregg v. Sup.Ct. (Jani-King)* (1987) 194 CA3d 134, 136, 239 CR 380, 381]

In such cases, however, California courts may refuse to entertain the later action on general principles of *comity*. But a stay on this ground is *discretionary*, not mandatory. [*Thomson v. Continental Ins. Co.* (1967) 66 C2d 738, 746-747, 59 CR 101, 107; *Caiafa Professional Law Corp. v. State Farm Fire & Cas. Co.* (1993) 15 CA4th 800, 804, 19 CR2d 138, 140]

1) **[7:77.2]** **Procedure:** The appropriate procedure in such a case is a *motion to stay or dismiss* the action on ground of forum non conveniens (CCP §§410.30, 418.10; see ¶3:408). [*Leadford v. Leadford* (1992) 6 CA4th 571, 575, 8 CR2d 9, 12; *County of Fresno v. Shelton* (1998) 66 CA4th 996, 1009, 78 CR2d 272, 279 (citing text)]

2) **[7:77.3]** **Motion to stay distinguished from demurrer:** The motion to stay is addressed to the court's inherent equitable power, and differs from a demurrer in these important respects:

- A motion to stay requires consideration of *matters outside the pleadings.* Declarations are admissible to show the status of the foreign action; the convenience of the parties; the seriousness of the threat of multiple litigation; and the competing interests of the two forums. [*Leadford v. Leadford* (1992) 6 CA4th 571, 575, 8 CR2d 9, 12]

- A motion to stay may be granted even if the parties do *not* stand in the same procedural relationship to each other in the sister-state lawsuit. But a demurrer will lie only if the same plaintiff is suing the same defendant in another California action. [See *Franchise Tax Bd. v. Firestone Tire & Rubber Co.* (1978) 87 CA3d 878, 883, 151 CR 460, 464]

(3) [7:78] **Defect or misjoinder of parties** [CCP §430.10(d)]

  (a) [7:79] **Application:** Demurrers on this ground lie only where it appears from the *face of the complaint* (or matters judicially noticed) that:

    1) [7:80] **Defect (nonjoinder) of parties**—some third person is a "necessary" or "indispensable" party to the action; and hence must be joined before the action may proceed. (*See discussion of "necessary" and "indispensable" parties at ¶2:151 ff.*)

    2) [7:81] **Misjoinder of parties**—plaintiffs lack sufficient unity of interest [CCP §378]; or there is no common question of law or fact as to the defendants [CCP §379]. (*See ¶2:207 ff.*)

    [7:82] It is rare that this ground for objection appears on the *face* of the complaint. More frequently, defendant must raise it as a plea in abatement in the answer.

    3) [7:82.1] **Compare—plaintiff uncertain which defendant responsible:** A demurrer on ground of misjoinder does *not* lie to challenge allegations that plaintiff is uncertain which defendant caused his or her injuries. (A motion for severance or for a protective order is the preferred remedy in such cases; see CCP §§379.5 and 1048.) [*Landau v. Salam* (1971) 4 C3d 901, 908, 95 CR 46, 51; *Geraci v. United*

*Services Auto. Ass'n* (1987) 188 CA3d 1245, 1252, 233 CR 896, 900, fn. 4]

(b) **[7:83]  Waiver:**  The Code states that unless raised by demurrer or answer, any objection for defect or misjoinder of parties is automatically waived. [CCP §430.80]

(c) **[7:83.1]  Prejudice from misjoinder required?** Where the ground for demurrer is misjoinder (improper parties), need the demurring party show prejudice? While the Code seemingly authorizes demurrer on this ground without any such showing, case law is apparently to the contrary: i.e., a demurrer for misjoinder will be overruled if the defendant shows no prejudice suffered or interests impaired by the misjoinder. [See *Anaya v. Sup.Ct. (Dow Chem. Co.)* (1984) 160 CA3d 228, 231, 206 CR 520, 522, fn. 1]

 1) **[7:83.2]  Comment:**  In practical effect, this means only *the persons improperly joined* can raise this ground for demurrer. (A proper party-defendant will rarely be injured by joinder of unnecessary or improper parties.) Moreover, such prejudice can rarely be determined at the demurrer stage; i.e., it rarely would appear on the face of plaintiff's complaint! [See *Royal Surplus Lines Ins. Co., Inc. v. Ranger Ins. Co.* (2002) 100 CA4th 193, 198, 122 CR2d 459, 462 (citing text)]

(4) **[7:84]  Uncertainty:**  "The pleading is uncertain. As used in this subdivision, 'uncertainty' includes ambiguous and unintelligible." [CCP §430.10(f)]

(a) **[7:85]  Disfavored ground:**  Demurrer for uncertainty will be sustained only where the complaint is so bad that the defendant *cannot reasonably respond*; i.e., he or she cannot reasonably determine what issues must be admitted or denied, or what counts or claims are directed against him. [*Khoury v. Maly's of Calif., Inc.* (1993) 14 CA4th 612, 616, 17 CR2d 708, 710 (citing text)]

 1) **[7:86]  Comment:**  Otherwise, judges usually make short shrift of demurrers for uncertainty. They expect counsel to clear up any ambiguities through discovery, or stipulations, rather than by demurrer.

 Thus, demurrers for uncertainty will almost certainly be overruled where:

- directed to *inconsequential* matters;

- the facts alleged in the complaint are *presumptively within the knowledge* of the demurring party or *ascertainable* by invoking discovery procedures; or

- not *dispositive* of one or more causes of action. [See *Khoury v. Maly's of Calif., Inc.,* supra, 14 CA4th at 616, 17 CR2d at 710]

2) [7:86.1] **Example—failure to identify parties and claims:** Where several claims or causes of action are joined, each should be captioned so as to identify the nature of the claim and the parties affected thereby (*see* ¶6:35).

A demurrer for uncertainty may lie if the failure to label the parties and claims renders the complaint so confusing defendant *cannot tell what he or she is supposed to respond to.* [*Williams v. Beechnut Nutrition Corp.* (1986) 185 CA3d 135, 139, 229 CR 605, 607, fn. 2]

But if the complaint contains *enough facts* to apprise defendant of the issues it is being asked to meet, failure to label each cause of action is not ground for demurrer: "Although inconvenient, annoying and inconsiderate, the lack of labels does not substantially impair (defendant's) ability to understand the complaint." [*Williams v. Beechnut Nutrition Corp.,* supra, 185 CA3d at 139, 229 CR at 607, fn. 2]

[7:87] *Reserved.*

(b) [7:88] **Form of demurrer—"uncertainties" must be specified:** Where a demurrer is made upon this ground, it must distinctly specify exactly how or *why* the pleading is uncertain, and *where* such uncertainty appears (by reference to page and line numbers of the complaint). [See *Fenton v. Groveland Community Services Dist.* (1982) 135 CA3d 797, 809, 185 CR 758, 765]

▭▷[7:88.1] *PRACTICE POINTER:* Although not specifically required by CRC 325(a), a demurrer for uncertainty should refer by *page* and *line number* to the particular allegations or part of the pleading that is uncertain (*see suggested form at* ¶7:109). Judges will not search the pleading to detect claimed uncertainties.

➡️[7:89] *FURTHER PRACTICE POINTER:* Don't waste your time and the court's time with special demurrers where the opposing party is represented by competent counsel. Telephone the attorney preparing the complaint, and point out the ambiguities or uncertainties that you see. You may be able to resolve the matter by stipulation or by the attorney filing a simple amendment to the complaint. (This is particularly true if the only uncertainty is the failure to check the proper box on one of the Official Form complaints!)

(c) [7:89.1] **Waiver:** Challenges to a pleading on ground of uncertainty or ambiguity must be timely raised in the trial court by demurrer or answer. Otherwise, the objection is deemed waived. It cannot be raised for the first time on appeal. [CCP §430.80(a); *Stockton Newspapers, Inc. v. Members of Redevelopment Agency* (1985) 171 CA3d 95, 103, 214 CR 561, 565]

(5) [7:90] **Failure to allege whether contract oral or written:** "In an action upon a contract, it cannot be ascertained from the pleading whether the contract is written, or whether it is oral, or whether it is implied by conduct." [CCP §430.10(g)]

(a) [7:91] **Application:** This ground is designed to flush out two potential defenses:

- **Statute of Frauds** (although the demurrer can be asserted even as to contracts not within the statute of frauds); and

- **Statute of Limitations** (if the contract is oral, it is subject to the shorter 2-year statute; *see* ¶7:54).

Once disclosed, the complaint may then be attacked by a *general* demurrer; ¶7:49 ff.

(b) [7:92] **Limitation—action "upon a contract":** Note that this ground for demurrer lies only where the action is "upon a contract." This means that the *right to recover must be based* on the contract in question.

1) [7:93] **Example:** If plaintiff sues for inducing a breach of contract (a tort action), a demurrer for failure to allege whether the contract was written or oral will *not* lie. The action is *not* "upon a contract" within the meaning of CCP §430.10(g).

(c) **[7:94] Limitation—pleading common counts:** Plaintiff can usually avoid a demurrer on this ground by pleading the contract via the common counts (with no separate cause of action on the contract). [*Moya v. Northrup* (1970) 10 CA3d 276, 285, 88 CR 783, 788]

In such a case, defendant will have to raise the statute of frauds (or statute of limitations) as an affirmative defense in his answer.

(6) **[7:95] Failure to attach attorney certificate in certain malpractice actions:** "No certificate was filed as required by Section 411.35." [CCP §430.10(h); see *Price v. Dames & Moore* (2001) 92 CA4th 355, 360, 112 CR2d 65, 69 (citing text)—failure to file certificate was curable and leave to amend should have been granted] (Note: This is also ground for a motion to strike; *see* ¶¶1:887, 7:174.)

(a) **[7:96] Application:** This ground enforces the requirement that an attorney certificate accompany complaints for malpractice against certain professionals (engineers, architects, etc.; *see* ¶1:874 ff.).

Basically, the attorney certificate must show that, unless excused for good cause defined in the statute, the attorney *consulted* with at least one recognized expert in the field before filing suit; and, based on such consultation, *believes the action is meritorious.* [CCP §411.35(b)]

(b) **[7:96.1] Limitation—in pro per complaints:** This ground may not lie where plaintiff sues in pro per. (CCP §411.35 seems limited to attorney-drawn complaints or cross-complaints.)

[7:96.2-96.4] *Reserved.*

(c) **[7:96.5] Leave to amend:** Leave to amend to add or correct the CCP §411.35 certificate *must* be granted if such is possible. [*Price v. Dames & Moore*, supra, 92 CA4th at 360-361, 112 CR2d at 69-70]

(7) **[7:97] Failure to attach attorney certificate in actions by "common interest development" against contractor:** Although CCP §430.10(i) provides that a special demurrer may raise the failure to comply with CCP §411.36, the latter section sunsetted in 1997.

[7:97.1-97.4] *Reserved.*

(8) **[7:97.5] Failure to attach prelawsuit ADR certificate in certain actions involving "common interest developments":** Although not specifically mentioned

in CCP §430.10, a demurrer (or motion to strike) also lies in actions to enforce CC&Rs or other documents governing a "common interest development" (condominiums, etc.) if plaintiff fails to attach a certificate that ADR was attempted before filing suit. [Civ.C. §1354(c); *see discussion at ¶1:899 ff.*]

(a) [7:97.6] **Application:** The requirements for filing a certificate that ADR was attempted only apply to actions for declaratory or injunctive relief, or for such relief in conjunction with a claim for damages of $5,000 or less. [Civ.C. §1354(c)]

1) [7:97.7] **Limitation—cross-complaints:** The certificate filing requirements do *not* apply to cross-complaints. [Civ.C. §1354(e)]

2) [7:97.8] **Limitation—statute of limitations soon to expire:** Likewise, the requirements do *not* apply where the applicable statute of limitations would run within 120 days. [Civ.C. §1354(b)]

[7:97.9-97.12] *Reserved.*

4. [7:97.13] **Demurrers to Judicial Council Form Pleadings:** Judicial Council form pleadings are not immune from demurrer. [*People ex rel. Department of Transp. v. Sup.Ct. (Verdeja)* (1992) 5 CA4th 1480, 1484, 7 CR2d 498, 500 (citing text)]

*Cross-refer:* Attacking improperly-executed official forms by demurrer is discussed at ¶6:219 ff.

5. [7:98] **Procedure—Moving Papers:** The procedure governing demurrers is generally the same applicable to motions. The Civil Law and Motion Rules (CRC 301-391) apply to demurrers (except where otherwise required by the context or subject matter of specific Rules). [CRC 303(c)]

The demurring party must file with the court, and serve on the other party, the following:

• Demurrer;

• Notice of Hearing (*see ¶7:111 ff.*);

• Memorandum of Points and Authorities; [CRC 312(a)]

• Proof of service. [CCP §1005(b); CRC 317(c)]

**FORMS**

• Demurrer to Complaint, Notice of Hearing, Points and Authorities, *see Form 7:A.*

• Checklist on Demurrer, *see Form 7:B.*

a. **Demurrer**

(1) [7:99] **Caption:** A demurrer should be captioned as such. The caption should also state the name of the party filing the demurrer, and the party whose pleading is the subject of the demurrer. [CRC 325(c)]

For example:

"DEMURRER BY BEA BAKER
TO FIRST AMENDED COMPLAINT
OF PLAINTIFF ALAN AMES"

(2) [7:100] **Grounds must be specified distinctly:** The Code provides that unless the grounds for a demurrer are *distinctly* specified, it may be disregarded. [CCP §430.60]

☞[7:101] *PRACTICE POINTER:* Most lawyers state their grounds for demurrer in the exact language of CCP §430.10, above. I.e., "The pleading does not state facts sufficient to constitute a cause of action"; or "There is a defect or misjoinder of parties," etc.

(3) [7:102] **Each ground separately stated:** Where there are several grounds for demurrer, each must be stated in a separate paragraph; *and* must state whether the challenge is to the entire pleading or to some specific cause of action therein. [CRC 325(a)]

(a) **Each ground in separate paragraph**

1) [7:103] **Caution—demurrer "trap":** If several grounds are stated conjunctively in the same paragraph (e.g., "the complaint is uncertain *and* fails to state facts sufficient to constitute a cause of action"), the demurrer violates CRC 325(a).

(b) [7:104] **Each ground directed to particular cause of action:** Although a demurrer may be taken to the entire complaint [CCP §430.50], most demurrers are directed at specified causes of action.

1) [7:105] **Caution—demurrer "trap":** If there are several causes of action in the complaint, a demurrer to the *entire* complaint may be overruled if *any* cause of action therein is properly stated. [*Warren v. Atchison, Topeka & Santa Fe Ry. Co.* (1971) 19 CA3d 24, 36, 96 CR 317, 326]

(c) [7:106] **Each paragraph consecutively numbered:** The paragraphs of the demurrer should be numbered consecutively throughout although pertaining to different causes of action. (This avoids several "Paragraph 3's" on different pages of the demurrer.)

(4) [7:107] **Which of several defendants:** Where there are several defendants, the demurrer should specify on which defendant's or defendants' behalf each ground is asserted. [CRC 325(c)]

(a) [7:108] **Caution—joint demurrer trap:** If counsel representing several defendants demurs on their behalf *jointly* (instead of "jointly *and severally*"), the demurrer may be overruled if the complaint is sufficient against *any one* of them . . . at least where only a special demurrer as to form is involved (the grounds for general demurrer are never waived). [*Majestic Realty Co. v. Pacific Lighting Corp.* (1974) 37 CA3d 641, 642, 112 CR 423, 424]

(5) [7:109] **Suggested format:** The following example illustrates the guidelines above, and avoids the demurrer "traps" noted above:

"Defendants ALAN AMES and AMY AMES jointly and severally demur to the complaint on each of the following grounds:

"Demurrer to First Cause of Action

"1. The First Cause of Action fails to state facts sufficient to constitute a cause of action.

"2. The First Cause of Action is uncertain because Paragraph 1 alleges plaintiff is a corporation (Complaint, page 2, line 10); while Paragraph 2 alleges it is a partnership (Complaint, page 2, line 22).

"Demurrer to Second Cause of Action

"3. The Second Cause of Action of the complaint fails to state facts sufficient to constitute a cause of action.

"Demurrer to Third Cause of Action

"4. The Third Cause of Action fails to state facts sufficient to constitute a cause of action."

(6) [7:109.1] **Signature:** The demurrer is usually signed by the attorney for the defendant.

b. [7:110] **Notice of hearing:** The demurring party must serve with his or her demurrer a notice of hearing thereon. [CRC 325(b)]

Rev. #1 2002

(1) [7:111] **Length of notice required:** The notice and all supporting papers must be served at least *21 calendar days* before the hearing, plus whatever additional time is required because of the manner of service:

— If served by fax, express mail or overnight courier, the 21-day notice period is extended by *2 court days*;

— If served by mail, papers must be served *26 days* before the hearing where both the place of mailing and address are within California; *31 days*, if either is in another state; and *41 days*, if either is in another country. [CCP §1005(b); CRC 325(b); *see* ¶*9:31*]

The demurrer must be noticed for hearing not more than 35 days after filing or on the first available court date thereafter. [CRC 325(b)]

(a) [7:112] **Order shortening or extending time:** For good cause shown, the court can order the hearing held at an earlier or later time, on such notice it may prescribe. [CCP §1005(b); CRC 325(b)]

[7:113] *Reserved.*

➡[7:114] *PRACTICE POINTER:* Common sense and courtesy suggest that you contact plaintiff's counsel *before* filing the demurrer to make sure that the date will be convenient on his or her calendar. This will avoid a lot of phone calls, requests for continuances, etc.

➡[7:115] *PRACTICE POINTER:* If you are not familiar with the law and motion calendar of the court in which you plan to file your demurrer, *call the clerk* of the judge who will hear the motion (or setting desk) and ask what dates and times are available. You may inquire whether any of the available dates has a particularly heavy calendar already, so that you can pick some other date. (It's often wise to avoid Mondays and days after holidays.)

Avoid setting motions in the same case in *different departments* on the same date (the file can't be in two places at the same time). Doing so may result in both motions being ordered off calendar.

c. [7:116] **Points and authorities:** A memorandum of points and authorities is required in support of each ground for demurrer. Failure to provide such memorandum may be construed by the court as an admission that any *special* demurrer is nonmeritorious and cause for its denial; and further as a "*waiver* of *all grounds not supported.*" [CRC 313(a)]

(The rule does not apply to general demurrers or demurrers based on lack of subject matter jurisdiction, since these grounds are never waived; see below.)

(1) [7:117] **Caption:** The memorandum of points and authorities usually is attached to the demurrer and notice of hearing. If filed separately, be sure to include the department number, and date and time of the hearing. (This helps prevent supporting papers from getting lost or misfiled.)

(2) [7:118] **Content:** Each ground for demurrer should be *separately stated* and *supported* in the points and authorities.

　(a) [7:119] **Reference to CCP §430.10 not enough:** There should be relevant case citations *and arguments* to support each ground. A mere cite to CCP §430.10, or any subparagraph, is *not* enough.

　(b) [7:120] **Grounds waived if not supported?** CRC 313(a) provides for waiver of all grounds not supported in the points and authorities. Technically, this cannot be applied to grounds for general demurrer, or for lack of subject matter jurisdiction . . . because these grounds cannot be waived. [CCP §430.80; *see ¶7:69*]

　　▷[7:120.1] *PRACTICE POINTER:* Even so, don't expect judges to be favorably impressed by a demurrer which simply states "the complaint fails to state sufficient facts to constitute a cause of action; see CCP §430.10(e)." The judge is *not* likely to scrutinize each line of the complaint to figure out what is wrong with it. It is your job to point out in your points and authorities *why* or *how* the facts are insufficient.

　(c) [7:120.2] **Effective arguments:** *See Law and Motion Practice discussion at ¶9:73 ff.*

(3) [7:120.3] **Length limitation:** A memorandum of points and authorities may not exceed 15 pages in length (exclusive of exhibits, attachments and/or table of contents) without a prior court order. The court may properly refuse to consider memoranda that exceed this limit. [CRC 313(d),(e) 317(d); *see ¶9:64.3 ff.*]

(4) [7:120.4] **Footers:** Footers are required on each page of the demurrer and must be at least 10-point type. [CRC 201(g); *see ¶6:20.1*]

d. [7:121] **Proof of service:** The moving party must file a proof of service of the moving papers *at least 5 calendar days* (not court days) before the hearing. [CRC 317(c)]

⇨[7:121.1] *PRACTICE POINTER:* The busier the court, the more rigidly this rule is applied. Many judges simply won't waste the time working up demurrers if no proof of service is on file 5 days before the hearing date. Watch out for long weekends!

e. [7:122] **Opposition papers:** Although not required, plaintiff will usually file points and authorities in opposition to the demurrer. The above comments as to format and content apply equally to points and authorities filed in opposition to the demurrer.

(1) [7:122.1] **Length limitation:** The same *15-page limit* applicable to the demurring party's memorandum (¶*7:120.3*) applies to any opposition memorandum. [CRC 313(d); *see ¶9:63.4*]

(2) [7:122.2] **Time requirement:** All opposition papers must be served on the demurring party and filed with the court *at least 10 calendar days* before the hearing. [CCP §1005; CRC 317(a)]

(3) [7:122.3] **Service requirement:** Opposition papers must be served in a manner "reasonably calculated" to ensure delivery not later than the *close of the next business day* after filing (e.g., by personal delivery, express mail, fax, etc.). [See CCP §1005(c), *discussed at* ¶*9:105.1*]

[7:122.4] *Reserved.*

f. [7:122.5] **Reply papers:** Although not required, the demurring defendant may file a memorandum in reply to whatever points are made in plaintiff's opposition memorandum.

(1) [7:122.6] **Length limitation:** A reply memorandum may not exceed 10 pages (excluding attachments, exhibits, etc.) without prior leave of court. [CRC 313(d)(e); *see ¶9:64.3 ff.*]

(2) [7:122.7] **Time requirement:** Any such reply memorandum must be served and filed *at least 5 calendar days* before the hearing. [CCP §1005(b)]

(3) [7:122.8] **Service requirement:** Like opposition papers, reply papers must be served in a manner "reasonably calculated" to ensure delivery not later than the *close of the next business day* after filing (e.g., by personal delivery, express mail, fax, etc.). [See CCP §1005(c), *discussed at ¶9:105.1*]

6. **[7:123] Attending the Hearing:** The court will proceed to rule on the demurrer at the request of whichever party appears at the hearing; i.e., the other side's failure to appear will not deter a ruling (unless the hearing is ordered continued for good cause). Moreover, failure to appear by the *demurring party* may be construed by the court as an admission that any *special* demurrer is not meritorious and as a waiver of all grounds thereof. [CRC 325(d)]

If *neither* party appears, the court may either dispose of the demurrer on its merits, or order it off calendar, or continue the hearing, whichever it deems appropriate. [CRC 325(d)]

a. **[7:123.1] Parties' stipulation that demurrer go off calendar equivalent to order sustaining demurrer:** Under certain circumstances, the parties' stipulation that a demurrer go off calendar may have the same effect as an order sustaining the demurrer:

(1) **[7:123.2] Stipulation coupled with agreement to amend:** A stipulation that a demurrer go off calendar and that plaintiff file an amended complaint, is equivalent to an order *sustaining* the demurrer with leave to amend. Thus, if plaintiff fails to amend within the stipulated time, a motion to dismiss will lie. [*Harding v. Collazo* (1986) 177 CA3d 1044, 1053, 223 CR 329, 333; see ¶11:277.2]

(2) **[7:123.3] Stipulation coupled with agreement to abate action:** Where the ground for demurrer is another action pending between the same parties on the same claim (CCP §430.10(c)), a stipulation that the demurrer go off calendar *may* be "the functional equivalent" of an order sustaining the demurrer. I.e., the stipulation may reflect the parties' agreement that the demurrer is well taken and that the action be abated pending the outcome of the other action. [See *Barragan v. Banco BCH* (1986) 188 CA3d 283, 298, 232 CR 758, 766]

[7:123.4] *Reserved.*

b. **[7:123.5] Right to oral argument if requested:** Oral argument on the demurrer must be afforded at the request of a party. [*Medix Ambulance Service, Inc. v. Sup.Ct. (Collado)* (2002) 97 CA4th 109, 115, 118 CR2d 249, 253]

7. **Ruling on Demurrer**

a. **[7:124] Policy to construe complaint liberally:** First of all, judges will not sustain a demurrer unless the objection is clearly well taken. The complaint will be construed "liberally . . . with a view to substantial justice between the parties." [CCP §452; see *Stevens v. Sup.Ct. (API Auto Ins. Services)* (1999) 75 CA4th 594, 601, 89 CR2d 370, 374]

(1) **[7:125] Impact:** A lot of poor pleading gets by. Demurrers based on pure technicalities, not affecting any real issue in the case, are often overruled. And, complaints which show *some* right to relief are held sufficient against demurrer—even though the facts are not clearly stated; or are intermingled with irrelevant matters; or the plaintiff has demanded relief to which he is not entitled. [*Gressley v. Williams* (1961) 193 CA2d 636, 639, 14 CR 496, 498]

b. **[7:126] If demurrer sustained, judge must specify ground:** Unless waived by the party against whom the demurrer is sustained (¶7:128a), the judge must specify the grounds upon which the ruling is based. It is sufficient, however, if the judge simply includes in the order or decision a reference to the appropriate pages and paragraphs of the demurrer. [CCP §472d]

(1) **[7:127] Sufficiency of statement:** Not much is required. The judge's statement from the bench is sufficient if entered in the clerk's *minute order* of the proceedings. (E.g., "The court adopted its tentative decision as set forth below. *Failure to state a cause of action.* Sustain without leave to amend.") No more detailed reasoning is required. [*Stevenson v. San Francisco Housing Authority* (1994) 24 CA4th 269, 275, 29 CR2d 398, 400]

- **[7:127.1]** Where such minute order exists, it is immaterial that the formal written order signed by the judge did not state any ground for the ruling. [*Stevenson v. San Francisco Housing Authority*, supra, 24 CA4th at 275, 29 CR2d at 400]

- **[7:127.2]** *Compare—failure to state statutory ground:* To satisfy CCP §472d, the order should specify one of the statutory grounds; e.g., "failure to state facts sufficient to constitute a cause of action," etc.

An order sustaining a demurrer "*based on* (cited cases)" does *not* clearly state the court's reasons. [*Crowley v. Katleman* (1994) 8 C4th 666, 676, 34 CR2d 386, 389]

▷**[7:128]** ***PRACTICE POINTER:*** If you're the demurring party, make sure the court's order *specifies* the grounds on which your demurrer was sustained. Otherwise, if the complaint is amended and you demur again, the judge may forget; or some new judge may be sitting, and he or she won't have any idea what the previous judge found wrong with the complaint. To avoid this, make sure the order you prepare for the judge's signature (CRC 391) *spells out in detail* each ground upon which your demurrer was sustained!

(2) **[7:128a]** **Waiver of specification:** The party against whom the demurrer is sustained may waive the judge's specification of grounds (CCP §472d). Indeed, failure to request a statement of reasons *constitutes a waiver.* [*Krawitz v. Rusch* (1989) 209 CA3d 957, 962, 257 CR 610, 612]

➡️**[7:128b]** *PRACTICE POINTER:* Be safe! Ask the court *at the time of the hearing* to specify the grounds on which its decision rests.

(3) **[7:128.1]** **Effect of failure to specify:** Where a demurrer is sustained without leave to amend (see below) and the case goes up on appeal, the judge's failure to specify grounds for sustaining the demurrer complicates the appellate process:

(a) **[7:128.2]** **Not reversible error:** The judge's failure to specify the ground is not reversible error per se: "The court sustained defendant's demurrer without leave to amend in general terms, contrary to CCP §472d. Regardless of this error, the court's ruling will be upheld if *any* of the grounds stated in the demurrer is well taken." [*Muraoka v. Budget Rent A Car, Inc.* (1984) 160 CA3d 107, 115, 206 CR 476, 479; *Beck v. American Health Group Int'l, Inc.* (1989) 211 CA3d 1555, 1566, 260 CR 237, 244]

(b) **[7:128.3]** **Special demurrers may be renewed:** When a demurrer is filed on both general and special grounds, and is sustained in general terms and without a statement of reasons as required by CCP §472d, "it will be *assumed on appeal that the court ruled only on the general demurrer* and not on the special demurrer . . . Thus, upon remand the parties and the court will not be precluded from further addressing the matter of specificity." [*Muraoka v. Budget Rent A Car, Inc.,* supra (emphasis added)]

c. **[7:129]** **Leave to amend routinely granted:** Even if a demurrer is sustained, leave to amend the complaint is routinely granted. Courts are very liberal in permitting amendments, not only where a complaint is defective in form, but also where substantive defects are apparent: "Liberality in permitting amendment is the rule, if a fair opportunity to correct any defect has not been given." [*Angie M. v. Sup.Ct. (Hiemstra)* (1995) 37 CA4th 1217, 1227, 44 CR2d 197, 204; *Stevens v. Sup.Ct. (API Auto Ins. Services)* (1999) 75 CA4th 594, 601, 89 CR2d 370, 375]

Indeed, in the case of an *original* complaint, plaintiff need not even request leave to amend: "Unless the complaint shows on its face that it is incapable of amendment, denial of leave to amend constitutes an abuse of discretion, irrespective of whether leave to amend is requested or not." [*McDonald v. Sup.Ct. (Flintkote Co.)* (1986) 180 CA3d 297, 303-304, 225 CR 394, 398]

(1) [7:129.1] **Error to deny leave if reasonable possibility exists to cure defect:** It is an abuse of discretion for the court to deny leave to amend where there is any *reasonable possibility* that plaintiff can state a good cause of action. [*Goodman v. Kennedy* (1976) 18 C3d 335, 349, 134 CR 375, 384; *Okun v. Sup.Ct. (Maple Properties)* (1981) 29 C3d 442, 460, 175 CR 157, 168]

(a) [7:129.2] **Request for leave to amend *not* required:** Ordinarily, failure to raise an issue in the trial court waives the point on appeal. However, an order sustaining a demurrer without leave to amend is reviewable for abuse of discretion "even though no request to amend (the) pleading was made." [CCP §472c(a) (parentheses added); see *Kolani v. Gluska* (1998) 64 CA4th 402, 412, 75 CR2d 257, 263]

- [7:129.3] Even so, absent such request, no abuse of discretion will be found unless a potentially effective amendment is "both *apparent* and consistent with plaintiff's theory of the case." [*CAMSI IV v. Hunter Technology Corp.* (1991) 230 CA3d 1525, 1542, 282 CR 80, 89 (emphasis added)]

(b) [7:130] **Burden on plaintiff to show reasonable possibility:** It is not up to the judge to figure out how the complaint can be amended to state a cause of action. Rather, the burden is on the plaintiff to show *in what manner* he or she can amend the complaint, and *how* that amendment will change the legal effect of the pleading. [*Goodman v. Kennedy*, supra, 18 C3d at 349, 134 CR at 384; *Hendy v. Losse* (1991) 54 C3d 723, 742, 1 CR2d 543, 555]

Where a demurrer is sustained without leave, such showing may be made in the first instance to the appellate court. [See *Careau & Co. v. Security Pac. Business Credit, Inc.* (1990) 222 CA3d 1371, 1386, 272 CR 387, 394; *Smith v. State Farm Mut. Auto. Ins. Co.* (2001) 93 CA4th 700, 711, 113 CR2d 399, 409]

(c) **[7:131] Comment:** Do not expect a judge to sustain a demurrer without leave to amend if, under the applicable substantive law, there is *any* theory on which plaintiff might proceed. Leave to amend (i.e., to cure the defect) will almost certainly be granted.

Leave to amend may be granted *notwithstanding* that *previous demurrers* have been sustained on the same ground. Courts often permit several efforts to cure a defect. (How long this continues depends on the patience of the particular judge.) [See *Stevenson v. San Francisco Housing Authority* (1994) 24 CA4th 269, 284, 29 CR2d 398, 406-407—"We find no error in the denial of appellant's request to amend after having seven previous chances to state a cause of action"]

(2) **[7:132] Compare—strictly legal issues; leave to amend may be denied:** However, there is no reluctance to sustain a demurrer without leave to amend where the *only* issues are legal ones, and the court decides against the plaintiff as a matter of law: "Leave to amend *should* be denied where the facts are not in dispute and the nature of the claim is clear but no liability exists under substantive law." [*Lawrence v. Bank of America* (1985) 163 CA3d 431, 436, 209 CR 541, 545; *Schonfeldt v. State of Calif.* (1998) 61 CA4th 1462, 1465, 72 CR2d 464, 465—if no liability as a matter of law, leave to amend should not be granted]

(3) **[7:132a] Compare—failure to "plead around" earlier admission:** Courts are also likely to sustain without out leave to amend where plaintiff has alleged facts in the original complaint that preclude the relief sought in an amended pleading: "Permitting plaintiff to amend the complaint would serve no useful purpose given the fact that the actions of petitioner, as set forth in plaintiff's original complaint, cannot give rise to a cause of action." [*Mercury Cas. Co. v. Sup.Ct. (Garcia)* (1986) 179 CA3d 1027, 1035, 225 CR 100, 104; *and see* ¶7:48]

d. **[7:132.1] Leave to amend may be granted conditionally:** In granting leave to amend the complaint, the court may impose "any terms as may be just." [CCP §472a(c)]

(1) [7:132.2] **Comment:** This may empower the judge to limit the type of amendment permitted, and even to *award expenses and fees* to the demurring party.

e. [7:132.2a] **Discovery may be stayed pending amendment:** It is not an abuse of discretion for a court to stay discovery pending the amendment . . . at least where plaintiff has had *ample opportunity* for discovery and fails to show the discovery sought would enable it to state a viable claim. Under such circumstances, "further discovery would only be an unnecessary and burdensome additional expense to (defendant)." [*Terminals Equipment Co. v. San Francisco* (1990) 221 CA3d 234, 247, 270 CR 329, 337—documents sought could not overcome claim of governmental privilege]

(1) [7:132.2b] **Comment:** A discovery stay would be improper, however, where plaintiff shows a *particularized need* for further discovery; e.g., to inspect documents or to depose witnesses *to determine whether* there is evidence upon which to base the amendment.

f. [7:132.3] **Sanctions:** Sanctions may be imposed where, after repeated demurrers have been sustained on the same ground, plaintiff files an amended complaint with only superficial changes. The amended complaint may violate the signing counsel's "certificate of merit" under CCP §128.7 (applicable to cases filed after 1994; *see* ¶9:1135 ff.).

g. [7:132.4] **Appellate review of order sustaining demurrer:** *See discussion at* ¶7:151 ff.

8. [7:133] **Time to Answer or Amend; Notice of Ruling:** If the court sustains a demurrer, *leave* to amend within *10 days* is deemed granted, unless the court orders otherwise. Similarly, if the demurrer is overruled, the answer is due within 10 days, unless ordered otherwise. [CRC 325(e)]

Where the demurrer challenged only certain causes of action and was overruled, defendant may demur, move to strike or otherwise plead to the remaining causes of action within the same 10-day period. [CRC 325(g)] (But "piecemeal" demurrers are discouraged; *see* ¶7:34.1.)

**Exception—unlawful detainer actions:** However, in actions for forcible entry, forcible detainer or unlawful detainer, the amended complaint or answer is due within *5 calendar days*, unless ordered otherwise. [CRC 325(e)]

**Comment:** Counsel often find the 10-day period insufficient. Therefore, in the past at least, judges routinely granted longer periods within which to answer or amend (typically 20 or 30 days). But this is changing in courts with "fast track" rules (¶12:4 ff.), and judges may require parties to replead within the statutory 10-day period.

a. **[7:134] Runs from service of notice of ruling by prevailing party:** The time within which to answer or amend runs not from the date of actual ruling, but from the date of service of *notice* of the court's decision or order . . . unless such notice is waived in open court and entered in the minutes of the court. [CCP §472b]

CRC 391 requires the prevailing party on "any motion" (presumably, including demurrers) to prepare an *order* for the court's signature—*unless the parties waive notice or the court orders otherwise* (*see Ch. 9(I)*).

(1) **[7:135] Impact:** Unless a proposed order is submitted with the moving papers, the prevailing party must prepare and serve such order on opposing counsel *within 5 days after* the ruling. Opposing counsel then has 5 days to inform counsel for the prevailing party of any objections as to form. Thereafter, the proposed order and any objection are submitted to the court for signature. Then, *after the court signs the order*, the "Notice of Ruling" required by CCP §472b must be served . . . a rather lengthy process, but an important one: The 10-day limit for filing a motion for reconsideration runs from service of this notice (CCP §1008(a)).

Even if the judge makes the ruling in open court before both counsel, the time within which to answer or amend does not begin to run until the prevailing party sends out a formal "Notice of Ruling" (unless waived). Thus, if the prevailing party forgets or delays sending out the requisite notice, it operates as an automatic extension of time to the other side!

(2) **[7:136] Clerk's notice sufficient?** If the demurrer is taken under submission, the court clerk usually mails a copy of the judge's ruling on the demurrer to each of the parties. *If this mailing is ordered by the court*, no separate "Notice of Ruling" need be served by the prevailing party. The time to amend or answer runs from service of the clerk's notice. [See CCP §664.5(d); CRC 309; and *Robbins v. Los Angeles Unified School Dist.* (1992) 3 CA4th 313, 318, 4 CR2d 649, 652—service of copy of minute order triggered time to amend: failure to amend justified dismissal]

☞ **[7:136a] *PRACTICE POINTER:*** It is a good idea to send out your own Notice of Ruling. This avoids any question whether the clerk's notice was ordered by the court.

**FORM:** Notice of Ruling on Demurrer, *see Form 7:C.*

(3) **[7:136.1] File-stamped copy of order as service:**
The copy of the court order mailed by the court clerk
does *not* constitute "service of notice" of the order sustaining the demurrer (see above). But the *prevailing
party* may serve a "file-stamped copy" of the order as
such notice: "(T)here can be no better notice of what an
order says than is provided by a file-stamped copy of the
order itself." [*Parris v. Cave* (1985) 174 CA3d 292, 294,
219 CR 871, 872; *see ¶9:320.3*]

(4) **[7:136.2] Extension for service by mail:** If the
address and place of mailing are both in California, time
is extended by 5 days. If either the address or place of
mailing is outside California, time is extended 10 days;
20 days, if either is outside the United States. [CCP
§1013(a); see *People v. $20,000 U.S. Currency* (1991)
235 CA3d 682, 692, 286 CR 746, 750]

b. **[7:137] Waiver of notice:** If all parties entitled to notice
are before the court, the judge may ask whether the losing
party agrees to waive notice of the ruling. If such waiver is
made (and entered in the court records), the time within
which to answer or amend will run from the date of the
judge's ruling on the demurrer.

However, no waiver may be implied simply from the losing
party's presence at the hearing. [*People v. $20,000 U.S. Cur-
rency* (1991) 235 CA3d 682, 692, 286 CR 746, 750]

⇨**[7:138] *PRACTICE POINTER:*** The Notice of Ruling is often a needless formality. This is particularly so
where both sides were in court when the judge made
the ruling. In such cases, many lawyers routinely waive
notice of the ruling.

Even so, if the judge has not yet indicated how much
time will be granted within which to answer or amend,
it is a good idea to ask about this *before* waiving notice!

c. **[7:138.1] Compare—after reversal on appeal:** Where
a demurrer is sustained *without leave* to amend but is reversed on appeal, any amended complaint must be filed
within 30 days after the appellate court clerk mails notice of
issuance of the remittitur. [CCP §472b]

[7:138.2-138.4] *Reserved.*

d. **[7:138.5] Effect of belated amendment:** After expiration of the time in which a pleading can be amended as a
matter of course, or after expiration of the time allowed by
the court after demurrer sustained with leave to amend, a
noticed motion must be made for permission to file the

pleading. [*Leader v. Health Industries of America, Inc.* (2001) 89 CA4th 603, 612-613, 107 CR2d 489, 496-497]

Unless properly challenged, however, an amended pleading filed after the time allowed still prevents default or dismissal. The opposing party's remedy is to file a noticed motion for an order *striking* the untimely amended pleading. [CRC 325(f); *see also ¶11:277*]

### 9. Subsequent Pleadings and Procedures

a. **[7:139] Successive demurrers:** If, after a demurrer is sustained with leave to amend, plaintiff files an amended complaint, it is treated as a *new* pleading; *see ¶6:688*. Defendant is therefore entitled to respond to the amended pleading as he or she did to the original—including another demurrer. [See *Clausing v. San Francisco Unified School Dist.* (1990) 221 CA3d 1224, 1232, 271 CR 72, 75]

No statute or rule specifically provides a time limit for demurring to an *amended* complaint. Presumably, the 30-day time limit for demurring to the "complaint" (CCP §430.40, ¶7:24) should apply to amended complaints. Alternatively, CCP §471.5, which gives defendant 30 days within which to *"answer"* an amended complaint (¶7:34.1), may be interpreted to mean defendant has 30 days to "respond" including a demurrer.

(1) **[7:140] No demurrer on grounds previously overruled:** Where a prior demurrer was sustained as to some causes of action but overruled as to others, and plaintiff then amends the complaint, defendants *may not demur again* on the same grounds to those portions of the amended pleading to which an earlier demurrer was overruled. [*Bennett v. Suncloud* (1997) 56 CA4th 91, 96, 65 CR2d 80, 83, fn. 1]

Instead, counsel may consider a motion for reconsideration under CCP §1008, which must be made within 10 days of notice of the earlier ruling. *See ¶7:155.2 ff., 9:324 ff.*

[7:141] *Reserved.*

(2) **[7:142] Contrary view:** There is authority allowing successive demurrers. [*Pavicich v. Santucci* (2000) 85 CA4th 382, 389, 102 CR2d 125, 131, fn. 3; *Pacific States Enterprises, Inc. v. City of Coachella* (1993) 13 CA4th 1414, 1420, 17 CR2d 68, 70, fn. 3]

⇨ **[7:143] *PRACTICE POINTER:*** This is a risky area! Successive demurrers are in effect motions to reconsider subject to the requirements of CCP §1008 (*see ¶9:324 ff.*), and failure to comply with §1008 is punishable by contempt. [CCP §1008(d); *see ¶9:333*]

Therefore, before renewing a demurrer that has been overruled, defendants should make a *motion for reconsideration* (which must be made within 10 days after notice of the earlier ruling; *see ¶7:155.3*).

b. **[7:144]** **Answer to remaining causes of action:** If the demurrer was sustained as to only certain causes of action, and the time to amend has expired, the case moves forward on the remaining causes of action. No motion to dismiss lies; defendant must answer the remaining causes of action.

Absent court order or stipulation with plaintiff, such answer is *due within 10 days* after expiration of the time to amend (or where the demurrer was sustained without leave, within 10 days after notice of the order sustaining the demurrer). [See CRC 325(e)]

(Note: The causes of action as to which the demurrer was sustained remain in the complaint, but they have no legal effect. At time of trial, they will be dismissed. Some judges may order interlocutory judgments of dismissal at the pleading stage.)

c. **[7:145]** **Dismissal of defendant whose demurrer sustained:** If the demurrer was sustained as to *all* causes of action against one of several codefendants, and the time to amend has expired, that defendant may obtain a dismissal by *ex parte* application to the court. [See CCP §581(f)(2); CRC 325(f); *see ¶7:150 ff., 9:355 ff.*]

10. **Alternatives Available to Losing Party**

a. **[7:146]** **Demurrer sustained with leave to amend:** If the demurrer is sustained with leave to amend, plaintiffs may either:

(1) **[7:147]** **Seek writ:** Plaintiffs may seek immediate review of the demurrer ruling by petitioning the appellate court for an *extraordinary writ* (prohibition or mandamus). To prevent entry of default, such petition should be filed before expiration of the time to amend.

(a) **[7:147.1]** **Drawback:** Such writs are *rarely* granted . . . on the premise that plaintiff has an adequate remedy by appeal from a subsequent judgment. (The only possible exception may be if "jurisdictional" objections—e.g., failure to state a cause of action—are involved.)

(2) **[7:148]** **Amend the complaint:** The second (and usual) alternative is simply to *amend* the complaint within the time allowed, and attempt to cure the defect.

(a) **[7:148.1]** **Drawback:** The amended complaint will supersede the original and, therefore, any error in the order sustaining the demurrer will be waived and *cannot be reviewed* on a later appeal.

The only possible exception is where the trial court *denied leave* to include *particular* allegations in the amended complaint. In that event, the appellate court *can* review the demurrer ruling on the earlier complaint. [*Committee on Children's Television, Inc. v. General Foods Corp.* (1983) 35 C3d 197, 208-209, 197 CR 783, 790]

(b) **[7:148.1a]** **Scope of permissible amendment:** Generally, where the court grants leave to amend, the scope of the amendment is limited by the cause of action to which the demurrer was sustained. [*People v. Clausen* (1967) 248 CA2d 770, 785-786, 57 CR 227, 238; *see ¶6:635.5 ff.*]

(3) **[7:148.2]** **Dismiss and refile:** Another alternative is to decline to amend and simply dismiss the action *without prejudice* during the time allowed for amendment, leaving the way open to filing a new action. [See *Parsons v. Umansky* (1994) 28 CA4th 867, 871, 34 CR2d 144, 146 (citing text); *see further discussion at ¶11:19.1 ff.*]

(a) **[7:148.3]** **Drawback:** Many "direct calendar" courts restrict dismissal and refiling by local rules requiring that actions on the same claim as a dismissed action be *assigned to the same court* in which the dismissed action was pending (*see ¶12:44*) . . . so the refiled action is heard by the same judge who sustained the demurrer.

(4) **[7:149]** **Refuse to amend; allow entry of judgment of dismissal:** The final (and most risky) alternative is to refuse to amend, allow entry of judgment of dismissal, and then *appeal* that judgment. [*Jeffers v. Screen Extras Guild, Inc.* (1951) 107 CA2d 253, 254, 237 P2d 51, 52]

(a) **[7:149.1]** **Drawback:** Plaintiffs' refusal to amend is deemed an *admission* that they have stated the case as strongly as they can, and that there are no more facts which could be alleged to cure the defect. Thus, if they lose the appeal, they *cannot* file a new lawsuit on the same cause of action. The judgment is *res judicata*. [*Logan v. Southern California Rapid Transit District* (1982) 136 CA3d 116, 127, 185 CR 878, 884]

And note: In determining whether the trial court abused its discretion in sustaining the demurrer, the rule favoring liberal construction of pleadings (CCP §452) is inapplicable. Any uncertainty is resolved *against* the plaintiff. Thus, if the demurrer could have been properly sustained on *any* ground, the judgment of dismissal will be upheld. [*Hooper v. Deukmejian* (1981) 122 CA3d 987, 994, 176 CR 569, 572; *Soliz v. Williams* (1999) 74 CA4th 577, 585, 88 CR2d 184, 189]

(b) [7:150] **Dismissal may be obtained ex parte:** Defendant may obtain dismissal of the action by ex parte application to the court after expiration of the time to amend. [CCP §581(f)(2); CRC 325(f); *see* ¶11:277.2]

No formal motion is required to obtain the order of dismissal. [*Sadler v. Turner* (1986) 186 CA3d 245, 250, 230 CR 561, 564]

1) [7:150a] **Informal notice to opposing counsel required:** However, the requirement of CRC 379 that, prior to making an ex parte application to the court, informal notice be given to opposing counsel *does* apply. [*Datig v. Dove Books, Inc.* (1999) 73 CA4th 964, 976, 87 CR2d 719, 728-729]

(c) [7:150.1] **No statement of reasons required:** No findings or statement of reasons need be given by the court in granting a motion to dismiss after expiration of time within which to amend. The CCP §472d requirement of a statement of reasons on sustaining a demurrer (*see* ¶7:126) does not apply in this situation. [*Harding v. Collazo* (1986) 177 CA3d 1044, 1056, 223 CR 329, 335]

b. [7:151] **Demurrer sustained *with* leave to amend as to *less than all* causes of action:** If there are several claims or causes of action in the complaint and the demurrer was sustained only as to some of the claims, plaintiff may:

• Seek to amend to correct the deficiencies identified by the trial court; or

• Challenge the order sustaining the demurrer by filing a petition for writ of mandate (in the court of appeal for unlimited jurisdiction cases, or in the appellate division of the superior court for limited jurisdiction cases); or

• Allow the causes of action to which demurrers have been sustained with leave to amend to be dismissed (*see* ¶7:149 ff.) and proceed to trial on the remaining claims. After a final judgment is obtained, an appeal will lie on whether the demurrer should have been sustained. (*Comment:* This alternative is obviously inefficient because obtaining a final judgment and resolving the issue on appeal may take years. This is particularly true where the major causes of action were demurred out, forcing plaintiff to go to trial on relatively minor claims.)

c. **[7:151.1]** **Demurrer sustained *without* leave to amend:** If a demurrer is sustained without leave to amend as to *all* causes of action, the court will enter a judgment dismissing the action. An immediate appeal lies from such judgment. The propriety of the demurrer ruling may be raised on appeal *even if no request for leave to amend* was made in the trial court. [CCP §472c(a); *Governing Bd. of ABC Unified School Dist. v. Haar* (1994) 28 CA4th 369, 375, 33 CR2d 744, 746; *Careau & Co. v. Security Pac. Business Credit, Inc.* (1990) 222 CA3d 1371, 1386, 272 CR 387, 394]

d. **[7:151.2]** **Demurrer sustained *without* leave to amend as to *less than all* causes of action:** No immediate appeal lies where a demurrer is sustained without leave to amend as to some but not all causes of action in the complaint. However, plaintiff may seek immediate review by extraordinary writ. While writ review is always discretionary with the appellate court, it is available "when it appears that the trial court has deprived a party of an opportunity to plead his cause of action or defense, and when extraordinary relief may prevent a needless and expensive trial and reversal." [*Taylor v. Sup.Ct. (Stille)* (1979) 24 C3d 890, 893, 157 CR 693, 695]

If the appellate court refuses a writ, plaintiff must either *dismiss* or *go to trial* on the remaining causes of action, and then appeal from the judgment entered. [CCP §472c]

*Cross-refer:* See further discussion of writ review in Eisenberg, Horvitz & Wiener, *Cal. Prac. Guide: Civil Appeals & Writs* (TRG), Ch. 15.

(1) **[7:151.3]** **New lawsuit improper:** Trying to shortcut the process by filing a new lawsuit on the causes of action as to which the demurrer was sustained has been held improper. [*Ricard v. Grobstein, Goldman, Stevenson, Siegel, LeVine & Mangel* (1992) 6 CA4th 157, 162, 8 CR2d 139, 142—new complaint stricken as sham]

(2) **[7:151.4]** **Compare—multiparty lawsuit:** A demurrer sustained without leave to amend as to one of several defendants can support a separate judgment of dismissal as to that defendant (assuming no other claims asserted against that defendant). The judgment is *final as to that defendant* and hence immediately appealable

by the plaintiff although the suit continues against the other defendants. [*Tinsley v. Palo Alto Unified School Dist.* (1979) 91 CA3d 871, 880, 154 CR 591, 596]

e. **[7:152]** **Demurrer *overruled* as to all causes of action:** If the demurrer is overruled as to every cause of action pleaded, defendant may either:

(1) **[7:153]** **Seek writ:** Defendant may petition an appellate court for an *extraordinary writ* (mandamus or prohibition) to review the demurrer ruling. Such petition does not extend defendant's time to answer.

(a) **[7:153.1]** **Drawback:** Such writs are almost never granted and, therefore, it is almost always a wasted effort to seek one. [See *Curry v. Sup.Ct. (Rialto Unified School Dist.)* (1993) 20 CA4th 180, 183, 24 CR2d 495, 497—such review given with "extreme reluctance" but may be appropriate "where a significant issue of law is raised, and where resolution of the issue in favor of the petitioner would result in a final disposition as to that party"]

(2) **[7:154]** **Answer:** The second (and usual) alternative is to answer the complaint within the time allowed.

(a) **[7:154.1]** **Drawback:** Doing so *waives* any *formal* defects in the complaint, so there is no basis for subsequent appeal on such grounds. But failure to state a cause of action, and lack of subject matter jurisdiction, are of course never waived. [CCP §430.80(a)]

**[7:155-155.1]** *Reserved.*

f. **[7:155.2]** **Motion for reconsideration:** Whichever party loses may move for reconsideration under CCP §1008(a) (*discussed in detail at ¶9:324 ff.*).

(1) **[7:155.3]** **Requirements:** A motion for reconsideration must be made to the same judge who made the original order and must be:

• made *within 10 days* after service of the notice of entry of the order or ruling; and

• based on *new or different facts, circumstances or law*; and

• accompanied by an *affidavit* (declaration) stating what previous "application" (demurrer) was made, the ruling thereon, and what new or different facts, circumstances or law are claimed to exist. [CCP §1008(a)]

(2) **[7:155.4]** **Comment:** A motion for reconsideration *cannot* be used simply to ask the court to change its mind. Claims of "new or different" law are not likely to be well received if the points were already argued to the court.

**[7:155.5]** *Reserved.*

(3) **[7:155.6]** **Proposed amended complaint as basis for motion to reconsider:** Where a demurrer has been sustained *without leave* to amend, it is proper to seek reconsideration based on a *proposed* amended complaint alleging different facts than the complaint to which the demurrer was sustained. The amended pleading itself constitutes a "different state of facts" to permit reconsideration under CCP §1008(a). [*Rains v. Sup.Ct. (Center Foundation)* (1984) 150 CA3d 933, 944, 198 CR 249, 257]

(a) **[7:155.7]** **Court must allow:** If the proposed amended complaint states *any* valid cause of action, the trial court *must* vacate its order sustaining the demurrer and grant plaintiffs leave to file the amended complaint. [*Careau & Co. v. Security Pac. Business Credit, Inc.* (1990) 222 CA3d 1371, 1387, 272 CR 387, 394; compare *McGettigan v. Bay Area Rapid Transit Dist.* (1997) 57 CA4th 1011, 1024, 67 CR2d 516, 524—untimely motion for reconsideration properly denied where proposed amended complaint failed to state valid cause of action]

## B. MOTIONS TO STRIKE

1. **[7:156]** **General Considerations:** Motions to strike can be used to reach defects or objections to pleadings that are *not* challengeable by demurrer. Complaints, cross-complaints, answers and demurrers are all subject to a motion to strike (CCP §435(a)(2)). Moreover, a motion to strike can be used to attack the entire pleading, or any part thereof—i.e., even single words or phrases (unlike demurrers). [*Warren v. Atchison, Topeka & Santa Fe Ry. Co.* (1971) 19 CA3d 24, 40, 96 CR 317, 329]

Note: There are a few situations in which *either* a demurrer or motion to strike can be used:
— for failure to file a certificate of merit in malpractice actions against certain construction professionals (CCP §411.35, *see* ¶1:887); and
— for failure to file an ADR compliance certificate in certain actions involving common interest developments (Civ.C. §1354(c), *see* ¶1:905.5).

a. **[7:157]** **As defendant's initial pleading:** If the defendant has not previously appeared in the action, filing a motion to strike the complaint constitutes a general appearance (thus subjecting defendant to the court's personal jurisdiction). [CCP §1014; *Goodwine v. Sup.Ct. (Goodwine)* (1965) 63 C2d 481, 484, 47 CR 201, 203]

  (1) [7:158] **Prevents entry of default:** So long as the motion is timely filed, no default can be taken while a motion to strike is pending. Defendant need not answer the complaint until after his motion is denied. [CCP §§585, 586]

b. [7:158.1] **Court may strike pleading on own motion:** Courts are specifically authorized to strike a pleading "upon a motion . . . or at any time in its discretion . . ." [CCP §436]

It is therefore proper for a court to strike a complaint and dismiss the action entirely on its own motion. [*Lodi v. Lodi* (1985) 173 CA3d 628, 631, 219 CR 116, 118]

c. [7:158.2] **Improper motion to strike as motion for judgment on pleadings:** As stated above, a motion to strike generally does *not* lie against a defect or objection that may be raised by demurrer. But a "motion to strike" for failure to state a cause of action (ground for general demurrer) *may* be treated by the court as a motion for judgment on the pleadings (*see ¶7:275 ff.*) and granted accordingly. [*Pierson v. Sharp Memorial Hosp.* (1989) 216 CA3d 340, 342-343, 264 CR 673, 674]

Alternatively, a "motion to strike" filed after defendant has answered and which is based on declarations and facts outside the pleadings may be treated as a *motion for summary judgment.* [*City & County of San Francisco v. Strahlendorf* (1992) 7 CA4th 1911, 1913, 9 CR2d 817, 818]

d. **Limitations on use**

  • [7:158.3] In limited civil cases, motions to strike are permitted only on limited grounds (CCP §92(d); *see* ¶7:189).

2. [7:159] **Time to File Motion to Strike:** A motion to strike any pleading must be filed "within the time allowed to respond to [the] pleading"—e.g., 30 days after service of the complaint or cross-complaint unless extended by court order. [CCP §435(b)] (This does not affect the court's power to strike *sua sponte*; *see* ¶7:158.1.)

Exception: This time limit does not apply to motions to strike pleadings after the time permitted by the court in granting judgment on the pleadings with leave to amend; *see* ¶7:352. [CCP §435(b)(1)]

[7:160-161] *Reserved.*

a. [7:162] **Motion to strike filed with demurrer:** Where there are grounds both for demurring and moving to strike, the two procedures must be filed together. Filing a motion to strike does *not* extend the time within which to demur. [CCP §585(f)]

(1) [7:162.1] **Separate documents:** Motions to strike and demurrers should be filed separately because they normally seek relief on different grounds.

(2) [7:163] **Must be heard concurrently:** If both a demurrer and motion to strike are to be filed, they must be

*(Text cont'd on p. 7-59)*

filed together and noticed for hearing at the same time. [CCP §435(b)(3); CRC 329]

(3) [7:164] **Same notice requirements:** The length of notice required on a demurrer hearing is the same as that on a motion to strike, and is governed by CCP §1005. [CRC 325; *see ¶7:191*]

(4) [7:165] **No extension of time if filed separately from demurrer:** If either a demurrer or motion to strike is filed separately, there is no extension of time to file the other. [CCP §435(d)]

(The policy is to require defendant to raise *all* of his or her challenges to the complaint at the same time; i.e., defendant is not permitted to demur, and then if he or she loses, file a motion to strike, etc.)

b. [7:166] **Compare—motion used to attack opposing demurrer:** If the motion is used to attack a demurrer (e.g., where the demurrer was not timely filed), it must be filed at or before the time an opposition to the demurrer is due—i.e., at least 10 calendar days before the hearing on the demurrer; and it must be set for hearing *concurrently* with the demurrer. [CCP §§435(b), 1005]

c. [7:166.1] **Motion to strike answer:** The only pleading allowed to an answer is a demurrer (which must be filed *within 10 days* after service; *see ¶7:27*). Thus, a motion to strike an answer must be filed within the same period of time. [CCP §435(b); CRC 329]

3. [7:167] **Grounds for Motion:** Unless the action is a limited civil case, the motion lies *either:*

- To strike any "*irrelevant, false or improper matter* inserted in any pleading"; or

- To strike any pleading or part thereof "*not drawn or filed in conformity with the laws of this state*, a court rule or order of court." [CCP §436]

(In limited civil cases, the motion can be made only on more limited grounds; *see ¶7:189*.)

*Compare—SLAPP suits:* A *broader* motion to strike is authorized against suits designed to "chill" the free exercise of speech. [CCP §425.16; *see ¶7:207*]

a. [7:168] **Grounds must appear on face of pleading or by judicial notice:** As with demurrers (*¶7:8*), the grounds for a motion to strike must appear on the face of the pleading under attack, or from matter which the court may judicially notice (e.g., the court's own files or records). [CCP §437]

(1) [7:169] **Extrinsic evidence generally improper:** Thus, for example, defendant *cannot* base a motion to strike the complaint on *affidavits or declarations* containing extrinsic evidence showing that the allegations are "false" or "sham." Such challenges lie only if these defects appear on the *face* of the complaint, or from matters judicially noticeable.

    (a) **Comment:** They rarely do . . . and hence a motion to strike can rarely be made successfully on this ground.

(2) [7:170] **Compare—motion for summary judgment:** Where the moving party needs to introduce extrinsic evidence to show the falsity of the pleading, the proper procedure is a *motion for summary judgment* under CCP §437c (*Ch. 10*)—rather than a motion to strike. The Code provisions for summary judgment are held to supersede all other "speaking" motions. [*Vesely v. Sager* (1971) 5 C3d 153, 167, 95 CR 623, 633]

[7:171-172] *Reserved.*

b. [7:173] **Grounds for striking entire pleading:** A motion to strike can be used where the complaint or other pleading has not been drawn or filed in conformity with applicable rules or court orders.

(1) [7:174] **Examples**

- Answer filed without verification, where complaint was verified (¶6:488 ff.);

- Amended pleading filed without leave of court, where required (¶6:611 ff.);

- Amended pleading filed after expiration of time granted by court within which to amend (¶7:133);

- Amended complaint alleging facts beyond permissible scope of amendment (e.g., setting up claim on different set of facts after statute of limitations has run; ¶6:715 ff.);

- Complaint filed by nonlawyer on behalf of another person or corporation (not acting in pro per);

- Complaint filed in malpractice actions against certain construction professionals without the required certificate of merit. [CCP §411.35(g); ¶1:887—also ground for demurrer]

- Complaint failed to state facts sufficient to constitute a cause of action (i.e., not drawn in conformity with CCP §425.10). [*Lodi v. Lodi* (1985) 173 CA3d 628,

631, 219 CR 116, 118—complaint stricken on court's own motion]

- Complaint filed in action to enforce CC&Rs governing a "common interest development" without the required certificate of attempt to resolve through ADR. [Civ.C. §1354(c); see ¶1:899 ff.]

- Complaint not signed by lawyer or pro per party as required by CCP §128.7. [*Vaccaro v. Kaiman* (1998) 63 CA4th 761, 767-768, 73 CR2d 829, 833 (citing text)]

(2) [7:175] **"False" pleadings:** The Code allows a motion to strike on the ground that the pleadings contain "irrelevant, false, or improper matter" or where the pleadings are drawn in violation of a law, rule or court order. [CCP §436]

Case law also permits a motion to strike "sham pleadings." [*Ricard v. Grobstein, Goldman, Stevenson, Siegel, LeVine & Mangel* (1992) 6 CA4th 157, 162, 8 CR2d 139, 142—suit "sham" because admittedly filed solely to circumvent court's adverse ruling in earlier suit]

(a) [7:176] **Limitation—no extrinsic evidence:** However, "falsity" must appear from the face of the pleadings or from matters *judicially noticed.* [*Garcia v. Sterling* (1985) 176 CA3d 17, 21, 221 CR 349, 352]

If "falsity" can be proven only by reference to extrinsic evidence (declarations, etc.), there is no ground for a motion to strike. The correct procedure is a motion for summary judgment (*see ¶7:168-172*).

c. [7:177] **Grounds for striking portions of pleading:** A motion to strike can also be used as a "scalpel"—to cut out any "irrelevant, false or improper" matters inserted therein. [CCP §436(a)]

(1) [7:178] **"Irrelevant matter":** This includes:
— allegations not essential to the claim or defense;
— allegations "neither pertinent to nor supported by an otherwise sufficient claim or defense"; or
— a demand for judgment "requesting relief not supported by the allegations of the complaint or cross-complaint." [CCP §431.10(b)]

(2) **Application**

(a) [7:179] **Conclusionary allegations:** A motion to strike can be used to attack legal conclusions in a pleading. For example, in a straight promissory note action, allegations that defendant's failure to pay was "wrongful, malicious and illegal." Such allegations are conclusions of the pleader and "irrelevant matter," subject to motion to strike.

➡️[7:180] ***PRACTICE POINTER:*** Why bother? It is rarely worth the effort and expense to file a motion to strike such allegations. The only conceivable purpose might be to prevent their being read to the jury at the time of trial. But pleadings are usually not admissible as evidence at trial; and even if they are, you can *object* then to whatever portions are improper.

1) [7:181] **Conclusory allegations permitted where supported by facts:** Moreover, conclusory allegations will *not* be stricken where they are supported by other, *factual* allegations in the complaint. Example: Allegation that defendant was guilty of "oppression, fraud and malice" could not be stricken where the complaint contained sufficient facts to support such allegation. [*Perkins v. Sup.Ct. (General Tel. Directory Co.)* (1981) 117 CA3d 1, 6, 172 CR 427, 430: "The distinction between conclusions of law and ultimate facts is not at all clear and involves at most a matter of degree."]

(b) [7:182] **Improper demands or damage claims:** A motion to strike can also be used to attack claims for damages that are *not supported by the cause of action pleaded.* (A demurrer would not lie because a valid cause of action is otherwise stated.) Examples:

1) [7:183] **Unauthorized attorney fees claims:** For example, in an unlawful detainer action, the complaint seeks attorney fees, although the lease was oral and no mention was made of such fees; and attorney fees are not otherwise authorized by statute.

➡️[7:184] ***PRACTICE POINTER:*** A motion to strike makes more sense in this situation. It provides an early ruling on the recoverability of the damages claimed. If granted, it will lessen the discovery burden, and possibly lead to a quicker settlement.

2) [7:185] **Punitive damages claims:** There are several situations in which a motion to strike

may be utilized in connection with punitive damages claims:

- [7:185.1] **Amounts:** First of all, the *amount or amounts* of punitive damages sought may not be alleged (Civ.C. §3295(e)); and if alleged, would be subject to motion to strike. *See ¶6:175.*

- [7:185.2] **Prior court order required:** A court order is required prior to pleading punitive damage claims against health care providers (CCP §425.13, *see ¶6:327 ff.*); or against religious corporations (CCP §425.14, *see ¶6:346 ff.*). Without such an order, the punitives claim is subject to a motion to strike. [*United Western Med. Ctrs. v. Sup.Ct. (Michelle Marie H.)* (1996) 42 CA4th 500, 49 CR2d 682, 685]

- [7:186] **Not legally recoverable:** A motion to strike punitive damage allegations may lie where the claim sued upon would not support an award of punitive damages *as a matter of law:* e.g., straight promissory note actions; claims against governmental entities, etc. [See Civ.C. §3294(a); *Commodore Home Systems, Inc. v. Sup.Ct. (Brown)* (1982) 32 C3d 211, 214-215, 185 CR 270, 272; and *Woodland Production Credit Ass'n v. Nicholas* (1988) 201 CA3d 123, 129, 251 CR 791, 794— federally-chartered credit institution immune from punitives claim]

  a) [7:187] **Comment:** Because of the higher burden of proof at trial ("clear and convincing evidence" of "despicable conduct," etc.), judges often strike claims for which punitive damages are not *clearly* authorized. I.e., "innovative" and "imaginative" theories are less likely to be allowed. [See *Woolstrum v. Mailloux* (1983) 141 CA3d Supp. 1, 11, 190 CR 729, 735]

3) [7:188] **Improper rent claims in unlawful detainer actions:** In unlawful detainer actions based on a 30-day notice to quit, pretermination rent is not recoverable (CCP §1174(b)), and allegations requesting such rent are subject to a motion to strike. [*Saberi v. Bakhtiari* (1985) 169 CA3d 509, 512, 215 CR 359, 361]

(c) **[7:188.1]** **Substantive defects in portion of claim:** A general demurrer does not lie to a portion of a cause of action (*see ¶7:42.2*). Thus, where there is a substantive defect affecting only a *portion* of a claim, the proper challenge is by motion to strike. [*PH II, Inc. v. Sup.Ct. (Ibershof)* (1995) 33 CA4th 1680, 1682-1683, 40 CR2d 169, 171—legal malpractice claim based on several incidents of alleged malpractice, one of which was not actionable as a matter of law]

This use of the motion must be "cautious and sparing": "We have no intention of creating a procedural 'line item veto' for the civil defendant." [*PH II, Inc. v. Sup.Ct. (Ibershof)*, supra, 33 CA4th at 1683, 40 CR2d at 171]

d. **[7:189]** **Limitation in limited civil cases:** Motions to strike are permitted in limited civil cases only on the ground that the damages or relief sought are not supported by the allegations of the complaint (e.g., punitive damages sought for simple nonpayment of promissory note). Any other ground for a motion to strike must be raised, if at all, as an affirmative defense in the answer. [CCP §92(d),(e)]

4. **[7:190]** **Moving Papers:** The regular noticed motion procedure applies. The moving party must serve and file on opposing counsel the following:

- Notice of Motion [CCP §1010]

- Declarations (if necessary)

- Points and Authorities [CRC 312(c), 313]

- Proposed Order (required only in courts still using attorney orders; *see discussion at ¶6:680*)

**FORMS**

- Notice of Motion to Strike Complaint; Points and Authorities in Support, *see Form 7:D*.

a. **Notice of motion**

(1) **[7:191]** **Notice required:** The notice and all supporting papers must be served *at least 21 calendar days* before the hearing. If served by mail, longer notice is required: 26 calendar days, if both the place of mailing and address are within California; 31 calendar days, if either the place of mailing or address is in another state; and 41 calendar days, if either is in another country. [CCP §§435(b), 1005(b); *see ¶9:31*]

If the motion to strike is filed concurrently with a demurrer, both must be set for hearing not more than 35 days from filing, or on the first available court date thereafter. [CRC 325(b)]

(2) [7:192] **Portion to be stricken quoted verbatim:** If only some sentences or phrases are sought to be stricken, these must be quoted verbatim in the notice of motion. But this does *not* apply where the motion to strike is directed to the entire pleading, or to some *paragraph*, count or cause of action therein. [CRC 329]

[7:193] *Reserved.*

b. **Declarations in support of motion**

(1) [7:194] **Not permitted:** Because the defect must appear on the face of the pleading and extraneous evidence is not permitted, declarations cannot be used to support the motion.

(2) [7:195] **Request for judicial notice:** The court may take judicial notice of facts under the same rules as for demurrers. *See ¶7:12 ff.*

c. [7:196] **Points and authorities in support:** Failure to include points and authorities supporting each ground for the motion may be treated as an admission that the motion is not meritorious, and as ground to deny it. [CRC 313(a); *and see ¶7:116*]

5. **Ruling on Motion**

a. [7:197] **Policy to construe pleadings liberally:** As with demurrers, motions to strike are disfavored. The policy of the law is to construe the pleadings "liberally . . . with a view to substantial justice" (CCP §452). Thus, purely technical objections generally receive short shrift.

[7:197.1-197.4] *Reserved.*

b. [7:197.5] **Allegations presumed true:** In ruling on a motion to strike, the allegations in the complaint are considered in context and presumed to be true: "(J)udges read allegations of a pleading subject to a motion to strike as a whole, all parts in their context, and assume their truth." [*Clauson v. Sup.Ct. (Pedus Services, Inc.)* (1998) 67 CA4th 1253, 1255, 79 CR2d 747, 748]

c. [7:198] **Motion to strike heard concurrently with demurrer:** The court will usually rule on one, and put the other off calendar.

(1) [7:199] If the judge decides the pleading has been improperly filed (e.g., late, or without leave of court, etc.), the judge will generally grant the motion to strike the entire pleading; and order any demurrers off calendar.

(2) **[7:200]** If there is no ground to strike the entire pleading, the court will usually deal with any general demurrer to the pleading. If such demurrer is sustained, any accompanying motion to strike will be put off calendar.

### d. Motion to strike granted

(1) **[7:201]** **If only a portion of pleading stricken:** Depending on how much is stricken, the judge may or may not require filing an amended pleading. If only a few words are involved, the judge may actually strike them from the original pleading, and initial same by interlineation. In such cases, defendant will then be ordered to *answer* the complaint (as stricken).

(2) **[7:202]** **If entire complaint stricken:** If the defect in the complaint is correctible, the judge will almost certainly grant *leave to amend* on terms it deems proper. Indeed, failure to do so is an abuse of discretion. [See CCP §472a(d); *Vaccaro v. Kaiman* (1998) 63 CA4th 761, 768-769, 73 CR2d 829, 833-834 (citing text)]

(a) **[7:203]** **Liberal policy re amendments:** The same liberal policy re amendment of pleadings applies as on sustaining demurrers (*see ¶7:129*). Therefore, as long as the defect is correctible, an amended pleading will usually be allowed. [See *Grieves v. Sup.Ct. (Fox)* (1984) 157 CA3d 159, 168, 203 CR 556, 561—relying on CCP §576 which authorizes court to allow amendment of pleadings at any time "in furtherance of justice"; *Price v. Dames & Moore* (2001) 92 CA4th 355, 360, 112 CR2d 65, 69 (citing text)]

(b) **[7:203.1]** **Conditions imposed:** A pleading may be stricken upon terms the court "deems proper." [See CCP §472a(d)]

As a condition of granting leave to amend, the court may order plaintiff to pay defendant's expenses on the motion to strike. [*Vaccaro v. Kaiman*, supra, 63 CA4th at 769, 73 CR2d at 834]

(c) **[7:204]** **Compare—noncorrectible defects:** Of course, not all defects are correctible (e.g., complaint filed by nonlawyer for another person; or "sham" complaint). In such cases, the court may grant a motion to strike *without* granting leave to amend; and the moving party should follow up with a motion for judgment of dismissal. [CCP §581(c); see *Vaccaro v. Kaiman*, supra, 63 CA4th at 768-769, 73 CR2d at 833-834 (citing text)]

➡️[7:205]  *PRACTICE POINTER:*  Few defects are not correctible, and therefore there's little chance that your motion to strike will end the litigation.

Therefore, it usually makes sense to discuss the defect with opposing counsel *before* filing your motion. The matter can often be resolved by stipulation . . . at considerable savings to all concerned!

(3) [7:205.1]  **If demurrer stricken:**  A plaintiff may file a motion to strike a defendant's demurrer (¶7:166). If the motion is granted and the defendant has not previously filed an answer, the court must allow an answer to be filed on terms that are just. [CCP §472a(c)]

e.  [7:206]  **Motion denied:**  If the motion is denied, the judge must allow defendant time to *answer* the complaint. [CCP §472a(d)]

No fixed time within which to answer is provided by statute or court rule, but courts generally permit the same number of days as upon overruling a demurrer (*see* ¶7:133).

No default for failure to answer can be taken against the defendant until expiration of whatever period of time has been granted. [CCP §586]

The time within which to answer runs from service of *notice of ruling.* [CCP §1019.5; *see* ¶5:62]

f.  [7:206a]  **Appellate review:**  When an entire pleading is stricken without leave to amend, a judgment of dismissal may be entered from which an appeal lies. But no immediate appeal lies when only a *portion* of a pleading is stricken; that ruling may be reviewed only by writ or on appeal from the final judgment. [CCP §472c(b)(3)]

## C. SPECIAL MOTION TO STRIKE SLAPP SUITS ("ANTI-SLAPP MOTIONS")

[7:207]  **Introduction:**  A special *broader* motion to strike is authorized against so-called "SLAPP" suits (standing for "Strategic Litigation Against Public Participation")—i.e., lawsuits brought "primarily to chill the valid exercise of constitutional rights of freedom of speech and petition for the redress of grievances." [CCP §425.16 (a)] (But no intent to "chill" or actual "chilling" of such rights is required; *see* ¶7:244.6.)

CCP §425.16 provides a summary procedure by which defendants may dispose of such lawsuits *at the pleading stage* and thus avoid the cost and delays of lengthy litigation. In lieu of answering or demurring, defendant may file a "special motion to strike" the complaint, which has the following effects:

- may prevent entry of default (*see ¶7:159*);

- automatically *stays discovery* until ruling on the motion (*see ¶7:258*);

- forces plaintiff to establish a "probability" that plaintiff will prevail on the claim (*see ¶7:245*);

- pierces the pleadings and requires an *evidentiary showing* (*see ¶7:249*); and

- creates an incentive to early settlement by exposing plaintiff to a fee award if the motion is granted (*see ¶7:259*).

*Comment:* As will be seen, a §425.16 motion is more than merely an attack on the pleadings. It is *more akin to a motion for summary judgment* and indeed has been called "reverse summary judgment."

[7:207.1-207.4] *Reserved.*

1. **[7:207.5] Interpretation and Limitations:** The statute expressly provides that it "shall be construed broadly" (CCP §425.16(a)). But CCP §425.17, effective 2004, limits application of §425.16 by excluding certain (but not all) actions brought in the public interest and certain (but not all) causes of action arising from commercial conduct. *See ¶7:209 ff.*

2. **[7:208] What Constitutes SLAPP Suit—In General:** There are four categories of suits to which the anti-SLAPP statute applies:

   (a) statements or writings made *before a legislative, executive, or judicial or other official proceeding* (CCP §425.16(e)(1); *see ¶7:220 ff.*);

   (b) statements or writings made *in connection with* an issue under consideration or review by a legislative, executive, or judicial body, or any other legally authorized official proceeding (CCP §425.16(e)(2); *see ¶7:225 ff.*);

   (c) statements or writings made in a *place open to the public* or in a public forum, in connection with an *issue of public interest* (CCP §425.16(e)(3); *see ¶7:229 ff.*);

   (d) any other *conduct* in furtherance of the exercise of the *constitutional right* of petition or the constitutional right of free speech *in connection with an issue of public interest* (CCP §425.16(e)(4); *see ¶7:233 ff.*).

   [7:208.1-208.4] *Reserved.*

   a. **[7:208.5] Differences:** There are significant differences between the four categories of SLAPP suits:

      — Categories (c) and (d) are *limited* to *issues of public interest;* categories (a) and (b) are not.

— Category (d) is expressly limited to the exercise of a *constitutional right;* categories (a), (b) and (c) are not.

— Category (b) requires a *nexus* between the statement or writing and an issue under consideration by a *public body;* categories (a), (c) and (d) do not.

— Category (c) requires the statement or writing to be made in a *public forum;* categories (a), (b) and (d) do not.

— Categories (a), (b) and (c) pertain to oral or written *statements;* category (d) pertains to *conduct.*

[7:209-211] *Reserved.*

3. **[7:212] Exemptions (Actions Not Subject to SLAPP Statute):** Even though an action otherwise qualifies as a SLAPP suit, the following cases are *not subject to dismissal* under the anti-SLAPP statute:

a. **[7:212.1] Public enforcement actions:** An enforcement action brought in the name of the state by the Attorney General, a district attorney or a city attorney, acting as a *public prosecutor* is exempt from §425.16. [CCP §425.16(d); see *People ex rel. Lockyer v. Brar* (2004) 115 CA4th 1315, 1318, 9 CR3d 844, 847]

- **[7:212.2]** This includes *civil* actions by a governmental agency to enforce a law. [*City of Long Beach v. California Citizens for Neighborhood Empowerment* (2003) 111 CA4th 302, 304, 3 CR3d 473, 475—City's action against fundraising group to enforce campaign expenditure laws exempt from anti-SLAPP statute]

[7:212.3-212.4] *Reserved.*

b. **[7:212.5] Actions for public benefit:** Actions brought *solely in the public interest* or on behalf of *the general public* are exempt from §425.16, provided *all* of the following conditions are met:

— plaintiff does not seek any relief *greater than* or *different from* the relief sought for the general public or a class of which plaintiff is a member (a claim for attorney fees does not constitute greater of different relief);

— the action, if successful, would enforce an important right affecting the *public interest*, and would confer a significant benefit on the *general public* or a *large class of persons;*

— private enforcement is necessary; *and*

— the action places a *disproportionate* financial burden on plaintiff in relation to his or her stake in the matter. [CCP §425.17(b) (added 2003)]

(1) **[7:212.6] Application:** Possible examples include actions brought by litigants acting as private attorneys general (see ¶1:298).

- **[7:212.7]** *Bus. & Prof. C. §17200 actions?* Plaintiffs may sue under Bus. & Prof.C. §17200 "on behalf of the general public" for unfair competition or false advertising. It is not clear, however, whether all such suits meet the above requirements for exemption from the anti-SLAPP statute.

  [7:212.8-212.9] *Reserved.*

c. **[7:212.10] Certain claims against business entities:** Also exempt from the anti-SLAPP statute are claims against a person or entity *primarily engaged* in the business of selling or leasing *goods* or *services* based on statements or conduct where *all* of the following conditions are met:

- the statement or conduct consists of *representations of fact* about that person's or a competitor's business operation, goods or services;

- the statement or conduct occurred *in connection with a commercial transaction* (i.e., for the purpose of promoting or securing sales or leases of the person's goods or services; or in the course of delivering such person's goods or services); *and*

- the *intended audience* is an actual or potential customer, or a person likely to influence an actual or potential customer, *or* the statement or conduct arose in connection with a *regulatory approval* process, proceeding or investigation. [CCP §425.17(c) (added 2003)] (An exception is provided for statements or conduct by a telephone company in proceedings before the Public Utilities Commission which are the subject of a competitor's lawsuit; see CCP §425.17(c), last sent.)

(1) **[7:212.11] Application:** Thus, a business entity cannot use an anti-SLAPP motion to challenge claims of *false advertising* and *unfair business practices* based on its advertisements and labeling. [See *Brenton v. Metabolife Int'l, Inc.* (2004) 116 CA4th 679, 689, 10 CR3d 702, 710—§425.17 applies to pending actions]

d. **[7:213] Limitation—certain claims protected despite exemptions:** Even though an action otherwise falls within one of the above exemptions (¶7:212 ff.), certain claims are *excepted:* An anti-SLAPP motion *can* be used to strike lawsuits against a person or entity based on "the creation, dissemination, exhibition, advertisement, or other promotion of *dramatic, literary, musical, political, or artistic work,*" including movies, TV programs, and magazine articles. [CCP §425.17(d)(2) (emphasis added) (added 2003)]

e. **[7:214] Limitation—certain parties protected despite exemptions:** Even though an action otherwise falls within one of the exemptions enumerated above (*¶7:212 ff.*), the following parties *can* file an anti-SLAPP motion when sued in connection with protected activities:

- **[7:214.1]** *News media:* Persons connected with or employed by a newspaper, magazine, other periodical, wire service, radio or television news, or who have been so connected or employed (persons identified in Cal. Const. Art. I, §2(b) and Ev.C. §1070) (see CCP §425.17 (d)(1) (added 2003));

- **[7:214.2]** *Publishers:* Persons engaged in dissemination of ideas or expression in any book or academic journal while engaged in gathering or processing information for communication to the public (see CCP §425.17(d)(1) (added 2003));

- **[7:214.3]** *Nonprofits:* Nonprofit organizations that receive more than 50% of their annual revenue from federal, state or local government grants, awards, programs or reimbursements (see CCP §425.17(d)(3) (added 2003)).

[7:215] *Reserved.*

4. **[7:216] "Persons" Protected by Anti-SLAPP Statute:** Any "person" (defendant) sued for acts in furtherance of free speech or petition activities is protected. [CCP §425.16(b)]

*Comment:* As will be seen, SLAPP suits are not limited to suits by "big guys" against "little guys." Even "deep pocket" defendants can invoke §425.16 when sued for free speech activities! [See *Yu v. Signet Bank/Virginia ("Yu II")* (2002) 103 CA4th 298, 316, 126 CR2d 516, 528—debtors' action against Bank was subject to anti-SLAPP motion because it arose from petitioning activity by Bank]

☞**[7:216.1]** *CAUTION re Pre-2004 case law:* Cases decided before 2004 must be tested against the provisions of CCP §425.17. This statute creates significant exemptions from the anti-SLAPP statute (*see ¶7:212 ff.*), preventing its application in many commercial settings.

a. **[7:216.2] Corporations:** "Person" as used in §425.16 includes both natural persons and corporations. [*Mattel, Inc. v. Luce, Forward, Hamilton & Scripps* (2002) 99 CA4th 1179, 1188, 121 CR2d 794, 800; *Lafayette Morehouse, Inc. v. Chronicle Pub. Co.* (1995) 37 CA4th 855, 862, 44 CR2d 46, 50 (news media defendant)]

b. [7:216.3] **Nonprofits:** A nonprofit corporation is a "person" within the meaning of §425.16. [See *Governor Gray Davis Committee v. American Taxpayers Alliance* (2002) 102 CA4th 449, 456, 125 CR2d 534, 539]

c. [7:216.4] **Public entities and officials:** A public entity that is sued for constitutionally-protected activities by its officials or representatives may file a CCP §425.16 motion. [*Bradbury v. Sup.Ct. (Spencer)* (1996) 49 CA4th 1108, 1114, 57 CR2d 207, 210—County and District Attorney sued for defamation could file §425.16 motion]

d. [7:216.5] **Political candidates:** Similarly, a candidate for public office sued for protected speech may file an anti-SLAPP motion. [*Beilenson v. Sup.Ct. (Sybert)* (1996) 44 CA4th 944, 949-950, 52 CR2d 357, 361—§425.16 available to candidate sued for distributing allegedly libelous campaign literature; see also *Matson v. Dvorak* (1995) 40 CA4th 539, 548, 46 CR2d 880, 885-886—§425.16 available to contributor to political organization]

[7:216.6-216.9] *Reserved.*

e. [7:216.10] **Attorney in earlier litigation?** Dictum in one case suggests that, depending on the circumstances, the attorney for a party to earlier litigation is *not* a "person" protected under CCP §425.16 in a later suit based on that earlier litigation (e.g., malicious prosecution). [See *Shekhter v. Financial Indem. Co.* (2001) 89 CA4th 141, 151-154, 106 CR2d 843, 851-852]

However, other cases hold an attorney who is sued based upon written or oral statements made on behalf of clients in a prior action or in connection with an issue under review by a court, may have standing to bring an anti-SLAPP motion. [*Jespersen v. Zubiate-Beauchamp* (2003) 114 CA4th 624, 629, 7 CR3d 715, 718-719; see *Briggs v. Eden Council for Hope & Opportunity* (1999) 19 C4th 1106, 1116, 81 CR2d 471, 471—rejecting argument that statute was limited to persons acting on their own behalf; and *White v. Lieberman* (2002) 103 CA4th 210, 220-221, 126 CR2d 608, 614-615—invoking anti-SLAPP statute protection in favor of attorneys without discussing any distinction between them and their clients]

[7:217-218] *Reserved.*

5. [7:219] **Activities Protected by Anti-SLAPP Statute:** CCP §425.16 protects the following acts "in furtherance of a person's right of petition or free speech . . . in connection with a public issue," including (without limitation):

a. [7:220] **Statements or writings in official proceedings:** The statute protects statements and writings made before a *legislative, executive or judicial proceeding,* "or any other official proceeding authorized by law." [CCP §425.16(e)(1)]

[7:220.1-220.4]  *Reserved.*

(1) [7:220.5]  **Need not concern public issue:**  The anti-SLAPP statute protects *all* petition-related activity before a governmental body whether or not the statements involve a public issue: "(A)ll that matters is that the First Amendment activity take place in an official proceeding or be made in connection with an issue being reviewed by an official proceeding." [*Briggs v. Eden Council for Hope & Opportunity* (1999) 19 C4 1106, 1116, 81 CR2d 471, 477 (disapproving earlier cases contra)]

    (a) [7:220.6]  **Rationale:**  "Any matter pending before an official proceeding possesses some measure of 'public significance' owing solely to the public nature of the proceeding, and free discussion of such matters furthers effective exercise of the petition rights section 425.16 was intended to protect." [*Briggs v. Eden Council for Hope & Opportunity,* supra, 19 C4th at 1118, 81 CR2d at 478]

(2) [7:220.7]  **Constitutionally-protected activity:**  Any such statement or writing before an official proceeding is *deemed to be* an exercise of the defendant's right of free speech and petition—i.e., "an act in furtherance of a person's right of petition and speech under the United States or California Constitution." [CCP §425.16(e)]

(3) [7:220.8]  **No nexus required:**  Note, however, that §425.16(e) does not require a nexus between the statement or writing and any issue under consideration by the public body: "The Legislature's stated intent is best served . . . by a construction of section 425.16 that broadly encompasses participation in official proceedings, generally, whether or not such participation remains strictly focused on 'public' issues." [*Briggs v. Eden Council for Hope & Opportunity,* supra, 19 C4th at 1118, 81 CR2d at 478]

(4) [7:221]  **Application—statements or writings in** *judicial proceedings:*  Statements and writings made during judicial proceeding are protected by the anti-SLAPP statute. Filing a lawsuit is an exercise of a party's constitutional right to petition for grievances. A claim for relief filed in court is "indisputably a statement or writing made before a judicial proceeding." [*Navellier v. Sletten* (2002) 29 C4th 82, 90, 124 CR2d 530, 537; *Briggs v. Eden Council for Hope & Opportunity,* supra, 19 C4th at 1115, 81 CR2d at 476]

Thus, an anti-SLAPP motion lies to strike lawsuits that seek to penalize earlier litigation or to inhibit future litigation. [*Navellier v. Sletten*, supra, 29 C4th at 89, 124 CR2d at 536-537; *Chavez v. Mendoza* (2001) 94 CA4th 1083, 1087, 114 CR2d 825, 828]

(a) **[7:221.1]** **Malicious prosecution action as SLAPP suit:** An action for malicious prosecution based on a party's or attorney's statements or writings in an earlier judicial proceeding is subject to being stricken as a SLAPP suit: "(B)y its terms, section 425.16 potentially may apply to every malicious prosecution action, because every such action arises from an underlying lawsuit, or petition to the judicial branch." [*Jarrow Formulas, Inc. v. LaMarche* (2003) 31 C4th 728, 735, 3 CR3d 636, 641]

  1) **[7:221.2]** **Effect:** Malicious prosecution plaintiffs must be prepared to show at the outset a probability of prevailing—i.e., that the earlier suit was filed "maliciously" and "without probable cause." This does *not* "unduly burden ( ) plaintiffs' access to court." [*Jarrow Formulas, Inc. v. LaMarche*, supra, 31 C4th at 740, 3 CR3d at 645, fn. 8]

  **[7:221.3-221.4]** *Reserved.*

(b) **[7:221.5]** **Compare—attorney malpractice actions:** A "garden variety" malpractice action based on an attorney's *negligent conduct* in an *earlier lawsuit* (e.g., failure to conduct discovery, failure to comply with court orders, missed deadlines, etc.) is *not* a SLAPP action. Negligent representation of the client is not constitutionally-protected speech. [*Jespersen v. Zubiate-Beauchamp* (2003) 114 CA4th 624, 632, 7 CR3d 715, 720-721]

**[7:221.6]** *Reserved.*

(c) **[7:221.7]** **Compare—retaliatory lawsuits:** A cross-complaint or independent lawsuit is not a SLAPP suit merely because filed in response to pending litigation. As long as the claims asserted are *based on activities that preceded the pending litigation*, the cross-complaint or independent suit cannot be regarded as burdening the opposing party's constitutional right to seek judicial redress. [*Kajima Eng. & Const., Inc. v City of Los Angeles* (2002) 95 CA4th 921, 929, 116 CR2d 187, 193—in Contractor's action to enforce construction contract, City's cross-complaint charging Contractor with fraud in procuring contract was *not* subject to anti-SLAPP motion]

[7:221.8-221.9] *Reserved.*

(d) [7:221.10] **Compare—tort actions based on attorney conduct unrelated to judicial proceedings:** Similarly, a tort action against attorneys based on preparing documents for use in a *nonlitigation matter* (e.g., drafting a trust) is not subject to dismissal under §425.16(e)(1) . . . because the statements are not made in a judicial proceeding. [*Moore v. Shaw* (2004) 116 CA4th 182, 197, 10 CR3d 154, 164—attorney sued for drafting documents that enabled client to breach trust agreement]

(e) [7:222] **Protection extends to certain nonjudicial proceedings:** Other types of litigation may be treated as "official proceedings" under the anti-SLAPP statute, including:

1) [7:222.1] **Administrative proceedings:** [See *Briggs v. Eden Council for Hope & Opportunity* (1999) 19 C4th 1106, 1115, 81 CR2d 471, 476—"petitioning activity includes . . . seeking administrative action"]

2) [7:222.2] **Arbitration:** [See *Paul v. Friedman* (2002) 95 CA4th 853, 866-868, 117 CR2d 82, 92-93—earlier litigation was proceeding before an arbitrator]

(5) [7:223] **Application—statements or writings in *legislative or executive proceedings:*** Statements or writings presented before a governmental body in legislative or executive proceedings are also protected under CCP §425.16(a)(1). Such statements and writings in the course of official proceedings are deemed to have public significance *per se.* [See *Briggs v. Eden Council for Hope & Opportunity* (1999) 19 C4th 1106, 1122, 81 CR2d 471, 480-481]

(a) **Application**

- [7:223.1] Landlords sued Tenants' Rights Advocacy Group for defamations ("racist" and "rednecks") allegedly uttered by Advocacy Group while assisting tenants in small claims court and in administrative proceedings Advocacy Group moved to strike Landlords' suit as a SLAPP suit. Its statements were protected under §425.16 because connected with official proceedings even if the alleged defamations did not involve a public issue. [*Briggs v. Eden Council for Hope & Opportunity,* supra, 19 C4th at 1122-1123, 81 CR2d at 480-481]

- [7:223.2] Reporting another person's unlawful conduct to the police, with the intention of prompting his or her arrest (as distinguished from making a citizen's arrest), may constitute a protected "petition" to an official body. [See *Wang v. Hartunian* (2003) 111 CA4th 744, 749, 3 CR3d 909, 912]

[7:224] *Reserved.*

b. [7:225] **Statements or writings *in connection with issue under consideration* in official proceeding:** The anti-SLAPP statute also protects communications "made in connection with an issue under consideration or review by a legislative, executive, or judicial body, or any other official proceeding authorized by law." [CCP §425.16(e)(2)]

Effect: The same protection for statements and conduct made *during* an official proceeding extends to statements and conduct outside the proceedings *if sufficiently related* to matters under consideration by the official body.

[7:225.1-225.4] *Reserved.*

(1) [7:225.5] **Need not concern public issue:** Again, a bright-line test applies: As long as the statements or conduct are made "in connection with an issue under consideration" by a government body, they are protected. They are deemed to pertain to a public issue by virtue of being considered by a public body. *See discussion at ¶7:220.5.*

(2) [7:225.6] **Constitutionally-protected activity:** Although §425.16(e)(2) does not expressly require that the statements or writings involve the exercise of a constitutional right, the presentation of such a statement or writing to a public body necessarily implicates the rights of free speech. *See discussion at ¶7:220.7.*

(3) [7:225.7] **Nexus required:** The statement or writing *need not be made before the official body.* But a nexus is required between the statement or writing and an issue under consideration by the public body. [CCP §425.16(e)(2)]

"(S)ection 425.16 does not accord anti-SLAPP protection to suits arising from any act having any connection, however remote, with an official proceeding. The statements or writings in question must occur in connection with 'an issue under consideration or review' in the proceeding." [*Paul v. Friedman* (2002) 95 CA4th 853, 866, 117 CR2d 82, 92; see also *Blackburn v. Brady* (2004) 116 CA4th 670, 677, 10 CR3d 696, 701]

(4) **Application**

- [7:226]   Defendant petitioned the city council to refuse a permit being sought by Charitable Organization to establish a group home in defendant's neighborhood. She also urged her employer not to support Charitable Organization. Charitable Organization sued Defendant for libel *based on her statements to her employer* (carefully crafting the suit to exclude her comments to the city council). An anti-SLAPP motion was granted. It was enough that the allegedly slanderous statements "arose in the context of a public issue." [*Averill v. Sup.Ct. (Eli Home, Inc.)* (1996) 42 CA4th 1170, 1175, 50 CR2d 62, 65]

- [7:226.1]   Law Firm sent a letter to celebrities who made a recording for charities, soliciting their support for Attorney General's investigation of Charitable Organization's operations. Charitable Organization sued Law Firm for defamation. Law Firm's communication was protected under the anti-SLAPP statute because it was made in connection with a proposed complaint to the Attorney General seeking an investigation: "The fact that the communication was made to other private citizens rather than to the official agency does not exclude it from the shelter of the anti-SLAPP suit statute." [*Dove Audio, Inc. v. Rosenfeld, Meyer & Susman* (1996) 47 CA4th 777, 784, 54 CR2d 830, 835]

- [7:227]   *Compare:* Fraudulent activities that depress the bid price at a *Sheriff's sale* are not protected by the anti-SLAPP statute: "The ministerial event of a Sheriff's sale or auction simply does not concern an issue under review or determine some disputed matter as contemplated under the anti-SLAPP law." [*Blackburn v. Brady*, supra, 116 CA4th at 677, 10 CR3d at 701]

  [7:228]   *Reserved.*

c. [7:229]   **Statements or writings in public place or forum:**   The anti-SLAPP statute also protects statements and writings "made in a place open to the public or a public forum in connection with an issue of public interest" [CCP §425.16(e)(3)]

(1) [7:229.1] **Must concern "issue of public interest":** Unlike statements made before a public body, statements and writings in a public place or forum are protected under the anti-SLAPP statute only if they are made "in connection with an issue of public interest." [CCP §425.16(e)(3)]

*Cross-refer:* What constitutes an "issue of public interest" is discussed at ¶7:233 ff.

(2) [7:229.2] **Constitutionally-protected activity:** Although §425.16(e)(3) does not expressly require that the statements or writings in a public place or forum involve the exercise of a constitutional right, the presentation of such a statement or writing to a public body necessarily implicates the rights of free speech. *See discussion at ¶7:220.7.*

(3) [7:229.3] **No nexus required:** No nexus or connection is required between the statement or writing in a public place and any issue under consideration by a public body.

(4) [7:230] **"Public forum":** This term has been construed broadly to include settings and contexts beyond those protected by the First Amendment. [See *Seelig v. Infinity Broadcasting Corp.* (2002) 97 CA4th 798, 807, 119 CR2d 108, 115—on-air discussion between talk-radio cohosts; *ComputerXpress, Inc. v. Jackson* (2001) 93 CA4th 993, 1006, 113 CR2d 625, 638—Internet Web site]

- [7:230.1] Streets, parks and other public places are considered "public forums." [*Zhao v. Wong* (1996) 48 CA4th 1114, 1125-1126, 55 CR2d 909, 916 (overruled on other grounds in *Briggs v. Eden Council for Hope & Opportunity* (1999) 19 C4th 1106, 1123, 81 CR2d 471, 482, fn. 10)]

- [7:230.2] Speech *by mail* (e.g., in a campaign flyer mailed to potential voters) is a "public forum." [*Macias v. Hartwell* (1997) 55 CA4th 669, 674, 64 CR2d 222, 225]

- [7:230.3] Conventional Internet venues constitute a "public forum" or a place "open to the public" within the meaning of §425.16: "Considering that the Internet provides the most participatory form of mass speech yet developed, it is not surprising that courts have uniformly held . . . that Internet venues to which members of the public have relatively easy access constitute a 'public forum' or a place 'open to the public' within the meaning of §425.16." [*Barrett v. Rosenthal* (2004) 114 CA4th 1379, 1388,

9 CR3d 142, 149; *ComputerXpress, Inc. v. Jackson* (2001) 93 CA4th 993, 1006, 113 CR2d 625, 638— Internet Web message board or "chat room" was "public forum"]

d. **[7:231] Other conduct in furtherance of free speech right:** The anti-SLAPP statute also protects "*any other conduct* in furtherance of the exercise of the constitutional right of petition or the constitutional right of free speech in connection with a public issue or an issue of public interest." [CCP §425.16(e)(4) (emphasis added)]

(1) **[7:231.1] Must concern "public issue or issue of public interest":** The statute expressly requires that the conduct be "in connection with a public issue or an issue of public interest. [CCP §425.16(e)(4)]

*Cross-refer:* What constitutes a "public issue" or "issue of public interest" is discussed at ¶7:233 ff.

(2) **[7:231.2] Constitutionally-protected activity:** The statute expressly requires that the conduct be "in furtherance of the right of free speech or petition," thus establishing a constitutionally-protected activity. [CCP §425.16(e)(4)]

(3) **[7:231.3] No nexus required:** No nexus is required between the conduct and any issue under consideration by a public body.

(4) **Application**

- [7:232] Television Station's *gathering of information* to be used in a broadcast news report regarding a doctor who was allegedly unlawfully dispensing controlled substances was "conduct in furtherance of its free speech rights" within the meaning of the anti-SLAPP statute. [*Lieberman v. KCOP Television, Inc.* (2003) 110 CA4th 156, 163, 1 CR3d 536, 540-541]

- [7:232.1] Optometrist's *arranging meetings* with other optometrists to discuss legislation and legal actions affecting their business was "conduct in furtherance of" protected speech. [See *1-800 Contacts, Inc. v. Steinberg* (2003) 107 CA4th 568, 583, 132 CR2d 789, 801]

e. **[7:233] What constitutes "public issue" or "issue of public interest":** Statements, writings or conduct *not* made or occurring in an official proceeding (or in connection with an issue under consideration in such a proceeding) are protected only if made in a public place and "in connection with an issue of public interest" (CCP §425.16(e)(3)). Other conduct in furtherance of the right of free speech is protected only if made "in connection with a *public issue* or an issue of public interest" (CCP §425.16(e)(4) (emphasis added)).

*Comment:* Although §425.16(e)(4) uses these terms disjunctively, there appears to be no substantive difference between them. [See *Du Charme v. International Broth. of Elec. Workers, Local 45* (2003) 110 CA4th 107, 118, 1 CR3d 501, 510—applying same standard to "the public issue/issue of public interest requirement of subdivisions (e)(3) and (4)"]

[7:233.1-233.4]  *Reserved.*

(1) **[7:233.5]  Broadly construed:**  "Public interest" within the meaning of the anti-SLAPP statute includes "not only governmental matters, but also private conduct that impacts a broad segment of society and/or that affects a community in a manner similar to that of a governmental entity." [*Damon v. Ocean Hills Journalism Club* (2000) 85 CA4th 468, 479, 102 CR2d 205, 212]

"Although matters of public interest include legislative and governmental activities, they may also include activities that involve private persons and entities, especially when a large, powerful organization may impact the lives of many individuals." [*Du Charme v. International Broth. of Elec. Workers, Local 45* (2003) 110 CA4th 107, 115-116, 1 CR3d 501, 507-508]

(2) **[7:233.6]  Includes matters of interest to limited segment of public:**  In cases where the issue is not of interest to the public at large, but rather to a *limited, but definable portion of the public* (a private group, organization or community), the constitutionally-protected activity must occur, at a minimum, "*in the context of an ongoing controversy, dispute or discussion* . . . (thus embodying) the public policy of encouraging participation in matters of public significance." [*Du Charme v. International Broth. of Elec. Workers, Local 45,* supra, 110 CA4th at 119, 1 CR3d at 510 (emphasis and parentheses added)]

(3) **[7:234]  Application:**  A statement or activity has been held "in the public interest" when it involves:
— a person or entity in the public eye;
— conduct that could affect large numbers of people beyond the direct participants; or
— a topic of widespread interest. [*Rivero v. American Fed. of State, County & Mun. Employees, AFL-CIO* (2003) 105 CA4th 913, 924, 130 CR2d 81, 89]

• [7:234.1]  Defendant made allegedly defamatory statements about Manager of a homeowners association governing 3,000 individuals in 1,633 homes at a board of directors meeting and in a newsletter. Manager's defamation suit was subject to an anti-SLAPP motion: "(B)ecause each of the statements concerned the manner in which a large residential community would be governed, they concerned 'issues of public interest.'" [*Damon v. Ocean Hills Journalism Club*, supra, 85 CA4th at 474-475, 102 CR2d at 209 (emphasis added)]

[7:234.2-234.4] *Reserved.*

• [7:234.5] Developer of a large bayfront property sued Defendants for inducing breach of contract based on their contacts with City employees while City was subject to an exclusive negotiating agreement with Developer. Developer's action was subject to an anti-SLAPP motion because the proposed development with its potential commercial and environmental impacts "is plainly a matter of public interest." [*Tuscher Develop. Enterprises, Inc. v. San Diego Unified Port Dist. (*2003) 106 CA4th 1219, 1234, 132 CR2d 57, 68]

• [7:234.6] Political Consultant sued for defamation based on a magazine article accusing him of domestic violence. The issue was of "public interest" because Political Consultant was a public figure and had made the prevention of domestic violence a cornerstone in his advertising campaigns for politicians known around the world. [*Sipple v. Foundation for Nat'l Progress* (1999) 71 CA4th 226, 236-240, 83 CR2d 677, 683-685]

— [7:234.7] *Compare:* Slanders regarding a *nonpublic* figure in private conversations and in a newsletter reaching no more than 700 people have been held *not* of "public interest." [*Weinberg v. Feisel* (2003) 110 CA4th 1122, 1135, 2 CR3d 385, 395]

[7:234.8-234.9] *Reserved.*

• [7:234.10] *Compare:* Union accused Janitorial Supervisor of dishonesty and favoritism in supervising a staff of eight persons at a public university. Supervisor's slander suit against Union was *not* subject to dismissal as a SLAPP suit. Not every workplace dispute is a matter of "public interest." [*Rivero v. American Fed. of State, County & Mun. Employees, AFL-CIO,* supra, 105 CA4th at 924, 130 CR2d at 90; see also *Du Charme v. International Broth. of Elec. Workers, Local 45,* supra, 110

CA4th at 118, 1 CR3d at 510—Internet Web site posting stating plaintiff had been fired from his union job because of financial irregularities did *not* constitute information "in the public interest"]

[7:234.11-234.14]  *Reserved.*

(4) **[7:234.15]**  **Compare—purely commercial speech not protected:**  Speech that does no more than propose a business transaction ("commercial speech") does not raise a "public issue" within the meaning of §425.16. Therefore, false advertising claims cannot be stricken as SLAPP suits. [*Rezec v. Sony Pictures Entertainment, Inc.* (2004) 116 CA4th 135, 140, 10 CR3d 333, 337]

What constitutes "commercial speech" requires consideration of three elements: the *speaker*, the *intended audience*, and the *content of the message*. Advertising a product or service based on economic motivation falls in this category. [See *Rezec v. Sony Pictures Entertainment, Inc.*, supra, 116 CA4th at 140, 10 CR3d at 337]

(a) **[7:234.16]**  **Public interest in advertised product not sufficient:**  That there is a public interest in the product or service advertised does not mean the advertisement is of "public interest" within the meaning of the anti-SLAPP statute: "Just because you are selling something that is intrinsically important does not mean that the public is interested in the fact that you are selling it." [*Commonwealth Energy v. Investor Data Exch., Inc.* (2003) 110 CA4th 26, 34, 1 CR3d 390, 395—telemarketers' offering investors protection against investment scams was *not* "in the public interest"]

- [7:234.17]  Similarly, advertising a product that contains *protected speech* (e.g., a book, film or television program) is not "in the public interest" for purposes of the anti-SLAPP statute even though the speech itself may be protected. [See *Rezec v. Sony Pictures Entertainment, Inc.*, supra, 116 CA4th at 146, 10 CR3d at 341]

[7:234.18-234.19]  *Reserved.*

(b) **[7:234.20]**  **Compare—"educational" activities:**  An advertisement may be protected if its primary purpose is "educational" rather than purely economic.

Example: Drug Co.'s advertising claimed that "more than 1.8 million Americans have purchased (Drug

Co.'s product), an anti-coagulation medication, for the prevention and treatment of blood clots . . ." A competitor's suit for false advertising was subject to an anti-SLAPP motion. The *number of persons allegedly affected* and the *seriousness* of the condition treated made the advertising one of "public interest." [*DuPont Merck Pharmaceutical Co. v. Sup.Ct. (Newman)* (2000) 78 CA4th 562, 567, 92 CR2d 755, 759]

1) [7:234.21] **Comment:** *DuPont* can be distinguished on the basis that Drug Co. was also engaged in lobbying and educational activities. Even so, the case has been questioned and no subsequent case has adopted *DuPont's* approach. [See *Martinez v. Metabolife Int'l, Inc.* (2003) 113 CA4th 181, 192, 6 CR3d 494, 502]

   In any event, *DuPont* would probably be decided differently under current law because the false advertising claim would appear to be exempt from the anti-SLAPP statute; see ¶7:212.6 ff.

   [7:234.22-234.24] *Reserved.*

(c) **Application**

* [7:234.25] Credit card solicitations mailed to a target audience of consumers were *not* "in the public interest." This was purely commercial speech. It was not an attempt to educate or inform on an issue of importance to large numbers of people, and thus not entitled to protection under the anti-SLAPP statute. [*Jewett v. Capital One Bank* (2003) 113 CA4th 805, 815, 6 CR3d 675, 682]

* [7:234.26] A manufacturer's advertising of a *specific consumer product* on its labels or in public advertising, for the purpose of selling the product, is not an "issue of public interest" under §425.16. [*Scott v. Metabolife Int'l, Inc.* (2004) 115 CA4th 404, 420, 9 CR3d 242, 253; see *Consumer Justice Ctr. v. Trimedica Int'l, Inc.* (2003) 107 CA4th 595, 601, 132 CR2d 191, 194-195—advertising claims made about the effectiveness of an herbal supplement promising breast enlargement did not involve a "public issue" or an "issue of public interest"; *Nagel v. Twin Laboratories, Inc.* (2003) 109 CA4th 39, 47, 134 CR2d 420, 425—list of ingredients on product label was "commercial speech," not

information "of public interest" under anti-SLAPP statute]

— [7:234.27]   Comment: On the other hand, claims made about herbal supplements or alternative medicine *in general,* rather than a particular product, might be regarded as a matter of "public interest." [*Consumer Justice Ctr. v. Trimedica Int'l, Inc.*, supra, 107 CA4th at 601, 132 CR2d at 194]

6.  [7:235]   **Causes of Action Subject to Being Stricken:**   The anti-SLAPP statute applies to causes of action "arising from any act . . . in furtherance of (a) person's right of petition or free speech under the United States or California Constitution in connection with a public issue." [CCP §425.16(b)(1)]

The cause of action may appear in either a complaint, petition or cross-complaint. [CCP §425.16(h); see *Kajima Eng. & Const., Inc. v. City of Los Angeles* (2002) 95 CA4th 921, 929, 116 CR2d 187, 193]

The theory or type of plaintiff's action (i.e., contract or tort) is not dispositive: "Nothing in the statute . . . excludes any particular type of action from its operation." [*Navellier v. Sletten* (2002) 29 C4th 82, 92, 124 CR2d 530, 539]

a.  [7:235.1]   **"Arising from":**   In the anti-SLAPP context, the critical consideration is whether the cause of action is *based on* defendant's protected free speech or petitioning activity. Whether plaintiff's lawsuit was *intended* to chill or *actually* chilled defendant's protected conduct is immaterial: "(T)he statutory phrase 'cause of action . . . arising from' means simply that the defendant's act underlying the plaintiff's cause of action must *itself* have been an act in furtherance of the right of petition or free speech." [*City of Cotati v. Cashman* (2002) 29 C4th 69, 78, 124 CR2d 519, 527 (emphasis added); *Navellier v. Sletten,* supra, 29 C4th at 88, 124 CR2d at 535]

In determining this matter, the court may look to the pleadings and supporting and opposing affidavits stating the acts upon which the liability or defense is based. [CCP §425.16(b); *Navellier v. Sletten,* supra, 29 C4th at 88, 124 CR2d at 535]

[7:235.2-235.4]   *Reserved.*

(1)  [7:235.5]   **Determined by "principal thrust" of plaintiff's claim:**   Whether the anti-SLAPP statute applies is determined by the "principal thrust or gravamen" of plaintiff's claim. It cannot be invoked where allegations of protected activity are only *incidental* to a

cause of action based on nonprotected activity. [*Martinez v. Metabolife Int'l, Inc.* (2003) 113 CA4th 181, 187, 6 CR3d 494, 499]

- **[7:235.6]** Consumer complained of physical injury resulting from consuming Manufacturer's herbal product. Although the complaint alleged various advertising claims made by Manufacturer for its product (a protected activity), the "gravamen" of the suit was for injury resulting from *manufacturing and distribution of a defective product*—conduct *not* protected by the First Amendment: "(C)ollateral allusions to protected activity should not subject the cause of action to the anti-SLAPP statute." [*Martinez v. Metabolife Int'l, Inc.*, supra, 113 CA4th at 187, 6 CR3d at 499; see also *Scott v. Metabolife Int'l, Inc.*(2004) 115 CA4th 404, 420, 9 CR3d 242, 253; *Brenton v. Metabolife Int'l, Inc.* (2004) 116 CA4th 679, 686, 10 CR3d 702, 707]

- **[7:235.7]** An action for damages resulting from an intrusive investigation and disclosures regarding plaintiff's personal life that bore no relationship to the issues pending before the tribunal (here, arbitration) did not *arise from* the litigation. [*Paul v. Friedman* (2002) 95 CA4th 853, 866-868, 117 CR2d 82, 92-93]

- **[7:235.8]** The fact that *evidence* supporting plaintiff's complaint was obtained in connection with administrative proceedings does not by itself qualify the suit under the anti-SLAPP statute. [*Gallimore v. State Farm Fire & Cas. Ins. Co.* (2002) 102 CA4th 1388, 1398, 126 CR2d 560, 568]

(2) **[7:236] Sequence not determinative:** That the lawsuit was filed *after* defendant's protected activity took place does not establish that it "arose from" a protected activity for purposes of the anti-SLAPP statute. [*City of Cotati v. Cashman*, supra, 29 C4th at 77, 124 CR2d at 526; *Navellier v. Sletten,* supra, 29 C4th at 88, 124 CR2d at 535]

Nor is it enough to show that the action was "triggered by" or filed *in response to* or in *retaliation for* a party's exercise of free speech rights. A cause of action may be "triggered by" protected activity without necessarily "arising from" such protected activity. [*City of Cotati v. Cashman*, supra, 29 C4th at 77, 124 CR2d at 526— defendant's act underlying plaintiff's cause of action *must itself* have been an act in furtherance of the right of petition or free speech]

- [7:236.1]   Plaintiff's state court action, filed *after* defendant initiated a federal suit relating to the same issues, was *not* subject to §425.16. The state action did not "arise from" the federal action; rather, it was based on a dispute concerning the constitutionality of a statute [*City of Cotati v. Cashman*, supra, 29 C4th at 78, 124 CR2d at 527]

- [7:236.2]   After Landlord commenced statutory procedures to increase the rents on his rent-controlled apartments, Rent Control Board sued him for violating the rent control ordinance. Even if Board's suit was "triggered by" Landlord's petitioning activity (seeking the rent adjustments), it was *not* a SLAPP suit because it was *not based on* his petitioning activity but rather on his charging illegal rent. [*Santa Monica Rent Control Bd. v. Pearl Street, LLC* (2003) 109 CA4th 1308, 1318, 135 CR2d 903, 910]

b.   [7:237]   **Typical claims:**   The "favored" causes of action in SLAPP suits include:
— *defamation;*
— *interference with prospective economic advantage* and other business torts;
— *nuisance;* and
— *intentional (or negligent) infliction of emotional distress.* [*Gallimore v. State Farm Fire & Cas. Co.* (2002) 102 CA4th 1388, 1400, 126 CR2d 560, 569, fn. 9]

Any of these causes of action could support damage awards that would be ruinous to the defendant and therefore "chill" defendant's exercise of constitutionally-protected rights. [See *Conroy v. Spitzer* (1999) 70 CA4th 1446, 1451, 83 CR2d 443, 446]

- [7:237.1]   A *defamation* action by a large land developer against environmental activists or homeowners who oppose the developer's plans, intended to "chill" their opposition to his plans, is the "paradigm SLAPP" suit. [See *Wilcox v. Sup.Ct. (Peters)* (1994) 27 CA4th 809, 815, 33 CR2d 446, 449 (overruled on other grounds in *Equilon Enterprises, L.L.C. v. Consumer Cause, Inc.* (2002) 29 C4th 53, 124 CR2d 507)]

- [7:237.2]   Businessman sued Attorney who opposed his development plans for defamation, unfair competition and unfair business practices. [*Kashian v. Harriman* (2002) 98 CA4th 892, 907-908, 120 CR2d 576, 587-588]

[7:237.3-237.9]   *Reserved.*

c. **Other actions subject to anti-SLAPP statute**

- **[7:237.10]** Oil Company's suit against Consumer Group for *declaratory and injunctive* relief in response to Consumer Group's filing a statutorily-required notice of intent to sue (under the Safe Drinking Water and Toxic Enforcement Act) was subject to an anti-SLAPP motion because it *arose from* Consumer Group's exercise of its constitutional right of free speech and petition. [*Equilon Enterprises, L.L.C. v. Consumer Cause, Inc.* (2002) 29 C4th 53, 67, 124 CR2d 507, 518]

  — **[7:237.11]** Note: It is an open question whether a "pure" declaratory relief action seeking mere clarification of *past* speech or petitioning (and alleging no liability or remedy that would impair future exercise of defendant's free speech or petition rights) might evade a §425.16 motion. [*Equilon Enterprises, L.L.C. v. Consumer Cause, Inc.,* supra, 29 C4th at 67, 124 CR2d at 519, fn. 4]

- **[7:237.12]** An action for *breach of contract* and *fraud* was subject to §425.16 because a counterclaim filed in an earlier action *arose from* the exercise of the right to litigate: "Conduct alleged to constitute breach of contract may also come within constitutionally protected speech or petitioning." [*Navellier v. Sletten* (2002) 29 C4th 82, 92, 124 CR2d 530, 539]

- **[7:237.13]** Plaintiff's suit against Broadcasting Company for slander and *invasion of privacy,* and for negligent hiring, retention and supervision of its employees who made on-the-air comments regarding plaintiff, was subject to §425.16. [*Seelig v. Infinity Broadcasting Corp.* (2002) 97 CA4th 798, 807, 119 CR2d 108, 115]

- **[7:237.14]** Debtors' *abuse of process* action against Bank based on its practice of filing collection actions against debtors in a distant forum is a SLAPP suit because it is based on Bank's petitioning activity. [*Yu v. Signet Bank/Virginia ("Yu II")* (2002) 103 CA4th 298, 316, 126 CR2d 516, 528—"It is ironic that a lawsuit challenging distant forum abuse—a practice calculated to prevent (Debtors') 'public participation" in the collection action against them—should itself meet the threshold definition of a SLAPP suit, but that is the result under the anti-SLAPP statute" (parentheses added)]

  **[7:237.15-237.19]** *Reserved.*

d. **[7:237.20]** **Compare—oppressive litigation tactics not enough:** A cross-complaint or independent action is not subject to the anti-SLAPP statute simply because it may be viewed as an oppressive litigation tactic: "No lawsuit is properly subject to a motion to strike unless its allegations arise from acts in furtherance of the right of petition or free speech." [*Kajima Eng. & Const., Inc. v. City of Los Angeles* (2002) 95 CA4th 921, 924, 116 CR2d 187, 189—allegedly meritless cross-complaint not subject to §425.16 motion because it was not related to any free speech or petitioning activity]

7. **Effect of Joining Non-SLAPP Claims**

a. [7:238] **Separate non-SLAPP causes of action:** An anti-SLAPP motion may be directed at individual causes of action (see CCP §425.16(b)(1)). Thus, where a complaint contains both SLAPP and non-SLAPP causes of action, the SLAPP claim alone may be stricken: "The fact that other claims remain does not bar a trial judge from granting a §425.16 special motion to strike." [*Shekhter v. Financial Indem. Co.* (2001) 89 CA4th 141, 150, 106 CR2d 843, 849]

b. [7:239] **Protected and nonprotected activities alleged in same cause of action ("mixed" cause of action):** An anti-SLAPP motion challenges a cause of action, rather than individual allegations or theories supporting the cause of action (see CCP §425.16(b)(1)). Thus, where a single cause of action alleges both acts protected under the statute and nonprotected acts, the entire cause of action may be stricken under §425.16. Plaintiffs "cannot frustrate the purposes of the SLAPP statute through a pleading tactic of combining allegations of protected and non-protected activity under the label of one 'cause of action.'" [*Fox Searchlight Pictures, Inc. v. Paladino* (2001) 89 CA4th 294, 308, 106 CR2d 906, 918]

(1) [7:239.1] **Contra authority:** There is contrary dictum in *M.G. v. Time Warner, Inc.* (2001) 89 CA4th 623, 629, 107 CR2d 504, 509. But the holding dealt with plaintiff's probability of success on the merits rather than whether the cause of action was subject to the statute.

[7:239.2] *CAUTION:* This issue is presently before the California Supreme Court in *Kids Against Pollution v. California Dental Ass'n*, Case No. S117156; and *Finke v. Walt Disney Co.*, Case No. S118936.

8. [7:240] **Procedure:** Except as otherwise provided in CCP §425.16, the procedures on motions to strike generally (¶7:190 ff.) presumably apply:

a. [7:241] **Timing of motion:** The anti-SLAPP motion must be filed within 60 days after service of the complaint or amended complaint. Thereafter, a motion may be permitted in the court's discretion "upon terms it deems proper." [CCP §425.16(f)]

(1) [7:241.1] **Extension for service by mail:** Where an amended complaint is served by mail, the time for filing an anti-SLAPP motion is extended pursuant to CCP §1013(a) (*see ¶9:87.5*)—i.e., an extra 5 days if the mailing address is in California. [*Lam v. Ngo* (2001) 91 CA4th 832, 842, 111 CR2d 582, 589-590]

[7:241.2-241.4] *Reserved.*

(2) [7:241.5] **After amended complaint:** Amending the complaint "reopens" the time period for an anti-SLAPP motion. The 60-day period for filing the motion runs from service of the most recent amended complaint, rather than from the original complaint. [*Yu v. Signet Bank/ Virginia ("Yu II")* (2002) 103 CA4th 298, 314, 126 CR2d 516, 527]

b. [7:242] **Notice of motion:** The motion shall be noticed for hearing *not more than 30 days* after service (unless the court's docket requires a later hearing). [CCP §425.16(f); see *Decker v. U.D. Registry, Inc.* (2003) 105 CA4th 1382, 1390, 129 CR2d 892, 897—30-day hearing requirement mandatory]

c. [7:243] **Declarations required:** The motion must be supported (and opposed) by declarations stating *facts* upon which the liability or defense is based. [CCP §425.16(b)]

d. [7:244] **Defendant's burden of proof:** The only thing that defendant needs to show to invoke the protection of the SLAPP statute is that plaintiff's lawsuit *"arises from"* defendant's exercise of free speech or petition rights as defined in CCP §425.16(e). [*Equilon Enterprises, L.L.C. v. Consumer Cause, Inc.* (2002) 29 C4th 53, 61, 124 CR2d 507, 513]

(1) [7:244.1] *Prima facie* **showing sufficient:** Defendant need only make a prima facie showing that plaintiff's complaint "arises from" defendant's constitutionally-protected free speech or petition activity. The burden shifts to plaintiff to establish *as a matter of law* that no such protection exists. [See *Governor Gray Davis Committee v. American Taxpayers Alliance* (2002) 102 CA4th 449, 458-459, 125 CR2d 534, 541-542]

[7:244.2-244.4] *Reserved.*

(2) [7:244.5] **No "intent-to-chill" required:** Although the statute refers to "lawsuits brought primarily to chill exercise" of rights of free speech and petition, defendant *need not show* that the lawsuit was brought with the subjective intent to "chill" these rights. [*Equilon Enterprises, L.L.C. v. Consumer Cause, Inc.*, supra, 29 C4th at 58, 124 CR2d at 511-512]

(3) **[7:244.6]** **No actual "chilling" required:** Nor need defendant demonstrate that plaintiff's complaint actually had a "chilling" effect on his or her First Amendment rights. [*Equilon Enterprises, L.L.C. v. Consumer Cause, Inc.*, supra, 29 C4th at 59, 124 CR2d at 512; *City of Cotati v. Cashman* (2002) 29 C4th 69, 74, 124 CR2d 519, 524; *Navellier v. Sletten* (2002) 29 C4th 82, 88, 124 CR2d 530, 535]

e. **[7:245]** **Plaintiff's burden of proof:** Once defendant makes such a prima facie showing, the burden shifts to plaintiff to establish a "probability" that plaintiff will prevail on whatever claims are asserted against defendant. [See CCP §425.16(b)]

The burden is on plaintiff to produce evidence that would be admissible at trial—i.e., to proffer a prima facie showing of facts supporting a judgment in plaintiff's favor. [*Chavez v. Mendoza* (2001) 94 CA4th 1083, 1087, 114 CR2d 825, 828]

(1) **[7:246]** **What constitutes "probability":** Plaintiff must show:
— a *legally sufficient* claim (i.e., a claim which, if supported by facts, is sustainable as a matter of law); and
— that the claim is *supported* by competent, *admissible* evidence within the declarant's *personal knowledge*. [*DuPont Merck Pharmaceutical Co. v. Sup.Ct. (Newman)* (2000) 78 CA4th 562, 568, 92 CR2d 755, 760]

**[7:247]** Put another way, plaintiff must demonstrate that the complaint is both:
— *legally sufficient;* and
— supported by a sufficient *prima facie showing of facts* to sustain a favorable judgment if the evidence submitted by plaintiff is credited. [*Wilson v. Parker, Covert & Chidester* (2002) 28 C4th 811, 821, 123 CR2d 19, 26; also see *Navellier v. Sletten* (2002) 29 C4th 82, 87, 124 CR2d 530, 536]

(a) **[7:248]** **Summary judgment standards:** The "probability of prevailing" is tested by the same standard governing a motion for summary judgment. I.e., in opposing a SLAPP motion, it is plaintiff's burden to make a *prima facie* showing of *facts* that would support a judgment in plaintiff's favor. [*Kyle v. Carmon* (1999) 71 CA4th 901, 907, 84 CR2d 303, 306]

The court will consider the pleadings and evidentiary submissions of both plaintiff and defendant but *does not weigh credibility or comparative strength of the evidence.* The court considers defendant's evidence only to determine if it defeats plaintiff's showing *as a matter of law.* [*Kashian v. Harriman* (2002) 98 CA4th 892, 906 120 CR2d 576, 586]

(2) **[7:249] Evidentiary considerations:** In opposing an anti-SLAPP motion, plaintiff must present *admissible evidence* and cannot rely on the allegations of the complaint. [*Roberts v. Los Angeles County Bar Ass'n* (2003) 105 CA4th 604, 613-614, 129 CR2d 546, 551]

(a) **[7:250] Hearsay affidavits:** Affidavits or declarations "on information and belief" are hearsay and hence inadmissible evidence to show a "probability" that plaintiff will prevail. [*Evans v. Unkow* (1995) 38 CA4th 1490, 1497, 45 CR2d 624, 628]

[7:250.1-250.4] *Reserved.*

(b) **[7:250.5] Preliminary injunction shows "probability" of prevailing on merits:** Evidence showing that plaintiffs are entitled to injunctive relief (which requires a finding of probability of success, *see ¶9:527*) may also show a "probability" of prevailing on the merits sufficient to withstand an anti-SLAPP motion. [*Slauson Partnership v. Ochoa* (2003) 112 CA4th 1005, 1022, 5 CR3d 668, 680— no error in considering same evidence both for preliminary injunction and on motion to strike]

[7:250.6-250.9] *Reserved.*

(c) **[7:250.10] Denial of summary judgment in earlier lawsuit as bar to malicious prosecution claim:** Plaintiffs may be unable to establish a "probability" of prevailing in a malicious prosecution action where, as defendants in the earlier lawsuit, they lost a motion for summary judgment: "Because denial of summary judgment is a sound indicator of probable cause, it is sensible to accept it as *establishing probable cause* defeating a later malicious prosecution suit." [*Slaney v. Ranger Ins. Co.,* (2004) 115 CA4th 306, 319, 8 CR3d 915, 925 (emphasis added)]

1) **[7:250.11] Compare—defense summary judgment *not* proof of lack of probable cause:** On the other hand, malicious prosecution plaintiffs cannot establish *lack of probable cause* based on their having obtained, as defendants in the earlier action, a defense summary judgment based on insufficiency of the evidence: "(S)uccessfully defending a lawsuit

does not establish that the suit was brought without probable cause." [*Jarrow Formulas, Inc. v. LaMarche* (2003) 31 C4th 728, 742, 3 CR3d 636, 647—nor does a defense summary judgment establish the malice required for malicious prosecution; see *Slaney v. Ranger Ins. Co.*, supra, 115 CA4th at 319, 8 CR3d at 925]

(3) **Application**

- [7:251]   Plaintiff could not show a "probability" that he would prevail in a libel action where the allegedly libelous article was shown to be *absolutely privileged* under Civ.C. §47(d) (privilege for fair report in a public journal of a judicial proceeding). [*Sipple v. Foundation For Nat'l Progress* (1999) 71 CA4th 226, 240-241, 83 CR2d 677, 685-686]

- [7:251.1]   Plaintiffs could not show probability of prevailing on their libel action against newspaper that published "fair and true reports" of SEC proceedings against them. [*Colt v. Freedom Communications, Inc.* (2003) 109 CA4th 1551, 1556, 1 CR3d 245, 249]

- [7:252]   Plaintiffs could show a reasonable probability of success in an invasion of privacy suit against news media defendants based on publication of photographs identifying plaintiffs as victims of sexual molestation. [*M.G. v. Time Warner, Inc.* (2001) 89 CA4th 623, 632, 107 CR2d 504, 511]

(4) [7:253]   **Where higher standard of proof required:** Where plaintiff's claim must be proved by "*clear and convincing evidence*" at trial (e.g., claims for defamation or punitive damages), plaintiff's opposition evidence must meet this higher standard. [*Conroy v. Spitzer* (1999) 70 CA4th 1446, 1451-1454, 83 CR2d 443, 447-448; *Rosenaur v. Scherer* (2001) 88 CA4th 260, 273, 105 CR2d 674, 683]

[7:254-255]   *Reserved.*

f.   [7:256]   **Ruling:**   The court must engage in a two-step process:

— First, the court decides whether defendant has made a threshold showing that the challenged cause of action is one arising from protected activity (i.e., that the act or acts of which plaintiff complains were taken "in furtherance of defendant's right of petition or free speech");

— If such a showing has been made, the court then determines whether plaintiff has demonstrated a "probability" of prevailing on the claim. [CCP §425.16(b); see

*Equilon Enterprises, L.L.C. v. Consumer Cause, Inc.*
(2002) 29 C4th 53, 66, 124 CR2d 507, 518]

(1) [7:256.1] **Matters considered:** In making its determination, "the court shall consider the pleadings, and supporting *and opposing* affidavits stating the facts upon which the liability or defense is based." [CCP §425.16(b)(2) (emphasis added)]

Only evidence admissible at trial may be considered. [*Evans v. Unkow* (1995) 38 CA4th 1490, 1497, 45 CR2d 624, 628]

(a) [7:256.2] **Including opposing evidence:** When assessing plaintiff's showing, the court must also consider evidence presented by the defendant—i.e., "opposing affidavits." [See CCP §425.16(b)(2)]

(b) [7:256.3] **No weighing of evidence:** The court does *not*, however, weigh defendant's evidence against plaintiff's in terms of either credibility or persuasiveness. Rather, defendant's evidence is considered only to determine whether it defeats plaintiff's claims *as a matter of law*—e.g., by establishing a defense or the absence of a necessary element. [*1-800 Contacts, Inc. v. Sternberg* (2003) 107 CA4th 568, 585, 132 CR2d 789, 802; *see also* ¶7:248]

(2) [7:257] **Motion granted:** If the court grants the motion, its order results in a judgment striking the complaint and should be supported by a *statement of decision.* [*DuPont Merck Pharmaceutical Co. v. Sup.Ct. (Newman)* (2000) 78 CA4th 562, 564, 92 CR2d 755, 757]

(a) [7:257a] **No leave to amend:** If the motion is granted, the court may not grant leave to amend. [*Simmons v. Allstate Ins. Co.* (2001) 92 CA4th 1068, 1073, 112 CR2d 397, 400; *see discussion at* ¶6:665.5]

Rationale: Amendments could frustrate the Legislature's objective of providing a "quick and inexpensive method of unmasking and dismissing such suits." [*Simmons v. Allstate Ins. Co.,* supra, 92 CA4th at 1073, 112 CR2d at 400]

(3) [7:257.1] **Motion denied:** If the court determines that plaintiff has established a "probability" of recovery, the action proceeds (unless an appeal is taken, *see* ¶7:267).

(a) [7:257.2] **Limited effect:** That determination, however, does *not* affect the burden of proof at trial.

Nor is it admissible in evidence at any later stage of the case. [CCP §425.16(b)]

It *bars* any later malicious prosecution action, however, because plaintiff has established probable cause. [*Wilson v. Parker, Covert & Chidester* (2002) 28 C4th 811, 820, 123 CR2d 19, 26]

☞[7:257.3]  ***PRACTICE POINTER:***  For this reason, before bringing an anti-SLAPP motion, defense counsel should advise the client that if the motion fails, any claim for malicious prosecution will be precluded.

(b)  [7:257.4]  **Later amendment disregarded for appellate review:**  If defendant appeals denial of the motion (an order granting or denying a SLAPP motion is immediately appealable, *see* ¶7:267), plaintiff cannot avoid appellate review by amending the complaint. The operative pleading for purposes of appeal is the former complaint. [*Roberts v. Los Angeles County Bar Ass'n* (2003) 105 CA4th 604, 612, 129 CR2d 546, 550]

g.  [7:258]  **Discovery stayed:**  Unless the court orders otherwise for "good cause shown," all discovery proceedings shall be stayed *upon filing* of a notice of motion under CCP §425.16. The stay remains in effect until notice of entry of order ruling on the motion. [CCP §425.16(g)]

Effect: A SLAPP defendant is protected from the potential costs of protracted litigation and the burden of traditional discovery pending resolution of the motion. [*Mattel, Inc. v. Luce, Forward, Hamilton & Scripps* (2002) 99 CA4th 1179, 1190, 121 CR2d 794, 801]

(1)  [7:258.1]  **Procedure where discovery needed:**  Because a §425.16 motion may be made within 60 days after service of the complaint (and must be heard within 30 days thereafter), plaintiff may need additional discovery to oppose defendant's motion. If so, it must move for an order allowing such discovery (and, if necessary, a *continuance* of the hearing). It *cannot* merely oppose the motion for lack of opportunity to obtain such information. [*Lafayette Morehouse, Inc. v. Chronicle Pub. Co.* (1995) 37 CA4th 855, 867, 44 CR2d 46, 53-54; *Robertson v. Rodriguez* (1995) 36 CA4th 347, 357, 42 CR2d 464, 469]

To establish "good cause" for an order permitting discovery prior to the ruling on the anti-SLAPP motion, plaintiff must show:

— that a defendant or witness possesses evidence needed by plaintiff *to establish a prima facie case*; and

— an explanation of what additional facts plaintiff expects to recover. [*1-800 Contacts, Inc. v. Sternberg* (2003) 107 CA4th 568, 593, 132 CR2d 789, 809]

If discovery is allowed, it will be *limited* to the issues raised by the motion to strike; i.e., information that would help plaintiff establish a prima facie case, and not merely to impeach defendant's credibility. [See *Sipple v. Foundation For Nat'l Progress* (1999) 71 CA4th 226, 247, 83 CR2d 677, 690]

h. **[7:259] Fees and costs:** The "prevailing defendant" on the motion to strike "shall be *entitled*" to recover his or her attorney fees and costs. [CCP §425.16(c)]

The fee award is mandatory: "(A)ny SLAPP defendant who brings a successful motion to strike is entitled to mandatory attorney fees." [*Ketchum v. Moses* (2001) 24 C4th 1122, 1131, 104 CR2d 377, 381; see *Bernardo v. Planned Parenthood Fed. of America* (2004) 115 CA4th 322, 364, 9 CR3d 197, 232—rejecting due process and equal protection challenges]

But if the motion is found to be "frivolous or solely intended to cause unnecessary delay," plaintiff is entitled to an award of costs and fees as sanctions (see below). [CCP §425.16(c)]

[7:260-260.4] *Reserved.*

(1) **[7:260.5] Recovery of fees and costs on dismissal:** Plaintiff's voluntary dismissal of a suit after a §425.16 motion to strike has been filed neither prevents nor mandates an award of attorney fees and costs under §425.16(c). [*Moore v. Liu* (1999) 69 CA4th 745, 750-751, 81 CR2d 807, 812]

Rather, defendant is entitled to its fees and costs if plaintiff's case is shown to be a "pure SLAPP suit." [*Kyle v. Carmon* (1999) 71 CA4th 901, 918, 84 CR2d 303, 314]

(a) **[7:260.6] Showing required?** One case holds that the trial court must adjudicate the merits of the motion to strike before it may rule on defendant's request for fees and costs. [*Moore v. Liu*, supra, 69 CA4th at 751, 81 CR2d at 812]

But another case holds that the voluntary dismissal creates a *presumption* that defendants "prevailed"; plaintiffs may show they dismissed because they substantially achieved their goals through settlement or other means, or for other reasons unrelated to a probability of success on the merits. [*Coltrain v. Shewalter* (1998) 66 CA4th 94, 107, 77 CR2d 600, 608]

Comment: The latter view effectively shifts the customary burden of proof; *see ¶7:244 ff.*

(b) **[7:260.7] Court-ordered dismissal before SLAPP motion heard:** Similarly, the court may award fees to a prevailing defendant whose SLAPP motion was not heard because the complaint was dismissed on other grounds before the hearing on the motion. [*White v. Lieberman* (2002) 103 CA4th 210, 220, 126 CR2d 608, 614—case dismissed after sustaining demurrer without leave to amend; *Pfeiffer Venice Properties v. Bernard* (2002) 101 CA4th 211, 215, 123 CR2d 647, 650—case dismissed under doctrine of *de minimus non curat lex*]

"(R)esolution of the underlying action does not moot a fee request under the SLAPP statute." [*Moraga-Orinda Fire Protection Dist. v. Weir* (2004) 115 CA4th 477, 480, 10 CR3d 13, 17—action dismissed for lack of standing and because not timely filed]

[7:260.8-260.9] *Reserved.*

(c) **[7:260.10] Dismissal of appeal from order granting motion:** Where an anti-SLAPP motion is granted, and plaintiff appeals but then voluntarily dismisses the appeal, defendant is entitled to attorney fees without any further showing: "The dismissal of an appeal from the trial court's determination leaves intact the judicial finding that the action was a SLAPP suit." [*Wilkerson v. Sullivan* (2002) 99 CA4th 443, 447, 121 CR2d 275, 278]

(2) **[7:261] "Fees and costs" recoverable:** Section 425.16(c) is ambiguous as to what "fees and costs" are recoverable. But legislative history shows it was intended to allow only fees and costs incurred *on the motion* to strike (not the entire litigation). [*Lafayette Morehouse, Inc. v. Chronicle Pub. Co.* (1995) 39 CA4th 1379, 1383, 46 CR2d 542, 544]

(a) **[7:261.1] Partially successful motion:** If defendant successfully strikes only a part of the complaint, costs and fees are awarded only as to the causes of action that were stricken. [*ComputerXpress, Inc. v. Jackson* (2001) 93 CA4th 993, 1020, 113 CR2d 625, 648-649]

(b) [7:262] **Appellate fees and costs:** The statute also permits recovery of costs and fees on an appeal from the court's ruling on a §425.16 motion: "A statute authorizing an attorney fee award at the trial court level includes appellate attorney fees unless the statute specifically provides otherwise." [*Evans v. Unkow* (1995) 38 CA4th 1490, 1499, 45 CR2d 624, 630; *Dove Audio, Inc. v. Rosenfeld, Meyer & Susman* (1996) 47 CA4th 777, 785, 54 CR2d 830, 835]

(3) [7:263] **Only reasonable fees:** Again, although the statute does not expressly so provide, it is interpreted to allow awards of only such fees as the court deems reasonable. [*Robertson v. Rodriguez* (1995) 36 CA4th 347, 362, 42 CR2d 464, 472; *Dove Audio, Inc. v. Rosenfeld, Meyer & Susman*, supra, 47 CA4th at 785, 54 CR2d at 835—although "generous," $27,000 award was not abuse of discretion]

(a) [7:263.1] **"Lodestar" approach:** Courts generally apply a lodestar approach (i.e., number of hours reasonably expended multiplied by the reasonable hourly rate prevailing in the community for similar work) in setting a fee award under CCP §425.16. [*Ketchum v. Moses* (2001) 24 C4th 1122, 1136, 104 CR2d 377, 387]

*Cross-refer: See detailed discussion at ¶1:267 ff.*

[7:263.2-263.4] *Reserved.*

(4) [7:263.5] **Pro bono representation:** Because CCP §425.16(c) says prevailing defendants are "entitled to recover" attorney fees, they are entitled to such recovery even if their attorney represents them *pro bono*. [*Rosenaur v. Scherer* (2001) 88 CA4th 260, 283, 105 CR2d 674, 690]

(5) [7:264] **Procedure to obtain fees:** There are three *alternative* procedures by which a successful defendant may obtain a fee award under CCP §425.16(c):
— request fees as part of the anti-SLAPP motion;
— make a noticed motion for fees after the anti-SLAPP motion has been granted; or
— include the fee request in the cost bill after entry of judgment. [*American Humane Ass'n v. L.A. Times Communications* (2001) 92 CA4th 1095, 1103, 112 CR2d 488, 494]

i. [7:265] **Compare—sanctions for "frivolous" motion:** If the court finds a special motion to strike is "frivolous or is solely intended to cause unnecessary delay," it is *required* to award costs and reasonable attorney fees "pursuant to Section 128.5" to a "plaintiff prevailing on the motion." [CCP §425.16(c); see *Ketchum v. Moses*, supra, 24 C4th at 1131, 104 CR2d at 383]

    (1) [7:265.1] **"Pursuant to §128.5" means standards of former statute:** Although §425.16(c) mandates an award "pursuant to Section 128.5," that statute has only limited application (*see ¶9:1010*). The reference to §128.5 means a court "must use the procedures and apply the substantive standards of CCP §128.5 in deciding whether to award fees under the anti-SLAPP statute." [*Decker v. U.D. Registry, Inc.* (2003) 105 CA4th 1382, 1392, 129 CR2d 892, 898—although untimely CCP §425.16 motion was not "frivolous" under §128.5 standards; *Moore v. Shaw* (2004) 116 CA4th 182, 199, 10 CR3d 154, 166, fn. 9]

    (2) [7:266] **"Frivolous":** Attorney fees can be assessed against defendant only if the anti-SLAPP motion was "totally and completely without merit" (see CCP §128.5(b)(2)). This requires a finding that "*any reasonable attorney would agree* such motion is totally devoid of merit." [*Moore v. Shaw*, supra, 116 CA4th at 199, 10 CR3d at 166 (emphasis in original; internal quotes omitted)]

j.  [7:267] **Appellate review:** Orders granting or denying an anti-SLAPP motion under CCP §425.16 are immediately appealable *except* for denials based one of the *exemptions* enumerated in CCP §425.17 (*¶7:212 ff.*). (In the latter case, counsel may consider seeking discretionary writ relief.) [See CCP §§425.17(e), 425.16(j), 904.1(a)(13)]

    (1) [7:267.1] **Automatic stay of action:** The appeal automatically stays proceedings in the trial court where the SLAPP claim is the only cause of action in the complaint, so that the appeal "embraces the entirety of the action." [*Mattel, Inc. v. Luce, Forward Hamilton & Scripps* (2002) 99 CA4th 1179, 1190, 121 CR2d 794, 801]

       (a) [7:267.2] **Comment:** This may create an incentive to appeal the denial of even a patently *frivolous* anti-SLAPP motion: i.e., "the defendant gets a very cheap hiatus in the proceedings." To prevent delay, however, the appellate court has discretion to *dismiss* the appeal rather than hear it on the merits. [*People ex rel Lockyer v. Brar* (2004) 115 CA4th 1315, 1319, 9 CR3d 844, 847]

    (2) [7:267.3] **Compare—other joined claims stayed?** It is not clear whether an appeal from the ruling on the

SLAPP cause of action automatically stays proceedings on the remaining claims.

***Caution:*** This issue is presently before the California Supreme Court in *Varian Medical Systems, Inc. v. Delfino*, Case No. S121400.

[7:267.4] *Reserved.*

(3) [7:267.5] **Compare—stay of judgment awarding fees and costs:** A prevailing SLAPP defendant's enforcement of a judgment awarding fees and costs under CCP §425.16(c) is *not automatically stayed* by plaintiff's appeal. Rather, a SLAPP plaintiff must post an appropriate appeal bond or undertaking or petition for writ of supersedeas to stay enforcement. [*Dowling v. Zimmerman* (2001) 85 CA4th 1400, 1434, 103 CR2d 174, 200-201]

*Cross-refer:* See further discussion in Eisenberg, Horvitz & Wiener, *Cal. Prac. Guide: Civ. Appeals & Writs* (TRG), Ch. 7.

k. [7:268] **Fax or e-mail copies to Judicial Council:** The party *filing or opposing* an anti-SLAPP motion must "promptly" *fax or e-mail* the following to the Judicial Council (which will maintain this information as a public record for at least 3 years):
— a copy of the "endorsed filed" caption page of the motion or opposition;
— a "conformed copy" of any order granting or denying the anti-SLAPP motion, discovery or fees; and
— any related notice of appeal or writ petition. [CCP §425.16(k)]

[7:269-274] *Reserved.*

## D. MOTION FOR JUDGMENT ON THE PLEADINGS

1. [7:275] **In General:** A motion for judgment on the pleadings has the same function as a general demurrer but is made after the time for demurrer has expired. Except as provided by statute (CCP §438, below), the rules governing demurrers apply. [*Cloud v. Northrop Grumman Corp.* (1998) 67 CA4th 995, 999, 79 CR2d 544, 546 (citing text); see *Smiley v. Citibank (South Dakota) N.A.* (1995) 11 C4th 138, 145-146, 44 CR2d 441, 446]

a. [7:276] **Statutory basis:** CCP §438 became effective in 1994 and sets forth grounds and procedures for the motion.

Before 1994, there was no statutory basis for this motion, although its use was well recognized by case law. [*Colberg, Inc. v. State of Calif. ex rel. Dept. of Pub. Works* (1967) 67 C2d 408, 412, 62 CR 401, 403]

Pre-1994 case law, not in conflict with the statute, should generally be applicable to a motion based on CCP §438.

b. [7:277] **Nonstatutory motion survives:** CCP §438 imposes major limitations on the motion; e.g., it does not lie on grounds that previously were or could have been raised by demurrer unless there has been a material change in the law (*see ¶7:305*). It also imposes time limits (*see ¶7:280*). However, these limitations are essentially meaningless because a nonstatutory motion for judgment on the pleadings survives *without* such limitations:

— "A motion for judgment on the pleadings may be made at any time either prior to the trial or at the trial itself." [*Stoops v. Abbassi* (2002) 100 CA4th 644, 650, 122 CR2d 747, 752 (citing pre-CCP §438 case of *Ion Equip. Corp. v. Nelson* (1980) 110 CA3d 868, 877, 168 CR 361); see also *Smiley v. Citibank (South Dakota) N.A.* (1995) 11 C4th 138, 145, 44 CR2d 441, 445, fn. 2— "*common law motion* for judgment on the pleadings" upheld despite fact CCP §438 had been enacted during course of proceedings; and *Saltarelli & Steponovich v. Douglas* (1995) 40 CA4th 1, 5, 46 CR2d 683, 686— treating defective motion for summary judgment as "*nonstatutory motion* for judgment on the pleadings"]

2. [7:278] **Motion by Party or Court:** A motion for judgment on the pleadings may be made by any party to the action or by the court *sua sponte.* [CCP §438(b)(2)]

3. [7:279] **Time for Motion:** A *defendant's* motion for judgment on the pleadings may be made after the time to demur has expired and an answer has been filed. A *plaintiff's* motion for judgment on the pleadings may be made after expiration of the time to demur to defendant's answer. [CCP §438(f)]

a. [7:280] **Deadline:** Unless the court orders otherwise, the statutory motion for judgment on the pleadings cannot be "made" after entry of a pretrial conference order (see CRC 212; CCP §575) or *30 days before the initial trial date* ("the date the action is initially set for trial"), whichever is later. [CCP §438(e)]

Comment: The statutory reference to a "pretrial conference order" should be interpreted to mean the "case management order" (CRC 212(i); *see ¶12:84*).

[7:281-284] *Reserved.*

b. [7:285] **Compare—nonstatutory motion:** The nonstatutory motion could be made *at any time* during the lawsuit, even during trial, since the grounds for general demurrer are never waived (*see ¶7:33*). [See *Sofias v. Bank of*

*America* (1985) 172 CA3d 583, 586, 218 CR 388, 389—motion made shortly before trial]

It is unclear whether CCP §438 supersedes the nonstatutory motion (*see* ¶7:277) and therefore whether a nonstatutory motion may be made *after* the deadline for a CCP §438 motion.

*(Text cont'd on p. 7-89)*

**RESERVED**

c. **[7:286] Compare—other challenges:** Although "irregular," failure to state a cause of action may also be raised by a *motion in limine* or *motion for nonsuit* during trial. Trial courts have inherent power to control litigation and conserve judicial resources through whatever procedural vehicle reaches that result. [*Lucas v. County of Los Angeles* (1996) 47 CA4th 277, 284-285, 54 CR2d 655, 661]

⇨**[7:287]** ***PRACTICE POINTER:*** Don't count on this! If there are grounds for a motion for judgment on the pleadings, make your motion *as early as possible.* Trial judges are often reluctant to grant "last minute" challenges to the pleadings, because they disrupt the court's trial calendar and may result in unnecessary trial preparation expenses for both sides.

**[7:288-289]** *Reserved.*

4. **[7:290] Grounds:** A motion by defendant (or cross-defendant) can be made on the ground that:

— the court "lacks jurisdiction of the subject of one or more of the causes of action alleged"; or

— the complaint (or any cause of action therein) "does not state facts sufficient to constitute a cause of action against that defendant." [CCP §438(c)]

A motion by plaintiff (or cross-complainant) can be made on the ground *that the complaint states facts sufficient* to constitute a cause of action against the defendant (or cross-defendant) and "the answer does not state facts sufficient to constitute a defense to the complaint." [CCP §438(c)]

**[7:291]** *Compare:* The statute permits plaintiff (or cross-complainant) to obtain a ruling that the complaint states a valid cause of action. But there is *no parallel provision* permitting defendant (or cross-defendant) to obtain a ruling that the answer or defenses contained therein state facts sufficient to constitute a defense to the complaint.

a. **[7:292] Ground must appear on face of complaint or from facts judicially noticeable:** The grounds for a motion for judgment on the pleadings must appear on the face of the challenged pleading or be based on facts which the court may judicially notice. Where the motion is based on matters the court may judicially notice (under Ev.C. §§452, 453), such matters must be specified in the notice of motion or supporting points and authorities. [CCP §438(d); compare *Saltarelli & Steponovich v. Douglas* (1995) 40 CA4th 1, 5, 46 CR2d 683, 686—on "nonstatutory" motion for judgment on the pleadings, court took judicial notice of matters in parties' *exhibits*]

(1) **Application**

- [7:293]   A motion for judgment on the pleadings lies where the complaint shows on its face it is barred by the *statute of limitations,* and therefore does not state facts sufficient to constitute a cause of action. [See *Hunt v. County of Shasta* (1990) 225 CA3d 432, 440, 275 CR 113, 118]

- [7:294]   A motion for judgment on the pleadings was granted where the court took judicial notice of a prior action between parties as the basis for collateral estoppel in the present action. [See *Barker v. Hull* (1987) 191 CA3d 221, 227, 236 CR 285, 289]

  [7:295-299]   *Reserved.*

b. [7:300]   **Matters set forth in answer not considered:** The motion for judgment on the pleadings is often made after defendant has filed an answer. But matters pleaded in the answer *cannot* be considered in ruling on the motion. Therefore, plaintiff's failure to negate some defense raised by the defendant is *not* ground for the motion. [*Hughes v. Western MacArthur Co.* (1987) 192 CA3d 951, 957, 237 CR 738, 742]

- [7:301]   Widow sued D for Husband's wrongful death. D's answer alleged Husband had been D's employee, so that Widow's exclusive remedy was through workers' compensation. D moved for judgment on the pleadings on the theory that Widow had not pleaded any exception to the exclusive remedy rule. "However, on motion for judgment on the pleading, *the complaint cannot be attacked by reference to matters set forth in the answer.*" [*Hughes v. Western MacArthur Co.*, supra, 192 CA3d at 957, 237 CR at 742]

  [7:301.1]   Comment: D could presumably proceed by *motion for summary judgment,* presenting evidence that Husband was an employee.

  [7:302-304]   *Reserved.*

c. [7:305]   **Limitation—*change in law* required where same ground raised by demurrer:**   The statutory motion for judgment on the pleadings does not lie on grounds previously raised by demurrer unless there has been a "material change in applicable case law or statute" since the demurrer was overruled. [CCP §438(g)(1); see *Yancey v. Sup.Ct. (Neil)* (1994) 28 CA4th 558, 562, 33 CR2d 777, 779, fn. 1 (citing text)]

(1) [7:306]   **Compare—nonstatutory motion:**   There was no such requirement under the nonstatutory motion for judgment on the pleadings.

If the statutory motion *supersedes* the previous case-law motion, this could be a significant limitation. But CCP §430.80 provides that grounds for a general demurrer are *never waived* (*see ¶7:69*). Thus, it seems likely that the *nonstatutory* motion for judgment on the pleadings will still be available to challenge failure to state a cause of action in cases where there has been no change in applicable law since the time for demurrer.

*Cross-refer:* The issue of whether the nonstatutory motion survived enactment of CCP §438 is discussed at ¶7:277.

(2) [7:307] **Compare—demurrer on different ground:** The above rule does not apply where defendant demurred to the complaint on *different* grounds than raised in the motion for judgment on the pleadings. No material change in law is required for a CCP §438 motion in such cases.

(3) [7:308] **Compare—same ground raised by other motions:** The rule prohibiting CCP §438 motions on the same grounds as an overruled demurrer should not affect defendant's right to use other motions to renew those grounds: e.g., motion for summary judgment; motion to exclude evidence; motion for nonsuit, directed verdict, etc.

[7:309] *Reserved.*

5. [7:310] **Procedure:** The normal noticed motion procedure (*see Ch. 9(I)*) applies to motions under CCP §438. The moving party must file and serve on opposing parties:

- Notice of Motion;
- Points and Authorities.

**FORMS**

- Notice of Motion for Judgment on the Pleadings; Request to Take Judicial Notice; Points and Authorities in Support, *see Form 7:F.*
- Checklist: Judgment on the Pleadings, *see Form 7:G.*

a. [7:311] **Notice directed to entire or part of pleading:** The notice of motion should state whether judgment on the pleadings is sought as to the entire pleading or some particular portion thereof. [CCP §438(c)]

⇨[7:312] **PRACTICE POINTER:** Even if challenging the entire pleading, your Notice should state the motion is directed *both* to the pleading as a whole *and to each* (separately identified) cause of action or defense. Otherwise, your motion may be denied if *any one* cause of action or defense is held to state facts sufficient to constitute a cause of action or a defense.

[7:313-314]   *Reserved.*

b.   [7:315]   **Requesting judicial notice:**   Where the court is being asked to take judicial notice of any matter (e.g., files in other actions, etc.), the particular matters to be noticed must be specified *either* in the notice of motion or supporting points and authorities, or otherwise by court order. (No separate formal request for judicial notice is required.) [CCP §438(d); compare *Saltarelli & Steponovich v. Douglas* (1995) 40 CA4th 1, 5, 46 CR2d 683, 686—on "*nonstatutory*" motion for judgment on the pleadings, court took judicial notice of matters in parties' *exhibits*]

(Judicial notice on demurrer hearings is discussed further at ¶*7:12 ff.*)

⇨[7:316]   ***PRACTICE POINTER:***   Although not required, it is a good idea to file a *separate* "Request That Court Take Judicial Notice" where numerous documents are involved because it is easier for the judge to handle and review. However, since CCP §438 specifically requires that the request be made in the notice of motion or points and authorities, be sure to repeat your request in one of these, preferably the notice of motion. (*Also see discussion at* ¶*7:12 ff.*)

c.   [7:317]   **Compare—*sua sponte* motion:**   CCP §438(b) specifically authorizes judgment on the pleadings on the court's own motion but does not specify the procedure to be followed in such cases.

•   [7:318]   **Comment:**   Due process requires that the party against whom judgment is to be entered have adequate notice and opportunity to be heard. Presumably, therefore, the court would issue an order to show cause or otherwise notice a hearing where the matter could be argued.

[7:319]   *Reserved.*

d.   [7:320]   **Compare—motion at time of trial:**   As stated above (¶*7:280*), prior to the enactment of CCP §438, a motion for judgment on the pleadings could be made even as late as the time of trial (*see* ¶*7:285*).

•   [7:321]   Such a motion was usually made *in limine* (at the outset of trial). As such, it could be made *orally*, without prior notice. [*Kortmeyer v. California Ins. Guar. Ass'n* (1992) 9 CA4th 1285, 1293, 12 CR2d 71, 76—made during course of OSC hearing]

If the nonstatutory motion for judgment on the pleadings survived enactment of CCP §438 (*see ¶7:277*), the same procedure may still be followed. This seems likely in view of CCP §430.80, which provides that grounds for a general demurrer are never waived. [See *Lucas v. County of Los Angeles* (1996) 47 CA4th 277, 284-285, 54 CR2d 655, 661—granting *in limine* motion for judgment proper exercise of court's discretion to control litigation]

e. **[7:322] No extrinsic evidence:** The motion normally lies only for defects fully disclosed on the *face* of the pleading under attack or by matters for which judicial notice may be taken. Declarations or other extrinsic matters are improper. Therefore, the judge hearing the motion *cannot* consider discovery admissions or other evidence controverting the pleadings. Rather, the pleading under attack must be accepted as true. [CCP §438(d), *see ¶7:292*; *Gerawan Farming, Inc. v. Lyons* (2000) 24 C4th 468, 515-516, 101 CR2d 470, 504—factual allegations accepted as true and given liberal construction; *Lance Camper Mfg. Corp. v. Republic Indem. Co. of America* (1996) 44 CA4th 194, 198, 51 CR2d 622, 625; *Cloud v. Northrop Grumman Corp.* (1998) 67 CA4th 995, 999, 79 CR2d 544, 546 (citing text)]

(1) **[7:323] Compare—summary judgment:** If you need to *controvert* any material fact in the pleading under attack in order to make your motion good, the proper procedure is a motion for summary judgment . . . *not* a motion for judgment on the pleadings. (And, of course, different standards apply to summary judgment motions; *see detailed discussion at Ch. 10.*) [*Christian v. County of Los Angeles* (1986) 176 CA3d 466, 468, 222 CR 76—court relied on extrinsic evidence in granting motion for judgment on the pleadings; on appeal, treated as summary judgment; *Taylor v. Lockheed Martin Corp.* (2000) 78 CA4th 472, 479, 92 CR2d 873, 877—same]

• **[7:324]** Where an *ambiguous writing* is set out in the complaint (or attached as an exhibit), *parol evidence* to clarify its meaning *cannot* be presented on a motion for judgment on the pleadings. Such extrinsic evidence may be presented, however, by a motion for summary judgment. [*Columbia Cas. Co. v. Northwestern Nat'l Ins. Co.* (1991) 231 CA3d 457, 468-469, 282 CR 389, 395]

**[7:325]** *Reserved.*

(2) **[7:326]** **Summary judgment motion treated as motion for judgment on the pleadings:** Although summary judgment motions are designed to test the sufficiency of evidence rather than pleadings (*see Ch. 10*), they may effectively operate as motions for judgment on the pleadings. [*Hejmadi v. Amfac, Inc.* (1988) 202 CA3d 525, 535-536, 249 CR 5, 9—error for court on summary judgment motion to grant plaintiff leave to amend cause of action while summarily adjudicating the underlying issues: on appeal, treated as judgment on the pleadings; *see further discussion at ¶10:6 ff.*]

## 6. Ruling on Motion

a. **[7:327]** **Effect that general demurrer overruled:** A motion for judgment on the pleadings under CCP §438 may *not* be granted if a demurrer on the same ground was previously overruled *unless* there is an intervening change in the law. [CCP §438(g)(1); see *Yancey v. Sup.Ct. (Neil)* (1994) 28 CA4th 558, 562, 33 CR2d 777, 779, fn. 1 (citing text)]

(1) **[7:328]** **Compare—nonstatutory motion:** The rule was contra prior to enactment of CCP §438: A motion for judgment on the pleadings could be granted even if defendant's previous demurrer on the same ground had been overruled . . . thus permitting defendant "two bites at the apple"!

The justification is that grounds for general demurrer are never waived and the interests of the parties and the court are advanced by avoiding trial and reversal on appeal. [*Ion Equip. Corp. v. Nelson* (1980) 110 CA3d 868, 877, 168 CR 361, 365; *Donohue v. State of Calif.* (1986) 178 CA3d 795, 800-801, 224 CR 57, 59-60—motion granted despite fact complaint had been upheld against general demurrer and two prior motions for judgment on the pleading; see also *Stoops v. Abbassi* (2002) 100 CA4th 644, 650, 122 CR2d 747, 752]

**[7:329]** *Reserved.*

(2) **[7:330]** **Caution re judicial reaction:** Even assuming the motion lies after overruling of a demurrer on the same ground, the judge who previously overruled the demurrer may not be disposed to change his or her mind. Further, when the motion is heard by a different judge, that judge is often reluctant to "second guess" the judge who ruled on the demurrer.

➡️**[7:331]** ***PRACTICE POINTER:*** You will probably have an uphill battle. Your best bet will be to *try to come up with new arguments and legal authority* to support your position. It will make it easier for the judge to change his or her mind; or for the new judge to conclude the first judge had not been fully briefed, etc.

(3) [7:332] **Prior demurrer ruling should be disclosed in moving papers:** Counsel for the moving party should file a declaration in support of the motion, disclosing whether a demurrer had previously been taken on the same ground. If it was, counsel should identify the judge before whom the demurrer was heard, and the *grounds* upon which the ruling was based.

   (a) [7:333] **Sanctions for failure to disclose?** Conceivably, failure to disclose that a prior demurrer on the same ground had been overruled might lead a judge to conclude that the present motion violates an implied "certification" as to its legal and factual merit. In that event, sanctions might be imposed under CCP §128.7 (*see discussion at ¶9:1135 ff.*). (Note also that failure to disclose similar information in connection with a motion for reconsideration or the renewal of a prior motion under CCP §1008 is punishable as a *contempt* of court.)

b. [7:334] **Motion may be granted with or without leave to amend:** If the motion for judgment on the pleadings is granted, it may be granted with or without leave to amend. [CCP §438(h)(1)]

   (1) [7:335] **Leave to amend routinely granted:** The same standards apply in granting leave to amend as for demurrers and leave is routinely granted (*see ¶7:129*). [*People v. $20,000 U.S. Currency* (1991) 235 CA3d 682, 692, 286 CR 746, 750]

   "Where a demurrer is sustained or a motion for judgment on the pleadings is granted as to the original complaint, denial of leave to amend constitutes an abuse of discretion if the pleading does not show on its face that it is *incapable* of amendment." [*Virginia G. v. ABC Unified School Dist.* (1993) 15 CA4th 1848, 1852, 19 CR2d 671, 673 (emphasis added)]

   (a) [7:336] **Comment:** Even so, particularly when a motion for judgment on the pleadings is granted shortly before trial, before granting leave to amend the court usually must be satisfied the proposed amendment is *bona fide* and *supported by the facts* of the case.

   (2) **Application**

   • [7:337] Where no previous demurrer had been interposed (and the complaint was not obviously barred by the statute of limitations or other absolute defense), it was an abuse of discretion to deny leave to amend after granting a motion for judgment on the pleadings. Pleaders should have the same opportunity to cure defects in their pleadings as they would have had after a normal ruling on demurrer. [*MacIsaac v. Pozzo* (1945) 26 C2d 809, 815, 161 P2d 449, 452]

- [7:338] Where a previous demurrer had been *overruled* (i.e., complaint held legally sufficient), it would be an even clearer abuse of discretion to grant judgment on the pleadings without leave to amend. Plaintiff will have justifiably assumed the complaint was legally sufficient. [*Higgins v. Del Faro* (1981) 123 CA3d 558, 566, 176 CR 704, 708—trial judge who granted motion for judgment on pleadings was same judge who had previously overruled demurrer on same ground]

- [7:339] *Compare—strictly legal issues:* Notwithstanding the above, leave to amend is properly denied where the issue raised on the motion is strictly a legal one and no further amendment can alter that issue. [*La Jolla Village Homeowners' Ass'n, Inc. v. Sup.Ct. (Quality Roofing, Inc.)* (1989) 212 CA3d 1131, 1141, 261 CR 146, 151; *Schonfeldt v. State of Calif.* (1998) 61 CA4th 1462, 72 CR2d 464—leave to amend properly denied where no duty owed as a matter of law]

  (The same result obtains at the demurrer stage; *see* ¶*7:132.*)

c. [7:340] **Time to amend:** Under CCP §438, if leave to amend is granted, the party against whom the motion is granted *must* be given *30 days* to file an amended pleading. [See CCP §438(h)(2)—"the court *shall* grant 30 days"]

  (1) [7:341] **Effect:** Since the statutory motion may be made as late as 30 days before trial, this creates the possibility the case may not be at issue at commencement of trial.

  - [7:342] **Comment:** Although the language of the statute requiring 30 days to amend appears to be mandatory, it will probably be interpreted to give the court inherent power to shorten this time to avoid the anomalous result of either commencing trial before the case is at issue or delaying the start of trial.

  (2) [7:343] **Compare—nonstatutory motion:** If the nonstatutory motion for judgment on the pleadings

survives (*see ¶7:277*), there is no equivalent time allot-ment. I.e., courts could require that an amended plead-ing be served and filed within a substantially shorter period of time.

(3) **[7:344] Computing time to amend:** The same rules apply as on a demurrer: i.e., if leave to amend is granted, the time to amend runs from service of the notice of ruling (notice of judgment on the pleadings); and is extended where such notice is served by mail. [CCP §1013(a); *People v. $20,000 U.S. Currency* (1991) 235 CA3d 682, 692, 286 CR 746, 750]

[7:345-349] *Reserved.*

7. **[7:350] Entry of Judgment:** Entry of judgment depends on whether the motion was granted as to the entire complaint and whether granted with or without leave to amend:

a. **[7:351] Where leave to amend denied:** If the motion is granted *without* leave to amend and pertains to the *entire* pleading, judgment "shall be entered forthwith" for the moving party. [CCP §438(h)(3)]

On the other hand, if the motion is granted without leave to amend only as to *certain* causes of action or defenses, no judgment is usually entered. The case goes to trial on the remaining claims. The ruling on the motion is reviewable by writ or on appeal from the final judgment.

b. **[7:352] Where leave granted but no amended pleading filed:** If leave to amend is granted as to the entire com-plaint and an amended complaint is not filed within the time allowed, judgment "shall be entered forthwith" in favor of the moving party. [CCP §438(h)(4)(C)]

But the entry of judgment is not automatic; the prevailing party must make a motion for entry of judgment. [CCP §438(i)(1)(B)]

c. **[7:353] Where leave granted but amended pleading *filed late:*** Where an amended complaint is filed after the time to amend (or otherwise in violation of the court's ruling in granting leave to amend), the prevailing party must make a separate *motion to strike* the pleading (under CCP §1010) in addition to the motion for entry of judgment. [CCP §438(h)(4)(A) & (i)(1)(A)]

Entry of judgment is *not* automatic because the court has *discretion* whether to strike the late complaint. [CCP §438(h)(4)(A)—"the court *may* strike the complaint"]

• **[7:354] Comment:** It is not entirely clear whether this applies to an amendment filed *after a motion for entry of judgment* has been filed (but before the hearing on that motion). Arguably it should, so that entry of judgment would be discretionary, rather than mandatory.

➡️ **[7:355]** ***PRACTICE POINTER:*** If opposing a motion to strike a late amendment, attempt to make the same factual showing required for relief under CCP §473(b) ("mistake, inadvertence, surprise, excusable neglect"; *see ¶5:282 ff.*).

[7:356-369] *Reserved.*

## E. MOTION TO DISMISS

1. **[7:370]** **No Statutory Basis for Challenging Pleadings:** There is no statutory authority for using a motion to dismiss as a method to challenge opposing pleadings. Under the Code, dismissal motions lie only on specified grounds, including nonjoinder of necessary parties (CCP §389(b), *see ¶2:188*) and delay in service of summons or prosecution of the action (see CCP §§581, 583.110 et seq., *discussed in Ch. 11*).

   But several cases hold a motion to dismiss may serve the same function as a general demurrer. Despite lack of statutory authority, courts may assert their *inherent judicial power* to dismiss cases in which no valid cause of action or defense is stated.

   "(W)here the question is whether a complaint states a cause of action against a defendant, that question is always available whether demurrer be filed or not." [*McKay v. County of Riverside* (1959) 175 CA2d 247, 249, 345 P2d 949, 950]

   a. **[7:371]** **Other applications:** Some cases suggest the nonstatutory motion can also be used in other circumstances.

      For example, where a complaint was filed *without* the authority of some of the named plaintiffs, "the appropriate remedy is not a motion to quash service, but perhaps a nonstatutory motion to dismiss." [*Baker v. Boxx* (1991) 226 CA3d 1303, 1312, 277 CR 409, 414]

   b. **[7:372]** **Compare—federal practice:** Demurrers are not used in federal practice (see FRCP 7(c)). A motion to dismiss is the primary method for challenging pleadings (see FRCP 12(b)).

2. **[7:373]** **As Defendant's Initial Pleading:** According to case law, a motion to dismiss may be substituted for a demurrer as the defendant's first pleading. [*Barragan v. Banco BCH* (1986) 188 CA3d 283, 299, 232 CR 758, 767]

   a. **[7:374]** **Caution re entry of default:** However, it is not clear whether a motion to dismiss would be recognized by a court clerk as one of the "permitted responses" to prevent entry of default (*see ¶5:31*).

b. [7:375] **Bar to later demurrer?**  If the motion to dismiss is denied, one court says it is treated as "a demurrer over-ruled without leave to amend" (whatever that is!). [*Barragan v. Banco BCH*, supra, 188 CA3d at 299, 232 CR at 767]

**Comment:**  It is not clear why a motion to dismiss should foreclose later demurrers on the same or different grounds. But the matter is very unclear. It is better to avoid the problem and stick to demurrers!

3. [7:376] **No "Speaking" Motions:**  As a substitute for general demurrer, the motion to dismiss should be confined to matters appearing on the face of the pleading under attack, or of which the court can take judicial notice. Affidavits and discovery responses should *not* be relied upon.

Of course, a court might treat a "speaking" motion to dismiss as a *motion for summary judgment* . . . but that would necessitate denial if any triable issue of material fact were raised (*see ¶10:3*).

**RESERVED**

# DEMURRER TO COMPLAINT; NOTICE OF HEARING; POINTS AND AUTHORITIES IN SUPPORT

```
1   ............................
    State Bar No. ..............
2   ............................
    ............................
3   ............................
    ............................
4   ............................
5   Attorneys for ..............
6
7
8            SUPERIOR COURT OF THE STATE OF CALIFORNIA
9                      COUNTY OF .........
10
11  ............................,  ) CASE NO. ....................
                                   )
12              Plaintiff,         ) HEARING DATE/TIME: ..........
                                   ) DEPT. NO. ...................
13  vs.                            ) HEARING JUDGE: ...... (if known)
                                   )
14  ............................,  ) DEMURRER BY DEFENDANT ..... TO
                                   ) FIRST AMENDED COMPLAINT BY
15              Defendant.         ) PLAINTIFF; NOTICE OF HEARING;
                                   ) DECLARATION OF .....; POINTS AND
16                                 ) AUTHORITIES; PROPOSED ORDER
                                   )
17                                 ) DATE ACTION FILED: ...........
                                   ) DATE SET FOR TRIAL: ... (if set)
18  _____ )
```

19    Defendant ..............., individually and not jointly with

20 any other party to this action, hereby demurs to the First

21 Amended Complaint filed by plaintiff .......... on each of the

22 following grounds:

23                  <u>Demurrer to First Cause of Action</u>

24    1.   The First Cause of Action fails to state facts

25 sufficient to constitute a cause of action.

26    2.   The First Cause of Action for Defamation is uncertain

27 because it cannot be ascertained therefrom whether plaintiff is

28 claiming to be a public figure. Paragraph 7 (page 3, lines 10-15)

1

---

DEMURRER TO COMPLAINT; NOTICE OF HEARING;
SUPP. DECL'N OF .......; POINTS & AUTH.

1 of the complaint alleges only that plaintiff is a "former city
2 councilwoman." But there is no allegation in said paragraph or
3 elsewhere in the complaint as to whether she is currently holding
4 any public office, or has otherwise achieved such widespread fame
5 or notoriety in the community that she can be considered a public
6 figure for defamation purposes.

7                    Demurrer to Second Cause of Action

8      3.   The Second Cause of Action fails to state facts
9 sufficient to constitute a cause of action.

10 DATED: ............., .....

11                               By /s/_____
                                 Attorneys for ............
12

13

14

15

16

17

18

19

20

21

22

23

24

25

26

27

28                                2
_____
                DEMURRER TO COMPLAINT; NOTICE OF HEARING;
                SUPP. DECL'N OF .......; POINTS & AUTH.

```
 1  ..............................
    State Bar No. ...............
 2  ..............................
    ..............................
 3  ..............................
    ..............................
 4  ..............................

 5  Attorney for: .............

 6

 7

 8              SUPERIOR COURT OF THE STATE OF CALIFORNIA

 9                      COUNTY OF .........

10

11  ........................,    ) CASE NO. ...................
                                 )
12              Plaintiff,       ) HEARING DATE/TIME: ..........
                                 ) DEPT. NO....................
13  vs.                          ) HEARING JUDGE: ...... (if known)
                                 )
14  ........................,    ) NOTICE OF HEARING ON DEMURRER
                                 ) BY DEFENDANT ........ TO FIRST
15              Defendant.       ) AMENDED COMPLAINT
                                 )
16                               ) DATE ACTION FILED: ...........
                                 ) DATE SET FOR TRIAL: ... (if set)
17  _____    )

18  TO EACH PARTY AND ATTORNEY OF RECORD IN THIS ACTION:

19      PLEASE TAKE NOTICE THAT the demurrer served and filed

20  herewith has been set for hearing on ............., ....., at 9:00

21  a.m., or as soon thereafter as counsel can be heard, in Department

22  ..... of this Court, at the County Courthouse, ..... (address)

23  ....., (city) ....., California.

24  DATED: ............., .....

25                               /s/_____
                                 Attorney for .............
26

27

28                               3
```

---

DEMURRER TO COMPLAINT; NOTICE OF HEARING;
SUPP. DECL'N OF ........; POINTS & AUTH.

```
 1   ........................
     State Bar No. ...........
 2   ........................
     ........................
 3   ........................

 4

 5   Attorneys for ..........

 6

 7

 8              SUPERIOR COURT OF THE STATE OF CALIFORNIA

 9                     COUNTY OF .........

10   .........................,  ) CASE NO. .....................
                                 )
11              Plaintiff,       ) HEARING DATE/TIME: ...........
                                 ) DEPT. NO. ....................
12   vs.                         ) HEARING JUDGE: ...... (if known)
                                 )
13   .........................,  ) POINTS AND AUTHORITIES
                                 ) SUPPORTING DEMURRER BY ........
14              Defendant.       ) TO FIRST AMENDED COMPLAINT
                                 )
15                               )
                                 ) DATE ACTION FILED: ...........
16   ─────────────────────────── ) DATE SET FOR TRIAL: ... (if set)

17        Plaintiff .............. has filed a First Amended complaint

18   herein seeking damages for defamation, invasion of privacy and

19   infliction of emotional distress. Said First Amended Complaint is

20   subject to the same infirmities as her original complaint and is

21   demurred to on the same grounds.  This court sustained this

22   defendant's demurrer to said plaintiff's original complaint on

23   ..................., ......., on these same grounds.

24        SUPPORTING THE DEMURRER TO THE FIRST CAUSE OF ACTION

25        1.   The First Cause of Action fails to state facts sufficient

26   to constitute a cause of action, and hence is subject to demurrer

27   under CCP §430.10(e).

28   /////
                              4
```

---

1  The First Cause of Action is captioned as an action "For

2  Defamation", but it fails to allege that the claimed defamatory

3  statements were untrue; or that they were uttered maliciously or

4  with reckless disregard for the truth of the matters alleged.

5  Plaintiff alleges she is a "former city councilwoman" and

6  "widely known in the community" (Complaint, Paragraph 9, page 4,

7  lines 12-18); and that defendants alleged utterances have caused

8  substantial harm and damages to her reputation in the community

9  (Complaint, Paragraphs 15-16, page 6, line 10 ff.).  However, if

10  plaintiff is in fact a "former city councilwoman"..."widely known

11  in the community," she may be a public figure within the meaning of

12  the Constitutional limitation on defamation actions involving

13  public figures.  If so, the complaint fails to allege the requisite

14  "malice" in publication (knowledge of falsity or reckless disregard

15  for the truth) of the matters published. [New York Times v.

16  Sullivan (1964) 376 U.S. 254; and Gertz v. Welch (1974) 418 U.S.

17  323]  Hence, it fails to state a cause of action for defamation.

18  [FOLLOW WITH ARGUMENTS AND CITES SUPPORTING EACH OTHER GROUND FOR

19  DEMURRER]

20                          Respectfully submitted,

21

22                          By/s/ _____
                            Attorney for .................

23

24

25

26

27

28                              5
_____
        DEMURRER TO COMPLAINT; NOTICE OF HEARING;
        SUPP. DECL'N OF ........; POINTS & AUTH.

## CHECKLIST
## DEMURRER

*[Ed. Note:   This form or similar forms are used by many courts. Counsel should use this as a checklist when preparing a motion or opposition because it may raise factors of concern to the court. Declarations or points and authorities should be prepared to address each of the points on the checklist.]*

| **DEMURRER**<br>[CCP §430.10 et. seq.  CRC 325,  LASC 9.18] | | | |
|---|---|---|---|
| ____ Complaint _____ Answer ____ Amended Pleading ___ Cross-Complaint | | | |
| Calendar:<br>Date:<br>Notice: | Discovery cutoff date (CCP §2024(a)):<br>Motion cutoff:<br>Trial Date: | | Case No: |
| Moving Party: | | | |
| Responding Party: | | | |
| Address: | | Proof of service | |
| CRC 201, 311, 313 | | LASC Rules | |
| 15/20 day lapse(CCP §1005) | | Pleading served on: | |
| Pleading filed on: | | Demurrer filed on:<br>w/in 30 days?<br>w/in 10 days? (answer) | |
| Relief Requested: | | | |
| Causes of Action: | | Summary of Facts: | |
| GROUNDS FOR MOTION: | | GROUNDS FOR OPPOSITION: | |
| ANALYSIS | | | |
| TENTATIVE RULING: _____ Sustain w/ leave to amend<br>_____ Sustain w/o leave to amend<br>_____ Overrule | | | |

Rev. #1 2000

# NOTICE OF RULING ON DEMURRER

```
 1    .........................
      State Bar No. ...........
 2    .........................
      .........................
 3    .........................

 4

 5   .Attorney for Defendant
      DONALD E. DALTON
 6

 7

 8           SUPERIOR COURT OF THE STATE OF CALIFORNIA

 9                  COUNTY OF .........

10   ....................,        )    CASE NO. ...........
                                  )
11              Plaintiffs,       )    NOTICE OF RULING ON DEMURRER
                                  )
12   vs.                          )
                                  )
13   ....................,        )
                                  )
14              Defendants.       )
     _____ )
15

16        TO: PLAINTIFF PAMELA PHILLIPS AND HER ATTORNEY OF RECORD

17        PLEASE TAKE NOTICE THAT on November 15, ......, the Court in

18   Department 81 thereof, sustained the demurrer of DONALD E. DALTON

19   to the First Amended Complaint, and granted said plaintiff thirty

20   (30) days from date of service of this notice within which to amend

21   said complaint.   The Court sustained the said demurrer on the

22   following grounds:

23        The First Cause of Action fails to allege facts sufficient to

24   state a cause of action against the demurring defendant; The First

25   Cause of Action is uncertain because it cannot be ascertained

26   therefrom whether plaintiff is claiming defamation as a public

27   /////

28   /////
                                    1
     _____
                     NOTICE OF RULING ON DEMURRER
```

```
 1 │ figure or private individual; the Second Cause of Action fails to
 2 │ allege facts sufficient to state a cause of action.
 3 │ DATED:  ..............,  .....
 4 │                                    By:  /s/
 5 │                                    Attorney for Defendant
   │                                    DONALD E. DALTON
 6 │
 7 │
 8 │
 9 │
10 │
11 │
12 │
13 │
14 │
15 │
16 │
17 │
18 │
19 │
20 │
21 │
22 │
23 │
24 │
25 │
26 │
27 │
28 │
```

2

NOTICE OF RULING ON DEMURRER

# NOTICE OF MOTION TO STRIKE;
## POINTS AND AUTHORITIES IN SUPPORT

```
 1  ...........................
    State Bar No. ..............
 2  ...........................
    ...........................
 3  ...........................

 4

 5  Attorney for ..............

 6              SUPERIOR COURT OF THE STATE OF CALIFORNIA

 7                     COUNTY OF ...........

 8  .............................,   )   CASE NO. ........................
 9                                   )
              Plaintiff,             )   HEARING DATE/TIME: ..............
10                                   )   DEPT. NO. ......................
    vs.                              )   HEARING JUDGE: ....... (if known)
11                                   )
    .............................,   )   NOTICE OF MOTION TO STRIKE
12                                   )   PORTIONS OF COMPLAINT;
              Defendant.             )   DECLARATIONS OF ......; POINTS AND
13                                   )   AUTHORITIES; PROPOSED ORDER
                                     )
14                                   )   DATE ACTION FILED: ..............
                                     )   DATE SET FOR TRIAL: ..... (if set)
15  _____)
```

16  TO EACH PARTY AND ATTORNEY OF RECORD:

17      PLEASE TAKE NOTICE THAT on October 21, ....., at 9:00 a.m., or as soon

18  thereafter as counsel can be heard, defendants ............... will move this

19  court in Department 81 thereof, at the County Courthouse, 111 N. Hill Street,

20  Room 833, Los Angeles, California, for an order striking: (1) paragraph 12 of

21  the first cause of action and (2) the final paragraph of the prayer for relief

22  which seeks punitive damages. Said motion will be made on the grounds that

23  paragraph 12 and the related punitive damages paragraph in the prayer for

24  relief seek damages which are not recoverable as a matter of law and will be

25  based on this notice, the attached points and authorities, and the complaint.

26  DATED: .....................

                                     /s/_____
27                                   Attorney for ...............

28                          1

```
_____
        MOTION TO STRIKE PORT'NS OF COMPLAINT;
        SUPP. DECL'N OF .......; POINTS & AUTH.
```

```
 1    ....................................
      State Bar No. ...............
 2    ....................................
      ....................................
 3    ....................................

 4

 5    Attorney for ...............

 6

 7

 8              SUPERIOR COURT OF THE STATE OF CALIFORNIA

 9                     COUNTY OF .........

10    ..........................,   ) CASE NO. ...................
                                    )
11              Plaintiff,          ) HEARING DATE/TIME: ..........
                                    ) DEPT. NO. .................
12    vs.                           ) HEARING JUDGE: ...... (if known)
                                    )
13    ..........................,   ) POINTS AND AUTHORITIES IN
                                    ) SUPPORT OF MOTION TO STRIKE
14              Defendant.          ) PORTIONS OF COMPLAINT
                                    )
15                                  ) DATE ACTION FILED: ...........
                                    ) DATE SET FOR TRIAL: ... (if set)
16    _____ )
```

17    Paragraph 12 of the First Cause of Action in the Complaint in
18  this action alleges in substance that defendant "willfully,
19  deliberately and maliciously" refused to pay the payments due
20  under the promissory note sued upon "with intent and for the
21  purpose of damaging plaintiff's financial interest" and "with
22  conscious disregard for the plaintiff's expectation and need for
23  prompt payment in order to discharge on his own obligations"
24  constituting "oppression, fraud and malice" as to plaintiff.
25  (Complaint, page 2, line 20, to page 3, line 15) the prayer of the
26  complaint seeks $50,000.00 damages against defendants "to punish
27  for the oppression, fraud and malice" allegedly pleaded in the
28  aforesaid Paragraph 12.

                                   2
      _____
              MOTION TO STRIKE PORT'NS OF COMPLAINT;
              SUPP. DECL'N OF ........; POINTS & AUTH.

1.  Exemplary Damages Not Recoverable in Contract Actions:
Civil Code Section 3294(a) provides that exemplary damages shall be
allowable "In an action for the breach of an obligation not arising
from contract..." (emphasis added).

2.  Action for Non-Payment of Promissory Note is a Contract
Action:  "It is settled that punitive damages may not be awarded in
action based on a breach of contract even though the defendant's
breach was wilful or fraudulent."  [Contractor's Safety Assoc. v.
Calif. Comp. Ins. Co. (1957) 48 C2d 71, 77, 307 P2d 626]

[ADD OTHER APPROPRIATE CITES]

Respectfully submitted,

By _____/s/_____
Attorneys for .....................

3

MOTION TO STRIKE PORT'NS OF COMPLAINT;
SUPP. DECL'N OF ........; POINTS & AUTH.

**RESERVED**

Rev. #1 1999

## NOTICE OF MOTION FOR JUDGMENT ON THE PLEADINGS;
## REQUEST TO TAKE JUDICIAL NOTICE;
## POINTS AND AUTHORITIES IN SUPPORT

```
 1  ......................
    State Bar No. ...........
 2  ......................
    ......................
 3  ......................

 4

 5  Attorneys for ..........

 6

 7

 8              SUPERIOR COURT OF THE STATE OF CALIFORNIA

 9                      COUNTY OF .........

10  ......................,  ) CASE NO. ....................
                             )
11              Plaintiff,   ) HEARING DATE/TIME: ..........
                             ) DEPT. NO. ..................
12  vs.                      ) HEARING JUDGE: ...... (if known)
                             )
13  ......................,  ) NOTICE OF MOTION FOR JUDGMENT
                             ) ON THE PLEADINGS; DECLARATIONS
14              Defendant.   ) OF .......; POINTS AND
                             ) AUTHORITIES; PROPOSED ORDER
15                           )
                             ) DATE ACTION FILED: ..........
16  _____) DATE SET FOR TRIAL: ... (if set)

17  TO EACH PARTY AND ATTORNEY OF RECORD IN THIS ACTION:

18       PLEASE TAKE NOTICE THAT on ..........., ...... at ..... a.m.,

19  or as soon thereafter as counsel can be heard, defendant .........

20  ......... will, through its attorneys of record herein, move this

21  Court in Department 81 thereof, at the County Courthouse, 111 N.

22  Hill Street, Room 833, Los Angeles, California for judgment on the

23  pleadings in this action in favor of said defendant, including an

24  award of reasonable attorneys fees and costs.  This motion will be

25  made on the ground that plaintiff's complaint does not state facts

26  sufficient to constitute a cause of action against this moving

27  defendant for the reason that the action is barred by the effect of

28  res judicata.   The motion will be based on this notice, the
```
                                    1

                 MOTION FOR JUDG'MT ON PLEADINGS; REQUEST FOR JUD'L NOTICE;
                         SUPP. DECL'N OF ........; POINTS & AUTH.

```
 1 │ attached points and authorities, and the complete files and records
 2 │ of this action and the matters of which judicial notice is
 3 │ requested to be taken as per Request to Take Judicial Notice served
 4 │ and filed herewith.
 5 │
 6 │ DATED:   ................, ......
 7 │                                   By /s/_____
 8 │                                   Attorneys for ...............
 9 │
10 │
11 │
12 │
13 │
14 │
15 │
16 │
17 │
18 │
19 │
20 │
21 │
22 │
23 │
24 │
25 │
26 │
27 │
28 │
```

2

MOTION FOR JUDG'MT ON PLEADINGS; REQUEST FOR JUD'L NOTICE;
SUPP. DECL'N OF ........; POINTS & AUTH.

```
 1  ........................
    State Bar No. ...........
 2  ........................
    ........................
 3  ........................

 4

 5  Attorneys for ..........

 6

 7

 8              SUPERIOR COURT OF THE STATE OF CALIFORNIA

 9                     COUNTY OF .........

10  ........................,    ) CASE NO. ....................
                                 )
11              Plaintiff,       ) HEARING DATE/TIME: ..........
                                 ) DEPT. NO. ...................
12  vs.                          ) HEARING JUDGE: ...... (if known)
                                 )
13  ........................,    ) REQUEST TO TAKE JUDICIAL NOTICE
                                 )
14              Defendant.       ) DATE ACTION FILED: ..........
                                 ) DATE SET FOR TRIAL: ... (if set)
15  _____)

16       Defendant ....................... hereby requests that this

17  court take judicial notice of the findings of fact, conclusions of

18  law and judgment rendered by the ......... Court of California,

19  ......... County, on .........., ......, in the action entitled

20  ................................. being Case No. .............

21  in the files and records of the said Court.  Attached to this

22  notice, marked Exhibits "A", "B" and "C", respectively, are

23  certified copies of the said findings of fact, conclusions of law

24  and judgment in the said action.

25  DATED:  ................, ......

26
                                    /s/_____  _____
27                                  Attorneys for ...............

28  _____
                                   3
         MOTION FOR JUDG'MT ON PLEADINGS; REQUEST FOR JUD'L NOTICE;
                SUPP. DECL'N OF ........; POINTS & AUTH.
```

7-109

```
 1   ..............................
     State Bar No. ...............
 2   ..............................
 3   ..............................
     ..............................
 4

 5   Attorney for ...............

 6

 7

 8              SUPERIOR COURT OF THE STATE OF CALIFORNIA

 9                       COUNTY OF .........

10   .........................,   ) CASE NO. ...................
                                  )
11                 Plaintiff,     ) HEARING DATE/TIME: ..........
                                  ) DEPT. NO. ..................
12   vs.                          ) HEARING JUDGE: ...... (if known)
                                  )
13   .........................,   ) POINTS AND AUTHORITIES IN
                                  ) SUPPORT OF MOTION FOR JUDGMENT
14                 Defendant.     ) ON THE PLEADING
                                  )
15                                ) DATE ACTION FILED: ...........
                                  ) DATE SET FOR TRIAL: ... (if set)
16   _____)

17        Plaintiff's complaint seeks damages against defendant .......

18   ......... for alleged defective workmanship in the production of

19   certain  aluminum  alloy  castings  delivered  by  defendant  to

20   plaintiff between .........., ..... and ........., ..... (See

21   Complaint, Paragraphs 7 through 9, inclusive.)

22        The identical claim has been fully litigated and adjudicated

23   in an action in ........ County between the same parties (Case No.

24   ....... in the files and records of said Court, as disclosed by

25   the records which this Court is requested to judicially notice.

26   (See request to Take Judicial Notice attached hereto and served

27   and filed herewith.) The judgment in the aforesaid ........ County

28   /////
                                   4
     _____
       MOTION FOR JUDG'MT ON PLEADINGS; REQUEST FOR JUD'L NOTICE;
            SUPP. DECL'N OF ........; POINTS & AUTH.
```

action is now final, no appeal having been taken.  Hence, it is res

judicata of the claims asserted by plaintiff in this action.

1.  Judgment on the Pleadings may be Granted After Time for

Demurrer Expired:  A motion for judgment on the pleadings may be

made at any time, even after the time for demurrer or answer to the

complaint.  [Ion Equipment Co. v. Nelson (1981) 110 CA3d 868, 168

CR 361]

2.  Judgment on the Pleadings May be Granted on Same Ground

as General Demurrer:  A motion for judgment on the pleadings may be

made on the ground that the opposing pleading fails to state facts

sufficient to constitute a claim or defense under the appropriate

substantive law.  (Colberg v. California (1971) 67 C2d 408, 412, 62

CR 401]

3.  General Demurrer Lies Where Facts Judicially Noticeable

Disclose Complete Bar to Action:  A general demurrer will lie for

defects apparent on the face of the pleading under attack or on the

basis of matters of which the court can take judicial notice.  [CCP

¶430.30(a)]

4.  Court May Take Judicial Notice of Judgment in Other Civil

Action:  The court may take judicial notice of the truth of the

facts asserted in documents such as findings of fact, conclusions

of law and judgments in other court actions.  [Day v. Sharp (1975)

50 CA3d 904, 914, 123 CR 918]

5.  When Facts Judicially Noticed Constitute Complete Defense

to Present Action General Demurrer or Judgment on Pleadings may be

Granted:  Where the matters judicially noticed establish a complete

bar to the present action, the complaint fails to allege facts suf-

ficient to constitute a cause of action.  It is treated as if the

5

1 | contrary allegations in the complaint did not exist, and hence the
2 | general demurrer, or motion for judgment on the pleadings is prop-
3 | erly granted. [Dryden v. Tri-Valley Growers (1977) 65 CA3d 990,
4 | 997, 135 CR 720]
5 | In light of the above authorities, and upon review of the
6 | findings and judgment in the ........ County case, it is submitted
7 | that plaintiff is suing on the identical cause of action previously
8 | litigated; and therefore, the judgment in that action is a complete
9 | bar to the present proceeding. Hence, the motion for judgment on
10 | the pleading should now be granted.

Respectfully submitted,

By /s/ _____
Attorney for .....................

6

MOTION FOR JUDG'MT ON PLEADINGS; REQUEST FOR JUD'L NOTICE;
SUPP. DECL'N OF ........; POINTS & AUTH.

Rev. #1 1999

# CHECKLIST
# JUDGMENT ON THE PLEADINGS

*[Ed. Note: This form or similar forms are used by many courts. Counsel should use this as a checklist when preparing a motion or opposition because it may raise factors of concern to the court. Declarations or points and authorities should be prepared to address each of the points on the checklist.]*

Discovery Cut-off: _____        Calendar: _____

Motion Cut-off: _____            Date: _____

Trial Date: _____                  Notice: _____

### JUDGMENT ON THE PLEADINGS
### (CCP § 438)
### (CONFIDENTIAL COURT DOCUMENT WHEN COMPLETED)

NAME OF MOVING PARTY: _____

NAME OF RESPONDING PARTY: _____

CORRECT ADDRESS IN PROOF OF SERVICE (CCP §§ 1013, 1013a): _____

21- DAY LAPSE UNDER CCP § 1005: _____

TIME FOR ANSWER OR DEMURRER EXPIRED (CCP §438(f))

PREVIOUS DEMURRER BY MOVING PARTY (CCP § 438(g)(1)):

    ❑ Yes    ❑ No

    Disposition: _____ Date: _____

SUMMARY OF COMPLAINT:

GROUNDS FOR MOTION:

    ❑ Statutory (CCP §438(c)(1))

    ❑ Common law (Weil & Brown, §7:277)

OPPOSITION:

RECOMMENDED RULING:

    ❑ Grant without leave to amend

    ❑ Grant with 30 days' leave to amend

    ❑ Deny

        ❑ w/o prejudice

    ❑ Enter judgment

# CHECKLIST
# MOTION TO STRIKE

*[Ed. Note: This form or similar forms are used by many courts. Counsel should use this as a checklist when preparing a motion or opposition because it may raise factors of concern to the court. Declarations or points and authorities should be prepared to address each of the points on the checklist.]*

| MOTION TO STRIKE<br>[ CCP §§435 et. seq. , CRC 329, LASC 9.18] | | | |
|---|---|---|---|
| ____ Amended Pleading ____ Complaint ____ Cross-Complaint ____ Answer | | | |

| | | |
|---|---|---|
| Calender:<br>Date:<br>Notice: | Discovery cut-off:<br>Motion cut-off:<br>Trial Date: | Case No: |
| Moving Party: | Responding Party: | |
| Address: | Proof of service: | |
| CRC 201<br>CRC 311, 313 | LASC Rules: | |
| 15/20 day lapse? | Pleading served on: | |
| Pleading filed on: | Motion to strike filed on: | |

**Relief Requested:**

| Causes of Action: | Summary of Facts: |
|---|---|
| | |

| GROUNDS FOR MOTION: | GROUNDS FOR OPPOSITION: |
|---|---|
| | |

| ANALYSIS |
|---|
| |

TENTATIVE RULING: ____ Grant Motion to Strike the whole pleading
____ Grant Motion to Strike portions of the pleading as follows:
____ Deny Motion to Strike
____ Off-calendar

Rev. #1 2003

# CHECKLIST
# DEMURRER DISMISSAL

*[Ed. Note: This form or similar forms are used by many courts. Counsel should use this as a checklist when preparing a motion or opposition because it may raise factors of concern to the court. Declarations or points and authorities should be prepared to address each of the points on the checklist.]*

Discovery Cut-off: _____  Calendar: _____

Motion Cut-off: _____  Date: _____

Trial Date: _____  Notice: _____

### DEMURRER DISMISSAL
#### (CCP § 581(f), CRC 325)
##### (CONFIDENTIAL COURT DOCUMENT WHEN COMPLETED)

NAME OF MOVING PARTY: _____

NAME OF RESPONDING PARTY: _____

CORRECT ADDRESS IN PROOF OF SERVICE (CCP §§ 1013, 1013a): _____

21-DAY LAPSE UNDER CCP § 1005: _____ OR EX PARTE NOTICE UNDER CRC Rule 325(f)_____

1.  DEMURRER TO _____; ENTIRE CASE: _____

2.  DEMURRER WAS TO ONLY SOME CAUSES OF ACTION (CRC Rule 325(g)):

    Count 1 _____

    Count 2 _____

    Count 3 _____

    Count 4 _____

    Count 5 _____

    Count 6 _____

3.  GROUNDS FOR RULING: _____

    _____

    _____

4.  DATE OF ORDER SUSTAINING DEMURRER: _____

5.  LEAVE TO AMEND: _____ DAYS.

6.  EXPIRING: _____

7.  NOTICE GIVEN _____ OR WAIVED _____

8.  TIME UP? _____

9.  DOES CCP § 597 APPLY? _____

DECLARATION OF MOVING PARTY (CCP § 2015.5; CRC 315(a)):

OPPOSITION:

RECOMMENDED RULING:

    ❑ Grant

    ❑ Deny

    ❑ w/o prejudice

**RESERVED**